The 1997-98   Official PFA

FOOTBALLERS
FACTFILE

Edited by
Barry J Hugman

Photographs by
Colorsport

Queen Anne Press

First published in 1997

© Barry J Hugman

Barry J Hugman has asserted his right under
the Copyright, Designs and Patent Act, 1988
to be identified as the author of this work

First published in Great Britain in 1997 by
Queen Anne Press
a division of Lennard Associates Limited
Mackerye End, Harpenden
Hertfordshire AL5 5DR

A CIP catalogue record for this book
is available from the British Library

ISBN 1 85291 581 1

Typeset and designed by Typecast (Artwork & Design)
West Country Marketing, 8 Mudford Road
Yeovil, Somerset BA21 4AA

Printed and bound in Great Britain by
Butler & Tanner, London and Frome

PICTURE ACKNOWLEDGEMENTS

The editor and publishers would also like to thank the
following for providing additional photographs for the book:
Empics Sports Photo Agency; *Rotheram Advertiser*;
Nottingham Evening Post; *Lincolnshire Echo*; *Scunthorpe
Evening Telegraph* and Paul Huddart from the *Exeter Express
& Echo.*

Acknowledgements

In introducing the third PFA Footballers' Factfile, I would like to start by thanking **Gordon Taylor**, chief executive, and those at the PFA, including **Brendon Batson** and **Brian Marwood**, now departed for pastures new, for their wholehearted support. I have known Gordon and his team for a long time now and the one thing that always comes across is his great enthusiasm for the game. Also excellent back up came in the shape, when needed, of the players themselves.

The level of accurate information available at both the Football League and the Premier League continues to improve and is now as good as you are going to find, especially in the areas of appearances, so long the bane of the football statistician's existence. For that I am extremely grateful to **Sheila Andrew, Debbie Birch,** and **Jonathan Hargreaves** (Football League), and **Mike Foster** and **Mike Kelleher** of the Premiership.

As in previous editions, tracking down international honours at all levels of the game is not an easy task, and I was again happy to have the help of **David Barber** (English FA), **Kitty Barlers** (FA of Ireland), **Scott McIntosh** (Scottish FA), and **John Watson** (Scottish Schools FA). However, without the work done by others it is almost certain that vital information would just not pass down to the man in the street. Thus, I would like to add my thanks to **Ceri Stennett** (official FAW statistician), **Sean Creedon** (official FA of Ireland statistician), and **Marshall Gillespie** (editor of the Northern Ireland Football Yearbook). All three do a spendid job, being much appreciated at this end, and it is such a great pity that after seven editions the Northern Ireland Football Yearbook may not appear again. This excellent publication needs urgent support and, hopefully, will get it before it is too late.

Once again, I was lucky to be able to call upon **Mike Featherstone** and **Alan Platt**. Mike audited the season's appearances, subs' and goals information, as well as helping to supply missing heights and weights, while Alan came in to help with the construction of the late biographical entries. Both also continued to assess historical information applying to current players. And, with the time factor always working against completing a work of this nature, a friend of mine, **Bob Lonkhurst**, came to the rescue when certain contributors failed to deliver on time.

For the third year, **Jonathan Ticehurst**, managing director of Windsor Insurance Brokers' Sports Division, has thrown his weight behind the Factfile, both financially and vocally. His and Windsor's support, as with the British Boxing Board of Control Yearbook, is greatly appreciated.

For details provided on players, I have listed below, in alphabetical order, the names of the "team", without whose help this book would not have been possible to produce. Once again, I thank every one of them for all the hard work they put in.

Audrey Adams *(Watford):* Producer and statistician for BBC Radio Sport and a Watford supporter since the days of Cliff Holton, Audrey is also the club statistician for the *Ultimate Football Guide.*

Steve Adamson *(Scarborough):* Having supported Scarborough for 26 years, during which time he has been the programme editor (1984-1992), Steve continues to contribute to the programme as well as being the club's historian. In his spare time he runs his own junior football team.

Denise Allibone *(Aston Villa):* In her own words, Denise is a mad, crazy Villa supporter, who follows them up-and-down the country without fail. Her only previous football work was to help me with the club's profiles required for the *Premier League: The Players* publication.

Geoff Allman *(Walsall):* A university lecturer by trade, he saw his first ever game in February 1944, Walsall versus Wolves. Has written for Walsall's programme for the last 29 seasons and, at one time or another, has provided articles for more than half of the clubs currently in the Premiership and Football League. Geoff is also a Methodist local preacher and press officer.

Lawrence Appleby *(Hereford United):* In supporting Hereford for more than 26 years, for the past 17 he has collected stats and club history and has provided the data for the *Ultimate Football Guide.* Currently writing two club histories.

Stuart Basson *(Chesterfield):* Is the author of *The Definitive Chesterfield FC,* which was published by the Association of Football Statisticians, of which he has been a member for 11 years. His comprehensive Who's Who of the club is also nearing completion.

Ian Bates *(Bradford):* Has followed City since 1951 and refereed in amateur football up until 1995-96. A member of the AFS, this is the first publication that Ian has been involved in.

David Batters *(York City):* A supporter since 1948, he is the club historian, a contributor to the programme and author of *York City: The Complete Record 1922-1990.* Also commentates on matches at York Hospital.

Harry Berry *(Blackburn Rovers):* Author of the club centenary history, *A Century of Soccer* and other books on Rovers, and co-author of the *Preston North End* history, along with several books on athletics.

Simon Bowden *(Barnet):* As sports editor of the *Barnet Advertiser,* he has followed the club home and away for the past four seasons.

Peter Bower and **Ken Craig** *(Colchester United):* The former, a life-long fan since the mid 1950s, worked with Ken to produce the input for the enclosed. The latter currently edits a monthly newsletter for all United fans living away from the area called *U's from 'Ome.*

Eddie Brennan *(Sunderland):* A regular at Roker since 1976 (aged nine) and currently the club statistician for the *Ultimate Football Guide.*

Stuart Brennan *(Stockport County):* As sports editor of the *Stockport Express* newspaper from 1989 to 1994, he covered the club's fortunes both home and away and was a programme contributor. Also County's statistician for the *Ultimate Football Guide.*

Jonathan Brewer *(Plymouth Argyle):* Currently the Argyle statistician for the *Ultimate Football Guide,* Jonathan also writes articles for the *Pasty News,* a publication run by the London branch of the supporters' club.

Jim Brown *(Coventry City):* The club's official statistician and contributor to the programme, he also pens a column for the local newspaper answering readers' queries.

Trevor Bugg *(Hull City):* A supporter of the Tigers for 28 years, Trevor is a major contributor to Hull City's much respected matchday programme.

Graham Caton *(Bournemouth):* Into his third year with the *Factfile,* Graham is a committed Cherries' supporter who has always enjoyed collating facts and figures relating to the club.

Wallace Chadwick *(Burnley):* A supporter for over 30 years, he has seen all the extremes in the period from the great days of the '60s, including the championship of all four divisions and a narrow escape from relegation to the Conference. Wallace is a regular contributor to the Clarets' programme.

Dennis Chapman *(Manchester City):* Now retired, Dennis has followed City since 1937-38. Has worked on several publications, including the *FA Carling Premier League: The Players* and the *Ultimate Football Guide.* Possesses possibly the largest collection of City programmes, the earliest being 1902-03.

Paul Clayton *(Charlton Athletic):* Writes in the club's matchday programme and various other publications connected with Athletic. A Charlton season ticket-holder, despite living in Wiltshire, and a member of the AFS, Paul also compiles the statistics for the *Ultimate Football Guide.*

Grant Coleby *(Exeter City):* A member of both Exeter City's Supporters' Club and the Association of Football Statisticians, Grant has been the official contributor to the Factfile since its inception.

Eddie Collins *(Nottingham Forest):* A Forest supporter since 1956, and a member of the Associated Football Statisticians, this is the first publication he has been involved in.

David Copping *(Barnsley):* The writer of the past meetings column in the Barnsley programme for the last seven seasons, he also commentated live hospital broadcasts from Oakwell between 1978 and 1991 and has since narrated for the club videos.

Frank Coumbe *(Brentford):* Frank, who has not missed a Brentford home game since 1977, has been the Bees' statistician for the Ultimate Football Guide for the last 13 years, as well as writing for many club programmes.

Peter Cullen *(Bury):* Peter is a former Bury FC Supporters' Club secretary, who also acted as the programme editor between 1983-1991. Editor of the *Bury Centenary Brochure* in 1985, he is currently, along with Paul Greenless, working on a definitive club history.

Carol Dalziel *(Tranmere Rovers):* The electronic scoreboard operator at Prenton Park on matchdays, club liaison officer, and contributor to the matchday programme, Carol has supported Tranmere faithfully since 1968.

Mike Davage *(Norwich City):* Author of the ultimate Who's Who, *Glorious Canaries,* and co-author of *Canary Citizens.* Presently involved in the ninth volume of the *Norwich City handbook* and is a regular contributor to local and national TV, radio and newspapers. As a contributor to over 60 books, Mike is currently working with Jim Creasy on a 1919-1939 supplemental book to the author's *Football League Players' Records, 1946-1992.*

Gareth Davies *(Wrexham):* Assists in the much acclaimed club

programme, the editor of which, **Geraint Parry**, also helped on heights and weights, etc, for this publication. Gareth has written and published the *Coast of Soccer Memories*, the centenary history of the *North Wales Coast FA (1995)*, and co-authored with Ian Garland the *Who's Who of Welsh International Soccer Players (1991)*. Also heavily involved in Wrexham, *A Complete Record 1872-1992*, written by Peter Jones. Currently researching *Wrexham FC's Who's Who* at the moment, he still finds time to compile the club section for the *Ultimate Football Guide*.

David Downs (*Reading*): Teaches in a local primary school and works part-time for Reading FC at their Centre of Excellence. The official historian and statistician for the club, David is the author of *Biscuits & Royals*, the history of Reading.

Ray Driscoll (*Chelsea*): A life-long Blues' fan born and bred two miles away from Stamford Bridge, before moving to Woking, Ray was fortunate enough to witness Chelsea's first FA Cup win in 27 years, and Woking's third FA Trophy triumph in four years, all in the space of 24 hours at Wembley last season. A contributor to many football books, he also wrote articles for the Euro '96 programmes.

Mark Evans (*Leeds United*): Has supported United for the last 29 years and describes his association with the club as one of the loves of his life. The Leeds' statistician for the *Ultimate Football Guide* for nearly nine years, he was also involved in my two editions of the *FA Carling Premiership: The Players*.

Keith Evemy (*Fulham*): Long-standing supporter who was unfortunately away on military service when the club won its only post-war honour, the second division championship in 1948-49. Highly regarded at Craven Cottage, he contributes to the matchday programme and is never far from the ground.

Colin Faiers (*Cambridge United*): A 38-year-old chartered accountant, Colin, a fan for over 27 years, is the recognised club statistician and currently writes the historical features for the programme.

Harold Finch (*Crewe Alexandra*): The club's historian and a supporter for over 60 years, Harold has been the programme editor for more than 40 of them. A one-club man, he has travelled extensively to watch them play.

Paul Gilligan (*Doncaster Rovers*): A keen follower of Rovers for over 30 years, Paul has written three books on the club and is a regular contributor in the matchday programme. Also the official club photographer.

Dave Goody (*Southend United*): United historian, statistician and collector, he co-authored *Southend United: The Official History of the Blues* and is a regular contributor to the programme.

Frank Grande (*Northampton Town*): Author of *The Cobblers, A History of Northampton Town FC* and a *Who's Who* on the club. Has contributed a regular column to the club programme for the past 17 seasons.

Roy Grant (*Oxford United*): Formerly assistant secretary at Oxford United and club programme editor and statistician, he also handled the Clubline telephone service. A contributor to the Ultimate Football Guide, and, in the past, the Official Football League Yearbook, Roy kindly stepped in to help, regarding work on other clubs as well as Oxford, following difficulties caused by holidays. His efforts were much appreciated.

Bert and **Michael Green** (*Bolton Wanderers*): The commercial executive at Altrincham, Bert, who is a life member of the AFS, is currently writing a history of Horwich RMI (now Leigh RMI) of the Unibond League. His son, 24-year-old Michael, despite supplying the majority of the input, just like his dad is a fanatical Newcastle United supporter. This is the first attempt by either in this field and Michael will be raring to go on next year's *Factfile*.

Don Hales (*Leyton Orient and Luton Town*): A management consultant in financial services, Don has contributed to *World Soccer*, *Team Talk* and the *Ultimate Football Guide*, as well as compiling the obituary column for the AFS. In compiling the Orient and Luton information, he was assisted by **Paul Morant**, a 20-year-old O's fan, and his son, **Daniel Hales**, currently studying at Warwick University.

Roger Harris (*Brighton & Hove Albion*): A life-long enthusiast of Brighton, and football in general, Roger co-authored *Seagulls: The Story of Brighton and Hove Albion FC* and is a life member of the Association of Football Statisticians.

Roger Harrison (*Blackpool*): Life-long supporter who has seen the Pool play every other league side both home and away. Joint programme editor and club statistician, Roger also contributes to other publications, including the *Ultimate Football Guide*.

Richard and **Janey Heyhoe** (*Tottenham Hotspur*): In a season of mixed fortunes for Spurs, the highlight for Janey and Richard was 14 September 1996, the day they were married. The team also celebrated

that day, following a 1-0 win at Southampton.

Ron Hockings (*International football*): Has now published five books involving the history of Chelsea, European and South American Cups. *The Nations of Europe*, currently available in two volumes, includes every line-up for all the European countries' matches up until 1993, with volume three envisaged being ready shortly and has recently completed *90 Years of the "Blues"*, the statistical history of Chelsea. Provided all the international appearances for non-British teams in this year's *Factfile*.

Mike Jay (*Bristol Rovers*): Apart from helping out on other publications, notably the *Ultimate Football Guide*, Mike has had two books of his own published on Bristol Rovers, namely *The Complete Record (1883-1987)* and *Pirates in Profile, A Who's Who of the Players 1920-1995*.

Alan Jenkins (*Cardiff City*): A life-long Cardiff supporter, who has been involved in several other publications, and is currently the City statistician for the Ultimate Football Guide, sadly, Alan will no longer be available to the *Factfile*.

Colin Jones (*Swansea City*): A fan since the early 1960s and a contributor to the club programme during the last five years. Played non-league football, before being involved in training and coaching.

Gordon Lawton (*Oldham Athletic*): Employed as the public relations officer at the club and Athletic's official photographer. Other publications contributed to, include *Carling Premiership: The Players*, *Rothmans Yearbook*, *Ultimate Football Guide* and *News of the World* annual.

Geoffrey Lea (*Wigan Athletic*): The club statistician for the *Ultimate Football Guide*, Geoffrey has been following the Latics for over 20 years and is a major contributor to the matchday programme that won the 'Third Division Programme of the Year' award in 1993-94. Also assists with the match commentary on the Clubcall.

Richard Lindsay (*Millwall*): Author of *Millwall: The Complete Record (1885-1991)*, and currently in the process of helping establish the Millwall FC Museum at the New Den.

John Lovis (*Torquay United*): A supporter since 1955, and a regular contributor to the club programme, he is also United's statistician for the *Ultimate Football Guide*.

Steve McGhee (*Derby County*): A collector of Derby memorabilia and a fan since 1969. Earlier involved in a bi-monthly historical magazine on County, he currently compiles the club section for the *Ultimate Football Guide*.

Peter Macey (*Portsmouth*): Currently undertaking the third year of a BSc in computer science at the University of Wolverhampton, Peter is a member of the AFS, as well as contributing to the Ultimate Football Guide.

John Maguire (*Manchester United*): A member of the AFS, and a qualified FA coach, John has been working on several sports related projects during the past 12 months, including a new booklet on Sir Matt Busby's record in the FA Cup.

John Martin (*Chester City*): Club statistician for both the *Rothmans Yearbook* and *Ultimate Football Guide*, he also contributes for various other publications. Was City's programme editor for ten years up until 1993-94, winning the 'Third Division Programme of the Year" award that same season.

Wade Martin (*Stoke City*): For many years a major contributor to the club programme, as well as writing *A Potters Tale* and the *Master Potters'* series of books.

Tony Matthews (*West Bromwich Albion*): Official statistician and curator of Albion, his publications include, *the complete records of Aston Villa, Birmingham City, WBA, Wolves, Walsall and Stoke City*. Has also compiled *Who 's Whos* on the first four clubs listed above, plus Manchester United, and currently contributes to several programmes.

Ian Mills, Richard and **Sarah Taylor** (*Notts County*): Ian supplied the County stats, Richard the words, and Sarah the typing. Having seen his first game at Gay Meadow in 1959-60, Ian, who runs the matchday programme sales, has been hooked ever since, missing just one game since 1970. The Taylors, both recent additions to the *Factfile* "team", follow a similar family tradition. Richard (father) began watching County in the mid 1950s and needs to visit just five more league grounds to join the 92 Club, while Sarah (daughter) has been an avid fan for over ten years.

Ian Nannestad (*Lincoln City*): A past contributor to the Imps' programme and co-author of the *Who's Who of Lincoln City, 1892-1994* publication.

John Northcutt (*West Ham United*): Has supported the Hammers since 1959 and is the co-author of West Ham books, *The Complete Record* and the *Illustrated History*. A regular contributor to the club programme and the club adviser to the *Ultimate Football Guide*.

Michael Norton *(Scunthorpe United):* A former matchday programme editor (1986-1993), Michael has followed Scunthorpe's fortunes since the late 1950s. As a member of the AFS, other football interests include collecting programmes and various memorabilia.

Brian Pead *(Liverpool):* Author of three editions of *Liverpool, A Complete Record, Liverpool: Champion of Champions* (1990) and *Ee Aye Addio - We've Won the Cup (1993)*, Brian was the statistician for the *Rush for Glory* video and has contributed to many publications, including the *Footballer* magazine and the *Ultimate Football Guide*.

Steve Peart and **Dave Finch** *(Wycombe Wanderers):* A former programme editor of the club and a supporter for over 20 years, Steve put together the player profiles, while the club statistics were supplied by Dave, the official Wycombe statistician.

Steve Phillips *(Rochdale):* A Dale fan of over 30 years standing, he is the club's official statistician and author of *The Survivors: The Story of Rochdale AFC.*

Paul Plowman *(Swindon Town):* Football historian, statistician, freelance journalist, and a member of the AFS.

David Prentice *(Everton):* Everton correspondent for the *Liverpool Echo* since 1993 and author of a club history five years earlier, when he was reporting both Everton and Liverpool for the Daily Post, he completed his Mersey set when reporting on Tranmere Rovers for three years from 1990. Currently on his fourth manager at Goodison and hoping for a period of stability!

Mike Purkiss *(Crystal Palace):* Having supported Palace since 1950 and produced stats on them since 1960, Mike is the author of *Complete History of Crystal Palace, 1905-1989*, the club statistician for the *Ultimate Football Guide*, and contributed to *Premier League: The Players.*

Mike Renshaw *(Sheffield Wednesday):* Has followed Wednesday for over 40 years and is a great supporter of European soccer. Currently produces the club section for the *Ultimate Football Guide.*

Jack Retter *(Mansfield Town):* First saw the team play over 60 years ago. Author of *Who's Who - The Stags,* and a regular contributor to the matchday programme. Currently working on a comprehensive centenary history of the club, due to be published shortly, he is a member of the AFS and contributes to a number of publications.

Robert Ringsell *(Wimbledon):* A life-long Dons' supporter, and from a family who have seen the side through thick and thin, Robert enjoyed one of the club's most impressive seasons. Is currently working for WH Smith and hoping for a career in retail management.

Mick Robinson *(Peterborough United):* Another life-long fan, for a number of years Mick has contributed to the club programme and was the joint editor of the *Official Peterborough History*. Also the club statistician for the *Ultimate Football Guide.*

Phil Sherwin *(Port Vale):* As Vale's statistician, Phil works on a number of other publications and has contributed to the club programme for 16 years. A fan since 1968, he follows them home and away.

Andy Shute *(Queens Park Rangers):* Life-long QPR supporter and compiler of the QPR and Tottenham details for the *Ultimate Football Guide.*

Derrick Slasor *(Middlesbrough):* First saw the Boro play in December 1946 and, as Managing Director of Trapezium Transport Services, is well known in the area for sponsoring various club activities.

Mike Slater *(Wolverhampton Wanderers):* Mike has attended almost 1,000 Wolves' matches and, in 1988, wrote and published a book on their history called *Molineux Memories*. From 1989 to 1995 he compiled the annual *Brain of Wolves' Quiz*, prior to producing a booklet containing all the club's competitive results.

Gordon Small *(Hartlepool Unlted):* Has supported United since October 1965, experiencing two promotions, two relegations, six re-elections and several close calls, not least the 1996-97 season. Is the statistician for the *Ultimate Football Guide.*

Dave Smith *(Leicester City):* A regular columnist in the programme, co-author of *Fossils & Foxes* and the *Foxes Alphabet,* he assists with several other club handbooks.

Gerry Somerton *(Rotherham United):* Workwise, the deputy sports editor of the *Rotherham Advertiser*, and part-time sports reporter for *Hallam FM*, the local commercial radio station, Gerry is also the author of *Now we are United,* the official history of Rotherham United, and co-editor of the matchday programme. Last season he completed 50 years of watching the club.

Richard Stead *(Huddersfield Town):* Has supported his hometown team, Huddersfield, since the early '70s and, despite living in Manchester these days, continues to do so. Also contributes to the *Ultimate Football Guide.*

David Steele *(Carlisle United):* A regular contributor to the club programme for several years now, his current interest is in tracking down ex-United players.

Richard Stocken *(Shrewsbury Town):* A supporter of 39 years and a collector of club programmes and memorabilia, Richard is an annual contributor to the *Ultimate Football Guide* and other publications.

Bill Swan *(Newcastle United):* A supporter since the early 1950s, he is now a shareholder in the club, as are his wife and children. Is a keen collector of programmes and other memorabilia and long-term member of the AFS. Although the author of numerous published scientific papers, and assisting in the production of the club's volume in the *Complete Record* series, this is his first involvement in this kind of work.

Alan Tait *(Scottish clubs):* A regular contributor to Tony Brown's ultimate *Scottish League* book, and a compiler of statistics appertaining to that country, Alan is currently working on a project, probably still several years down tbe road, that will give line-ups for all Scottish League matches since 1890.

Colin Tattum *(Birmingham City):* Colin has reported the fortunes of Birmingham City and west midlands' clubs for the *Birmingham Evening Mail* and *Sports Argus* newspapers for almost a decade. A native of the second city, he also covers the national side.

Chris Thompson *(Arsenal):* Born in Greenwich the week before Charlton won the FA Cup, Chris has held season tickets for both the Valley and Highbury. Publications worked on, include *FA Carling Premiership: The Players* and, currently, the *Ultimate Football Guide.*

Andrew Treherne *(Sheffield United):* Contributor to the *Ultimate Football Guide, The Premier League: The Players* and *Sheffield United: The first Hundred Years.* Also a member of the AFS.

Les Triggs *(Grimsby Town):* First became involved with the statistical side of the club when asked to assist with Town's centenary exhibition in 1978. A retired librarian, Les, who first saw the Mariners in a wartime league match, is the co-author of the Grimsby Town volume in the *Complete Record* series and has been club statistician to the *Ultimate Football Guide* since its inception.

Roger Triggs *(Gillingham):* Has written three books on the club, *Gillingham FC - A Chronology 1893-1984, Priestfield Profiles 1950-1988* and the centenary publication, *Home of the Shouting Men,* which he co-authored with Andy Bradley. Also a feature writer in the programme since 1975.

Frank Tweddle *(Darlington):* The club's official historian and statistician, Frank is the author of *Darlington's Centenary History* and the programme editor since 1975. Also a contributor for various other publications, including the *Ultimate Football Guide.*

Paul Voller *(Ipswich Town):* A Town supporter since 1963-64, Paul works at the ground on matchdays and is a member of the supporters' management committee. Other publications worked on include the *FA Carling Premier League: The Players* and the *Ultimate Football Guide.*

Tony Woodburn and **Martin Atherton** *(Preston North End):* Tony started watching the club in the late 1960s and is a life member of the AFS, the Ninety-Two club and the Scottish 38 club. Martin, a fan for over 30 years, lives within a long throw-in of Deepdale and has been able to watch the development of the ground from his front doorstep.

David Woods *(Bristol City):* Has supported Bristol City since 1958, becoming a shareholder in the old company in the early '70s and in the new organisation in the dark days of 1982. However, as a life member of the AFS, David's main interest is in the early days of the game through to the end of the First World War. Author of the *Bristol Babe,* as well as the complete *Record of Bristol City* (with Andrew Crabtree), he is currently working on the official *Bristol City Centenary A-Z* and is a regular contributor to the City programme. Has also written for *Bristol Rovers,* the Footballer magazine, and is the City statistician for the *Ultimate Football Guide.*

Dick Wright *(Southampton):* Although supporting Saints for over 20 years, Dick has never undertaken work of this kind before the previous edition and hopes fans will forgive him for any oversight made in the *Factfile*. He also lives in hopes of avoiding a nervous breakdown and starting the season with the same manager, as in the previous term. Away from the Dell, he is the president of Goldsworth Park Rangers, Woking, which he helped form 14 years ago, and was delighted that the teams, which start from seven through to adult, had such a marvellous 1996-97 season, winning several trophies.

Finally, on the production side of the book, my thanks go to Jean Bastin, of Typecast (Artwork & Design), for her patience and diligent work on the typesetting and design, which again went far beyond the call of normal duty and was much appreciated. She was ably supported by Paul Bastin (Fintan Design) and Nina Whatmore (Orchard Design) who were called in to help at a crucial time and performed admirably.

If you get carried off...

The rewards of a sporting life can be high – but so are the risks involved. One bad tackle can end a career that is already short by conventional standards. Which is why all the F.A. Premier and Football League clubs have Windsor Sports Insurance behind them to protect their players.

Why Windsor?

Because professional sport needs professional advice and the best advice comes from Windsor Sports Insurance – insurance consultants to The Football League, The F.A. Premier League and The Football Association.

Windsor is one of the world's largest specialist sports, leisure and entertainment brokers covering players, clubs, leagues and national sports associations throughout the UK, Europe and world-wide.

Beyond Personal Accident Insurance, we provide cover for Stadium Risks, Legal Liabilities, Event Cancellation, Prize Performance and Incentive Indemnities and other insurance-protected sponsorship enhancements and marketing initiatives.

A separate Group company also provides consultancy on Group Pensions, Pension Scheme Administration and Personal Financial Planning.

So whatever the sport, whatever the risk, we are here to help you carry on.

...we're here to help you carry on.

For further information call The Sports Division on:-

Tel: +44(0) 171 407 7144
Fax: +44(0) 171 378 7961

WINDSOR
Sports Insurance Brokers

Professionals Dealin With Professionals

Forewords

I am extremely pleased to give the PFA's full endorsement and recommendation to Footballer's Factfile, which I consider to be the finest work of its kind, presenting a comprehensive coverage on statistics and profiles of every one of the 2,000 plus members of the PFA who played in first-team football throughout the Premier League and Football League in England and Wales during 1996-97.

The publication has again been sponsored by Windsor Insurance Brokers, key players in our industry with regard to the protection of players against injury, and is written and compiled once more by Barry Hugman whose record in this field is unsurpassed. The unique aspect of this book which makes it a must for every football enthusiast, manager, administrator, and commentator, is that there is a team of almost 100 people providing Barry with invaluable aspects of local information, thus giving the book that much more informative comment to underline the statistics.

Its coverage is wider than ever and reflects the present popularity of our game and its good health as we approach the next Millennium. We can also reflect on the success of Euro '96 and look forward to the World Cup campaign in Paris next summer with full anticipation, bearing in mind our success in the Tournoi de France and the development of some of our fine young players led by the PFA Young Player of the Year, David Beckham, and the continued quality of such as Alan Shearer helping to combine a fine blend of experience and youth.

We now have some of the finest stadiums in the world and, it is hoped, that with the increasing amount of money coming from television the game will prosper at all levels and pay due regard to the need to develop our own talent to compete with the foreign players who have been attracted to these shores.

It is hoped that the differences in income between the Premier League and the Football League do not cause a diminution in the viability of the lower division clubs and that those such as Crewe Alexandra can continue to prosper and continue the conveyor belt of talent that they have provided over recent years.

New retain and transfer rules since the Bosman decision will mean that in 1998 players aged 24 and over at the end of their contract will be literally free domestically and internationally, which should help to redress the balance when clubs are looking to assess whether to buy from abroad or, as in the past, pick up some "rough diamonds" amongst the lower division clubs.

The book is a must for everyone connected with football and will occupy a prominent position on my desk. I promise that anybody who purchases a copy will not be disappointed.

Gordon Taylor,
Chief Executive of the Professional Footballers' Association.

Yet again, Barry Hugman and his research team have produced what is quickly becoming regarded as the definitive authority on the facts and figures of professional footballers currently in the game.

The Windsor Insurance Group has been closely involved with professional football for 25 years and there is not an English player currently in the game who has not been insured for injury and sickness through our offices since the day he signed professional forms as an 18 year old.

Our close links with the Professional Football Association and the clubs, leagues, and national associations, give us tremendous pleasure and we are more than happy to continue to support and again lend our name as sponsors to this excellent publication.

Jonathan Ticehurst,
Managing Director of the Sports Division, Windsor Insurance Brokers Limited.

Editorial Introduction

Following on from last year's edition, the Factfile portrays the statistical career record of every FA Carling Premiership and Nationwide League player who made an appearance in 1996-97, whether it be in league football, the Football League (Coca-Cola) Cup, FA Cup (Sponsored by Littlewoods Pools), Charity Shield, European Cup, European Cup Winners' Cup, UEFA Cup, Auto Windscreen's Shield, or in the Play Offs. Not included are Inter-Toto Cup matches. It goes beyond mere statistics, however, with a write up on all of the 2,300 plus players involved and also records faithfully last season's playing records separately by club.

The work falls into two sections, both inter-relating. Firstly, the main core, PFA Footballers' Factfile: A-Z (pages 9 to 300), and secondly, FA Carling Premiership and Nationwide League Clubs: Summary of Appearances and Goals for 1996-97 (pages 301 to 316). Below is an explanation on how to follow the PFA Footballers' Factfile.

As the title suggests, all players are listed in alphabetical order and are shown by Surnames first, followed by full Christian names, with the one the player is commonly known by shown in **bold.** Any abbreviation or pseudonym is bracketed.

Birthplace/date: You will note that several players who would be predominately classified as British, were born in places like Germany and India, for example. My book, Football League Players' Records (last edition: 1992), which covered every man who had played league football since the war, has, in the past, used the family domicile as a more realistic "birthplace". But, for our purposes here, I have reverted to that which has been officially recorded.

Height and Weight: Listed in feet and inches, and stones and pounds, respectively. It must be remembered that a player's weight can frequently change and, on that basis, the recorded data should be used as a guide only, especially as they would have been weighed several times during the season.

Club Honours: Those shown, cover careers from the Conference and FA Trophy upwards. For abbreviations, read:- European Honours: EC (European Cup), ESC (European Super Cup), ECWC (European Cup Winners' Cup). English Honours: FAC (FA Cup), FLC (Football League Cup), CS (Charity Shield), FMC (Full Members Cup, which takes in the Simod and Zenith Data sponsorships), AMC (Associated Members Cup - Freight Rover, Sherpa Van, Leyland DAF, Autoglass and Auto Windscreen), AIC (Anglo-Italian Cup), GMVC (GM Vauxhall Conference), FAT (FA Trophy), FAYC (FA Youth Cup). Scottish Honours: SPD (Scottish Premier Division), S Div 1/2 (Scottish Leagues), SC (Scottish Cup), SLC (Scottish League Cup). Welsh Honours: WC (Welsh Cup). Note that honours applicable to players coming in from abroad are not shown, but the position will be reviewed in future editions.

International Honours: For abbreviations, read:- E (England), NI (Northern Ireland), S (Scotland), W (Wales)

and Ei (Republic of Ireland). Under 21 through to full internationals give total appearances (inclusive of subs), while schoolboy (U16s and U18s) and youth representatives are just listed. Not included are U20 matches, which will be recorded in future editions. The cut off date used for appearances was 30 June.

Player Descriptions: Gives position and playing strengths and, in keeping the work topical, a few words on how their season went in 1996-97. This takes into account, in a positive fashion, key performances, along with value to the team, injuries, honours, and other points of interest, etc. To allow for play off and international input to be included, and the publication date to be maintained, the cut-off date used was 30 June. Transfers, however, are shown as stop press if they took place after 18 May, the cut-off date used by the Football and Premier Leagues to produce the close season retained and free transfer lists. The decision was taken on the grounds that the May/June Registration and Transfer booklets would not be available until after going to press.

Career Records: Full appearances, plus substitutes and goals, are given for all Carling Premiership and Nationwide League games and, if a player who is in the book has played in any of the senior Scottish Leagues, his appearances with the club in question will also be recorded. Other information given, includes the origination of players (clubs in the non-leagues, junior football, or from abroad), registered signing dates (if a player signs permanently following a loan spell, for our purposes, we have shown the initial date as being the point of temporary transfer. Also, loan transfers are only recorded if an appearance is made), transfer fees (these are the figures that have been reported in newspapers and magazines and should only be used as a guide to a player's valuation), and a breakdown of matches by P/FL (Premiership and Football League), PL (Premier League), FL (Football League), FLC (Football League Cup), FAC (FA Cup), and Others. Other matches will take in the Welsh Cup, play offs, Anglo-Italian Cup, Auto Windscreen Shield, Charity Shield, and any major European competition. All of these matches are lumped together for reasons of saving space. Scottish appearances for players on loan to P/FL clubs in 1996-97 are shown at the point of transfer and do not include games following their return to Scotland.

Career statistics are depicted as
Appearances + Substitutes/Goals

Whether you wish to analyse someone for your fantasy football team selection or would like to know more about a little-known player appearing in the lower reaches of the game, the *PFA Footballers' Factfile* should provide you with the answer.

Barry J. Hugman, Editor, PFA Footballers' Factfile

PFA Footballers' Factfile : A-Z

ABLETT Gary Ian
Born: Liverpool, 19 November 1965
Height: 6'2" Weight: 12.7
Club Honours: Div 1 '88, '90; CS '88, '90, '95; FAC '89; '95
International Honours: E: B-1; U21-1
A distinguished natural left-footed player signed from Everton during the 1996 close season, Gary started 1996-97 for Birmingham at left back due to the injury to Martin Grainger, but was more settled and effective when moved to the centre of defence, where his experience proved crucial, his consistent, steady performances earning him the Clubman of the Year award, decided upon by manager, Trevor Francis. Missed a few games through injury, and captained the side in the absence of Steve Bruce and Barry Horne.
Liverpool (From apprentice on 19/11/83) FL 103+6/1 FLC 10+1 FAC 16+2 Others 9
Derby Co (Loaned on 25/1/85) FL 3+3 Others 2
Hull C (Loaned on 10/9/86) FL 5
Everton (£750,000 on 14/1/92) F/PL 128/5 FLC 12 FAC 12/1 Others 4
Sheffield U (Loaned on 1/3/96) FL 12
Birmingham C (£390,000 on 21/6/96) FL 39+3/1 FLC 4 FAC 3

Gary Ablett

ABRAHAMS Paul
Born: Colchester, 31 October 1973
Height: 5'9" Weight: 11.3
Colchester born Paul rejoined the U's from Brentford last October, for his third spell at Layer Road. He instantly reclaimed his position as a crowd favourite, largely operating on the left-hand side of the attack, scoring many vital goals in the promotion

challenge, including memorable efforts against Fulham, Rochdale and Swansea. Also bagged the winner at his old club, Brentford, in the AWS, but will be immortalised at Layer Road for scoring a stirring Golden Goal against Peterborough that sent United to Wembley.
Colchester U (From trainee on 11/8/92) FL 30+25/8 FLC 2+3 FAC 4/2 Others 3/2
Brentford (£30,000 on 9/3/95) FL 26+9/8 FLC 1+2 Others 1
Colchester U (Loaned on 29/12/95) FL 8/2 Others 1
Colchester U (£20,000 on 23/10/96) FL 27+2/7 FAC 1 Others 5+1/2

ADAMS Kieran Charles
Born: Cambridge, 20 October 1977
Height: 5'11" Weight: 11.6
A product of the YTS, the ball-playing Barnet midfielder grew in strength in 1996-97, but failed to make the full breakthrough into the first team, having just one start. Loaned to Hayes earlier in the campaign and St Albans in March, the coming season will be an important one for the skilful youngster.
Barnet (From trainee on 3/7/96) FL 4+4 FLC 0+1

ADAMS Michael (Micky) Richard
Born: Sheffield, 8 November 1961
Height: 5'8" Weight: 11.11
International Honours E: Yth
Injury and the success of players in his position restricted Micky to just five appearances for Fulham in 1996-97, but he more than compensated by guiding the club to their first promotion since 1982, his first full season in charge. Considering they were 71st in Football League when he took over in February 1996, and there was not a great deal of money available, his election as Third Division Manager of the Year was well deserved.
Gillingham (From apprentice on 1/11/79) FL 85+7/5 FLC 5 FAC 6
Coventry C (£75,000 on 19/7/83) FL 85+5/9 FLC 9/1 FAC 7 Others 2
Leeds U (£110,000 on 23/1/87) FL 72+1/2 FLC 4 FAC 6/1 Others 6
Southampton (£250,000 on 14/3/89) F/PL 141+3/7 FLC 16 FAC 8 Others 6
Stoke C (Free on 24/3/94) FL 10/3
Fulham (Free on 14/7/94) FL 25+4/8 FLC 4 FAC 2/4 Others 3/1

ADAMS Neil James
Born: Stoke, 23 November 1965
Height: 5'8" Weight: 10.12
Club Honours: CS '86; Div 1 '87, Div 2 '91
International Honours: E: U21-1
On reaching his 100th league game for Norwich during 1996-97, Neil became one of the most experienced players on the club's books, and a regular in the first team, who had his best scoring season in ten years when finishing with a very respectable total of 16. He also took over as the new penalty-kick king, claiming a 100 per-cent career record, leaving the manager, Mike Walker, to enthuse that he was the best he had ever

seen from the spot. A right winger with plenty of pace and enthusiasm, who is the master of the early cross, he runs at defenders to drive balls in, as well as going all the way himself on occasions. The epitome of consistency, he missed just one game, and that as a result of flu.
Stoke C (Signed on 1/7/85) FL 31+1/4 FLC 3 FAC 1 Others 3
Everton (£150,000 on 7/7/86) FL 17+3 FLC 4+1/1 Others 5+1
Oldham Ath (Loaned on 11/1/89) FL 9
Oldham Ath (£100,000 on 21/6/89) F/PL 93+36/23 FLC 13+2/1 FAC 10+2/2 Others 1+1
Norwich C (£250,000 on 17/2/94) P/FL 119+15/18 FLC 12+1/3 FAC 6/1

Tony Adams

ADAMS Tony Alexander
Born: Romford, 10 October 1966
Height: 6'3" Weight: 13.11
Club Honours: Div 1 '89, '91; FLC '87, '93; FAC '93; ECWC '94
International Honours: E: 47; B-4; U21-5; Yth
Unfortunately, the knee injury that the Arsenal and England centre back carried through Euro '96 kept him out of the 1996-97 season until late September. Still as determined and as inspirational as ever, Tony came back, putting his well-documented drinking problems well and truly behind him to enjoy a wonderful campaign, as Arsene Wenger's system released him as a potent attacking force. Included among his three strikes was a traditional one in the derby game against arch-rivals, Tottenham, and another when he started and finished a move with a diving header at Leicester. As rock solid as ever, both on the ground and in the air, his never-say-die spirit getting him to block ons and

recovering tackles, it was hardly surprising that he was part of a defence that conceded just 32 goals, the lowest total in the Premiership. Yet again voted by his fellow professionals as being worthy of a place in the PFA award winning Premiership side, the Gunners would surely struggle without his invigorating presence. Also specialises in striking long balls behind the opposition.
Arsenal (From apprentice on 30/1/84) F/PL 391+4/27 FLC 56+1/5 FAC 34+1/5 Others 29/3

ADCOCK Anthony (Tony) Charles
Born: Bethnal Green, 27 February 1963
Height: 5'10" Weight: 11.9
Once again Tony finished a season as Colchester's top goalscorer, despite an untypically slow start to 1996-97 and a three-month spell out of the side, marking his return to action in January with a brace at Millwall in the AWS, following which normal service was resumed and the goals flowed more regularly. Is now only six league goals away from an all-time United record.
Colchester U (From apprentice on 31/3/81) FL 192+18/98 FLC 16+1/5 FAC 12+2/3 Others 9/6
Manchester C (£75,000 on 1/6/87) FL 12+3/5 FLC 2+1/1 FAC 2 Others 2/3
Northampton T (£85,000 on 25/1/88) FL 72/30 FLC 6/3 FAC 1 Others 4/1
Bradford C (£190,000 on 6/10/89) FL 33+5/6 FLC 1 FAC 0+1 Others 2
Northampton T (£75,000 on 11/1/91) FL 34+1/10 FLC 1 FAC 1/1 Others 2/1
Peterborough U (£35,000 on 30/12/91) FL 107+4/35 FLC 8+1/3 FAC 5/1 Others 3+2
Luton T (£20,000 on 4/8/94) FL 0+2 FAC 0+1
Colchester U (Free on 3/8/95) FL 67+10/23 FLC 5+1/2 FAC 1+1 Others 9+1/6

ADCOCK Paul Malcolm
Born: Ilminster, 2 May 1972
Height: 5'8" Weight: 10.2
Freed by Bath during the 1996 close season, having dropped off their goalscoring standard, Paul joined Torquay and played in two of the first three games of 1996-97 as a sub. Although quick off the mark and fairly sharp, competition for forward places at that time was tough due to the good form of Rodney Jack and Paul Baker and he left the league to play for Gloucester City in November.
Plymouth Arg (From trainee on 7/8/90) FL 11+10/2 FLC 1+1 FAC 3 Others 0+1 (Free to Bath C during 1993 close season)
Torquay U (Free on 16/8/96) FL 0+1 FLC 0+1

ADEBOLA Bamberdele (Dele)
Born: Lagos, Nigeria, 23 June 1975
Height: 6'3" Weight: 12.8
Despite having two spells out through injury, Dele finished 1996-97 as Crewe's leading scorer with 18 to his credit as the club moved into the first division for the first time in its history, via the play offs. Deceptively quick for a big man, and steadily improving, his strike rate of one in every two games last season compared favourably with many of his counterparts and included four braces. Is good in the air and a natural left footer.
Crewe Alex (From trainee on 21/6/93) FL 72+25/32 FLC 3+2/2 FAC 7+2/3 Others 10+1/2

ADEKOLA David Adeolu
Born: Nigeria, 19 May 1968
Height: 5'11" Weight: 12.10
International Honours: Nigeria: 1
Brought to Brighton for a month's trial from Cologne based club, Preussain, last September, this widely travelled former Nigerian international did not enjoy the best of times at the Goldstone. Drafted into the forward line for the home game with Cambridge on 12 October, he suffered a knee injury in the second half and was substituted as Albion went down 2-1. Was released at the end of his trial period and rejoined one of his former clubs, Bishop's Stortford.
Bury (Signed on 15/1/93) FL 21+14/12 FLC 0+1 FAC 1 Others 3+1
Exeter C (Loaned on 18/2/94) FL 1+2/1
Bournemouth (Free on 29/9/94) FLC 0+1
Wigan Ath (Free on 14/10/94) FL 1+3 FAC 0+1 Others 0+1
Hereford U (Free on 2/2/95. Free to Bath C during 1995 close season)
Cambridge U (Free on 18/8/95) FL 1+4/1 FLC 2 Others 1+1/1 (Free to Preussain in December 1995)
Brighton & HA (Free on 11/10/96) FL 1

AGANA Patrick Anthony (Tony)
Born: Bromley, 2 October 1963
Height: 6'0" Weight: 12.2
Club Honours: AIC '95
International Honours: E: SP-1
A very powerful left-sided attacker, and the former partner of Leeds' Brian Deane before becoming Notts County's record signing back in 1991, the hugely popular Tony was allowed to join struggling Hereford on transfer deadline day. Still adept at holding the ball up for his team mates, his two goals from the subs' bench were not enough to keep the side in the Football League and he seems certain to be playing in the Conference this coming term.
Watford (£35,000 from Weymouth on 13/8/87) FL 12+3/1 FLC 1+1/2 FAC 2 Others 1
Sheffield U (£45,000 on 19/2/88) FL 105+13/42 FLC 12/3 FAC 14/5 Others 4+1/1
Leeds U (Loaned on 27/2/92) FL 1+1
Notts Co (£750,000 on 12/11/91) FL 114+31/15 FLC 8+1/2 FAC 7+3/4 Others 17+1/3
Hereford U (Free on 28/3/97) FL 3+2/2

AGNEW Paul
Born: Lisburn, 15 August 1965
Height: 5'9" Weight: 10.12
International Honours: NI: U23-1; Yth; Sch
Unfortunately, West Brom's left back was again hampered by injury during the first half of last season (like he had been in 1995-96) and when he did return to action early in the New Year he found it difficult to hold down a first team place, as well as being plagued by more niggling injuries. A strong tackler, who loves joining up with the attack, he was ever reliable, nevertheless, despite being released during the summer.
Grimsby T (£4,000 from Cliftonville on 15/2/84) FL 219+23/3 FLC 17+1 FAC 23+1 Others 12+2
West Bromwich A (£65,000 on 23/2/95) FL 38+1/1 FLC 1 FAC 0+1

AGNEW Stephen (Steve) Mark
Born: Shipley, 9 November 1965

Height: 5'10" Weight: 11.9
Club Honours: Div 1 '96
Midfielder Steve endured a frustrating season at Sunderland in 1996-97, due to constant injury problems. Managed two goals, however, both of which came against Coventry City – a tremendous left-foot volley at Roker Park and a penalty at Highfield Road – before a badly-broken wrist at Arsenal in January meant that he could only watch from the sidelines as the club were relegated from the Premiership. Has great passing ability and vision to match and is always dangerous at free kicks.
Barnsley (From apprentice on 10/11/83) FL 186+8/29 FLC 13/3 FAC 20/4 Others 6+1
Blackburn Rov (£700,000 on 25/6/91) FL 2 FLC 2
Portsmouth (Loaned on 21/11/92) FL 3+2 Others 2
Leicester C (£250,000 on 9/2/93) F/PL 52+4/4 FLC 4+1 FAC 2 Others 2
Sunderland (£250,000 on 11/1/95) P/FL 53+7/9 FLC 3 FAC 2+1/1

Steve Agnew

AGOSTINO Paul
Born: Woodville, Australia, 9 June 1975
Height: 6'0" Weight: 12.12
International Honours: Australia: 2
Paul was a regular in the Bristol City side throughout most of last season, forming an excellent partnership with Shaun Goater and was in great form, especially during December, notching four goals against St Albans in the FA Cup and putting on a brilliant display in the league game against Bristol Rovers at Ashton Gate. Unfortunately, City lost the services of this talented player at the end of the campaign, when he exercised his rights under freedom of contract and signed for the German club, Munich 1860.
Bristol C (£50,000 from Young Boys of Berne on 18/7/95) FL 63+21/19 FLC 6+2/2 FAC 4/5 Others 4+2

Paul Agostino

AINSWORTH Gareth
Born: Blackburn, 10 May 1973
Height: 5'10" Weight: 12.5
A fast and skilful right-sided winger with the knack of scoring goals, he was Lincoln's only ever present in 1996-97 and finished as leading scorer after becoming the first City player to reach 20 league goals in a season since 1982-83. Hugely popular with the fans who voted him Player of the Year, Gareth was also selected for the PFA division three team and finished second to Wigan's Graeme Jones in the division's scoring charts.
Preston NE (Signed from Northwich Vic, via Blackburn Rov YTS, on 21/1/92) FL 2+3 Others 1/1
Cambridge U (Free on 17/8/92) FL 1+3/1 FLC 0+1
Preston NE (Free on 23/12/92) FL 76+6/12 FLC 3+2 FAC 3+1 Others 8+1/1
Lincoln C (£25,000 on 31/10/95) FL 77/34 FLC 6/2 FAC 2 Others 4/1

AISTON Samuel (Sam) James
Born: Newcastle, 21 November 1976
Height: 6'1" Weight: 12.10
Club Honours: Div 1 '96
International Honours: E: Sch
This promising left winger made a handful of substitute appearances for Sunderland early on in 1996-97, before moving to Chester on loan in February and staying for the remainder of the season. Quickly becoming a favourite of the fans at the Deva, his tremendous pace often leaving full backs standing, Sam made an indelible contribution to City's play-off push and surely has a great future ahead of him.
Sunderland (Free from Newcastle U juniors on 14/7/95) P/FL 4+12 FLC 0+1 FAC 0+2
Chester C (Loaned on 21/2/97) FL 14 FLC 1 Others 2

AKINBIYI Adeola (Ade) Peter
Born: Hackney, 10 October 1974
Height: 6'1" Weight: 12.9
Tony Pulis, finally got his man after many months, despite the fact he had to pay a club record fee of £250,000 to acquire his services from Brighton last January. A fleet-footed striker, he scored a tremendous first goal for Gillingham on his home debut against Plymouth Argyle and Pulis went on record to say that the supporters would not see the best of him until the coming season. Most Gills fans can hardly wait!
Norwich C (From trainee on 5/2/93) P/FL 22+27/3 FLC 2+4/2 FAC 1+2 Others 0+1
Hereford U (Loaned on 21/1/94) FL 3+1/2
Brighton & Hove A (Loaned on 24/11/94) FL 7/4
Gillingham (£250,000 on 13/1/97) FL 19/7

ALBERT Philippe
Born: Bouillon, Belgium, 10 August 1967
Height: 6'3" Weight: 13.7
International Honours: Belgium: 42
The Belgian international is a tall, cultured, central defender for whom last season was his third in Newcastle's colours, following his signing of an extended four-year contract. Calm and confident under pressure, and a player who enjoys using his skill on the ball to join the attack where his powerful shooting poses a constant threat to the opposition, he started the campaign in the side, but after three games was dropped for the visit to Sunderland when Darren Peacock was preferred. An injury to Steve Howey led to his recall in October and he turned in a class performance against Derby, form he subsequently maintained to make him a regular in the side. His goals were rarer than in 1995-96, but he scored with an exquisite 20-yard chip over Peter Schmeichel in the victory against Manchester United, and his counter in the rout of Spurs was Newcastle's 600th league goal. While the arrival of Mark Lawrenson and Kenny Dalglish at the club resulted in him curbing his attacking flair, he proved himself a top-class defender until a knee injury necessitated a minor operation at the end of March and put him out of action for all but the remaining three games.
Newcastle U (£2,650,000 from Anderlecht, via Charleroi and Mechelen, on 10/8/94) PL 63+4/8 FLC 8+1/2 FAC 4/1 Others 12+1/1

ALCIDE Colin James
Born: Huddersfield, 14 April 1972
Height: 6'2" Weight: 12.9
Powerful left-sided Lincoln midfielder who was also used as a target man up front in 1996-97. Although only in his second season as a full-time professional, Colin showed himself to be a very effective team player with the ability to score goals, including two effective equalisers and two in each leg of a 5-4 aggregate win over Hartlepool in the Coca-Cola Cup.
Lincoln C (£15,000 from Emley on 5/12/95) FL 60+9/14 FLC 4+2/2 FAC 1 Others 2

ALDRIDGE John William
Born: Liverpool, 18 September 1958
Height: 5'11" Weight: 12.3
Club Honours: WC '80; Div 2 '85, Div 1 '88; FLC '86; CS '88; FAC '89
International Honours: Ei: 69
In his first full season as Tranmere's player/ manager, John passed the milestone of 468 career goals, surpassing the record previously held by Jimmy Greaves and, once again, he ended a campaign as the club's highest goalscorer, with a total of 20 in all competitions. However, to allow himself more time to concentrate on the job of managing Rovers, he decided to retire from international football with Eire, just one goal short of equalling their scoring record, and, although he named himself as substitute on 11 occasions, he shows no sign of hanging up his boots at club level just yet. Always a passionate and committed player, the striker was sent off in the third round FA Cup tie at Carlisle.
Newport Co (£3,500 from South Liverpool on 2/5/79) FL 159+11/69 FLC 11/5 FAC 12+1/7 Others 4/2
Oxford U (£78,000 on 21/3/84) FL 111+3/72 FLC 17/14 FAC 5/2 Others 5/2
Liverpool (£750,000 on 27/1/87) FL 69+14/50 FLC 7+1/3 FAC 12/8 Others 1/2 (£1,000,000 to Real Sociedad on 1/9/89)
Tranmere Rov (£250,000 on 11/7/91) FL 214+14/133 FLC 25/22 FAC 8+1/4 Others 18/10

ALDRIDGE Martin James
Born: Northampton, 6 December 1974
Height: 5'11" Weight: 12.2
Last season, Martin battled with Paul Moody for the Oxford strikers' role alongside Nigel Jemson and enjoyed some success, notably a 15-minute hat trick against Sheffield United. Worked hard and coped well with the higher division and celebrated most of his goals with a backwards somersault. Also developed his long throw as an added attacking force for the United forwards. Finished as second top scorer with nine goals and would probably have notched more if a series of minor knocks had not hampered him.
Northampton T (From trainee on 27/8/93) FL 50+20/17 FLC 1+2 FAC 1+1/1 Others 5+2/4
Oxford U (Free on 22/12/95) FL 33+15/17 FLC 5+2/1 FAC 2+2

ALEXANDER Graham
Born: Coventry, 10 October 1971
Height: 5'10" Weight: 12.7
An industrious, fierce-tackling midfielder who was an automatic choice for Luton in their bid to regain division one status last season, missing just two games. Although capable of tearing the opposition's midfield apart when at his best, he occasionally found the game passing him by. But for sheer effort and honesty he was one of the first names on the team sheet week in and week out. Although scoring comparatively few goals for a player with attacking flair and excellent shot, he was always a danger when in shooting distance. Also combined well with others.
Scunthorpe U (From trainee on 20/3/90) FL 149+10/18 FLC 11+1/2 FAC 12/1 Others 13+3/3
Luton T (£100,000 on 8/7/95) FL 79+3/4 FLC 8 FAC 3+1 Others 4+2

ALLAN Derek Thomas
Born: Irvine, 24 December 1974
Height: 6'0" Weight: 12.1
International Honours: S: Yth

A most reliable defender, Derek missed only a handful of games through injury during 1996-97 and developed a good understanding with Gary Hobson at the heart of the Brighton defence. The 23-year-old Scot displayed admirable qualities and was particularly impressive during Albion's resurgence in the latter half of the campaign, though he missed the hectic run in due to an injury.

Ayr U (Trainee) SL 5
Southampton (£75,000 on 16/3/93) PL 0+1
Brighton & Hove A (Free on 28/3/96) FL 39 FLC 2 Others 1

ALLEN Bradley James
Born: Romford, 13 September 1971
Height: 5'7" Weight: 10.7
International Honours: E: U21-8; Yth

Another season plagued with injuries saw Bradley only start in a third of Charlton's fixtures, being out of the side from last November until late April. Comfortable on the ball, and with good awareness, he found the net on six occasions, before suffering a foot ligament injury which ultimately required an operation. Has proved his capabilities whilst in the team and when fully fit should continue to find the net on a regular basis.

Queens Park R (From juniors on 30/9/88) F/PL 56+25/27 FLC 5+2/5 FAC 3+2 Others 1
Charlton Ath (£400,000 on 28/3/96) FL 23+5/7 FLC 3/2 Others 1+1

ALLEN Christopher (Chris) Anthony
Born: Oxford, 18 November 1972
Height: 5'11" Weight: 12.2
International Honours: E: U21-2

Having hoped to sign for Nottingham Forest the previous season, when he had a spell on loan at the City Ground, Chris finally got his chance to move from Oxford following a tribunal agreed fee in the summer of 1996. However, he failed to secure a regular berth on the left wing, playing sporadically, apart from a run of six games, but scored in the 3-0 FA Cup win over Ipswich. Has tremendous pace and uses this to beat his man, although he may need to add guile to speed in order to drop the more capable defenders.

Oxford U (From trainee on 14/5/91) FL 110+40/12 FLC 11+2/4 FAC 5+5/1 Others 5+3
Nottingham F (Loaned on 24/2/96) PL 1+2/1
Nottingham F (£300,000 on 3/7/96) PL 16+8 FAC 1/1

ALLEN Graham
Born: Bolton, 8 April 1977
Height: 6'1" Weight: 12.8
International Honours: E: Yth

A determined and aggressive Everton footballer, Graham is equally at home in central defence or when employed as a defensive midfielder. Although regularly sitting on the substitutes' bench during 1996-97, he actually appeared on the field of play only briefly, coming on as a 14th minute substitute at Middlesbrough during the height of an injury crisis before making way for Marc Hottiger. Looks to be a good un though.

Everton (From trainee on 10/12/94) PL 0+1

ALLEN Martin James
Born: Reading, 14 August 1965
Height: 5'10" Weight: 11.0
International Honours: E: U21-2; Yth

The battling Portsmouth midfielder's season was interrupted for the most part by injuries in 1996-97, but his reappearance on the bench towards the end of the campaign added some much needed experience to the squad in their surge for a play-off spot. From a famous footballing family, his dad, Dennis, played for Charlton, Reading and Bournemouth, uncle Les was at Chelsea, Spurs and QPR, and of his cousins, Clive has now retired, whilst Bradley and Paul are still going strong. Nicknamed "Mad Dog", Martin loves to be involved and, although physical, is also very constructive. He also packs a good shot in his boots.

Queens Park R (From apprentice on 27/5/83) FL 128+8/16 FLC 15+3/1 FAC 9/1 Others 2/1
West Ham U (£675,000 on 24/8/89) F/PL 163+27/26 FLC 15+3/5 FAC 14/4 Others 10
Portsmouth (Loaned on 11/9/95) FL 15/3
Portsmouth (£500,000 on 22/2/96) FL 15+1/1 FAC 0+1

Paul Allen

ALLEN Paul Kevin
Born: Aveley, 28 August 1962
Height: 5'7" Weight: 11.4
Club Honours: FAC '80, '91; CS '91; Div 2 '96
International Honours: E: U21-3; Yth (UEFAYC '80)

The veteran midfielder started last season for Swindon in his familiar right-wing back role before losing his place after three games. Recalled to first-team duty in

September and October, but only briefly, and with little prospect of regular Football League action, he was allowed to move on to Bristol City in mid term. Ironically, for an infrequent scorer, he netted on his final appearance for the club - his first and last goal for the Robins. For Bristol City, his foraging runs down the right flank quickly made him a favourite of the Ashton Gate crowd and it was a little surprising that he was released without an offer of a new contract at the end of the campaign.

West Ham U (From apprentice on 29/8/79) FL 149+3/6 FLC 20+4/2 FAC 15+3/3 Others 2+1
Tottenham H (£400,000 on 19/6/85) F/PL 276+16/23 FLC 42+2/4 FAC 26+1/1 Others 12+2
Southampton (£550,000 on 16/9/93) PL 40+3/1 FLC 4 FAC 2
Luton T (Loaned on 9/12/94) FL 4
Stoke C (Loaned on 20/1/95) FL 17/1 Others 2
Swindon T (Free on 11/10/95) FL 30+7/1 FLC 2 FAC 5/1 Others 1
Bristol C (Free on 16/1/97) FL 13+1 Others 3

ALLEN Rory William
Born: Beckenham, 17 October 1977
Height: 5'11" Weight: 11.2

Predatory Tottenham striker who, with four goals in so few appearances in 1996-97, won praise from Teddy Sheringham who described him as "massively talented and having tremendous potential". Composed and intelligent in his use of the ball, Rory made his Premiership debut when coming off the bench a minute into the second half at Wimbledon in September and impressed enough to warrant a full outing three days later at White Hart Lane against Newcastle. Despite the team suffering a 2-1 home defeat, Rory opened his scoring account and later added two more against Preston in the Coca-Cola Cup, plus another during a 2-1 home defeat at the hands of Manchester United, and definitely has the ability to eventually establish himself as a regular first teamer.

Tottenham H (From trainee on 28/3/96) PL 9+3/2 FLC 2+1/2 FAC 1

ALLISON Neil James
Born: Hull, 20 October 1973
Height: 6'2" Weight: 11.10

Surprisingly released by Hull City at the end of last October, the uncomplicated centre back then lived a nomadic existence, which included a trial at Swindon Town, a month with Sligo Rovers in Ireland and helping North Ferriby United on their way to the FA Carlsberg Vase final before joining Chesterfield on a short-term contract, soon after their FA Cup quarter-final win.

Hull C (From trainee on 13/7/92) FL 95+11/3 FLC 7+1/1 FAC 3 Others 6+1
Swindon T (Free on 25/11/96 - Released to Sligo Rov in December 1996)
Chesterfield (Free from North Ferriby U on 11/3/97) FL 0+2

ALLISON Wayne Anthony
Born: Huddersfield, 16 October 1968
Height: 6'1" Weight: 13.5
Club Honours: Div 2 '96

Once again Swindon's top scorer in 1996-97 with 13 League and Cup goals, but, although a regular first-choice striker throughout the

campaign his strike rate was disappointing after Christmas (having netted ten beforehand), with only three more goals to his credit. A hard-working forward who is strong in the air, he is always ready to lend his support to the defence when necessary.
Halifax T (From trainee on 6/7/87) FL 74+10/23 FLC 3/2 FAC 4+1/2 Others 8+1/3
Watford (£250,000 on 26/7/89) FL 6+1
Bristol C (£300,000 on 9/8/90) FL 149+46/48 FLC 4+5/2 FAC 12+1/5 Others 6+2/2
Swindon T (£475,000 on 22/7/95) FL 82+3/28 FLC 7/3 FAC 7/2 Others 3

ALLON Joseph (Joe) Ball
Born: Gateshead, 12 November 1966
Height: 5'11" Weight: 13.6
Club Honours: FAYC '85
International Honours: E: Yth
Although he was again the club's top goalscorer in 1996-97, it was an up-and-down season for Hartlepool's opportunist striker. Began in good form, but was then troubled by a run of minor injuries which caused him to lose his edge and saw him transfer listed. At that stage of the campaign, he looked to be out of the picture until making a dramatic return at Darlington when coming on as substitute in the 83rd minute to score a last-gasp goal which clinched a vital 2-1 win. The following week he further proved his worth by scoring two goals in the 4-0 defeat of Barnet, which confirmed Pool's safety from relegation.
Newcastle U (From trainee on 16/11/84) FL 9/2 FLC 1
Swansea C (Free on 6/8/87) FL 27+7/11 FLC 2 FAC 2 Others 2/1
Hartlepool U (Free on 29/11/88) FL 112+48 FLC 5/2 FAC 6+1/5 Others 7/2
Chelsea (£250,000 on 14/8/91) FL 3+11/2 FLC 0+2 Others 1+1/1
Port Vale (Loaned on 27/2/92) FL 2+4
Brentford (£275,000 on 19/11/92) FL 38+7/19 FLC 2 FAC 2/2 Others 7/7
Southend U (Loaned on 16/9/93) FL 2+1
Port Vale (Signed on 24/3/94) FL 13+10/9 FLC 0+1 FAC 2/1
Lincoln C (£42,500 on 17/7/95) FL 3+1 FLC 1
Hartlepool U (£42,500 on 13/10/95) FL 49+3/17 FLC 2/2 FAC 1 Others 3/1

ALLOTT Mark Stephen
Born: Manchester, 3 October 1977
Height: 5'10" Weight: 11.6
The 19-year-old centre forward burst onto the Football League scene for Oldham last October when scoring a spectacular goal at Bolton on his debut. Having come off the bench with 13 minutes left and with Latics 3-0 down, within eight minutes he had bent the ball round the 'keeper with the outside of his foot for a superb strike. Four more subs' appearances followed and the youth side's top scorer is reckoned to have a tremendous future in the game. Holds the ball up exceptionally well for the lay off.
Oldham Ath (From trainee on 14/10/95) FL 0+5/1

ALSFORD Julian
Born: Poole, 24 December 1972
Height: 6'2" Weight: 13.7
An ever improving Chester central defender, Julian had a tremendous season in 1996-97, making 43 league appearances and scoring

his first goals for a club that only failed at the final hurdle to climb out of the third division, via the play offs. Voted the Best Away Player of the Year, he has progressed continuously since arriving from Watford. Can also play at full back if required.
Watford (From trainee on 30/4/91) FL 9+4/1 FLC 1 Others 2
Chester C (Free on 11/8/94) FL 97+5/2 FLC 6+1 FAC 6 Others 7

ALSOP Julian Mark
Born: Nuneaton, 28 May 1973
Height: 6'4" Weight: 13.0
Julian, a powerful targetman, made a remarkable transition from part-time football to the professional game after joining Bristol Rovers from Tamworth last February. Opened his goal account in only his second appearance as a substitute at Burnley and showed promise for the future as he became used to full time training and attained match fitness. His aerial ability will certainly test most second division defences in 1997-98.
Bristol Rov (£15,000 from Halesowen on 14/2/97) FL 10+6/3

Kwame Ampadu

AMPADU Patrick Kwame
Born: Bradford, 20 December 1970
Height: 5'10" Weight: 11.10
Club Honours: AMC '94
International Honours: Ei: U21-4; Yth
Despite signing a new contract for Swansea prior to the start of last season, "Paddy" struggled to show consistency and was demoted to the reserves. He soon regained some form, however, and, after being

brought back into the first team, produced a high standard of play, also scoring vital goals from midfield. Not only attack minded, he is equally sound where defensive duties are concerned.
Arsenal (From trainee on 19/11/88) FL 0+2
Plymouth Arg (Loaned on 31/10/90) FL 6/1 Others 1
West Bromwich A (£50,000 on 24/6/91) FL 27+22/4 FLC 6+1 FAC 1 Others 5/1
Swansea C (£15,000 on 16/2/94) FL 112+17/12 FLC 6+1/1 FAC 5/1 Others 16/1

ANDERSEN Lief Erik
Born: Fredrickstad, Norway, 19 April 1971
Height: 6'5" Weight: 14.10
Started last season in the Crystal Palace first-team squad, scoring his first goal for the club in the 3-1 home win over Manchester City, before several leaks in the defence found him demoted to the reserves. At 6'5" the tallest Palace player ever, although his headwork was undoubted as you would expect, his ability on the ground failed to match up and he was offered a free transfer in February by the then manager, Dave Bassett. Stayed on in the reserves, however, before an injury, followed by an operation, saw him return to Norway.
Crystal Palace (£120,000 from Moss FK on 18/1/96) FL 19+11/1 FLC 3 FAC 1 Others 1

ANDERSON Ijah Massai
Born: Hackney, 30 December 1975
Height: 5'8" Weight: 10.6
This left back with plenty of pace was an ever present for Brentford in the league in 1996-97. Also good going forward to join up with the midfielders and strikers, he scored in a 2-1 defeat at Bournemouth after cutting in from the flank to beat the 'keeper. Not only an attacking player, but is defensively sound when the need be.
Southend U (Free from Tottenham H juniors on 2/8/94)
Brentford (Free on 31/7/95) FL 71/3 FLC 6/1 FAC 3+2 Others 4+1

ANDERSON Lee Charles
Born: Tottington, 4 October 1973
Height: 5'9" Weight: 11.3
Lee started out with Bury in 1991, playing 38 times, before stepping out of the league to join Altrincham during the 1995 close season. A player who is small in stature but not lacking in bravery, he came back to the Football League with Doncaster on transfer deadline day last March, via Southport, and immediately settled into the left-back slot, showing good, quick feet in the six games played. Signed on non-contract terms, he was not retained.
Bury (From trainee on 16/10/91) FL 27+2 FLC 5 FAC 2 Others 1+1 (Free to Altrincham during 1995 close season)
Doncaster Rov (Free from Southport on 27/3/97) FL 6

ANDERTON Darren Robert
Born: Southampton, 3 March 1972
Height: 6'1" Weight: 12.0
International Honours: E: 16; U21-12; Yth
Quick, intelligent winger who made a terrific contribution to England's Euro '96

campaign despite being injured for much of 1995-96. Alas, the story of 1996-97 was similar, with his season wrecked by groin and hamstring injuries, rare appearances only rubbed salt into the wounds of the Tottenham faithful when Darren displayed the sheer brilliance so badly missing from the attack. When scoring against West Ham and Liverpool, he reminded the Premier League and Glenn Hoddle that a fully fit Darren Anderton is not only a pleasure to watch, but a must for inclusion at club and international level and both Gerry Francis and Hoddle will be hoping that his summer trip to Sweden for medical treatment pays dividends for 1997-98 and the World Cup Finals in France which follow.

Portsmouth (From trainee on 5/2/90) FL 53+9/7 FLC 3+2/1 FAC 7+1/5 Others 2
Tottenham H (£1,750,000 on 3/6/92) PL 124+8/229 FLC 13/4 FAC 13+1/2

ANDREWS Philip (Phil)
Born: Andover, 14 September 1976
Height: 5'11" Weight: 11.0
Having warmed Brighton's bench on a regular basis during the first half of last season, this 20-year-old striker made the starting line up in the absence of Ian Baird for the New Years Day fixture at Torquay and bagged his first senior goal with a well taken header as Albion went down 2-1. Despite being a lively lad who showed fair promise, he was released during the summer.

Brighton & Hove A (From trainee on 17/5/95) FL 2+23/1 FLC 1+2 FAC 1+2 Others 1+2

ANDREWS Wayne Michael Hill
Born: Paddington, 25 November 1977
Height: 5'11" Weight: 11.6
The promising young Watford striker confirmed the good impression he made in his debut season when establishing himself in the first team squad in 1996-97. Possessing a strong physical presence and a startling turn of foot, he was seen to best effect when running on to through passes. Scored six goals, including a winner in stoppage time at Notts county.

Watford (From trainee on 5/7/96) FL 16+10/4 FLC 3/1 FAC 0+2 Others 2/1

ANELKA Nicolas
Born: Versailles, France, 27 March 1979
Height: 5'11" Weight: 12.3
In following Patrick Vieira and Remi Garde to Arsenal to join up with the Gunners' French manager, Arsene Wenger, last March, young Nicolas merely strengthened that country's foothold at Highbury. Having made his name with Paris St Germain, but unable to sign professional forms until he was 18, the 17-year-old striker was still very much a free agent, which allowed Wenger to move in and spark fury at what the French club called ungentlemanly conduct. The issue was eventually resolved when it was recognised that the youngster never intended settling in France, despite the bait of a six-year contract. Came off the bench at Chelsea to make his Premier League bow and immediately impressed with his

excellent touch and pace, so much so that he made three further subs' appearances before the campaign ended. Could take the Premiership by storm in 1997-98.

Arsenal (£500,000+ from Paris St Germain on 6/3/97) PL 0+4

Nicolas Anelka

ANGEL Mark
Born: Newcastle, 23 August 1975
Height: 5'8" Weight: 11.1
A tricky winger in his second term with Oxford, Mark had to wait until the mid point of 1996-97 for a run in the side and started back with a goal against Stoke. Equally at home on either flank, he also likes to cut inside and test 'keepers with his long-range attempts. For a small player, it was unusual to see him score at Portsmouth with a towering header.

Sunderland (From Walker Central on 31/12/93)
Oxford U (Free on 9/8/95) FL 31+20/3 FLC 2+2 FAC 4+1 Others 2+1/1

ANGELL Brett Ashley
Born: Marlborough, 20 August 1968
Height: 6'2" Weight: 13.11
The tall striker made a triumphant return to Stockport, the club where he began his career at the start of 1996-97 and, after scoring a hatful of goals during his loan period from Sunderland, Brett was signed on a permanent basis in November. Continued to grab vital goals in County's amazing Coca-Cola Cup run and promotion chase, his 20th of the season clinched promotion to the first division in the penultimate match at Chesterfield.

Portsmouth (From trainee on 1/8/86)
Derby Co (£40,000 from Cheltenham T on 19/2/88)
Stockport Co (£33,000 on 20/10/88) FL 60+10/28 FLC 3 FAC 3/1 Others 8/4

Southend U (£100,000 on 2/8/90) FL 109+6/47 FLC 7+1/4 FAC 3/2 Others 9+1/10
Everton (£500,000 on 17/1/94) PL 16+4/1 FLC 0+1
Sunderland (£600,000 on 23/3/95) FL 10 FLC 1/1
Sheffield U (Loaned on 30/1/96) FL 6/2
West Bromwich A (Loaned on 28/3/96) FL 0+3
Stockport Co (£120,000 on 19/8/96) FL 30+4/15 FLC 8+2/3 FAC 3/1 Others 4+1/1

ANGUS Terence (Terry) Norman
Born: Coventry, 14 January 1966
Height: 6'0" Weight: 13.9
A great favourite with the Fulham crowd, Terry's defensive qualities were a big asset in the team's successful promotion bid in 1996-97. Selected as Man of the Match in the Cottagers' 1-1 home leg against Ipswich Town in the Coca-Cola Cup, the centre back also scored a vital equaliser against Exeter at Craven Cottage on Boxing Day. Is equally as competent at full back.

Northampton T (£15,000 from VS Rugby on 22/8/90) FL 115+1/6 FLC 7 FAC 5+1 Others 9
Fulham (Free on 12/7/93) FL 107+15/5 FLC 7+2 FAC 6/1 Others 12/1

ANSAH Andrew (Andy)
Born: Lewisham, 19 March 1969
Height: 5'10" Weight: 11.1
A centre forward, cum right winger, Andy joined Leyton Orient on a non-contract basis last October after being released by Gillingham and then trialling at a number of clubs without success. Tricky, with the ability to run at an opponent and able to cross from either foot, he made a couple of appearances as a sub before being released and signing for Hayes.

Brentford (Free from Dorking on 21/3/89) FL 3+5/2 FLC 0+1
Southend U (Free on 29/3/90) FL 141+16/33 FLC 7+2 FAC 4 Others 7+3/5
Brentford (Loaned on 4/11/94) FL 2+1/1 Others 2/1
Brentford (Loaned on 15/11/95) FL 6/1 Others 1
Peterborough U (Free on 15/3/96) FL 0+2/1
Gillingham (Free on 28/3/96) FL 0+2
Leyton Orient (Free on 19/12/96) FL 0+2

ANTHONY Graham John
Born: South Shields, 9 August 1975
Height: 5'9" Weight: 10.8
A talented young midfielder with good passing skills, his chances of first-team action in his fourth season as a professional at Sheffield United in 1996-97 seemed more and more remote, despite two outings from the bench. He was thus allowed to move to Swindon on trial on transfer deadline day, making his debut on Easter Monday in the traumatic 5-1 defeat by relegated Oldham. Two further appearances followed, but it was hard for an inexperienced newcomer to make his mark in a struggling team and he was released at the end of the season.

Sheffield U (From trainee on 7/7/93) FL 0+3 FLC 1 Others 2
Scarborough (Loaned on 1/3/96) FL 2
Swindon T (Free on 26/3/97) FL 3

ANTHROBUS Stephen (Steve) Anthony
Born: Lewisham, 10 November 1968
Height: 6'2" Weight: 14.11
A striker and real crowd favourite. Very strong and impressive in the air, Steve's displays for Shrewsbury in 1996-97 also

showed improving ball skills, these additional attributes being recognised by Crewe, who signed him in transfer deadline week. Not a prolific scorer himself, more of a provider for others in fact, he quickly built up an understanding with Dele Adebola. Can also operate effectively in central defence in emergencies.
Millwall (From juniors on 4/8/86) FL 19+2/4 FLC 3 Others 1
Wimbledon (£150,000 on 16/2/90) F/PL 27+1 FLC 1 FAC 2
Peterborough U (Loaned on 21/1/94) FL 2
Chester C (Loaned on 26/8/94) FL 7
Shrewsbury T (£25,000 on 8/8/95) FL 60+12/16 FLC 4+1 FAC 5+3/1 Others 7+2/1
Crewe Alex (£75,000 on 24/3/97) FL 10

APPLEBY Matthew (Matty) Wilfred
Born: Middlesbrough, 16 April 1972
Height: 5'10" Weight: 11.5
Signed from Darlington during the 1996 close season, the young sweeper settled in well at Barnsley in 1996-97, reading the game impressively, while his passing and ability to bring the ball forward from the back were of the highest quality. In a great season, promotion to the Premiership being achieved for the first time in the club's history, Matty missed very few games, but was unfortunate to suffer ankle ligament damage which kept him out of the final three of the campaign. Is the brother of Swansea's Richard.
Newcastle U (From trainee on 4/5/90) F/PL 18+2 FLC 2+1 FAC 2 Others 2+2
Darlington (Loaned on 25/11/93) FL 10/1 Others 1
Darlington (Free on 15/6/94) FL 77+2/7 FLC 2 FAC 4 Others 8/3
Barnsley (£200,000 on 19/7/96) FL 35 FLC 4 FAC 1

APPLEBY Richard (Richie) Dean
Born: Middlesbrough, 18 September 1975
Height: 5'8" Weight: 10.6
International Honours: E: Yth
Signed from Ipswich during the summer of 1996, Richie started last season for Swansea operating as a wing back who produced many telling crosses. However, knee problems kept him out of the team for long periods in mid term, but after he had regained match fitness and was a regular inclusion in Jan Molby's squad, an horrific head injury, which required 24 stitches, during a reserve game against Bristol Rovers, kept him on the sidelines again until the final match against Hartlepool, which he celebrated by scoring his first goal for the club.
Newcastle U From trainee on 12/8/93) Others 2
Ipswich T (Free on 12/12/95) FL 0+3 Others 1
Swansea C (Free on 16/8/96) FL 8+3/1 FLC 2 Others 1

APPLETON Michael Antony
Born: Salford, 4 December 1975
Height: 5'9" Weight: 11.13
A young right-sided midfielder with excellent passing and ball-winning skills, Michael came into the Manchester United squad for the Premiership game against Aston Villa in September, before making his bow in the Coca-Cola Cup against Swindon at Old Trafford and giving an excellent

account of himself when playing alongside Roy Keane, before leaving the field with a second-half injury. Although he also played in the Coca-Cola Cup against Leicester in November, the lack of first-team opportunities limited his progress and he went on loan to Grimsby in January. Quickly established himself as a favourite at Blundell Park, scoring his first league goal in his second game at home to Barnsley and, although a price was agreed between the two clubs to make the move permanent, he preferred to return to Manchester with a view to eventually breaking into the senior squad.
Manchester U (From trainee on 1/7/94) FLC 1+1
Lincoln C (Loaned on 15/9/95) FL 4 Others 1
Grimsby T (Loaned on 17/1/97) FL 10/3

ARCHDEACON Owen Duncan
Born: Greenock, 4 March 1966
Height: 5'7" Weight: 11.0
Club Honours: SPD '86; AMC '97
International Honours: S: U21-1; Yth
The latest in the long line of Scots-born footballers to shine at Carlisle, Owen was recruited from Barnsley in the 1996 close season and quickly settled into the fashionable role of wing back, being a model of consistency throughout the campaign in missing only one fixture. Forays into his opponents' half were one of the most striking features of his game and he ended the term as club's top scorer with 14 goals, all but three of them coming from open play. As a result he was voted United's Player of the Year and nominated for the PFA division three select side.
Glasgow Celtic (From Gourock U on 20/8/82) SL 38+38/7 SLC 1+4/1 SC 3+1 Others 1+3
Barnsley (£80,000 on 7/7/89) FL 222+11/23 FLC 15+1/2 FAC 14+1/2 Others 9+1/4
Carlisle U (Free on 12/7/96) FL 46/7 FLC 4/1 FAC 4/2 Others 6/4

ARCHER Lee
Born: Bristol, 6 November 1972
Height: 5'6" Weight 9.6
On 31 August 1996, Lee scored the memorable first-ever goal at Bristol Rovers' new Memorial Ground home in a 1-1 draw against Stockport County. The 24-year-old left winger added two other goals to his season's total in the first ten matches, but then did not enjoy the best of fortunes, a persistent knee affecting his form, plus a lack of opportunities to make any impression on new player-manager, Ian Holloway. Despite that, he declined the chance to join Torquay United on loan in March.
Bristol Rov (From trainee on 18/7/91) FL 104+22/15 FLC 7/1 FAC 5+1/2 Others 10+2/1

ARDLEY Neal Christopher
Born: Epsom, 1 September 1972
Height: 5'11" Weight: 11.9
International Honours: E: U21-10
Another development from the very successful youth policy at Wimbledon, which just goes to prove that a team does not have to spend millions when it comes to finding talent, the former England U21 international is a natural right-sided winger with a talent to deliver accurate crosses to

the target men. Also at home in midfield and defensive positions, Neal is exceptional in dead-ball situations which was evidenced when he caught Neville Southall off guard with a 40-yard free kick against Everton last September. Strangely, his second and final goal of the season came when he beat Chelsea's Kevin Hitchcock with a hopeful shot, again from 40 yards out.
Wimbledon (From trainee on 29/7/91) F/PL 92+13/8 FLC 13+3/2 FAC 13+2

ARIS Steven (Steve)
Born: London, 27 April 1978
Height: 5'10" Weight: 11.3
After graduating from the Millwall youth side to first team action as a substitute at Hereford (AWS) last season, Steve, who can play at right back or in midfield, suffered a broken bone in his foot during a reserve game at Watford in December which set back his breakthrough.
Millwall (From juniors on 12/7/94) Others 0+1

ARKINS Vincent (Vince)
Born: Dublin, 18 September 1970
Height: 6'2" Weight: 11.10
International Honours: Ei: B-1; U21-8: Yth
The tall, blond striker started last season for Notts County alongside Gary Martindale, but did not get on the scoresheet until the end of November and scored just once more before leaving for Portadown in February. During his time at Meadow Lane, Vince showed himself to be an intelligent passer of the ball with a hard shot to match.
Dundee U (Signed from Home Farm on 9/12/87. Transferred back on 11/10/89)
St Johnstone (Signed on 25/11/91) SL 38+10/11 SLC 1 SC 7/2 (Transferred to Shelbourne on 15/10/93)
Notts Co (£100,000 on 12/9/95) FL 30+8/8 FLC 2+2 FAC 4+1/1 Others 4

ARMSTRONG Alun
Born: Gateshead, 22 February 1975
Height: 6'1" Weight: 11.13
The young Geordie striker attracted interest from Sunderland and Newcastle after a typically hard-working and impressive campaign for Stockport in 1996-97. Whether it was partnering Brett Angell, Andy Mutch, or Ken Charlery, fans appreciated his endeavour, even through an 18-game goal drought during the run in to the end of the season. Earlier, however, he had a scoring burst of five goals in three games, followed by four consecutive scoring matches.
Newcastle U (From trainee on 1/10/93)
Stockport Co (£50,000 on 23/6/94) FL 122+8/36 FLC 19/6 FAC 8+1/4 Others 7

ARMSTRONG Christopher (Chris) Peter
Born: Newcastle, 19 June 1971
Height: 6'0" Weight: 13.3
Club Honours: Div 1 '94
International Honours: E: B-1
The latter part of 1995-96 saw Chris in top form for Tottenham and he was, no doubt, relishing the prospect of mounting a challenge to the likes of Alan Shearer, Robbie Fowler, and Ian Wright, as one of the Premiership's top scorers in 1996-97.

Alas, injury, following 15 games and six goals, finally wrecked any prospect of that and he spent many months battling for fitness and as news of comebacks would appear they would only be dashed by that of breakdowns. Gerry Francis's frustration at having such talents as Chris, Darren Anderton and Ruel Fox injured began to show and must have reached its peak soon into the New Year as Teddy Sheringham joined the growing list of unfit. Looking forward to 1997-98, the strong striker remains a terrific prospect for Spurs and will undoubtedly make a big impact this coming campaign if available.

Wrexham (Free from Llay Welfare on 3/3/89) FL 40+20/13 FLC 2+1 FAC 0+1 Others 5+1/3
Millwall (£50,000 on 16/8/91) FL 11+17/5 FLC 3+1/2 FAC 0+1 Others 0+1
Crystal Palace (£1,000,000 on 1/9/92) F/PL 118/45 FLC 8/6 FAC 8/5 Others 2/1
Tottenham H (£4,500,000 on 30/6/95) PL 48/20 FLC 6/4 FAC 6/4

Christopher Armstrong

ARMSTRONG Steven **Craig**
Born: South Shields, 23 May 1975
Height: 5'11" Weight: 12.10
Unable to get a break at Nottingham Forest, Craig, a left-sided utility player, had loan spells at Gillingham and Watford (twice) during 1996-97 before returning to the City Ground. A player with the ability to get forward, he made 13 appearances for the Gills between October and December, playing mainly as a left winger, before having two spells at Vicarage Road where he impressed at left back in 15 games. Left-wing back would seem to be his best position.

Nottingham F (From trainee on 2/6/92)
Burnley (Loaned on 29/12/94) FL 4
Bristol Rov (Loaned on 8/1/96) FL 4
Bristol Rov (Loaned on 28/3/96) FL 9+1

Gillingham (Loaned on 18/10/96) FL 10 FLC 2 Others 1
Watford (Loaned on 24/1/97) FL 3
Watford (Loaned on 14/3/97) FL 12

ARMSTRONG Gordon Ian
Born: Newcastle, 15 July 1967
Height: 6'0" Weight: 12.11
Club Honours: Div 3 '88
Signed from Sunderland in the 1996 close season, "Stretch" missed large chunks of Bury's campaign in 1996-97, due to a re-occurring hamstring injury. However, featuring regularly in Bury's division two championship winning side from March onwards, playing at left-wing back in the absence of injured skipper, Dave Pugh, he went one better than his medal winning performance of 1988.

Sunderland (From apprentice on 10/7/85) FL 331+18/50 FLC 25+4/3 FAC 19/4 Others 18+1/4
Bristol C (Loaned on 24/8/95) FL 6
Northampton T (Loaned on 5/1/96) FL 4/1 Others 1
Bury (Free on 16/7/96) FL 16+16/2 FLC 2 FAC 0+1 Others 1+1

ARNOTT Andrew (Andy) John
Born: Chatham, 18 October 1973
Height: 6'1" Weight: 12.0
A versatile player who played in every position for Leyton Orient last season, including goalkeeper for the last 20 minutes in the home game with Exeter after Luke Weaver went off with a bad cut to his forehead, he finished the campaign in midfield, where he looks to be most comfortable. Always a danger at set plays, Andy will be hoping to utilise his natural attacking instincts in order to increase his goalscoring in 1997-98.

Gillingham (From trainee on 13/5/91) FL 50+23/12 FLC 2+3 FAC 10+2/1 Others 3+2
Leyton Orient (£15,000 on 25/1/96) FL 47+3/6 FLC 2 FAC 2 Others 1

Carl Asaba

ASABA Carl
Born: London, 28 January 1973
Height: 6'2" Weight: 13.0
Strong Brentford striker who is extremely difficult to shake off the ball when in possession. Completed a wonderful season in 1996-97 after two quiet years at Griffin Park, scoring 11 goals in the first 11 games of the campaign and finishing as the Bees' top league goalscorer with 23. Highlights included a seven minute hat trick at Shrewsbury, plus two in a game against York (twice) and Wrexham, and being voted into the PFA second division team by his fellow professionals..

Brentford (Free from Dulwich Hamlet on 9/8/94) FL 49+5/25 FLC 5 FAC 4 Others 7/2
Colchester U (Loaned on 16/2/95) FL 9+3/2

ASANOVIC Aljosa
Born: Croatia, 14 December 1965
Height: 5'10" Weight: 12.6
International Honours: Croatia
Probably the single most important factor in keeping Derby out of the relegation zone, the Croatian international signed after Euro 96 from Hajduk Split. A left-sided mid-fielder who can dictate the pace of any game, he impressed with his ability at dead-ball situations, as well as playing some of the most incisive passes in the Premiership. Taking over as the club's regular penalty taker from Paul Simpson, this deceptively strong player, who is difficult to shake off the ball, has signed for County till the year 2000.

Derby Co (£950,000 from Hadjuk Split on 11/7/96) PL 34/6 FLC 1 FAC 3

ASHBEE Ian
Born: Birmingham, 6 September 1976
Height: 6'1" Weight: 12.10
International Honours: E: Yth
Having had a spell on loan in Iceland, Ian was Roy McFarland's first Cambridge signing from his old club, Derby County, when he joined in December. A utility defender, he played mainly as a right-wing back, although also appearing in midfield, eventually becoming a first team regular. Thought he had scored his first goal for the club in the home game against Chester, his shot going in off a defender to bring about a 2-2 draw, however, it was generally recognised to have been an own goal.

Derby Co (From trainee on 9/11/94) FL 1
Cambridge U (Free on 13/12/96) FL 16+2

ASHBY Barry John
Born: Park Royal, 21 November 1970
Height: 6'2" Weight: 13.2
Club Honours: FAYC '89
An extremely competent centre back for Brentford who, with Jamie Bates, formed probably the best central defensive partnership in division two in 1996-97. As in 1995-96, it was yet another good season for Barry, despite him missing the last few games through injury, his headed equaliser in the 1-1 draw at Notts County, which came in the 86th minute, proving a valuable point saver for the Bees and one that helped them into the play offs.

Watford (From trainee on 1/12/88) FL 101+13/3 FLC 6 FAC 4 Others 2+1
Brentford (Signed on 22/3/94) FL 119+2/4 FLC 11 FAC 9/1 Others 11+1

ASHCROFT Lee
Born: Preston, 7 September 1972
Height: 5'10" Weight: 11.10
International Honours: E: U21-1

Lee's return to his hometown club was welcomed by the Preston supporters, after signing from West Brom last November, having been on loan earlier in the season. His speed on the right wing finally restored the balance that the side had missed during Lee Cartwright's long absence through injury, and his goals were vital to a low-scoring side. Suffered a hamstring injury in February which kept him out for six weeks.
Preston NE (From trainee on 16/7/91) FL 78+13/13 FLC 3 FAC 5 Others 6+2/1
West Bromwich A (£250,000 on 1/8/93) FL 66+24/17 FLC 2+3 FAC 3+1/1 Others 8+3
Notts Co (Loaned on 28/3/96) FL 4+2
Preston NE (£150,000 on 5/9/96) FL 26+1/8 FAC 2/3 Others 0+1

Neil Aspin

ASPIN Neil
Born: Gateshead, 12 April 1965
Height: 6'0" Weight: 12.6
Club Honours: AMC '93

The Port Vale team captain once again had an excellent campaign at the heart of the defence in 1996-97. Often seen making last -ditch clearances from the danger zone when all hope seemed lost, his spirit never wavered whatever the situation, and, having now completed eight years service at Vale Park, is a certainty for a best-ever XI. Also played at right back in some games, proving a real headache for opposing left wingers.
Leeds U (From apprentice on 6/10/82) FL 203+4/5 FLC 9/1 FAC 17 Others 11
Port Vale (£200,000 on 28/7/89) FL 289+3/3 FLC 17 FAC 21 Others 18

Warren Aspinall

ASPINALL Warren
Born: Wigan, 13 September 1967
Height: 5'9" Weight: 11.12
Club Honours: AMC '85, '97
International Honours: E: Yth

A busy Carlisle midfielder whose battling style endears him to the crowd, Warren missed only a handful of games during last season and was another club nominee for the PFA third division select team. He was also voted Away Player of the Year, while his brilliant solo effort at Brighton was chosen as the Goal of the Season by United fans.
Wigan Ath (From apprentice on 31/8/85) FL 21+12/10 FLC 1 FAC 2+3/2 Others 1+5/2
Everton (£150,000 on 4/2/86) FL 0+7 FLC 0+1 Others 0+2
Wigan Ath (Loaned on 6/2/86) FL 18/12 Others 2/2
Aston Villa (£300,000 on 19/2/87) FL 40+4/14 FLC 4/2 FAC 1+1
Portsmouth (£315,000 on 26/8/88) FL 97+35/21 FLC 8+3/3 FAC 4+5/2 Others 6+1/2
Bournemouth (Loaned on 27/8/93) FL 4+2/1
Swansea C (Loaned on 14/10/93) FL 5 Others 1
Bournemouth (£20,000 on 31/12/93) FL 26+1/8 FLC 4 FAC 1 Others 1
Carlisle U (Free on 8/3/95) FL 81+8/12 FLC 4/2 FAC 5 Others 10+1/1

ASPRILLA Hinestroza **Faustino (Tino)** Hernan
Born: Tulua, Colombia, 10 November 1969
Height: 5'9" Weight: 11.9
International Honours: Colombia: 45

Tino is a popular if unorthodox Newcastle striker, whose ambling gait with one sock at half mast disguises his extravagant skills and exciting pace. Even his team mates found it difficult to read him in 1996-97, due to of his unpredictability, and this probably explains why he was not a regular in the

side. However, although his skills are very individualistic he does work to harness them to the benefit of the side and, as the season progressed, there were encouraging signs that he and the team were beginning to come together more. His biggest impact came in UEFA Cup games where he scored five times, each marked with his trademark somersault. Against Metz he hung his shirt on a corner post and raised it as a flag in celebration of his first goal, for which he was booked and thus banned from the first leg against Monaco. A torn right hamstring suffered later in the Metz game put him on the sidelines for eight weeks, but he returned in the home game against Everton when coming off the bench to help turn a 1-0 deficit into a 4-1 victory with a dazzling display over the last 18 minutes. Still appears regularly for Colombia, and scored a hat trick in the World Cup qualifier against Chile in September.
Newcastle U (£7,500,000 from Parma, via Cueuta Deportivo and Atletico Nacional de Medellin, on 10/2/96) PL 28+10/6 FLC 2 Others 6+1/5

Tino Asprilla

ATHERTON Peter
Born: Orrell, 6 April 1970
Height: 5'11" Weight: 13.12
International Honours: E: U21-1; Sch

Peter was a virtual ever present for Sheffield Wednesday in 1996-97, missing just one game. A solid defender at full back or in central defence, he ended up also appearing in a midfield holding role, and, as an inspirational captain and leader, he epitomised the Owls' spirit, playing a big part in their revival. Strong tackling and positionally sound, but also capable of getting down the line to cross, his one goal in an early season game at Newcastle doubled his Wednesday career tally.

Wigan Ath (From trainee on 12/2/88) FL 145+4/1 FLC 8 FAC 7 Others 12+1
Coventry C (£300,000 on 23/8/91) F/PL 113+1 FLC 4 FAC 2
Sheffield Wed (£800,000 on 1/6/94) PL 114/3 FLC 10 FAC 8

ATKIN Paul Anthony
Born: Nottingham, 3 September 1969
Height: 6'0" Weight: 12.11
International Honours: E: Yth; Sch

In his sixth season with York in 1996-97, the central defender made only a handful of senior appearances and spent the last couple of months on loan at Leyton Orient before returning just before the end of the campaign. Ever reliable, and a player who rarely gets phased, he was surprisingly released during the summer.

Notts Co (From trainee on 6/7/87)
Bury (Signed on 22/3/89) FL 14+7/1 Others 2+1
York C (Free on 1/7/91) FL 131+22/3 FLC 5+4 FAC 6 Others 10+1
Leyton Orient (Loaned on 21/3/97) FL 5

ATKINS Mark Nigel
Born: Doncaster, 14 August 1968
Height: 6'0" Weight: 12.5
Club Honours: PL '95
International Honours: E: Sch

The strong midfielder spent much of last season as a sweeper, looking comfortable with more time on the ball as Wolves usually played with five at the back. When they did revert to a flat back four in January he lost his ever-present record, but quickly returned, calmly adapting to the various tactical changes, and over the last seven matches he occupied a more advanced role, netting four times. Reads the game well and again saved Wanderers more than once with clearances off the goal line.

Scunthorpe U (From juniors on 9/7/86) FL 45+5/2 FLC 3+1 FAC 5 Others 6+1
Blackburn Rov (£45,000 on 16/6/88) F/PL 224+33/35 FLC 20+2/4 FAC 11+3 Others 17+2/1
Wolverhampton W (£1,000,000 on 21/9/95) FL 70+7/6 FLC 7/2 FAC 5 Others 2/1

ATKINSON Brian
Born: Darlington, 19 January 1971
Height: 5'10" Weight: 12.5
International Honours: E: U21-6

A vastly experienced midfielder signed from Sunderland during the 1996 close season after seven years at Roker Park, injuries prevented him from extended spells in the Darlington side in 1996-97. A tough tackler, he scored four goals, two of them resulting in matches being saved.

Sunderland (From trainee on 21/7/89) FL 119+22/4 FLC 8+2 FAC 13/2 Others 2+3
Carlisle U (Loaned on 19/1/96) FL 2 Others 1
Darlington (Free on 10/8/96) FL 25+5/4 FLC 4 FAC 0+1 Others 1

ATKINSON Dalian Robert
Born: Shrewsbury, 21 March 1968
Height: 6'0" Weight: 13.10
Club Honours: FLC '94
International Honours: E: B-1

After successful years in the early '90s as a striker with Sheffield Wednesday and Aston Villa, Dalian drifted away to Spain and Turkey where he spent most of last season.

However, with his contract at Fenerbahce up in February, he was invited to train at Manchester City, with a view to staying permanently and played for the reserves at York in a six pointer Pontins League match, netting the winner, before making his first-team debut at home to Stoke City, and scoring the first goal with a spectacular header. Despite being released, he appeared to have lost none of his close footwork skills and his height and robust build should be a big asset to any number of forward lines.

Ipswich T (From apprentice on 4/6/85) FL 49+11/18 FLC 5+1/3 Others 2+1
Sheffield Wed (£450,000 on 16/6/89) FL 38/10 FLC 3/3 FAC 2/1 Others 2/1 (£1,700,000 to Real Sociedad on 1/8/90)
Aston Villa (£1,600,000 on 11/7/91) F/PL 79+8/23 FLC 15/11 FAC 4 Others 8/2 (?)
Manchester C (Free on 19/3/97) FL 7+1/2

ATKINSON Graeme
Born: Hull, 11 November 1971
Height: 5'8" Weight: 11.3
Club Honours: Div 3 '96

Preston's utility midfielder started 1996-97 as a first choice, but spent the rest of the campaign in and out of the side. Although his thunderbolt shots of the previous season were not seen too often, his commitment remained obvious, even when experiencing a dip in form. Apart from his shooting ability with either foot, Graeme enjoys the passing game.

Hull C (From trainee on 6/5/90) FL 129+20/23 FLC 6+3/2 FAC 4+1/1 Others 9
Preston NE (Signed on 7/10/94) FL 62+14/6 FLC 5/1 FAC 2+1 Others 5/2

ATKINSON Jonathon (Jon) David
Born: Ashington, 18 September 1972
Height: 5'11" Weight: 12.4

Signed on a monthly basis from Northern League side, Morpeth, just before the transfer deadline, the young striker made his Darlington debut as a substitute at home to Hull when coming on for Glenn Naylor after 81 minutes. Will be looking to be offered a long-term contract.

Darlington (Free from Morpeth on 27/3/97) FL 2+3

ATKINSON Patrick (Paddy) Darren
Born: Singapore, 22 May 1970
Height: 5'9" Weight: 11.6

In his first full season at York in 1996-97, Paddy was unable to establish himself at senior level, partly due to injury problems, but also because of stiff competition from Wayne Hall and Gary Himsworth. On his day a capable left back, he will be hoping for a better run in 1997-98.

Hartlepool U (Free from Sheffield U juniors on 23/8/88) FL 9+12/3 FLC 0+1 FAC 2 Others 1+1 (Free to Gateshead during 1990 close season)
York C (Free from Workington, via Newcastle Blue Star and Barrow on 17/11/95) FL 33+3 FAC 3 Others 4

AUSTIN Dean Barry
Born: Hemel Hempstead, 26 April 1970
Height: 5'11" Weight: 12.4

A right-sided Tottenham defender whose 1996-97 season was dogged by injury and

match fitness problems, Dean found it hard to break into the side, even when available to be picked. However, rare first team appearances showed that he had lost none of his determination and speed, along with his willingness to bring the ball out of defence and take opponents on. With the introduction of John Scales and Ramon Vega, and the fine early form of Stephen Carr, came rumours of him being unsettled and anxious to play first-team football on a regular basis, fuelling speculation of a summer move. Despite all that, he was still recognised as an important member of the first-team squad, either playing or sitting on the bench for 20 of the final 21 games of the campaign.

Southend U (£12,000 from St Albans C on 22/3/90) FL 96/2 FLC 4/1 FAC 2 Others 7
Tottenham H (£375,000 on 4/6/92) PL 117+7 FLC 7+2 FAC 16+1

AUSTIN Kevin Levi
Born: London, 12 February 1973
Height: 6'0" Weight: 14.0

A central defender signed from Leyton Orient during the summer of 1996, following an appeal to the City supporters for cash, Kevin immediately established himself at the heart of Lincoln's defence in 1996-97, going on to produce some outstanding displays. Missing just three games, his speed and power were big assets to the City back four.

Leyton Orient (Free from Saffron Walden on 19/8/93) FL 101+8/3 FLC 4/1 FAC 6 Others 7
Lincoln C (£30,000 on 31/7/96) FL 44 FLC 6 Others 1

AWFORD Andrew (Andy) Terence
Born: Worcester, 14 July 1972
Height: 5'10" Weight: 12.0
International Honours: E: U21-9; Yth; Sch

The ball-playing Portsmouth central defender took over the captaincy from Martin Allen in 1996-97, due to the latter's absence from the team and was the lynchpin of a defence which improved as the campaign went on, his performances being calm and assured alongside younger team mates. His passing and reading of the game was also second to none and before last season, he had never had to serve a suspension, but was unlucky to be dismissed twice, both for two bookable offences. During the run in, Andy missed a couple of games due to a groin injury, which required surgery during the summer.

Portsmouth (From trainee on 24/7/89) FL 192+11/1 FLC 22+1 FAC 14 Others 12

AYORINDE Samuel (Sam) Tayo
Born: Lagos, Nigeria, 20 October 1974
Height: 5'11" Weight: 12.5

A Leyton Orient centre forward who will trouble defences with his pace, although still trying to adjust to the English game, Sam scored a spectacular overhead bicycle kick at Exeter last season and will surely become a consistent goalscorer with experience. Spent loan spells at Rushden & Diamonds and Altrincham to help him adjust.

Leyton Orient (Signed from Nigerian amateur football on 24/4/96) FL 7+6/2 FLC 1+1 FAC 1

B

BAARDSEN Espen
Born: San Rafael, USA, 7 December 1977
Height: 6'5" Weight: 13.13
International Honours: USA: Yth. Norway U21

Having been signed from the American side, San Francisco All Blacks during the 1996 close season, Espen made his debut in goal against Liverpool last May and, in showing great confidence in his ability, soon had the admiration of Tottenham fans and critics alike. Replacing the injured Ian Walker in the second half of the Liverpool game he made three crucial saves from the Premiership's leading strikers and, in his full debut, he ably demonstrated to Gerry Francis that he was up to the challenge of big occasions and that Francis could rely on him in Walker's absence to produce a confident performance of good quality. Spurs' fans will rest assured, having seen the quality available in Ian Walker's understudy.

Tottenham H (Free from San Francisco All Blacks on 16/7/96) PL 1+1

BABB Philip (Phil) Andrew
Born: Lambeth, 30 November 1970
Height: 6'0" Weight: 12.3
Club Honours: FLC '95
International Honours: Ei: 21; B-1

Although starting last season as a regular in the Liverpool side, having a consistent run until the end of October, by the time the campaign had ground to a halt he had lost his way following the advent of Bjorn Tore Kvarme at right back and Pool's reversion to just two centre backs. He had also lost his way with the Republic only playing just once. Despite remaining a stylish defender who, on his day passed with immaculate precision and set up attacking moves, Phil found it difficult to fall back on the kind of consistency and form of previous years, which marked him out as a defender of the highest order. Scored just one goal — the winner at Coventry in September.

Millwall (From trainee on 25/4/89)
Bradford C (Free on 10/8/90) FL 73+7/14 FLC 5+1 FAC 3 Others 3+1
Coventry C (£500,000 on 21/7/92) PL 70+7/3 FLC 5/1 FAC 2
Liverpool (£3,600,000 on 1/9/94) PL 82+2/1 FLC 14 FAC 11 Others 8+1

BADDELEY Lee Matthew
Born: Cardiff, 12 July 1974
Height: 6'1" Weight: 12.7
International Honours: W: U21-2; Yth

A central defender who showed plenty of class in previous seasons, Lee was not part of Cardiff's plans in 1996-97, playing just ten times and being behind Scott Young, Lee Jarman and Jason Perry in the pecking order for regular places. Transferred to Exeter in February, although not letting the side down, he struggled to make an impact and will be looking to establish himself this coming term.

Cardiff C (From trainee on 13/8/91) FL 112+21/1 FLC 4+2 FAC 8 Others 24
Exeter C (Free on 6/2/97) FL 8+3

BAILEY Danny Stephen
Born: Leyton, 21 May 1964
Height: 5'8" Weight: 12.11
Club Honours: Div 4 '90

The midfield anchor man and ball winner, Danny, who is in his second spell at Exeter, was a consistently high performer and virtually ever present in 1996-97 as he helped City avoid relegation. Not often on the scoring charts, but when he does hit the target it is often spectacular.

Bournemouth (Apprentice) FL 1+1
Torquay U (Free from Walthamstow Ave on 1/3/84) FL 1
Exeter C (Free from Wealdstone, via Grays Ath, Harringey Bor and Kingsbury T, on 1/8/89) FL 63+1/2 FLC 8 FAC 7/1 Others 4+1/1
Reading (£50,000 on 26/12/90) FL 49+1/2 FAC 3
Fulham (Loaned on 29/7/92) FL 2+1
Exeter C (Free on 7/12/92) FL 143+9/4 FLC 10 FAC 9/1 Others 16/1

BAILEY Dennis Lincoln
Born: Lambeth, 13 November 1965
Height: 5'10" Weight: 11.6

Season 1996-97 was a disappointing time for Dennis. A regular for most of the time on Gillingham's bench, his goalscoring ability and close control deserted him when the club needed him most, although he did score the winning goal in the first away victory at Shrewsbury — a brave diving header. He reserved his two best performances for the Coca-Cola cup ties against Coventry City, when he got the room to show that on his day he can be a first class performer. Top scored for the reserves in the Capitol League.

Fulham (Free from Barking on 8/11/86)
Crystal Palace (£10,000 from Farnborough T on 2/12/87) FL 0+5/1
Bristol Rov (Loaned on 27/2/89) FL 17/9 Others 1+1/1
Birmingham C (£80,000 on 3/8/89) FL 65+10/23 FLC 6/2 FAC 6 Others 3+3
Bristol Rov (Loaned on 28/3/91) FL 6/1
Queens Park R (£175,000 on 2/7/91) FL 32+7/10 FLC 5/3 FAC 1+1 Others 1
Charlton Ath (Loaned on 29/10/93) FL 0+4 Others 2
Watford (Loaned on 24/3/94) FL 2+6/4
Brentford (Loaned on 26/1/95) FL 6/3
Gillingham (£25,000 on 15/8/95) FL 56+19/10 FLC 7+2/1 FAC 4+1/1 Others 1

BAILEY John Andrew
Born: Lambeth, 6 May 1969
Height: 5'8" Weight: 10.8

John had another excellent season in 1996-97 on the right-hand side of Bournemouth's midfield, always giving 100 per cent and, although not particularly tall, proving to be strong in the air. Also a strong tackler, he is quick and not afraid to run at defenders in order to deliver telling crosses.

Bournemouth (£40,000 from Enfield on 5/7/95) FL 76+8/5 FLC 4+1 FAC 4 Others 3+1

BAILEY Mark
Born: Stoke, 12 August 1976
Height: 5'9" Weight: 10.12

The former Stoke trainee, who signed last

October, quickly made his mark in Rochdale's successful reserve side before gaining a first team place on the wing in the absence of Mark Stuart. He also figured at full back in the reserves and his strong running earned him a first team recall in midfield towards the end of the season. Mark is the son of former Port Vale skipper, Terry.

Stoke C (From trainee on 12/7/94)
Rochdale (Free on 10/10/96) FL 13+2 FAC 1 Others 1

BAIN Kevin
Born: Kirkcaldy, 19 September 1972
Height: 6'0" Weight: 11.9
International Honours: S: U21-4; Yth; Sch

Joined Rotherham in 1996-97 after a brief trial spell from Dundee and went straight into the team, making his debut in a midfield role. However, Kevin played out the rest of the season in a central defensive role, where he displayed a coolness under pressure and an ability to use the ball intelligently.

Dundee (From Abbey Star on 28/6/89) SL 74+7/1 SLC 5+1 SC 5 Others 8+1/1
Rotherham U (Free on 4/3/97) FL 10+2

BAIRD Ian James
Born: Rotherham, 1 April 1964
Height: 6'1" Weight: 12.12
Club Honours: Div 2 '90
International Honours: E: Sch

Particularly strong in the air, this widely-travelled striker added some much needed steel to Brighton's front line last season, after joining the club from Plymouth during the summer. Following a quiet start, Ian underwent surgery in October, having played an entire game with a broken knee cap, but returned to form a fine twin spearhead with Craig Maskell as Albion struggled gallantly for survival under new manager, Steve Gritt, finishing the season as second highest goalscorer with 13. Inherited the captaincy from George Parris in the New Year.

Southampton (From apprentice on 5/4/82) FL 20+2/5 FLC 1+1
Cardiff C (Loaned on 1/11/80) FL 12/6
Newcastle U (Loaned on 1/12/86) FL 4+1/1
Leeds U (£75,000 on 10/3/85) FL 84+1/33 FLC 4 FAC 5/4 Others 7
Portsmouth (£285,000 on 12/8/87) FL 20/1 FLC 1 FAC 1
Leeds U (£120,000 on 4/3/88) FL 76+1/17 FLC 5/1 FAC 3/2 Others 6
Middlesbrough (£500,000 on 29/1/90) FL 60+3/19 FLC 5+1 FAC 3/1 Others 4/1
Heart of Midlothian (£400,000 on 31/7/91) SL 64/15 SLC 5/2 SC 7/1 Others 3/1
Bristol C (£295,000 on 6/7/93) FL 45+12/11 FLC 3 FAC 2/1 Others 2
Plymouth Arg (Free on 29/9/95) FL 24+3/6 FAC 1+1/1
Brighton & Hove A (£35,000 on 31/7/96) FL 34+1/13 FLC 2 FAC 1+1 Others 1

BAKER Joseph (Joe) Philip
Born: London, 19 April 1977
Height: 5'7" Weight: 10.4

Exciting Leyton Orient winger and a real crowd favourite, he is an excellent crosser of the ball who can play on either wing but favours the right-hand side. Yet another player who will be looking to become a

regular in 1997-98, Joe always looks to be enjoying himself.

Leyton Orient (Free from Charlton Ath juniors on 24/5/95) FL 19+21 FLC 0+2 FAC 0+2 Others 0+2

BAKER David **Paul**
Born: Newcastle, 5 January 1963
Height: 6'1" Weight: 13.2

A big, strong striker whose mere physical presence can often unsettle defences, he started the first 12 games for Torquay last season, scoring seven goals, including a hat trick against Bristol City, before signing for Scunthorpe in October. At Glanford Park it was much of the same, 14 goals in 26 games, before he was surprisingly allowed to move to Hartlepool on transfer deadline day, despite the fact that he had been sidelined by a minor knee ligament operation. In a deal that saw Sean McAuley move in the opposite direction, Paul rejoined United as player/coach and, despite not being fully match fit, scored two important goals, while helping his team mates pull off some important results that ultimately averted relegation to the GMVC.

Southampton (£4,000 from Bishop Auckland on 1/7/94)
Carlisle U (Free on 2/7/85) FL 66+5/11 FLC 4/1 FAC 3 Others 2+1
Hartlepool U (Free on 31/7/87) FL 192+5/67 FLC 12/4 FAC 16/6 Others 16/5
Motherwell (£77,500 on 1/8/92) SL 5+4/1 SLC 1
Gillingham (£40,000 on 7/1/93) FL 58+4/16 FAC 5/1 Others 2
York C (£15,000 on 1/10/94) FL 36+12/18 FLC 2+2/2 FAC 3 Others 5+1/1
Torquay U (£25,000 on 19/1/96) FL 30/8 FLC 2/3
Scunthorpe U (£15,000 on 4/10/96) FL 21/9 FAC 3/5 Others 2
Hartlepool U (Signed on 27/3/97) FL 6/2

BALDRY Simon
Born: Huddersfield, 12 February 1976
Height: 5'11" Weight: 11.6

The pacy Huddersfield forward, a home-grown product who has found it difficult to establish himself in the first team, he was offered a new two-year contract at the end of last season, during which time he will hope to make an impact. A good passer of the ball, whose subs' appearances outweighed his starts in 1996-97, Simon is still young enough to make the breakthrough.

Huddersfield T (From trainee on 14/7/94) FL 23+19/2 FLC 2+1 Others 1+2/1

BALL Kevin Anthony
Born: Hastings, 12 November 1964
Height: 5'10" Weight: 12.6
Club Honours: Div 1 '96

Skipper "Bally" will no doubt have felt relegation harder than anyone at Sunderland in 1996-97. The midfielder's season was once again epitomised by gritty whole-hearted displays and he finished the campaign as the club's joint top-scorer with four goals, two of which were brilliant efforts against Chelsea in December and Nottingham Forest in March. He also overcame a broken jaw against Derby on Boxing Day and if the Rokerites are to make a quick return to the top flight then

committed characters such as him will be important to the cause. Can also play in central defence if required.

Portsmouth (Free from Coventry C juniors on 6/10/82) FL 96+9/4 FLC 8+1 FAC 8 Others 6
Sunderland (£350,000 on 16/7/90) P/FL 252+3/16 FLC 17+1/3 FAC 15 Others 4/1

BALL Michael John
Born: Liverpool, 2 October 1979
Height: 5'10" Weight 11.2
International Honours: E: Yth

Handed a testing debut in a crucial Everton relegation crunch against Tottenham last season, Michael showed maturity and composure well beyond his 17 years. Such was the quality of his performance after coming on as a first-half substitute, caretaker boss, Dave Watson, had no qualms about introducing him just 23 minutes into a fierce Merseyside derby and then handing him a full Premiership appearance at West Ham. A sharp-tackling, over-lapping left back, he is equally at home in central defence and also possesses the useful weapon of an enormous long throw. Guaranteed a promising career in the game

after the club swiftly offered him a five-year professional contract during his first year as a YTS trainee at Goodison.

Everton (From trainee on 17/10/96) PL 2+3

BALMER Stuart Murray
Born: Falkirk, 20 September 1969
Height: 6'1" Weight: 12.4
International Honours: S: Yth; Sch

Right-footed Charlton central defender who can also play at full back. Comfortable on the ball, with good distribution, and good in the air, Stuart also scored the winning goals against QPR and WBA in 1996-97, with well taken volleys from the edge of the penalty area. Captaining the side until injury forced him to miss several games in mid season, he formed a solid partnership with Richard Rufus in the centre of the defence.

Glasgow Celtic (From juniors in 1987)
Charlton Ath (£120,000 on 24/8/90) FL 188+23/8 FLC 13 FAC 9 Others 11+1

BANGER Nicholas (**Nicky**) Lee
Born: Southampton, 25 February 1971
Height: 5'9" Weight: 11.6

A busy little forward who twists and turns well on the edge of the box and always

Kevin Ball

causes defenders problems with his quick, darting runs, Nicky started in 12 of Oldham's first 15 games last season, but from then on only appeared sporadically. Although six goals seemed a fair return, including winners at Tranmere and QPR, and at Boundary Park against Manchester City, with competition for places and injuries taken into consideration, the club released him during the summer.

Southampton (From trainee on 25/4/89) F/PL 18+37/8 FLC 2+2/3 FAC 0+2 Others 1
Oldham Ath (£250,000 on 4/10/94) FL 44+20/10 FLC 6/1 FAC 2+1 Others 0+1

BANKOLE Ademola
Born: Abeokuta, Nigeria, 9 September1969
Height: 6'3" Weight: 13.0
Having had trials with both Doncaster and Leyton Orient during 1995-96, the Nigerian goalkeeper joined Crewe early last season as cover for the injured Mark Gayle, but was deemed too inexperienced to risk at that stage, the club sticking with Martin Taylor on loan from Derby until signing Everton's Jason Kearton. Extremely agile for such a big man, he made his league debut in a 1-1 draw at Wrexham, following an injury to Kearton, before playing the final game of the campaign, following a spell on loan at Hyde United.

Doncaster Rov (Free from Nigerian football on 30/11/95)
Leyton Orient (Free on 27/12/95)
Crewe Alex (Free on 25/9/96) FL 3

BANKS Steven (Steve)
Born: Hillingdon, 9 February 1972
Height: 6'0" Weight: 13.2
Steve had an outstanding season for Blackpool in 1996-97, his reward being a new two-year contract. Cool and commanding, two tremendous saves in the home game against Preston summed up just how valuable he is to the Seasiders and he was often the main difference between winning and losing or getting a point. Voted Player of the Year, he was the only man to have started every game for Pool.

West Ham U (From trainee on 24/3/90) Others 1
Gillingham (Free on 25/3/93) FL 67 FAC 7 Others 2
Blackpool (£60,000 on 18/8/95) FL 70 FLC 5 FAC 5 Others 7

BARACLOUGH Ian Robert
Born: Leicester, 4 December 1970
Height: 6'1" Weight: 12.2
International Honours: E: Yth
Notts County's regular first choice left back in 1996-97, Ian's experience in midfield at previous clubs saw him naturally converted to wing back under new manager, Sam Allardyce. Highly popular with the fans who enjoyed his thrusting runs into the opposition's penalty area, he got himself on the scoring charts in home games against Millwall and Stockport.

Leicester C (From trainee on 15/12/88) FAC 1 Others 0+1
Wigan Ath (Loaned on 22/3/90) FL 8+1/2
Grimsby T (Loaned on 21/12/90) FL 1+3
Grimsby T (Free on 13/8/91) FL 1
Lincoln C (Free on 21/8/92) FL 68+5/10 FLC 7/1 FAC 4 Others 7
Mansfield T (Free on 6/6/94) FL 47/5 FLC 7 FAC 4 Others 4
Notts Co (Signed on 13/10/95) FL 71+2/4 FLC 2 FAC 6 Others 4

BARBARA Daniel
Born: France, 12 October 1974
Height: 5'6" Weight: 12.7
A diminutive French forward, having experience with Monaco and Lourosa of Portugal, Daniel arrived at Darlington on a short-term contract last December, making two full appearances and five as a substitute. Interestingly, the two spectacular goals he scored came in his two full games at Bury, in the AWS, and Exeter.

Darlington (Signed from Lourosa on 13/12/96) FL 1+5/1 Others 1/1

BARKER Simon
Born: Farnworth, 4 November 1964
Height: 5'9" Weight: 11.7
Club Honours: FMC '87
International Honours: E: U21-4
Now in the veteran stage, in 1996-97 Simon continued to show the form everyone has come to expect of him at QPR, putting many of the younger players to shame with his energy and workrate as the side's driving force from the centre of midfield. A player with a good footballing brain, who is capable of opening defences up with sound passing technique, he only missed eight league games throughout the campaign, all through injury, and managed to add four more goals, including two penalties, to his career total. Still has a year left to run on his contract.

Blackburn Rov (From apprentice on 6/11/82) FL 180+2/35 FLC 11/4 FAC 12 Others 8/2
Queens Park R (£400,000 on 20/7/88) F/PL 271+21/30 FLC 27+2/5 FAC 22+1/3 Others 7

BARLOW Andrew (Andy) John
Born: Oldham, 24 November 1965
Height: 5'9" Weight: 11.1
Club Honours: Div 2 '91
Despite performing consistently well at left back for Blackpool in 1996-97, his injury problems of the past seemingly behind him as he missed few games, he was surprisingly freed during the summer. As a player with attacking flair his two-footed ability allows him to cross well, while, at the back, he remains cool under pressure. Also has a good long throw.

Oldham Ath (From juniors on 31/7/84) F/PL 245+16/5 FLC 22 FAC 19 Others 6
Bradford C (Loaned on 1/11/93) FL 2
Blackpool (Free on 13/7/95) FL 77+3/2 FLC 4+2 FAC 4 Others 6

BARLOW Martin David
Born: Barnstaple, 25 June 1971
Height: 5'7" Weight: 10.3
Martin was a consistent performer for Plymouth throughout the last campaign, forming part of a three-man midfield in a formation which included wing backs. Originally a winger, the central midfield berth suits his neat passing and determined battling. Scored the second goal in a vital 2-0 win over Walsall with relegation looming large.

Plymouth Arg (From trainee on 1/7/89) FL 190+30/15 FLC 7+1/2 FAC 10 Others 15+1

Martin Barlow

BARLOW Stuart
Born: Liverpool, 16 July 1968
Height: 5'10" Weight: 11.0
Stuart was Oldham's top scorer in the league in 1996-97, with 12 from 35 games, nine of which were made from the subs' bench. A busy, hard-working and extremely quick front-line player who is likened to greased lightning over the first five yards, he got off the mark with a hat trick in a 3-0 win at Bradford in early November and cracked in another later in the campaign during a 5-1 home victory over Swindon. However, with the club hugging the foot of the first division for much of the season, his goals were not enough to save Latics from the drop. Is also good in the air for a small man.

Everton (Free from Sherwood Park on 6/6/90) F/PL 24+47/10 FLC 3+5/1 FAC 4+3/2 Others 0+2
Rotherham U (Loaned on 10/1/92) Others 0+1
Oldham Ath (£450,000 on 20/11/95) FL 47+14/19 FLC 3+1 FAC 3 Others 1

BARMBY Nicholas (Nick) Jonathan
Born: Hull, 11 February 1974
Height: 5'7" Weight: 11.3
International Honours: E: 10; B-1; U21-3; Yth; Sch
Became Everton's record signing last season, just 13 months after Middlesbrough had also paid out a record transfer fee to Tottenham for his services. A lively player with excellent vision and the ability to deliver damaging passes and crosses, he prefers to play behind two strikers. When employed in that role he lived up to his price tag, but was all too often played up front or in midfield where he never looked as comfortable. Although scoring the first goal of Glenn Hoddle's career as England coach

21

Nick Barmby

BARNES David
Born: Paddington, 16 November 1961
Height: 5'10" Weight: 11.4
International Honours: E: Yth (UEFAYC '80)
Signed from Watford in the summer of 1996 to fill a weakness at left back for Colchester, having previously played alongside U's manager, Steve Wignall, at Aldershot. Looked very impressive in pre-season, but competitive appearances were restricted by injury and he never got an extended run in the side, his contract being cancelled by mutual consent in March.
Coventry C (From apprentice on 31/5/79) FL 9 FAC 4
Ipswich T (Free on 12/4/82) FL 16+1
Wolverhampton W (£35,000 on 3/10/84) FL 86+2/4 FLC 7 FAC 6 Others 6
Aldershot (£25,000 on 22/8/87) FL 68+1/1 FLC 2 FAC 2+2 Others 4
Sheffield U (£50,000 on 11/7/89) F/PL 82/1 FLC 6 FAC 14 Others 4
Watford (£50,000 on 14/1/94) FL 16 FAC 1+1
Colchester U (Free on 5/8/96) FL 11 FLC 1 Others 1

BARNES John Charles Bryan
Born: Jamaica, 7 November 1963
Height: 5'11" Weight: 12.7
Club Honours: FAYC '82; Div 1 '88, '90; FAC '89; CS '88, '89, '90; FLC '95
International Honours: E: 79; U21-3
As Liverpool's club captain, and a likely future candidate for management, John used all his consummate skill, pin-point, accurate passing, athleticism and strength to keep his place in midfield during 1996-97. Also provided a strong anchor role at the back, linking midfield with defence, while often initiating some excellent attacking thrusts when finding team mates with immaculate, intelligent passes. Among his goals in 1996-97 was one on the opening day of last season in a 3-3 draw at Middlesbrough, the winner at Southampton, and three in Pool's European Cup Winners Cup run to the semi finals. Now in the twilight of a brilliant career, aged 33, his huge experience allows him to hold up play and then set the side swiftly on to the offensive.
Watford (Free from Sudbury Court on 14/7/81) FL 232+1/65 FLC 21/7 FAC 31/11 Others 7
Liverpool (£900,000 on 19/6/87) F/PL 310+4/84 FLC 26/3 FAC 51/16 Others 16/5

BARNES Paul Lance
Born: Leicester, 16 November 1967
Height: 5'10" Weight: 12.9
Following his club record transfer from Birmingham last September, Paul struggled to find the target at first, failing to score in his first eight games for Burnley, before getting off the mark spectacularly with all five against Stockport. From then on, his regular appearances on the scoresheet, together with the development of a potentially fine partnership with Andy Cooke, ensured his place in the fans' hearts. Is a skilful striker who holds the ball up well.
Notts Co (From apprentice on 16/11/85) FL 36+17/14 FAC 0+1 Others 4+6/5
Stoke C (£30,000 on 23/3/90) FL 10+14/3 FLC 0+2 Others 3+1/2

in Moldova, by the end of the campaign he had lost his international place, but that aside, Nick looks to have an outstanding future in the game.
Tottenham H (From trainee on 9/4/91) PL 81+6/20 FLC 7+1/2 FAC 12+1/5
Middlesbrough (£5,250,000 on 8/8/95) PL 42/8 FLC 4/1 FAC 3/1
Everton (£5,750,000 on 2/11/96) PL 22+3/4 FAC 2/1

BARNARD Darren Sean
Born: Rintein, Germany, 30 November 1971
Height: 5'10" Weight: 12.0
International Honours: E: Sch
1996-97 was another great season for this gifted Bristol City player who, as in 1995-96, operated from the left-back berth. Blessed with the skill to go past opponents, and a good crosser of the ball as well as the possessor of excellent long-range shooting ability, it was no surprise that Darren made his presence felt on the goal sheet this term. The goals flowed, many from his role as the club's free-kick specialist as well as penalty taker, plus great strikes that either won or saved matches, especially winners in the Coca-Cola Cup against Torquay and Bury in the league. Voted the Young Reds' Player of the Year.
Chelsea (£50,000 from Wokingham T on 25/7/90) F/PL 18+11/2 FLC 1+1 FAC 1+1
Reading (Loaned on 18/11/94) FL 3+1
Bristol C (£175,000 on 6/10/95) FL 77+1/15 FLC 4/1 FAC 6 Others 6/1

BARNARD Mark
Born: Sheffield, 27 November 1975
Height: 5'11" Weight: 11.10
Establishing himself in the left-back spot at Darlington in 1996-97, his second season at the club, Mark is a wing back who loves to get forward. Surprisingly, he failed to score after getting three goals in 1995-96.
Rotherham U (From trainee on 13/7/94. Free to Worksop T during 1995 close season)
Darlington (Free on 27/9/95) FL 72+2/3 FLC 5 FAC 2 Others 6

Chesterfield (Loaned on 8/11/90) FL 1 FAC 1/1
York C (£50,000 on 15/7/92) FL 147+1/76 FLC 10/5 FAC 5 Others 16/4
Birmingham C (£350,000 on 4/3/96) FL 15/7
Burnley (£350,000+ on 6/9/96) FL 39+1/24 FLC 2 FAC 3/1

BARNES Philip Kenneth
Born: Sheffield, 2 March 1979
Height: 6'1" Weight: 11.1

Just over a month past his 18th birthday this young trainee goalkeeper came into a Rotherham side already destined to play in the third division in 1997-98, for the final two matches of last season and showed outstanding form which belied his inexperience. Good in the air, and possessing remarkable shot-stopping ability, Philip is a real star of the future, make no mistake. Having started 1996-97 as second choice junior 'keeper, his rave notices were all the more remarkable, and his magnificent display at Bristol Rovers earned him a well-deserved ovation from a sporting crowd.
Rotherham U (Trainee) FL 2

BARNESS Anthony
Born: Lewisham, 25 March 1973
Height: 5'10" Weight: 13.1

Anthony rejoined his first club, Charlton Athletic, in the 1996 close season from Chelsea and missed only one game during the 1996-97 campaign. Although predominately right footed, he can play in either full back position and, in fact, made the majority of his appearances in the left-back spot. Likes to get forward and scored a couple of useful goals, including a brilliant solo effort against Oxford. Is a strong tackler with good distribution and very calm when under pressure.
Charlton Ath (From trainee on 6/3/91) FL 21+6/1 FLC 2 FAC 3 Others 1+1/1
Chelsea (£350,000 on 8/9/92) PL 12+2 FLC 2 Others 2+1
Middlesbrough (Loaned on 12/8/93) Others 1
Southend U (Loaned on 2/2/96) FL 5
Charlton Ath (£165,000 on 8/8/96) FL 45/2 FLC 4 FAC 2

BARNETT David (Dave) Kwame
Born: Birmingham, 16 April 1967
Height: 6'1" Weight: 12.8
Club Honours: AMC '95; Div 2 '95

A deceptively quick Birmingham centre back whose main strength is his ability in the air, David returned unexpectedly last March after two years' out with a twice-snapped Achilles tendon. Although playing with sufficient aggression, determination, and success to keep his place for a further five games, following the arrival of Darren Wassall, on loan from Derby, however, he lost his place and was given a free transfer during the Summer.
Colchester U (Signed from Windsor & Eton on 25/8/88) FL 19+1 FLC 2 FAC 3+2 Others 3 (Freed in June 1988)
West Bromwich A (Free from Edmonton Oilers on 13/10/89)
Walsall (Free on 17/7/90) FL 4+1 FLC 2 (Free to Kidderminster Harriers on 1/10/90)
Barnet (£10,000 on 29/2/92) FL 58+1/3 FLC 5 FAC 3 Others 5
Birmingham C (£150,000 on 20/12/93) FL 45+1 FLC 1 FAC 5 Others 8

BARNETT Jason Vincent
Born: Shrewsbury, 21 April 1976
Height: 5'9" Weight: 12.4

Versatile Lincoln player who developed into a great favourite with the fans in 1996-97 thanks to superb attitude. A real battler who appeared in both full-back positions as well as in midfield. Jason was the most improved City player of the campaign and won the club's Young Player of the Year award for the second successive season.
Wolverhampton W (From trainee on 4/7/94)
Lincoln C (£5,000 on 26/10/95) FL 60+8/2 FLC 3 FAC 2 Others 4

BARNWELL-EDINBORO Jamie
Born: Hull, 26 December 1975
Height: 5'10" Weight: 11.6

Much was expected from this Cambridge centre forward in 1996-97, but he struggled to find the back of the net and did not get on to the scoresheet until November, with a goal in the FA Cup against Welling. Still only 21, he needed an experienced player to bring him through and it is to be hoped that playing alongside John Taylor will help him develop into the goalscorer that he promises to be.
Coventry C (From trainee on 1/7/94) PL 0+1
Swansea C (Loaned on 15/12/95) FL 2+2
Wigan Ath (Loaned on 2/2/96) FL 2+8/1
Cambridge U (Signed on 29/3/96) FL 42+5/8 FLC 2 FAC 2/1 Others 0+1

BARR William (Billy) Joseph
Born: Halifax, 21 January 1969
Height: 5'11" Weight: 10.8

Again proved his versatility for Crewe, this time in 1996-97, filling a variety of positions, including those at right back and outside left, in a side that would eventually reach the first division for the first time in its history, via the play offs. Sidelined after the 1-0 defeat at Stockport, he had earlier scored four goals, one of which being the winner against Rotherham at Gresty Road. Released during the summer, apart from his ability to play anywhere on the park, he is extremely hard working.

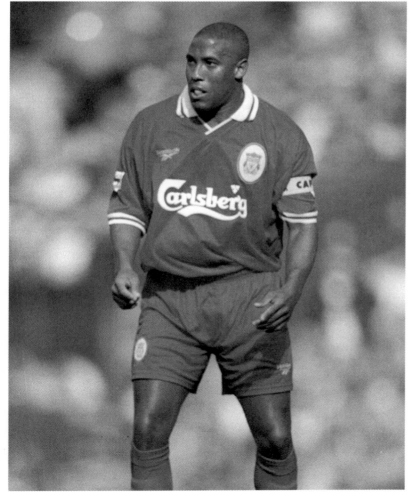

John Barnes

Halifax T (From trainee on 6/7/87) FL 178+18/13 FLC 8+1/2 FAC 11+1/2 Others 14+3
Crewe Alex (Free on 17/6/94) FL 73+12/6 FLC 2 FAC 4 Others 8+1

BARRAS Anthony (Tony)
Born: Billingham, 29 March 1971
Height: 6'0" Weight: 13.0
York City's captain and only ever present in 1996-97, Tony again proved to be a commanding central defender, having an outstanding season and being elected Clubman of the Year. Also scored an important goal, City's second in the 3-2 FA Cup victory at Preston.
Hartlepool U (From trainee on 6/7/89) FL 9+3 FLC 2 FAC 1 Others 1
Stockport Co (Free on 23/7/90) FL 94+5/5 FLC 2 FAC 7 Others 19+1
Rotherham U (Loaned on 25/2/94) FL 5/1
York C (Signed on 18/7/94) FL 105+4/5 FLC 12/1 FAC 7/1 Others 7+1/1

BARRETT Earl Delisser
Born: Rochdale, 28 April 1967
Height: 5'10" Weight: 11.7
Club Honours: Div 2 '91; FLC '94; CS '95
International Honours: E: 3; B-4; U21-4
Having recovered from a career-threatening knee injury which wiped out all but the first two months of the 1995-96 season, Earl bounced back to become Everton's most reliable defensive performer in 1996-97. An ever present all the way through to April, he was a paragon of consistency, usually at right back, although sometimes seen as an effective wing back, his excellent performances effectively ending the Everton careers of Marc Hottiger and Matt Jackson. Is still seeking his first Everton goal, despite a couple of close shaves.
Manchester C (From trainee on 26/4/85) FL 2+1 FLC 1
Chester C (Loaned on 1/3/86) FL 12
Oldham Ath (£35,000 on 24/11/87) FL 181+2/7 FLC 20/1 FAC 14/1 Others 4
Aston Villa (£1,700,000 on 25/2/92) F/PL 118+1/1 FLC 15/1 FAC 9 Others 7
Everton (£1,700,000 on 30/1/95) PL 61 FLC 4 FAC 2 Others 3

BARRETT Scott
Born: Ilkeston, 2 April 1963
Height: 6'0" Weight: 13.8
Club Honours: GMVC '92; FAT '92
Continued as Cambridge's first-choice goalkeeper in 1996-97, missing just one game all season. Although criticised for some poor performances, it should be noted that he played behind a very young defence and made many crucial stops that kept United alive, including one reflex save in the televised Sky game against Carlisle United in February.
Wolverhampton W (Signed from Ilkeston T on 27/9/84) FL 30 FLC 1 FAC 1 Others 3
Stoke C (£10,000 on 24/7/87) FL 51 FLC 2 FAC 3 Others 4
Colchester U (Loaned on 10/1/90) FL 13
Stockport Co (Loaned on 22/3/90) FL 10 Others 2
Gillingham (Free on 14/8/92) FL 51 FLC 7 FAC 4 Others 4
Cambridge U (Free on 2/8/95) FL 76 FLC 4 FAC 3 Others 2

BARRICK Dean
Born: Hemsworth, 30 September 1969
Height: 5'9" Weight: 12.0
Club Honours: Div 3 '96
A left back who lost his previously ever-present place in the Preston first team in 1996-97, following a back injury, Dean is a good overlapper and crosser, as well as a committed tackler. However, he did not feature as often when the team adopted a wing-back formation.
Sheffield Wed (From trainee on 7/5/88) FL 11/2
Rotherham U (£50,000 on 14/2/91) FL 96+3/7 FLC 6 FAC 8 Others 5/1
Cambridge U (£50,000 on 11/8/93) FL 90+1/3 FLC 7/1 FAC 7/1 Others 6
Preston NE (Signed on 11/9/95) FL 69+7 FAC 4 FAC 2 Others 3

BARRON Michael James
Born: Chester le Street, 22 December 1974
Height: 5'11" Weight: 11.9
A skilful Middlesbrough central defender, Michael had a successful three-month loan spell with Hartlepool early on in 1996-97. Although he played at a difficult time, during which there was a change of manager, he was probably Pool's most outstanding player in the first half of the season, impressing everyone with his confident play, which gave him plenty of time on the ball. Despite the Hartlepool manager, Mick Tait, making a number of attempts to sign him permanently, Boro failed to take the bait.
Middlesbrough (From trainee on 2/2/93) P/FL 2+1 FLC 1 Others 3+3
Hartlepool U (Loaned on 6/9/96) FL 16

BARROW Lee Alexander
Born: Belper, 1 May 1973
Height: 5'11" Weight: 13.0
Once again one of Torquay United's most dependable players and an ever-present, if you include substitutions, he added a coolness to his steely central defensive play in 1996-97, a season which promised so much but fell away badly. Intercepts well and has good pace for a defender.
Notts Co (From trainee on 9/7/91)
Scarborough (Free on 3/8/92) FL 11 FLC 2 Others 1
Torquay U (Free on 18/2/93) FL 154+8/5 FLC 11/2 FAC 10/1 Others 6

BARTLETT Neal
Born: Southampton, 7 April 1975
Height: 5'9" Weight: 12.2
International Honours: E: Sch

Chris Bart-Williams

Having once experienced the Premiership with Southampton, Neal returned to England following a spell in Scandinavia and landed at Hereford last September. Capable of playing in midfield or up front, but now a defender, he was only given three subs' appearances to show his wares and although trying hard it was not enough in a struggling side and he departed in March.

Southampton (From trainee on 2/7/93) PL 4+4 FLC 0+1 (Free to Fareham on 2/12/94)
Hereford U (Free from BK Haken on 12/9/96) FL 0+3

BARTON Warren Dean
Born: Stoke Newington, 19 March 1969
Height: 6'0" Weight: 12.0
International Honours: E: 3; B-3

Last season was a disappointing one for Warren, as he struggled to gain a regular spot in the Newcastle side. Confident on the ball, with a good turn of pace, and enjoying joining in with the attack whenever possible, Steve Watson's fine form, however, limited his appearances to occasional cup ties and substitutions. Despite this he never lost his self belief and he was rewarded on the arrival of Kenny Dalglish, following which he won regular selection. His versatility was an asset as he was chosen at both right back and midfield, proving himself an able deputy for David Batty in the latter role. Scored his first Premiership goal for the club in the dramatic 4-3 defeat by Liverpool at Anfield.

Maidstone U (£10,000 from Leytonstone on 28/7/89) FL 41+1 FLC 0+2 FAC 3/1 Others 7
Wimbledon (£300,000 on 7/6/90) F/PL 178+2/10 FLC 16/1 FAC 11 Others 2
Newcastle U (£4,500,000 on 5/6/95) PL 44+5/1 FLC 6/1 FAC 3+1 Others 4+2

BART-WILLIAMS Christopher (Chris) Gerald
Born: Freetown, Sierra Leone, 16 June 1974
Height: 5'11" Weight: 11.11
International Honours: E: B-1; U21-16; Yth

Chris was played in a more forward role at Nottingham Forest in 1996-97, his second with the club, and showed good stamina as he covered most of the pitch in each game he played, giving good honest, no-nonsense performances, reminiscent of his previous form at Sheffield Wednesday. Out of the side from the end of October through to January, he finally broke his duck when scoring his first Premiership goal in a 2-0 win over Chelsea, but sadly that was to be his only one. Unfortunately injured against Aston Villa, he was out of action for the remainder of the campaign and, in a season that finished disastrously for the club, he must be hoping that he can pick up the pieces in 1997-98.

Leyton Orient (From trainee on 18/7/91) FL 34+2/2 FLC 4 Others 2
Sheffield Wed (£275,000 on 21/11/91) F/PL 95+29/16 FLC 14+2/4 FAC 9+3/2 Others 1+3/2
Nottingham F (£2,500,000 on 1/7/95) PL 49/1 FLC 5 FAC 9 Others 7+1

BASHAM Michael (Mike)
Born: Barking, 27 September 1973
Height: 6'2" Weight: 13.2
Club Honours: AMC '94
International Honours: E: Yth; Sch

In yet another injury-hit season for the Peterborough defender, the former England schoolboy international made just seven appearances in 1996-97, two of them coming from the bench. Freed during the summer, when fit, Mike is a central defender who can play on either flank at the back and is a strong tackler with excellent distribution.

West Ham U (From trainee on 3/7/92)
Colchester U (Loaned on 18/11/93) FL 1
Swansea C (Free on 24/3/94) FL 27+2/1 FAC 6 Others 8+2
Peterborough U (Free on 18/12/95) FL 17+2/1 FLC 1 FAC 0+1

BASHAM Steven
Born: Southampton, 2 December 1977
Height: 5'11" Weight: 11.3

A young Southampton striker who came through the youth team as a trainee to sign professional forms prior to the start of last season, Steve obviously made a good impression, starting in the squad on the opening day and coming on as a sub against Chelsea. Rather an old-fashioned type centre forward who holds the ball up well, with a good shot in either foot and strong in the air, he made his only start of the campaign in a 2-1 defeat at Manchester United and stayed the full 90 minutes. Able to play on either flank also, although yet to open his scoring account for the first team, he has a good strike rate for the reserves.

Southampton (From trainee on 24/5/96) PL 1+5

BASS David
Born: Frimley, 29 November 1974
Height: 5'11" Weight: 12.7

Although David eventually made a return to first-team football with Reading in 1996-97, after a series of injuries had disrupted his career, he made only a handful of substitute appearances and was given a free transfer at the end of the season. A solid performer in midfield for the reserves, he spent a month on loan at Basingstoke Town during the early part of the campaign, and also had a trial with Colchester United.

Reading (From trainee on 14/7/93) FL 0+2

BASS Jonathan (Jon) David
Born: Bristol, 1 January 1976
Height: 6'0" Weight: 12.2
International Honours: E: Sch

A Birmingham City youth product and former England schoolboy international, Jon made his debut against Blackburn Rovers in the Coca-Cola Cup as a teenager, his next appearance coming 16 months later in the semi final of the same competition against Leeds United. Perseverance and enthusiasm earned him his chance in the problem right-back position last March and he performed with great maturity, playing a big part in the Blues' unbeaten ten-match run to the end of the season.

Birmingham C (From juniors on 27/6/94) FL 16+2 FLC 2 FAC 1
Carlisle U (Loaned on 11/10/96) FL 3

BATES James (Jamie) Alan
Born: Croydon, 24 February 1968
Height: 6'1" Weight: 13.0
Club Honours: Div 3 '92

Strong, powerful centre half and captain of Brentford. A great leader of the side again in 1996-97, he continued his central defensive partnership with Barry Ashby, a pairing that had few equals in the second division, after coming back from a hernia operation at the end of September, having missed nine games. After 11 seasons at Griffin Park, Jamie is now in the top five in the all-time Brentford appearances' chart.

Brentford (From trainee on 1/6/87) FL 332+20/16 FLC 29+3/2 FAC 15+1/1 Others 41/1

BATTERSBY Anthony (Tony)
Born: Doncaster, 30 August 1975
Height: 6'0" Weight: 12.7

Signed by Colin Murphy for Notts County in January 1996, Tony made only few appearances under new manager, Sam Allardyce, last season, before going to Bury on loan in March. A lively striker who is a good passer and powerful in possession, he joined the Shakers at the height of an injury crisis and earned a regular place in the closing months of the season, his full debut at Gigg Lane against Gillingham seeing him score before being sent off for a second bookable offence. Ironically, although one game short of winning a second division championship medal with Bury, he returned to Meadow Lane to find County relegated to the third. *Stop Press:* Joined Bury on a permanent basis on 22 May.

Sheffield U (From trainee on 5/7/93) FL 3+7/1 FLC 1+1 Others 2+1/1
Southend U (Loaned on 23/3/95) FL 6+2/1
Notts Co (£200,000 on 8/1/96) FL 20+19/8 FLC 1 FAC 0+3 Others 4
Bury (Loaned on 3/3/97) FL 9+2/2

BATTY David
Born: Leeds, 2 December 1968
Height: 5'8" Weight: 12.0
Club Honours: Div 2 '90, Div 1 '92
International Honours: E: 25; B-5; U21-7

David became a key player in the Newcastle set up in 1996-97, admirably filling the central midfield anchor role. With his battling instincts and ball-winning ability he formed a sound, protective screen in front of the defence, while his composure on the ball and his fine distribution skills enabled him to operate as a highly effective link between defence and attack. Goals remain something of a rarity, however, but he scored the club's first of the season with a precision chip from 40 yards after three minutes against Wimbledon in the second game of the campaign. Although known for his combative approach, his sending off at Chelsea was his first dismissal in senior football and when his fine, consistent form persuaded Glenn Hoddle to recall him to the England colours he responded by giving a Man of the Match performance in Georgia in November. The regard with which he is held by his fellow professionals was demonstrated by his selection for the Premiership XI at the PFA annual awards dinner.

Leeds U (From trainee on 3/8/87) F/PL 201+10/4 FLC 17 FAC 12 Others 17
Blackburn Rov (£2,750,000 on 26/10/93) PL 53+1/1 FLC 6 FAC 5 Others 6
Newcastle U (£3,750,000 on 2/3/96) PL 43/2 FLC 2 FAC 3 Others 8

David Batty

BAYES Ashley John
Born: Lincoln, 19 April 1972
Height: 6'1" Weight: 13.5
International Honours: E: Yth
Signed in the 1996 close season from Torquay, Ashley took over Exeter's number one spot in 1996-97 from Peter Fox, who virtually stood down. After a shaky start, he really came into his own and proved to be a reliable 'keeper, especially good at reflex saves. Is also a great enthusiast.
Brentford (From trainee on 5/7/90) FL 4 FLC 5 FAC 2 Others 1
Torquay U (Free on 13/8/93) FL 97 FLC 7 FAC 9 Others 6
Exeter C (Free on 31/7/96) FL 41 FLC 2 FAC 2 Others 1

BAYLISS David (Dave) Anthony
Born: Liverpool, 8 June 1976
Height: 5'11" Weight: 12.4
Briefly used as one of three centre backs in 1996-97, Dave, Rochdale's Young Player of the Year the previous term, then gained a regular slot at full back before an achilles tendon injury curtailed his season.
Rochdale (From trainee on 10/6/95) FL 48+5 FLC 3 FAC 2+1 Others 3

BAZELEY Darren Shaun
Born: Northampton, 5 October 1972
Height: 5'10" Weight" 11.2
International Honours: E: U21-1
On Watford's books as a defender, but more a right-sided utility player, at his best, Darren operates as an orthodox winger. Enjoyed his most effective season yet in 1996-97, providing a potent source of goals

with his accurate crossing and scoring seven himself to equal his best tally. Quick, athletic, and an increasing influence on the team.
Watford (From trainee on 6/5/91) FL 137+47/16 FLC 12+4/2 FAC 11+1/3 Others 6+1/1

Darren Bazeley

BEADLE Peter Clifford
Born: Lambeth, 13 May 1972
Height: 6'1" Weight: 13.7
Powerful and popular with the Bristol Rovers' fans, Peter spent last season as the main striker while the club tried to replace Marcus Stewart. On the credit side, he scored an impressive hat trick on 30 November in a remarkable ten-minute spell against high riding Bury to secure an exciting 4-3 victory, and also an important last-minute equaliser in the derby at Bristol City. Unfortunately, in the return match against City, he had the disappointment of his penalty, Rovers' only one of the campaign, being saved as the visitors ran out 2-1 winners. His form improved noticeably, following the signing of big target man, Julian Alsop, in February.
Gillingham (From trainee on 5/5/90) FL 42+25/14 FLC 2+4/2 FAC 1+1 Others 1
Tottenham H (£300,000 on 4/6/92)
Bournemouth (Loaned on 25/3/93) FL 9/2
Southend U (Loaned on 4/3/94) FL 8/1
Watford (Signed on 12/9/94) FL 12+11/1 FLC 1
Bristol Rov (£50,000 on 17/11/95) FL 62+7/24 FLC 1 FAC 1 Others 3

BEAGRIE Peter Sydney
Born: Middlesbrough, 28 November 1965
Height: 5'8" Weight: 12.0
International Honours: E: B-2; U21-2
A very patient Manchester City winger, even after the end of 1995-96 his problems continued throughout the summer of 1996 as he received treatment to both hernia and skin complaints. However, carefully nurtured through the "A" and reserve sides, Peter eventually made the first team as a substitute against Sheffield United at the end of last January, receiving a rapturous applause. He next came on as a sub at home to Middlesbrough in the FA Cup and there were glimpses of his old attacking form, but the manager sensibly continued to pace him slowly. With his ability to run at defenders and pass them, coupled to tight control and good shooting ability, if fully fit, he will be welcomed back with open arms in 1997-98.
Middlesbrough (From juniors on 10/9/83) FL 24+9/2 FLC 1 Others 1+1
Sheffield U (£35,000 on 16/8/86) FL 81+3/11 FLC 5 FAC 5 Others 4
Stoke C (£210,000 on 29/6/88) FL 54/7 FLC 4 FAC 3/1
Everton (£750,000 on 2/11/89) F/PL 88+26/11 FLC 7+2/3 FAC 7+2 Others 5+1/1
Sunderland (Loaned on 26/9/91) FL 5/1
Manchester C (£1,100,000 on 24/3/94) F/PL 46+6/3 FLC 8/1 FAC 4+1/1

BEALL Matthew John
Born: Enfield, 4 December 1977
Height: 5'7" Weight: 10.6
Having broken into the Cambridge team in 1995-96, last season saw the right-footed midfielder become a first-team regular, working tirelessly and benefiting from playing alongside older, more experienced players. Only scored three goals, but, with good luck, can continue to add to that tally and go on to become an excellent midfield player.
Cambridge U (From trainee on 28/3/96) FL 48+3/6 FLC 2 FAC 2/1 Others 1+1

BEARD Mark
Born: Roehampton, 8 October 1974
Height: 5'10" Weight: 11.3
This young Sheffield United midfielder or defender did not appear in the first team until last November, having gone on the transfer list at the start of the season. Despite that, while failing to challenge for a regular full back slot, he performed well in midfield when called upon to become a valuable squad member. Tenacious and a good tackler, although still transfer listed, he would prefer to stay and win a regular first-team slot.
Millwall (From trainee on 18/3/93) FL 32+13/2 FLC 3+1 FAC 4/1
Sheffield U (£117,000 on 18/8/95) FL 22+14 FLC 2 FAC 1

BEARDSLEY Peter Andrew
Born: Newcastle, 18 January 1961
Height: 5'8" Weight: 11.7
Club Honours: Div 1 '88, '90; FAC '89; CS '88, '89, '90
International Honours: E: 59; B-2
One of Newcastle's all-time great players, club captain Peter continued in 1996-97 to perform as a model professional both on and off the field and was a fine ambassador for his club and for the game in general. As the side searched for shape, he was asked to play in a range of roles, including midfield and attack, but was most effective when operating in the space just behind the front players, where his sharp mind and good ball control make him expert at creating opportunities for himself or others. Started the season on the bench, but was recalled for the derby against Sunderland to inspire an important victory, before leading the side to a further four consecutive wins until a calf injury caused him to miss a couple of matches. Although he turned 36 during the campaign, his enthusiasm and energy remain undiminished and he continued to score with some stunning strikes, most notably an audacious chip in the home UEFA Cup tie against Halmstads. Two personal milestones were passed during home matches in November, in that the game against Middlesbrough was the 700th league and cup appearance of his career and, when he typically jinked his way into the box to score a point saver against West Ham, it was his 200th league goal. Received a Merit Award for his outstanding contribution to football at the PFA annual dinner.
Carlisle U (Free from Wallsend BC on 9/8/79) FL 93+11/22 FLC 6+1 FAC 15/7 (£275,000 to Vancouver Whitecaps on 1/4/82)
Manchester U (£300,000 on 9/9/82) FLC 1 (Free to Vancouver Whitecaps on 1/3/83)
Newcastle U (£150,000 on 23/9/83) FL 146+1/61 FLC 10 FAC 6 Others 1
Liverpool (£1,900,000 on 24/7/87) FL 120+11/46 FLC 13+1/1 FAC 22+3/11 Others 5/1
Everton (£1,000,000 on 5/8/91) F/LP 81/25 FLC 8/5 FAC 4/1 Others 2/1
Newcastle U (£1,400,000 on 16/7/93) PL 126+3/47 FLC 11/4 FAC 11/3 Others 11/4

BEARDSMORE Russell Peter
Born: Wigan, 28 September 1968
Height: 5'7" Weight 10.4
Club Honours: ESC '91
International Honours: E: U21-5

After playing at left back for the majority of 1995-96, Russell reverted to his more accustomed role in Bournemouth's midfield for the 1996-97 campaign, appearing mainly in the centre. Again having a very consistent season, he is a very busy player who closes opponents quickly and seems to be involved in every move.
Manchester U (From apprentice on 2/10/86) FL 30+26/4 FLC 3+1 FAC 4+4 Others 2+5
Blackburn Rov (Loaned on 19/12/91) FL 1+1
Bournemouth (Free on 29/6/93) FL 139+10/3 FLC 13/1 FAC 7 Others 5+1

BEASANT David (Dave) John
Born: Willesden, 20 March 1959
Height: 6'4" Weight: 14.3
Club Honours: Div 4 '83, Div 2 '89; FAC '88; FMC '90
International Honours: E: 2; B-7
Despite being Southampton's Player of the Year in 1995-96, last season saw Dave take a back seat first to Neil Moss, then Chris Woods, and finally, Maik Taylor, who came into the side from Barnet. The giant goalkeeper had started in the side, but once Taylor arrived he was excluded from thereon, although sitting on the bench, his sum total of 19 appearances making it a disappointing campaign. One of those appearances even came from the bench when Woods broke his leg at Blackburn after just 16 minutes and with a likely rout on the cards, the away team, especially the replacement goalie, performed most

bravely, and it was not his fault that the score ended 2-1 in favour of Rovers. Still a good 'keeper, even if a little eccentric, he can still be relied upon to do well when called up.
Wimbledon (£1,000 from Edgware T on 7/8/79) FL 340 FLC 21 FAC 27 Others 3
Newcastle U (£800,000 on 13/6/88) FL 20 FLC 2 FAC 2 Others 1
Chelsea (£725,000 on 14/1/89) F/PL 133 FLC 11 FAC 5 Others 8
Grimsby T (Loaned on 24/10/92) FL 6
Wolverhampton W (Loaned on 12/1/93) FL 4 FAC 1
Southampton (£300,000 on 4/11/93) PL 86+2 FLC 8 FAC 9

BEATTIE James Scott
Born: Lancaster, 27 February 1978
Height: 6'1" Weight: 12.0
Thrust into the Blackburn side in 1996-97 due to an injury crisis, the first year professional striker, a product of the youth team, made his Premiership debut at Ewood against Arsenal early in October and followed that up with an appearance on the same ground against Stockport in the Coca-Cola Cup. Unfortunately, unable to take his considerable scoring exploits into the first team as the season passed, he fell behind the youth-team centre forward, James Thomas, in the reserve-team pecking order and will be looking to adjust to the rigours of that level in 1997-98.
Blackburn Rov (From trainee on 7/3/95) PL 1 FLC 1

Dave Beasant

BEAUCHAMP Joseph (Joey) Daniel
Born: Oxford, 13 March 1971
Height: 5'10" Weight: 12.5
Despite being an Oxford regular for most of last season, it was not one of the winger's most memorable. It started well enough with a brace against Southend, and also a cracker against Reading in a derby game, but, as the season wore on, Joey was more often seen coming off the bench to chase the game as United struggled in the final third of the campaign. On his day, he can leave most full backs in his wake, but most defences had done their homework last season and he often was marked by two men. Returned with a vengeance in the final game, with two goals against promoted Barnsley, and several times came close to a hat trick.
Oxford U (From trainee on 16/5/89) FL 117+7/20 FLC 6+1/2 FAC 8/3 Others 5+1
Swansea C (Loaned on 30/10/91) FL 5/2 Others 1
West Ham U (£1,000,000 on 22/6/94)
Swindon T (£850,000 on 18/8/94) FL 39+6/3 FLC 7+2/1 FAC 2 Others 4
Oxford U (£300,000 on 4/10/95) FL 61+16/14 FLC 8 FAC 3+2/1 Others 0+2

Joey Beauchamp

BEAUMONT Christopher (Chris) Paul
Born: Sheffield, 5 December 1965
Height: 5'11" Weight: 11.7
Chesterfield's 1996 summer signing from Stockport found it difficult to make an early impression but he dug in, worked hard, and became an important member of the midfield by Christmas. Chris contributed greatly to the Spireites' epic FA Cup run, intelligently crafting the defence-splitting pass that led to the penalty against Forest and showing strength, imagination and anticipation to score the goal that beat Wrexham in the sixth round.
Rochdale (Free from Denaby U on 21/7/88) FL 31+3/7 FLC 0+1/1 FAC 2/1 Others 2

Stockport Co (£8,000 on 21/7/89) FL 238+20/39 FLC 14+3/3 FAC 15/2 Others 34+2/7
Chesterfield (£30,000 on 22/7/96) FL 29+4/1 FLC 2 FAC 3+2/1 Others 1

BECK Mikkel
Born: Arhus, Denmark, 12 May 1973
Height: 6'2" Weight: 12.9
International Honours: Denmark: 13
Arrived almost unnoticed at Middlesbrough last September, his legal wrangle with the German second division club, Fortuna Koln, preventing a straightforward conventional transfer. However, Mikkel quickly put all of that behind him when he eventually made Boro's first team, proving his worth as a brilliant opportunist striker and provider in the successful domestic cup runs. While his Premiership appearances underlined his goalscoring prowess and an international game for Denmark (v. Finland) saw him record his first national representative goal, other initial Boro appearances, against Huddersfield (reserves) and Hereford (Coca-Cola Cup), also proved fruitful, with debut goals on each occasion. Now fully acclimatised to the high-speed English game, the Dane could well be a high-scoring package in the first division this coming term.
Middlesbrough (Free from Fortuna Cologne on 13/9/96) PL 22+3/5 FLC 6+1/4 FAC 5+1/2

BECKFORD Darren Richard
Born: Manchester, 12 May 1967
Height: 6'1" Weight: 13.6
International Honours: E: Yth; Sch
A hard-running, bustling centre forward, Darren left Oldham for Heart of Midlothian during the 1996 close season in an effort to get regular first-team football but, unable to settle in Scotland, he came back down south early in the New Year to try his luck with Preston, playing just three games. Following that, another trial period, this time with Fulham, offered nothing tangible and he signed a monthly contract with Walsall where he appeared eight times before being released.
Manchester C (From apprentice on 21/8/84) FL 7+4 FLC 0+1
Bury (Loaned on 10/10/85) FL 12/5
Port Vale (£15,000 on 26/3/87) FL 169+9/72 FLC 12/3 FAC 14/4 Others 9+1/3
Norwich C (£925,000 on 14/6/91) F/PL 32+6/8 FLC 3+2/3 FAC 4+1/1 Others 1/1
Oldham Ath (£300,000 on 25/3/93) P/FL 31+21/11 FLC 2/1 FAC 6+3/4 Others 1+1
Heart of Midlothian (Free on 14/8/96) SL 5+2 SLC 1+3/1
Preston NE (Free on 17/1/97) FL 0+2 Others 1
Fulham (Free on 10/2/97)
Walsall (Free on 25/3/97) FL 3+5

BECKHAM David Robert
Born: Leytonstone, 2 May 1975
Height: 6'0" Weight: 11.2
Club Honours: FAYC '92; PL '96, '97; FAC '96; CS '97
International Honours: E: 9; U21-9; Yth
An excellent midfielder with a wonderful range of passing and shooting skills, David started last season in spectacular fashion for Manchester United, scoring a brilliant goal against Newcastle at Wembley in the Charity Shield, before netting what Alex Ferguson described as the goal of the season in the opening Premiership game at Wimbledon – chipping the 'keeper from the half-way line. Having been named the first Carling Player of the Month for August, and promoted to the full England side under Glenn Hoddle, his season went from strength to strength, especially as a regular scorer of outstanding goals, none more important than those against Rapid Vienna in the Champions' League and Spurs in the FA Cup. Although a niggling ankle injury threatened to disrupt his form in January, he made an excellent recovery to play a major part in United's continuing quest for honours, winning a further championship medal, and being voted the PFA Young Footballer of the Year as well as being selected for the PFA award-winning Premiership side, as a tribute for his superb efforts.
Manchester U (From trainee on 29/1/93) PL 61+12/15 FLC 5+1 FAC 6+1/2 Others 14/4
Preston NE (Loaned on 28/2/95) FL 4+1/2

David Beckham

BEDEAU Anthony (Tony) Charles Osmond
Born: Hammersmith, 24 March 1979
Height: 5'10" Weight: 11.0
A second-year Torquay YTS who impressed on his limited first team outings in 1996-97, he seemed happier as an out-and-out winger rather than deeper in midfield. Has good pace and is comfortable on the ball.
Torquay U (Trainee) FL 4+8/1 FAC 0+1

BEECH Christopher (Chris) Stephen
Born: Blackpool, 16 September 1974
Height: 5'11" Weight: 11.4
Released by Blackpool during the 1996 close season, the hard working, if unspectacular, midfielder began last season at Hartlepool well, forming a good partnership with fellow signing, Mark Cooper. As he himself admitted he then went off the boil, but, in mid term, he

cracked down to become a much more constructive player, maintaining a high level of fitness and scoring some important long-range goals. In practice, he was Pool's most consistent player, being rewarded when voted the Supporters' Player of the Season.
Blackpool (From trainee on 9/7/93) FL 53+29/4 FLC 4+4 FAC 1 Others 3+3/2
Hartlepool U (Free on 18/7/96) FL 42/8 FLC 2/1 FAC 2 Others 1

BEENEY Mark Raymond
Born: Tunbridge Wells, 30 December 1967
Height: 6'4" Weight: 14.7
Club Honours: GMVC '89
International Honours: E: SP-1
A good shot stopper and a Leeds' goalkeeper of undoubted ability, Mark, the longtime understudy to John Lukic, last season found himself as back up to the superb Nigel Martyn. With the former Crystal Palace man in such commanding form, he made his only appearance against Derby County in January after the latter picked up a back injury in training and let no one down in keeping a clean sheet. Under contract until June 1998, he is a good man to have as first team cover
Gillingham (From juniors on 17/8/85) FL 2 FLC 1
Maidstone U (Free on 31/1/87) FL 50 FLC 3 FAC 11 Others 6
Aldershot (Loaned on 22/3/90) FL 7
Brighton & Hove A (£30,000 on 28/3/91) FL 68+1 FLC 6 FAC 7 Others 6
Leeds U (£350,000 on 22/4/93) PL 34 FLC 3 FAC 4

BEESLEY Paul
Born: Liverpool, 21 July 1965
Height: 6'1" Weight: 12.6
A seasoned Manchester City central defender, Paul was signed from Leeds United early last February after making 14 appearances under George Graham, but was cup tied. Having played under Frank Clark before, his City debut at home to Southend was very impressive and he soon began to stabilise and strengthen the defence. Unfortunately, after six league games, he was injured at Birmingham, which unsettled the defence and brought the good run of results to an end. Is definitely a player the manager will be building on to form a strong squad for this coming season.
Wigan Ath (Free from Marine on 22/9/84) FL 153+2/3 FLC 13 FAC 6 Others 11
Leyton Orient (£175,000 on 20/10/89) FL 32/1 FAC 1 Others 2/1
Sheffield U (£300,000 on 10/7/90) F/PL 162+6/7 FLC 12+1 FAC 9+2/1 Others 3/1
Leeds U (£250,000 on 2/8/95) PL 19+3 FLC 5+1 FAC 5 Others 2+2
Manchester C (£500,000 on 7/2/97) FL 6

BEESTON Carl Frederick
Born: Stoke, 30 June 1967
Height: 5'10" Weight: 12.4
Club Honours: Div 2 '93
International Honours: E: U21-1
Local Stoke midfielder who started last season in the side, playing in the first seven games, before an injury cost him his place. On top of that, the former England U21 international also appeared to fall from favour, but a mid-term loan spell at Hereford boosted his confidence and resulted in a

return to the team, prior to him being released in the summer. At his best, he combines play-making skills with tough tackling.
Stoke C (From apprentice on 1/7/85) FL 224+12/13 FLC 12/1 FAC 7+1/1 Others 15/2
Hereford U (Loaned on 23/1/97) FL 9/2

BEIRNE Michael Andrew
Born: Manchester, 21 September 1973
Height: 5'9" Weight: 11.0
An ex Manchester City trainee, Michael came to Doncaster last season on non-contract forms from Droylesden, having been with any number of clubs previously, including Congleton Town, Winsford United, Rossendale United and Ashton United. A prolific scorer with Abbey Hay in the Manchester League, who has been unable to translate that ability at higher levels, he made his league debut at home to Barnet in February before returning to Droylesden.
Doncaster Rov (Free from Droylesden on 14/2/97) FL 1

BELL Michael (Mickey)
Born: Newcastle, 15 November 1971
Height: 5'10" Weight: 11.4
Mickey had an outstanding season as an ever present at left back and then left-wing back for Wycombe in 1996-97, deservedly winning both Player of the Season awards and firmly establishing himself as the club's most talented player. Solid when defending, beautifully balanced, and with the ability to glide past players, he laid on many goals with his teasing outswinging crosses.
Northampton T (From trainee on 1/7/90) FL 133+20/10 FLC 7+1 FAC 5/1 Others 9+2/1
Wycombe W (£45,000 on 21/10/94) FL 117+1/5 FLC 5 FAC 9/2 Others 3+1

BELLAMY Craig Douglas
Born: Cardiff, 13 July 1979
Height: 5'8" Weight: 10.5
International Honours: W: U21-4; Yth; Sch
Yet to experience a Norwich first-team win bonus, Craig had only walk on parts when introduced in 1996-97 – 90 seconds versus Crystal Palace; a cameo 19 minutes against Manchester City when he made a nuisance of himself with good touches, plus a game for every player and fan to forget at Boundary Park. Having scored over 100 goals for his junior school and heavily for City youths, this Welsh schoolboy international became the youngest ever player to represent Wales at U21 level when he played against San Marino. An attacking central midfielder who enjoys running at defenders, he possesses fleetness of foot good passing skills, and can score goals. Those in the know at Carrow Road predict a great future for this bright youngster.
Norwich C (From trainee on 20/1/97) FL 0+3

BENALI Francis (Franny) Vincent
Born: Southampton, 30 December 1968
Height: 5'10" Weight: 11.0
International Honours: E: Sch
Tough-tackling Southampton player, who can play with equal ability at left back, in the

centre of defence, or in midfield, and never lets the side down. Having spent the first part of 1996-97 on the bench before being called into the side for his seasonal debut at the Dell against Derby, Francis missed very few games from thereon, his total commitment being invaluable as the Saints struggled to avoid relegation. An excellent striker of the ball, despite being able to get forward down the left flank into crossing positions he still awaits his first goal, and that after more than 260 appearances. At the club since his schooldays, Francis was awarded a well-deserved testimonial at the end of last season.
Southampton (From apprentice on 5/1/87) F/PL 193+27 FLC 17+6 FAC 19 Others 3+1

BENJAMIN Trevor Junior
Born: Kettering, 8 February 1979
Height: 6'2" Weight: 13.2
Limited to substitute appearances for Cambridge in 1995-96, before making his full debut on the final day of last season, Trevor was again mainly consigned to coming off the bench, despite scoring his first league goal against Scarborough in September. A regular in the youth team, and previously seen as a left winger, he is now a very strong centre forward and, almost certainly, will be a handful to opposing defences in 1997-98.
Cambridge U (From trainee on 21/2/97) FL 1+11/1 FLC 0+1

BENNETT Dean
Born: Wolverhampton, 13 December 1977
Height: 5'10" Weight: 11.0
Introduced by West Bromwich manager, Ray Harford, as a late substitute against Grimsby in Albion's final home match of last season, he looked to be a useful footballer, having done well in the reserve and intermediate sides as a wide midfielder. Was signed on a monthly basis after coming to the club on trial in February 1996, following a spell at Aston Villa.
West Bromwich A (Free from Aston Villa juniors on 19/12/96) FL 0+1

BENNETT Frank (Frankie)
Born: Birmingham, 3 January 1969
Height: 5'7" Weight: 12.1
A pacy winger, Frankie impressed against Bristol Rovers during a loan spell with Shrewsbury Town last season and was snapped up from Southampton in November for a small fee. Unfortunately, after just two starts he suffered a repeat of a previous niggling knee injury which kept him out of the side until the new year. Later scored his first and only league goal for Rovers, an impressive 30-yard strike on 20 April, which proved to be the match winner against Notts County.
Southampton (£7,500 from Halesowen T on 24/2/93) PL 5+14/1 FLC 1+2 FAC 0+1
Shrewsbury T (Loaned on 25/10/96) FL 2+2/3
Bristol Rov (£15,000 on 22/11/96) FL 6+5/1

BENNETT Gary Ernest
Born: Manchester, 4 December 1961
Height: 6'1" Weight: 13.0
Club Honours: Div 3 '88

An elegant central defender, powerful in the air and strong in the tackle, although now in the veteran stage of his career, Gary joined Scarborough in the summer of 1996, having been freed by Carlisle, and enjoyed a magnificent campaign. Playing in every match, he was named North East Player of the Year by the Newcastle based *Sunday Sun* newspaper.

Manchester C (Free from Ashton U on 8/9/79)
Cardiff C (Free on 16/9/81) FL 85+2/11 FLC 6/1 FAC 3
Sunderland (£65,000 on 26/7/84) FL 362+7/23 FLC 34+1/1 FAC 17+1 Others 21/1
Carlisle U (Free on 16/11/95) FL 26/5 Others 5/1
Scarborough (Free on 2/8/96) FL 46/9 FLC 4/2 FAC 3 Others 1

Gary Bennett (Scarborough)

BENNETT Gary Michael
Born: Liverpool, 20 September 1962
Height: 5'11" Weight: 12.0
Club Honours: AMC '85; WC '95

A pre-season shin fracture kept Gary out of first-team action for Preston until last October and on his return, he was clearly not fully fit and his form suffered as a consequence. Used more often as a substitute than a starter, he scored two goals from the bench against the old enemy in the 3-0 home win over Blackpool, before being transferred to former club, Wrexham, in February. Although not making an immediate mark, it is to be hoped that he will continue his goalscoring ways at the Racecourse in 1997-98.

Wigan Ath (Free from Kirby T on 9/10/84) FL 10+10/3 FAC 1 Others 3+1/1
Chester C (Free on 22/8/85) FL 109+17/36 FLC 6+4/1 FAC 8+1/5 Others 10/5
Southend U (Signed on 11/11/88) FL 36+6/6 FLC 4/4 FAC 1 Others 2+1
Chester C (£20,000 on 1/3/90) FL 71+9/15 FLC 8/2 FAC 5/1 Others 4+1/1
Wrexham (Free on 12/8/92) FL 120+1/77 FLC 17/9 FAC 7/3 Others 9/9
Tranmere Rov (£300,000 on 13/7/95) FL 26+3/9 FLC 4
Preston NE (£200,000 on 27/3/96) FL 15+9/4 Others 1
Wrexham (£100,000 on 28/2/97) FL 15/5 FAC 0+1

BENNETT Ian Michael
Born: Worksop, 10 October 1971
Height: 6'0" Weight: 12.0
Club Honours: Div 2 '95; AMC '95

One of the best shot stoppers outside the Premier Division, Ian's superb reflexes and positional skills gave great confidence to the Birmingham defence in 1996-97, his stop from Charlton's Shaun Newton in March being one of the best saves ever seen at St Andrews. Had another fine season with 17 clean sheets, including seven in the last nine matches and holds the club record of nine consecutive clean sheets (in 1994).

Newcastle U (Free from Queens Park R juniors on 20/3/89)
Peterborough U (Free on 22/3/91) FL 72 FLC 10 FAC 3 Others 4
Birmingham C (£325,000 on 17/12/93) FL 132 FLC 16 FAC 10 Others 11

BENNETT Michael (Micky) Richard
Born: Camberwell, 27 July 1969
Height: 5'11" Weight: 11.11

Released by Millwall during the 1996 close season, Micky joined Cardiff on non-contract terms at the start of 1996-97, coming into the side on the wide right for the opening six games before being relegated to a subs' role. However, having opened his scoring account at home to Rochdale, and apparently winning over the fans, he was surprisingly released just prior to Christmas.

Charlton Ath (From apprentice on 27/4/87) FL 24+11/2 FLC 4 FAC 1 Others 6+1
Wimbledon (£250,000 on 9/1/90) FL 12+6/2 FLC 1+1 FAC 0+1 Others 1+1
Brentford (£60,000 on 14/7/92) FL 40+6/4 FLC 4+1 FAC 1 Others 6+1
Charlton Ath (Free on 24/3/94) FL 19+5/1 FAC 1
Millwall (Free on 16/5/95) FL 1+1
Cardiff C (Free on 14/8/96) FL 5+9/1 FLC 2 FAC 1+1 Others 0+1

BENNETT Thomas (Tom) McNeill
Born: Falkirk, 12 December 1969
Height: 5'11" Weight: 11.8

In missing just three league games for Stockport in 1996-97, the Scottish midfielder had a marvellous season, drawing praise from many, especially for his displays in County's televised Coca-Cola Cup games. A cultured player, he also showed good combativeness as a campaign that culminated in the club being promoted to the first division, reached its climax.

Aston Villa (From apprentice on 16/12/87)
Wolverhampton W (Free on 5/7/88) FL 103+12/2 FLC 7 FAC 5+2 Others 3+1
Stockport Co (£75,000 on 23/6/95) FL 67/4 FLC 16/2 FAC 7 Others 6+1

BENNETT Troy
Born: Barnsley, 25 December 1975
Height: 5'9" Weight: 11.13
International Honours: E: Yth

A young Barnsley midfielder who normally plays wide on either flank, Troy's career to date has been decimated by injury, a bone graft operation in January 1996 putting him out of action until last October. On coming back, he pressed on in the reserves until being loaned to Scarborough on transfer deadline day, playing five games and

scoring from a superbly taken free kick from the edge of the area for his first league goal before returning to Oakwell. Was released during the summer.

Barnsley (From trainee on 23/12/93) FL 2
Scarborough (Loaned on 27/3/97) FC 4+1/1

BENT Junior Antony
Born: Huddersfield, 1 March 1970
Height: 5'6" Weight: 10.9

After a early season spell on loan with Shrewsbury last October, Junior came back refreshed and wrested the Bristol City right-wing position from Greg Goodridge. He looked like a new player in reaching new heights of excellence, but, unfortunately, towards the end of the campaign, wingers fell out of favour at Ashton Gate and opportunities became limited. While his speed still remains his greatest asset, and it is encouraging to find that his crossing has improved immensely, the fans want to see him become the finished article he had promised to be, in finding opponents' nets more often.

Huddersfield T (From trainee on 9/12/87) FL 25+11/6 FLC 1 FAC 3+1/1 Others 4
Burnley (Loaned on 30/11/89) FL 7+2/3
Bristol C (£30,000 on 22/3/90) FL 142+39/20 FLC 10+1 FAC 12+3/2 Others 7+3
Stoke C (Loaned on 26/3/92) FL 1
Shrewsbury T (Loaned on 24/10/96) FL 6

BENT Marcus Nathan
Born: Hammersmith, 19 May 1978
Height: 6'2" Weight: 12.4

Tall Brentford right winger with good speed and ball control. Despite being only 18 years old, Marcus was a regular throughout last season, scoring a fine goal against Plymouth in September to clinch a victory and also converting a well-taken effort against Bristol City in the play offs. Shows the same level of promise as the former Bee, Marcus Gayle, did at the same age.

Brentford (From trainee on 21/7/95) FL 37+9/4 FLC 4 FAC 6/3 Others 5+1/1

BERESFORD David
Born: Middlesbrough, 11 November 1976
Height: 5'8" Weight: 11.4
International Honours: E: Yth; Sch

A tricky, pacy right winger, David was a regular for Oldham last season before transferring to Huddersfield on transfer deadline day, a move that saw Paul Reid go in the opposite direction. Missed just one of the last seven matches, while showing himself to have excellent crossing ability and always looking to create chances for others. He also provided a good outlet when playing on the break and using his pace to pressure opposing defenders, scoring his first goal for Town in a 2-1 win at Southend.

Oldham Ath (From trainee on 22/7/94) P/FL 32+32/2 FLC 3+3 FAC 0+1 Others 3
Swansea C (Loaned on 11/8/95) FL 4+2
Huddersfield T (£350,000 on 27/3/97) FL 6/1

BERESFORD John
Born: Sheffield, 4 September 1966
Height: 5'6" Weight: 10.12
Club Honours: Div 1 '93
International Honours: E: B-2; Yth; Sch

John is a Newcastle left back whose skill on the ball and speed and eagerness to join the attack equip him well for the modern role of wing back. Started the opening game of last season, but then gave way to Robbie Elliott when the latter signed a new contract, before being brought back for the match against Blackburn in September to combat the pace of Georgios Donis and playing so well he re-established himself in the team. Competing with Elliott throughout 1996-97 for a first-team place, he never let the side down when selected and it was a blow when a hip injury sidelined him for a period early in 1997, although he did return to the side again to play soundly in the closing matches of the campaign to earn a new two-year contract.

Manchester C (From apprentice on 16/9/83)
Barnsley (Free on 4/8/86) FL 79+9/5 FLC 5+2/2 FAC 5/1
Portsmouth (£300,000 on 23/3/89) FL 102+5/8 FLC 12/2 FAC 11 Others 2
Newcastle U (£650,000 on 2/7/92) F/PL 159+2/1 FLC 14 FAC 15/1 Others 10+1

BERESFORD Marlon
Born: Lincoln, 2 September 1969
Height: 6'1" Weight: 13.6

It was another consistent season for Burnley's goalkeeper, still one of the best shot stoppers outside the Premiership, as he maintained his fine penalty-saving record during 1996-97. Occasionally criticised for poor distribution, he nevertheless remained unchallenged as the Clarets' first choice, keeping 14 clean sheets as the club made a run for the play offs.

Sheffield Wed (From trainee on 23/9/87)
Bury (Loaned on 25/8/89) FL 1
Northampton T (Loaned on 27/9/90) FL 13 Others 2
Crewe Alex (Loaned on 28/2/91) FL 3
Northampton T (Loaned on 15/8/91) FL 15
Burnley (£95,000 on 28/8/92) FL 206 FLC 14 FAC 18 Others 13

BERG Henning
Born: Eidsvell, Norway, 1 September 1969
Height: 6'0" Weight: 12.7
Club Honours: PL '95
International Honours: Norway: 45

Whether playing at right back or alongside Colin Hendry for Blackburn in 1996-97, Henning was seldom less than superb. An intelligent reader of the game, with a keen positional sense, he is a natural sealer of the defence whose timing and judgement are impeccable. Always one to join the attack for set pieces, the Norwegian international opened the scoring at West Ham in October, before spectacularly heading a Stan Lazaridis cross into his own net for the Hammers' winner. Other attempts brought little reward until he scored the vital first goal in the crucial game at home to Sheffield Wednesday, which ultimately resulted in a 4-1 win for Rovers and Premiership football in 1997-98.

Blackburn Rov (£400,000 from Lillestrom on 26/1/93) PL154+5/4 FLC 16 FAC 10 Others 9

BERGER Patrik
Born: Prague, Czechoslovakia, 10 November 1973
Height: 6'1" Weight: 12.6

International Honours: Czechoslovakia: 26

Following the success of the Czech Republic in Euro '96, Patrik followed his friend Karel Poborsky into Premiership football when joining Liverpool at the start of last season. He made an immediate impact, scoring twice in his second outing at Leicester, and showed excellent, accurate shooting ability, especially from long range. Going on to score five goals in three consecutive games in September, it was his incisive runs into the opposition's penalty area that took the eye. However, following that super start he found it difficult to maintain a first-team place due to the strength in depth of the squad, often losing out to Jamie Redknapp and Stan Collymore and having to settle for a place on the bench. A strong runner from midfield, despite notching nine goals in 23 starts, he sometimes proved a luxury when Pool's main problems stemmed from a shortage of hard-tackling midfielders.

Liverpool (£3,250,000 from Borussia Dortmund on 15/8/96) PL 13+10/6 FLC 3/1 FAC 1+1 Others 6/2

BERGKAMP Dennis
Born: Amsterdam, Holland, 18 May 1969
Height: 6'0" Weight: 12.5
International Honours: Holland: 55

Playing in a more advanced role at Arsenal in 1996-97 than previously, Dennis had a superb season, despite suffering from early injury problems. Indeed, it was mainly down to the Dutchman's brilliance that the Gunners were able to sustain a realistic championship challenge until late April, while his partnership with the mercurial Ian Wright continued to improve to a degree that it was right up there with all other leading pairings. Memorable goals included a late strike that ensured a home victory over arch-rivals, Tottenham and, arguably, the goal of the season at Sunderland – taking a

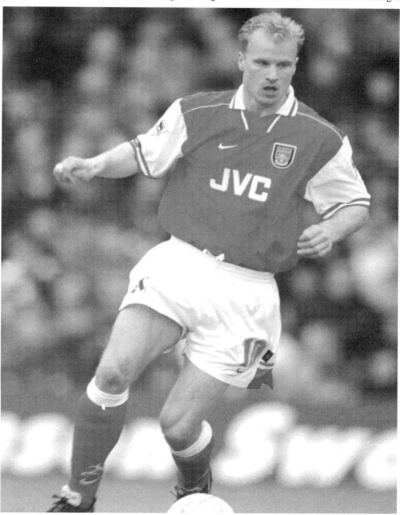

Dennis Bergkamp

pass from Paul Merson, turning two defenders, and chipping the ball into the top corner of the net – that took the club into the fourth round of the FA Cup. A regular for Holland, it is felt that he will play a pivotal role in the expected Arsenal championship challenge this coming term.

Arsenal (£7,500,000 from Inter Milan, via Ajax, on 3/7/95) PL 61+1/23 FLC 9/6 FAC 3/1 Others 1

BERGSSON Gudni
Born: Iceland, 21 July 1965
Height: 6'1" Weight: 12.3
Club Honours: CS '91; Div 1 '97
International Honours: Iceland: 74

Although starting last season on the bench, Gudni again proved a dependable member of the Bolton rearguard, operating in both the full-back and centre-back positions. The height of the captain of the Icelandic national team makes him an ominous presence in the opponents' penalty area, particularly from set pieces, and this was seen to good effect when he scored two goals in the 7-0 drubbing of Swindon Town.

Tottenham H (£100,000 from Valur on 15/12/88) F/PL 51+20/2 FLC 4+2 FAC 2+2 Others 5+1
Bolton W (£65,000 on 21/3/95) P/FL 72+3/7 FLC 9+1 FAC 2 Others 3

BERKLEY Austin James
Born: Dartford, 28 January 1973
Height: 5'9" Weight: 11.6

Very tricky Shrewsbury left winger. On his day, an exciting provider who can cause opposing defences continual problems, his 1996-97 season was unfortunately interrupted by injury, which saw him sidelined on three separate occasions. For all his work, it would be nice to see him find the net more often, one goal in the AWS being his sole total for the campaign.

Gillingham (From trainee on 13/5/91) FL 0+3 Others 0+3
Swindon T (Free on 16/5/92) FL 0+1 FLC 0+1 Others 3+1/1
Shrewsbury T (Free on 29/7/95) FL 56+6/1 FLC 4+1 FAC 5+1 Others 9/1

BERKOVIC Eyal
Born: Haifa, Israel, 2 April 1972
Height: 5'7" Weight: 10.2
International Honours: Israel: 43

What an excellent signing, the Israeli international turned out to be for Southampton in 1996-97. Brought to the club by Graeme Souness in October, the classy midfielder proved to be one of the Premiership bargains of the season, his great ball control, vision and passing skills, plus an ability to retain possession in dangerous areas, seeing him become an integral part of a side that ultimately staved off relegation by the skin of its teeth. Although not a prolific scorer, he still popped in six invaluable goals after making a sensational scoring debut in his second game for the club at the Dell against Manchester United, notching two in a great 6-3 victory over the prospective champions. A regular for Israel, Eyal's excellent form gave the manager a continuous problem of selection, with both him and Matt le Tissier vying for the same midfield slot. *Stop Press:* Having been

signed on a lease deal, with a fee of £1.2 million to change hands once the Israeli signed a long-term contract, it was reported during the summer that he had joined West Ham.

Southampton (Leased from Maccabi Tel Aviv on 11/10/96) PL 26+2/4 FLC 5+1/2 FAC 1

BERNAL Andrew (Andy)
Born: Canberra, Australia, 16 May 1966
Height: 5'10" Weight: 12.5
International Honours: Australia: 18

Andy completed another season in 1996-97 as a combative, reliable Reading defender, and skippered the team on several occasions. An eventful campaign included a run of appearances in midfield, three sendings off and an acrobatic display as substitute goalkeeper after Bobby Mihailov had been sent off in the match at Ipswich. Again proving capable of playing anywhere across the back four, he was one of the more consistent performers for the Royals.

Ipswich T (Free from Sporting Gijon on 24/9/87) FL 4+5 Others 0+2
Reading (£30,000 from Sydney Olympic on 26/7/94) FL 108/2 FLC 8+1 FAC 4 Others 3

BERRY Gregory (Greg) John
Born: Grays, 5 March 1971
Height: 6'0" Weight: 12.0

In 1996-97, Greg overcame the bad injuries which had threatened his Millwall career after being drafted in at left back in February, following injuries to others, and keeping his place. And, while trying to curb his usual attacking style of play, he put in some exceptional work in the Lions' rearguard. Surprisingly released during the summer, his speed and control also make him a candidate for most midfield roles if required.

Leyton Orient (£2,000 from East Thurrock on 3/7/89) FL 68+12/14 FLC 6/3 FAC 8+2/2 Others 5+3/1
Wimbledon (£250,000 on 17/8/92) PL 6+1/1 FAC 0+1
Millwall (£200,000 on 24/3/94) FL 23+11/1 FLC 1/2 FAC 1 Others 1/1
Brighton & HA (Loaned on 24/8/95) FL 6/2
Leyton Orient (Loaned on 22/3/96) FL 4+3

BERRY Trevor John
Born: Haslemere, 1 August 1974
Height: 5'7" Weight: 10.8
Club Honours: AMC '96
International Honours: E: Yth

Despite the fact that a role wide on the right had previously been accepted as his best position, Trevor was often used more as a central midfielder for Rotherham in 1996-97, although he was unable to carve out a regular spot and had to settle for a substitute's place on several occasions. A hard-working player, his speed and ability to run down opposing forwards, has often proved invaluable.

Aston Villa (£50,000 from Bournemouth juniors on 3/4/92)
Rotherham U (£20,000 on 8/9/95) FL 52+14/11 FLC 1+1 FAC 1+1 Others 8/1

BETTNEY Christopher (Chris) John
Born: Chesterfield, 27 October 1977
Height: 5'10" Weight: 10.10

A young first-year Sheffield United professional who made a surprise appearance at Tranmere last April, due to the loss of first-choice strikers through injuries, Chris acquitted himself well. Still learning the game, he uses his pace to take defenders on, mainly down the right-hand side, and looks to be a good prospect for the future.

Sheffield U (From trainee on 15/5/96) FL 0+1

BETTS Simon Richard
Born: Middlesbrough, 3 March 1973
Height: 5'7" Weight: 11.4

Simon alternated between both full-back positions at Colchester in the early months of last season, before scoring his first goal from the penalty spot at Lincoln at the end of October. Unfortunately, he tore groin muscles in taking the penalty and missed the rest of the season, after suffering a nasty ankle injury in his first comeback reserve run out in March. Approaching full fitness as the campaign finished, his accuracy from 12 yards was sadly missed in the Wembley AWS shoot out!

Ipswich T (From trainee on 2/7/91)
Wrexham (Free on 13/8/92)
Scarborough (Free on 3/11/92)
Colchester U (Free on 11/12/92) FL 143+3/9 FLC 7 FAC 6+1 Others 10/2

BIBBO Salvatore (Sal)
Born: Basingstoke, 24 August 1974
Height: 6'2" Weight: 13.5

Sal came on trial from Sheffield United at the start of last season and did well enough in friendly games to be given a two-year contract. However, he was never able to establish himself in the first team, only playing when the senior goalkeepers were unavailable through injury, suspension or international calls. Is a good shot stopper, kicks well, and used his spare time coaching the youngsters at the club's school of excellence.

Sheffield U (Free from Crawley T on 18/8/93) Others 2
Chesterfield (Loaned on 10/2/95) FL 0+1
Reading (Free on 15/8/96) FL 5 FAC 1

BIGGINS Wayne
Born: Sheffield, 20 November 1961
Height: 5'11" Weight: 13.0
Club Honours: AMC '92; Div 3 '97

Playing under manager, John Deehan, for the third time, the Wigan player relished his new central midfield role in 1996-97, chipping in with some vital goals. Although his astute skills and vision were invaluable when called upon, he was released at the end of the season, after his 33 league games ensured him of a third division championship medal.

Lincoln C (From apprentice on 22/11/79) FL 8/1 (Free to Kings Lynn during 1981 close season)
Burnley (£7,500 from Matlock on 4/2/84) FL 78/29 FLC 6/1 FAC 3/1 Others 7/5
Norwich C (£40,000 on 17/10/85) FL 66+13/16 FLC 6/2 FAC 4 Others 6+2/3
Manchester C (£150,000 on 15/7/88) FL 29+3/9 FLC 4/1 FAC 2
Stoke C (£250,000 on 10/8/89) FL 120+2/46 FLC 10/2 FAC 6 Others 10/5
Barnsley (£200,000 on 2/10/92) FL 44+3/16 FAC 3+1

Glasgow Celtic (Signed on 25/11/93) SL 4+5 SC 0+1
Stoke C (£125,000 on 24/3/94) FL 18+9/6 FLC 1+1 Others 3+1/2
Luton T (Loaned on 20/1/95) FL 6+1/1 FAC 2/1
Oxford U (Free on 6/7/95) FL 8+2/1 FLC 3+1/1 Others 0+1
Wigan Ath (Free on 17/11/95) FL 35+16/5 FLC 1+1 FAC 1 Others 0+1

BILIC Slaven
Born: Croatia, 11 September 1968
Height: 6'2" Weight: 13.8
International Honours: Croatia: 30

The West Ham and Croatian international defender enjoyed an outstanding season at the heart of West Ham's defence in 1996-97, only missing three Premiership games and being voted runner up in the end of season Hammer of the Year award, which he might have won but for speculation about his future commitment to the club. A strong tackler with good distribution abilities and powerful in the air, both in defence and at set pieces with two headed goals to his credit in the home matches with Liverpool and Sunderland, his consistency was a major factor in the Hammers' preservation of Premier League status. *Stop Press:* Transferred to Everton for a fee of £4.5 million soon after the end of the campaign
West Ham U (£1,300,000 from Karlsruhe on 4/2/96) PL 48/2 FLC 5/1 FAC 1

BILLING Peter Graham
Born: Liverpool, 24 October 1964
Height: 6'1" Weight: 13.12
Club Honours: AMC '93

Given a free transfer by Hartlepool during the 1996 close season, this seasoned defender had his second spell at Crewe when signing on a 12-month contract, making a useful contribution when needed, mainly from left or right back. Reliable in the air and solid on the ground, he never let the side down.
Everton (Free from South Liverpool on 15/1/86) FL 1 Others 4
Crewe Alex (£12,000 on 23/12/86) FL 83+5/1 FLC 1+1 FAC 5 Others 9
Coventry C (£120,000 on 28/6/89) F/PL 51+7/1 FLC 9+1 FAC 7 Others 2
Port Vale (£35,000 on 26/2/93) FL 23+3 FLC 1 Others 3+2
Hartlepool U (Free on 8/8/95) FL 35+1 FLC 4 FAC 1 Others 2
Crewe Alex (Free on 23/8/96) FL 9+6 FAC 1+1 Others 3

BILLINGTON David James
Born: Oxford, 15 January 1980
Height: 5'8" Weight: 10.2

A young utility player who can perform anywhere on the field with equal ability, David made his Peterborough debut when coming off the bench at Southampton in the Coca-Cola Cup last September and showed real class. Still a trainee, he appeared six more times in the first team, while continuing to impress many shrewd judges, before being transferred to Sheffield Wednesday in early April. Is very quick, with two good feet, and an excellent passer.
Peterborough U (Trainee) FL 2+3 FLC 1+1
Sheffield Wed (£500,000+ on 3/4/97)

Chris Billy

BILLY Christopher (Chris) Anthony
Born: Huddersfield, 2 January 1973
Height: 5'11" Weight: 11.8

Had an outstanding season for Plymouth in 1996-97 as a right-wing back, after being forced into the position by an early injury to Mark Patterson and making the slot his own. A natural attacker, this came to the fore from his new role in the side, and he collected eight out of ten Player of the Year awards. Not much of a goalscorer, but a double in a 3-2 win at Shrewsbury in March was something to cheer about.
Huddersfield T (From trainee on 1/7/91) FL 76+18/4 FLC 8+2 FAC 5 Others 15+2/2
Plymouth Arg (Signed on 10/8/95) FL 66+11/7 FLC 4 FAC 6/1 Others 4+1

BIMSON Stuart James
Born: Liverpool, 29 September 1969
Height: 5'11" Weight: 11.12

Unable to beat off competition from Gordon Armstrong, Ian Hughes and David Pugh for the left-back slot at Bury, following just one league game for the Shakers in 1996-97, Stuart signed for Lincoln on a free transfer in December, following a short period on loan. Suffered a ligament injury in the home match with Wigan, which eventually kept him out of action until the final match of the season. Not only a strong tackler, but an adventurous sort, also.
Bury (£12,500 from Macclesfield T on 6/2/95) FL 36 FLC 5 Others 3
Lincoln C (Free on 29/11/96) FL 13+2 Others 1

BIRCH Paul
Born: Birmingham, 20 November 1962
Height: 5'6" Weight: 11.0
Club Honours: FAYC '80; ESC '82

Although approaching the veteran stage of his career, Paul remains superbly fit, which was surely one of the reasons why Doncaster signed him during the 1996 close season following his release from Wolves.

A right-sided, hard-working, bustling midfielder with a wealth of experience, he played 31 games before joining Exeter on transfer deadline day, possibly with a view to eventually going into coaching.
Aston Villa (From apprentice on 15/7/80) FL 153+20/16 FLC 21+4/5 FAC 9+5/3 Others 5+2/1
Wolverhampton W (£400,000 on 1/2/91) FL 128+14/15 FLC 11+1/3 FAC 2+1 Others 8+1/1
Preston NE (Loaned on 7/3/96) FL 11/2
Doncaster Rov (Free on 20/7/96) FL 26+1/2 FLC 2 FAC 1 Others 1
Exeter C (Free on 27/3/97) FL 2

BIRCHAM Marc Stephen John
Born: Wembley, 11 May 1978
Height: 5'10" Weight: 10.12

A Millwall youth team product whose first-team debut in 1996-97 was at right back, settled down right away with no-nonsense tackling, good touch and passing ability. Unfortunately sent off at Stockport when a goal bound shot careered off his chest, only for the referee to award a penalty and a red card for handball, Marc proved his versatility when he played the second half of a reserve game at Swansea in goal and kept a clean sheet. Deservedly voted the club's Young Player of the Year.
Millwall (From trainee on 22/5/96) FL 6

BISHOP Charles (Charlie) Darren
Born: Nottingham, 16 February 1968
Height: 6'0" Weight: 12.11
Club Honours: Div 3 '97

Unfortunate to snap his ankle ligaments just 125 minutes into last season, after joining Wigan Athletic in the close season from Barnsley, he returned to the team for the first match in the New Year with a Man of the Match performance against Shrewsbury in the Auto Windscreen trophy. Extremely strong, with powerful heading ability, Charlie proved to be a valuable member of the defensive line up and was delighted to win his first major honour, a third division championship medal.
Watford (Free from Stoke C juniors on 17/4/86)
Bury (Free on 10/8/87) FL 104+10/6 FLC 5 FAC 4/1 Others 12+1
Barnsley (£50,000 on 24/7/91) FL 124+6/1 FLC 11+1 FAC 9 Others 5
Preston NE (Loaned on 12/1/96) FL 4
Burnley (Loaned on 28/3/96) FL 9
Wigan Ath (£20,000 on 28/6/96) FL 20+1 FLC 1 Others 1

BISHOP Ian William
Born: Liverpool, 29 May 1965
Height: 5'9" Weight: 10.12
International Honours: E: B-1

Completed his eighth season at Upton Park in 1996-97 as a midfield dynamo for West Ham. Although forced to miss the start with a groin injury, he was a regular performer after winning back his place in the first team from late September. An excellent passer, he always tries to play with flair and imagination, while an infrequent scorer, his rare goals are usually memorable, such as the one against Derby in November when he won the ball in a midfield tackle, ran forward, and blasted the ball into the top corner from 25 yards.

Everton (From apprentice on 24/5/83) FL 0+1
Crewe Alex (Loaned on 22/3/84) FL 4
Carlisle U (£15,000 on 11/10/84) FL 131+1/14 FLC 8/1 FAC 5/1 Others 4
Bournemouth (£35,000 on 14/7/88) FL 44/2 FLC 4 FAC 5 Others 1
Manchester C (£465,000 on 2/8/89) FL 18+1/2 FLC 4/1 Others 1
West Ham U (£500,000 on 28/12/89) F/PL 237+14/12 FLC 21/1 FAC 22+1/3 Others 4+1/1

BJORNEBYE Stig-Inge
Born: Norway, 11 December 1969
Height: 5'10" Weight: 11.9
Club Honours: FLC '95
International Honours: Norway: 54

1996-97 was possibly the Norwegian international's best season in a Liverpool shirt, his dependability, powerful tackling, strong running, and amazingly accurate crosses that were whipped in with some venom, providing the side with an added extra. An ever present, he made the left-wing back role his own and was often used for corners and free kicks, simply because of his wonderful accuracy, and, as a defender who gave his all to the cause, there was no doubting his right to be named the club's Player of the Year. All this and four goals as well, including the first of the season after just four minutes at Middlesbrough and two in the run to the European Cup Winners Cup semi final.
Liverpool (£600,000 from Rosenborg on 18/12/92) PL 88+3/2 FLC 11 FAC 9+2 Others 8/2

BLACK Kingsley Terence
Born: Luton, 22 June 1968
Height: 5'9" Weight: 11.12
Club Honours: FLC '88; FMC '92
International Honours: E: Sch. NI: 30; B-2; U21-1

The Northern Ireland international winger transferred to Grimsby from Nottingham Forest during the 1996 close season in an attempt to revive a flagging career. After a bright start, he found himself out of favour following the departure of former City Ground team-mate, Brian Laws, as manager and Kenny Swain's decision to blood the brilliant John Oster on the left flank. Still a class player, however, with good control and crossing skills.
Luton T (From juniors on 7/7/86) FL 123+4/26 FLC 16+2/1 FAC 5+1/2 Others 3+2/1
Nottingham F (£1,500,000 on 2/9/91) F/PL 80+18/14 FLC 19+1/5 FAC 4 Others 4+2/1
Sheffield U (Loaned on 2/3/95) FL 8+3/2
Millwall (Loaned on 29/9/95) FL 1+2/1 FLC 0+1
Grimsby T (£25,000 on 16/7/96) FL 19+5 FLC 2 FAC 1

BLACKMORE Clayton Graham
Born: Neath, 23 September 1964
Height: 5'8" Weight: 11.12
Club Honours: FAC '90; CS '90; ECWC '91; ESC '91; PL '93; Div 1 '95
International Honours: W: 39; U21-3; Yth; Sch

On his recall to Middlesbrough after a short loan spell with Bristol City last November, Clayton inspired everyone at the Riverside with his brilliant form, while playing probably the best football of his illustrious career in the

midfield, or on both flanks, and scoring with a tremendous 30-yard screamer against Everton, he won consistently high ratings on every outing. Although the highlight of his season must surely have been his recall to international duty for Wales in the World Cup qualifier against Holland, he emerged from all appearances made in the Premiership, FA and Coca-Cola Cups with enormous credit, adding an FA cup finalists medal to his collection along the way.
Manchester U (From apprentice on 28/9/82) F/PL 150+36/19 FLC 23+2/3 FAC 15+6/1 Others 19/4
Middlesbrough (Free on 11/7/94) P/FL 44+7/4 FLC 3+2 FAC 4+1 Others 1
Bristol C (Loaned on 1/11/96) FL 5/1

Clayton Blackmore

BLACKWELL Dean Robert
Born: Camden, 5 December 1969
Height: 6'1" Weight: 12.7
International Honours: E: U21-6

A former England U21 international, Dean has become a top-quality defender for Wimbledon, reading the game well and coping commendably with the hottest Premier League strikers around. Although his main strength is in the air, he displays a catalogue of additional skills, such as accuracy, stamina, and pace, being yet another player cultivated from the Dons' very successful youth policy. With the side in great form in 1996-97, reaching two cup semi finals and finishing very creditably in the league, Dean's form made it difficult for the defensive formation to break down and he deserves credit from everyone at the club.
Wimbledon (From trainee on 7/7/88) F/PL 97+22/1 FLC 11 FAC 16+1 Others 1
Plymouth Arg (Loaned on 15/3/90) FL 5+2

BLACKWELL Kevin Patrick
Born: Luton, 21 December 1958
Height: 5'11" Weight: 12.10
Club Honours: GMVC '87

An excellent professional, Kevin took time off from his normal duties of youth development officer at Plymouth to fill in between the sticks for the club in 1996 while Bruce Grobbelaar was on international duty, or James Dungey was also indisposed. Appearing four times, he showed that he had lost none of his shot-stopping qualities in keeping two clean sheets and being on the losing side just once.
Scarborough (Signed from Barnet on 1/11/86) FL 44 FLC 11 FAC 2 Others 2
Notts Co (£15,000 on 8/11/89)
Torquay U (Free on 15/1/93) FL 18 Others 2
Huddersfield T (Free on 5/8/93) FL 3+2 FLC 0+1 FAC 1 Others 3
Plymouth Arg (Free on 11/8/95) FL 24 FAC 3

BLADES Paul Andrew
Born: Peterborough, 5 January 1965
Height: 6'0" Weight: 12.0
Club Honours: Div 2 '87; AMC '96
International Honours: E: Yth

A summer knee operation kept him out of action until the end of last November and he only started nine games for Rotherham before the trouble flared up again, leading to his premature retirement in April. His experience and tackling ability at the heart of the defence was sorely missed during the club's troubled season.
Derby Co (From apprentice on 29/12/82) FL 157+9/1 FLC 9+3 FAC 12 Others 8+2
Norwich C (£700,000 on 18/7/90) FL 47 FLC 8 FAC 2 Others 5
Wolverhampton W (£325,000 on 14/8/92) FL 103+4/2 FLC 4+1 FAC 9/1 Others 6
Rotherham U (£110,000 on 18/7/95) FL 43/2 FLC 3 FAC 1 Others 7+1

BLAKE Mark Antony
Born: Nottingham, 16 December 1970
Height: 5'11" Weight: 12.9
International Honours: E: U21-9; Yth; Sch

Signed from Leicester at the start of 1996-97, Mark had a mixed first season at Walsall with spells both in midfield and defence. Getting off to a solid start, he was approaching his best form in mid term, snapping up a fine goal in the 3-1 win over champions elect, Bury, before his impetuosity cost the side dearly when he was sent off at Millwall and again, in the penultimate away game at Gillingham. A former Leicester record signing, he is at his best when going forward.
Aston Villa (From trainee on 1/7/89) FL 26+5/2 FLC 1+1 FAC 2 Others 2
Wolverhampton W (Loaned on 17/1/91) FL 2
Portsmouth (£400,000 on 5/8/93) FL 15 Others 4+1
Leicester C (£360,000 on 24/3/94) F/PL 42+7/4 FLC 4 Others 3
Walsall (Free on 23/8/96) FL 35+3/4 FLC 1 FAC 0+2 Others 1

BLAKE Mark Christopher
Born: Portsmouth, 17 December 1967
Height: 6'1" Weight: 12.8
International Honours: E: Yth

Fulham's "Mr Reliable" missed only five games as one of the markers in a three-man central defence which conceded the least goals in division three in 1996-97 and under the old goal difference system, the Cottagers

would have won the championship. A player who has impressive aerial strength and the ability to get forward at set pieces, Mark's cool head and accurate shot also resulted in a seven out of seven record from the penalty spot.

Southampton (From apprentice on 23/12/85) FL 18/2 FLC 2 FAC 3 Others 1+2
Colchester U (Loaned on 5/9/89) FL 4/1
Shrewsbury T (£100,000 on 22/3/90) FL 142/3 FLC 12 FAC 9 Others 12
Fulham (Free on 16/9/94) FL 109+5/15 FLC 10/1 FAC 7/1 Others 4+1

BLAKE Nathan Alexander
Born: Cardiff, 27 January 1972
Height: 5'11" Weight: 13.12
Club Honours: WC '92, '93; Div 3 '93, Div 1 '97
International Honours: W: 6; B-1; U21-5; Yth
The powerful striker came into his own last season after a somewhat unspectacular start to his Bolton career midway through 1995-96, re-discovering his scoring touch to become one half of the most prolific goalscoring partnership, alongside John McGinlay, in the English leagues. His strength on the ball and his turn of pace will be certain to cause defenders problems when Wanderers return to the Premiership for the new season, something that will undoubtedly keep him a firm favourite with the fans.

Cardiff C (Free from Chelsea juniors on 20/8/90) FL 113+18/35 FLC 6+2 FAC 10/4 Others 13+2/1
Sheffield U (£300,000 on 17/2/94) P/FL 55+14/34 FLC 3+1/1 FAC 1 Others 1
Bolton W (£1,500,000 on 23/12/95) F/PL 56+4/22 FLC 5/3 FAC 5/2

BLAKE Noel Lloyd George
Born: Jamaica, 12 January 1962
Height: 6'1" Weight: 14.2
As Exeter's assistant manager, Noel's presence in 1996-97 was important as he helped steady a sometimes shaky defence. Contributing more goals than he had ever scored in a season before and one of the top scorers, his experience proved invaluable as he helped the young squad in the battle to avoid the drop.

Aston Villa (Signed from Sutton Coldfield T on 1/8/79) FL 4
Shrewsbury T (Loaned on 1/3/82) FL 6
Birmingham C (£55,000 on 15/9/82) FL 76/5 FLC 12 FAC 8
Portsmouth (£150,000 on 24/4/84) FL 144/10 FLC 14/1 FAC 10/2 Others 5/1
Leeds U (Free on 4/7/88) FL 51/4 FLC 4+1 FAC 2 Others 4
Stoke C (£175,000 on 9/2/90) FL 74+1/3 FLC 6 FAC 3+1 Others 4+1
Bradford C (Loaned on 27/2/92) FL 6
Bradford C (Free on 20/7/92) FL 38+1/3 FLC 2+1 FAC 5/1 Others 4
Dundee (Free on 10/12/93) SL 52+2/2 SLC 2 SC 5 Others 3
Exeter C (Free on 18/8/95) FL 90/8 FLC 4 FAC 3 Others 2

BLAKE Robert (Robbie) James
Born: Middlesbrough, 4 March 1976
Height: 5'10" Weight: 12.0
Having again impressed at Darlington last season, scoring in the two opening games and notching a further nine goals, despite

missing several matches due to injury, the highly-rated young striker was transferred to Bradford for a Quakers' record fee on transfer deadline day. Strong running and hard working, he was given five outings, two of them from the bench, in a struggling side and showed enough to suggest that he will become a crowd favourite before too long.

Darlington (From trainee on 1/7/94) FL 54+14/21 FLC 4+2/1 FAC 3+1 Others 3+1/1
Bradford C (£300,000 on 27/3/97) FL 3+2

BLAMEY Nathan
Born: Plymouth, 10 June 1977
Height: 5'10" Weight: 11.5
Right-sided Shrewsbury full back. Signed on a free transfer from Southampton last February, Nathan made his full league debut in a 2-1 home victory against Burnley in April and maintained his place for the rest of the season. It was a very promising start to his career, looking instantly at home, and perhaps the best testimony is to ask why he was not used earlier.

Southampton (From trainee on 1/7/95)
Shrewsbury T (Free on 14/2/97) FL 6

BLATHERWICK Steven (Steve) Scott
Born: Nottingham, 20 September 1973
Height: 6'1" Weight: 14.0
Steve, a centre back, started for Nottingham Forest for the first time since September 1993 when he played in ten games last season. A tough-tackling, no-nonsense defender he liked to get forward at set pieces, his first game coming at Wycombe, a club where he had been on loan in the Coca-Cola Cup and made the majority of his appearances in the matches just after this. Spent the last months of the season on loan at Reading, making a total of seven appearances and clearing his lines well, despite playing on occasion with niggling injuries. He also showed neat touches and good control when pushed forward into midfield and attacking situations.

Nottingham F (Free from Notts Co juniors on 2/8/92) FL 10 FLC 2 FAC 1 Others 2
Wycombe W (Loaned on 18/2/94) FL 2 Others 1
Hereford U (Loaned on 11/9/95) FL 10/1 Others 2
Reading (Loaned on 27/3/97) FL 6+1

BLINKER Reginald (Regi) Waldie
Born: Surinam, 4 June 1969
Height: 5'8" Weight: 11.7
International Honours: Holland: 3
Reggi started 1996-97 as a regular on the left of the Sheffield Wednesday midfield, being very adept in a winger's role where he could tease defenders with his skill. However, as the season moved on he missed games through injury and suspension and had to conform to a more rigid midfield position, but by the close of the campaign, he was more often than not used as a substitute when Richie Humphries moved back into midfield. Not the best of times for the Dutchman, just one goal being a disappointing return for a very exciting player.

Sheffield Wed (£275,000 from Feyenoord on 5/3/96) PL 24+18/3 FLC 2 FAC 1

Regi Blinker

BLUNT Jason
Born: Penzance, 16 August 1977
Height: 5'8" Weight: 10.10
International Honours: E: Yth
A young Leeds' midfielder, and yet another of the crop of emerging youngsters at Elland Road who have tasted first-team football, Jason's only appearance last season was as a substitute in George Graham's first game as manager at Coventry. However, as a regular member of the reserve team throughout 1996-97, and a player who is highly thought of at the club, he should not have to wait too long for a run of games.

Leeds U (From trainee on 1/1/95) PL 2+2 FLC 0+1

BOCHENSKI Simon
Born: Worksop, 6 December 1975
Height: 5'8" Weight: 11.13
The skilful young striker joined Scarborough from Barnsley in the summer of 1996, scoring regularly for the reserves, and occupying the subs' bench for much of last season, although never letting the side down when called upon for first-team action. A player with good movement and pace, his only senior goal was in the 3-2 defeat at Brighton.

Barnsley (From trainee on 6/7/94) FL 0+1 FAC 0+1
Scarborough (Free on 16/8/96) FL 5+14/1 FLC 2+1 Others 0+1

BODIN Paul John
Born: Cardiff, 13 September 1964
Height: 6'0" Weight: 13.1
Club Honours: Div 2 '96
International Honours: W: 23; U21-1; Yth
Although Paul was a regular in the left-back spot for the first half of last season, having signed from Swindon during the summer, a dip in form, plus the emergence of younger

players, meant that his Reading appearances became less frequent as the campaign progressed. Struggling for pace in some games, but still showing he could cross the ball accurately, he scored his only goal with a stunning volley at Crystal Palace.

Newport Co (Free from Chelsea juniors on 28/1/82)
Cardiff C (Free on 1/8/82) FL 68+7/4 FLC 11 FAC 4 (Free to Bath C during 1985 close season)
Newport Co (£15,000 on 27/1/88) FL 6/1
Swindon T (£30,000 on 7/3/88) FL 87+6/9 FLC 12 FAC 6 Others 8/1
Crystal Palace (£550,000 on 20/3/91) FL 8+1 FLC 1
Newcastle U (Loaned on 5/12/91) FL 6
Swindon T (£225,000 on 10/1/92) F/PL 140+6/28 FLC 14 FAC 10/1 Others 8/1
Reading (Free on 11/7/96) FL 37/1 FLC 2

BODLEY Michael (Mick) John
Born: Hayes, 14 September 1967
Height: 6'1" Weight: 13.2
Club Honours: GMVC '91

Signed from Southend during the 1996 close season, the ball-playing Peterborough central defender showed great skill on occasion in 1996-97. As a regular, Mick only missed games when unavailable, his wholehearted displays being a welcome boost to a struggling side. Strong in the air, rather than just clearing his lines, his way forward was all about constructive passing.

Chelsea (From apprentice on 17/9/85) FL 6/1 FLC 1 Others 1
Northampton T (£50,000 on 12/1/89) FL 20 Others 2
Barnet (£15,000 on 1/10/89) FL 69/3 FLC 2 FAC 10 Others 9
Southend U (Free on 15/7/93) FL 66+1/2 FLC 3 FAC 2 Others 7
Gillingham (Loaned on 23/11/94) FL 6+1 Others 1
Birmingham C (Loaned on 23/1/95) FL 3
Peterborough U (£75,000 on 27/7/96) FL 31 FLC 3 FAC 5 Others 4

BOERE Jeroen Willem
Born: Arnhem, Holland, 18 November 1967
Height: 6'3" Weight: 13.5

Jeroen endured a battle for his place with Andy Rammell at Southend in 1996-97, a season which brought some excellent goals. Very tall and strong in the air, he is also skilful on the ground, although his lack of application on occasions tended to turn the crowd against him. More of a support forward than a striker, the Dutchman always looked more accomplished when the team were playing well as a whole.

West Ham U (£250,000 from Go Ahead Eagles on 22/9/93) PL 15+10/6 FLC 1+1/1 FAC 2
Portsmouth (Loaned on 24/3/94) FL 4+1
West Bromwich A (Loaned on 8/9/94) FL 5
Crystal Palace (£375,000 on 7/9/95) FL 0+8/1
Southend U (£150,000 on 1/3/96) FL 33+9/11 FLC 1+1 FAC 0+1

BOGIE Ian
Born: Newcastle, 6 December 1967
Height: 5'7" Weight: 12.0
International Honours: E: Sch

As the central midfield playmaker with Port Vale, Ian is usually the hub of any creativity in the side and performed his part well in the club's rise to the verge of the play offs last season, as well as scoring two goals, both

away from home, at Crewe in the Coca-Cola Cup and Bolton in the league. Signed a new three-year contract at the end of the season to take him to the next millennium in a Vale shirt.

Newcastle U (From apprentice on 18/12/85) FL 7+7 FLC 0+1 FAC 1+2 Others 3/1
Preston NE (Signed on 9/2/89) FL 67+12/12 FLC 3+1 FAC 3 Others 4+1
Millwall (£145,000 on 16/8/91) FL 44+7/1 FLC 1 FAC 2 Others 3
Leyton Orient (Signed on 14/10/93) FL 62+3/5 FLC 2 FAC 2 Others 8+1
Port Vale (£50,000 on 23/3/95) FL 62+10/6 FLC 6/1 FAC 5+2/2 Others 8

BOHINEN Lars
Born: Vadso, Norway, 8 September 1969
Height: 6'0" Weight: 12.2
International Honours: Norway: 47

Suffering from injury early on last season, the central midfielder failed to secure his Blackburn place, despite giving an outstanding display at Old Trafford where he scored a magnificent goal. Even when Tony Parkes took over as caretaker manager he found that his intermittent skills were not so much in demand as was total effort and he was reduced to occasional appearances in the role of deputy. Following on from that, Lars then criticised the Norwegian selectors for lack of opportunities, only to find that they concurred with Parkes' views, something that saw him dropped from the national squad. A player with tremendous vision and skill, he is bound to be back and should be very much in the plans of the new manager, Roy Hodgson.

Nottingham F (£450,000 from Young Boys of Berne on 5/11/93) F/PL 59+5/7 FLC 7+1/2 FAC 2/1 Others 1
Blackburn Rov (£700,000 on 14/10/95) PL 34+8/6 FLC 2+1 FAC 2/1

BOLAND William (Willie) John
Born: Ennis, Ireland, 6 August 1975
Height: 5'9" Weight: 11.2
International Honours: Ei: U21-9; Yth; Sch

The young Irish midfielder, a patient understudy to Kevin Richardson in 1996-97, played only seven minutes in the Coventry first team as a sub at Newcastle and was often left unused on the bench. A product of the club's youth scheme, Willie is a skilful midfielder who rarely wastes the ball, but found it difficult to get a chance in a struggling side that ultimately had to rely on the combative side of the game to avoid relegation. Still a regular for the Republic's U21 side, he played in three of the four internationals last season.

Coventry C (From juniors on 4/11/92) PL 35+9 FLC 4

BONETTI Ivano
Born: Brescia, Italy, 1 August 1964
Height: 5'10" Weight: 11.0
International Honours: Italy: 1

Signed from Grimsby Town on a free transfer last August, Ivano started his Tranmere career in sparkling fashion, scoring in the Coca-Cola Cup tie at Shrewsbury. However, unable to hold down a first-team place for any prolonged spell, he spent part of the campaign in Italy, in an

attempt to find a club there. He later returned to Prenton Park, before being released on a free transfer in May 1997.

Grimsby T (Signed from Torino, via Brescia, Atalanta and Sampdoria, on 29/9/95) FL 19/3 FLC 1 FAC 2/1
Tranmere Rov (Free on 9/8/96) FL 9+4/1 FLC 2/1

BONNER Mark
Born: Ormskirk, 7 June 1974
Height: 5'10" Weight: 11.0

Although still a regular choice for Blackpool when fit, this skilful right-sided midfielder, who is also noted for his workrate and surging forward runs, had a disappointing time of it in 1996-97 when suffering with injury problems. Hopefully, it will be all systems go for 1997-98.

Blackpool (From trainee on 18/6/92) FL 124+22/11 FLC 11+3 FAC 9 Others 9+3/1

BOOTH Andrew (Andy) David
Born: Huddersfield, 6 December 1973
Height: 6'0" Weight: 12.6
International Honours: E: U21-3

Andy had a good first season in the Premiership with Sheffield Wednesday in 1996-97, following his big money summer move from Huddersfield Town during the previous summer. A big striker, he may lack extreme pace, but is good in the air as well as on the ground and his 13 goals (top scored) was a just reward for his efforts. His settling in period was not helped in having to play alongside different partners, Richie Humphries and David Hirst both taking turns, but, despite the lack of continuity, he hardly missed a game, and will have benefited from the experience. Just out of interest, when becoming Wednesday's third 'keeper in ten minutes during the final match against Liverpool at Hillsborough, after Kevin Pressman was injured and Matthew Clarke was sent off, he unfortunately conceded the equalising goal with just seven minutes left on the clock, but recovered to make some good saves before the final whistle.

Huddersfield T (From trainee on 1/7/92) FL 109+14/54 FLC 6+1/3 FAC 8/3 Others 12+1/4
Sheffield Wed (£2,700,000 on 8/7/96) PL 32+3/10 FLC 2 FAC 4/3

BOOTHROYD Adrian (Aidey) Neil
Born: Bradford, 8 February 1971
Height: 5'10" Weight: 11.6

Having been released by Mansfield during the summer of 1996, Aidey started 1996-97 as Peterborough's right back, but had an in-and-out time of it before being unfortunate to break a leg late on in the campaign. Obviously hoping to get back into the swing of things as early as possible in 1997-98, he scored his one and only goal for the club, a penalty, in a 2-1 home win against Watford in February.

Huddersfield T (From trainee on 1/7/89) FL 9+1
Bristol Rov (£30,000 on 20/6/90) FL 10+6 FLC 1 FAC 0+1
Heart of Midlothian (Free on 19/11/92) SL 0+4 SC 0+2/2
Mansfield T (Free on 9/12/93) FL 99+3/3 FLC 7 FAC 6 Others 5+1
Peterborough U (Free on 6/7/96) FL 24+2/1 FLC 2 FAC 4+1 Others 4

BOOTY Martyn James
Born: Kirby Muxloe, 30 May 1971
Height: 5'8" Weight: 11.2
Although one of the younger players on whom Reading will base their hopes for the future, he missed large chunks of last season through a succession of injuries. However, when he did play he showed himself to be a neat defender who made up for what he lacked in height with aggression and, more importantly, one who could distribute the ball well. Returned to the team as captain towards the end of the campaign.
Coventry C (From trainee on 30/5/89) FL 4+1 FLC 2 FAC 2
Crewe Alex (Free on 7/10/93) FL 95+1/5 FLC 6 FAC 8/1 Others 13
Reading (£75,000 on 18/1/96) FL 31/1 FLC 2 FAC 2

BORLAND John Robert
Born: Lancaster, 28 January 1977
Height: 5'8" Weight: 11.6
Released by Burnley during the 1996 close season, the young midfielder was taken on by Scunthorpe at the start of the 1996-97 campaign. Slightly built in appearance but a hard worker and strong tackler, John failed to command a regular place and was freed during the summer.
Burnley (From trainee on 6/7/95) FL 1 FLC 2 FAC 0+1
Scunthorpe U (Free on 16/8/96) FL 0+2

BORROWS Brian
Born: Liverpool, 20 December 1960
Height: 5'10" Weight: 11.12
International Honours: E: B-1
The veteran Coventry full back was not reckoned to be a regular choice following the purchase of Regis Genaux at the start of last season, but the Belgian's injury opened the door for "Bugsy" again. With the adoption of the wing-back system he was more at home in the centre of defence and although not a regular, rarely let the side down. Unlucky to be sent off at Newcastle for a clumsy challenge after coming on as a sub, having served his suspension, he returned with some outstanding performances at centre back towards the end of the campaign. Reached 400 league appearances for Coventry during 1996-97 and has now played 12 seasons for the club.
Everton (From juniors on 23/4/80) FL 27 FLC 2
Bolton W (£10,000 on 24/3/83) FL 95 FLC 7 FAC 4 Others 4
Coventry C (£80,000 on 6/6/85) F/PL 396+13/11 FLC 42/1 FAC 26/1 Others 10+1
Bristol C (Loaned on 17/9/93) FL 6

BOS Gijsbert
Born: Spakenburg, Holland, 22 February 1973
Height: 6'4" Weight: 12.7
Tall and skilful Lincoln central striker who began last season as first choice. Netted in both legs of the Coca-Cola Cup win over Manchester City, but the goals failed to materialise in the league and he was loaned out to Gateshead during the second half of the campaign and restricted to reserve appearances on his return.
Lincoln C (£10,000 from Ijsselmeervogels on 19/3/96) FL 28+6/6 FLC 6/3 FAC 1/1 Others 1

BOSANCIC Jovo
Born: Novi Sad, Portugal, 7 August 1970
Height: 5'11" Weight: 12.4
Having joined Barnsley from Iniao Madeira during the 1996 close season, the Portuguese midfielder had his best spell at the start of 1996-97, his passing and ability to drift past the opposition in the middle of the park being his strengths. A tremendous character who always gave 100 per cent whenever called upon, he filled in on a number of occasions and never let the side down. Opened his scoring account at Barnsley when converting a penalty in a 2-0 home win against Manchester City.
Barnsley (Free from Iniao Madeira on 2/8/96) FL 17+8/1 FLC 3+1 FAC 2

BOSNICH Mark John
Born: Sydney, Australia, 13 January 1972
Height: 6'2" Weight: 13.7
Club Honours: FLC '94, '96
International Honours: Australia: 9
1996-97 was an eventful season for the Aussie 'keeper and he appeared in just half of Aston Villa's fixtures. The campaign started with him suffering from a knee injury picked up in training, which looked as though it might have needed surgery but, luckily, that proved not to be the case and he made a belated return to the team in a game at Tottenham, which gave him headlines of a different sort. Then, in his fourth game back he damaged his knee again, thus putting himself out until near Christmas when he returned for a long run in the side. Unfortunately, after injuring himself in a game for Australia, Mark was again out of the side and again caused headlines of a different sort before coming back for the last three games. Still, 12 clean sheets in 24 games proved that he was right up there amongst the leading Premiership custodians.
Manchester U (Free from Sydney Croatia on 5/6/89) Fl 3
Aston Villa (Free on 28/2/92) F/PL 134 FLC 19+1 FAC 13 Others 2

BOULD Stephen (Steve) Andrew
Born: Stoke, 16 November 1962
Height: 6'4" Weight: 14.2
Club Honours: Div 1 '89, '91; ECWC '94
International Honours: E: 2; B-1
A tall, determined and reliable Arsenal centre back, Steve had a welcome injury-free campaign in 1996-97 and, at the same time, adapted well to the three-man defensive system, alongside Tony Adams and Martin Keown, that the new manager, Arsene Wenger, much enjoys, revelling in the freedom to go forward when appropriate. Extremely good in the air and still very much a threat in the opposition's penalty area, where his thoughtful flicks cause havoc, he is an integral part of the meanest defence in the Premiership that conceded just 32 goals. Had an excellent game against Chelsea's Gianluca Vialli towards the end of the campaign, the world-renowned Italian being reduced to a peripheral figure who faded completely when tightly marked.
Stoke C (From apprentice on 15/11/80) FL 179+4/6 FLC 13/1 FAC 10 Others 5

Torquay U (Loaned on 19/10/82) FL 9 FAC 2
Arsenal (£390,000 on 13/6/88) F/PL 236+8/5 FLC 30/1 FAC 20 Others 14+4/2

BOUND Matthew Terence
Born: Melksham, 9 November 1972
Height: 6'2" Weight: 14.6
The big, tough-tackling defender was one of the unluckiest men at Stockport in 1996-97 when, after starting the season as first choice, he was unluckily sent off in the second game and his subsequent suspension saw him lose his place to Jim Gannon. Apart from the odd game, he failed to regain the number six shirt, but will undoubtedly be in contention during the coming campaign.
Southampton (From trainee on 3/5/91) F/PL 2+3
Hull C (Loaned on 27/8/93) FL 7/1
Stockport Co (£100,000 on 27/10/94) FL 44/5 FLC 1 FAC 3/1 Others 3/1
Lincoln C (Loaned on 11/9/95) FL 3+1 Others 1

BOWATER Jason
Born: Chesterfield, 5 April 1978
Height: 5'10" Weight: 10.10
A promising midfielder, Jason completed the second year of his traineeship in 1997, having made his Chesterfield debut (and, to date, his only appearance) as a 70th minute substitute at Bournemouth last March.
Chesterfield (Trainee) FL 0+1

BOWEN Jason Peter
Born: Merthyr Tydfil, 24 August 1972
Height: 5'6" Weight: 9.0
Club Honours: AMC '94
International Honours: W: 2; B-1; U21-5; Yth; Sch
After making a bright start to last season, Jason earned a recall to the Welsh side which faced Holland in a World Cup qualifier. Unfortunately, his play at Birmingham lacked consistency and, after being dropped, the club agreed on a £600,000 move to Huddersfield, only for him to reject it. On form he is a strong, attacking player who is at home either in midfield or on the wing, and being technically sound with good vision, he is rated as one of the most gifted players at St Andrews.
Swansea C (From trainee on 1/7/90) FL 93+31/26 FLC 6+1/2 FAC 9+2/1 Others 15+3/8
Birmingham C (£350,000 on 24/7/95) FL 35+13/7 FLC 4+6/2 FAC 1+4 Others 2/2

BOWEN Mark Rosslyn
Born: Neath, 7 December 1963
Height: 5'8" Weight: 11.11
International Honours: W: 41; U21-3; Yth; Sch
Signing the Welsh international and former Norwich City left back on a free seemed like a scoop for West Ham's manager, Harry Redknapp, last summer. In the event, Mark was unable to break the stranglehold on the left-back slot exerted by Julian Dicks and had to be content in the role of squad player, dividing his appearances almost equally between right back and midfield, scoring his only goal of the season, a header, away to Nottingham Forest in September. Released in March to take up an offer from a Japanese club, ironically, shortly afterwards, Dicks

was injured and the left-back slot became available!

Tottenham H (From apprentice on 1/12/81) FL 14+3/2 FAC 3 Others 0+1
Norwich C (£97,000 on 23/7/87) F/PL 315+5/24 FLC 34/1 FAC 28/1 Others 17/1
West Ham U (Free on 10/7/96) PL 15+2/1 FLC 3

BOWLING Ian
Born: Sheffield, 27 July 1965
Height: 6'3" Weight: 14.8

The giant Mansfield goalie had a much better season in 1996-97 than in his first campaign at the Field Mill Ground, but refused to renew his contract for a time. Once that was resolved, however, he put in some good performances, including no less than five penalty saves by the end of the campaign.

Lincoln C (£2,000 from Gainsborough Trinity on 23/10/88) FL 59 FLC 3 FAC 2 Others 4
Hartlepool U (Loaned on 17/8/89) FL 1
Bradford C (Loaned on 25/3/93) FL 7
Bradford C (£27,500 on 28/7/93) FL 29 FLC 2 FAC 2+1 Others 1
Mansfield T (Free on 11/8/95) FL 90 FLC 4 FAC 4 Others 2

BOWMAN Robert (Rob)
Born: Durham City, 21 November 1975
Height: 6'1" Weight: 11.12
International Honours: E: Yth

Unable to fulfil his youthful promise at Leeds, Robert stepped down the divisions to kick start his career with Rotherham last February. Going straight into the team at right back, he soon created a good impression with his ability to use the ball well and in getting up to support the attack. Also showed his versatility when playing in the centre of the defence, before being surprisingly released during the summer.

Leeds U (From trainee on 20/11/92) PL 4+3 FLC 0+1 Others 1
Rotherham U (Free on 21/2/97) FL 13

BOWRY Robert (Bobby)
Born: Croydon, 19 May 1971
Height: 5'9" Weight: 10.8
Club Honours: Div 1 '94

Promoted to captain after the injury to Keith Stevens early last season, the Millwall midfield missed his steadying influence and pinpoint passes after he succumbed to a broken wrist at Walsall, this after he had given the Lions the lead with a ferocious right-foot volley. A strong-running, all-action player, it is expected that he will continue his improving form in 1997-98.

Queens Park R (Signed on 8/8/90)
Crystal Palace (Free from Carshalton on 4/4/92) F/PL 36+14/1 FLC 10 FAC 1
Millwall (£220,000 on 5/7/95) FL 59+7/3 FLC 5 FAC 4

BOWYER Gary David
Born: Manchester, 22 June 1971
Height: 6'0" Weight: 12.13
Club Honours: WFAC '90; AMC '96

A strong, forceful Rotherham midfielder, Gary unfortunately had yet another season of fits and starts due to several injuries, which restricted his appearances in 1996-97, and he failed to make more than four in

succession. However, whenever he played, he brought a better balance to the team with his strong left foot. Is the son of Ian, who played for a number of clubs, including Manchester City and Nottingham Forest. Was freed during the summer.

Hereford U (Free from Westfields on 2/12/89) FL 12+2/2
Nottingham F (Free on 15/9/90)
Rotherham U (Free on 2/8/95) FL 33+5/2 FLC 3 Others 5

BOWYER Lee David
Born: London, 3 January 1977
Height: 5'9" Weight: 9.11
International Honours: E: U21-8; Yth

Lee found himself the country's most expensive teenager when joining Leeds from Charlton in the 1996 close season, beginning very promisingly and scoring on his debut at Derby on the opening day. Unfortunately, he then sustained an horrific eye injury in the game against Manchester United in September, which temporarily caused the loss of sight in his right eye. Sidelined for two months, on his return he was arguably the club's most consistent outfield player, weighing in with some valuable goals from midfield, his performances earning him a place in the England squad for the friendly with Mexico in March and the captaincy of the U21's against Switzerland just four days later. A classy young midfielder, who is so strong in the tackle for someone of his size, he is also very quick and extremely comfortable on the ball, coupled with great vision when in possession, and has settled in very well at Elland Road. Should have a big future in the game.

Charlton Ath (From trainee on 13/4/94) FL 46/8 FLC 6+1/5 FAC 3/1 Others 2
Leeds U (£2,600,000 on 5/7/96) PL 32/4 FAC 4/2

BOXALL Daniel James
Born: Croydon, 24 August 1977
Height: 5'8" Weight: 10.5

Having made his Crystal Palace debut in the final match of 1995-96, big things were expected of this talented young defender last season. Unfortunately, although starting promisingly enough as an attacking right-wing back in the opening fixture and playing six more times, a serious injury laid him low and resulted in a cruciate knee ligament operation. Recovering well, however, Danny came back for an outing in the reserves on the last day of the campaign and looks forward to picking up the pieces in 1997-98.

Crystal Palace (From trainee on 19/4/95) FL 5+2 FLC 0+1

BOYLAN Lee Martin
Born: Chelmsford, 2 September 1978
Height: 5'6" Weight: 11.2
International Honours: Ei: Yth

Leading scorer for the West Ham youth team and a Republic of Ireland youth international, Lee was still a trainee when he made his Premiership debut as a last-minute substitute against Sheffield Wednesday in May. A member of the Hammers' Youth Cup final team in 1996, he signed a

professional contract in the summer and the club have high expectations of him for the future.

West Ham U (Trainee) PL 0+1

BOYLE Wesley Samuel
Born: Portadown, 30 March 1979
Height: 5'8" Weight: 10.1
Club Honours: FAYC '97
International Honours: NI: Yth; Sch

A Northern Ireland youth international and a player who has come through Leeds' junior ranks, he made his debut as a substitute against Newcastle United at Elland Road last September. Wesley, a talented winger, and yet another of the club's youngsters to benefit from the spin off of the horrendous injury list around that time, continued to be a regular member of the successful youth side.

Leeds U (From trainee on 26/4/96) PL 0+1

BRABIN Gary
Born: Liverpool, 9 December 1970
Height: 5'11" Weight: 14.8
International Honours: E: SP-4

Signed from Bury during the 1996 close season, Gary made his debut for Blackpool in a 1-0 win at Bristol City on 24 August. Totally committed to the cause, while again running into disciplinary problems, his wholehearted endeavour and hard tackling more than compensated and he can always be relied upon to weigh in with the odd goal or two.

Stockport Co (From trainee on 14/12/89) FL 1+1 Others 1+1
Doncaster Rov (£45,000 from Runcorn on 26/7/94) FL 58+1/11 FLC 2 FAC 2 Others 4
Bury (£125,000 on 29/3/96) FL 5
Blackpool (£200,000 on 30/7/96) FL 30+2/2 FLC 3 FAC 1 Others 2

BRACE Deryn Paul John
Born: Haverfordwest, 15 March 1975
Height: 5'8" Weight: 10.6
Club Honours: WC '95
International Honours: W: U21-7; Yth

Fast becoming a hero at Wrexham with his never-say-die spirit and totally committed displays in 1996-97, Deryn is a left back who also likes to get forward whenever possible. Unfortunately tends to be injury prone, due no doubt to his wholehearted play, but could be challenging for a place in the full Welsh international side in the near future, having furthered his claims with two more U21 appearances during the season.

Norwich C (From trainee on 6/7/93)
Wrexham (Free on 28/4/94) FL 53+4/2 FLC 3 FAC 5 Others 6

BRACEWELL Paul William
Born: Heswall, 19 July 1962
Height: 5'9" Weight: 12.5
Club Honours: CS '84, '85; ECWC '85; Div 1 '85, '93, '96
International Honours: E: 3; U21-13 (UEFAC '84)

The veteran midfielder and assistant manager was Sunderland's only ever present in the Premiership last term, but suffered the trauma of relegation for the second time in his Roker career. At times, Paul's vast

experience proved invaluable to the Rokerites' cause, but signs were also there that, in terms of the top level, time is beginning to catch up with him. Whether he decides to concentrate solely on his managerial duties in the future remains to be seen. At his best, a brave, industrious ball winner with good control and passing ability.

Stoke C (From apprentice on 6/2/80) FL 123+6/5 FLC 6 FAC 6/1
Sunderland (£250,000 on 1/7/83) FL 38/4 FLC 4 FAC 2
Everton (£425,000 on 25/5/84) FL 95/7 FLC 11/2 FAC 19+2 Others 17+2/1
Sunderland (£250,000 on 23/8/89) FL 112+1/2 FLC 9 FAC 10 Others 6
Newcastle U (£250,000 on 16/6/92) F/PL 64+9/3 FLC 3+1/1 FAC 6+2 Others 2
Sunderland (£100,000 on 23/5/95) P/FL 76 FLC 6 FAC 3

Paul Bracewell

BRADBURY Lee Michael
Born: Isle of Wight, 3 July 1975
Height: 6'0" Weight: 12.7
International Honours: E: U21-1

After a spell on loan to Exeter in 1995-96, Lee made the step up to a regular place in the Portsmouth first team during 1996-97 and formed effective partnerships up front with firstly John Durnin, and then, most impressively, with Mathias Svensson, being rewarded for a number of fine performances with a starting place in the Nationwide League U21 team that faced the Italian Serie "B". Other highlights for him, included his first hat trick for the club in a 4-2 victory over Barnsley, a call up for the England U21 squad for the game against Georgia in April and, the final accolade, Pompey's Player of the Year award.

Portsmouth (Free from Cowes on 14/8/95) FL 41+13/15 FLC 1+2 FAC 4/2
Exeter C (Loaned on 1/12/95) FL 14/5

BRADLEY Darren Michael
Born: Birmingham, 24 November 1965
Height: 5'11" Weight: 13.2
International Honours: E: Yth

In 1996-97, his second season at Walsall since moving from West Bromwich on a free transfer, Darren had a few injury problems, something he has been used to since the cruciate knee operation, and was forced onto the sidelines for two separate spells. Released during the summer, when fit, however, he proved himself still to be a controlling influence in midfield and a master of floated free kicks or made-to-measure corners.

Aston Villa (From apprentice on 19/12/83) FL 16+4 FAC 3
West Bromwich A (Signed on 14/3/86) FL 236+18/9 FLC 13/1 FAC 10/2 Others 11/1
Walsall (Free on 3/8/95) FL 66+5/1 FLC 4 FAC 7/2 Others 3

BRADLEY Russell
Born: Birmingham, 28 March 1966
Height: 6'2" Weight: 13.0
Club Honours: WC '90

The Scunthorpe central defender had an in-and-out season for the club in 1996-97 and was sidelined a couple of times by niggling injuries. Unable to win back his place when fit again, Russell finished the campaign on loan to Hartlepool. Settled in well at Pool, especially in holding the back line together, his outstanding form impressing manager, Mick Tait, immensely, but, at the time of going to press, a permanent deal had not been struck, despite him being released in May.

Nottingham F (Signed from Dudley T on 20/5/88)
Hereford U (Loaned on 13/11/88) FL 12/1 FAC 1 Others 3
Hereford U (£15,000 on 26/7/89) FL 75+2/3 FLC 7 Others 5+1
Halifax T (£45,000 on 6/9/91) FL 54+2/3 FLC 2 FAC 3 Others 4
Scunthorpe U (Free on 30/6/93) FL 116+3/5 FLC 6 FAC 11 Others 9
Hartlepool U (Loaned on 14/2/97) FL 12/1

BRADSHAW Carl
Born: Sheffield, 2 October 1968
Height: 5'11" Weight: 11.11
International Honours: E: Yth

Began his defensive career at Bramall Lane, having earlier been a winger, Carl is now an uncomplicated, enthusiastic defender who adds stability to the Norwich side. Unfortunately, he suffered a succession of injuries in 1996-97, the worst being a ripped thigh muscle and, consequently, he only started 11 games. Following an altercation, at Oxford that saw him sent off for retaliation in injury time, it took him until March to have a run of eight consecutive games. Offered a new contract, at the time of going to press he was undecided about his future.

Sheffield Wed (From apprentice on 23/8/86) FL 16+16/4 FLC 2+2 FAC 6+1/3 Others 1
Barnsley (Loaned on 23/8/86) FL 6/1
Manchester C (£50,000 on 30/9/88) FL 1+4 FAC 0+1 Others 0+1
Sheffield U (£50,000 on 7/9/89) F/PL 122+25/8 FLC 10+1/2 FAC 12+1/3 Others 4
Norwich C (£500,000 on 28/7/94) P/FL 54+10/2 FLC 5+1/1 FAC 2

BRADSHAW Darren Shaun
Born: Sheffield, 19 March 1967
Height: 5'11" Weight: 11.4
International Honours: E: Yth

Placed on the transfer list halfway through the 1996-97 campaign, Darren did not make his seasonal debut for Blackpool until the end of October, and then as a substitute. A player who can perform equally well in defence and midfield, and good on the ball, he followed that up with a handful of games in defence. Is another Seasider who has been unlucky with injuries.

Chesterfield (On trial from Matlock T on 12/8/87) FL 18 FLC 2
York C (Free from Matlock T on 14/11/87) FL 58+1/3 FLC 2 FAC 2 Others 3
Newcastle U (£10,000 on 16/8/89) FL 32+6 FLC 3 FAC 2+1 Others 3
Peterborough U (Free on 13/8/92) FL 70+3/1 FLC 7/1 FAC 4 Others 2
Plymouth Arg (Loaned on 18/8/94) FL 5+1/1 FLC 1
Blackpool (£35,000 on 20/10/94) FL 55+6/1 FLC 2 FAC 4 Others 6

BRADY Matthew John
Born: Marylebone, 27 October 1977
Height: 5'11" Weight: 11.0

Yet another product of the Barnet YTS scheme, Matthew is neat and tidy on the ball and added a determined streak to his other left-sided midfield attributes in 1996-97. Mainly used from the bench, apart from an outing at Wigan, he should be pushing for a place this coming season.

Barnet (From trainee on 3/7/96) FL 2+8

BRAITHWAITE Leon Jerome
Born: Hackney, 17 December 1972
Height: 5'11" Weight: 12.0

Forward. As the Exeter fans' favourite, Leon's natural pace, together with improved touch and control, helped him gain a first-team place for a large chunk of last season, although a lack of consistency and experience saw him replaced towards the end of the campaign. Can only improve as he is still young and new to the game in what was his first full season as a pro.

Exeter C (Free from Bishops Stortford on 3/11/95) FL 40+21/8 FLC 2 FAC 0+2 Others 1+1

BRAMMER David
Born: Bromborough, 28 February 1975
Height: 5'10" Weight: 12.0

Although not yet realising his undoubted promise, David was more involved in the Wrexham first-team squad in 1996-97 than previously. A strong central midfielder who, with the right attitude and commitment, would be a big asset at the Racecourse, still has time on his side. Not afraid to try his luck at goal, being the possessor of a powerful shot.

Wrexham (From trainee on 2/7/93) FL 58+12/6 FLC 4+1 FAC 3+2 Others 6+2

BRANAGAN Keith Graham
Born: Fulham, 10 July 1966
Height: 6'0" Weight: 13.2
Club Honours: Div 1 '97
International Honours: Ei: 1; B-1

In winning his first full cap for the Republic of Ireland in 1996-97, Keith again showed

he is a consistent and sometimes spectacular goalkeeper and, at the age of 30, is in his prime between the sticks. Shared Bolton's number one jersey with Gavin Ward, though having the lions share between the sticks, and remained a firm favourite with the Burnden fans, while playing a major role in Wanderers return to the big time. Keith is thought of by many as being one of the best 'keepers outside of the Premier League and should be up there with the best of them in 1997-98.

Cambridge U (From juniors on 4/8/83) FL 110 FLC 12 FAC 6 Others 6
Millwall (£100,000 on 25/3/88) FL 46 FLC 1 FAC 5 Others 1
Brentford (Loaned on 24/11/89) FL 2 Others 1
Gillingham (Loaned on 1/10/91) FL 1
Bolton W (Free on 3/7/92) P/FL 166 FLC 26 FAC 10 Others 6

BRANCH Graham

Born: Liverpool, 12 February 1972
Height: 6'2" Weight: 12.2
The cousin of Everton's teenage striker, Michael, Graham continued to either delight or frustrate Rovers' supporters in equal measure in 1996-97. A fast wing forward, he continued to be a stalwart of the Pontins League team, while regularly appearing in the first team, and decided to remain at Tranmere after being unable to agree personal terms with Oldham Athletic in March. He still has all the attributes to become a leading front man.

Tranmere Rov (Free from Heswall on 2/7/91) FL 39+38/7 FLC 3+5/1 FAC 0+2 Others 2+1
Bury (Loaned on 20/11/92) FL 3+1/1 Others 1

BRANCH Paul Michael

Born: Liverpool, 18 October 1978
Height: 5'10" Weight: 11.7
International Honours: E: U21-2; Yth; Sch
A livewire Everton striker with outstanding pace, and an England U21 international, Michael established himself last season as a Premiership forward with a very bright future. Still only 18, he has forged a promising looking partnership with Duncan Ferguson and scored his first senior goal at Stamford Bridge on 7 December. Despite being brought in for half games and substitute appearances, Michael added two more goals, both in important matches, to underline his natural predatory instincts, and seems assured of an excellent future.

Everton (From trainee on 24/10/95) PL 14+14/3 FLC 0+1 FAC 1

[BRANCO] LEAL Claudio Ibraim Vaz

Born: Brazil, 4 April 1964
Height: 5'11" Weight: 12.6
International Honours: Brazil: 73
Branco was sensationally released by Middlesbrough last October just a few weeks into the new season, having arrived on Teesside in a blaze of publicity and excitement just a few months earlier after buying himself out of his contract with Internacional in order to join the Boro. A very versatile left-full back whose appearances this term were strictly limited, he still managed to find the back of the net in both of his Coca-Cola Cup outings against

Hereford United, but left the club and returned to Brazil under a cloud. His consummate skill and ice coolness under pressure were never in doubt, but he seemed to struggle noticeably to achieve the match fitness required for the demanding levels of the FA Carling Premiership.

Middlesbrough (Free from Genoa, via Fluminese, Porto Alegre, FC Porto and Brescia, on 2/3/96) PL 6+3 FLC 2/2

BRANNAN Gerard (Ged) Daniel

Born: Prescot, 15 January 1972
Height: 6'0" Weight: 12.3
Another potentially good buy for Manchester City last season, Ged's contract at Tranmere had been due to expire at the end of the campaign and, with the Merseysiders keen to act as quickly as possible in light of the Bosman ruling , he transferred in March for a sum felt to be well below his current valuation. A six footer, who is equally competent either at full back or midfield, and extremely difficult to knock off the ball, he has a great future ahead of him. Made his City debut at Grimsby, slotting quickly into the action, but, eager to impress, picked up a booking, before being back in action a week later at his old ground, Prenton Park, in a 1-1 draw.

Tranmere Rov (From trainee on 3/7/90) FL 227+11/20 FLC 26+1/4 FAC 10+1 Others 26+1/1
Manchester C (£750,000 on 12/3/97) FL 11/1

BRASS Christopher (Chris) Paul

Born: Easington, 24 July 1975
Height: 5'10" Weight: 12.6
Used mainly at right back in the previous two seasons when he was a fringe member of the first team, Chris established himself as a commanding central defender in 1996-97 and won most of Burnley's Player of the Year awards. Strong in the tackle, unflappable, and with excellent distribution skills, he is one of the players the club will hope to hold on to as they bid for promotion next time round.

Burnley (From trainee on 8/7/93) FL 46+7 FLC 2+1 FAC 3+1 Others 4
Torquay U (Loaned on 14/10/94) FL 7 FAC 2 Others 1
\

BRAYSON Paul

Born: Newcastle, 16 September 1977
Height: 5'4" Weight: 10.10
International Honours: E: Yth
Unable to get a game at Newcastle, Paul was loaned out to Swansea last January and scored on his debut against Cambridge. Although small in stature, he showed a lot of promise, claiming five league goals during his spell at the Vetch, before a back injury suffered at the start of his third month at the club forced the speedy striker to return to St James' Park. Shows excellent first touch and awareness on the ball, which enables him to turn defenders despite there being little room.

Newcastle U (From trainee on 1/8/95) FLC 1
Swansea C (Loaned on 30/1/97) FL 11/5

BRAZIER Matthew Ronald

Born: Leytonstone, 2 July 1976
Height: 5'8" Weight: 11.6

The hard-running QPR midfielder continued where he left off in 1995-96 when making good his threat to not only mount a challenge for a first team place in 1996-97, but to actually hold a regular spot down. Very busy and always looking to be involved, he also scored his first goals for the club, the opener coming in a 3-1 Coca-Cola Cup defeat at home to Swindon, followed by two winning league goals, one at home to Bradford and the other at Huddersfield. Apart from having an eye for goal, Matthew is comfortable on the ball and looks to bring others into the game.

Queens Park R (From trainee on 1/7/94) P/FL 28+10/2 FLC 3+1/1 FAC 3

BRAZIL Gary Nicholas

Born: Tunbridge Wells, 19 September 1962
Height: 5'11" Weight: 11.3
Released by Fulham during the 1996 close season, Gary joined Cambridge on non-contract terms at the start of 1996-97, scoring their first goal of the campaign against Barnet. However, unable to command a first-team place, the skilful, hard-running striker was released in September and moved to Barnet, where he scored just twice before moving out of the league with St Albans City.

Sheffield U (Free from Crystal Palace juniors on 11/8/80) FL 39+23/9 FLC 4+1 FAC 4+5/1 Others 1+1
Port Vale (Loaned on 24/8/84) FL 6/3
Preston NE (£12,500 on 15/2/85) FL 163+3/58 FLC 13/6 FAC 10/3 Others 13/5
Newcastle U (Signed on 9/2/89) FL 7+16/2 FLC 1+1/1 FAC 0+1 Others 0+1
Fulham (£110,000 on 6/9/90) FL 207+7/48 FLC 13+1/4 FAC 9/5 Others 17/3
Cambridge U (Free on 8/8/96) FL 1/1 FLC 1
Barnet (Free on 5/9/96) FL 15+4/2 FAC 0+1

BREACKER Timothy (Tim) Sean

Born: Bicester, 2 July 1965
Height: 6'0" Weight: 13.0
Club Honours: FLC '88
International Honours: E: U21-2
A tenacious right back with the ability to break forward and deliver telling crosses, Tim had a fragmented season for West Ham in 1996-97, finding himself frequently sidelined with injury. After his longest run of consecutive games (12) from January to March his campaign came to a premature end following another injury, this time sustained at Coventry. He enjoyed an outstanding game at Newcastle in November, keeping David Ginola at bay and also providing the cross for Keith Rowland's goal which earned the Hammers a valuable point. Now entering his eighth season at Upton Park, he will be hoping for better luck with his fitness in 1997-98.

Luton T (From apprentice on 15/5/83) FL 204+6/3 FLC 22+2 FAC 21 Others 7
West Ham U (£600,000 on 12/10/90) F/PL 209+9/8 FLC 16 FAC 24 Others 7

BRECKIN Ian

Born: Rotherham, 24 February 1975
Height: 6'0" Weight: 12.9
Club Honours: AMC '96
As Rotherham's most consistent player in 1996-97, he often showed a maturity beyond

his years when having to try and hold the defence together. It was also noticeable that Ian had grown much stronger in the air and he played the majority of his games in a central role, although moving to right back on numerous occasions, and developed his attacking play, while he also proved useful in scoring goals from dead-ball situations. Finishing the season as skipper of his hometown team, he is the nephew of former United captain, John.
Rotherham U (From trainee on 1/11/93) FL 130+2/6 FLC 6 FAC 5 Others 11

BREEN Gary Patrick
Born: Hendon, 12 December 1973
Height: 6'1" Weight: 12.0
International Honours: Ei: 10; U21-9
Signed at the end of January from Birmingham City, the Eire international made a good impression on his Coventry debut at Hillsborough, despite carrying an arm injury sustained in an off the field incident. Although solid performances followed, crucial errors at Old Trafford and in the West Ham home defeat cost him his place in the run in. A skilful, right-footed central defender, who likes to bring the ball out of defence and is also very good in the air, he is considered an excellent prospect for the future when he adjusts to the Premier League.
Maidstone U (Free from Charlton Ath juniors on 6/3/91) FL 19
Gillingham (Free on 2/7/92) FL 45+6 FLC 4 FAC 5 Others 1
Peterborough U (£70,000 on 5/8/94) FL 68+1/1 FLC 6 FAC 6 Others 6/1
Birmingham C (£400,000 on 9/2/96) FL 37+3/2 FLC 4 FAC 1
Coventry C (£2,400,000 on 1/2/97) PL 8+1

BRENNAN James (Jim) Gerald
Born: Toronto, Canada, 8 May 1977
Height: 5'9" Weight: 12.5
The young wing back made a promising Bristol City debut in a 2-1 win at Bournemouth last season and by the end of the campaign had the benefit of adding seven more games to make it a highly satisfactory start to his Football League career. Had earlier come to City's attention thanks to the club's former assistant manager, Tony Taylor, who was coaching in Canada and, following a trial, when he scored against Spurs' reserves, he was signed from Toronto club, Sora Lazio.
Bristol C (Free from Sora Lazio on 25/10/94) FL 7+1

BREVETT Rufus Emanuel
Born: Derby, 24 September 1969
Height: 5'8" Weight: 11.0
After spending most of his time at QPR previously being in and out of the side, Rufus had an excellent season in 1996-97, at last realising his potential in giving some outstanding performances in the left-back position and occasionally as a wing back. Missing just two games throughout the campaign, due to injury, and a strong candidate for the Player of the Year award, he proved to be defensively strong, his tackling sound, and very quick to link up

with the attack when coming out with the ball. His crossing ability was also much improved.
Doncaster Rov (From trainee on 8/7/88) FL 106+3/3 FLC 5 FAC 4 Others 10+1
Queens Park R (£250,000 on 15/2/91) F/PL 121+8/1 FLC 7+1 FAC 6

BRIDGES Michael
Born: North Shields, 5 August 1978
Height: 6'1" Weight: 10.11
Club Honours: Div 1 '96
International Honours: E: U21-1
The highly-rated teenage striker was used mainly as a substitute last term and came off the bench to score twice in one of Sunderland's best results of the season, a 3-1 win at Everton in November. He was also a regular for the England U18s, before making his U21 debut against Switzerland. With Sunderland dropping back into division one, the future of the club lies with players such as Michael, a young man with pace and skill who has the potential to become one of the best strikers in the country. Is adept at holding up play.
Sunderland (From trainee on 9/11/95) P/FL 12+28/7 FLC 1+1 FAC 2

Michael Bridges

BRIEN Anthony (Tony) James
Born: Dublin, 10 February 1969
Height: 6'0" Weight: 13.2
International Honours: Ei: Yth
An experienced centre back, Tony joined Hull City during the 1996 close season, a year after turning down a similar move. Became a fixture in City's strong five-man

defence, but missed out from January when a back four was employed. A good tackler, his return was further hindered by a hip injury.
Leicester C (From apprentice on 13/2/87) FL 12+4/1 FLC 1 FAC 1 Others 3
Chesterfield (£90,000 on 16/12/88) FL 201+3/8 FLC 14 FAC 7 Others 14
Rotherham U (Signed on 8/10/93) FL 41+2/2 FLC 2 FAC 4 Others 6
West Bromwich A (Free on 13/7/95) FL 2 FLC 1 Others 1
Mansfield T (Loaned on 16/2/96) FL 4
Chester C (Loaned on 22/3/96) FL 8
Hull C (Free on 12/7/96) FL 29 +3/1 FLC 2 FAC 3 Others 2

BRIGHT Mark Abraham
Born: Stoke, 6 June 1962
Height: 6'0" Weight: 12.12
Club Honours: FMC '91
Having failed to make an impression in David Pleat's Sheffield Wednesday team selections last season, apart from just one substitute appearance at home to one of his former clubs, Leicester, the experienced striker was loaned out to Millwall in mid-December and scored on his debut at Bournemouth with a neat far-post header, before going back to Hillsborough three games later. Still unable to get a game, however, he was then released from his contract at the end of January and joined the Swiss side, Sion, on a short-term contract. Next it was back to England to join Charlton on transfer deadline day where, following a couple of subs' appearances, he made his full debut against Huddersfield at the Valley, scoring both goals in a 2-1 win, and showing great awareness and unselfishness up front while blending well into the pattern of play.
Port Vale (Free from Leek T on 15/10/81) FL 18+11/10 FLC 1+1 FAC 0+1/1 Others 2
Leicester C (£33,000 on 19/7/84) FL 26+16/6 FLC 3+1 FAC 1
Crystal Palace (£75,000 on 13/11/86) F/PL 224+3/92 FLC 22/11 FAC 13+1/2 Others 23/9
Sheffield Wed (£1,375,000 on 11/9/92) PL 112+21/48 FLC 20+1/11 FAC 13/7 (Free to Sion on 27/1/97)
Millwall (Loaned on 13/12/96) FL 3/1 Others 1
Charlton Ath (Free on 4/4/97) FL 4+2/2

BRIGHTWELL David John
Born: Lutterworth, 7 January 1971
Height: 6'2" Weight: 13.5
A strong centre back, who can perform equally well at full back, David appeared in just two first-team games for Bradford last season due to injuries and loss of form and was loaned out to Blackpool in December, starting just once. The reserve team captain, and brother to Manchester City's Ian, his mother (Ann Packer) and father, Robbie, both won medals in the Tokyo Olympics of 1964. Released during the summer, he has good aerial power and should find another club without too much difficulty.
Manchester C (From juniors on 11/4/88) F/PL 35+8/1 FLC 2+1 FAC 5+2/1
Chester C (Loaned on 22/3/91) FL 6
Lincoln C (Loaned on 11/8/95) FL 5 FLC 2
Stoke C (Loaned on 11/9/95) FL 0+1 Others 1
Bradford C (£30,000 on 22/12/95) FL 23+1 FAC 1 Others 2
Blackpool (Loaned on 12/12/96) FL 1+1

BRIGHTWELL Ian Robert
Born: Lutterworth, 9 April 1968
Height: 5'10" Weight: 12.5
International Honours: E: U21-4; Yth
Ian is a sound and reliable midfield player, who somehow manages to fit into the plans of the various managers who have been in charge of Manchester City during the last three seasons. Is equally effective when called to fill the back positions. Had a particularly impressive game at home to Middlesbrough in the FA Cup last season, where he was detailed to close down the world-renowned skills of Fabrizio Ravanelli. This he did very well, although a big disappointment was in having a goal disallowed for offside, prior to the TV replays showing it to have been legitimate. Finished the season with a very impressive run at full back, especially when coming forward and complimenting the winger by overlapping.
Manchester C (From juniors on 7/5/86) F/PL 266+34/18 FLC 27+2 FAC 17+4/1 Others 4+3

BRISCOE Anthony Maurice
Born: Birmingham, 16 August 1978
Height: 5'11" Weight: 11.10
Still only 18, the well-built Shrewsbury trainee forward was thrust into the squad at Bristol Rovers last February, due to an injury crisis and came off the bench for the final 12 minutes. A promising youngster whom the club obviously have hopes for, he must be considered as one for the future.
Shrewsbury T (Trainee) FL 0+1

BRISCOE Lee Stephen
Born: Pontefract, 30 September 1975
Height: 5'11" Weight: 10.9
International Honours: E: U21-5
After an encouraging time in 1995-96, Lee had a disappointing 1996-97 season for Sheffield Wednesday, coming into the new campaign with an injury carried over from the previous term and not featuring until the end of November, and that just for a solitary start. The England U21 full back, cum midfielder, could not break back into the side except at the end of the campaign when he seemed to be back on song, no doubt waiting for a new start in 1997-98. At his best, he is capable of adding drive and pace to the club's left flank.
Sheffield Wed (From trainee on 22/5/94) PL 33+6 FLC 1

BRISSETT Jason Curtis
Born: Wanstead, 7 September 1974
Height: 5'10" Weight: 12.7
A quick and tricky Bournemouth left winger, Jason started last season well, scoring in the first three league games before being unfortunately injured. Able to attack defenders with penetrating runs in order to deliver quality crosses, although returning in November, was unable to recapture his early form.
Peterborough U (Free from Arsenal juniors on 14/6/93) FL 27+8 FLC 5+1/1 FAC 2+1/1 Others 3+1/1
Bournemouth (Free on 23/12/94) FL 83+10/7 FLC 5 FAC 3 Others 4/2

BRODIE Stephen (Steve) Eric
Born: Sunderland, 14 January 1973
Height: 5'6" Weight: 10.6
Initially joining Scarborough on loan from Sunderland last December, having earlier impressed during some reserve team outings for the club in a previous loan spell, the pacy young striker settled down well to make the transfer permanent seven weeks later. Slotting in, and scoring some vital goals as the Boro chased a promotion play-off slot, he will be a key ingredient in the coming campaign.
Sunderland (From trainee on 1/7/91) FL 1+11
Doncaster Rov (Loaned on 31/8/95) FL 5/1
Scarborough (Free on 20/12/96) FL 23+1/5

BROOKE David
Born: Barnsley, 23 November 1975
Height: 5'8" Weight: 11.2
A talented midfielder, David made the move from hometown club, Barnsley, to third division Scarborough, during the 1996 close season, having been a regular in Barnsley's Pontins league side in 1995-96. His senior debut came in the opening game of the campaign and, despite remaining a regular for much of the time, he was released during the summer.
Barnsley (From trainee on 7/7/93)
Scarborough (Free on 5/8/96) FL 28+6/2 FLC 3 FAC 1+1 Others 1

BROOKER Paul
Born: Hammersmith, 25 November 1976
Height: 5'8" Weight: 10.0
His attacking runs at defences and eye for a goal made this exciting right-sided midfielder, cum striker, a great favourite with the Fulham fans in 1996-97. Micky Adams continued to bring him along slowly and he did not start a single league match, despite coming off the subs' bench on no less than 26 occasions, often to great advantage. Top scored in the reserves with 11 goals.
Fulham (From trainee on 1/7/95) FL 9+37/4 FLC 0+1/1 FAC 1+3/1 Others 1+1

BROOMES Marlon Charles
Born: Birmingham, 28 November 1977
Height: 6'0" Weight: 12.12
International Honours: E: U21-2; Yth; Sch
A highly-rated young central defender with Blackburn Rovers, he was farmed out to Swindon Town last January for first team experience, making his Football League debut in a 3-3 home draw with Grimsby. In forming an effective tri-partite defensive partnership with Mark Seagraves and Ian Culverhouse, the highlight of his two-month stay was a long-range, wind assisted goal from 40 yards in a 3-1 victory over Birmingham City, although it was also marred by a collective nightmare - a 7-0 defeat by first division champions elect, Bolton Wanderers. Rovers have very high hopes that he will prove to be one of their graduates who can make the breakthrough to Premier League standard. Was also capped for the England U21 side as a measure of his progress in the game.
Blackburn Rov (From trainee on 28/11/94)
Swindon T (Loaned on 22/1/97) FL 12/1

BROUGH John Robert
Born: Ilkeston, 8 January 1973
Height: 6'0" Weight: 12.10
Hereford utility player who can be relied upon to play anywhere and give 100 per cent regardless. Most efficient in the centre of defence, forming an excellent partnership with Dean Smith and Trevor Matthewson in 1996-97, he was cool, calm and calculating, and a must for this coming season with the Conference beckoning. Always attacks the ball and is an excellent tackler.
Notts Co (From trainee on 9/7/91)
Shrewsbury T (Free on 6/7/92) FL 7+9/1 FLC 1+1 FAC 1 Others 1
Hereford U (Free from Telford on 4/11/94) FL 70+9/3 FLC 5 FAC 4/1 Others 4+3

BROUGHTON Drewe Oliver
Born: Hitchin, 25 October 1978
Height: 6'3" Weight: 12.0
A scorer at youth and reserve levels for Norwich last season, Drewe was given a first-team debut when coming off the bench at Crystal Palace in March, before scoring with a stylish volley at Molineux, plus getting in an angled header that almost beat the 'keeper. Educated at Bedford Public School and representing Milton Keynes and Border Counties, he has risen rapidly through the ranks to turn professional this past summer. Possessing a willowy frame, at 6'3", he overcame persistent knee problems at the start of the campaign and it is expected that he will be given an extended run in the side in 1997-98 to see if he can produce the goods.
Norwich C (From trainee on 6/5/97) FL 3+5/1

Andrew Brown

BROWN Andrew Stewart
Born: Edinburgh, 11 October 1976
Height: 6'3" Weight: 13.10
Signed on a free transfer in May 1996, the lanky Hull City striker rejoined former youthful Leeds' colleagues, Jamie Marks

and Paul Wharton, at Boothferry last season, becoming a true "Braveheart" in a remarkable full league debut as he took over in goal for the last 20 minutes from the injured Roy Carroll to secure a 1-0 win at Lincoln. Donned the replacement gloves again against Northampton after spending much of his first season on City's bench.
Leeds U (Signed from St Johnstone juniors on 1/4/95)
Hull C (Free on 13/5/96) FL 17+19/1 FLC 0+1 FAC 2

BROWN Grant Ashley
Born: Sunderland, 19 November 1969
Height: 6'0" Weight: 11.12
Although the Lincoln club captain and central defender missed both the start and the finish of last season through injury, he still took his career tally for the Imps past the 300 mark during the campaign. Solid and reliable, and easily the longest-serving player at the club, he is a crucial part of the foundation that the side is built on.
Leicester C (From trainee on 1/7/88) FL 14 FLC 2
Lincoln C (£60,000 on 20/8/89) FL 288/12 FLC 18/1 FAC 11 Others 17/2

BROWN Gregory (Greg) Jonathan
Born: Manchester, 31 July 1978
Height: 5'10" Weight: 11.6
A product of Chester's youth policy, having turned professional during the 1996 close season, Greg unfortunately missed most of 1996-97 due to injuries and made just two subs' appearances, one in the league and the other in the FA Cup. Disappointingly, the promising midfielder, who had been expecting to follow up the excellent start he made while still a trainee in 1995-96, was released in the summer.
Chester C (From trainee on 20/6/96) FL 1+3 FAC 0+1 Others 0+1

BROWN Kenneth (Kenny) James
Born: Upminster, 11 July 1967
Height: 5'9" Weight: 11.6
Yet again failing to get a game with West Ham, Kenny went on loan to Reading for the second season running last September, playing five times as an effective full back who won the ball cleanly and linked up well with midfield players. Later in the year, he was transferred to Birmingham after on-loan Matt Jackson joined Norwich and immediately went into the right-back slot, being extremely useful as a wing back. However, having lost his position to Jon Bass towards the end of the campaign, he went on the transfer list after being told that a regular place could not be guaranteed.
Norwich C (From juniors on 10/7/85) FL 24+1 Others 3
Plymouth Arg (Free on 10/8/88) FL 126/4 FLC 9 FAC 6 Others 3
West Ham U (£175,000 on 2/8/91) F/PL 55+8/5 FLC 2+1 FAC 7+2/1 Others 2+2
Huddersfield T (Loaned on 7/9/95) FL 5
Reading (Loaned on 27/10/95) FL 12/1 FLC 3
Southend U (Loaned on 1/3/96) FL 6
Crystal Palace (Loaned on 28/3/96) FL 5+1/2 Others 3/1
Reading (Loaned on 9/9/96) FL 5
Birmingham C (£75,000 on 27/12/96) FL 11 FAC 1

BROWN Linton James
Born: Hull, 12 April 1968
Height: 5'9" Weight: 11.0
Suspension and ankle injuries disrupted Linton's first full season at Swansea in 1996-97, as he struggled to command a regular place in the line up. Showed his electric pace, however, when called into the first team, scoring important goals, but was sent off twice at Scarborough and Northampton. In favouring his right foot, he can play in wide or central roles.
Halifax T (Free from Guisley on 18/12/92) FL 3
Hull C (Free on 8/1/93) FL 111+10/23 FLC 6 FAC 4+1/1 Others 4
Swansea C (£60,000 on 22/3/96) FL 16+9/3 FLC 1+1 FAC 1 Others 1+2

BROWN Michael (Mickey) Antony
Born: Birmingham, 8 February 1968
Height: 5'9" Weight: 11.12
Club Honours: Div 3 '94
The right winger returned home to Shrewsbury, his first club, for the third time last December, initially on loan before a permanent transfer, following a disappointing spell at Preston. A player with excellent speed on the run who can produce superb crosses from the line, he took some time to show signs of the form of his previous spell at the club, but hopes are high that 1997-98 will see Mickey return to his former achievements. Prior to rejoining Town, he had performed well on loan at Rochdale, his debut coinciding with their first win of the season.
Shrewsbury T (From apprentice on 11/2/86) FL 174+16/9 FLC 17/2 FAC 10/1 Others 11
Bolton W (£100,000 on 15/8/91) FL 27+6/3 FLC 0+1 FAC 3 Others 2
Shrewsbury T (£25,000 on 23/12/92) FL 66+1/11 FLC 8/1 FAC 3 Others 2
Preston NE (£75,000 on 30/11/94) FL 11+5/1 FLC 0+1 Others 1
Rochdale (Loaned on 13/9/96) FL 5
Shrewsbury T (£20,000 on 12/12/96) FL 17+2/1 Others 3

BROWN Michael Robert
Born: Hartlepool, 25 January 1977
Height: 5'8" Weight: 11.8
International Honours: E: U21-4
Started 1996-97 well, playing in six out of the first seven league games for Manchester City, before his season appeared to fall away. Other than the occasional outing, Michael was unable to push his way back into contention, but following a meeting with the chairman, Francis Lee, he was lifted to understand that hard work and dedication would bring back his opportunities. The firm-tackling midfielder came back for the home FA Cup tie against Middlesbrough, but was subbed after 65 minutes mainly through exhaustion in giving his all during a hard game. On the last day for transfers, having been given a long-term contract by City, he was allowed to join Hartlepool on loan for one month to gain further experience. It was no easy ride at his hometown club, but he added that extra touch of class to a makeshift side which had a real battle on its hands to avoid relegation, something that was ultimately averted.
Manchester C (From trainee on 13/9/94) F/PL 23+9 FLC 1+3 FAC 6
Hartlepool U (Loaned on 27/3/97) FL 6/1

BROWN Steven (Steve) Byron
Born: Brighton, 13 May 1972
Height: 6'1" Weight: 13.10
Tall, strong right-sided Charlton defender who is equally comfortable at right back or in central defence and can also play in midfield. Good in the air, with a liking for going forward, and possessing a powerful shot, Steve was once again called upon to don the 'keeper's jersey, this time against Wolves in 1996-97, when Mike Salmon was injured. For those in the know, it was no great surprise that he proceeded to make two excellent saves to preserve a clean sheet.
Charlton Ath (From trainee on 3/7/90) FL 99+9/3 FLC 5 FAC 10 Others 3

BROWN Steven (Steve) Ferold
Born: Northampton, 6 July 1966
Height: 6'1" Weight: 11.8
Left-footed Wycombe midfielder who was a regular until losing his place last December. Suffered an ankle injury in February before his return to the side in the final weeks added a much needed edge to midfield. Having scored the club's first goal of the 1996-97 campaign he got back in the groove with six goals, some long-range specials, including a brilliantly executed 35-yard drive in the 2-1 win at Notts County.
Northampton T (From juniors on 11/8/83) FL 14+1/3 (Free to Irthlingborough T in December 1985)
Northampton T (Free on 21/7/89) FL 145+13/19 FLC 10/1 FAC 12/2 Others 10+1/1
Wycombe W (£60,000 on 9/2/94) FL 112+9/8 FLC 9+1 FAC 7+1 Others 2+2

BROWN Steven (Steve) Robert
Born: Southend, 6 December 1973
Height: 6'0" Weight: 12.7
A strong-running Lincoln front man who spent most of last season, either in the reserves or on the substitutes' bench, Steve rediscovered his form following a loan move to Dover and won his place back on his return, appearing in the final nine matches. He also scored two goals, including the first in a 3-3 draw at Exeter.
Southend U (From trainee on 10/7/92) FL 10/2 FAC 0+1 Others 1
Scunthorpe U (Free on 5/7/93)
Colchester U (Free on 27/8/93) FL 56+6/17 FLC 2 FAC 5/1 Others 4/1
Gillingham (Signed on 22/3/95) FL 8+1/2
Lincoln C (£20,000 on 6/10/95) FL 31+10/5 FLC 0+3 FAC 1 Others 3/1

BROWN Wayne Larry
Born: Southampton, 14 January 1977
Height: 6'1" Weight: 11.6
Owing to Keith Welch's continued good form at Bristol City, this young goalkeeper, with just one league appearance behind him, was allowed to leave the club during the 1996 close season. However, spotted playing for Weston super Mare early in 1996-97, Wayne signed for Chester following a trial and later stood in twice for Ronnie Sinclair as City moved towards the play offs.
Bristol C (From trainee on 3/7/95) FL 1 (Free to Weston super Mare during 1996 close season)
Chester C (Free on 30/9/96) FL 2

BROWNING Marcus Trevor
Born: Bristol, 22 April 1971
Height: 6'0" Weight: 12.10
International Honours: W: 5

The powerful ball-winning Welsh international midfielder was the subject of an unsuccessful bid by Wimbledon prior to his transfer to Huddersfield last February, where he linked up with former Bristol Rovers' team mate, Marcus Stewart, and assistant manager, Dennis Booth. Earlier in 1996-97, however, while still a Rover, he was involved in one of the season's strangest incidents when the Brentford goalie, Kevin Dearden, having believed he had heard the referee's whistle for an infringement, placed the ball for the kick, and Marcus promptly despatched the ball into the net to claim an important victory for the Pirates. Has yet to score for Town.
Bristol Rov (From trainee on 1/7/89) FL 152+22/13 FLC 7+3 FAC 8/1 Others 13+5/3
Hereford U (Loaned on 18/9/92) FL 7/5
Huddersfield T (£500,000 on 17/2/97) FL 13

Steve Bruce

BRUCE Stephen (Steve) Roger
Born: Corbridge, 31 December 1960
Height: 6'0" Weight: 13.0
Club Honours: Div 2 '86, PL '93, '94, '96; FLC '85, '92; FAC '90, '94; CS '90, '93, '94; ECWC '91; ESC '91;
International Honours: E: B-1; Yth

A very experienced and consistent central defender who was appointed Birmingham's captain after his free transfer capture from Manchester United during the 1996 close season. His leadership and reading of the game was first class, and he was soon an integral part of the Blues' defence in 1996-97, again proving himself to be a great competitor who attacks everything on the

ground and in the air. Fractured an eye socket in mid March which put him out for a month, but it did not stop him from finishing runner up for the Player of the Season award.
Gillingham (From apprentice on 27/10/78) FL 203+2/29 FLC 15/6 FAC 14/1
Norwich C (£125,000 on 24/8/84) FL 141/14 FLC 20/5 FAC 9/1 Others 10
Manchester U (£800,000 on 18/12/87) F/PL 309/36 FLC 32+2/6 FAC 41/3 Others 32+2/7
Birmingham C (Free on 17/6/96) FL 30+2 FLC 4 FAC 3/1

BRUMWELL Phillip (Phil)
Born: Darlington, 8 August 1975
Height: 5'8" Weight: 11.0

A tenacious Darlington defender and utility midfielder, he appeared in the majority of games last season, without ever commanding any one position. Scoring in the 4-1 win at Runcorn in the FA Cup, his strength is in his tackling.
Sunderland (From trainee on 30/6/94)
Darlington (Free on 11/8/95) FL 47+19/1 FLC 5+1 FAC 5/2 Others 3+3

BRYAN Marvin Lee
Born: Paddington, 2 August 1975
Height: 6'0" Weight: 12.2

An attacking full back who likes to get down Blackpool's right flank, Marvin dropped out of the side after suffering injury early into last season, before coming back strongly to regain his place. As you would expect from a former out-and-out wingman, his speed, coupled to strength, made him difficult to pass, and, at the same time, it gave the team an added dimension up front.
Queens Park R (From trainee on 17/8/92)
Doncaster Rov (Loaned on 8/12/94) FL 5/1
Blackpool (£20,000 on 10/8/95) FL 78+2/2 FLC 4+2 FAC 4 Others 8

BRYANT Matthew (Matt)
Born: Bristol, 21 September 1970
Height: 6'1" Weight: 13.2

Signed from Bristol City in August 1996, he soon settled into the heart of the Gillingham defence and had only missed one game when, on a shooting expedition back in Bristol in late November, he unfortunately shot himself in the leg. The fact that he missed a whole month because of the incident, resulted in Tony Pulis banning all of his players from any field sports apart from football!
Bristol C (From trainee on 1/7/89) FL 201+2/7 FLC 9+1 FAC 11 Others 9
Walsall (Loaned on 24/8/90) FL 13 FLC 4
Gillingham (£65,000 on 8/8/96) FL 38+1 FLC 6 FAC 2

BRYDON Lee
Born: Stockton, 15 November 1974
Height: 5'11" Weight: 11.0

Released by Liverpool, having been at Anfield for four years, Lee signed for Darlington during the 1996 close season and deputised in the centre of their defence on a number of occasions throughout 1996-97. Fast in recovery and composed on the ball, he made his debut as a sub at home to Swansea in the third game of the campaign.

Liverpool (From trainee on 24/6/92)
Darlington (Free on 14/8/96) FL 17+8 FLC 0+1 FAC 0+1 Others 1

BRYSON James Ian Cook
Born: Kilmarnock, 26 November 1962
Height: 5'11" Weight: 12.12
Club Honours: Div 3 '96

Preston's captain remained an important member of the first-team squad in 1996-97, although more often on the bench than starting in the early part of the season. Regained his wide left midfield place and was one of the most consistent performers in a difficult season, using his experience to good effect, prior to being released during the summer.
Kilmarnock (Signed from Hurlford in 1981) SL 194+21/40 SLC 12+7/1 SC 14+2/3
Sheffield U (£40,000 on 24/8/88) F/PL 138+17/36 FLC 11+2/1 FAC 18+4/4 Others 7/3
Barnsley (£20,000 on 12/8/93) FL 16/3 FLC 2/1 Others 2
Preston NE (£42,500 on 29/11/93) FL 141+10/19 FLC 6+1/1 FAC 7+2 Others 12/1

Ian Bryson

BUCKLE Paul John
Born: Hatfield, 16 December 1970
Height: 5'8" Weight: 11.2
Club Honours: Div 3 '92

Picked up as a free agent from Wycombe just after they knocked Colchester out of the FA Cup, having previously been with Northampton after being released by Exeter during the 1996 close season, Paul quickly established himself in the first team and kept his place for the rest of the campaign. An Auto Windscreen goal spectacular with U's first ever Golden Goal at Millwall, the winner against Northampton, and the aggregate equaliser in the southern area final, he was most unlucky to miss the big Wembley showpiece with a pre-match suspension. Is a bustling midfielder and dead-ball expert who promises great things for 1997-98.
Brentford (From trainee on 1/7/89) FL 42+15/1 FLC 5+1 FAC 3+1 Others 6+5

Torquay U (Free on 3/2/94) FL 57+2/9 FLC 8 FAC 3 Others 1
Exeter C (Free on 13/10/95) FL 22/2 FAC 1 Others 2
Northampton T (Free on 30/8/96)
Wycombe W (Free on 18/10/96)
Colchester U (Free on 28/11/96) FL 24 Others 5/3

BULL Garry William
Born: West Bromwich, 12 June 1966
Height: 5'10" Weight: 12.2
Club Honours: GMVC '91

Although his scoring touch deserted him in 1996-97, Garry still had a good season at York, impressing with his skill, ball control, passing ability, and tremendous workrate up front. However, one vital goal he did score helped to knock Everton out of the Coca-Cola Cup. Is the cousin of Wolverhampton's Steve.

Southampton (Signed from Paget R on 15/10/86)
Cambridge U (Signed on 29/3/88) FL 13+6/4 FLC 0+1 Others 0+2
Barnet (£2,000 on 1/3/89) FL 83/37 FLC 4/4 FAC 11/3 Others 8/2
Nottingham F (Free on 21/7/93) F/PL 4+8/1 FLC 2 FAC 0+3
Birmingham C (Loaned on 12/9/94) FL 10/6 Others 2/1
Brighton & Hove A (Loaned on 17/8/95) FL 10/2 Others 1/2
Birmingham C (Free on 29/12/95) FL 3+3 FLC 0+1 FAC 0+2 Others 1/1
York C (Free on 4/3/96) FL 48+8/10 FLC 4+1/1 FAC 4

Garry Bull

BULL Stephen (Steve) George
Born: Tipton, 28 March 1965
Height: 5'11" Weight: 12.11
Club Honours: Div 4 '88, Div 3 '89; AMC '88
International Honours: E: 13; B-5; U21-5

The expertly taken hat trick on the opening day of 1996-97 at Grimsby was his 17th, a Wolves' club record, while the winner at Manchester City made him the highest-scoring west midlands-based player ever. It was a typical Bull strike in that he was clearly going to shoot, yet did so a fraction earlier than the goalkeeper anticipated. After a poor spell the goals flowed again from the captain, including a rasping drive from outside the area to set up a vital win at Barnsley and a 45-seconds strike at Birmingham, when he controlled the ball, beat his man, and neatly found the corner of the net. A tenth goal in ten games at Oldham was a prelude to a harsh dismissal, the subsequent three-match suspension possibly costing the club promotion. Steve would have been top scorer in the first division, but for the penalties of John McGinlay, while his career total for club and country is now 303. No wonder the Wolves' Fanzine is named after him! Off the field he had a noisy "This is your life" at Wolverhampton Civic Hall as part of a testimonial year, which culminated in a Molineux sell out.

West Bromwich A (Free from Tipton T on 24/8/85) FL 2+2/2 FLC 2/1 Others 1+2
Wolverhampton W (£35,000 on 21/11/86) FL 426+2/239 FLC 25+1/13 FAC 17/7 Others 33+1/32

BULLIMORE Wayne Alan
Born: Sutton in Ashfield, 12 September 1970
Height: 5'9" Weight: 12.1
International Honours: E: Yth

Out of contention for first-team places at Bradford in 1996-97, following a cruciate ligament operation, Wayne was loaned out to Doncaster in September, playing four games, before signing for Peterborough the day before the transfer deadline. Came off the bench to make his debut at London Road against Bristol Rovers, eventually appearing in six of the final eight games of the campaign. Is obviously hoping to get back to his best as a skilful left-footed midfielder who is excellent at set pieces and capable of scoring an occasional cracker.

Manchester U (From trainee on 16/9/88)
Barnsley (Free on 9/3/91) FL 27+8/1 FLC 2+1 FAC 1+1
Stockport Co (Free on 11/10/93)
Scunthorpe U (Free on 19/11/93) FL 62+5/11 FLC 2+2/1 FAC 7/1 Others 5/1
Bradford C (£40,000 on 15/12/95) FL 1+1
Doncaster Rov (Loaned on 20/9/96) FL 4
Peterborough U (Free on 26/3/97) FL 2+4

BULLOCK Darren John
Born: Worcester, 12 February 1969
Height: 5'8" Weight: 12.7

A combative midfield powerhouse for Huddersfield, sadly a sequence of events saw his "star on the wane", following a well documented incident. In the circumstances, Terriers' manager, Brian Horton, concluded that an early parting of the ways was in the best interests of all concerned and sold him last February in a cut-price deal to Swindon, who needed to augment their midfield strength following the departure of Kevin Horlock. Despite scoring in the 13th minute of his debut (a 3-1 victory over Birmingham City), Darren struggled to make an immediate impact at the County Ground and was unable to counteract the Robins' late-term slump in form. He will probably need to put last season's events well behind him before he reveals his true form for Swindon.

Huddersfield T (£55,000 from Nuneaton Borough on 19/11/93) FL 127+1/16 FLC 11/1 FAC 8/2 Others 9/1
Swindon T (£400,000 on 24/2/97) FL 12+1/1

BULLOCK Martin John
Born: Derby, 5 March 1975
Height: 5'5" Weight: 10.7

Again used mainly from the subs' bench for Barnsley in 1996-97, his pace and close control terrorising tired defenders when unleashed. A natural winger who has adapted his style to the modern game, playing a number of times in the free role behind the front two, last season was a disappointment to him in that he felt he deserved more than nine starting opportunities. Good enough, however, to be selected for the Nationwide League U21s against the Italian Serie "B", as in 1995-96, Martin only scored the one goal, a saviour in the FA Cup against Oldham.

Barnsley (£15,000 from Eastwood T on 4/9/93) FL 49+49/1 FLC 3+2 FAC 1+4/1 Others 1

BURGESS Daryl
Born: Birmingham, 24 January 1971
Height: 5'11" Weight: 12.4

Daryl played at right back, centre half, and as a sweeper in West Brom's back line in 1996-97 and did very well, being one of the most consistent members of the team, especially when forming a dual partnership at the heart of the defence with Paul Raven and more latterly, Shaun Murphy. Troubled by injury early in 1997, eventually he came through without too much bother. Has pace and strength in the tackle to go with his aerial ability.

West Bromwich A (From trainee on 1/7/89) FL 251+5/8 FLC 13+2/3 FAC 8 Others 14

BURLEY Craig William
Born: Irvine, 24 September 1971
Height: 6'1" Weight: 12.13
International Honours: S: 20; U21-7; Yth; Sch

An all-action, attacking midfielder with a powerful shot, Chelsea's Craig has been a regular in Craig Brown's Scotland teams of the past two seasons, being employed as a right-sided wing back and featuring in the bizarre World Cup qualifier in Tallinn in October 1996 when Estonia failed to appear and the match was abandoned after three seconds! He began 1996-97 in the central midfield position and was instrumental in ruining Sheffield Wednesday's 100 per-cent start when he broke away for a fine individual goal and set up Andy Myers for the Blues' second in the 2-0 victory at Hillsborough, he also scored a neatly-taken goal against West Bromwich in the FA Cup third round. Another Chelsea player whose season was interrupted he was stretchered off against Derby County in January with a nasty ankle injury which sidelined him for nine matches, following an impressive spell either side of the Christmas period when he played some of the best football of his career. With Dan Petrescu injured for the FA Cup semi final, Craig moved to the right

side of midfield and his shrewd overlapping kept the Wimbledon defence at full stretch.
Chelsea (From trainee on 1/9/89) F/PL 85+28/7 FLC 8 FAC 12+5/4 Others 3

BURNETT Wayne
Born: Lambeth, 4 September 1971
Height: 6'0" Weight: 12.6
International Honours: E: Yth
Joined Huddersfield just after the start of last season from Bolton, initially on loan, and showed enough promise to be offered a permanent contract. A skilful midfielder who has also been called upon to play as a sweeper, he has the ability to pick out fellow players with excellent passes, but sometimes drifts in and out of games and, as a result, often finds himself substituted.
Leyton Orient (From trainee on 13/11/89) FL 34+6 FLC 3+1/1 FAC 3+1 Others 4
Blackburn Rov (£90,000 on 19/8/92)
Plymouth Arg (Signed on 9/8/93) FL 61+9/3 FLC 3 FAC 8 Others 4+1
Bolton W (£100,000 on 12/10/95) F/PL 0+2
Huddersfield T (Signed on 6/9/96) FL 33+2 FLC 3 FAC 1+1

BURNS Christopher (Chris)
Born: Manchester, 9 November 1967
Height: 6'0" Weight: 14.0
An attacking midfielder, first team outings for Northampton were far and few for Chris in 1996-97 with so many midfielders on the books, and he decided to concentrate on his family business in the south west of England, signing for Gloucester City in October.
Portsmouth (£25,000 from Cheltenham T on 15/3/91) FL 78+12/9 FLC 7+2/2 FAC 7 Others 9+1/1
Swansea C (Loaned on 17/12/93) FL 4 Others 1/1
Bournemouth (Loaned on 11/3/94) FL 13+1/1
Swansea C (Free on 25/11/94) FL 3+2 FAC 0+1
Northampton T (Free on 13/1/95) FL 62+4/9 FLC 3/1 FAC 2 Others 3/1

BURRIDGE John
Born: Workington, 3 December 1951
Height: 5'11" Weight: 13.3
Club Honours: FLC '77; Div 2 '79; SLC '91
The veteran 45-year-old goalkeeper played regularly for Unibond League club, Blyth Spartans, last season, whilst also working as a goalkeeping coach for Leeds United and Newcastle United. Signed on non-contract forms for Scarborough in December, John made one appearance in the Auto Windscreen shield game against Notts County when the regular 'keeper, Ian Ironside, was out injured.
Workington (From apprentice on 2/1/70) FL 27 FLC 1 FAC 4
Blackpool (£10,000 on 1/4/71) FL 134 FLC 10 FAC 4 Others 17
Aston Villa (£100,000 on 1/9/75) FL 65 FLC 9 FAC 6
Southend U (Loaned on 20/1/78) FL 6
Crystal Palace (£65,000 on 9/3/78) FL 88 FLC 7 FAC 7
Queens Park R (£200,000 on 19/12/80) FL 39 FLC 4 FAC 2
Wolverhampton W (£75,000 on 26/8/82) FL 74 FLC 2 FAC 5
Derby Co (Loaned on 21/9/84) FL 6 FLC 2
Sheffield U (£10,000 on 26/10/84) FL 109 FLC 6 FAC 6 Others 4

Southampton (£30,000 on 11/8/87) FL 62 FLC 7 FAC 4 Others 2
Newcastle U (£25,000 on 3/10/89) FL 67 FLC 4 FAC 7 Others 5
Hibernian (Free during 1991 close season) SL 65 SLC 5 SC 5 Others 2
Newcastle U (Free on 13/8/93)
Scarborough (Free on 29/10/93) FL 3 Others 1
Lincoln C (Free on 24/12/93) FL 4 (Free to Enfield in February 1994)
Aberdeen (Free in March 1994) SL 3 SC 1 (Free to Barrow in September 1994)
Dumbarton (Free in October 1994) SL 3
Falkirk (Free in November 1994) SL 3
Manchester C (Free on 15/12/94) PL 3+1
Notts Co (Free on 11/8/95. Free to Witton A on 1/10/95)
Darlington (Free on 17/11/95) FL 3 FAC 2
Grimsby T (Free on 20/12/95. Free to Gateshead in January 1996)
Northampton T (Free on 26/1/96 - Free to Blyth Spartans during the 1996 close season)
Scarborough (Free on 9/12/96) Others 1

BURROWS David
Born: Dudley, 25 October 1968
Height: 5'10" Weight: 11.8
Club Honours: CS '89 '90; Div 1 '90; FAC '92
International Honours: E: B-3; U21-7
A left-sided or central defender, David had a frustrating season for Coventry in 1996-97 as hernia injuries kept him sidelined from October through to April, but whenever he played in the centre of defence, City looked more solid with his tough tackling, good positional play and strength in the air giving them additional options. Gave an excellent display in the win at Anfield, his first full game back, and followed up with a solid performance at the Dell.
West Bromwich A (From apprentice on 8/11/86) FL 37+9/1 FLC 3+1 FAC 2 Others 1
Liverpool (£550,000 on 20/10/88) F/PL 135+11/3 FLC 16 FAC 16+1 Others 14
West Ham U (Signed on 17/9/93) PL 29/1 FLC 3/1 FAC 3
Everton (Signed on 6/9/94) PL 19 FLC 2 FAC 2
Coventry C (£1,100,000 on 2/3/95) PL 39+1 FLC 2 FAC 1

BURTON Deon John
Born: Ashford, 25 October 1976
Height: 5'8" Weight: 11.9
Started last season as Portsmouth's first-choice striker, but, following an indifferent run of form, was left out of the side in favour of Lee Bradbury and was loaned out to Exeter in December. Delighted the fans with a double in a 2-0 home win over Torquay on his debut, but five games later was back at Fratton Park and, although still playing second fiddle, scored against Chelsea in the FA Cup and the winner at West Bromwich. However, it was not until Mathias Svensson was injured with a few games to go that Deon got another run, this time linking effectively with Bradbury.
Portsmouth (From trainee on 15/2/94) FL 42+20/10 FLC 3+2/2 FAC 0+2/1
Cardiff C (Loaned on 24/12/96) FL 5/2 Others 1

BUSHELL Stephen (Steve) Paul
Born: Manchester, 28 December 1972
Height: 5'9" Weight: 11.6
Although injury setbacks have proved a big problem to Steve in recent years, the busy,

hard-working midfielder finally re-established himself in the York senior side during the closing months of 1996-97, finishing the campaign in good form. Also scored a few goals, including a 20-yard cracker that brought a vital equaliser at home to Plymouth.
York C (From trainee on 25/2/91) FL 116+18/8 FLC 4+1/1 FAC 3 Others 10+2/1

BUTLER Philip Anthony (Tony)
Born: Stockport, 28 September 1972
Height: 6'2" Weight: 12.0
Signed from Gillingham during the 1996 close season, the tall central defender immediately got down to the business of forming a formidable partnership with David Linighan at the heart of the Blackpool defence. Dominant in the air, there are not many forwards who can claim to get the better of him in goalmouth tussles.
Gillingham (From trainee on 13/5/91) FL 142+6/5 FLC 12 FAC 12+1 Others 5+1/1
Blackpool (£225,000 on 30/7/96) FL 41+1 FLC 3 FAC 1 Others 2/1

Tony Butler (right)

BUTLER John Edward
Born: Liverpool, 7 February 1962
Height: 5'11" Weight: 12.1
Club Honours: AMC '92; Div 2 '93, Div 3 '97
As Wigan Athletic's "Mr Dependable", John completed his 300th league start for the club in the draw at Chester City last season. One of the most popular players to ever represent the club, he now holds a unique record, winning promotion in his first and most recent seasons at the club, having played in the previous promotion-winning side of 1982. Released during the summer, he may have lost a yard of pace, but counters that with sound positional sense.
Wigan Ath (Free from Prescot Cables on 15/1/82) FL 238+7/15 FLC 17+1 FAC 20+1/2 Others 18
Stoke C (£75,000 on 23/12/88) FL 258+4/7 FLC 19 FAC 11 Others 26+1/2
Wigan Ath (Free on 17/6/95) FL 53+4/1 FLC 1 FAC 4 Others 4

BUTLER Lee Simon
Born: Sheffield, 30 May 1966
Height: 6'2" Weight: 14.4
Club Honours: Div 3 '97

A goalkeeper very much in the David Seaman mould, it took him a while to win over the Wigan Athletic fans after his transfer from Barnsley during the 1996 close season, but that all changed when he hit peak form following the turn of the year, his consistent performances keeping the club in more than a few games during the promotion run in. An agile shot stopper and ever present during the campaign, Lee's reward for his super work was a third division championship medal.

Lincoln C (Free from Haworth Colliery on 16/6/86) FL 30 FLC 1 FAC 1
Aston Villa (£100,000 on 21/8/87) FL 8 Others 2
Hull C (Loaned on 18/3/91) FL 4
Barnsley (£165,000 on 22/7/91) FL 118+2 FLC 5 FAC 9 Others 4
Scunthorpe U (Loaned on 5/2/96) FL 2
Wigan Ath (Free on 5/7/96) FL 46 FLC 2 FAC 1 Others 1

BUTLER Martin Neil
Born: Wordsley, 15 September 1974
Height: 5'11" Weight: 11.9

In 1996-97, his fourth season of being in and out of the Walsall team, Martin got an equaliser on the opening day against Rotherham, but did not score again, his all-out efforts not always being appreciated by fans. Predominately, a striker, and a lively one at that, in the latter part of the campaign he showed up well as a wing back.

Walsall (From trainee on 24/5/93) FL 43+31/8 FLC 2+1 FAC 2+5/2 Others 2+2/2

BUTLER Paul John
Born: Manchester, 2 November 1972
Height: 6'2" Weight: 13.0
Club Honours: Div 2 '97

A summer signing from Rochdale in July 1996, Paul featured in 41 of Bury's division two championship games alongside Chris Lucketti and Andy Woodward, who replaced Michael Jackson in the side following his move to Preston, in the Shakers' three-man central defence. A powerful centre half, who has great aerial presence and is a constant danger in dead-ball situations, he proved to be a very shrewd capture for the club.

Rochdale (From trainee on 5/7/91) FL 151+7/10 FLC 8+1 FAC 6+2 Others 12+1
Bury (£100,000 on 22/7/96) FL 40+1/2 FLC 4 FAC 1 Others 3/1

BUTLER Peter James
Born: Halifax, 27 August 1966
Height: 5'9" Weight: 11.1

Injury struck Peter in a West Brom pre-1996-97 season friendly versus Coventry and he was out of action for over five months. Albion had been hoping that his tackling would be a key feature in their midfield engine room, but, alas, he was absent for a crucial period, although coming back for a few outings during the second half of the campaign. At his best, he enjoys both the tackling and passing aspects of the game.

Huddersfield T (From apprentice on 21/8/84) FL 0+5
Cambridge U (Loaned on 24/1/86) FL 14/1 Others 1
Bury (Free on 8/7/86) FL 9+2 FLC 2/1 FAC 1
Cambridge U (Free on 10/12/86) FL 55/9 FLC 4 FAC 2 Others 2
Southend U (£75,000 on 12/2/88) FL 135+7/9 FLC 12/1 FAC 2 Others 2
Huddersfield T (Loaned on 24/3/92) FL 7
West Ham U (£125,000 on 12/8/92) F/PL 70/3 FLC 4 FAC 3 Others 1
Notts Co (£350,000 on 4/10/94) FL 20 FLC 2 FAC 2 Others 3
Grimsby T (Loaned on 30/1/96) FL 3
West Bromwich A (£175,000 on 28/3/96) FL 21+5 FAC 0+1

BUTLER Stephen (Steve)
Born: Birmingham, 27 January 1962
Height: 6'2" Weight: 12.12
Club Honours: GMVC '89
International Honours: E: SP-3

1996-97 was a bit of an up and down season for Steve. The veteran striker missed the early part of the campaign, only to come back and injure himself at Luton in early September, before returning for the home match against Millwall in mid October, where he scored two penalties (only the fourth Gillingham player to do so in a league game). Then, just when he was showing his best form, he went down with appendicitis on the eve of the Bristol Rovers game on 8 February. Amazingly, he was back within a month and towards the end of the term he netted five goals in six games to finish as the club's second highest league scorer.

Brentford (Free from Windsor & Eton on 19/12/84) FL 18+3/3 Others 2
Maidstone U (Free on 1/8/86) FL 76/41 FLC 4/3 FAC 18/7 Others 10/4
Watford (£150,000 on 28/3/91) FL 40+22/9 FLC 4+3 FAC 1 Others 2+1
Bournemouth (Loaned on 18/12/92) FL 1
Cambridge U (£75,000 on 23/12/92) FL 107+2/51 FLC 4+1 FAC 6/5 Others 3
Gillingham (£100,000 on 15/12/95) FL 43+15/14 FLC 4+1/1 FAC 3/1

BUTT Nicholas (Nicky)
Born: Manchester, 21 January 1975
Height: 5'10" Weight: 11.3
Club Honours: FAYC '92; CS '94, '97; PL '96, '97; FAC '96
International Honours: E: 2; U21-7; Yth (UEFA Yth '93); Sch

A gritty Manchester United midfielder with neat skills and a hardened edge, Nicky made a spectacular start to last season, scoring a brilliantly headed goal against Newcastle in the Charity Shield at Wembley, before leaving the field with concussion. Although he carried the effects of that injury into United's opening Premiership game against Wimbledon, he made an excellent recovery and missed only three league games up to the turn of the year. Having doubled his goal tally from the previous season, scoring his first against Leeds in September, hitting a brace against Leicester in November, and adding two in successive games against Sunderland and Nottingham Forest in December, after playing against Aston Villa on New Years Day, he missed six games with a long-standing ankle injury, which included United's ill-fated FA Cup

campaign. Once recovered, however, he showed the kind of form that earned him the captaincy of the England U21 side in November, and was elevated to the full England squad for the friendly against Mexico in March. The winner of another championship medal, his future continues to look bright both at club and international level, something reflected in him signing a new five-year contract in September.

Manchester U (From trainee on 29/1/93) PL 66+16/8 FLC 3 FAC 10+2/1 Others 16+2/1

BUTTERS Guy
Born: Hillingdon, 30 October 1969
Height: 6'3" Weight: 13.0
International Honours: E: U21-3

Having been signed from Portsmouth last October, Guy took a little time to settle into his central defensive position at Gillingham, but, once he had got going, he proved to be a valuable asset, being strong in the tackle, supreme in the air and always a danger at corners and long throws. An experienced defender, he should prove invaluable as the Gills look to maintain a second division place.

Tottenham H (From trainee on 5/8/88) FL 34+1/1 FLC 2+1 FAC 1
Southend U (Loaned on 13/1/90) FL 16/3 Others 2
Portsmouth (£375,000 on 28/9/90) FL 148+6/6 FLC 15+1/1 FAC 7 Others 7+2
Oxford U (Loaned on 4/11/94) FL 3/1 Others 1
Gillingham (£225,000 on 18/10/96) FL 30 FAC 3

BYRNE Paul Peter
Born: Dublin, 30 June 1972
Height: 5'11" Weight: 13.0
International Honours: Ei: U21-1; Yth; Sch

1996-97 was a disappointing season at Southend for Paul, as his reported off-field problems seemed to lead to a lack of confidence on the pitch. An exceptionally talented winger on his day, he turned in some indifferent performances and found it hard to create the form that earned him rave notices in 1995-96. However, his jinking touchline runs were more in evidence towards the end of the campaign and the fans will be hoping that he will return to his full form in 1997-98.

Oxford U (From trainee on 4/7/89) FL 4+2 (Free to Bangor in September 1991)
Glasgow Celtic (Signed on 26/5/93) SL 24+4/4 SLC 1+1 SC 1 Others 2
Brighton & Hove A (Loaned on 10/3/95) FL 8/1
Southend U (£50,000 on 25/8/95) FL 61+12/6 FLC 3/1 FAC 2 Others 4

BYRNE Wesley John
Born: Dublin, 9 February 1977
Height: 5'10" Weight: 11.6
International Honours: Ei: Yth; Sch

Released by Middlesbrough during the 1996 close season, Wesley joined Stoke on non-contract terms, before moving to Darlington on the same basis in December. A strong tackler with fair speed, the young left back made just one full appearance and one as a substitute, prior to signing for non-league Gateshead a month later.

Middlesbrough (From trainee on 24/2/94) Others 1
Stoke C (Free on 18/7/96)
Darlington (Free on 23/12/96) FL 1+1

Carling Black Label

CARLING Black. Label
Position: No. 1
Nationality: British
Strength: 4.1% volume
Appearances: Every Carling Premiership game
Record: Sponsor of the Carling Premiership: 1993 to present. Sponsor of the Professional Footballers' Association: 1993 to present.
Honours: The Carling No.1 Awards - the only football awards in which fans representatives get a vote
The Carling Manager of the Month
The Carling Player of the Month
The Carling No.1 Award
The Carling Manager of the Year
The Carling Player of the Year

Ever-present in the top flight since 1993, Carling is a natural leader and a consistent crowd pleaser. Carling's main assets are: pace - 44 pints are served every second; strength - 4.1%abv and its distribution - 27,000 pubs and clubs nationwide. Constantly in demand, Carling is a refreshing all-rounder suited to all occasions.

CARLING BLACK LABEL, THE BEST SELLING BEER IN BRITAIN... A FACT WORTH REMEMBERING NEXT TIME YOU HIT THE BAR

carling net @
www.fa-carling.com

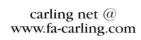

C

CADAMARTERI Daniel (Danny) Leon
Born: Bradford, 12 October 1979
Height: 5'7" Weight:11.12
A pacy, dreadlocked winger with more than a passing resemblance to QPR's Trevor Sinclair, Danny turned pro with Everton last October, when he was handed a five-year contract, and made his debut when coming off the bench for the final 45 minutes of the season against Chelsea, making a big impact with the home supporters. Interestingly, he possesses the unusual distinction of being eligible for international selection as far as six countries - Nigeria, Italy, England, Ireland, Scotland and Jamaica - are concerned, with England being the first to court his services in inviting him to youth training camp. Is a confident youngster who seems set for an exciting future.
Everton (From trainee on 15/10/96) PL 0+1

CADETTE Richard Raymond
Born: Hammersmith, 21 March 1965
Height: 5'8" Weight: 12.0
Club Honours: B&QC '94
Richard was unfortunately dogged by injuries in 1996-97 and only returned to first team action in January. An exciting forward with excellent close control and speed, he was seen to good effect against Rotherham when he jinked past two defenders in the box, his cross shot being deflected in for the second goal of Millwall's 2-0 win. Was freed during the summer.
Leyton Orient (Free from Wembley on 25/8/84) FL 19+2/4 FLC 4 FAC 1/1 Others 2
Southend U (Free on 15/8/85) FL 90/48 FLC 5+1/1 FAC 4/5 Others 5/1
Sheffield U (£130,000 on 20/7/87) FL 26+2/7 FLC 1 FAC 2 Others 2
Brentford (£80,000 on 22/7/88) FL 67+20/20 FLC 10+3/6 FAC 9/1 Others 14/4
Bournemouth (Loaned on 23/3/90) FL 4+4/1
Falkirk (Signed on 9/1/92) SL 82+10/31 SLC 6/7 SC 4/2 Others 4/6
Millwall (£135,000 on 13/10/94) FL 19+5/5 FLC 2/1 FAC 1

CAIG Antony (Tony)
Born: Whitehaven, 11 April 1974
Height: 6'1" Weight: 13.4
Club Honours: Div 3 '95; AMC '97
Tony was the only Carlisle player to be ever present in all 61 league and cup fixtures last season. A goalkeeper with safe hands and a good shot stopper, he improved on other aspects of his game in 1996-97 and was deservedly chosen for the third division PFA select side, his finest moment coming in the AWS final at Wembley when two splendid saves in the penalty shoot out helped clinch the trophy for United.
Carlisle U (From trainee on 10/7/92) FL 140 FLC 10 FAC 11 Others 24

CALDERWOOD Colin
Born: Stranraer, 20 January 1965
Height: 6'0" Weight: 12.12
Club Honours: Div 4 '86
International Honours: S: 20; Sch

A strong, reliable central defender who figured in Scotland's Euro '96 campaign, added consistency and good aerial ability saw him continue to improve his performances in 1996-97 to become an essential part of both Tottenham and Scotland's plans. Paired with Sol Campbell, Colin controlled the heart of the Spurs' defence and applied his height at set pieces, while his ability to place a dead ball saw him called upon for free kicks and joining attacks. And, as an accurate passer, he continued to show his ability to read the game well and gain a crucial half a yard on opponents. Despite an underlying knee injury, the Scot played on to all but the last game of the season before going for surgery.
Mansfield T (Signed on 19/3/82) FL 97+3/1 FLC 4 FAC 6/1 Others 7
Swindon T (£30,000 on 1/7/85) FL 328+2/20 FLC 35 FAC 17/1 Others 32
Tottenham H (£1,250,000 on 22/7/93) PL 120+5/3 FLC 13 FAC 14

CALDWELL Garrett Evan James
Born: Princeton, USA, 6 November 1973
Height: 6'2" Weight: 13.0
Colchester's Olympic international goalkeeper, Garrett enjoyed an excellent build up for 1996-97 and managed to displace the previous first-choice 'keeper, Carl Emberson for the opening of the season. Unfortunately, he sustained a serious thigh injury in only his sixth game and only played twice more, once in an emergency in January and then at Barnet during the last game of the campaign, where, after a shaky start, he showed United followers what they had been missing with a really solid display.
Colchester U (Free from Princeton, USA on 25/9/95) FL 6 FLC 2 Others 1

CALDWELL Peter James
Born: Dorchester, 5 June 1972
Height: 6'1" Weight: 13.0
International Honours: E: Sch
A good shot stopper, Peter started 1996-97 as second choice at Leyton Orient after being unable to dislodge Les Sealey and then had his season virtually ended by injury just as he returned to the number-one spot for two games, prior to being released in mid March.
Queens Park R (From trainee on 9/3/90)
Leyton Orient (Free on 3/7/95) FL 31 FLC 2 Others 1

CAMPBELL Andrew (Andy) Paul
Born: Stockton, 18 April 1979
Height: 5'11" Weight: 11.7
International Honours: E: Yth
A young Middlesbrough striker who was blooded as sub towards the end of 1995-96 against Sheffield Wednesday and, at 17, one of Boro's youngest ever debutants, Andy developed steadily through the club's reserve teams in 1996-97, and was given further Premiership experience when coming off the bench at Aston Villa, Liverpool and Coventry. A prolific goalscorer who is held in high esteem by all of his coaches, he is expected to breakthrough this coming season in the less demanding atmosphere of the first division.
Middlesbrough (From trainee on 4/7/96) PL 1+4

CAMPBELL Jamie
Born: Birmingham, 21 October 1972
Height: 6'1" Weight: 12.11
Jamie played in a number of positions for Barnet last season, but looked at his most comfortable playing up front as a second striker. Despite being equally at home in midfield and defence, it was in this position that he scored against Wycombe in the FA Cup match shown live on Sky TV, one of the six he netted during the campaign.
Luton T (From trainee on 1/7/91) FL 10+26/1 FLC 1+1 FAC 1+3 Others 1+2
Mansfield T (Loaned on 25/11/94) FL 3/1 FAC 2
Cambridge U (Loaned on 10/3/95) FL 12
Barnet (Free on 11/7/95) FL 50+17/5 FLC 3+3/1 FAC 4+2/1 Others 1

CAMPBELL Kevin Joseph
Born: Lambeth, 4 February 1970
Height: 6'1" Weight: 13.8
Club Honours: FAYC '88; FLC '93; FAC '93; ECWC '94
International Honours: E: B-1; U21-4
A much maligned striker in his first season at Forest, Kevin started 1996-97 in the best possible way with a hat trick on the opening day at Coventry. Another goal followed against Southampton in game four before he received an injury which kept him out for some time and after coming back in November he was never the same, scoring just twice more before losing his place to Nigel Clough, and latterly Pierre Van Hooijdonk. A strong striker with plenty of pace, despite finding the net just six times, he was joint top scorer for Forest, merely indicative of the club's continuing struggles to avoid the drop.
Arsenal (From trainee on 11/2/88) F/PL 124+42/46 FLC 14+10/6 FAC 13+6/2 Others 15+4/5
Leyton Orient (Loaned on 16/1/89) FL 16/9
Leicester C (Loaned on 8/11/89) FL 11/5 Others 1/1
Nottingham F (£3,000,000 on 1/7/95) PL 37+1/9 FAC 10/3 Others 3

CAMPBELL Neil Andrew
Born: Middlesbrough, 26 January 1977
Height: 6'2" Weight: 13.7
Neil is a strong, well-built young York striker who made his league debut during last season when standing in for Neil Tolson. A promising lad, he found it difficult at times to adjust to senior level but will have gained from the experience. Scored his first goal for the club, a header, in a 3-1 defeat at Wycombe.
York C (From trainee on 21/6/95) FL 5+6/1 FAC 0+2 Others 2

CAMPBELL Stuart Pearson
Born: Corby, 9 December 1977
Height: 5'10" Weight:10.8
Club Honours: FLC '97
A right-sided Leicester midfielder, Stuart made his debut in a Coca-Cola Cup tie at Scarborough last September, followed by a handful of first-team appearances, usually being thrown in on the big occasions, against Manchester United at Old Trafford, Liverpool at Anfield, and Chelsea in the FA

Sol Campbell

Cup, the latter as an emergency wing back. In not letting the team down at all and looking to have a bright future, his Scottish parentage could also make him a target for Scotland U21 honours in the very near future.

Leicester C (From trainee on 4/7/96) PL 4+6 FLC 0+2 FAC 2

CAMPBELL Sulzeer (Sol) Jeremiah
Born: Newham, 18 September 1974
Height: 6'2" Weight: 14.1
International Honours: E: 9; B-1; U21-11; Yth (UEFA Yth '93)

Probably the most versatile player in the Tottenham line up, Sol, a natural defender, found himself in midfield and even playing as a striker in an injury-ravaged Tottenham side during 1996-97, his outstanding defensive performances being rewarded with a regular England first-team spot. Maturing into a reliable and intelligent defender for club and country, he gained confidence in his ability on the ball, resulting in some fine attacking runs. He will no doubt remember the 2-0 defeat of Georgia as one of his best performances and, more importantly, one that earned him the reputation as one of the finest players in his position in the country. Speculation of a move to Liverpool was proved unfounded with the player himself expressing his happiness at White Hart Lane and signing a new four-year contract in May.

Tottenham H (From trainee on 23/9/92) PL 125+9/2 FLC 14/2 FAC 11+2

CANHAM Scott Walter
Born: Newham, 5 November 1974
Height: 5'7" Weight: 11.7
A central midfield playmaker who specialises with free kicks and corners, Scott joined Brentford last August from West Ham, following a successful loan spell in 1995-96. Although used very sparingly by David Webb in 1996-97, he scored his first league goal at Griffin Park against Stockport in November and generally impressed when on the park

West Ham U (From trainee on 2/7/93)
Torquay U (Loaned on 3/11/95) FL 3
Brentford (Loaned on 19/1/96) FL 14
Brentford (£25,000 + on 29/8/96) FL 13/1 FLC 2 FAC 1 Others 0+2

CANOVILLE Dean
Born: Perrivale, 30 November 1978
Height: 6'1" Weight: 11.10
Related to Paul who played for Chelsea, Dean was introduced to Millwall first team football last March after overcoming a serious injury suffered against Norwich reserves in 1995-96, which led to a cruciate ligament operation. Tall and rangy, mainly right footed, having excelled as a striker in Lions' youth teams, but now operating in midfield, he has both the skill and energy to go all the way.

Millwall (From juniors on 6/12/95) FL 0+2

CANTONA Eric
Born: Nimes, France, 24 May 1966
Height: 6'2" Weight: 14.3
Club Honours: Div 1 '92; PL '93, '94, '96, '97; CS '93, '94, '97; FAC '94, '96
International Honours: France: 45
One of the most naturally gifted talents to play in the Premiership, Eric's great skill, vision, and spectacular goals helped Manchester United through another action-packed campaign in 1996-97. Having led the club to their second league and cup double, and writing a best-selling book and starring in a movie, he began the season in excellent fashion, netting a goal in the opening game at Wimbledon, plus further strikes against Leeds – a game in which he missed his first-ever penalty – Nottingham Forest (2) and Fenerbahce. Although he endured some unfair criticism during a lean spell by the club in October, when some leading experts suggested his Gallic flair had gone, he answered his critics with some brilliant performances, his strike rate during December being of particular importance, with a vital goal against Rapid Vienna in the Champions' League, and two against Sunderland in the Premiership. Having scored in the quarter final of the European Cup against Porto in March, his decisive strike against Everton in the Premiership set

the stage for one of the most exciting finales in the club's history that ended with another championship medal, prior to his premature retirement from the game. He will be missed.

Leeds U (£900,000 from Nimes on 6/2/92) F/PL 18+10/9 FLC 1 Others 6/5
Manchester U (£1,200,000 on 27/11/92) PL 142+1/64 FLC 6/1 FAC 17/10 Others 19/7

CARBON Matthew (Matt) Phillip
Born: Nottingham, 8 June 1975
Height: 6'2" Weight: 12.4
International Honours: E: U21-4
Young Derby utility player whose best position is at the centre of defence. Fierce competition for places limited his appearances in 1996-97, but he should have learned much from the influence of Paul McGrath and is definitely a player for the future, making occasional appearances both at right back and central defence. Left footed with good ball skills, Matt is excellent in the air, his timing invaluable at both ends of the park. Also added three more England U21 caps to his collection.
Lincoln C (From trainee on 13/4/93) FL 66+3/10 FLC 4/1 FAC 3 Others 4+3
Derby Co (£385,000 on 8/3/96) P/FL 8+8 FLC 1 FAC 0+1

Benito Carbone

CARBONE Benito
Born: Italy, 14 August 1971
Height: 5'6" Weight: 10.8
Benito became one of the increasing band of Italian imports in the English game when he joined Sheffield Wednesday from Inter-Milan part way into last season, after, ironically, being forced out of Inter's side by foreign imports, making his debut against Blackburn and scoring his first goal a few matches later against Nottingham. A midfield playmaker, who made up for his lack of inches with an abundance of skill, he scored six goals in his first Premiership season and much is expected from the crowd favourite in 1997-98 as the Owls look to improve on their encouraging campaign.
Sheffield Wed (£3,000,000 from Inter Milan on 18/10/96) PL 24+1/6 FAC 2

CARDEN Paul
Born: Liverpool, 29 March 1979
Height: 5'8" Weight: 11.10
Still a Blackpool trainee, the young striker was given an opportunity to impress in an AWS match at Rotherham last December and showed enough to suggest that he has a future with the Seasiders.
Blackpool (Trainee) FL 0+1 FAC 0+1 Others 1

CAREY Brian Patrick
Born: Cork, 31 May 1968
Height: 6'3" Weight: 14.4
International Honours: Ei: 3; U21-1
When the Northern Ireland international centre half, Barry Hunter, was sold to Reading doubts were raised at Wrexham about finding a suitable replacement. However, signed from Leicester during the 1996 close season, Brian soon allayed those fears with his assured displays at the heart of the defence and the involved transfer fee becoming more apparent as the season wore on as being something of a bargain. In his third spell at the Racecourse, having had two earlier loan periods, he feels very much at home at Wrexham.
Manchester U (£100,000 from Cork C on 2/9/89)
Wrexham (Loaned on 17/1/91) FL 3
Wrexham (Loaned on 24/12/91) FL 13/1 FAC 3 Others 3
Leicester C (£250,000 on 16/7/93) F/PL 51+7/1 FLC 3 FAC 0+1 Others 4
Wrexham (£100,000 on 19/7/96) FL 38 FLC 2 FAC 9 Others 1

CAREY Louis Anthony
Born: Bristol, 22 January 1977
Height: 5'10" Weight: 11.10
This young Bristolian continued the excellent progress he had made in 1995-96 to hold down a first-team berth with Bristol City throughout last season, missing very few games and linking well with others down the right flank. A cool-headed defender or wing-back, to use the modern idiom, he has the ability to become a key player with City.
Bristol C (From trainee on 3/7/95) FL 62+3 FLC 3 FAC 6 Others 1+2

CAREY Shaun Peter
Born: Kettering, 13 May 1976
Height: 5'9" Weight: 10.10
International Honours: Ei: U21-2
A Norwich associate schoolboy from December 1990, after being at Aston Villa's School of Excellence, Shaun has the vision to see and make the pass and also do a fair amount of tracking back while playing in the holding position just in front of the defence. Unlucky to make just 17 appearances in 1996-97, eight of them from the bench, the young Irish U21 star suffered a six-week absence with an ankle injury and regularly wore the Number 12 shirt in the first three months of the campaign, four starts in January being his best run. An excellent tackler and distributor, his services are going to be needed more plentifully in 1997-98 if City are to launch a determined assault on the Premiership.
Norwich C (From trainee on 1/7/94) FL 14+9 FLC 2+2 FAC 1+1

CARPENTER Richard
Born: Sheerness, 30 September 1972
Height: 6'0" Weight: 13.0
Signed from Gillingham towards the end of last September, Richard fitted in well to the Fulham midfield as well as having the occasional game at right-wing back in 1996-97. A strong tackler, and dangerous at free kicks, especially from long range, he opened his scoring account at Darlington two days after joining the club and went on to net four more before the season was over.
Gillingham (From trainee on 13/5/91) FL 107+15/4 FLC 2+1 FAC 9+1 Others 7/1
Fulham (£15,000 on 26/9/96) FL 34/5 FAC 1

CARR Darren John
Born: Bristol, 4 September 1968
Height: 6'2" Weight: 13.7
The big man returned to the centre of Chesterfield's defence in 1996-97 after more than a year out with injury and dropped straight back into the groove, displaying his usual commanding dominance and power, never once looking stretched by difficult opponents. The ease with which he returned surprised and delighted everyone and his effective combination with Sean Dyche and Mark Williams greatly enhanced the Spireites' highly effective defence.
Bristol Rov (From trainee on 20/8/86) FL 26+4 FLC 2+2 FAC 3 Others 2
Newport Co (£3,000 on 30/10/87) FL 9
Sheffield U (£8,000 on 10/3/88) FL 12+1/1 FLC 1 FAC 3+1 Others 1
Crewe Alex (£35,000 on 18/9/90) FL 96+8/5 FLC 8 FAC 12/2 Others 10
Chesterfield (£30,000 on 21/7/93) FL 76/3 FLC 8 FAC 6+2 Others 8

CARR Stephen
Born: Dublin, 29 August 1976
Height: 5'7" Weight: 12.2
International Honours: Ei: U21-11; Yth; Sch
The Spurs' wing back made a big impression in his first season as a regular in 1996-97, having appeared just once previously, and would have benefited enormously from facing the likes of Eric Cantona and Alan Shearer, something which should add confidence to future performances. A hard-working player who demonstrated good stamina and the ability to pick out attackers, his speed and an enthusiasm to run with the ball, being his major assets,

Steve will be an obvious contender in the battle for places in 1997-98. Already an U21 international, he is expected to challenge for full Republic caps this coming campaign.
Tottenham H (From trainee on 1/9/93) PL 25+2 FLC 4 FAC 1

CARR-LAWTON Colin
Born: South Shields, 5 September 1978
Height: 5'11" Weight:11.7
A tall teenage striker who only turned pro last January and is still progressing through Burnley's youth ranks, Colin made his first team debut as a sub in the Auto Windscreens Shield game against Stockport. Obviously promising, he had been on the bench twice previously without getting a call, prior to having a spell on loan at Leek Town.
Burnley (From trainee on 21/1/97) Others 0+1

CARRAGHER James (Jamie) Lee
Born: Bootle, 28 January 1978
Height: 6'0" Weight: 12.0
Club Honours: FAYC '96
International Honours: E: U21-4; Yth
Having sat on the Liverpool bench for a handful of games in 1996-97, the young first-year professional made his debut in the quarter final of the Coca-Cola Cup at Middlesbrough in February and did well enough to be selected for the following two matches. Showing the potential to become a strong and powerful midfield dynamo, Jamie marked his first full appearance, against Aston Villa at Anfield, with a firm header into the Kop End net from a Stig Bjorneybe corner to open the scoring in a 3-0 win. Although he has plenty of time on his hands, after winning four England U21 caps there is no doubt that he will be pressing for further opportunities in 1997-98.
Liverpool (From trainee on 9/10/96) PL 1+1/1 FLC 0+1

CARRAGHER Matthew (Matty)
Born: Liverpool, 14 January 1976
Height: 5'9" Weight: 10.7
Club Honours: Div 3 '97
The youngest player ever to make a century of league starts for Wigan, the strong-tackling right back failed to live up to expectations in 1996-97, after twice winning the Young Player of the Year award. Although his 18 league games were good enough for him to pick up a third division championship medal after Athletic pipped Fulham for the title, he was given a free transfer during the summer. Hopefully, Matthew can get back on track with a fresh start elsewhere in 1997-98.
Wigan Ath (From trainee on 25/11/93) FL 102+17 FLC 6+1/1 FAC 10+1/2 Others 7+1

CARROLL David (Dave) Francis
Born: Paisley, 20 September 1966
Height: 6'0" Weight: 12.0
Club Honours: FAT '91, '93; GMVC '93
International Honours: E: Sch
1996-97 was another marvellous season for this skilful and very hard-working, two-footed Wycombe midfielder and he ended the campaign on 442 appearances and 86

goals, the fifth longest-serving player in the club's history. Top scorer with ten goals, including four penalties, and Wanderers' all-time top scorer in the Football League (30 goals), Dave looks to continue the good work in 1997-98.
Wycombe W (£6,000 from Ruislip Manor in 1988 close season) FL 170+1/30 FLC 14 FAC 12/2 Others 10/3

Dave Carroll

CARROLL Roy Eric
Born: Enniskillen, 30 September 1977
Height: 6'2" Weight: 12.9
International Honours: NI: 1; Yth
An outstanding young Hull City goal-keeping prospect, Roy got his first full inter-national call up last October (for Northern Ireland's World Cup qualifier against Armenia) as understudy to ex-Tiger, Alan Fettis. Unfortunately, shoulder and hand injuries led to two spells on the sidelines, before he was surprisingly transferred to Wigan near the end of the season in order to help the club out of a financial dilemma.
Hull C (From trainee on 7/9/95) FL 46 FLC 2 FAC 1 Others 1
Wigan Ath (£350,000 on 16/4/97)

CARRUTHERS Martin George
Born: Nottingham, 7 August 1972
Height: 5'11" Weight: 11.9
After a number of seasons on the fringe of the Stoke first team and out of contract, Martin transferred to Peterborough last November. An extremely hard-working and skilful striker, he made his debut for Posh against Gillingham, before scoring twice in a 6-2 home win over Rotherham three

games later. Unfortunately, having scored six goals and looking good for a few more, a hernia injury saw him sidelined for two months following an operation. Although coming back for four matches towards the end of the campaign, he lacked match fitness and was rested up, but is fully expected to put the wind up a few defences in 1997-98.
Aston Villa (From trainee on 4/7/90) F/PL 2+2 FAC 0+1 Others 0+1
Hull C (Loaned on 31/10/92) FL 13/6 Others 3
Stoke C (£100,000 on 5/7/93) FL 60+31/13 FLC 7+3/1 FAC 3+1 Others 10+4/6
Peterborough U (Signed on 18/11/96) FL 13+1/4 FAC 3/2 Others 2

CARSLEY Lee Kevin
Born: Birmingham, 28 February 1974
Height: 5'10" Weight: 11.11
International Honours: Ei: U21-1
A tough and tenacious Derby midfielder, Lee built on his extended first-team run in 1995-96 to claim a regular place during the second half of last season. Battling non-stop in the centre of midfield, allowing the more creative players to flourish, he is a Republic of Ireland U21 international. Equally capable of performing well in defence, his good ability on the ground helping others out of trouble, he is surely a County player for the future.
Derby Co (From trainee on 6/7/92) P/FL 68+14/3 FLC 6+2 FAC 5 Others 3

CARSS Anthony John
Born: Alnwick, 31 March 1976
Height: 5'10" Weight: 12.0
A left-sided Darlington forward or midfielder, his appearances with the club in 1996-97 were restricted due to injury, although he came back strongly towards the end of the campaign. Despite having the ability to score cracking goals, he failed to find the net last season and was released during the summer.
Blackburn Rov (Free from Bradford C juniors on 29/8/94)
Darlington (Free on 11/8/95) FL 33+24/2 FLC 5/1 FAC 2+1 Others 4

CARTER Darren (Danny) Stephen
Born: Hackney, 29 June 1969
Height: 5'10" Weight: 11.12
Unfortunately, Danny's 1996-97 season for Peterborough was badly affected by injury and he made just 11 appearances before being freed during the summer. A tricky, wide, right-sided attacking player, who also has the ability to go past defenders to pin-point crosses into the box, he was earlier given two opportunities to leave London Road, but struggled on hoping to turn things around.
Leyton Orient (Signed from Billericay T on 4/7/88) FL 168+20/22 FLC 13+3/2 FAC 10/3 Others 17+2/1
Peterborough U (£25,000 on 21/6/95) FL 33+12/1 FLC 3+2 FAC 2+1 Others 3

CARTER James (Jimmy) William Charles
Born: Hammersmith, 9 November 1965
Height: 5'10" Weight: 11.1
Club Honours: Div 2 '88

Jimmy started last season in the Portsmouth team and was a regular until the end of November, before being left out of the side due to injury. However, due to Pompey's form, and the impressive Paul Hall, he was unable to regain his place until April, marking his return with a goal against Grimsby Town. A tricky right winger with pace and the ability to go past his marker to release superb crosses for the front men, he is sure to be in contention for a place in 1997-98.

Crystal Palace (From apprentice on 15/11/83)
Queens Park R (Free on 30/9/85)
Millwall (£15,000 on 12/3/87) FL 99+11/10 FLC 6+1 FAC 6+1/2 Others 5+1
Liverpool (£800,000 on 10/1/91) FL 2+3 FAC 2 Others 0+1
Arsenal (£500,000 on 8/10/91) F/PL 18+7/2 FLC 1 FAC 2+1
Oxford U (Loaned on 23/3/94) FL 5
Oxford U (Loaned on 23/12/94) FL 3+1
Portsmouth (Free on 6/7/95) FL 54+8/5 FLC 5+1/1 FAC 0+1

CARTER Mark Colin
Born: Liverpool, 17 December 1960
Height: 5'9" Weight: 12.6
Club Honours: Div 2 '97
International Honours: E: SP-11

In his fourth season at Bury, this prolific goalscorer was once again the Shakers' top scorer with 15 league and cup goals (four from the penalty spot) in 1996-97, despite approaching his 37th birthday. In the latter half of the campaign, "Spike" was utilised mainly as a substitute, but, nevertheless, played a big part in the club's elevation to division one and, at the same time, winning his first Football League honours, before being released during the summer.

Barnet (£40,000 from Runcorn on 20/2/91) FL 62+20/30 FLC 5/2 FAC 4+1/6 Others 7+2/8
Bury (£6,000 on 10/9/93) FL 113+21/62 FLC 10+1/4 FAC 5 Others 12+1/2

CARTER Timothy (Tim) Douglas
Born: Bristol, 5 October 1967
Height: 6'2" Weight: 12.8
International Honours: E: Yth

It was another steady season for Tim in the Millwall goal in 1996-97, despite the seemingly endless defensive changes owing to injuries. Consistent to a fault, he only missed the AWS game against Colchester after injuring his hand in the warm up before the home match with Peterborough at the Den on Boxing Day and being replaced by Andrew Iga after 20 minutes. Adept, with quick reactions at close range, he saved Millwall's goal on numerous occasions.

Bristol Rov (From apprentice on 8/10/85) FL 47 FLC 2 FAC 2 Others 2
Newport Co (Loaned on 14/12/87) FL 1
Sunderland (£50,000 on 24/12/87) FL 37 FLC 9 Others 4
Carlisle U (Loaned on 18/3/88) FL 4
Bristol C (Loaned on 15/9/88) FL 3
Birmingham C (Loaned on 21/11/91) FL 2 FLC 1
Hartlepool U (Free on 1/8/92) FL 18 FLC 4 FAC 1 Others 2
Millwall (Free on 6/1/94) FL 4 FLC 0+1
Blackpool (Free on 4/8/95)
Oxford U (Free on 18/8/95) FL 12 FLC 4 Others 1 Others 2
Millwall (Free on 6/12/95) FL 50 FLC 2 FAC 3 Others 1

CARTWRIGHT Lee
Born: Rawtenstall, 19 September 1972
Height: 5'9" Weight: 11.0
Club Honours: Div 3 '96

Lee's return to Preston first-team action at Burnley last February ended a nightmare 11 months out injured, following a cruciate ligament operation. His speed and penetration on the right side of midfield had been sorely missed and all North End fans rejoiced in his return. Began by filling the right-wing-back role, before sustaining another, fortunately minor, injury to his other knee, resulting in a short spell back in the treatment room. A strong tackler and good marker, he also enjoys the passing side of the game.

Preston NE (From trainee on 30/7/91) FL 174+22/14 FLC 7/2 FAC 12+1/1 Others 11+4

CARTWRIGHT Mark Neville
Born: Chester, 13 January 1973
Height: 6'2" Weight: 13.6

Goalkeeper. "Patience is a virtue" must be Mark's theme song, as his Wrexham first-team appearances were a rarity in 1996-97, due to Andy Marriot's consistency. However, during November he was handed his chance when the latter was injured and did not let anyone down, making a number of fine reflex saves in his four appearances and will now be looking for more chances to prove himself in 1997-98.

Stockport Co (Free from York C juniors on 17/8/91 - Released during 1992 close season)
Wrexham (Signed from USA soccer scholarship on 5/3/94) FL 3 FAC 1

CASEY Ryan Peter
Born: Coventry, 3 January 1979
Height: 6'1" Weight:11.2
International Honours: Ei: Yth

A very promising tall 17-year-old YTS, Ryan was given his opportunity at Swansea last season with regular inclusions on the substitutes' bench. Showing good skill on the ball, and capable of producing accurate crosses, he signed a two-year contract immediately prior to the end of the campaign.

Swansea C (From trainee on 7/5/97) FL 3+7

CASKEY Darren Mark
Born: Basildon, 21 August 1974
Height: 5'8" Weight: 11.9
International Honours: E: Yth (UEFAYC '93); Sch

Despite being Reading's record signing, he really failed to establish himself in the team until the second half of last season, when his ability to hit long, penetrating passes set up so many of the team's attacks. A good competitor and a strong tackler, Darren has yet to make much of a reputation as a goalscorer, though his one strike of the season set up an important FA Cup victory over Southampton.

Tottenham H (From trainee on 6/3/92) PL 20+12/4 FLC 3+1/1 FAC 6+1
Watford (Loaned on 27/10/95) FL 6/1
Reading (£700,000 on 28/2/96) FL 41+9/2 FLC 1 FAC 2/1

Darren Caskey

CASPER Christopher (Chris) Martin
Born: Burnley, 28 April 1975
Height: 6'0" Weight: 11.11
Club Honours: FAYC '92; CS '94
International Honours: E: U21-1; Yth (EUFAC '93)

An elegant Manchester United central defender who reads the game well, Chris gave such a good account of himself in the Coca-Cola Cup against Swindon last October, and then Middlesbrough in the Premiership in November, that Alex Ferguson promoted him to the side for the Champions' League game against Rapid Vienna in December and the FA Cup tie against Wimbledon in January. Although he came through those games with flying colours, his chances of a regular place were limited once United's regular centre backs had recovered from injuries. That said, his chance will surely come again. Is the son of former Burnley striker, Frank.

Manchester U (From trainee on 3/2/93) PL 0+2 FLC 3 FAC 1 Others 0+1
Bournemouth (Loaned on 11/1/96) FL 16/1

CASTLE Stephen (Steve) Charles
Born: Barking, 17 May 1966
Height: 5'11" Weight: 12.10

Used primarily as a stop gap at Birmingham in 1996-97 by manager, Trevor Francis, the strong, bustling, competitive midfielder was never one to shirk in defence or attack, despite opportunities being few and far between. However, in a bid to get regular first-team football under his belt, Steve went on loan to Leyton Orient in February, playing four matches and scoring against his old favourites, Rochdale, having struck four

past them in a previous match, before unfortunately having his season ended by a knee injury. Stop press: Released by Brum, he joined his old manager, Barry Fry, at Peterborough during the summer.

Leyton Orient (From apprentice on 18/5/84) FL 232+11/55 FLC 15+1/5 FAC 23+1/6 Others 18+2
Plymouth Arg (£195,000 on 30/6/92) FL 98+3/35 FLC 5/1 FAC 8/2 Others 6/1
Birmingham C (£225,000 on 21/7/95) FL 16+7/1 FLC 11 FAC 1 Others 3/1
Gillingham (Loaned on 15/2/96) FL 5+1/1
Leyton Orient (Loaned on 3/2/97) FL 4/1

CASTLEDINE Stewart Mark
Born: Wandsworth, 22 January 1973
Height: 6'1" Weight: 12.13

A well-liked Wimbledon striker who had a part in helping the reserves to win the Avon Insurance Combination League in 1996-97, Stewart is a tall player who is very good in the air and more than capable of losing his marker. Made seven first team appearances, including two from the bench, scoring with a 15-yard volley in the 2-0 win against Leeds, and a brave header in the crucial Coca-Cola Cup game against Luton Town. Outside football, like Dean Holdsworth, he has taken up modelling.

Wimbledon (From trainee on 2/7/91) F/PL 14+7/4 FAC 1+1
Wycombe W (Loaned on 25/8/95) FL 7/3

CAVACO Luis Miguel Pasaro
Born: Portugal, 1 March 1972
Height: 5'9" Weight: 11.5

Picked up during Stockport's Portuguese 1996 summer tour, the former Estoril player's pace and attacking nature made him a big hit with the fans in 1996-97. Although never a regular fixture in the team, Luis made a big impact until a sickening double leg fracture in early April forced him to miss the season's climax.

Stockport Co (Free from Estoril on 27/8/96) FL 19+8/5 FLC 7+1/2 FAC 3 Others 3+2/1

CAWLEY Peter (Pete)
Born: Walton on Thames, 15 September 1965
Height: 6'4" Weight: 15.7

Big Pete had a mixed season with Colchester in 1996-97, missing many games through injury, but performing as inspirationally as ever when fully fit. His years of experience as a defensive kingpin also stood him in good stead when he took over in goal against Northampton in the AWS semi final, one of three outfield men to try on the green jersey during United's cup exploits. However, his worst nightmare was realised when he had the misfortune to have a crucial penalty saved against Carlisle at Wembley, but, as all U's supporters know, the club captain will bounce back again for 1997-98.

Wimbledon (Signed from Chertsey T on 26/1/87) FL 1 Others 1
Bristol Rov (Loaned on 26/2/87) FL 9+1
Fulham (Loaned on 14/12/88) FL 3+2
Bristol Rov (Free on 17/7/89) FL 1+2
Southend U (Free on 6/7/90) FL 6+1/1 FLC 1 FAC 1 Others 1
Exeter C (Free on 22/11/90) FL 7
Barnet (Free on 8/11/91) FL 3 Others 1
Colchester U (Free on 9/10/92) FL 151+2/8 FLC 6 FAC 9 Others 12+1/1

CECERE Michele (Mike) Joseph
Born: Chester, 4 January 1968
Height: 6'0" Weight: 12.12

Signed on a short-term contract in July 1996, Mike scored Rochdale's first goal of last season when coming on as substitute in the opening game, but then fell foul of the injuries which had dogged his spell at Exeter. A player with an ability to strike from midfield, he made a couple of brief re-appearances, before being released after Christmas.

Oldham Ath (From apprentice on 17/1/86) FL 35+17/8 FLC 4+1 FAC 1+2/1 Others 2+1/1
Huddersfield T (£100,000 on 11/11/88) FL 50+4/8 FLC 4/1 FAC 7+1/3 Others 5/1
Stockport Co (Loaned on 22/3/90) FL 0+1
Walsall (£25,000 on 23/8/90) FL 92+20/32 FLC 10+1 FAC 4+2 Others 12/2
Exeter C (Signed on 13/1/94) FL 34+9/11 FLC 3/1 FAC 2/1 Others 3+1/2
Rochdale (Free on 12/7/96) FL 2+2/1 FLC 0+1 FAC 1 Others 1

Martyn Chalk

CHALK Martyn Peter Glyn
Born: Louth, 30 August 1969
Height: 5'6" Weight: 10.0

A tricky little Wrexham winger who, on his day, poses many problems for defenders, did not figure on the scoresheet often enough last season and perhaps suffered as a result of the more cautious approach in club tactics. However, the league goal he scored at Blackpool in October was enough to secure a valuable point in a 3-3 draw.

Derby Co (£10,000 from Louth U on 23/1/90) FL 4+3/1 FAC 3/1 Others 0+1
Stockport Co (£40,000 on 30/6/94) FL 29+14/6 FLC 7+1/2 FAC 2+3 Others 2+2
Wrexham (Signed on 19/2/96) FL 53+9/5 FLC 2 FAC 6 Others 1

CHALLINOR David (Dave) Paul
Born: Chester, 2 October 1975
Height: 6'1" Weight: 13.0
International Honours: E: Yth; Sch

The possessor of one of the longest throws in the Football League, the 21 year old broke into Tranmere's first team towards the end of last season after giving a number of impressive performances at centre back in the reserves. Made his debut at home to Stoke in February, when standing in for John McGreal, later deputising for Andy Thorn, and shows great promise for the future. Has appeared for the England U19 side.

Tranmere Rov (Signed from Brombrough Pool on 18/7/94) FL 4+1

CHALLIS Trevor Michael
Born: Paddington, 23 October 1975
Height: 5'8" Weight: 11.0
International Honours: E: U21-1; Yth

After making his first team breakthrough at QPR in 1995-96, it was expected that Trevor would make the left-back position his own last season, but, unfortunately, fate determined otherwise. Following selection for early September games against West Bromwich and Norwich, having been substituted in both, it was discovered that he needed an operation to repair an injured knee and, at the same time, remove cysts. A good tackler with spring who reads the game well, hopefully, his excellent attitude will see him back in fine fettle for 1997-98.

Queens Park R (From trainee on 1/7/94) F/PL 12+1 FAC 2

CHAMBERLAIN Alec Francis Roy
Born: March, 20 June 1964
Height: 6'2" Weight: 13.9
Club Honours: Div 1 '96

An experienced goalkeeper signed from Sunderland prior to the start of last season, his first team opportunities at Watford were limited because of the consistency of Kevin Miller, but, despite that, he proved a reliable deputy. Although suffering a broken foot in February, he recovered to return to first-team duty at the end of the campaign, playing in the final three matches. Tall and commanding and an excellent shot stopper.

Ipswich T (Free from Ramsey T on 27/7/81)
Colchester U (Free on 3/8/82) FL 188 FLC 11 FAC 10 Others 12
Everton (£80,000 on 28/7/87)
Tranmere Rov (Loaned on 1/11/87) FL 15
Luton T (£150,000 on 27/7/88) FL 138 FLC 7 FAC 7 Others 7
Sunderland (Free on 8/7/93) FL 89+1 FLC 9 FAC 8 Others 1
Watford (£40,000 on 10/7/96) FL 4

CHAMBERLAIN Mark Valentine
Born: Stoke, 19 November 1961
Height: 5'9" Weight" 12.0
International Honours: E: 8; U21-4 (UEFA U21 '84); Sch

Used mainly as a right back last season, Mark was troubled by hamstring injuries which ensured that he was never an Exeter first-team regular. A good squad player who could be called upon for his vast experience, he left City in April to become player/

manager at Dr Martens League side, Fareham.

Port Vale (From apprentice on 1/5/79) FL 90+6/17 FLC 4 FAC 10/2
Stoke C (£135,000 on 24/8/82) FL 110+2/17 FLC 9 FAC 4/1
Sheffield Wed (£300,000 on 13/9/85) FL 32+34/8 FLC 5+2/1 FAC 1+11/1 Others 2+1
Portsmouth (£200,000 on 2/8/88) FL 143+24/20 FLC 11+2/1 FAC 7+1/1 Others 9+1
Brighton & Hove A (Free on 20/8/94) FL 12+7/2 FLC 3/1 FAC 1 Others 1
Exeter C (Free on 11/8/95) FL 51+8/4 FLC 4 FAC 1 Others 3

CHANDLER Dean Andrew Robert
Born: Ilford, 6 May 1976
Height: 6'2" Weight: 11.10
A tall Charlton central defender, Dean was again very unlucky with injuries last season and failed to make a first-team appearance. A strong tackler, and commanding in the air, he was denied a place when Kevin Scott was signed on loan to cover for injury to Stuart Balmer and was himself loaned to Torquay just before the transfer deadline, immediately making his debut for The Gulls and playing four times before returning to London and being released during the summer.

Charlton Ath (From trainee on 13/4/94) FL 1+1/1
Torquay U (Loaned on 27/3/97) FL 4

CHANNING Justin Andrew
Born: Reading, 19 November 1968
Height: 5'10" Weight: 11.7
International Honours: E: Yth
An attacking midfielder signed on a free transfer from Bristol Rovers during the 1996 close season, Justin picked up his fair share of goals for Leyton Orient in 1996-97, scoring the winner at Scunthorpe with a free kick from the edge of the box. Fitted in well when asked to replace Ian Hendon at right back after the latter departed towards the end of the campaign and, at the same time, continued his goalscoring habit.

Queens Park R (From apprentice on 27/8/86) F/PL 42+13/5 FLC 4+1 FAC 2 Others 5
Bristol Rov (£250,000 on 24/10/92) FL 121+9/10 FLC 5 FAC 4+1 Others 11+1
Leyton Orient (Free on 25/7/96) FL 40/5 FLC 1 FAC 2/1 Others 1

CHAPMAN Daniel (Danny) Graham
Born: Deptford, 21 November 1974
Height: 5'11" Weight: 13.6
Defensive midfielder who also played at right back and centre half for Leyton Orient in 1996-97. Scored both of his goals away from Brisbane Road, one of which was a spectacular 35-yard chip over the advancing Scarborough goalkeeper, before being released at the end of the season.

Millwall (From trainee on 18/3/93) FL 4+8 FLC 0+1
Leyton Orient (Free on 3/7/95) FL 69+9/4 FLC 2+1 FAC 2+1 Others 3

CHAPMAN Ian Russell
Born: Brighton, 31 May 1970
Height: 5'9" Weight: 12.5
A free transfer signing from Brighton & Hove Albion at the start of last season, Ian was a Gillingham first team regular until the

2-0 defeat at Blackpool on 12 October. Regaining his place in February, which was all the more surprising as he was the only natural left-footed player, apart from Guy Butters, in the squad, he impressed when taking on opposing full backs to get in crosses.

Brighton & Hove A (From trainee on 5/6/87) FL 265+16/14 FLC 18+2 FAC 12+2/2 Others 12+4
Gillingham (Free on 1/8/96) FL 20+3/1 FLC 5 FAC 1+2 Others 1

CHAPPLE Philip (Phil) Richard
Born: Norwich, 26 November 1966
Height: 6'2" Weight: 12.7
Club Honours: Div 3 '91
A right-sided Charlton central defender who is excellent in the air, a strong tackler, and very dangerous at corners and set pieces, Phil is always likely to grab a goal. Captained the side on several occasions in 1996-97 and could be relied upon to give 100 per cent when vying with Richard Rufus and Stuart Balmer for a first team place in the centre of the Addicks' defence, partnering both at various times.

Norwich C (From apprentice on 10/7/85)
Cambridge U (Signed on 29/3/88) FL 183+4/19 FLC 11/2 FAC 23/1 Others 17
Charlton Ath (£100,000 on 13/8/93) FL 99+8/11 FLC 10 FAC 6 Others 5

CHAPPLE Shaun Ronald
Born: Swansea, 14 February 1973
Height: 5'11" Weight: 12.3
International Honours: W: B-1; U21-10; Sch
Shaun made an impressive start to last season for Swansea before being injured against Fulham, which set him back for a number of matches. An influential midfielder, and an excellent passer of the ball, he turned down an opportunity of a loan spell at Exeter in mid season, having earlier suffered a bad leg injury at Hartlepool, an incident that saw Jan Molby sent off from the dug out.

Swansea C (From trainee on 15/7/91) FL 69+34/9 FLC 4+2/1 FAC 8+2 Others 9+3/1

CHARLERY Kenneth (Kenny)
Born: Stepney, 28 November 1964
Height: 6'1" Weight: 13.3
Despite his strike rate in 1996-97 not being as good as in his previous two spells at Peterborough, he was still a great crowd favourite with Posh fans who were surprised to see him sold to Stockport in transfer deadline week, especially after he had scored in every round of the FA Cup. At County, Kenny had a tough time being accepted as the injured Brett Angell's replacement after failing to hit the net, but with that experience now behind him, the big striker will obviously be hoping to show off his undoubted power and ability in 1997-98.

Maidstone U (£35,000 from Fisher on 1/3/89) FL 41+18/11 FLC 1+3/1 FAC 0+3 Others 5+4
Peterborough U (£20,000 on 28/3/91) FL 45+6/19 FLC 10/5 FAC 3/1 Others 11/7
Watford (£350,000 on 16/10/92) FL 45+3/13 FLC 3 FAC 1 Others 0+1
Peterborough U (£150,000 on 16/12/93) FL 70/24 FLC 2 FAC 2+1/3 Others 2/1

Birmingham C (£350,000 on 4/7/95) FL 8+9/4 FLC 3+1/2 Others 2+1
Southend U (Loaned on 12/1/96) FL 2+1
Peterborough U (Signed on 9/2/96) FL 55+1/12 FLC 4/1 FAC 6/6 Others 6/1
Stockport Co (£85,000 on 25/3/97) FL 8+2

CHARLES Lee
Born: Hillingdon, 20 August 1971
Height: 5'11" Weight: 12.4
Began last season on the sub's bench, making three appearances for QPR in that capacity before being given his first start for the club in a 1-0 home win over Bradford on 16 October. The following game at Tranmere it was back to the bench for Lee, but after being called into action for Danny Dichio he put the finishing touch to a Trevor Sinclair cross that eventually won the match for Rangers, 3-2. Not long out of non-league football, he is a confident forward with good first touch and pace, who shows a willingness to take on opponents.

Queens Park R (£67,500 from Chertsey on 4/7/95) P/FL 6+10/1 FLC 0+1
Barnet (Loaned on 22/9/95) FL 2+3 Others 0+1

Simon Charlton

CHARLTON Simon Thomas
Born: Huddersfield, 25 October 1971
Height: 5'8" Weight: 11.10
International Honours: E: Yth
A solid and reliable, natural left back, Simon adapted well to the wing-back role for Southampton in 1996-97, his forceful forward runs more often than not ending with accurate crosses. Starting the season well, he retained his place in the side at the expense of Francis Benali, apart from the odd injury, until being sidelined with seven games left and relegation (ultimately staved off) staring Saints in the face. The proud possessor of a long throw, an added weapon

which was used to place the ball in the opponent's danger area, he will be hoping for an even better run in 1997-98.
Huddersfield T (From trainee on 1/7/89) FL 121+3/1 FLC 9/1 FAC 10 Others 14
Southampton (£250,000 on 8/6/93) PL 102+9/2 FLC 8+3/1 FAC 8+1

CHARNOCK Philip (Phil) Anthony
Born: Southport, 14 February 1975
Height: 5'11" Weight: 11.2
Unable to make it into the Liverpool first-team squad, Phil spent three months on loan at Crewe early last season before signing on a permanent basis in December. A hard-working midfielder, who also played at full back when required, he quickly settled into the Dario Gradi pattern of things at Gresty Road and was a member of the side that reached the first division, via the play offs. Scored his first ever league goal in a 3-0 home win over Notts County.
Liverpool (From trainee on 16/3/93) FLC 1 Others 0+1
Blackpool (Loaned on 9/2/96) FL 0+4
Crewe Alex (Signed on 30/9/96) FL 24+8/1 FAC 2 Others 6

CHEESEWRIGHT John Anthony
Born: Romford, 12 January 1973
Height: 6'0" Weight: 14.0
Having began last season as understudy to Brian Parkin in the Wycombe goal the new manager, John Gregory, unexpectedly called him up for his debut at York in October. An excellent shot stopper and particularly brave and effective in one-on-one situations, John held his place for 23 games before Parkin was recalled. Released during the summer, having had experience at several league clubs, he had joined Wanderers in March 1996 from non-league football.
Southend U (Free from Tottenham H juniors on 28/3/91)
Birmingham C (Free on 28/11/91) FL 1 Others 1
Colchester U (£10,000 from Braintree T, via Redbridge F and Cohb Ramblers, on 13/1/94) FL 40 FLC 1 FAC 3 Others 2
Wimbledon (Free on 12/6/95 - Free to Braintree T on 11/8/95)
Wycombe W (Free on 27/3/96) FL 18 FAC 4 Others 1

CHERRY Steven (Steve) Reginald
Born: Nottingham, 5 August 1960
Height: 6'1" Weight: 13.0
Club Honours: AIC '95
International Honours: E: Yth
After being released by Plymouth during the 1996 close season and joining Rotherham – he had nearly done that the previous summer – Steve started last season as automatic choice before losing his place at the end of October. However, he was soon back, only to go out of favour again, leaving the club by mutual consent in March and moving into non-league football with Rushden & Diamonds. An experienced 'keeper, he could well turn to coaching in the future.
Derby Co (From apprentice on 22/3/78) FL 77 FLC 5 FAC 8
Port Vale (Loaned on 26/11/80) FL 4 FAC 4
Walsall (£25,000 on 10/8/84) FL 71 FLC 10 FAC 7 Others 6
Plymouth Arg (£17,000 on 23/10/86) FL 73 FLC 4 FAC 5 Others 1

Chesterfield (Loaned on 1/12/88) FL 10 Others 3
Notts Co (£70,000 on 16/2/89) FL 266 FLC 17 FAC 14 Others 31
Watford (Free on 14/7/95) FL 4
Plymouth Arg (Signed on 19/2/96) FL 16 Others 3
Plymouth Arg (Free on 20/5/96)
Rotherham U (Free on 15/7/96) FL 20 FLC 2 Others 1

CHETTLE Stephen (Steve)
Born: Nottingham, 27 September 1968
Height: 6'1" Weight: 13.3
Club Honours: FMC '89, '92; FLC '90
International Honours: E: U21-12
The centre back, had a steady if not spectacular season for Nottingham Forest in 1996-97, being a regular in the side and not missing a game from December onwards. Although happy on the ball, his goalscoring form deserted him and he did not find the net all season, while apart from a few games, his partnership with Colin Cooper was as reliable as ever, the club's problem being more in the scoring goals department than in conceding them. Recognised for his positional play and timely interventions, it would be difficult to imagine Forest without him, especially in the light of him having played almost 450 games for them.
Nottingham F (From apprentice on 28/8/86) F/PL 311+14/7 FLC 39+3/1 FAC 34+1 Others 21+2/2

CHILDS Gary Paul Colin
Born: Birmingham, 19 April 1964
Height: 5'7" Weight: 10.9
International Honours: E: Yth
A clever, quick-thinking and creative Grimsby player, at home in midfield or up front, Gary did not enjoy one of his better seasons in 1996-97, playing few full games and often being substituted or left on the bench. Released during the summer, many supporters feel he was unfairly made the scapegoat for the Mariners' poor season and that his role as playmaker was sadly missed.
West Bromwich A (From apprentice on 13/2/82) FL 2+1
Walsall (£15,000 on 7/10/83) FL 120+11/17 FLC 14+2/2 FAC 9+1/2 Others 7/2
Birmingham C (£50,000 on 8/7/87) FL 39+16/2 FLC 0+2 FAC 3 Others 2
Grimsby T (Free on 20/7/89) FL 204+29/26 FLC 16/1 FAC 15/1 Others 7+2

CHRISTIE Iyseden
Born: Coventry, 14 November 1976
Height: 6'0" Weight: 12.6
Although this young striker had made his Coventry debut in 1995-96, he was to be afforded no further opportunities last season, especially with the club's back against the Premiership wall and, consequently, spent spells on loan at Bournemouth (November) and Mansfield (February). Performed reasonably well at Bournemouth in four games played, while his constant foraging at Mansfield made him a constant menace to third division defences, who found it difficult to combat his ability. Unfortunately, he had to return to Highfield Road early due to injury. *Stop Press:* Freed by Coventry, it was reported that he had signed on a permanent basis for Mansfield during the summer.

Coventry C (From trainee on 22/5/95) PL 0+1 FLC 0+1
Bournemouth (Loaned on 18/11/96) FL 3+1
Mansfield T (Loaned on 7/2/97) FL 8

CLAPHAM James (Jamie) Richard
Born: Lincoln, 7 December 1975
Height: 5'9" Weight: 10.11
In making his Premiership debut in Tottenham's final game of last season at home to Coventry, due to the absence of Colin Calderwood, Jamie proved to be a strong, and enthusiastic competitor who performed well under pressure. A name to watch for the future, he had earlier spent loan spells at first Leyton Orient (January) and then Bristol Rovers (March), playing at left back and impressing all around him. Not frightened to attack, especially on the overlap, Jamie gets the ball to the front men, via a sweet left foot.
Tottenham H (From trainee on 1/7/94) PL 0+1
Leyton Orient (Loaned on 29/1/97) FL 6
Bristol Rov (Loaned on 27/3/97) FL 4+1

CLARIDGE Stephen (Steve) Edward
Born: Portsmouth, 10 April 1966
Height: 5'11" Weight: 12.10
Club Honours: Div 3 '91, Div 2 '95; AMC '95; FLC '97
Bustling right-footed Leicester striker. Signed from Birmingham towards the end of 1995-96, his transfer fee has now risen to a final figure of £1.2 million, having reached 50 appearances. Proved many pundits wrong in 1996-97 when looking thoroughly at home at the highest level, and a real handful for all defenders, setting up super strikes away at Sheffield Wednesday and Blackburn Rovers, whilst his volley at home to Manchester United in the Coca-Cola Cup was voted the club's Goal of the Season. Always willing to work harder than anyone for the team, being rewarded by a regular supply of goals and finishing the campaign as City's leading marksman, Steve capped his season with the winner in the League Cup final replay at Hillsborough, a typical volley from a ball that came to him at an awkward height.
Bournemouth (Signed from Fareham on 30/11/84) FL 3+4/1 Others 1 (£10,000 to Weymouth in October 1985)
Crystal Palace (Signed on 11/10/88)
Aldershot (£14,000 on 13/10/88) FL 58+4/19 FLC 2+1 FAC 6/1 Others 5/2
Cambridge U (£75,000 on 8/2/90) FL 56+23/18 FLC 2+4/2 FAC 1 Others 6+3/1
Luton T (£160,000 on 17/7/92) FL 15+1/2 FLC 2/3 Others 2/1
Cambridge U (£195,000 on 20/11/92) FL 53/18 FLC 4/3 FAC 4 Others 3
Birmingham C (£350,000 on 7/1/94) FL 86+2/35 FLC 14+1/2 FAC 7 Others 9+1/5
Leicester C (£1,200,000 on 1/3/96) P/FL 43+3/17 FLC 8/2 FAC 4/1 Others 3/1

CLARK Ian David
Born: Stockton, 23 October 1974
Height: 5'11" Weight: 11.7
Last season has proved to be a disappointing one for Ian, who failed to cement a regular place in Doncaster's attack. His involvement was largely as a playing substitute, a role he filled on over a dozen occasions. A

Steve Claridge (left)

throw back to the days of the old-fashioned winger, keen to take players on, he also played in a deeper position when required.
Doncaster Rov (Free from Stockton on 11/8/95) FL 22+21/3 FLC 1+2 FAC 1+1 Others 4/1

CLARK Lee Robert
Born: Wallsend, 27 October 1972
Height: 5'8" Weight: 11.7
Club Honours: Div 1 '93
Local boy Lee's wholehearted endeavour in Newcastle's midfield, either in a defensive or an attacking role, has made him a favourite with the crowd. He displays good close control, is always available to receive the ball from colleagues, and his distribution over both long and short distances is excellent. However, the wealth of talent available at St James' Park limited his first-team opportunities in 1996-97 and led him to request to be made available for transfer, which was granted in November. Most of

his appearances were as substitute, although he was a starter in several games in the second half of the season. Whatever the circumstances he is a player who can always be relied upon to give of his best and, while never being a frequent scorer, he hit purple patch in January when netting in three successive games. *Stop Press:* Reportedly signed by Sunderland for £2.5 million, their record transfer fee, in early June.
International Honours: E: U21-11; Yth; Sch
Newcastle U (From trainee on 9/12/89) F/PL 153+42/23 FLC 17 FAC 14+2/3 Others 7+5/1

CLARK Simon
Born: Boston, 12 March 1967
Height: 6'1" Weight: 12.12
A hard-tackling player who is equally at home at full back or in central defence, Simon had an up-and-down season for Peterborough in 1996-97 and never really produced a settled run in a struggling side that were ultimately relegated. However, out

injured earlier on in the campaign, he came back and celebrated with goals in big-scoring wins against Wycombe and Preston.
Peterborough U (Free from Stevenage Borough on 25/3/94) FL 102+5/3 FLC 5 FAC 12 Others 7+1/1

CLARK William (Billy) Raymond
Born: Christchurch, 19 May 1967
Height: 6'0" Weight: 12.4
An experienced central defender with 250 league games behind him, Billy lost his place in the Bristol Rovers' team, having featured in 26 consecutive league matches in 1996-97, before his most unfortunate sending off at Chesterfield on 11 January. In making a return to the squad in the later stages of the season, the club's longest serving player completed nine seasons with Rovers.
Bournemouth (From apprentice on 25/9/84) FL 4
Bristol Rov (Signed on 16/10/87) FL 235+13/14 FLC 11+1 FAC 8+1 Others 19+2/1

CLARKE Adrian James
Born: Cambridge, 28 September 1974
Height: 5'10" Weight: 11.0
Club Honours: FAYC '94
International Honours: E: Yth; Sch

A loan signing from Arsenal last March, after failing to get a game for the Gunners in 1996-97, and following one start at Rotherham on a similar basis a few months earlier, Adrian proved very popular with the Southend fans who enjoyed his Steve McManaman-type runs and crosses. Although joining the club at a very difficult stage of the season, he proved himself with a number of fully committed performances in an unfamiliar wing-back position before returning to Highbury. Released during the summer.

Arsenal (From trainee on 6/7/93) PL 4+3 FAC 1+1
Rotherham U (Loaned on 2/12/96) FL 1+1 Others 1
Southend U (Loaned on 27/3/97) FL 7

CLARKE Andrew (Andy) Weston
Born: Islington, 22 July 1967
Height: 5'10" Weight: 11.7
Club Honours: GMVC '91
International Honours: E: SP-2

A popular player taken from non-league Barnet in 1991, Andy was unable to burst onto the scene for Wimbledon last season, but still managed a goal in a rare appearance at Upton Park earlier in the campaign. A very quick forward, who torments defenders with his characteristic runs and is able to take on three or four players, although playing in the successful reserve team in 1996-97, he does not quite fit into Joe Kinnear's plans at the present time.

Wimbledon (£250,000 from Barnet on 21/2/91) F/PL 73+83/17 FLC 11+11/3 FAC 9+4/2

CLARKE Darrell James
Born: Mansfield, 16 December 1977
Height: 5'10" Weight: 12.0

Won a place in Mansfield's senior team on merit by the second half of last season and maintained it as the Stags pushed for a play-off place. Having made his league debut in 1995-96 while still a trainee, the young midfielder signed pro forms during the 1996 close season, scoring his first goal for the club in a 2-0 home win over Doncaster in January.

Mansfield T (From trainee on 3/7/96) FL 18+4/2 FAC 0+1 Others 0+1

CLARKE Matthew (Matt) John
Born: Sheffield, 3 November 1973
Height: 6'3" Weight: 11.7

Matt, a 1996 close season signing from Rotherham had an eventful debut in goal for Sheffield Wednesday when, after coming on for Kevin Pressman following an injury, he was sent off nine minutes later for handling outside the area in the final game of last season against Liverpool. The number two 'keeper for the entire campaign, he had little chance to show the form which nearly earned him England U21 honours in 1995-96. Although a good shot stopper, and well placed to command his area, with Pressman

in such fine form he will have to be patient a little while yet.

Rotherham U (From trainee on 28/7/92) FL 123+1 FLC 4 FAC 3 Others 3
Sheffield Wed (£325,000 + on 10/7/96) PL 0+1

CLARKE Stephen (Steve)
Born: Saltcoats, 29 August 1963
Height: 5'10" Weight: 12.5
Club Honours: Div 2 '89; FAC '97
International Honours: S: 6; B-3; U21-8; Yth

Chelsea's long-serving Steve just seems to play better as h e gets older. Elevated to club captain in 1996-97 and playing his second season as a centre back, his unflappability and positional sense made him an integral part of Blues' three-centre-back strategy which gave the defence their most solid look for many years. Awarded a pre-season testimonial against PSV Eindhoven in recognition of his ten years at the Bridge, he is a good passer of the ball and sets many of Chelsea's attacks in motion by calmly striding out of defence, looking to play probing passes to the front players. After five goalless seasons, Steve must have been mortified when, during the FA Cup sixth round victory at Portsmouth, his goal-bound header was tapped over the line from a few inches by Dennis Wise who promptly claimed the goal – Steve has not scored since April 1992! Showed his adaptability by switching to an unfamiliar left-wing-back role against Wimbledon in the FA Cup semi final, where Chelsea's victory was sweet compensation for Steve, following his first-half injury 12 months previously when he had to limp off against Manchester United in the 1996 semi final at Villa Park. The proud possessor of a FA Cup winners medal following the 2-0 win over Middlesbrough, Steve has signed a new contract that will keep him at Chelsea until 1999.

St Mirren (Free from Beith Juniors in 1981) SL 151/6 SLC 21 SC 19/1 Others 6
Chelsea (£422,000 on 19/1/87) F/PL 299+5/6 FLC 20/1 FAC 33+2/1 Others 21/1

CLARKE Timothy (Tim) Joseph
Born: Stourbridge, 19 September 1968
Height: 6'3" Weight: 13.7
Club Honours: AMC '96

Having been released by Shrewsbury during the 1996 close season, Tim signed for York last September, making his debut at Bristol City (11 October) and appearing regularly until being replaced by Andy Warrington as the club slipped into the relegation zone. Signing for Scunthorpe, initially on loan in February and permanently on transfer deadline week, the imposing goalie's physical presence and confident approach had much to do with restoring confidence in a previously shaky defence.

Coventry C (£25,000 from Halesowen T on 22/10/90)
Huddersfield T (£15,000 on 22/7/91) FL 70 FLC 7 FAC 6 Others 8 (Free to Halesowen on 19/8/93)
Rochdale (Loaned on 12/2/93) FL 2
Shrewsbury T (Free from Altrincham on 21/10/93) FL 30+1 FLC 3 Others 1 (Free to Witton A during 1996 close season)

York C (Free on 7/9/96) FL 17 FLC 1 FAC 4 Others 1
Scunthorpe U (Signed on 21/2/97) FL 15

CLARKSON Ian Stewart
Born: Solihull, 4 December 1970
Weight: 5'11" Weight: 12.0
Club Honours: AMC '91

An attacking right back, Ian joined Northampton on a free transfer from Stoke during the 1996 close season and quickly became a crowd favourite with his powerful forward runs. The supporters' Player of the Year, he is also a strong tackler when defending.

Birmingham C (From trainee on 15/12/88) FL 125+11 FLC 12 FAC 5+1 Others 17+1
Stoke C (£40,000 on 13/9/93) FL 72+3 FLC 6 FAC 5 Others 8+2
Northampton T (Free on 2/8/96) FL 45 FLC 4 FAC 1 Others 6

CLARKSON Philip (Phil) Ian
Born: Garstang, 13 November 1968
Height: 5'9" Weight: 11.13

Top scorer at Scunthorpe at the time of his transfer to Blackpool last February, it took him seven games to find the net for his new club, before two close-range strikes made him a local hero and gained three home points against Preston. Good in the air, he can also perform equally well in midfield.

Crewe Alex (£22,500 from Fleetwood T on 15/10/91) FL 76+22/27 FLC 6+2/1 FAC 3+2/2 Others 7+4/1
Scunthorpe U (Loaned on 30/10/95) FL 4/1
Scunthorpe U (Free on 13/2/96) FL 45+3/18 FLC 2/1 FAC 3/2 Others 1
Blackpool (£80,000 on 6/2/97) FL 17/5

CLAYTON Gary
Born: Sheffield, 2 February 1963
Height: 5'10" Weight: 12.3
International Honours: E: SP-1

1996-97 was a frustrating season for the senior pro at Plymouth as he missed almost all of the campaign with a knee injury, before returning for one substitute appearance in the penultimate game. Freed during the summer, Gary is a utility player who can perform anywhere you need him, although having a preference for a midfield role.

Doncaster Rov (Signed from Burton A on 23/8/86) FL 34+1/5 FLC 2 FAC 3 Others 2
Cambridge U (£10,000 on 2/7/87) FL 166+13/17 FLC 17+1/3 FAC 9 Others 7/2
Peterborough U (Loaned on 25/1/91) FL 4
Huddersfield T (£20,000 on 18/2/94) FL 15+4/1 FAC 0+1 Others 4/2
Plymouth Arg (Signed on 10/8/95) FL 32+5/2 FLC 2 FAC 2 Others 1

CLEAVER Christopher (Chris) William
Born: Hitchin, 24 March 1979
Height: 5'11" Weight: 11.3

A young Peterborough striker who came through the youth team to make his debut when coming off the bench at London Road against Shrewsbury last October, Chris showed much promise for the future as a non-stop, wholehearted trier. Having scored his first goal for Posh in the 90th minute of a 5-1 defeat at Blackpool, he signed professional forms and with a little more

experience could become a more than useful member of the side.

Peterborough U (From trainee on 22/3/97) FL 6+7/1 FAC 0+1 Others 1

CLEGG David Lee
Born: Liverpool, 23 October 1976
Height: 5'9" Weight: 10.4
Described by Kenny Dalglish as the bargain free transfer signing of the 1996 close season, this young midfielder struggled to establish himself at Hartlepool after being released by Liverpool. A quick player, who is also a good crosser of the ball, he was a member of the first-team squad throughout 1996-97, but, on many occasions, was named as substitute and with the manager, Mick Tait forced to trim down the size of his first-team squad, he was released at the end of the campaign.

Liverpool (From trainee on 22/5/95)
Hartlepool U (Free on 4/7/96) FL 24+11/2 FLC 1 FAC 2 Others 1

CLEGG Michael Jamie
Born: London, 3 July 1977
Height: 5'8" Weight: 11.8
Club Honours: FAYC '95
A very able Manchester United full back, who is good in the tackle and excellent on the overlap, Michael had a tough start to his professional career, having been seen as an average player among the glittering stars of United's youth team. His perseverance, however, finally paid off when he gave a solid performance on his Premiership debut against Middlesbrough last November, which earned him rave reviews. Although he faces an uphill struggle in competing with the likes of Denis Irwin and the Neville brothers for a regular place in the team, his chance should come again. Was named the Pontins' League Player of the Year.

Manchester U (From trainee on 1/7/95) PL 3+1 FLC 1 FAC 1

CLEMENT Neil
Born: Reading, 3 October 1978
Height: 5'10" Weight: 10.0
International Honours: E: Yth; Sch
Saturday, 21 December 1996. A capacity crowd begins to stream in to Stamford Bridge to watch a tense London derby between Chelsea and West Ham with so much at stake for both sides. Ruud Gullit calls a team talk at 1.30pm and at its completion the young defender was thinking of grabbing his coat and taking his customary seat in the stand when Ruud whispered to him "By the way, you're playing today!" – leaving Neil no time to develop pre-match nerves. He took the field with household names such as Gullit, Roberto Di Matteo, Gianfranco Zola and Mark Hughes, and gave an assured performance. His potential was recognised by England boss, Glenn Hoddle, when, in February, he was one of two youth internationals called up to join the England squad's preparations for the World Cup qualifier against Italy. Son of the late Queens Park Rangers and England full back, Dave, he is just one of a galaxy of talent

waiting in the wings at the Bridge and much is expected of him.

Chelsea (From trainee on 8/10/95) PL 1

CLIFFORD Mark Robert
Born: Nottingham, 11 September 1977
Height: 5'10" Weight: 10.5
Having debuted for Mansfield while a trainee, Mark made his first senior appearances for two seasons in 1996-97 and performed well at right back when called upon. Surprisingly released during the summer, injuries permitting, he could still have a future in the game.

Mansfield T (From trainee on 3/7/96) FL 4 FLC 1

CLODE Mark James
Born: Plymouth, 24 February 1973
Height: 5'10" Weight: 10.10
Club Honours: AMC '94
Mark recaptured his adventurous attacking style of play for Swansea during the early part of 1996-97, giving many fine displays at full back. However, hamstring problems suffered during the campaign prevented him from making regular first-team appearances and a broken ankle in a reserve game against Bristol Rovers towards the end of March saw his season come to a premature end, thus missing the run in to the play offs.

Plymouth Arg (From trainee on 30/3/91)
Swansea C (Free on 23/7/93) FL 100+9/3 FLC 7+2 FAC 5 Others 8+2

CLOUGH Nigel Howard
Born: Sunderland, 19 March 1966
Height: 5'10" Weight: 12.3
Club Honours: FLC '89, '90; FMC '89, '92
International Honours: E: 14; B-3; U21-15
Missed Manchester City's first game of last season at home to Ipswich Town, but then had a continuous run through to the home defeat against Oxford in mid November, following which he came in for a lot of unfair criticism. This appeared to be the beginning of the end of his career at Maine Road and, after playing three more games as a substitute, he went on loan to Nottingham Forest for three months, a move that was expected to be permanent. However, negotiations broke down and he returned to Maine Road and now that Frank Clark is in charge there is a strong possibility that Nigel will come good again. A deep-lying old-fashioned centre forward who can make and take goals, he is the son of Brian, a man who had two great careers in soccer as both a player and a manager. Was placed on the transfer list during the summer.

Nottingham F (Free from Heanor T on 15/9/84) F/PL 307+4/101 FLC 46/22 FAC 28/6 Others 11+3/1
Liverpool (£2,275,000 on 7/6/93) PL 29+10/7 FLC 3/2 FAC 2
Manchester C (£1,500,000 on 24/1/96) P/FL 33+5/4 FLC 2 FAC 3/1
Nottingham F (Loaned on 21/12/96) PL 10+3/1

COADY Lewis
Born: Liverpool, 20 September 1976
Height: 6'1" Weight: 11.1
Unable to hold down a place at Wrexham in 1996-97, Lewis was freed early this year and joined Doncaster on non-contract terms

in transfer deadline week, immediately coming into the side for the home game against Hereford. A composed left-sided player who can perform in defence or midfield, he was not retained.

Wrexham (From trainee on 4/7/95) FL 2
Doncaster Rov (Free on 20/3/97) FL 1

COATES Jonathan Simon
Born: Swansea, 27 June 1975
Height: 5'8" Weight: 10.4
International Honours: W: U21-4; Yth
Jonathan showed excellent form throughout last season on the left-hand side of Swansea's midfield, showing good close ball skills, along with good defensive ability, and was regularly included in the Welsh U21 squad, despite being sent off against Holland for two bookable offences. An automatic choice, in what was his first full season as a regular at the Vetch, he also scored three times, thus trebling his previous total.

Swansea C (From trainee on 8/7/93) FL 45+22/4 FLC 2+1 FAC 3 Others 7

COCKERILL Glenn
Born: Grimsby, 25 August 1959
Height: 5'10" Weight: 12.4
Given a free by Leyton Orient in the summer of 1996, Micky Adams knew his qualities from his days at Southampton and stepped in to sign him for Fulham on a one-year contract. Did so well in the midfield as both ball winner and distributor that, despite his age, another productive season in division two beckons. Is thought of so highly by his fellow pros that the likes of Tim Flowers, Alan Shearer and Matt Le Tissier, as well as several other international former team mates, turned out against Fulham in a benefit match for him.

Lincoln C (Free from Louth U on 1/11/76) FL 65+6/10 FLC 2 FAC 2
Swindon T (£11,000 on 6/12/79) FL 23+3/1 FLC 3
Lincoln C (£40,000 on 12/8/81) FL 114+1/25 FLC 16/1 FAC 7 Others 1
Sheffield U (£125,000 on 23/3/84) FL 62/10 FLC 6/1 FAC 1
Southampton (£225,000 on 17/10/85) F/PL 272+6/35 FLC 35+2/5 FAC 20+2/2 Others 1/2
Leyton Orient (Free on 10/12/93) FL 89+1/7 FLC 4/1 FAC 3 Others 10
Fulham (Free on 5/7/96) FL 27+5/1 FLC 3 FAC 1

CODNER Robert George
Born: Walthamstow, 23 January 1965
Height: 5'11" Weight: 13.1
International Honours: E: SP-1
A pass and move central midfielder with attacking flair, Robert was unable to settle at Barnet in 1996-97 and following a long spell in the reserves he was allowed to move on to Southend. Scored two goals during his stay at Underhill, one of them being the winner at Darlington last October.

Leicester C (Free from Tottenham H juniors on 17/9/83)
Brighton & Hove A (£125,000 from Barnet, via Dagenham, on 8/9/88) FL 257+9/39 FLC 18+2/1 FAC 11+1/4 Others 16+1/3
Reading (Free on 22/9/95) FL 3+1 FLC 1
Peterborough U (Free on 8/3/96) FL 1+1
Barnet (Free on 28/3/96) FL 28+4/1 FLC 4/1 FAC 4
Southend U (Free on 27/3/97) FL 3+1

COLCOMBE Scott

Born: West Bromwich, 15 December 1971
Height: 5'6" Weight: 10.6

Not featuring in Doncaster's first team on a regular basis in 1996-97, although a permanent member of the first team squad, he often failed to make the starting line up, and then a chronic foot injury proved to be a further set back. When fit, he had much to offer, being able to play in attack or defence, although having a personal preference for the full-back position. Was released at the end of the season.

West Bromwich A (From trainee on 5/7/90)
Torquay U (Free on 14/8/91) FL 78+11/1 FLC 8+1 FAC 4+1/1 Others 5
Doncaster Rov (Free on 10/7/95) FL 30+12/4 FLC 1 FAC 2 Others 2+1/1

COLDICOTT Stacy

Born: Redditch, 29 April 1974
Height: 5'8" Weight: 11.2

A competent West Brom midfielder, determined, aggressive, and totally committed, Stacy battled for a place in the side in 1996-97, with at least six other players of similar style, but never really established himself as a first teamer until late on in the campaign. Had a spell on loan at Cardiff early last season, before returning to the Hawthornes.

West Bromwich A (From trainee on 4/3/92) FL 57+25/3 FLC 7+1 FAC 2+1/1 Others 7+3
Cardiff C (Loaned on 30/8/96) FL 6

COLE Andrew (Andy) Alexander

Born: Nottingham, 15 October 1971
Height: 5'11" Weight: 11.2
Club Honours: Div 1 '93; PL '96, '97; FAC '96
International Honours: E: 2; B-1; U21-8; Yth, Sch

A quick and elusive Manchester United striker, with lightening speed and good skills to match, Andy was struck down with pneumonia at the start of last season, having been a target of both Blackburn and Everton in the wake of the Alan Shearer transfer saga. He made an excellent recovery, however, playing in five Premiership games before he was injured again, and was just about to make another comeback in a reserve game against Liverpool at Anfield, when a challenge by Neil Ruddock left him nursing two fractured shins. With gritty determination, he celebrated his return to the side in December with a goal against Nottingham Forest at the City Ground, appeared in both of United's FA Cup ties against Spurs and Wimbledon in January, before forming a new and prolific partnership with Ole Solskjaer in February, which yielded four goals in five games. Although a hamstring problem ruled him out again, he made a good recovery and important strikes in successive games against Blackburn and Liverpool helped to turn the championship United's way. His good form saw him recalled by England for the Tournoi de France game against Italy in June.

Arsenal (From trainee on 18/10/89) FL 0+1 Others 0+1
Fulham (Loaned on 5/9/91) FL 13/3 Others 2/1
Bristol C (£500,000 on 12/3/92) FL 41/20 FLC 3/4 FAC 1 Others 4/1
Newcastle U (£1,750,000 on 12/3/93) F/PL 69+1/55 FLC 7/8 FAC 4/1 Others 3/4
Manchester U (£6,000,000 on 12/1/95) PL 59+13/30 FLC 1 FAC 9+1/2 Others 3+3/1

COLEMAN Christopher (Chris)

Born: Swansea, 10 June 1970
Height: 6'2" Weight: 14.6
Club Honours: WC '89, '91; Div 1 '94
International Honours: W: 15; U21-3; Yth; Sch

Starting 1996-97 alongside Colin Hendry on the right-hand side of Blackburn's defence, he only once played in a winning side, a 2-0 home Coca-Cola Cup win over Brentford, before an achilles tendon injury cut short his season and left him on the sidelines. A natural athlete with the perfect build for a defender, hopefully, the Welsh international can recover full fitness in time for 1997-98. With a superb left foot and capable of making both long and short passes, Chris loves to move up with the attack.

Swansea C (From Manchester C juniors on 1/9/87) FL 159+1/2 FLC 8 FAC 13/1 Others 15
Crystal Palace (£275,000 on 19/7/91) F/PL 143+11/13 FLC 24+2/2 FAC 8/1 Others 2
Blackburn Rov (£2,800,000 on 16/12/95) PL 27+1 FLC 1 FAC 2

COLEMAN Simon

Born: Worksop, 13 March 1968
Height: 6'0" Weight: 10.8

Unfortunately, in 1996-97, Simon never really re-discovered the form he showed for Bolton prior to breaking a leg at Derby in February 1995 and, with Gerry Taggart and Chris Fairclough in excellent fettle in the Wanderers' defence, he found it very difficult to regain a place in the first team, being only named as a substitute on a handful of occasions. Played in the number five shirt in the FA Cup third round at Luton and was named as one of the substitutes, without taking the field, in the shock 3-2 defeat against Chesterfield in the fourth round at Burnden Park in February, but was never really involved after that match, though a regular with the reserves. A steady defender who, at his best, can be relied upon to create problems in opponents' penalty areas in dead-ball situations.

Mansfield T (From juniors on 29/7/85) FL 96/7 FLC 9 FAC 7 Others 7/1
Middlesbrough (£600,000 on 26/9/89) FL 51+4/2 FAC 5 Others 10/1
Derby Co (£300,000 on 15/8/91) FL 62+8/2 FLC 5+1 FAC 5 Others 12
Sheffield Wed (£250,000 on 20/1/94) PL 11+5/1 FLC 3 FAC 2
Bolton W (£350,000 on 5/10/94) P/FL 34/5 FLC 4 FAC 2

COLGAN Nicholas (Nick) Vincent

Born: Drogheda, Eire, 19 September 1973
Height: 6'1" Weight: 13.6
International Honours: Ei: U21-8; Yth; Sch

Having been a pro for over four years, and having to wait in the wings as a whole succession of goalkeepers came and went at Chelsea, Nick finally got his main chance against West Ham last March with Dmitri Kharine, Frode Grodas and Kevin Hitchcock all out injured. A young man who reads the game well, and is competent in the handling and kicking aspects of the game, he stepped up to give a confident performance in a 3-2 defeat, only being beaten by a penalty and two deflections. Will find it even tougher this coming season following Blues' signing Ed de Goey, the Dutch number one.

Chelsea (From trainee on 1/10/92) PL 1

COLKIN Lee

Born: Nuneaton, 15 July 1974
Height: 5'11" Weight: 12.4

A left-sided Northampton defender or midfielder, injury robbed a lot of last season for the club's longest-serving player. However, he always gave 100 per cent and showed both pace and aggression. Is a good squad player.

Northampton T (From trainee on 31/8/92) FL 74+25/3 FLC 6+3/1 FAC 2+2 Others 3+2

COLL Owen Oliver

Born: Donegal, 9 April 1976
Height: 6'1" Weight: 11.7
International Honours: Ei: U21-5

After joining Bournemouth towards the end of 1995-96, Owen started last season well, playing for the Republic of Ireland at U21 level, before a knee injury in November put him out of action for almost the rest of the campaign. Still only 21, but a commanding centre back who is strong in the air and able to move forward with the ball, he will be looking forward to an injury-free 1997-98.

Tottenham H (From Enfield R on 1/7/94)
Bournemouth (Signed on 28/3/96) FL 24 FLC 2 FAC 1

COLLETT Andrew (Andy) Alfred

Born: Stockton, 28 October 1973
Height: 5'11" Weight: 12.0

Agile, brave, and confident, Andy, enjoyed his first full season as first-choice Bristol Rovers' goalkeeper in 1996-97, missing just one match due to injury. Selected as Player of the Year, he managed 15 clean sheets and certainly was a match winner on numerous occasions with his inspirational performances. Rovers' management and the club's supporters are justifiably pleased he has signed a new two-year contract to remain at the club.

Middlesbrough (From trainee on 6/3/92) PL 2 Others 3
Bristol Rov (£10,000 on 18/10/94) FL 74 FLC 2 FAC 2 Others 7

COLLINS Lee

Born: Bellshill, 3 February 1974
Height: 5'8" Weight: 10.2

The young Scottish midfielder made three unconsecutive appearances for Swindon in mid season in 1996-97, whilst deputising for Kevin Watson, without suggesting he was on the brink of a first-team breakthrough. However, he was offered a new contract in December to the end of this coming season which suggests that Robins' manager, Steve McMahon, still has faith in him. Very much in the mould of his manager, Lee is a tigerish tackler who does not leave opponents alone for long periods.

Albion Rov (Signed from Pollock on 25/11/93) SL 43+2/1 SLC 2 SC 2 Others 2
Swindon T (£15,000 on 15/11/95) FL 5+4 FAC 2 Others 1

COLLINS Michael Thomas
Born: Belfast, 6 September 1977
Height: 5'10" Weight: 12.7
International Honours: NI: Yth
At Sheffield United as a trainee, the young Irish midfielder was released in June 1996, before joining Coleraine and then having trials at Darlington prior to the start of 1996-97. Making only one substitute appearance in a 3-1 defeat at Northampton, he was released in December and signed for Cliftonville.
Darlington (Free from Sheffield U juniors on 16/8/96) FL 0+1

COLLINS Samuel (Sam) Jason
Born: Pontefract, 5 June 1977
Height: 6'2" Weight: 13.7
The brother of Simon, he is another home-grown Huddersfield youngster who made his debut in 1996-97, managing to break in to the first team at centre half in September. Strong in the air and elegant in the tackle, he is one to watch for the future.
Huddersfield T (From trainee on 6/7/94) FL 3+1 FLC 1+1

COLLINS Simon
Born: Pontefract, 16 December 1973
Height: 5'11" Weight: 13.0
A homegrown Huddersfield product and elder brother of Sam, the combative and hard-working midfielder found it difficult to establish himself in 1996-97, starting as many games on the bench as he did in the starting line up. Despite much praise from the manager for his commitment he was allowed to leave the club in March as the replacement for Micky Evans at Plymouth, scoring once in 12 appearances, and it seems likely that he will revert to a natural midfield role in 1997-98.
Huddersfield T (From trainee on 1/7/92) FL 31+21/3 FLC 6+3/2 FAC 1+4 Others 1+3
Plymouth Arg (£60,000 on 6/3/97) FL 11+1/1

COLLINS Wayne Anthony
Born: Manchester, 4 March 1969
Height: 6'0" Weight: 12.0
Wayne joined Sheffield Wednesday from Crewe during the summer of 1996 and started his first season in the Premiership as a regular in the Owl's midfield, helping them to four straight wins and the leadership of the table. Unfortunately injured in his next match and out of the side until December when it was difficult to regain his place, he made just three more starts and a few more as a sub before the end of the campaign, but remained good cover both for a midfield spot and also as a full back, where he spent most of his time with the Alex. Pacy, with an eye for goal, he opened his league account in a 2-2 draw at Derby and will be looking for more of the same in 1997-98.

Crewe Alex (£10,000 from Winsford U on 29/7/93) FL 102+15/14 FLC 5/1 FAC 8+1 Others 14+1/2
Sheffield Wed (£600,000 on 1/8/96) PL 8+4/1 FAC 1

COLLYMORE Stanley (Stan) Victor
Born: Cannock, 22 January 1971
Height: 6'4" Weight: 14.10
International Honours: E: 2
Despite being in and out of the Liverpool side in 1996-97, Stan, still an idol of the crowd, was occasionally used in the role of a substitute who would come on just at the right time to score and gain valuable points for the Reds. There was no doubting his ability to run at defenders in order to unsettle them and turn them inside out, to either lay on goals for his main striking partner, Robbie Fowler, or to crash in a shot himself that would turn a game around. Can also score spectacularly from headers. However, this gifted striker never fully realised his potential at Anfield, his tempestuous nature not allowing him to settle and hold down an automatic place on the team sheet. *Stop Press:* In signing for Aston Villa during the summer, £7,000,000 reportedly changing hands, he became the midland club's most expensive acquisition ever.
Wolverhampton W (From trainee on 13/7/89)
Crystal Palace (£100,000 from Stafford R on 4/1/91) FL 4+16/1 FLC 2+3/1
Southend U (£100,000 on 20/11/92) FL 30/15 FAC 3/3
Nottingham F (£2,000,000 on 5/7/93) F/PL 64+1/41 FLC 9/2 FAC 2/1 Others 2/1
Liverpool (£8,500,000 on 3/7/95) PL 55+6/26 FLC 2+2 FAC 9/7 Others 5+2/2

Sean Connelly

CONNELLY Sean Patrick
Born: Sheffield, 26 June 1970
Height: 5'10" Weight: 11.10
A solid Stockport right back with plenty of attacking flair, Sean continued to improve in 1996-97, to the point where he became one of the first names on the team sheet. Also doubling as the club's assistant physio, he missed just one league match as County eventually reached the first division as runners up to Bury. All in all a great season.
Stockport Co (Free from Hallam on 12/8/91) FL 161+5 FLC 20/1 FAC 10+1 Others 15+1

CONNOLLY David James
Born: Willesden, 6 June 1977
Height: 5'8" Weight: 11.4
International Honours: Ei: 6
The promising young Watford striker is already a regular in the full Irish team and linked with various bigger clubs. Pacy, with good close control, and the ability to turn quickly, unfortunately his 1996-97 season was disrupted by persistent hamstring trouble, which saw him make just 18 appearances, although he did score a 13-minute FA Cup hat trick after coming on as substitute against Ashford. Also scored a hat trick for the Republic in a 5-0 win over Liechtenstein in a home World Cup qualifier in May, all three goals coming in the space of 11 minutes prior to half time.
Watford (From trainee on 15/11/94) FL 19+7/10 FLC 1 FAC 3+3/4 Others 1/1

CONNOLLY Karl Andrew
Born: Prescot, 9 February 1970
Height: 5'10" Weight: 11.2
Club Honours: WC '95
The general feeling among fans at the Racecourse in 1996-97 was that if Karl was on song, the whole team responded. For half the season, up until around Christmas, his skilful darting runs were always a feature, along with the goals, until a general loss of form, together with a niggling injury, frustrated him to the point of asking for a move just prior to the transfer deadline. Although a number of clubs showed interest in the central striker, nothing was forth-coming and the fans can only hope that he can be persuaded to stay at the club.
Wrexham (Free from Napoli, in local Sunday League, on 8/5/91) FL 228+10/61 FLC 16/2 FAC 24/5 Others 25+1/5

CONROY Michael (Mike) Kevin
Born: Glasgow, 31 December 1965
Height: 6'0" Weight: 13.3
Club Honours: Div 4 '92
The first Fulham player to hit 20 goals in a season since Gordon Davies 13 years ago, Mike reached that milestone at the end of last January when he was the leading scorer in the country. Unfortunately, injuries to key players then forced a change in tactics which resulted in far less scoring opportunities, although, despite an injury, he still managed three more, including the vital equaliser at Carlisle. His contribution to the club's promotion won him a place in the PFA divisional team and the supporters' Player of the Year award.

Clydebank (Free from Coventry C juniors in 1984) SL 92+22/38 SLC 4+1 SC 5+2
St Mirren (Signed in Dec 1987) SL 9+1/1 SC 0+1
Reading (£50,000 on 28/9/88) FL 65+15/7 FLC 3+2 FAC 8+2/1 Others 2+2
Burnley (£35,000 on 16/7/91) FL 76+1/30 FLC 4/1 FAC 9+1/4 Others 7+1/4
Preston NE (£85,000 on 20/8/93) FL 50+7/22 FLC 2+1 FAC 7/2 Others 2+3
Fulham (£75,000 on 9/8/95) FL 78+5/30 FLC 8/4 FAC 5+1/3 Others 4/1

CONSTANTINOU Costakis
Born: Limasol, Cyprus, 24 September 1968
Height: 6'0" Weight: 12.4
International Honours: Cyprus: 32

Arriving on loan at Barnet from Omonia Nicosia last October, with a view to a £60,000 transfer, the Greek Cypriot played just once at centre half against Cardiff City at Underhill, before being released in January. At his best, capped more than 30 times for Cyprus.
Barnet (Loaned from Omonia Nicosia on 4/10/96) FL 1

CONWAY Paul James
Born: Wandsworth, 17 April 1970
Height: 6'1" Weight: 12.10
Club Honours: Div 3 '95; AMC '97
International Honours: USA: U21

A gifted Carlisle footballer with the ability to both create and take chances, Paul's 1996-97 season was again somewhat disrupted by injury problems. However, he turned in some memorable performances, including a hat trick in the AWS tie against Hull City, only the third United player to achieve this feat in 12 years. He then netted twice in the following league game and, with 13 strikes, ended the campaign as the club's second top scorer.
Carlisle U (Signed on 29/10/93) FL 75+14/22 FLC 5+1 FAC 8+1/3 Others 14+3/4

COOK Andrew (Andy) Charles
Born: Romsey, 10 August 1969
Height: 5'9" Weight: 12.0

Unable to hold down a place at Swansea in 1996-97, Andy was transferred to Portsmouth last December, being an ideal replacement for Alan McLoughlin on the occasions the latter was unavailable. A versatile player who is comfortable at full back or in midfield, his progress in the game has been unfortunately held back by injuries, but in full flow he can be an exciting attacking extra, who can come through from deep or get in good crosses to the front men.
Southampton (From apprentice on 6/7/87) FL 11+5/1 FLC 4 FAC 1 Others 1
Exeter C (£50,000 on 13/9/91) FL 70/1 FLC 2 FAC 7/1 Others 6/1
Swansea C (£125,000 on 23/7/93) FL 54+8 FLC 2 FAC 3 Others 9+1/2
Portsmouth (£35,000 on 20/12/96) FL 6+2

COOK Garry John
Born: Northampton, 31 March 1978
Height: 6'1" Weight: 12.5

A young midfielder, Garry made his Hereford debut when coming off the bench at Darlington last September and then went on to play a further 23 games when being

thrown in at the deep end. Despite needing an old head to guide him earlier on he showed some fine touches, the quality of his passing improving game by game, and looks to be a gem in the making.
Hereford U (From trainee on 15/7/96) FL 17+3 FLC 0+2 FAC 1 Others 1

COOK Paul Anthony
Born: Liverpool, 22 February 1967
Height: 5'11" Weight: 11.0

Although plagued by injury at several stages during last season, Paul still managed to make 41 appearances in a Tranmere shirt, scoring three goals in the process, including a double in a 3-1 home win over Norwich. A left-sided player, he favours sending in long-range shots and lengthy passes, and always proved dependable wherever called upon to play.
Wigan Ath (Signed from Marine on 20/7/84) FL 77+6/14 FLC 4 FAC 6+1 Others 5+1/1
Norwich C (£73,000 on 23/5/88) FL 3+3 Others 1+1
Wolverhampton W (£250,000 on 1/11/89) FL 191+2/19 FLC 7/1 FAC 5+2 Others 6+1/1
Coventry C (£600,000 on 18/8/94) PL 35+2/3 FLC 3 FAC 3
Tranmere Rov (£250,000 on 29/2/96) FL 45+6/4 FLC 4 FAC 1

COOKE Andrew (Andy) Roy
Born: Shrewsbury, 2 January 1974
Height: 6'0" Weight: 12.8

Starting last season in Burnley's first team, Andy became the regular sub following the signing of Paul Barnes, but regained his place after the departure of Kurt Nogan. A good eye for goal, a talent for the spectacular (his overhead kick against Gillingham was one of the Clarets' goals of the season), and a fine understanding with Barnes should ensure that he is in the side to stay. Ended 1996-97 with a hat trick against Watford.
Burnley (Signed from Newtown on 1/5/95) FL 29+25/17 FLC 1+2/1 FAC 1+3 Others 3+2

COOKE Terence (Terry) John
Born: Birmingham, 5 August 1976
Height: 5'7" Weight: 9.9
Club Honours: FAYC '95
International Honours: E: U21-4; Yth

A talented Manchester United right winger with lightning pace and excellent skills, Terry's hopes of a first-team place in 1996-97 were dashed during the 1996 close season by the arrival of Karel Poborsky. Despite having shown great promise during the Coca-Cola Cup tie at Leicester, where he came off the bench, he was loaned out to Birmingham two days later, making four appearances before his time was up. From a family of Blues' fans, his jinking performances were more than well received, his most effective spell coming at Southend when he created Paul Devlin's 88th minute equaliser. Great things are still expected from him from those who matter at Old Trafford.
Manchester U (From trainee on 1/7/94) PL 1+3 FLC 1+2/1 Others 0+1
Sunderland (Loaned on 29/1/96) FL 6
Birmingham C (Loaned on 29/11/96) FL 1+3

COOPER Colin Terence
Born: Sedgefield, 28 February 1967
Height: 5'10" Weight: 11.9
International Honours: E: 2; U21-8

As Forest's most consistent player throughout 1996-97, the tough-tackling no-frills defender played mainly in his favoured centre-back position, although he did start the season at full back. Always a threat in opposing penalty areas, with his ability at set pieces, he was able to add some fire power to the attack scoring two vital league goals in draws with Blackburn and Leicester. And, in missing just two games and captaining the side in Stuart Pearce's absence, his accomplished performances could well see him selected for England again in the future, despite the club's relegation to division one.
Middlesbrough (From juniors on 17/7/84) FL 183+5/6 FLC 18 FAC 13 Others 19+1/2
Millwall (£300,000 on 25/7/91) FL 77/6 FLC 6 FAC 2 Others 2
Nottingham F (£1,700,000 on 21/6/93) F/PL 144+1/15 FLC 13/2 FAC 11/1 Others 7

Colin Cooper

COOPER Kevin Lee
Born: Derby, 8 February 1975
Height: 5'7" Weight: 10.7

This Derby reserve team left winger made two further appearances from the bench in 1996-97, but with little prospect of further promotion he went on loan to Stockport County before signing permanently to assist their ultimately successful promotion charge. An instant hit at Edgley Park with his busy play, Kevin scored two vital goals in 1-0 wins over Crewe and Bristol City during the run in.
Derby Co (From trainee on 2/7/93) FL 0+2 FLC 0+2 Others 1
Stockport Co (Loaned on 24/3/97) FL 11+1/3 Others 1

COOPER Mark David
Born: Watford, 5 April 1967
Height: 6'4" Weight: 14.0
An out-and-out striker, signed from Barnet during the 1996 close season, Mark's strength was his ability to hold the ball while his new Northampton team mates got into position. Although lacking in pace he more than made up for that with his aerial power and strong shooting ability, which saw him score his 100th league goal during the season. Was released in the summer.
Cambridge U (From apprentice on 16/10/84) FL 62+9/17 FLC 7/3 FAC 4 Others 2
Tottenham H (Signed on 2/4/87)
Shrewsbury T (Loaned on 10/9/87) FL 6/2
Gillingham (£105,000 on 9/10/87) FL 38+11/11 FLC 2+1 FAC 3+1 Others 4
Leyton Orient (Signed on 2/2/89) FL 117+33/45 FLC 6/2 FAC 8+2/4 Others 10+2/4
Barnet (Free on 13/7/94) FL 58+9/19 FLC 2+3/2 FAC 4/2 Others 3/2
Northampton T (Free on 2/8/96) FL 37+4/10 FLC 3 FAC 1 Others 1

COOPER Mark Nicholas
Born: Wakefield, 18 December 1968
Height: 5'8" Weight" 11.4
Club Honours: Div 4 '90
Released by Exeter during the 1996 close season, this influential midfielder looked to be a bargain free-transfer signing for Hartlepool early in 1996-97. As the most experienced of Keith Houchen's summer signings, he was praised for his battling displays and accurate passing and was also a regular goalscorer, his powerful right-foot shot making him especially deadly as a penalty taker. Unfortunately, he lost his way as the campaign progressed and was transfer listed.
Bristol C (From trainee on 10/9/87)
Exeter C (Free on 3/10/89) FL 46+4/12 FLC 4+1 FAC 3+1/1 Others 5
Southend U (Loaned on 22/3/90) FL 4+1
Birmingham C (Signed on 5/9/91) FL 30+9/4 FAC 2 Others 3/1
Fulham (£40,000 on 21/11/92) FL 10+4 FLC 2 Others 3
Huddersfield T (Loaned on 25/3/93) FL 10/4
Wycombe W (Free on 10/1/94) FL 0+2/1
Exeter C (Free on 11/2/94) FL 78+10/20 FLC 3 FAC 2 Others 4/1
Hartlepool U (Free on 26/7/96) FL 33/9 FLC 2 FAC 1 Others 1

COPE James Andrew
Born: Solihull, 4 October 1977
Height: 6'0" Weight: 11.0
Having signed pro forms for Shrewsbury during the 1996 close season, the young midfielder spent most of last season playing reserve-team football, apart from the odd sitting on the subs' bench, before getting his chance at Plymouth. Followed that up with appearances against Walsall and Bristol Rovers and will be looking to improve on that in 1997-98.
Shrewsbury T (From trainee on 12/7/96)) FL 3+1

CORAZZIN Giancarlo (Carlo) Michele
Born: Canada, 25 December 1971
Height: 5'11" Weight: 12.7
International Honours: Canada: 27
Signed as a forward, Carlo spent a lot of his time for Plymouth in 1996-97 in a midfield

berth and, in showing ample skill and passing ability, the new position seemed to suit his style. Missed a number of games due to international call ups for Canada, but still had time to score some valuable goals for Argyle, including the season's opener against York and an equaliser in the return, along with winner, via the penalty spot, against Rotherham.
Cambridge U (£20,000 from Vancouver 86ers on 10/12/93) FL 104+1/39 FLC 4/2 FAC 5 Others 3/2
Plymouth Arg (£150,000 on 28/3/96) FL 23+13/6 FLC 1+1 FAC 0+2/1 Others 2+1

CORDEN Simon **Wayne**
Born: Leek, 1 November 1975
Height: 5'9" Weight: 10.6
The Port Vale left winger who is now hoping to step into Steve Guppy's shoes, played on the left, despite being predominantly right footed, and caused problems to defences whenever he drifted inside. Started five games towards the end of the campaign and signed a three year contract to tie him to the club until the year 2000
Port Vale (From trainee on 20/9/94) FL 7+8 FLC 1

CORICA Stephen (Steve) Christopher
Born: Cairns, Australia, 24 March 1973
Height: 5'8" Weight: 10.10
International Honours: Australia: 14
The right-sided Wolves' midfielder played a part in the first 16 matches of 1996-97, before being omitted from the next four. Returning in style at Crystal Palace, with well-timed runs helping him to get two early goals, rounding the 'keeper for the latter, he only missed two more matches up until April but still did not win the fans over completely. His off the ball running showed his awareness and he was often able to receive it then change the direction of play, however, he had already been replaced in 17 games when a bad knee injury at Port Vale ended his campaign.
Leicester C (£325,000 from Marconi on 11/8/95) FL 49+3/4 FLC 2 FAC 3
Wolverhampton W (£700,000 on 16/2/96) FL 17

CORNFORTH John Michael
Born: Whitley Bay, 7 October 1967
Height: 6'1" Weight: 12.11
Club Honours: Div 3 '88; AMC '94
International Honours: W: 2
Unable to get into the side at Birmingham last season, this influential central midfield distributor with excellent passing skills, was transferred to Wycombe in December, only to find his debut delayed by a hamstring injury. For a player who has suffered badly from injuries during the last few years, it was probably no surprise to him that when he finally appeared on Boxing Day against Walsall he limped off after only 17 minutes with an achilles tendon problem. Reappeared in March and, although clearly not fully match fit, began to show glimpses of the form that had earlier won him two Welsh caps.
Sunderland (From apprentice on 11/10/85) FL 21+11/2 FLC 0+1 Others 1+3
Doncaster Rov (Loaned on 6/11/86) FL 6+1/3 Others 2
Shrewsbury T (Loaned on 23/11/89) FL 3 Others 2

Lincoln C (Loaned on 11/1/90) FL 9/1
Swansea C (£50,000 on 2/8/91) FL 147+2/16 FLC 14 FAC 11/1 Others 19/1
Birmingham C (£350,000 on 26/3/96) FL 8
Wycombe W (£50,000 on 5/12/96) FL 8+2

CORT Carl Edward Richard
Born: London, 1 November 1977
Height: 6'2" Weight: 12.0
A tall Wimbledon striker, and a first-year professional, Carl was given a Premier League debut against Aston Villa last April at Selhurst Park and did not look out of place in the Dons' line up when coming off the bench for Efan Ekoku with 20 minutes still left on the clock. Definitely a youngster to watch out for, he held the ball up well and displayed both skill and pace. Had earlier spent time on loan at Lincoln, scoring on his Football League debut against Wigan, where he created plenty of problems for third division defenders despite his inexperience
Wimbledon (From trainee on 7/6/96) PL 0+1
Lincoln C (Loaned on 3/2/97) FL 5+1/1

COTON Anthony (Tony) Philip
Born: Tamworth, 19 May 1961
Height: 6'2" Weight: 13.7
International Honours: E: B-1
Goalkeeper Tony arrived at Sunderland in the summer of 1996 from Manchester United, no doubt relishing the opportunity to re-establish himself in the Premiership. However, an accidental collision with the Southampton striker, Egil Ostenstad, in October, saw him fracture a leg in five places and his season was over after only 12 games. Has good positional sense, is brave, with good hands, and not afraid to come for crosses.
Birmingham C (Free from Mile Oak Rov on 13/10/78) FL 94 FLC 10 FAC 10
Watford (£300,000 on 27/9/84) FL 233 FLC 18 FAC 32 Others 8
Manchester C (£1,000,000 on 20/7/90) F/PL 162+1 FLC 16 FAC 12 Others 3
Manchester U (£500,000 on 31/1/96)
Sunderland (£600,000 on 18/7/96) PL 10 FLC 2

COTTEE Anthony (Tony) Richard
Born: West Ham, 11 July 1965
Height: 5'8" Weight: 11.5
International Honours: E: 7; U21-8; Yth
After a long and distinguished career (in two spells) with West Ham, the near-veteran striker said his goodbyes to Upton Park last October to join up with the top Malaysian club, Selangor. At his best, a live-wire striker with excellent pace, who had the ability to lose his marker in the box to get on the end of difficult chances, his last goal for the club, at Barnet in August, saved the Hammers from an embarrassing defeat in the Coca-Cola Cup.
West Ham U (From apprentice on 1/9/82) FL 203+9/92 FLC 19/14 FAC 24/11 Others 1/1
Everton (£2,300,000 on 2/8/88) F/PL 161+23/72 FLC 19+4/11 FAC 15+6/4 Others 11+2/12
West Ham U (Signed on 7/9/94) PL 63+4/23 FLC 8/4 FAC 5/1

COTTERELL Leo Spencer
Born: Cambridge, 2 September 1974
Height: 5'9" Weight: 10.0
International Honours: E: Yth, Sch

Arriving in the summer of 1996 from Ipswich, Leo struggled to find his form at Bournemouth in 1996-97, due in no small part to persistent injury. Able to play in defence, but considered more of a midfielder, he will be looking for opportunities during 1997-98 to command a regular first-team spot. Can get forward well and shows much enthusiasm.

Ipswich T (From trainee on 1/7/93) PL 0+2 FLC 0+1
Bournemouth (Free on 19/6/96) FL 2+7

COUGHLAN Graham
Born: Dublin, 18 November 1974
Height: 6'2" Weight: 13.4

A young Irish central defender with Blackburn Rovers, he was farmed out to Swindon for experience just before last March's transfer deadline (perhaps in replacement for the returning Marlon Broomes whose loan period had elapsed), making his Football League debut in a 3-0 home defeat by Norwich City. It was probably a case of joining the wrong club at the wrong time as his third and final appearance for the Robins was a 4-0 home defeat by Ipswich. However, with a contract dated to 1999, he still has plenty of time to make his mark at Ewood Park.

Blackburn Rov (£100,000 from Bray W on 14/10/95)
Swindon T (Loaned on 25/3/97) FL 3

Jason Cousins

COUSINS Jason Michael
Born: Hayes, 14 October 1970
Height: 5'11" Weight: 12.4
Club Honours: GMVC '93; FAT '93

Probably the most improved player at Wycombe last season, and relishing his role as a right-wing back and stand-in captain, Jason is nearing 300 appearances for the club. A much tidier defender these days, allied to tough tackling, his commitment to the cause ensures his enduring popularity with the fans. Can also play in central defence if required.

Brentford (From trainee on 13/7/89) FL 20+1 Others 2+2
Wycombe W (Free on 1/7/91) FL 142+3/3 FLC 12/1 FAC 17 Others 13

COUZENS Andrew (Andy)
Born: Shipley, 4 June 1975
Height: 5'10" Weight: 11.11
Club Honours: FAYC '93
International Honours: E: U21-3

The local-born versatile youngster appeared in a number of roles for Leeds in 1996-97, after his breakthrough the previous season, playing in 13 of the first 15 games, and scoring after just 51 seconds of George Graham's first match in charge at Coventry City in September. Initially, Andy made a big impression on his new manager, but after a poor defeat at Arsenal in October he was left out and thereafter he had to contend with reserve team football, before being transfer listed at his own request in March. Capable of playing in defence or in midfield, and a good passer of the ball, he could still have a bright future in the game.

Leeds U (From trainee on 5/3/93) PL 17+11/1 FLC 4+1/1 Others 0+2

Tom Cowan

COWAN Thomas (Tom)
Born: Bellshill, 28 August 1969
Height: 5'8" Weight: 11.10

A wholehearted competitor who has made the Huddersfield left-back position his own, despite his height he is a tremendous header of the ball and his forward runs and crossing ability meant he was the third highest assists provider last season. Always consistent, even down to being sent off at least once a season, Tom scored four goals, including a tremendous 25-yard effort in a 1-1 draw at West Bromwich and the winner in the home game against Sheffield United, his former team.

Clyde (Free from Netherdale BC in 1988-89) SL 16/2 SC 2
Glasgow R (Signed in February 1989) SL 8+4 SC 0+1 Others 2

Sheffield U (£350,000 on 1/8/91) F/PL 45 FLC 5 FAC 2 Others 1
Stoke C (Loaned on 1/10/93) FL 14 FLC 1 Others 3
Huddersfield T (£150,000 on 24/3/94) FL 132/7 FLC 13/1 FAC 7/1 Others 6

COWANS Gordon Sidney
Born: Cornforth, 27 October 1958
Height: 5'7" Weight: 10.6
Club Honours: FLC '77; Div 1 '81; CS '81; EC '82; ESC '82
International Honours: E: 10; B-2; U21-5; Yth

After joining Bradford during the 1996 close season, having been released by Sheffield United, the still classy former England midfielder came into the side for the first 17 matches and looked good until further City signings in that area of the field saw him alternating between an occasional appearance or a seat on the bench. Offered the chance of a move to promotion-chasing Stockport in transfer deadline week, Gordon initially provided a calming influence when the club were struck down by injuries, but, on finding the physical demands a little too much at the age of 37, he was eventually replaced by the returning Chris Marsden.

Aston Villa (From apprentice on 1/9/76) FL 276+10/42 FLC 23+4/5 FAC 19+1/3 Others 23+1/2 (£500,000 to Bari on 1/7/85)
Aston Villa (£250,000 on 13/7/88) FL 114+3/7 FLC 15 FAC 9 Others 11+1
Blackburn Rov (£200,000 on 28/11/91) F/PL 49+1/2 FLC 4 FAC 5/1 Others 3
Aston Villa (Free on 5/7/93) PL 9+2 FLC 2 Others 4
Derby Co (£80,000 on 3/2/94) FL 36 FLC 3 Others 5+1/1
Wolverhampton W (£20,000 on 19/12/94) FL 31+6 FLC 2 FAC 5/1 Others 2
Sheffield U (Free on 29/12/95) FL 18+2 FAC 3
Bradford C (Free on 17/7/96) FL 23+1 FLC 2
Stockport Co (Free on 24/3/97) FL 6+1 Others 0+1

COWE Steven (Steve) Mark
Born: Gloucester, 29 September 1974
Height: 5'7" Weight: 10.2

An energetic Swindon Town striker who competed with Peter Thorne and Steve Finney for the second forward slot in partnership with Wayne Allison in 1996-97, Steve usually had the edge over his rivals, participating in 38 of the clubs 46 league games, either as first choice or on the bench. Unfortunately, he did not score consistently enough to be sure of automatic selection and of his meagre haul of six goals only two were matchwinners but, with a difficult first full season behind him, he should now have the confidence to improve his scoring output in the coming campaign.

Aston Villa (From trainee on 7/7/93)
Swindon T (£100,000 on 22/3/96) FL 32+17/7 FLC 3+1 FAC 1

COX Ian Gary
Born: Croydon, 25 March 1971
Height: 6'0" Weight: 12.2

Came to Bournemouth in 1995-96 as a midfielder, but was converted to a centre back earlier in 1996-97 with effective results, giving some excellent displays at the heart of the defence, leading to numerous Man of the Match awards, as well as winning the Player of the Year award. His

aerial ability and tough tackling, coupled with his coolness on the ball, led to him becoming a formidable defender and, as well as his defensive capabilities, he showed an eye for goal, scoring eight times in 48 appearances.
Crystal Palace (£35,000 from Carshalton on 8/3/94) F/PL 2+13 FAC 1+2/1
Bournemouth (Free on 28/3/96) FL 52/8 FLC 2 FAC 1 Others 1

COX Neil James
Born: Scunthorpe, 8 October 1971
Height: 6'0" Weight: 13.2
Club Honours: FLC '94; Div 1 '95
International Honours: E: U21-6

"Coxy" amply repaid his manager's faith when becoming Middlesbrough's first £1m signing, being almost an ever present following his arrival from Aston Villa, his strong tackling, ball winning, and determination, added to his pace going forward as a very forceful wing back, making him a threat to Premiership defenders. Switched easily to the centre back position in 1996-97 when called on during Nigel Pearson's enforced absence through injury and consistently won acclaim for his star performances. Stop Press: Left to assist Colin Todd's bid to restore the fortunes of Bolton Wanderers on their return to Premiership duty on 27 May, following Boro's disastrous end of season.
Scunthorpe U (From trainee on 20/3/90) FL 17/1 FAC 4 Others 4+1
Aston Villa (£400,000 on 12/2/91) F/PL 26+16/3 FLC 5+2 FAC 4+2/1 Others 2
Middlesbrough (£1,000,000 on 19/7/94) P/FL 103+3/3 FLC 14+1 FAC 5/1 Others 2

COYNE Daniel (Danny)
Born: Prestatyn, 27 August 1973
Height: 5'11" Weight: 13.0
International Honours: W: 1; U21-9; Yth; Sch

A product of Tranmere's impressive youth policy, Danny started last season as the undisputed first choice between the posts, but was displaced by his mentor, Eric Nixon, towards the end of November. His return, in December, unfortunately proved to be short lived as the New Year began on a sour note when, on 1 January, the young goalie was involved in an horrendous clash at West Bromwich Albion, that left him with badly-torn neck ligaments which took several months to heal. However, he had played himself back to full match fitness with the reserves as the campaign ended. Blessed with exceptional positional awareness, he continued to be a member of Bobby Gould's Welsh squad, making one appearance for Wales during the footballing year.
Tranmere Rov (From trainee on 8/5/92) FL 77+1 FLC 8 FAC 1 Others 2

CRADDOCK Jody Darryl
Born: Bromsgrove, 25 July 1975
Height: 6'2" Weight: 12.4

Despite missing the start of 1996-97 with a hamstring injury sustained in a summer friendly, once in the Cambridge first team he was a consistent performer throughout the campaign and attracted the attention of higher division clubs. Again proving

excellent in the air, the central defender was rewarded with a place in the PFA third division team and celebrated the accolade with his first goal of the season at Hartlepool on 12 April.
Cambridge U (Free from Christchurch on 13/8/93) FL 142+3/4 FLC 3/1 FAC 6 Others 5

CRAMB Colin
Born: Lanark, 23 June 1974
Height: 6'0" Weight: 13.0
Club Honours: B&Q '93

Colin was Doncaster's top goalscorer by a distance in 1996-97, scoring a number of memorable goals, not least a brace at Scunthorpe which will live long in the memory. Currently attracting the interest of some of the bigger clubs, he is a firm favourite with the Rovers' faithful, who would be more than disappointed should he leave Belle Vue.
Hamilton Academical (From juniors on 1/6/93) SL 27+18/8 SC 0+1 Others 1+3
Southampton (£75,000 on 8/6/93) PL 0+1
Falkirk (Signed on 30/8/94) SL 6+2/1 SLC 0+1
Heart of Midlothian (Signed on 1/3/95) SL 3+3/1
Doncaster Rov (£25,000 on 15/12/95) FL 60+2/25 FLC 2/1 FAC 1/1 Others 1/1

CRANE Steven (Steve) John
Born: Orsett, 3 June 1972
Height: 5'9" Weight: 12.0

A former Charlton and Gillingham forward who had spent the previous two years in New Zealand, Steve returned to this country last December and signed non-contract forms with Torquay. However, following two subs' appearances in the league that brought him just 35 minutes playing time, plus an AWS start, he moved on shortly after the arrival of Andy McFarlane.
Charlton Ath (From trainee on 3/7/90 - Released in February 1991)
Gillingham (Signed from USA on 19/3/93) FL 3+10/1 FLC 0+2 Others 2 (Free to Hornchurch from USA during 1994 close season)
Torquay U (Free from New Zealand on 24/12/96) FL 0+2 Others 1

CRANSON Ian
Born: Easington, 2 July 1964
Height: 5'11" Weight: 13.4
Club Honours: AMC '92; Div 2 '93
International Honours: E: U21-5

Over the past seven seasons, Ian had been a tremendous servant to Stoke, that was until his long-suffering knees finally got the better of him early on in 1996-97 and he retired. His leadership, tremendous consistency, and determination, won him many fans at the Victoria Ground and he will be rewarded with a testimonial year. Strong in the air and an excellent tackler, he had stoically been fighting off injuries for many years.
Ipswich T (From apprentice on 5/7/82) FL 130+1/5 FLC 15 FAC 11+1 Others 7
Sheffield Wed (£450,000 on 24/3/88) FL 29+1 FLC 2 FAC 2 Others 1
Stoke C (£450,000 on 25/7/89) FL 220+3/9 FLC 16+1/1 FAC 14/1 Others 27/1

CRAWFORD James (Jimmy)
Born: Chicago, USA, 1 May 1973
Height: 5'11" Weight: 11.6
International Honours: Ei: U21-2

A player who is able to play in a wide role or in a more conventional midfield position, and one being groomed for the future, he was on the Newcastle bench quite often during the latter half of last season, but was only called upon to make two substitute appearances. Earlier, last September, Jimmy had a successful loan spell at Rotherham, but just when he looked like playing a major part in reviving their fortunes and very much wanted at Millmoor, he had to return to St James' Park when the clubs failed to agree terms to make the move permanent.
Newcastle U (£75,000 from Bohemians on 23/3/95) PL 0+2 FLC 0+1
Rotherham U (Loaned on 27/9/96) FL 11

CRAWFORD Stephen (Steve)
Born: Dunfermline, 9 January 1974
Height: 5'10" Weight: 10.7
International Honours: S: 1; U21-19

Signed by Millwall from Raith Rovers during the summer of 1996, Steven is both pacy and skilful and loves taking defenders on. The Lions' top scorer, with some excellent strikes from both right or left foot, he started end of the season games from midfield, thus allowing him to dribble through from midfield.
Raith Rov (Free from Rosyth Rec on 13/8/92) SL 83+33/22 SLC 4+3/1 SC 6/3 Others 7+2/2
Millwall (Signed on 4/7/96) FL 40+2/11 FLC 1 FAC 2/1 Others 2/3

Steve Crawford

CREANEY Gerard (Gerry) Thomas
Born: Coatbridge, 13 April 1970
Height: 5'11" Weight: 13.6
International Honours: S: B-1; U21-11

1996-97 was another spasmodic season for Gerry, with only a handful of appearances for Manchester City, mainly as a substitute, despite scoring a good goal at home to Charlton Athletic in September to clinch victory in the last three minutes. His career at Maine Road has been extremely

disappointing to quote himself and he joined Ipswich on loan for one month in October and felt refreshed to play some first-team football, scoring in Town's home win over Swindon. Since returning, he has been in the squad, but mainly as a substitute. Placed on the transfer list during the summer, at his best, he is a skilful forward with a good strike rate and a player who holds up the ball well.

Glasgow Celtic (From juniors on 15/5/87) SL 85+28/36 SLC 9+1/7 SC 9/8 Others 6+3/3
Portsmouth (£500,000 on 25/1/94) FL 60/32 FLC 7/3 FAC 2/1
Manchester C (£2,000,000 on 8/9/95) P/FL 7+13/4 FAC 0+4/1
Oldham Ath (Loaned on 28/3/96) FL 8+1/2
Ipswich T (Loaned on 25/10/96) FL 6/1

CRESSWELL Richard Paul Wesley
Born: Bridlington, 20 September 1977
Height: 6'0" Weight: 11.0
The tall, young York striker was unable to maintain the promise he showed for York in 1995-96 and had a spell on loan at Mansfield Town in the closing weeks of last season, opening his scoring account with the Stags in a 1-0 win at Rochdale. Back at City, and with age on his side, it is hoped Richard has a bright future at Bootham Crescent.
York C (From trainee on 15/11/95) FL 18+15/1 FLC 1+2 FAC 0+1 Others 2
Mansfield T (Loaned on 27/3/97) FL 5/1

CRICHTON Paul Andrew
Born: Pontefract, 3 October 1968
Height: 6'1" Weight: 12.2
Paul took over between the posts from the ageing (and injured) Nigel Spink at West Brom and did well initially, following his transfer from Grimsby last September. A good shot stopper, he lacked confidence at times, especially with his kicking, and the fans got on his back which led to him being replaced by Alan Miller (March). On song, his sound anticipation and quick reflexes generally save the day.
Nottingham F (From juniors on 23/5/86)
Notts Co (Loaned on 19/9/86) FL 5
Darlington (Loaned on 30/1/87) FL 5
Peterborough U (Loaned on 27/3/87) FL 4
Darlington (Loaned on 28/9/87) FL 3 FLC 1 Others 1
Swindon T (Loaned on 24/12/87) FL 4
Rotherham U (Loaned on 9/3/88) FL 6
Torquay U (Loaned on 25/8/88) FL 13 FLC 2
Peterborough U (Signed on 3/11/88) FL 47 FAC 5 Others 3
Doncaster Rov (Free on 25/8/90) FL 77 FLC 5 FAC 3 Others 5
Grimsby T (Free on 9/7/93) FL 133 FLC 7 FAC 8 Others 2
West Bromwich A (£250,000 on 9/9/96) FL 30 FAC 1

CROFT Gary
Born: Burton on Trent, 17 February 1974
Height: 5'9" Weight: 11.8
International Honours: E: U21-4
Having been signed in March 1996, predominately as first team cover and insurance against injury, Gary made his debut for Blackburn last September against Brentford in the Coca-Cola Cup, before appearing in six of the next seven games. Unfortunately, despite being quick footed and thoughtful in his use of the ball, the stylish left back's lack

of experience was exploited by Premiership opposition and he spent the rest of the season in the reserves. A strong tackler and a versatile player, who is able to play in midfield and further up the flank if required, he will be back.
Grimsby T (From trainee on 7/7/92) FL 139+10/3 FLC 7 FAC 8+2/1 Others 3
Blackburn Rov (£1,700,000 on 29/3/96) PL 4+1 FLC 2

CROOK Ian Stuart
Born: Romford, 18 January 1963
Height: 5'8" Weight: 10.6
International Honours: E: B-1
A dramatic pre-season day in June 1996 saw Ian paraded as Ipswich Town's new signing at the same time as Mike Walker was reinstated as manager at Norwich. However, a change of mind ensued and he continued his Canary career, becoming the eighth city player to reach 400 games. Always good for a goal or two, his two last term were both 25 yarders - A measured side footer and a hopeful shot which beat a bemused 'keeper. Originally expected to take up a coaching position at Carrow Road, he signed a one-year contract with Sanfrece Hiroshima in Japan as the 1996-97 campaign drew to a close. Once again proving his ability to dictate a game from midfield, his vision, flair, and passing ability standing out, he will be remembered as one on City's finest.
Tottenham H (From apprentice on 1/8/80) FL 10+10/1 FLC 1 FAC 0+1 Others 1+1
Norwich C (£80,000 on 13/6/86) F/PL 314+27/18 FLC 31+5/4 FAC 19+4/1 Others 16+1/1

CROOKS Lee Robert
Born: Wakefield, 14 January 1978
Height: 5'11" Weight: 12.1
International Honours: E: Yth
A strong young Manchester City lad who graduated through the "A" and reserve teams at Maine Road to catch the eye with very positive displays in 1996-97, following his debut, he appeared to enjoy being at the back. His stature is ideal and an asset is that he can go forward and cross well into the opposing goalmouth, something he did to great effect in the games away at Wolverhampton and at home to Watford, in the FA Cup. Having given a very mature performance against the big names of Middlesbrough in the home FA Cup game, Lee was selected for the England U21 squad, but, unfortunately, had to withdraw through injury.
Manchester C (From trainee on 14/1/95) FL 8+7 FLC 0+1 FAC 2

CROSBY Andrew (Andy) Keith
Born: Rotherham, 3 March 1973
Height: 6'2" Weight: 13.7
Stalwart Darlington central defender and captain. Commanding in the air and strong on the ground, and a player who rarely finds the net, despite being a handful at corners, Andy followed up his 1995-96 solitary league goal with another last season – the equaliser at home to Chester.
Doncaster Rov (Free from Leeds U juniors on 4/7/91) FL 41+10 FLC 1+1 FAC 2 Others 4+1/1
Darlington (Free on 10/12/93) FL 147/2 FLC 8 FAC 7/1 Others 8

Andy Crosby

CROSBY Gary
Born: Sleaford, 8 May 1964
Height: 5'8" Weight: 9.13
Club Honours: FLC '90; FMC '92
A skilful Huddersfield winger who forced his way back into the side at the start of last season for an extended run, using his experience to good effect, Gary scored the club's fastest goal of the season at Bradford City. Having lost his place towards the end of the campaign, due to the recurrence of a niggling injury, he was released during the summer. Still quick off the mark and has a surprisingly long throw for one so small.
Lincoln C (Free from Lincoln U on 23/8/86) FL 6+1 FLC 2 (Free to Grantham in November 1986)
Nottingham F (£20,000 on 21/12/87) F/PL 139+13/12 FLC 29+1/6 FAC 18+3/3 Others 10+1/4
Grimsby T (Loaned on 23/8/93) FL 2+1
Huddersfield T (Free on 27/9/94) FL 35+9/6 FLC 2 FAC 3/1 Others 5+2/1

CROSS Jonathan Neil
Born: Wallasey, 2 March 1975
Height: 5'10" Weight: 11.7
Another talented player on Wrexham's books who failed to impose himself last season, he was loaned out to Hereford in December to hopefully rekindle his form. Jonathan, a strong forceful player, who can play a part in attack, midfield, and defence, can still figure prominently in the club's future plans, but needs to become more involved with the squad. However, he showed his versatility when filling in at left back for the last four games of the campaign.
Wrexham (From trainee on 15/11/92) FL 90+27/12 FLC 4+3/1 FAC 4+1/1 Others 9+6/1
Hereford U (Loaned on 2/12/96) FL 5/1 Others 1

CROSSLEY Mark Geoffrey
Born: Barnsley, 16 June 1969
Height: 6'0" Weight: 16.0
International Honours: E: U21-3. W: 1
Remained the number one 'keeper at

Nottingham Forest in 1996-97, despite it being a disappointing season, and missed very few games – the first being in March, after he was dismissed for bringing down Jon Howard during Forest's shock FA Cup defeat at Chesterfield, the winner coming from the resultant penalty. Despite being a Yorkshireman, Mark made his full international debut for Wales after representing England at U21 level and declaring his desire to play for Scotland, courtesy of a Scottish grandmother. Another grandparent had Welsh ancestry hence the change. A big, strong goalie, who makes scoring past him difficult, being at his best in one-to-one situations, he completed ten seasons with the club during the 1997 close season. Kicks the ball well from his hands.

Nottingham F (From trainee on 2/7/87) F/PL 270+1 FLC 34 FAC 32 Others 18

CROSSLEY Matthew (Matt) John William
Born: Basingstoke, 18 March 1968
Height: 6'2" Weight: 13.12
Club Honours: FAT '91, '93; GMVC '93

Reliable two-footed central defender and Wycombe's longest-serving player, Matt came back into favour when new manager, John Gregory, joined last October. However, it was to be short lived and, on losing his place in November, he then had a spell on loan at Rushden & Diamonds before being sadly forced to retire from full-time football at the end of the season with a persistent back injury.

Wycombe W (Signed from Overton U in 1987-88) FL 93+3/3 FLC 7/1 FAC 16 Others 9+1

CROWE Glen Michael
Born: Dublin, 25 December 1977
Height: 5'10" Weight: 13.1
International Honours: Ei: U21-1; Yth

A persistent striker who came on for club colleague, Dominic Foley, in an Eire U21 match in October, he started three games for Wolves that month before going on loan to Exeter in a bid to sharpen up. It is no exaggeration to say that the arrival of Glen for the final three months of last season played a big part in helping the club avoid relegation. His physical presence up front, coupled with his heading and shooting power, proved a handful for third division defenders as he showed that he was more than capable of operating in a higher class of football. A highlight for the fans was his second goal in the away win at Doncaster. Back at Molineux, however, he played in the final two league games, rendered meaningless by the play-off results.

Wolverhampton W (From trainee on 3/7/96) FL 6+2/1
Exeter C (Loaned on 21/2/97) FL 10/5

CRUYFF Jordi
Born: Holland, 9 February 1974
Height: 6'0" Weight: 11.0
Club Honours: PL '97; CS '97
International Honours: Holland: 8

Signed from Barcelona prior to the start of last season, the highly versatile front-line Dutch international, with excellent skills and a terrific shot in either foot, made a promising start to his Manchester United career, notching two goals in his opening three Premiership games, against Everton and Blackburn. But as 1996-97 progressed, he was troubled by persistent knee ligament problems which kept him out of the side from November until February, while his main problems on the pitch appeared to be adjusting to the English style of play, which confined him to the bench for several periods throughout the campaign. Seen as a long-term investment by Alex Ferguson, the United boss remarked, "Jordi is young and can play in several positions. He's a developing player." The son of former Dutch superstar, Johann, he is now the proud winner of a championship medal, following United's title success.

Manchester U (£1,400,000 from Barcelona on 12/8/96) PL 11+5/3 FLC 1 Others 3+1

CULLEN David Jonathan (Jon)
Born: Durham, 10 January 1973
Height: 6'0" Weight: 12.0

A right-sided midfielder, Jon was perhaps the least well known of Hartlepool's signings on transfer deadline day last March. After several years of non-league football, following a spell with Doncaster, he was thrown in at the deep end and did not let the side down and played an important role as a provider for the forwards. As a non-contract player his game benefited from full-time training and, in May 1997, he was offered a new contract to continue his promising return to senior soccer.

Doncaster Rov (From trainee on 16/9/91) FL 8+1 FLC 2+1/1 FAC 0+1 Others 1 (Free to Spennymoor in September 1993)
Hartlepool U (Free from Morpeth on 27/3/97) FL 5+1

CULLIP Daniel (Danny)
Born: Bracknell, 17 September 1976
Height: 6'1" Weight: 12.7

Signed in the summer of 1996 from Oxford as central defensive cover, Danny did so well in pre-season games that he went straight into the Fulham side, making his league debut at home to Hereford. A good header of the ball, and learning all the time, his positional sense improved match by match as he pressed for a regular place in the side. Scored his first goal at the Cottage in the 6-0 January thumping of Darlington.

Oxford U (From trainee on 6/7/95)
Fulham (Free on 5/7/96) FL 23+6/1 FLC 4 FAC 1 Others 1

CULVERHOUSE Ian Brett
Born: Bishops Stortford, 22 September 1964
Height: 5'10" Weight: 11.2
Club Honours: Div 2 '86, '96
International Honours: E: Yth

Ever present in Swindon's second division championship team the previous season, he did not enjoy such a commanding year in division one in 1996-97, with injuries and suspension disrupting his progress. Although partnering Mark Seagraves in central defence in a flat back four in the early months of the season, after dropping out of the team through injury in October he

returned in December in his previous role of sweeper. He next lost his place through injury after Easter, sharing in the collective collapse of confidence in the Robins' defence, following the heavy defeats at Bolton and Oldham, and must hope to be back to full fitness for the coming term.

Tottenham H (From apprentice on 24/9/82) FL 1+1
Norwich C (£50,000 on 8/10/85) F/PL 295+1/1 FLC 23 FAC 28 Others 22/1
Swindon T (£250,000 on 9/12/94) FL 86 FLC 9 FAC 9 Others 1

CUNDY Jason Victor
Born: Wandsworth, 12 November 1969
Height: 6'1" Weight: 13.13
International Honours: E: U21-3

Unable to make it at Spurs, Jason went out on loan to Bristol City last August and performed well in his six games played, scoring in the 5-0 success against Luton before returning to White Hart Lane. Next stop was another loan transfer, this time at Ipswich in October. The well-built defender who is good in the air, with a fast turn of pace, brought much needed stability to the Town defence, the deal becoming permanent in time for him to play in the Coca-Cola Cup against Gillingham, which was curtailed when he received a nasty facial injury and had to leave the field. Injury then halted his season in mid February when a shin problem turned septic and while recovering he was diagnosed as having cancer. At the time of writing, he appears to have made a great recovery and is expecting to resume his career this coming season.

Chelsea (From trainee on 1/8/88) FL 40+1/1 FLC 6 FAC 6 Others 4
Tottenham H (£750,000 on 26/3/92) F/PL 23+3/1 FLC 2
Crystal Palace (Loaned on 14/12/95) FL 4
Bristol C (Loaned on 23/8/96) FL 6/1
Ipswich T (£200,000 on 29/10/96) FL 13/2 FLC 2 FAC 1

CUNNINGHAM Daniel Harvey
Born: Manchester, 11 September 1968
Height: 5'9" Weight: 11.0

Another non-league signing for Doncaster in 1996-97, this right-sided winger, cum full back, who joined from Droylesden in February, became the third Rovers' player to make his debut in the game with Barnet at Belle Vue, later that month. Having previously played for a number of clubs outside the league, including Southport and Winsford United, "Cunny" openly admits that his best moment in football came when arriving at Belle Vue for the first time.

Doncaster Rov (Free from Droylesden on 14/2/97) FL 11

CUNNINGHAM Kenneth (Kenny) Edward
Born: Dublin, 28 June 1971
Height: 6'0" Weight: 11.8
International Honours: Ei: 10; B-2; U21-4; Yth

A Republic of Ireland international who joined Wimbledon from Millwall in November 1994, Kenny is not only a comfortable defender but also a very useful attacking right back whose overlapping runs

were of a real benefit to the Dons' forward play last season. A great deal of the goals scored in open play were due to his awareness of other players and his precision in finding them with accurate passes or well flighted crosses. A reliable player, he fits very well into the Premiership scene.

Millwall (Signed from Tolka Rov on 18/9/89) FL 132+4/1 FLC 10 FAC 1 Others 5+1/1
Wimbledon (Signed on 9/11/94) PL 96+1 FLC 9 FAC 19

Kenny Cunningham

CUNNINGTON Shaun Gary
Born: Bourne, 4 January 1966
Height: 5'9" Weight: 11.12
Club Honours: WC '86

Knee and ankle injuries once again ruined Shaun's season at West Bromwich in 1995-96, his aggressive, tough-tackling style of play in midfield being missed, but when recovered and unable to maintain a place in the side he was sold to Notts County last March. Had to overcome a nightmare debut at Rotherham in a side already destined for relegation, before giving some solid performances and impressing as a leader and ball winner in the middle of the park.

Wrexham (From juniors on 11/1/84) FL 196+3/12 FLC 13 FAC 9/1 Others 21/2
Grimsby T (£55,000 on 19/2/88) FL 182/13 FLC 11 FAC 11/3 Others 9
Sunderland (£650,000 on 17/7/92) FL 52+6/8 FLC 3 FAC 2/1 Others 2
West Bromwich A (£220,000 on 11/8/95) FL 8+5 FLC 1+2 Others 2
Notts Co (£25,000 on 14/3/97) FL 6+2

CURCIC Sasa
Born: Belgrade, Yugoslavia, 14 February 1972
Height: 5'9" Weight: 10.7
International Honours: Yugoslavia: 12

Sasa became Aston Villa's record signing when moving from Bolton early last season, but, after an encouraging start, he fell out of favour for long spells, prompting calls from the player that he was wrong to leave Bolton and led to him submitting an official transfer request at the end of February. At his best,

Sasa Curcic

an attacking midfielder with silky skills, he struggled to make the impression that he had the previous season as the star of a struggling Wanderers' side and, despite making 20 starts, plus a few more as sub, he failed to score. At the time of going to press, it was being debated whether he had played enough games within the guidelines laid down in the regulations.

Bolton W (£1,500,000 from Partizan Belgrade on 28/10/95) PL 28/4 FLC 3/1 FAC 2/2
Aston Villa (£4,000,000 on 23/8/96) PL 17+5 FLC 1 FAC 2/1

CURETON Jamie
Born: Bristol, 28 August 1975
Height: 5'8" Weight: 10.7
International Honours: E: Yth

A diminutive and popular striker, Jamie made a magnificent impression at Bristol Rovers in 1996-97, having come on loan from Norwich, when scoring four goals in as many matches. With the transfer firmed up, he returned to his home city after spending six years at Carrow Road to become a firm favourite with the Memorial Ground fans, his stunning goal on 5 October from long range against Crewe Alexandra being followed by an even more impressive volley past Plymouth Argyle goalkeeper, Bruce Grobbelaar, on 25 February. Formed a promising understanding with fellow strike-partner, Peter Beadle, and contributed 11 goals as Rovers remained clear of the bottom four. Voted the club's Young Player of the Season.

Norwich C (From trainee on 5/2/93) P/FL 13+16/6 FLC 0+1 FAC 0+2
Bournemouth (Loaned on 8/9/95) FL 0+5 Others 0+1
Bristol Rov (£250,000 on 20/9/96) FL 33+5/11 FAC 1 Others 1

Keith Curle

CURLE Keith
Born: Bristol, 14 November 1963
Height: 6'0" Weight: 12.12
Club Honours: AMC '86; FMC '88
International Honours: E: 3; B-4

Arriving from Manchester City during the 1996 close season, the well-respected central defender was signed by Wolves to replace Adrian Williams, who had been injured before making his full debut. A friendly at Cardiff was his first appearance and he got a calf strain which developed into achilles tendonitis, lingering on until he came on as sub at Oxford in early September. However, he was still not right and surgery was needed, so it was January before he made his full debut. Not deterred by an own goal in his first away match at Bolton, his organisational skills soon becoming apparent, Keith proved to be fast, competitive and eager to venture forward with telling effect. Scored his first goals for the club in successive matches from penalties and after being rested for the last league match he was outstanding in the play offs.

Bristol Rov (From apprentice on 20/11/81) FL 21+11/4 FLC 3 FAC 1
Torquay U (£5,000 on 4/11/83) FL 16/5 FAC 1/1 Others 1
Bristol C (£10,000 on 3/3/84) FL 113+8/1 FLC 7+1 FAC 5 Others 14+1
Reading (£150,000 on 23/10/87) FL 40 FLC 8 Others 5
Wimbledon (£500,000 on 21/10/88) FL 91+2/3 FLC 7 FAC 5 Others 6/1
Manchester C (£2,500,000 on 14/8/91) F/PL 171/11 FLC 18/2 FAC 14 Others 1
Wolverhampton W (£650,000 on 2/8/96) FL 20+1/2 Others 2

CURRAN Christopher (Chris)
Born: Birmingham, 17 September 1971
Height: 5'11" Weight: 12.4

A speedy Plymouth central defender who can play anywhere in the defence and even as a midfielder, Chris was in and out of the side in 1996-97 with a number of central defenders in the squad. Very combative, and a player who keeps going, when selected he always looked an accomplished performer.

Torquay U (From trainee on 13/7/90) FL 144+8/4 FLC 15 FAC 8 Others 10/1
Plymouth Arg (£40,000 on 22/12/95) FL 26+4 FLC 1+1 FAC 1 Others 4

CURRIE Darren Paul
Born: Hampstead, 29 November 1974
Height: 5'8" Weight: 11.10

The Shrewsbury Town left winger, cum midfielder, continued to please the crowd in 1996-97 with surging runs at opposition defences, coupled with pinpoint crosses. Speedy and accurate, he also has a devastating shot and is equally effective roving in midfield. Disappointingly, despite giving some promising displays, he was not always given the opportunity to show his skills.

West Ham U (From trainee on 2/7/93)
Shrewsbury T (Loaned on 5/9/94) FL 10+2/2
Shrewsbury T (Loaned on 3/2/95) FL 5
Leyton Orient (Loaned on 16/11/95) FL 9+1
Shrewsbury T (£70,000 on 7/2/96) FL 36+14/4 FLC 1+1 FAC 2

CURRIE David Norman
Born: Stockton, 27 November 1962
Height: 6'0" Weight: 12.13
Club Honours: Div 2 '91, Div 3 '95

A vastly experienced striker, he joined Scarborough, initially on loan from Carlisle United last January, but then moved permanently to the Seasiders on a month-to-month contract. Became only the second Boro forward to score a Football League hat trick, in a 4-1 win over Darlington on 8 February, and totalled six goals for the club, before being released towards the end of the season.

Middlesbrough (Signed on 5/2/82) FL 94+19/31 FLC 6/1 FAC 5+1 Others 2
Darlington (Free on 17/6/86) FL 76/33 FLC 6 FAC 3 Others 5/3
Barnsley (£150,000 on 26/2/88) FL 80/30 FLC 3/1 FAC 5/4 Others 1
Nottingham F (£750,000 on 19/1/90) FL 4+4/1
Oldham Ath (£460,000 on 23/8/90) FL 17+14/3 FLC 2+1/2 FAC 1 Others 0+1
Barnsley (£250,000 on 5/9/91) FL 53+22/12 FLC 2+1 FAC 4+1 Others 1+1/1
Rotherham U (Loaned on 15/10/92) FL 5/2
Huddersfield T (Loaned on 10/1/94) FL 7/1 Others 1
Carlisle U (Free on 18/7/94) FL 84+5/13 FLC 5+2 FAC 4/1 Others 13+1/5
Scarborough (Signed on 24/1/97) FL 16/6

CURTIS Thomas (Tom) David
Born: Exeter, 1 March 1973
Height: 5'8" Weight: 11.7

Tom has become one of Chesterfield's most experienced players, with more than 150 appearances to his name at the end of the 1996-97 season, despite being only 24 years old and having been a full professional for just a year. The livewire midfielder's hustling style often conceals his more creative side, but he is no mere stopper: he

has a gift for intelligent passing and support play, and is developing an ability to read the game well. Tom in one of many of the current team to have recently agreed a new contract with the Spireites.

Derby Co (From juniors on 1/7/91)
Chesterfield (Free on 12/8/93) FL 160+2/8 FLC 11+1 FAC 13/1 Others 10

CUSACK Nicholas (Nicky) John
Born: Maltby, 24 December 1965
Height: 6'0" Weight: 12.8

A former Fulham striker who was voted Player of the Year in 1995-96 for his exploits in midfield, Nicky was pressed into service as a sweeper at the start of last season and took to it so well that he was retained in that spot throughout in the meanest defence in the third division. Always carries the ball out of defence, if possible, and is a very good passer.

Leicester C (Signed from Alvechurch on 18/6/87) FL 5+11/1 FAC 0+1 Others 1+1
Peterborough U (£40,000 on 29/7/88) FL 44/10 FLC 4/1 FAC 4/1 Others 2
Motherwell (£100,000 on 2/8/89) SL 68+9/17 SLC 5/4 SC 3+1/2 Others 1+1/1
Darlington (£95,000 on 24/1/92) FL 21/6
Oxford U (£95,000 on 16/7/92) FL 48+13/10 FLC 3/2 FAC 4+2/1 Others 2+1
Wycombe W (Loaned on 24/3/94) FL 2+2/1
Fulham (Free on 4/11/94) FL 108+6/14 FLC 5+3/1 FAC 7+1/1 Others 5+2/3

CUTLER Neil Anthony
Born: Birmingham, 3 September 1976
Height: 6'1" Weight: 12.0
International Honours: E: Yth; Sch

Signed by Crewe from West Bromwich during the 1996 close season as goalkeeping cover for Mark Gayle, he was on loan at Chester when the latter was injured and, despite coming back, he found his way blocked first by Martin Taylor, on loan from Derby, and then by Jason Kearton, a new signing from Everton. However, still very much a 'keeper for the future, his five games at City saw him keep two clean sheets, before he joined non-league Leek Town on a temporary basis in March to gain further experience.

West Bromwich A (From trainee on 7/9/93)
Chester C (Loaned on 27/3/96) FL 1
Crewe Alex (Signed on 30/7/96)
Chester C (Loaned on 30/8/96) FL 5

CYRUS Andrew
Born: Lambeth, 30 September 1976
Height: 5'8" Weight: 10.7

Having come through the Crystal Palace ranks as a trainee, Andrew turned professional early into 1995-96 and, after impressing in youth and reserve team games, was given a first-team opportunity at Manchester City last January when a number of regulars were unavailable. A talented and skilful left-wing back who gets up the line well to cross to the front men, and can defend resolutely if the need be, he had a trial with Bristol Rovers at the tail-end of the season before being released during the summer.

Crystal Palace (From trainee on 22/8/95) FL 1

DA COSTA Hugo Alexandre
Born: Tramagal, Portugal, 4 November 1973
Height: 6'1" Weight: 13.6
A loan signing from Benfica at the start of last season, the central defender made a handful of appearances in the heart of the Stoke defence, deputising for Ian Cranson and John Dreyer, although never really became accustomed to the pace of the English game. Good distribution and strong in the air, he returned home in October.
Stoke C (Loaned from Benfica on 28/8/96) FL 1+1 FLC 1+1

DAILLY Christian Eduard
Born: Dundee, 23 October 1973
Height: 6'0" Weight: 12.10
International Honours: S: 3; B-1; U21-34; Yth; Sch
Highly promising Derby defender, cum midfielder, signed in the 1996 close season from Dundee United after a move to the continent broke down, and the holder of a record number of Scottish U21 caps, he started off 1996-97 in a defensive midfield role before withdrawing into the back line following an injury to Igor Stimac. His sterling performances were noted by Scotland manager, Craig Brown, who gave him his first Scottish cap in a May friendly versus Wales. Scored in his second full international against Malta a week later, before playing in the Belgian match.
Dundee U (From juniors on 2/8/90) SL 110+33/18 SLC 9/1 SC 10+2 Others 8+1/1
Derby Co (£1,000,000 on 12/8/96) PL 31+5/3 FLC 2 FAC 4

DAILLY Marcus Graham
Born: Dundee, 1 October 1975
Height: 5'9" Weight: 11.6
The brother of Derby's Christian, Marcus arrived at Exeter on a free transfer from Dundee at the start of last season. Unfortunately, it was only injuries that prevented him from establishing a first-team place in the midfield, before he moved back to his native Scotland towards the end of the campaign.
Dundee (Signed from Dundee U-N/C - 6/7/94) SL 1 Others 2
Exeter C (Free on 16/8/96) FL 8+9 FLC 1 FAC 2 Others 1

DAIR Jason
Born: Dunfermline, 15 June 1974
Height: 5'11" Weight: 10.8
International Honours: S: Sch
Signed by Millwall from Raith Rovers during the summer of 1996, Jason operated last season on the left of midfield or as a striker, showing neat touches and a quick turn of pace to go wide to produce crosses. Currently at Hearts on trial.

Raith Rov (Free from Castlebridge on 3/7/91) SL 80+15/11 SLC 5+1 SC 3+1 Others 6+1/1
Millwall (Signed on 4/7/96) FL 21+3/1 FLC 2 FAC 2 Others 1/2

DAISH Liam Sean
Born: Portsmouth, 23 September 1968
Height: 6'2" Weight: 13.5
Club Honours: Div 3 '91, B-1; Div 2 '95; AMC '95
International Honours: Ei: 5; B-1; U21-5
A committed no-nonsense Coventry central defender, who was almost an ever present before suffering a knee injury in training last January, an injury that ruled him out for the rest of the season, Liam scored two goals, one of them a vital late equaliser against his old team, Birmingham, in the Coca-Cola Cup. Possessing a strong left foot and tough in the air, although sometimes challenged for speed by faster strikers, he makes up for any deficiencies with wholehearted effort. Sent off twice early in the season, first at Chelsea for dissent after the controversial first goal, and then at St Andrews for two bookable offences, the second an ill-timed sliding tackle which looked worse than it was, he will be looking to get back into contention for 1997-98. Is always dangerous at set pieces.
Portsmouth (From apprentice on 29/9/86) FL 1 Others 1+1
Cambridge U (Free on 11/7/88) FL 138+1/4 FLC 11 FAC 17 Others 15/3
Birmingham C (£50,000 on 10/1/94) FL 72+1/3 FLC 10/3 FAC 7 Others 8
Coventry C (£1,500,000 on 24/2/96) PL 31/2 FLC 3/1

DALE Carl
Born: Colwyn Bay, 29 April 1966
Height: 5'9" Weight: 12.0
Club Honours: WC '92, '93; Div 3 '93
Although dogged by injuries throughout 1996-97, the old Cardiff warhorse still managed to get among the goals, scoring 11, including the one that brought City's first win of the season at home to Northampton and three in successive games on two separate occasions. A natural goalscorer, who struck up a good partnership with newcomer Steve White, two of his last four strikes were quite probably the main reasons for the club scraping into the play-off places. Always dangerous, even when not fully fit.
Chester C (£12,000 from Bangor C on 19/5/88) FL 106+10/41 FLC 7+1 FAC 9/5 Others 6/2
Cardiff C (£100,000 on 19/8/91) FL 172+16/67 FLC 10+1/5 FAC 8/2 Others 21+1/20

DALTON Paul
Born: Middlesbrough, 25 April 1967
Height: 5'11" Weight: 12.7
Despite being predominantly left footed, Paul can play on either wing, creating a number of chances with his ability to cut inside opposing full backs. However, while finding it difficult to establish himself at Huddersfield in 1996-97, often participating in many games from the substitutes' bench, he still scored his quota of goals, including a magnificent 30-yard shot at Leeds Road against Bradford. With Town 3-0 down, his goal stopped the rot in a game that ultimately finished 3-3.

Manchester U (£35,000 from Brandon U on 3/5/88)
Hartlepool U (£20,000 on 4/3/89) FL 140+11/37 FLC 10/2 FAC 7/1 Others 9/3
Plymouth Arg (£275,000 on 11/6/92) FL 93+5/25 FLC 5/2 FAC 7/5 Others 6
Huddersfield T (Signed on 11/8/95) FL 46+12/9 FLC 5+2/1 FAC 3+1

DANIEL Raymond (Ray) Christopher
Born: Luton, 10 December 1964
Height: 5'8" Weight: 12.5
Ray had an unhappy season at Walsall in 1996-97, being in and out of the team in the first half and then sustaining an achilles injury that kept him out from January onwards, though he returned to score a fine goal in the reserves near the end of the campaign. Having spent two seasons at Bescot, this strong left-flank defender was released during the summer.
Luton T (From apprentice on 7/9/82) FL 14+8/4 FLC 2 FAC 5+1
Gillingham (Loaned on 1/9/83) FL 5
Hull C (Free on 30/6/86) FL 55+3/3 FLC 1 FAC 1+1 Others 0+1
Cardiff C (£40,000 on 22/8/89) FL 56/1 FLC 5 FAC 5 Others 1
Portsmouth (£80,000 on 9/11/90) FL 91+9/4 FLC 7+2 FAC 6 Others 6+1/1
Notts Co (Loaned on 28/10/94) FL 5 Others 1
Walsall (Free on 9/8/95) FL 31+4 FLC 4 FAC 3 Others 1

DARBY Duane Anthony
Born: Birmingham, 17 October 1973
Height: 5'11" Weight: 12.6
A goalscoring vulture often feeding off scraps, Hull City's Duane enjoyed a marvellous 1996-97 season, highlighted by his opening-day hat trick against Darlington and six goals in the FA Cup replay win against Whitby Town, which saw him become the first-ever Tiger to hit a sextet (only the 12th in the entire history of The Cup). Voted the supporters' Player of the Year, he is a Steve Bull lookalike, who strongly favours his right side.
Torquay U (From trainee on 3/7/92) FL 60+48/26 FLC 4+4 FAC 1+4 Others 5+3/2
Doncaster Rov (£60,000 on 19/7/95) FL 8+9/4 FLC 2 FAC 0+1 Others 1+1
Hull C (Signed on 27/3/96) FL 48+1/14 FLC 2 FAC 3/6 Others 2/1

DARBY Julian Timothy
Born: Bolton, 3 October 1967
Height: 6'0" Weight: 11.4
Club Honours: AMC '89
International Honours: E: Sch
A hard-working midfielder who also played at left back and in the centre of West Brom's defence in 1996-97, Julian was never a regular in the side, injuries plaguing him early in the campaign, but he always gave 100 per cent when he did turn out. Scored many useful goals while at Bolton, but has yet to make his mark in that area of the field at Albion.
Bolton W (From trainee on 22/7/86) FL 258+12/36 FLC 25/8 FAC 19/3 Others 31+1/5
Coventry C (£150,000 on 28/10/93) PL 52+3/5 FLC 3/1 FAC 2+2
West Bromwich A (£200,000 on 24/11/95) FL 32+7/1 FAC 1 Others 4

DARRAS Frederic Guy Albert
Born: Calais, France, 19 August 1974
Height: 5'11" Weight: 11.5
A little known, but highly experienced French player, Frederic joined Swindon Town in the summer of 1996 from the Corsican club, AS Bastia, following previous spells with Auxerre (1986-92) and Sochaux (1992-94). Essentially a utility player, he started last season at right back before losing his place to Mark Robinson in September. Thereafter, he was deployed in separate spells in midfield, central defence, and left back, usually covering for injuries or loss of form to other players. This versatility makes him a very useful squad player, but the lack of a fixed position may further limit his appearances in 1997-98.
Swindon T (Free from Bastia on 9/8/96) FL 30+5 FLC 4

DARTON Scott Richard
Born: Ipswich, 27 March 1975
Height: 5'11" Weight: 11.3
Only figured in Blackpool's starting line up once before the New Year, in the centre of the defence, before coming back for a spell in January and February and scoring his first goal for the club in a 3-0 home win over Millwall. A player with good technique and better known as a left back, he now sits mainly in midfield. Was released during the summer.
West Bromwich A (From trainee on 28/10/92) FL 15 FLC 1 Others 5/1
Blackpool (£7,500 on 20/1/95) FL 31+11/1 Others 2+1

D'AURIA David Alan
Born: Swansea, 26 March 1970
Height: 5'9" Weight: 11.11
Club Honours: WC '94
International Honours: W: Yth
A busy Scunthorpe midfielder who likes to be involved, always wanting the ball, David also loves getting forward for goalscoring opportunities, again scoring a handful of goals for the Irons in 1996-97 as the side consolidated a mid-table position. Also has excellent distribution qualities.
Swansea C (From trainee on 2/8/88) FL 27+18/6 FLC 2+2 FAC 1 Others 4 (Free transfer to Merthyr Tydfil during 1991 close season)
Scarborough (Signed from Barry T on 22/8/94) FL 49+3/8 FLC 3+2/1 FAC 4+1 Others 2
Scunthorpe U (£40,000 on 6/12/95) FL 66/8 FLC 2 FAC 3/1 Others 1+1

DAVEY Simon
Born: Swansea, 1 October 1970
Height: 5'10" Weight: 12.2
Club Honours: Div 3 '95, '96
The hard-working Preston midfielder lost his place temporarily in mid season, before returning to display his tenacity in the centre of the field and contributing his usual quota of valuable goals, including a brace at Millwall and winners against Gillingham and Wycombe. An excellent passer and dead-ball specialist, Simon is also recognised as a strong tackler.
Swansea C (From trainee on 3/7/89) FL 37+12/4 FLC 1 FAC 1+2/1 Others 2+3

Carlisle U (Free on 5/8/92) FL 105/18 FLC 10/1 FAC 7/2 Others 15/2
Preston NE (£125,000 on 22/2/95) FL 80+8/19 FLC 4/1 FAC 2+1 Others 7

DAVIDSON Ross James
Born: Chertsey, 13 November 1973
Height: 5'9" Weight: 12.4
Since signing from Sheffield United in March 1996, Ross has made the Chester right-back slot his own, playing 46 times last season and being one of the key factors in the club's progress towards the play offs. An assured defender, he also proved very effective when going forward and provided many telling crosses for the front men, while also finding the time to pop in a couple of goals himself.
Sheffield U (Signed from Walton & Hersham on 5/6/93) FL 2 Others 2
Chester C (Free on 26/1/96) FL 59/3 FLC 1 FAC 2 Others 3

DAVIES Gareth Melville
Born: Hereford, 11 December 1973
Height: 6'1" Weight: 11.12
International Honours: W: U21-8
Prior to the return of Steve Coppell to Selhurst Park, this ginger-haired Crystal Palace defender's 1996-97 season was spent mainly on the treatment table or in the reserves, and he was even loaned out to Cardiff last February by Palace manager, Dave Bassett, before his resignation. However, with Coppell back in the fold, and Gareth again in contention for a first-team place, he came into the side for six of the last nine games, which included the home play-off leg against Wolves. Although at home as an attacking midfielder, his tackling strengths and aerial ability saw him at the back, mainly in central defence.
Hereford U (From trainee on 10/4/92) FL 91+4/1 FLC 5+2 FAC 4 Others 5
Crystal Palace (£120,000 on 1/7/95) FL 22+4/2 FAC 2 Others 1
Cardiff C (Loaned on 21/2/97) FL 6/2

DAVIES Glen
Born: Brighton, 20 July 1976
Height: 6'1" Weight: 12.10
Released by Burnley during the 1996 close season, this promising central defender joined Hartlepool for his first taste of senior football. Began 1996-97 well in a three-man central defence but, as the campaign progressed, he struggled to find his best form and was in and out of the side, before being transfer listed. However, when gradually regaining his confidence during the closing weeks, he was seen at his best, playing alongside a number of different defensive partners.
Burnley (From trainee on 18/7/94)
Hartlepool U (Free on 19/6/96) FL 30+2/1 FLC 2/1 Others 1

DAVIES Kevin Cyril
Born: Sheffield, 26 March 1977
Height: 6'1" Weight: 13.5
International Honours: E: Yth
The most naturally gifted member of Chesterfield's squad struggled against injury and loss of form during 1996-97. Even so, his willingness to take men on and his

ability to cause problems to other defences by doing the unexpected made him a regular in the side, when fit. Kevin went through his highest and lowest points, scoring a fine hat trick in the FA Cup to demolish Bolton and gain nationwide attention, but being one of five men sent from the field during the infamous Plymouth match. Kevin is the sort of thoughtful young man who will learn from these experiences and emerge a better player for it. *Stop Press:* Signed for Southampton on 14 May.
Chesterfield (From trainee on 18/4/94) FL 113+16/22 FLC 7+2/1 FAC 10/6 Others 9+2/1

DAVIES Simon Ithel
Born: Winsford, 23 April 1974
Height: 6'0" Weight: 11.11
Club Honours: FAYC '92
International Honours: W: 1
A talented Manchester United midfielder with excellent skills and wonderful vision, Simon was another young player who found chances hard to come by at Old Trafford in 1996-97, making just two solid Coca-Cola Cup appearances against Swindon and Leicester. Sandwiched between those two games, and with a view to gaining more experience, he had a three-match spell at Huddersfield on loan and was involved in the comeback of the season, a 3-3 draw against Bradford after Town had been three goals down. Highly promising, he will be looking for further opportunities in 1997-98.
Manchester U (From trainee on 6/7/92) PL 4+7 FLC 4+2 Others 2+1/1
Exeter C (Loaned on 17/12/93) FL 5+1/1 FAC 1
Huddersfield T (Loaned on 29/10/96) FL 3

DAVIS Kelvin Geoffrey
Born: Bedford, 29 September 1976
Height: 6'1" Weight: 14.0
International Honours: E: U21-3; Yth
With Ian Feuer in outstanding form in goal for Luton in 1996-97, Kelvin was restricted to just one first-team appearance in a relatively insignificant 2-1 victory over Leyton Orient in the Auto Windscreen Cup. However, he played steadily in the reserves and was again included in the Football League U21 squad against the Italians, although he did not appear in the match. After a promising start to his goalkeeping career as a teenager, he is in danger of becoming a forgotten figure and desperately needs regular football if he is to reach the potential shown in those early days. Loaned out to Doncaster in February, he returned to Kenilworth Road without an appearance to his name.
Luton T (From trainee on 1/7/94) FL 16 Others 5
Torquay U (Loaned on 16/9/94) FL 2 FLC 1 Others 1

DAVIS Neil
Born: Bloxwich, 15 August 1973
Height: 5'8" Weight: 11.0
Unable to stake a claim to a place at Aston Villa in 1996-97, Neil began a three-month loan spell at Wycombe in October when his former manager, John Gregory, joined the Bucks side. Although desperately unlucky not to score in his 14 appearances, the striker contributed much to an improving

team, proving to be very hard working, fast, with good close control, and able to link up well with his team mates.

Aston Villa (£25,000 from Redditch on 4/5/91) PL 0+2 FAC 0+1
Wycombe W (Loaned on 25/10/96) FL 13 Others 1

DAVIS Sean
Born: Clapham, 20 September 1979
Height: 5'10" Weight: 12.0

A first-year Fulham trainee, the young midfielder made his first-team debut as a sub in the home league match against Cambridge United in October after the manager, Micky Adams, had explained to the young lads that any player, regardless of age, would be given an early opportunity at the club if good enough. Sean did not let him down and showed up impressively before returning to the juniors, where he finished as the second top scorer. Is definitely one for the future.

Fulham (Trainee) FL 0+1

DAVIS Stephen (Steve) Mark
Born: Hexham, 30 October 1968
Height: 6'2" Weight: 14.7
Club Honours: Div 4 '92

After a tame start to last season with Luton, Steve went on to enjoy an outstanding campaign after relinquishing the captain's armband. Excellent in the air, he was rock solid in defence at centre back and weighed in with nine goals, making him the club's second highest league scorer behind the prolific Tony Thorpe. His excellent form was such that he was elected to the PFA second division XI by his fellow professionals.

Southampton (From trainee on 6/7/87) FL 5+1
Burnley (Loaned on 21/11/89) FL 7+2
Notts Co (Loaned on 28/3/91) FL 0+2
Burnley (£60,000 on 17/8/91) FL 162/22 FLC 10/2 FAC 18/1 Others 13
Luton T (£750,000 on 13/7/95) FL 79+1/10 FLC 8 FAC 3 Others 8/1

DAVIS Steven (Steve) Peter
Born: Birmingham, 26 July 1965
Height: 6'0" Weight: 12.12
International Honours: E: Yth

Formed a crucial partnership with Arjan de Zeeuw at the heart of the Barnsley defence in 1996-97 until his season was cruelly ended in January when he suffered a broken leg in the game at QPR, following a challenge by John Spencer, a man who was on his way to a hat trick in a 3-1 win over the Reds. Good in the air, and a menace at set pieces, he scored a number of crucial goals, notably the winner in a 3-2 home victory over Portsmouth, and is working hard to be fit in time for the coming Premiership campaign.

Crewe Alex (Free from Stoke C juniors on 17/8/83) FL 140+5/1 FLC 10 FAC 3 Others 7+1
Burnley (£15,000 on 3/10/87) FL 147/11 FLC 7 FAC 9 Others 19/1
Barnsley (£180,000 on 26/7/91) FL 103+4/10 FLC 9 FAC 3

DAVISON Aidan John
Born: Sedgefield, 11 May 1968
Height: 6'1" Weight: 13.12
International Honours: NI: 2; B-1

Unable to get a place in the Bolton line up last season, being behind Keith Branagan and Gavin Ward in the goalkeeping pecking order, Aidan was loaned out to Hull City in November for two months and gave some reliable and solid, if unspectacular, displays while covering for Roy Carroll, who had suffered a shoulder injury and was indisposed. Later, with Bradford having lost three vital games and in danger of being relegated, the Northern Ireland international moved on a short-term contract in order to help them out. In becoming an overnight hero, he did more than that, pulling off some incredible saves and keeping four clean sheets in the last ten matches as the Bantams maintained their first division place on the very last day of the campaign.

Notts Co (Signed from Billingham Synthonia on 25/3/88) FL 1
Bury (£6,000 on 7/10/89)
Millwall (Free on 14/8/91) FL 34 FLC 3 FAC 3 Others 2
Bolton W (£25,000 on 26/7/93) P/FL 35+2 FAC 8 Others 4
Hull C (Loaned on 29/11/96) FL 9 Others 1
Bradford C (Free on 14/3/97) FL 10

DAWS Anthony (Tony)
Born: Sheffield, 10 September 1966
Height: 5'8" Weight: 11.10
International Honours: E: Yth; Sch

Released by Lincoln during the summer of 1996, the hard-working striker with a good scoring record joined Scarborough at the start of 1996-97. Unfortunately, his progress was hampered by a pre-season stress fracture of his tibia, and he was out injured for a lengthy period, prior to being released from his contract in December. Had a brief spell with Altrincham before moving on to Unibond League club, Bradford Park Avenue.

Notts Co (From apprentice on 18/9/84) FL 6+2/1
Sheffield U (Free on 21/8/86) FL 7+4/3 FAC 1 Others 0+1
Scunthorpe U (Free on 2/7/87) FL 166+17/63 FLC 15+1/4 FAC 9/2 Others 23+1/3
Grimsby T (£50,000 on 25/3/93) FL 14+2/1 FLC 2 Others 1+1/1
Lincoln C (£50,000 on 15/2/94) FL 42+9/13 FAC 1+1 Others 2
Scarborough (Free on 2/8/96) FL 4+2 FLC 1/1 FAC 1+1 Others 1

DAWS Nicholas (Nick) John
Born: Manchester, 15 March 1970
Height: 5'11" Weight: 13.2
Club Honours: Div 2 '97

A wholehearted midfield battler whose non-stop running has made him a firm favourite at Bury, he competed in all 46 of the Shakers' league games in their division two championship season of 1996-97. Although goals from the midfielder were infrequent, Nick scored in successive matches over Easter, including an all-important spectacular winner against top of the table Brentford at Griffin Park, which was subsequently voted as Bury's Goal of the Season.

Bury (£10,000 from Altrincham on 13/8/92) FL 177+13/7 FLC 12+3/1 FAC 10 Others 13+2/1

DAY Christopher (Chris) Nicholas
Born: Whipps Cross, 28 July 1975
Height: 6'2" Weight: 13.6

International Honours: E: U21-6, Yth

Transferred from Spurs to Crystal Palace during the 1996 close season, following Nigel Martyn's move to Leeds, the young England U21 international goalkeeper made his league debut on the opening day of last season at Birmingham and went on to appear 28 times in all, keeping eight clean sheets in a defence that ended joint best in the first division. Although eventually replaced by Carlo Nash, Chris, in his first term of league football, had proved an agile shot stopper and excellent dead-ball kicker.

Tottenham H (From trainee on 16/4/93)
Crystal Palace (£225,000+ on 9/8/96) FL 24 FLC 2 FAC 2

DEAN Michael James
Born: Weymouth, 9 March 1978
Height: 5'10" Weight: 11.12

After breaking into Bournemouth's first team in 1995-96, Michael established himself as a squad member last season, making intermittent appearances in the team mostly as cover for injuries and suspensions. Playing mainly in the centre of midfield and a good passer of the ball, he showed enough ability to suggest it will not be long before he commands a regular first team place.

Bournemouth (From trainee on 4/7/96) FL 14+3 FAC 1

DEANE Brian Christopher
Born: Leeds, 7 February 1968
Height: 6'3" Weight: 12.7
International Honours: E: 3; B-3

Began 1996-97 at Leeds in his usual central role, only to suffer a bad groin injury during the game at Derby, which resulted in him missing the first three months of the season. Upon his return, he added power and strength to the front line, something which was sorely missed in his absence, being particularly impressive when scoring fine goals against Chelsea and Sunderland in the victories at Elland Road, results which enabled the club to move away from the relegation zone. Having worked tirelessly in a campaign where the side struggled for goals, Brian again proved to be an excellent target man, his skill unsettling defenders, thus allowing others to take advantage.

Doncaster Rov (From juniors on 14/12/85) FL 59+7/12 FLC 3 FAC 2+1/1 Others 2+2
Sheffield U (£30,000 on 19/7/88) F/PL 197/82 FLC 16/11 FAC 23+1/11 Others 2/2
Leeds U (£2,900,000 on 14/7/93) PL 131+7/32 FLC 8+3/2 FAC 13+3/4 Others 3

DEARDEN Kevin Charles
Born: Luton, 8 March 1970
Height: 5'11" Weight: 12.8

Extremely reliable Brentford goalkeeper who has few peers at second division level. A fine shot stopper, one he saved low to his left against Shrewsbury being particularly impressive, but, unfortunately, 1996-97 will always be remembered for the game at Bristol Rovers in October when he heard a whistle, subsequently blamed on a spectator, and put the ball down only for a Rovers' forward to dribble the ball in for a goal. The incident was later featured on A Question of Sport. In a season when Bees went close to

promotion, via the play offs, Kevin missed just three games, while keeping 20 clean sheets.

Tottenham H (From trainee on 5/8/88) PL 0+1 FLC 1
Cambridge U (Loaned on 9/3/89) FL 15
Hartlepool U (Loaned on 31/8/89) FL 10
Swindon T (Loaned on 23/3/90) FL 1
Peterborough U (Loaned on 24/8/90) FL 7
Hull C (Loaned on 10/1/91) FL 3
Rochdale (Loaned on 16/8/91) FL 2
Birmingham C (Loaned on 19/3/92) FL 12
Brentford (Free on 30/9/93) FL 163 FLC 12 FAC 10 Others 16

Kevin Dearden

DEARY John Steele
Born: Ormskirk, 18 October 1962
Height: 5'9" Weight: 12.4
Club Honours: Div 4 '92

A midfield battler who liked to get forward in 1996-97, John was again a model of consistency and professionalism for Rochdale. Also had a successful season on the scoring front, and even managed to stay out of trouble with referees (while training to be one himself!), before being released during the summer.

Blackpool (From apprentice on 13/3/80) FL 285+18/43 FLC 20/5 FAC 16+2/4 Others 14/1
Burnley (£30,000 on 18/7/89) FL 209+6/23 FLC 13+3/1 FAC 20+1/2 Others 21/1
Rochdale (£25,000 on 30/1/95) FL 90+1/10 FLC 3/1 FAC 5/3 Others 7/1

DEBONT Andrew (Andy) Cornelius
Born: Wolverhampton, 7 February 1974
Height: 6'2" Weight: 15.6

Having played on loan at Hereford at the tail end of 1995-96, Andy joined them

permanently on being freed by Wolves during the summer and started 1996-97 where he left off as their first choice goalkeeper. Playing in 32 successive games before being injured, he eventually came back for the final game of the campaign only to be part of the side that plummeted into the Conference. Showed himself to be an agile all-rounder, though.

Wolverhampton W (From trainee on 7/7/92)
Hartlepool U (Loaned on 13/10/95) FL 1
Hereford U (Loaned on 21/3/96) FL 8
Hereford U (Free on 12/8/96) FL 27 FLC 4 FAC 1 Others 1

DELAP Rory John
Born: Sutton Coldfield, 6 July 1976
Height: 6'0" Weight: 12.3
Club Honour: AMC '97
International Honours: Ei: U21-3

One of the most versatile players in the Carlisle squad. Rory appeared equally at home as a striker or as a right-wing back for the club in 1996-97, his attributes including a powerful right-foot shot, good ball control, and a long throw that caused problems for many an opposing defence. Now an established member of the Eire U21 squad, he is yet another young player at the club who can look forward to the future with confidence.

Carlisle U (From trainee on 18/7/94) FL 32+24/7 FLC 3+1 FAC 0+3 Others 10+2

DEMPSEY Mark Anthony
Born: Dublin, 10 December 1972
Height: 5'7" Weight: 12.5
International Honours: Ei: U21-5; Yth

Where does he play next, that was the question all Shrewsbury fans were asking in 1996-97. Capable of playing on the left wing, or in midfield, and a complete revelation at left back after he switched there in the autumn, he looked very comfortable and was one of the most consistent players at Gay Meadow. It was from there that he was able to show his attacking roots on many occasions with speedy runs to the line, matched by fine crosses, and how the fans loved it.

Gillingham (From trainee on 9/8/90) FL 27+21/2 FLC 0+1 FAC 5 Others 6
Leyton Orient (Free on 4/7/94) FL 43/1 FLC 2 FAC 1+1 Others 5/1
Shrewsbury T (£25,000 on 4/7/95) FL 54+14/2 FLC 2+3 FAC 5+3/2 Others 7+1/1

DENNIS John Anthony (Tony)
Born: Maidenhead, 1 December 1963
Height: 5'8" Weight: 13.0
Club Honours: Div 3 '91

A veteran midfield player signed on a free transfer from Colchester United in the summer of 1996, Tony lost his Lincoln place early on last season and then had to battle with Mark Hone for a first-team spot. Released on a free transfer at the end of the campaign, he proved a useful acquisition, scoring two goals and looking quite lively on occasions.

Plymouth Arg (From apprentice on 3/12/81) FL 7+2 FLC 1/1 FAC 0+1
Exeter C (Free on 15/8/83) FL 3+1 FLC 1 (Free to Bideford on 1/10/83)

Cambridge U (£15,000 from Slough T, via Taunton, on 22/2/89) FL 89+22/10 FLC 6+2 FAC 2+4 Others 7+2/1
Chesterfield (£20,000 on 15/6/93) FL 4+6 FLC 2 Others 2
Colchester U (Free on 10/8/94) FL 56+9/5 FLC 2 FAC 1+3 Others 5+1
Lincoln C (Free on 30/7/96) FL 23+5/2 FLC 1+2 Others 1

DENNIS Kevin Jason
Born: Islington, 14 December 1976
Height: 5'10" Weight: 12.0

An outside left who is a good crosser of the ball, Kevin joined Brentford in the 1996 close season after being released by Arsenal, but, apart from three brief appearances, did not get into the team until late March. However, when in the side he made some good contributions, appearing in 12 of the final 14 matches, including the second leg of the play offs, and gave signs of better things to come.

Brentford (Free from Arsenal juniors on 23/7/96) FL 9+3 Others 3

DENNISON Robert (Robbie)
Born: Banbridge, 30 April 1963
Height: 5'7" Weight: 12.0
Club Honours: AMC '88; Div 4 '88, Div 3 '89
International Honours: NI: 18; B-1; Yth

The veteran Wolves' left winger joined proceedings in October, when he occupied a deeper role than previously used to, setting up a goal for Steve Corica at Palace with a long pass, then against Manchester City venturing up to curl in a beauty with his left foot. This turned the clock back a few years for those who had followed his career, it being his 50th goal for the club. He then began eight successive games up until January, even returning from the Northern Ireland international wilderness to come on as sub for the last ten minutes in Italy, but, from then on, just two brief outings saw his campaign wind down prior to his release during the summer.

West Bromwich A (£40,000 from Glenavon on 13/9/85) FL 9+7/1 FLC 1 FAC 2 Others 1
Wolverhampton W (£20,000 on 13/3/87) FL 264+29/40 FLC 12+4/3 FAC 16+2/2 Others 24+2/4
Swansea C (Loaned on 5/10/95) FL 9 Others 2

DERRY Shaun Peter
Born: Nottingham, 6 December 1977
Height: 5'10" Weight: 10.13

After breaking through for Notts County at the tail end of 1995-96 as a right back, he reverted to his preferred central midfield role during 1996-97, missing very few games, and was repeatedly watched by a number of Premiership clubs. An excellent passer of the ball, Shaun is tipped to have a bright future.

Notts Co (From trainee on 13/4/96) FL 49+2/2 FLC 2 FAC 4 Others 3

DESOUZA Miquel Juan
Born: Newham, 11 February 1970
Height: 6'0" Weight: 13.8

After the previous season's 20-goal haul for Wycombe, his seven in 38 starts in 1996-97 was a little disappointing. First choice

central striker for most of 1996-97 before rejoining his former manager, Barry Fry, at Peterborough during the transfer deadline week, his devastating acceleration, on occasion, caused havoc, particularly when playing down the wings. His ability to get in behind the opposing defences saw him get off to a flier at London Road with two goals in the final eight games and he will almost certainly be one of the players Posh will be looking to, regards a quick return to the second division.

Charlton Ath (Signed from Clapton on 4/7/89)
Bristol C (Free on 1/8/90)
Birmingham C (£25,000 from Dagenham & Redbridge, via Yeovil T, Dorchester T and Bashley, on 1/2/94) FL 5+10 FLC 2 Others 1
Bury (Loaned on 25/11/94) FL 2+1
Wycombe W (£80,000 on 27/1/95) FL 73+10/29 FLC 8/2 FAC 6/2 Others 3
Peterborough U (£50,000 on 26/3/97) FL 8/2

Sean Devine

DEVINE Sean Thomas
Born: Lewisham, 6 September 1972
Height: 6'0" Weight: 13.0
Plagued by injury since last Christmas, it was a measure of his ability that he still finished as Barnet's top goalscorer. Lightning quick and aggressive, he happily scored the spectaculars and the tap ins alike, his hat trick in the 3-0 defeat of Exeter being merely typical, a header, a touch and a tremendous 20-yard left foot drive doing the business.

Barnet (£10,000 from Famagusta on 5/10/95) FL 65+1/30 FLC 4/1 FAC 5/5 Others 3

DEVLIN Mark Andrew
Born: Irvine, 18 January 1973
Height: 5'10" Weight: 11.3
International Honours: S: Yth
A versatile midfielder whose appearances

for Stoke in 1996-97 were again mainly from the substitutes' bench, Mark found himself still unable to command a regular first-team place after a number of seasons on the fringes. Having come back from serious injury, he will be hoping to break through in 1997-98.

Stoke C (From trainee on 6/4/91) FL 39+16/2 FLC 4+1 Others 3+2

DEVLIN Paul John
Born: Birmingham, 14 April 1972
Height: 5'9" Weight: 11.5
Club Honours: AIC '95
A life-long Birmingham fan, Paul can play either down the middle or wide on the right. As a brave and aggressive tackler whose spiky style has made him a favourite with the fans, but has also resulted in the occasional red card, he was leading goalscorer during 1996-97 season, and easily won the Blues' Player of the Year award. Also scored the Goal of the Season at QPR in January, and hit a rich vein of form with eight in as many games.

Notts Co (£40,000 from Stafford R on 22/2/92) FL 132+9/25 FLC 11+1/1 FAC 8/1 Others 17+2/4
Birmingham C (Signed on 29/2/96) FL 48+6/23 FLC 3+1/1 FAC 3/2

DEVOS Jason Richard
Born: Canada, 2 January 1974
Height: 6'4" Weight: 13.7
A Canadian Olympic Games' player, signed from Montreal Impact in November 1996, Jason established himself in the heart of the Darlington defence in 1996-97, before a broken foot curtailed his season and saw him back in Canada for treatment. Has extended his short-term contract and will return for this season.

Darlington (Free from Montreal Impact on 29/11/96) FL 7+1 FAC 1

DEWHURST Robert (Rob) Matthew
Born: Keighley, 10 September 1971
Height: 6'3" Weight: 14.0
Fought back strongly in 1996-97 from the broken leg suffered in December 1995, resuming full training in April, to finally re-establish himself as the kingpin of the Hull City defence last October. Left-footed, Rob is strong in the air and the tackle and fully deserves the contract which keeps him at Boothferry to the end of 1998-99.

Blackburn Rov (From trainee on 15/10/90) FL 13 FLC 2 Others 1
Darlington (Loaned on 20/12/91) FL 11/1 Others 1
Huddersfield T (Loaned on 2/10/92) FL 7
Hull C (Free on 5/11/93) FL 104+2/10 FLC 5 FAC 7 Others 5

DE ZEEUW Adrianus (Arjan) Johannes
Born: Holland, 16 April 1970
Height: 6'1" Weight: 13.11
In 1996-97, Arjan again showed why he is considered by many to be one of the best central defenders outside of the Premiership and, with Barnsley having been promoted as runners up to Bolton, this coming season will see him able to pit his skills against the best the division has to offer. As a tall, quick player who can pass, tackle and head with equal success, his ability to read a situation

got the Reds out of a number of tight situations with the minimum amount of fuss. Is also a good man to have at set pieces, two headers in consecutive games being a useful addition to the scoring charts.

Barnsley (£250,000 from Telstar on 3/11/95) FL 74/3 FLC 4 FAC 4

DIA Aly
Born: Daker, Senegal, 20 August 1965
Height: 5'10" Weight: 11.2
Signed by Southampton on a reported personal recommendation to Graeme Souness given by George Weah, Aly came to the Dell on a monthly contract last November and just a day later made his first-team debut as a sub, replacing Matt le Tissier in the 33rd minute, during the home game against Leeds. Unfortunately, having shone on the training ground as a player who could be used up front, his form was such that he himself had to be replaced 52 minutes later. Following his trial period, he joined non-league Gateshead.

Southampton (Free from Lubeck on 22/11/96) PL 0+1

DIAZ Isidro (Izzy)
Born: Valencia, Spain, 15 May 1972
Height: 5'7" Weight: 9.6
Club Honours: Div 3 '97
The pacy Wigan Athletic right winger continued to be a thorn in the side of many defenders with his speed in 1996-97, despite not being as consistent as in the previous season. On his day, the best wide forward outside the Premiership, two wonder strikes at Carlisle ensured Latics of their most impressive away win of the campaign, his first goal picking up the Away Goal of the Season award. Also produced the pass that saw David Lowe make sure that a third division championship medal came his way, when scoring the second goal in the 2-0 win over Mansfield on the final day of the campaign.

Wigan Ath (Free from Balaguer on 25/7/95) FL 57+19/16 FLC 2+1 FAC 4+1/2 Others 3

DIBBLE Andrew (Andy) Gerald
Born: Cwmbran, 8 May 1965
Height: 6'2" Weight: 13.7
International Honours: W: 3; U21-3; Yth; Sch
After a complete season in the wilderness at Manchester City, Andy came back into the first team at home to Barnsley under temporary manager, Asa Hartford, in 1996-97. To hopefully produce more dialogue in the penalty area, the experienced goalie had a run of 14 league and cup games before being relegated to the reserve team. During this run, it is fair to say that he turned in some good performances and indeed contributed to the few successes the team had in the first half of the season. Spent the last six weeks of the Bells Scottish Premier League at Glasgow Rangers on loan, starting with the Old Firm derby away at Celtic Park, while looking to establish his career in first-team football. Is a good clubman.

Cardiff C (From apprentice on 27/8/82) FL 62 FLC 4 FAC 4

Luton T (£125,000 on 16/7/84) FL 30 FLC 4 FAC 1 Others 1
Sunderland (Loaned on 21/2/86) FL 12
Huddersfield T (Loaned on 26/3/87) FL 5
Manchester C (£240,000 on 1/7/88) F/PL 113+3 FLC 14 FAC 8+1 Others 2
Aberdeen (Loaned on 20/10/90) SL 5
Middlesbrough (Loaned on 20/2/91) FL 19 Others 2
Bolton W (Loaned on 6/9/91) FL 13 Others 1
West Bromwich A (Loaned on 27/2/92) FL 9

DICHIO Daniele (Danny) Salvatore Ernest
Born: Hammersmith, 19 October 1974
Height: 6'3" Weight: 12.3
International Honours: E: U21-1; Sch

For a striker who is very good in the air, packs a fair wallop in his boots, has some nice touches, and brings his team mates into the game, Danny failed to notch as many goals for Queens Park Rangers in 1996-97 as in the previous season, although among those he did score some were certainly spectacular. Having opened his seasonal account with the winner at Loftus Road against Oxford, his next strike was a tremendous 30-yard shot that crashed into the Wolves' net for the equaliser, and five goals later he signed off the campaign with the first in a 2-0 home win over Tranmere. Stop Press: With his contract up during the summer it was reported that he had agreed a three-year deal with the Italian side, Sampdoria.

Queens Park R (From trainee on 17/5/93) P/FL 56+19/20 FLC 6/2 FAC 3+3
Barnet (Loaned on 24/3/94) FL 9/2

DICKINSON Patrick James
Born: Vancouver, Canada, 6 May 1978
Height: 5'10" Weight: 10.8
International Honours: Canada: Yth

Following a fine run of performances for Hull City reserves, the second-year trainee was handed his debut when coming on as a half-time substitute at Doncaster last March. Is a left-sided midfielder who has earned the reputation of being an excellent crosser.
Hull C (Trainee) FL 0+1

DICKOV Paul
Born: Livingston, 1 November 1972
Height: 5'6" Weight: 11.9
Club Honours: ECWC '94
International Honours: S: U21-4; Yth; Sch

Signed by Alan Ball from Arsenal last August and making his Manchester City debut as a substitute at Stoke City, the game which led to the departure of Ball, he came with a steady report. Small in stature, but making up for it with determination and tenacity and working hard for the 90 minutes, Paul had a good run through until Christmas under various managers, scoring four goals. Following Frank Clark's arrival he was often overlooked, but came back into first-team contention in February and March, giving his all, before being subbed usually in the last quarter of the games.
Arsenal (From trainee on 28/12/90) PL 6+15/3 FLC 2+2/3
Luton T (Loaned on 8/10/93) FL 8+7/1
Brighton & Hove A (Loaned on 23/3/94) FL 8/5
Manchester C (£1,000,000 on 23/8/96) FL 25+4/5 FLC 2 FAC 0+1

DICKS Julian Andrew
Born: Bristol, 8 August 1968
Height: 5'10" Weight: 13.0
International Honours: E: B-2; U21-4

The West Ham captain and hard-tackling left back had another inspirational season in 1996-97, leading by example and, as one of Upton Park's all-time favourite sons, he was unsurprisingly voted Hammer of the Year by the supporters. Perhaps more surprisingly, detailed computer analysis comparing different players in the same position and published in the Observer newspaper late in the season indicated that he was the most effective left back in the Premier League. Despite that, his belligerent style may not have endeared him to England manager, Glenn Hoddle! In scoring six league goals, five from the penalty spot, and all but one matchwinners or point savers, he enjoyed a superb game against Tottenham in February, scoring twice, including the clinching goal from a penalty in a see-saw 4-3 epic, which proved to be the turning point of Hammers' season. Although missing the closing matches through injury, the club were, by then, well on their way to safety. His amazing record of 64 goals (from 314 games) for the Hammers alone, makes him one of the highest-scoring full backs of all time in league football.
Birmingham C (From apprentice on 12/4/86) FL 83+6/1 FLC 5+1 FAC 5 Others 2
West Ham U (£300,000 on 25/3/88) FL 159/29 FLC 19/5 FAC 14/2 Others 11/4
Liverpool (£1,500,000 on 17/9/93) PL 24/3 FLC 3 FAC 1
West Ham U (£1,000,000 on 20/10/94) PL 94/21 FLC 10/3 FAC 7

Julian Dicks

DIGBY Fraser Charles
Born: Sheffield, 23 April 1967
Height: 6'1" Weight: 12.12
Club Honours: Div 2 '96
International Honours: E: U21-5; Yth; Sch

Swindon Town's longest-serving player by far, Fraser completed his tenth and testimonial season at the County Ground in 1996-97 and, barring injury or transfer, should make his 500th appearance for the Robins during the coming term. Usurped by Frank Talia as first-choice 'keeper for the first three months of the campaign, he was restored to first-team duty in November and held his place, even surviving the two defensive disasters at Bolton and Oldham, which suggested that the manager, Steve McMahon, felt that the culpability lay elsewhere in the team. A testimonial match against his former club, Manchester United, was scheduled for the past summer.
Manchester U (From apprentice on 25/4/85)
Swindon T (£32,000 on 25/9/86) F/PL 379 FLC 32 FAC 20 Others 33+1

DILLON Paul William
Born: Limerick, 22 October 1978
Height: 5'9" Weight: 10.11
International Honours: Ei: Yth

Skipper of the successful Rotherham junior team, Paul got his first-team chance earlier than expected, but made an immediate impact with his commendable never-say-die attitude. Given his debut at Millwall last February, he became an automatic choice for the rest of the season and, to cap it all, he smashed home Rotherham's goal of the season, beating Gillingham's Jim Stannard from all of 40 yards. Definitely a star of the future.
Rotherham U (From trainee on 7/3/97) FL 11+2/1

DI MATTEO Roberto
Born: Switzerland, 29 May 1970
Height: 5'10" Weight: 12.5
Club Honours: FAC '97
International Honours: Italy: 26

Three days after the capture of Frank Leboeuf during the 1996 close season, Chelsea smashed their transfer record when paying Lazio £4.9 million for Italian international midfield star, Roberto. Born in Switzerland of Italian parents, he was voted Swiss Player of the Year in 1993 for his part in FC Aarau's first post-war championship, before moving on to Lazio and becoming a fixture in the Italian national team. The complete midfield player, he became one of the most effective in the Premiership. He can tackle firmly, pass superbly and, to use *Coachspeak*, the lad has a good engine which enables him to get upfield to shoot dynamically, his match winner at Tottenham in February being a prime example. Was instrumental in Chelsea's two January victories over Liverpool at the Bridge – striding forward to score the only goal in the league match on New Year's day with a crisp shot and dominating midfield in the epic fourth-round FA Cup victory. One of his most effective matches during 1996-97, to the chagrin of England supporters, came in the World Cup qualifier at Wembley, when he played, superbly in Italy's 1-0 victory. Three days later, in the televised fifth-round FA Cup tie at Filbert Street, he scored another superb goal, dribbling in from the left wing and hitting a fierce right-footed shot into the far corner of the net and played magnificently in the next two rounds

Roberto di Matteo (left)

as Ruud Gullit's cosmopolitan Chelsea ultimately lifted the FA Cup for the second time. Voted Man of the Match at Wembley, following his record-breaking 43-second goal in the 2-0 win over Middlesbrough, the Italian's season was complete.
Chelsea (£4,900,000 from Lazio, via FC Aarac, FC Zurich and Schaffhausen, on 17/7/96) PL 33+1/7 FLC 3 FAC 7/2

DINNING Anthony (Tony)
Born: Wallsend, 12 April 1975
Height: 6'0" Weight: 12.11
Although a fringe player at Stockport in 1996-97, Tony played an important part in the club's fine season. Regularly stepping in as a defensive midfielder or central defender, and proving versatile as a substitute, he brought solidity and composure to many hectic situations in an incredible season for County. He also got himself on the scoresheet three times.
Newcastle U (From trainee on 1/10/93)
Stockport Co (Free on 23/6/94) FL 51+19/4 FLC 4+4 FAC 0+6 Others 6+1/2

DIUK Wayne John
Born: Nottingham, 26 May 1980
Height: 5'11" Weight: 11.0
Following some consistent and skilful midfield displays in a highly successful Notts County youth team in 1996-97, Wayne made his league debut when coming off the bench for the final eight minutes of the season, a home fixture against Chesterfield. Still a trainee, he looks to be a real prospect.
Notts Co (Trainee) FL 0+1

DIXON Benjamin (Ben) Marcus
Born: Lincoln, 16 September 1974
Height: 6'1" Weight: 11.0

Signed during the summer of 1996 from Lincoln, Ben's Blackpool appearances at left back last season were somewhat limited due to the good form of Andy Barlow. Able to play in midfield as well as on the wing, his height was often useful to have at both ends of the park.
Lincoln C (From trainee on 4/11/92) FL 33+10 FLC 2 FAC 0+1 Others 2+1
Blackpool (£20,000 on 12/7/96) FL 3+8 FLC 2 FAC 1 Others 2

DIXON Kerry Michael
Born: Luton, 24 July 1961
Height: 6'0" Weight: 13.10
Club Honours: Div 2 '84, '89; FMC '90
International Honours: E: 8; U21-1
Appointed Doncaster Rovers' player/manager just one hour before the opening game of 1996-97, having been at Watford previously, the former Chelsea and England striker had a fairly traumatic time of it during his first season in the hot seat at Belle Vue, there being a number of problems to deal with both on and off the field. On the playing front, his appearances were limited by ill health and injury - although a super glancing header in a 3-2 home win over Darlington for his opening goal showed that he could still do it when required - and he may now decide that the time is now right to concentrate on the management side of things. Is a firm favourite with the fans who wish him nothing but goodwill.
Tottenham H (From apprentice on 1/7/78)
Reading (£20,000 from Dunstable on 22/7/80) FL 110+6/51 FLC 6+1 FAC 2+1
Chelsea (£175,000 on 4/8/83) FL 331+4/147 FLC 40+1/24 FAC 18+2/8 Others 25/12
Southampton (£575,000 on 19/7/92) PL 8+1/2 FLC 2 FAC 1
Luton T (Free on 19/2/93) FL 66+9/19 FLC 2 FAC 7+2 Others 2/1

Millwall (£5,000 on 23/3/95) FL 24+7/9 FLC 1+2 FAC 1
Watford (£25,000 on 12/1/96) FL 8+3
Doncaster Rov (Free on 19/8/96) FL 13+3/3 FLC 2 FAC 1 Others 1

DIXON Lee Michael
Born: Manchester, 17 March 1964
Height: 5'9" Weight: 11.8
Club Honours: Div 1 '89, '91; FAC '93; ECWC '94
International Honours: E: 21; B-4
The two-footed right-wing back enjoyed a new lease of life for Arsenal in 1996-97 under the new manager, Arsene Wenger, his attacking instincts being given more freedom within the three-man defensive system. A player who has always been able to get forward to cross the ball to his front men and occasionally to get into good shooting positions himself, he scored the vital first goal in a 2-1 win at Newcastle in November as ten men overcame the Magpies for what turned out to be an important result. Also scored in a 3-0 home win over Leeds. Although recognised for his attacking talents, one must not forget that he was an integral part of a defence that conceded less goals than any other Premiership team during the campaign, 14 away from home being outstanding. Will complete ten years at Highbury this coming season.
Burnley (From juniors on 21/7/82) FL 4 FLC 1
Chester C (Free on 16/2/84) FL 56+1/1 FLC 2 FAC 1 Others 3
Bury (Free on 15/7/85) FL 45/5 FLC 4 FAC 8/1 Others 1
Stoke C (£40,000 on 18/7/86) FL 71/5 FLC 6 FAC 7 Others 4
Arsenal (£400,000 on 29/1/88) F/PL 320+4/20 FLC 42 FAC 29/1 Others 29

DOBBIN James (Jim)
Born: Dunfermline, 17 September 1963
Height: 5'10" Weight: 10.7
International Honours: S: Yth
Signed by Rotherham after being released by Grimsby during the 1996 close season, being brought to the club in the hope that his experience would prove invaluable, he had to wait until the end of September to get his chance. His debut coincided with the team's first win of the season and he immediately took over as skipper, before losing his place in December and being released during the summer when the rebuilding process started to take place. A midfielder with shooting ability, Jim's passing skills have never gone unrecognised.
Glasgow Celtic (Free from Whitburn BC on 9/10/80) SL 1+1 SLC 4/1
Motherwell (Loaned on 1/2/84) SL 1+1
Doncaster Rov (£25,000 on 19/3/84) FL 56+8/13 FLC 5/1 FAC 2 Others 3
Barnsley (£35,000 on 19/9/86) FL 116+13/12 FLC 3+1 FAC 11 Others 4/1
Grimsby T (£55,000 on 15/7/91) FL 154+10/21 FLC 13/3 FAC 7+1/1 Others 5/1
Rotherham U (Free on 2/8/96) FL 17+2 FLC 0+1 FAC 1 Others 1

DOBIE Robert **Scott**
Born: Workington, 10 October 1978
Height: 6'1" Weight: 11.12
A YTS trainee who made substitute

appearances for Carlisle in the final two games of last season, Scott marked his debut with a well-taken goal after coming on against Rochdale at Brunton Park with 22 minutes left on the clock. Racing on to a Warren Aspinall pass to finish clinically from 16 yards was a dream start for the young forward who has recently been rewarded with a five-year contract and he is sure to be given further chances in 1997-98.

Carlisle U (From trainee on 10/5/97) FL 0+2/1

DOBSON Anthony (Tony) John
Born: Coventry, 5 February 1969
Height: 6'1" Weight: 13.6
Club Honours: FAYC '87
International Honours: E: U21-4

Portsmouth's perennial substitute who is solid and reliable when called upon as cover for one of the three centre halves, Tony started just five games in 1996-97, prior to being released in the summer. However, as in previous seasons, the former England U21 man never let the side down and could always be relied upon to do the job in hand, his fierce tackling and defensive capability being up to the task in hand. Can also play at left back.

Coventry C (From apprentice on 7/7/86) FL 51+3/1 FLC 5+3 Others 0+1
Blackburn Rov (£300,000 on 17/1/91) F/PL 36+5 FLC 5 FAC 2 Others 1
Portsmouth (£150,000 on 22/9/93) FL 48+5/2 FLC 6 FAC 1+2 Others 4/1
Oxford U (Loaned on 15/12/94) FL 5
Peterborough U (Loaned on 29/1/96) FL 4

DODD Jason Robert
Born: Bath, 2 November 1970
Height: 5'11" Weight: 12.3
International Honours: E: U21-8

An outstanding Southampton player, and eyed by many of the leading Premiership clubs, Jason, who was once recognised exclusively as a right back, has since become more versatile, being able to perform with equal ability as a wing back, in midfield, or as a central defender, whenever the need. In short, he is the perfect clubman and one of the first names on the team sheet whenever fit. A great reader of the game, he was back to his very best towards the end of 1996-97, his fitness worries of earlier weeks seemingly behind him as Saints successfully fought off relegation to the first division. Able to defend, pass the ball well, and win aerial battles, hopefully, he will stay injury free this coming term as the club prepares to consolidate.

Southampton (£50,000 from Bath C on 15/3/89) F/PL 179+16/6 FLC 25+1 FAC 21/1 Others 5

DOHERTY Thomas (Tommy) Edward
Born: Bristol, 17 March 1979
Height: 5'8" Weight: 9.13

This young midfielder had the distinction of making his Bristol City debut in the 9-2 win over St Albans in the FA Cup last December, while still a trainee, when coming on as substitute after 60 minutes when City were 6-0 ahead. Renowned in the reserves for his enthusiastic style and sharp tackling, it is hoped that he will soon be challenging strongly for a regular spot in the Robins' midfield.

Bristol C (Trainee) FAC 0+1

DOLBY Tony Christopher
Born: Greenwich, 16 June 1974
Height: 5'11" Weight: 13.0
Club Honours: FAYC '91

Tony played mainly on the left-hand side of midfield for Millwall in 1996-97, scoring with a tremendous free kick at Luton which he flighted in at the angle of bar and post. Although his quickness in the tackle saw him collect a number of bookings last season, more through impetuosity than petulance, his neat and tidy control more than compensated. Released during the summer.

Millwall (From trainee on 29/10/91) FL 38+28/3 FLC 5+1 FAC 0+1 Others 3+1
Barnet (Loaned on 16/2/94) FL 13+3/2

DOLING Stuart James
Born: Newport, IOW, 28 October 1972
Height: 5'7" Weight: 11.6
International Honours: E: Yth

Stuart has barely figured in first team affairs since joining Doncaster Rovers from non-league Lymington in October, 1995, his continuing problems with a groin injury delaying his full league debut until last November – more than a year after moving to Belle Vue. A strong midfielder with good passing skills, he was unfortunate to suffer further injuries, which again blighted his season, and he was released in April.

Portsmouth (From trainee on 25/6/90) FL 20+17/4 FLC 4+3 FAC 1 Others 4+3/1 (Free to Lymington on 3/7/95)
Doncaster Rov (Free on 30/10/95) FL 3+3

Jason Dodd

DONALDSON O'Neill McKay
Born: Birmingham, 24 November 1969
Height: 6'0" Weight: 11.8
The past season was just as frustrating for O'Neill as was his first at Sheffield Wednesday, with just a handful of appearances being made. The bubbly, pacy striker could not make progress but, after just two subs' appearances, he made a breakthrough with a few games to go and inspired the Owls to a win over Wimbledon when he scored his second goal for the club, and followed that with Wednesday's final goal of the season in the last day draw with Liverpool. On his day a match winner, he can only hope for a breakthrough in 1997-98, but certainly ended 1996-97 in the right mood.
Shrewsbury T (Free from Hinckley T on 13/11/91) FL 15+13/4 Others 1
Doncaster Rov (Free on 10/8/94) FL 7+2/2 FLC 2 Others 0+1
Mansfield T (Loaned on 23/12/94) FL 4/6 FAC 1/1
Sheffield Wed (£50,000 on 9/1/95) PL 3+6/3

DONCEL-VARCARCEL Antonio
Born: Lugo, Spain, 31 January 1967
Height: 6'0" Weight: 12.1
Signed during the 1996 close season, and the first Spaniard to represent Hull City, Antonio is a right-footed player who displayed the assured style common amongst his countrymen. Used at right back and in the centre of midfield, but looking most accomplished in the sweeper role, an encouraging start came to a shuddering halt when he damaged knee ligaments at Swansea in September. Had previously played for Deportivo la Coruna (over 100 appearances between 1988 and 1994), Burgos, Levante, and El Ferrol in Spain.
Hull C (Free from Ferrol on 8/8/96) FL 22+4/2 FLC 2 FAC 1+1 Others 1

DONIS Georgios
Born: Frankfurt, 22 October 1969
Height: 6'0" Weight: 12.6
International Honours: Greece: 24
Brought to Blackburn from Panathanaikos during the 1996 close season in order to provide the crosses for Alan Shearer, the speedy left winger could well be excused for feeling bemused at what happened at Ewood in 1996-97. Possessing electrifying pace and a fine crosser of the ball, he perhaps became discouraged when the strikers failed to turn his good work into goals. Opened his scoring account, however, with a memorable solo goal at Everton, having earlier hit the Derby crossbar with a shot that was timed at 86 mph. By the time that Ray Harford resigned as manager the club was faced with a long fight against relegation and Georgios was left out so that an extra midfielder could be included. A player capable of moving inside and running at defenders, the Greek international will obviously be awaiting the arrival of the new manager, Roy Hodgson, with more than a passing interest.
Blackburn Rov (Free from Panathanaikos on 5/7/96) PL 11+11/2 FLC 3 FAC 0+1

DONNELLY Mark Paul
Born: Leeds, 22 December 1979
Height: 6'0" Weight: 12.0
Still a YTS, Mark made his league debut for Doncaster in the penultimate game of last season, the crunch affair at Brighton, when he came off the bench as a second-half substitute, a role he repeated in the final match at home to Torquay. An 18-year-old midfielder, Mark is certainly one to watch out for in the future.
Doncaster Rov (Trainee) FL 0+2

DONOVAN Kevin
Born: Halifax, 17 December 1971
Height: 5'8" Weight: 11.2
As a wide midfielder, playing down the right, Kevin did not have the greatest of seasons for West Brom in 1996-97. In and out of the side early on, at Christmas time he went on the transfer list, but when new boss, Ray Harford, took over, he withdrew his request and he was brought back into the first team, performing much better late on. The possessor of a great right-foot shot, he loves running at defenders before getting his crosses in.
Huddersfield T (From trainee on 11/10/89) FL 11+9/1 FLC 1+1 FAC 1/2 Others 4
Halifax T (Loaned on 13/2/92) FL 6
West Bromwich A (£70,000 on 1/10/92) FL 139+29/19 FLC 9+2/6 FAC 7+1/3 Others 15+1/4

DONOWA Brian **Louis** (Louie)
Born: Ipswich, 24 September 1964
Height: 5'9" Weight: 12.2
Club Honours: FAYC '83; FLC '85; Div 2 '95; AMC '95
International Honours: E: U21-3
A fast left winger who was popular with the fans at Birmingham, Louie's six-year association with the club came to an end in anti-climatic fashion in 1996-97, spending much of the season on loan because the manager, Trevor Francis, showed a reluctance to use players who were on a week-to-week contract. Loaned to Walsall in October, he looked good in six games, before going to Peterborough on similar terms and scoring one of the goals that put the Saddlers out of the Auto Windscreen trophy. At his best, a thrill-a-minute winger, he eventually joined the Posh on a permanent basis in March and despite still having the ability to leave defenders standing, was released during the summer.
Norwich C (From apprentice on 28/9/82) FL 56+6/11 FLC 3+2/3 FAC 1+2/1 (£400,000 to Real Deportivo on 1/2/86)
Stoke C (Loaned on 23/12/85) FL 4/1 FAC 0+1
Ipswich T (Free from Willem 1 on 14/8/89) FL 17+6/1 FLC 0+2 FAC 2 Others 2+1/1
Bristol C (£55,000 on 10/8/90) FL 11+13/3 FLC 1 FAC 0+1
Birmingham C (£60,000 on 30/8/91) FL 78+38/18 FLC 16+6 FAC 8/1 Others 9+3/2
Burnley (Loaned on 15/1/93) FL 4 Others 2
Shrewsbury T (Loaned on 27/1/94) FL 4
Walsall (Loaned on 14/10/96) FL 6/1
Peterborough U (Free on 13/12/96) FL 16+6/1 Others 4+1/2

DOOLAN John
Born: Liverpool, 7 May 1974
Height: 6'1" Weight: 13.0

Fully recovered from the broken ankle sustained in Mansfield's final match of 1995-96, John again had a good season for the Stags in 1996-97, but probably showed up best when used in the role of sweeper earlier on in the campaign.
Everton (From trainee on 1/6/92)
Mansfield T (Free on 2/9/94) FL 104+3/9 FLC 6 FAC 5/2 Others 4+1/1

DORIGO Anthony (Tony) Robert
Born: Australia, 31 December 1965
Height: 5'9" Weight: 10.10
Club Honours: Div 2 '89, Div 1 '92; FMC '90; CS '92
International Honours: E: 15; B-7; U21-11
Unfortunately, this most unlucky of Leeds' players had yet another season that was decimated by injuries in 1996-97. On his day, arguably one of the best left backs in the business - a point that was highlighted by George Graham, who, on his return to first-team action, compared him to the "signing of a three million pound defender", - he had to suffer a lengthy period out of the side, caused by damaged knee and hamstring problems, and was rarely able to put any kind of run of games together. Tony, who oozes class when in possession, was sorely missed when unavailable and the club and its supporters can only hope for better fortunes in his future.
Aston Villa (From apprentice on 19/7/83) FL 106+5/1 FLC 14+1 FAC 7 Others 2
Chelsea (£475,000 on 3/7/87) FL 146/11 FLC 14 FAC 4 Others 16/1
Leeds U (£1,300,000 on 6/6/91) F/PL 168+3/5 FLC 12+1 FAC 16 Others 9/1

DOUGLAS Stuart Anthony
Born: Enfield, 9 April 1978
Height: 5'9" Weight: 11.5
A promising attacking Luton midfielder, Stuart received few chances during 1996-97, but remains an important squad member, earmarked for a more prominent role in future seasons. Fast and tricky, he probably needs to develop his stamina if he is to bid for a regular place in 1997-98.
Luton T (From trainee on 2/5/96) FL 5+12/1 FLC 0+1 FAC 1 Others 0+1

DOWE Jens
Born: Rostock, Germany, 1 June 1968
Height: 5'11" Weight: 12.5
Arriving from Hamburg last October, the midfielder became Wolves' first German player and it was hoped he would have their familiar traits of power, ability, and discipline. His debut at Southend in September was promising enough, apart from when the speed and ferocity of a Mike Marsh challenge caught him out and led to a goal, but he only played another 90 minutes before being replaced in the next three games. Following that, his interest petered out and, unable to settle, having been signed on loan for £200,000 until the end of the season, he went to Sturm Graz for £100,000, making the deal an expensive one for Wanderers.
Wolverhampton W (Loaned from Hamburg on 11/10/96) FL 5+3

DOWELL Wayne Anthony
Born: Durham, 28 December 1973
Height: 5'10" Weight: 12.6
After playing in the 1996-97 pre-season games, following his transfer from Burnley, Wayne had to endure a long injury lay off before finally making his league debut for Rochdale. Unfortunately, after some excellent performances at left back, further injuries ruled him out again and he was released during the summer.
Burnley (From trainee on 27/3/93) FL 6 FLC 1 FAC 2
Carlisle U (Loaned on 29/3/96) FL 2+5
Rochdale (Free on 25/7/96) FL 6+1

DOWIE Iain
Born: Hatfield, 9 January 1965
Height: 6'1" Weight: 13.11
International Honours: NI: 44; U23-1; U21-1
West Ham's target man in 1996-97 at times looked out of place amongst the host of foreign imports that Harry Redknapp brought to Upton Park during the summer, but, unlike some of his more illustrious colleagues, he could never be faulted for lack of effort and commitment. Unfortunately, apart from one outstanding game against Nottingham Forest in the Coca-Cola Cup in October when he scored twice in a 4-1 victory, he was unable to hit the target and, after 15 Premiership games without a goal, Redknapp felt obliged to drop him in December and bring in first, Mike Newell on loan, and later, John Hartson and Paul Kitson, to solve the Hammers' debilitating goal famine. He enjoyed more success for Northern Ireland, however, being appointed captain for the game against Albania and celebrated the honour with two goals!
Luton T (£30,000 from Hendon on 14/12/88) FL 53+13/16 FLC 3+1 FAC 1+2 Others 5/4
Fulham (Loaned on 13/9/89) FL 5/1
West Ham U (£480,000 on 22/3/91) FL 12/4
Southampton (£500,000 on 3/9/91) F/PL 115+7/30 FLC 8+3/1 FAC 6/1 Others 4
Crystal Palace (£400,000 on 13/1/95) P/FL 19/6 FAC 6/4
West Ham U (£500,000 on 8/9/95) PL 51+5/8 FLC 8/2 FAC 3/1

DOWNING Keith Gordon
Born: Oldbury, 23 July 1965
Height: 5'8" Weight: 11.5
Club Honours: Div 4 '88, Div 3 '89; AMC '88
Having suffered from injury all last season, the inspirational, tough-tackling Hereford midfielder returned for a spell of games early in the New Year and, as ever, never let the team down. Tragically, for both the player and a club that was ultimately relegated to the Conference, Keith was forced to retire at the end of March, due to a chronic back ailment, and will be sadly missed.
Notts Co (Free from Mile Oak Rov on 16/5/84) FL 23/1
Wolverhampton W (Free on 6/8/87) FL 169+22/8 FLC 9+3 FAC 7/2 Others 15+3/1
Birmingham C (Free on 22/7/93) FL 1 FLC 1
Stoke C (Free on 9/8/94) FL 16 FLC 2 FAC 1 Others 3+2
Cardiff C (Free on 21/8/95) FL 3+1 FLC 0+1
Hereford U (Free on 15/9/95) FL 45 FLC 3 FAC 3 Others 4

DOYLE Maurice
Born: Ellesmere Port, 17 October 1969
Height: 5'8" Weight: 10.7
Scored his first goal for Millwall last February with a last-minute volley from just outside the penalty area to equalise in the match at Shrewsbury. A tenacious midfielder who is quick to mark the opposition, under John Docherty he retained his first team role in the Lions' side.
Crewe Alex (From trainee on 11/7/88) FL 6+2/2
Queens Park R (£120,000 on 21/4/89) PL 6
Crewe Alex (Loaned on 17/1/91) FL 6+1/2 FAC 2
Millwall (Signed on 16/5/95) FL 34+12/1 FLC 2 Others 1+1

DOZZELL Jason Alvin Winans
Born: Ipswich, 9 December 1967
Height: 6'1" Weight: 13.8
Club Honours: Div 2 '92
International Honours: E: U21-9; Yth
Midfield creative player who experienced a difficult time at Tottenham last season. Still looking lively, alert, and enthusiastic, Jason had little trouble silencing his critics with crucial goals and gained the endorsement of his manager when being offered a new deal. Good in the air, his excellent first touch on the ball giving him both time and space to run at defenders, his desire to hold a regular first-team place fuelled rumours of a possible move abroad under the Bosman ruling. However, with a great deal to offer, Gerry Francis will be keen to keep a player who copes admirably with the intense pressure put on him by an expectant White Hart Lane crowd.
Ipswich T (From apprentice on 20/12/84) F/PL 312+20/52 FLC 29+1/3 FAC 22/12 Others 22/4
Tottenham H (£1,900,000 on 1/8/93) PL 68+16/13 FLC 8+2 FAC 4+1/1

DRAPER Mark Andrew
Born: Long Eaton, 11 November 1970
Height: 5'10" Weight: 12.4
Club Honours: FLC '96
International Honours: E: U21-3
A regular in the Aston Villa midfield for most of last season, Mark was to be part of the "dream" midfield with Sasa Curcic and Andy Townsend which ultimately failed, although not on his part. However, he continued his good form and earned a late call up for the England squad for the World Cup tie with Moldova, making the bench but not getting on for his debut. A good consistent player, and a key link between defence and attack, most of his matches missed were in a spell early in the new year, which cost him seven games.
Notts Co (From trainee on 12/12/88) FL 206+16/40 FLC 14+1/2 FAC 10/2 Others 21+2/5
Leicester C (£1,250,000 on 22/7/94) PL 39/5 FLC 2 FAC 2
Aston Villa (£3,250,000 on 5/7/95) PL 64+1/2 FLC 9+1/1 FAC 5/2 Others 2

DREYER John Brian
Born: Alnwick, 11 June 1963
Height: 6'1" Weight: 13.2
Transferred to Bradford last November, much to the surprise of the Stoke faithful, who felt that he was playing his best football for the club and that his departure would

leave a distinct lack of defensive cover, he quickly got down to business with the Bantams, scoring on his debut in a 3-3 draw at Huddersfield. An experienced left-sided defender, with a good left foot and equally at home in midfield, John works for 90 minutes of every game and never gives less than 100 per cent. Always dangerous at set pieces, his other three City goals came in FA Cup matches at Wycombe and Everton.
Oxford U (Signed from Wallingford on 8/1/85) FL 57+3/2 FLC 10+1 FAC 2 Others 3
Torquay U (Loaned on 13/12/85) FL 5
Fulham (Loaned on 27/3/88) FL 12/2
Luton T (£140,000 on 27/6/88) FL 212+2/13 FLC 13+1/1 FAC 14 Others 8/1
Stoke C (Free on 15/7/94) FL32+17/3 FLC 5 FAC 1 Others 4+1/1
Bolton W (Loaned on 23/3/95) FL 1+1 Others 1+1
Bradford C (£25,000 on 6/11/96) FL 27+1/1 FLC 2 FAC 3/3

DRUCE Mark Andrew
Born: Oxford, 3 March 1974
Height: 5'11" Weight: 12.8
Mark made a devastating impact when he joined Rotherham on loan from Oxford last September, scoring in each of his first four games. But, after signing on a permanent basis, the goals dried up as injuries restricted his appearances and he was in and out of the team with a string of different partners up front, making it difficult to establish an automatic place. A striker with pace, he will do well if he can only keep free of injuries.
Oxford U (From trainee on 3/12/91) FL 18+34/4 FLC 1+3 Others 2+1
Rotherham U (£50,000 on 26/9/96) FL 16+4/4

DRURY Adam James
Born: Cambridge, 29 August 1978
Height: 5'9" Weight: 10.13
Having signed professional forms for Peterborough during the summer of 1996, following on from his league debut when still a trainee in 1995-96, Adam came into the side for six further appearances last season and again never let anyone down, performing with maturity and confidence. He even scored the winning goal in the final game of the campaign and, if able to continue improving at the same rate, could well find himself the regular left back in 1997-98.
Peterborough U (From trainee on 3/7/96) FL 5+1/1 FLC 1

DRYDEN Richard Andrew
Born: Stroud, 14 June 1969
Height: 6'0" Weight: 13.0
Club Honours: Div 4 '90
Signed from Bristol City prior to the start of 1996-97, Richard came straight into the Southampton defence for the home match against Chelsea. Having spent his whole career in the lower divisions, the left-sided central defender was a revelation, especially when you realise that he had suffered badly with injuries in 1995-96, being strong, comfortable on the ball, and reliable to a fault. Would have been an automatic choice, injuries and suspensions aside, and only two players made more appearances for a team struggling against adversity for much of the

Richard Dryden

campaign. Excellent at corners and free kicks, his opening goal, and only one in the Premiership, came at the Dell against Nottingham Forest when he headed in a Simon Charlton corner to begin a fight back that eventually ended at 2-2.

Bristol Rov (From trainee on 14/7/87) FL 12+1 FLC 2+1 FAC 0+2 Others 2
Exeter C (Loaned on 22/9/88) FL 6
Exeter C (Signed on 8/3/89) FL 86/13 FLC 7/2 FAC 2 Others 4
Notts Co (£250,000 on 9/8/91) FL 30+1/1 FLC 1+1 FAC 2+1 Others 2
Plymouth Arg (Loaned on 18/11/92) FL 5 Others 1
Birmingham C (£165,000 on 19/3/93) FL 48 FLC 5 FAC 1
Bristol C (£140,000 on 16/12/94) FL 32+5/2 FLC 4 FAC 1+1 Others 2
Southampton (£150,000 on 6/8/96) PL 28+1/1 FLC 6/3

DRYSDALE Jason
Born: Bristol, 17 November 1970
Height: 5'10" Weight: 12.0
Club Honours: FAYC '89; Div 2 '96
International Honours: E: Yth

1996-97 was another disappointing season for the Swindon Town full back who was injured in a Coca-Cola Cup match at Wolverhampton in early September and made two short-lived comeback attempts in January and March. When fully fit, however, he should be the Robins' first-choice left back for the coming term, but may face fierce competition from Gary Elkins and the recently signed Phil King.

Watford (From trainee on 8/9/88) FL 135+10/11 FLC 8+1/2 FAC 2 Others 4
Newcastle U (£425,000 on 2/8/94)
Swindon T (£340,000 on 23/3/95) FL 24+4 FLC 2 FAC 2+3 Others 2

DUBERRY Michael Wayne
Born: Enfield, 14 October 1975
Height: 6'1" Weight: 13.6
International Honours: E: U21-3

This magnificent young Chelsea centre back continued his meteoric rise to become one of the outstanding young defenders in the country in 1996-97, being regarded as an international prospect in the near future.

Sadly, he joined the club's long-term injury list in January when he snapped an achilles tendon in training and missed the remainder of the season. This was particularly unfortunate for Blues as he had produced a string of mature performances and had settled into a fine understanding with fellow centre backs, Frank Leboeuf and Steve Clarke. Built like a heavyweight boxer, he is surprisingly fast and agile for such a big man and is a threat in the air at set pieces, ably demonstrated at Old Trafford in November when he rose head and shoulders above everybody else to head past Peter Schmeichel to notch Chelsea's first goal in the match that smashed United's long unbeaten home run. Having made his delayed debut for the England U21 side against Moldova in August, he again showed his prowess in the opposition penalty area by scoring the only goal of the game in Georgia to clinch victory for England in his third match. All Blues' fans will be hoping that he makes a complete recovery to resume his place in Chelsea's back three which has given the club its most stable defence for many years.

Chelsea (From trainee on 7/6/93) PL 36+2/1 FLC 2 FAC 9/2
Bournemouth (Loaned on 29/9/95) FL 7 Others 1

DUBLIN Dion
Born: Leicester, 22 April 1969
Height: 6'1" Weight: 12.4
Club Honours: Div 3 '91; CS '94

1996-97 was a mixed season for the big Coventry striker. He lost the captaincy after early defeats and struggled to score, only getting his first goal in his 11th game against Southampton after he had been relegated to the bench. His move to centre back coincided with the team's excellent run in December and Dion scored four in four games from set pieces. Although sent off in successive games, against Sunderland and Blackburn, and suffering a seven-match ban, on his return he played in defence with mixed results, despite finding goals easier to come by. Scored the dramatic late winner at Anfield and subsequently reverted to his striking role for the final games, but then picked up a knee injury against Arsenal, having scored an excellent early goal.

Norwich C (From Oakham U on 24/3/88)
Cambridge U (Free on 2/8/88) FL 133+23/52 FLC 8+2/5 FAC 21/11 Others 14+1/5
Manchester U (£1,000,000 on 7/8/92) PL 4+8/2 FLC 1+1/1 FAC 1+1 Others 0+1
Coventry C (£2,000,000 on 9/9/94) PL 98+1/40 FLC 7+2/2 FAC 8/1

Keith Dublin (right)

DUBLIN Keith Barry
Born: High Wycombe, 29 January 1966
Height: 6'0" Weight: 12.10
International Honours: E: Yth

It was another season of chop and change at Southend in 1996-97 for Keith, who appeared in all the back four positions, plus emergency centre forward in times of need. Strong in the air, and always giving 100 per cent wherever chosen to play, he ended the season as the club's only ever present.
Chelsea (From apprentice on 28/1/84) FL 50+1 FLC 6 FAC 5 Others 5+1
Brighton & Hove A (£3,500 on 14/8/87) FL 132/5 FLC 5 FAC 7/1 Others 7
Watford (£275,000 on 17/7/90) FL 165+3/2 FLC 12 FAC 4 Others 6
Southend U (Signed on 21/7/94) FL 128+1/5 FLC 6 FAC 3 Others 2

DUCROS Andrew John
Born: Evesham, 16 September 1977
Height: 5'4" Weight: 9.8
International Honours: E: Yth; Sch

An outstanding prospect developed through Coventry's youth policy, the young striker made his debut in 1996-97 as a sub in the opening-day defeat by Forest and brought some spark to a lack-lustre attack. Four days later he made his first start, setting up Gary McAllister's goal with some great work on the right wing and generally giving a good account of himself. He next made three further sub appearances before suffering a groin injury which kept him out for a large part of the campaign, re-appearing on the bench towards the end of the season. His lack of height may be a disadvantage, but his speed and eye for goal should more than compensate.
Coventry C (From trainee on 16/9/94) PL 1+4

DUDLEY Craig Bryan
Born: Newark, 12 September 1979
Height: 5'10" Weight: 11.2

The young striker broke into the Notts County side last March when coming off the bench at Meadow Lane against Brentford, while still a trainee. Given the chance after poaching over 20 goals for the youth side, Craig showed himself to be quick off the mark and having a natural eye for goal in his ten games, scoring the first in a 2-1 win at York and the effective equaliser in a 1-1 home draw against Burnley. Now a professional and an excellent prospect for the coming term.
Notts Co (From trainee on 2/4/97) FL 6+4/2

DUFF Damien Anthony
Born: Ballyboden, 2 March 1979
Height: 5'10" Weight: 9.7
International Honours: Ei: Yth; Sch

Signed from Irish junior football, Damien is an outstanding young left-sided Blackburn player who is expected to go all the way by the management. Introduced in the final game of last season, a 4-2 home defeat at the hands of Leicester, it is expected that he will be afforded further opportunities in 1997-98, where his capabilities which include intelligence, pace, and good crossing skills, will be seen to good effect.

Blackburn Rov (Signed from Lourdes Celtic on 5/3/97) PL 1

DUGUID Karl Anthony
Born: Hitchin, 21 March 1978
Height: 5'11" Weight: 11.7

A young and exciting Colchester attacker, Karl was successfully building on the previous season's foundations with a good goalscoring run last autumn, before being sidelined with a kidney infection. His appearances were limited afterwards as a long recovery period ensued, but he made the substitutes' bench at Wembley and was an extra-time replacement for Paul Abrahams, being brave enough to volunteer for one of the penalties in the shoot out, ahead of many more experienced men. Unfortunately, for him, his shot was well saved, his disconsolate reactions will never be forgotten by the Sky viewers or United's blue army of fans.
Colchester U (From trainee on 16/7/96) FL 17+19/4 FLC 0+2 FAC 0+1 Others 1+2

DUMITRESCU Ilie
Born: Bucharest, Romania, 6 January 1969
Height: 5'9" Weight: 10.7
International Honours: Romania: 56

Ever since the bright start to his English career with Spurs in the opening weeks of the 1994-95 season, the Romanian international striker has looked a misfit in the Premier League. However, a move to West Ham in March 1996 offered him the chance of a fresh start, but, in the event, he only made five starting line ups for the Hammers in 1996-97 and although he played well in his final game, a 2-2 draw at Old Trafford, manager Harry Redknapp had already decided to cut his losses and transferred him to the Mexican side, Futbol America, in January. A sad waste of a once great talent.
Tottenham H (£2,600,000 from Steau Bucharest on 3/8/94) PL 16+2/4 FLC 2/1
West Ham U (£1,500,000 on 9/3/96) PL 5+5 FLC 2+1

DUNGEY James Andrew
Born: Plymouth, 7 February 1978
Height: 5'10" Weight: 12.0
International Honours: E: Yth; Sch

A young Plymouth goalkeeper who understudied Bruce Grobbelaar in 1996-97, James proved to be very agile and an excellent shot stopper. Sure to have learned a lot from his illustrious mentor, he appeared nine times and kept five clean sheets, including three in a row during a season when Argyle faced the threat of relegation for much of the time.
Plymouth Arg (Trainee) FL 9+1 Others 4

DUNN Iain George
Born: Goole, 1 April 1970
Height: 5'10" Weight: 12.0
International Honours: E: Sch

Iain returned to Chesterfield, via Huddersfield, last March, having previously been discarded in 1992 without being given much of a chance, bringing more options to the left-hand side of the midfield and able to fit in behind a forward or take a more attacking role himself. With the side busy

chasing FA Cup and play-off glory, Iain did not get too many starts in 1996-97, but will be able to press a strong claim for inclusion during the pre-season period. Earlier last season, had a spell on loan at Scunthorpe.
York C (From juniors on 7/7/88) FL 46+31/11 FLC 3+1 FAC 3+1 Others 1+3
Chesterfield (Free on 14/8/91) FL 8+5/1
Scarborough (Free on 27/8/92)
Peterborough U (Free on 29/9/92) Others 0+1
Scarborough (Free on 9/10/92)
Huddersfield T (Free from Goole T on 4/12/92) FL 62+58/14 FLC 6+4/3 FAC 7+3/3 Others 11+7/9
Scunthorpe U (Loaned on 20/9/96) FL 3
Chesterfield (£30,000 on 28/2/97) FL 10+1 FAC 0+1

DUNNE Joseph (Joe) John
Born: Dublin, 25 May 1973
Height: 5'9" Weight: 11.6
International Honours: Ei: U21-1; Yth; Sch

A junior and U21 Irish international right back who is equally comfortable performing in midfield, Joe scored one of Colchester's goals in that superb Coca-Cola Cup win at West Bromwich last season and came within inches of being a Wembley hero when his last-second-of-extra-time 20-yard shot whistled just over the Carlisle crossbar. His cool and composed display at Wembley was typical of a man on form, and he will be looking to claim a permanent place in 1997-98.
Gillingham (From trainee on 9/8/90) FL 108+7/1 FLC 7 FAC 5+1 Others 4+2
Colchester U (Free on 27/3/96) FL 25+15/1 FLC 3/1 FAC 1 Others 2+1

DUNNE Richard Patrick
Born: Dublin, 21 September 1979
Height: 6'2" Weight:15.0
International Honours: Ei: Yth; Sch

A giant centre half who topped six feet two inches and 15 stone before his 16th birthday, Richard's professional progress has been almost as meteoric as his physical development. The first product of Everton's sponsorship links with famous Irish club, Home Farm, he made history last January when becoming the youngest Everton player to play in a first-team match at Goodison Park, making an impressive debut in the FA Cup tie against Swindon at 17 years and 106 days of age. Two months later, after giving a typically composed performance in the passion of a Merseyside derby, he was called up to the full Republic of Ireland squad. Guaranteed a promising career in the game, the club swiftly offered him a five-year professional contract during his first year as a YTS trainee at Goodison.
Everton (From trainee on 8/10/96) PL 6+1 FAC 1

DUNWELL Richard Kirk
Born: Islington, 17 June 1971
Height: 6'0" Weight: 13.0

A keen, hard-working centre forward in his second season at Barnet, Richard made just two appearances in 1996-97, starting the opening game at Cambridge and coming off the bench at Exeter in the Coca-Cola Cup, before being loaned to Walton & Hersham (August) and later Cheltenham Town

(March). Released during the summer, he is a player who is always looking to be involved.

Millwall (From trainee on 6/7/89)
Aldershot (Free on 19/11/90) FL 0+1 (Released during 1991 close season)
Barnet (Free from Collier Row on 5/10/95) FL 4+10/1 FLC 0+1

DURKAN Kieran John
Born: Chester, 1 December 1973
Height: 5'11" Weight: 12.0
Club Honours: WC '95
International Honours: Ei: U21-3

The Stockport right winger won over many sceptical fans with some effective displays in 1996-97. Not the quickest or trickiest of wide men, his excellent delivery of a football and occasional spectacular goal, more than compensated. Had an outstanding game at Mansfield in the FA Cup, having a hand in all three winning goals – a corner that ended up in the net via a Town defender, a tremendous right-footed shot on the run, and a curling left-foot free kick from 18 yards.

Wrexham (From trainee on 16/7/92) FL 43+7/3 FLC 3+1 FAC 4+2/2 Others 15/1
Stockport Co (£95,000 on 16/2/96) FL 47+10/3 FLC 9 FAC 4/3 Others 4+2

DURNIN John Paul
Born: Bootle, 18 August 1965
Height: 5'10" Weight: 11.10

Failed to hold down a regular place at Portsmouth last season following the arrival of Matthias Svensson in December, but proved a more than capable replacement for either the latter or Lee Bradbury when called upon. In consequence, his appearances from the bench overtook his league starts. Capable of playing in midfield as a biting tackler who gives opponents no room to manoeuvre, or as a bustling front runner, John is a wholehearted player who never gives anything less than his best.

Liverpool (Free from Waterloo Dock on 29/3/86) FLC 1+1
West Bromwich A (Loaned on 20/10/88) FL 5/2
Oxford U (£225,000 on 10/2/89) FL 140+21/44 FLC 7/1 FAC 7/1 Others 4+1/1
Portsmouth (£200,000 on 15/7/93) FL 77+42/14 FLC 9+1/2 FAC 4+1 Others 4+2

DURSUN Peter Muhamet Ali
Born: Arhus, Denmark, 8 January 1975
Height: 5'10" Weight: 12.0

Signed from Danish football at the end of last November and contracted until June 1997, Peter was given his one and only opportunity of league football at Queens Park Rangers, when coming off the bench for the last 36 minutes. Despite being decidedly quick over short distances and able to hold the ball up well, the young striker was unable to settle and soon departed.

Southend U (Signed from Arhus Fremad on 29/11/96) FL 0+1

DUXBURY Lee Edward
Born: Keighley, 7 October 1969
Height: 5'9" Weight: 11.13

Having missed just one game for Bradford throughout last season, and proving to be an inspirational captain who led by example from central midfield, Lee was transferred to Oldham in early March. Although it took a few people by surprise, with both clubs in the first division free-fall area, it seemed excellent business for a Latics' side desperately in need of inspiration. Despite arriving too late to halt the slide, this hard-working, hard-tackling battler immediately built up a good partnership with Lee Richardson which augurs well for the coming season. A scorer of vital goals, two of his four during the campaign just gone proved the point.

Bradford C (From trainee on 4/7/88) FL 204+5/25 FLC 18+1/3 FAC 11 Others 13
Rochdale (Loaned on 18/1/90) FL 9+1 FAC 1
Huddersfield T (£250,000 on 23/12/94) FL 29/2 FLC 1 Others 3
Bradford C (£135,000 on 15/11/95) FL 63/7 FLC 2 FAC 5 Others 3
Oldham Ath (£350,000 on 7/3/97) FL 11+1/1

Sean Dyche

DYCHE Sean Mark
Born: Kettering, 28 June 1971
Height: 6'0" Weight: 13.2

Firmly established as the regular first choice at the heart of Chesterfield's defence in 1996-97, Sean plays as if that has always been his position, using a mature and unhurried approach to make the best of his strength in the tackle and his powers of anticipation. Since moving from right back, he has come on greatly, adding a necessary aerial presence to his range of skills and developing the knack of holding up a forward without committing himself to a tackle on every occasion. Fans feel that, if Sean's name is on the teamsheet, then Chesterfield are in with a chance against anyone.

Nottingham F (From trainee on 20/5/89)
Chesterfield (Free on 1/2/90) FL 219+12/8 FLC 9 FAC 13/1 Others 16

DYER Bruce Antonio
Born: Ilford, 13 April 1975
Height: 6'0" Weight: 11.3
International Honours: E: U21-9

In performing at a very high standard in 1996-97, Bruce had his best season yet for Crystal Palace. Whether it was playing wide or attacking through the middle, his skill shone through and his quick, strong running continually caused problems for the opposition, his 18 goals being suitable testament to his ability and effort. His good form also saw him represent the Football League against the Italian Serie "B" and add to his collection of England U21 caps, while the club's, if not his, crowning moment came via the Wembley play offs that ended in a 1-0 victory over Sheffield United and Premiership football this coming term.

Watford (From trainee on 19/4/93) FL 29+2/6 FLC 4/2 FAC 1 Others 2/1
Crystal Palace (£1,100,000 on 10/3/94) F/PL 69+36/31 FLC 7+3/1 FAC 3+3/2 Others 3+2

DYER Keiron Courtney
Born: Ipswich, 29 December 1978
Height: 5'7" Weight: 9.7
International Honours: E: Yth

One of the new breed of players coming through Ipswich's revitalised youth policy, Keiron made his full debut in the FA Cup defeat at Nottingham Forest last January and went on to play in a further 15 games, 12 of them from the subs' bench. A slightly built player who can play in a number of positions, including midfield and wing back, he is predominantly right footed, a good passer of the ball, and has the ability to run at players from midfield to set up chances for others.

Ipswich T (From trainee on 3/1/97) FL 2+11 FAC 1 Others 1+1

DYSON Jonathan (Jon) Paul
Born: Mirfield, 18 December 1971
Height: 6'1" Weight: 12.9

Is a versatile player whose preferred position is either at right back or in the centre of defence, although he also deputised in midfield for Huddersfield in 1996-97. Again found it difficult to establish a consistent spell in the side, often sitting on the substitutes' bench, his longest run being just eight games. An intelligent player with a degree from the local university, he is also the clubs PFA representative.

Huddersfield T (From juniors on 29//12/90) FL 90+15/2 FLC 11+2 FAC 5 Others 7+4

At The Royal Bank of Scotland we're delighted to give our continued support to a wide variety of sporting events throughout the U.K.

The Royal Bank of Scotland

FOR MORE INFORMATION ON THE FULL RANGE OF SERVICES AVAILABLE FROM THE ROYAL BANK OF SCOTLAND PLEASE CONTACT BILL GILLINGS ON 01204 525474,

E

EADEN Nicholas (Nicky) Jeremy
Born: Sheffield, 12 December 1972
Height: 5'9" Weight: 11.9
For the second successive season, the end of which saw Barnsley promoted to the Premiership, this attacking right-wing back remained an ever present for the club, having had a highly successful 1996-97 campaign, his attacking play being encouraged by the manager. Although his crosses were a constant threat and the side scored its fair share of goals from them, he also had an eye for goal himself, twice netting important effective equalisers at Wolves and Norwich. A player who should do well in the Premiership, his good form was rewarded with selection in the PFA divisional team.
Barnsley (From juniors on 4/6/91) FL 173+3/8 FLC 10+1 FAC 9 Others 2

Darren Eadie

EADIE Darren Malcolm
Born: Chippenham, 10 June 1975
Height: 5'8" Weight: 11.6
International Honours: E: U21-6; Yth
A fit, feisty, and fiery Darren literally ran amok in last season's Norwich campaign to regain a Premiership place. The First Division Team of the Year, in the eyes of his fellow professionals, rightly had him in their ranks and further goal-laden England U21 games followed, before a call up to the full England squad versus South Africa brought a disappointing injury in training. There

were bookings, sending offs, and 17 goals that could have been more, while his thrilling runs and hurdling of defenders was worth the admission alone. A left winger with terrific pace who runs at defenders, happily for Canary supporters he has pledged another year with the club.
Norwich C (From trainee on 5/2/93) P/FL 102+12/28 FLC 17+1/2 FAC 6+1/1 Others 1+1

EARLE Robert (Robbie) Gerald
Born: Newcastle under Lyme, 27 January 1965
Height: 5'9" Weight: 10.10
A Wimbledon player with immense talent, Robbie had another outstanding season in 1996-97, being one of the highest-scoring midfielders in the league. Very consistent, and enjoying the FA Cup run which saw him score in every round up to the semi final, including a 90th minute equaliser against Manchester United at Old Trafford, his physical presence, stamina, and competence to get forward means that he can not be far off gaining a full England cap, a point made when he was put on stand by for England's World Cup qualifying squad against Italy. Since his move from Port Vale in 1991, Robbie has become a legend at the club.
Port Vale (From juniors on 5/7/82) FL 284+10/77 FLC 21+2/4 FAC 20+1/4 Others 18+1/5
Wimbledon (£775,000 on 19/7/91) F/PL 202/48 FLC 20/5 FAC 28/7 Others 1/1

EASTON Clint Jude
Born: Barking, 1 October 1977
Height: 5'9" Weight: 10.8
A predominantly left-sided Watford midfield player who made his debut last season at the age of 18 and went on to claim a permanent place in the first-team squad. Although needing to fill out a bit, but already showing the confidence and passing ability to act as a playmaker, he ended 1996-97 in style by scoring his first senior goal and earning selection for the England U19 squad.
Watford (From trainee on 5/7/96) FL 17/1 FAC 2+1 Others 2

EBBRELL John Keith
Born: Bromborough, 1 October 1969
Height: 5'9" Weight: 11.9
Club Honours: CS '95
International Honours: E: B-1; U21-14; Yth; Sch
A committed and technically adept midfielder, John endured a topsy-turvy season at Everton in 1996-97, going from captain in a 2-2 draw at Manchester United to a frustrated sub at Tottenham four days later. Although bouncing back to reclaim his place, he then fell foul of the injury curse which plagued the club throughout the campaign, before signing for Sheffield United in March, having been tracked by Howard Kendall for some time. Unfortunately, his debut was delayed due to an ankle injury and when he did get on the field of play at Bramall Lane against Reading he lasted just 45 minutes, a broken rib putting him out of action until the coming term.
Everton (From trainee on 7/11/86) F/PL 207+10/13 FLC 17/1 FAC 20/3 Others 9+2/2
Sheffield U (£1,000,000 on 3/3/97) FL 1

EBDON Marcus
Born: Pontypool, 17 October 1970
Height: 5'9" Weight: 12.4
International Honours: W: U21-2; Yth
The former Welsh U21 international joined Chesterfield from Peterborough last March, slotting straight into the creative heart of the midfield, where his crisp, accurate passing came to the fore. Despite his fee, his arrival was somewhat overshadowed by the club's involvement in the FA Cup (for which he was ineligible), but he is certain to stamp his class on the team with great effect in 1997-98.
Everton (From trainee on 16/8/89)
Peterborough U (Free on 15/7/91) FL 136+11/15 FLC 14+2 FAC 12+3/1 Others 11+1
Chesterfield (£100,000 on 21/3/97) FL 11+1/1

ECKHARDT Jeffrey (Jeff) Edward
Born: Sheffield, 7 October 1965
Height: 6'0" Weight: 11.7
Transferred to Cardiff from Stockport immediately following the start of last season, Jeff showed himself a very determined, hard-working player who brought much needed steel to a defence that needed bolstering. Extremely versatile, being able to play in midfield or up front as well, and a good tackler with excellent powers of recovery, he scored on his debut and put away another four in the chase for a play-off place. Will be one of City's key men if the second division beckons.
Sheffield U (From juniors on 23/8/84) FL 73+1/2 FLC 7 FAC 2 Others 5
Fulham (£50,000 on 20/11/87) FL 245+4/25 FLC 13 FAC 5+1 Others 15/3
Stockport Co (£50,000 on 21/7/94) FL 56+6/7 FLC 6+2/1 FAC 5/4 Others 2
Cardiff C (£30,000 on 22/8/96) FL 34+1/5 FLC 1 FAC 2 Others 4/1

EDINBURGH Justin Charles
Born: Brentwood, 18 December 1969
Height: 5'10" Weight: 11.6
Club Honours: FAC '91; CS '91
Competitive left back who continued to find a regular Tottenham first-team place hard to come by in 1996-97. Justin's enthusiasm and reliability was still evident when called upon and his commitment to maintaining personal fitness helped him overcome some minor difficulties to add much needed experience when Spurs, ravaged by injury problems, were forced to field young, inexperienced sides. Signing a new three-year contract put paid to rumours of a move and is sure to give Justin renewed self confidence in Gerry Francis' commitment to him. Still has a great deal to offer at Premiership level.
Southend U (From trainee on 5/8/88) FL 36+1 FLC 2+1 FAC 2 Others 4+1/1
Tottenham H (£150,000 on 30/7/90) F/PL 156+17/1 FLC 17+4 FAC 22 Others 3

[EDINHO] Amaral Neto Edon Do
Born: Brazil, 21 February 1967
Height: 5'10" Weight: 12.9
Signed from the Portuguese side, VSC Guimaraes on a two-and-a-half year contract last February, this strong, bustling Brazilian forward became a great favourite at Bradford, scoring five goals, three of

them vital in the battle against relegation. A player with typical Brazilian skills and tricks, prior to arriving at Valley Parade, Edinho had scored 95 goals in 192 games in Portuguese football after moving from Brazil in 1990. Quickly established as City's penalty taker in just his third game, scoring from the spot after being bundled over at Manchester City, as you would expect he is already a key player.

Bradford C (£250,000 from VSC Guimaraes on 6/2/97) FL 15/5 FAC 1

EDMONDSON Darren Stephen
Born: Coniston, 4 November 1971
Height: 6'0" Weight: 12.11
Club Honours: Div 3 '95; AMC '97

A positive performer whose wholehearted attitude made him a Carlisle crowd favourite and a regular at either full back or in central defence until a surprise move to Huddersfield last March. Still only 25, but a veteran of more than 200 league games, Darren quickly settled in at Leeds Road in giving some very assured and skilful performances in the centre-half position. He also showed his versatility when deputising at right back.

Carlisle U (From trainee on 17/7/90) FL 205+9/8 FLC 15/1 FAC 15/3 Others 22/3
Huddersfield T (£200,000 + on 3/3/97) FL 10

Andy Edwards

EDWARDS Andrew (Andy) David
Born: Epping, 17 September 1971
Height: 6'3" Weight: 13.7

A strong and decisive central defender who can also play on either side of the back four, Andy is good in the air and deceptively quick. The third costliest player in Birmingham's history, following the arrival of Steve Bruce and Gary Ablett, however, there was no permanent place in the side for him in 1996-97 and, in November, he moved to Peterborough to rejoin his old boss, Barry Fry. Quickly became a favourite of the fans at London Road, his ability to play the ball out, rather than clearing his lines, helping to shore up a leaky defence.

Southend U (From trainee on 14/12/89) FL 141+6/5 FLC 5 FAC 4 Others 9/2
Birmingham C (£400,000 on 6/7/95) FL 37+3/1 FLC 12/1 FAC 2 Others 5/1
Peterborough U (Signed on 29/11/96) FL 25 FAC 4 Others 5

EDWARDS Christian (Chris) Nicholas Howells
Born: Caerphilly, 23 November 1975
Height: 6'3" Weight: 11.9
International Honours: W: 1; U21-6

Missed the start of last season, but, on returning to first team duty at the heart of Swansea's defence early September, showed consistent form. A regular in the Welsh U21 side, playing against West Germany, Holland and Belgium, he was selected for the full team against Eire, but withdrew because the Swans were playing Fulham on the same night. Impressing as a commanding presence in aerial challenges, his form brought him to the attention of several top clubs in 1996-97.

Swansea C (From trainee on 20/7/94) FL 81+2/2 FLC 3 FAC 3 Others 9+1

EDWARDS Neil Ryan
Born: Aberdare, 5 December 1970
Height: 5'9" Weight: 11.10
International Honours: W: U21-1; Yth; Sch

Stockport's hugely popular young Welsh 'keeper was extremely unlucky to find himself fighting for the number one jersey with the magnificent Paul Jones in 1996-97 and being restricted to just two Auto Windscreen Shield appearances, when he got the biggest cheer of the night from the County fans on both occasions! An excellent shot stopper, and a man who works extremely hard at his game, Neil will be back.

Leeds U (From trainee on 10/3/89) Others 1
Stockport Co (£5,000 on 3/9/91) FL 163+1 FLC 11 FAC 11 Others 31

EDWARDS Paul
Born: Liverpool, 22 February 1965
Height: 5'11" Weight: 13.2
Club Honours: Div 3 '94

Shrewsbury Town goalkeeper. Kept out of the side at the start of last season, following the introduction of Benny Gall, Paul returned after a heavy home defeat by Luton, playing 18 games before being replaced by the latter. Always a confident 'keeper, with reflex saves and brave on the ground, although his kicking sometimes let him down, he came back for the last eight matches and the spiral into the third division.

Crewe Alex (Free from Leek T on 24/2/89) FL 29 FLC 4 FAC 3 Others 4
Shrewsbury T (Free on 6/8/92) FL 169 FLC 11 FAC 15 Others 15

EDWARDS Robert (Rob)
Born: Manchester, 23 February 1970
Height: 5'9" Weight: 12.4

A midfielder in his first full season at Huddersfield, although failing to emulate the goalscoring form he showed during his explosive start for the club at the end of 1995-96, he still proved he had an eye for creating and taking chances when coming second in the assists and third in the scorers'

charts. Is equally at home in aerial tussles as he is on the ground.

Crewe Alex (From trainee on 11/7/88) FL 110+45/44 FLC 8/5 FAC 13+5/5 Others 9+8/4
Huddersfield T (£150,000 on 8/3/96) FL 37+9/10 FLC 4+1/1 FAC 2/1

EDWARDS Robert (Rob) William
Born: Kendal, 1 July 1973
Height: 6'0" Weight: 12.2
International Honours: W: B-2; U21-17; Yth

Niggling injuries disrupted this midfielder's season in 1996-97, but each time he managed to quickly regain his place in the Bristol City side. Although his sweet left foot often outshines his right, he had his best campaign at Ashton Gate and, at long last, gave consistent evidence of the ability that brought about his signing from Carlisle United six years ago. His call up into the full Welsh squad at the end of the season was a suitable reward for all his effort and City fans hope that it will not be too long before he wins his first full cap. Not only a ball winner, but is intelligent in distribution.

Carlisle U (From trainee on 10/4/90) FL 48/5 FLC 4 FAC 1 Others 2+1
Bristol C (£135,000 on 27/3/91) FL 135+21/3 FLC 12+1/1 FAC 12+2 Others 11+1/2

EDWORTHY Marc
Born: Barnstaple, 24 December 1972
Height: 5'8" Weight: 11.10

This fast-raiding Crystal Palace right back, who also had a spell as a sweeper, impressed all with his exciting runs and accurate crossing that, on occasion in 1996-97, led to goals. Also scored his first for the club in a 3-1 Coca-Cola Cup win at Bury in September. In a season that ultimately saw Palace go back to the Premiership after a 1-0 Wembley play-off win over Sheffield United, Marc missed just one game and his sterling efforts were recognised when being named as joint runner up in the club's Player of the Year award. Is a versatile player who can easily turn up in midfield if required.

Plymouth Arg (From trainee on 30/3/91) FL 52+17/1 FLC 5+2 FAC 5+2 Others 2+2
Crystal Palace (£350,000 on 9/6/95) FL 86+3 FLC 7/1 FAC 4 Others 6

Ugo Ehiogu

EHIOGU Ugochuku (Ugo)
Born: Hackney, 3 November 1972
Height: 6'2" Weight: 13.3
Club Honours: FLC '96
International Honours: E: 1; B-1; U21-15

1996-97 was another good, solid season for Ugo, which saw him appear in every game in Aston Villa's defence, usually alongside Gareth Southgate or Carl Tiler and Steve Staunton. A well-built centre back, quick and good in the air, he continued to improve and he became the lynch pin in that area after seeing off the challenge of his long-time mentor Paul McGrath. He also had his best goalscoring season, finding the net four times, including a vital winner at Everton in September, and if his current form persists he could soon become a regular in the England side.

West Bromwich A (From trainee on 13/7/89) FL 0+2
Aston Villa (£40,000 on 12/7/91) F/PL 131+11/7 FLC 14+1/1 FAC 10+2/1 Others 7/1

Efan Ekoku

EKOKU Efangwu (Efan) Goziem
Born: Manchester, 8 June 1967
Height: 6'1" Weight: 12.0
International Honours: Nigeria: 4

The Nigerian international once again proved to be worth every penny of the fee Wimbledon paid to Norwich in 1994, especially after last season. With superb close control, the striker chipped in with 12 goals in 1996-97 after teaming up with Marcus Gayle in what was surely one of the partnerships in the Premiership. His terrific speed enables him to leave defenders for dead before unleashing an explosive finish, thus making him one of the most feared opponents around, a feature of his game that was highlighted at West Ham in September when he robbed Julian Dicks 40 yards from

goal before racing through to slot past the 'keeper for the Dons' second in a 2-0 win.
Bournemouth (£100,000 from Sutton U on 11/5/90) FL 43+19/21 FLC 0+2 FAC 5+2/2 Others 3+1/2
Norwich C (£500,000 on 26/3/93) PL 26+11/15 FLC 3/1 FAC 1+1 Others 3/1
Wimbledon (£900,000 on 14/10/94) PL 80+5/27 FLC 6/1 FAC 16/3

ELKINS Gary
Born: Wallingford, 4 May 1966
Height: 5'9" Weight: 11.13
International Honours: E: Yth

With no first-team action at Wimbledon since a knee injury suffered in November 1995, Gary had hoped to reactivate his career with a move to Swindon Town (in late September 1996), who needed a replacement left back for the injured Jason Drysdale. However, things did not go all his way at the County Ground and after just nine games he found himself in and out of the team, swapping the position with Drysdale, Ty Gooden, Frederic Darras and latterly, Phil King. Manager Steve McMahon also tried him out in central defence, from which position, ironically, he scored his first goal for the Robins - a close-range header - against Sheffield United in February. With King and Drysdale also competing for the number three shirt, and the team's chronic late season problems in central defence, it may be that his best chances in the coming term lie in this hitherto unfamiliar position. Has a smart left foot to go with a super range of quality passes.

Fulham (From apprentice on 3/12/83) FL 100+4/2 FLC 6 FAC 2+2 Others 7+1
Exeter C (Loaned on 23/12/89) FL 5
Wimbledon (£20,000 on 20/8/90) F/PL 100+10/3 FLC 8 FAC 7/1 Others 1+1
Swindon T (£100,000 on 18/9/96) FL 19+4/1 FLC 2 FAC 1

ELLINGTON Lee Simon
Born: Bradford, 3 July 1980
Height: 5'10" Weight: 11.0

Having played against Hull City in a friendly for Eccleshill United a year earlier, the first-year trainee was plucked from the Tigers' junior team for occasional outings on the senior's bench during 1996-97. Lee, a powerfully built midfielder, has become the club's third youngest-ever player.

Hull C (Trainee) FL 0+2 Others 0+1

ELLIOTT Andrew (Andy)
Born: Newcastle, 2 May 1974
Height: 5'9" Weight: 11.10

A part-time midfielder whose career appeared to be on the rocks when he was holidaying in Tenerife, having been released by Unibond League team, Spennymoor United, on his return last February he was offered a contract by Hartlepool's Mick Tait, who had been impressed by his attacking wing play in a pre-season friendly for Dunston Federation. Andy was immediately promoted to the senior side, but after a short first-team run he was unable to win a regular place and was released.

Hartlepool U (Free from Spennymoor on 10/2/97) FL 2+2

ELLIOTT Anthony (Tony) Robert
Born: Nuneaton, 30 November 1969
Height: 6'0" Weight: 13.7
Club Honours: WC '90
International Honours: E: Yth; Sch

Released by Carlisle during the 1996 close season, this confident goalkeeper started superbly well at Cardiff by keeping four clean sheets in the opening five games of 1996-97. Unfortunately, a back problem rendered him unfit early in December and having got back after missing nine games, of which City only won two, a calf injury brought his campaign to a premature close in April. Created an excellent impression, his ability to react quickly helping the defence out on numerous occasions.

Birmingham C (From apprentice on 3/12/86) FLC 1
Hereford U (Free on 22/12/88) FL 75 FLC 5 FAC 6 Others 9
Huddersfield T (Free on 29/7/92) FL 15 FLC 2 FAC 3 Others 3
Carlisle U (Free on 28/6/93) FL 21+1 FAC 1 Others 5
Cardiff C (Free on 4/7/96) FL 36 FLC 2 FAC 1

ELLIOTT Matthew (Matt) Stephen
Born: Wandsworth, 1 November 1968
Height: 6'3" Weight: 14.10

A right-footed central defender, and commanding in the air, Matt was signed from Oxford United last January for a club record fee. Made his debut in the home win over Wimbledon and scored his first goal in a thrilling 4-3 defeat at St James' Park, before collecting a brace to help City to a double over Wimbledon at Selhurst Park. Missing out on Wembley through being cup tied, he looked to be one of the best buys of the season anywhere in the Premiership and earned his glory by netting the goal against Sheffield Wednesday that ensured survival. At Oxford, where he had organised their defence and helped them to many clean sheets, as well as scoring ten goals, his loss was immeasurable.

Charlton Ath (£5,000 from Epsom & Ewell on 9/5/88) FLC 1
Torquay U (£10,000 on 23/3/89) FL 123+1/15 FLC 9/2 FAC 9/2 Others 16/1
Scunthorpe U (£50,000 on 26/3/92) FL 61/8 FLC 6 FAC 2 Others 8
Oxford U (£150,000 on 5/11/93) FL 148/21 FLC 16/1 FAC 11/2 Others 6
Leicester C (£1,600,000 on 18/1/97) PL 16/4 FAC 2

ELLIOTT Robert (Robbie) James
Born: Newcastle, 25 December 1973
Height: 5'10" Weight: 11.6
International Honours: E: U21-2; Yth

Now established as an important member of the Newcastle squad, where his flexibility is highly valued, Robbie is a confident young player who is strong in the tackle, uses the ball well, and enjoys joining the attack when the opportunity arises. Began 1996-97 on a weekly contract and in discussion with Blackburn over a big money transfer, thus missing the Charity Shield match and the opening league game. However, the move fell through and, after signing a new two-year contract, he immediately returned to the side to become a regular, playing in most of the subsequent games. Appeared mostly

in the left-back position, though he was also used as a useful central defender on occasion, but ended the campaign operating in midfield. With a keen eye for scoring opportunities, he netted seven times in 17 matches during the latter half of the season, including a goal direct from a corner against Derby. *Stop Press:* Was reported to have signed for Bolton, an initial £2.2 million fee, rising to £2.5, securing the deal.

Newcastle U (From trainee on 3/4/91) F/PL 71+15/2 FLC 5 FAC 7+3 Others 5+1

ELLIOTT Stuart Thomas
Born: London, 27 August 1977
Height: 5'8" Weight: 11.5

Yet to play for Newcastle, despite being on the first-team bench, this combative midfielder joined Hull City on loan last February and experienced a league debut he would never forget when sent off in injury time against Northampton at Boothferry. Returned to United after two more games at City and can be expected to progress in the game.

Newcastle U (From trainee on 28/8/95)
Hull C (Loaned on 28/2/97) FL 3

ELLIS Anthony (Tony) Joseph
Born: Salford, 20 October 1964
Height: 5'11" Weight: 11.0

Continued his run as a consistent goalscorer for Blackpool last season, scoring in three successive games and grabbing a hat trick at Peterborough, while, at the same time, working tremendously hard for his team mates. As the other half of the strike partnership with Jimmy Quinn, he also scored twice in a 3-1 League Cup win over the Premiership's Chelsea.

Oldham Ath (Free from Horwich RMI on 22/8/86) FL 5+3 FLC 1 Others 1
Preston NE (£23,000 on 16/10/87) FL 80+6/27 FLC 3 FAC 5 Others 11+1/5
Stoke C (£250,000 on 20/12/89) FL 66+11/19 FLC 5+1/1 FAC 1+4 Others 3+2
Preston NE (£140,000 on 14/8/92) FL 70+2/48 FLC 4/2 FAC 6/3 Others 6/3
Blackpool (£165,000 on 25/7/94) FL 122+6/47 FLC 8/6 FAC 5 Others 8/3

ELLISON Anthony Lee
Born: Bishop Auckland, 13 January 1973
Height: 5'11" Weight: 12.3
Club Honours: Div 4 '91

Started last season at Crewe on a non-contract basis, playing four games, and, despite scoring twice early on at Peterborough, was not offered a contract and released. Following that, the 22-year-old forward turned up at Hereford, where he was restricted to just one subs' appearance before trialling at Mansfield, prior to going out of the league.

Darlington (From trainee on 8/11/90) FL 54+18/17 FLC 2+1 FAC 4+2/2 Others 3+1/1
Hartlepool U (Loaned on 25/3/93) FL 3+1/1
Leicester C (Free on 12/8/94)
Crewe Alex (Free on 23/8/95) FL 3+1/2 FLC 1 Others 0+1 (Free to Halifax during 1996 close season)
Hereford U (Free on 11/10/96) FL 0+1

EMBERSON Carl Wayne
Born: Epsom, 13 July 1973
Height: 6'2" Weight: 14.7

The previous season's first-choice Colchester goalkeeper, Carl lost his place to Garrett Caldwell at the start of 1996-97 and could little have imagined that he would be starring in a Wembley final only months later. With Caldwell injured and Carl back in the side he produced a series of fine displays throughout the rest of the campaign as his command of the penalty area developed, giving many excellent performances, including a penalty save at Wembley. Is now well past 100 league appearances for the U's and aiming for the longevity of Mike Walker in the United goal.

Millwall (From trainee on 4/5/91) Others 1
Colchester U (Loaned on 17/12/92) FL 13
Colchester U (£25,000 on 6/7/94) FL 95+1 FLC 5 FAC 3 Others 11

EMBLEN Neil Robert
Born: Bromley, 19 June 1971
Height: 6'2" Weight: 13.11

Having torn his hamstring on the Wolves' summer tour, the injury lingered on and it was not until the end of last September that Neil's season began properly, and then he took a blow on the head at Swindon and went off at half time. In November, however, he began a settled run in the team, though his job was not always the same, as he could be the central defender he was originally, or the strong-running midfielder he had developed into. He produced some good away performances, but always looked more confident going forward rather than chasing back. Also played as an orthodox full back, while perhaps a sweeper role would have suited him best. All such arguments and a run of 22 games was ended by a tackle at Bradford in March, causing medial ligament trouble, and although he started a match a month later his season really ended there.

Millwall (£175,000 from Sittingbourne on 8/11/93) FL 12 Others 1
Wolverhampton W (£600,000 on 14/7/94) FL 80+8/9 FLC 2+2/1 FAC 7+2 Others 2+1

EMERSON Moises Costa
Born: Rio de Janeiro, Brazil, 12 April 1972
Height: 6'0" Weight: 14.5

Signed from Porto during the 1996 close season, the brilliant Brazilian with the deceptive ambling gait and electrifying pace, developed a love-hate relationship with the Middlesbrough fans during his well documented absences from the club in 1996-97. The "love" part far outweighed the "hate" when he paraded his astute foot-balling brain and super soccer skills to carve gaping holes in many of the best Premiership defences, while his ferocious dead-ball kicking, powerful running, and delightful dribbling, coupled to his ability to shrug off the most savage tackles, made him a delight to watch. Although able to lay claim to many Man of the Match awards, which bear testimony to the powerful impact he made at the club during his initial introduction to the Premiership, at the time of going to press it was still early days to know whether he would be playing first division football at the Riverside this coming term.

Emerson

Middlesbrough (£4,000,000 from Porto on 26/7/96) PL 32/4 FLC 8/2 FAC 5/1

ERIKSSON Jan
Born: Sunsdvall, Sweden, 24 August 1967
Height: 6'0" Weight: 13.0
International Honours: Sweden: 35

Defender Jan arrived at Roker last January having helped his former club Helsingborg knock Aston Villa out of the UEFA Cup earlier in the season. However, having made an impressive Sunderland debut, ironically at Villa Park, the Swedish international was surprisingly confined to the substitutes' bench for the rest of the campaign as the Rokerites slid towards division one. Many fans are hoping he is given the chance to establish himself at the club next term.

Sunderland (£250,000 from Helsingborg on 11/1/97) PL 1

ESDAILLE Darren
Born: Manchester, 4 November 1974
Height: 5'8" Weight: 10.7

Joined Doncaster Rovers from non-league Hyde United last January, making his debut at Swansea later that month, Darren proved he could play either at full back or in midfield. Signed until July 1998, there should be no shortage of opportunities for him.

Doncaster Rov (Free from Hyde U on 27/1/97) FL 16+2/1

ETHERINGTON Matthew
Born: Truro, 14 August 1981
Height: 5'10" Weight: 10.1

Matthew became Peterborough's third youngest league player ever when making

his debut in the number 11 shirt at Brentford in the final game of last season. Still an associate schoolboy, big things are predicted for this speedy young attacker.

Peterborough U (Associated Schoolboy) FL 1

EUELL Jason Joseph
Born: Lambeth, 6 February 1977
Height: 6'0" Weight: 12.7
An exciting young Wimbledon attacker who has been with the club since his schooldays, and is worshipped by the fans who have very high hopes for him, Jason is not afraid to made a challenge, is full of pace, and has a very similar style of play to that of Ian Wright. With youth on his side, but still needing valuable experience, he made just five starts in 1996-97, scoring in the final two matches of the campaign, a header in a 2-1 win over Liverpool and an 86th minute strike that consigned Sunderland to the first division.
Wimbledon (From trainee on 1/6/95) PL 8+8/4 FLC 1 FAC 1+5

EUSTACE Scott Douglas
Born: Leicester, 13 June 1975
Height: 6'0" Weight: 14.2
The young Mansfield central defender continued to improve in 1996-97 and was certainly one of the better anchor men in the third division. Fully dependable, he had a very good season indeed.
Leicester C (From trainee on 9/7/93) FL 0+1
Mansfield T (Free on 9/6/95) FL 66+3/5 FLC 1 FAC 3/1 Others 3

EVANS Michael (Micky) James
Born: Plymouth, 1 January 1973
Height: 6'0" Weight: 13.4
A strong centre forward who likes to take on defenders, causing many a torrid time, he improved no end over the past two seasons, catching the eye of many managers before being snapped up by Southampton's Graeme Souness last March, having already scored 15 times for second division Plymouth in 41 appearances during 1996-97. Came into a struggling Saints' side for the final 12 games, immediately impressing with his pace and ability to hit the target, his first goals in a red and white shirt could not have been more welcome. Brought off the bench after 68 minutes in the Premiership dog fight at Nottingham Forest to replace the god-like Matt le Tissier, he sealed a 3-1 victory and Forest's ultimate fate with two goals in the final three minutes. Two more strikes followed in crucial games and he looks set to become a regular scorer.
Plymouth Arg (From trainee on 30/3/91) FL 130+33/38 FLC 8+1 FAC 10+2/3 Others 10/2
Southampton (£500,000 on 4/3/97) PL 8+4/4

EVANS Paul Simon
Born: Oswestry, 1 September 1974
Height: 5'6" Weight: 12.0
Club Honours: Div 3 '94
International Honours: W: U21-4; Yth
A midfielder terrier in the middle of the park for Shrewsbury, and always in the action, Paul played in the vast majority of games last season. Hard tackling, with a superb

shot, with the ability to score a number of spectacular goals, if he finds a little more composure to go with his distribution, he will create even more danger to the opposition's defences in 1997-98.
Shrewsbury T (From trainee on 2/7/93) FL 109+18/14 FLC 8+2/1 FAC 9+1/2 Others 10/4

EVANS Terence (Terry) William
Born: Hammersmith, 12 April 1965
Height: 6'5" Weight: 15.7
Club Honours: Div 3 '92
Giant central defender and Wycombe club captain, Terry gave some particularly memorable performances away from home in 1996-97 when he appeared to single handedly repel all comers. Although losing his place briefly to the more mobile Paul McCarthy in January, and again in April, it still came as a shock when he was released at the end of the season, especially when one remembers it was his 86th minute do-or-die goal that brought Wanderers a 4-3 victory at Bristol Rovers after being 3-1 down.
Brentford (£5,000 from Hillingdon Borough on 22/7/85) FL 228+1/23 FLC 15+1/4 FAC 17/2 Others 23/1
Wycombe W (£40,000 on 26/8/93) FL 128+8/16 FLC 8/2 FAC 7+1 Others 4/1

EVANS Duncan Wayne
Born: Abermule, 25 August 1971
Height: 5'10" Weight: 12.5
Walsall's Wayne had the bad luck to suffer an early season groin strain at Chesterfield in 1996-97, in what was his 100th appearance for his one and only league club. A strong tackler, he came back well to give his usual wholehearted displays, mainly on the left flank of the defence, after playing on the right in previous seasons.
Walsall (Free from Welshpool on 13/8/93) FL 124+5 FLC 8+1/1 FAC 10+1 Others 5

EVERS Sean Anthony
Born: Hitchin, 10 October 1977
Height: 5'9" Weight: 9.11
Although spending most of last season as a leading member of the Luton reserve side, the clever midfield player was given just two first-team games, helping the side to a point in a 2-2 draw at home to Plymouth in the league and making an appearance in the AWS. Sean is yet another young player developed by the Hatter's youth policy, which has produced Mark Pembridge, John Hartson, and Matthew Upson in recent years. Not only a provider, he can also be a hard-tackling ball winner.
Luton T (From trainee on 16/5/96) FL 2 Others 2

EVTUSHOK Aleksandr (Alex)
Born: Ukraine, 11 January 1970
Height: 6'2" Weight: 12.10
International Honours: Ukraine: 7
A Ukrainian international central defender who impressed during trials and was signed from Karpaty last February, he made his debut for Coventry at Old Trafford, a match that saw City two down in five minutes, before being withdrawn after half an hour. Having given notice in the Leicester home game of his timing and skill on the ball,

despite the obvious signs that his positional sense will need to adapt to the English game, Alex gave notice that he will be very much in the running for team selection this coming season. Incidentally, according to a good source, the English translation of his surname should be Yevtutchok.
Coventry C (£800,000 from Karpaty on 6/2/97) PL 3

EYRE John Robert
Born: Hull, 9 October 1974
Height: 6'1" Weight: 12.7
1996-97 was an up-and-down season for the Scunthorpe striker as he showed only glimpses of his true form. However, with skilful touches and good positional play being his main assets, he still found the net at vital times after opening his account in a 1-1 draw at Swansea in October.
Oldham Ath (From trainee on 16/7/93) P/FL 4+6/1 FLC 0+2
Scunthorpe U (Loaned on 15/12/94) FL 9/8
Scunthorpe U (£40,000 on 4/7/95) FL 77+4/18 FLC 4/2 FAC 6/1 Others 3/1

EYRES David
Born: Liverpool, 26 February 1964
Height: 5'10" Weight: 11.8
David's talents were employed almost exclusively from the position of left-wing back at Burnley during 1996-97, and he fitted in well with the new system introduced by Adrian Heath. Although some fans missed his more attacking skills and spectacular goal attempts, his performances were good enough to win him a place in the PFA second division side for the season.
Blackpool (£10,000 from Rhyl on 15/8/89) FL 147+11/38 FLC 11+1/1 FAC 11/2 Others 13+2/4
Burnley (£90,000 on 29/7/93) FL 158+4/36 FLC 13/6 FAC 14/8 Others 9/3

David Eyres

EAT FOOTBALL.
SLEEP FOOTBALL.
DRINK COCA-COLA.©1996

Coca-Cola plays a unique role in supporting Football at all levels of the game – adding enjoyment to a young player's first kick through to the World Cup Final.

Starting with the **Coca-Cola FA Grassroots Development Programme** which invests in the future of the sport and ensures young players receive top quality coaching to improve their performance, knowledge and enjoyment of our national game.

The Coca-Cola Cup gives supporters of all the regional clubs throughout England and Scotland the chance to enjoy the excitement and calibre of play that only a cup competition can give.

Moving into the international arena, Coca-Cola supports **the England Team** which competed in **Euro 96™** – the biggest sporting event to be held in England since the 1966 World Cup. As one of the main supporters of **Euro 96™**, Coca-Cola enhanced the event by bringing fans closer to the action.

In 1998 the **World Cup** takes place in France and, as sponsors, Coca-Cola will ensure fans are given the opportunity to enjoy the World's premier sporting occasion.

F

FACEY Delroy Michael
Born: Huddersfield, 22 April 1980
Height: 5'11" Weight: 11.10
The fifth youngest player in Huddersfield's history, Delroy was yet another homegrown product to have made his debut last season, when coming off the bench at home to Portsmouth in March. A big, strong, bustling striker, he proved himself very good in the air after being pressed in to service much sooner than expected, due to injuries, but showed himself to be more than capable and will be one to watch in the future. Signed a three-year contract in May.
Huddersfield T (From trainee on 13/5/97) FL 1+2

FAHY Alan
Born: Liverpool, 27 January 1973
Height: 5'10" Weight: 11.7
Alan joined Doncaster Rovers from Barrow on transfer deadline day, 1997, on non-contract forms, basically to act as cover from the subs' bench and, in the process, came on to the field of play five times. A tough-tackling central midfielder with a wealth of experience in non-league football, his job done, he moved to Droylesden at the end of the campaign.
Doncaster Rov (£1,500 from Barrow on 27/3/97) FL 0+5

Chris Fairclough

FAIRCLOUGH Courtney (Chris) Huw
Born: Nottingham, 12 April 1964
Height: 5'11" Weight: 11.7
Club Honours: Div 2 '90, Div 1 '92, '97; CS '92
International Honours: E: B-1; U21-7
A tower of strength in Bolton's number six shirt alongside Gerry Taggart, the duo forming an excellent partnership on which

the whole side thrived in 1996-97, Chris produced many top-quality displays and his strong tackling gave a number of opposing forwards a torrid time. He also weighed in with some important goals and loved to go foraging in the opponents' penalty area, his first goal of the season coming in the 6-1 thrashing of Grimsby. However, his most important goal was the one that brought Wanderers back to 1-1 against Queens Park Rangers in April, followed by John McGinlay scoring the winner to ensure Bolton of Premiership football for 1997-98.
Nottingham F (From apprentice on 12/10/81) FL 102+5/1 FLC 9+1/1 FAC 6 Others 9+2
Tottenham H (£387,000 on 3/7/87) FL 60/5 FLC 7 FAC 3
Leeds U (£500,000 on 23/3/89) FL 187+6/21 FLC 17+2/2 FAC 14+1 Others 14
Bolton W (£500,000 on 4/7/95) F/PL 79/6 FLC 11 FAC 5

FARRELL Andrew (Andy) James
Born: Colchester, 7 October 1965
Height: 5'11" Weight: 12.3
Club Honours: Div 4 '92
An experienced defender or midfielder whom Rochdale boss, Graham Barrow, signed from his former club, Wigan, during the 1996 close season, Andy put in consistently professional performances at left back, centre back, or in midfield, as the situation demanded. Scored twice at Northampton after being pushed up from full back.
Colchester U (From apprentice on 21/9/83) FL 98+7/5 FLC 9 FAC 8 Others 6
Burnley (£13,000 on 7/8/87) FL 237+20/19 FLC 17+4/1 FAC 19+2 Others 27+3/3
Wigan Ath (£20,000 on 22/9/94) FL 51+3/1 FLC 3 FAC 4+1 Others 5/1
Rochdale (Free on 3/7/96) FL 37+3/2 FLC 2 FAC 2

FARRELL David (Dave) William
Born: Birmingham, 11 November 1971
Height: 5'11" Weight: 11.9
Was first-choice Wycombe left winger until the new manager, John Gregory, arrived last October and chose Mickey Bell to be the left-wing back in his new formation. On his day an exciting player, quick, with close control, and two good feet, Dave was released on a free transfer at the end of the season. Scored his only goal of the campaign in a 2-1 defeat at Bournemouth.
Aston Villa (£45,000 from Redditch U on 6/1/92) F/PL 5+1 FLC 2
Scunthorpe U (Loaned on 25/1/93) FL 4+1/1 Others 2
Wycombe W (£100,000 on 14/9/95) FL 44+16/6 FLC 6 FAC 3+2 Others 2

FARRELL Sean Paul
Born: Watford, 28 February 1969
Height: 6'0" Weight: 13.7
Unable to hold down a regular place at Peterborough, despite having already scored four goals in nine games last season, Sean jumped at the opportunity of joining Notts County in October. Although the big centre forward scored prolifically in the reserves, gaining two hat tricks, he was just one of several players used in the first team's number nine shirt and was never able to put a proper run together. A never-say-die kind

of player whose efforts are appreciated by his team mates, he is good in the air and on the ground and helps to defend set pieces well.
Luton T (From apprentice on 5/3/87) FL 14+11/1 FAC 2+1/1 Others 1+2/2
Colchester U (Loaned on 1/3/88) FL 4+5/1
Northampton T (Loaned on 13/9/91) FL 4/1
Fulham (£100,000 on 19/12/91) FL 93+1/31 FLC 5+1/3 FAC 2/3 Others 8/1
Peterborough U (£120,000 on 5/8/94) FL 49+17/20 FLC 4+2/1 FAC 4+1/3 Others 3+1/1
Notts Co (£80,000 on 14/10/96) FL 10+4/1 FAC 3 Others 1

FARRELLY Gareth
Born: Dublin, 28 August 1975
Height: 6'1" Weight: 12.7
International Honours: Ei: 3; U21-8; Yth; Sch
Gareth eventually increased his Aston Villa first-team experience in 1996-97 with a late season start and two more when coming on as a sub, having spent long spells on the bench without getting a game. The midfielder also increased his Republic of Ireland honours, following a non-playing game against Liechtenstein, with further "B" and U21 caps coming his way, but, despite that, was a disappointing campaign for a player who had seemed set for a major breakthrough into the side, but then Villa's midfield does look strong!
Aston Villa (From trainee on 21/1/92) PL 2+6 FLC 0+1
Rotherham U (Loaned on 21/3/95) FL 9+1/2

FARRELLY Stephen (Steve)
Born: Liverpool, 27 March 1965
Height: 6'5" Weight: 15.7
International Honours: E: SP
A giant of a goalkeeper who made his Rotherham debut at Brentford last October at the ripe old age of 31, his second season at Millmoor, Steve was unable to hold on to a first-team place and moved to non-league Barrow in January, before coming back into the Football League with Scunthorpe on transfer deadline day as non-contract first-team cover.
Rotherham U (£20,000 from Macclesfield on 13/7/95) FL 7 FAC 1 (Free to Barrow on 9/1/97)
Scunthorpe U (Free on 27/3/97)

FAULKNER David Peter
Born: Sheffield, 8 October 1975
Height: 6'1" Weight: 12.13
International Honours: E: Yth, Sch
A former England youth central defender who joined Darlington from Sheffield Wednesday in the 1996 close season, he failed to establish himself in the first team and was released before the end of the season after just four appearances. David enjoys the physical side of the game, being a sound tackler, and could return to the league before too long.
Sheffield Wed (From trainee on 23/12/92)
Darlington (Free on 15/8/96) FL 2+2

FEAR Peter Stanley
Born: Sutton, 10 September 1973
Height: 5'10" Weight: 11.7
International Honours: E: U21-3

Les Ferdinand

Nicknamed "The Rash" because of his man-marking ability, Peter made 22 appearances, including nine from the bench, for Wimbledon last season and scored a vital extra-time winner in the Coca-Cola Cup at Luton in November. Although used mainly in central midfield, he is just as capable in defence where he tackles solidly and cuts opponents' space down well. Also a good passer in an attacking role, his pace takes him clear of defenders, while he is more than useful to have around for set pieces.

Wimbledon (From trainee on 2/7/92) PL 46+17/2 FLC 7+2/1 FAC 2

FENN Neale Michael
Born: Edmonton, 18 January 1977
Height: 5'10" Weight: 11.2
International Honours: Ei: U21-1; Yth

In a baptism of fire, Neale, a regular scorer for the reserves, made his Tottenham debut in the injury-ravaged line up against Manchester United in the third round of the FA Cup last January, proving extremely composed for a player of such inexperience. The young target man also showed strength when holding the ball up, complimenting his powerful running and shooting, and ably demonstrated the quality of the youth outfit at White Hart Lane. Already a Republic of Ireland youth international, his good form in 1996-97 saw him elevated to the U21 side, when playing against Romania in April.

Tottenham H (From trainee on 1/7/95) PL 0+4 FAC 1

FENSOME Andrew (Andy) Brian
Born: Northampton, 18 February 1969
Height: 5'8" Weight: 11.2
Club Honours: Div 3 '91, '96

One of several new defenders signed by Rochdale during the summer of 1996, Andy immediately made the right-back position his own with some solid performances, missing only a handful of games. Originally with Preston, where he was recognised as a long-throw expert, he can both defend well and get forward when the need arises.

Norwich C (From apprentice on 16/2/87)
Cambridge U (Free from Bury T on 21/11/89) FL 122+4/1 FLC 11 FAC 17+2 Others 9+1
Preston NE (Signed on 8/10/93 FL 93/1 FLC 3/1 FAC 9 Others 11
Rochdale (Free on 3/7/96) FL 38+2 FLC 2 FAC 2 Others 1

FENTON Graham Anthony
Born: Wallsend, 22 May 1974
Height: 5'10" Weight: 12.10
Club Honours: FLC '94, '96
International Honours: E: U21-1

After his Blackburn goalscoring exploits at the end of 1995-96, Graham started three of the first ten games of last season and came off the bench in the other seven, before going down with a badly torn hamstring in a reserve game against Sheffield Wednesday that put him out of action until January. Returning somewhat overweight, he was a frequent visitor to the Ewood treatment table as the injury continually reappeared and played little football from then on. A quick, all-purpose forward who shows coolness under pressure in tight areas, he will be hoping to put 1996-97 well behind him come the new campaign.

Aston Villa (From trainee on 13/2/92) PL 16+16/3 FLC 2+5
West Bromwich A (Loaned on 10/1/94) FL 7/3
Blackburn Rov (£1,500,000 on 7/11/95) PL 9+18/7 FLC 0+2 FAC 0+1

FERDINAND Leslie (Les)
Born: Acton, 8 December 1966
Height: 5'11" Weight: 13.5
Club Honours: Turkish Cup '89 (During loan spell in 1988-89 with Besiktas)
International Honours: E: 13

A natural striker whose game is based upon exploiting his strength, his pace, and his power in the air, Les gave up the number nine shirt when Alan Shearer arrived at Newcastle, switching to number ten. Many thought this was symbolic of the fact that he would now be surplus to requirements and soon on his way. However, Kevin Keegan was adamant that the two could play effectively together, and the strikers proved him right. With Alan Shearer as the focal point of the attack in 1996-97, Les was encouraged to bring more width into his game, which he did to good effect, being rewarded with another healthy tally of goals, including one in each of his four UEFA Cup ties. Early on he netted in six consecutive matches, and his form earned him a recall to the England side against Poland and Georgia, scoring against the latter. Unfortunately, his season was interrupted by injury and he suffered a depressed fracture of the cheekbone against West Ham in November. A hamstring injury in March was a further upset and although he returned as a sub-stitute against Liverpool at Anfield, he lasted only ten minutes, before resuming his place in the side for the final few matches of the campaign. Having scored a brace against Nottingham Forest in the final game, he reached 50 goals for United and went beyond 100 in the Premiership to secure his position as second only to Alan Shearer in the all-time Premier League scoring charts. Is a cousin to West Ham's rising young star, Rio Ferdinand.

Queens Park R (£15,000 from Hayes on 12/3/87) F/PL 152+11/80 FLC 11+2/7 FAC 6+1/3 Others 1
Brentford (Loaned on 24/3/88) FL 3
Newcastle U (£6,000,000 on 7/6/95) PL 67+1/41 FLC 6/3 FAC 4+1/2 Others 5/4

FERDINAND Rio Gavin
Born: Peckham, 7 November 1978
Height: 6'2" Weight: 12.1
International Honours: E: U21-2; Yth

The brightest star in West Ham's youth academy, and strongly tipped as a future England international, the teenage central defender made occasional appearances from the bench in the first half of last season and after scoring his first Premiership goal as a substitute forward at Blackburn in February he remained a permanent member of the first-team squad for the rest of the season. To illustrate his versatility, he filled in as a central defender, midfielder, and left back (covering for the injured Julian Dicks) in the closing weeks of the campaign, during which he added England U21 honours to his youth caps. Very composed on the ball, it remains to be seen if he can graduate to the full England squad quickly enough to make an international appearance at the same time as his illustrious cousin, Les, of Newcastle United.

West Ham U (From trainee on 27/11/95) PL 11+5/2 FLC 0+1 FAC 1
Bournemouth (Loaned on 8/11/96) FL 10 Others 1

Rio Ferdinand

FERGUSON Darren
Born: Glasgow, 9 February 1972
Height: 5'10" Weight: 11.10
Club Honours: PL '93
International Honours: S: U21-5; Yth

A tidy midfield player, Alex Ferguson's son was involved in the opening three games for Wolves in 1996-97, but only started one of the first ten, before being named in the side at Swindon and running through to get a neat goal. Although this was followed with a good first-time strike with the outside of his left foot to score against Bolton, before the 90 minutes was up his season had turned sour when he was sent off and involved in a melee that ensued. Despite this, he kept his place for one further game, but, with his suspension imminent, he was not seen again until January, when he came on and scored

in the FA Cup tie against Portsmouth. Had started only four games all season before being selected for the last nine, a run highlighted by a lovely free kick against Southend, as well as an improved workrate.
Manchester U (From trainee on 11/7/90) F/PL 20+7 FLC 2+1
Wolverhampton W (£250,000 on 13/1/94) FL 70+17/4 FLC 8/1 FAC 7+2/2 Others 6

FERGUSON Duncan
Born: Stirling, 27 December 1971
Height: 6'3" Weight: 13.5
Club Honours: SL '94; SLC '94; FAC '95
International Honours: S: 7; B; U21-7; Yth; Sch

On his day an unstoppable centre forward of intimidating physical presence and awesome aerial ability, Duncan is idolised by the Everton supporters and reserves his best performances for the big matches, scoring spectacular goals last season at Old Trafford against Manchester United and in the Goodison derby match against Liverpool. He also came back for Scotland, winning caps against Austria and Estonia in World Cup qualifying matches. Despite the excessive publicity given to his ability in the air, he is also remarkably nimble on the floor for such a tall player and possesses excellent pace.
Dundee U (Signed from Carse Thistle on 1/2/90) SL 75+2/27 SLC 2+1/2 SC 6/4

Glasgow R (£4,000,000 on 20/7/93) SL 8+6/2 SLC 2+2/3 SC 0+3 Others 1
Everton (£4,400,000 on 4/10/94) PL 69+5/22 FLC 2 FAC 7+1/4

FERNANDES Tamer Hasan
Born: Paddington, 7 December 1974
Height: 6'3" Weight: 13.7
International Honours: E: Yth

A tall and reliable Brentford reserve goalkeeper who was again understudy to Kevin Dearden in 1996-97, Tamer played just three games, sitting on the bench as an unused substitute for the remaining 56. However, when called upon the former England youth international did well, keeping two clean sheets and conceding just one goal as the Bees aimed for an automatic promotion place.
Brentford (From trainee on 12/7/93) FL 10+2 FAC 2 Others 2+1

FESTA Gianluca
Born: Cagliari, Italy, 12 March 1969
Height: 6'0" Weight: 12.8

Making his first appearance on Teeside in a friendly match when Inter-Milan visited Teeside last August, his principal adversary that day was destined to be his future Boro colleague and team mate, fellow countryman, Fabrizio Ravanelli. Joining Middlesbrough in January, the Sardinian-born Gianluca must be considered one of

Duncan Ferguson

Bryan Robson's most inspired signings, being vastly experienced, having helped his hometown club, Cagliari, to promotion from Serie "C" to Serie "A" in consecutive seasons. Although ignored by the national coach, he had played in over 300 Italian league, cup, and UEFA Cup games before his transfer. Once settled into Robson's side, his defensive skills were loudly applauded by the fans and he scored a brilliant goal on his debut (against Sheffield Wednesday) at the Riverside Stadium. With sound defensive ability, being excellent in the air, a hard tackler, and more than capable of adding to the attack, the Italian won his spurs so far as Boro fans were concerned with a string of games that (although it was not to be) sparked hope that the desperate battle for Premiership survival might be won.

Middlesbrough (£2,700,000 from Inter Milan on 18/1/97) PL 13/1 FLC 4 FAC 5/1

FETTIS Alan William
Born: Newtonards, 1 February 1971
Height: 6'1" Weight:11.8
International Honours: NI: 18; B-2; Yth; Sch

Having sat on the bench for most of his time at the City Ground, Alan eventually made his Nottingham Forest debut last season in difficult circumstances, when coming on as sub for Mark Crossley at Chesterfield in the FA Cup after the former had been sent off. Thus, the first shot he had to face was the resultant penalty, which turned out to be the match winner. Following that, he had to wait until a few games from the end of the campaign to make his Premiership debut, keeping a clean sheet in the east midland derby at Derby in his second game. Also increased his Northern Ireland international caps by playing in the World Cup ties.

Hull C (£50,000 from Ards on 14/8/91) FL 131+4/2 FLC 7+1 FAC 5 Others 7
West Bromwich A (Loaned on 20/11/95) FL 3
Nottingham F (£250,000 on 13/1/96) PL 4 FAC 0+1

FEUER Anthony **Ian**
Born: Las Vegas, USA, 20 May 1971
Height: 6'7" Weight: 15.6

The giant Luton goalkeeper was once again in brilliant form throughout last season, frequently saving the club single handedly, especially in the early months before the defence steadied. Dominating in the air, as his height would suggest, he is also an excellent shot saver with a long throw and kick to match. An uncharacteristic hesitation in the divisional play-off semi final, meant that the club will face second division football again in 1997-98, but they may not be able to hold on to one of the best 'keepers outside the Premier League. Voted Young Supporters Player of the Year, Ian was surprisingly overlooked for the PFA divisional award.

West Ham U (£70,000 from Los Angeles Salsa on 23/3/94)
Peterborough U (Loaned on 20/2/95) FL 16
Luton T (£580,000 on 11/9/95) FL 84 FLC 6 FAC 4 Others 3

FEWINGS Paul John
Born: Hull, 18 February 1978
Height: 6'0" Weight: 12.6

A re-occurring hamstring injury severely restricted Paul's 1996-97 season until March, thus halting the promise he had shown for Hull City during the previous season. Hoping to resurrect his progress in 1997-98, the young right-footed forward is highly thought of by the Tigers' management.

Hull C (From trainee on 4/8/95) FL 19+20/2 FLC 3+1/1 FAC 2 Others 0+1/1

FICKLING Ashley
Born: Sheffield, 15 November 1972
Height: 5'10" Weight: 11.6
International Honours: E: Sch

The versatile Grimsby central defender or full back, took the opportunity afforded by long-term injuries to establish himself as a regular member of the senior squad in 1996-97. Though probably not as skilful a player as some of his fellow defenders, this was compensated for by 100 per-cent effort and enthusiasm, allied to tough tackling.

Sheffield U (From juniors on 26/7/91) FLC 2+1 Others 3
Darlington (Loaned on 26/11/92) FL 14 Others 1
Darlington (Loaned on 12/8/93) FL 1 FLC 1
Grimsby T (Free on 23/3/95) FL 26+13/2 FLC 2+1 FAC 2+1

FILAN John Richard
Born: Sydney, Australia, 8 February 1970
Height: 5'11" Weight: 13.2
International Honours: Australia: U21

As Coventry's deputy 'keeper, John sat on the bench all last season whilst Steve Ogrizovic performed miracles, being called on just once, at Highbury, after the big man was carried off and then having to keep the Gunners at bay for the final six minutes. Called into the Australian national squad by Terry Venables towards the end of the

Gianluca Festa

campaign, he is a goalie who comes for the ball confidently and clears his lines well.

Cambridge U (£40,000 from Budapest St George on 12/3/93) FL 68 FLC 6 FAC 3 Others 3
Coventry C (£300,000 on 2/3/95) PL 15+1 FLC 2

FINNAN Stephen (Steve) John
Born: Limerick, 20 April 1976
Height: 5'10" Weight: 12.0
International Honours: Ei: U21-5

Having impressed on loan at Notts County during the closing months of 1995-96, and surplus to requirements at Birmingham, the talented right winger signed for the Magpies on a permanent basis last November. Skilful on the ball and pacy down the flanks, despite County being relegated, Steve's efforts were rewarded when he was selected for the Republic of Ireland squad, after being a regular at U21 level.

Birmingham C (£100,000 from Welling U on 12/6/95) FL 9+6/1 FLC 2+2 Others 2+1
Notts Co (Loaned on 5/3/96) FL 14+3/2 Others 3/1
Notts Co (£300,000 on 31/10/96) FL 18+5 FAC 4 Others 1

FINNEY Stephen (Steve) Kenneth
Born: Hexham, 31 October 1973
Height: 5'10" Weight: 12.0
Club Honours: Div 2 '96

Despite a brilliant start to his Swindon Town career in 1995-96, Steve has been unable to recapture that goalscoring form since suffering a broken leg in March 1996 and last season must have been hugely disappointing, both for him and his manager. Although starting the campaign as first-choice striking partner for Wayne Allison, he soon lost his place and made only occasional appearances in the starting line up thereafter, playing third fiddle to Steve Cowe and Peter Thorne as support striker to Allison. His two goals, at Southend in August and at home to Barnsley in November, while being late strikes in matches already in the bag, proved his intent to force his way back in to the side on a permanent basis. Runs well off the ball and is more than capable of producing excellent crosses from wide positions.

Preston NE (From trainee on 2/5/92) FL 1+5/1 FAC 0+1 Others 1+1
Manchester C (Free on 12/2/93)
Swindon T (Free on 15/6/95) FL 30+20/14 FLC 5+1/1 FAC 2+4/2 Others 2+1/1

FISHER Neil John
Born: St Helens, 7 November 1970
Height: 5'10" Weight: 11.0

This constructive and creative Chester midfielder had an indifferent time of it in 1996-97 after promising so much. Having started the season as first choice, a series of injuries restricted his appearances, especially from January onwards, before he returned to the side as a sub in the penultimate league game at Exeter. Hopefully, he can put all that behind him this coming term.

Bolton W (From trainee on 12/7/89) FL 17+7/1 FLC 4 FAC 1
Chester C (Free on 5/6/95) FL 62+11/3 FLC 6 FAC 4 Others 2

FISHLOCK Murray Edward
Born: Marlborough, 23 September 1973
Height: 5'8" Weight: 10.8

Hereford left back who enjoys surging runs down the flank to produce excellent crosses into the box. Started 1996-97 as a regular before being sidelined nine games into the season and then coming back at the end of December, he scored in a 3-1 home win over Wigan for his customary goal. Is also a determined tackler.

Hereford U (Free from Trowbridge on 30/9/94) FL 67+4/4 FLC 5 FAC 3 Others 6

FITZGERALD Scott Brian
Born: Westminster, 13 August 1969
Height: 6'0" Weight: 12.12
International Honours: Ei: B-1; U21-4

The cultured central defender was brought to Millwall on loan from Wimbledon last October, playing seven games before a fractured ankle sustained at Bristol City delayed him signing permanently. Unfortunately, for both club and player, by the time Scott was fully recovered, the Football League had imposed a transfer veto on the club, thus scuppering any plans of a deal. Is a very useful centre back who reads the game well, can pass long and short, and takes up good covering positions.

Wimbledon (From trainee on 13/7/89) F/PL 95+11/1 FLC 13 FAC 5 Others 1
Sheffield U (Loaned on 23/11/95) FL 6
Millwall (Loaned on 11/10/96) FL 7

Jan-Aage Fjortoft

FJORTOFT Jan-Aage
Born: Aalesund, Norway, 10 January 1967
Height: 6'3" Weight: 13.4
International Honours: Norway: 70

Following the further influx of foreigners at Middlesborough in 1996-97, Jan finally made his Premiership bow when coming off the bench in the home game against Leicester at the beginning of December. However, seven games and nearly two months later, the Norwegian international had been transferred to Sheffield United, having endeared himself to the Boro fans by his resolution and determination to fight for his place. After a quiet debut against his old club, Swindon, he proceeded to score eight goals in the next eight games, including a hat trick against Grimsby, and became an instant hero with the fans for his familiar "aeroplane" goal celebration. Was within seconds of a return Premiership ticket, being denied in the dying moments of the Wembley play-off final against Crystal Palace.

Swindon T (£500,000 from Rapid Vienna on 29/7/93) P/FL 62+10/28 FLC 9/9 FAC 3+1/2 Others 1+1
Middlesbrough (£1,300,000 on 31/3/95) P/FL 37+4/10 FLC 7/2 FAC 0+2/1
Sheffield U (£700,000 on 31/1/97) FL 15+2/10 Others 3/1

FLACK Steven (Steve) Richard
Born: Cambridge, 29 May 1971
Height: 6'2" Weight: 14.4

Steve joined Exeter in the early part of last season from Cardiff and quickly made an impression up front with his presence in the air and at set pieces. A strong player who can hold the ball up well, he scored an important goal at Bristol Rovers in the FA Cup, before struggling with a shoulder injury towards the end of the campaign.

Cardiff C (£10,000 from Cambridge C on 13/11/95) FL 6+5/1
Exeter C (£10,000 on 13/9/96) FL 20+7/4 FAC 2/1 Others 2

FLAHAVAN Aaron Adam
Born: Southampton, 15 December 1975
Height: 6'1" Weight: 11.12

Started last season as Portsmouth's number one 'keeper at Bradford, but was unfortunately sent off on what was his league debut, along with team-mate Andy Awford. Played in over half the league games, but after a dramatic loss of form he lost his place to long-serving Alan Knight. Tall and commanding, in the long term he may prove to be a dependable replacement for Knight in the Pompey goal.

Portsmouth (From trainee on 15/2/94) FL 24 FLC 4

FLASH Richard Garfield
Born: Birmingham, 8 April 1976
Height: 5'9" Weight: 11.10

Young Watford midfield player signed during the summer of 1996 on a free transfer from Wolves, having earlier been on Manchester United's books. After a string of good performances in the reserves, Richard made his first-team debut as a second-half substitute in the very last match of the 1996-97 season, a 4-1 defeat at Burnley.

Manchester U (From trainee on 1/7/94)
Wolverhampton W (Free on 22/9/95)
Watford (Free on 25/7/96) FL 0+1

FLECK Robert William
Born: Glasgow, 11 August 1965
Height: 5'8" Weight: 11.9
Club Honours: SPD '87; SLC '87, '88
International Honours: S: 4; U21-6; Yth
Without doubt one of the most popular players ever to wear a Norwich shirt, despite scoring just four goals in 39 outings in 1996-97, Robert is now third in the club's all-time scoring charts behind the two centurions, Johnny Gavin and Terry Allcock. Although appearing to have lost a little pace due to the sands of time, the management retained their faith in his abilities, his experience counteracting any deficiencies in that area and, at the same time, helping to bring out the best from such promising youngsters as Darren Eadie, Keith O'Neill, Craig Bellamy, and Drewe Broughton. At his best, he can still unsettle defenders.
Glasgow R (Free from Possil YM in 1983) SL 61+24/29 SLC 3+5/2 SC 1+1 Others 3+4/3
Partick Thistle (Loaned in November 1983) SL 1+1/1
Norwich C (£580,000 on 17/12/87) FL 130+13/40 FLC 13/11 FAC 16+2/11 Others 7/4
Chelsea (£2,100,000 on 13/8/92) PL 35+5/3 FLC 7/1 FAC 1
Bolton W (Loaned on 17/12/93) FL 6+1/1 Others 1
Bristol C (Loaned on 12/1/95) FL 10/1
Norwich C (£650,000 on 29/8/95) FL 70+7/14 FLC 7+2/2 FAC 2

Craig Fleming

FLEMING Craig
Born: Halifax, 6 October 1971
Height: 6'0" Weight: 11.7
As solid as a rock, Craig missed just two league games for Oldham last season, his hard tackling and deceptive speed making him ideal for the man-for-man marking role. Given crucial tasks and carrying them out, it was no fault of his that the club ended in the

second division and, as in previous campaigns, he was always prepared to hold the ball up until others were free. A player who always takes up good positions himself, he appeared either at right back or in central defence. *Stop Press:* According to late reports, Craig has signed for Norwich, a fee of £600,000 securing the deal.
Halifax T (From trainee on 21/3/90) FL 56+1 FLC 4 FAC 3 Others 3+2
Oldham Ath (£80,000 on 15/8/91) F/PL 158+6/1 FLC 12+1 FAC 11 Others 4

FLEMING Curtis
Born: Manchester, 8 October 1968
Height: 5'11" Weight: 12.8
Club Honours: Div 1 '95
International Honours: Ei: 8; U23-2; U21-5; Yth
The brilliant Middlesbrough full back enjoyed his best ever season in the top flight in 1996-97, displaying total commitment in the Boro's ultimately unsuccessful fight for Premiership survival and playing no small part in the successful league and cup runs. In a most trying season, his strong tackling, followed by his coming away with the ball from the most impossible of situations was his trademark and he fully deserved the adulation of the fans for his many sterling performances. Is now considered to be an integral part of the Republic of Ireland squad.
Middlesbrough (£50,000 from St Patricks on 16/8/91) F/PL 144+12/1 FLC 15+2/1 FAC 12+1 Others 7+1

Curtis Fleming (right)

FLEMING Haydn Valentine
Born: Islington, 14 March 1978
Height: 5'5" Weight: 9.11
Having turned pro for Cardiff during the 1996 close season after impressing in 23 starts in 1995-96 while still a trainee, the young right back came into the side in early

October before being loaned out to Inter Cable Tel. Unfortunately, whilst there, Haydn suffered a terrible knee injury which brought his career to a halt and ended in him being freed during the summer. Hopefully, he can remain in the game.
Cardiff C (From trainee on 3/7/96) FL 29+3 FAC 2 Others 1

FLEMING Terence (Terry) Maurice
Born: Marston Green, 5 January 1973
Height: 5'9" Weight: 10.9
An all-action midfield man who occasionally appeared at left back for Lincoln in 1996-97, Terry missed several matches due to suspension, but was one of City's most effective players in creating many goals from his long throw ins. Able to play in a number of positions, his pace allows him to play in a more forward, wide attacking role if required.
Coventry C (From trainee on 2/7/91) F/PL 8+5 FLC 0+1
Northampton T (Free on 3/8/93) FL 26+5/1 FLC 2 FAC 0+1 Others 0+1
Preston NE (Free on 18/7/94) FL 25+7/2 FLC 4 FAC 0+1 Others 3+2
Lincoln C (Signed on 7/12/95) FL 54+5 FLC 6/1 FAC 1 Others 1

FLETCHER Steven (Steve) Mark
Born: Hartlepool, 26 July 1972
Height: 6'2" Weight: 14.9
After the frustrations of injuries in 1995-96, Steve was hoping for better with Bournemouth in 1996-97, but, unfortunately, suffered a hamstring problem in March which ruled him out for the rest of the campaign. Up until that point he had had a good season, playing with a succession of striking partners, proving to be very strong in the air and excellent at holding the ball when necessary, attributes that were sorely missed by the team when he was unavailable.
Hartlepool U (From trainee on 23/8/90) FL 19+13/4 FLC 0+2/1 FAC 1+2 Others 2+2/1
Bournemouth (£30,000 on 28/7/92) FL 133+16/24 FLC 13/2 FAC 5 Others 3

FLITCROFT David (Dave) John
Born: Bolton, 14 January 1974
Height: 5'11" Weight: 13.5
Employed to great effect on the right-hand side of Chester's midfield in 1996-97, Dave provided many crosses for the forwards to turn into goals, as well as scoring six himself, one of them being the last-minute winner at Hereford. Unfortunately, for both him and the club, his season was disrupted by two spells of injuries, which resulted in him making just 35 starts from a possible 54. Is the brother of Blackburn's Garry.
Preston NE (From trainee on 2/5/92) FL 4+4/2 FLC 0+1 Others 0+1
Lincoln C (Loaned on 17/9/93) FL 2 FLC 0+1
Chester C (Free on 9/12/93) FL 61+20/8 FLC 4+1 FAC 4 Others 6

FLITCROFT Garry William
Born: Bolton, 6 November 1972
Height: 6'0" Weight: 12.9
International Honours: E: U21-10; Yth; Sch
An early injury restricted the young Blackburn midfielder last season, but when

the caretaker manager, Tony Parkes, made it clear that he wanted a "dogs of war" midfield, Garry came into his element. A prodigious worker, who can also play in defence and has a bit of everything – good skills, strong in the tackle and comfortable on the ball – he came back at Sheffield Wednesday, having a run of eight games before picking up a further injury and then being ruled out until after Christmas. Very much a regular from then on, he finally got on the scoresheet with a stunning last-minute equaliser at Arsenal which effectively ended the Gunners' title hopes and, at the same time, lifted Rovers further away from relegation.

Manchester C (From trainee on 2/7/91) PL 109+6/13 FLC 11+1 FAC 14/2
Bury (Loaned on 5/3/92) FL 12
Blackburn Rov (£3,200,000 on 26/3/96) PL 30+1/3 FLC 2/1 FAC 1

FLOWERS Timothy (Tim) David
Born: Kenilworth, 3 February 1967
Height: 6'2" Weight: 14.0
Club Honours: PL '95
International Honours: E: 8; U21-3; Yth
Having lost his place in the England squad and appearing to be on the decline in the early part of last season, the Blackburn goalkeeper displayed typical confidence when challenged for his club spot by Shay Given and around the turn of the year began to play with all of his old authority, continuing to be a fine shot stopper and a positive influence on the defence. In a difficult campaign, with Rovers forced to battle their way out of the Premiership danger zone, Tim kept four successive clean sheets, which included away matches at Everton and Sunderland, and certainly played his part as relegation was ultimately averted. Came back for England, as cover for David Seaman, to keep a clean sheet in the 2-0 Tournoi de France win over Italy in June.

Wolverhampton W (From apprentice on 28/8/84) FL 63 FLC 5 FAC 2 Others 2
Southampton (£70,000 on 13/6/86) F/PL 192 FLC 26 FAC 16 Others 8
Swindon T (Loaned on 23/3/87) FL 2
Swindon T (Loaned on 13/11/87) FL 5
Blackburn Rov (£2,400,000 on 4/11/93) PL 141 FLC 10 FAC 10 Others 10

FLYNN Michael (Mike) Anthony
Born: Oldham, 23 February 1969
Height: 6'0" Weight: 11.0
The inspirational Stockport captain thoroughly deserved his place in the PFA second division select side in 1996-97. An ever present, apart from one Auto Windscreen Shield game, Mike's commitment and bravery did not flag throughout a long season, which culminated in the club reaching the first division as runners up to Bury. His long throws also created several important goals.

Oldham Ath (From apprentice on 7/2/87) FL 37+3/1 FLC 1+1/1 FAC 1 Others 2
Norwich C (£100,000 on 22/12/88)
Preston NE (£125,000 on 4/12/89) FL 134+2/7 FLC 6 FAC 6+1/1 Others 13
Stockport Co (£125,000 on 25/3/93) FL 190+1/11 FLC 22/1 FAC 13/1 Others 19

FLYNN Sean Michael
Born: Birmingham, 13 March 1968
Height: 5'8" Weight: 11.8
Another of Derby's utility men who are at home either in midfield or at full back, Sean found it difficult to win back his first-team place in 1996-97, but when he did for the latter part of the year he showed the same determination which had persuaded Jim Smith to sign him from Coventry. After losing his place again, Sean went on loan to Stoke City in March for the remainder of the season, where he occupied a right-sided position in strengthening an inconsistent midfield. Enthusiastic and robust, with a great workrate, he is also a player who can win balls at either end of the field.

Coventry C (£20,000 from Halesowen T on 3/12/91) F/PL 90+7/9 FLC 5/1 FAC 3
Derby Co (£250,000 on 11/8/95) F/PL 39+20/3 FLC 3 FAC 3
Stoke C (Loaned on 27/3/97) FL 5

FOLEY Dominic Joseph
Born: Cork, 7 July 1976
Height: 6'1" Weight: 12.8
International Honours: Ei: U21-6
The tall Wolves' forward made his 1996-97 seasonal debut last September when coming off the bench after 77 minutes at Swindon, a ground the club had never won on, chesting the ball down and scoring with just five minutes remaining. He made three more appearances as a sub in October before fading from the picture, although the month did see him score for Eire U21 as they beat Macedonia 4-0. Added to his subs' collection in May, showing composure and some deft touches, especially with his lay offs.

Wolverhampton W (£35,000 from St James' Gate on 31/8/95) FL 1+9/1 FLC 0+1 FAC 0+1 Others 0+2

FORAN Mark James
Born: Aldershot, 30 October 1973
Height: 6'4" Weight: 14.3
Obviously not part of Barry Fry's plans at Peterborough in 1996-97, Mark only started twice and was loaned first to Lincoln and then to Oldham before returning to London Road. At both, having been brought in to add height to the defences, he was used just once, apart from an extra subs' appearance for the Imps, and failed to make much progress. Very tall and commanding, he can win aerial battles at both ends of the park.

Millwall (From trainee on 3/11/90)
Sheffield U (£25,000 on 28/8/93) FL 10+1/1 FLC 1 Others 0+1
Rotherham U (Loaned on 26/8/94) FL 3
Wycombe W (Loaned on 11/8/95) FL 5 FLC 2
Peterborough U (£40,000 on 8/2/96) FL 19+2/1 Others 1
Lincoln C (Loaned on 22/1/97) FL 1+1
Oldham Ath (Loaned on 3/3/97) FL 0+1

FORBES Adrian Emmanuel
Born: London, 23 January 1979
Height: 5'7" Weight: 11.0
International Honours: E: Yth
After playing in youth games and then making appearances in a truncated Avon Insurance Combination League, Adrian

became yet another teenager in the Norwich set up to make his appearance in the first team in 1996-97. Of similar build and stature to Ruel Fox, and learning to concentrate for the full 90 minutes of every match, he made his debut from the subs' bench on the last day of August in a 1-0 Carrow Road win over Wolves. Given more games, he was magnificent in the FA Cup tie at Leicester, producing a cool and combative display just two days after turning 18. Although the programme listed him as 21-year-old Steve Forbes, City feel that it will not be long before everyone has heard of him.

Norwich C (From trainee on 21/1/97) FL 3+7 FAC 1

FORBES Steven (Steve) Dudley
Born: Stoke Newington, 24 December 1975
Height: 6'2" Weight: 12.6
Unable to hold down a place at Millwall, Steve, a deadline week signing for Colchester last March, only got into the team for the last game at Barnet, but certainly made an impression, with an all-action, tireless midfield display, capped with a fine individual goal. A memorable debut, and United fans will look forward to more of the same this coming season if terms can be agreed.

Millwall (£45,000 from Sittingbourne on 11/7/94) FL 0+5 FLC 0+1 FAC 0+1
Colchester U (Signed on 14/3/97) FL 1/1

FORD Anthony (Tony)
Born: Grimsby, 14 May 1959
Height: 5'10" Weight: 13.0
Club Honours: Div 3 '80; FLGC '82
International Honours: E: B-2
Although 37 years old when he joined Mansfield last October from non-league, Barrow, as player/coach, he was soon drafted into first-team action and showed such exemplary talent playing in the wing-back role, that he had no serious challenger for the position. Still very much a force to be reckoned with.

Grimsby T (From apprentice on 1/5/77) FL 321+34/54 FLC 31+3/4 FAC 15+4/2 Others 2
Sunderland (Loaned on 27/3/86) FL 8+1/1
Stoke C (£35,000 on 8/7/86) FL 112/13 FLC 8 FAC 9 Others 6/1
West Bromwich A (£145,000 on 24/3/89) FL 114/14 FLC 7 FAC 4/1 Others 2+1
Grimsby T (£50,000 on 21/11/91) FL 59+9/3 FLC 1 FAC 3
Bradford C (Loaned on 16/9/93) FL 5 FLC 2
Scunthorpe U (Free on 2/8/94) FL 73+3/9 FLC 4/1 FAC 7/1 Others 4 (Free to Barrow on 22/8/96)
Mansfield T (Free on 25/10/96) FL 25+2/2 FAC 2/1 Others 1

FORD Jonathan (Jon) Steven
Born: Birmingham, 12 April 1968
Height: 6'2" Weight: 13.4
Club Honours: AMC '94
Signed by Gillingham from Bradford during the 1996 close season, Jon failed to get going at the Prestfield Stadium, making just six starts, before moving to Barnet on transfer deadline day, following a month on loan at Underhill. Quickly impressing at his new club, whether playing as a composed

sweeper or as a centre half, he scored the equaliser at Exeter to open his account and will be looking for more of the same in 1997-98.

Swansea C (£5,000 from Cradley T on 19/8/91) FL 145+15/7 FLC 12+1 FAC 8+5/2 Others 15+5
Bradford C (£21,000 on 26/7/95) FL 18+1 FLC 4 FAC 2 Others 1
Gillingham (£15,000 on 16/8/96) FL 2+2 FLC 3 FAC 0+1 Others 1
Barnet (£25,000 on 21/2/97) FL 13/1

FORD Mark
Born: Pontefract, 10 October 1975
Height: 5'8" Weight: 10.8
Club Honours: FAYC '93
International Honours: E: U21-2; Yth

The player many Leeds' supporters compare to David Batty, Mark is a tenacious tackler whose stamina seems never ending. This stocky midfielder began 1996-97 in the midfield holding role and commanded a place in the first team until mid season, whereupon George Graham began introducing his own signings, which then limited him to a squad place. A Leeds' player through and through, he also had the distinction of scoring his first goal for the club, with a close range header in the victory over Sunderland in November, and did he celebrate. Won a further England U21 cap against Moldova in August.

Leeds U (From trainee on 5/3/93) PL 27+2/1 FLC 7 FAC 5 Others 0+1

FORD Michael (Mike) Paul
Born: Bristol, 9 February 1966
Height: 6'0" Weight: 12.6
Club Honours: WC '88

Oxford United's skipper had another consistent campaign in 1996-97 and knocked in five goals, his best return for the club, despite not playing as a wing back. Always eager to get down the left wing from his full back spot to put in a cross or play a one-two, he was a valuable member of the squad and always around to give advice to the youngsters. Ever present until February, prior to being injured, next season will be his tenth at the Manor Ground.

Leicester C (From apprentice on 11/2/84)
Cardiff C (Free from Devizes T on 19/9/84) FL 144+1/13 FLC 6 FAC 9 Others 7
Oxford U (£150,000 on 10/6/88) FL 251+16/16 FLC 25+1/2 FAC 11+1/1 Others 8/1

FORD Robert (Bobby) John
Born: Bristol, 22 September 1974
Height: 5'9" Weight: 11.0

Performed better for Oxford last season when given a free role in midfield to wreak havoc. Often played wide on the wing where he was less effective, but his excellence on the ball, allied to good pace and skill, proved that he still has the capabilities to be a very good player and, perhaps, eventually destined for the Premier League. Surprisingly, he scored just once, but that was a great goal at Southampton in the Coca-Cola Cup. Suffered with a series of minor knocks, a back injury keeping him out for over a month in October.

Oxford U (From trainee on 6/10/92) FL 87+11/5 FLC 8+2/1 FAC 10/2 Others 7/1

FORMBY Kevin
Born: Ormskirk, 22 July 1971
Height: 5'10" Weight: 12.0

Like his old partner Andy Thackeray, Kevin lost his full-back spot for Rochdale at the start of last season and had to wait until after the turn of the year for another first-team chance in midfield. Released during the summer, he scored the first goal of his career at Hartlepool.

Rochdale (Free from Burscough on 24/3/94) FL 59+8/1 FLC 5 FAC 5 Others 10

FORREST Craig Lorne
Born: Vancouver, Canada, 20 September 1967
Height: 6'4" Weight: 14.4
Club Honours: Div 2 '92
International Honours: Canada: 37

When the Canadian international joined Chelsea from Ipswich on a month's loan last March, it was initially as cover to help the club over the busy end-of-season period, with the Blues having just two fit 'keepers available. Even so, he could not have imagined playing an active part in Chelsea's season, but, as in November, a mini-goalkeeping crisis struck after Frode Grodås stretched a hamstring vainly trying to prevent Alan Shearer's second goal at Newcastle, Craig coming off the bench to replace him to become Chelsea's fifth goalkeeper, and 30th player to be used in the Premiership – both surely a record. Kept his place for the next fixture, at home to Leicester, playing confidently as the side ended a run of four consecutive league defeats, before returning to Portman Road.

Ipswich T (From apprentice on 31/8/85) F/PL 263 FLC 19 FAC 16 Others 14
Colchester U (Loaned on 1/3/88) FL 11
Chelsea (Loaned on 26/3/97) PL 2+1

FORRESTER Jamie Mark
Born: Bradford, 1 November 1974
Height: 5'6" Weight: 10.4
Club Honours: FAYC '93
International Honours: E: Yth (UEFAYC '93); Sch

Following the departure of player/manager, Brian Laws, Jamie found himself out of favour with the new management team at Grimsby in 1996-97, his first team opportunities being limited. It was no surprise, therefore, when shortly before the transfer deadline he moved the 30 miles inland to join Laws at Scunthorpe. The fact that he scored in each of his first three outings for the Iron, obviously cast some doubt on Town's decision to let him go, especially in the light of his quick-thinking abilities both on and off the ball.

Leeds U (£60,000 from Auxerre on 20/10/92) PL 7+2 FAC 1+1/2
Southend U (Loaned on 1/9/94) FL 3+2
Grimsby T (Loaned on 10/3/95) FL 7+2/1
Grimsby T (Signed on 17/10/95) FL 27+14/6 FLC 0+2 FAC 3+1/3
Scunthorpe U (Signed on 21/3/97) FL 10/6

FORSTER Nicholas (Nicky) Michael
Born: Caterham, 8 September 1973
Height: 5'10" Weight: 11.5
International Honours: E: U21-4

A very quick, natural goalscorer, Nicky joined Birmingham from Brentford last January, coming into the side the following month when Paul Devlin was suspended and scoring three times in his first four starts. Scored a crucial goal at Grimsby, ending a dismal spell of six consecutive defeats for the Blues, before seriously damaging his knee ligaments a week later, an injury which will keep him out of action until well into the 1997-98 season. Earlier in the campaign, having had a quiet 1995-96, Nicky burst into action for Brentford, scoring twice in a game in successive away matches, and it was felt keenly by the fans that his transfer to St Andrews ultimately cost the Bees promotion.

Gillingham (Signed from Horley T on 22/5/92) FL 54+13/24 FLC 3+2 FAC 6/2
Brentford (£100,000 on 17/6/94) FL 108+1/39 FLC 11/3 FAC 8/1 Others 7+1/4
Birmingham C (£700,000 on 31/1/97) FL 4+3/3

FORSYTH Michael (Mike) Eric
Born: Liverpool, 20 March 1966
Height: 5'11" Weight: 12.2
Club Honours: Div 2 '87
International Honours: E: B-1; U21-1; Yth

Out of action through injury in 1995-96, Mike proved to be a bargain signing from Notts County last January, the left-footed central defender becoming the great unsung hero of Wycombe's successful fight against relegation. Very cool under pressure, with a knack of making crucial tackles, and dangerous when coming up for corners, he also scored two goals. Earlier in the season, he played 12 games on loan at Hereford and formed an excellent defensive partnership with Dean Smith before returning to Meadow Lane.

West Bromwich A (From apprentice on 16/11/83) FL 28+1 FLC 1 FAC 2 Others 1
Derby Co (£25,000 on 28/3/86) FL 323+2/8 FLC 36/1 FAC 15+1 Others 29/1
Notts Co (£200,000 on 23/2/95) FL 7
Hereford U (Loaned on 27/9/96) FL 12
Wycombe W (£50,000 on 6/12/96) FL 22+1/2 FAC 1 Others 1

FORSYTH Richard Michael
Born: Dudley, 3 October 1970
Height: 5'11" Weight: 12.4
International Honours: E: SP-2

Signed from Birmingham City during the 1996 close season, Richard was seen by many at Stoke as the replacement for the departing Nigel Gleghorn, being a goal-scoring midfielder, and his series of excellent long-range goals (particularly in the home game against Wolves, the club his family supported) confirmed this belief. Despite defensive duties limiting his scoring output in the second half of the campaign, the former England semi-pro international showed up well in the other side of his game – hard tackling.

Birmingham C (£50,000 from Kidderminster Hrs on 13/7/95) FL 12+14/2 FLC 7+2 FAC 2 Others 3+1
Stoke C (£200,000 on 25/7/96) FL 40/8 FLC 3 FAC 1

FORTUNE-WEST Leo Paul
Born: Stratford, 9 April 1971
Height: 6'3" Weight: 13.10

In continuing his form of 1995-96, he had the misfortune to break his ankle in the 2-1 win at Walsall last September. The injury was more complicated than first feared and it was not until the end of March that he had a full 90 minutes for the reserves. Oddly, he was then loaned to Leyton Orient on transfer deadline day for the rest of the season, with Tony Pulis stating it was better for him to get match action in league games rather than playing for the reserves.

Gillingham (£5,000 from Stevenage Borough on 12/7/95) FL 43+4/14 FLC 3/2 FAC 3/2
Leyton Orient (Loaned on 27/3/97) FL 1+4

FOSTER Adrian Michael
Born: Kidderminster, 19 March 1971
Height: 5'9" Weight: 11.0
Signed by Hereford on a free, having been released by Gillingham immediately prior to 1996-97 getting underway, Adrian missed just four games on his way to finishing the season as his new side's leading scorer. Unfortunately, with the campaign being an uphill battle, this hard-working forward spent most of his time up front on his own. Apart from his scoring ability, is also good at holding the ball up for others.

West Bromwich A (From trainee on 20/7/89) FL 13+14/2 FLC 1+3 FAC 0+2
Torquay U (Free on 3/7/92) FL 55+20/24 FLC 5+1/3 FAC 3/1 Others 4+3
Gillingham (£60,000 on 11/8/94) FL 28+12/9 FLC 2+2 FAC 3 Others 3/2
Exeter C (Loaned on 22/3/96) FL 4+3
Hereford U (Free on 12/8/96) FL 42+1/16 FLC 4/1 FAC 1 Others 1

FOSTER Colin John
Born: Chislehurst, 16 July 1964
Height: 6'4" Weight: 14.1
Having missed much of last season at Watford through injury, the tall central defender joined Cambridge United on loan in March, the day before the transfer deadline was up. A player who is still good in the air, either defensively or at set plays, he made a fine impression in seven games as he strove to bolster a defence badly shaken by the transfer of Danny Granville to Chelsea. Was released by the Hornets during the summer.

Leyton Orient (From apprentice on 4/2/82) FL 173+1/10 FLC 12 FAC 19/5 Others 5/1
Nottingham F (Signed on 4/3/87) FL 68+4/5 FLC 8/1 FAC 5 Others 2
West Ham U (Signed on 22/9/89) F/PL 88+5/5 FLC 5 FAC 9/2 Others 2+2
Notts Co (Loaned on 10/1/94) FL 9 Others 2
Watford (£100,000 on 23/3/94) FL 66/7 FLC 6/1 FAC 6
Cambridge U (Loaned on 26/3/97) FL 7

FOSTER Ian James
Born: Liverpool, 11 November 1976
Height: 5'7" Weight: 10.7
International Honours: E: Sch
A former England schoolboy international, and a prolific scorer in Liverpool reserves, Ian was released from Anfield after he had reached the end of his YTS period and signed for Hereford during the 1996 close season. An aggressive lad who will develop with a longer run in the side, he was used mainly from the bench. A tough tackler, he could eventually play in a more defensive role.

Hereford U (Free from Liverpool juniors on 15/7/96) FL 4+15 FLC 2+1 Others 0+1

FOSTER John Colin
Born: Manchester, 19 September 1973
Height: 5'11" Weight: 13.2
International Honours: E: Sch
A disappointing season saw John come into the Manchester City first team at right back for the two home games against Charlton Athletic and Barnsley last September, before being injured in the latter. Returned three weeks later as the stand in for Kit Symons at number five at Sheffield United, but was then dogged with more injuries and was out of contention until late February. A player who always tries to play the ball out of defence, he was named as an unused substitute in a few games to the end of the season. Hopefully, will be back at his best in 1997-98.

Manchester C (From trainee on 15/7/92) P/FL 17+2 FLC 2+1 FAC 2+1

FOTIADIS Andrew
Born: Hitchin, 6 September 1977
Height: 5'11" Weight: 11.7
International Honours: E: Sch
A young striker of great promise, Andrew took his first-team opportunities at Luton with much success in 1996-97. Full of pace, he ran his heart out and contributed well to the efforts of his team mates and it says much for his skill that he figured so strongly in a squad containing Tony Thorpe, David Oldfield, Kim Grant, Dwight Marshall and Bontcho Guentchev as fellow strikers. Finished the season by scoring twice, once after coming on as a substitute in a difficult match as the Hatters contested a promotion place, before making a vital goal for Oldfield in the first leg of the semi final play off which kept the Town in the hunt.

Luton T (Free from juniors on 26/7/96) FL 9+8/3 FLC 0+2 Others 1+2

FOWLER Jason Kenneth
Born: Bristol, 20 August 1974
Height: 6'0" Weight: 11.12
Freed by Bristol City in the summer of 1996, Jason signed for Cardiff, starting 1996-97 as a regular and, although losing his place on a couple of occasions when loan signings were brought in, he always came back strongly. An attacking midfielder, he ultimately missed very few games and scored six goals, including one to no avail in the second leg of the play-off semi finals at Northampton. All in all, a useful campaign for the newcomer.

Bristol C (From trainee on 8/7/93) FL 16+9 FLC 1+2 Others 1+1
Cardiff C (Signed on 19/6/96) FL 37/5 FLC 2 FAC 2 Others 3/1

FOWLER Robert (Robbie) Bernard
Born: Liverpool, 9 April 1975
Height: 5'11" Weight: 11.10
Club Honours: FLC '95
International Honours: E: 6; B-1; U21-8; Yth (UEFAYC '93)

Last season was another one of immense personal triumph for the young Liverpool striker. Once again the scourge of all Premierhsip defences, Robbie was the side's top scorer with 31 to his credit and such was his powerful impact in the red shirt that few mourned the passing of Ian Rush to Leeds. It mattered little to him who was his strike partner, since he was able to score with either foot or head, or from outside the penalty area, or within the six-yard box. Goal poacher supreme, a master craftsman of his trade, plundering goals wherever he went, he scored against Mexico when wearing an England shirt and is likely to become a regular in the international squad before too long. He also won many friends with his honesty at Arsenal in a crucial Premiership match, when telling the referee that he had not been brought down by David Seaman and therefore felt the penalty award incorrect. Incidentally, Robbie actually had his spot kick saved, although Jason McAteer followed up to score. Out for the last three games of the campaign, after being sent off against Everton, he was sorely missed as the Reds, who were still in the championship chase, gained just four points and ultimately finished in fourth position. Was also elected to the PFA Premiership Team of the Year.

Liverpool (From trainee on 23/4/92) FL 137+3/83 FLC 21/17 FAC 16/9 Others 10+1/7

Robbie Fowler

FOX Mark Stephen
Born: Basingstoke, 17 November 1975
Height: 5'11" Weight: 10.9
This former trainee performed a fringe role at Brighton in 1996-97, being selected as a substitute sporadically throughout the season. A tenacious midfielder, he came off the bench on two occasions (along with his younger brother Simon), but had little opportunity to impress as Brighton battled for survival and was released during the summer.

Brighton & Hove A (From trainee on 21/7/94) FL 8+17/1 Others 1

FOX Peter David
Born: Scunthorpe, 5 July 1957
Height: 5'11" Weight: 13.10
Club Honours: AMC '92; Div 2 '93

In order to concentrate on the manager's job, Peter gave up his first-team place at Exeter last season to Ashley Bayes and only played in a handful of league matches. However, his record in the game meant that he could still be relied upon in times of emergency to show some of the shot-stopping skills amassed in a career that has spanned more than 20 years.

Sheffield Wed (From apprentice on 1/6/75) FL 49 FAC 3
Barnsley (Loaned on 22/12/77) FL 1 FLC 1
Stoke C (£15,000 on 4/3/78) FL 409 FLC 32 FAC 22 Others 14
Exeter C (Free on 15/7/93) FL 107+1 FLC 7 FAC 6 Others 5

FOX Ruel Adrian
Born: Ipswich, 14 January 1968
Height: 5'6" Weight: 10.0
International Honours: E: B-2

This lively winger was yet another Tottenham star plagued by injury in 1996-97. Ruel had little opportunity to display the tenacity and ball skills which had led to him becoming a crowd favourite in 1995-96, despite still being able, when fit, to single-handedly break down the best of defences. A player who can inject urgency into Spurs' attack, that feature of his game was best demonstrated against Chelsea in February when Tottenham were unlucky not to get a point, eventually losing 2-1 to their London rivals in an exciting derby. Speculation as to his future came about with Gerry Francis' preference to play with wing backs as opposed to out-and-out wingers, but, that aside, Ruel still has a great deal to offer in attack at Premiership level.

Norwich C (From apprentice on 20/1/86) F/PL 148+24/22 FLC 13+3/3 FAC 11+4 Others 12+4
Newcastle U (£2,250,000 on 2/2/94) PL 56+2/12 FLC 3/1 FAC 5 Others 4/1
Tottenham H (£4,200,000 on 6/10/95) PL 45+6/7 FLC 3+1 FAC 6

FOX Simon Michael
Born: Basingstoke, 28 August 1977
Height: 5'11" Weight: 10.2

A graduate of Brighton's trainee scheme, this 19-year-old striker was a regular member of the first team squad last season. Employed mainly in a substitute role, Simon was placed on the transfer list along with several other youngsters in November, but regained favour under new manager, Steve Gritt, and played his part well as the Albion improved dramatically in the latter part of the campaign. Despite that, along with his brother, he was released during the summer.

Brighton & Hove A (From trainee on 17/5/95) FL 6+15 FLC 0+1 Others 1+1

FOYLE Martin John
Born: Salisbury, 2 May 1963
Height: 5'10" Weight: 11.2
Club Honours: AMC '93

An experienced striker with Port Vale, Martin spent the majority of last season on the bench in setting a new club record with 30 substitute appearances, the form of Tony Naylor and Lee Mills keeping him out of the starting line up for virtually the whole campaign. Always got on with the job in hand, whatever was required of him, and never complained, despite not being first choice and still managed four goals. Was the only Port Vale player sent off last season, at Carlisle in the Coca-Cola Cup.

Southampton (From apprentice on 13/8/80) FL 6+6/1 FLC 0+2/2
Aldershot (£10,000 on 3/8/84) FL 98/35 FLC 10/5 FAC 8/5 Others 6
Oxford U (£140,000 on 26/3/87) FL 120+6/36 FLC 16/4 FAC 5/3 Others 3+1/1
Port Vale (£375,000 on 25/6/91) FL 162+38/59 FLC 17+1/7 FAC 13+2/9 Others 13+3/9

FRAIN John William
Born: Birmingham, 8 October 1968
Height: 5'8" Weight: 11.9
Club Honours: AMC '91

A left-sided midfielder or defender, John joined Northampton last season, firstly on loan, and then on a permanent basis on transfer deadline day. Prior to the move, he had been Birmingham's longest-serving player, it was hoped his experience would help the club in their final bid for the promotion push. Scored the last-gasp winner at Wembley that secured Town's promotion drive to division two, via the play offs.

Birmingham C (From apprentice on 10/10/86) FL 265+9/23 FLC 28/1 FAC 12 Others 22/2
Northampton T (Free on 24/1/97) FL 13 Others 6/1

FRANCIS John Andrew
Born: Dewsbury, 21 November 1963
Height: 5'8" Weight: 12.13
Club Honours: Div 4 '92

Released by Burnley during the summer of 1996, John signed non-contract forms for Scunthorpe immediately prior to the start of last season. Unfortunately, having never been able to get back to his speedy best following the serious injury suffered during the 1994 play offs, after just six appearances and no goals, he left in February to play for non-league, Halifax Town.

Halifax T (On trial from Emley on 8/2/85) FL 1+3 Others 2
Sheffield U (£10,000 from Emley on 15/9/88) FL 14+28/6 FLC 0+2 FAC 0+1 Others 3+2/1
Burnley (£90,000 on 24/1/90) FL 99+2/26 FLC 6 FAC 8 Others 11+1/4
Cambridge U (£95,000 on 13/8/92) FL 15+14/3 FLC 2+2/1 FAC 0+1 Others 0+1
Burnley (£70,000 on 25/3/93) FL 44+32/10 FLC 3+4/1 FAC 4+2 Others 4+4/2
Scunthorpe U (Free on 12/8/96) FL 1+4 FLC 0+1

FRANCIS Kevin Michael
Born: Birmingham, 6 December 1967
Height: 6'7" Weight: 15.8
Club Honours: Div 2 '95; AMC '95

A Birmingham fan who was brought up at Small Heath just minutes away from the St Andrews ground, at 6'7", Kevin is the tallest striker in the Football League. Suffered an ankle injury whilst on holiday during the 1996 close season, which kept him out until January, when he made his first start of 1996-97 in the third round of the F A Cup against Stevenage and scored. Despite scoring against Stockport County in the next

round, he was used sparingly from then on, managing only three more starts during the remainder of the campaign. Hopefully, he will have an injury-free 1997-98.

Derby Co (Free from Mile Oak Rov on 2/2/89) FL 0+10 FLC 1+2 FAC 1+2/1 Others 0+1
Stockport Co (£45,000 on 21/2/91) FL 147+5/88 FLC 12/5 FAC 9/6 Others 25/18
Birmingham C (£800,000 on 20/1/95) FL 30+23/12 FLC 6/4 FAC 3+1/2 Others 4/1

FRANCIS Stephen (Steve) Stuart
Born: Billericay, 29 May 1964
Height: 6'0" Weight: 14.0
Club Honours: FMC '86, '88
International Honours: E: Yth

Still one of the most consistent goalkeepers in the first division, Steve always seems to pull off near impossible saves and would almost certainly have been an ever present for Huddersfield were it not for an injury which caused him to miss a handful of games in the middle of last season. Apart from keeping 16 clean sheets during a campaign in which Town finished one place away from relegation, his good form saw the former Sunderland 'keeper, Tony Norman, again consigned to the reserves.

Chelsea (From apprentice on 28/4/82) FL 71 FLC 6 FAC 10 Others 1
Reading (£20,000 on 27/2/87) FL 216 FLC 15 FAC 15 Others 13
Huddersfield T (£150,000 on 1//8/93) FL 174 FLC 16 FAC 9 Others 12

FRANDSEN Per
Born: Copenhagen, Denmark, 6 February 1970
Height: 5'8" Weight: 12.6
Club Honours: Div 1 '97
International Honours: Denmark-12

Signed during the 1996 close season from FC Copenhagen in a joint deal involving Michael Johansen, both players being members of the side which won the Danish Cup following a 5-0 victory over AB Alaa, as well as Danish internationals, Per came straight into Bolton's midfield, scoring his first goal one game later in the 1-0 win over Manchester City. A forceful type with a powerful shot, and also able to be used up front if required, as a key member of the first division championship winning side he missed just five games, while scoring five goals – an excellent start.

Bolton W (£1,250,000 from F.C. Copenhagen on 7/8/96) FL 40+1/5 FLC 4+1 FAC 2+1

FREEDMAN Douglas (Dougie) Alan
Born: Glasgow, 21 January 1974
Height: 5'9" Weight: 11.2
International Honours: S: U21-8; Sch

Started last season for Crystal Palace very much as he had ended the previous campaign, scoring regularly and reaching double figures by November, including four in four successive games. Surprisingly, though, Dougie was to add only two more before the campaign came to a close, due mainly to loss of form and 15 subs' appearances. However, with Palace into the play offs, he came into his own, even in the knowledge that he would be suspended for the final. Having started just two games in

the previous two months, the striker came off the bench with just 17 minutes to go in the first-leg tie at home to Wolves and scored twice in the 89th and 90th minutes to give Palace a 3-1 aggregate lead, which was ultimately good enough to take them to Wembley and then regain their Premiership place.

Queens Park R (From trainee on 15/5/92)
Barnet (Free on 26/7/94) FL 47/27 FLC 6/5 FAC 2 Others 2
Crystal Palace (£800,000 on 8/9/95) FL 70+13/31 FLC 2+1/1 FAC 2+1 Others 3+2/2

FREEMAN Darren Barry Andduet
Born: Brighton, 22 August 1973
Height: 5'11" Weight: 13.0
Signed by Fulham from Gillingham during the 1996 close season, Darren was a constant menace to opposing defences in 1996-97 with his tremendous pace. Playing on either flank, he scored nine goals and created numerous chances for himself as well as for others. A crowd pleaser, with his flowing locks making him easily identifiable, he will score even more goals once he calms down in the penalty area. Was voted Division Three's Player of the Season in a poll carried out by the National Review.
Gillingham (Free from Horsham on 31/1/95) FL 4+8 FAC 0+1 Others 2/1
Fulham (£15,000 + on 4/7/96) FL 32+7/9 FLC 2 Others 1

FREESTONE Christopher (Chris) Mark
Born: Nottingham, 4 September 1971
Height: 5'11" Weight: 11.7
Club Honours: AMC '97
The speedy young Middlesbrough striker with a keen eye for goal, fully merited his inclusion in the senior squad in 1996-97 after being recalled from a loan spell with Carlisle United, where he scored twice in seven appearances. On standby during the Boro's injury crisis, he made his presence felt when taking the field as a substitute in the thriller at Old Trafford against Champions elect, Manchester United, while his 69th minute appearance at Elland Road against Leeds United in the final match of the campaign was too late for him to have been expected to save the day, although dutifully giving of his best. He could do rather well this coming term and his ability to run both on and off the ball could give quite a few first division defences problems.
Middlesbrough (£10,000 from Arnold T on 2/12/94) P/FL 2+5/1 FAC 0+2
Carlisle U (Loaned on 3/3/97) FL 3+2/2 Others 2

FREESTONE Roger
Born: Newport, 19 August 1968
Height: 6'3" Weight: 14.6
Club Honours: Div 2 '89; AMC '94
International Honours: W: U21-1; Yth; Sch
Rated for many years as one of the top goalkeepers outside of the Premier League, Roger's form suffered towards the end of last season as he produced several uncharacteristic slip ups, albeit keeping 13 clean sheets for Swansea in the league. A good shot stopper, he also possesses a safe pair of hands when dealing with crosses into the penalty area.

Newport Co (From trainee on 2/4/86 FL 13 Others 1
Chelsea (£95,000 on 10/3/87) FL 42 FLC 2 FAC 3 Others 6
Swansea C (Loaned on 29/9/89) FL 14 Others 1
Hereford U (Loaned on 9/3/90) FL 8
Swansea C (£45,000 on 5/9/91) FL 268+1/3 FLC 16 FAC 18 Others 32

FRENCH Jonathan (Jon) Charles
Born: Bristol, 25 September 1976
Height: 5'10" Weight: 10.10
A striker or midfielder, Jon, the 20-year-old captain of Bristol Rovers' reserves, managed to add just three full and three substitute appearances to his career total as he found it difficult to make much impression in 1996-97. Eventually, the club's former Young Player of the Year spent the final three months of the season on loan to GM Conference club, Bath City.
Bristol Rov (From trainee on 15/7/95) FL 6+8/1 FLC 0+1 FAC 0+1 Others 2+1/1

FROGGATT Stephen (Steve) Junior
Born: Lincoln, 9 March 1973
Height: 5'10" Weight: 11.11
International Honours: E: U21-2
The left winger completed his transition to wing back in 1996-97, which did not stop him being involved in the all three goals Wolves scored on the opening day. Had a similar impact in the 4-2 win at Albion in September, but for most of the time supporters felt he was too deep, especially at home. Played in all 15 games up until the visit to Portsmouth, when he got inflammation of the knee, and returned for a ten-match run, where he again relied on speed on the break, sidefooting the ball home at Huddersfield to complete a flowing move and claiming a goal at Barnsley, after his curling free kick went in off the head of a defender. Elected by his fellow professionals for the PFA award-winning first division side, injuries continued to disrupt his career though.
Aston Villa (From trainee on 26/1/91) F/PL 30+5/2 FLC 1+1 FAC 5+2/1
Wolverhampton W (£1,000,000 on 11/7/94) FL 60+5/5 FLC 5/1 Others 2

FRONTZECK Michael
Born: Germany, 26 March 1964
Height: 5'11" Weight: 12.12
International Honours: Germany: 19
Started last season at left back for Manchester City, but was unfortunately sent off in the opening home game against Ipswich. It was not a particularly bad challenge, but as the Ipswich player had a clear run on goal it was adjudged that Michael had baulked Paul Mason. After this, under three different managers, he appeared spasmodically and made his last appearance at home to Tranmere Rovers as a substitute at the end of November. He then returned home to Germany for personal reasons and in early January completed a £80,000 move to SC Freiburg in the German League.
Manchester C (£350,000 from Borussia Munchengladbach on 31/1/96) P/FL 19+4 FLC 1 FAC 1

FRY Christopher (Chris) David
Born: Cardiff, 23 October 1969
Height: 5'9" Weight: 10.7
International Honours: W: Yth
A lightweight, but lightning fast right winger, Chris enjoyed another excellent season for Colchester in 1996-97, which was correctly rewarded with two of the Player of the Year awards. Always a crowd favourite with his buccaneering runs and crosses, he also scored eight goals during the campaign, many of them spectacular, long-range strikes. He also scored United's first goal in their fight back against Peterborough in the AWS southern final. "Twiggy for Wales" is a common chant at Layer Road, the U's fans believing he would not be out of place on the opposite wing to Ryan Giggs.
Cardiff C (From trainee on 3/8/88) FL 22+33/1 FLC 1+2 FAC 0+2 Others 0+2
Hereford U (Free on 2/8/91) FL 76+14/10 FLC 6+2 FAC 8+2/1 Others 6+1
Colchester U (Signed on 24/10/93) FL 102+28/16 FLC 3+3/1 FAC 3+1 Others 12+2/1

FURLONG Paul Anthony
Born: Wood Green, 1 October 1968
Height: 6'0" Weight: 13.8
Club Honours: FAT '88
International Honours: E: SP-5
The big, powerful and naturally aggressive striker became Birmingham's most expensive signing when he moved from Chelsea during the 1996 close season, and managing to stay clear of injuries during 1996-97, he was an automatic choice, making more appearances than any other player at St Andrews. Although Paul's goal tally of 12 was disappointing, his all-round, wholehearted play was much appreciated by both management and fans, alike, but, on a personal front, a 20-goal target this coming term is a must.
Coventry C (£130,000 from Enfield on 31/7/91) FL 27+10/4 FLC 4/1 FAC 1+1 Others 1
Watford (£250,000 on 24/7/92) FL 79/37 FLC 7/4 FAC 2 Others 4
Chelsea (£2,300,000 on 26/5/94) PL 44+20/13 FLC 3+1 FAC 5+4/1 Others 7/3
Birmingham C (£1,500,000 on 17/7/96) FL 37+6/10 FLC 4/1 FAC 2/1

FUTRE Paulo Jorge
Born: Portugal, 28 February 1966
Height: 5'10" Weight: 12.0
International Honours: Portugal: 41
The legendary Portugese international forward joined West Ham during the 1996 close season on a free transfer from Italian giants, AC Milan, with doubts over his fitness. After four early 1996-97 starts he was sidelined with a hamstring injury and, on his return in October, suffered from knee problems, at which point, by mutual agreement, Paolo announced his retirement from the game. In becoming yet another victim of Harry Redknapp's wretched luck in the transfer market he brought to an end a brilliant career of which Hammers' fans saw only the briefest of glimpses.
West Ham U (Free from AC Milan on 16/7/96) PL 4+5

101

G

GABBIADINI Marco
Born: Nottingham, 20 January 1968
Height: 5'10" Weight: 13.4
Club Honours: Div 3 '88
International Honours: E: B-1; FL-1; U21-2
One of the longest serving players at Derby and still strong and alert in the penalty box, he started off last season competing for a first-team spot before the partnership of Dean Sturridge and Ashley Ward left him sidelined. Preferring to play first-team football, he had loan spells at both Birmingham City (October) and Oxford United (January). Spent an ill-fated three weeks at St Andrews, making just two subs' appearances before being sent home with a cartilage problem, which required an operation, and, when fit again, his trip to Oxford resulted in just five games and a goal. Arriving back at the Baseball Ground, Marco had to be content with reserve team football, followed by an almost inevitable free transfer during the summer.
York C (From apprentice on 5/9/85) FL 42+18/14 FLC 4+3/1 Others 4/3
Sunderland (£80,000 on 23/9/87) FL 155+2/74 FLC 14/9 FAC 5 Others 9/4
Crystal Palace (£1,800,000 on 1/10/91) FL 15/5 FLC 6/1 FAC 1 Others 3/1
Derby Co (£1,000,000 on 31/1/92) F/PL 163+25/50 FLC 13/7 FAC 8+1/3 Others 16+1/8
Birmingham C (Loaned on 14/10/96) FL 0+2
Oxford U (Loaned on 31/1/97) FL 5/1

GAGE Kevin William
Born: Chiswick, 21 April 1964
Height: 5'10" Weight: 12.11
Club Honours: Div 4 '83
International Honours: E: Yth
Injured in the first half of last season's opening fixture, Kevin was unable to regain a regular place at right back for Preston, following further injuries and illness. Sound when he did play, as always, he gave 100 per-cent effort and remained cool under pressure.
Wimbledon (From apprentice on 4/1/82) FL 135+33/15 FLC 7+2/1 FAC 8+3/1 Others 0+1
Aston Villa (£100,000 on 17/7/87) FL 113+2/8 FLC 13/3 FAC 9/1 Others 8
Sheffield U (£150,000 on 15/11/91) F/PL 107+5/7 FLC 6 FAC 10+2 Others 1
Preston NE (Free on 28/3/96) FL 20+3 FAC 1

GALE Shaun Michael
Born: Reading, 8 October 1969
Height: 6'0" Weight: 11.10
A reliable Barnet full back, who can play on either flank, Shaun took on the difficult wing-back role when called upon in 1996-97. With great crossing ability he is an important source of goals for Barnet, while scoring two himself last season. Is the club's number one corner-kick specialist, an accurate passer, especially with the right foot, and can run all day.
Portsmouth (From trainee on 12/7/88) FL 2+1 Others 0+1

Barnet (Free on 13/7/94) FL 109+5/5 FLC 10 FAC 6 Others 3

GALL Benny
Born: Copenhagen, Denmark, 14 March 1971
Height: 6'1" Weight: 13.11
In sharing the custodian's role with Paul Edwards, following his pre-1996-97 season transfer from Holland, the Dane became Shrewsbury's first import. Confident in the air, a strong kicker of the ball, and looking quite at home when playing the ball at feet to his defenders, even when under pressure, he started the campaign with this tactic quite successfully, but, strangely, this strength was rarely seen in the later stages.
Shrewsbury T (Free from Dordrecht De Grashaarp on 16/8/96) FL 23 FLC 2 Others 2

Kevin Gallacher

GALLACHER Kevin William
Born: Clydebank, 23 November 1966
Height: 5'8" Weight: 11.0
International Honours: S: 31; B-2; U21-7; Yth
No man contributed more than Kevin did to get Blackburn out of the relegation zone in 1996-97, his prodigious energy enabling him to operate wide on the right, drift in alongside the lone striker and still track back to assist the defence. Without him and his vital goals – all three in a 3-1 win at Ewood against Wimbledon and at least six others that either won games or saved them – the club would surely have been unable to play the formation they adopted. Is a player who is always difficult to keep track of, his skill, quick, darting movements and elusive running off the ball continuously making him a threat to defenders. Another highlight for him last season, was in scoring both of Scotland's goals against Austria.

Dundee U (Signed from Duntocher BC in 1983) SL 118+13/27 SLC 13/5 SC 20+3/5 Others 15+6/3
Coventry C (£900,000 on 29/1/90) F/PL 99+1/28 FLC 11/7 FAC 4 Others 2
Blackburn Rov (£1,500,000 on 22/3/93) PL 85+5/25 FLC 7/1 FAC 8/1 Others 1+1

GALLAGHER Ian
Born: Hartlepool, 30 May 1978
Height: 5'10" Weight: 11.7
A young Hartlepool midfielder, Ian was signed as a first-year professional in the 1996 close season, being given the chance of a contract because fellow YTS player, Paul Conlon, had opted for a move to Sunderland. Unfortunately, he was not able to make the most of this opportunity, and was completely out of the first-team picture, except for six minutes play as a substitute in the Auto Windscreens Shield match against Burnley.
Hartlepool U (From trainee on 2/7/96) FL 1 Others 0+1

GALLAGHER Thomas (Tommy) Duncan
Born: Nottingham, 25 August 1974
Height: 5'10" Weight: 11.8
Club Honours: AIC '95
A very skilful Notts County right back and right-sided midfield player, who always looked comfortable in possession, Tommy recovered well after suffering a broken leg at the end of 1995-96 to come back at Bristol City last October. However, he made just two more appearances in the AWS competition before being released in February after failing to agree to a new contract.
Notts Co (From trainee on 1/6/92) FL 42+1/2 FLC 1 FAC 3 Others 9+3/1

GALLEN Kevin Andrew
Born: Chiswick, 21 September 1975
Height: 6'0" Weight: 12.10
International Honours: E: U21-4; Yth (EUFAC '93); Sch
A great deal was expected of Kevin at QPR last season, and he started superbly, a goal against Oxford on the opening day being followed by two on Portsmouth. Unfortunately, for both him and the club, he damaged his knee while scoring the second at Fratton Park and was ruled out for the rest of the campaign. Almost an old-fashioned forward in many respects, despite him having difficulties finding the net on a regular basis in a relegation doomed side in 1995-96, he had been expected to lead the charge back to the Premiership, his predatory instincts around the box being vital to the cause. An England U21 international, he will be hoping for a clean bill of health in 1997-98.
Queens Park R (From trainee on 22/9/92) P/FL 59+10/21 FLC 3+1/2 FAC 4/1

GALLIMORE Anthony (Tony) Mark
Born: Crewe, 21 February 1972
Height: 5'11" Weight: 12.12
Club Honours: Div 3 '95
Having had the opportunity to adjust to higher grade football, Tony firmly established himself as first choice in Grimsby's left-back position last season, despite having a hard act to follow in the

departed Gary Croft. His strength in defence, and his penchant for going forward, overcame the initial reluctance of the Blundell Park crowd to accept him as he went from strength to strength.

Stoke C (From trainee on 11/7/90) FL 6+5
Carlisle U (Loaned on 3/10/91) FL 8
Carlisle U (Loaned on 26/2/92) FL 8
Carlisle U (£15,000 on 25/3/93) FL 124/9 FLC 8/1 FAC 8 Others 24/1
Grimsby T (£125,000 on 28/3/96) FL 46+6/2 FLC 2 FAC 1

GALLOWAY Michael (Mick) Anthony
Born: Nottingham, 13 October 1974
Height: 5'11" Weight: 11.5
A local lad who impressed in reserve team football at Notts County last season, he made a handful of appearances in his favoured left-sided midfield slot, before being loaned to Gillingham on transfer deadline day. Also able to play up front, the attacking midfielder came in for the last nine games for the Gills and scored his first ever league goal in a 3-2 home defeat at the hands of Blackpool, before going back to Meadow Lane.

Notts Co (From trainee on 15/6/93) FL 17+4 FLC 2 FAC 0+1 Others 4
Gillingham (Loaned on 27/3/97) FL 6+3/1

GANNON James (Jim) Paul
Born: Southwark, 7 September 1968
Height: 6'2" Weight: 13.0
The tall Irish defender claimed his Stockport place after Matthew Bound's suspension six games into 1996-97, and never relinquished it, his aerial power and composure being important elements in a season that culminated with the club being promoted to the first division. As the club's longest-serving player, Jim came back remarkably well from the broken leg suffered in 1995-96.

Sheffield U (Signed from Dundalk on 27/4/89)
Halifax T (Loaned on 22/2/90) FL 2
Stockport Co (£40,000 on 7/3/90) FL 271+9/51 FLC 27+2/3 FAC 15/1 Others 37+2/8
Notts Co (Loaned on 14/1/94) FL 2

GANNON John Spencer
Born: Wimbledon, 18 December 1966
Height: 5'9" Weight: 11.10
This unlucky player always seemed to be recovering from one injury after another in 1996-97 and made just one appearance for Oldham, a stormer against Tranmere. A confident and creative midfielder who always wants to be involved in the game, and who has a superb left foot and some nice touches, John was released during the summer. Could still do a good job if able to achieve a reasonable level of match fitness.

Wimbledon (From apprentice on 19/12/84) FL 13+3/2 FLC 1+1 Others 1
Crewe Alex (Loaned on 19/12/86) FL 14+1 Others 1
Sheffield U (Signed on 23/2/89) F/PL 162+12/6 FLC 13+1 FAC 14 Others 6/1
Middlesbrough (Loaned on 5/11/93) FL 6+1 Others 2
Oldham Ath (Free on 8/3/96) FL 6

GARCIA Alexander Calvo
Born: Ordizia, Spain, 1 January 1972
Height: 5'10" Weight: 11.0

Alexander became the first Spaniard to appear for Scunthorpe, following his move to Glanford Park last October. Despite the anticipation, the 24-year-old midfielder failed to set the town alight and, although producing skilful touches on occasion, he lacked the physical strength required for the third division and failed to gain a regular place in the side.

Scunthorpe U (Free from Eibar on 4/10/96) FL 7+6/1 FAC 2 Others 1

GARDE Remi
Born: L'arbresle, France, 3 April 1966
Height: 5'9" Weight: 11.7
International Honours: France: 5
Remi was another Arsene Wenger signing, albeit he arrived at Arsenal before his mentor when joining from Strasbourg during the 1996 close season. Much troubled by injuries, the sweeper, cum midfielder, played just 11 times, following his first-team debut against Leeds at Highbury last October, and impressed every time he appeared. A superb passer of the ball, he always seemed to have time to spare, the sign of a good player, but it was his tackling that took the eye, especially in the game at Chelsea. If the Frenchman can stay free of injuries in 1997-98 he could be an important component in the new Gunners' machine. Is a former French international.

Arsenal (Free from Strasbourg on 14/8/96) PL 7+4

GARDNER David (Dave) Scott
Born: Salford, 17 September 1976
Height: 5'9" Weight: 11.0
Recommended to Wrexham by Ryan Giggs, who asked Brian Flynn to give him a trial, Dave was previously a trainee with both Manchester City and United. Very good when going forward, and an excellent passer of the ball, the midfielder signed as a non-contract player until the end of the campaign.

Manchester C (Free from Manchester U juniors on 1/7/95 - Released during 1996 close season and going on Pontins' Forms to Blackpool, Birmingham C, Bury and Barnsley)
Wrexham (Free on 27/1/97) Others 0+1

GARDNER James (Jimmy)
Born: Dunfermline, 27 September 1967
Height: 5'10" Weight: 10.2
An orthodox winger and capable of playing on either flank, once again Jimmy proved to be a fine crosser of the ball at Cardiff, in 1996-97, but injury and loss of confidence saw him dropped and, unable to regain his place apart from the odd subs' appearance, he was released during the summer. Two footed and happy to take on the full back, he may not be finished with league football yet.

Queens Park (Free from Ayresome North AFC on 1/4/87) SL 1+2
Motherwell (Signed on 1/7/88) SL 8+8 SC 0+1
St Mirren (Signed on 7/9/93) SL 31+10/1 SLC 1 SC 0+2 Others 2
Scarborough (Free on 25/8/95) FL 5+1/1
Cardiff C (Free on 28/9/95) FL 51+12/5 FLC 0+1 FAC 3 Others 4+1

GARLAND Peter John
Born: Croydon, 20 January 1971
Height: 5'10" Weight: 12.0
International Honours: E: Yth
A bustling midfielder with a great vision for passing, having been released by Charlton during the 1996 season Peter joined Leyton Orient on a free transfer after impressing in a friendly against Wales, during which he scored what proved to be the winner. Unlucky not to have played more games in 1996-97, due to injury and the competition for places, he was released at the end of the season.

Tottenham H (From trainee on 1/7/89) FL 0+1
Newcastle U (£35,000 on 24/3/92) FL 0+2 Others 0+1
Charlton Ath (Signed on 18/12/92) FL 40+13/2 FLC 5/1 FAC 2 Others 4+1/1
Wycombe W (Loaned on 18/3/95) FL 5
Leyton Orient (Free on 25/7/96) FL 13+8 FLC 1 FAC 2

GARNER Darren John
Born: Plymouth, 10 December 1971
Height: 5'9" Weight: 12.7
Club Honours: AMC '96
After starting last season as an automatic choice in Rotherham's midfield, Darren's future at the club looked gloomy when he had a dispute with the management. However, he showed his good character by putting that behind him and soon became a regular again, with his ability to control midfield. Scored a cracking goal which gave the Millers their first away win of the season at Bristol City in mid March.

Plymouth Arg (From trainee on 15/3/89) FL 22+5/1 FLC 2+1 FAC 1 (Free to Dorchester T on 19/8/94)
Rotherham U (£20,000 on 26/6/95) FL 61/3 FLC 5 FAC 1 Others 6/1

GARNETT Shaun Maurice
Born: Wallasey, 22 November 1969
Height: 6'3" Weight: 13.4
Club Honours: AMC '90
Having struggled to find his form at Swansea following his move from Tranmere towards the end of 1995-96, within a month of the start of last season he was transferred to first division Oldham. Stepping straight into the Latics' defence on arriving at Boundary Park, Shaun showed his worth as a more than dependable centre back, slotting in well alongside Steve Redmond. Unfortunately, he was sorely missed when suffering a torn muscle in the right leg and being forced out of action for 17 games, the club continuing its slide into the second division, before coming back strongly for the final six matches.

Tranmere Rov (From trainee on 15/6/88) FL 110+12/5 FLC 13/1 FAC 4 Others 15+2
Chester C (Loaned on 1/10/92) FL 9
Preston NE (Loaned on 11/12/92) FL 10/2 Others 1
Wigan Ath (Loaned on 26/2/93) FL 13/1
Swansea C (£200,000 on 11/3/96) FL 15 FLC 2
Oldham Ath (£150,000 on 19/9/96) FL 22+1/1 FAC 1

GARVEY Stephen (Steve) Hugh
Born: Stalybridge, 22 November 1973
Height: 5'9" Weight: 11.1
A fringe player rather than a first-team

regular at Crewe in 1996-97, his 11 starts being equalled by his appearances from the bench, he operated from either wing and could always be relied upon to cause defences some problems. At the end of the campaign, having been out of the side for several weeks, Steve came on as a sub in both of the remaining two play-off matches to participate in the games that ultimately took the club into the first division for the first time in its history.

Crewe Alex (From trainee on 25/10/91) FL 60+35/6 FLC 6+5/2 FAC 3+4/2 Others 8+3/1

GAUGHAN Steven (Steve) Edward
Born: Doncaster, 14 April 1970
Height: 5'11" Weight: 11.2
John Duncan had been keeping tabs on Steve for some years and Darlington turned down a Chesterfield bid far in excess of the £30,000 eventually paid for him a season or two ago, so his 1996 close-season capture was a good deal on Duncan's part. A busy, scheming link between defence and attack, he is a strong runner and is difficult to dispossess – two qualities that led to his inclusion in the forward line as injury and suspension deprived the Spireites of their first choices in that department. One feels that the club still has to find Steve's key role in the overall pattern of the side and that, when that happens, he will become a regular and important team member.

Doncaster Rov (Free from Hatfield Main Colliery on 21/1/88) FL 42+25/3 FLC 2+2 FAC 4+1 Others 5+1
Sunderland (Free on 1/7/90)
Darlington (£10,000 on 21/1/92) FL 159+12/15 FLC 8 FAC 6/1 Others 10+1
Chesterfield (£30,000 on 16/8/96) FL 14+4 FLC 1/1 FAC 0+1 Others 1

GAVIN Mark Wilson
Born: Bailleston, 10 December 1963
Height: 5'8" Weight: 11.1
A much-travelled wide midfield player who has sampled football at high level, and having been released by Exeter at the end of 1995-96, Mark signed for Scunthorpe last August, hoping that he had shrugged off the injury problems that had beset him during his time at St James' Park. It was not to be, however, as an early season hamstring pull put him on the sidelines yet again and badly affected his appearances.

Leeds U (From apprentice on 24/12/81) FL 20+10/3 FLC 4+1/1 FAC 0+1
Hartlepool U (Loaned on 29/3/85) FL 7/1
Carlisle U (Free on 4/7/85) FL 12+1/1 FLC 2/1 Others 1
Bolton W (Free on 27/3/86) FL 48+1/3 FLC 1 FAC 5/1 Others 10/1
Rochdale (£20,000 on 14/8/87) FL 23/6 FLC 3 FAC 1 Others 2
Heart of Midlothian (£30,000 on 3/2/88) SL 5+4
Bristol C (£30,000 on 4/10/88) FL 62+7/6 FLC 8 FAC 13/1 Others 6/1
Watford (Signed on 9/8/90) FL 8+5
Bristol C (£60,000 on 6/12/91) FL 34+7/2 FLC 0+1 FAC 4 Others 4
Exeter C (Signed on 11/2/94) FL 73+4/4 FLC 3 FAC 3 Others 5
Scunthorpe U (Free on 23/8/96) FL 10+1 FLC 1 Others 1+1

GAYLE Brian Wilbert
Born: Kingston, 6 March 1965
Height: 6'1" Weight: 13.12
Released by Sheffield United during the 1996 close season, Brian joined Exeter on a monthly basis, before being brought to Rotherham in October after goals had been conceded on a far too regular basis. Quickly showing all his experience to shore up the defence, his leadership was invaluable until he bowed out in favour of youth in March, when moving on deadline transfer day to Bristol Rovers on loan and being freed during the summer.

Wimbledon (From apprentice on 31/10/84) FL 76+7/3 FLC 7/1 FAC 8/1 Others 2
Manchester C (£325,000 on 6/7/88) FL 55/3 FLC 8 FAC 2 Others 1
Ipswich T (£330,000 on 19/1/90) FL 58/4 FLC 3 FAC 0+1
Sheffield U (£750,000 on 17/9/91) F/PL 115+2/9 FLC 9 FAC 11/1 Others 1/1
Exeter C (Free on 14/8/96) FL 10 FLC 1

Rotherham U (Free on 10/10/96) FL 19+1 FAC 1 Others 1
Bristol Rov (Loaned on 27/3/97) FL 7

GAYLE John
Born: Bromsgrove, 30 July 1964
Height: 6'2" Weight: 15.4
Club Honours: AMC '91
A powerful, pacy striker with excellent aerial power, John made a promising start to the 1996-97 season at Stoke, partnering Mike Sheron, prior to moving to Northampton in February. The ideal target man also had the unique record of scoring a bizarre own goal for Northampton before joining them when the Cobblers and Stoke met earlier in the Littlewoods Cup. Always works hard on his fitness.

Wimbledon (£30,000 from Burton A on 1/3/89) FL 17+3/2 FLC 3
Birmingham C (£175,000 on 21/11/90) FL 39+5/10 FAC 2 Others 8+1/4
Walsall (Loaned on 20/8/93) FL 4/1
Coventry C (£100,000 on 13/9/93) PL 3 FLC 1+2

Scot Gemmill

Burnley (£70,000 on 17/8/94) FL 7+7/3 FLC 1+1/1 FAC 1+1/1
Stoke C (£70,000 on 23/1/95) FL 14+12/4 FLC 2 FAC 0+1 Others 3+1
Gillingham (Loaned on 14/3/96) FL 9/3
Northampton T (£25,000 on 10/2/97) FL 9+4/1 Others 5/2

GAYLE Marcus Anthony
Born: Hammersmith, 27 September 1970
Height: 6'1" Weight: 12.9
Club Honours: Div 3 '92
International Honours: E: Yth
A front man who was without doubt Wimbledon's revelation of last season, Marcus played out of his skin in giving 100 pe- cent effort in every match. Rarely has the club been in possession of a player with such energy, skill, aplomb, and confidence, and since his move from Brentford he has shown signs of possibly playing at international level before too long. A man of real class who is able to execute venomous shots with the minimum of fuss, the born-again Christian has been the scorer of some memorable strikes, including the Pele style goal at Stamford Bridge and the bullet-like header which knocked Manchester United out of the FA Cup.
Brentford (From trainee on 6/7/89) FL 118+38/22 FLC 6+3 FAC 6+2/2 Others 14+6/2
Wimbledon (£250,000 on 24/3/94) PL 87+16/15 FLC 11/4 FAC 12+2/2

GAYLE Mark Samuel Roye
Born: Bromsgrove, 21 October 1969
Height: 6'2" Weight: 12.3
Started last season as Crewe's number one goalkeeper, playing in the first six matches, before an injury unfortunately sidelined him for most of the campaign. Tall and commanding, and an excellent shot stopper, Mark was unlucky to come back at a time when his replacement, Jason Kearton, was in such great form, and in order to get match practice he was loaned to Birmingham. Not required at St Andrews, however, he returned to Gresty Road and looks forward to receiving an early first division opportunity.
Leicester C (From trainee on 1/7/88)
Blackpool (Free on 15/8/89) FLC 1 (Free to Worcester C in July 1990)
Walsall (£15,000 on 8/5/91) FL 74+1 FAC 8 FAC 1 Others 8
Crewe Alex (£35,000 on 21/12/93) FL 82+1 FLC 6 FAC 5 Others 9

GEMMILL Scot
Born: Paisley, 2 January 1971
Height: 5'11" Weight: 11.6
Club Honours: FMC '92
International Honours: S: 11; B-2; U21-4
1996-97 was an in-and-out season at Nottingham Forest for the Scottish international midfielder, his best run of games not coming until March, but then playing as a regular until the end of the campaign. Always giving 100 per-cent effort and covering a lot of ground in his central midfield role, despite his indifferent spell, Scot retained his place in the Scotland side for their World Cup matches. At his best, is always looking to play one-twos around the box.

Nottingham F (From trainee on 5/1/90) F/PL 167+14/19 FLC 24+2/3 FAC 17+2/1 Others 13+1/4

GENAUX Regis Herve
Born: Charleroi, Belgium, 31 August 1973
Height: 5'9" Weight: 11.8
International Honours: Belgium: 14
A Belgian full back signed from Standard Liege on the eve of last season, Regis made his Coventry debut at West Ham, looking comfortable on the ball and strong in the tackle. Started the next two games but then suffered a groin injury which kept him out until December, when he made his final appearance in a City shirt, as a sub against Spurs, before being transferred to Italian club, Udinese, for the same fee that City had paid for him. Having made some derogatory comments about Gordon Strachan as he left, it was no great surprise to hear that he had been sent off for dissent after three minutes of Udinese's game at Juventus in April.
Coventry C (£750.000 from Standard Liege on 21/8/96) PL 3+1

GERRARD Paul William
Born: Heywood, 22 January 1973
Height: 6'2" Weight: 13.1
International Honours: E: U21-18
Following a move from Oldham in the 1996 close season, the highly-sought after goalie had to wait patiently for his first taste of Premiership football for Everton. It came, surprisingly, at Neville Southall's instigation. Leading Southampton 5-1 at half time, Southall volunteered to make way for Paul, who played the second half of a match the Blues won 7-1! His full debut came two months later at Newcastle, but after three successive starts and two clean sheets, he developed a niggling thigh strain and had to step down again. Recalled for a high profile game against Manchester United and suffering the embarrassment of making two mistakes that led to goals, he is a talented and promising young keeper and is sure to learn from the experience rather than let it haunt him.
Oldham Ath (From trainee on 2/11/91) P/FL 118+1 FLC 7 FAC 7 Others 2+1
Everton (£1,000,000 + on 1/7/96) PL 4+1

GHAZGHAZI Sufyan
Born: Honiton, 24 August 1977
Height: 5'9" Weight: 11.7
International Honours: E: Yth; Sch
Forward. The current Exeter Young Player of the Year, teenager Sufyan had a brief taste of first team action in 1996-97. Having played for England youth, he will be hoping that he can produce his U18 side form (where he is leading scorer) for the first team this coming season.
Exeter C (From trainee on 31/7/96) FL 1+5 FLC 0+1

GIBB Alistair (Ally) Stuart
Born: Salisbury, 17 February 1976
Height: 5'9" Weight: 11.7
A right-sided Northampton midfielder, who is both speedy and excellent at free kicks, injury robbed him of a lot of last season.

When fully fit, his pacy runs make him a crowd favourite.
Norwich C (From trainee on 1/7/94)
Northampton T (Loaned on 22/9/95) FL 9/1
Northampton T (£30,000 on 5/2/96) FL 9+23/2 FLC 3+1 Others 2+1

GIBBS Nigel James
Born: St Albans, 20 November 1965
Height: 5'7" Weight: 11.11
Club Honours: FAYC '82
International Honours: E: U21-5; Yth
The Watford right back provided one of the happiest stories of last season. After 14 years with the club, and a two-year struggle with a persistent knee injury, Nigel was given a free transfer at the end of the 1995-96 season. Somehow he never left and soon he was back in the first team, going on to enjoy one of his best seasons and winning a well-deserved new contract. Indeed, he ended up playing more matches than anyone else. One of the Hornets' most popular players, he has now made more than 400 senior appearances, placing him ninth in the club's all-time list.
Watford (From apprentice on 23/11/83) FL 328+8/4 FLC 19/2 FAC 34+1 Others 16

GIBBS Paul Derek
Born: Gorleston, 26 October 1972
Height: 5'10" Weight: 11.3
An athletic Colchester left back who missed the start of last season with injury, he recovered to replace David Barnes and then Simon Betts, following their injury problems, playing from Christmas right through to Easter until losing his place to the new signing, Scott Stamps. Having starred vocally on United's Wembley CD, Paul played his last game for the club in the final before being released at the end of the campaign.
Colchester U (Signed from Diss T on 6/3/95) FL 39+14/3 FAC 1+1 Others 8+1

GIGGS Ryan Joseph
Born: Cardiff, 29 November 1973
Height: 5'11" Weight: 10.9
Club Honours: ESC '91; FAYC '92; FLC '92; PL '93, '94, '96, '97; CS '93, '94, '97; FAYC '94, '96
International Honours: W: 19; U21-1; Yth. E: Sch
A highly skilled Welsh international left winger, who darts past defenders and packs a tremendous left-footed shot, Ryan missed Manchester United's opening game of last season at Wimbledon, having sustained a hamstring injury in the Charity Shield against Newcastle at Wembley. Once recovered, however, he came back with a vengeance, scoring his first goal of the campaign against Nottingham Forest in September, before other injury problems surfaced. Unfortunately, he missed both of United's Champions' League games against Fenerbahce, but returned in time for the European tie against Juventus, a game that was the prelude to his longest unbroken spell in the side, with two more important goals against Rapid Vienna in the Champions' League and Coventry in the Premiership. His greatest game of 1996-97

came against Porto at Old Trafford, a performance that was compared with George Best's legendary night against Benfica, some 31 years earlier. Now at the peak of his form, he was an inspirational figure during United's vital run in that ended with him winning another championship medal. Signed a new five-year contract in October.

Manchester U (From trainee on 1/12/90) F/PL 189+18/41 FLC 16+4/6 FAC 27+2/5 Others 20+2/4

GILBERT David (Dave) James
Born: Lincoln, 22 June 1963
Height: 5'4" Weight: 10.8
Club Honours: Div 4 '87

Dave did not have the greatest of seasons at West Brom in 1996-97, injuries not helping his cause. Playing wide on the left-hand side of midfield, he was in and out of the team throughout the campaign and following the departure of Alan Buckley, early in the New Year, was confined to the reserves before joining York City on loan in early March. A hard-working player, his ball skills and crossing ability make him great entertainment value.

Lincoln C (From apprentice on 29/6/81) FL 15+15/1 FLC 5 FAC 3
Scunthorpe U (Free on 18/8/82) FL 1 FLC 1 (Free to Boston U in September 1982)
Northampton T (Signed on 30/6/86) FL 120/21 FLC 10/2 FAC 6/3 Others 9/1
Grimsby T (£55,000 on 23/3/89) FL 259/41 FLC 18/4 FAC 11/2 Others 9
West Bromwich A (£50,000 on 8/8/95) FL 46+12/6 FLC 6 FAC 1 Others 7
York C (Loaned on 7/3/97) FL 9/1

GILBERT Kenneth (Kenny) Robert
Born: Aberdeen, 8 March 1975
Height: 5'8" Weight: 10.7
International Honours: S: Yth; Sch

Returned to Scotland last February to join Ross County for a nominal fee, after his fiancee had failed to settle in Hull. A gritty right-sided midfielder, Kenny always gave of his best in his year with City, playing 23 times and scoring one goal in 1996-97.

Aberdeen (Free from East End "A" on 7/6/91)
Hull C (Free on 12/1/96) FL 21+11/1 FLC 1 FAC 0+1 Others 1+1

GILCHRIST Philip (Phil) Alexander
Born: Stockton on Tees, 25 August 1973
Height: 5'11" Weight: 13.4

Missed his central defensive partner at Oxford when Matt Elliott moved on and had to play with several different men for the remainder of last season. With lots of pace, and his long throw adding to the attacking options, Phil had two spells out with injury but other than that he was again a regular who was happier with a big man alongside him – proof being the number of clean sheets the defence kept in the early part of the campaign.

Nottingham F (From trainee on 5/12/90)
Middlesbrough (Free on 10/1/92)
Hartlepool U (Free on 27/11/92) FL 77+5 FLC 4+1 FAC 4 Others 5
Oxford U (£100,000 on 17/2/95) FL 98/6 FLC 9 FAC 6 Others 3

GILES Martin William
Born: Shrewsbury, 1 January 1979
Height: 5'10" Weight: 10.13

Following injuries to senior players last January, Martin became yet another of Chester's fine youngsters to break into the first team when coming off the bench at Middlesbrough in the third round of the FA Cup. A midfielder, and still a trainee, he had already proved very effective in the reserves and looks to have a good future in the game.

Chester C (Trainee) FAC 0+1

GILKES Michael Earl
Born: Hackney, 20 July 1965
Height: 5'8" Weight: 10.10
Club Honours: FMC '88; Div 3 '86, Div 2 '94

Following a 13-year stint at Reading, Michael eventually left Elm Park bound for Wolves on transfer deadline day last March, having played more than 500 games and scored 50 goals. Despite managing just one goal, at home to Southend, in 1996-97, his flair and pace were much missed by Royals' supporters. Arriving at Molineux, the left-footed forward showed some clever touches on his debut, but his return to Reading the next week was an unhappy one for him, when injured. Came back to score with a neatly-placed right footer against Grimsby, but his season ended when he badly hurt his knee at Port Vale, during his fifth appearance for the club.

Reading (Free from Leicester C juniors on 10/7/84) FL 348+45/43 FLC 25+7/6 FAC 31+2/1 Others 26+2/2

Chelsea (Loaned on 28/1/92) FL 0+1 Others 0+1
Southampton (Loaned on 4/3/92) FL 4+2
Wolverhampton W (£155,000 on 27/3/97) FL 5/1

GILLESPIE Keith Robert
Born: Bangor, 18 February 1975
Height: 5'10" Weight: 11.3
Club Honours: FAYC '92; CS '94
International Honours: NI: 17; U21-1; Yth; Sch

Keith is a speedy young winger who has continued to improve, adapting to the requirements of the modern game and learning to operate as a right-wing back for Newcastle when the need arises. Although not a natural defender he has applied himself well to this role, working hard at tackling back and performing creditably. However, he is seen to best effect when on the attack where his blistering pace and ability to cross on the run cause potent threats to any opposition whatever their quality. Disappointed to make only a substitute appearance in the Charity Shield match, he played in the first game of last season, was then dropped, but won his place back in late September to become a virtual regular in the side. Is now established as an important member of the Northern Ireland squad. His only goal of the season came at Liverpool when he triggered a comeback from 3-0 down to 3-3 before Robbie Fowler scored an injury-time winner.

Manchester U (From trainee on 3/2/93) PL 3+6/1 FLC 3 FAC 1+1/1

David Ginola

Wigan Ath (Loaned on 3/9/93) FL 8/4 Others 2
Newcastle U (£1,000,000 on 12/1/95) PL 64+13/7 FLC 5/1 FAC 4+1/2 Others 6+3

GINOLA David

Born: Gossin, France, 25 January 1967
Height: 6'0" Weight: 11.10
International Honours: France:17

Despite rumours of a close-season move to Barcelona, David began last season playing on Newcastle's left wing, again displaying his style and flair. Often criticised by some pundits for not working harder in defence, his game is all about using his consummate skill on the ball and his vision and creativity to cause havoc in the opposition's penalty area, and he remained extremely popular with the Newcastle crowd. Dangerous when raiding down the wing and crossing, as he demonstrated to good effect in the home UEFA Cup tie against Halmstads, when his centres resulted in three goals. He also likes to cut inside onto his right foot for a strike himself, scoring superb goals against Manchester United and Ferencvaros which were selected third and first, respectively, in BBC's October Goal of the Month competition, the first time one player has had two of the top three places in any one month. Reportedly unhappy at being left on the bench by Kenny Dalglish, he had a transfer request granted and has attracted the attention of Marseilles, among others, for a possible close season transfer.
Newcastle U (£2,500,000 from Paris St Germain, via Toulon, Racing Paris and Brest, on 6/7/95) PL 54+4/6 FLC 6 FAC 4 Others 7+1/1

GITTENS Jonathan (Jon) Antoni

Born: Birmingham, 22 January 1964
Height: 5'11" Weight: 12.10

Released by Portsmouth during the 1996 close season, the hard tackling and pacy central defender could not be faulted for his on-field displays at Torquay, his new club, but two sendings off and a difficult relationship with the management saw him out of favour during the latter part of the campaign. Good in the air, a right-foot shot from ten yards saw him score the club's first goal of the season in 1996-97.
Southampton (£10,000 from Paget R on 16/10/85) FL 18 FLC 4 FAC 1
Swindon T (£40,000 on 22/7/87) FL 124+2/6 FLC 15+1 FAC 9 Others 13+1/1
Southampton (£400,000 on 28/3/91) FL 16+3 FLC 4 Others 1
Middlesbrough (Loaned on 19/2/92) FL 9+3/1
Middlesbrough (£200,000 on 27/7/92) PL 13 FLC 0+1 FAC 1
Portsmouth (Free on 9/8/93) FL 81+2/2 FLC 10 FAC 3 Others 3/1
Torquay U (Free on 5/8/96) FL 33/3 FLC 2 FAC 1 Others 1

GIVEN Seamus (Shay) John

Born: Lifford, 20 April 1976
Height: 6'2" Weight: 13.4
Club Honours: Div 1 '96
International Honours: Ei: 9; U21; Yth

Although taking over as Eire's goalkeeper, Shay lost his place because he was not playing regular first-team football at Blackburn in 1996-97. However, when granted his Rovers' debut at Wimbledon in

December after Tim Flowers went down with an injury, he merely confirmed his exceptional agility, poise and confidence, and then further substantiated that when keeping a clean sheet in the 2-0 win at Derby. Unfortunately for him, with the side too close to the relegation zone for comfort, the caretaker manager, Tony Parkes, preferred to go with a proven 'keeper and he made way for Flowers. Desperate for first team football, he is sure to be granted his wish before too long. *Stop Press:* Out of contract at Ewood during the summer, the Irishman signed a four-year contract for Newcastle with a tribunal set to decide a fee.
Blackburn Rov (Free from Glasgow Celtic juniors on 8/8/94) PL 2 FLC 0+1
Swindon T (Loaned on 4/8/95) FL 5
Sunderland (Loaned on 19/1/96) FL 17

GLASGOW Byron Fitzgerald

Born: Clapham, 18 February 1979
Height: 5'7" Weight: 10.7

A talented young Reading midfield player, Byron graduated through the club's youth and reserve teams to make his debut in the FA Cup tie against Southampton last season, and then added four league appearances at the end of the campaign. Given a three-year contract, his play is characterised by excellent control and a wide range of passes.
Reading (From trainee on 24/8/96) FL 2+2 FAC 0+1

GLASS James (Jimmy) Robert

Born: Epsom, 1 August 1973
Height: 6'1" Weight: 13.4

Started 1996-97 well enough for Bournemouth, but suffered a loss in confidence during the middle of the season when he was replaced by Andy Marshall, who came on loan from Norwich. However, Jimmy regained his place with the departure of Marshall and never looked back, producing some brilliant displays in what was a difficult season off the pitch for the Cherries. He commands his area well and is a good shot stopper who is not afraid to come off his line and, on occasions, out of his area!
Crystal Palace (From trainee on 4/7/91)
Portsmouth (Loaned on 10/2/95) FL 3
Bournemouth (Free on 8/3/96) FL 48 FLC 2 FAC 1 Others 1

GLEGHORN Nigel William

Born: Seaham, 12 August 1962
Height: 6'0" Weight: 13.7
Club Honours: AMC '91; Div 2 '93

Signed from Stoke during the 1996 close season, Nigel captained Burnley in the early stages of 1996-97 and looked to be the skilful left-sided midfield provider that the club needed in Steve Thompson's absence. However, a loss of form was already threatening his place before a knee injury at Bournemouth in February all but brought his campaign to an end. A free kick and corner specialist, and a player who enjoys the passing game, he is also good in the air.
Ipswich T (Free from Seaham RS on 30/8/85) FL 54+12/11 FLC 3+2 FAC 3+1 Others 7+2/2
Manchester C (£47,500 on 4/8/88) FL 27+7/7 FLC 2+1/2 FAC 0+1/1 Others 1/1

Birmingham C (£175,000 on 9/9/89) FL 142/33 FLC 13/5 FAC 7/3 Others 14/2
Stoke C (£100,000 on 24/10/92) FL 162+4/26 FLC 10/2 FAC 10 Others 22/3
Burnley (Free on 15/7/96) FL 32+1/4 FLC 4 FAC 4/1 Others 2

GLOVER Dean Victor

Born: West Bromwich, 29 December 1963
Height: 5'10" Weight: 11.13
Club Honours: AMC '93

An experienced central defender who had an excellent season in the Port Vale back four in 1996-97, helping the club to within two games of the play offs, he came back strongly after missing the first four matches of the campaign to play in all but two from then on, taking his career total to 500 in the final match. Classy on the ball, his best game was probably against Wolves in April and twice scored two in a match, both in live TV games, versus QPR and Birmingham City.
Aston Villa (From apprentice on 30/12/81) FL 25+3 FLC 7/1 FAC 3 Others 1
Sheffield U (Loaned on 17/10/86) FL 5
Middlesbrough (Signed on 17/6/87) FL 44+6/5 FLC 4 FAC 5 Others 7/2
Port Vale (£200,000 on 3/2/89) FL 333+5/14 FLC 25/1 FAC 19/1 Others 22/3

GLOVER Edward Lee

Born: Kettering, 24 April 1970
Height: 5'10" Weight: 12.1
Club Honours: FMC '92
International Honours: S: U21-3; Yth

A Rotherham 1996 close season signing for a joint club record, the former Port Vale striker was expected to be able to bring a scoring touch to the team, but had to wait until January before hitting his one and only goal. Probably playing when less than 100 per-cent fit, his ability to hold the ball was not enough to get the team out of trouble and he moved on loan to Huddersfield Town in March. Is a skilful player who holds the ball up well and brings team mates into the game.
Nottingham F (From apprentice on 2/5/87) F/PL 61+15/9 FLC 6+5/2 FAC 8+2/1 Others 4+1/1
Leicester C (Loaned on 14/9/89) FL 3+2/1
Barnsley (Loaned on 18/1/90) FL 8 FAC 4
Luton T (Loaned on 2/9/91) FL 1
Port Vale (£200,000 on 2/8/94) FL 38+14/7 FLC 5+1/4 FAC 0+2 Others 3+2/2
Rotherham U (£150,000 on 15/8/96) FL 16+6/1 FLC 2 FAC 1 Others 0+1
Huddersfield T (Loaned on 3/3/97) FL 11

GOATER Leonard Shaun

Born: Hamilton, Bermuda, 25 February 1970
Height: 6'1" Weight: 12.0
Club Honours: AMC '96
International Honours: Bermuda: 8

Shaun gave Bristol City fans what had long been wanted at Ashton Gate – an effective goalscorer. This Burmudian international was certainly that, his 23 league goals haul in 1996-97 making him City's highest scorer since Bob Taylor seven years ago. Very good on the turn, his speed, together with an often languid style, created many chances for himself, including a hat trick in a 4-0 home win over Notts County and several

doubles that were savoured by the fans. Very single minded as far as goalscoring was concerned, and not one to hold the ball up for others, he hit the net in four of the last seven games of the campaign.
Manchester U (From juniors on 8/5/89)
Rotherham U (Free on 25/10/89) FL 169+40/70 FLC 13+4/4 FAC 12+3/7 Others 15+5/5
Notts Co (Loaned on 12/11/93) FL 1
Bristol C (£175,000 on 17/7/96) FL 39+3/23 FLC 4/1 FAC 3 Others 4/1

GODDARD-CRAWLEY Richard Lewis
Born: Hammersmith, 31 March 1978
Height: 6'4" Weight: 14.2
Released by Arsenal at the end of his YTS contract during the 1996 close season, Richard moved across London, along with team mate, Kevin Dennis, and joined Brentford. A tall centre back, apart from the odd occasion as an unused sub, he was confined to the reserves until coming off the bench for the last 12 minutes of the 1996-97 season to make his first team debut at Griffin Park in a 1-0 defeat at the hands of Peterborough.
Brentford (Free from Arsenal juniors on 23/7/96) FL 0+1

GOODEN Ty Michael
Born: Canvey Island, 23 October 1972
Height: 5'8" Weight: 12.6
Club Honours: Div 2 '96
After advancing his claims considerably to a first-team slot in 1995-96, the left winger, cum midfield, player must have been disappointed to be confined to the reserves for most of last season, with Kevin Horlock holding down his favourite left-wing slot. His first appearance in 1996-97 came at left back in November, when displacing Gary Elkins for three games, and from which position he scored his only goal of the campaign, a long-range blast against Barnsley. However, manager Steve McMahon decided against prolonging the experiment and he returned to the reserves and was out of favour even after the departure of Horlock to Manchester City, before reappearing on the left wing in the closing weeks of the campaign.
Swindon T (Free from Wycombe W on 17/9/93) P/FL 36+23/6 FLC 2+1/1 FAC 3+1 Others 3+1

GOODHIND Warren Ernest
Born: Johannesburg, South Africa, 16 August 1977
Height: 5'11" Weight: 11.2
Although spending most of last season in the reserves at Barnet, he was often used as cover on the subs' bench. Tough and tenacious in the tackle at centre half or in midfield, Warren made his full first-team debut in the final game of the campaign at home to Colchester.
Barnet (From trainee on 3/7/96) FL 1+2

GOODING Michael (Mick) Charles
Born: Newcastle, 12 April 1959
Height: 5'9" Weight: 10.7
Club Honours: Div 3 '81, '89, Div 2 '94
Mick clearly relished his second full season as joint player/manager at Reading in 1996-

97, missing only three games, as well as coping with administrative and coaching duties and remaining, at the age of 38, one of the fittest players on the books. Still a very consistent midfield performer, and an excellent example in terms of enthusiasm and urgency to those around him, along with Jimmy Quinn he left the club by mutual agreement following a long and tenuous campaign.
Rotherham U (Signed from Bishop Auckland on 18/7/79) FL 90+12/10 FLC 9/3 FAC 3
Chesterfield (Signed on 24/12/82) FL 12
Rotherham U (Signed on 9/9/83) FL 149+7/33 FLC 18/3 FAC 13/4 Others 7
Peterborough U (£18,000 on 13/8/87) FL 47/21 FLC 8/2 FAC 1/2 Others 4/2
Wolverhampton W (£85,000 on 20/9/88) FL 43+1/4 FLC 4 Others 5+1/1
Reading (£65,000 on 26/12/89) FL 303+11/26 FLC 19 FAC 18+1/2 Others 16/2

Don Goodman

GOODMAN Donald (Don) Ralph
Born: Leeds, 9 May 1966
Height: 5'10" Weight: 13.2
Club Honours: Div 3 '85
The strong, gritty Wolves' striker made a remarkable recovery from a fractured skull in April 1996, returning to the reserves last October, albeit wearing a headguard. He was twice a sub at the end of the month then scored on his proper return against Barnsley, a simple but important goal. He was soon heading the ball as bravely as before and also set up a goal against Oxford with a neat back heel. The circumstances usually dictated whether he or Iwan Roberts were selected to partner Steve Bull, but he kept working hard and rarely let the side down. He was in good form when he endured a calf strain, and that kept him out for three weeks until the very last match.
Bradford C (Free from Collingham on 10/7/84) FL 65+5/14 FLC 1+1/2 FAC 2+3/4 Others 4+1/2
West Bromwich A (£50,000 on 27/3/87) FL 140+18/60 FLC 11/1 FAC 7/1 Others 5/1

Sunderland (£900,000 on 6/12/91) FL 112+4/40 FLC 9/1 FAC 3/1 Others 4/2
Wolverhampton W (£1,100,000 on 6/12/94) FL 86+9/25 FLC 6/3 FAC 10+1/1 Others 3

GOODMAN Jonathan (Jon)
Born: Walthamstow, 2 June 1971
Height: 5'11" Weight: 12.11
International Honours: Ei: 4
A classy out-and-out striker whose overall aim must be to gain a regular Wimbledon first-team place this coming season, although he played in the Eire international clash against Wales at Cardiff Arms Park, he made only a few appearances for the club in 1996-97. Fleet of foot, hard running, and a good finisher, Jon can be relied upon when given the opportunity, scoring at Sheffield Wednesday when coming off the bench, but with Efan, Ekoku, Marcus Gayle, and Dean Holdsworth in contention for places, he has a difficult time ahead of him.
Millwall (£50,000 from Bromley on 20/8/90) FL 97+12/35 FLC 5+4/2 FAC 5+1 Others 3
Wimbledon (Signed on 9/11/94) PL 28+31/11 FLC 1+1 FAC 3+4/3

GOODRIDGE Gregory (Greg) Ronald St Clair
Born: Barbados, 10 July 1971
Height: 5'6" Weight: 10.0
International Honours: Barbados: 5
Signed from QPR at the start of 1996-97, this international winger made an electrifying scoring debut for Bristol City in the 5-0 home win over Luton Town on 27 August. Unfortunately, his performances away from home, where the onus was on defence more than attack, coupled to the heavier grounds later in the season, reduced his effectiveness and he left for a couple of weeks in late season to captain Barbados in a tournament against Grenada, Trinidad, and Guyana. A player of undoubted ability and great pace, he will be working hard to find more consistency as well as greater workrate in 1997-98.
Torquay U (Free from Lambada on 24/3/94) FL 32+6/4 FLC 4/1 FAC 2+1 Others 3+1/1
Queens Park R (£350,000 on 9/8/95) PL 0+7/1 FLC 0+1 FAC 0+1
Bristol C (£50,000 on 19/8/96) FL 19+9/6 FLC 3 FAC 3+1/1 Others 0+3

GOODWIN Shaun
Born: Rotherham, 14 June 1969
Height: 5'8" Weight: 11.4
Club Honours: Div 4 '89; AMC '96
Much hope was placed at his feet in his testimonial season at Rotherham last season and prospects looked bright when he scored in a 1-1 draw at Walsall on the opening day. But he once more was plagued by injuries and did his cause no good by falling out with the management, although he did settle his differences before suffering a stomach muscle injury which ruled him out from the end of January. Released during the summer, fully fit, he would be an asset with his ability to run at defences.
Rotherham U (From trainee on 1/7/87) FL 250+17/37 FLC 18+7/1 FAC 17+1/3 Others 21+2/4

GORDON Dale Andrew
Born: Great Yarmouth, 9 January 1967
Height: 5'10" Weight: 11.8

Club Honours: SC '92; SPD '92, '93; SLC '93
International Honours: E: B-2; U21-4; Yth; Sch

Released by West Ham during the 1996 close season, Dale joined Bournemouth in time for the start of 1996-97, coming into the side for the opening game of the campaign and quickly settling in. At his best a skilful and pacy right winger who could damage the best of defences, unfortunately, however, the knee problem that had persistently set him back was aggravated yet again and he was forced to call a halt on the surgeon's advice early in the New Year.

Norwich C (From apprentice on 17/1/84) FL 194+12/31 FLC 21/3 FAC 19/6 Others 14+2/3
Glasgow R (£1,200,000 on 8/11/91) SL 41+4/6 SLC 1+1/1 SC 6+1/1 Others 1
West Ham U (£750,000 on 20/7/93) PL 8+1/1 FLC 1 FAC 0+1
Peterborough U (Loaned on 23/3/95) FL 6/1
Millwall (Loaned on 21/3/96) FL 6
Bournemouth (Free on 16/8/96) FL 14+2/1 FLC 2 FAC 1

GORDON Dean Dwight
Born: Croydon, 10 February 1973
Height: 6'0" Weight: 13.4
Club Honours: Div 1 '94
International Honours: E: U21-13

An extremely athletic Crystal Palace left back who is strong in the tackle and adept at hitting long balls behind defenders, Dean missed the start of 1996-97 when carrying an injury over from the previous term. Came back into the side just as Palace were having a bad patch in mid season and quickly regained his high standard to become an ever present for the remaining 30 games, while scoring three goals, something that had certain Premiership clubs casting envious eyes in his direction. Following the Eagles' 1-0 win over Sheffield United in the play-off final at Wembley, Dean can look forward to being back among the big boys in 1997-98.

Crystal Palace (From trainee on 4/7/91) F/PL 145+19/18 FLC 14+3/2 FAC 10+1/1 Others 5+1

GORDON Kenyatta Gavin
Born: Manchester, 24 June 1979
Height: 6'1" Weight: 12.0

The second youngest-ever Tiger, Gavin became the first-choice partner for Duane Darby in Hull City's attack last season, only for a troublesome hamstring injury to betray his tender years. A big forward, the former Manchester City schoolboy continued to show a fine turn of speed, culminating in him earning the club's Young Player of the Year award.

Hull C (From trainee on 3/7/96) FL 22+11/7 FLC 1+3/1 Others 1+1

GORE Ian George
Born: Prescot, 10 January 1968
Height: 5'11" Weight: 12.4

A stalwart in the centre of Doncaster's back four alongside Darren Moore for most of last season, Ian proved again to be quick footed and strong in the air, being a seasoned professional with over 250 league games to his credit.

Birmingham C (From trainee on 1/5/86)

Blackpool (Free from Southport on 21/1/88) FL 196+4 FLC 15+1 FAC 11 Others 20+2
Torquay U (Free on 11/8/95) FL 25/2 FLC 4 FAC 1/1 Others 2
Doncaster Rov (£5,000 on 22/3/96) FL 40+1/1 FLC 2 FAC 1 Others 1

GOUCK Andrew (Andy) Scott
Born: Blackpool, 8 June 1972
Height: 5'9" Weight: 11.2

Andy took some time to establish himself in the team after signing for Rochdale from Blackpool in the 1996 close season, but eventually came good with some battling midfield performances. With a liking to get forward, he came off the bench to score a remarkable winner after Dale had been reduced to nine men against Doncaster.

Blackpool (From trainee on 4/7/90) FL 121+27/12 FLC 9+3 FAC 4+1 Others 11+1/3
Rochdale (Free on 25/7/96) FL 22+6/3 FAC 1

GOULD Jonathan (Jon) Alan
Born: Paddington, 18 July 1968
Height: 6'1" Weight: 13.7

Started last season as Bradford's first-choice goalkeeper, but suffered an horrific injury at Wolverhampton in the third match when having 18 stitches inserted in a facial wound after colliding with a home forward. Replaced first by Eric Nixon, on loan from Tranmere, and then by Mark Schwarzer, apart from injuries, Jon also missed games through suspension after being sent off twice. Had a spell at Gillingham on loan himself in October, playing three games, before returning to Valley Parade and getting in a few games towards the end of the campaign. The son of the Welsh manager, Bobby, he is a brave shot stopper who relies heavily on reflex saves.

Halifax T (Free from Clevedon T on 18/7/90) FL 32 FLC 2 FAC 5 Others 5
West Bromwich A (Free on 30/1/92)
Coventry C (Free on 15/7/92) PL 25 FLC 1+1
Bradford C (Free on 29/3/96) FL 18 FLC 2 Others 3
Gillingham (Loaned on 28/10/96) FL 3

GRAHAM Mark Roland
Born: Newry, 24 October 1974
Height: 5'7" Weight: 10.12
International Honours: NI: B-3; Yth; Sch

A pro at QPR since 1993, and originally a winger, Mark has since been converted with some success to the right-back position and it was there that he finally made his first-team start at home to Swindon in the Coca-Cola Cup last September, having come off the bench for his league debut against the same club on the same ground four days earlier. An attack minded player, who is also very strong in the tackle, and with skill to match, he settled down to give some outstanding performances and showed much promise for the future. His good form also saw him capped for Northern Ireland at "B" level in March, Portugal being on the end of a 2-0 battering in Glenavon.

Queens Park R (From trainee on 26/5/93) FL 16+2 FLC 2 FAC 2

GRAHAM Richard Ean
Born: Dewsbury, 28 November 1974
Height: 6'2" Weight: 12.1

Starting 1996-97 promisingly in the centre of Oldham's defence, where he had performed the previous season, Richard was unfortunately struck down by an horrendous catalogue of injuries. It was all the more frustrating in the knowledge that he was playing well and, at the same time, being continuously tracked by a host of Premiership clubs. He was also selected for the Football League side. A danger at set pieces and having the ability to unhinge opposing defences with forward runs, he is quick, agile, and excellent in the air. In short, he has the lot, if he can remain free of injuries that is.

Oldham Ath (From trainee on 16/7/93) P/FL 80+8/5 FLC 8 FAC 6 Others 2

GRAINGER Martin Robert
Born: Enfield, 23 August 1972
Height: 5'11" Weight: 12.0

A strong, aggressive left-sided Birmingham player, Martin missed the first half of 1996-97 due to a knee injury picked up in a pre-season game against Everton. Resumed at full back, but a move to midfield proved much more effective and he scored winning goals at Crystal Palace and Barnsley in the space of three games, the latter seeing his dramatic 30-yard curling free kick ensuring another 1-0 win. The very next match, at Oldham, then saw him strike another bending free kick over the defensive wall, this time from 25 yards, to bring about an effective equaliser in a 2-2 draw as he continued to end the campaign on a high.

Colchester U (From trainee on 28/7/92) FL 37+9/7 FLC 3 FAC 3+2 Others 3/1
Brentford (£60,000 on 21/10/93) FL 100+1/12 FLC 6/1 FAC 9/1 Others 8/2
Birmingham C (£400,000 on 25/3/96) FL 29 +2/3 FAC 2

GRANT Anthony (Tony) James
Born: Liverpool, 14 November 1974
Height: 5'10" Weight: 10.2
Club Honours: CS '95

A supremely gifted midfield artist in Everton's very best traditions, there were initial fears that Tony would prove too slight to establish himself in the Premiership. Those fears proved groundless as he became a regular in Joe Royle's side until sustaining a damaging ankle injury shortly after last Christmas. Despite several attempts to persevere with the problem, he was eventually forced to concede that he would not play again that season. A childhood friend of Liverpool's Robbie Fowler, he has occasionally become frustrated at the speed with which his friend's career has progressed compared to his own, but he seems certain to mark himself down as a Premiership star of the future.

Everton (From trainee on 8/7/93) PL 23+13/1 FLC 3 FAC 0+3 Others 2+2/1
Swindon T (Loaned on 18/1/96) FL 3/1

GRANT Kim Tyrone
Born: Ghana, 25 September 1972
Height: 5'10" Weight: 10.12
International Honours: Ghana: 5

After making a promising start to his Luton career at the end of 1995-96, this hard-

working striker failed to build upon his club reputation last season. Although he scored some opportunist goals in the first half of the campaign, he was often substituted and, with competition for places intense, eventually his rare first-team opportunities came mainly from the bench. However, there was light at the end of the tunnel and he impressed as a member of Ghana's international squad, gaining his first cap, and then winning a regular place and scoring his first international goal. There is no doubt that if given a settled run he will score goals, four in six reserve matches lending weight to that theory.

Charlton Ath (From trainee on 6/3/91) FL 74+49/18 FLC 3+9/1 FAC 8+5/5 Others 5+2/1
Luton T (£250,000 on 15/3/96) FL 18+17/5 FLC 4/2 FAC 0+2 Others 2+1/1

GRANVILLE Daniel (Danny) Patrick
Born: Islington, 19 January 1975
Height: 5'11" Weight: 12.5
International Honours: E: U21-2

A talented left-sided defender who made the step up to the Premiership when he joined Chelsea from Cambridge last March, Danny made his debut as a half-time substitute against his schoolboy heroes, Arsenal, and four matches later started his first full game against Leicester, playing impressively and creating the Blues' winning goal for Mark Hughes with a pinpoint cross. Extremely versatile, being able to play on the left side of the back three, or as a pushed-on left-wing back with an eye for goal, within weeks of arriving at Stamford Bridge, he had been capped for England U21s, starring against Georgia at the Valley. Bought as one for the future, he will, along with Celestine Babayaro (the Nigerian international signed in April for £2.25 million from Anderlecht), give the Chelsea squad extra competition for places on the left flank in 1997-98.

Cambridge U (From trainee on 19/5/93) FL 89+10/7 FLC 3+2 FAC 2+2 Others 4+2
Chelsea (£300,000 + on 21/3/97) PL 3+2

GRAY Alan Muir
Born: Carlisle, 2 May 1974
Height: 6'0" Weight: 12.2

Initially a Carlisle associate schoolboy, Alan arrived back in this country in 1996 after completing a four-year soccer scholarship with Richmond University in Augusta, Georgia. Recommended to Doncaster, the hard-tackling right back signed immediately prior to the start of last season and was given two first-team games before leaving at the end of December and seeing the rest of the campaign out with non-league Bishop Auckland.

Doncaster Rov (Signed from Richmond University on 1/8/96) FL 1 Others 1

GRAY Andrew (Andy) David
Born: Harrogate, 15 November 1977
Height: 6'1" Weight: 12.8
International Honours: S: Yth

Having burst on to the scene at Leeds the previous season, the quick and skilful young winger started 1996-97 in the first team squad, only to unluckily suffer his fair share of injuries. In fact, Andy was selected for the Scotland U21 squad on three occasions,

before having to withdraw each time. However, on managing to force his way back into the first-team picture towards the end of the campaign, he again proved to be a young man of genuine talent who will, undoubtedly, be compared to his more famous relatives, father Frank and uncle Eddie, though he looks to have the necessary attitude and ability to make a name for himself in his own right. Is a great crosser of the ball.

Leeds U (From trainee on 1/7/95) PL 13+9 FLC 3+1 FAC 0+2

GRAY Ian James
Born: Manchester, 25 February 1975
Height: 6'2" Weight: 12.0

Back to fitness after a long lay off the previous term, Ian was soon attracting the scouts again with some terrific perform-ances in goal for Rochdale in 1996-97. An ever present, he was selected for the Nationwide League side to meet the Italian Serie "B", but had to miss the game as it clashed with a rearranged league match. Good on crosses, with safe hands, his agility saved the day on numbers of occasions.

Oldham Ath (From trainee on 16/7/93)
Rochdale (Loaned on 18/11/94) FL 12 Others 3
Rochdale (£20,000 on 17/7/95) FL 66 FLC 4 FAC 5 Others 4

GRAY Kevin John
Born: Sheffield, 7 January 1972
Height: 6'0" Weight: 14.0

Consistent Huddersfield centre half who is very experienced despite his age. Most assured, he is a quality player who made one of the centre-back positions his own in 1996-97, before losing his place at the end of the season due to a drop in form which may have been connected to the controversy surrounding his tackle on Gordon Watson of Bradford City and subsequent publicity. Scored his first ever goal for the club at home to Oldham in September, his close-range header from a corner proving to be the winner.

Mansfield T (From trainee on 1/7/90) FL 129+12/3 FLC 8/1 FAC 6+1 Others 12+2/2
Huddersfield T (Signed on 18/7/94) FL 79+3/1 FLC 4 FAC 4 Others 3

GRAY Martin David
Born: Stockton on Tees, 17 August 1971
Height: 5'9" Weight: 11.4

His first full season at Oxford in 1996-97 saw him as a regular member of the midfield and even captaining the side on occasions. A ball winner, who covers every blade of grass, he scored a couple of times after pushing forward to help the forwards and proved more than adept at the sideways, rather than the defence splitting ball. Is a player full of enthusiasm and spirit.

Sunderland (From trainee on 1/2/90) FL 46+18/1 FLC 6+2 FAC 0+3 Others 3+1
Aldershot (Loaned on 9/1/91) FL 3+2 Others 1
Fulham (Loaned on 20/10/95) FL 6 Others 1
Oxford U (£100,000 on 28/3/96) FL 47+3/2 FLC 7 FAC 1

Michael Gray

GRAY Michael
Born: Sunderland, 3 August 1974
Height: 5'7" Weight: 10.10
Club Honours: Div 1 '96
Michael operated in his usual position on the left-hand side of midfield for most of the 1996-97 campaign, but switched to left back for the final month following the arrival of Chris Waddle. Despite Sunderland's relegation, Michael could be reasonably satisfied with his season's work, his highlights including the club's first goal of the campaign away at Nottingham Forest and other important strikes at Newcastle and at Roker against Manchester United. Quick and skilful, he can also offer sound defensive qualities.
Sunderland (From trainee on 1/7/92) P/FL 126+19/10 FLC 8+3 FAC 5+1/1

GRAYSON Neil
Born: York, 1 November 1964
Height: 5'10" Weight: 12.9
A striker, who can also play on the left side of midfield, "Larry" is a great favourite at Northampton with his very high workrate, his commitment, and his flair for goals. Broke the club record last season with a four-minute hat trick against Hartlepool.
Doncaster Rov (Free from Rowntree Mackintosh on 22/3/90) FL 21+8/6 FAC 1+1 Others 2+1/1
York C (Free on 28/3/91) FL 0+1
Chesterfield (Free on 16/8/91) FL 9+6 FLC 2 FAC 1 Others 1
Northampton T (Free from Boston U, via Gateshead, on 19/6/94) FL 103+17/31 FLC 7+1 FAC 3 Others 10/3

GRAYSON Simon Nicholas
Born: Ripon, 16 December 1969
Height: 6'0" Weight: 12.10
Club Honours: FLC '97
Right-sided Leicester full back and occasional midfielder. In 1996-97, Simon was a revelation, having clearly learned from previous Premiership experience and his occasional forays into the opponents' box brought goals in the Coca-Cola Cup ties against York and Wimbledon, the latter being a quality header that took the Foxes to Wembley. Also able to operate as a man marker when required, he adapted well to the wing-back role and was a regular threat in the League Cup final replay at Hillsborough, carrying off a cup winners' medal following the club's victory over Middlesbrough. An outstanding campaign ended in him being an obvious choice as the Foxes' Player of the Year. *Stop Press:* Out of contract during the summer, he reportedly signed for Aston Villa.
Leeds U (From trainee on 13/6/88) FL 2 Others 1+1
Leicester C (£50,000 on 13/3/92) F/PL 175+13/4 FLC 16+2/2 FAC 9 Others 13+1

GRAZIOLI Giuliano Stefano Luigi
Born: Marylebone, 23 March 1975
Height: 5'11" Weight: 12.11
The young Peterborough striker who looked to be moving to Woking before suffering a broken bone in his foot towards the end of last year, has promised to be back in action at London Road as soon as possible, despite problems in getting back to match fitness. Although making nine appearances from the bench without starting a game, Giuliano scored in extra time at Cheltenham in the FA Cup and many believe he would score on a regular basis if given an extended run. Is a player who thinks on his feet and picks up the pieces around the box.
Peterborough U (Free from Wembley on 19/10/95) FL 2+5/1 FLC 0+2 FAC 0+3/1

GREAVES Mark Andrew
Born: Hull, 22 January 1975
Height: 6'1" Weight: 13.0
Having impressed as a member of Brigg Town's 1996 FA Carlsberg Vase winning team, Hull City captured Mark's signature ahead of a number of interested clubs during the 1996 close season. Previously played for Gainsborough Trinity after supporting City as a boy, he is fleet of foot and quick in though and could shine at a higher level. Used in midfield, but looked most comfortable in central defence.
Hull C (Free from Brigg T on 17/6/96) FL 23+7/2 FAC 1 Others 1

GREEN Richard Edward
Born: Wolverhampton, 22 November 1967
Height: 6'1" Weight: 13.7
The fractured arm he sustained at the end of the 1995-96 season, meant he did not play in Gillingham's first team until 26 October. However, he soon made up for lost time, immediately displaying his consistency at the heart of the Gills defence, his form being such that he signed a new two-year contract with the club. A good man to have at set-piece situations, Richard can always be expected to unsettle defences in dangerous areas.
Shrewsbury T (From trainee on 19/7/86) FL 120+5/5 FLC 11/1 FAC 5 Others 5/1
Swindon T (Free on 25/10/90)
Gillingham (Free on 6/3/92) FL 189+2/16 FLC 11 FAC 16+1/1 Others 6

GREEN Scott Paul
Born: Walsall, 15 January 1970
Height: 5'10" Weight: 12.5
Club Honours: Div 1 '97
A highly versatile and valuable Bolton squad member who can operate in virtually any area of the park when required, he was confined to the subs' bench for much of last season, despite playing in the opening three matches, making only seven league starts in all. However, he scored three goals, including the first in an important 2-2 league draw at Swindon and one in the 6-2 drubbing of Luton in the third round of the FA Cup. *Stop Press:* Having just played the requisite amount of games to earn a first division championship medal, Scott was reported to have signed for newly-promoted Wigan for a fee of £300,000.
Derby Co (From trainee on 20/7/88)
Bolton W (£50,000 on 17/3/90) P/FL 166+54/25 FLC 19+4/1 FAC 20+3/4 Others 16+4/1

GREENACRE Christopher (Chris) Mark
Born: Halifax, 23 December 1977
Height: 5'11" Weight: 12.8
One of the many young professionals on Manchester City's books, Chris came through the "A" and reserve teams to be given his first-team debut in a 3-0 home win against Swindon last February, coming on as a substitute for Paul Dickov 15 minutes from the end and impressing immediately. In fact, he was unlucky not to score when he received a pass with his back to goal, swivelled, and unleashed a fierce shot that the visiting 'keeper only just saved. Since then he was only used as a substitute and performed well each time. Well built, tall, and looking to be busy in the opponents' half, he is a player to be watched and bears some comparison with Colin Bell, both in style and positional play.
Manchester C (From trainee on 1/7/95) FL 0+4

GREENALL Colin Anthony
Born: Billinge, 30 December 1963
Height: 5'11" Weight: 12.12
Club Honours: Div 3 '97
International Honours: E: Yth
Captain fantastic and the hub of Wigan Athletic's most successful team in more than a decade in 1996-97, Colin, a towering, dependable figure at the heart of the defence, went through the season as an ever present without picking up a single booking. His leadership and organisational skills were rewarded when he collected a third division championship medal, his first honour after 16 years in the game. Crowned a great campaign when winning the Shareholders and Supporters Player of the Year and the Players' Player of the Year awards.
Blackpool (From apprentice on 17/1/81) FL 179+4/9 FLC 12/2 FAC 9 Others 2
Gillingham (£40,000 on 10/9/86) FL 62/4 FLC 3/1 FAC 6/1 Others 9/2
Oxford U (£285,000 on 15/2/88) FL 67/2 FLC 4 FAC 1 Others 2
Bury (Loaned on 4/1/90) FL 3 Other 1
Bury (£125,000 on 16/7/90) FL 66+2/5 FLC 3 FAC 1 Others 8/1
Preston NE (£50,000 on 27/3/92) FL 29/1
Chester (Free on 13/8/93) FL 42/1 FLC 2 FAC 4/1 Others 4
Lincoln C (Free on 27/7/94) FL 43/3 FLC 6 FAC 3/1 Others 2
Wigan Ath (£45,000 on 19/9/95) FL 83/4 FLC 1+1/1 FAC 4 Others 3+1

GREENE David Michael
Born: Luton, 26 October 1973
Height: 6'2" Weight: 13.5
International Honours: Ei: U21-14
A towering former Irish U21 centre half, the most capped at that level for his country, David joined Colchester from Luton in the summer of 1996, after a very successful three-month loan midway through the previous season. Virtually an ever present, missing only three games through suspension, and equally at home in a three-centre half or flat back four formation, he scored three important goals, and also thundered home a penalty in the AWS Wembley shoot out.
Luton T (From juniors on 3/9/91) FL 18+1 FLC 2 FAC 1 Others 0+1
Colchester U (Loaned on 23/11/95) FL 14/1 Others 2
Brentford (Loaned on 1/3/96) FL 11
Colchester U (£30,000 on 21/6/96) FL 44/2 FLC 4 FAC 1 Others 6/1

GREENING Jonathan
Born: Scarborough, 2 January 1979
Height: 5'11" Weight: 11.7
A very promising York City youngster who turned professional during the 1996-97 campaign, Jonathan can play either in midfield or up front. Having impressed in the handful of substitute appearances he made towards the end of the season he is sure to be offered further opportunities.
York C (From trainee on 23/12/96) FL 0+5

GREGAN Sean Matthew
Born: Guisborough, 29 March 1974
Height: 6'2" Weight: 14.0
A dominating centre half signed by Preston from Darlington last November, Sean has a wealth of experience despite his age. Cool under pressure, a decisive tackler, and commanding in the air, he distributed the ball well and with a powerful shot was a threat at set pieces. Scored his first goal for the club, a 30-yard thunderbolt at Shrewsbury, and was also used to great effect in midfield where he seems destined to play at the highest level.
Darlington (From trainee on 20/1/91) FL 129+7/4 FLC 8 FAC 7 Others 10+1/1
Preston NE (£350,000 on 29/11/96) FL 21/1 Others 1

GREGG Matthew Stephen
Born: Cheltenham, 30 November 1978
Height: 5'11" Weight: 12.0
Having made his Torquay debut in 1995-96, the second-year trainee goalkeeper went back to youth and reserve team football before getting the call for the final game of last season, following injuries to both Rhys Wilmot and Ray Newland. Despite having come back from injury himself, Matthew performed well in a 2-1 defeat at Doncaster and could not be faulted for any of the goals.
Torquay U (Trainee) FL 2

GREGORY David Spencer
Born: Sudbury, 23 January 1970
Height: 5'10" Weight: 12.8
Having struggled to establish himself in midfield for Colchester in 1995-96, he looked more comfortable in his limited games early last season and scored a cracking long-distance goal against eventual champions, Wigan, in October. Inspired management then saw him switched to right back where he began to look a natural, holding that position for most of the second half of the campaign. The only ever present throughout the AWS run, David is the brother of Ipswich Town striker, Neil.
Ipswich T (From trainee on 31/3/87) F/PL 16+16/2 FLC 3+2 FAC 1 Others 3+2/4
Hereford U (Loaned on 9/1/95) FL 2 Others 1
Peterborough U (Free on 4/7/95) FL 0+3 FLC 1 FAC 1 Others 2
Colchester U (Free on 8/12/95) FL 39+9/1 FLC 1+1 FAC 1 Others 7

GREGORY Neil Richard
Born: Ndola, Zambia, 7 October 1972
Height: 5'11" Weight: 11.10
Despite the absence of Ian Marshall (transferred) and Alex Mathie (long-term

injury) last season, Neil was unable to force himself into the Ipswich side and had to content himself in the reserves, while the club brought in loan strikers. He made his now customary substitute goalkeeper appearance against Huddersfield, playing for 75 minutes after Richard Wright was injured, before going off on loan to Torquay in November and playing five games prior to returning to Portman Road. His regular goalscoring for the reserves finally brought him back into the limelight and strikes against QPR and Bradford, when coming on as substitute, earned him a full recall to the team, while the visit of Sheffield United brought his first ever hat trick for the senior side. Although the goals dried up somewhat he retained his place in the side and appeared in both play-off semi finals.
Ipswich T (From trainee on 21/2/92) P/FL 16+21/8 FLC 2+1 FAC 0+1 Others 4+3/2
Chesterfield (Loaned on 3/2/94) FL 2+1/1
Scunthorpe U (Loaned on 6/3/95) FL 10/7
Torquay U (Loaned on 22/11/96) FL 5

GRIDELET Philip (Phil) Raymond
Born: Hendon, 30 April 1967
Height: 5'11" Weight: 13.0
International Honours: E: SP-5
With Southend virtually always anchored near the bottom of division one, in 1996-97, it was a tough season for Phil and his battling qualities were unable to lift the club for any long period of time. On his day a match-winning midfield general, his lack of goals was particularly disappointing and he will hope to get a better return in 1997-98.
Barnsley (£175,000 from Barnet on 21/1/90) FL 3+3 FAC 1 Others 1
Rotherham U (Loaned on 5/3/93) FL 9
Southend U (Free on 25/9/93) FL 118+21/8 FLC 2 FAC 2 Others 7/1

GRIEMINK Bart
Born: Holland, 29 March 1972
Height: 6'4" Weight: 15.4
Unable to get further opportunities in goal at Birmingham due to the excellent form of Ian Bennett, Bart moved to Peterborough in October to join up with his former manager, Barry Fry. Apart from a disastrous start, giving away a goal in both of his first two games, the giant 'keeper came back strongly to prove a more than useful buy, showing great agility for such a big man. Will benefit from a settled defence this coming term.
Birmingham C (Free from WK Emmen on 9/11/95) FL 20 FLC 3 FAC 1 Others 1+1
Peterborough U (£25,000 on 11/10/96) FL 27 FAC 4 Others 4

GRIFFIN Andrew
Born: Billinge, 7 March 1979
Height: 5'9" Weight: 10.10
International Honours: E: Yth
A product of Stoke's improving youth policy, Andrew burst into the first team aged 17 in the 1996-97 season, keeping Northern Ireland international, Nigel Worthington, on the sidelines. The left back's potential was rewarded with a professional contract and a series of England youth international call ups. Scored his first goal for the club at home to Grimsby in March when storming

into the penalty area and finishing with an unstoppable left-footed drive.
Stoke C (From trainee on 5/9/96) FL 29+5/1 FLC 0+1 FAC 1

GRIFFITHS Carl Brian
Born: Welshpool, 16 July 1971
Height: 6'0" Weight: 12.6
International Honours: W: B-1; U21-2; Yth
The Peterborough record buy when purchased from Portsmouth, Carl failed to get a proper run with Posh in 1996-97, appearing more from the bench than making starts, and was loaned to Leyton Orient in October. A classy centre forward, he made such an impact with his unselfish running and his goalscoring that he became an instant hit with the fans and it was the vital boost to both the team and fans when he joined the club permanently towards the end of the season.
Shrewsbury T (From trainee on 26/9/88) FL 110+33/54 FLC 7+4/3 FAC 6/2 Others 7+3/3
Manchester C (£500,000 on 29/10/93) PL 11+7/4 FLC 0+1 FAC 2
Portsmouth (£200,000 on 17/8/95) FL 2+12/2 FLC 0+1
Peterborough U (£225,000 on 28/3/96) FL 6+10/2 FLC 0+2/1 FAC 1+1/1 Others 0+1
Leyton Orient (Loaned on 31/10/96) FL 5/3
Leyton Orient (£100,000 on 7/3/97) FL 8/3

GRIFFITHS Gareth John
Born: Winsford, 10 April 1970
Height: 6'4" Weight: 14.0
A tall central defender with Port Vale whose season ended last January, thanks to a knee injury, having done well during the first half of 1996-97. Tipped for a move to higher echelons, after limping off against QPR in January with just seven minutes gone it became a long fight to get fit again. Returned for the reserves in April before playing in the final game at Crystal Palace, but may still need an operation to cure the problem.
Port Vale (Signed from Rhyl on 8/2/93) FL 87+4/4 FLC 8 FAC 7/1 Others 7

GROBBELAAR Bruce David
Born: Durban, South Africa, 6 October 1957
Height: 6'1" Weight: 14.2
Club Honours: Div 1 '82, '83, '84, '86, '88, '90; FLC '82, '83, '84, '90; FAC '86, '89, '92; CS '82, '86, '88, '89; EC '84
International Honours: Zimbabwe: 20
Signed from Southampton in the 1996 close season on a 12-month contract, Bruce proved he was still a top-class goalkeeper, turning in some excellent performances for Plymouth, even though his mind must have regularly been elsewhere. As eccentric as ever he often appeared to be a stand-in sweeper, while missing only ten league games largely due to call ups from Zimbabwe. Hopefully, his well publicised off-field problems can be sorted sooner, rather than later, in order for him to concentrate on what he does best – keeping goal with a smile on his face.
Crewe Alex (On trial from Vancouver Whitecaps on 18/12/79) FL 24/1

Liverpool (£250,000 from Vancouver Whitecaps on 12/3/81) F/PL 440 FLC 70 FAC 62 Others 56
Stoke C (Loaned on 17/3/93) FL 4
Southampton (Free on 11/8/94) PL 32 FLC 3 FAC 5
Plymouth Arg (Free on 12/8/96) FL 36 FLC 2 FAC 3

GRODAS Frode

Born: Sogndal, Norway, 24 October 1964
Height: 6'2" Weight: 14.7
Club Honours: FAC '97
International Honours: Norway: 30

In desperate need of experienced goal-keeping cover after Dmitri Kharine's serious knee injury, and Nick Colgan's broken arm, left just Kevin Hitchcock with any senior experience on Blues' staff, goalkeeping coach, Eddie Niedzwiecki, made a special trip to Lillestrom last September to watch Norway's number one 'keeper, Frode Grodås, who was due to sign for Sturm Graz of Austria and persuaded him to join his compatriot, Erland Johnsen, at the Bridge on loan until his transfer was finalised. He must have wondered what he let himself in for when he made his debut in a wretched Chelsea performance at home to Blackpool in a second leg Coca-Cola Cup tie as the Seasiders outplayed Chelsea to win 3-1 and almost dump the Blues out of the competition. Hitchcock came back for the next six matches until a serious elbow injury ruled him out and Frode literally grabbed his chance with both hands, impressing Ruud Gullit so much that he offered him a two-year contract following a free transfer. Confident and agile, he has acclimatised remarkably well to Premiership football and gave a solid performance in the FA Cup semi final against Wimbledon when the Dons put high balls, and bodies, into the box as they desperately tried to claw their way back into the match, prior to picking up an FA Cup winners medal following the 2-0 Wembley win over Middlesbrough.
Chelsea (Free from Lillestrom on 21/9/96) PL 20+1 FLC 1 FAC 5

GROVES Paul

Born: Derby, 28 February 1966
Height: 5'11" Weight: 11.5

A strongly built right-footed midfielder, Paul was first choice in the West Brom side under Alan Buckley after being signed from Grimsby during the 1996 close season and did reasonably well, but the supporters never totally accepted him, and when Ray Harford took over as manager he lost his place in the side. He did, however, reach a personal milestone during the season, making his 350th consecutive appearance at club level. Is a player who can always be relied upon to score vital goals, as well as being an excellent provider.
Leicester C (£12,000 from Burton A on 18/4/88) FL 7+9/1 FLC 1/1 FAC 0+1 Others 0+1
Lincoln C (Loaned on 20/8/89) FL 8/1 FLC 2
Blackpool (£60,000 on 25/1/90) FL 106+1/21 FLC 6/1 FAC 9/4 Others 13/3
Grimsby T (£150,000 on 12/8/92) FL 183+1/38 FLC 10+1/2 FAC 12/2 Others 4/1
West Bromwich A (£600,000 on 8/7/96) FL 27+2/4 FLC 2/1 FAC 1

GUDMUNDSSON Niklas

Born: Sweden, 29 February 1972
Height: 5'11" Weight: 12.9
International Honours: Sweden: 10

Unable to find himself a place in the Blackburn line up, apart from a couple of subs' appearances in 1996-97, Nicklas spent the last two months of the season on loan at Ipswich, during which time he scored three goals – a tap in at Swindon, a long-range effort in the Birmingham game, and a header in the second leg of the play-off semi final. Although not an out-and-out centre forward, he has the ability to hold the ball up well and possesses some neat touches.
Blackburn Rov (Signed from Halmstads on 2/12/95) PL 1+5
Ipswich T (Loaned on 21/3/97) FL 2+6/2 Others 1+1/1

Frode Grodas

Bontcho Guentchev

GUENTCHEV Bontcho Lubomisov
Born: Tchoshevo, Bulgaria, 7 July 1964
Height: 5'10" Weight: 11.7
International Honours: Bulgaria: 14

Although highly talented and immensely skilful, Bontcho failed to make very much impact for Luton Town in the second division in 1996-97, displaying a certain lack of appetite for the hurly burly of life in the lower reaches. After losing his penalty-taking role, following a miss on the opening day in a 2-1 home defeat against Burnley, he scored just one goal during the campaign, despite being involved in most of the matches, although frequently as a substitute, and was released on a free transfer during the summer.

Ipswich T (£250,000 from Sporting Lisbon on 29/12/92) PL 39+22/6 FLC 6 FAC 6+2/5
Luton T (Free on 23/8/95) FL 40+22/10 FLC 5+2 FAC 2+1 Others 4+1/2

GUINAN Stephen (Steve)
Born: Birmingham, 24 December 1975
Height: 6'1" Weight: 13.7

A promising young Nottingham Forest striker who was unable to command a regular place in the line up last season, despite promising much in 1995-96, Steve was limited to just two subs' appearances before joining Burnley on loan in transfer deadline week. At Turf Moor, disappointingly, his six games were again only from the bench, and he made no real impression as the side struggled, before returning to the City Ground.

Nottingham F (From trainee on 7/1/93) PL 1+3
Darlington (Loaned on 14/12/95) FL 3/1
Burnley (Loaned on 27/3/97) FL 0+6

GULLIT Ruud
Born: Surinam, 1 September 1962
Height: 6'2" Weight: 13.0
International Honours: Holland: 64

Newly installed during the 1996-97 close season as Chelsea's player/manager, Ruud set about revamping the squad by signing the continental trio of Gianluca Vialli, Frank Leboeuf and Roberto Di Matteo and, in November, acquiring Gianfranco Zola. August saw his first competitive matches as the boss, and success, as Chelsea overcame Nottingham Forest and Ajax to win the Umbro Trophy. Unfortunately, that match also brought further surgery to his damaged knee which prevented him from playing until late October in the Coca-Cola Cup tie at Burnden Park, a traumatic night for the club as millionaire benefactor and vice-president, Matthew Harding, was tragically killed in a helicopter crash after the match. Three days later, showing tremendous dignity and humility, he led the team out at an emotion-packed Stamford Bridge for the derby against Tottenham and, perhaps fittingly, scored the first goal of the game. Has shown himself to be tactically astute, often changing the sweeper system to a flat back four during the course of a game to great effect. This was particularly evident in the FA Cup and he became the first overseas manager to lead a club to a Wembley win, following Chelsea's 2-0 victory over Middlesbrough in the final, after just 11

months in the job. The most disappointing aspect of an exciting season was the tiny amount of first-team football that Ruud was able to play. A fractured ankle sustained at Derby in March, which put him out for the rest of the season, meant that he only started six Premiership matches and the Dutchman in full flow is still one of the finest sights in football. In the space of 12 months Ruud has made his side one of the most glamorous as he tries to mould a team in his own image: skilful, entertaining and articulate. At last a style and swagger has returned to Stamford Bridge, and, not before time, Chelsea fans can look to the future with optimism.

Chelsea (Free from Sampdoria, via Haarlem, PSV Eindhoven and AC Milan, on 1/7/95) PL 37+6/4 FLC 3 FAC 7+1/3

GUNN Bryan James
Born: Thurso, 22 December 1963
Height: 6'2" Weight: 13.13
International Honours: S: 6; B-4; U21-9; Yth; Sch

Now standing fourth in Norwich City's all-time list of appearance makers, Bryan had a very successful testimonial year of events in 1996-97, with his decade-long contribution earning him the respect of fans and colleagues alike. Despite 14 goals being put past him in three successive December games, this was followed by five consecutive wins, including three clean sheets. Later, under immense pressure for the goalkeeping position from the emerging Andy Marshall, he turned down the club's offer of a new one-year contract, but is now considering a dual role that allows him to be available to play, plus having involvement on the commercial side.

Aberdeen (Signed from Invergordon BC in 1980) SL 15 SLC 4 SC 1 Others 1
Norwich C (£150,000 on 23/10/86) F/PL 386 FLC 38 FAC 27 Others 22

GUPPY Stephen (Steve)
Born: Winchester, 29 March 1969
Height: 5'11" Weight: 12.0
Club Honours: FAT '91, '93; GMVC '93
International Honours: E: SP-1

Prior to departing to Leicester last February, the left-sided midfielder had a very good season with Port Vale, helping the club to challenge for the play offs and only missing one game, at Oxford in the Coca-Cola Cup when he injured his back during the warm up. Made his debut for City in the league victory at Wimbledon, appearing as an emergency left back, and impressed with his accurate crossing ability. However, from then on, he had little opportunity to play in his normal role due to the club's injury crisis, but in gradually adapting to the demands of Premiership football, Steve is likely to be an influential performer in 1997-98.

Wycombe W (Signed in 1989-90) FL 41/8 FLC 4 FAC 8/2 Others 10
Newcastle U (£150,000 on 2/8/94) FLC 0+1
Port Vale (£225,000 on 25/11/94) FL 102+3/12 FLC 7 FAC 8 Others 7+1/1
Leicester C (£850,000 + on 28/2/97) PL 12+1

GURNEY Andrew (Andy) Robert
Born: Bristol, 25 January 1974
Height: 5'11" Weight: 12.2

Andy started last season on the right-hand side of midfield, scoring three goals in the opening 17 matches for Bristol Rovers. However, after being sent off at Bury on 26 October, he was unable to reclaim his first team place on a regular basis and was subsequently transfer listed. Completed his 100th league appearance for Rovers on 1 March against Walsall, but turned down an offer of a further contract.

Bristol Rov (From trainee on 10/7/92) FL 100+8/9 FLC 7/1 FAC 5 Others 15

Bryan Gunn

A WARM WELCOME
TO FOOTBALL FOOTBALL™
LONDON
a unique footballing experience

FOOTBALL FOOTBALL™ is an exciting new restaurant situated in the heart of Central London, close to Piccadilly Circus tube station. The aim of the restaurant is to provide a total and dynamic football experience. In addition to the internationally themed food, service and futuristic interior design, the restaurant also features a myriad of special effects. Imagine emerging from a continental style tunnel accompanied by the sound of studs on concrete, to be welcomed by the roar of a packed stadium!

The state of the art audio visual system provides thrilling entertainment with clips from memorable matches and magical moments.

On display is one of the world's largest collections of football memorabilia, including personal mementos of the great heroes and their cup winning medals.

"Football Football"™ is open from 12 noon 7 days a week and provides a unique entertainment facility - including live football matches on two video walls and 14 TV monitors.

For football fans everywhere, "Football Football"™ is the restaurant to be seen at with star players such as George Best, Jamie Redknapp, Chris Armstrong, Richard Gough all being regular visitors.

BOOKINGS AND INFORMATION,
CONTACT THE RESTAURANT ON:

TEL: 0171 930 9970

FOOTBALL FOOTBALL™
57-60 HAYMARKET
LONDON
SW1Y 4QX

FOOTBALL FOOTBALL ™
supports the Bobby Moore Fund
for Imperial Cancer Research

H

HAALAND Alf-Inge Rasdal
Born: Stavanger, Norway, 23 November 1972
Height: 5'10" Weight: 12.12
International Honours: Norway: 24
Alf had his best season for Nottingham Forest in 1996-97 and scored six times, four of them vital, including both against Arsenal in Stuart Pearce's first game as manager. This made him joint top scorer. Missing very few games throughout the campaign, he established himself in a central midfield role, despite making the occasional appearance at the back. Yet to agree to a new contract, he showed good form, having settled into one specific role as many thought he would, after spending two seasons in various positions. Is a player who can mix strong tackling to powerful surging runs which often end in searing long-range shots. *Stop Press:* Reported to have signed for Leeds during the summer with a tribunal set to decide the fee.
Nottingham F (Signed from Bryne on 25/1/94) F/PL 66+9/7 FLC 2+5 FAC 5+1 Others 2+3

HACKETT Warren James
Born: Plaistow, 16 December 1971
Height: 6'0" Weight: 12.5
Club Honours: FAYC '90
The Mansfield full back suffered a long-lasting injury early on last season, but came back in strength by mid term, being outstanding in a defensive midfield role. A classy player, Warren also enjoys the attacking side of the game.
Leyton Orient (Free from Tottenham H juniors on 3/7/90) FL 74+2/3 FLC 4 FAC 8/2 Others 7
Doncaster Rov (Free on 26/7/94) FL 46/2 FLC 4 FAC 1 Others 4
Mansfield T (£50,000 on 20/10/95) FL 67+1/4 FLC 2 FAC 3 Others 1

HADDOW Paul Andrew
Born: Blackpool, 11 October 1978
Height: 5'8" Weight: 10.10
As one of two trainees given a first team opportunity for Blackpool last season in the AWS competition at Rotherham (10 December), the young midfielder will be hoping that he impressed enough to be offered professional terms for this coming season.
Blackpool (Trainee) Others 1

HADLEY Stewart
Born: Dudley, 30 December 1973
Height: 6'0" Weight: 13.2
Stewart had a disappointing season for Mansfield in 1996-97 and seemed unable to find his old scoring touch. However, never short of enthusiasm and energy, after falling out of favour in mid term, the hard-running forward came back strongly towards the end of the campaign.
Derby Co (Free from Halesowen T on 6/7/92)
Mansfield T (Signed on 9/2/94) FL 100+22/31 FLC 6+2 FAC 7/1 Others 5+1/3

HAILS Julian
Born: Lincoln, 20 November 1967
Height: 5'10" Weight: 11.1
A real team player, Julian always gave 100 per cent, whichever position he was thrust into during a difficult season for Southend in 1996-97, and more often than not, came out with credit. Good neat touches and tough tackling for a small frame, allied to strong running down the left made him a very useful squad player, although he never seemed to manage to hold down a permanent first-team slot.
Fulham (Signed from Hemel Hempstead on 29/8/90) FL 99+10/12 FLC 5+1 FAC 2 Others 9/1
Southend U (Free on 2/12/94) FL 91+14/6 FLC 3+1 FAC 1+1 Others 3

HALL Gareth David
Born: Croydon, 12 March 1969
Height: 5'8" Weight: 12.0
Club Honours: Div 2 '89; Div 1 '96; FMC 90
International Honours: E: Sch. W: 9; U21-1
The Welsh international utility man established himself as Peter Reid's first-choice right back at Sunderland last September and remained there for the rest of the season. Unfortunately, he became a target for some criticism from the terraces, but to his credit, he never hid from his responsibilities, despite looking uncomfortable at times in the full-back role. Is a player who likes to get forward in support of the attack and has good long-range shooting ability.
Chelsea (From apprentice on 25/4/86) F/PL 120+18/4 FLC 12+1 FAC 6 Others 10+4/1
Sunderland (£300,000 on 20/12/95) P/FL 40+6 FLC 3 FAC 2

HALL Marcus Thomas
Born: Coventry, 24 March 1976
Height: 6'1" Weight: 12.2
International Honours: E: U21-5
The previous season's hernia injury still bothered him at the start of 1996-97 and after a handful of Coventry games he was sidelined again. Returned after Christmas and, although performing reasonably well, found the new wing-back role hard to adjust to and, being very much a confidence player, his performances at Derby in the cup and at Old Trafford did not help him. A classy defender who is equally capable in central defence, and who comes out well looking to make the right pass, Marcus was selected for England U21s and played four times without letting the side down.
Coventry C (From trainee on 1/7/94) PL 36+7 FLC 6 FAC 5

HALL Paul Anthony
Born: Manchester, 3 July 1972
Height: 5'9" Weight: 11.0
Paul had by far his best season at Portsmouth in 1996-97 after finding a role within the team playing just behind the front two, having started the campaign up front alongside Deon Burton. A player with great pace, verve, and control, he also contributed 15 goals, including one apiece in the FA Cup games against Wolves and Reading and a double in a 3-1 league win at Huddersfield. Also twice found the net in three

consecutive matches as Pompey made an ultimately unsuccessful run for the play offs.
Torquay U (From trainee on 9/7/90) FL 77+16/1 FLC 7 FAC 4+1/2 Others 5+1/1
Portsmouth (£70,000 on 25/3/93) FL 126+33/32 FLC 9+3/1 FAC 5+1/2 Others 6+2/2

Paul Hall

HALL Richard Anthony
Born: Ipswich, 14 March 1972
Height: 6'2" Weight: 13.11
International Honours: E: U21-11
Yet another 1996 summer signing by West Ham's manager Harry Redknapp to be sidelined by injury for most of last season, the former Southampton central defender was injured in a pre-season friendly and, after a foot operation, did not make his debut until early April against Middlesbrough, holding his place to assist in the fight against relegation. With the departure of Slaven Bilic in the close season, Richard now has every chance to establish himself in the heart of the Hammers' defence as a strong tackling defender, who is commanding in the air.
Scunthorpe U (From trainee on 20/3/90) FL 22/3 FLC 2 FAC 3 Others 4
Southampton (£200,000 on 13/2/91) F/PL 119+7/12 FLC 11+1/1 FAC 15/3 Others 3
West Ham U (£1,400,000 + on 19/7/96) PL 7

HALL Wayne
Born: Rotherham, 25 October 1968
Height: 5'8" Weight: 10.6
Last season was a frustrating one for York City's experienced and reliable left back as a series of troublesome injuries limited his senior appearances to just 16 league and cup games. The highlight of Wayne's abbreviated campaign was when he kept a tight rein on Andrei Kanchelskis in the Coca-Cola Cup win over Everton.

York C (Free from Hatfield Main Colliery on 15/3/89) FL 257+15/8 FLC 17+1 FAC 10+1/1 Others 19/1

HALLE Gunnar
Born: Oslo, Norway, 11 August 1965
Height: 5'11" Weight: 11.2
Club Honours: Div 2 '91
International Honours: Norway: 54

A versatile Norwegian international with over 50 caps to his name, Gunnar was originally due to sign for Leeds from Oldham following talks at Elland Road on 6 September, but, unfortunately, the 4-0 defeat at the hands of Manchester United the next day resulted in the sacking of manager, Howard Wilkinson, just one day later. However, the club remained interested and, in December, he became George Graham's first signing, going straight into the side and filling a number of positions. A wing back with pace and skill, who also played in central defence where he was equally adept, he proved to be a player of international class and an excellent acquisition.
Oldham Ath (£280,000 from Lillestrom on 15/2/91) F/PL 185+3/17 FLC 16/2 FAC 8/2 Others 4
Leeds U (£400,000 on 13/12/96) PL 20 FAC 3

HALLIDAY Stephen William
Born: Sunderland, 3 May 1976
Height: 5'10" Weight: 12.3

The young Hartlepool forward began 1996-97 on a low, with Sunderland having refused to pay the £375,000 fee which had been set by the transfer tribunal. Understandably, he made a quiet start and was just beginning to get back to his best form when he suffered a serious knee injury. Out for a long spell, Stephen then took a few games to regain his confidence, but during the end of season games he was again seen to best effect, running at speed at opposition defences as Pool battled to hold on to their Nationwide League status.
Hartlepool U (From trainee on 5/7/94) FL 90+19/20 FLC 7+2 FAC 4/1 Others 3+1

HALLWORTH Jonathan (Jon) Geoffrey
Born: Stockport, 26 October 1965
Height: 6'1" Weight: 14.3
Club Honours: Div 2 '91

Started last season as Oldham's first choice goalkeeper but, having received a knee injury after just six matches, he was replaced by the new signing, Gary Kelly, and, with the latter in such splendid form throughout the rest of the campaign, failed to win his place back. Kelly had joined the Latics just two weeks earlier as a replacement for second-string 'keeper, Paul Gerrard, recently sold to Everton. A reliable and confident custodian for a number of years, Jon was given a free transfer during the summer.
Ipswich T (From apprentice on 26/5/83) FL 45 FLC 4 FAC 1 Others 6
Bristol Rov (Loaned on 1/1/85) FL 2 Others 1
Oldham Ath (£75,000 on 3/2/89) F/PL 171+3 FLC 20 FAC 20 Others 3

HAMILTON Derrick (Des) Vivian
Born: Bradford, 15 August 1976
Height: 5'11" Weight: 13.0
International Honours: E: U21-1

Des Hamilton

Made a quiet start for Bradford last season before being moved to the right-wing back position and becoming a revelation, his surging runs creating many opportunities for his team mates. Such was his form that he was selected for the Nationwide U21 League side against the Italian League, a match that ended in a 1-1 draw, and began to draw bigger clubs' scouts to Valley Parade, something that saw him eventually transferred to Newcastle on transfer deadline day for a £1.5 million fee that could rise by £8,000 per each match played to a total of £2 million. Yet to make his debut for United, Des' newly found status saw him honoured at England U21 level when capped in the Poland away game in the European Championships. Is strong, aggressive, and hard working.
Bradford C (From trainee on 1/6/94) FL 67+21/5 FLC 6/1 FAC 6 Others 4+1/2
Newcastle U (£1,500,000 + on 27/3/97)

HAMILTON Ian Richard
Born: Stevenage, 14 December 1967
Height: 5'9" Weight: 11.3

Ian had a fine season for West Brom in 1996-97, his prompting play and probing exploits from midfield certainly pleasing his two managers (Alan Buckley and Ray Harford) as well as the fans. With a penchant for coming through from deep positions, he skippered the team late on and hardly ever lost his composure, producing several outstanding performances. Was voted Albion's 1997 Player of the Year.
Southampton (From apprentice on 24/12/85)
Cambridge U (Signed on 29/3/88) FL 23+1/1 FLC 1 FAC 2 Others 2
Scunthorpe U (Signed on 23/12/88) FL 139+6/18 FLC 6 FAC 6+1 Others 14+1/3
West Bromwich A (£160,000 on 19/6/92) FL 200+3/22 FLC 10/1 FAC 8+1/1 Others 14+2/3

HAMMOND Nicholas (Nicky) David
Born: Hornchurch, 7 September 1967
Height: 6'0" Weight: 11.13

A serious back injury meant that Nicky made only one first-team appearance for Reading in 1996-97, a 3-2 defeat away to West Bromwich, though he had recovered sufficiently to appear in the reserve team during the closing months of the season. Obviously hoping to contest the first-team jersey with Steve Mautone next campaign, he did excellent work coaching the schoolboy goalkeepers at the club.

Arsenal (From apprentice on 12/7/85)
Bristol Rov (Loaned on 23/8/86) FL 3
Swindon T (Free on 1/7/87) F/PL 65+2 FLC 11
FAC 10 Others 6
Plymouth Arg (£40,000 on 14/8/95) FL 4 FLC 2
Others 1
Reading (£40,000 on 13/2/96) FL 6 FAC 1

HANBY Robert (Rob) James
Born: Pontefract, 24 December 1974
Height: 5'8" Weight: 11.9
A defender and occasional midfielder, Rob joined Scarborough from Barnsley in the summer of 1996 but found first-team opportunities limited, making just three starts, including two against Leicester City in the Coca-Cola Cup, before being released on a free transfer at the end of the season.
Barnsley (From trainee on 6/7/93)
Scarborough (Free on 15/8/96) FL 1+3 FLC 2

HANCOX Richard
Born: Wolverhampton, 4 October 1968
Height: 5'10" Weight: 13.0
Started last season in the left-wing-back role for Torquay, but, although fine in going forward, when the results started to go against the side, the defensive part of his game was not up to the same standard and he was released in December. The chairman, Mike Bateson's son in law, Richard is currently with Taunton Town.
Torquay U (Free from Stourport Swifts on 18/3/93) FL 56+26/10 FLC 8+1/3 FAC 3+3/2 Others 2

HANDYSIDE Peter David
Born: Dumfries, 31 July 1974
Height: 6'1" Weight: 13.0
International Honours: S: U21-7
A Grimsby right-footed central defender, Peter is a highly-rated graduate of the club's youth scheme. Strong, both in the air and on the ground, and an effective distributor of the ball from defence, injury, however, sidelined him for most of last season and his long-term absence undoubtedly contributed greatly to the Mariners' abysmal campaign.
Grimsby T (From trainee on 21/11/92) FL 94+4/1 FLC 7 FAC 4 Others 4

HANLON Richard (Richie) Kenneth
Born: Wembley, 26 May 1978
Height: 6'1" Weight: 13.7
A player who can operate in midfield or as a forward, Richie found opportunities at Southend few and far between after signing from Chelsea in the 1996 close season and had a spell on loan with Dover. Making his debut in a 3-0 defeat at Sheffield United was not the best of starts and he went back to the reserves before being freed during the summer.
Southend U (Free from Chelsea juniors on 10/7/96) FL 1+1

HANSON David (Dave) Paul
Born: Huddersfield, 19 November 1968
Height: 6'0" Weight: 13.7
A big, strong Leyton Orient centre forward who scored two away goals at Mansfield in 1996-97, and another player to have his season interrupted by injuries and the competition for places, he spent a month on

loan at Chesterfield prior to the end of the campaign before returning to play the last couple of games with Orient. With good control and turning ability, which make him particularly adept at playing with his back to the goal, Dave will have benefited from the experience and will be a vital squad player this year.
Bury (Free from Farsley Celtic on 19/7/93) FL 1 FLC 2 (Free to Halifax T on 18/8/94)
Leyton Orient (£50,000 from Hednesford T on 4/10/95) FL 22+14/4 FLC 1+1 Others 2
Chesterfield (Loaned on 10/3/97) FL 3/1

HAPGOOD Leon Duane
Born: Torbay, 7 August 1979
Height: 5'6" Weight: 10.0
Still a second-year trainee midfielder, he made an encouraging start for Torquay when coming off the bench for the final 20 minutes of last season at Doncaster. Incidentally, Leon was one of seven YTS boys who made the first team – surely a record, even by third division standards.
Torquay U (Trainee) FL 0+1

HARDY Philip (Phil)
Born: Ellesmere Port, 9 April 1973
Height: 5'8" Weight: 11.2
Club Honours: WC '95
International Honours: Ei: U21-9
This young "hardy perennial" seems to have been around the Wrexham scene for so long that he has become part of the furniture! Unfortunately, 1996-97 was not one of his better seasons as he had the ever-improving Derwyn Brace to contend with for the left-back slot, while also being out for a spell with injury. Although requesting a transfer during the campaign, Phil was eventually happy to be taken off the list and stay to fight for his place.
Wrexham (From trainee on 24/11/90) FL 230+1 FLC 16 FAC 23 Others 32

HARDYMAN Paul George
Born: Portsmouth, 11 March 1964
Height: 5'8" Weight: 11.12
International Honours: E: U21-2
Released by Wycombe during the 1996 close season, Paul signed for Barnet, becoming an important left-full back under manager, Ray Clemence, before being injured just before Christmas and failing to win his place back. Prior to being released before the end of the campaign, he continued to show good passing skills, while his strong shooting ability saw him score twice at Underhill against Wigan and Rochdale. Also had a spell on loan at Slough in February.
Portsmouth (Free from Waterford on 8/7/83) FL 113+4/3 FLC 5 FAC 6 Others 8/1
Sunderland (£130,000 on 25/7/89) FL 101+5/9 FLC 11/2 FAC 8+1/1 Others 3
Bristol Rov (£160,000 on 3/8/92) FL 54+13/5 FLC 3 FAC 3+1 Others 3/1
Wycombe W (Free on 8/8/95) FL 12+3 FLC 4 Others 1
Barnet (Free on 2/8/96) FL 13+3/2 FLC 3 FAC 4

HARE Matthew
Born: Barnstaple, 26 December 1976
Height: 6'1" Weight: 13.0

Exeter defender. Matthew made the first-team breakthrough last season, proving exceptional at man marking and long-range throw ins, and will be looking to book himself a regular place in 1997-98.
Exeter C (From trainee on 4/8/95) FL 26+12/1 FLC 0+1 FAC 2+1 Others 4

Mick Harford

HARFORD Michael (Mick) Gordon
Born: Sunderland, 12 February 1959
Height: 6'2" Weight: 14.5
Club Honours: FLC '88
International Honours: E: 2; B-1
A strong, old-fashioned Wimbledon centre forward who, at the age of 38, showed no signs of tiredness in 1996-97 and was still a major threat from set pieces. Spent most of the season on the subs' bench, but, when brought on, his physical presence and little flicks were of great benefit on a number of occasions and he was delighted to score in the home draw against West Ham with a typical header that has been his trade mark over the years. The much-travelled player's career has taken him to 11 clubs and youngsters should well look up to Mick as a role model.
Lincoln C (Free from Lambton Street BC on 6/7/77) FL 109+6/41 FLC 8/5 FAC 3
Newcastle U (£180,000 on 24/12/80) FL 18+1/4
Bristol C (£160,000 on 24/8/81) FL 30/11 FLC 5/1 FAC 5/2
Birmingham C (£100,000 on 26/3/82) FL 92/25 FLC 10/6 FAC 7/2
Luton T (£250,000 on 13/12/84) FL 135+4/57 FLC 16/10 FAC 27/11 Others 4/3
Derby Co (£450,000 on 18/1/90) FL 58/15 FLC 7/3 FAC 1 Others 2
Luton T (£325,000 on 12/9/91) FL 29/12 FLC 1 Others 1
Chelsea (£300,000 on 13/8/92) PL 27+1/9 FLC 5/2 FAC 1
Sunderland (£250,000 on 18/3/93) FL 10+1/2
Coventry C (£200,000 on 12/7/93) PL 0+1/1
Wimbledon (£50,000 on 18/8/94) PL 37+24/8 FLC 2+7/1 FAC 9+4/1

HARGREAVES Christian (Chris)
Born: Cleethorpes, 12 May 1972
Height: 5'11" Weight: 12.2

With Hereford battling against the elements, Chris missed just three games last season after transferring from West Bromwich on a permanent basis, following on from his loan spell at the tail end of 1995-96. At his best playing just behind the forwards, which gives him the room to run at the opposition, although forming a good understanding with Adrian Foster, he will undoubtedly be looking for more goals in 1997-98.

Grimsby (From trainee on 6/12/89) FL 15+36/5 FLC 2+2/1 FAC 1+2/1 Others 2+4
Scarborough (Loaned on 4/3/93) FL 2+1
Hull C (Signed on 26/7/93) FL 34+15 FLC 1 FAC 2+1/1 Others 3+1
West Bromwich A (Free on 13/7/95) FL 0+1 Others 0+1
Hereford U (Free on 19/2/96) FL 57+4/5 FLC 3+1 FAC 1 Others 2

HARKIN Maurice Presley
Born: Derry, 16 August 1979
Height: 5'10" Weight: 11.11
International Honours: NI: Yth

A promising right winger who made further appearances for the Northern Ireland youth team last season, he also became Wycombe's youngest ever player in a first class match, at 17 years and 113 days, when coming on as a substitute in a difficult FA Cup tie at Barnet, the first of six appearances from the bench. Even at this age he possessed a certain class when on the ball and, after signing a 30-month contract in February, clearly much is expected of him.

Wycombe W (From trainee on 14/2/97) FL 0+4 FAC 0+2

HARKNESS Steven (Steve)
Born: Carlisle, 27 August 1971
Height: 5'10" Weight: 11.2
International Honours: E: Yth

Despite missing most of last season, due to him recovering from the broken leg sustained at Coventry in 1995-96, Steve finally got back in a Liverpool shirt towards the end of the campaign, making ten appearances, including two from the bench. A steady utility player who does the simple things well, and able to perform in defence or midfield with equal reliability, he gradually played his way back into contention and the fans will be looking for him to return to the form that saw him keeping Rob Jones out of the side, his strong tackling making him a must.

Carlisle U (From trainee on 23/3/89) FL 12+1
Liverpool (£75,000 on 17/7/89) F/PL 62+9/2 FLC 8+2/1 FAC 3 Others 11+2
Huddersfield T (Loaned on 24/9/93) FL 5 Others 1
Southend U (Loaned on 3/2/95) FL 6

HARLE Michael (Mike) James
Born: Lewisham, 31 October 1972
Height: 5'11" Weight: 12.6

A fearless tackler who likes to get forward to put in telling crosses, Mike finally got into the Millwall first team at the start of 1996-97 and, although a left back, he scored the Lions' first goal at Watford with his right foot. Unfortunately, just after coming on as a substitute at Walsall a clash of heads, needing stitches, put him out for two months, rendering his season almost all but over.

Gillingham (Trainee) FL 1+1
Millwall (£100,000 from Sittingbourne on 8/11/93) FL 12+9/1 FLC 1+1 FAC 1 Others 1
Bury (Loaned on 8/12/95) FL 0+1

HARPER Lee Charles Phillip
Born: London, 30 October 1971
Height: 6'1" Weight: 13.11

Well-built young Arsenal goalkeeper who was signed from non-league football three years ago. Having waited patiently in the wings at Highbury, understudying David Seaman, Vince Bartram and, more recently, John Lukic, Lee finally made his Premiership debut at Southampton last March following a spate of injuries at Highbury that saw him being one of five reserves selected. Made a great start in keeping a clean sheet in a vital 2-0 win, showing instinctive reactions to block a perfect volley from Matt le Tissier from the edge of the six-yard box, and looks to be a 'keeper who will do well in the game.

Arsenal (£150,000 from Sittingbourne on 16/6/94) PL 1

HARPER Steven (Steve) James
Born: Newcastle under Lyme, 3 February 1969
Height: 5'10" Weight: 11.12
Club Honours: Div 4 '92

Playing Steve as a wing back, really brought out the talent which Mansfield supporters had not seen in the previous 12 months and he enjoyed a very productive season in 1996-97, his jinking runs down the wing being a delight to behold.

Port Vale (From trainee 29/6/87) FL 16+12/2 FLC 1+2 Others 1+1
Preston NE (Signed on 23/3/89) FL 57+20/10 FLC 1+1 FAC 1+2 Others 6+1/1
Burnley (Free on 23/7/91) FL 64+5/8 FLC 1+2 FAC 10/3 Others 8
Doncaster Rov (Free on 7/8/93) FL 56+9/11 FLC 2+1/1 FAC 3 Others 4
Mansfield T (£20,000 on 8/9/95) FL 66+3/7 FLC 2 FAC 4/1 Others 3

HARRIS Andrew (Andy) David Douglas
Born: Springs, 26 February 1977
Height: 5'10" Weight: 11.11

A 1996 close season signing from Liverpool, he soon made a spot in Southend's defence his own in 1996-97, with good heading ability and positional sense. Whether asked to perform at full back or centre half, Andy always gave 100 per cent, although he must curb his tendency to over-commit himself, and is one to watch for the future.

Liverpool (From trainee on 23/3/94)
Southend U (Free on 10/7/96) FL 43+1 FLC 2 FAC 1

HARRIS Jason Andre Sebastian
Born: Sutton, 24 November 1976
Height: 6'1" Weight: 11.7

A professional signing during the summer of 1995, Jason is one of the new breed of young strikers to come out of the successful Crystal Palace youth team. Aged 20, he made his Eagles' debut from the bench in a fine 6-1 win at Reading last September, prior to coming on again during the next match against Southend at Selhurst Park, which was won by the same scoreline. Loaned to Bristol Rovers two months later in order to gain further experience, he scored on his first appearance at Luton and added two more in a further six games before going back to Selhurst. The elder brother of Richard, an associate schoolboy currently at Palace, this promising youngster top scored in the reserve team and is definitely one to watch.

Crystal Palace (From trainee on 3/7/95) FL 0+2 FLC 0+2
Bristol Rov (Loaned on 22/11/96) FL 5+1/2 Others 1/1

HARRIS Mark Andrew
Born: Reading, 15 July 1963
Height: 6'3" Weight: 14.6
Club Honours: AMC '94

A Gillingham regular at the start of last season, before losing his place when Guy Butters arrived from Portsmouth, he did not let the side down when selected, as was shown in the Coca-Cola cup ties at Coventry and Ipswich, when he was outstanding. He also showed his versatility, when replacing the injured 'keeper, Jim Stannard, at Peterborough and kept a clean sheet for the whole time he was in goal – nearly an hour! Was released during the summer.

Crystal Palace (£25,000 from Wokingham T on 29/2/88) FL 0+2
Burnley (Loaned on 7/8/89) FL 4 FLC 2
Swansea C (£22,500 on 22/9/89) FL 228/14 FLC 16/1 FAC 18/1 Others 26/2
Gillingham (£50,000 on 11/8/95) FL 63+2/3 FLC 8 FAC 5+1 Others 0+1

HARRISON Gerald (Gerry) Randall
Born: Lambeth, 15 April 1972
Height: 5'10" Weight: 12.12
International Honours: E: Sch

An automatic and often essential choice among Burnley's varying centre-back line up in 1996-97, Gerry maintained the promise of the previous season, but was unable to dislodge either Chris Brass, Jamie Hoyland or Mark Winstanley on his return for the last few matches following injury, and proved less effective in midfield. Is a good tackler and a useful player to have for a man-to-man marking role.

Watford (From trainee on 18/12/89) FL 6+3 Others 1
Bristol C (Free on 23/7/91) FL 25+13/1 FLC 2+2 FAC 1 Others 4+1
Cardiff C (Loaned on 24/1/92) FL 10/1
Hereford U (Loaned on 19/11/93) FL 6 FAC 1 Others 1
Huddersfield T (Free on 24/3/94)
Burnley (Free on 5/8/94) FL 83+6/3 FLC 5+1 FAC 6 Others 4+1

HARRISON Lee David
Born: Billericay, 12 September 1971
Height: 6'2" Weight: 12.7

Signed by Barnet during the 1996 close season, having been released by Fulham, Lee waited a long time for his chance, before finally getting it when first-team goalkeeper, Maik Taylor, was sold to

Southampton in January. A revelation between the sticks, and an ever present from the moment he made the team, his shot stopping, along with his ability in the air, made him a strong favourite for Player of the Year, despite only playing in 22 games.
Charlton Ath (From trainee on 3/7/90)
Fulham (Loaned on 18/11/91) Others 1
Gillingham (Loaned on 24/3/92) FL 2
Fulham (Free on 18/12/92) FL 11+1 FAC 1 Others 6
Barnet (Free on 15/7/96) FL 21 Others 1

HARRISON Thomas (Tommy) Edward
Born: Edinburgh, 22 January 1974
Height: 5'10" Weight: 12.7
International Honours: S: Yth; Sch
Having been released by Clyde, the former Hearts' midfielder spent the second half of last season on a short-term contract as a triallist at York, trying to make an impression. A hard-working player, he made a couple of substitute appearances at senior level without setting Bootham Crescent alight, before moving on at the end of the campaign.
Heart of Midlothian (Free from Salveson BC on 25/4/90) SL 5+5/1 SLC 0+2
Dunfermline (Loaned on 1/1/95) SL 1+1
Clyde (Signed on 4/8/95) SL 24+10/4 SLC 1 SC 3+1/1 Others 1
York C (Free on 31/1/97) FL 0+1 Others 0+1

HARTE Ian Patrick
Born: Drogheda, 31 August 1977
Height: 5'11" Weight: 11.8
International Honours: Ei: 11; U21-2
The nephew of Garry Kelly, Ian had the distinction of starting 1996-97 with more international than Leeds' appearances to his name. Has a really strong left foot and, arguably, his best position is the left-wing-back role, but as with a number of the younger players at the club, he has filled several different slots in his progress to the first team. Having come on as substitute at Derby on the first day of the season and scored with a cracking 20-yard shot, the young Irishman followed that up by scoring the winner at Blackburn three games later. A regular with the first team and the Republic of Ireland squad, after appearing in all seven full internationals during the past term, he should have a big future at Elland Road.
Leeds U (From trainee on 15/12/95) PL 12+6/2 FLC 2+2/1 FAC 1

HARTFIELD Charles (Charlie) Joseph
Born: Lambeth, 4 September 1971
Height: 6'0" Weight: 12.2
International Honours: E: Yth
There were limited opportunities at Sheffield United in 1996-97 for this hard-tackling midfielder, as he continued his recovery from a serious knee injury, making only one start, plus two substitute appearances, before being transfer listed in January and then loaned to Fulham in February. With several regulars injured, he made his debut for the Cottagers in a 2-0 defeat at Lincoln, followed by a subs' appearance at home to Wigan, but, not fitting in to Micky Adams' plans, returned to Bramall Lane. Given a free transfer at the end of the season.

Arsenal (From trainee on 20/9/89)
Sheffield U (Free on 6/8/91) F/PL 45+11/1 FLC 2+1 FAC 4+1 Others 1
Fulham (Loaned on 5/2/97) FL 1+1

HARTLEY Paul
Born: Glasgow, 19 October 1976
Height: 5'9" Weight: 10.4
International Honours: S: U21-1
Known to his team mates as "J.R.", Paul moved to Millwall from Hamilton during the summer of 1996 and, although starting as a substitute, quickly became a firm crowd favourite with his tricky ball skills and quick turn of pace. Played as a right winger, he was very unlucky not to have had more goals to his credit, his best being the club's second at Luton, coming after he had dribbled wide into the box to smash home a cross shot.
Hamilton Acc (Free from Mill BC on 9/9/94) SL 39+8/11 SLC 1+1 SC 1 Others 1+2
Millwall (£400,000 on 4/7/96) FL 35+9/4 FLC 1+1 FAC 2 Others 1

John Hartson (left)

HARTSON John
Born: Swansea, 5 April 1975
Height: 6'1" Weight: 14.6
International Honours: W: 11; U21-9; Yth
Although a regular member of Arsenal's first-team squad last season, the Welsh international forward's short-term prospects at Highbury were not too bright, with two of Europe's finest strikers - Dennis Bergkamp and Ian Wright - in the driving seat. Furthermore, his poor disciplinary record may have persuaded the Gunners' manager, Arsene Wenger, to accept West Ham's offer of £5 million - a record fee for the Hammers to pay out - in February, his signing, along with that of Paul Kitson from Newcastle, representing a last desperate throw of the dice for the beleaguered Harry Redknapp. Happily, the gamble paid off almost immediately, with both players scoring in their second game - a 4-3 epic against London rivals, Spurs - a victory which proved to be the turning point of the

Hammers' season. John also scored a brace of goals against Coventry and Sheffield Wednesday to help the team ease their way to safety, while continuing his international career with Wales.
Luton T (From trainee on 19/12/92) FL 32+22/11 FLC 0+1 FAC 3+3/2 Others 2
Arsenal (£2,500,000 on 13/1/95) PL 43+10/14 FLC 2+4/1 FAC 2+1/1 Others 8+1/1
West Ham U (£3,200,000 + on 14/2/97) PL 11/5

HARVEY Lee Derek
Born: Harlow, 21 December 1966
Height: 5'11" Weight: 11.7
International Honours: E: Yth
Extremely reliable right-sided midfield player for Brentford. Surprisingly, only a regular substitute for the Bees during the first three months of last season, the third game he started (versus Preston) he sustained a bad leg injury and did not play again for the rest of the campaign. Although released during the summer, his presence was badly missed as the team looked for an automatic promotion place.
Leyton Orient (From apprentice on 5/12/84) FL 135+49/23 FLC 13+3/3 FAC 10+4/2 Others 19+4/3
Nottingham F (Free on 4/8/93) FL 0+2 FLC 0+1
Brentford (Free on 18/11/93) FL 87+18/6 FLC 6+3/1 FAC 7+3 Others 6

HARVEY Richard George
Born: Letchworth, 17 April 1969
Height: 5'10" Weight: 11.10
International Honours: E: Yth; Sch
A strong-tackling, dependable Luton full back who lost virtually the whole of last season through injury – he did not play his first game for the reserves until March! However, he did not let the Hatters down in one substitute and one full league appearance, both coming during the crucial run in to the play offs. Released on a free transfer during the summer he will surely have little difficulty attracting a new club if he can attain a good level of fitness.
Luton T (From apprentice on 10/1/87) FL 129+26/4 FLC 8/1 FAC 6+2 Others 9
Blackpool (Loaned on 30/10/92) FL 4+1

HATELEY Mark Wayne
Born: Wallasey, 7 November 1961
Height: 6'2" Weight: 13.0
Club Honours: SPD '91, '92, '93, '94, '95; SC '92, '93; SLC '90, '92, '93
International Honours: E: 32; U21-10; Yth
After starting the opening game of last season for Queens Park Rangers before being substituted, following a hostile reception from the fans, Mark was immediately loaned to Leeds to partner Ian Rush, an injury to Brian Deane causing a crisis at Elland Road. Although the former England man eventually returned to Loftus Road, having played six times for United without getting on the scoresheet, it would never be the same again, despite him notching three goals, including an 88th minute equaliser in the FA Cup at home to Huddersfield, and he rejoined his old club, Glasgow Rangers, in March. The son of the former goalscoring star of the 1960s, Tony, while not quite emulating his dad's terrific

strike rate, at his best, his ability on the ground as well as in the air brought him more recognition at the highest level.

Coventry C (From apprentice on 1/12/78) FL 86+6/25 FLC 8/3 FAC 10+1/6
Portsmouth (£220,000 on 6/6/83) (£1,000,000 to AC Milan on 28/6/84) FL 38/22 FLC 4/2 FAC 2/1
Glasgow R (Signed from AS Monaco on 19/7/90) SL 158+7/85 SLC 15+3/11 SC 16/10 Others 17/7
Queens Park R (£1,500,000 on 3/11/95) P/FL 18+9/3 FLC 0+1 FAC 3+2/2
Leeds U (Loaned on 19/8/96) PL 5+1

HATHAWAY Ian Ashley
Born: Wordsley, 22 August 1968
Height: 5'7" Weight: 11.4
The talented Torquay left winger, cum midfield player, occasionally showed glimpses of his wonderful skills, but 1996-97 must go down as yet another disappointing one for both him and the club. Known for his crosses under pressure and superb strikes, just one goal was forthcoming, a 20-yard left footer in a 2-1 win at Mansfield, prior to him being released during the summer.

Mansfield T (£8,000 from Bedworth U on 8/2/89) FL 21+23/2 FLC 1+1 FAC 1 Others 3+1/1
Rotherham U (Signed on 22/3/91) FL 5+8/1 Others 0+1
Torquay U (Free on 30/7/93) FL 114+26/14 FLC 9+1/1 FAC 9+1/2 Others 4+3/1

HAWES Steven Robert
Born: High Wycombe, 17 July 1978
Height: 5'8" Weight: 11.4
The youngest player to have appeared for Sheffield United, Steven continued to further his career in the reserves last season, whilst making only two brief substitute appearances in the league. A central midfielder who can also play at right back, he works hard and has excellent stamina. Is also a good passer of the ball.

Sheffield U (From trainee on 2/3/96) FL 1+3

HAWORTH Simon Owen
Born: Cardiff, 30 March 1977
Height: 6'3" Weight: 13.8
International Honours: W: 1; U21-3; Yth
Following his Cardiff debut the previous season, Simon went back to the reserves to bide his time before storming back to first-team football and playing in the last 22 matches of 1996-97. Tall, strong, and skilful with it, the young striker made a meteoric rise to stardom, scoring some superb goals, including two match winners and a sweet 90th minute 20 yarder at Northampton in the play offs. Expected to join Coventry during the summer, the day after a proposed transfer to Norwich on deadline day fell through when he failed a medical, he scored for the Welsh U21 side against Belgium. After winning a full cap against Scotland at the end of May, he looks to be a star of the future.

Cardiff C (From trainee on 7/8/95) FL 27+10/9 FLC 4 FAC 0+1 Others 4/1

HAWTHORNE Mark
Born: Glasgow, 31 October 1973
Height: 5'9" Weight: 11.9
A combative Torquay midfielder who undoubtedly improved during the course of last season, never giving less than 100 per cent in all his appearances for the club, prior to being released in the summer. Having waited 40 games to open his league account, Mark scored twice at Darlington to secure a 3-2 win for United.

Crystal Palace (From juniors on 26/6/92)
Sheffield U (Free on 16/8/94) Others 3/1
Walsall (Free on 23/1/95)
Torquay U (Free on 23/3/95) FL 43+15/2 FLC 3+1/1 FAC 3 Others 3

HAY Darran Andrew
Born: Hitchin, 17 December 1969
Height: 6'0" Weight: 13.8
With Cambridge in need of cover for the front men, the club's former forward returned for a loan spell last October, making just four subs' appearances before going back to non-league football. Came back to the Abbey as a member of the Woking team that knocked United out of the FA Cup.

Cambridge U (Free from Biggleswade T on 11/3/94) FL 7+22/3 FAC 4/1 Others 1+1/1 (Free to Woking on 30/3/95)
Cambridge U (Loaned on 11/10/96) FL 0+4

HAYDON Nicholas (Nicky)
Born: Barking, 18 August 1978
Height: 5'10" Weight: 11.6
Colchester's youth team captain and a highly promising midfielder, Nicky finally got his first-team chance as a late substitute in the final game of last season. And what an impression he made! Booked within a minute of coming on, and possibly fortunate not to get a red card, within another three minutes he had scored United's fourth and clinching goal. Brother-in-law of fellow United starlet, Karl Duguid, he is yet another youngster of whom the U's management have high hopes.

Colchester U (From trainee on 10/8/95) FL 0+1/1

HAYES Adrian (Adi) Michael
Born: Norwich, 22 May 1978
Height: 6'1" Weight: 12.10
A cultured left-footed central midfielder who had a good run in the Cambridge side during the middle of last season, also appearing as a left-wing back, Adi again looked good on the ball, showing nice touches, before being replaced by Ian Ashbee. Improving all the while, he will be challenging strongly for a place in 1997-98.

Cambridge U (From trainee on 9/7/96) FL 20+6 FLC 0+1 FAC 2 Others 1

HAYFIELD Matthew (Matt) Anthony
Born: Bristol, 8 August 1975
Height: 5'11" Weight: 12.2
A highly competitive ball-winning Bristol Rovers' midfielder, Matt returned last November after a year out due to a knee injury, with a typical all-action display against Luton Town. A versatile attacking or defensive player, he showed with goals for Rovers' reserves that he could play up front when asked to and was successfully used as a stand-in striker on 22 February in the 2-2 draw at Burnley.

Bristol Rov (From trainee on 13/7/94) FL 15+8 FAC 1 Others 2+1

HAYTER James Edward
Born: Newport, 9 April 1979
Height: 5'9" Weight: 10.7
A product of Bournemouth's youth policy, James made the transition from youth-team football and the reserve side, before making two substitute appearances for the first team in 1996-97. Having become a regular scorer for the reserves, where he has shown a great deal of ability, there is no reason why that form should not transcend at senior level before too long.

Bournemouth (Trainee) FL 0+2

HAYWARD Andrew (Andy) William
Born: Barnsley, 21 June 1970
Height: 6'0" Weight: 11.2
Club Honours: AMC '96
A player who can always be relied upon to give his utmost for Rotherham, Andy willingly played in whatever role he was asked to in 1996-97, flitting from midfield to up front. He probably did not get on the scoresheet as often as he might have done, but that should not detract from his approach to the game, and he never gave less than maximum effort, even when asked to play up front with a succession of different partners.

Rotherham U (Free from Frickley Ath on 10/8/94) FL 87+20/12 FLC 4+2/3 FAC 2+1 Others 6+3/2

HAYWARD Steven (Steve) Lee
Born: Pelsall, 8 September 1971
Height: 5'10" Weight: 12.5
Club Honours: AMC '97
International Honours: E: Yth
Steve succeeded David Reeves as Carlisle's club skipper when he moved to Preston last October and he too led the side by example. A hard-working midfielder who wears his heart on his sleeve, he gave some fine displays, notably in the FA Cup against Premier League, Sheffield Wednesday. Always on the look out for scoring opportunities, especially from free kicks within range of goal, his greatest moment came in the AWS final when his successful strike sealed the game for United in the penalty shoot out. He thus became the first Carlisle captain to lift a trophy at Wembley, thereby securing his place in the club's history.

Derby Co (From juniors on 17/9/88) FL 15+11/1 FLC 0+2 FAC 1 Others 3+4
Carlisle U (£100,000 on 13/3/95) FL 88+2/14 FLC 6/1 FAC 4 Others 15/1

HEALD Gregory (Greg) James
Born: Enfield, 26 September 1971
Height: 6'1" Weight: 13.1
International Honours: E: Sch
Effectively a regular at the heart of Peterborough's defence last season, Greg lost his place through injury towards the end of March before coming back as a sub in the penultimate game. Deceptively pacy, and a fine header of the ball who clears his lines with the minimum of fuss, he continued to be a danger at set pieces, his two headed goals, coming via a corner and free kick, respectively. Can also play at full back.

Peterborough U (£35,000 from Enfield on 8/7/94) FL 101+4/6 FLC 8 FAC 8+1 Others 11/2

HEALD Paul Andrew
Born: Wath on Dearne, 20 September 1968
Height: 6'2" Weight: 14.0
Paul has become a very popular player amongst the Wimbledon fans since his move from Leyton Orient in 1995, despite being kept out of the side in 1996-97 by Neil Sullivan's excellent form. A good 'keeper to have in the wings, he made two appearances, one coming in the Coca-Cola Cup game against Portsmouth, and the other in the Premier league clash against Coventry City, in which he was outstanding. Able to stand up well, he has very quick reactions which allow him to pull off some breathtaking saves.
Sheffield U (From trainee on 30/6/87)
Leyton Orient (Signed on 2/12/88) FL 176 FLC 13 FAC 9 Others 21
Coventry C (Loaned on 10/3/92) PL 2
Swindon T (Loaned on 24/3/94) PL 1+1
Wimbledon (£125,000 on 25/7/95) PL 20 FLC 3

HEANEY Neil Andrew
Born: Middlesbrough, 3 November 1971
Height: 5'9" Weight: 11.13
Club Honours: FAYC '88
International Honours: E: U21-6; Yth
Signed by Manchester City caretaker manager, Phil Neal, from Southampton last November, Neil, a natural left winger with speed and close ball control, made a very promising debut at home to West Brom in a bruising 3-2 win, his pace and trickery causing many problems. Following that, however, he failed to show the form the club had hoped for, but this should be balanced against the fact that he was used as a wing back helping in the middle third of the pitch. Having earlier scored his debut goal, the first against Watford at home in the FA Cup fourth round, he found opportunities limited in March due to added competition for places and was later placed on the transfer list.
Arsenal (From trainee on 14/11/89) F/PL 4+3 FLC 0+1
Hartlepool U (Loaned on 3/1/91) FL 2+1
Cambridge U (Loaned on 9/1/92) FL 9+4/2 FAC 1
Southampton (£300,000 on 22/3/94) PL 42+19/5 FLC 4+2 FAC 6/2
Manchester C (£500,000 on 25/11/96) FL 10+5/1 FAC 2/1

HEARY Thomas Mark
Born: Dublin, 14 February 1979
Height: 5'9" Weight: 11.3
International Honours: Ei: Yth; Sch
Another Huddersfield player with an Irish background, Thomas would have played more games in 1996-97 were it not for injury. Having made his debut when coming off the bench at Leeds Road against Reading at the end of September, he proved to be a very elegant midfielder who showed his versatility when putting in some competent performances in defence. Recognised at junior international level, he will be one to watch for the future.
Huddersfield T (From trainee on 17/2/96) FL 2+3 FAC 1

HEATH Adrian Paul
Born: Stoke, 11 January 1961
Height: 5'6" Weight: 11.0
Club Honours: Div 1 '85, '87; FAC '84; CS '84, '85, '86, '87

International Honours: E: B-1; U21-8 (UEFAC '82)
Burnley's manager made just two brief appearances as a sub early on in 1996-97, and it now seems clear that his distinguished playing career is over, leaving him free to concentrate on getting the side out of the second division. He will be remembered mainly as a midfield player with vision and an ability to get forward to score goals, as well as being a former record signing for Everton.
Stoke C (From apprentice on 12/1/79) FL 94+1/16 FLC 9 FAC 4/1
Everton (£700,000 on 7/1/82) FL 206+20/71 FLC 33+2/11 FAC 24+5/6 Others 14+3/5 (£600,000 to Espanol on 15/11/88)
Aston Villa (£360,000 on 14/8/89) FL 8+1 FLC 1+1 FAC 0+1
Manchester C (£300,000 on 23/2/90) FL 58+17/4 FLC 7+1/2 FAC 2+1 Others 1+2
Stoke C (£50,000 on 27/3/92) FL 5+1 Others 3+1
Burnley (Free on 21/8/92) FL 109+6/29 FLC 8+1 FAC 12/6 Others 7
Sheffield U (Free on 15/12/95) FL 0+4 FAC 0+1
Burnley (Free on 7/3/96) FL 1+4

HEATH Stephen Dennis
Born: Hull, 15 November 1977
Height: 6'1" Weight: 12.11
International Honours: E: Yth
A central defender who was recruited from Leeds in the 1996 close season, his only first-team action for Carlisle in 1996-97 was confined to a single substitute appearance, lasting seven minutes, in the October home match against Colchester. Contracted for one year, he was released during the summer.
Leeds U (From trainee on 15/11/94)
Carlisle U (Free on 17/7/96) FL 0+1

HEATHCOTE Michael (Mick)
Born: Kelloe, 10 September 1965
Height: 6'2" Weight: 12.5
The rock at the centre of Plymouth's defence, Mick had an indifferent start to last season, but showed what a true professional he was by suggesting he should be dropped. The Argyle captain eventually returned as the solid, reliable defender he is renowned for, missing just two of the remaining 44 games, and proving inspirational to a side struggling to avoid relegation for much of the campaign.
Sunderland (£15,000 from Spennymoor on 19/8/87) FL 6+3 Others 0+1
Halifax T (Loaned on 17/12/87) FL 7/1 FAC 1
York C (Loaned on 4/1/90) FL 3 Others 1
Shrewsbury T (£55,000 on 12/7/90) FL 43+1/6 FLC 6 FAC 5 Others 4
Cambridge U (£150,000 on 12/9/91) FL123+5/13 FLC 7/1 FAC 5+2/2 Others 7/2
Plymouth Arg (£100,000 on 27/7/95) FL 85+1/5 FLC 4/1 FAC 6/1 Others 7

HEGGS Carl Sydney
Born: Leicester, 11 October 1970
Height: 6'1" Weight: 12.10
Struggled to find a regular place in the Swansea first team last season, but top scored for the club in combination football, netting four times at Wimbledon. On the transfer list for most of 1996-97, the striker

missed many games in mid term with a broken ankle, having treatment at Lilleshall. Showed his goalscoring talent when coming off the bench at Mansfield to score twice, thus assuring Swans of a play-off place.
West Bromwich A (£25,000 from Leicester U on 22/8/91) FL 13+27/3 FLC 2 FAC 0+1 Others 6+3/1
Bristol Rov (Loaned on 27/1/95) FL 2+3/1
Swansea C (£60,000 on 27/7/95) FL 33+13/7 FLC 2 FAC 2 Others 4+1/1

HEIDENSTROM Bjorn
Born: Porsgrunn, Norway, 15 January 1968
Height: 5'10" Weight: 12.0
Signed on a month's trial from Norwegian side, Odd Grenland, last December, the defensive midfielder unfortunately struggled to adjust to English football, playing just four times for Leyton Orient before returning home.
Leyton Orient (Free from Odd Grenland on 20/12/96) FL 3+1

HELDER Glenn
Born: Leiden, Holland, 28 October 1968
Height: 5'11" Weight: 11.7
International Honours: Holland: 4
Despite being very quick and an excellent crosser of the ball from the left flank, Glenn never quite fitted in at Arsenal and following just four appearances from the bench early in 1996-97, and the arrival of the new manager, Arsene Wenger, was allowed to leave the club, moving to Benfica until the end of the campaign. At his best when running at and taking on defenders, the classy Dutchman was used mainly as a substitute during his time with the Gunners, but found it difficult to sustain the physical endeavours of the Premiership, his form thus suffering.
Arsenal (£2,300,000 from Vitesse Arnhem on 14/2/95) PL 27+12/1 FLC 4+2 FAC 2 Others 0+2

HELLIWELL Ian
Born: Rotherham, 7 November 1962
Height: 6'3" Weight: 14.8
Out of the Burnley side due to a cartilage operation in January 1996, Ian was nursed back into action on loan at Mansfield last September, scoring his 101st senior goal in his second game of five for Town, before returning to Turf Moor. Then, following another loan period, this time at Chester, where he scored just once in nine games, he found himself down the Clarets' pecking order behind the likes of Kurt Nogan, Paul Barnes and Andy Cooke and , consequently, was consigned to the reserves. Big and strong, it is his considerable aerial ability that makes him a threat to opposition defences, especially at set pieces.
York C (£10,000 from Matlock T on 23/10/87) FL 158+4/40 FLC 8/1 FAC 5 Others 9+1/7
Scunthorpe U (£80,000 on 16/8/91) FL 78+2/22 FLC 8/5 FAC 4/2 Others 9/2
Rotherham U (£50,000 on 1/8/93) FL 47+5/4 FLC 4+1 FAC 1+2/1 Others 2+1/1
Stockport Co (Signed on 12/1/95) FL 35+4/13 FLC 4/1 FAC 2/1 Others 1
Burnley (£30,000 on 9/2/96) FL 3+1
Mansfield T (Loaned on 6/9/96) FL 4+1/1
Chester C (Loaned on 11/10/96) FL 8+1/1

HENDON Ian Michael
Born: Ilford, 5 December 1971
Height: 6'1" Weight: 12.10
Club Honours: FAYC '90; CS '91
International Honours: E: U21-7; Yth

An attacking right-wing back who is excellent at taking on opposing defenders and supplying pinpoint crosses, and also an excellent free-kick specialist, Ian scored a last minute winner for Leyton Orient at Lincoln with a thunderbolt from the edge of the box. Transferred to Notts County at the end of February, having never let Orient down in over three and a half seasons, he continued his good form at Meadow Lane showing his versatility when appearing at centre back. Was selected as a member of the PFA third division team by his fellow professionals.
Tottenham H (From trainee on 20/12/89) FL 0+4 FLC 1 Others 0+2
Portsmouth (Loaned on 16/1/92) FL 1+3
Leyton Orient (Loaned on 26/3/92) FL 5+1
Barnsley (Loaned on 17/3/93) FL 6
Leyton Orient (£50,000 on 9/8/93) FL 130+1/5 FLC 8 FAC 7 Others 12/1
Birmingham C (Loaned on 23/3/95) FL 4
Notts Co (£50,000 on 24/2/97) FL 12

Ian Hendon

HENDRIE John Grattan
Born: Lennoxtown, 24 October 1963
Height: 5'8" Weight: 12.3
Club Honours: Div 3 '85, Div 2 '90, Div 1 '95
International Honours: S: Yth

Unable to hold down a place in the rebuilt Middlesbrough side in 1996-97, and with a view to playing regular first team football, John signed for a Barnsley side whose early form had dipped a shade. Transferred in October, once match fit his partnership with Paul Wilkinson flourished and his ability in finding space in crowded penalty areas to produce excellent finishes brought in many points for the Reds. With the Boro being relegated and Barnsley gaining promotion to the Premiership, he must be the bargain buy of the season and his popularity was such that the fans named him as their Player of the Year.
Coventry C (From apprentice on 18/5/81) FL 15+6/2 FLC 2
Hereford U (Loaned on 10/1/84) FL 6
Bradford C (Free on 2/7/84) FL 173/46 FLC 17/3 FAC 11/6 Others 11/4
Newcastle U (£500,000 on 17/6/88) FL 34/4 FLC 2/1 FAC 4 Others 3
Leeds U (£600,000 on 20/6/89) FL 22+5/5 FLC 1 FAC 1 Others 2
Middlesbrough (£550,000 on 5/7/90) F/PL 181+11/44 FLC 22+2/6 FAC 10+2/2 Others 6/3
Barnsley (£250,000 on 11/10/96) FL 36/15 FAC 2/1

John Hendrie

HENDRIE Lee Andrew
Born: Birmingham, 18 May 1977
Height: 5'8" Weight: 10.3
International Honours: E: U21-1; Yth

A hard-working young Aston Villa forward, Lee was unable to win himself a regular place in the side in 1996-97, making just one start, while coming off the bench six times. From a football family, being the son of Paul, a former Birmingham star, and the cousin of John, currently with Barnsley, in continuing to give encouraging displays whenever called upon, however, he proved a valuable squad player who could be relied upon and there is still plenty of time for him to make his mark in the game. Was also called up to the England U21 side, but failed to add to the previous season's cap.
Aston Villa (From trainee on 18/5/94) PL 2+5 FAC 1+2

HENDRY Edward **Colin** James
Born: Keith, 7 December 1965
Height: 6'1" Weight: 12.7
Club Honours: FMC '87; PL '95
International Honours: S: 27; B-1

The heart of Ewood Park, Colin continued to play with huge passion and commitment for Blackburn in 1996-97 as the club battled against relegation fears for much of the season. He also collected six further Scottish caps. A fearsome opponent when the ball is both in the air or on the ground, he dominated the majority of the men he came up against and this, despite a groin injury that niggled him throughout the campaign and forced him to miss four games in October. Although scoring with a bullet-type header at Tottenham – it was not enough, Rovers eventually going down 2-1 – there were to be no more goals for the big man. Having delayed surgery in order to aid the team, hopefully, the operation that repaired the damage during the summer will put things right for 1997-98.
Dundee (Signed from Islavale in 1983) SL 17+24/2 SC 2+3/1
Blackburn Rov (£30,000 on 11/3/87) FL 99+3/22 FLC 4 FAC 3 Others 13/1
Manchester C (£700,000 on 16/11/89) FL 57+6/5 FLC 4+1/1 FAC 5/2 Others 4/2
Blackburn Rov (£700,000 on 8/11/91) F/PL 195+5/11 FLC 22 FAC 13+1 Others 11

Colin Hendry

HENRY Nicholas (Nicky) Ian
Born: Liverpool, 21 February 1969
Height: 5'6" Weight: 10.8
Club Honours: Div 2 '91

The Oldham club captain for many years and a midfield stalwart, Nicky missed eight games for the Latics, due to injury in October and November last year, before fighting his way back into contention to play

in the next 16. However, with Sheffield United looking to add some missing bite as they eyed the Premiership, he moved to Bramall lane in February in exchange for Doug Hodgson, only to have his debut delayed by a two-match suspension. His ability to break up attacks and keep the ball flowing was very much in evidence at his new club, but, unfortunately, a further sending off at the play-off semi-final stage against Ipswich saw him miss the Wembley final.
Oldham Ath (From trainee on 6/7/87) F/PL 264+9/19 FLC 30+4/3 FAC 21 Others 5
Sheffield U (£500,000 on 28/2/97) FL 9 Others 2

HERRERA Roberto (Robbie)
Born: Torquay, 12 June 1970
Height: 5'7" Weight: 10.6
Robbie was having another excellent season in the left-wing-back berth for pace-setters Fulham in 1996-97, until a shoulder injury sustained in a match at his hometown of Torquay in January put him out for the remainder of the campaign. He was badly missed, as his forays down the left and accurate centres had led to many of the Cottager's goals up to that time.
Queens Park R (From trainee on 1/3/88) FL 4+2 FLC 1+2 Others 1+1
Torquay U (Loaned on 17/3/92) FL 11
Torquay U (Loaned on 24/10/92) FL 5
Fulham (Signed on 29/10/93) FL 117+2/1 FLC 11 FAC 10 Others 6+1

HESKEY Emile William Ivanhoe
Born: Leicester, 11 January 1978
Height: 6'2" Weight: 13.12
Club Honours: FLC '97
International Honours: E: U21-4; Yth
Two-footed Leicester striker with power and pace. Affectionately nicknamed "Bruno" by City fans, he has the potential to go right to the very top, scoring some stunning goals in 1996-97, his first Premiership season, including a powerful long-range effort at home to Southampton and another blockbuster at Blackburn. Sometimes used in a wide midfield role where his pace could trouble full backs, notably in a victory at White Hart Lane, he also scored a fine goal at St James' Park in a televised thriller, when breaking from the halfway line. Promoted to the England U21 team during the campaign, Emile scored the vital last ditch equaliser at Wembley in the Coca-Cola Cup final against Middlesbrough after previously hitting the bar twice. Again struck the woodwork in the replay, on his way to a cup winners' medal, having been particularly influential.
Leicester C (From trainee on 3/10/95) P/FL 56+10/17 FLC 9+2/2 FAC 3 Others 3

HESSENTHALER Andrew (Andy)
Born: Dartford, 17 August 1965
Height: 5'7" Weight: 11.5
International Honours: E: SP-1
In signing for a then Gillingham club record fee from Watford last August, Andy returned to his native county. An inspirational captain, working tirelessly in the midfield department, he does not score many goals, but had an extra cause for

celebration when netting against his former club in March. Has turned out to be a sound investment for the Gills' future and it came as no surprise when he was voted the club's Player of the Year, as well as winning the Away Player award also.
Watford (£65,000 from Redbridge Forest on 12/9/91) FL 195/11 FLC 13/1 FAC 5/2 Others 4
Gillingham (£235,000 on 7/8/96) FL 38/2 FLC 7 FAC 3/1

Jamie Hewitt

HEWITT James (Jamie) Robert
Born: Chesterfield, 17 May 1968
Height: 5'10" Weight: 11.9
1996-97 was, for Jamie, his finest season for a long time. He has always been valuable to the Chesterfield side for his ability to play anywhere in defence and anywhere else, at a push, but last season he looked every inch the experienced professional that he is. He has come on as a great reader of the game and his unflappable nature came to the fore during the highly-charged atmosphere of the club's run to the FA Cup semi-finals, oozing a coolness that had a great steadying effect on those around him, and netting that memorable late equaliser against Middlesbrough. Of all the current players, he has played the most matches for the club, standing 11th in the list of all-time appearance makers.
Chesterfield (From trainee on 22/4/86) FL 240+9/14 FLC 10/1 FAC 8+1 Others 11+2
Doncaster Rov (Free on 1/8/92) FL 32+1 FLC 3+1/1 FAC 1 Others 3
Chesterfield (Signed on 8/10/93) FL 125+7/9 FLC 7 FAC 10/1 Others 10

HEWLETT Matthew (Matt) Paul
Born: Bristol, 25 February 1976
Height: 6'2" Weight: 11.3
International Honours: E: Yth

Having made an excellent start to 1996-97 at Bristol City, Matt earned a call up to the England U21 squad for the game against Italy at Ashton Gate in February, but did not gain selection on the day. A midfield player with much skill and ability, he has become almost a fixture in the Bristol City side during the past two seasons, having now made over 75 league appearances, and has impressed many a shrewd judges in the game. Will probably develop into a more attacking player once fully grown.
Bristol C (From trainee on 12/8/93) FL 71+5/4 FLC 5+2 FAC 2+1/2 Others 4

HIBBARD Mark Andrew
Born: Hereford, 12 August 1977
Height: 5'6" Weight: 9.9
A young first-year professional, Mark was given a taste of first-team soccer at Hereford when making his debut at left back in the home fixture against Rochdale last September and impressed enough to be given eight further opportunities. Showing himself to be an intelligent player with good all-round ability, he also proved sound.
Hereford U (From trainee on 15/7/96) FL 5+2/1 FLC 1 FAC 1

HICKS Stuart Jason
Born: Peterborough, 30 May 1967
Height: 6'1" Weight: 13.0
This commanding central defender never gives less than 100 per cent and is a great favourite with the Scarborough fans. Player of the Year in 1995-96, he was runner up last season after another consistent campaign, despite missing several games with an ankle injury. Has given the club great service but, with the manager looking to rebuild the side, Stuart was given a free transfer at the end of the campaign.
Peterborough U (From apprentice on 10/8/84)
Colchester U (Free from Wisbech on 24/3/88) FL 57+7 FLC 2 FAC 5/1 Others 5
Scunthorpe U (Free on 19/8/90) FL 67/1 FLC 4 FAC 4/1 Others 8
Doncaster Rov (Free on 10/8/92) FL 36 FLC 2 FAC 1 Others 2
Huddersfield T (Signed on 27/8/93) FL 20+2/1 FLC 3 FAC 3 Others 1
Preston NE (Signed on 24/3/94) FL 11+1 FLC 2 Others 1/1
Scarborough (Signed on 22/2/95) FL 81+4/2 FLC 5 FAC 4 Others 3

HIGGINS David (Dave) Anthony
Born: Liverpool, 19 August 1961
Height: 6'0" Weight: 11.7
Club Honours: AMC '90
Having completed ten years in his second spell at the club, this uncompromising defender was given a free transfer by Tranmere and granted a well-deserved testimonial game. A crowd favourite because of his totally committed approach whenever he was recalled to the first team in 1996-97, he turned in a series of rock-steady performances, even taking over as substitute goalkeeper at the Hawthorns on New Year's day. Once again, he suffered his annual fate of being sent off at Oxford United.

Tranmere Rov (Free from Eagle FC on 22/8/83) FL 27+1 FAC 2 Others 5 (Free to South Liverpool during 1985 close season)
Tranmere Rov (Free from Caernarfon on 20/7/87) FL 315+4/12 FLC 28 FAC 18 Others 34

HIGGS Shane Peter
Born: Oxford, 13 May 1977
Height: 6'2" Weight: 12.12

The tall, commanding Bristol Rovers' goalkeeper had to be very patient before being called up to make his league debut at home to Burnley last November, having spent some two years on the bench as a substitute. Making a favourable impression, Shane almost capped his big day with a stunning goal from one of his huge goal kicks, for which he is now noted. Is strongly expected to challenge Andy Collett for the number one jersey this coming campaign.
Bristol Rov (From trainee on 17/7/95) FL 2
Swansea C (Loaned on 30/1/97) FL 2

HIGNETT Craig John
Born: Prescot, 12 January 1970
Height: 5'9" Weight: 11.10
Club Honours: Div 1 '95

Craig should be nicknamed the "Phoenix" for resurrecting his career in 1996-97 when all of the signs were that his Middlesbrough playing days were over. He staked his claim to being retained by asking for a salary cut, and then went out to prove to his manager that he was the equal of anyone else in the Premiership, regaining his first-team place on pure merit and never looking back. The workrate of this dedicated and skilful midfielder was way beyond reproach, while his goals, especially from the penalty spot, were executed with all the coolness associated with top-class strikers. In a dramatic campaign, which ended in relegation and defeats in both the FA and Coca-Cola Cups, Craig could always be seen in the heart of the action and looks to star in the first division this coming term.
Crewe Alex (Free from Liverpool juniors on 11/5/88) FL 108+13/42 FLC 9+1/4 FAC 11+1/8 Others 6+1/3
Middlesbrough (£500,000 on 27/11/92) F/PL 98+22/26 FLC 15+2/9 FAC 8+1/2 Others 5+1

HILEY Scott Patrick
Born: Plymouth, 27 September 1968
Height: 5'9" Weight: 11.5
Club Honours: Div 4 '90

Picking up from the previous season, Scott continued his encouraging form for Manchester City at the start of 1996-97 with competent displays in the first two games. Unfortunately, in the next home match against Charlton he was stretchered off with what proved to be a very serious leg problem and similar to the injuries received by Paul Lake and Niall Quinn. A classy right back who catches the eye with quality crosses, he has not played since, though the reports are that he hopes to be fully fit in time for the start of 1997-98.
Exeter C (From trainee on 4/8/86) FL 205+5/12 FLC 17 FAC 14 Others 16+2
Birmingham C (£100,000 on 12/3/93) FL 49 FLC 7 FAC 1 Others 2
Manchester C (£250,000 on 23/2/96) P/FL 4+5

HILL Andrew (Andy) Rowland
Born: Maltby, 20 January 1965
Height: 5'11" Weight: 12.0
International Honours: E: Yth

The regular right back, who was as dependable as ever in the Port Vale defence in 1996-97, Andy missed only a handful of games, all through injury, and was one of the main reasons that the club almost made the play offs. Scored one goal, against Grimsby Town early on in the campaign, but his main attribute was his solid tackling. Has now topped 500 career appearances.
Manchester U (From apprentice on 16/1/83)
Bury (Free on 4/7/84) FL 264/10 FLC 22/1 FAC 12 Others 19/1
Manchester C (£200,000 on 21/12/90) F/PL 91+7/6 FLC 11 FAC 2+1 Others 1
Port Vale (£150,000 on 25/8/95) FL 71+2/1 FLC 5 FAC 6 Others 6

HILL Colin Frederick
Born: Uxbridge, 12 November 1963
Height: 6'0" Weight: 12.11
Club Honours: FLC '97
International Honours: NI: 22

A right-footed Leicester central defender, Colin was on the bench throughout 1996-97, but failed to hold a regular position due to injury, illness, and stiff competition. At his best, a player with pace who reads the game well and invariably picks out the right pass to make in the circumstances, he captained the team at Arsenal, but ended the game by being carried off. Also added to his Northern Ireland caps, in defence and midfield, where he remained a regular choice for Bryan Hamilton.
Arsenal (From apprentice on 7/8/81) FL 46/1 FLC 4 FAC 1 (Free to Maritimo during 1986 close season)
Colchester U (Free on 30/10/87) FL 64+5 FLC 2 FAC 7/2 Others 3+1
Sheffield U (£85,000 on 1/8/89) FL 77+5/1 FLC 5 FAC 10+2 Others 3
Leicester C (£200,000 on 26/3/92) F/PL 140+5 FLC 10+2/1 FAC 8 Others 9+1

HILL Keith John
Born: Bolton, 17 May 1969
Height: 6'0" Weight: 12.6

One of new manager, Graham Barrow's first signings for Rochdale during the 1996 close season, the former Plymouth Argyle player formed a successful centre-back partnership with Alan Johnson. Capable of playing anywhere across the back four, with pace, the only games he missed were due to suspensions, following two sendings off.
Blackburn Rov (From juniors on 9/5/87) F/PL 89+7/4 FLC 6/1 FAC 5+1 Others 3+2
Plymouth Arg (Signed on 23/9/92) FL 117+6/2 FLC 9 FAC 10 Others 9
Rochdale (Free on 3/7/96) FL 43/3 FLC 2 FAC 2 Others 1

HILLIER David
Born: Blackheath, 19 December 1969
Height: 5'10" Weight: 12.5
Club Honours: FAYC '88; Div 1 '91
International Honours: E: U21-1

Arriving at Portsmouth from Arsenal last November, despite being sent off on his debut at Oldham, David came back strongly to produce a series of fine performances in

becoming an integral part of the midfield. His ball-winning skills, coupled with fine passing, were noticeable as Pompey's league position improved and equally as impressive was his stamina and general wholehearted play. He also scored three goals, one more than he had managed during his time at Highbury, and looks set to be part of the structure that the club will build on in their efforts to reach the Premiership.
Arsenal (From trainee on 11/2/88) F/PL 82+22/2 FLC 13+2 FAC 13+2 Others 5+4
Portsmouth (£250,000 on 2/11/96) FL 21/2 FAC 4/1

HILLS John David
Born: Blackpool, 21 April 1978
Height: 5'8" Weight: 10.8

A hugely promising left back, John caused a stir when he was transferred to Everton from Blackpool in November 1995 only a week after signing professional forms! Quickly making a name as one of the best athletes at the club, joining the pre-1996-97 season training group headed by speed kings like Andrei Kanchelskis and Anders Limpar, he sat on the substitutes' bench several times, but only saw first team action for ten torrid minutes against Wimbledon on 28 December, when the Blues were already trailing 3-1. Following that outing he went to Swansea on loan to develop his experience and made a big impact at the Vetch Field, especially with his overlapping and attacking play, before returning to Goodison.
Blackpool (From trainee on 27/10/95)
Everton (£90,000 on 4/11/95) PL 1+2
Swansea C (Loaned on 30/1/97) FL 11

HIMSWORTH Gary Paul
Born: Pickering, 19 December 1969
Height: 5'8" Weight: 11.0

Having recovered from injury, Gary had a good season in 1996-97 for York, proving to be most consistent. A skilful and tricky utility player with good acceleration, he did well in midfield, but his best displays were at left back where he got forward to good effect.
York C (From trainee on 27/1/88) FL 74+14/8 FLC 5 Others 5+2
Scarborough (Free on 5/12/90) FL 83+9/6 FLC 7+2/1 FAC 1+1 Others 6+1
Darlington (Free on 16/7/93) FL 86+8/8 FLC 5+1 FAC 6 Others 7/4
York C (£25,000 on 16/2/96) FL 39+2/2 FLC 4 FAC 4/1 Others 2/1

HINCHCLIFFE Andrew (Andy) George
Born: Manchester, 5 February 1969
Height: 5'10" Weight: 13.7
Club Honours: FAC '95; CS '95
International Honours: E: 3; U21-1; Yth

An attacking Everton left back with a supremely cultivated left foot, Andy was enjoying the most outstanding season of his career in 1996-97, until sustaining cruciate knee ligament damage in a home match against Leeds on 21 December. Surprisingly called up by England coach, Glenn Hoddle, to fill the left wing-back role in Moldova, and doing his job so effectively he retained his place in Georgia and against Poland at

Wembley, Italian spies watching England ahead of the Wembley World Cup qualifier identified him as the player they were most concerned about. Sadly, however, his injury meant he was not available to Hoddle. Having spent the summer working on his fitness and looking to be fully fit to reclaim his England spot this season, his contribution to Everton's attacking efforts meant that he remained their most productive goal creator until the closing weeks of 1996-97 – four months after he last kicked a ball!

Manchester C (From apprentice on 13/2/86) FL 107+5/8 FLC 11/1 FAC 12/1 Others 4/1
Everton (£800,000 on 17/7/90) F/PL 155+10/6 FLC 18+2/1 FAC 12+2/1 Others 8

HINSHELWOOD Daniel (Danny) Martin
Born: Bromley, 12 December 1975
Height: 5'9" Weight: 11.13
International Honours: E: Yth

Unable to break into the Portsmouth side last season, due to injuries and a number of players holding their form, Danny was loaned out to Torquay at the beginning of March and was unfortunate to make his debut in the 5-1 defeat at the hands of Carlisle before returning to Fratton Park eight games later. From a footballing family, his father Martin, uncle Paul, and grandfather Danny, all playing for professional clubs, the young right back, who can also perform in midfield, will be hoping for better in 1997-98.

Nottingham F (From trainee on 14/12/92)
Portsmouth (Free on 28/2/96) FL 5
Torquay U (Loaned on 3/3/97) FL 7+2

David Hirst

HIRST David Eric
Born: Cudworth, 7 December 1967
Height: 5'11" Weight: 13.10
Club Honours: FLC '91

International Honours: E: 3; B-3; U21-7; Yth

David was still a class striker in the Sheffield Wednesday side of 1996-97, but missed a lot of the season with a series of minor injuries, with his first goal not coming until the turn of the year. Five more followed in quick succession, but, overall, it will go down as a disappointing campaign for a player who leads the line well and who has an excellent left foot and a lot of pace. Despite that, he continued to remain very popular with the fans and many believe that the side is better with him in it.

Barnsley (From apprentice on 8/11/85) FL 26+2/9 FLC 1
Sheffield Wed (£200,000 on 11/8/86) F/PL 258+30/106 FLC 26+9/11 FAC 12+7/6 Others 8/5

HISLOP Terence **Kona**
Born: London, 21 December 1970
Height: 5'11" Weight: 12.2

An extremely fast left-sided attacker with a good first touch and, like his more famous brother, Shaka, a US College graduate, Kona first joined Hartlepool as a triallist early last season. In his initial games, he looked to be a major discovery, while proving to be a real livewire for division three defences. Unfortunately, although he always looked dangerous, he was not as effective as manager Mick Tait would have liked and he was released on a free transfer in May 1997.

Hartlepool U (Free from Livingston on 18/9/96) FL 23+4 FAC 2 Others 1

HISLOP Neil (Shaka)
Born: Hackney, 22 February 1969
Height: 6'4" Weight: 14.4
Club Honours: Div 2 '94

A giant of a goalkeeper who equals the height of Newcastle's tallest ever players, an important attribute in dealing with crosses, Shaka's quick reflexes and agility make him a good shot stopper and one who uses impressive pace to extend his area of influence to the whole penalty area and beyond. Disappointed to miss out on last season's Charity Shield match, he played in the opening Premiership fixture, but was then dropped before being recalled for the 7-1 drubbing of Spurs and grasping the opportunity to establish himself as first choice for the rest of the season, turning in a string of performances which showed a steady improvement as his confidence returned. His double save from Dwight York's penalty and follow up, helped grasp the initiative back from Villa to earn an important point in the first Premiership match following the departure of Kevin Keegan, while his best game was probably at the Riverside Stadium when he shut out Middlesbrough in windy conditions to help United to an important 1-0 win. Unfortunately, flu cost him his place for the final four games.

Reading (Signed from US college soccer on 9/9/92) FL 104 FLC 10 FAC 3 Others 9
Newcastle U (£1,575,000 on 10/8/95) PL 40 FLC 5 FAC 3 Others 2

HITCHCOCK Kevin Joseph
Born: Canning Town, 5 October 1962
Height: 6'1" Weight: 13.4
Club Honours: AMC '87; FAC '97

A popular, long-serving Chelsea goalkeeper who started last season as number two to Dmitri Kharine, he came off the bench at Hillsborough when the Russian was carried off after badly twisting his knee in an awkward fall and played superbly as Sheffield Wednesday poured forward in an effort to maintain their 100 per-cent record. First choice for the next seven Premiership matches, playing brilliantly at Old Trafford in the last of these which destroyed United's unbeaten home league record – stretching back 35 matches. In fact, Manchester United were Kevin's jinx club, picking up an elbow injury during Chelsea's impressive 2-1 victory and missing the next 11 matches and then dislocating a shoulder in the return match at the Bridge in February, which required an operation and put paid to his season. Following that, he joined the ranks of long-term injured and now faces an intriguing battle with international 'keepers Kharine and Frode Grodås for the goalkeeping jersey. Despite being an unused sub at Wembley, he won an FA Cup winners medal, following Blues' 2-0 win over Middlesbrough.

Nottingham F (£15,000 from Barking on 4/8/83)
Mansfield T (£14,000 on 1/2/84) FL 182 FLC 12 FAC 10 Others 20
Chelsea (£250,000 on 25/3/88) F/PL 90+3 FLC 10 FAC 14 Others 13
Northampton T (Loaned on 28/12/90) FL 17 Others 1

HOBSON Gary
Born: Hull, 12 November 1972
Height: 6'1" Weight: 13.3

A transfer deadline signing from his hometown club, Hull City, in 1995-96, Gary continued to show good form for Brighton throughout 1996-97. A classy left-footed defender, noted for his cool distributive skills, he missed only a handful of games through injury and netted his first ever league goal with an excellent header in a 5-0 demolition of Hartlepool United in the much-publicised "Fans United" match at the Goldstone in February.

Hull C (From trainee on 17/7/91) FL 135+7 FLC 13+1 FAC 2+2/1 Others 6
Brighton & Hove A (£60,000 on 27/3/96) FL 44+2/1 FLC 2 FAC 2 Others 2

HOCKLEY Wayne
Born: Paignton, 6 September 1978
Height: 5'8" Weight: 11.0

A young Torquay YTS striker who will remember the first of two substitute appearances, at Scarborough, last season, for a missed goal, Wayne did not let it get him down and gave a spirited display that augered well for the future.

Torquay U (Trainee) FL 0+2

HOCKTON Daniel (Danny) John
Born: Barking, 7 February 1979
Height: 5'10" Weight: 11.11

Having joined Millwall whilst still at school,

before graduating through the youth ranks, his height, lightning pace, and skill on the ball bode well for the future of this talented striker. A prolific goalscorer in the youth team, he made his debut against Stockport as a substitute and was unlucky not to score.

Millwall (From trainee on 8/3/97) FL 0+2

HODGE John
Born: Skelmersdale, 1 April 1969
Height: 5'7" Weight: 11.3
Club Honours: AMC '94

Signed from Swansea last September, John had an outstanding season for Walsall, always ready to take on defenders down the left flank and scoring several spectacular goals, such as the last-minute equaliser against Blackpool and the match winner against Luton. That apart, there were his many made-to-measure crosses for Kyle Lightbourne, to go with his crowd-pleasing appeal. Is sure to become a firm favourite at Bescot.

Exeter C (Signed from Falmouth T on 12/9/91) FL 57+8/10 FLC 3/1 FAC 2 Others 8+2/1
Swansea C (Signed on 14/7/93) FL 87+25/10 FLC 6+2/3 FAC 6 Others 13+4
Walsall (Free on 23/9/96) FL 32+5/4 FAC 4 Others 0+1

HODGES Kevin
Born: Bridport, 12 June 1960
Height: 5'8" Weight: 11.2

As Torquay United's head coach, Kevin showed up well in his only match last season, a brief substitute appearance in the home match against Scarborough. Incidentally, it was the 601st game for the 37-year-old midfielder in a career stretching back to 1977-78.

Plymouth Arg (From apprentice on 2/3/78) FL 502+28/81 FLC 32+3 FAC 39/3 Others 9+2/2
Torquay U (Loaned on 21/1/92) FL 3
Torquay U (Free on 7/12/92) FL 49+19/4 FLC 2 FAC 2+3 Others 8/1

HODGES Lee Leslie
Born: Plaistow, 2 March 1978
Height: 5'5" Weight: 10.2

Unable to get a game at West Ham in 1996-97, Lee was loaned out first to Exeter (December) and then to Leyton Orient (February). A creative, attacking left-sided midfielder, and an excellent passer, he proved to be an exciting player in both stints, and one who enjoyed taking on defenders and crossing. Unfortunate to have his season ended by a knee injury, he is most definitely one for the future.

West Ham U (From trainee on 2/3/95)
Exeter C (Loaned on 13/9/96)
Exeter C (Loaned on 12/12/96) FL 16+1
Leyton Orient (Loaned on 28/2/97) FL 3

HODGES Lee Leslie
Born: Epping, 4 September 1973
Height: 6'0" Weight: 12.1
International Honours: E: Yth

A classy midfielder with good ball skills and workrate to match, Lee was the vital link between Barnet's midfield and attack in 1996-97. Although going through a sticky patch during the club's hard winter, he had regained his place before the end of the season, with seven goals to his credit and was back to his best.

Tottenham H (From trainee on 29/2/92) PL 0+4
Plymouth Arg (Loaned on 26/3/93) FL 6+1/2
Wycombe W (Loaned on 31/12/93) FL 2+2 FAC 1 Others 1
Barnet (Free on 31/5/94) FL 94+11/26 FLC 6+1 FAC 6+1/4 Others 3+1

HODGSON Douglas (Doug) John
Born: Frankston, Australia, 27 February 1969
Height: 6'2" Weight: 13.10

A tough-tackling centre back, Doug started last season at Sheffield United as cover for Michel Vonk and David Holdsworth, making just six appearances before going on loan to Burnley in October. Unfortunately, his stay at Turf Moor was even shorter than expected when he sustained a neck injury near the end of his first game and was forced to return to United. However, having regained his place following an injury to Vonk, he scored his first league goal, at Bradford, before being placed on the transfer list and being allowed to move to Oldham as part of the deal that saw Nicky Henry go in the opposite direction. A very good header of the ball who hates to lose, his 12 games for the Latics promised a good return for the coming term.

Sheffield U (£30,000 from Heidelberg Alex on 22/7/94) FL 24+6/1 FLC 3+1 FAC 2+1 Others 1
Plymouth Arg (Loaned on 10/8/95) FL 3+2
Burnley (Loaned on 17/10/96) FL 1
Oldham Ath (Signed on 28/2/97) FL 11+1

HOGG Graeme James
Born: Aberdeen, 17 June 1964
Height: 6'1" Weight: 12.4
Club Honours: AIC '95
International Honours: S: U21-4; Yth

The vastly experienced Notts County centre back who started his career at Manchester United, played as one of three centre backs for the club in 1996-97, a season that ultimately saw the club relegated to the third division. Sound and reliable in the air, and a solid tackler with a good left foot, he should be invaluable in 1997-98 as County look to reclaim their former status.

Manchester U (From apprentice on 1/6/82) FL 82+1/1 FLC 7+1 FAC 8 Others 12
West Bromwich A (Loaned on 3/11/87) FL 7 Others 1
Portsmouth (£150,000 on 25/8/88) FL 97+3/2 FLC 2 FAC 6 Others 2
Heart of Midlothian (£200,000 on 23/8/91) SL 50+8/3 SLC 6 SC 1/1 Others 4
Notts Co (£75,000 on 27/1/95) FL 62 FLC 3 FAC 3 Others 4

HOLBROOK Leigh William
Born: Belper, 6 August 1979
Height: 5'9" Weight: 10.0

This promising Mansfield second-year trainee central defender was given his league baptism in the final six minutes of 1996-97, when coming off the subs' bench at Wigan, who claimed the third division championship following their 2-0 victory. One of several promising youngsters at the club, Leigh will be looking for further opportunities and a professional contract this coming term.

Mansfield T (Trainee) FL 0+1

HOLCROFT Peter Ian
Born: Liverpool, 3 January 1976
Height: 5'9" Weight: 11.0

With no prospect of breaking into the spotlight at Goodison Park, the young Everton midfielder was allowed to join Swindon Town on a free last November, making his league debut as a substitute shortly after signing. However, he had to wait until late February for his first full appearance in a 3-0 defeat at Manchester City, and only made one further start in late season. There is no reason for him to be downhearted as with two seasons left on his contract he has plenty of time to make his mark at the County Ground.

Everton (From trainee on 1/7/94)
Swindon T (Free on 11/11/96) FL 2+1

HOLDSWORTH David Gary
Born: Walthamstow, 8 November 1968
Height: 6'1" Weight: 12.4
International Honours: E: U21-1; Yth

Signed from Watford last October, following his recovery from injury the centre back became an instant fixture in the Sheffield United first team, forming a strong partnership with Michel Vonk. Having scored his first goal for the club at Swindon, after conceding an own goal earlier in the match, he gave away a further own goal in the following match against Norwich, before being appointed captain of the team in succession to Mark Patterson. A classy defender who is good in the air and marshalls the troops well, he enjoyed an excellent first season with United. Is the twin brother of Wimbledon's Dean.

Watford (From apprentice on 8/11/86) FL 249+9/10 FLC 20/2 FAC 14+1/1 Others 8+2
Sheffield U (£450,00 on 8/10/96) FL 37/1 FAC 1 Others 3

HOLDSWORTH Dean Christopher
Born: Walthamstow, 8 November 1968
Height: 5'11" Weight: 11.13
Club Honours: Div 3 '92
International Honours: E: B-1

A regular in the Wimbledon side since 1992, Dean was kept out in 1996-97 for the most part due to the impressive form of Marcus Gayle and Efan Ekoku. But nobody can doubt his energy when it comes to poaching, which he proved by scoring some vital goals, even though appearances worked against him. Finally put all the transfer speculation behind him when he signed a new contract and won back the fans by scoring in the 1-0 win over Blackburn Rovers in December. The brother of Sheffield United's David, he also has interests outside football with a modelling career.

Watford (From apprentice on 12/11/86) FL 2+14/3 Others 0+4
Carlisle U (Loaned on 11/2/88) FL 4/1
Port Vale (Loaned on 18/3/88) FL 6/2
Swansea C (Loaned on 25/8/88) FL 4+1/1
Brentford (Loaned on 13/10/88) FL 2+5/1
Brentford (£125,000 on 29/9/89) FL 106+4/53 FLC 7+1/6 FAC 6/7 Others 12+2/9
Wimbledon (£720,000 on 20/7/92) PL 144+20/58 FLC 16+2/11 FAC 13+7/7

HOLLAND Christopher (Chris) James
Born: Whalley, 11 September 1975
Height: 5'9" Weight: 11.5
International Honours: E: U21-10; Yth
A very fit, attacking Birmingham mid-fielder, Chris was signed from Newcastle at the end of last October, following an impressive loan spell at St Andrews. A busy and inventive player, he was also a regular with the England U21 side and often showed great flashes of skill. Unfortunately, in what was his first full season at first-team level, his form tailed off, but, nevertheless, the Blues have high hopes of him in the years to come. Also played for the Football League U21 side that drew with the Italian Serie "B" equivalent in February.
Preston NE (Trainee) FL 0+1 Others 1
Newcastle U (£100,000 on 20/1/94) PL 2+1 FLC 0+1
Birmingham C (£600,000 on 5/9/96) FL 28+4 FAC 3

HOLLAND Matthew (Matt) Rhys
Born: Bury, 11 April 1974
Height: 5'9" Weight: 11.12
Matt, the Bournemouth captain, started last season in his familiar role in central midfield, producing his normal outstanding displays, but following the long-term injury of regular defender, Owen Coll, he moved to the centre of defence where he again produced some good performances. A very strong player who makes some penetrating runs from midfield and is adept at free kicks, he displayed his defensive qualities during his spell at the back to underline his versatility.
West Ham U (From trainee on 3/7/92)
Bournemouth (Signed on 27/1/95) FL 97+7/18 FLC 6 FAC 3 Others 3

HOLLAND Paul
Born: Lincoln, 8 July 1973
Height: 5'11" Weight: 12.10
International Honours: E: U21-4; Yth; Sch
Last season, Paul was given more starts in the sort of forward midfield role for Chesterfield that best suits his aggressive, attacking style. It was ironic, then, that his best performance should have come as an emergency centre half against Forest in the FA Cup. This probably surprised everyone except Kevin Randall, the Spireites' assistant manager, who remembered Paul's ability in that position from their days at Field Mill, and whose very good idea it was to play him there on the day.
Mansfield T (From juniors on 4/7/91) FL 149/25 FLC 11 FAC 7/3 Others 9/1
Sheffield U (£250,000 on 20/6/95) FL 11+7/1 FLC 2/1
Chesterfield (Signed on 5/1/96) FL 40+2/5 FLC 2 FAC 7 Others 1

HOLLOWAY Ian Scott
Born: Kingswood, 12 March 1963
Height: 5'8" Weight: 10.10
Club Honours: Div 3 '90
Released by QPR during the 1996 close season, Ian signed on for Bristol Rovers as player/manager. A hard-working midfielder, by his own admission he found life very difficult during the first five months of

1996-97, his own playing form being patchy and, after collecting eight bookings, he was duly suspended. Adapted well, having changed the team's playing style and personnel on and off the pitch and scored an emotional first and only goal of the season on 15 February against high-riding Luton in a vital 3-2 victory, a result which helped lift Rovers at a time games were not going their way.
Bristol Rov (From apprentice on 18/3/81) FL 104+7/14 FLC 10/1 FAC 8/2 Others 5
Wimbledon (£35,000 on 18/7/85) FL 19/2 FLC 3 FAC 1
Brentford (£25,000 on 12/3/86) FL 27+3/2 FLC 2 FAC 3 Others 0+1
Torquay U (Loaned on 30/1/87) FL 5
Bristol Rov (£10,000 on 21/8/87) FL 179/26 FLC 5 FAC 10/1 Others 20/3
Queens Park R (£230,000 on 12/8/91) F/PL 130+17/4 FLC 12+1 FAC 7+1/1 Others 1+1
Bristol Rov (Free on 22/7/96) FL 29+2/1 FLC 2 FAC 1

Ian Holloway

HOLMES Paul
Born: Stocksbridge, 18 February 1968
Height: 5'10" Weight: 11.3
Paul added a new dimension to West Brom's play in 1996-97 as an over-lapping right back with good technique. Always willing to get into the opponents' half of the field, with a good turn of pace, at ease with the ball, and good at running the opposition down, he is something of a utility player.
Doncaster Rov (From apprentice on 24/2/86) FL 42+5/1 FAC 3+1/1 Others 1
Torquay U (£6,000 on 12/8/88) FL 127+11/4 FLC 9 FAC 9+2 Others 13+3
Birmingham C (£40,000 on 5/6/92) FL 12 FAC 1
Everton (£100,000 on 19/3/93) PL 21 FLC 4 FAC 1 Others 0+2
West Bromwich A (£80,000 on 12/1/96) FL 55+1/1 FLC 2 FAC 1 Others 3

HOLMES Steven (Steve) Peter
Born: Middlesbrough, 13 January 1971
Height: 6'2" Weight: 13.0
A Lincoln right back whose 1996-97 season was badly disrupted by a knee injury at Scunthorpe last October, Steve was out of action for three months, but returned to play a key role in the run in to the end of the campaign, scoring some vital goals in the process. Strong in the air and on the ground, his presence at set pieces keeps the opposition on their toes.
Lincoln C (From trainee on 17/7/89)
Preston NE (£10,000 from Guisborough T, via Gainsborough Trinity, on 14/3/94) FL 13/1 FAC 3 Others 1
Hartlepool U (Loaned on 10/3/95) FL 5/2
Lincoln C (Loaned on 20/10/95) FL 12/1 Others 2
Lincoln C (£30,000 on 15/3/96) FL 38+1/5 FLC 4/2

HOLSGROVE Paul
Born: Telford, 26 August 1969
Height: 6'1" Weight: 11.10
1996-97 was a disappointing season for Paul, who struggled with injuries and a loss of form to the extent that he made very few first-team appearances for Reading, though he did include two well-taken goals, against Stoke City and Birmingham City, in those games. A strong midfielder with a wide range of passing skills, he still has to fulfil the obvious potential he first showed when he came to the club. Is the son of John, the former Swindon and Wolves' player.
Aldershot (From trainee on 9/2/87) FL 0+3 Others 1 (Free to Wokingham T in 1990 close season)
Luton T (£25,000 on 1/1/91) FL 1+1 (Free to Heracles in November 1991)
Millwall (Free on 13/8/92) FL 3+8 FLC 0+1 FAC 0+1 Others 2
Reading (Free on 10/8/94) FL 62+6/6 FLC 8+2/1 FAC 5

HOLT Andrew (Andy)
Born: Stockport, 21 April 1978
Height: 6'1" Weight: 12.7
Another product of the Oldham youth side who came through in 1996-97, Andy had already showed himself to be a young central defender of some promise before making his debut at Bolton in April. Steady and composed, good in the air, as you would expect of a youngster over six foot and a strong tackler, he was blooded in league football when coming on for the last seven minutes at Burnden. However, what is even more remarkable about him is the fact that his throw, which must be the longest in the game, regularly reaches the far post and is propelled more like a missile than a drop. Is expected to be a regular before too long.
Oldham Ath (From trainee on 23/7/96) FL 0+1

HOLT Michael Andrew
Born: Burnley, 28 July 1977
Height: 5'9" Weight: 10.9
A young striker signed by Preston during the summer of 1996 with a view to the future, he received an early chance last season through injuries to senior players, scoring a 90th minute equaliser on his full debut against Spurs in the Coca-Cola Cup, and becoming an immediate hit with fans with his all-

action style. Occasionally a little over-enthusiastic in his attempts to close down defenders, he continued to show great promise when he returned to the reserves after a good run in the first team.
Preston NE (Free from Blackburn Rov juniors on 16/8/96) FL 8+11/3 FLC 2/1 FAC 1+1

HOLWYN Jermaine Titano Benito
Born: Amsterdam, Holland, 16 April 1973
Height: 5'10" Weight: 11.8
Having arrived from Ajax the previous season, the Dutch defender made his Port Vale debut last January as a sub against QPR, unfortunately heading in an own goal in a remarkable 4-4 draw, after the Vale had led 4-0. That seemed to affect his confidence a bit, although he started five games as cover for injuries, four of them at right back, his best performance coming at Bradford when playing in his favoured centre-half position. Signed a one year contract extension in March to enable him to continue his football education.
Port Vale (£5,000 from Ajax on 31/7/95) FL 5+2

HOMER Christopher (Chris)
Born: Stockton, 16 April 1977
Height: 5'9" Weight: 11.5
1996-97 was another disappointing season for this young Hartlepool midfielder, especially after his health problems in 1995-96. Given another opportunity to prove himself, in the event, he made just one first-team appearance when coming on as a substitute and playing half a game before being released in December.
Hartlepool U (From trainee on 11/7/95) FL 2+5 FLC 0+1 Others 0+1

HONE Mark Joseph
Born: Croydon, 31 March 1968
Height: 6'1" Weight: 13.1
International Honours: E: SP-4
A skilful and hard-tackling midfielder signed on a free transfer from Southend in the summer of 1996, Mark soon established a first-team place for himself at Lincoln before being hit by a series of injuries in the second half of the season. Good in the air, with a liking to get forward, his only goal came in the Coca-Cola Cup tie at Southampton.
Crystal Palace (From juniors on 3/11/85) FL 4 FLC 0+1
Southend U (£50,000 from Welling U on 11/8/94) FL 50+6 FLC 2+2 FAC 1 Others 2
Lincoln C (Free on 30/7/96) FL 26+3 FLC 5+1/1 FAC 1

HOPE Christopher (Chris) Jonathan
Born: Sheffield, 14 November 1972
Height: 6'1" Weight: 12.7
At his best when operating as a central defender, where his strength in the tackle and aerial ability continued to be seen to good effect in Scunthorpe's colours during 1996-97, Chris can also be used at right back if required. Carried on where he left off the previous season in scoring useful goals.
Nottingham F (Free from Darlington juniors on 23/8/90)
Scunthorpe U (£50,000 on 5/7/93) FL 143+8/6 FLC 5+1 FAC 10/1 Others 10/2

HOPE Mark Bryan
Born: Isleworth, 13 June 1970
Height: 6'2" Weight: 13.0
Signed on non-contract terms from non-league Porthleven last January, the young central defender played just one first-team game for Darlington before being released. Unfortunately, the game in question was the club's worst defeat of the season, a 6-0 shellacking at Fulham, and Mark, who was standing in for Andy Crosby, was taken off following the third goal.
Darlington (Free from Porthleven on 9/1/97) FL 1

HOPE Richard Paul
Born: Middlesbrough, 22 June 1978
Height: 6'2" Weight: 12.6
The son of former Darlington goalkeeper, John, Richard joined his father's old club from Blackburn, on loan last January, before signing permanently. A tall central defender, who established himself in the first team as the eventual replacement for Sean Gregan, he made his league debut at home to Cambridge and thereafter was ever present.
Blackburn Rov (From trainee on 9/8/95)
Darlington (Free on 17/1/97) FL 20

David Hopkin

HOPKIN David
Born: Greenock, 21 August 1970
Height: 5'9" Weight: 13.0
International Honours: S: 2
Powerful, wide midfielder, or front player, strong in the air, with an excellent right foot shot and a good early crosser of the ball, David has really blossomed at Crystal Palace since leaving Chelsea. Only missing games in 1996-97 because of unavailability and injury, the vice captain scored 17 goals from midfield to put himself in line for a call up to the Scottish squad and, at the same time, powered Palace into the Premiership via the play-off victory over Sheffield United at Wembley, his wonderfully curled

25 yarder in the dying embers of the game winning it for the Londoners. Twice capped for Scotland during the summer, he was voted Palace's Player of the Year.
Morton (Signed from Port Glasgow BC in 1989-90) SL 33+15/4 SLC 2/2 SC 2/1
Chelsea (£300,000 on 25/9/92) PL 21+19/1 FLC 0+1 FAC 3+2
Crystal Palace (£850,000 on 29/7/95) FL 79+4/21 FLC 6/6 FAC 3 Others 4/2

HOPKINS Jeffrey (Jeff)
Born: Swansea, 14 April 1964
Height: 6'0" Weight: 12.12
Club Honours: Div 2 '94
International Honours: W: 16; U21-5; Yth
Jeff was rather unlucky to be given a free transfer by Reading before the end of last season, having performed consistently well whenever he was in the side, especially when being recalled for a late run of appearances at centre back after injuries to other defenders. Is a model professional, dedicated to the game and another player who coaches at the club's school of excellence.
Fulham (From apprentice on 10/9/81) FL 213+6/4 FLC 26/2 FAC 12 Others 3
Crystal Palace (£240,000 on 17/8/88) FL 70/2 FLC 7/1 FAC 4/1 Others 12
Plymouth Arg (Loaned on 24/10/91) FL 8 Others 1
Bristol Rov (Free on 5/3/92) FL 4+2
Reading (Free on 13/7/92) FL 127+4/3 FLC 9+1/1 FAC 6+1 Others 6+2

HOPPER Anthony (Tony)
Born: Carlisle, 31 May 1976
Height: 5'10" Weight: 11.13
Club Honours: AMC '97
A product of the Carlisle youth system, Tony continued to improve in 1996-97 and his positive approach earned him a number of first-team starts. Although he can operate in midfield, most of his appearances were at right back and, it is from there that he will probably be in contention for a regular place in the side next term.
Carlisle U (From trainee on 18/7/94) FL 17+14/1 FAC 2/1 Others 3+1

HORACE Alain
Born: Madagascar, 4 December 1971
Height: 5'6" Weight: 10.1
A diminutive Madagascan-born midfielder, he joined Hartlepool as a triallist last October and made just one first-team appearance, playing half a match when coming on as a substitute against Northampton. Recognised as a tricky midfielder with plenty of talent, he was subsequently released as manager, Mick Tait, did not believe he was up to the rigours of English division three football.
Hartlepool U (Free from Mulhouse on 25/10/96) FL 0+1

HORLOCK Kevin
Born: Bexley, 1 November 1972
Height: 6'0" Weight: 12.0
Club Honours: Div 2 '96
International Honours: NI: 9; B-2
Signed from Swindon Town last January, his impressive debut for Manchester City at Oxford was seen in front of the TV cameras,

but being cup tied he could not play in the two rounds against Watford and Middlesbrough. With a good reputation as a hard-working midfield player, Kevin operated from the number three spot, being busy over most of the field, supporting the defence one minute and then to be seen in the opposing penalty area when instinctively picking up crosses which resulted in valuable goals. A great clubman suited to Frank Clark's style of play, he is a member of the Northern Ireland squad and at the age of 24 his future must be promising for club and country.

West Ham U (From trainee on 1/7/91)
Swindon T (Free on 27/8/92) F/PL 151+12/22 FLC 15+2/1 FAC 12/3 Others 5+2
Manchester C (£1,250,000 on 31/1/97) FL 18/4

HORNE Barry

Born: St Asaph, 18 May 1962
Height: 5'10" Weight: 12.2
Club Honours: WC '86; FAC '95; CS '95
International Honours: W: 59

Another Birmingham bargain buy from the premiership, having joined the club from Everton during the 1996 close season, the experienced midfielder was inspirational during the first half of 1996-97, his industry and astute reading of a game earning him a number of man of the match awards. Ever present until March, when the sheer slog of matches finally caught up with him, Barry was all set to re-sign for Everton on transfer deadline day, before the deal was unfortunately scuppered due to Joe Royle's resignation. Continuing play for Wales during the campaign, although he later relinquished the captaincy, the Brum fans love his tigerish tackling and all-action style.

Wrexham (Free from Rhyl on 26/6/84) FL 136/17 FLC 10/1 FAC 7/2 Others 15/3
Portsmouth (£60,000 on 17/7/87) FL 66+4/7 FLC 3 FAC 6
Southampton (£700,000 on 22/3/89) FL 111+1/6 FLC 15+2/3 FAC 15/3 Others 7/1
Everton (£675,000 on 1/7/92) PL 118+5/3 FLC 12+1 FAC 11+1 Others 3
Birmingham C (£250,000 on 10/6/96) FL 33 FLC 3 FAC 3

HOTTIGER Marc

Born: Lausanne, Switzerland, 7 November 1967
Height: 5'10" Weight: 12.9
International Honours: Switzerland: 65

After featuring in two of Switzerland's three Euro 96 matches in the summer of 1996, right back Marc endured a desperately frustrating club season in 1996-97. Left out of Everton's starting line up, following the return from injury of Earl Barrett, he figured in the first team on only a handful of occasions, way below the figure required for the Department of Employment for him to have his work permit renewed. With two years still remaining on his Everton contract, there could still be time for the attack-minded full back, a player who is good on the ball and can produce dangerous crosses from the wide right, to make his name at the club.

Newcastle U (£520,000 from Sion on 4/8/94) PL 38+1/1 FLC 6+1 FAC 4/1 Others 4
Everton (£700,000 on 9/3/96) PL 13+4/1 FLC 1

HOUCHEN Keith Morton

Born: Middlesbrough, 25 July 1960
Height: 6'2" Weight: 13.7
Club Honours: FAC '87

1996-97 was a disappointing final season for this outstanding goalscorer who had achieved much in his two spells with Hartlepool, having made it clear that he would be winding down his playing career. However, the end came sooner than expected when he announced his retirement after failing to overcome a long-standing knee injury in September. This meant that he was able to concentrate fully on being the club's manager, but, following a bad run of results, he was out of a job just six weeks later.

Hartlepool U (Free from Chesterfield juniors on 9/2/78) FL 160+10/65 FLC 8/1 FAC 4+1
Leyton Orient (£25,000 on 26/3/82) FL 74+2/20 FLC 3/1 FAC 3 Others 0+1
York C (£151,000 on 23/3/84) FL 56+11/19 FLC 6/3 FAC 9+2/3 Others 4/2
Scunthorpe U (£40,000 on 28/3/86) FL 9/3
Coventry C (£60,000 on 3/7/86) FL 43+11/7 FLC 2+1 FAC 5+1/5 Others 2+1
Hibernian (£100,000 on 29/3/89) SL 51+6/11 SLC 5/1 SC 6/4 Others 4/1
Port Vale (£100,000 on 9/8/91) FL 44+5/10 FLC 2+1/1 FAC 2 Others 1+1
Hartlepool U (Free on 1/8/93) FL 104+5/27 FLC 9+1/1 FAC 2 Others 3

Ray Houghton

HOUGHTON Raymond (Ray) James

Born: Glasgow, 9 January 1962
Height: 5'7" Weight: 10.10
Club Honours: FLC '86, '94; Div 1 '88, '90; CS '88, '90; FAC '89, '92
International Honours: Ei: 69

An industrious, experienced Crystal Palace midfielder with superb vision and excellent passing skills that can unlock the best defences, the club captain had two spells out through injury and suspension in 1996-97, making just 24 appearances. Regardless of a

lack of games, his form was still good enough to see him recalled to the Republic of Ireland squad and adding to his caps. Replaced after 62 minutes in the first semi-final leg of the play offs, when obviously under strain, his calm and controlled influence was noticeable by his absence and it was David Hopkin who stepped up to lift the trophy at Wembley, following the 1-0 victory over Sheffield United that took the club back to the Premiership.

West Ham U (From juniors on 5/7/79) FL 0+1
Fulham (Free on 7/7/82) FL 129/16 FLC 12/2 FAC 4/3
Oxford U (£147,000 on 13/9/85) FL 83/10 FLC 13/3 FAC 3 Others 6/1
Liverpool (£825,000 on 19/10/87) FL 147+6/28 FLC 14/3 FAC 26+1/4 Others 8/3
Aston Villa (£900,000 on 28/7/92) PL 83+12/6 FLC 11+2/2 FAC 7/2 Others 4+2/1
Crystal Palace (£300,000 on 23/3/95) P/FL 69+3/7 FLC 6 FAC 4 Others 4/1

HOUGHTON Scott Aaron

Born: Hitchin, 22 October 1971
Height: 5'7" Weight: 12.4
Club Honours: FAYC '90
International Honours: E: Yth; Sch

Captured from Walsall during the 1996 close season, Scott soon proved his value in Peterborough's midfield in 1996-97 when finishing as the club's leading scorer with nine to his credit. This, despite suffering a hernia problem which resulted in an operation and kept him out of several more matches as he strove for match fitness. A busy player, who is at his best in wide positions when using his speed to take defenders on, he can either deliver excellent crosses for the front men or cut inside to get in shots of his own.

Tottenham H (From trainee on 24/8/90) FL 0+10/2 FLC 0+2 Others 0+2
Ipswich T (Loaned on 26/3/91) FL 7+1/1
Gillingham (Loaned on 17/12/92) FL 3
Charlton Ath (Loaned on 26/2/93) FL 6
Luton T (Free on 10/8/93) FL 7+9/1 FLC 2+1 FAC 0+1 Others 2
Walsall (£20,000 on 2/9/94) FL 76+2/14 FLC 0+1/1 FAC 10/3 Others 4
Peterborough U (£60,000 + on 12/7/96) FL 26+6/8 FLC 2+2 FAC 5/1 Others 0+1

HOULT Russell

Born: Leicester, 22 November 1972
Height: 6'3" Weight: 14.9

Prior to 1996-97, the former Leicester 'keeper seemed likely to be Derby's long-term choice, using his height well at crosses and agile enough to be able to get down quickly enough to deal with anything along the ground. However, some less than consistent performances towards the season's end, including a 6-1 defeat by Middlesbrough and a mistake at Newcastle sapped his confidence and the signing of Matt Poom, who displaced him at the end of the campaign, will mean he may find it difficult to hold on to his place.

Leicester C (From trainee on 28/3/91) FL 10 FLC 3 Others 1
Lincoln C (Loaned on 27/8/91) FL 2 FLC 1
Bolton W (Loaned on 3/11/93) FL 3+1 Others 1
Lincoln C (Loaned on 12/8/94) FL 15 Others 1
Derby Co (£300,000 on 17/2/95) F/PL 86+2 FLC 4 FAC 4

HOUSHAM Steven (Steve) James
Born: Gainsborough, 24 February 1976
Height: 5'10" Weight: 11.8
Beginning last season at right back for Scunthorpe, before moving to his preferred role in midfield, Steve continued to show as an aggressive, busy player who covered plenty of ground. Always looking to get forward, unfortunately, suspension interrupted his run in the side.
Scunthorpe U (From trainee on 23/12/93) FL 56+10/3 FLC 0+1 FAC 3 Others 4+1/1

HOWARD Jonathan (Jon)
Born: Sheffield, 7 October 1971
Height: 5'11" Weight: 12.6
Easily Chesterfield's most improved player in 1996-97, Jon's strong running up front was never in question, but he further developed his ability to read the game and worked hard to improve concentration and anticipation. Now has the poacher's knack of being in the right place at the right time, as experience lends a coolness to his finishing and his confidence grows, he will be able to take games by the scruff of the neck and put away many more of the sort of chances that led to his being the club's top scorer last season.
Rotherham U (From trainee on 10/7/90) FL 25+11/5 FLC 0+1 FAC 4/2 Others 3+1 (Free to Buxton on 11/11/94)
Chesterfield (Free on 9/12/94) FL 43+34/12 FLC 3 FAC 8+1/2 Others 5+3/2

HOWARD Steven (Steve) John
Born: Durham, 10 May 1976
Height: 6'2" Weight: 13.7
It was a mixed season for this young Hartlepool utility player in 1996-97. Despite struggling with injuries and loss of form in the first half of the campaign, by mid term he looked to have found his best position, playing as an old-fashioned centre forward, his awkward style of play certainly causing the opposition defences plenty of problems. Unfortunately, his goalscoring record was patchy, although he ended the season on a high with two goals at Swansea when playing as a midfielder.
Hartlepool U (Free from Tow Law on 8/8/95) FL 58+13/14 FLC 4 FAC 2 Others 3/2

HOWARTH Lee
Born: Bolton, 3 January 1968
Height: 6'2" Weight: 13.8
Is a no-nonsense centre half whose commitment to the cause is appreciated by the Barnet fans. Good in the air, and with the ability to use the ball to effect on the deck, Lee was very rarely missing from the first team line up in 1996-97 and was delighted to open his scoring account for the club with the winner at Torquay in April.
Peterborough U (Free from Chorley on 16/8/91) FL 56+6 FLC 8 FAC 3 Others 3+2/1
Mansfield T (£15,000 on 5/8/94) FL 56+1/2 FLC 7 FAC 4 Others 5
Barnet (Signed on 26/1/96) FL 56+1/1 FLC 4 FAC 3 Others 1

HOWE Edward (Eddie) John Frank
Born: Amersham, 29 November 1977
Height: 5'11" Weight: 11.10

The 1996-97 season was one of limited opportunity for Eddie who, after breaking into the Bournemouth first team in the latter stages of the previous season, was unable to command a regular first team place, despite establishing himself as a member of the squad. Playing mainly as a right-sided defender, although he can perform well as a centre back or in midfield, his confidence and ability should see him establish himself before too long.
Bournemouth (From trainee on 4/7/96) FL 11+7

HOWE Stephen **Robert (Bobby)**
Born: Annitsford, 6 November 1973
Height: 5'7" Weight: 10.4
International Honours: E: Yth
With a lot expected from the young Nottingham Forest striker, last season was a bit of a disappointment with one fleeting subs' appearance in a 4-2 defeat at Liverpool before he was loaned out to Ipswich, following their FA Cup exit at the City Ground. Recognised as being a skilful midfielder who passes the ball well and gets forward to assist the attack, he was played further up front than he would have favoured and subsequently played in just four games before returning home.
Nottingham F (From trainee on 5/12/90) P/FL 6+8/2 FLC 1 Others 1+1
Ipswich T (Loaned on 17/1/97) FL 2+1 FLC 1

HOWELL James (Jamie) Alexander
Born: Rustington, 19 February 1977
Height: 5'8" Weight: 11.2
Club Honours: FAYC '94
International Honours: E: Yth
Having been released by Arsenal and Portsmouth, this hard-working diminutive midfielder performed well for Torquay following his introduction to the team last April. Signed on non-contract forms, he will be hoping to make his mark at this level. Has a good attitude to the game.
Arsenal (From trainee on 1/7/95)
Portsmouth (Free on 22/8/96)
Torquay U (Free on 26/3/97) FL 2+2

HOWELLS David
Born: Guildford, 15 December 1967
Height: 5'11" Weight: 12.4
Club Honours: FAC '91; CS '91
International Honours: E: Yth
Midfield anchor man at Tottenham with both defensive and attacking instincts. In 1996-97, his testimonial year, David held the team together with sturdy performances in the absence of experienced squad members out with injuries. Still showing a keen eye for goal, he produced the poise and confidence to take a match to the opponents when others might have opted for a purely defensive approach. The fans would be the first to agree that, whilst his performances are rarely spectacular, his workrate and commitment make him a true team player. It would also be amiss not to mention his concentration, having a truly traumatic time off the field in helping his wife overcome cancer and suffering the tragic loss of his father in February. He is a much respected player from all corners of the game.

Tottenham H (From apprentice on 28/1/85) F/PL 224+33/22 FLC 25+5/4 FAC 18+3/1 Others 7

HOWES Shaun Colin
Born: Norwich, 7 November 1977
Height: 5'10" Weight: 12.3
A young left back who followed Tommy Taylor to Leyton Orient from Cambridge on a free transfer last November, Shaun spent the early part of the season gaining experience on loan at Billericay, before playing a handful of games and returning to Billericay once again on loan for the last few games of the campaign. Whilst with the non leaguers he was unfortunate to gain a nasty leg injury which brought his appearances to a close.
Cambridge U (From trainee on 9/7/96) FL 0+1
Leyton Orient (Free on 18/11/96) FL 3+2

HOWEY Lee Matthew
Born: Sunderland, 1 April 1969
Height: 6'2" Weight: 13.9
Club Honours: Div 1 '96
A locally-born centre back, and the elder brother of Newcastle's Steve, Lee was restricted in his first-team opportunities at Sunderland in 1996-97, due to the good form of Richard Ord and Andy Melville. However, following an injury to the latter, he came in for the final seven games of the season, performing especially well in the away derbies at Newcastle and Middlesbrough. As a life-long Sunderland fan, he was no doubt especially hurt by the Rokerites' relegation and will be determined to play his part in a quick return to the Premiership. Is more than capable of playing up front where he can get among the goals as a bustling centre forward.
Ipswich T (From trainee on 2/10/86 - Free to Blyth Spartans in March 1988)
Sunderland (Free from Bishop Auckland on 25/3/93) P/FL 39+30/8 FLC 1+4/2 FAC 2+4/1 Others 0+1

HOWEY Stephen (Steve) Norman
Born: Sunderland, 26 October 1971
Height: 6'2" Weight: 11.12
Club Honours: Div 1 '93
International Honours: E: 4
The younger brother of Sunderland striker, Lee, central defender Steve's career has been badly disrupted by injury. A training accident, in which he turned an ankle, caused him to miss Euro 96 and having recovered he opened last season in Newcastle's side, and played well enough to be selected for the England squad for the Moldova game. However, he suffered problems with both his calves and, after scoring in the 4-3 win over Villa in September, he sought medical help, subsequently undergoing two operations on each leg, and it was March before he was able to train again. Tall and good in the air, but also skilled and confident on the ground, and rarely exposed for pace, he is likely to be a central figure in United's defence this coming season, when he will also be seeking to re-establish himself in the England squad.
Newcastle U (From trainee on 11/12/89) F/PL 135+19/6 FLC 13+2/1 FAC 11+2 Others 9

HOYLAND Jamie William
Born: Sheffield, 23 January 1966
Height: 6'0" Weight: 14.0
International Honours: E: Yth

Jamie had two extended runs in Burnley's first team at the start and end of last season, showing much of the composure and dominance at the back that had marked his early days at Turf Moor, particularly during the latter run. Still showing plenty of stamina, his trademark, he regained the captaincy of the side, even finding time to score the first two goals in a 3-0 win at Brentford, and will be looking to lead the side out of the second division in 1997-98. Is the son of Tommy, who played for Sheffield United and Bradford between 1949 and 1961.
Manchester C (From apprentice on 12/11/83) FL 2 FLC 0+1/1
Bury (Free on 11/7/86) FL 169+3/35 FLC 14+1/5 FAC 6 Others 12/2
Sheffield U (£250,000 on 4/7/90) F/PL 72+17/6 FLC 5+3/1 FAC 8+2/1 Others 5/1
Bristol C (Loaned on 4/3/94) FL 6
Burnley (£130,000 on 14/10/94) FL 75+3/4 FLC 5 FAC 7 Others 3

Darren Huckerby

HUCKERBY Darren Carl
Born: Nottingham, 23 April 1976
Height: 5'10" Weight: 11.12
International Honours: E: U21-4

A young striker bought from Newcastle in November after an earlier loan period at Millwall, Darren made his Coventry debut as a sub in the Villa home game, where he set up one goal and another good chance in his 16 minutes on the pitch. His speed and close control are his strengths and he seems to ghost past players when he goes to the byline, something adequately demonstrated

in the Villa game when he set up Dion Dublin's goal. A prodigious talent, the coaching staff will no doubt work on his tendency to be caught offside and his occasional lack of awareness when on one of his deadly runs. Touted as one of the buys of the season, his arrival sparked off an excellent run of results and his contribution resulted in superb goals against his former club, a 2-1 home win, and a 3-1 Boxing Day victory over Leeds. Later, he was to score other good goals at Blackburn in the cup and at Old Trafford. Was selected for the England U21 side and capped twice.
Lincoln C From trainee on 14/7/93) FL 20+8/5 FLC 2 Others 1/2
Newcastle U (£400,000 on 10/11/95) PL 0+1 FAC 0+1
Millwall (Loaned on 6/9/96) FL 6/3
Coventry C (£1,000,000 on 23/11/96) PL 21+4/5 FAC 4/2

HUGHES Andrew John
Born: Manchester, 2 January 1978
Height: 5'11" Weight: 12.1

Still one for the future, Andrew took a bit of a step back in 1996-97, making only nine appearances after such an excellent start the previous season. Extremely pacy, and having a great motor, which more than comes in handy when patrolling the midfield engine room, he came back strongly to play in three of the final five games of the campaign, with Latics already on their way to the second division. Is sure to figure prominently in 1997-98.
Oldham Ath (From trainee on 20/1/96) FL 17+6/1 FLC 0+1 FAC 3 Others 0+2

HUGHES Bryan
Born: Liverpool, 19 June 1976
Height: 5'10" Weight: 11.2
Club Honours: WC '95

Bryan was right back to his best in central midfield last season and became a major influence in Wrexham's FA Cup run to the quarter finals, scoring a number of important goals – one of them against Birmingham, who were so impressed that manager, Trevor Francis, made a successful bid of close on a million pounds as soon as the run was over at Chesterfield. With careful supervision and coaching the lad should have a superb future, having a fine first touch, keen awareness, and being a good passer of the ball with an eye for goal. Without hopefully putting too much pressure on him he has been likened to none other than Bryan Robson in some quarters. Appeared for the Nationwide Football League U21 XI versus their Italian counterparts in February – testimony to his promise. Was also recognised by his fellow professionals when elected to the PFA award-winning second division team.
Wrexham (Trainee) FL 71+23/12 FLC 2 FAC 13+3/7 Others 14+1/3
Birmingham C (£750,000 + on 12/3/97) FL 10+1

HUGHES Ceri Morgan
Born: Pontypridd, 26 February 1971
Height: 5'10" Weight: 12.7
International Honours: W: 6; B-2; Yth

As a change from previous campaigns, Ceri

managed to avoid suspension and (until the very end) injuries, thus making a far greater contribution to Luton's season in 1996-97. Indeed, his authoritative midfield performances on both flanks, plus his corner-taking ability were one of the main reasons for the club's sustained challenge at the top of the division. In particular, his vastly improved control of his previously volatile temper meant that his fierce tackles, allied to his ball skills, allowed him to dominate the midfield and create many opportunities for his forwards. Rewarded with a recall to the Welsh team in the friendly against Republic of Ireland, coming on as a substitute for Vinny Jones, unfortunately, injury struck again at the end of the term when a thigh problem was eventually revealed as a hernia and he missed the concluding matches, including the play offs. Had he played, the Hatters might well have been able to clinch promotion to the first division. *Stop Press:* Was reported to have joined Wimbledon during the summer for an initial fee of around £400,000.
Luton T (From trainee on 1/7/89) FL 157+18/17 FLC 13/1 FAC 11/2 Others 6

HUGHES Darren John
Born: Prescot, 6 October 1965
Height: 5'11" Weight: 13.1
Club Honours: FAYC '84

Exeter left back. Unfortunately troubled by injuries last season, which accounted for his sporadic appearances, when playing, Darren still looked good, especially in linking up with the midfield. Still has a penchant for whipping in crosses from the left-hand side.
Everton (From apprentice on 8/10/83) FL 3
Shrewsbury T (Free on 13/6/85) FL 34+3/1 FLC 5+1 FAC 1 Others 2
Brighton & Hove A (£35,000 on 30/9/86) FL 26/2 FAC 2 Others 1
Port Vale (£10,000 on 4/9/87) FL 183+1/4 FLC 12 FAC 14 Others 12
Northampton T (Signed on 12/1/95) FL 19+2 Others 1
Exeter C (Free on 3/11/95) FL 58+4/1 FLC 2 FAC 2 Others 1

HUGHES Robert David
Born: Wrexham, 1 February 1978
Height: 6'4" Weight: 13.6
International Honours: W: U21-6; Yth

David, a young Aston Villa centre back, made his debut when coming on as a sub at Villa Park against Liverpool last March and put together a little run of games when appearing in place of the injured Steve Staunton. Being new to the professional game, he still had a lot to learn, but his encouraging displays showed that he could be ready for an even better run in the side in 1997-98, especially now that he has won Welsh U21 caps.
Aston Villa (From trainee on 5/7/96) PL 4+3

HUGHES David Robert
Born: St Albans, 30 December 1972
Height: 5'10" Weight: 11.8
International Honours: W: U21-1. E: Sch

A hard-working, attacking Southampton midfielder who is extremely versatile, David has yet to fulfil his potential, having been

extremely unfortunate with injuries during his short career, 1996-97 being no exception. Making just one start in six Premiership appearances, a 1-0 win at Middlesbrough in January, he was unlucky not to increase the scoreline, but was thwarted by a stunning save by the 'keeper. Confident on the ball, passing and moving well, his great strength is in tackling back when dispossessed.

Southampton (From juniors on 2/7/91) PL 9+22/3 FLC 3+1 FAC 0+5/1

HUGHES Ian
Born: Bangor, 2 August 1974
Height: 5'10" Weight: 12.8
Club Honours: Div 2 '97
International Honours: W: U21-12; Yth

Equally at home at full back, central defence, or in midfield, Ian has been used in a utility role for Bury for several seasons, meaning that a regular place in the team has not always been forthcoming. Once again in 1996-97, the club's longest-serving player was utilised in various roles and much of the campaign was spent on the substitutes' bench, although he made enough appearances to warrant a second division championship medal as Bury pipped Stockport for the title. The son of a former Bury player, he is composed and comfortable on the ball.

Bury (From trainee on 19/11/91) FL 125+22/1 FLC 11+1 FAC 6+2 Others 14+4/1

Mark Hughes

HUGHES Leslie **Mark**
Born: Wrexham, 1 November 1963
Height: 5'11" Weight: 13.0
Club Honours: FAC '85, '90, '94, '97; ECWC '91; ESC '91; FLC '92; PL '93, '94; CS '93, '94
International Honours: W: 65; U21-5; Yth; Sch

Still one of the most feared strikers in the Premiership – certainly the best in the business at laying the ball off with his back to goal – the Welsh international played probably the best football of his illustrious career in 1996-97. Remained scoreless for

the first six matches of the campaign as his partnership with Gianluca Vialli took time to develop but broke his duck with a blinder from the edge of the box at Bloomfield Road in the Coca-Cola Cup. Following Vialli's tweaked hamstring in December, Mark formed an almost-telepathic understanding with Gianfranco Zola when the Sardinian sorcerer was pushed further forward, but despite hitting top form, he was surprisingly left on the bench for the pulsating fourth round FA Cup tie at home to Liverpool – making way for the return of Vialli. At half-time, with Blues 2-0 down, Ruud Gullit shuffled his pack and brought "Sparky" off the bench. His appearance galvanised Chelsea and within five minutes he had reduced the deficit with a typical Hughes goal; receiving the ball with his back to goal, holding off a defender and turning in one movement to lash a fierce drive past David James. Leading the line magnificently, his sheer physical presence lifted the team as they completed a remarkable comeback to win 4-2. In the next round at Filbert Street he scored a classic breakaway goal, ramming a shot across Kasey Keller after a sweeping Chelsea move from their own penalty area. Then, in March, he picked up magnums of Champagne on successive Sundays after being named Sky Sports Man of the Match with storming performances against Portsmouth and Sunderland, Mark's contribution being three goals plus two assists. He continued his great record in the FA Cup with two goals against Wimbledon in the semi final, becoming Blues' top scorer with five goals as they reached their fifth FA Cup Final, before creating a 20th-century record with his fourth FA Cup winners medal, following the 2-0 victory over Middlesbrough.

Manchester U (From apprentice on 5/11/80) FL 85+4/37 FLC 5+1/4 FAC 10/4 Others 14+2/2 (£2,500,000 to Barcelona on 1/7/86)
Manchester U (£1,500,000 on 20/7/88) F/PL 251+5/82 FLC 32/12 FAC 34+1/13 Others 27+1/8
Chelsea (£1,500,000 on 6/7/95) PL 63+3/16 FLC 4/1 FAC 12+1/9

HUGHES Michael Eamonn
Born: Larne, 2 August 1971
Height: 5'7" Weight: 10.13
International Honours: NI: 37; U23-2; U21-1; Yth; Sch

After two seasons on loan from the French club, Strasbourg, the Northern Ireland international winger finally made the move permanent by signing a three-year contract for West Ham in the summer of 1996. He started last season on fire, with three goals in the first seven games, two of them contributing to victories, but the best - from 30 yards - being merely a consolation goal in a 4-1 defeat at Middlesbrough. Although that was the end of his scoring exploits for the campaign, he remained an automatic first choice, playing on either flank, although traditionally a more left-sided player.

Manchester C (From trainee on 17/8/88) FL 25+1/1 FLC 5 FAC 1 Others 1 (£450,000 to RS Strasbourg in 1992 close season)
West Ham U (Loaned on 29/11/94) PL 15+2/2 FAC 2

West Ham U (Loaned on 2/10/95) PL 28 FLC 2 FAC 3/1
West Ham U (Free on 12/8/96) PL 31+2/3 FLC 4 FAC 2

HUGHES John Paul
Born: Hammersmith, 19 April 1976
Height: 6'0" Weight: 11.7
International Honours: E: Sch

Whilst Chelsea created back-page headlines in 1996-97 by signing a string of big-name continental stars, their famous footballing "production line" is still producing young talent good enough for the Premiership, with five homegrown youngsters making their full debuts in the 1996-97 season. The fourth of these debutants made a stunning entrance into big-time football when coming on as a half-time substitute for Dennis Wise against Derby at the Bridge on 18 January. Picking the ball up in his own half in the left-back position, he played three give and goes with different players, continued to run into the penalty area, drew the Rams' 'keeper and calmly slid the ball past him with the aplomb of a veteran to score one of the goals of the season. Five weeks later he made his full debut away to the same opposition and created Chelsea's first goal with a superb defence-splitting pass. Paul's career has been hampered by a series of serious injuries, including shin splints, ankle injuries and, most recently, a pelvic strain which sidelined him for 11 months. With developing talent such as Paul and Jody Morris challenging the international players for midfield places the future looks very bright for Chelsea.

Chelsea (From trainee on 11/7/94) PL 8+4/2 FAC 2

Paul Hughes

HUGHES Stephen (Steve) John
Born: Reading, 18 September 1976
Height: 6'0" Weight: 12.12
Club Honours: FAYC '94
International Honours: E: U21-4; Yth; Sch

Classy left-sided Arsenal midfielder who graduated to captaining the England U21 side in 1996-97, as well as impressing the

Steve Hughes

HULBERT Robin James
Born: Plymouth, 14 March 1980
Height: 5'9" Weight: 10.5
International Honours: E: Yth; Sch

A first year trainee and England schoolboy international with Swindon Town, the teenage midfielder made a surprisingly early first-team debut at the age of 16 years and 195 days when he was selected as a substitute for the second-leg Coca-Cola Cup tie at Queens Park Rangers last September, entering the fray in the closing minute of extra time.
Swindon T (Trainee) FLC 0+1

HUMES Anthony (Tony)
Born: Blyth, 19 March 1966
Height: 5'11" Weight: 11.0

As captain of Wrexham, Tony enjoyed another very committed successful season in 1996-97, alongside Brian Carey in the heart of the defence. Epitomising the word battler, his strong, aggressive, but fair play endeared him to the fans, and he was a fine example to younger players in giving 100 per cent for their clubs. Also popped up with a few goals and looks to be one of Brian Flynn's best buys
Ipswich T (From apprentice on 26/5/83) FL 107+13/10 FLC 6 FAC 4/1 Others 10/1
Wrexham (£40,000 on 27/3/92) FL 159+4/8 FLC 7 FAC 18/1 Others 13

HUMPHREY John
Born: Paddington, 31 January 1961
Height: 5'10" Weight: 11.4
Club Honours: FMC '91; Div 1 '94

A former colleague of new manager, Steve Gritt, at Charlton, the veteran right back was signed from Gillingham on a free transfer last January to add some experienced support to Brighton's youthful back line. Taking over the number two berth from an out-of-touch Peter Smith in March, John performed well during the crucial run in as the Seagulls battled successfully for Football League survival, before being given a free transfer during the summer.
Wolverhampton W (From apprentice on 14/2/79) FL 149/3 FLC 8 FAC 7
Charlton Ath (£60,000 on 22/7/85) FL 194/3 FLC 13 FAC 9 Others 15/1
Crystal Palace (£400,000 on 16/8/90) F/PL 153+7/2 FLC 23+2 FAC 8+1 Others 8+1
Reading (Loaned on 9/12/93) FL 8 Others 1
Charlton Ath (Free on 13/7/95) FL 28 FLC 6 FAC 2
Gillingham (Free on 16/8/96) FL 9 FLC 3 Others 1
Brighton & Hove A (Free on 14/1/97) FL 11

HUMPHREYS Richard (Richie) John
Born: Sheffield, 30 November 1977
Height: 5'10" Weight: 11.3
International Honours: E: U21-3

Richie had a great start to his first full season in the Sheffield Wednesday side in 1996-97, scoring three goals in his first four games when playing as an out-and-out striker. He lost his place to a fit David Hirst, but continued to remain a regular member of the squad, making further appearances in a left-sided midfield role and also as a regular on the bench, plus further games up front.

new manager at Highbury, Arsene Wenger. Showing great skills from midfield, running at defenders and producing quality passes to set the front men up in the reserve side, Steve came off the bench at Sunderland in January to make his seasonal Premiership debut and continued his progress on the same ground four days later in the third round FA Cup replay, scoring his first goal for the club in a 2-0 win. Appearing 14 times in all from then on, mainly when standing in for Paul Merson, the youngster continued his rise to celebrity when scoring the first in a 2-0 win at Southampton, a result that kept the Gunners on target for championship challenge. Looks an excellent bet for future honours in the game.
Arsenal (From trainee on 15/7/95) PL 10+6/1 FLC 0+1 FAC 2/1

Richie Humphreys

His early form also saw him gain England U21 recognition and he looks to have a good career ahead of him.

Sheffield Wed (From trainee on 8/2/96) PL 15+19/3 FLC 1+1 FAC 3+1/2

HUNT Andrew (Andy)
Born: Thurrock, 9 June 1970
Height: 6'0" Weight: 12.0

Andy did not have a brilliant season for West Brom in 1996-97 on his own admittance, but he grafted hard and long and always gave 100 per-cent effort up front, sometimes being the lone attacker. He did well alongside both Bob Taylor and Paul Peschisolido, always working his socks off, no matter what the circumstances. Tall and rangy, he has the knack of being in the right place at the right time, finishing the campaign as the club's leading scorer with 16 goals, including a smartly-taken hat trick in the 3-2 home win over Reading.

Newcastle U (£150,000 from Kettering T on 29/1/91) FL 34+9/11 FLC 3/1 FAC 2/2 Others 3
West Bromwich A (£100,000 on 25/3/93) FL 163+11/63 FLC 8/3 FAC 5/2 Others 8+1/3

HUNT David
Born: Durham, 5 March 1980
Height: 5'7" Weight: 12.0

A first-year Darlington trainee, David impressed so much at Feethams last season that he was given the chance to come of the first-team subs' bench, albeit for just two minutes, at Exeter on 22 February, still 11 days short of his 17th birthday. Strong, very quick, comfortable on the ball, and a super passer, informed insiders rate the young left back an exciting prospect.

Darlington (Trainee) FL 0+1

HUNT James Malcolm
Born: Derby, 17 December 1976
Height: 5'8" Weight: 10.3

After progressing quite well towards the end of 1995-96, the Notts County central midfielder was released during the summer of 1997, despite having impressed in the reserves, and played in 12 first team games, which included a 90th minute equaliser at Scunthorpe in the AWS competition. Quick and a good passer, he will be looking to stay in the Football League.

Notts Co (From trainee on 15/7/94) FL 15+4/1 FAC 0+1 Others 2+2/1

HUNT Jonathan Richard
Born: Camden, 2 November 1971
Height: 5'10" Weight: 12.3
Club Honours: Div 2 '95; AMC '95

As Birmingham's Player of the Season and top scorer in 1995-96, Jon looked to be a key member of Trevor Francis' side until damaging his knee against Ipswich at St Andrews last October. Despite being a good all-round player, stylish with a fair shot in either boot, he failed to regain his first-team place and was condemned to reserve football after Francis decided to sign Anders Limpar and use the more predictable Andy Legg and Martin Grainger in wide areas. *Stop Press:* Joined Derby County for £500,000 during the summer, in a deal that saw Darren Wassall travelling in the other direction.

Barnet (From juniors in 1989-90) FL 12+21 FLC 1 FAC 0+1 Others 6+2
Southend U (Free on 20/7/93) FL 41+8/6 FLC 1+3 FAC 1 Others 6+1
Birmingham C (£50,000 on 16/9/94) FL 67+10/18 FLC 10+5/2 FAC 3+1/1 Others 8/4

HUNTER Barry Victor
Born: Coleraine, 18 November 1968
Height: 6'3" Weight: 12.9
Club Honours: WC '95
International Honours: NI: 11; B-1; Yth

Signed from Wrexham during the 1996 close season to replace Adrian Williams, Barry quickly established himself at the heart of Reading's defence and also became club captain. A dominant centre back, who leads by example, and also a regular in the Northern Ireland side, a patella tendon injury meant that he was unable to play after the 2-0 win at QPR in March. The nephew of Alan Hunter, the former Ipswich and Northern Ireland international, he has good awareness, is a sound tackler, and has a good touch for such a big man.

Newcastle U (Signed from Coleraine on 2/11/87 - Freed during 1988 close season)
Wrexham (£50,000 from Crusaders on 20/8/93) FL 88+3/4 FLC 6 FAC 7+1/1 Others 15/1
Reading (£400,000 on 12/7/96) FL 26+1/2 FLC 1 FAC 1

HUNTER Roy Ian
Born: Middlesbrough, 29 October 1973
Height: 5'10" Weight: 12.8

Is a Northampton midfielder who can convert to defence when needed. Another busy player, who has become a favourite at Sixfields, Roy missed a large portion of last season through injury. Is the club penalty taker, with a 100 per-cent record, and a long-throw expert.

West Bromwich A (From trainee on 4/3/92) FL 3+6/1 Others 4+1
Northampton T (Free on 2/8/95) FL 52+18/6 FLC 4 FAC 3 Others 8/1

HURDLE Augustus (Gus) Athel
Born: Kensington, 14 October 1973
Height: 5'8" Weight: 11.11
International Honours: Barbados: 2

A Brentford right back noted for his speed, Gus was the regular full back until last

January when injury and then Carl Hutchings' fine form forced him onto the sidelines. Went abroad to make his international debut for Barbados before returning for the Bees' three play-off games. Can also play in midfield and central defence if required.
Fulham (From trainee on 3/7/92)
Brentford (Free on 5/10/93) FL 46+8 FLC 8 FAC 2+1 Others 5

HURST Glynn
Born: Barnsley, 17 January 1976
Height: 5'10" Weight: 11.6
With the introduction of a number of new faces at Barnsley in 1996-97, Glyn found his first team chances limited to a bare minimum, his one start being in the unaccustomed left-wing back position. With a view to playing first team football, the hard-running striker had a spell on loan at Mansfield before being released during the summer.
Barnsley (Free from Tottenham H juniors on 13/7/94) FL 0+8 FLC 1
Swansea C (Loaned on 15/12/95) FL 2/1
Mansfield T (Loaned on 18/11/96) FL 5+1 Others 0+1

HURST Paul Michael
Born: Sheffield, 25 September 1974
Height: 5'7" Weight: 10.4
Club Honours: AMC '96
Small in stature but big in heart, Paul is one of the Rotherham crowd's favourites and he was yet another player who was called upon to fulfil a variety of different roles in 1996-97. Essentially left footed, he can play at the back and in midfield, where he also has an eye for goal, an ability that was demonstrated at Shrewsbury in March when he nipped in to score with all the aplomb of a natural striker. Can run all day and never knows when he is beaten.
Rotherham U (From trainee on 12/8/93) FL 68+19/4 FLC 2 FAC 3/1 Others 9+1

HUTCHINGS Carl Emil
Born: Hammersmith, 24 September 1974
Height: 5'11" Weight: 11.0
Wholehearted Brentford player who is now maturing into an extremely talented second division footballer. Had an early season run in central midfield in 1996-97 and scored his first ever goal (versus Walsall) in his 100th league appearance, following it up with another two games later. Took over at right back in January, having an excellent spell in that position, before ending the campaign at centre back due to Barry Ashby's injury and being, arguably, the Bees' Man of the Match in all three play-off games. He certainly took the eye when clearing shots off the line twice in the final at Wembley.
Brentford (From trainee on 12/7/93) FL 101+18/2 FLC 5+1 FAC 9+1 Others 11+3

HUTCHISON Donald (Don)
Born: Gateshead, 9 May 1971
Height: 6'2" Weight: 11.8
International Honours: S: B-1
The skilful Sheffield United player once again enjoyed a mixed season at the club in 1996-97, putting in some excellent

performances from central midfield but being less involved when asked to play wide right, due to injuries and suspensions of others. At his best when coming from midfield to link up with the attack, Don scored three goals, including the winner at West Bromwich, but again had problems with bookings which led to accumulating 45 penalty points during the season. Was unluckily injured in the play-off final, a factor that may well have contributed to United's eventual defeat.
Hartlepool U (From trainee on 20/3/90) FL 19+5/2 FLC 1+1 FAC 2 Others 1
Liverpool (£175,000 on 27/11/90) F/PL 33+12/7 FLC 7+1/2 FAC 1+2 Others 3+1/1
West Ham U (£1,500,000 on 30/8/94) PL 30+5/11 FLC 3/2 FAC 0+1
Sheffield U (£1,200,000 on 11/1/96) FL 56+4/5 FLC 3+1 FAC 1 Others 2+1

HUTT Stephen Graham
Born: Middlesbrough, 19 February 1979
Height: 6'3" Weight: 12.0
Promising midfielder who has established a good reputation playing for the Hartlepool junior and reserve sides. So far, Stephen has had to be content with only brief tastes of first-team football – he played only five minutes in 1995-96, then last season played just a further six minutes when coming on as substitute against Burnley in the Auto Windscreens Shield match. He is one of five second-year YTS players to be offered professional terms by the Pool.
Hartlepool U (Trainee) FL 0+1 Others 0+1

HUXFORD Richard John
Born: Scunthorpe, 25 July 1969
Height: 5'11" Weight: 12.2
Unable to break into Bradford's team on a regular basis in 1996-97, having previously been first choice, Richard had a spell at Peterborough on loan in October, hardly putting a foot wrong in seven games, before signing for Burnley in January. Predominately a full back, he was initially used as the right-wing back in place of the injured Gary Parkinson, but failed to hold his place and was subsequently employed mainly from the bench, playing either in defence or in midfield. Is a reliable and wholehearted player who never gives up the cause.
Barnet (Signed from Kettering T on 6/8/92) FL 33/1 FLC 2 FAC 2 Others 2+1
Millwall (Free on 16/7/93) FL 25+7 FLC 1+1/1 FAC 1 Others 3
Birmingham C (Loaned on 21/2/94) FL 5
Bradford C (£50,000 on 7/10/94) FL 55+6/2 FLC 5+1 FAC 3+1 Others 1
Peterborough U (Loaned on 4/10/96) FL 7
Burnley (Free on 21/1/97) FL 2+7 Others 1

HYDE Graham
Born: Doncaster, 10 November 1970
Height: 5'8" Weight: 11.11
A Yorkshireman, and thus well liked by the Sheffield Wednesday fans, Graham had to wait a while before breaking into the side last season, but when he did he again became a regular in the midfield as a combative player who always gave 100 per cent. He retained his spot until a couple of injuries ended his campaign early, the second coming in the FA Cup sixth round tie with Wimbledon. Having improved the

passing side of his game to good effect, and also become a player who can be relied upon to score an important goal or two, Graham now approaches 200 games as an unsung hero for his only professional club.
Sheffield Wed (From trainee on 17/5/88) F/PL 112+37/10 FLC 17+3/2 FAC 12+5/2 Others 4/1

HYDE Micah Anthony
Born: Newham, 10 November 1974
Height: 5'9" Weight: 11.5
1996-97 was an excellent season for this classy Cambridge midfield player, his good form bringing him to the attention of a number of bigger clubs. A right-footed, skilful ball player, with real passing ability, he also attacked well and was joint leading scorer for the team, many of his goals being winners or equalisers.
Cambridge U (From trainee on 19/5/93) FL 89+18/13 FLC 3 FAC 7+2 Others 4+1

Micah Hyde (left)

HYDE Paul David
Born: Hayes, 7 April 1963
Height: 6'1" Weight: 15.5
Club Honours: GMVC '93; FAT '93
Another experienced goalkeeper who joined Leyton Orient, originally on a non-contract basis from Leicester, as cover for the injuries to Peter Caldwell, Peter Shilton and Luke Weaver, he made a good impression in four games before a brief return to Leicester. Came back just 14 days later, signing a two-year contract, and soon made the first team number one spot his own. An excellent shot stopper, he is equally good at taking crosses.
Wycombe W (£15,000 from Hayes on 6/7/93) FL 105 FLC 10 FAC 13 Others 13
Leicester C (Free on 15/2/96)
Leyton Orient (Free on 3/2/97) FL 4
Leicester C (Free on 28/2/97)
Leyton Orient (Free on 14/3/97) FL 9

Professional Footballers Association
2 Oxford Court
Bishopsgate
Manchester
M2 3WQ

Tel: 0161 236 0575
Fax: 0161 228 7229

* * * * *

PFA Financial Management
91 Broad Street
Birmingham
B15 1AU

Tel: 0121 644 5277
Fax: 0121 644 5288

* * * * *

PFA Enterprises Ltd
Suite 9, 4th Floor
52 Haymarket
London
SW1Y 4RP

Tel: 0171 839 8663
Fax: 0171 839 2097

IGA Andrew
Born: Kampala, Uganda, 9 December 1977
Height: 6'1" Weight: 12.3
Andrew made a surprise debut for Millwall in 1996-97, coming on as a substitute after Tim Carter had earlier injured his hand in a pre-match warm up, before starting the AWS game against Colchester. Came through the Lions' youth set up and had been in excellent form for the reserves, showing himself to be quick and agile and a good shot stopper. Was surprisingly released at the beginning of April.
Millwall (From juniors on 13/6/95) FL 0+1 Others 1

IGOE Samuel (Sammy) Gary
Born: Spelthorne, 30 September 1975
Height: 5'6" Weight: 10.8
Having made just four starts before the 1996-97 season began, Sammy became an integral part of the Portsmouth squad, starting nearly half of the games during the course of the campaign and scoring two goals in the process. His all-round play, awareness of others, and first touch, show he has a good future in the game and maybe he could become a regular fixture in the starting line up in 1997-98.
Portsmouth (From trainee on 15/2/94) FL 26+37/2 FLC 3+3 FAC 0+2

ILLINGWORTH Jeremy Marcus
Born: Huddersfield, 20 May 1977
Height: 5'10" Weight: 11.11
One of a crop of promising homegrown Huddersfield youngsters, Jeremy made his debut after coming on as a substitute at Reading last January, and went on to start the final two games of the season. A left-sided full back or midfielder, his style of play is to win the ball and pass it.
Huddersfield T (From trainee on 27/6/95) FL 2+1

ILLMAN Neil David
Born: Doncaster, 29 April 1975
Height: 5'9" Weight: 11.5
Having his first full season in the Football League with Plymouth in 1996-97, Neil proved to be a very quick and lively centre forward, always pursuing defenders and causing havoc. The possessor of a strong left foot, which was often used to deliver some telling corner kicks and crosses, he scored his first league goal against Gillingham in October and looks ready to step up in 1997-98.
Middlesbrough (From trainee on 23/3/93) FL 0+1 FLC 0+1 Others 3+1 (Free to Eastwood T on 26/2/94)
Plymouth Arg (£15,000 on 27/3/96) FL 12+13/4 FAC 2 Others 1+1/1
Cambridge U (Loaned on 28/3/96) FL 1+4

IMMEL Eike
Born: Marburg, Germany, 27 November 1960
Height: 6'2" Weight: 13.5

International Honours: West Germany: 19
Having kept goal for Manchester City in all league and cup matches in 1995-96, and proving to be sound and reliable, if unspectacular, Eike started the first four league games of last season. When Alan Ball left, the stand-in manager, Asa Hartford, retained him for the home game against Charlton, but from then on he was left out on the promise that more talking was needed between goalkeeper and defence. It then transpired that he had carried a long-running shoulder injury and was allowed to go back to Germany for treatment at his own expense. Returned in early spring, but unable to regain first team recognition and with his contract up on 30 June, he departed at the end of the season.
Manchester C (£400,000 from VFB Stuttgart on 17/8/95) P/FL 42 FLC 3 FAC 5

IMPEY Andrew (Andy) Rodney
Born: Hammersmith, 30 September 1971
Height: 5'8" Weight: 11.2
International Honours: E: U21-1
In comparison to 1995-96, last season had to go down as a disappointing one, as injuries, loss of form, and suspension, prevented him from having a prolonged run in the QPR side. A pacy wide player, who is probably more at home on the left-hand side, and loves taking defenders on in order to get in telling crosses, Andy scored twice in the league, including an equaliser in a 1-1 draw at Norwich and another in an incredible fight back from 4-0 down to 4-4 at Port Vale. Finishing the campaign in good form, appearing in the final 12 games, he looks to hold down a regular place this coming season as Rangers try to rejoin the elite. *Stop Press:* Was reported to have signed a four-year contract for West Ham during the summer.
Queens Park R (£35,000 from Yeading on 14/6/90) F/PL 177+10/13 FLC 15+1/3 FAC 7+3/1 Others 0+2/1

INGLETHORPE Alexander (Alex) Matthew
Born: Epsom, 14 November 1971
Height: 5'11" Weight: 11.6
An attacking Leyton Orient midfielder converted from centre forward by Tommy Taylor, he had a knack of arriving late in the box and getting into goalscoring positions. Despite spending much of the first part of last season injured, only returning in early December, Alex finished the campaign as top scorer with eight, a sum which included a goal in each of the last four games.
Watford (From juniors on 1/7/90) FL 2+10/2 FLC 1+2 Others 1+1/1
Barnet (Loaned on 23/3/95) FL 5+1/3
Leyton Orient (Signed on 19/5/95) FL 40+6/17 FLC 2 FAC 0+1 Others 1+1

INGRAM Stuart Denevan (Denny)
Born: Sunderland, 27 June 1976
Height: 5'10" Weight: 12.1
For most of 1996-97, Denny looked the ideal team member, playing with total commitment when turning out for Hartlepool in a variety of defensive and midfield positions. Unfortunately, late in the season a minor disagreement with some

supporters soured things and in the closing weeks he was no longer an automatic choice. Hopefully, this is all behind him now, as he is ample proof that the youth scheme can produce quality players.
Hartlepool U (From trainee on 5/7/94) FL 114+4/3 FLC 8+1 FAC 4 Others 5

INGRAM Rae
Born: Manchester, 6 December 1974
Height: 5'11" Weight: 12.8
Following a promising debut for Manchester City in 1995-96, after which he received a foot injury and played no more, last season was almost a repeat. Again selected by caretaker manager, Asa Hartford, he played four full games before dropping out of contention for no particular reason. Then, having received a nasty nose injury in a home reserve game against York, he had to have his nose rebuilt. Although coming back into the first team under new manager, Frank Clark, and holding the number three spot down with an impressive run of eight league and cup games, Rae was yet another young player who had to make way for experienced signings. Good on the overlap and an excellent crosser of the ball, he can also play in the centre of defence if required.
Manchester C (From trainee on 9/7/93) P/FL 18+5 FLC 1 FAC 4

Rae Ingram

INMAN Niall Edward
Born: Wakefield, 6 February 1978
Height: 5'8" Weight: 10.6
International Honours: Ei: U21-1

Having made his first-team debut for Peterborough while still a trainee in 1995-96, Neil signed professional forms for the club during the 1996 close season, but was used most sparingly, making just one start and four subs' appearances, and being loaned out to Cambridge City. A recent Republic of Ireland U21 international, this tricky youngster who can play on either flank and can deliver excellent crosses for the big men, is sure to figure strongly in 1997-98.

Peterborough U (From trainee on 3/7/96) FL 1+3 FLC 1 FAC 0+1

INNES Gary John
Born: Consett, 7 October 1977
Height: 5'7" Weight: 11.7
International Honours: E: Yth

An England U18 international and recently out of time as a Sheffield United trainee, Gary signed for Darlington during the 1996 close season. However, after making only one first team start, plus 15 appearances as a substitute, mainly in midfield, he was released in March and joined Gateshead.

Darlington (Free from Sheffield U juniors on 30/7/96) FL 1+14 FLC 0+1

IRELAND Simon Piers
Born: Barnstaple, 23 November 1971
Height: 5'11" Weight: 11.12
International Honours: E: Sch

Simon joined Doncaster on a permanent basis from Mansfield Town last January, after spending a couple of months on loan at Belle Vue. His ability to take on opposing defenders and deliver quality crosses soon made him a valued member of the first team. Scored his first league goal for the Rovers, at home to Cambridge United in November, having failed to score for Mansfield earlier in the season.

Huddersfield T (From juniors on 1/7/90) FL 10+9 FLC 1/1 FAC 0+1 Others 1+1
Wrexham (Loaned on 11/3/92) FL 2+3
Blackburn Rov (£200,000 on 3/11/92) PL 0+1
Mansfield T (£60,000 on 8/3/94) FL 89+5/11 FLC 9/1 FAC 6+1/1 Others 4+1
Doncaster Rov (Loaned on 18/10/96) FL 9/1
Doncaster Rov (£10,000 on 28/1/97) FL 18/1

IRONS Kenneth (Kenny)
Born: Liverpool, 4 November 1970
Height: 5'10" Weight: 12.2

At his happiest and most effective when playing in a "Libero" type role just behind the front line, Kenny still managed to contribute five goals to Tranmere's league campaign in 1996-97, while picking up five Man of the Match awards in the local evening paper. Despite his lack of searing pace, he possesses the ability to read the game well and never shirks a tackle.

Tranmere Rov (From trainee on 9/11/89) FL 234+31/35 FLC 18+4/4 FAC 11+2/3 Others 28+3/3

IRONSIDE Ian
Born: Sheffield, 8 March 1964
Height: 6'2" Weight: 13.10

A consistent goalkeeper, who is very agile and an excellent taker of high balls, he made his 200th senior appearance for Scarborough at Wigan last January. Enjoyed another fine season, despite missing several games due to a knee injury sustained at Chesterfield in the FA Cup. However, with young Kevin Martin emerging to contest the number one jersey, Ian was offered a free transfer at the end of the campaign.

Barnsley (From juniors on 17/9/82)
Scarborough (Free from North Ferriby U on 8/3/88) FL 88 FLC 2 FAC 2 Others 10
Middlesbrough (£80,000 on 15/8/91) F/PL 12+1 FLC 2
Scarborough (Loaned on 5/3/92) FL 7
Stockport Co (Signed on 23/9/93) FL 17+2 FAC 1 Others 1
Scarborough (Free on 23/3/95) FL 88 FLC 4 FAC 4 Others 2

IRVINE Stuart Christopher
Born: Hartlepool, 1 March 1979
Height: 5'9" Weight: 11.10

A quick and tenacious young striker who had just one substitute appearance for Hartlepool when he grabbed the local sports headlines by scoring on his full debut for his hometown club against Exeter City last November. Unfortunately, he was not able to build on this great start and, shortly after, his progress was slowed by a stress fracture. One of several promising second-year YTS players, he has been offered professional terms for 1997-98.

Hartlepool U (Trainee) FL 2+2/1 FAC 0+1 Others 0+1

IRWIN Joseph Denis
Born: Cork, 31 October 1965
Height: 5'8" Weight: 11.0
Club Honours: CS '90, '93, '97; ECWC '91; ESC '91; FLC '92; PL '93, '94, '96, '97; FAC '94, '96
International Honours: Ei: 45; B-1; U23-1; U21-3; Yth; Sch

A highly experienced Manchester United defender, who is a model of consistency, and a specialist goalscorer from set plays, Denis started last season in tremendous fashion, netting a goal in the opening Premiership game against Wimbledon before allowing John O'Kane a run out in the Coca-Cola Cup against Swindon. Returning to complete 14 consecutive Premiership games before he was struck down by injury, unfortunately, his omission from the side coincided with United's home defeat to Juventus in the Champions' League, although once recovered he missed only one other Premiership game, that against Spurs in January. With games coming thick and fast at the end of another hectic campaign, his experience was an invaluable asset as the club continued its search for major honours that ended with another championship medal for the effervescent Irishman.

Leeds U (From apprentice on 3/11/83) FL 72/1 FLC 5 FAC 3 Others 2
Oldham Ath (Free on 22/5/86) FL 166+1/4 FLC 19/3 FAC 13 Others 5
Manchester U (£625,000 on 20/6/90) F/PL 252+4/15 FLC 28+2 FAC 32/6 Others 31

ISAIAS Marques Soares
Born: Rio de Janeiro, Brazil, 17 November 1963
Height: 5'10" Weight: 12.10

The former Benfica star played only ten minutes of first-team football for Coventry in 1996-97, as a sub in an early season game against Liverpool, despite having a lively summer. Largely out of favour with the management, Marques then suffered a knee injury playing for the reserves in November and was unfit until April. Silky skills and fierce shooting ability are among his trademarks.

Coventry C (£500,000 from Benfica on 2/8/95) PL 9+3/2 FLC 2

IVERSON Steffen
Born: Oslo, Norway, 10 November 1976
Height: 6'1" Weight: 11.2
International Honours: Norway: U21

Signed from Rosenborg towards the end of last year, the Norwegian youngster made his debut in December at Coventry and, as an extremely talented striker, did not take long to demonstrate the skill, pace, and accuracy, which had led to Gerry Francis battling for his signature against the likes of Premiership rivals, Liverpool and Leeds. An awesome prospect, Steffen, despite his youth, showed poise and quick thinking that could turn a game and threaten the sharpest defence. His ability to run with the ball deep into the box, paired with his enthusiasm to strike from long range, being shown in early appearances against Manchester United, (the crossbar denying a spectacular goal) and at Sunderland, where his hat trick in the 4-0 win contributed to Spurs' best away performance of the season. Expect to see him hitting the headlines in 1997-98 for both Tottenham and his native Norway.

Tottenham H (£2,700,000 from Rosenborg, via Nationalkam, on 7/12/96) PL 16/6

IZZET Mustafa (Muzzy) Kemmel
Born: Mile End, 31 October 1974
Height: 5'10" Weight: 10.12
Club Honours: FLC '97

A right-footed Leicester midfielder, signed during the 1996 close season from Chelsea, having been on loan in the latter stages of 1995-96, Muzzy was a regular choice for the club in 1996-97. One drawback, however, although City would not have viewed it as such, was that his transfer fee which carried certain conditions escalated to £800,000. He also might have been called into the Turkish squad, due to his father's nationality, had he not rejected the compulsory national service that would have gone hand in hand with the footballing call up. Scored a fine goal to clinch the points at Aston Villa and another with a real piledriver at Middlesbrough, having earlier set the Foxes off on their Coca-Cola Cup run to Wembley with the opener at Scarborough back in round two. One of the midfield driving forces during an up and down campaign, his season was made complete following the 1-0 replay victory over Middlesbrough that brought the Coca-Cola Cup to Filbert Street for the first time in the club's history.

Chelsea (From trainee on 19/5/93)
Leicester C (£650,000 + on 28/3/96) P/FL 42+2/4 FLC 8/1 FAC 3 Others 3

Muzzy Izzet

PFA Enterprises Ltd
18 Oxford Court
Bishopsgate
Manchester
M2 3WQ

Tel: 0161 228 2733
Fax: 0161 236 4496

* * * * *

Football in the Community
11 Oxford Court
Bishopsgate
Manchester
M2 3WQ

Tel: 0161 236 0583
Fax: 0161 236 4459

* * * * *

F.F.E. & V.T.S. Ltd
2 Oxford Court
Bishopsgate
Manchester
M2 3WQ

Tel: 0161 236 0637
Fax: 0161 228 7229

JACK Rodney Alphonso
Born: St Vincent, 28 September 1972
Height: 5'7" Weight: 10.9
International Honours: St Vincent: 15
The St Vincent international proved to be one of the fastest and most exciting players in the lower division in 1996-97, his undoubted talents catching the eye of both Newcastle and Sunderland, where he spent brief training periods. However, with the work permit rules probably affecting both clubs reluctance to sign him, he remained at Torquay, alternating as a striker or wide midfielder.
Torquay U (Free from Lambada, St Vincent on 10/10/95) FL 42+5/12 FLC 2 FAC 3 Others 2

JACKSON Elliot
Born: Swindon, 27 August 1979
Height: 6'1" Weight: 13.0
A first-year professional at Oxford, the young goalkeeper kept a clean sheet on his debut at Tranmere last season, but dropped out on the return of the fit-again Phil Whitehead. Had a couple of further opportunities later in the campaign, but it was unfortunately at a time when the defence was leaking goals. A confident 'keeper, he takes his crosses well, is a good shot stopper, and is definitely one for the future.
Oxford U (From trainee on 2/7/96) FL 3

JACKSON Kirk Stewart
Born: Doncaster, 16 October 1976
Height: 5'11" Weight: 11.6
Striker. Freed by Sheffield Wednesday during the summer of 1996, having had no first-team opportunities at Hillsborough, Kirk signed for Scunthorpe and, although showing promise in pre-season games, was never given a proper run, appearing only five times. However, when coming on as a sub for David D'Auria at Hereford, he scored his solitary league goal within five minutes of a match ultimately lost 3-2. Was released at the end of the campaign.
Sheffield Wed (From trainee on 15/5/95)
Scunthorpe U (Free on 23/7/96) FL 0+4/1 Others 0+1

JACKSON Mark Graham
Born: Leeds, 30 September 1977
Height: 6'0" Weight: 11.3
International Honours: E: Yth
Yet another promising youngster at Leeds, locally-born Mark was given his full debut at Leicester City last September. Considering most of his reserve and junior appearances had been in central defence, his rise to prominence can only be measured in that he was a regular member of George Graham's squad, and that all of his first-team games were in midfield. A good passer of the ball, and really strong in the tackle, although he was rested in February after a run of 12 games, he appears to have a big future at Leeds.
Leeds U (From trainee on 1/7/95) PL 11+7 FAC 4

JACKSON Matthew (Matt) Alan
Born: Leeds, 19 October 1971
Height: 6'0" Weight: 12.12
Club Honours: FAC '95; CS '95
International Honours: E: U21-10; Sch
Unable to hold down a place at Everton last season, Matt went out on loan to Queens Park Rangers in August, playing seven games before returning to Goodison. His next loan stop was Birmingham at the end of October. After excelling in ten appearances at right back, finishing on the losing side just once, a permanent deal failed to materialise when the Blues dithered and his former Everton boss, Mike Walker, now at Norwich, nipped in to sign him on Christmas Eve. A composed right back, he arrived at Carrow Road, striking up an instant rapport with John Polston and Rob Newman, in immediately helping to plug up defensive gaps, and even scored a rare goal to put the gloss on a win over Portsmouth. Having made a great start with City, his composed and often superb displays augur well for the coming term.
Luton T (From juniors on 4/7/90) FL 7+2 FLC 2 Others 0+1
Preston NE (Loaned on 27/3/91) FL 3+1 Others 1
Everton (£600,000 on 18/10/91) F/PL 132+6/4 FLC 9 FAC 14/2 Others 4
Charlton Ath (Loaned on 26/3/96) FL 8 Others 2
Queens Park R (Loaned on 20/8/96) FL 7
Birmingham C (Loaned on 31/10/96) FL 10
Norwich C (£450,000 on 24/12/96) FL 19/2 FAC 2

JACKSON Michael James
Born: Runcorn, 4 December 1973
Height: 6'0" Weight: 13.8
Club Honours: Div 2 '97
International Honours: E: Yth
A regular performer in defence for Bury in 1996-97, Michael was utilised on the right-hand side of central defender, Chris Lucketti, but a desire to hold down a central role of his own saw the talented and highly popular defender, who also has an eye for a goal, move on to Preston in March for a surprisingly low fee. In playing seven games for North End, he immediately slotted in, proving strong and effective in the tackle, and producing powerful headers at both ends of the park.
Crewe Alex (From trainee on 29/7/92) FL 5 FLC 1 FAC 1 Others 2
Bury (Free on 13/8/93) FL 123+2/9 FLC 9/1 FAC 3 Others 12
Preston NE (£125,000 on 26/3/97) FL 7

JACKSON Peter Allan
Born: Bradford, 6 April 1961
Height: 6'0" Weight: 13.6
Club Honours: Div 3 '85
A vastly experienced Chester central defender, Peter made his 100th league appearance for the club at home to Barnet last March, immediately prior to being ruled out of any further action that season due to a hernia operation. Ironically, with him being given a free transfer during the summer, that was to be his last game for City. The Player of the Year in 1995-96 and captain again last season, he will be missed.
Bradford C (From apprentice on 7/4/79) FL 267+11/24 FLC 27/1 FAC 10+1 Others 4

Newcastle U (£250,000 on 23/10/86) FL 60/3 FLC 3 FAC 6 Others 3
Bradford C (£290,000 on 15/9/88) FL 55+3/5 FLC 7 FAC 4 Others 2
Huddersfield T (Free on 6/9/90) FL 152+3/3 FLC 11 FAC 13/1 Others 18/1
Chester C (Free on 29/9/94) FL 100/3 FLC 5 FAC 4 Others 3

JACOBS Wayne Graham
Born: Sheffield, 3 February 1969
Height: 5'9" Weight: 11.2
Had an outstanding season for Bradford in 1996-97, playing in the wing-back position, despite being out of action for four weeks with a broken collar bone. Taking over the captaincy when Lee Duxbury moved to Oldham in March, Wayne scored three spectacular goals, two of them in vital 1-1 draws, and was a vital element during the final weeks of a long, hard campaign as City ultimately saw off the threat of relegation. Voted Player of the Year, he shows great flair going forward and is very strong defensively.
Sheffield Wed (From apprentice on 3/1/87) FL 5+1 FLC 3 Others 1
Hull C (£27,000 on 25/3/88) FL 127+2/4 FLC 7 FAC 8 Others 6
Rotherham U (Free on 5/8/93) FL 40+2/2 FLC 4 FAC 1 Others 2
Bradford C (Free on 5/8/94) FL 103+2/4 FLC 9 FAC 7/2 Others 5

JAMES Anthony (Tony) Craig
Born: Sheffield, 27 June 1967
Height: 6'3" Weight: 14.7
A bargain buy from Hereford at the start of last season, Tony proved to be a superb central defender for Plymouth in a difficult campaign, being strong, quick, and good in the air. Very consistent, he would have been a regular apart from two injuries, the latter a serious knee problem which required an operation and is likely to keep him out of the team until around this coming Christmas. Having formed a good partnership with Mick Heathcote, he will be sorely missed.
Lincoln C (£6,000 from Gainsborough Trinity on 22/8/88) FL 24+5 FLC 2 Others 0+1
Leicester C (£150,000 on 23/8/89) FL 79+28/11 FLC 6 FAC 2/1 Others 3+1
Hereford U (Free on 25/7/94) FL 35/4 FLC 4 FAC 1 Others 5/1
Plymouth Arg (£60,000 + on 13/8/96) FL 34/1 FLC 1 FAC 3 Others 1

JAMES David Benjamin
Born: Welwyn Garden City, 1 August 1970
Height: 6'5" Weight: 14.5
Club Honours: FAYC '89; FLC '95
International Honours: E: 1; B-1; U21-10
Now established in the Liverpool goal, in the main, David continued to perform brilliantly in 1996-97, making breathtaking saves and keeping his team in the game when all seemed lost. His good form was also recognised at international level when selected by England for the Mexican match at the end of March and he was obviously delighted to keep a clean sheet in a 2-0 win. Unfortunately, the spotlight fell on him at the end of the campaign when, with the Reds aiming for the championship and not being in a position to drop points, he was blamed for occasionally rushing off his line

and not claiming the ball, which led to the opposition scoring several crucial goals. However, he has not lost his ability overnight and, with more work from the goalkeeping coach at Anfield, Joe Corrigan, this imposing figure will be back better than ever in 1997-98. An honest pro, David blamed his moments of madness on a love of personal computer games.

Watford (From trainee on 1/7/88) FL 89 FLC 6 FAC 2 Others 1
Liverpool (£1,000,000 on 6/7/92) PL 160+1 FLC 17 FAC 16 Others 13

JAMES Julian Colin
Born: Tring, 22 March 1970
Height: 5'10" Weight: 12.4
International Honours: E: U21-2

Generally had a sound season for Luton in 1996-97 as the regular right back. Good in the air and a hard tackler, Julian also showed promise when going forward, his 15-yard blaster defeating Derby in the first leg of the Coca-Cola Cup at Kenilworth Road in September. Missing just two league games, his was a major role in keeping the Hatters on course for promotion. Unfortunately, the term ended on a sour note when he was sent off for a second bookable offence in the first play-off semi final, the referee's decision allowing Crewe to dominate a game they could easily have lost.

Luton T (From trainee on 1/7/88) FL 239+19/13 FLC 15+1/1 FAC 20+1 Others 12+1
Preston NE (Loaned on 12/9/91) FL 6

JAMES Martin Joseph
Born: Crosby, 18 May 1971
Height: 5'10" Weight: 11.10

A serious back injury meant that he was restricted to just three appearances as a substitute for Rotherham in 1996-97 and a subsequent retirement from the full-time professional game. Extremely versatile, he had originally come to Millmoor as a left winger before moving to full back, where his ability to get forward was utilised to the full.

Preston NE (From trainee on 19/7/89) FL 92+6/11 FLC 6 FAC 4 Others 8+1
Stockport Co (£50,000 on 16/3/93) FL 13+19 FLC 2 FAC 0+1 Others 0+2
Rotherham U (£50,000 on 3/8/94) FL 40+4 FLC 2 FAC 3 Others 3

JANNEY Mark
Born: Romford, 2 December 1977
Height: 5'10" Weight: 11.5

A first year Spurs' professional, having left the YTS ranks during the 1996 close season, in order to further his experience, he was loaned to Brentford on transfer deadline day. With the Bees gunning for a second division promotion place, the young right winger stepped off the bench for his league debut just four days later and, with his very first touch, headed home the first goal in a 2-1 win at Gillingham. Made just one start before returning to White Hart Lane and being released during the summer.

Tottenham H (From trainee on 4/7/96)
Brentford (Loaned on 27/3/97) FL 1+1/1

JANSEN Matthew (Matt) Brooke
Born: Carlisle, 20 October 1977
Height: 5'11" Weight:10.13
Club Honours: AMC '97
International Honours: E: Yth

An inside forward of great promise, Matt is another of the cadre of Cumbrians who have come through into the Carlisle first team in recent years. In a memorable first appearance as a substitute last October, he transformed the team's display with an electric performance and in subsequent games he seldom failed to impress. Already an England U19 player, he is another who has a bright future in the game.

Carlisle U (From trainee on 18/1/96) FL 4+15/1 FLC 0+1 FAC 0+3 Others 1+3

JANSSON Jan
Born: Kalmar, Sweden, 26 January 1968
Height: 5'10" Weight: 11.2
International Honours: Sweden: 7

A former Swedish international midfielder who spent three months on loan at Port Vale from Norrkoping last season, Jan made an impressive debut at West Bromwich and helped to stiffen the midfield area, particularly away from home. He scored an excellent goal in the 4-4 draw with QPR, but after his best game, at Bradford City, he returned to Sweden to prepare for their new campaign. Although a permanent deal was discussed with a fee in the region of £250,000 mentioned, it never came to fruition.

Port Vale (Loaned from Norrkoping on 4/11/96) FL 10+1/1 FAC 1

JARMAN Lee
Born: Cardiff, 16 December 1977
Height: 6'2" Weight: 12.9
International Honours: W: U21-5; Yth

Although not as commanding in the centre of Cardiff's defence as in previous seasons at the start of 1996-97, once his confidence returned in the right-back position he began to blossom again, his passes being a joy to watch. Good in the air, as you would expect from one so tall, he is equally competent on the ground and should go a long way in the game. Continued to add to his Welsh U21 caps with appearances against San Marino, Holland (twice), and Belgium during the campaign.

Cardiff C (From trainee on 23/8/95) FL 58+6 FLC 2 FAC 3/1 Others 3+2

JEAN Earl Jude
Born: St Lucia, 9 October 1971
Height: 5'8" Weight: 11.4
International Honours: St Lucia: 4

A West Indian-born St Lucian international striker spent six years playing in Portugal before coming to Rotherham, via Ipswich, on a monthly basis last January, he scored on his debut in a substitute's role. For a small player, his ability to win the ball in the air was quite remarkable and he soon won the crowd's approval with his quick running and eye for goal.

Ipswich T (Free from Uniao de Coimbra Felgueiras on 6/12/96) FL 0+1
Rotherham U (Free on 23/1/97) FL 7+11/6

JEFFERS John Joseph
Born: Liverpool, 5 October 1968
Height: 5'10" Weight: 11.10
International Honours: E: Sch

The tricky left-winger was often a victim of the competition for places at Stockport in 1996-97, his inconsistency being his worst enemy, as he varied from brilliant – winning games on his own at times – to anonymous. However, he proved a good man to have on the bench, especially when coming on to score the winner against Watford at Edgeley Park, an important result in a run of end of season games that saw County ultimately promoted to the first division.

Liverpool (From apprentice on 13/10/86)
Port Vale (£30,000 on 11/12/88) FL 147+33/10 FLC 8+1 FAC 13+2 Others 13+2/1
Shrewsbury T (Loaned on 6/1/95) FL 3/1 Others 2
Stockport Co (Free on 16/11/95) FL 46+11/6 FLC 6+2 FAC 4+1 Others 3

JEMSON Nigel Bradley
Born: Hutton, 10 August 1969
Height: 5'10" Weight: 12.10
Club Honours: FLC '90; AMC '96
International Honours: E: U21-1

A striker signed from Notts County during the 1996 close season, Nigel turned out to be an inspired buy for Oxford and had the most productive period of his career, scoring five in the Coca-Cola Cup, including the winner against one of his former clubs, Sheffield Wednesday. Held play up well and worked hard, often coming a long way back for the ball, and showed excellent finishing skills too, scoring several headers, free kicks, and penalties – they all go in when your confidence is back and you are playing regularly.

Preston NE (From trainee on 6/7/87) FL 28+4/8 FAC 2/1 Others 5+1/5
Nottingham F (£150,000 on 24/3/88) FL 45+2/13 FLC 9/4 FAC 3+1/3 Others 1
Bolton W Loaned on 23/12/88) FL 4+1
Preston NE (Loaned on 15/3/89) FL 6+3/2 Others 2/1
Sheffield Wed (£800,000 on 17/9/91) F/PL 26+25/9 FLC 3+4 FAC 3+3/1 Others 2+2/1
Grimsby T (Loaned on 10/9/93) FL 6/2 Others 1
Notts Co (£300,000 on 8/9/94) FL 7+7/1 FLC 2+2/1 Others 1
Watford (Loaned on 12/1/95) FL 3+1
Rotherham U (Loaned on 15/2/96) FL 16/5 Others 2
Oxford U (£60,000 on 23/7/96) FL 44/18 FLC 7/5 FAC 1

JENKINS Iain
Born: Whiston, 24 November 1972
Height: 5'9" Weight: 11.9
International Honours: NI: 2; B-1

In 1996-97, Iain undoubtedly had the season of his life, making 46 appearances at left back for Chester, having missed most of the previous campaign due to injuries sustained in a car crash. Only 24 years old, and looking destined for greater things, his solid performances brought him to the attention of the Northern Ireland's manager, Bryan Hamilton, who promptly capped him twice after he had impressed with the "B" side. Ended the campaign as City's captain, following the injury to Peter Jackson.

Everton (From trainee on 4/6/91) PL 3+2 FLC 0+1

Bradford C (Loaned on 31/12/92) FL 6 Others 1
Chester C (Free on 13/8/93) FL 121+5 FLC 5+2
FAC 9+1 Others 11

JENKINS Lee David
Born: Pontypool, 28 June 1979
Height: 5'9" Weight: 11.0
International Honours: W: Yth; Sch
In making a goalscoring debut against Hereford last September, the 17-year-old trainee midfielder became Swansea's find of the season. Retaining his place in the team, he proved to be a real competitor and showed great maturity for one so young, before suffering a depressed fracture of the cheek bone against Bristol City in an AWS game, an injury which kept him on the sidelines for two months. His good form was also recognised by Wales who capped him at U18 level and included him in an U21 squad. Signed pro forms in December.
Swansea C (From trainee on 20/12/96) FL 21+2/2 FAC 1 Others 1

JENKINS Stephen (Steve) Robert
Born: Merthyr, 16 July 1972
Height: 5'11" Weight: 12.3
Club Honours: AMC '94
International Honours: W: 6; U21-2; Yth
In 1996-97, his first full season at Huddersfield after his transfer from Swansea, he established himself as first-choice right back where he was both solid and dependable and used his ability to read the game well. Originally a right winger, which would explain his pace and recovery capability, and now established as a Welsh international, Steve increased his tally of caps during the campaign.
Swansea C (From trainee on 1/7/90) FL 155+10/1 FLC 12+1 FAC 10+1 Others 26
Huddersfield T (£275,000 on 3/11/95) FL 64/1 FLC 5 FAC 6

JEPSON Ronald (Ronnie) Francis
Born: Stoke, 12 May 1963
Height: 6'1" Weight: 13.7
Club Honours: Div 2 '97
An experienced striker who was signed by Bury in July 1996 for a bargain basement fee from Huddersfield, his experience played an important role in helping to guide the Shakers to the division two championship in his first season at Gigg Lane in 1996-97. A particularly troublesome hamstring injury and an inflamed disc in his back, unfortunately, limited Ronnie's appearances during the campaign, but he was still able to chip in with 11 league and cup goals on his way to a medal and first division football in 1997-98.
Port Vale (Free from Nantwich T on 23/3/89) FL 12+10 FLC 1+1 FAC 1+1
Peterborough U (Loaned on 25/1/90) FL 18/5
Preston NE (£80,000 on 12/2/91) FL 36+2/8 FLC 2 Others 3/4
Exeter C (£60,000 on 29/7/92) FL 51+3/21 FLC 6/2 FAC 3/1 Others 4/1
Huddersfield T (£80,000 on 7/12/93) FL 95+12/36 FLC 6+1/2 FAC 4/3 Others 6/1
Bury (£40,000 on 27/7/96) FL 24+7/9 FLC 3 FAC 0+1 Others 1+1/2

Ronnie Jepson

JERKAN Nicola
Born: Croatia, 8 December 1964
Height: 6'4" Weight: 14.3
International Honours: Croatia: 31
The Croatian international was a big money signing for Nottingham Forest when they captured him from Real Ovieado in the summer of 1996, following some impressive displays in the European Championships. With the group games being played at the City Ground, Forest fans had also an early opportunity to see the defender/midfielder. Having started last season in defence, often playing as sweeper, he struggled as the side struggled and the best was not seen of him. A player whose obvious asset in his height, despite being a typical continental and comfortable on the ball, he had a few games in midfield and was another not to find the net.
Nottingham F (£1,000,000 from Real Oviedo on 26/7/96) PL 14

Eoin Jess

JESS Eoin
Born: Aberdeen, 13 December 1970
Height: 5'9" Weight: 11.6
Club Honours: SLC '89
International Honours: S: 13; B-2; U21-14
Season 1996-97 was disappointing for Coventry's Scottish international midfielder. A slight player who has superb ball skills, an excellent first touch and a good turn of speed, he started brightly but lost his place, somewhat unluckily, following the 4-0 defeat at Middlesbrough, after his lack of strength had been exposed a number of times and he seemed to need too much time on the ball. He struggled to score in the league, but netted vital FA Cup goals against Woking, and at Blackburn, when he had his best game of the season in the 2-1 victory. Normally played in midfield but, on occasion, he was used up front without great effect.
Aberdeen (Free from Glasgow Rangers juniors on 13/11/87) SL 167+34/50 SLC 19+2/4 SC 14+2/3 Others 8+2/6
Coventry C (£1,750,000 on 24/2/96) PL 28+11/1 FLC 1 FAC 4/2

Julian Joachim

JOACHIM Julian Kevin
Born: Peterborough, 20 September 1974
Height: 5'6" Weight: 12.11
International Honours: E: U21-9; Yth (UEFAC '93)
1996-97 was another frustrating term for the exciting Aston Villa forward as he spent much of his time on the first-team bench, making just five starts, having hoped for better in his second term at Villa Park. Able to be used on the right-hand side of midfield, or as a striker with speed in abundance and good feet, he opened his scoring account against Derby in the third match of the campaign, also scoring in the return at the Baseball Ground, before netting from what had seemed an impossible angle at Coventry in November. A regular scorer at reserve-team level, however, as you would expect, he will be looking to push for

the place vacated by Tommy Johnson's move to Celtic.

Leicester C (From trainee on 15/9/92) F/PL 77+22/25 FLC 7+2/3 FAC 4+1/1 Others 4+2/2
Aston Villa (£1,500,000 on 24/2/96) PL 7+19/5 FLC 1 FAC 1

JOBLING Kevin Andrew
Born: Sunderland, 1 January 1968
Height: 5'8" Weight: 12.0

After missing most of 1995-96 through injury, Kevin returned to full fitness last season, although kept out of his customary place on the left of defence by the consistency of Tony Gallimore, and took up the position on the other flank during the absence of John McDermott. Following the return of the latter to fitness, he moved to his former midfield role and, during the fight against relegation, was given the task of man marking key players and, in doing so, rendered ineffective some of the division's most highly-rated creators, before returning to the right of defence as the club's injury problems continued.

Leicester C (From apprentice on 9/1/86) FL 4+5 FAC 0+1 Others 3/2
Grimsby T (Signed on 19/2/88) FL 234+21/19 FLC 12+1 FAC 5+3/1 Others 5+4
Scunthorpe U (Loaned on 10/1/94) Others 1

JOBSON Richard Ian
Born: Holderness, 9 May 1963
Height: 6'1" Weight: 13.5
Club Honours: Div 2 '91
International Honours: E: B-2

Richard seemed determined to make his mark at Leeds in 1996-97 and fully justify the expectancy of the large fee paid to Oldham Athletic the previous October, when, having initially settled in quietly and efficiently, a knee ligament injury decimated his first season at the club. Therefore it was no surprise when he began the campaign in good form and appeared in the first ten games. Unfortunately, and frustratingly, he then suffered problems with the same knee before an exploratory operation in November revealed some quite serious damage, an injury which caused him to take no further part in the action. Hopefully, he can return in 1997-98 as new.

Watford (£22,000 from Burton A on 5/11/82) FL 26+2/4 FLC 2 FAC 0+1 Others 5+1
Hull C (£40,000 on 7/2/85) FL 219+2/17 FLC 12 FAC 13/1 Others 9
Oldham Ath (£460,000 on 30/8/90) F/PL 188+1/10 FLC 19/1 FAC 13 Others 4
Leeds U (£1,000,000 on 26/10/95) PL 22/1 FLC 3 FAC 1

JOHANSEN Michael Bro
Born: Glostrup, Denmark, 22 July 1972
Height: 5'10" Weight: 10.5
Club Honours: Div 1 '97
International Honours: Denmark: 3

An exciting winger signed from FC Copenhagen in the 1996 close season as part of a £2.25 million deal which included Per Frandsen, Michael soon established himself as a Bolton favourite, largely due to his attacking style of play when on the ball and his electric turn of pace. This gifted young player also likes a shot on goal, a fact highlighted by his double in the 6-1

hammering of Grimsby early on, and is certainly a name to watch out for in next season's Premiership campaign. Is a full Danish international.

Bolton W (£1,250,000 from FC Copenhagen on 14/8/96) FL 24+9/5 FLC 3 FAC 1+1

JOHNROSE Leonard (Lenny)
Born: Preston, 29 November 1969
Height: 5'10" Weight: 12.6
Club Honours: Div 2 '97

Only suspensions prevented the Bury midfield man from completing an ever-present season in 1996-97. Like his midfield partner Nick Daws, Lenny's game revolves around non-stop running and an ability to time his tackling to perfection, and he also scored some important goals, including one in the final game of the campaign at home to Millwall, the club's second, which made sure that the second division championship came to Gigg Lane.

Blackburn Rov (From trainee on 16/6/88) FL 20+22/11 FLC 2+1/1 FAC 0+3 Others 2
Preston NE (Loaned on 21/1/92) FL 1+2/1
Hartlepool U (£50,000 on 28/2/92) FL 59+7/11 FLC 5+1/4 FAC 5/1 Others 5
Bury (Signed on 7/12/93) FL 111+6/15 FLC 7+2 FAC 6/1 Others 9/1

JOHNSEN Erland
Born: Fredrikstad, Norway, 5 April 1967
Height: 6'1" Weight: 14.4
International Honours: Norway: 24

Remember the scene? 16 February 1997 and the FA Cup fifth round replay at Stamford Bridge between Chelsea and Leicester City. After 118 goalless minutes, Blues' substitute, Erland, goes on a buccaneering run into the Leicester penalty area and crashes to the ground, referee Mike Reed points to the spot, Frank Leboeuf calmly strokes home the penalty and Chelsea are through to the sixth round and controversy rages in the sports pages of the national press. Perhaps all the fuss was a little unfair on the big Norwegian because goalscoring and Erland are hardly synonymous. Later, playing in the FA Cup semi final, the popular, tough-tackling central defender gave a towering performance, winning everything in the air against the tall Wimbledon strike force. Played in the first six matches of the season but dropped to the subs' bench once Michael Duberry returned from injury and did not start the next 20 matches. Out of contract, he has now returned home to Norway to play his future football.

Chelsea (£306,000 from Bayern Munich on 6/12/89) F/PL 135+10/1 FLC 7 FAC 16+4 Others 12

JOHNSEN Jean Ronny
Born: Norway, 10 June 1969
Height: 6'2" Weight: 12.8
Club Honours: PL '97; CS '97
International Honours: Norway: 30

A classy midfielder or central defender, Ronny was one of Alex Ferguson's most inspirational signings, when he joined Manchester United from Besiktas in the 1996 close season. After showing his immense versatility when standing in for the injured Nicky Butt in the opening game of

the season at Wimbledon, the Norwegian international assumed a role in the centre of defence, where his timing in the pass and tackle were of the highest quality. Having missed only seven games up to the turn of the year, he kept his place in the side, despite a niggling hamstring injury, and was one of United's key players during their quest for major honours that ended in him winning a championship medal.

Manchester U (£1,200,000 from Besiktas on 26/7/96) PL 26+5 FAC 2 Others 9

JOHNSON Alan Keith
Born: Wigan, 19 February 1971
Height: 6'0" Weight: 12.0

Signed on the eve of the 1996-97 season from Lincoln, Alan became the strong man of the Rochdale defence and a huge favourite with the fans for his wholehearted approach. An ever present and Player of the Year, his power in the air also earned him his share of goals from set pieces.

Wigan Ath (From trainee on 1/4/89) FL 163+17/13 FLC 7+2/2 FAC 14+2/1 Others 14+3/3
Lincoln C (Signed on 15/2/94) FL 57+6 FLC 2 FAC 3 Others 3+1/1
Preston NE (Loaned on 1/9/95) FL 2
Rochdale (Free on 16/8/96) FL 46/4 FLC 2 FAC 2/1 Others 1

JOHNSON Andrew (Andy) James
Born: Bristol, 2 May 1974
Height: 6'0" Weight: 12.0
International Honours: E: Yth

Norwich City never lost when Andy scored in 1996-97 and five goals in his first nine appearances during the season left everyone with high hopes for the campaign. A key figure when fit, which was not very often, his two goals against Ipswich Town were offset by his stunning the fans with a March transfer request. Able to play in defence and midfield, as well as up front he is extremely quick and an excellent passer who links with his team mates superbly well. *Stop press:* Reportedly transferred back to Nottingham Forest during the summer for £2.2 million.

Norwich C (From trainee on 4/3/92) F/PL 56+10/13 FLC 6+1/2 FAC 2

JOHNSON Christopher (Chris)
Born: Brighton, 25 January 1979
Height: 5'8" Weight: 11.2

A young Watford midfield player and still a trainee at the time, Chris made an assured debut at the age of 17 against Plymouth at Vicarage Road last August, showing good passing skills. An identical twin, his brother Andy is also on Watford's books as a striker, both lads signed professional terms during last season.

Watford (From trainee on 13/2/97) FL 1 FAC 0+1

JOHNSON David Anthony
Born: Kingston, Jamaica, 15 August 1976
Height: 5'6" Weight: 12.3
Club Honours: FAYC '95; Div 2 '97

The diminutive Bury striker has now enjoyed promotion in both his two seasons with the Shakers so far, since arriving from Manchester United, and is an exciting prospect with a low centre of gravity, possessing great pace, who will undoubtedly

continue to improve in future years. Although his main aim will be to improve upon his final 1996-97 goal tally of eight league goals, three of them – at Peterborough, at home to Chesterfield, and the return with Posh – earned the club seven points and was an immense help on the road to the first division title.

Manchester U (From trainee on 1/7/94)
Bury (Free on 5/7/95) FL 55+25/12 FLC 4+3/1 FAC 1+1 Others 3+2/1

JOHNSON Gavin
Born: Stowmarket, 10 October 1970
Height: 5'11" Weight: 11.12
Club Honours: Div 2 '92; Div 3 '97

Flexible Wigan Athletic player who can play anywhere down the left flank, either at full back or in wide midfield. Dogged by groin problems towards the end of last season, which often meant playing through the pain barrier, Gavin was a threat when coming forward to score some spectacular goals from dead-ball situations, including the winner in the away victory at Exeter. Despite not being available for the final game, his 37 league appearances fully warranted the third division championship medal that came his way.

Ipswich T (From trainee on 1/3/89) F/PL 114+18/11 FLC 10+1/2 FAC 2/2 Others 3+1/1
Luton T (Free on 4/7/95) FL 4+1
Wigan Ath (£15,000 on 15/12/95) FL 64/6 FLC 2 FAC 1 Others 1

JOHNSON Marvin Anthony
Born: Wembley, 29 October 1968
Height: 6'0" Weight: 13.6

Good in the air and a solid tackler, Marvin enjoyed another successful season at centre back for Luton in 1996-97, playing effectively alongside Steve Davis. A favourite with the crowd, due to his whole-hearted displays and ability to recover situations, he was an automatic choice and missed matches only when unavailable. Unfortunately, he missed the first leg play-off match through injury, where his fighting defensive qualities were sorely missed, especially late in the game when the Hatters were reduced to ten men.

Luton T (From apprentice on 12/11/86) FL 233+13/4 FLC 16+2/1 FAC 11+1/1 Others 12

JOHNSON Michael Owen
Born: Nottingham, 4 July 1973
Height: 5'11" Weight: 11.12
Club Honours: AIC '95

Nicknamed "Magic", Michael is a cultured Birmingham central defender who can play anywhere in the back line, having good man-marking ability and impressive aerial powers. At one stage last season it was thought that he would be surplus to Trevor Francis' requirements, due to the availability of Steve Bruce, Garry Ablett, and Gary Breen but, able to use his pace to cut out danger in tight situations, he continued to shine as the campaign wore on, making 39 first-team appearances in all, while still searching for his first senior goal. Predominantly a left-sided player, he also showed up well on the overlap.

Notts Co (From trainee on 9/7/91) FL 102+5 FLC 9 FAC 4 Others 15+1
Birmingham C (£225,000 on 1/9/95) FL 59+9 FLC 5+2 FAC 2+1 Others 4

JOHNSON Richard Mark
Born: Newcastle, Australia, 27 April 1974
Height: 5'10" Weight: 12.0

An aggressive, strong-tackling Watford midfield player whose best asset is a searing shot. Remained largely injury free in 1996-97, so had the benefit of an extended run in the first team to boost his confidence, though his goal return of just two was disappointing.

Watford (From trainee on 11/5/92) FL 102+20/6 FLC 8+1/1 FAC 6+1 Others 2+1

JOHNSON Ross York
Born: Brighton, 2 January 1976
Height: 6'0" Weight: 12.4

A local lad, in 1996-97, Ross continued to show the tremendous promise he displayed for Brighton during 1995-96, despite suffering a hamstring injury in mid season. Initially employed as a deputy for the regular central defenders, he broke into the side under new manager, Steve Gritt, and performed with such aplomb that he was named Player of the Month for January by the Brighton Evening Argus. His prodigious throw in often proved as effective as a corner.

Brighton & Hove A (From trainee on 22/7/94) FL 41+10 FLC 0+1 FAC 2 Others 3+1

JOHNSON Seth Art Maurice
Born: Birmingham, 12 March 1979
Height: 5'10" Weight: 10.7
International Honours: E: Yth

Just 18 years of age and a first year Crewe professional, Seth originally came to the club from Dawlish as an associate schoolboy, completing his education locally. Able to play in defence or midfield, he made his first-team debut in the left-back slot against Preston at Gresty Road on the last day of March, his form being such that he forced his way into the side for the remaining games, including a Wembley sub appearance, as Alex went into the first division via the play offs. Also scored in a 1-1 draw at Wrexham.

Crewe Alex (From trainee on 12/7/96) FL 8+3/1 Others 0+3

JOHNSON Thomas (Tommy)
Born: Newcastle on Tyne, 15 January 1971
Height: 5'11" Weight: 12.4
Club Honours: FLC '96
International Honours: E: U21-7

Although always on the fringe of the Aston Villa side last year, with Savo Milosevic unsettled, Tommy started the first three games and scored the club's first goal of the new campaign, a superb header in a 2-1 defeat at Sheffield Wednesday. From then on until the New Year, however, he was only in the side when Milosevic was unavailable, his next spell coming when he returned for four games after Mark Draper was injured in January. A hard working and pacy forward, with a reputation for jumping on half

chances and keeping the line moving, he completed a £2.4 million transfer to Celtic on transfer deadline day.

Notts Co (From trainee on 19/1/89) FL 100+18/47 FLC 7+2/5 FAC 3+2/1 Others 14+3/4
Derby Co (£1,3000,000 on 12/3/92) FL 91+7/30 FLC 9+1/2 FAC 5/1 Others 16/8
Aston Villa (Signed on 6/1/95) PL 38+19/13 FLC 5/2 FAC 5+2/1 Others 1+1/1

JOHNSTON Allan
Born: Glasgow, 14 December 1973
Height: 5'10" Weight: 11.0
International Honours: S: U21-3

Signed from the French club, Rennes, last April, "Magic" immediately impressed the Sunderland fans with his clever wing play. He is also able to operate in midfield, and opened his goalscoring account for the Rokermen with a header in the 3-0 win over Everton at home in May – a goal that will go down in Roker folklore as the last ever scored at the famous old ground. Following the club's relegation, the fans will be looking to players such as Allan to fire them to promotion at the first attempt.

Heart of Midlothian (Free from Tynecastle BC on 23/6/90) SL 46+38/12 SLC 3+2/2 SC 4+1 (Signed for Rennes during 1996 close season)
Sunderland (£550,000 on 27/3/97) PL 4+2/1

JONES Barry
Born: Prescot, 20 June 1970
Height: 5'11" Weight: 11.12
Club Honours: WC '95

Very much in the background at Wrexham in 1996-97, Barry had earlier looked to be a permanent fixture in the side, with a bright future predicted by many. However, failure to command a regular place at right back or in central defence seems to have left him unsettled, but, all that aside, he is a very useful squad member.

Liverpool (Signed from Prescot Cables on 19/1/89) Others 0+1
Wrexham (Free on 10/7/92) FL 172+9/4 FLC 12+1/1 FAC 10+1 Others 21+1

JONES Gary
Born: Huddersfield, 6 April 1969
Height: 6'1" Weight: 12.9

A strong Notts County centre forward who gets his share of goals and then some from outside the penalty area, Gary had a dip in form during the second half of last season and was allowed to go on loan to Scunthorpe in February. Remaining until the end of the campaign, both the confidence and the goals returned, five strikes in 11 games being ample testament. Is lively, mobile, and a good passer.

Doncaster Rov (Free from Rossington Main Colliery on 26/1/89) FL 10+10/2 FLC 1 (Free to Grantham on 1/11/89)
Southend U (£25,000 from Boston U, via Kettering T, on 3/6/93) FL 47+23/16 FLC 3/1 FAC 2 Others 6+1/2
Lincoln C (Loaned on 17/9/93) FL 0+4/2 Others 0+1
Notts Co (£140,000 on 1/3/96) FL 37+8/8 FLC 1/1 FAC 2/1 Others 1+1
Scunthorpe U (Loaned on 21/2/97) FL 9+2/5

JONES Gary Steven
Born: Chester, 10 May 1975
Height: 6'3" Weight: 14.0

Although handicapped by a series of niggling injuries during last season, and starting matches more often on the bench as cover for John Aldridge than on the field itself, Gary nonetheless finished up as Tranmere's second highest league scorer, with six goals. Due to his size, he will never be able to run the length of the pitch in possession, but has a neat first touch to go with accurate passing ability and is especially valuable to the club for his versatility – he can play at either centre half, centre forward, or in a pivotal role in midfield.

Tranmere Rov (From trainee on 5/7/93) FL 38+40/12 FLC 4+2/2 FAC 2+1 Others 1+1

Graeme Jones

JONES Graeme Anthony
Born: Gateshead, 13 March 1970
Height: 6'0" Weight: 12.12
Club Honours: Div 3 '97

A record signing from Doncaster at the start of last season, the Wigan Athletic centre forward ended 1996-97 as the Football League's highest scorer with 33 goals to his credit, a total that included four hat tricks. Voted the club's Player of the Year, the hard-running, out-and-out striker was a handful for any defence and was honoured by selection for the third division team at the PFA awards night. Surely destined to play at a higher level in the not-too-distant future, Graeme was delighted to cap a wonderful campaign with a third division championship medal.

Doncaster Rov (£10,000 from Bridlington T on 2/8/93) FL 80+12/26 FLC 4+1/1 FAC 2+1/1 Others 5/1
Wigan Ath (£150,000 on 8/7/96) FL 39+1/31 FLC 1+1/1 FAC 1 Others 1/1

JONES Jonathan (Jon) Berwyn
Born: Wrexham, 27 October 1978
Height: 5'11" Weight: 11.5

Having played for Chester in the AWS competition only in 1995-96, and still a trainee, Jon was promoted to the first-team

bench on a regular basis during the second half of last season and made quite an impact when scoring on his home debut with a penalty against Doncaster. A forward with tremendous pace, the club has high hopes of this youngster and rewarded him with a two-year pro contract following his elevation from the youth side in March.

Chester C (From trainee on 27/3/97) FL 3+14/1 Others 0+2

JONES Keith Aubrey
Born: Dulwich, 14 October 1965
Height: 5'9" Weight: 10.11
International Honours: E: Yth; Sch

A competitive Charlton midfielder, who is hard working and a tenacious tackler, Keith is predominantly right footed with good distribution, and likes to get forward whenever possible. Missed a large chunk of last season due to a knee injury sustained against Reading in September, which required an operation, but returned to put in some outstanding performances, particularly in the away games at Birmingham and West Bromwich Albion.

Chelsea (From apprentice on 16/8/83) FL 43+9/7 FLC 9+2/3 FAC 1 Others 4+1
Brentford (£40,000 on 3/9/87) FL 167+2/13 FLC 15/2 FAC 13/4 Others 16/1
Southend U (£175,000 on 21/10/91) FL 88+2/11 FLC 4 FAC 5 Others 9/1
Charlton Ath (£150,000 on 16/9/94) FL 69+6/1 FLC 2+1 FAC 2+1

JONES Lea David
Born: Liverpool, 25 September 1977
Height: 6'0" Weight: 14.5

The son of the Stockport boss, Lea made his debut for County as a substitute in the Auto Windscreen Shield game at Burnley last February. Seen by the Edgeley Park backroom staff as a sound bet for a future first-team place, he is a big, strong, uncompromising central defender who is good in the air and clears his line well. As a regular in the reserves during 1996-97, the first year professional also showed he could play a bit when required.

Stockport Co (From trainee on 29/7/96) Others 0+1

JONES Philip Lee
Born: Wrexham, 29 May 1973
Height: 5'9" Weight: 10.8
International Honours: W: 1; B-1; U21-14

Again failing to hold down a place in the Liverpool first team, although appearing a couple of times from the bench in 1996-97, Lee had a couple of loan spells, firstly at Wrexham (January) and then at Tranmere (March). Having his second loan period at Wrexham, his first club, the pacy striker remained goaless in six appearances, before joining up with an old team-mate, John Aldridge, at Tranmere. There he quickly established himself as a favourite with the Prenton Park faithful and scored five goals in eight starts, showing both skill and vision. Keen to further his Welsh international career, having won his first full cap against Scotland, and despite being tracked by a number of Premier League clubs, he was presented with a petition from Rovers'

supporters, urging him to make the move permanent, before returning to the Pool. *Stop Press:* Signed for Tranmere at the end of May, £100,000 closing the deal.

Wrexham (From trainee on 5/7/91) FL 24+15/10 FLC 2 FAC 1+2/1 Others 4+1/2
Liverpool (£300,000 on 12/3/92) PL 0+3 FLC 0+1
Crewe Alex Loaned on 3/9/93) FL 4+4/1
Wrexham (Loaned on 26/1/96) FL 20/8
Wrexham (Loaned on 31/1/97) FL 2+4
Tranmere Rov (Loaned on 27/3/97) FL 8/5

JONES Lee
Born: Pontypridd, 9 August 1970
Height: 6'3" Weight: 14.4
Club Honours: AMC '94

Besides having to play as number two behind Roger Freestone at Swansea, Lee also had to contend with cartilage problems earlier last season. With an imposing build for a goalkeeper, his only appearance for Swans in 1996-97, came in the final match of the campaign, as in 1995-96, and he will obviously be hoping for a change of fortune in the future.

Swansea C (£7,500 from AFC Porth on 24/3/94) FL 4 Others 1

JONES Mark
Born: Havering, 4 August 1979
Height: 5'8" Weight: 11.7

Having impressed at left back in Southend's junior and reserve sides, the young trainee came off the bench to make his debut at Grimsby, playing the final 32 minutes of last season. A player who can link up well with the attack, and even score himself on occasion, Mark has vision and a good turn of pace to match an educated left foot.

Southend U (Trainee) FL 0+1

JONES Paul Philip
Born: Birkenhead, 2 October 1976
Height: 5'11" Weight: 11.8

Paul graduated through Wrexham's fine youth policy in 1996-97 to make his Football League debut on Good Friday versus Millwall at the Racecourse, after injuries had deprived the club of all regular squad left backs. Manager Brian Flynn summed up his performance after the game by saying: "Sometimes you throw people in at the deep end and they come out swimming, that is what Paul did." With a good left foot and strong in the tackle, his manager had no problem in selecting him for the next match. Was surprisingly released during the summer.

Wrexham (From trainee on 4/7/95) FL 6

JONES Paul Steven
Born: Chirk, 18 April 1967
Height: 6'3" Weight: 14.8
International Honours: W: 1

Signed by Stockport during the 1996 close season, the former Wolves goalkeeper had a stunning 1996-97 campaign, which was rightly recognised by his call up to the Welsh international squad and resulted in an appearance against Scotland in May. Widely seen as County's Player of the Year, Paul proved remarkably agile for a big man and was a calm and assertive figure in the

defence, while keeping Neil Edwards, the 1995-96 first-choice 'keeper, on the sidelines. Instrumental in the club's promotion to the first division, he kept seven consecutive clean sheets during the critical last few weeks.

Wolverhampton W (£40,000 from Kidderminster Harriers on 23/7/91) FL 33 FLC 2 FAC 5 Others 4
Stockport Co (£60,000 on 25/7/96) FL 46 FLC 11 FAC 4 Others 4

JONES Robert (Rob) Marc
Born: Wrexham, 5 November 1971
Height: 5'11" Weight: 11.0
Club Honours: FAC '92; FLC '95
International Honours: W: Sch. E: 8; U21-2; Yth

Hampered by injury throughout 1996-97, Liverpool's Rob played just three times and was only available for the bench sporadically. And to rub salt into the wounds, with Stig Bjornebye and Jason McAteer now established down the right-hand side, the once brilliant right back will need to be in outstanding form in 1997-98 if he is to wrest his old slot back. At his best, the complete full back, decisive in the tackle, winning balls cleanly, passing accurately, and not afraid to get down the line to cross to the front men, it will be ironic if he gets back into the side at the expense of others' injuries.

Crewe Alex (From trainee on 20/12/88) FL 59+16/2 FLC 9 FAC 0+3 Others 3
Liverpool (£300,000 on 4/10/91) F/PL 162 FLC 19+1 FAC 27 Others 4

JONES Scott
Born: Sheffield, 1 May 1975
Height: 5'10" Weight: 11.6

With Barnsley in full flow last season on their way to Premiership football for the first time in the club's 99-year history, Scott made the best of his limited opportunities at left-wing back. Having said that, he certainly made progress, his performances improving with each game, and he will be looking for further chances in 1997-98. Is a strong tackler and good passer of the ball.

Barnsley (From trainee on 1/2/94) FL 16+6 FAC 0+2

JONES Stephen (Steve) Gary
Born: Cambridge, 17 March 1970
Height: 6'0" Weight: 12.12

Strong and deceptively quick, but having little opportunity to shine at Upton Park, Steve joined Charlton from West Ham United last February, immediately making his debut up front against Barnsley at The Valley. Although unfortunate to sustain a knee injury in the following game at home to Norwich, and playing no further part in the season, there are great expectations for him next season. Is a striker who not only hits the net on a regular basis, but one who delights in scoring spectacular goals.

West Ham U (£22,000 from Billericay T on 16/11/92) PL 8+8/4 FAC 2+2/1 Others 1+1
Bournemouth (£150,000 on 21/10/94) FL 71+3/26 FLC 4/3 FAC 3/1 Others 3
West Ham U (Signed on 16/5/96) PL 5+3 FLC 0+1 FAC 2
Charlton Ath (£400,000 on 14/2/97) FL 2

Steve Jones (Swansea)

JONES Stephen (Steve) Robert
Born: Bristol, 25 December 1970
Height: 5'10" Weight: 12.2

1996-97 was an excellent season for Swansea's Steve, either as an attacking wing back, or in central defence. A tremendous header of the ball for a player of his size, he matured as the campaign wore on, producing consistent performances week in and week out on his way to becoming Swans' only ever present. He was further recognised when being voted the Vetch Player of the Year.

Swansea C (£25,000 from Cheltenham T on 14/11/95) FL 62+1/1 FLC 2 FAC 2 Others 4

JONES Vincent (Vinny) Peter
Born: Watford, 5 January 1965
Height: 6'0" Weight: 11.12
Club Honours: FAC '88 DIV 2 '90
International Honours: W: 9

Vinnie's infamous career has now reached an all-time high, not only gaining the Wimbledon captaincy, but also leading his adopted country, Wales. Part of the team's success in 1996-97 must be put down to "Jonah's" superb motivation and organisation skills. Despite the reputation, his disciplinary record during the season was a credit to the man and it is safe to say that he has proved the doubters wrong by not only showing the powerful and uncompromising side to his game but producing moments of subtlety and skill as well. He also scored a few goals during the campaign, the best coming in the 1-0 victory over Arsenal at Highbury. And, in continuing to lead an active life outside football with public speaking at universities among his many pursuits, the Dons' hard man currently presents his own chat show on Satellite TV.

Wimbledon (£10,000 from Wealdstone on 20/11/86) FL 77/9 FLC 6+2 FAC 11+2/1 Others 3
Leeds U (£650,000 on 20/6/89) FL 44+2/5 FLC 2 FAC 1 Others 4
Sheffield U (£700,000 on 13/9/90) FL 35/2 FLC 4 FAC 1 Others 1
Chelsea (£575,000 on 30/8/91) F/PL 42/4 FLC 1 FAC 4/1 Others 5/2
Wimbledon (£700,000 on 10/9/92) F/PL 149+4/12 FLC 20/2 FAC 18

Vinny Jones

JORDAN Roy Antony
Born: Plymouth, 17 April 1978
Height: 5'10" Weight: 11.0
Still a second-year trainee and one of the stars of the Hereford reserve side in 1996-97, with the club struggling for selection, Roy made his league debut at the beginning of March in a home fixture against Exeter. Without a doubt a star of the future, he is an intelligent youngster who can play either in midfield or up front.
Hereford U (Trainee) FL 1

JORDAN Scott Douglas
Born: Newcastle, 19 July 1975
Height: 5'10" Weight: 11.2
1996-97 was a rather frustrating season for this talented York City midfielder. Injuries did not help but, that aside, he was still not able to command a regular place in the line up and spent much of the campaign on the subs' bench. At his best, is composed on the ball and a good passer.
York C (From trainee on 21/10/92) FL 58+21/5 FLC 4+1/1 FAC 2+1 Others 4+4

JOSEPH Marc Ellis
Born: Leicester, 10 November 1976
Height: 6'0" Weight: 12.5
1996-97 was a disappointing season for Marc after the excitement of a loan spell at Premier League Coventry in 1995-96. A defender who can also play as sweeper, he was sidelined with a groin injury early on and, without full match fitness, he found it difficult to break into the first-team squad until returning for the last game of the campaign. Is not only good on the ground, but makes full use of aerial ability also.
Cambridge U (From trainee on 23/5/95) FL 15+5 FLC 1 Others 1+1

JOSEPH Matthew (Matt) Nathan Adolphus
Born: Bethnal Green, 30 September 1972
Height: 5'8" Weight: 10.7
International Honours: E: Yth
A steadying influence on the Cambridge team all through last season, the sweeper was often highlighted as Man of the Match and rewarded with his consistency as the fans' Player of the Season. Ever present until the last two games, when he suffered a groin injury against Brighton, he was sorely missed and without him the team struggled and lost both matches. Able to play at full back or up front, Matt is a hard-tackling ball winner who can release others.
Arsenal (From trainee on 17/11/90)
Gillingham (Free on 7/12/92 - Free to Ilves during 1993 close season)
Cambridge U (Signed on 19/11/93) FL 152/6 FLC 6 FAC 7 Others 4

JOSEPH Roger Anthony
Born: Paddington, 24 December 1965
Height: 5'11" Weight: 11.0
International Honours: E: B-2
Recruited by West Brom manager Ray Harford on a short-term trial period last February after spending the early part of the season training with Chelsea, followed by a spell at Leyton Orient, Roger played in just two games, both as a second-half substitute, before receiving a groin injury. In his prime, had great pace and the ability to strike long balls behind the opposing full back.
Brentford (Free from Southall on 4/10/85) FL 103+1/2 FLC 7 FAC 1 Others 8
Wimbledon (£150,000 on 25/8/88) F/PL 155+7 FLC 17+2 FAC 11+1 Others 6
Millwall (Loaned on 2/3/95) FL 5
Leyton Orient (Free on 22/11/96) FL 15 Others 1
West Bromwich A (Free on 28/2/97) FL 0+2

JOYCE Warren Garton
Born: Oldham, 20 January 1965
Height: 5'9" Weight: 12.0
Rejoined Hull City in the summer of 1996 after an earlier loan spell, and was immediately awarded the captain's armband. The son of Walter (now at Bury FC), Joyce junior has become the senior Tiger, having passed the 500 league appearances milestone in February. Still outstandingly fit, he is a midfielder who loves to get forward.
Bolton W (From juniors on 23/6/82) FL 180+4/17 FLC 14+1/1 FAC 11/1 Others 11/2
Preston NR (£35,000 on 16/10/87) FL 170+7/34 FLC 8/2 FAC 6/1 Others 19/7
Plymouth Arg (£160,000 on 19/5/92) FL 28+2/3 FLC 6/1 FAC 2 Others 2
Burnley (£140,000 on 7/7/93) FL 65+5/9 FLC 8/1 FAC 4/1 Others 8/1
Hull C (Loaned on 20/1/95) FL 9/3
Hull C (£30,000 on 10/7/96) FL 45/5 FLC 2 FAC 3/1 Others 2/1

JULES Mark Anthony
Born: Bradford, 5 September 1971
Height: 5'8" Weight: 11.1
Mark has been performing so well for Chesterfield at left back for so long now, that it is easy to take his contribution for granted. Consistency was his strong point last season, and it is impossible to remember a bad game. Not one of the club's most demonstrative players, his quiet nature supports a power of concentration that is vital in his marking role. The job of looking after Juninho in the FA Cup semi final fell to Mark, but he was not overawed and emerged from the game with great credit.
Bradford C (From trainee on 3/7/90) FLC 0+1
Scarborough (Free on 14/8/91) FL 57+20/16 FLC 6+2/2 FAC 1+1 Others 6/4
Chesterfield (£40,000 on 21/5/93) FL 107+23/3 FLC 7+2/2 FAC 9+2 Others 8

[JUNINHO] JUNIOR Oswaldo Giroldo
Born: Sao Paulo, Brazil, 22 February 1975
Height: 5'5" Weight: 9.10
International Honours: Brazil: 35
Middlesbrough's brilliant Brazilian play-maker is without doubt one of the greatest footballers in the world today. Small of stature, but with a heart bigger than himself, he epitomises everything that is beautiful in the beautiful game, his skills and masterful control of the ball being a sheer joy to behold, while his deceptive body swerves and catch me if you can style of running at the opposition, left many Premiership defenders bewildered in 1996-97. Throughout a most difficult campaign, his whole-hearted enthusiasm and genuine sportsmanship endeared him to all true football fans everywhere and the stamina in one so small of stature often seemed to be of unbelievable proportions. The media, albeit grudgingly on occasion, were ultimately obliged to acknowledge the undeniable talent that graced the English game, and his ability to shrug off the most bone-crushing tackles by restarting the game from free-kick situations awarded to his side without the usual lamentable appeals to the referee, was refreshing in the extreme. Almost certain to leave the English game following the disastrous end of season results, his talent will be sorely missed by the Boro faithful who acknowledge that he must, perforce, seek new pastures in order to retain his status in the Brazilian national side.
Middlesbrough (£4,750,000 from Sao Paulo on 3/11/95) PL 54+2/14 FLC 9/1 FAC 6/2 Others 3

Juninho

JUPP Duncan Alan
Born: Haslemere, 25 January 1975
Height: 6'0" Weight: 12.12
International Honours: S: U21-10
Signed by Wimbledon during the 1996 close season, the former Fulham trainee was seen as a replacement for Roger Joseph. A Scottish U21 international right back, Duncan is an impressive and versatile defender who likes to make forward runs, being given his full debut in September against Portsmouth in the Coca-Cola Cup in which the Dons ran out 1-0 victors. Despite having had few Premier League run outs, when on the park, he seemed solid and composed and very much a player for the future.
Fulham (From trainee on 12/7/93) FL 101+4/2 FLC 10+2 FAC 9+1/1 Others 9+1/1
Wimbledon (£125,000 + on 27/6/96) PL 6 FLC 1 FAC 0+2

KAAMARK Pontus Sven
Born: Vasteras, Sweden, 5 April 1969
Height: 5'11" Weight: 12.7
Club Honours: FLC '97
International Honours: Sweden: 29

Having returned to action with Leicester last December, after a year out with a knee ligament injury, the right-footed Swedish defender, and occasional midfielder, was pressed into service at left back due to an injury crisis. Unfortunately, just when he was finding the best form of his English career, he suffered a broken arm in an FA Cup tie against Norwich, being out of action until coming back in March, his arm in light plaster, for a 2-2 draw at Southampton. The next game, operating as a man marker, he effectively shut out Middlesbrough's Juninho at Wembley in the Coca-Cola Cup final and repeated the process in the replay, a game that brought him a cup winners' medal following City's 1-0 victory. A top-class performer, who regained his Swedish international place in May, Pontus will surely blossom in the Premiership this coming season.
Leicester C (£840,000 from IFK Gothenberg on 2/11/95) P/FL 10+1 FLC 4 FAC 2

KANCHELSKIS Andrei
Born: Kirovograd, USSR, 23 January 1969
Height: 5'10" Weight: 13.3
Club Honours: ESC '91; FLC '92 PL '93, '94; CS '93, '94; FAC '94
International Honours: USSR: 43

At his best, a world-class right winger with the ability to terrorise any defence, but at worst a frustrating under-achiever, Andrei never regained the awesome heights he reached with Everton in 1995-96. Top scorer that season, the Russian took ten matches to score his first league goal last term, amid rumours that he was unsettled and wanted a move to the continent. His wish was granted after Everton's traumatic FA Cup exit to Bradford, when he was responsible for giving the ball away for Bradford's crucial second goal. Just four days later (29 January) he was transferred to Serie A side, Fiorentina, for an Everton transfer record of £8m.
Manchester U (£650,000 from Shakhtyor Donetsk on 26/3/91) F/PL 96+27/28 FLC 15+1/3 FAC 11+1/4 Others 10/1
Everton (£5,000,000 on 25/8/95) PL 52/21 FLC 2/1 FAC 6/1

KATCHOURO Petr
Born: Urss, Belarus, 2 August 1972
Height: 5'11" Weight: 11.5
International Honours: Belarus: 18

Signed from Dinamo Minsk during the 1996 close season, following a brief trial in 1995-96, the Belarus international striker came to Sheffield United in preference to CSKA Moscow or Spanish football, but started the new campaign on the bench and then suffered the indignity of being a substituted substitute. Just as the doubts were setting in, a storming performance at Wolverhampton signalled a change of fortune which ultimately led to 12 league goals and the Player of the Year trophy at the Lane. Although his pace was his undoubted strength, towards the end of 1996-97 tiredness took its toll and he was used in short bursts to good effect, this ability to move defenders out of position being helpful to the promotion push. Was very disappointed at being pulled off after only 25 minutes of the play-off final due to a change of tactics.
Sheffield U (£650,000 from Dinamo Minsk on 19/7/96) FL 28+12/12 FLC 2+2/1 FAC 1 Others 3/1

KAVANAGH Graham Anthony
Born: Dublin, 2 December 1973
Height: 5'10" Weight: 12.11
International Honours: Ei: U21-9; Yth; Sch

Despite being a big signing from Middlesborough last season, following a spell on loan, Graham had an up-and-down time at Stoke. Possessing what Lou Macari described as the hardest shot in football, he scored a wonder goal against Grimsby, but was eventually rested from the team as his confidence sagged in the face of some criticism. A strong and fearless midfielder, with excellent ball control and passing skills, he will come back stronger than ever.
Middlesbrough (Signed from Home Farm on 16/8/91) F/PL 22+13/3 FLC 1 FAC 3+1/1 Others 7
Darlington (Loaned on 25/2/94) FL 5
Stoke C (£250,000 + on 13/9/96) FL 32+6/4 FLC 2 FAC 1

KAVANAGH Jason Colin
Born: Meriden, 23 November 1971
Height: 5'9" Weight: 12.7
International Honours: E: Yth; Sch

An extremely versatile, solid right-sided defender who was unable to make it into the Derby side in 1996-97, Jason was a bargain signing for Wycombe in November and quickly established himself in central defence, although equally at home as a wing back or midfielder. In becoming one of the most consistent players at Wanderers, missing games only when unfit, he not only showed himself to be a tenacious ball winner, but more than comfortable when going forward.
Derby Co (From trainee on 9/12/88) FL 74+25/1 FLC 3+2 FAC 7 Others 8+8
Wycombe W (£25,000 on 1/11/96) FL 27 FAC 2 Others 1

KAVELASHVILI Mikhail
Born: Tbilisi, Georgia, 22 July 1971
Height: 6'0" Weight: 12.1
International Honours: Georgia: 14

Started last season as Manchester City's first choice striker alongside Uwe Rosler, playing the first three games during Alan Ball's brief stay. Following that, he spent most of 1996-97 as a playing substitute under all the other four managers who were in charge. With recommendations from various sources in Georgia before he was signed, Mikhail has yet to show his best form in England, his style and ability on the ball being used to a slower pace, and is often baulked off the ball in the fast and physical style of the first division. That aside, he had an impressive game in the 1-1 draw at Grimsby, where he scored with a brave header from a cross by Rosler – one of the best goals scored by the team during the campaign. Remains a key member of the Georgian World Cup squad.
Manchester C (£1,400,000 from Sporting Vladikavkaz on 28/3/96) P/FL 9+19/3 FLC 0+1

KAY John
Born: Great Lumley, 29 January 1964
Height: 5'9" Weight: 11.6
Club Honours: Div 3 '88

The vastly experienced full back, who has experienced promotion with Wimbledon and Sunderland (twice), joined Scarborough last September, after injury problems had seen him released by Sunderland. Made the right back position his own and enjoyed a successful campaign with the Seasiders, even scoring a rare goal in a 1-0 FA Cup victory over Shrewsbury. Prior to arriving at the McCain Stadium, John had spent a month at Preston, covering for both injured right backs and, as you would expect, performing with credit.
Arsenal (From apprentice on 7/8/81) FL 13+1
Wimbledon (£25,000 on 20/7/84) FL 63/2 FLC 3 FAC 3 Others 1
Middlesbrough (Loaned on 8/1/85) FL 8
Sunderland (£22,500 on 22/7/87) FL 196+3 FLC 19 FAC 12 Others 6
Shrewsbury T (Loaned on 28/3/96) FL 7 Others 1
Preston NE (Free on 23/8/96) FL 7 FLC 3
Scarborough (Free on 27/9/96) FL 34 FAC 2/1

KAYE Peter John
Born: Huddersfield, 4 February 1979
Height: 5'8" Weight: 11.1

Yet another young player introduced by Huddersfield last season, Peter signed pro forms during the summer, having come through the youth team as a trainee. A promising forward who made his debut when coming off the bench for the last 29 minutes of the final game of the season, a 0-0 home draw against Swindon, he will obviously be hoping to press for further recognition in 1997-98.
Huddersfield T (From trainee on 6/9/96) FL 0+1

KEANE Roy Maurice
Born: Cork, 10 August 1971
Height: 5'10" Weight: 12.10
Club Honours: FMC '92; CS '93, '97; PL '94, '96, '97; FAC '94, '96
International Honours: Ei: 35; U21-4; Yth; Sch

An inspirational Republic of Ireland and Manchester United midfielder, with excellent skills and a hardened edge, Roy was one of Bobby Robson's main targets for Barcelona in the 1996 close season, before he signed a new four-year contract with United in August. Having played in the opening game of 1996-97 at Wimbledon, he went into hospital for an exploratory knee operation, which kept him out for six games and, on his return, played against Aston

Villa in the Premiership and Rapid Vienna in the Champions' League, before injury struck again. After missing another four games, came back for United's Coca-Cola Cup victory against Swindon, but was then sent off in the Premiership against Southampton at the Dell. Following that, he scored his first Premiership goal of the season against Middlesbrough, which coincided with his longest spell in the side, and although the injury jinx struck again during the return leg against Rapid Vienna, the New Year brought a better run of luck. Whether fit, or struggling with injury, no player works harder for United's cause than Roy. And Alex Ferguson put his value into perspective in August when he said, "I believe we have secured the heart of Manchester United for the next four years. I wouldn't swap him for anyone." At the end of another long, hard campaign, Roy was the proud possesser of a third championship medal as United surged to their fourth title win in five years, and was also selected for the award-winning Premiership side.

Nottingham F (£10,000 from Cobh Ramblers on 12/6/90) F/PL 114/22 FLC 17/6 FAC 18/3 Others 5/2
Manchester U (£3,750,000 on 22/7/93) PL 107+5/15 FLC 9+2 FAC 22+1/1 Others 17/4

KEARTON Jason Brett
Born: Ipswich, Australia, 9 July 1969
Height: 6'1" Weight: 11.10
Club Honours: FAC '95

Released by Everton last October, the Australian-born Jason signed for Crewe, a side who had lost their first-choice goalkeeper, Mark Gayle, through injury and had borrowed first Steve Mautone (West Ham), then Martin Taylor (Derby), to tide them over. Apart from the last three league games, when out of the side through injury, he was a regular, proving to be popular with both fans and team mates alike when keeping 16 clean sheets and enjoying himself no end as the club reached the first division, via the play offs. Comes out for crosses well and is a good shot stopper.

Everton (Free from Brisbane Lions on 31/10/88) PL 3+3 FLC 1 FAC 1
Stoke C (Loaned on 13/8/91) FL 16 Others 1
Blackpool (Loaned on 9/1/92) FL 14
Notts Co (Loaned on 19/1/95) FL 10 Others 2
Crewe Alex (Free on 16/10/96) FL 30 FAC 4 Others 6

KEATES Dean Scott
Born: Walsall, 30 June 1978
Height: 5'5" Weight: 10.6

This highly promising Walsall defender made a big impression in his one and only full game against Notts County last January and was immediately labelled by his manager as a little fellow with a heart bigger than his size. Look out for him in 1997-98.

Walsall (From trainee on 14/8/96) FL 1+1

KEEN Kevin Ian
Born: Amersham, 25 February 1967
Height: 5'6" Weight: 10.10
International Honours: E: Yth; Sch

1996-97 was yet another immensely frustrating season for Stoke's Kevin, this

Roy Keane

time due to a series of injuries, including ankle ligament damage and a broken fibula sustained at Swindon in a comeback game. Although his high point came when scoring in the local derby at Vale Park, he will be looking to be back to his hard-working best on the right-hand side of the Potters' midfield, come 1997-98.

West Ham U (From apprentice on 8/3/84) FL 187+32/21 FLC 21+1/5 FAC 15+7/1 Others 14+2/3
Wolverhampton W (£600,000 on 7/7/93) FL 37+5/7 FLC 2+1 FAC 5/1 Others 4/1
Stoke C (£300,000 on 19/10/94) FL 47+23/6 FLC 4+2 FAC 2 Others 2

KEISTER John Edward Samuel
Born: Manchester, 11 November 1970
Height: 5'8" Weight: 11.0
International Honours: Sierra Leone: 1

The tenacious Walsall midfielder had an outstanding season in 1996-97, his all-action displays being very popular with the fans. Unlucky to be sent off in the home game against Bury, he returned in time to score a tremendous goal against Watford in December, only his second in league football, before going on to pick up a Sierra Leone cap in a World Cup qualifier in April.

Walsall (Free from Faweh FC on 18/9/93) FL 65+25/2 FAC 9+2 Others 2+2

KELLER Kasey
Born: Washington, USA, 27 November 1969
Height: 6'2" Weight: 13.12
Club Honours: FLC '97
International Honours: USA: 35

Signed from Millwall at the beginning of 1996-97, the big goalkeeper was quickly into the action with Leicester, keeping a clean sheet at Sunderland on the opening day and making some outstanding saves, particularly in the home win over Newcastle. Deservedly voted Man of the Match in the Coca-Cola Cup semi-final win over Wimbledon, after he had again thwarted the Dons almost single handedly at times, he made at least three top-class saves in the Hillsborough replay, Leicester and Middlesbrough having drawn the Wembley final, especially the one from Emerson in extra time that preserved a 1-0 lead and ultimately brought a cup to Filbert Street for the first time in the club's history. Regularly called across the Atlantic to boost the USA World Cup bid, Kasey jetted back to the States following the epic cup win to take part in another World Cup qualifier.

Millwall (Free from Portland University on 20/2/92) FL 176 FLC 14 FAC 8 Others 4
Leicester C (£900,000 on 17/8/96) FL 31 FLC 8 FAC 4

Kasey Keller

KELLY Alan Thomas
Born: Preston, 11 August 1968
Height: 6'2" Weight: 14.3
International Honours: Ei: 18; U23-1; Yth

The Sheffield United goalkeeper, who relinquished the club captaincy prior to the start of 1996-97, once again performed heroics when required, his talents being recognised by his inclusion in the PFA first division team selected by fellow professionals. Only surrendered his first-team place due to injuries, which invariably arrived when the team had no substitute 'keeper on the bench, a point elaborated upon through the play-off second leg when he was virtually on one leg for 80 minutes following a knee injury which forced him to miss the Wembley final. From a footballing family with a goalkeeping background, his dad playing for Preston and the Republic, while his brother, Gary, is currently at Oldham, Alan regained his Irish jersey during the season and can be considered one of the top 'keepers in the country.

Preston NE (From apprentice on 25/9/85) FL 142 FLC 1 FAC 8 Others 13
Sheffield U (£200,000 on 24/7/92) P/FL 172+3 FLC 12 FAC 13 Others 2

KELLY Nyrere Anthony (Tony)
Born: Meriden, 14 February 1966
Height: 5'11" Weight: 11.6

A right winger who on his day can be a match winner, Tony played only ten games for Leyton Orient in 1996-97, due to competition for places, and, despite scoring once against Hartlepool, he was released by Tommy Taylor and finished the season playing for St Albans. Had a spell on loan at Colchester in October, having impressed when playing against them a month earlier, but that too petered out.

Bristol C (Apprentice) FL 2+4/1
Stoke C (£20,000 from St Albans C, via Dulwich Hamlet, Cheshunt and Enfield, on 29/1/90) FL 33+25/5 FLC 5+4/3 Others 3+3
Hull C (Loaned on 30/1/92) FL 6/1
Cardiff C (Loaned on 30/10/92) FL 5/1
Bury (£10,000 on 17/9/93) FL 53+4/10 FLC 0+1 FAC 1+1 Others 8/3
Leyton Orient (£30,000 on 7/7/95) FL 32+2/3 FLC 1 FAC 1 Others 2
Colchester U (Loaned on 11/10/96) FL 2+1

KELLY David Thomas
Born: Birmingham, 25 November 1965
Height: 5'11" Weight: 12.1
Club Honours: Div '93
International Honours: Ei: 23; B-3; U23-1; U21-3

The Republic of Ireland international began last season as Sunderland's first-choice striker but, following an injury, his return to the side saw him occupying the right-midfield berth where, at times, he looked out of sorts. His unfamiliarity with such a role probably contributed to him failing to find the net in 1996-97 – surely the first time this has happened to him and following the final game, it was revealed in the local press that David was likely to leave the club in the summer.

Walsall (Signed from Alvechurch on 21/12/83) FL 115+32/63 FLC 11+1/4 FAC 12+2/3 Others 14+3/10

West Ham U (£600,000 on 1/8/88) FL 29+12/7 FLC 11+3/5 FAC 6 Others 2+1/2
Leicester C (£300,000 on 22/3/90) FL 63+3/22 FLC 6/2 FAC 1 Others 2/1
Newcastle U (£250,000 on 4/12/91) FL 70+35 FLC 4/2 FAC 5/1 Others 4/1
Wolverhampton W (£750,000 on 23/6/93) FL 76+7/26 FLC 5/2 FAC 11/6 Others 4/2
Sunderland (£1,000,000 on 19/9/95) P/FL 32+2/2 FLC 2+1 FAC 3

KELLY Garry
Born: Drogheda, 9 July 1974
Height: 5'9" Weight: 13.3
International Honours: Ei: 21; U21-5; Yth; Sch

Regarded as one of the best right backs in the Premiership, although still only in his fourth full season at Leeds in 1996-97, Garry found himself to be one of the longest serving players at Elland Road at the age of 22. There appeared to be some occasions where he seemed somewhat jaded, probably . due to the non-stop football he has played since his breakthrough. Even so he still produced performances of the highest quality and again proved to be equally adept in defence and attack, scoring his first goal for the club at Southampton, followed with a superb curling free kick at West Ham. With his quick-silver speed and recovery making him an exceptional man marker and defender, one of the biggest surprises on the international front was his consistent omission from the Republic of Ireland squad. Their loss, however, is Leeds United's gain and the player himself would surely benefit from a football-free close season.

Leeds U (Signed from Home Farm on 24/9/91) PL 152+4/2 FLC 15+1 FAC 16 Others 4

KELLY Gary Alexander
Born: Preston, 3 August 1966
Height: 5'11" Weight: 13.6
Club Honours: FAYC '85
International Honours: Ei: B-1; U23-1; U21-8

Displaced by Dean Kiely as the number one goalkeeper at Bury at the start of 1996-97, Gary, the son of the former Preston and Eire 'keeper, Alan, and brother of Alan junior, the current Sheffield United and Eire 'keeper, transferred to Oldham following a spell on loan. Despite playing in a side that was ultimately doomed for relegation to the second division he could not be faulted, keeping four successive clean sheets at one stage and giving the Latics every chance to stay adrift. Reckoned to be the bargain of the season and voted Player of the Year by his colleagues, the supporters, and the junior fans.

Newcastle U (From apprentice on 20/6/84) FL 53 FLC 4 FAC 3 Others 2
Blackpool (Loaned on 7/10/88) FL 5
Bury (£60,000 on 5/10/89) FL 236 FLC 14 FAC 13 Others 29
Oldham Ath (£10,000 on 27/8/96) FL 42 FLC 3 FAC 1

KELLY Russell
Born: Ballymoney, 10 August 1976
Height: 5'11" Weight: 11.2
International Honours: Ei: Yth; Sch

This Irish youth international midfielder was signed by Darlington on non-contract terms and made his debut at Leyton Orient, a team he had been on loan with in 1995-96, in September. A player with pace and fair skill, he was released prior to the end of the season, despite scoring two goals.

Chelsea (From trainee on 4/7/95)
Leyton Orient (Loaned on 28/3/96) FL 11+4/1 FLC 1
Darlington (Free on 16/8/96) FL 13+10/2 FLC 0+1

KENNA Jeffrey (Jeff) Jude
Born: Dublin, 27 August 1970
Height: 5'11" Weight: 12.2
International Honours: Ei: 17; B-1; U21-8; Yth; Sch

Starting 1996-97 for Blackburn, deputising for Graeme le Saux at left back, Jeff struggled on his weaker side, especially when in opposition to Everton's Andrei Kanchelskis, but following the loss of Chris Coleman to injury and the return of Le Saux, he was able to move back to his recognised position of right back. It took some time for the Eire international to re-establish himself, but he developed gradually, exhibiting good skills on the ball when coming out of defence, and will be remembered for a fine hooked clearance to move the ball away from the danger area. Gets his foot in well in defensive situations.

Southampton (From trainee on 25/4/89) F/PL 110+4/4 FLC 4 FAC 10+1 Others 3
Blackburn Rov (£1,500,000 on 15/3/95) PL 78/1 FLC 7 FAC 4 Others 6

KENNEDY Mark
Born: Dublin, 15 May 1976
Height: 5'11" Weight: 11.9
International Honours: Ei: 12; U21-7; Yth; Sch

Mark spent most of last season sitting on the Liverpool bench, making just eight rare appearances as a sub, mainly to give added width in an effort to unlock a durable defence. Still a quality player, and still a regular in the Republic of Ireland side, with a preference for the left-hand side, his speed and powerful running, if coupled with added aggression, could make him a regular in future Reds' configurations. With great potential, he has much to fulfil.

Millwall (From trainee on 6/5/92) FL 37+6/9 FLC 6+1/2 FAC 3+1/1
Liverpool (£1,500,000 on 21/3/95) PL 5+10 FLC 0+2 FAC 0+1 Others 0+2

KENNEDY Peter Henry James
Born: Lurgan, 10 September 1973
Height: 5'11" Weight: 11.11
International Honours: NI: B-1

Signed from Portadown early on in 1996-97, the speedy left winger soon made his debut for Notts County, coming off the bench against York on the last day of August at Meadow Lane. In settling down quickly, he proved to be comfortable on the ball and a provider of excellent crosses, while showing up well with Steve Finnan on the opposite flank. Broke his scoring duck against Newcastle Town in the FA Cup and impressed enough to be selected for the Northern Ireland squad, having been capped for the "B" side in March.

Notts Co (£100,000 from Portadown on 28/8/96) FL 20+2 FLC 1 FAC 2+1/1 Others 0+1

KEOWN Martin Raymond
Born: Oxford, 24 July 1966
Height: 6'1" Weight: 12.4
International Honours: E: 15; B-1; U21-8; Yth

Martin was probably Arsenal's most improved player last season, being a permanent fixture in the back three and captaining the side in the absence of Tony Adams. Interestingly, the only boyhood Gunners' fan in the first team, he improved his distribution out of all recognition under the new manager, Arsene Wenger, his new found skills beginning to match his excellent aerial and tackling strengths, and being one of the reasons for his occasional appearances in an England shirt under Glenn Hoddle. Although the team ultimately failed to lift the championship, it was his defensive partnership with Tony Adams and Steve Bould – the best in the top flight, conceding a measly 32 goals – that was instrumental in the Gunners finishing in third place and gaining a UEFA Cup spot this coming term.

Arsenal (From apprentice on 2/2/84) FL 22 FAC 5
Brighton & Hove A (Loaned on 15/2/85) FL 21+2/1 FLC 2/1 Others 2/1
Aston Villa (£200,000 on 9/6/86) FL 109+3/3 FLC 12+1 FAC 6 Others 2
Everton (£750,000 on 7/8/89) F/PL 92+4 FLC 11 FAC 12+1 Others 6
Arsenal (£2,000,000 on 4/2/93) PL 129+18/2 FLC 14+2/1 FAC 8+2 Others 11+5

KERNAGHAN Alan Nigel
Born: Otley, 25 April 1967
Height: 6'1" Weight: 14.1
International Honours: NI: Sch. Ei: 22

A tried and trusted defender, and still a valuable Manchester City squad member, Alan returned to first-team duty at Stoke City in 1996-97, quickly showing his old form with a solid display alongside Kit Symons at the heart of the defence. This looked as though it would become the backbone of the team, but, sadly, it was not to be, as in the next match at home to Charlton he received a back injury which kept him out of football until late January. Having returned, he next played in two FA Cup and two league games before dropping out again through injuries, thus adding to the disappointment of losing his place in the Northern Ireland squad for the same reason.

Middlesbrough (From apprentice on 8/3/85) F/PL 172+40/16 FLC 22+7/1 FAC 7+4/3 Others 14+2/2
Charlton Ath (Loaned on 17/1/91) FL 13
Manchester C (£1,600,000 on 20/9/93) P/FL 54+8/1 FLC 7 FAC 7/1
Bolton W (Loaned on 18/8/94) FL 9+2
Bradford C (Loaned on 2/2/96) FL 5

KERR David William
Born: Dumfries, 6 September 1974
Height: 5'11" Weight: 12.7

Having signed permanently for Mansfield during the 1996 close season after his successful loan spell in 1995-96, the former Manchester City man suffered a double fracture of the leg early in October and took no further part in the remainder of the campaign. A strong tackler who can play in midfield and defence, he was badly missed.

Manchester C (From trainee on 10/9/91) PL 4+2
Mansfield T (Loaned on 22/9/95) FL 4+1 Others 1
Mansfield T (£20,000 on 31/7/96) FL 9 FLC 1

KERR Dylan
Born: Valetta, Malta, 14 January 1967
Height: 5'9" Weight: 11.4
Club Honours: Div 2 '94

Released by Reading at the end of 1995-96, he made just one substitute appearance for Carlisle in 1996-97, while on trial, before moving on to Kilmarnock. For the record, Dylan is an attacking left back who packs a powerful shot, which often brings him spectacular goals.

Sheffield Wed (From juniors on 1/9/84)
Leeds U (Free from Arcadia Shepherds on 8/2/89) F/PL 6+7 FLC 2 FAC 1 Others 0+4
Doncaster Rov (Loaned on 22/8/91) FL 7/1
Blackpool (Loaned on 31/12/91) FL 12/1 Others 1
Reading (£75,000 on 15/7/93) FL 84+5/5 FLC 8+1 FAC 2 Others 3+1
Carlisle U (Free on 16/9/96) FL 0+1

KERSLAKE David
Born: Stepney, 19 June 1966
Height: 5'9" Weight: 12.3
International Honours: E: U21-1; Yth; Sch

Since leaving the County Ground for Leeds United in March 1993, David's career has been very much on hold. Unable to make much impact at Premier League level, either at Leeds or with his current club, Tottenham Hotspur, and totally out of favour with Spurs' manager, Gerry Francis, who did not sign him, he was kicking his heels in the reserves when given the chance to return to the scene of his greatest triumphs, joining Swindon on a two-month loan last November. Sadly, Spurs did not agree to a permanent move and the right back returned to the obscurity of reserve-team football at White Hart Lane before being released during the summer. A player with pace, and a quality crosser of the ball, David was expected to sign for the Robins prior to the start of 1997-98.

Queens Park R (From apprentice on 1/6/83) FL 38+20/6 FLC 6+2/4 FAC 2+2 Others 2+2
Swindon T (£110,000 on 24/11/89) FL 133+2/1 FLC 12 FAC 8 Others 10
Leeds U (£500,000 on 11/3/93) PL 8
Tottenham H (£450,000 on 24/9/93) PL 34+3 FLC 5 FAC 1+1
Swindon T (Loaned on 29/11/96) FL 8

KEWELL Harold (Harry)
Born: Smithfield, Australia, 22 September 1978
Height: 6'0" Weight: 11.10
Club Honours: FAYC '97

After his initial breakthrough the previous season, this young Australian left back was again a regular member of the Leeds' youth and reserve sides in 1996-97 and made his one appearance for the first team as a substitute against Tottenham in December. Also gaining international recognition when selected for the Australian U20s for a tournament in Tahiti, before joining Terry Venables' full squad for a game with

Macedonia in March, Harry is another of the youngsters who should have a good future at Elland Road.

Leeds U (Signed from the Australian Academy of Sport on 23/12/95) PL 2+1

KEY Daniel (Danny) Charles
Born: Darlington, 2 November 1977
Height: 5'7" Weight: 12.0
A local-born midfield player who came through Darlington's junior ranks to make his first-team debut at Runcorn in the FA Cup last November, following a handful of appearances, he was released a month or so later and joined Gateshead.

Darlington (From trainee on 5/7/96) FL 0+3 FAC 1

KHARINE Dmitri Victorvitch
Born: Moscow, Russia, 16 August 1968
Height: 6'2" Weight: 13.9
International Honours: Russia: 34
A superb goalkeeper who played for Russia in the Euro 96 Championship, his 1996-97 season was cruelly curtailed in the fifth Premiership match at Hillsborough when he ruptured a cruciate ligament in his left knee and was carried off in the 18th minute of the game which saw Chelsea smash Sheffield Wednesday's 100 per-cent league record. This was particularly disappointing for Chelsea as the Moscow-born 'keeper had started in great form, keeping a clean sheet in each of the first three matches. Very agile and a tremendous shot stopper, upon his recovery, Dmitri faces an intriguing battle to keep his number one spot ahead of his old mate Kevin Hitchcock, the Norwegian international, Frode Grodås, and the new signing, Holland's Ed de Goey.

Chelsea (£200,000 from CSKA Moscow on 22/12/92) PL 107 FLC 8 FAC 12 Others 4

KIDD Ryan Andrew
Born: Radcliffe, 6 October 1971
Height: 6'1" Weight: 13.0
Club Honours: Div 3 '96
Ryan was a key figure in the adoption of the wing-back system by Preston manager, Gary Peters, last season, before his absence with a groin injury in February corresponded with a poor run of results that merely emphasised his vital part on the left side of the team's defensive formation. Good in the air, and a strong tackler, he continues to improve.

Port Vale (From trainee on 12/7/90) FL 1 FLC 0+2 Others 0+1
Preston NE (Free on 15/7/92) FL 136+12/4 FLC 8+1/1 FAC 7 Others 10+1/1

KIELY Dean Laurence
Born: Salford, 10 October 1970
Height: 6'1" Weight: 13.5
Club Honours: Div 2 '97
International Honours: E: Yth; Sch
A goalkeeper who was rated as one of the best in the lower divisions when he was signed from York City last August, Dean gained an immediate place in Bury's 1996-97 line up, managing to keep 22 clean sheets, saving two penalties and being voted as runner up in the fans' Player of the Season poll. Obviously a good move, while York finished 20th and missed relegation by

one place, the Shakers won the second division title and Dean picked up a championship medal, hopefully, the first of many.

Coventry C (From trainee on 30/10/87)
York C (Signed on 9/3/90) FL 210 FLC 9 FAC 4 Others 16
Bury (Signed on 15/8/96) FL 46 FLC 4 FAC 1 Others 3

Dean Kiely

[KIKO] CHARANA Manuel Henrique
Baptista Gomes
Born: Portugal, 24 October 1976
Height: 5'10" Weight: 12.5
Stockport finally signed this Portuguese midfielder last December after he had been at Edgeley Park on trial in 1995-96. A talented dribbler, Kiko's appearances were restricted to just one start and four from the bench, by fitness and injury problems, following his first team debut as a sub at Doncaster in the AWS competition and it is difficult to see where he goes from here.

Stockport Co (Signed from Belenenses on 10/12/96) FL 0+3 Others 1+1

KILBANE Kevin Daniel
Born: Preston, 1 February 1977
Height: 6'0" Weight: 12.10
International Honours: Ei: U21-4
An enigmatic young Eire U21 international who, at his best, has the pace and ability to trouble the tightest defences. His speed and crossing from the Preston left wing last season caused problems for many opponents, but a loss of form, coupled with a nagging groin injury, did not always see him at his best. Despite this, North End still received a bid of £900,000 from West Brom, which was rejected. Is young enough to mature into a very good player. *Stop Press:* Was reported to have become West Brom's first £1 million signing in early June.

Preston NE (From trainee on 6/7/95) FL 39+9/3 FLC 4 FAC 1 Others 1+1

KILCLINE Brian
Born: Nottingham, 7 May 1962
Height: 6'2" Weight: 12.10
Club Honours: FAC '87; Div 1 '93

International Honours: E: U21-2
A central defender of proven ability, Brian had an outstanding season for Mansfield in 1996-97, dominating the centre of the park, producing some of the best football of his long career and playing no small part in successfully shoring up a leaky defence. Despite that, however, he and Town parted company in the summer.

Notts Co (From apprentice on 1/4/80) FL 156+2/9 FLC 16/1 FAC 10/2
Coventry C (£60,000 on 11/6/84) FL 173/28 FLC 16+1/4 FAC 15/3 Others 8
Oldham Ath (£400,000 on 1/8/91) FL 8 FLC 2
Newcastle U (£250,000 on 19/2/92) F/PL 20+12 FLC 3+2 FAC 1+2 Others 5
Swindon T (£90,000 on 20/1/94) P/FL 16+1 FLC 3 Others 4
Mansfield T (Free on 1/12/95) FL 48+2/3 FLC 1 FAC 2 Others 1

KILFORD Ian Anthony
Born: Bristol, 6 October 1973
Height: 5'10" Weight: 11.0
Club Honours: Div 3 '97
Without a doubt, Ian enjoyed his best season for Wigan Athletic in 1996-97 since his arrival from Nottingham Forest, a season that culminated in him winning a third division championship medal. Labelled by his manager, John Deehan, as his midfield "Rolls Royce", the graceful playmaker with a lovely touch did not disappoint, his versatility and important goals, eight in total, were vital as he was called on to fill a number of roles from right back to left wing.

Nottingham F (From trainee on 3/4/91) FL 0+1
Wigan Ath (Loaned on 23/12/93) FL 2+1/2 FAC 0+1
Wigan Ath (Free on 13/7/94) FL 82+18/17 FLC 5 FAC 3+1/1 Others 6/1

KIMBLE Alan Frank
Born: Dagenham, 6 August 1966
Height: 5'9" Weight: 12.4
Club Honours: Div 3 '91
A very reliable Wimbledon left back who arrived from Cambridge in July 1993. His emergence as a top quality defender made him a regular force in the Wimbledon line up in 1996-97. Alan is not only solid at the back but shows a fair amount of pace when coming forward and with that pace he is able to add another dimension to Joe Kinnear's assaults on the opposing team's goal. With his well-focused mind and superb ability at set piece routines he has become a valuable acquisition.

Charlton Ath (From juniors on 8/8/84) FL 6
Exeter C (Loaned on 23/8/85) FL 1 FLC 1
Cambridge U (Free on 22/8/86) FL 295+4/24 FLC 23+1 FAC 29/1 Others 22
Wimbledon (£175,000 on 27/7/93) PL 99+3 FLC 14 FAC 17

KINDER Vladimir (Vlad)
Born: Bratislava, Czechoslovakia, 9 March 1969
Height: 5'10" Weight: 13.0
International Honours: Czechoslovakia: 29
A late arrival during the 1996-97 season, but one who was welcomed in the dour struggle to stave off the threat of relegation and help Middlesbrough's beleaguered injury and illness situation, Vlad played his heart out in

Vlad Kinder

Georgiou Kinkladze

ten appearances, while scoring a vital goal in the Premiership game against Derby County. The Boro fans will hope that the hard-tackling defender's introduction to the English game has whetted his appetite for more of the same next season, and that he will be part of the side that attempts to reach the Premiership at the first time of asking. Will unfortunately be remembered as the player who was sent off during the thrilling FA Cup semi-final clash against second division, Chesterfield. Has played for both Czechoslovakia and Slovakia at international level.

Middlesbrough (£1,000,000 from Slovan Bratislava on 18/1/97) PL 4+2/1 FLC 1 FAC 2+1

KING Philip (Phil) Geoffrey
Born: Bristol, 28 December 1967
Height: 5'8" Weight: 12.7
Club Honours: FLC '91
International Honours: E: B-1

Very much a forgotten player at Aston Villa,

following a cruciate ligament injury sustained with West Bromwich in 1995-96, his nightmare was ended with a free transfer to one of his former clubs, Swindon Town, just before the transfer deadline last season. Played five games in his familiar position of left back and, although it was a bad time to rejoin the club, in the throes of a defensive reforming, he can hardly be blamed for that. This coming term should see him re-establish his credentials, although he will face fierce competition for the left-back slot from Jason Drysdale and Gary Elkins. Capable of producing quality passes and crosses, Phil can be used as an extra forward when the occasion demands.

Exeter C (From apprentice on 7/1/85) FL 24+3 FLC 1 Others 1+2
Torquay U (£3,000 on 14/7/86) FL 24/3 FLC 2 FAC 1 Others 2
Swindon T (£155,000 on 6/2/87) FL 112+4/4 FLC 11 FAC 5 Others 13
Sheffield Wed (£400,000 on 30/11/89) F/PL 124+5/2 FLC 17 FAC 9 Others 4

Notts Co (Loaned on 22/10/93) FL 6 Others 2
Aston Villa (£250,000 on 1/8/94) PL 13+3 FLC 3 Others 4
West Bromwich A (Loaned on 30/10/95) FL 4 Others 1
Swindon T (Free on 26/3/97) FL 5

KING Robert David
Born: Merthyr Tydfil, 2 September 1977
Height: 5'8" Weight: 10.6
International Honours: W: Yth

Having earlier been released by Torquay, where he had been a trainee, Robert impressed during Swansea's summer tour of Denmark and signed professional forms for the club. Although captaining the reserves for most of the season, the young right back was given two first-team starts (at Cambridge and at the Vetch against Doncaster) and will be looking for more of the same in 1997-98.

Swansea C (Free from Torquay U juniors on 1/7/96) FL 2 FAC 0+1 Others 0+1

KINKLADZE Georgiou
Born: Tbilisi, Georgia, 6 November 1973
Height: 5'8" Weight: 10.9
International Honours: Georgia: 23

Following on from 1995-96, many people were interested to see how Georgiou would fare in the first division last season. As it happened, he did have a bit of a torrid time, particularly in the first half of the campaign. However, after the New Year, the young Georgian came back well, showing all his old flair, something that was obviously generated by new manager, Frank Clark, and also rubbed off on to other players in the squad. Ever present in the league until the home FA Cup game against Middlesbrough, following some hard treatment by defenders, he missed the next five games with a groin injury. A highly entertaining dribbler from midfield, with the vision and control to create goalscoring opportunities for himself and others, it was a modest season by his standards, but he still reached

double figures, albeit half of his goals came from the penalty spot, whilst the game at Oxford was his highlight with two brilliant individual goals watched by many live on TV. Elected by his fellow professionals to the PFA award-winning first division team.
Manchester C (£2,000,000 from Dinamo Tbilisi on 17/8/95) P/FL 76/16 FLC 4 FAC 7/1

KINSELLA Mark Anthony
Born: Dublin, 12 August 1972
Height: 5'9" Weight: 11.8
Club Honours: GMVC '92; FAT '92
International Honours: Ei: U21-8; Yth
An immensely talented right-sided Millwall midfield player, Mark signed from Colchester last September and immediately made his Charlton debut against Oldham at The Valley, keeping his place throughout the season. Very clever on the ball, with good vision, and an accurate passer, he scored from several spectacular long-range shots, including one against Newcastle in the FA Cup, and it can only be a matter of time before he is called into the full Republic of Ireland squad.
Colchester U (Free from Home Farm on 18/8/89) FL 174+6/27 FLC 11/3 FAC 11/1 Others 9+1/5
Charlton Ath (£150,000 on 23/9/96) FL 37/6 FAC 1/1

KIRBY Ryan Mark
Born: Chingford, 6 September 1974
Height: 5'11" Weight: 12.0
Released by Doncaster during the 1996 close season, Ryan had spells at Preston, Crewe, and Wigan, before joining Northampton on a non-contract basis as defensive cover for first team players. However, after a few months of reserve team football he opted to join Vauxhall Conference club, Stevenage, to help in their push towards the Football League. Created an unwanted record at Northampton in having the shortest first-team career of just three minutes, following his only appearance as a sub for the club.
Arsenal (From trainee on 6/7/93)
Doncaster Rov (Free on 6/7/94) FL 73+5 FLC 0+1 FAC 2 Others 5
Preston NE (Free on 31/7/96)
Crewe Alex (Free on 9/8/96)
Wigan Ath (Free on 23/8/96) FL 5+1
Northampton T (Free on 23/9/96) FL 0+1

KITSON Paul
Born: Murton, 9 January 1971
Height: 5'11" Weight: 10.12
International Honours: E: U21-7
Totally out in the cold at St James Park following the arrival of big guns, Les Ferdinand, Faustino Asprilla, and Alan Shearer, Paul had little prospect of starting a game for Newcastle, even after the shock departure of Kevin Keegan as manager and his replacement by Kenny Dalglish. Many critics questioned the judgement of West Ham manager, Harry Redknapp, and the size of the fee, when he signed Paul, along with John Hartson in February, in a desperate bid to solve the Hammers' goal drought. It was the most inspired gamble of the season with an immediate pay off. Both scored in their second game - the dramatic

4-3 victory over Spurs - and Paul went on to become the club's top scorer with eight goals (from only 14 games), a brace against both Chelsea and Everton, topped by a glorious hat trick against Sheffield Wednesday in May. Thus he answered his critics who claimed he was not Premier League class, whilst it was a long overdue vindication for the usually chipper, but increasingly beleaguered, Redknapp, whose previous signings had been cursed by bad luck.
Leicester C (From trainee on 15/12/88) FL 39+11/6 FLC 5/3 FAC 1+1/1 Others 5/1
Derby Co (£1,300,000 on 11/3/92) FL 105/36 FLC 7/3 FAC 5/1 Others 13+1/9
Newcastle U (£2,250,000 on 24/9/94) PL 26+10/10 FLC 3+2/1 FAC 6+1/3 Others 0+1
West Ham U (£2,300,000 on 10/2/97) PL 14/8

KIWOMYA Andrew (Andy) Derek
Born: Huddersfield, 1 October 1967
Height: 5'10" Weight: 10.10
International Honours: E: Yth
Known to Luton's manager, Lennie Lawrence, from their days together at Bradford, this clever midfielder played an important role in assisting them to the second division play offs, whilst on loan. He

was particularly impressive on his Town debut, when he helped the team to a 2-0 away victory over fellow-contenders, Burnley, whilst his 25-yard curling free kick against Walsall the following month was one of the Hatter's goals of the season.
Barnsley (From apprentice on 16/7/85) FL 1
Sheffield Wed (£5,000 on 7/10/86)
Dundee (Free in 1992-93) SL 11+10/1 SC 0+1
Rotherham U (Free on 1/10/93) FL 4+3 FLC 0+1 Others 0+2 (Free to Halifax during 1994 close season)
Scunthorpe U (Free on 23/3/93) FL 9/3
Bradford C (Free on 4/7/95) FL 27+16/3 FLC 1+1 FAC 3 Others 2+1
Luton T (Loaned on 27/3/97) FL 5/1

KNIGHT Alan Edward
Born: Balham, 3 July 1961
Height: 6'1" Weight: 13.11
Club Honours: Div 3 '83
International Honours: E: U21-2; Yth
Started last season as the number two 'keeper at Portsmouth behind Aaron Flahaven, but replaced him midway through the campaign, his return coinciding with the start of an impressive cup run and an improving league position. During the course of 1996-97, Alan surpassed 750

Paul Kitson

career games for Portsmouth, and 1997-98 will mark a landmark for him as April 1998 will represent the 20th anniversary of his first-team debut for the club. Is still an excellent shot stopper despite his 35 years.
Portsmouth (From apprentice on 12/3/79) FL 642 FLC 49 FAC 39 Others 21

KNILL Alan Richard
Born: Slough, 8 October 1964
Height: 6'3" Weight: 13.0
Club Honours: WC '89
International Honours: W: 1; Yth
The towering Scunthorpe central defender, obviously strong in the air and effective at set pieces, was again troubled by injuries, this time to the calf, during the first half of last season and consequently missed several games. A player who thrives on adversity, Alan came back as strong as ever, prior to being freed in the summer.
Southampton (From apprentice on 14/10/82)
Halifax T (Free on 13/7/84) FL 118/6 FLC 6 FAC 6 Others 6
Swansea C (£15,000 on 14/8/87) FL 89/3 FLC 4 FAC 5 Others 7
Bury (£95,000 on 18/8/89) FL 141+3/8 FLC 7 FAC 8/1 Others 14+1/1
Cardiff C (Loaned on 24/9/93) FL 4
Scunthorpe U (Signed on 5/11/93) FL 131/8 FLC 5 FAC 10 Others 8

KNOWLES Christopher (Chris) James
Born: Stone, 4 February 1978
Height: 5'10" Weight: 11.6
Released by Peterborough during the 1996 close season, having come to the end of his YTS period at the club, Chris joined Chester on a monthly contract and quickly made his league debut as a stand-in goalkeeper for Ronnie Sinclair, keeping a clean sheet in a 2-0 home win over Swansea. Although he appeared twice more, he was allowed to move on, later trialling at Hereford, and then Northampton, without further success.
Chester C (From Peterborough U juniors on 15/8/96) FL 2 FLC 1
Hereford U (Free on 8/11/96)
Northampton (Free on 20/1/97)

KNOWLES Darren Thomas
Born: Sheffield, 8 October 1970
Height: 5'6" Weight: 11.1
A reliable and consistent right back who lost his place at Scarborough when John Kay arrived at the club, he was surprisingly released on transfer deadline day to join Hartlepool. Playing in the final seven games of the season, he proved to be a keen tackler, whose terrier-like displays more than made up for his lack of inches, and immediately endeared himself to the Pool supporters with his wholehearted approach to the game.
Sheffield U (From trainee on 1/7/89)
Stockport Co (£3,000 on 14/9/89) FL 51+12 FLC 2+4 Others 14+1
Scarborough (Free on 4/8/93) FL 139+5/2 FLC 11+1 FAC 9 Others 7
Hartlepool U (Free on 27/3/97) FL 7

KOORDES Rogier
Born: Haarlem, Holland, 13 June 1972
Height: 6'1" Weight: 12.11
A left-sided midfield player who joined Port Vale in February from Dutch league outfit,

SC Telstar, as an eventual replacement for the soon-to-be departing Steve Guppy, although is not an out-and-out winger, he helped to solidify the midfield, especially away from home. Was particularly impressive during his first few games, despite having language difficulties, and should be a good asset to the club in the future.
Port Vale (£75,000 from Telstar on 12/2/97) FL 7+6

KOTTILA Mika
Born: Helsinki, Finland, 22 September 1974
Height: 6'1" Weight: 12.5
Mika joined Hereford last November from Finnish football and, at first glance, appeared to be the ideal target man for a side desperately seeking goals. Unfortunately, his 13 games only brought him one goal – his ball control being excellent, his lack of pace letting him down – and he returned home in February.
Hereford U (Free from Rops FC on 29/11/96) FL 11+2/1

KUBICKI Dariusz
Born: Warsaw, Poland, 6 June 1963
Height: 5'10" Weight: 11.12
Club Honours: Div 1 '96
International Honours: Poland: 49
The Polish right back had been a regular in the Sunderland side for two years, but was controversially dropped in favour of Gareth Hall in 1996-97 when poised to equal George Mulhall's consecutive appearances record for the club. Nevertheless, Dariusz typically battled his way back into the team in the left-back position, but was again left out for the remaining four games. The tough-tackling defender, who also enjoys the attacking game, has always been popular at Roker and many fans feel that he still has something to offer the club.
Aston Villa (£200,000 from Legia Warsaw on 28/8/91) F/PL 24+1 FLC 3 FAC 4+1 Others 1
Sunderland (£100,000 on 4/3/94) P/FL 135+1 FLC 7 FAC 7

KUHL Martin
Born: Frimley, 10 January 1965
Height: 5'11" Weight: 12.8
1996-97 was a disappointing time for the Bristol City midfielder, following on from a great campaign previously, his season being much disrupted by niggling injuries, and it was no surprise when he was released on a free transfer during the summer. A defensive player who provides stability as a midfield anchor, and having two good feet and a fine shot to match, Martin should have no difficulty finding another team.
Birmingham C (From apprentice on 13/1/83) FL 103+8/5 FLC 13 FAC 8/1 Others 1+1
Sheffield U (Signed on 20/3/87) FL 38/4 FLC 2 FAC 1 Others 1
Watford (Signed on 19/2/88) FL 4
Portsmouth (£125,000 on 30/9/88) FL 146+11/27 FLC 11/1 FAC 13 Others 3
Derby Co (£650,000 on 26/9/92) FL 68/1 FLC 6 FAC 6 Others 4/1
Notts Co (Loaned on 9/9/94) FL 2

Bristol C (£330,000 on 30/12/94) FL 85+9/7 FLC 6+2 FAC 8/2 Others 4

KULCSAR George
Born: Budapest, Hungary, 12 August 1967
Height: 6'2" Weight: 13.4
International Honours: Australia: 3
Signed from Royal Antwerp on a two-and-a-half year contract last March, although born in Hungary, George moved to Australia at the age of six and it was there that he learned the game and went on to play for Canberra and Australia in the 1983 World Youth Cup. Making his Bradford debut in the number eight shirt at home to Grimsby as a direct replacement for Lee Duxbury and missing just two games in the final 11 as relegation was averted, he proved to be a hard-working midfielder who never stopped running and could be counted upon to give 100 per cent. Is currently a member of Terry Venables' international squad.
Bradford C (£100,000 from Royal Antwerp on 7/3/97) FL 9

KVARME Bjorn Tore
Born: Trondheim, Norway, 17 June 1972
Height: 6'2" Weight: 12.9
Having made an outstanding start to his Premiership career after making his debut in a 3-0 win over Aston Villa at Anfield, just a day after signing on a free transfer from the Norwegian side, Rosenborg, last January, many would feel with some justification that Bjorn warrants the title of Liverpool's find of the decade. Quickly settling in at left back, he soon became a regular member of the defence, playing in 16 of the last 20 matches, and giving the impression that he had been in the side for years. With many similarities to the legendary Mark Lawrenson, he tackled back strongly to regain possession and provided further strength to the back three, his never-say-die spirit shining through. Sorely missed in the European Cup Winners Cup games because of already being cup tied, he also proved excellent when getting up the line to provide crosses for the front men.
Liverpool (Free from Rosenborg on 17/1/97) PL 15 FAC 1

KYD Michael Robert
Born: Hackney, 21 May 1977
Height: 5'8" Weight: 12.10
Spent the summer and early part of the 1996-97 season in Australia, where he scored an impressive 46 goals, before returning to England in October and netting in his first game back for Cambridge at Brighton. Fast and skilful, he struggled to achieve full fitness, but ended the campaign as joint-leading scorer, in spite of giving the others a two month start, scoring twice in the 3-2 win over Exeter at the Abbey. Only just turned 20, he has a promising career ahead of him.
Cambridge U (From trainee on 18/5/95) FL 35+21/9 FLC 1+1 FAC 2+1/1 Others 1+1

LACEY Damian James
Born: Ogur, 3 August 1977
Height: 5'9" Weight: 11.3
A first-year professional, Damien was given an early first-team opportunity in Swansea's midfield last season when stepping out for the opening game against Rochdale. Like Robert King, he had impressed during the summer tour of Denmark but, unfortunately, he went down with kidney trouble in mid term after making 11 appearances and was forced out of contention for three months. Is sure to be back though.
Swansea C (From trainee on 1/7/96) FL 9+1 FLC 1

LAIGHT Ellis Stanley
Born: Birmingham, 30 June 1976
Height: 5'10" Weight: 11.2
Initially released by Torquay during the 1996 close season, Ellis re-signed at the start of 1996-97 on a short-term contract, but following several opportunities as a striker, scoring just one goal, he left the club in December. A gutsy player who is more at home in midfield supplying the forwards, Ellis has still to find his way back into the league, despite trialling with Barnet and Exeter.
Torquay U (From trainee on 4/7/95) FL 18+23/3 FLC 0+2 FAC 2+1 Others 0+4/1

LAMBERT Christopher James
Born: Henley, 14 September 1973
Height: 5'7" Weight: 10.4
1996-97 was yet another in-and-out season for James, who was still not certain of a place in a Reading starting line up despite being one of the most perceptive players in the squad, contributing more than his fair share of goals from midfield and, at his best, an exciting match winner. However, having signed a new contract midway through the campaign after a lengthy wage dispute, he was voted "Young Player of the Season by the fans.
Reading (From juniors on 3/7/92) FL 43+47/13 FLC 2+3/1 FAC 6+2/1 Others 2+3/1

LAMPARD Frank James
Born: Romford, 21 June 1978
Height: 6'0" Weight: 13.7
International Honours: E: Yth
Son of the West Ham assistant manager and former full back of the same name, Frank is a young midfielder who made a handful of starts for the Hammers last season, with several more appearances coming off the bench. Very unfortunate to break his leg against Aston Villa in March, he will be hoping to regain full fitness for the start of the new season and become a more regular performer. An excellent prospect with good vision, ball control, and passing ability, he was a member of the Hammers' 1996 Youth Cup final team.

West Ham U (From trainee on 1/7/95) PL 3+12 FLC 1+1 FAC 1
Swansea C (Loaned on 6/10/95) FL 8+1/1 Others 1+1

LANCASHIRE Graham
Born: Blackpool, 19 October 1972
Height: 5'10" Weight: 11.12
Club Honours: Div 4 '92, Div 3 '97
A penalty box poacher, although the Wigan Athletic striker started 1996-97 in such tremendous form, scoring ten goals in the opening 12 games, and initiating the famed "G Force" partnership with Graeme Jones, tragically, for the second time in seven months, part of his season was wrecked by a serious knee injury. Happily, however, Graham returned to first-team action at the end of the campaign, scoring the opening goal in the 2-0 home victory over Mansfield in the final match, a victory which culminated in him winning a third division championship medal.
Burnley (From trainee on 1/7/91) FL 11+20/8 FLC 1+1 FAC 2+2/1 Others 2+4
Halifax T (Loaned on 20/11/92) FL 2 Others 1+1
Chester C (Loaned on 21/1/94) FL 10+1/7
Preston NE (£55,000 on 23/12/94) FL 11+12/2 Others 1+1
Wigan Ath (Loaned on 12/1/96) FL 4/3
Wigan Ath (£35,000 on 8/3/96) FL 16+9/9 FLC 2/4

LANCASTER David
Born: Preston, 8 September 1961
Height: 6'3" Weight: 14.0
Ousted by Mark Leonard at centre forward at the start of 1996-97, having been signed from Bury during the 1996 close season, Dave was Rochdale's regular substitute for a couple of months and figured at centre half in the reserves before leaving for Bamber Bridge in March, following an extended loan period. His strength is in knockdowns for others.
Blackpool (Free from Colne Dynamoes on 15/8/90) FL 7+1/1 FLC 2 Others 0+1
Chesterfield (Loaned on 26/2/91) FL 12/4
Chesterfield (£70,000 on 27/8/91) FL 66+3/16 FLC 5/3 FAC 2 Others 6/3
Rochdale (Free on 5/7/93) FL 37+3/14 FLC 4/1 FAC 2 Others 1 (£7,500 to Halifax T on 20/7/94)
Bury (Free on 12/3/95) FL 4+6/1 FLC 0+1 Others 0+1
Rochdale (Free on 19/2/96) FL 14+6/2 FLC 1

LANDON Richard John
Born: Worthing, 22 March 1970
Height: 6'3" Weight: 13.5
The big, tall striker was squeezed out by the tough competition for places at Stockport in 1996-97, making only three substitute appearances, which led to loan spells at Macclesfield and Rotherham. At Millmoor, having hoped to resurrect his career, Richard broke his hand following his first appearance, an injury which put him out of the next five games, before coming back to play in the last seven fixtures. Remained goalless, however.
Plymouth Arg (£30,000 from Bedworth U on 26/1/94) FL 21+9/12 FLC 0+1 FAC 0+1 Others 4
Stockport Co (£50,000 on 13/7/95) FL 7+6/4 FLC 0+1 FAC 0+1
Rotherham U (Loaned on 3/3/97) FL 7+1

LANGAN Kevin
Born: Jersey, 7 April 1978
Height: 5'11" Weight: 11.2
As a first-year professional, Kevin made an encouraging Bristol City debut at right back in the 1-0 win against Swansea City in the Auto Windscreens Shield last January, showing himself to be one for the future. He will be looking to add a run of consistent reserve performances in 1997-98, in order to produce further first-team opportunities.
Bristol C (From trainee on 4/7/96) Others 1

LANGE Anthony (Tony) Stephen
Born: West Ham, 10 December 1964
Height: 6'1" Weight: 14.6
Tony's second season at Fulham was a big disappointment to him as he jockeyed for the first team place with Mark Walton in 1996-97. Having lost his goalkeeping place in September, he regained it after a home defeat by Lincoln City, but lost it permanently after the televised 4-1 debacle against Cardiff City at the end of January and was released during the summer.
Charlton Ath (From apprentice on 15/12/82) FL 12 Others 1
Aldershot (Loaned on 22/8/85) FL 7
Aldershot (Free on 7/7/86) FL 125 FLC 5 FAC 10 Others 16
Wolverhampton W (£150,000 on 13/7/89) FL 8 FLC 2
Aldershot (Loaned on 23/11/90) FL 2 Others 1
Torquay U (Loaned on 12/9/91) FL 1
West Bromwich A (Free on 12/8/92) FL 45+3 FLC 3 FAC 1 Others 7
Fulham (Free on 27/7/95) FL 59 FLC 5 FAC 6 Others 2

LAPPER Michael (Mike) Steven
Born: California, USA, 28 August 1970
Height: 6'0" Weight: 12.2
International Honours: USA: 60
A strong, dominant Southend centre half, Mike seemed to suffer from the loss of Mike Bodley in 1996-97 and never quite reached the heights of the previous season. Still one of the most committed players in the squad, he was never found wanting in effort and encouragement, and he will be hoping to overcome the injuries that also affected him during the campaign.
Southend U (£150,000 from USSF on 11/8/95) FL 46+6/1 FLC 3 Others 4

LARMOUR David James
Born: Dundonald, 23 August 1977
Height: 5'9" Weight: 11.0
Club Honours: FAYC '96
Having been a member of the Liverpool FA Youth Cup winning team of 1996, David subsequently moved to Doncaster in July 1996. Not given too many opportunities to shine, he did not perhaps make all the progress he would have hoped for and will be eager to impress when his next chance comes along.
Doncaster Rov (Free from Liverpool juniors on 12/8/96) FL 3+17 FLC 0+2

LAUNDERS Brian Terence
Born: Dublin, 8 January 1976
Height: 5'10" Weight: 11.12
International Honours: Ei: U21-9; Yth

Released by Crystal Palace during the 1996 close season, the young Irish U21 star signed for Crewe in time for the start of 1996-97. Restricted to few games, due to healthy competition for forward places and then having to undergo surgery, Brian was eagerly awaiting the opportunity of playing first division football again following Alex's promotion via the play offs, prior to being freed during the summer. Very much a player who has yet to achieve his potential.

Crystal Palace (Signed on 2/9/93) P/FL 1+3 FLC 0+2
Crewe Alex (Free on 8/8/96) FL 6+3 FLC 1+1

LAURENT Pierre
Born: Tulle, France, 13 December 1970
Height: 5'10" Weight: 9.12

A right-sided midfielder, cum winger, the 24-year-old talented Frenchman was signed by Leeds from Bastia for a cut-price payment in transfer deadline week last March. He would have cost some two million pounds to join any other French side, come the end of the season, but, because he would have been out of contract and wanted to play in the Premier League, was allowed to move. Made his awaited debut against Blackburn Rovers in April and should be up and running for the start of 1997-98.

Leeds U (£500,000 from Bastia on 27/3/97) PL 2+2

Jacob Laursen

LAURSEN Jacob
Born: Denmark, 6 October 1971
Height: 5'11" Weight: 12.0
International Honours: Denmark: 19

This Danish international defender signed from Silkeborg during the 1996 close season, operated anywhere along the back four for Derby in 1996-97. Best utilised in a left-sided role, he started the campaign explosively with a superb goal from a free-kick against Manchester United, but did not find the net again. However, his consistent and understated performances made for a very successful first season in English football and he played a significant role in keeping Derby in the Premiership.

Derby Co (£500,000 from Silkeborg on 17/7/96) PL 35+1/1 FLC 2 FAC 2

LAVIN Gerard
Born: Corby, 5 February 1974
Height: 5'9" Weight: 11.0
International Honours: S: U21-7

Gerard's Millwall appearances were severely curtailed by an on-going patella tendon injury in 1996-97. Returned to his right back position in November but was then ruled out when it was discovered he had a cyst on the tendon. At his best, he is a tough tackler with good ball control.

Watford (From trainee on 11/5/92) FL 121+5/3 FLC 11/1 FAC 6 Others 2+1
Millwall (£500,000 on 23/11/95) FL 25+4 FAC 2+1 Others 1

Brian Law

LAW Brian John
Born: Merthyr Tydfil, 1 January 1970
Height: 6'2" Weight: 15.0
International Honours: W: 1; U21-2; Yth; Sch

Although the Wolves' central defender had his ankle reconstructed in the summer of 1996, stiffness continued and a small piece of bone was later removed, it being spring before he regained full fitness, almost going on loan to Oldham. Ironically, he then came on for the last minute of a match there. He next joined the fray before half time at QPR, where his fighting qualities helped steady the team, who drew having trailed 2-0, and began four games after Easter, even venturing upfield to hit the Portsmouth bar, before being released during the summer.

Queens Park R (From trainee on 15/8/87) FL 19+1 FLC 2+1 FAC 3 Others 1
Wolverhampton W (£134,000 on 23/12/94) FL 26+5/1 FLC 1+1 FAC 7

LAW Nicholas (Nicky)
Born: Greenwich, 8 September 1961
Height: 6'0" Weight: 13.5
International Honours: E: Sch

A vastly experienced central defender who served Chesterfield well for three years, despite playing in eight of the opening 13 games last season it was noticeable that his effectiveness at second division level had been severely impaired by injury and he was allowed to join Hereford last October. Although Nicky made 15 appearances for his new club, troubled by injuries and unable to settle, he left in early March bound for non-league Ilkeston, where he now combines a player/coach role.

Arsenal (From apprentice on 17/7/79)
Barnsley (Free on 4/8/81) FL 113+1/1 FLC 5 FAC 6
Blackpool (Free on 28/8/85) FL 64+2/1 FLC 2 FAC 2 Others 3
Plymouth Arg (£40,000 on 12/3/87) FL 37+1/5 FLC 2 FAC 2 Others 0+1
Notts Co (£70,000 on 17/6/88) FL 44+3/4 FLC 4 FAC 1 Others 4
Scarborough (Loaned on 10/11/89) FL 12 FLC 1
Rotherham U (£35,000 on 1/8/90) FL 126+2/4 FLC 12/1 FAC 12 Others 7
Chesterfield (Signed on 8/10/93) FL 108+3/11 FLC 4 FAC 3 Others 10/3
Hereford U (Free on 11/10/96) FL 14 FAC 1

LAWRENCE James (Jamie) Hubert
Born: Balham, 8 March 1970
Height: 6'0" Weight:12.11
Club Honours: FLC '97

A right-footed winger, who is often used in a wing-back role, Jamie was a regular on the Leicester bench throughout last season, making the majority of his appearances in that role. Scored in both legs of the Coca-Cola Cup tie against Scarborough, including a bullet-like header at Filbert Street that saw him concussed and stretchered off. Due to squad members being cup tied, most of his starts came in that competition, including a memorable appearance from the bench to replace Mike Whitlow during the extra-time period of the Coca-Cola Cup final replay at Hillsborough, the club's 1-0 victory handing him a cup winners medal. With good feet and pace, these qualities will serve him well in the Premiership in 1997-98. *Stop Press:* Was reported to have signed for Bradford City during the summer, a £50,000 fee changing hands.

Sunderland (Signed from Cowes on 15/10/93) FL 2+2 FLC 0+1
Doncaster Rov (£20,000 on 17/3/94) FL 16+9/3 FLC 2 FAC 1 Others 3
Leicester C (£125,000 on 6/1/95) P/FL 21+26/1 FLC 3+4/2 FAC 1+1

LAWRENCE Matthew James
Born: Northampton, 19 June 1974
Height: 5'10" Weight: 12.12

Able to play in attack, midfield or defence, he displayed some outstanding early-season form for Wycombe in 1996-97 as a tough-tackling midfielder, but, after an injury sidelined him, he was unable to re-establish himself and joined Fulham in February. With Paul Watson switching to the left for the injured Robbie Herrera, and with the manager, Micky Adams, needing a right-wing back with pace and crossing ability, Matt slotted into the berth as if he had played there for years, appearing in the final 11 games in which only one was lost and only two goals conceded.

Wycombe W (£20,000 from Grays Ath on 19/1/96) FL 13+3/1 FLC 4 FAC 1 Others 0+1
Fulham (Free on 7/2/97) FL 13+2

Matthew Lawrence

LAWS Brian
Born: Wallsend, 14 October 1961
Height: 5'8" Weight: 11.5
Club Honours: Div 3 '82; FLC '89, '90; FMC '89
International Honours: E: B-1
Started last season as Grimsby's player/manager, but following a disastrous 3-1 defeat at home to Wolves on the opening day, Brian picked himself only twice more before the club's declining fortunes led to his dismissal. Still a midfield anchor man when used, he signed for Scunthorpe in January on non-contract terms after a similar spell with Darlington, but was sidelined by a knee injury which required operation and then found himself appointed manager before resuming full fitness!
Burnley (From apprentice on 19/10/79) FL 125/12 FLC 14/2 FAC 15/1 Others 3
Huddersfield T (£10,000 on 26/8/83) FL 56/1 FLC 7 FAC 3
Middlesbrough (£30,000 on 15/3/85) FL 103+5/12 FLC 6+1/2 FAC 8+1 Others 2
Nottingham F (£120,000 on 7/7/88) F/PL 136+11/4 FLC 28+4 FAC 16+2/1 Others 11+1
Grimsby T (Free on 1/12/94) FL 30+16/2 FLC 2 FAC 4/1
Darlington (Free on 18/11/96) FL 10 FAC 1
Scunthorpe U (Free on 27/1/97) FL 2+2 Others 2

LAWSON Ian James
Born: Huddersfield, 4 November 1977
Height: 5'11" Weight: 11.5
One of a growing band of promising Huddersfield youngsters, this skilful and pacy forward made his debut when coming off the bench in a 3-0 home win over Wrexham early last season and would have made more appearances were it not for injury. Good in the air, with much expected of him in the future, the hope is that the club have unearthed the new Andy Booth. Opened his scoring account for Town in a

3-3 home draw against Bradford, his header pegging back the deficit to one goal, and picked up two more before the campaign closed.
Huddersfield T (From trainee on 26/1/95) FL 8+10/3 FLC 1+3 FAC 1+1

LAZARIDIS Stanley (Stan)
Born: Perth, Australia, 16 August 1972
Height: 5'9" Weight: 11.12
International Honours: Australia: 9
The flying Australian left winger became a more established member of the West Ham first-team squad last season, showing the ability to outpace his opponents down the flank, or to cut inside when the occasion demanded. His best performance came at Nottingham Forest in September, when his pace overwhelmed the Forest right back and paved the way to a 2-0 victory, while his first goal for the club in March, earned the Hammers an invaluable point away to Wimbledon.
West Ham U (£300,000 from West Adelaide on 8/9/95) PL 15+11/1 FLC 4+1 FAC 1+1

LEABURN Carl Winston
Born: Lewisham, 30 March 1969
Height: 6'3" Weight: 13.0
The tall striker was a regular in the Charlton side throughout 1996-97, despite refusing to sign a contract at the start of the season. Again, his main strengths were the ability to hold up the ball and lay it off, plus his heading accomplishment at corners and set pieces. Scored several valuable goals, but failed to improve on his career scoring ratio, despite being used on his own up front for several games towards the end of the campaign.
Charlton Ath (From apprentice on 22/4/87) FL 263+45/50 FLC 19/5 FAC 18+2/3 Others 9+5/4
Northampton T (Loaned on 22/3/90) FL 9

LEADBEATER Richard Paul
Born: Dudley, 21 October 1977
Height: 6'1" Weight: 11.7
After scoring four in midweek for Wolves' reserves, the young striker surprisingly came on for the closing minutes of a league match at Southend in October. Although not taking advantage of a half chance to score, he did not look out of his depth, being a useful header of the ball with an eye for goal. Finished equal top scorer in the Central League for the club, along with Dominic Foley and Glen Crowe.
Wolverhampton W (From trainee on 3/7/96) FL 0+1

LEADBITTER Christopher (Chris) Jonathan
Born: Middlesbrough, 17 October 1967
Height: 5'9" Weight: 10.6
Club Honours: Div 3 '91
Having started 1996-97 as a regular in the Plymouth team, the hard-working, tough-tackling midfielder's season was unfortunately brought to an end in January after it was learnt that he required an operation to repair cruciate ligament knee damage. Despite being out of contract during the summer, hopefully, with the problem

cleared up and back in training, Chris will be fit to return in time for the start of 1997-98.
Grimsby T (From apprentice on 4/9/85)
Hereford U (Free on 21/8/86) FL 32+4/1 FLC 2 FAC 2 Others 3
Cambridge U (Free on 2/8/88) FL 144+32/18 FLC 12/3 FAC 16+2/3 Others 11+2/1
Bournemouth (£25,000 on 16/8/93) FL 45+9/3 FLC 6+1 FAC 5 Others 2
Plymouth Arg (Free on 27/7/95) FL 46+6/1 FLC 2 FAC 6/1 Others 5+1/1

LEANING Andrew (Andy) John
Born: Goole, 18 May 1963
Height: 6'0" Weight: 14.7
A well-known 'keeper in the lower divisions, Andy came to Chesterfield last October for Billy Mercer, having been at Dundee on a non-contract basis. Those who got to games early enough often saw Andy coaching and helping with Billy's preparation, and it says much for his character that he would offer such help to the man who kept him out of the side.
York C (Free from Rowntree Mackintosh on 1/7/85) FL 69 FLC 4 FAC 8 Others 5
Sheffield U (Free on 28/5/87) FL 21 FLC 2 FAC 2
Bristol C (£12,000 on 27/9/88) FL 75 FLC 5 FAC 7 Others 2
Lincoln C (Free on 24/3/94) FL 36 FLC 6 FAC 3 Others 6 (Freed during 1996 season)
Dundee (Free during 1996 close season)
Chesterfield (Free on 1/10/96) FL 9 Others 1

LE BIHAN Neil Ernest
Born: Croydon, 14 March 1976
Height: 5'11" Weight: 12.13
The young Peterborough midfielder figured in the side just five times in 1996-97, before being freed during the past summer. When picked, however, despite lacking match fitness, the former Spurs' trainee continued to show a fine touch, coupled with excellent distribution, and will be looking for a way back to the league, maybe via the Conference. Also had a spell on loan with Bishop's Stortford during the season.
Peterborough U (Free from Tottenham H juniors on 13/7/94) FL 21+10 FLC 2+1/1 FAC 2+1/2 Others 5+2

Frank Leboeuf

LEBOEUF Frank
Born: France, 22 January 1968
Height: 6'1" Weight: 12.6
Club Honours: FAC '97
International Honours: France: 11

Understudy to Laurent Blanc in the French squad, this superb sweeper was snapped up by Chelsea just three days after the Euro 96 final. His influence on Chelsea's defence in 1996-97 was immense as the Blues opened the season with three consecutive clean sheets, and he moved upfield to open his goalscoring account with a bullet of a header against Coventry in the third of those games. Frank is the perfect example of the modern sweeper, being resolute in defence but also good on the ball. Possibly the most constructive defender in the Premiership, he often walks the ball out of defence to launch defence-splitting through balls to the forward players, his superb 30-yard pass to Mark Hughes for Chelsea's first goal in the FA Cup sixth round at Portsmouth being a prime example. He is also a regular goalscorer both from open play and coolly-taken, side-footed penalties, keeping his nerve in the frantic atmosphere at Stamford Bridge to roll home the controversial extra-time penalty against Leicester City in the FA Cup fifth round replay. Unlike some traditional stoppers who are content just to clear their lines, Frank is always looking to play his way out of trouble and to instigate counter attacks and his outstanding displays and calm air of authority have made him a cult figure amongst Chelsea fans. Finished an excellent first season in England with an FA Cup winners medal, following the 2-0 win over Middlesbrough.
Chelsea (£2,500,000 from Strasbourg on 12/7/96) PL 26/6 FLC 2 FAC 7/1

LEE Christian
Born: Aylesbury, 8 October 1976
Height: 6'2" Weight: 11.7

The tall Northampton striker was in and out of the first team last season, before starting to find the back of the net. Used sparingly, with more substitute appearances than starts, the manager, Ian Atkins, continues to refer to him as "One for the Future".
Northampton T (Free from Doncaster Rov YTS on 13/7/95) FL 13+21/7 FLC 1/2 FAC 1+2 Others 5+2

LEE David John
Born: Kingswood, 26 November 1969
Height: 6'3" Weight: 13.12
Club Honours: Div 2 '89
International Honours: E: U21-10; Yth

David suffered a frustrating 1996-97 campaign after showing the best form of his Chelsea career during 1995-96 when he settled into the sweeper position in Glenn Hoddle's 3-5-2 formation. Having lost his place to close season signing, Frank Leboeuf, and sitting out the first ten Premiership matches of the campaign, he replaced the injured French international for the emotional fixture against Tottenham, three days after the tragic death of club vice-president, Matthew Harding. In the 51st minute with the score at one apiece he

stepped up to slam a penalty past Ian Walker, but, unfortunately, 28 minutes later, his season was over when his right leg was broken by a heavy tackle. This was the latest setback in a career which has promised so much, but has resulted in this talented, ball-playing centre-back starting just 118 matches in his nine seasons at the club.
Chelsea (From trainee on 1/7/88) F/PL 118+32/11 FLC 13+5/1 FAC 10+4 Others 6+2/1
Reading (Loaned on 30/1/92) FL 5/5
Plymouth Arg (Loaned on 26/3/92) FL 9/1
Portsmouth (Loaned on 12/8/94) FL 4+1

LEE David Mark
Born: Blackburn, 5 November 1967
Height: 5'7" Weight: 11.0
Club Honours: Div 1 '97

David is still an invaluable member of the Bolton squad who figured in over half of their games last season, both in the starting line up and as a substitute. A speedy winger who can run all day and take players on with ease, one of his two goals came in the crucial 2-1 win over Bradford on New Year's Day. Although a regular in the Wanderers' side that reached the Premiership in 1993, this was his first (first division) championship medal, the club previously being promoted as runners up.
Bury (From juniors on 8/8/86) FL 203+5/35 FLC 15/1 FAC 6 Others 19+1/4
Southampton (£350,000 on 27/8/91) F/PL 11+9 FAC 0+1 Others 1+1
Bolton W (£300,000 on 2/11/92) P/FL 124+31/17 FLC 19+1/2 FAC 13+2 Others 8+1/1

Graeme Lee

LEE Graeme Barry
Born: Middlesbrough, 31 May 1978
Height: 6'2" Weight: 13.0

A well-built central defender who made great progress in his first full season as a professional with Hartlepool in 1996-97, having made his breakthrough to the first team in 1995-96, "Spike" was not rushed, but, on winning a regular place in mid term, he was probably Pool's most outstanding player. Although at times he was criticised

by the fans for his laid-back style, he held on to his place on merit, while other much more experienced players struggled.
Hartlepool U (From trainee on 2/7/96) FL 26+4 FLC 0+2 FAC 2 Others 1+1

LEE Jason Benedict
Born: Forest Gate, 9 May 1971
Height: 6'3" Weight: 13.8

Having got rid of the hairstyle for which he had become well known, and hoping for a long run in the Nottingham Forest side in 1996-97 after others had been given their chance, September and October was his best time and he scored in successive games, the second when coming on as a sub at Chelsea. However, after losing his place to Kevin Campbell, and spending time on the bench, the striker went out on loan to Grimsby, scoring twice, before having a similar spell at Charlton. There he made a welcome return to the club where he had started his career, and was immediately thrust into first team action partnering Carl Leaburn up front against Tranmere Rovers at The Valley. Big and strong, Jason found the net on three occasions, all from headers, and it was a big disappointment when he returned to Forest just before the transfer deadline.
Charlton Ath (From trainee on 2/6/89) FL 0+1 Others 0+2
Stockport Co (Loaned on 6/2/91) FL 2
Lincoln C (£35,000 on 1/3/91) FL 86+7/21 FLC 6 FAC 2+1/1 Others 4
Southend U (Signed on 6/8/93) FL 18+6/3 FLC 1 FAC 1 Others 5+3/3
Nottingham F (£200,000 on 4/3/94) F/PL 41+35/14 FLC 4+3/1 FAC 0+5 Others 4+2
Charlton Ath (Loaned on 5/2/97) FL 7+1/3
Grimsby T (Loaned on 27/3/97) FL 2+5/2 FAC 1

LEE Robert Martin
Born: West Ham, 1 February 1966
Height: 5'10" Weight: 11.13
Club Honours: Div 1 '93
International Honours: E: 13; B-1; U21-2

Robert was a powerful influence in Newcastle's midfield throughout last season, continuing to show his strength on the ball, difficult to dispossess, and liking nothing better than to make searching runs into the heart of the opposition's defence. Full of energy and workrate, he has a keen eye for goal, although his strike rate did not match that of the previous season as the team's changed style required him to adopt a more defensive game and restricted his opportunities for surging into the opposing box. However, he performed creditably when injuries and suspension led to him being called upon to play as a lone striker in the home UEFA Cup tie against Monaco and he scored in an emotional return to The Valley for a third round FA Cup tie against his former club, Charlton. His leadership qualities have also been recognised and he captained the side whenever Peter Beardsley was not playing. Having just missed out on selection for Euro 96, a great disappointment for him, he was recalled by Glenn Hoddle for the friendly against Mexico, and this clearly encouraged him as he turned in an outstanding display at right-wing back, enabling him to win further international honours into the summer.

Charlton Ath (Free from Hornchurch on 12/7/83) FL 274+24/59 FLC 16+3/1 FAC 14/2 Others 10+2/3
Newcastle U (£700,00 on 22/9/92) F/PL 180+1/39 FLC 13/3 FAC 14/4 Others 12/4

LEGG Andrew (Andy)
Born: Neath, 28 July 1966
Height: 5'8" Weight: 10.7
Club Honours: WC '89, '91; AIC '95
International Honours: W: 4

Andy, a fast and skilful winger with tremendous stamina, became a vital part of Birmingham's squad throughout last season,despite failing to win a regular place due to a series of niggling injuries hampering his progress, his ability to cross dangerously from wide and track back keeping him in the frame, while he also scored four goals, the joint highest of any recognised midfielder. Another great strength, and one that makes him a must for any squad, is his long-throw capability, although his world record throw of 44.54 metres was beaten by Tranmere Rover's Dave Challinor in 1996-97. A Welsh international, he added to his appearances in matches against Holland and the Republic of Ireland in 1996-97, the former being a World Cup qualifier.
Swansea C (Signed from Britton Ferry on 12/8/88) FL 155+8/29 FLC 9+1 FAC 16/4 Others 15+3/5
Notts Co (£275,000 on 23/7/93) FL 85+4/9 FLC 11 FAC 7+1 Others 13+2/6
Birmingham C (Signed on 29/2/96) FL 31+14/5 FLC 3+1 FAC 2+1

LEITCH Donald Scott
Born: Motherwell, 6 October 1969
Height: 5'9" Weight: 11.8

Following a successful loan period with Swindon at the end of 1995-96, the division two championship season, Scott signed a two-year contract for the Robins in July 1996. Again proved to be one of Town's most consistent performers, as the anchorman in midfield operating just in front of the defence, playing in all but ten of the club's league matches and only missing games through injury or suspension. His only goal came early in the campaign in a 2-0 Coca-Cola Cup victory over Wolves.
Dumfermline Ath (Free from Shettleston Juniors on 4/4/90) SL 72+17/16 SLC 6+1/3 SC 3 Others 1
Heart of Midlothian (Signed on 6/8/93) SL 46+9/2 SLC 1+2/1 SC 3 Others 2
Swindon T (Loaned on 29/3/96) FL 7
Swindon T (£15,000 on 30/7/96) FL 36 FLC 5/1 FAC 1

LENHART Sascha Daniel David
Born: Cologne, Germany, 16 December 1973
Height: 5'5" Weight: 9.7

A diminutive left winger signed on loan from Royal Antwerp last September, Sascha made just one solitary appearance as a sub for Leicester in the home Coca-Cola Cup tie against Scarborough, before suffering a broken foot during a reserve match and being sidelined for two months. Unable to fight his way into contention for a first team place, he returned home in mid January.
Leicester C (Loaned from Royal Antwerp on 21/9/96) FLC 0+1

LENNON Neil Francis
Born: Lurgan, 25 June 1971
Height: 5'9" Weight: 13.2
Club Honours: FLC '97
International Honours: NI: 15; B-3; U23-1; U21-2; Yth

Gradually becoming more and more important to Leicester as last season wore on, the fiery, right-footed dynamic midfielder had many moments to savour, among them a rasping drive for the first goal in the 2-0 Coca-Cola Cup win at York and a brilliant solo run that created the winner at home to Leeds in the league. It was not all roses, however, being fined by the FA after an alleged gesture following a match against Newcastle, sent off in the FA Cup win over Norwich, and playing the second half of the campaign carrying a broken toe. Currently a fixture in the Northern Ireland side, his impressive non-stop displays against Middlesbrough in the Coca-Cola Cup final at both Wembley and in the replay at Hillsborough, were a major factor in City lifting the trophy for the first time since the competition began.
Manchester C (From trainee on 26/8/89) FL 1
Crewe Alex (Free on 9/8/90) FL 142+5/15 FLC 8+1/1 FAC 16/1 Others 15+1
Leicester C (£750,000 on 23/2/96) P/FL 49+1/2 FLC 7/1 FAC 2 Others 3

Neil Lennon

LEONARD Mark Anthony
Born: St Helens, 27 September 1962
Height: 5'11" Weight: 13.3

In his second spell with Rochdale, and his third under manager Graham Barrow, having been signed from Wigan during the 1996 close season, Mark played either as the target man up front or as a bustling midfielder. After amazingly bad luck in front of goal, the veteran number nine finally broke his duck for the season when he scored the winner against Cardiff in January, the 112th senior goal of his career.
Everton (Signed from Witton A on 24/2/82)
Tranmere Rov (Loaned on 24/3/83) FL 6+1
Crewe Alex (Free on 1/6/83) FL 51+3/15 FLC 4/2 FAC 2 Others 3+1
Stockport Co (Free on 13/2/85) FL 73/23 FLC 5/2 FAC 1 Others 2/3
Bradford C (£40,000 on 27/9/86) FL 120+37/29 FLC 13+5/6 FAC 6+3/1 Others 6+5/3
Rochdale (£40,000 on 27/3/92) FL 9/1
Preston NE (£40,000 on 13/8/92) FL 19+3/1 FLC 2
Chester C (Free on 13/8/93) FL 28+4/8 FLC 2 FAC 3/1 Others 3
Wigan Ath (Signed on 15/9/94) FL 60+4/12 FLC 2 FAC 6/2 Others 6/2
Rochdale (Free on 3/7/96) FL 39/4 FLC 2 FAC 1

LEONHARDSEN Oyvind
Born: Norway, 17 August 1970
Height: 5'10" Weight: 11.13
International Honours: Norway: 53

A tireless player, who has the ability to shake off players in the most compact of midfields, Oyvind is strong and can hold the ball well, thus allowing for overlapping runs by defenders. As in 1995-96, the Norwegian international enjoyed an excellent season at Wimbledon in 1996-97, with moments of sheer magic which often turned an otherwise sterile game, whilst also displaying an uncompromising passion for the cause. A very popular player among the Dons' fans, he also scored some invaluable goals, including an equaliser at Liverpool and two more in 1-1 draws against Newcastle and Nottingham Forest. Stop Press: Reported to have joined Liverpool, a fee of £4.5 million changing hands during the summer.
Wimbledon (£660,000 from Rosenborg on 8/11/94) PL 73+3/13 FLC 7+2/1 FAC 17/2

LE SAUX Graeme Pierre
Born: Jersey, 17 October 1968
Height: 5'10" Weight: 12.2
Club Honours: PL '95
International Honours: E: 20; B-2; U21-4

A year after his horrific injury, Graeme returned to first team action with Blackburn last October and amazed all by the way he was able to reclaim his old form and his international spot. As confident as ever on the ball and able to twist and turn more easily than expected he looked the creative left back of old. However, no sooner had he won back his England place he became discontented with the lack of progress at Ewood and was omitted from the team. Three days later, however, he was restored and was soon back to his brilliant self, scoring his first goal of the campaign in the vital April game against Sheffield Wednesday. Skilful, very quick, a good crosser, and a creator of chances, he can play as a left-sided wing back or in midfield to equal effect.
Chelsea (Free from St Paul's, Jersey, on 9/12/87) F/PL 77+13/8 FLC 7+6/1 FAC 7+1 Others 8+1
Blackburn Rov (Signed on 25/3/93) PL 127+2/7 FLC 10 FAC 8 Others 6+1

LESTER Jack William
Born: Sheffield, 8 October 1975
Height: 5'10" Weight: 11.2
International Honours: E: Sch

A right-footed Grimsby striker, who, after several seasons in the reserves and following a spell on loan at Doncaster Rovers last September, at last earned himself a regular run in the senior squad as Kenny Swain's policy of blooding his youngsters in the attempt to stave off relegation took effect. He did not waste the opportunity, his speed and ability to lose his marker, establishing him as a regular goal-scorer in 1996-97.
Grimsby T (From juniors on 8/7/94) FL 17+17/5 FLC 0+2 FAC 0+2
Doncaster Rov (Loaned on 20/9/96) FL 5+6/1

Matt le Tissier

LE TISSIER Matthew (Matt) Paul
Born: Guernsey, 14 October 1968
Height: 6'1" Weight: 13.8
International Honours: E: 8; B-5; Yth

1996-97 was a traumatic season for Southampton's star player, ending with the side just avoiding relegation. Selected by Glenn Hoddle to play against Italy in the important World Cup qualifier at Wembley, following a September appearance versus Moldova, he was one of the players pilloried, in his case quite unfairly, by the press following England's 1-0 defeat. At club level, he was seriously affected by ankle and groin injuries throughout the campaign, being a regular sub as the season ground to a halt, although still managing to score 16 goals, far and away the biggest haul at the Dell. When fully fit, he remained outstanding. Brilliant with the ball at his feet, often leaving defenders for dead, his crossing, free kicks, and corners, creating numerous chances for others, the team was not the same without him. However, all is well that ends well and both Matt and Saints lived to fight another Premiership day together, it being unthinkable for many that he would ever leave, having publicly pledged himself to the club.

Southampton (From apprentice on 17/10/86) F/PL 321+36/140 FLC 36+6/23 FAC 29+1/12 Others 11+1/9

LEVER Mark
Born: Beverley, 29 March 1970
Height: 6'3" Weight: 13.5

Another of the excellent group of young defenders to come up through Grimsby's youth scheme, the right footer proved both strong in the tackle and in the air in 1996-97. The horrendous chapter of long-term injuries to the club's central defenders, and his suspension after a contentious sending off, limited his appearances and contributed to the dismal season the club experienced.
Grimsby T (From trainee on 9/8/88) FL 256+8/8 FLC 16+1 FAC 14+1 Others 9

LEWIS Neil Anthony
Born: Wolverhampton, 28 June 1974
Height: 5'8" Weight: 11.1
Club Honours: FLC '97

Left-footed Leicester midfielder or wing back. On the fringes of the first-team squad during the early part of last season, occasionally standing in as a left-wing back during City's injury crisis, he is a player whose obvious potential threatens to go unfilled, especially after a night club incident saw him jailed in January. A talented player, with super dribbling skills, Neil made just six starts prior to the incident that put him out of action for the rest of the campaign and the club can only hope that they can get him back to his best in time for 1997-98.
Leicester C (From trainee on 9/7/92) F/PL 53+14/1 FLC 6+1 FAC 2 Others 2

LIBURD Richard John
Born: Nottingham, 26 September 1973
Height: 5'9" Weight: 11.1

Having signed a new contract for Bradford at the beginning of last season, Richard showed more consistency this time round, playing really well in the club's new formation as a wing back, despite having to miss games when suffering a damaged shoulder. Equally at home on the right or left-hand side of the park, although lacking weight, he is strong in the challenge, does not lack commitment, and was a regular during the run in to the end of a campaign that saw City avert relegation in the last match, a 3-0 home win over QPR.
Middlesbrough (£20,000 from Eastwood T on 25/3/93) FL 41/1 FLC 4 FAC 2 Others 5
Bradford C (£200,000 on 21/7/94) FL 75+3/3 FLC 6+2 FAC 2+2 Others 2

LIDDELL Andrew Mark
Born: Leeds, 28 June 1973
Height: 5'8" Weight: 10.9
International Honours: S: U21-11

Set off like a house on fire for Barnsley in 1996-97, his goalscoring in the early games giving the Reds just the impetus they needed. However, the arrival of John Hendrie restricted him to the subs' bench for long periods after that, although he showed when starting a crucial match at Reading

that he had not lost any of his sharpness around the box. And, in a season that saw the club climb out of the first division for the first time in their history, Andrew was probably the unluckiest player at Oakwell. Small for a front man, but a tireless worker.
Barnsley (From trainee on 6/7/91) FL 126 +38/33 FLC 8+1/1 FAC 4+3 Others 2+1

LIDDLE Craig George
Born: Chester le Street, 21 October 1971
Height: 5'11" Weight: 12.7

The hard tackling and dedicated young Middlesbrough midfielder continued to work hard in an effort to force his way into the first-team squad in 1996-97, his apprenticeship with non-league Blyth Spartans having moulded his resolution. While his six meagre appearances during the season were due in no small measure to the invasion of the world-class stars engaged by the club in its ambitious attempt for honours, his application prevailed and he will be looking for a breakthrough this coming term, hopefully, with Boro. Extremely powerful in the air, Craig is more than capable of covering in at the back if required, something he did on a few occasions during the campaign, when standing in for Curtis Fleming.
Aston Villa (From trainee on 4/7/90 - Free to Blyth Spartans in August 1991)
Middlesbrough (Free from Blyth Spartans on 12/7/94) P/FL 18+1 FLC 2+1 FAC 2 Others 2

LIGHTBOURNE Kyle Lavince
Born: Bermuda, 29 September 1968
Height: 6'2" Weight: 12.4
International Honours: Bermuda: 24

The leading Walsall scorer for the third successive season, the tall striker missed only one game throughout 1996-97 and even gave up the chance of a Bermuda cap to help the club in their vain last-gasp bid for a play-off place. Interestingly, one of the many outstanding goals netted by Kyle during the campaign was unfortunately in the FA Cup replay at Burnley, when a power failure led to the game being called off at half time. His electrifying pace and finishing power with both head and feet brought a bid from Coventry last season and Saddlers' fans fear he may have moved on by the start of 1997-98.
Scarborough (Signed on 11/12/92) FL 11+8/3 FLC 1 Others 0+1
Walsall (Free on 17/9/93) FL 158+7/65 FLC 8/3 FAC 16+2/12 Others 7/5

LIGHTFOOT Christopher (Chris) Ian
Born: Warrington, 1 April 1970
Height: 6'2" Weight: 13.6

A more than useful Crewe utility player who can play in central defence or in midfield, and possessing good passing skills and strength in abundance, Chris was unfortunate to miss quite a chunk of last season due to an injury. However, he was delighted to be part of the club's rise to the first division, via the play offs, coming off the bench in two of the three matches, including the final at Wembley. Also scored his first goals for Alex.

Chester C (From trainee on 11/7/88) FL 263+14/32 FLC 15+2/1 FAC 16+2/1 Others 14+2/5
Wigan Ath (£87,500 on 13/7/95) FL 11+3/1 FLC 2 FAC 2 Others 3
Crewe Alex (£50,000 on 22/3/96) FL 21+10/1 FAC 1+1/1 Others 3+2

LILLEY Derek Symon
Born: Paisley, 9 February 1974
Height: 5'11" Weight: 12.7
International Honours: S: Yth

Derek is a 23-year-old Scottish striker whom Leeds' manager, George Graham, paid Greenock Morton in excess of half a million pounds for on transfer deadline day last March. A robust and physical type of player, he had been his club's top goalscorer for the previous three seasons and signed for United in the face of heavy competition from clubs both north and south of the border. Making his debut in the game with Blackburn Rovers in April, as an 85th minute sub' along with another new signing, Pierre Laurent, he played out the remainder of 1996-97 without getting on the scoresheet. Should, however, make his mark this coming season when fully acclimatised.
Greenock Morton (Free from Everton BC on 13/8/91) SL 157+23/56 SLC 5+1/4 SC 9+4/4 Others 6+4/5
Leeds U (£500,000+ on 27/3/97) PL 4+2

LIMPAR Anders Erik
Born: Solna, Sweden, 24 September 1965
Height: 5'8" Weight: 11.5
Club Honours: Div 1 '91; FAC '95; CS '95
International Honours: Sweden: 69

A crowd-pleasing winger who is equally at home on the right or left flanks, and possessing explosive pace and a powerful shot, Anders started only two matches for Everton last season, despite numerous pleas for his inclusion, his subs' appearance against Blackburn on New Year's Day was his last for the club. Leaving for Birmingham in January, it was a bold attempt by Trevor Francis to open up the play at St Andrews, but five games later the plan had backfired. Although he showed some hints of the skill he was capable of, niggling injuries often stopped him from completing a full game and he soon fell out of favour, having his contract cancelled before the campaign ended after he had failed to turn up for a reserve game.
Arsenal (£1,000,000 from Cremonese on 6/8/90) F/PL 76+20/17 FLC 9 FAC 7/2 Others 4/1
Everton (£1,600,000 on 24/3/94) PL 51+15/5 FLC 2 FAC 7+3/1 Others 4
Birmingham C (£100,000 on 20/1/97) FL 3+1 FAC 1

LING Martin
Born: West Ham, 15 July 1966
Height: 5'8" Weight: 10.8
Club Honours: Div 2 '96

Cultured Leyton Orient midfielder. Having played for Swindon under Glenn Hoddle during their rise to the Premier League, Martin arrived at Brisbane Road during the 1996 close season and went on to miss just two matches in 1996-97. Scored his only league goal (the winner) in the last home game against Hereford in what proved to be their final league defeat (voted by Sky Sports one of their best goals of the season) and often looked a class above the third division, showing many good touches and passing skills.
Exeter C (From apprentice on 13/1/84) FL 109+8/14 FLC 8 FAC 4 Others 5
Swindon T (£25,000 on 14/7/86) FL 2 FLC 1+1
Southend U (£15,000 on 16/10/86) FL 126+12/31 FLC 8/2 FAC 7/1 Others ll+1/3
Mansfield T (Loaned on 24/1/91) FL 3
Swindon T (£15,000 on 28/3/91) F/PL 132+18/10 FLC 11+1/1 FAC 10+1/1 Others 12+1/1
Leyton Orient (Free on 23/7/96) FL 39+5/1 FLC 2 FAC 2 Others 1/1

LINIGHAN Andrew (Andy)
Born: Hartlepool, 18 June 1962
Height: 6'3" Weight: 13.10
Club Honours: FLC '93; FAC '93; ECWC '94
International Honours: E: B-4

Started the opening nine games in central defence for Arsenal last season, effectively standing in for the injured Tony Adams and, despite being used to cover Martin Keown in November and December, the tough-tackling, consistent centre back was allowed to move to Crystal Palace at the end of January. Despite his age, he was still very fit and competitive, while his height gave Palace an edge both at the back and up front at set pieces, two headers against Bolton and Reading proving the latter point. An integral part of the team that went back to the Premiership via the play offs, Andy would have been delighted that the Eagle's goals against column was the joint best in the division.
Hartlepool U (Free from Henry Smiths BC on 19/9/80) FL 110/4 FLC 7+1/1 FAC 8 Others 1/1
Leeds U (£20,000 on 15/5/84) FL 66/3 FLC 6/1 FAC 2 Others 2
Oldham Ath (£65,000 on 17/1/86) FL 87/6 FLC 8/2 FAC 3 Others 4
Norwich C (£350,000 on 4/3/88) FL 86/8 FLC 6 FAC 10 Others 4
Arsenal (£1,250,000 on 4/7/90) F/PL 101+17/5 FLC 13+1/1 FAC 12+2/1 Others 9+1/1
Crystal Palace (£150,000 on 27/1/97) FL 19/2 Others 3

David Linighan

LINIGHAN David
Born: Hartlepool, 9 January 1965
Height: 6'2" Weight: 13.0
Club Honours: Div 2 '92

In his first full season (1996-97) at Blackpool, David again proved to be a true competitor in the middle of the Seasiders' defence, while forming a solid partnership with newcomer, Tony Butler. Dominant in the air, and a threat at set pieces, his experienced captaincy was of great importance to the wellbeing of the team.
Hartlepool U (From juniors on 3/3/82) FL 84+7/5 FLC 3+1/1 FAC 4 Others 2
Derby Co (£25,000 on 11/8/86)
Shrewsbury T (£30,000 on 4/12/86) FL 65/1 FLC 5 FAC 3 Others 1
Ipswich T (£300,000 on 23/6/88) F/PL 275+2/12 FLC 21 FAC 18/1 Others 11
Blackpool (£80,000 on 17/11/95) FL 71/5 FLC 3 FAC 1 Others 6

LINTON Desmond (Des) Martin
Born: Birmingham, 5 September 1971
Height: 6'1" Weight: 13.10

Once again injuries reduced his availability for selection at Luton in 1996-97 and when fit the versatile midfielder found it difficult to break into a largely settled team. He never let the side down when given a first-team opportunity, but his ball-winning skills were not seen to best advantage at Kenilworth Road and he joined Peterborough on transfer deadline day. Came into a side that would ultimately be doomed to the third division, playing in midfield or at right back and showed a calm assurance, even when results were going against Posh.
Leicester C (From trainee on 9/1/90) FL 6+5 FLC 0+1 Others 1
Luton T (Signed on 22/10/91) FL 65+18/1 FLC 4+1 FAC 8 Others 7
Peterborough U (£25,000 on 26/3/97) FL 8

LISBIE Kevin Anthony
Born: Hackney, 17 October 1978
Height: 5'10" Weight: 11.0
International Honours: E: Yth

An exciting young striker, Kevin made his debut for Charlton last season as a substitute in the Coca-Cola Cup tie at Burnley, before making his full debut against Swindon at The Valley. Exceptionally quick, with good ball control and all-round ability, and possessing a powerful shot, he opened the scoring for The Addicks against Reading in January. Already capped at U18 level, this youngster could go all the way to the top.
Charlton Ath (From trainee on 24/5/96) FL 4+21/1 FLC 0+3 FAC 0+1

LITTLE Colin Campbell
Born: Wythenshawe, 4 November 1972
Height: 5'9" Weight: 10.5

Coming to Crewe from non-league football with a goalscoring reputation early last year, although working hard to secure a regular first-team place in 1996-97, he was used mainly as a sub and, come the end of the league campaign, had yet to get off the mark. That was until the play offs. Selected for all three games, Colin scored in both semi-final legs against Luton, both goals coming at critical times, before basking in the Wembley sun following the 1-0 win over

Brentford that sent the club into the first division for the first time ever.
Crewe Alex (£50,000 from Hyde U on 7/2/96) FL 10+19/1 FLC 0+1 FAC 2 Others 5/3

LITTLE Glen Matthew
Born: Wimbledon, 15 October 1975
Height: 6'3" Weight: 13.0
Once with Crystal Palace, and more recently with Glentoran, the former Irish Player of the Year was signed by Adrian Heath last December and impressed on his occasional first-team appearances for Burnley. Usually playing just behind the front two, and showing good skills and workrate to suggest that he may play a more prominent part in 1997-98, Glen will hope to be less troubled by injuries this time round.
Crystal Palace (From trainee on 1/7/94 - Free to Glentoran on 11/11/94)
Burnley (£100,000 on 29/11/96) FL 5+4 FAC 1+1 Others 0+1

LITTLEJOHN Adrian Sylvester
Born: Wolverhampton, 26 September 1970
Height: 5'9" Weight: 10.5
International Honours: E: Yth
A Plymouth striker with lightning speed, which gets him in scoring positions, Adrian had a poor season by his standards in 1996-97, scoring only eight goals and lacking a real partner following the departure of Micky Evans to Southampton. With a liking to receive the ball to feet and run at defenders to utilise his pace, he gives other forwards options to take advantage of, especially when going wide to the flanks.
Walsall (Free from West Bromwich A juniors on 24/5/89) FL 26+18/1 FLC 2+1 FAC 1+1 Others 4+1
Sheffield U (Free on 6/8/91) F/PL 44+25/12 FLC 5+1 FAC 3+2/1 Others 2/1
Plymouth Arg (£100,000 on 22/9/95) FL 73+6/23 FLC 4 FAC 4+2/3 Others 6

LIVINGSTONE Stephen (Steve)
Born: Middlesbrough, 8 September 1969
Height: 6'1" Weight: 12.7
A right-footed Grimsby Town striker, who is strong and physical in the old centre-forward mould, Steve is a tireless worker with good timing in the air, a deft touch, and a sense of awareness in the box. During the past season, however, the club's mounting injury problems often saw him pressed into the role of central defender, a position which he filled to good effect with his usual enthusiasm and determination.
Coventry C (From trainee on 16/7/86) FL 17+14/5 FLC 8+2/10 Others 0+1
Blackburn Rov (£450,000 on 17/1/91) F/PL 25+5/10 FLC 2 FAC 1/1
Chelsea (£350,000 on 23/3/93) PL 0+1
Port Vale (Loaned on 3/9/93) FL 4+1
Grimsby T (£140,000 on 29/10/93) FL 112+19/28 FLC 4+1 FAC 4+2/2

LLOYD Kevin Gareth
Born: Llanidloes, 26 September 1970
Height: 6'0" Weight: 12.1
Freed by Hereford during the summer of 1996, Kevin joined Cardiff in time for the start of 1996-97, immediately slotting into the left-back spot and, despite a loss of confidence towards the end of the year, he

came back stronger than ever. A wing back, more than an out-and-out full back, his pace got him forward into good attacking positions and from one such move he scored against Carlisle, his lob beating the stranded 'keeper to put City on their way to the play offs.
Hereford U (Free from Caersws on 7/11/94) FL 49+2/3 FLC 2 FAC 1 Others 6
Cardiff C (Free on 2/8/96) FL 27+4/1 FLC 2 Others 3

LOCK Anthony (Tony) Charles
Born: Harlow, 3 September 1976
Height: 5'11" Weight: 13.0
A 20-year-old Colchester striker who missed all of 1995-96 with cruciate and medial ligament damage, and then spent the early part of last season at nearby Chelmsford City on loan, Tony made the occasional substitute appearance later in the campaign, before forcing his way in for his full first-team debut, marking it with his second career goal. Seemingly fully recovered, he will now be looking for an established place in 1997-98.
Colchester U (From trainee on 18/4/95) FL 1+8/2 Others 0+1

LOCKE Adam Spencer
Born: Croydon, 20 August 1970
Height: 5'11" Weight: 12.7
The Colchester crowd pleasing midfield powerhouse, who can also play down the right wing, Adam is at his best when running at defenders. He also has a good long-range shot, scoring four goals last season, all away from home, and featuring an excellent double strike at Exeter. However, given the depth of midfield talent at Layer Road, he found himself in and out of the starting line up and went on the transfer list at his own request in March.
Crystal Palace (From trainee on 21/6/88)
Southend U (Free on 6/8/90) FL 56+17/4 FLC 5 FAC 2+1 Others 6+1
Colchester U (Loaned on 8/10/93) FL 4 Others 1
Colchester U (Free on 23/9/94) FL 64+15/8 FLC 5+1 FAC 5 Others 8+5

LOCKWOOD Matthew (Matt) Dominic
Born: Southend, 17 October 1976
Height: 5'9" Weight: 10.12
A skilful and versatile player, Matt was one of three teenage players who moved to Bristol Rovers from Queens Park Rangers during the 1996 close season after Ian Holloway was appointed player/manager. Although able to operate comfortably in the left-back position or as a left-sided mid-fielder, he preferred the central midfield role usually occupied by Holloway and, towards the end of the campaign, was selected in place of his more experienced manager.
Queens Park R (Free from Southend U juniors on 2/5/95)
Bristol Rov (Free on 24/7/96) FL 36+3/1 FLC 2 FAC 1 Others 0+1

LOGAN Richard Anthony
Born: Barnsley, 24 May 1969
Height: 6'1" Weight: 13.3
A reliable squad member, Richard played most of last season in Plymouth's midfield,

proving to be a tough tackler who worked hard for his more creative partners. Also able to play as a central defender, and the proud possessor of a very long throw which is often used in an attacking role, he also scored some useful goals, including the equaliser in a 4-4 draw at Wrexham and winners in home games against Preston and Crewe, the last named coming in the 90th minute.
Huddersfield T (Free from Gainsborough Trinity on 15/11/93) FL 35+10/1 FLC 3 FAC 1 Others 9
Plymouth Arg (£20,000 on 26/10/95) FL 44+15/8 FLC 2 FAC 1+2 Others 7

LOMAS James Duncan
Born: Chesterfield, 18 October 1977
Height: 5'11" Weight: 10.12
This young midfielder graduated to full professional status from Chesterfield's youth scheme last August and became a regular member of the first-team squad, although much of his time was spent on the bench. When he did play, he looked comfortable on the ball, given his age and comparative lack of experience, and always seemed to be looking to make a constructive pass.
Chesterfield (From trainee on 16/9/96) FL 0+2 Others 0+1

Steve Lomas

LOMAS Stephen (Steve) Martin
Born: Hanover, Germany, 18 January 1974
Height: 6'0" Weight: 12.8
International Honours: NI: 22; B-1; Yth; Sch
After an excellent season in 1995-96 as a valuable member of the Manchester City midfield, despite there being a pre-season scare that he would be joining Wimbledon, Steve decided to stay and again proved consistent when playing under all five managers in charge. Having been disappointed at being sent off at Reading for

a debatable offence which meant he missed three league games, he benefited as others have under Frank Clark and gave 100 percent effort and guile in midfield, before surprisingly being transferred to West Ham on the day before the deadline. With three seasonal midfielders at City in Paul Beesley, Kevin Horlock and Ged Brannan, no doubt Steve thought it was a good opportunity to return to the Premiership, having being at Maine Road for over six years. Still a regular player with Northern Ireland, he is an excellent passer of the ball, with super touches, and will be an asset for the Londoners.

Manchester C (From trainee on 22/1/91) P/FL 102+9/8 FLC 15/2 FAC 10+1/1
West Ham U (£1,600,000 on 26/3/97) PL 7

LORMOR Anthony (Tony)
Born: Ashington, 29 October 1970
Height: 6'0" Weight: 13.6
Enthusiastic, hard working and committed, Tony was Chesterfield's top scorer for most of last season, until an ankle injury laid him low, causing him to miss the whole of March. The team missed his strong running, creative front play and won only one of seven games in his absence as their play-off chances receded, although this may have been due as much to the distraction presented by their fine FA Cup run. Tony spent a few matches in midfield before injury and performed well, improving the link between that department and the forwards.

Newcastle U (From trainee on 25/2/88) FL 6+2/3
Lincoln C (£25,000 on 29/1/90) FL 90+10/30 FLC 1+2/3 FAC 4/2 Others 6
Peterborough U (Free on 4/7/94) FL 2+3 FAC 1 Others 1+1
Chesterfield (Free on 23/12/94) FL 86+14/31 FLC 4/1 FAC 5/3 Others 7+1/3

LOVE Andrew (Andy) Mark
Born: Grimsby, 28 March 1979
Height: 6'1" Weight: 13.12
The rookie Grimsby goalkeeper was surprisingly pressed into first-team service last season in preference to the off-form Jason Pearcey. Another graduate of John Cockerill's football academy, after signing associate schoolboy forms at 14, he showed agility and good anticipation and, as the first division's youngest goalkeeper, had trials with the England U18 squad.

Grimsby T (From trainee on 6/7/96) FL 3

LOVE Michael John
Born: Stockport, 27 November 1973
Height: 5'11" Weight: 12.4
A left-sided midfielder, Michael forced his way into the Wigan side last October, making his league debut when coming off the bench at Colchester, and appearing twice more as a sub before leaving for Sligo of the Irish League in mid January. Came back to this country on transfer deadline day as a non-contract player on trial at Wycombe, but failed to make the first team prior to departing.

Wigan Ath (Free from Hinckley Ath on 15/1/96) FL 0+3 (Free to Sligo on 17/1/97)
Wycombe W (Free on 27/3/97)

LOVELL Stuart Andrew
Born: Sydney, Australia, 9 January 1972
Height: 5'10" Weight: 11.0
Club Honours: Div 2 '94
Spent a long time out of the Reading side at the start of last season, but worked hard to regain his place as a striker, specialising in late goals, scoring the 90th minute winner at home to Ipswich, and in the 91st and 96th minutes to earn an important 2-1 home victory over Wolves. He has now made over 200 appearances for the Royals, impressing with his workrate and love of having a crack at goal, and is still a great favourite with the fans.

Reading (From trainee on 13/7/90) FL 169+43/57 FLC 13/5 FAC 5+8/2 Others 7+3/2

LOW Joshua (Josh) David
Born: Bristol, 15 February, 1979
Height: 6'1" Weight: 12.0
International Honours: W: Yth
A long-striding and powerful Bristol Rovers' winger, Josh did not enjoy 1996-97, making just three brief substitute appearances before going down with an ankle injury which required an operation and subsequently saw him out of action for three months. Returning to the first team, and coming off the bench twice more, after resuming fitness in April and winning a further Welsh International youth cap, he signed a new two-year contract. Much is expected of him in the future.

Bristol Rov (Trainee) FL 0+4 FLC 0+2

LOWE David Anthony
Born: Liverpool, 30 August 1965
Height: 5'10" Weight: 11.9
Club Honours: AMC '85; Div 2 '92, Div 3 '97
International Honours: E: U21-2; Yth
One of the hardest working players at Wigan Athletic, David treated the Graeme Jones/Graham Lancashire partnership as a challenge and by last Christmas was a regular in the side. A right-footed striker, more of a creator than a scorer, he ended a long scoring drought in style with the vital winner over Carlisle United at Springfield Park in February. Celebrated his 300th league game for the club during the campaign, his goal in the final match of the season, which ensured the club the championship and him a medal, left him just one short of a half century of league goals for Wigan.

Wigan Ath (From apprentice on 1/6/83) FL 179+9/40 FLC 8 FAC 16+1/4 Others 18/9
Ipswich T (£80,000 on 26/6/87) FL 121+13/37 FLC 10/2 FAC 3 Others 10+2/6
Port Vale (Loaned on 19/3/92) FL 8+1/2
Leicester C (£250,000 on 13/7/92) F/PL 68+26/22 FLC 4+3/1 FAC 2+2 Others 3
Port Vale (Loaned on 18/2/94) FL 18+1/5
Wigan Ath (£125,000 on 28/3/96) FL 38+11/9 FLC 2 FAC 1 Others 1

LOWE Kenneth (Kenny)
Born: Sedgefield, 6 November 1961
Height: 6'1" Weight: 11.13
Club Honours: FAT '90
International Honours: E: SP-2
A much-travelled midfield player who was

signed from Gateshead last March, Kenny quickly became a steadying influence in Darlington's midfield with his control and good passing ability. Released during the summer, he was once described as the "Glenn Hoddle of non-league football".

Hartlepool U (From apprentice on 14/11/78) FL 50+4/3 FLC 1+1 FAC 2 Others 1 (Free to Billingham during 1984 close season)
Scarborough (Free from Barrow, via Spearwood, Australia, Gateshead and Morecambe, on 15/1/88) FL 4 (Free to Barrow in April 1989)
Barnet (£40,000 on 1/3/91) FL 55+17/5 FLC 2+1 FAC 5 Others 4
Stoke C (Free on 5/8/93) FL 3+6 FLC 2 Others 2
Birmingham C (£75,000 on 17/12/93) FL 16+7/3 FLC 0+1 FAC 3+1 Others 2+1 (Free to Gateshead on 10/1/96)
Carlisle U (Loaned on 22/9/94) FL 1+1
Hartlepool U (Loaned on 28/8/95) FL 13/3 FLC 2
Darlington (Free on 26/3/97) FL 5+2

LOWNDES Nathan Peter
Born: Salford, 2 June 1977
Height: 5'11" Weight: 10.6
A young red-headed Watford striker, yet to establish himself in the first team, Nathan has proved to be quick and direct. His progress in 1996-97 was hampered by back and foot injuries, but his long-term potential was recognised with the award of a new contract.

Leeds U (From trainee on 1/4/95)
Watford (£40,000 on 3/10/95) FL 0+3 FLC 0+1

LOWTHORPE Adam
Born: Hull, 7 August 1975
Height: 5'7" Weight: 11.3
An injured thigh denied Hull City of Adam's services during the first half of the 1996-97 campaign, but the best was seen of him as they switched to a flat-back four. A genuine right-full back, he is a reliable performer who retains the respect of fans and colleagues alike. Scored his first senior goal in the derby draw at Scunthorpe during April.

Hull C (From trainee on 2/7/93) FL 52+6/1 FLC 4 FAC 2 Others 2+1

LUCAS David Anthony
Born: Preston, 23 November 1977
Height: 6'2" Weight: 13.3
International Honours: E: Yth
Preston's young goalkeeper continued his steady progress in 1996-97, despite only playing one first-team game early in the season. A bright talent for the future, following a 4-4 Coca-Cola Cup draw with Wigan he spent loan spells at Darlington and Scunthorpe to gain further experience, before coming back to feature in the final two games of the campaign, keeping clean sheets in both of them.

Preston NE (From trainee on 12/12/94) FL 3 FLC 1
Darlington (Loaned on 14/12/95) FL 6
Darlington (Loaned on 3/10/96) FL 7
Scunthorpe U (Loaned on 23/12/96) FL 6 Others 2

LUCAS Richard
Born: Chapeltown, 22 September 1970
Height: 5'10" Weight: 12.6
At home in the left back or central defensive positions, Richard turned in several outstanding solid-tackling displays for

Scarborough, before being signed on a short-term contract shortly before last March's transfer deadline to add strength to Hartlepool's first team squad. Pleased with his performances in the last seven games of the campaign, he played his part in the club's revival and did enough to earn himself the offer of a contract for 1997-98. Like team-mate Darren Knowles, he will be anxious to prove that Scarborough were wrong in releasing him.

Sheffield U (From trainee on 1/7/89) FL 8+2 FAC 1 Others 0+1
Preston NE (£40,000 on 24/12/92) FL 47+3 FAC 4 Others 4+1
Lincoln C (Loaned on 14/10/94) FL 4 Others 2
Scarborough (Free on 5/7/95) FL 63+9 FLC 6 FAC 3+1 Others 2
Hartlepool U (Free on 27/3/97) FL 7

LUCKETTI Christopher (Chris) James
Born: Littleborough, 28 September 1971
Height: 6'0" Weight: 13.6
Club Honours: Div 2 '97

Despite suffering damaged knee ligaments when playing in the opening game of last season at home to Brentford and being out injured for six weeks, Bury's highly-rated central defender returned to action and immediately recaptured the consistent impressive form which is his trademark. Indeed, he played in every game after coming back, took over the captaincy mid season and went on to be voted Player of the Season for a record-breaking third successive year, as well as winning a second division championship medal as the Shakers fought their way to the title.

Rochdale (Trainee) FL 1
Stockport Co (Free on 23/8/90)
Halifax T (Free on 12/7/91) FL 73+5/2 FLC 2/1 FAC 2 Others 4
Bury (£50,000 on 1/10/93) FL 146/5 FLC 7 FAC 8/1 Others 15/1

LUDDEN Dominic James
Born: Basildon, 30 March 1974
Height: 5'8" Weight: 11.0
International Honours: E: Sch

Composed Watford left back who is solid in the tackle and strong going forward. Troubled by a niggling hamstring and back injuries that prevented him from confirming his first-team place in 1996-97, Dominic was sidelined from early March.

Leyton Orient (Signed from Billericay T on 6/7/92) FL 50+8/1 FLC 1 FAC 0+1 Others 6/1
Watford (£100,000 on 7/8/94) FL 28+5 FLC 3 FAC 2+1 Others 2

LUDLAM Craig
Born: Sheffield, 8 November 1976
Height: 5'11" Weight: 11.5

Unable to get on the team sheet at Sheffield Wednesday, the second year professional was loaned out to Notts County last October, making just one appearance at right back, his league debut at Burnley. Unfortunately, an injury sustained in that game forced the skilful youngster to return to Hillsborough, where it was back to reserve team football, prior to being released during the summer.

Sheffield Wed (From trainee on 15/5/95)
Notts Co (Loaned on 18/10/96) FL 1

LUKIC Jovan (John)
Born: Chesterfield, 11 December 1960
Height: 6'4" Weight: 13.12
Club Honours: Div 1 '89, '92; FLC '87; CS '89, '92
International Honours: E: B-1; EU21-7; Yth

Rejoining Arsenal during the 1996 close season, having been released by Leeds, it was an emotional return for "Big Johnny Goal kick" after six years at Elland Road. Signed to understudy David Seaman, the goalkeeper could hardly have expected to make 17 appearances but, following the latter's rib injury, he took full advantage of the situation and never let the Gunners down, keeping three clean sheets in a row as successive 2-0 victories were logged up against Everton, Nottingham Forest and Southampton in March. Still an outstanding shot stopper, John proved that when preserving the status quo at Tottenham in February, having been encouraged by the manager, Arsene Wenger, to take more risks in the penalty area. Extremely agile for a big man, he has safe hands and deals well with crosses.

Leeds U (From apprentice on 16/12/78) FL 146 FLC 7 FAC 9 Others 3
Arsenal (£50,000 on 25/7/83) FL 223 FLC 32 FAC 21 Others 4
Leeds U (£1,000,000 on 14/6/90) F/PL 209 FLC 23 FAC 19 Others 15
Arsenal (Free on 26/7/96) PL 15 FLC 1 FAC 1

LUND Gary James
Born: Grimsby, 13 September 1964
Height: 6'0" Weight: 12.8
International Honours: E: U21-1; Sch

With the ability to keep possession and hold the ball up, Gary would have fitted well into Chesterfield's attacking style, however, the experienced striker's 1996-97 season was a bits-and-pieces affair, really. Nagging injuries kept him out and, when fit, he often found himself in a queue behind other forwards. Frustrated with the lack of opportunity, he asked to be put on the list in October, but this did not effect his whole-hearted dedication to the club's fortunes. Was freed during the summer.

Grimsby T (From juniors on 27/7/83) FL 47+13/24 FLC 6+2/1 FAC 4/5 Others 2/1
Lincoln C (Free on 22/8/86) FL 41+3/13 FLC 4/1 FAC 1/1 Others 3/1
Notts Co (£40,000 on 17/6/87) FL 223+25/62 FLC 15+3/5 FAC 13+3/4 Others 28+6/8
Hull C (Loaned on 14/8/92) FL 5/2
Hull C (Loaned on 25/1/93) FL 6/1
Hull C (Loaned on 23/3/95) FL 11/3
Chesterfield (Free on 14/12/95) FL 13+5/1 FAC 1 Others 1

LUNDEKVAM Claus
Born: Norway, 22 February 1973
Height: 6'3" Weight: 12.10
International Honours: Norway: 4

Signed early into the 1996-97 season by the Southampton manager, Graeme Souness, from Norwegian football, Claus looked to be extremely comfortable on the ball and, as well as being a reliable and steadfast defender, found the time to combine with other players in attacking moves. One such move came at the Dell against West Ham when he ran fully 50 yards with the ball

before releasing it for Eyal Berkovic to score with a great diagonal shot, the second goal in a vital 2-0 win. Apart from all his natural ability, the Norwegian international also showed great fortitude when, in dislocating his shoulder at Sunderland after colliding with Lee Howey in the 11th minute, he pronounced himself fit to play in the two final crucial games. Now settled in the English game, a lot is expected from him this coming term.

Southampton (£400,000 from SK Brann on 3/9/96) PL 28+1 FLC 7+1 FAC 1

LYDIATE Jason Lee
Born: Manchester, 29 October 1971
Height: 5'11" Weight: 12.3

Although a regular in 1995-96, the strong Blackpool defender was used mainly last season to fill in for injuries and suspensions. Certainly, his pace and heading ability meant that he never looked out of place when playing and, if given further opportunities, could again become an integral member of the team.

Manchester U (From trainee on 1/7/90)
Bolton W (Free on 19/3/92) FL 29+1 FLC 4 FAC 2 Others 1
Blackpool (£75,000 on 3/3/95) FL 59+4/1 FLC 4+1 FAC 4/1 Others 3+1

LYNE Neil George Francis
Born: Leicester, 4 April 1970
Height: 6'1" Weight: 13.1

Released by Hereford during the 1996 close season, the left-sided winger joined Northampton on non-contract terms, but with his first team appearances limited to just one game, he threw in his lot with neighbouring non-leaguers, Kettering Town.

Nottingham F (Signed from Leicester U on 16/8/89) FLC 0+1
Walsall (Loaned on 22/3/90) FL 6+1
Shrewsbury T (Loaned on 14/3/91) FL 16/6
Shrewsbury T (Signed on 11/7/91) FL 61+3/11 FLC 6/2 FAC 3/2 Others 3
Cambridge U (£75,000 on 15/1/93) FL 5+12
Chesterfield (Loaned on 24/9/93) FL 3/1
Chesterfield (Loaned on 24/3/94) FL 2+1
Hereford U (Free on 27/7/94) FL 49+14/2 FLC 2 FAC 5 Others 9+1/1
Northampton T (Free on 30/8/96) FL 1

LYTTLE Desmond (Des)
Born: Wolverhampton, 24 September 1971
Height: 5'9" Weight: 12.13

Des had a reasonably sound season for Nottingham Forest in 1996-97, appearing mainly in the right back position although he fitted in well when the club operated the wing-back system. He was also used in midfield whenever a man-to-man marking job was required. Played in most of the matches after missing the first few games of the campaign and was an ever present from the opening day of 1997, scoring a vital goal at Sunderland in a 1-1 draw, only the third of his Forest career. Obviously a sound tackler, he can also be effective on the overlap.

Leicester C (From trainee on 1/9/90)
Swansea C (£12,500 from Worcester C on 9/7/92) FL 46/1 FLC 2 FAC 5 Others 5
Nottingham F (£375,000 on 27/7/93) F/PL 137+3/3 FLC 14 FAC 14 Others 8

MABBUTT Gary Vincent
Born: Bristol, 23 August 1961
Height: 5'10" Weight: 12.9
Club Honours: UEFA '84; FAC '91; CS '91
International Honours: E: 16; B-9; U21-7;
Yth

This massively experienced Tottenham central defender was to play no further part in the 1996-97 campaign after breaking his leg in the opening game against Blackburn and there was no doubting that the team missed his influence and organisational skill in defence and all-round inspiration. Late season reports had Gary aiming at full recovery in time for the commencement of the 1997-98 campaign, when he is sure to receive a massive welcome back from fans, players, and manager alike.
Bristol Rov (From apprentice on 9/1/79) FL 122+9/10 FLC 10/1 FAC 5+1/1
Tottenham H (£105,000 on 11/8/82) F/PL 450+16/27 FLC 59+2/2 FAC 45+2/3 Others 29+4/4

McALINDON Gareth Edward
Born: Hexham, 6 April 1977
Height: 5'10" Weight: 12.9
Club Honours: AMC '97

Formerly on the books of both Newcastle and Manchester United, Gareth made a number of substitute appearances for Carlisle in 1996-97, before achieving his full league debut at Cardiff near the end of the term. A front runner, he showed a predatory instinct in his play with some well-taken goals for the club, one of them at Chester saw him come off the bench with 18 minutes left to force an equaliser.
Carlisle U (Free from Newcastle U juniors on 10/7/95) FL 3+12/2 FAC 0+1/1 Others 0+2/1

McALLISTER Brian
Born: Glasgow, 30 November 1970
Height: 5'11" Weight: 12.5
International Honours: S: 3

A Scottish Womble who started his career with Wimbledon when they were at Plough Lane, Brian is a versatile and reliable defender who found it difficult to get into the side in 1996-97, with Chris Perry and Dean Blackwell in such good form. Held a regular place at the start of the season, making six consecutive appearances, before an injury saw him sidelined, he came back into contention for the last 27 matches, playing in 19 of them, and winning the first of three Scottish full caps in the match against Wales. Good in the air and possessing a strong left foot, the central defender is capable of hitting great long passes behind the opposing full backs.
Wimbledon (From trainee on 1/3/89) F/PL 70+8 FLC 5+1 FAC 5+3 Others 1
Plymouth Arg (Loaned on 5/12/90) FL 7+1
Crewe Alex (Loaned on 8/3/96) FL 13/1 Others 2

McALLISTER Gary
Born: Motherwell, 25 December 1964
Height: 6'0" Weight: 12.7
Club Honours: S Div 1 '85; Div 1 '92; CS '92
International Honours: S: 53; B-2; U21-1

The Scottish international captain joined Coventry City from Leeds in a sensational transfer deal in July 1996. Having shone in early season games with his excellent close control and silky passing ability, he assumed the captaincy after the club's poor start to the campaign, but failed to stamp his authority and class on games consistently. His ability was never in doubt, though, and he scored a magnificent goal at Goodison to earn a 1-1 draw, along with several other vital strikes, including two penalties, while his dead-ball activity was of a high level, perfectly illustrated at Anfield when his near-post corners resulted in both goals. There is no doubt that his performances in Euro 96 left him tired at times last season and a good rest in the summer should see him back to top form this coming term.
Motherwell (Signed from Fir Park BC in 1981) SL 52+7/6 SLC 3+1 SC 7/2
Leicester C (£125,000 on 15/8/85) FL 199+2/47 FLC 14+1/3 FAC 5/2 Others 4
Leeds U (£1,000,000 on 2/7/90) F/PL 230+1/31 FLC 26/5 FAC 24/6 Others 14/4
Coventry C (£3,000,000 on 26/7/96) PL 38/6 FLC 4/1 FAC 4

Gary McAllister

McANESPIE Stephen (Steve)
Born: Kilmarnock, 1 February 1972
Height: 5'9" Weight: 10.7
Club Honours: S Div 1 '95; SLC '95; Div 1 '97
International Honours: S: Yth

A competent right back, Steve played in five of Bolton's first eight games last season, eventually losing his place when Gudni Bergsson made the position his own. His next taste of first-team football coming as a substitute in the 3-2 defeat at Reading in February. Confident on the ball and suited to making probing runs into the opposing team's half, often resulting in pin-point crosses to feed Wanderers' forward line, his

13 league appearances were just enough to land him a first division championship medal as the Trotters headed for the Premiership.
Aberdeen (From juniors on 12/5/88. Transferred to Vasterhauringe on 30/6/93)
Raith Rov (Signed on 25/1/94) SL 37+3 SLC 4 SC 3 Others 5
Bolton W (£900,000 on 30/9/95) F/PL 18+4 FLC 4

McAREE Rodney (Rod) Joseph
Born: Dungannon, 19 August 1974
Height: 5'7" Weight: 10.9
International Honours: NI: Yth; Sch

Injuries badly restricted the midfielder's appearances in 1996-97, but he will carry happy memories of his only goal of the campaign, a superbly struck winner at Carlisle which convinced all present that Fulham were going up. Started the first four matches on the wide right and again showed good passing qualities.
Liverpool (From trainee on 21/8/91)
Bristol C (Free on 26/7/94) FL 4+2 FLC 2 (Free to Dungannon Swifts on 6/11/95)
Fulham (Free on 29/12/95) FL 21+5/3 FLC 1 Others 0+1

MACARI Michael (Mike)
Born: Kilwinning, 4 February 1973
Height: 5'7" Weight: 10.10

After a number of prolific seasons in Stoke's reserves and countless substitute appearances, the young striker reached the first team in the second half of 1996-97, scoring a memorable goal against Oxford at the Victoria Ground. Having been held back by his manager father, he finally seized his chance as the campaign drew to a close and looks a good bet for the future.
Stoke C (Free from West Ham U juniors on 31/7/91) FL 15+15/3 FLC 0+3 FAC 0+1

Jason McAteer

McATEER Jason Wynn
Born: Birkenhead, 18 June 1971
Height: 5'10" Weight: 11.12
International Honours: Ei: 22; B-1

Brave, courageous, and the epitome of a typical Liverpool player, that was Jason in 1996-97, once again being an indomitable figure in the side in missing just two games. Now firmly established as a right-wing back, despite the rumour that he will move into midfield to make way for Rob Jones in 1997-98, his strong, attacking runs down the flank and accurate crosses led to a number of goals. A regular in the Republic of Ireland side, his fighting spirit a valuable asset to both club and country, and it is hardly surprising to know that he comes from one of Britain's greatest boxing families, his uncles, Pat and Les being British professional champions. Scored his first league goal for the club at Arsenal when following up David Seaman's block on the famous Robbie Fowler penalty.
Bolton W (Signed from Marine on 22/1/92) P/FL 109+5/8 FLC 11/2 FAC 11/3 Others 8+1/2
Liverpool (£4,500,000 on 6/9/95) PL 63+3/1 FLC 7+1 FAC 9/3 Others 8

McAULEY Sean
Born: Sheffield, 23 June 1972
Height: 5'11" Weight: 11.7
International Honours: S: U21-1

An attacking left back who can also play in central defence or midfield, he was appointed Hartlepool captain at the start of 1996-97 and led by example, rarely having a bad game. Having scored an unforgettable long-range effort on the opening day at Colchester, it was a practical decision to let him join Scunthorpe, especially as he had been Pool's most consistent player, and he quickly made the position his own at Glanford Park.
Manchester U (From trainee on 1/7/90)
St Johnstone (Signed on 22/4/92) SL 59+3 SLC 3/1 SC 3 Others 1
Chesterfield (Loaned on 4/11/94) FL 1/1 FAC 1+1 Others 2
Hartlepool U (Free on 21/7/95) FL 84/1 FLC 6 FAC 3 Others 3
Scunthorpe U (Signed on 26/3/97) FL 9

MACAULEY Steven (Steve) Roy
Born: Lytham, 4 March 1969
Height: 6'1" Weight: 12.0
Club Honours: FAYC '86

A commanding Crewe central defender with over 200 first-team games to his credit, steady and reliable, he was almost ever present in 1996-97 and capped an excellent season with the Wembley play-off victory over Brentford that elevated the club into the first division. Ideal to have around at set pieces, being a powerful header of the ball, Steve always appears on the scoresheet, scoring three goals during the campaign, two of them proving vital.
Manchester C (From trainee on 5/11/87)
Crewe Alex (£25,000 from Fleetwood T on 24/3/92) FL 161+4/20 FLC 12 FAC 12/1 Others 20/3

McCALL Stephen (Steve) Harold
Born: Carlisle, 15 October 1960
Height: 5'11" Weight: 12.6
Club Honours: UEFAC '81

International Honours: E: B-1; U21-6; Yth
Signed from Plymouth during the 1996 close season, the Torquay team was never quite the same when the skilful midfielder was absent from the line up. Still one of the best passers of a ball in the game, his influence on the younger players as coach was immense and, following a summer operation, he should be again raring to go in 1997-98.
Ipswich T (From apprentice on 5/10/78) FL 249+8/7 FLC 29 FAC 23+1/1 Others 18+1/3
Sheffield Wed (£300,000 on 3/6/87) FL 21+8/2 FLC 2+3 FAC 1 Others 0+1
Carlisle U (Loaned on 8/2/90) FL 6
Plymouth Arg (£25,000 on 26/3/92) FL 97+3/5 FLC 5 FAC 6 Others 6
Torquay U (Free on 12/7/96) FL 23+1/1 FLC 2 Others 1

McCARTHY Alan James
Born: Wandsworth, 11 January 1972
Height: 5'11" Weight: 12.10
International Honours: E: Y-1. W: B-1; U21-3

A reliable left-sided Leyton Orient centre half who played a couple of games early in 1996-97 and was about to join Northampton before suffering an injury, he made a brief return at Brighton prior to being released at the end of the season. Comfortable on the ball, and a strong tackler, Alan will be looking to get back to full fitness in order to find another club for 1997-98.
Queens Park R (From trainee on 8/12/89) F/PL 8+3 FAC 0+1 Others 1
Watford (Loaned on 26/11/93) FL 8+1
Plymouth Arg (Loaned on 11/2/94) FL 1+1
Leyton Orient (Signed on 14/8/95) FL 43+4 FLC 2 Others 2

McCARTHY Anthony (Tony) Paul
Born: Dublin, 9 November 1969
Height: 6'1" Weight: 12.10
International Honours: Ei: U21-5; Yth

Another Irish U21 international in the Colchester defence, Tony enjoyed an excellent season in 1996-97, mainly at centre half, although also at right back at times. Had the misfortune to be sent off home and away against Hartlepool, the latter of which left him suspended from U's big day out at Wembley. However, he was twice honoured in the end-of-season awards, and United will be looking for more of the same in 1997-98.
Millwall (£100,000 from Shelbourne on 25/6/92) FL 20+1/1 FLC 3
Crewe Alex (Loaned on 9/12/94) FL 2
Colchester U (Free on 17/3/95) FL 88+1/1 FLC 5 FAC 1 Others 11

McCARTHY Jonathan (Jon) David
Born: Middlesbrough, 18 August 1970
Height: 5'9" Weight: 11.5
International Honours: NI: 4; B-1

This Port Vale right winger was once again one of the club's star players in 1996-97, his dazzling wing play, plus tenacious tackling back, went a long way to helping the club into one of their highest ever finishing positions. Scored six goals, five of them away from home, just missing one game, and that being because he was away on international duty with Northern Ireland.

Just to show his value to the club, they turned down a reported £1.5 million offer from Birmingham City in March.
Hartlepool U (From juniors on 7/11/87) FL 0+1 (Free to Shepshed Charterhouse in March 1989)
York C (Free on 22/3/90) FL 198+1/31 FLC 8/1 FAC 11/3 Others 15/3
Port Vale (£450,000 on 1/8/95) FL 89+1/12 FLC 8/2 FAC 7/1 Others 8/2

Jon McCarthy

McCARTHY Paul Jason
Born: Cork, 4 August 1971
Height: 6'0" Weight: 13.6
International Honours: Ei: U21-10; Yth; Sch

Wycombe central defender signed from Brighton in the summer of 1996. Predominantly left footed, cool under pressure, very strong in the air, and comfortable on the ball, he was unlucky to be replaced by Terry Evans for two spells after Christmas in the sweeper role, but is clearly going to be a key player this coming season. Scored his first and only goal for the club in the home Coca-Cola Cup tie against Nottingham Forest.
Brighton & Hove A (From trainee on 26/4/89) FL 180+1/6 FLC 11/1 FAC 13 Others 12/1
Wycombe W (£100,000 on 5/7/96) FL 36+4 FLC 4/1 FAC 4 Others 1

McCARTHY Sean Casey
Born: Bridgend, 12 September 1967
Height: 6'1" Weight: 12.5
International Honours: W: B-1

1996-97 was a disappointing season for both him, with just six goals in 25 appearances, and Oldham, who were eventually relegated to the second division. A bustling, hard-running striker who chases half chances and keeps defenders on their toes in doing so, he started well enough with five goals in the first ten games, including a double at

Huddersfield, before suffering a back injury and being sidelined for three months. Finished the campaign back in the side after Ian Ormondroyd was injured, but, apart from one in the final match, the goals dried up.
Swansea C (Signed from Bridgend T on 22/10/85) FL 76+15/25 FLC 4+1/3 FAC 5+2/4 Others 9+1/6
Plymouth Arg (£50,000 on 18/8/88) FL 67+3/19 FLC 7/5 FAC 3/1 Others 0+1/1
Bradford C (£250,000 on 4/7/90) FL 127+4/60 FLC 10+2/10 FAC 8/2 Others 8+1/7
Oldham Ath (£500,000 on 3/12/93) P/FL 101+14/36 FLC 9/2 FAC 3+1 Others 3/1

Sean McCarthy

McCLAIR Brian John
Born: Bellshill, 8 December 1963
Height: 5'10" Weight" 12.13
Club Honours: SC '85; SPD '86; FAC '90, '94; CS '90, '94, '97; ECWC '91; ESC '91; FLC '91; PL '93, '94, '96, '97
International Honours: S: 30; B-1; U21-8; Yth

A very experienced midfielder, or out-and-out striker, Brian kicked-off 1996-97, his testimonial year, as Manchester United's main man on the bench, but as the campaign progressed his contribution increased with each successive game. Although his play was exemplary, the only mute point was the lack of a first-team goal, something that has never happened before in his United career. On closer inspection, however, the reasons were obviously clear. Having made only seven full starts all season, his role was more of a roving forward, cum midfielder, cum defender. At 33, and now the club's most senior professional, the years have failed to dim his boy-like enthusiasm and given his contribution during another action-packed season that ended in him winning his fourth championship medal, he should be around at Old Trafford for a lot longer yet.

Motherwell (Free from Aston Villa juniors on 1/8/81) SL 32+7/15 SLC 9+1/4 SC 2/1
Glasgow Celtic (£100,000 on 1/7/83) SL 129+16/99 SLC 19+1/9 SC 14+4/11 Others 13+2/3
Manchester U (£850,000 on 30/7/87) F/PL 294+48/88 FLC 43+1/19 FAC 36+6/14 Others 23+3/7

McCLELLAND John
Born: Belfast, 7 December 1955
Height: 6'2" Weight: 13.2
Club Honours: SLC '84, '85
International Honours: NI: 53; E: Flge

Having been out of the game in a playing sense since 1992-93, certainly at league level, the vastly experienced Northern Ireland international defender joined Darlington as player/coach and made just one first team appearance before tragically breaking his leg at Hartlepool last October at the age of 40. John will almost certainly be sticking to management in the future.
Cardiff C (From Portadown on 1/2/74) FL 1+3/1 (Free to Bangor during 1975 close season)
Mansfield T (£8,000 on 18/5/78) FL 122+3/8 FLC 8+1/2 FAC 8/1
Glasgow R (£90,000 on 1/5/81) SL 96/4 SLC 29/2 SC 12/1 Others 14/1
Watford (£225,000 on 8/11/84) FL 184/3 FLC 12 FAC 32 Others 4+1
Leeds U (£100,000 on 16/6/89) FL 22+2 FLC 2+1 FAC 2
Watford (Loaned on 10/1/90) FL 1
Notts Co (Loaned on 5/3/92) FL 6
St Johnstone (Free during 1992 close season) SL 26+1 SLC 3 SC 4 (Free to Carrick R in December 1993)
Darlington (From retirement on 10/10/96) FL 1

McCONNELL Barry
Born: Exeter, 1 January 1977
Height: 5'10" Weight: 10.3

Forward. A product of the Exeter youth set up who has scored plenty of goals for the reserves, chances for Barry in 1996-97 were few, although appearances he did make showed that he was more than capable of holding his own.
Exeter C (From trainee on 4/8/95) FL 21+21 FLC 0+2 FAC 1+1

McDERMOTT Andrew
Born: Sydney, Australia, 24 March 1977
Height: 5'9" Weight: 11.3
International Honours: Australia

An Australian international right back and playing under the auspices of the Institute of Sport, after signing for QPR last August, Andrew made his first-team debut in the 4-0 home win over Southend on 14 December and impressed with his composure on the ball. Fast, a neat passer, and a player who is more than comfortable in midfield, his first goal for the club, which came in the home game against Norwich on Boxing Day, proved to be the winner. Summoned by the Australian squad in January, he returned to score one of Rangers' goals of the season, a 30 yarder in a 2-0 win over Huddersfield, before moving to West Bromwich on transfer deadline day. An excellent prospect and highly rated by Albion boss, Ray Harford, he quickly settled at the Hawthorns and looks good for 1997-98.
Queens Park R (Signed from Australian Institute of Sport on 4/8/95) FL 6/2
West Bromwich A (£400,000 on 27/3/97) FL 6

McDERMOTT John
Born: Middlesbrough, 3 February 1969
Height: 5'7" Weight: 10.6

Right-footed Grimsby defender and the club's senior professional. Surprisingly fast for a defender, and a strong tackler, he provided excellent service for the front runners in 1996-97 and was not adverse to going forward with the ball. Also very consistent, John re-established himself as first choice for the right-full-back position following the departure of Brian Laws and had one of his best season in recent years until sidelined through injury.
Grimsby T (From trainee on 1/6/87) FL 319+14/6 FLC 19+1 FAC 20+1 Others 11

McDONALD Alan
Born: Belfast, 12 October 1963
Height: 6'2" Weight: 13.11
International Honours: NI: 52; Sch

Into his 17th season at QPR in 1996-97, and still performing superbly at the heart of Rangers' defence as a rugged and uncom-promising, strong-tackling central defender, apart from the final five matches when Steve Yates came into the side, Alan was only missing when injured. Good in the air at both ends of the park, he scored two goals in televised league games against Bolton and Tranmere, the latter resulting in a 3-2 away win, before powering in a last-minute winner at Huddersfield in an FA Cup third round replay. With all of the above mentioned goals coming from aerial assaults, it merely emphasised his value to Rangers down the years. Was released during the summer.
Queens Park R (From apprentice on 12/8/81) F/PL 395+7/13 FLC 43/2 FAC 33/2 Others 5
Charlton Ath (Loaned on 24/3/83) FL 9

McDONALD Christopher (Chris)
Born: Edinburgh, 14 October 1975
Height: 6'0" Weight: 13.0
International Honours: S: Sch

A hard-working utility player who has struggled throughout his career with knee injuries, Chris joined Hartlepool as a triallist during the summer of 1996 and was sufficiently impressive that manager, Keith Houchen, offered him a six-month contract. Early in 1996-97 he was looking good on the left side of a three-man central defence, but, in October, his problems returned when his season was ended by a snapped cruciate ligament. Still anxious to make the grade, he was offered another one-month contract to prove his fitness.
Arsenal (From trainee on 13/12/93)
Stoke C (Free on 31/8/95)
Hartlepool U (Free on 17/8/96) FL 9 FLC 2

McDONALD Colin
Born: Edinburgh, 10 April 1974
Height: 5'7" Weight: 11.4
International Honours: S: U21-5; Sch

The little Scot struggled to impress in his three league starts for Swansea in 1996-97, his first full season at the Vetch, and, unable to find any sort of consistency even at reserve team level, he warranted just seven further appearances from the bench. At his

best, is a pacy striker who can also be used to good effect on either flank.
Hibernian (Signed from Musselburgh on 14/5/91)
Falkirk (Signed on 8/7/93) SL 35+21/10 SLC 2+2/1 SC 1+1 Others 2+2/2
Swansea C (£40,000 on 22/3/96) FL 6+12

MacDONALD David (Dave) Hugh
Born: Dublin, 2 January 1971
Height: 5'11" Weight: 12.5
International Honours: Ei: B-1; U21-3; Yth; Sch

Unfortunately, the hard-working Barnet full back suffered from injury problems throughout last season, which saw him mainly consigned to the subs' bench, his best spell being a run of six starts in October. Able to play on both sides of the park, apart from being a good tackler, Dave's other trademark is his long-passing skill.
Tottenham H (From trainee on 5/8/88) PL 2
Gillingham (Loaned on 27/9/90) FL 10 Others 2
Bradford C (Loaned on 28/8/92) FL 7
Reading (Loaned on 6/3/93) FL 11
Peterborough U (Free on 13/8/93) FL 28+1 FLC 4 FAC 2 Others 1
Barnet (Free on 24/3/94) FL 85+10 FLC 8+1 FAC 5 Others 4

McDONALD Martin Joseph
Born: Irvine, 4 December 1973
Height: 6'1" Weight: 11.12

As a hard-working Doncaster midfielder, Martin has much to offer, but a series of personal problems precluded his full participation in first-team affairs at Belle Vue in 1996-97. However, these problems would appear to have been settled and he looks to be keen to let his football speak for itself, having joined Rovers from non-league Southport last August and scoring his first league goal, against Brighton, in October.
Stockport Co (Free from Bramhall on 5/8/92 - Free to Macclesfield during 1993 close season)
Doncaster Rov (Signed from Southport on 1/8/96) FL 33/2 FLC 2 FAC 1

McDONALD Neil Raymond
Born: Wallsend, 2 November 1965
Height: 6'0" Weight: 13.0
International Honours: E: U21-5; Yth; Sch

At his best an accurate and incisive passer of the ball, Neil failed to gain the expected regular dominating midfield place for Preston in 1996-97, appearing more often from the bench. Suffered from a draining virus after Christmas, the high point of his season was undoubtedly the 20-yard volley which provided the equaliser against Wigan in the 123rd minute of the 4-4 Coca-Cola Cup tie. Was appointed youth team coach in March.
Newcastle U (From apprentice on 19/2/83) FL 163+17/24 FLC 12/3 FAC 10+1/1 Others 3
Everton (£525,000 on 3/8/88) FL 76+14/4 FLC 7/3 FAC 17 Others 10+1
Oldham Ath (£500,000 on 1/10/91) F/PL 19+5/1 FLC3 FAC2
Bolton W (Free on 20/7/94) FL 4 Others 2
Preston NE (£40,000 on 6/11/95) FL 20+13 FLC 0+2/1 FAC 3 Others 2

McDONALD Paul Thomas
Born: Motherwell, 20 April 1968
Height: 5'7" Weight: 10.0

Club Honours: S Div 1 '88; B&QC '92, '93
A tenacious little left winger, Paul found it difficult to hit form initially as Brighton struggled from the onset of last season, but his darting runs, fine ball control, and pin-point crosses were inspirational as the Seagulls improved tremendously after the turn of the year. As a provider, rather than a goalscorer, he nevertheless proved a cool spot kicker in the absence of regular penalty taker, Denny Mundee, and missed just one of the 52 competitive matches.
Hamilton Academical (Signed from Merry Street BC on 30/6/86) SL 187+28/26 SLC 8+2/2 SC 8+1 Others 8/3
Southampton (£75,000 on 8/6/93) PL 0+3 FAC 0+1
Burnley (Loaned on 15/9/95) FL 8+1/1 Others 2
Brighton & Hove A (£25,000 on 16/2/96) FL 45+5/4 FLC 2 FAC 2 Others 2/1

McDONALD Rodney (Rod)
Born: Westminster, 20 March 1967
Height: 5'10" Weight: 12.7

Following a stint in Scottish football with Partick Thistle, the former Walsall striker joined Chester last November, initially on trial, and immediately settled down to give the side more strength up front as well as acting as a provider on many occasions. A hard worker, Rod also chipped in with seven goals, including a couple of braces and one in the play-off semi final against Swansea. Is now contracted until June 1998.
Walsall (Signed from Colne Dynamoes on 24/8/90) FL 142+7/40 FLC 9/2 FAC 8/2 Others 10/1
Partick Thistle (£30,000 on 23/9/94) SL 40+9/11 SLC 2+1/1 SC 2 Others 0+1 (Free to Southport during 1996 close season)
Chester C (Free on 25/11/96) FL 22/6 Others 3/1

McDOUGALD David Eugene Junior
Born: Big Spring, Texas, USA, 12 January 1975
Height: 5'11" Weight: 12.6
International Honours: E: Yth

After joining from Brighton during the 1996 close season, this speedy striker scored on his Rotherham debut in August, but in the same game, suffered a serious back injury which proved to be a prolapsed disc. Battled back to fitness and returned to the team in the New Year, only to suffer a recurrence after just five more games. Fortunately, this was soon put behind him and he returned again, scoring in a rare away win at Shrewsbury with his first ever penalty kick for the club. Is also effective on the left-hand side of midfield, where his pace can unsettle defenders.
Tottenham H (From trainee on 12/7/93)
Brighton & Hove A (Signed on 12/5/94) FL 71+7/14 FLC 7/2 FAC 4/3 Others 6/3
Chesterfield (Loaned on 28/3/96) FL 9/3
Rotherham U (£50,000 on 30/7/96) FL 14+4/2 FAC 1 Others 1

McELHATTON Michael
Born: Killarney, 16 April 1975
Height: 6'1" Weight: 12.8
International Honours: Ei: Sch

An aggressive and determined midfielder who joined Scarborough last September, initially on loan from Bournemouth, the

move later becoming permanent, he quickly established a regular first team place, giving some excellent performances in Mick Wadsworth's much-changed team. Also donned the goalkeeper's jersey following an injury to Ian Ironside after 42 minutes of the game against Rochdale and pulled off some fine saves in a 2-2 draw.
Bournemouth (From trainee on 5/7/93) FL 21+21/2 FLC 3+1 FAC 1+2/1 Others 1
Scarborough (£15,000 on 20/9/96) FL 26+2/1 FLC 1 FAC 2+1 Others 1

McFARLANE Andrew (Andy) Antonie
Born: Wolverhampton, 30 November 1966
Height: 6'3" Weight: 13.8
Club Honours: AMC '94

Having failed to reproduce his goalscoring form of 1995-96 at Scunthorpe, the big centre forward lost his place and was transferred to Torquay last January to fill the gap left by Paul Baker, a player who had moved in the opposite direction some two months earlier. Had a mixed spell of form, but scored a spectacular goal in the vital 1-1 draw at Exeter in April.
Portsmouth (£20,000 from Cradley T on 20/11/90) FL 0+2
Swansea C (£20,000 on 6/8/92) FL 33+22/8 FLC 3/1 FAC 0+6 Others 3+4/3
Scunthorpe U (£15,000 on 4/8/95) FL 48+12/19 FLC 4/1 FAC 2+2/2 Others 3/2
Torquay U (£20,000 on 10/1/97) FL 19/3

McGARRIGLE Kevin
Born: Newcastle, 9 April 1977
Height: 5'11" Weight: 11.4

This tough-tackling, 19-year-old Geordie was a regular member of Brighton's first team squad during the first half of last season, usually performing the role of a substitute. Though normally a central defender, he was sometimes employed in midfield and performed his task very well, considering the plight that the Seagulls found themselves in, until losing favour in the New Year and being released during the summer.
Brighton & Hove A (From trainee on 21/7/94) FL 34+11/1 FLC 2 FAC 2 Others 1+2

McGAVIN Steven (Steve) James
Born: North Walsham, 24 January 1969
Height: 5'10" Weight: 12.8
Club Honours: GMVC '92; FAT '92; Div 2 '95

A skilful two-footed Wycombe forward, he was completely discarded by manager Alan Smith from the start of last season before finding a new lease of life under John Gregory. Having struggled to score regularly since arriving at Adams Park, he was converted into an extremely hard-working player, sitting just behind the front two and clearly relishing his football. Free from the pressure of having to score, he chipped in with a healthy nine goals.
Ipswich T (From trainee on 29/1/87 - Free to Thetford T in August 1987)
Colchester U (£10,000 from Sudbury T on 28/7/92) FL 55+3/17 FLC 2 FAC 6/2 Others 4
Birmingham C (£150,000 on 7/1/94) FL 16+7/2 FLC 1+1/1 FAC 3+1/2 Others 1+3
Wycombe W (£140,000 on 20/3/95) FL 67+11/12 FLC 3+1 FAC 4+1/1 Others 2+1

McGHEE David Christopher
Born: Worthing, 19 June 1976
Height: 5'10" Weight: 11.4
A wholehearted Brentford utility player who missed just one league game during 1996-97, he started the campaign in midfield before deputising for the injured Jamie Bates in nine games at centre back. Always a danger man at set pieces, David returned to midfield, alongside Paul Smith, for the rest of the league programme, but was moved up front to play in his original striker role in the play-off final at Wembley.
Brentford (From trainee on 15/7/94) FL 76+12/7 FLC 3+2/1 FAC 7/1 Others 8+1

McGIBBON Patrick (Pat)
Born: Lurgan, 6 September 1973
Height: 6'2" Weight: 13.2
International Honours: NI: 5; B-4; U21-1; Sch
Pat scored his first goal in the Football League with a header in the 1-0 home victory over Colchester, which ensured promotion for Wigan Athletic to division two. Another of the promising Manchester United youngsters, he arrived at Springfield Park in March on loan, following a series of injuries suffered earlier in the season and, after taking time to settle in, formed a solid centre half partnership with Colin Greenall. Dominant in the air, strong in the tackle, his composed and poised performances saw him recalled to the Northern Ireland side that played Thailand, following a "B" appearance against Portugal. Earlier in 1996-97, he played one game for Swansea on loan, before returning to Old Trafford.
Manchester U (£100,000 from Portadown on 1/8/92) FLC 1
Swansea C (Loaned on 20/9/96) FL 1
Wigan Ath (Loaned on 3/3/97) FL 10/1

McGINLAY John
Born: Inverness, 8 April 1964
Height: 5'9" Weight: 11.6
Club Honours: Div 1 '97
International Honours: S: 13; B-2
It would be fair to say that John can now be classed as a Bolton legend. A huge favourite with the fans, due to his wholehearted approach to the game and his superb goalscoring exploits, he found a blistering return to form last season after the previous year's disappointments in the Premiership. Come the end of a hugely successful campaign, and having won a first division championship medal, his 24 league goals also made him the leading goalscorer in the first division, while his partnership with Nathan Blake was the most prolific in all four of the English leagues. This form obviously helped him to add to his tally of international caps and he was a member of the Scotland squad for the farcical World Cup qualifier against Estonia, when the opponents failed to turn up! Was recognised by his fellow professionals when selected for the PFA award winning first division team.
Shrewsbury T (Signed from Elgin C on 22/2/89) FL 58+2/27 FLC 4 FAC 1/2 Others 3/2
Bury (£175,000 on 11/7/90) FL 16+9/9 FLC 1 FAC 1 Others 1+1

Millwall (£80,000 on 21/1/91) FL 27+7/10 FLC 2+1 FAC 2 Others 2/1
Bolton W (£125,000 on 30/9/92) P/FL 176+9/87 FLC 21+1/12 FAC 16+1/10 Others 11/7

John McGinlay

McGLASHAN John
Born: Dundee, 3 June 1967
Height: 6'1" Weight: 13.3
International Honours: S: Yth
A strong and powerful Rotherham midfield player, he was virtually an automatic choice in 1996-97, playing mainly on the left side of midfield until the last couple of months of the season. Released during the summer, unusually, his goalscoring let him down and he only managed one goal, in the FA Cup defeat at Scunthorpe United, although his height in both penalty areas often proved invaluable. Always sets a good example for those around him and never gives anything less than his best.
Montrose (Signed from Dundee Violet in 1988-89) SL 67+1/11 SLC 2 SC 4
Millwall (£50,000 on 22/8/90) FL 9+7 FAC 0+1 Others 1
Fulham (Loaned on 11/12/92) FL 5/1 Others 1
Cambridge U (Loaned on 15/1/93) FL 0+1
Peterborough U (£75,000 on 27/1/93) FL 44+2/3 FLC 4+1/1 FAC 1 Others 2/1
Rotherham U (Free on 4/11/94) FL 68+6/5 FLC 3+1/1 FAC 2/2 Others 2

McGLEISH Scott
Born: Barnet, 10 February 1974
Height: 5'10" Weight: 11.7
Unable to hold down a regular place at Peterborough, Scott went on loan to Cambridge last September and became an instant hit with the fans as he scored two goals in his first league game against Torquay, before being carried off with

damaged ankle ligaments. Returned to score five more goals in nine games, before following manager, Tommy Taylor, to Leyton Orient in November. The centre forward thus rejoined a club he had played for some 18 months earlier and ended the season as second top scorer and forming a good partnership with Carl Girffiths.
Charlton Ath (Free from Edgware T on 24/5/94) FL 0+6
Leyton Orient (Loaned on 10/3/95) FL 4+2/1 Others 1/1
Peterborough U (Free on 4/7/95) FL 3+10 FLC 0+1 FAC 0+1 Others 3+1/2
Colchester U (Loaned on 23/2/96) FL 10+5/6 Others 2
Cambridge U (Loaned on 2/9/96) FL 10/7 FLC 1
Leyton Orient (£50,000 on 22/11/96) FL 28/7 FAC 1 Others 1

McGOLDRICK Edward (Eddie) John
Born: Islington, 30 April 1965
Height: 5'10" Weight: 11.7
Club Honours: Div 4 '87; FMC '91; ECWC '94
International Honours: Ei: 15; B-1
Arriving at Manchester City as a loan player from Arsenal last September, before signing permanently a month later, Eddie made his debut at home to Birmingham. A useful and versatile player, who is equally at home at full back or midfield, he slotted in well and showed a steadying influence in midfield. Having joined when the team was at its lowest ebb, he proved to be an excellent organiser who talked throughout games, particularly to the younger players, thus creating a calming influence when under pressure. An ideal clubman, Eddie was one of the reasons that City began to make steady improvement following the New Year.
Northampton T (£10,000 from Nuneaton Borough on 23/8/86) FL 97+10/9 FLC 9 FAC 6+1/1 Others 7/1
Crystal Palace (£200,000 on 10/1/89) FL 139+8/11 FLC 21+1/2 FAC 5 Others 13+2/3
Arsenal (£1,000,000 on 18/6/93) PL 32+6 FLC 7+2 FAC 1+1 Others 4+4/1
Manchester C (£300,000 on 20/9/96) FL 33 FLC 1 FAC 3

McGORRY Brian Paul
Born: Liverpool, 16 April 1970
Height: 5'10" Weight: 12.8
This hard-working, strong-tackling mid-fielder had another frustrating season at Wycombe in 1996-97, sidelined with injury and reserve football, although his one and only appearance, in an Auto Windscreen tie at Swansea, did produce a goal. Putting that behind him, he joined Hereford on a free transfer at the end of March, playing in the last seven games of the campaign, enjoying surging runs from deep, and not afraid to have a go from long range as evidenced by his 35-yard free kick that whistled into the Colchester net to record a 1-0 victory.
Bournemouth (£30,000 from Weymouth on 13/8/91) FL 56+5/11 FLC 7 FAC 7+3/2 Others 5/1
Peterborough U (£60,000 on 10/2/94) FL 44+8/6 FLC 0+2 FAC 2 Others 2
Wycombe W (Free on 18/8/95) FL 0+4 FLC 1 Others 1
Cardiff C (Loaned on 22/3/96) FL 7
Hereford U (Signed on 26/3/97) FL 7/1

McGOWAN Gavin Gregory
Born: Blackheath, 16 January 1976
Height: 5'8" Weight: 11.10
Club Honours: FAYC '94
International Honours: E: Yth; Sch

Made just one appearance for Arsenal last season, playing in the right-wing back role in the absence of Lee Dixon at Nottingham Forest in December. At home on either flank and also able to play in central defence or midfield, this pacy youngster, who is a strong tackler and no mean passer of the ball, has been unlucky with injuries in his short career thus far and 1996-97 was no exception. Loaned out to Luton on transfer deadline day to kick start his career, despite helping the Hatters to a fine 2-0 win at Burnley and playing in the home game against Bristol City, on both occasions he was substituted before being diagnosed as suffering from a calf injury and returning to Highbury.

Arsenal (From trainee on 1/7/94) PL 3+2 FAC 1
Luton T (Loaned on 27/3/97) FL 2

McGRATH Paul
Born: Ealing, 4 December 1959
Height: 6'2" Weight: 14.0
Club Honours: FAC '85; FLC '94, '96
International Honours: Ei: 83

The veteran Eire international defender joined Derby in a surprise short-term transfer from Villa last October to add experience to the back line. Despite his veteran status, he showed on his debut against Newcastle, when marking Alan Shearer, that he had lost none of his ability to read the game and continued to play above himself for the rest of the season. Despite his success, Jim Smith declined to extend his contract to 1997-98, preferring to rely on younger players to move ahead. However, Paul won back his place in the Republic of Ireland squad, and could still do a useful job for any number of clubs.

Manchester U (£30,000 from St Patricks on 30/4/82) FL 159+4/12 FLC 13/2 FAC 15+2/2 Others 9
Aston Villa (£400,000 on 3/8/89) F/PL 248+5/9 FLC 29+1/1 FAC 23+1 Others 15+1
Derby Co (£100,000 + on 12/10/96) PL 23+1 FAC 2

McGREAL John
Born: Liverpool, 2 June 1972
Height: 5'11" Weight: 12.8

Appointed club captain by his predecessor in the role, Tranmere's player/manager, John Aldridge, this unruffled and cultured defender continued to impress in Rovers' back four in 1996-97. Frequently compared to his hero, Alan Hansen, for his coolness and vision, John revelled in bringing the ball out of defence to set up threatening attacks, while his confidence in his own ability to direct the side blossomed as the campaign progressed. A class act, he is often rumoured to be the target of the Premier League scouts spotted at Prenton Park.

Tranmere Rov (From trainee on 3/7/90) FL 115+2/1 FLC 10+1 FAC 4 Others 7+2

McGREGOR Mark Dale Thomas
Born: Chester, 16 February 1977
Height: 5'11" Weight: 11.5

Improving all the time in 1996-97, Wrexham's Mark impressed many with such maturity for a relative youngster and should have a very good future in the game if he continues at his present rate of progress. Always looked assured at right back, while also able to slot into a central defensive position with equal confidence.

Wrexham (From trainee on 4/7/95) FL 65+6/2 FLC 1 FAC 10+1 Others 3

McGREGOR Paul Anthony
Born: Liverpool, 17 December 1974
Height: 5'10" Weight: 11.6

1996-97 was a disappointing season for Paul, his only appearances for Nottingham Forest coming off the subs bench. Having promised so much in 1995-96, he would have been frustrated, especially as his knee injury required an operation. However, his time spent recuperating was not wasted as

Paul McGrath

he formed his own pop group – Merc – which earned him a few more plaudits. A winger, cum striker, with quick feet, he is at his best when taking defenders on.

Nottingham F (From trainee on 13/12/91) F/PL 7+23/3 FAC 0+3 Others 0+4/1

McGUCKIN Thomas **Ian**
Born: Middlesbrough, 24 April 1973
Height: 6'2" Weight: 14.2

1996-97 was very much a stop-start season for Hartlepool's longest serving player, who was unable to string together any significant run of consecutive appearances. He began on a week-to-week contract and, subsequently, was troubled by a knee injury which eventually needed surgery, but there was no doubting that Ian was back to his best form at the end of the season as the Pool fought for their Nationwide League survival.

Hartlepool U (From trainee on 20/6/91) FL 147+5/8 FLC 13+1/1 FAC 6 Others 6

Ian McGuckin

McKEEVER Mark Anthony
Born: Derry, 16 November 1978
Height: 5'8" Weight: 10.2
International Honours: NI: Yth

Despite still being a trainee, the young Irishman was given an early opportunity at Peterborough when coming on as a sub at London Road against York last September and impressed as an out-and-out left winger in three starts. His ability was quickly noted and, along with David Billington, he was signed by Sheffield Wednesday in April as one for the future. Is already a Northern Ireland youth international.

Peterborough U (Trainee) FL 2+1 FLC 1
Sheffield Wed (£500,000+ on 15/4/97)

McKENNA Paul Stephen
Born: Chorley, 20 October 1977
Height: 5'7" Weight: 11.5

A young Preston midfielder who broke into the first team last season, he marked his home debut with a goal, struck from outside the box versus Wycombe. A bustling, all-action player, his distribution and tackling belie his age and he looks to have a promising future.

Preston NE (From trainee on 2/2/96) FL 4+1/1 Others 2

McKENZIE Leon Mark
Born: Croydon, 17 May 1978
Height: 5'10" Weight: 11.2

The son of the former British boxing champion, Clinton, and the nephew of Duke, a world champion at three different weights, Leon continued his learning curve last season, following a brilliant start to his league career at Crystal Palace in 1995-96, making 24 appearances, 19 of them from the subs' bench. Although more was expected of him in some quarters, in scoring twice in succession, at home to Norwich and at Oldham, from four full games, the young centre forward proved that he had not lost the touch, but merely needed further experience. Fast, with good close control, you will be hearing more of him.

Crystal Palace (From trainee on 7/10/95) FL 8+25/2 FLC 4/1 FAC 1+3

MacKENZIE Neil David
Born: Birmingham, 15 April 1976
Height: 6'2" Weight: 12.5

Another promising young Stoke player who made his first-team breakthrough in 1996-97, Neil proved to be very confident and composed on the ball, always available for the pass, and possessing a strong shot as demonstrated by his goal against Oxford at the Victoria Ground. Also looks to be versatile, for after making his full debut as a number nine, his next two starts came in the right-back position when standing in for Ally Pickering.

Stoke C (Free from West Bromwich A juniors on 9/11/95) FL 5+17/1 FAC 0+1

McKENZIE Robert (Rob) Alexander
Born: Hexham, 22 March 1979
Height: 5'10" Weight: 11.5

Still a Rotherham trainee, Rob played for the junior team for most of last season, but his ability to hit accurate passes from midfield earned him a first-team call up in early March, after he had twice been named as a substitute. Essentially a strong midfielder, he also turned out in the wing-back position and is sure to become a regular next season, following the experience he has benefited from this time round.

Rotherham U (Trainee) FL 6+5

McKEOWN Gary Joseph
Born: Oxford, 19 October 1970
Height: 5'11" Weight: 11.8
International Honours: E: Yth; Sch

Signed on loan from Dundee last December, Gary went straight into the Exeter side at home to Swansea, playing consistently well

in three games before returning to Scotland. A defensive midfielder, cum central defender, who is a tackler and ball winner, despite being of Scottish parentage, he was born in Oxford and initially went to Arsenal after representing England schools.

Arsenal (From trainee on 8/11/88)
Shrewsbury T (Loaned on 5/3/92) FL 8/1
Dundee (Free on 31/7/92) SL 62+9/4 SLC 3+1 SC 1 Others 0+1
Exeter C (Loaned on 20/12/96) FL 3

McKINLAY William (Billy)
Born: Glasgow, 22 April 1969
Height: 5'9" Weight: 11.6
International Honours: S: 21; B-1; U21-6; Yth; Sch

Told by Ray Harford that he had little future at Blackburn, apart from a couple of subs' appearances, Billy was only given a regular place in the side after Tony Parkes took over as caretaker manager in 1996-97. Patrolling the area in front of the defence, he was a huge success with his tigerish tackling, key interceptions and his coolness on the ball, despite picking up unnecessary bookings. Scored his only goal of the season in the 3-2 home defeat at the hands of Manchester United in April, but with his ability to get forward the Scottish international will surely be looking to get himself on the scoresheets on a more regular basis in 1997-98.

Dundee U (Free from Hamilton Thistle on 24/6/85) SL 210+10/23 SLC 21/3 SC 23+3/4 Others 17/2
Blackburn Rov (£1,750,000 on 14/10/95) PL 36+8/3 FLC 1 FAC 3+1

McLAREN Paul Andrew
Born: High Wycombe, 17 November 1976
Height: 6'0" Weight: 13.4

A neat and methodical Luton midfielder who looks particularly comfortable when working the ball down the right flank, Paul established himself as a regular squad member in 1996-97 and played in almost half of all first team games. Certainly, if he can impose himself more and develop extra bite in midfield during crucial matches, he looks an outstanding prospect. Has excellent ball control and movement for a big fellow.

Luton T (From trainee on 5/1/94) FL 22+15/1 FLC 0+1 FAC 1 Others 5

McLEARY Alan Terry
Born: Lambeth, 6 October 1964
Height: 5'11" Weight: 11.9
Club Honours: FLT '83; Div 2 '88
International Honours: E: B-2; U21-1; Yth

Starting last season in the Bristol City team, this right-footed central defender soon fell out of favour and was released on a free transfer to join Millwall in February. A wholehearted, committed player, much admired by the fans at Ashton Gate for his refusal to give in when having to fight back from a number of serious injury problems whilst in the West Country, he soon showed all his old flair and skill at the New Den, often steadying a panicky defence. Appointed as team captain by John Docherty, Alan continued to read the game well and win important tackles.

Millwall (From apprentice on 12/10/81) FL 289+18/5 FLC 16+1 FAC 24+1/2 Others 22+1/2
Sheffield U (Loaned on 23/7/92) PL 3
Wimbledon (Loaned on 16/10/92) PL 4 FLC 2
Charlton Ath (Free on 27/5/93) FL 66/3 FLC 2 FAC 6 Others 3
Bristol C (Free on 31/7/95) FL 31+3 FLC 5
Millwall (Free on 21/2/97) FL 15

McLOUGHLIN Alan Francis
Born: Manchester, 20 April 1967
Height: 5'8" Weight: 10.0
International Honours: Ei: 28; B-3

Alan remained a regular fixture in the starting line up at Portsmouth in 1996-97 as a skilful midfielder with excellent passing ability and awareness. And, despite scoring less goals than in previous years, he continued to get forward into good attacking positions and yet again proved to be an effective member of the team, it being no surprise to many when he scored the opening goal in an excellent 3-2 fifth round FA Cup win at Leeds. However, the highlight of his season came when he was rewarded with the 1996 Republic of Ireland Player of the Year award, ahead of men like Roy Keane and Denis Irwin.

Manchester U (From apprentice on 25/4/85)
Swindon T (Free on 15/8/86) FL 101+5/19 FLC 11+3/5 FAC 4+2 Others 10/1
Torquay U (Loaned on 13/3/87) FL 21+3/4
Southampton (£1,000,000 on 13/12/90) FL 22+2/1 FLC 0+1 FAC 4 Others 1
Aston Villa (Loaned on 30/9/91) Others 1
Portsmouth (£400,000 on 17/2/92) FL 204+8/38 FLC 19/3 FAC 11+1/7 Others 9/1

McMAHON Gerard (Gerry) Joseph
Born: Belfast, 29 December 1973
Height: 5'11" Weight: 11.6
International Honours: NI: 14; B-2; U21-1; Yth; Sch

An early season signing from Spurs in 1996-97, the young winger found it difficult to establish the sort of consistent form that the Stoke manager, Lou Macari, sought. Whilst the skilful Northern Ireland international was undoubtedly the Man of the Match at home to Oxford United in front of the Sky TV cameras and scored twice against Portsmouth, the fans will be looking forward to the day that Gerry takes the game by the scruff of the neck in utilising his defence splitting passing skills and runs at the opposition.

Tottenham H (£100,000 from Glenavon on 31/7/92) PL 9+7 FLC 3 FAC 0+1
Barnet (Loaned on 20/10/94) FL 10/2 FAC 2/1 Others 1
Stoke C (£450,000 on 17/9/96) FL 31+4/3 FLC 3+1 FAC 1

McMAHON Stephen (Steve)
Born: Liverpool, 20 August 1961
Height: 5'9" Weight: 12.1
Club Honours: Div 1 '86, '88, '90; Div 2 '96; FAC '86, '89; CS '86, '88, '89
International Honours: E: 17; B-2; U21-6

Swindon Town's player/manager seemed to have decided that his playing career was over at the start of last season, but then recalled himself for two games in mid term after a year out of first-team action. In the second of these, against Sheffield United in February, he inspired the team to a 2-1

victory. Barring emergency, this was his "swan-song" and appropriately enough he was voted Man of the Match!

Everton (From apprentice on 29/8/79) FL 99+1/11 FLC 11/3 FAC 9
Aston Villa (£175,000 on 20/5/83) FL 74+1/7 FLC 9 FAC 3 Others 4
Liverpool (£375,000 on 12/9/85) FL 202+2/29 FLC 27/13 FAC 30/7 Others 16/1
Manchester C (£900,000 on 24/12/91) F/PL 83+4/1 FLC 8 FAC 3
Swindon T (£100,000 on 1/12/94) FL 38+3 FLC 4 FAC 3+1 Others 0+1

McMANAMAN Steven (Steve)
Born: Bootle, 11 February 1972
Height: 6'0" Weight: 10.10
Club Honours: FAC '92; FLC '95
International Honours: E: 18; U21-7; Yth

Sparkling intermittently for both Liverpool and England last season, Steve combined days of sheer brilliance, with those where little went right. At his peak, however, playing in a free role behind Robbie Fowler and Stan Collymore, he was dazzling, his mazy runs finding their way through tight-packed defences to help unlock games that appeared to be going nowhere and it was on those occasions that big foreign clubs cast envious eyes in his direction. Although scoring a more than useful ten goals, despite not possessing a lethal shot, it was his ability to conjure up chances for others that made him such an exciting player to watch and there was always the expectancy that he would provide the ammunition for Fowler and Collymore to fire. Tired and jaded at the end of a long, hard campaign, expect him to come back with a bang. Was also elected by his fellow professionals to the PFA award-winning Premiership team.

Liverpool (From trainee on 19/2/90) F/PL 197+11/31 FLC 27+1/10 FAC 27+1/5 Others 23/3

Steve McManaman

McMILLAN Lyndon Andre (Andy)
Born: Bloemfontein, South Africa, 22 June 1968
Height: 5'11" Weight: 11.9

In having another excellent season for York City in 1996-97, the regular right back missed just one senior game and was as consistent and reliable as ever. Polished and unhurried, he has now played over 400 matches for the Minstermen and looks set for many more.

York C (Signed on 17/10/87) FL 346+12/4 FLC 21 FAC 16 Others 25

McNALLY Mark
Born: Motherwell, 10 March 1971
Height: 5'9" Weight: 12.2
Club Honours: SC '95
International Honours: S: U21-2

Although only small in stature, Mark continually starred in the centre of Southend's defence in 1996-97, with immaculate timing in both heading and tackling. His distribution skills deserted him a little, probably due to the confidence crisis that affected the whole team throughout the season, but he has undoubted skill that should blossom as he matures. Was surprisingly reunited with former manager, Lou Macari, when becoming a deadline day signing for Stoke who were in urgent need of cover for Larus Sigurdsson and Justin Whittle.

Glasgow Celtic (From juniors on 15/5/87) SL 112+10/3 SLC 11+2/1 SC 10 Others 6+1
Southend U (£100,000 on 8/12/95) FL 52+2/2 FLC 2 FAC 2
Stoke C (£120,000 on 27/3/97) FL 3

McNIVEN David Jonathan
Born: Leeds, 27 May 1978
Height: 5'10" Weight: 11.4

One of twins at Oldham, and the son of the former Leeds' player, David senior, this one is built like a pocket battleship. Although his appearances from the bench far outweighed his starts in 1996-97, following his first-team debut in the first leg of the Coca-Cola Cup tie against Tranmere, big things are expected from a youngster who came into the side when Nicky Banger was having a thin time. Almost an old-fashioned inside forward, David attacks in short bursts, holds the ball up well, and, if given the opportunity, will score goals. Had a loan spell in the Irish League with Linfield (March), playing twice before returning to Boundary Park.

Oldham Ath (From trainee on 25/10/95) FL 2+6 FLC 0+2

McNIVEN Scott Andrew
Born: Leeds, 27 May 1978
Height: 5'10" Weight: 10.6
International Honours: S: U21-1; Yth

Following on from his successes in 1995-96, Scott became an Oldham first-team squad regular last season, continuing to improve and showing good passing skills and strong running, both on and off the ball. Recognised as being more suited to the right-back position, although he appeared comfortable in a number of roles, the twin

brother of David looks set for a fine career. When David came on in the last home game against Norwich, it was the first time in the club's history that twins had been on the field at the same time.

Oldham Ath (From trainee on 25/10/95) FL 26+2 FLC 3 FAC 2 Others 4

McPHERSON Keith Anthony
Born: Greenwich, 11 September 1963
Height: 5'11" Weight: 11.0
Club Honours: FAYC '81; Div 4 '87, Div 2 '94

Although approaching the veteran stage of his career in 1996-97, Keith battled back from injury to regain his Reading place at centre back, where he was one of the more reliable of the members of the team, so much so that he was runner up to Trevor Morley as the fans' Player of the Season. Is a solid defender, who heads and volleys the ball away with considerable power.

West Ham U (From apprentice on 12/9/81) FL 1
Cambridge U (Loaned on 30/9/85) FL 11/1
Northampton T (£15,000 on 23/1/86) FL 182/8 FLC 9/1 FAC 12 Others 13
Reading (Signed on 24/8/90) FL 227+5/8 FLC 13+1 FAC 11+1 Others 10+1

McPHERSON Malcolm
Born: Glasgow, 9 December 1974
Height: 5'10" Weight: 12.0

A neat right-sided midfielder, Malcolm came out of non-league football at the beginning of 1994, looking to make his mark at West Ham. Unfortunately, he never did get a first team opportunity and found himself freed during the 1996 close season, prior to signing for Brentford. Made his debut at Bristol Rovers in the AWS competition and looked a useful player in four further appearances.

West Ham U (£30,000 from Yeovil on 4/1/94)
Brentford (Free on 31/7/96) FL 2+1 Others 1+1

Lee McRobert

McROBERT Lee Peter
Born: Bromley, 4 October 1972
Height: 5'8" Weight: 10.12

A right-sided midfielder and fine ball winner, Lee returned to the Millwall first team at Hereford in the AWS tie last season, but, unfortunately, his appearances continued to be restricted by a series of injuries. Hopefully, he can pick up the pieces in 1997-98.

Millwall (£35,000 from Sittingbourne on 17/2/95) FL 8+10/1 FLC 1 FAC 1 Others 0+1

McSTAY Raymond (Ray)
Born: Hamilton, 16 May 1970
Height: 5'11" Weight: 11.0
International Honours: S: Sch

Following an unsuccessful loan period at Hereford last August, Ray was released by the Scottish League's Hamilton and joined Cardiff on non-contract forms towards the end of the year. Unfortunately, the creative midfielder, who showed himself to be a tidy passer and playmaker, never really settled, playing just once before returning to Scotland.

Glasgow Celtic (From juniors on 15/5/87)
Hamilton Academical (Free on 10/1/95) SL 25+5/5 Others 1
Cardiff C (Free on 19/12/96) FL 1

McVEIGH Paul
Born: Belfast, 6 December 1977
Height: 5'6" Weight: 10.5
International Honours: NI: Yth

A young Tottenham striker and first year professional, Paul impressed with a well-taken goal on his home debut in the final game of last season against Coventry, having made his initial appearance in a 1-1 draw at Aston Villa three weeks earlier. Reckoned to be a penalty box predator in the mould of Teddy Sheringham, since being converted from midfield, he has proved to be a busy, unselfish player, with good feet, who runs off the ball well and takes up excellent positions. Is also deceptively good in the air for one so small.

Tottenham H (From trainee on 10/7/96) PL 2+1/1

MADDISON Lee Robert
Born: Bristol, 5 October 1972
Height: 5'11" Weight: 12.4

Northampton left back, with a flair for going forward, like his right back partner, Ian Clarkson, he is still looking for his first goal for the club. Again, injury robbed him of part of last season and he was released during the summer.

Bristol Rov (From trainee on 18/7/91) FL 68+5 FLC 4 FAC 2 Others 6+1
Northampton T (£25,000 on 22/9/95) FL 55 FLC 3+1 FAC 3 Others 4+1

MADDISON Neil Stanley
Born: Darlington, 2 October 1969
Height: 5'10" Weight: 11.8

A versatile Southampton player who can play in a number of defensive or attacking positions, he was in and out of the side throughout last season, making just 22 appearances and scoring one goal. Despite having only one strike on target in a

campaign that was extremely tense, the Saints spending most of their time up against it near the foot of the Premiership, his goal was vital and was one which led to a remarkable fight back at home to Newcastle. With the side 2-0 down and with two minutes to go, first Neil struck, followed by Matt le Tissier smashing in a superb equaliser deep into extra time. An excellent clubman who can always be relied upon, he makes good runs off the ball, keeps his passing simple but effective, and, above all, puts the club first.

Southampton (From trainee on 14/4/88) F/PL 144+19/18 FLC 9+5 FAC 8+5 Others 1

MADDIX Daniel (Danny) Shawn
Born: Ashford, 11 October 1967
Height: 5'11" Weight: 11.7

Although not starting his first game for QPR until the end of last December, having been used from the bench up until that time, Danny held his place at right back and occasionally in the centre of defence, apart from a couple of games, for the remainder of the season. Despite his first-team opportunity being mainly due to Andrew McDermott joining the Australian national side in January, he showed no sign of relinquishing it, even when McDermott returned to Loftus Road, his man-to-man marking abilities and strength in the tackle giving Rangers an extra dimension. Is also good in the air.

Tottenham H (From apprentice on 25/7/85)
Southend U (Loaned on 1/11/86) FL 2
Queens Park R (Free on 23/7/87) F/PL 181+32/7 FLC 18/2 FAC 20+2/2 Others 2+3

MAGILTON Jim
Born: Belfast, 6 May 1969
Height: 6'0" Weight: 14.2
International Honours: NI: 36; U23-2; U21-1; Yth; Sch

The Southampton and Northern Ireland midfielder captained the Saints on many occasions in 1996-97 and, in missing just one league game, played a major role in keeping them in the Premiership. A skilful link-up man who scores goals, and was the penalty taker in Matt le Tissier's absence (he actually missed one in the 2-0 home win over West Ham), none was more dramatic or spectacular than the opener in a 3-1 life-saving win at Nottingham Forest. With little danger imminent on receiving the ball 25 yards out in a central position, he shot with such power and suddenness that the 'keeper was left rooted as the ball flashed past him into the net. Always a calming influence on the side, along with le Tissier, he was invaluable.

Liverpool (From apprentice on 14/5/86)
Oxford U (£100,000 on 3/10/90) FL 150/34 FLC 9/1 FAC 8/4 Others 6/3
Southampton (£600,000 on 11/2/94) PL 119+6/13 FLC 12+2/2 FAC 12/3

MAHON Alan Joseph
Born: Dublin, 4 April 1978
Height: 5'10" Weight: 11.5
International Honours: Ei: U21-3; Yth; Sch

In his first full season as a professional at Tranmere, Alan enjoyed a less than relaxing

summer break in 1996, managing to represent Eire at both U18 and U21 levels. In and out of the side from last October, he again proved to be an attacking midfield player with plenty of potential and definitely one to watch for the future, possessing creativity, vision, pace, skill and a never-say-die attitude. Scored his first goal for the club in the 4-0 home defeat of Charlton.

Tranmere Rov (From trainee on 7/4/95) FL 14+13/2 FLC 0+2

Alan Mahon

MAHON Gavin Andrew
Born: Birmingham, 2 January 1977
Height: 6'0" Weight: 13.2

Freed by Wolves during the summer of 1996, Gavin moved to Hereford and started last season on the wide left, playing in the first seven games. Although showing good touches and trickery on the ball in a further eight matches, it was a difficult time for him to settle in a club that ultimately finished in the Conference. Opening the scoring in a 3-0 home win over Rochdale would have undoubtedly been his high spot.

Wolverhampton W (From trainee on 3/7/95)
Hereford U (Free on 12/7/96) FL 10+1/1 FLC 4

MAHONEY-JOHNSON Michael Anthony
Born: Paddington, 6 November 1976
Height: 5'10" Weight: 12.0

Into his second full season without any first team experience, the pacy QPR striker was loaned out to Wycombe last August, making his Football League debut in a 0-0 draw at Blackpool and, although used sparingly at first, his final match for the club, a 6-3 defeat at Peterborough, saw him notch a double strike prior to returning to Loftus Road. Within a week, he had made his debut for Rangers, twice coming off the bench inside three days, before going back to the reserves to continue his soccer education.

Highly thought of, he looks certain to break through this coming season.

Queens Park R (From trainee on 11/4/95) FL 0+2
Wycombe W (Loaned on 30/8/96) FL 2+2/2

MAKEL Lee Robert
Born: Sunderland, 11 January 1973
Height: 5'10" Weight: 11.7

Midfield playmaker who took a time to settle in but has now established himself at Huddersfield. Top of the assists in 1996-97, he always looked to make the telling pass which would create an opportunity and, despite not being a prolific goalscorer, he continued to be dangerous at free kicks, from where most of his goals seemed likely to come. Unfortunately, his season was curtailed due to injury, during which Town seemed to lose much of their direction.

Newcastle U (From trainee on 11/2/91) FL 6+6/1 FLC 1 Others 0+1
Blackburn Rov (£160,000 on 20/7/92) PL 1+5 FLC 0+3 Others 1+3
Huddersfield T (£300,000 on 13/10/95) FL 52/5 FLC 3 FAC 6

MALKIN Christopher (Chris) Gregory
Born: Hoylake, 4 June 1967
Height: 6'3" Weight: 12.9
Club Honours: AMC '90

Signed from Millwall last October, Chris became Blackpool's record signing, ironically scoring his first goal for his new club against his old one. Fast, with an excellent workrate, the tall striker's appearances were unfortunately restricted by injury problems, something that will hopefully be ironed out in time for the coming season.

Tranmere Rov (Free from Stork AFC on 27/7/87) FL 184+48/60 FLC 20+5/6 FAC 9+4/3 Others 26+7/7
Millwall (£400,000 on 13/7/95) FL 46+6/13 FLC 5/1 FAC 2/1
Blackpool (£275,000 on 14/10/96) FL 8+7/3 FAC 2 Others 0+2

MANN Neil
Born: Nottingham, 19 November 1972
Height: 5'10" Weight: 12.1

This midfielder is arguably the most naturally gifted player in the Hull City camp. Left-footed Neil's stop-start 1996-97 season was hindered by injuries, suspension and loss of form, but Arthur Mann's son can do good things and has the will to do them more often in 1997-98. Showed his true potential with a sensational goal against Leyton Orient in April, having taking the ball from near his own area and chipping the 'keeper from 25 yards.

Grimsby T (Free from Notts Co juniors on 6/9/90)
Hull C (Free from Grantham T, via Spalding, on 30/7/93) FL 89+17/5 FLC 6+2 FAC 4+2/1 Others 2

MANUEL William (Billy) Albert James
Born: Hackney, 28 June 1969
Height: 5'8" Weight: 12.0
Club Honours: Div 3 '92

Not a regular in Gillingham's first team, he only came in when injuries and suspensions took their toll during 1996-97, being used in midfield, where his terrier-like tackling was always noticeable, and also filling the left-back position. Unfortunately, he broke his

ankle in training in January and was later released.

Tottenham H (From trainee on 28/7/87)
Gillingham (Signed on 10/2/89) FL 74+13/5 FLC 2 FAC 3 Others 5
Brentford (£60,000 on 14/6/91) FL 83+11/1 FLC 7+1/1 FAC 4 Others 8+2
Peterborough U (Free on 16/9/94)
Cambridge U (Free on 28/10/94) FL 10 FAC 2
Peterborough U (Free on 28/2/95) FL 27/2 FLC 4/3 FAC 1+1 Others 2
Gillingham (Free on 26/1/96) FL 9+12 FAC 1 Others 1

MARCELLE Clinton Sherwin
Born: Trinidad, 9 November 1968
Height: 5'4" Weight: 10.0
International Honours: Trinidad & Tobago: 6

A summer signing for Barnsley from Felgueiras, Clinton had the pace to frighten even the quickest of first division defenders in 1996-97, his running both with and without the ball from midfield being a constant danger. The Trinidad and Tobago international also showed he had the temperament and technique to succeed and scored his fair share of goals, including the first on the opening day of last season, his debut at West Bromwich, and one against Bradford that clinched promotion to the Premiership.

Barnsley (Free from Felgueiras on 8/8/96) FL 26+14/8 FLC 3+1 FAC 2/1

MARDON Paul Jonathan
Born: Bristol, 14 September 1969
Height: 6'0" Weight: 12.0
International Honours: W: 1

Not a happy 1996-97 season for West Brom defender Paul who tore a thigh muscle early on in the proceedings and was on the treatment table from October to late March. He then managed only a handful of reserve and senior games from towards the end of the season, but is hoping to be back to peak fitness for the start of the new campaign. Also capable of playing in midfield, he has fair pace, and is good in the air and on the ground.

Bristol C (From trainee on 29/1/88) FL 29+13 FLC 3+3/1 Others 1
Doncaster Rov (Loaned on 13/9/90) FL 3
Birmingham C (£115,000 on 16/8/91) FL 54+10 FLC 11+1 FAC 1 Others 3
West Bromwich A (£400,000 on 18/11/93) FL 95+8/2 FLC 6 FAC 3 Others 2

MARGETSON Martyn Walter
Born: Neath, 8 September 1971
Height: 6'0" Weight: 14.0
International Honours: W: B; U21-7; Yth; Sch

Although the goalkeeper has been at Manchester City since 1990, prior to the away game at Portsmouth last season, he had not played in a league game for three and a half years, but got his chance when Andy Dibble was dropped after the Oxford home defeat, playing in ten consecutive games until the arrival of Tommy Wright in late January. However, with Wright cup tied, he excelled as a shot stopper in three FA Cup games, before returning to the league side towards the end of the campaign. Clears his line well and kicks long and hard.

Manchester C (From trainee on 5/7/90) F/PL 23 FLC 0+2 FAC 3 Others 1
Bristol Rov (Loaned on 8/12/93) FL 2+1

MARKER Nicholas (Nicky) Robert
Born: Budleigh Salterton, 3 May 1965
Height: 6'0" Weight: 12.11

Able to fill in at full back, centre back or in midfield, Nicky was the rock on which the Blackburn reserve side was built upon in 1996-97 and his diligence and application also made him an automatic choice for the first-team bench. In that capacity, he also made several starts when standing in for a number of players and, as in 1995-96, he never let the side down, always performing with commitment and enthusiasm. Is a good man to be able to call up.
Exeter C (From apprentice on 4/5/83) FL 196+6/3 FLC 11/1 FAC 8 Others 8/3
Plymouth Arg (£95,000 on 31/10/87) FL 201+1/13 FLC 15/3 FAC 9/1 Others 7/1
Blackburn Rov (£500,000 on 23/9/92) PL 41+13/1 FLC 3+1 FAC 4+1 Others 1+1

MARKMAN Damien Liam
Born: Ascot, 7 January 1978
Height: 5'8" Weight: 11.1

A young Wycombe striker with a proven eye for goal in the reserves, he was restricted to just two substitute appearances last August and was released later in the season. Fast and compact, and a player who runs well off the ball, he will obviously be hoping for further Football League opportunities.
Wycombe W (Free from Slough T on 29/11/95) FL 0+4

MARKS Jamie
Born: Belfast, 18 March 1977
Height: 5'9" Weight: 10.13
International Honours: NI: Yth; Sch

As a valuable member of Hull City's squad in 1996-97, the former Leeds United trainee proved an able deputy for the injured Simon Trevitt on the right-wing-back berth. Enjoys going forward and has the physique to look after himself.
Leeds U (From trainee on 1/4/95)
Hull C (Free on 13/2/96) FL 11+4 FAC 2 Others 1

MARQUIS Paul Raymond
Born: Enfield, 29 August 1972
Height: 6'2" Weight: 13.0

Paul continued to struggle in 1996-97 with the injuries that have plagued his tenure at Doncaster, a foot injury limiting his involvement. Released during the summer, his cultured skills at the heart of the Rovers were sadly missed in what was a traumatic season for the club.
West Ham U (From trainee on 1/7/91) PL 0+1
Doncaster Rov (Free on 10/3/94) FL 28+1/1

MARRIOTT Andrew (Andy)
Born: Sutton in Ashfield, 11 October 1970
Height: 6'0" Weight: 12.6
Club Honours: Div 4 '92; FMC '92; WC '95
International Honours: E: U21-1; Yth; Sch. W: 2

Andy continued to impress for Wrexham in 1996-97 as a superb shot stopper and may soon be pressing for the number one slot in the Welsh jersey, having made his debut against Scotland in May, and following Neville Southall's indication that he may soon stand down from the international side. Working hard on his decision making, he is a big asset to Wrexham, keeping over 20 clean sheets throughout a season that saw the club reach the sixth round of the FA Cup. Qualifies for Wales through his maternal grandfather who was born in Bangor.
Arsenal (From trainee on 22/10/88)
Nottingham F (£50,000 on 20/6/89) F/PL 11 FLC 1 Others 1
West Bromwich A (Loaned on 6/9/89) FL 3
Blackburn Rov (Loaned on 29/12/89) FL 2
Colchester U (Loaned on 21/3/90) FL 10
Burnley (Loaned on 29/8/91) FL 15 Others 2
Wrexham (£200,000 on 8/10/93) FL 171 FLC 8 FAC 18 Others 20

MARSDEN Christopher (Chris)
Born: Sheffield, 3 January 1969
Height: 5'11" Weight: 10.12

Ultra competitive and possessing deft touches, Chris had an outstanding season at Stockport in 1996-97, partnering Tom Bennett in midfield. Although his fiery temper brought him a cascade of disciplinary points, resulting in a five-match ban in the crucial later stages of the campaign, he was a major influence in a side that won promotion to the first division. Was also recognised by his fellow professionals when elected to the PFA award-winning second division side.
Sheffield U (From apprentice on 6/1/87) FL 13+3/1 FLC 1 Others 1
Huddersfield T (Signed on 15/7/88) FL 113+8/9 FLC 15+1 FAC 6+2 Others 10
Coventry C (Loaned on 2/11/93) PL 5+2
Wolverhampton W (£250,000 on 11/1/94) FL 8 FAC 3
Notts Co (£250,000 on 15/11/94) FL 10 FLC 1 Others 1
Stockport Co (£70,000 on 12/1/96) FL 53+2/3 FLC 9 FAC 4 Others 4/1

MARSH Christopher (Chris) Jonathan
Born: Sedgley, 14 January 1970
Height: 5'11" Weight: 13.2

1996-97 was Chris's benefit season and he passed the 300 appearance mark, despite struggling at times with niggling injuries, although failing to score for the first time in seven years. A popular captain both on and off the field, his versatility, which has been a feature of his career, was shown again in August when he performed bravely at Chesterfield after Jimmy Walker had been sent off early in the game. The midfielder is at his best when coming out with the ball.
Walsall (From trainee on 11/7/88) FL 232+34/21 FLC 15+2/1 FAC 25+1/3 Others 14+1/3

MARSH Michael (Mike) Andrew
Born: Liverpool, 21 July 1969
Height: 5'8" Weight: 11.0
Club Honours: FAC '92

Mike's absence from the Southend midfield due to a knee operation between last November and January was a big factor in the failure of the team during 1996-97. By the time he returned, bringing his class and ability to bear, it was almost too late and he could do nothing to halt the slide. Despite that, his passing and distribution was a joy to watch, and it was his influence that led to many of Southend's goals during the season.
Liverpool (Free from Kirby T on 21/8/87) F/PL 42+27/2 FLC 10+1/3 FAC 6+2 Others 12+1/1
West Ham U (Signed on 17/9/93) PL 46+3/1 FLC 6 FAC 6/1
Coventry C (£450,000 on 30/12/94) PL 15/2 FAC 4 (£500,000 to Galatasaray on 13/7/95)
Southend U (£500,000 on 4/9/95) FL 75/10 FLC 4 FAC 2 Others 3/1

MARSH Simon Thomas Peter
Born: Ealing, 29 January 1977
Height: 5'11" Weight: 11.6

The young Oxford full back had more chances than previous to break into the side last season and looked a very accomplished player. He would have been disappointed not to have played more, but many feel that he will be more of a regular this coming season. Scored his first goal against Crystal Palace in a rare experiment as a wing back, but lost his place when Mike Ford returned. Impressive at set pieces, he will undoubtedly bounce back.
Oxford U (From trainee on 22/11/94) FL 16+5/1 FLC 2+2 FAC 2 Others 2

MARSHALL Andrew (Andy) John
Born: Bury St Edmunds, 14 April 1975
Height: 6'2" Weight: 13.7
International Honours: E: U21-4

An England U21 goalkeeper with an outstanding future, Andy showed remarkable maturity at Norwich in 1996-97, his handling improving all the time. Looks to have finally broken into the first team after a number of years as Bryan Gunn's understudy, following a displaced pelvis being clicked back into place by a London specialist in March, and manager Mike Walker picking him to play in seven of the last 12 games as City fell away from a play-off spot. Earlier in the campaign, in an effort to get match practice, the young goalie had loan spells at Bournemouth (September) and Gillingham (November), playing 18 invaluable matches, while, at the same time, serving notice that he was ready for regular first-team football. Is good on crosses, commands the penalty area well, and kicks long and hard. Also played for the Football League U21s against the Italian Serie "B" equivalent in February.
Norwich C (From trainee on 6/7/93) P/FL 30+1 FLC 2 FAC 2+1
Bournemouth (Loaned on 9/9/96) FL 11
Gillingham (Loaned on 21/11/96) FL 5 FLC 1 Others 1

MARSHALL Dwight Wayne
Born: Jamaica, WI, 3 October 1965
Height: 5'7" Weight: 11.8

His recovery from a badly-broken leg in February 1996 meant that he was unable to force his way back into the Luton first-team squad before last November. When he did get back in, however, he showed that he had lost none of his pace or goal finishing ability, scoring five goals in his first four full matches back and immediately re-establishing himself as a crowd favourite. Although his ability to attack from a wide position excited the fans and upset defences,

he found it difficult to maintain his form and, once deposed, could not win back a regular place with Tony Thorpe and David Oldfield established as first-choice strikers. That aside, he remained a key squad member, often coming on as a substitute and providing a new dimension to Town's attack.

Plymouth Arg (£35,000 from Grays Athletic on 9/8/91) FL 93+6/27 FLC 8/1 FAC 7+2/4 Others 7+1/4
Middlesbrough (Loaned on 25/3/93) PL 0+3
Luton T (£150,000 on 15/7/94) FL 68+27/24 FLC 3+1/2 FAC 7+1/5 Others 4+3/2

MARSHALL Ian Paul
Born: Liverpool, 20 March 1966
Height: 6'1" Weight: 12.12
Club Honours: CS '86; Div 2 '91

Signed from Ipswich two weeks into 1996-97, the burly Leicester striker was occasionally pressed into action in central defence, his original position, but, in the main, was used as an added threat up front, alongside Emile Heskey and Steve Claridge. Opening his City account with a headed winner at Tottenham, and going on to notch a late equaliser at Blackburn, the highlight of his season came in the 4-2 home win over Derby in February when he scored a hat trick in the space of 21 minutes. Unfortunate to be cup tied as far as the Coca-Cola Cup went, therefore missing the Foxes' run to Wembley, Ian scored in both the third and fourth rounds of the FA Cup before the club went out to Chelsea, the victims of a debatable penalty decision. Yet again proved himself to be a wholehearted team player.

Everton (From apprentice on 23/3/84) FL 9+6/1 FLC 1+1/1 Others 7
Oldham Ath (£100,000 on 24/3/88) F/PL 165+5/36 FLC 17 FAC 14/3 Others 2+1/1
Ipswich T (£750,000 on 9/8/93) P/FL 79+5/32 FLC 4/3 FAC 9/3
Leicester C (£875,000 on 31/8/96) PL 19+9/8 FAC 4/2

MARSHALL John Philip
Born: Balham, 18 August 1964
Height: 5'10" Weight: 12.6

After 14 years as a pro with his only club, during which he played in every position except goal for Fulham, John took over coaching the youth team as well as adding his experience to the Capital League side on a regular basis in 1996-97, making his only first-team appearance in the second-leg Coca-Cola Cup tie at Ipswich. An all-rounder, even today he could show some of the youngsters home.

Fulham (From apprentice on 20/8/82) FL 393+18/29 FLC 33+1/1 FAC 19+1/3 Others 21/2

MARSHALL Scott Roderick
Born: Edinburgh, 1 May 1973
Height: 6'1" Weight: 12.5
International Honours: S: U21-5; Yth

Arsenal's classy Scottish U21 central defender found opportunities limited in 1996-97, making just eight appearances, when competing with three England internationals for a place in the back three. The son of a former Hearts' goalie and brother to Gordon, the Celtic custodian,

Scott reads the game very well and prefers to come out of defence with the ball, looking for the pass rather than just clear his lines. Is also sound in the air.

Arsenal (From trainee on 18/3/91) PL 18+3/1
Rotherham U (Loaned on 3/12/93) FL 10/1 Others 1
Sheffield U (Loaned on 25/8/94) FL 17

MARSHALL Shaun Andrew
Born: Fakenham, 3 October 1978
Height: 6'0" Weight: 12.12

A Cambridge youth team goalkeeper, Shaun was given his first taste of league action following an injury to Scott Barrett in the 2-2 home draw against Rochdale last October and played well enough to suggest that he is a good prospect for the future. Having signed professional terms in February, he is now officially Barrett's understudy at the Abbey.

Cambridge U (From trainee on 21/2/97) FL 1

MARTIN Alvin Edward
Born: Bootle, 29 July 1958
Height: 6'1" Weight: 13.9
Club Honours: FAC '80; Div 2 '81
International Honours: E: 17; B-2; Yth

An experienced Leyton Orient centre half signed during the summer of 1996 on a free transfer from West Ham, he used all his experience to marshal the young defence and, along with Les Sealey, they kept five clean sheets in the first ten matches before injuries virtually put paid to his season. Despite making some brief returns, but not doing himself or the club justice, Alvin decided to retire from league football after a long and distinguished career.

West Ham U (From apprentice on 1/7/76) F/PL 462+7/27 FLC 71/6 FAC 40 Others 16/1
Leyton Orient (Free on 6/7/96) FL 16+1 FLC 2

MARTIN David
Born: East Ham, 25 April 1963
Height: 6'1" Weight: 13.1
Club Honours: FAYC '79; FLT '83; FAT '92
(On loan at Colchester U)
International Honours: E: Yth

Released by Gillingham during the 1996 close season, the hard-tackling midfielder, cum defender, joined Leyton Orient before signing for Northampton midway through last season. Despite a successful loan period with the club two years ago, his second spell was dogged with injury and suspension and he joined Brighton on loan on the transfer deadline. Scored twice for Town, both times in the Auto Windscreen competition.

Millwall (From apprentice on 10/5/80) FL 131+9/6 FLC 10+2/3 FAC 7/1 Others 4/1
Wimbledon (£35,000 on 14/9/84) FL 30+5/3 FLC 2 FAC 2+1
Southend U (Free on 23/8/86) FL 212+9/19 FLC 25/4 FAC 9+1 Others 10+1/3
Bristol C (Free on 19/7/93) FL 36+2/1 FAC 5 Others 2
Northampton T (Loaned on 13/2/95) FL 7/1
Gillingham (Free on 4/8/95) FL 27+4/1 FLC 1 FAC 4/1 Others 1
Leyton Orient (Free on 30/7/96) FL 8 FLC 2
Northampton T (Free on 11/10/96) FL 10+2 Others 3/2
Brighton & Hove A (Loaned on 27/3/97) FL 1

MARTIN Dean Stacey
Born: Halifax, 9 September 1967
Height: 5'11" Weight: 11.10

A regular midfielder in 1995-96, Dean made only one league appearance for Rochdale, as substitute in the first game of last season, before going on to have two loan spells with his former club, Halifax, in the Conference. Released at the end of the campaign, he can also play up front if required.

Halifax T (From apprentice on 10/9/85) FL 149+4/7 FLC 7 FAC 10 Others 12/3
Scunthorpe U (Free on 8/7/91) FL 100+6/7 FLC 8/1 FAC 7 Others 13+1/1
Rochdale (Free on 13/1/95) FL 45+8 FLC 0+1 FAC 4/1 Others 2+1

MARTIN Jae Andrew
Born: Hampstead, 5 February 1976
Height: 5'11" Weight: 12.4

A fast wingman who signed permanently for Lincoln in November after a three-month loan spell from Birmingham, Jae was noted for his solo efforts, but lost form in the second half of the season and finished the campaign out of the team. Scored some valuable goals though, including the winner at home to Barnet and one apiece in 3-2 wins over Hartlepool and Colchester.

Southend U (From trainee on 7/5/93) FL 1+7 FLC 1+1 Others 0+1
Leyton Orient (Loaned on 9/9/94) FL 1+3 Others 1
Birmingham C (Free on 1/7/95) FL 1+6 Others 0+2
Lincoln C (Signed on 21/8/96) FL 29+5/4 FLC 5/1 FAC 1 Others 0+1

MARTIN Kevin
Born: Bromsgrove, 22 June 1976
Height: 6'1" Weight: 12.9

A safe and reliable young goalkeeper who never let the side down, Kevin had to bide his time in Scarborough's reserve side for most of last season due to the excellence of Ian Ironside, but always impressed when given his chance. This was typified when he gave a splendid Man of the Match performance in the 3-1 win at Colchester in February, the first league match the home side had lost in 1996-97. Looks to be an outstanding prospect for the future.

Scarborough (From trainee on 5/7/95) FL 3 FAC 0+1

MARTIN Lee Andrew
Born: Hyde, 5 February 1968
Height: 5'10" Weight 11.5
Club Honours: FAC '90; ESC '91
International Honours: E: U21-2

An experienced full back, Lee, the stylish former Manchester United defender, returned to English league football during the 1996 close season after an absence of three years, having been released by Glasgow Celtic. Made a confident debut for Bristol Rovers, in what was the last ever league match at Twerton Park, before making his next home appearance in Rovers' opening fixture at the Memorial Ground on their emotional return to Bristol after a decade away. Switched from right back to his more comfortable left-back position in November, he lost his place in the latter stages of the campaign due to injury.

Manchester U (From trainee on 14/5/86) F/PL 56+17/1 FLC 8+2 FAC 13+1/1 Others 7+6
Glasgow Celtic (Signed on 18/1/94) SL 19 SLC 1
Bristol Rov (Free on 8/8/96) FL 25 FLC 2 Others 1

Lee Martin

MARTINDALE Gary
Born: Liverpool, 24 June 1971
Height: 5'11" Weight: 12.1
A naturally talented Notts County striker who passes the ball well, Gary went on loan to Mansfield last February, but, when recalled after scoring in his first two matches, the Stags' request for a further extension was answered with a "buy him or lose him" ultimatum. Back at the Field Mill Ground, he was still looking to produce the form that won him the second division Golden Boot award in 1995-96. As County's penalty king, four of his seven goals came from the spot in 1996-97.
Bolton W (Signed from Burscough on 24/3/94)
Peterborough U (Signed on 4/7/95) FL 26+5/15 FLC 4/1 FAC 4 Others 4/2
Notts Co (£175,000 on 6/3/96) FL 29+15/12 FLC 2 FAC 2 Others 2/1
Mansfield T (Loaned on 7/2/97) FL 5/2

MARTINEZ Roberto
Born: Balaguer Lerida, Spain, 13 July 1973
Height: 5'10" Weight: 12.2
Club Honours: Div 3 '97
A skilful and combative right-footed midfielder, who may have not taken the division by storm in 1996-97 as he did in his first season, he once again proved to be Wigan Athletic's most exciting player. With the ability to create something out of nothing, and a tireless worker, Roberto was named in the PFA division three team for the second time running, an honour that reflected his part in helping the club to the third division title.
Wigan Ath (Free from Balaguer on 25/7/95) FL 80+5/13 FLC 4/1 FAC 5/3 Others 2+1/1

MARTYN Antony Nigel
Born: St Austell, 11 August 1966
Height: 6'2" Weight: 14.7
Club Honours: Div 3 '90, FMC '91; Div 1 '94
International Honours: E: 4; B-6; U21-11
Easily Leeds' best signing of last season, and one of the finest goalkeepers in the country, Nigel is a commanding and imposing goalkeeper who is deceptively agile for a man of his size. He is also a superb kicker of the ball. The amount of times that he kept his side in the game in 1996-97 were too numerous to mention, but almost every week saw him produce saves of the highest quality on his way to keeping more clean sheets than any other Premiership goalie and winning the club's Player of the Year award. Having won three international caps while at Crystal Palace, he was widely tipped for a return to the England set up and after his surprise omission from the squad for the World Cup qualifier with Italy (considering four goalkeepers were selected), he was finally rewarded for his efforts with a place for the friendly with Mexico in March. As Leeds' most consistent performer, again it was a surprise when he was not chosen for the side.
Bristol Rov (Free from St Blazey on 6/8/87) FL 101 FLC 6 FAC 6 Others 11
Crystal Palace (£1,000,000 on 21/11/89) F/PL 272 FLC 36 FAC 22 Others 19
Leeds U (£2,250,000 on 26/7/96) PL 37 FLC 3 FAC 4

Nigel Martyn

MASKELL Craig Dell
Born: Aldershot, 10 April 1968
Height: 5'10" Weight: 11.11
Brighton's leading marksman in the past campaign with 16 goals, and a deceptively good ball player, Craig struggled to find his scoring touch initially in 1996-97, but played a big part in the team's revival in the New Year. The highlight of his season was undoubtedly the fine threesome registered in a 5-0 beating of Hartlepool United in the "Fans United" match at the Goldstone in

February, making him the first player to bag a hat trick for the Seagulls in 35 months. Was named Player of the Month for December by the Evening Argus.
Southampton (From apprentice on 15/4/86) FL 2+4/1
Huddersfield T (£20,000 on 31/5/88) FL 86+1/43 FLC 6/4 FAC 8/3 Others 7/4
Reading (f250,000 on 7/8/90) FL 60+12/26 FLC 2 FAC 5+1 Others 1
Swindon T (£225,000 on 9/7/92) F/PL 40+7/22 FLC 3+1/1 FAC 2+1 Others 4+1/4
Southampton (£250,000 on 7/2/94) PL 8+9/1 FAC 1+1
Bristol C (Loaned on 28/12/95) FL 5/1
Brighton & Hove A (£40,000 on 1/3/96) FL 52+18 FLC 2 FAC 2/1 Others 2/1

Craig Maskell

MASON Andrew (Andy) John
Born: Bolton, 22 November 1974
Height: 6'0" Weight: 12.0
Ended a long spell in the Hull City wilderness with a splendid two-goal salvo on his December return against Doncaster, going on to hit three in six games before being discarded and becoming a Chesterfield deadline capture. A cheerful character, the young striker thoroughly deserved another chance, but was freed during the summer.
Bolton W (From trainee on 21/5/93)
Hull C (Free on 27/6/95) FL 14+12/4 FLC 1+3 Others 1+2
Chesterfield (Signed on 26/3/97) FL 1+1

MASON Paul David
Born: Liverpool, 3 September 1963
Height: 5'8" Weight: 12.1
Club Honours: SLC '90; SC '90
With the absence of experienced strikers at Ipswich for much of last season, the responsibility for scoring goals was shared throughout the team and Paul played his part well, ending up as the leading scorer with 15 to his credit. Most of his strikes could be described as spectacular and were normally volleys from the edge of the penalty area, his best being the one scored against Crystal Palace on Boxing Day when he ran on to a Mauricio Taricco throw in and chipped the

ball past Chris Day into the net. This goal not only put the game virtually outside of Palace's reach, but also earned him the supporters' club "Goal of the Season" award.

Aberdeen (£200,000 from FC Groningen on 1/8/88) SL 138+20/27 SLC 13+2/8 SC 11+1/1 Others 7/1
Ipswich T (£400,000 on 18/6/93) P/FL 102+10/25 FLC 9/4 FAC 4+3/3 Others 4/3

MASSEY Stuart Anthony
Born: Crawley, 17 November 1964
Height: 5'11 " Weight: 12.7

Not a regular for Oxford last season, with half of his 36 appearances coming as a sub, but, when playing, Stuart did not let the side down. A hard-working midfield player who was happy both in the middle or out wide, he enjoyed scoring a vital equaliser when returning to his former club, Crystal Palace. Is a good team man who always encourages others.

Crystal Palace (£20,000 from Sutton U on 17/7/92) F/PL 1+1 Others 1
Oxford U (Free on 5/7/94) FL 68+18/7 FLC 9+3/1 FAC 7+1/4 Others 3

MATHIE Alexander (Alex)
Born: Bathgate, 20 December 1968
Height: 5'10" Weight: 11.7
International Honours: S: Yth

Alex found that the burden of responsibility for the majority of Ipswich's goals in 1996-97 fell upon him soon after the campaign started, once Ian Marshall had moved on. He bore it well, scoring nine times in 17 appearances, including doubles against Oldham, Fulham and Crystal Palace, until a dislocated shoulder in the Crystal Palace game ended his season prematurely in October. Tests proved that operations were needed on both shoulders, but the nature of things meant that they had to be carried out individually, thus doubling the time of his absence. Hopefully, he should be fit for the start of 1997-98.

Glasgow Celtic (From juniors on 15/5/87) SL 7+4 SC 1 Others 0+1
Morton (£100,000 on 1/8/91) SL 73+1/31 SLC 2/1 SC 5/3 Others 7/9
Port Vale (Loaned on 30/3/93) FL 0+3
Newcastle U (£285,000 on 30/7/93) PL 3+22/4 FLC 2+2
Ipswich T (£500,000 on 24/2/95) P/FL 63+1/24 FLC 6/5 FAC 2 Others 4/1

MATTEO Dominic
Born: Dumfries, 28 April 1974
Height: 6'1" Weight: 11.12
International Honours: E: U21-3; Yth

Established in the Liverpool defence right through to last November, and earning a call up for Glenn Hoddle's England in the process, he eventually fell away, making 38 appearances from a possible 52. However, there was no doubt that his maturity and dependability during those early months had given the Reds an added dimension and enabled them to maintain a strong position near the top of the Premiership table. Whilst his cause was certainly not helped by the impressive form of the newcomer, Bjorn Kvarme, Dominic still proved capable of distributing the ball intelligently and

running powerfully through the middle of the park or down the left-hand side to set up attacking moves. Will certainly be in contention for a place this coming term.

Liverpool (From trainee on 27/5/92) PL 40+9 FLC 5 FAC 3+1 Others 7
Sunderland (Loaned on 28/3/95) FL 1

MATTHEW Damian
Born: Islington, 23 September 1970
Height: 5'11" Weight" 10.10
Club Honours: Div 1 '94
International Honours: E: U21-9

Signed from Crystal Palace during the summer of 1996, Damian was more or less a midfield regular during his first season at Turf Moor, seldom offering less than 100 per-cent effort, but occasionally looked a shade lightweight in the weakest department of the Burnley side. He provided his share of goals, however, and they were often spectacular, including one direct from a corner at Notts County, and a brilliant overhead kick at Brentford.

Chelsea (From trainee on 13/6/89) F/PL 13+8 FLC 5 Others 1
Luton T (Loaned on 25/9/92) FL 3+2 Others 1
Crystal Palace (£150,000 on 11/2/94) F/PL 17+7/1 FLC 2+1 FAC 1
Bristol Rov (Loaned on 12/1/96) FL 8 Others 2/1
Burnley (£65,000 on 23/7/96) FL 29+3/6 FLC 3/1 FAC 2/1 Others 1

MATTHEWS Robert (Rob) David
Born: Slough, 14 October 1970
Height: 6'0" Weight: 13.0
Club Honours: Div 2 '97
International Honours: E: Sch

1996-97 was something of an unlucky season for Bury's tricky winger, who, having worked hard to earn a regular place in the side and was just reaching the peak of his form, limped out of the away game at Preston on 1 March with a badly swollen knee and did not feature again in the club's run in to the division two title. Indeed, he learned of his colleagues' success courtesy of a hospital TV after undergoing a late season knee operation. However, the good news was that Rob won a championship medal and will, hopefully, be back to his best in 1997-98.

Notts Co (Free from Loughborough University on 26/3/92) FL 23+20/11 FLC 0+2 FAC 3+2/2 Others 4+3
Luton T (£80,000 on 17/3/95) FL 6+5 FLC 0+1
York C (£90,000 on 8/9/95) FL 14+3/1 FAC 1 Others 3
Bury (£100,000 on 12/1/96) FL 33+10/9 FLC 1+3 FAC 1 Others 3

MATTHEWSON Trevor
Born: Sheffield, 12 February 1963
Height: 6'4" Weight: 13.6
Club Honours: GMVC '88; AMC '91

Having left Bury for non-league Witton Albion during the 1996 close season, Trevor quickly came back into the league fray when signing for Hereford last October. Soon formed a good relationship with Dean Smith and John Brough in the United rearguard, showing himself to be an ever reliable player who stood his ground when the going got rough. Also showed excellent heading ability.

Sheffield Wed (From apprentice on 12/2/81) FL 3 FAC 2
Newport Co (Free on 15/10/83) FL 73+2 FLC 2 FAC 7 Others 6
Stockport Co (Free on 27/9/85) FL 79+1 FLC 3 FAC 2 Others 3
Lincoln C (£13,000 on 1/8/87) FL 43/2 FLC 3 FAC 3 Others 3
Birmingham C (£45,000 on 3/8/89) FL 167+1/12 FLC 11 FAC 8 Others 16/1
Preston NE (Signed on 20/8/93) FL 12/1 FLC 1 Others 1
Bury (£10,000 on 2/9/94) FL 34 FLC 4 FAC 5 Others 6 (Free to Witton A during 1996 close season)
Hereford U (Free on 11/10/96) FL 35/2 FAC 1 Others 1

MAUGE Ronald (Ronnie) Carlton
Born: Islington, 10 March 1969
Height: 5'10" Weight: 11.10

1996-97 was a difficult season for the hero of the previous year's campaign as he spent the majority of the time on Plymouth's transfer list. At his best, an excellent midfielder with an eye for goal, Ronnie was in and out of the team, despite making 40 appearances and, with him out of contract during the summer, it will be interesting to see where and when he starts 1996-97.

Charlton Ath (From trainee on 22/7/87)
Fulham (Free on 21/9/88) FL 47+3/2 FLC 4 FAC 1 Others 2
Bury (£40,000 on 30/7/90) FL 92+16/10 FLC 8+2/2 FAC 8/2 Others 10+2
Manchester C (Loaned on 26/9/91) Others 0+1
Plymouth Arg (£40,000 on 22/7/95) FL 65+7/9 FLC 3 FAC 6/2 Others 4+1/3

MAUTONE Steven (Steve)
Born: Myrtleford, Australia, 10 August 1970
Height: 6'1" Weight: 12.0

Signed from Australian football towards the end of 1995-96, this tall, courageous goalkeeper started last season on the bench at West Ham, standing in for Ludek Miklosko, before being loaned to Crewe, following an injury to Mark Gayle. Having made three appearances and conceded just a single goal, he was recalled to Upton Park when Miklosko was unavailable and repeated that statistic before being allowed to leave for Reading in early February, also on loan. Quickly into the action, he stabilised a position that had been an acute problem for the Royals in recent years and even saved the only two penalties faced, against Ipswich and Oldham. Impressed so much at Elm Park that it is on the cards that he will sign permanently during the summer.

West Ham U (£30,000 from Canberra Cosmos on 29/3/96) PL 1 FLC 2
Crewe Alex (Loaned on 6/9/96) FL 3
Reading (Loaned on 17/2/97) FL 15

MAXFIELD Scott
Born: Doncaster, 13 July 1976
Height: 5'8" Weight: 11.6

A highly-rated Hull City utility man, the left-sided Scott fought his way into first-team contention in 1996-97, only for knee ligament damage picked up in a March reserves game, to rule him out for the rest of the season. A rather slight figure disguises a competitive edge.

Doncaster Rov (From trainee on 8/7/94) FL 22+7/1 FAC 0+1 Others 1
Hull C (Signed on 27/3/96) FL 13+8 FLC 1+1 FAC 1 Others 0+1

MAY David
Born: Oldham, 24 June 1970
Height: 6'0" Weight: 12.10
Club Honours: CS '94, '97; PL '96, '97; FAC '96

A very able Manchester United central defender with good recovery skills, and excellent heading ability, David's emergence as a major force was one of the main highlights of last season as far as Alex Ferguson was concerned. Having kept faith in his ability since signing him from Blackburn in 1994, the United boss put his performances on a par with the man he replaced, Steve Bruce. Only one of four players to appear in all competitions, his goal tally was also impressive with four to his credit, his most important coming against Porto in the quarter-final of the European Cup, a goal which opened the floodgates in an unforgettable night at Old Trafford. It certainly helped David to forget that unfortunate incident in the Champions' League in October, when an attempted shot by a Fenerbahce player went in off his shoulder and ended United's 40-year unbeaten home record in European competition. Having also played with a troublesome hernia for much of the campaign, he was deservedly recognised with an England call up by Glenn Hoddle for the friendly against Mexico in March. Ended the campaign with another championship medal, following United's fourth title win in five years.
Blackburn Rov (From trainee on 16/6/88) F/PL 123/3 FLC 12+1/2 FAC 10/1 Others 5
Manchester U (£1,400,000 on 1/7/94) PL 54+10/6 FLC 4/1 FAC 4 Others 13+1/1

MAYO Kerry
Born: Cuckfield, 21 September 1977
Height: 5'10" Weight: 11.7

A product of Brighton's associate schoolboy scheme, this flame-haired, dynamic midfielder graduated through the youth and reserve teams to make his senior debut as a second half substitute for skipper George Parris during the 3-1 home defeat by Carlisle United last November. He impressed sufficiently to be retained as a regular squad member and merited a lengthy run in the side under new manager, Steve Gritt, as the Seagulls miraculously came back from the dead.
Brighton & Hove A (From trainee on 3/7/96) FL 22+2 FAC 0+1 Others 1+1

MEAKER Michael John
Born: Greenford, 18 August 1971
Height: 5'11" Weight: 11.5
International Honours: W: B-1; U21-2

It was another season of inconsistency for the Reading midfielder, who spent much of the campaign in the reserves and had to wait until the final match, away to Manchester City, to score his first goal for the club. At his best, a player who runs well with the ball and very quick off the mark, in 1996-97,

again there were only glimpses of his ability to take on players and whip in crosses. Hopefully, 1997-98 will see him back on song.
Queens Park R (From trainee on 7/2/90) F/PL 21+13/1 FLC 2/1 FAC 3/1 Others 0+1
Plymouth Arg (Loaned on 20/11/91) FL 4 Others 1
Reading (£550,000 on 19/7/95) FL 30+16/1 FAC 0+1

MEDLIN Nicholas (Nicky) Ryan Maxwell
Born: Camborne, 23 November 1976
Height: 5'7" Weight: 10.7

Returning from a broken leg, Nicky was consistent in his Exeter midfield appearances in 1996-97, showing all of the ball-winning qualities that had earlier earmarked him as one to watch. One of the highlights of his season was his superb performance in the relegation battle at Doncaster where he helped City come from behind to take the three points.
Exeter C (From trainee on 4/8/95) FL 9+8/1 Others 1+2

MELLON Michael Joseph
Born: Paisley, 18 March 1972
Height: 5'9" Weight: 11.3

A Blackpool midfielder with a goalscoring record to go with good skills and a high workrate, Michael was disappointed not to have found the net with greater frequency last season. Always likely to pop up in dangerous positions, there are plenty more left in the tank, however.
Bristol C (From trainee on 6/12/89) FL 26+9/1 FLC 3 FAC 1+1 Others 5+3
West Bromwich A (£75,000 on 11/2/93) FL 38+7/6 FLC 3+2 FAC 0+1 Others 6/1
Blackpool (£50,000 on 23/11/94) FL 114/14 FLC 6/1 FAC 4 Others 7/2

MELVILLE Andrew (Andy) Roger
Born: Swansea, 29 November 1968
Height: 6'0" Weight: 13.10
Club Honours: WC '89; Div 1 '96
International Honours: W: 31; B-1; U21-2

Sunderland's Welsh international defender acquitted himself well in the Premiership before a badly-broken nose last March caused him to miss the final seven games of the season. Andy's partnership with Richard Ord was once again impressive for much of the campaign and he weighed in with his usual couple of goals, one of which saved a late point against Sheffield Wednesday at Roker. Powerful in the air and a player who always looks to use the ball intelligently.
Swansea C (From trainee on 25/7/86) FL 165+10/22 FLC 10 FAC 14+1/5 Others 13/2
Oxford U (£275,000 on 23/7/90) FL 135/13 FLC 12/1 FAC 6 Others 6/1
Sunderland (Signed on 9/8/93) P/FL 150/11 FLC 12+1 FAC 9 Others 2

MENDEZ Gabriel
Born: Buenos Aires, Argentina, 12 March 1973
Height: 5'9" Weight: 11.10

Loaned from Parrametta during transfer deadline week last March, "Chi Chi" appeared in just three games for Notts County before departing and leaving both the fans and management wishing for more. A highly skilled midfield playmaker, his set

pieces were reminiscent of the much revered Don Masson
Notts Co (Loaned from Parrametta on 24/3/97) FL 2+1

MENDONCA Clive Paul
Born: Tullington, 9 September 1968
Height: 5'10" Weight: 12.6

A talented right-footed Grimsby striker, who, having spent most of 1995-96 struggling against an injury which many thought had ended his career, returned to full fitness last season. Although struggling to recapture his old flair, he was once again the leading scorer in a campaign when goals were often hard to come by. *Stop Press:* Persistent rumours linking his name with other clubs, notably West Ham, proved unfounded, but, with his contract up at the end of the season, he signed for Charlton on 23 May.
Sheffield U (From apprentice on 10/9/86) FL 8+5/4 FLC 0+1 Others 1
Doncaster Rov (Loaned on 26/2/88) FL 2
Rotherham U (£35,000 on 25/3/88) FL 71+13/27 FLC 5+2/1 FAC 4+1/2 Others 4+2/1
Sheffield U (£110,000 on 1/8/91) FL 4+6/1 FLC 0+2 Others 0+1
Grimsby T (Loaned on 9/1/92) FL 10/3
Grimsby T (£85,000 on 13/8/92) FL 151+5/57 FLC 10+1/3 FAC 8/2 Others 2/1

MERCER William (Billy)
Born: Liverpool, 22 May 1969
Height: 6'2" Weight: 13.5

Chesterfield's number-one 'keeper played through the early part of last season with a groin injury that prevented him from training fully and slightly hampered his ability to get down to ground shots. As that cleared up, Billy resumed the excellent form to which Saltergate regulars have become accustomed, but a week before playing at Old Trafford in the FA Cup semi final, he was in hospital, coughing up blood, after being kneed in the abdomen during a game. That says all you need to know about Bill's courage and commitment. On a goals conceded per game basis, Billy stands fifth on the all-time list of 'keepers and as his team made their heroic run to the FA Cup semis, it is believed that he equalled the record for clean sheets in the competition proper.
Liverpool (From trainee on 21/8/87)
Rotherham U (Signed on 16/2/89) FL 104 FLC 12 FAC 12 Others 10
Sheffield U (Signed on 12/10/94) FL 4
Chesterfield (Loaned on 15/9/95) FL 11 Others 2
Chesterfield (£93,000 on 12/12/95) FL 58 FLC 2 FAC 8 Others 2

MERSON Paul Charles
Born: Harlesden, 20 March 1968
Height: 6'0" Weight: 13.2
Club Honours: Div 1 '89, '91; FLC '93; FAC '93; ECWC '94
International Honours: E: 15; B-3; U21-4; Yth

Paul was another Arsenal favourite who flourished under the new manager, Arsene Wenger, last season, playing regularly in what was probably his most effective role, a floating one, and getting an England call up for the World Cup qualifier against Italy in

February. Despite carrying a hernia injury, which ultimately required surgery in the second half of the campaign, his performances continued to be consistent and such was his natural level of fitness that he was back in the team for the last three matches. Nearing the unique 100-goal Gunners' club, he scored in both legs of the UEFA Cup against Borussia Monchengladbach and included among his other strikes was his almost traditional goal against boyhood idols, Chelsea. A top drawer attacking winger, cum forward, who has close control and runs well with the ball and favouring his right foot, he will regularly come inside to show off his explosive finishing power. *Stop Press:* Surprisingly, was reported to have signed for Middlesbrough as the replacement for Juninho, a £4.5 million transfer tag being the inducement.

Arsenal (From apprentice on 1/12/85) F/PL 289+38/78 FLC 38+2/9 FAC 28+3/4 Others 27+2/7
Brentford (Loaned on 22/1/87) FL 6+1 Others 1+1

Paul Merson

MESSER Gary Michael
Born: Consett, 22 September 1979
Height: 6'1" Weight: 12.0
Having impressed in the youth side in 1996-97, this first-year Doncaster trainee was drafted onto the first-team subs' bench at Chester, coming on after 58 minutes with Rovers already four goals down and on their way to a 6-0 defeat. Hardly an auspicious debut, but, with time on his side, Gary is highly thought of as an all-purpose forward who can play down the middle or out wide with equal ability.
Doncaster Rov (Trainee) FL 0+1

MICHAEL James (Jamie) David
Born: Pontypridd, 28 October 1978
Height: 5'11" Weight: 11.12
International Honours: W: Yth
Still a trainee, Jamie was given a run out with the Cardiff first team at Ninian Park against Mansfield last December when he came off the subs' bench after 75 minutes to directly replace an off key Jimmy Gardner on the left flank. A good crosser of the ball who can play on either wing, the youngster showed himself to be both skilful and quick and may get further opportunities before too long.
Cardiff C (Trainee) FL 0+1

MIDDLETON Craig Dean
Born: Nuneaton, 10 September 1970
Height: 5'9" Weight: 10.13
Released by Cambridge during the 1996 close season, Craig moved down to Wales to sign for Cardiff, coming into the side early in September and remaining a regular throughout the campaign, despite going through a shallow patch around Christmas. A useful attacking midfielder who makes intelligent forward runs and provides chances for others, he quickly got on the scoresheet himself, scoring four goals in eight outings, before drying up. Is the twin brother of Lee, formerly with Coventry, Swindon, and Cambridge.
Coventry C (From trainee on 30/5/89) F/PL 2+1 FLC 1
Cambridge U (Free on 20/7/93) FL 55+4/10 FLC 3 FAC 1 Others 1
Cardiff C (Free on 30/8/96) FL 40+1/4 FLC 0+1 FAC 2/1 Others 3+1

MIDGLEY Craig Steven
Born: Bradford, 24 May 1976
Height: 5'8" Weight: 10.13
As the Bradford reserve team's front runner, Craig got through a lot of work in 1996-97, but was only offered limited opportunities for the first team, two subs' appearances being his sum total. In order to get some first team games under his belt, and having impressed during a previous loan period at Scarborough, he signed up for a further spell at the McCain Stadium in March, displaying some fine touches in six matches before returning to City. Skilful and creative, and a player who is at home in wide positions, he has age on his side.
Bradford C (From trainee on 4/7/95) FL 0+9/1 FAC 0+3 Others 1
Scarborough (Loaned on 7/12/95) FL 14+2/1
Scarborough (Loaned on 14/3/97) FL 6/2

MIHAILOV Borislav (Bobby) Biserov
Born: Bulgaria, 12 February 1963
Height: 6'0" Weight: 12.10
International Honours: Bulgaria: 103
Bobby made intermittent appearances in goal for Reading in 1996-97, though none could doubt his bravery after a knee injury sustained against Bolton Wanderers ended his Elm Park career. Then, having completed 100 international appearances for Bulgaria, he returned to that country early in April after a mainly disappointing stay with the Royals.
Reading (£300,000 from Botev Plovdiv on 19/9/95) FL 24 FLC 2 FAC 2

MIKE Adrian (Adie) Roosevelt
Born: Manchester, 16 November 1973
Height: 6'0" Weight: 11.9
International Honours: E: Yth; Sch
The ex-Manchester City player failed to make his mark at Stockport for the second season running in 1996-97, making just one start and two subs' appearances and being loaned out to first Hartlepool and then Doncaster. A speedy striker whose good first touch makes him a danger to defences, his seven games for Pool brought him just one solitary goal, while at Rovers it took two games less, before injuries again let him down. *Stop Press:* Was released during the summer.
Manchester C (From trainee on 15/7/92) F/PL 5+11/2 FLC 1+1 FAC 0+1
Bury (Loaned on 25/3/93) FL 5+2/1
Stockport Co (£60,000 on 18/8/95) FL 4+5 FAC 0+1 Others 1+1
Hartlepool U (Loaned on 4/10/96) FL 7/1
Doncaster Rov (Loaned on 14/2/97) FL 5/1

MIKLOSKO Ludek (Ludo)
Born: Ostrava, Czechoslovakia, 9 December 1961
Height: 6'5" Weight: 14.0
International Honours: Czechoslovakia: 44
West Ham's Czech international goalkeeper completed his eighth season at Upton Park in 1996-97 with another series of consistent displays, being absent (through injury) for only two games. His most outstanding performances were in the away games at Newcastle (1-1) and Sheffield Wednesday (0-0) in November, and at Liverpool (0-0) in January where the Hammers picked up unexpected and invaluable points in their fight against relegation. Late in the season he made his 300th Premier League appearance against Sheffield Wednesday - the team appropriately celebrating the occasion with a 5-1 victory!
West Ham U (£300,000 from Banik Ostrava on 19/2/90) F/PL 302 FLC 23 FAC 25 Others 8

MILDENHALL Stephen (Steve) James
Born: Swindon, 13 May 1978
Height: 6'5" Weight: 13.5
As Swindon Town's third choice (and youth team) goalkeeper, Steve signed a one-year professional contract in July 1996, but probably did not expect any further first-team action so early in his career. Strangely, he was selected as a suitable substitute for the match at Tranmere in January - the only time that manager, Steve McMahon, deployed a 'keeper on the bench - and, even more bizarrely, was sent on for the last five minutes to replace an outfield player, even though McMahon was also available! Offered a new contract in the summer, he gained additional first-team experience on loan to Dr Martens League clubs, Gloucester City (November) and Salisbury City (March).
Swindon T (From trainee on 19/7/96) FL 0+1 FLC 2

MILLEN Keith Derek
Born: Croydon, 26 September 1966
Height: 6'2" Weight: 12.4
Club Honours: Div 3 '92

Consistent central defender whose partnership with Robert Page was a major factor in Watford's impressive 22-match unbeaten run and excellent defensive record in 1996-97. Had the great quality of bringing out the best in his team mates, despite being hampered by groin problems towards the end of the campaign.

Brentford (From apprentice on 7/8/84) FL 301+4/17 FLC 26/2 FAC 18/1 Others 30+1
Watford (Signed on 22/3/94) FL 115+1/4 FLC 7 FAC 10 Others 1

Keith Millen

MILLER Alan John
Born: Epping, 29 March 1970
Height: 6'3" Weight: 14.6
Club Honours: FAYC '88; ECWC '94; Div 1 '95
International Honours: E: U21-4; Sch

A well-built, commanding goalkeeper with good reflexes and a safe pair of hands, in 1996-97 Alan became the first player ever to join West Brom for two separate loan spells. When he came to the club second time round, from Middlesbrough, having had a spell on loan at Grimsby, he was immediately introduced to the first team (in place of Paul Crichton) and his presence made Albion's defence look a lot more confident.

Arsenal (From trainee on 5/5/88) PL 6+2
Plymouth Arg (Loaned on 24/11/88) FL 13 FAC 2
West Bromwich A (Loaned on 15/8/91) FL 3
Birmingham C (Loaned on 19/12/91) FL 15 Others 1
Middlesbrough (£500,000 on 12/8/94) P/FL 57 FLC 3 FAC 2 Others 2
Grimsby T (Loaned on 28/1/97) FL 3
West Bromwich A (£400,000 on 28/2/97) FL 12

Kevin Miller

MILLER Kevin
Born: Falmouth, 15 March 1969
Height: 6'1" Weight: 13.0
Club Honours: Div 4 '90

Kevin had an outstanding season in 1996-97, several good judges, including the PFA, rating him the best goalkeeper in the second division, and he was deservedly voted Watford's Player of the Year. A good shot stopper, sound on crosses, and having excellent rapport with his defence, it was only his kicking that occasionally let him down. Reportedly tracked by several Premiership clubs and is surely destined for greater things. *Stop Press:* Was reported to have signed for Crystal Palace, a fee of £1.55 million being involved.

Exeter C (Free from Newquay on 9/3/89) FL 163 FLC 7 FAC 12 Others 18
Birmingham C (£250,000 on 14/5/93) FL 24 FLC 4 Others 2
Watford (£250,000 on 7/8/94) FL128 FLC 10 FAC 10 Others 3

MILLER Paul Anthony
Born: Woking, 31 January 1968
Height: 6'0" Weight: 11.7

Paul started last season for Bristol Rovers as one of the first-choice strikers, but after just one goal he was replaced by new signings and was transfer listed in November, although turning down the opportunity of a move to York City. However, to his credit, the hard-working striker or midfielder managed to break back into the side again in the New Year and added a further goal to a career total of 22 in just over a century of league appearances for the club.

Wimbledon (From Yeovil T on 12/8/87) F/PL 65+15/10 FLC 3+3 FAC 3 Others 1
Newport Co (Loaned on 20/10/87) FL 6/2
Bristol C (Loaned on 11/1/90) FL 0+3 Others 2
Bristol Rov (£100,000 on 16/8/94) FL 100+5/22 FLC 7/1 FAC 5/4 Others 11/2

MILLIGAN Michael (Mike) Joseph
Born: Manchester, 20 February 1967
Height: 5'8" Weight: 11.0
International Honours: Ei: 1; B-2; U23-1; U21-1

As in previous years, Mike always attempted to deny the opposition the time and space to play in 1996-97, being something of an unsung hero at Norwich. A tremendous season saw him as an effective barrier in front of the defence in all-action displays, while his sending off at Southend was the club's eighth red card of the campaign, a statistic which meant that Norwich were often short handed and was definitely a factor in their failure to reach the Premiership. A great competitor and midfield general, and an experienced tenacious performer, he is a great man to have on your side, especially in breaking down your opponent's rhythm.

Oldham Ath (From apprentice on 2/3/85) FL 161+1/17 FLC 19+1/1 FAC 12/1 Others 4
Everton (£1,000,000 on 24/8/90) FL 16+1/1 FLC 0+1 FAC 1 Others 4+1/1
Oldham Ath (£600,000 on 17/7/91) F/PL 117/6 FLC 11/1 FAC 9 Others 1/1
Norwich C (£800,000 on 27/6/94) P/FL 83+8/5 FLC 10 FAC 5

MILLS Daniel (Danny) John
Born: Norwich, 18 May 1977
Height: 5'11" Weight: 11.9
International Honours: E: Yth

An automatic Norwich choice to replace the unfortunate Carl Bradshaw, his 1996-97 performances in an unfamiliar berth at left back were reckoned by many to be one of a disappointing season's plus points, while his manager, Mike Walker, rates his ability to get in front of people with good recovery being an especial skill. His two dismissals against Queens Park Rangers and West Brom and were more a young man learning his trade, rather than that of malicious intent, something that was reflected in his May call up into the England U21 squad's European Championship qualifier in Poland. Shows great awareness for one so young and seems almost certain to reach the top of the rung. Along with Andy Marshall, Danny was another City player selected for the Football League U21 side that played the Italian Serie "B" equivalent in February.

Norwich C (From trainee on 1/11/94) FL 35+11 FLC 3+2/1 FAC 1

MILLS Daniel (Danny) Raymond
Born: Sidcup, 13 February 1975
Height: 6'0" Weight: 11.6

A speedy and tricky Barnet winger, who can play on both flanks, Danny came off the bench three times early last season before a hamstring injury sidelined him and saw him spend the rest of the campaign in the reserves on recovery. Hopefully, 1997-98 will see him back to full match fitness and raring to go.

Charlton Ath (From trainee on 1/7/93) Others 0+2
Barnet (Free on 29/9/95) FL 5+16 FAC 1+2 Others 0+1

MILLS Rowan Lee
Born: Mexborough, 10 July 1970
Height: 6'1" Weight: 12.11

Although the Port Vale striker could not hold down a regular place during the first half of 1996-97, being left out away from

home as the team maintained a 4-5-1 formation as opposed to 4-4-2, he still maintained a good goals-to-games ratio, but a burst of seven goals in six games in March made him the number one striker, even ousting Tony Naylor away from home. A big, strong player, he was always a threat to the opposition and scored 15 goals in just 25 games, enough to win him the supporters' Player of the Year award.

Wolverhampton W (Signed from Stocksbridge on 9/12/92) FL 12+13/2 FLC 1 FAC 3+1/1 Others 3/1
Derby Co (£400,000 on 24/2/95) FL 16/7
Port Vale (£200,000 on 1/8/95) FL 42+25/21 FLC 5+3/3 FAC 0+2 Others 6/4

Lee Mills

MILNER Andrew (Andy) John

Born: Kendal, 10 February 1967
Height: 6'0" Weight: 11.0

Andy had his best season since joining Chester, ending 1996-97 as top scorer with 14 goals and breaking a personal record when notching four in the 6-0 victory over Doncaster at the Deva in February. A player with the ability to attack through the centre or down the flanks, where his pace can be seen to advantage, he is also a skilful provider for others, being responsible for ten assists during a campaign where the club reached the semi-final stage of the play offs.

Manchester C (£7,000 from Netherfield on 24/1/89)
Rochdale (£20,000 on 18/1/90) FL 103+24/25 FLC 9+4/5 FAC 6+2/1 Others 4/2
Chester C (Free on 12/8/94) FL 105+19/24 FLC 5+1/3 FAC 5+1/4 Others 4+1

MILOSEVIC Savo

Born: Bijeljina, Yugoslavia, 2 September 1973
Height: 6'1" Weight: 13.4
Club Honours: FLC '96
International Honours: Yugoslavia: 18

Savo's early season in 1996-97 at Aston Villa was taken up with a prolonged will he, won't he transfer to Perugia in Italy which eventually fell through. The left-footed

striker started the campaign well enough with two goals at Highbury in his second game, but his next goals did not come until the end of December after he had pledged his future to Villa. Coming back well after a hat trick for Yugoslavia in the World Cup ties he scored a further eight goals to reach double figures again, having only missed one match since the end of November, this after being injured on further international duty. A player of undoubted talent, he has great presence on the ball, links well with play and gets himself into excellent positions and really should be up there with the country's top scorers.

Aston Villa (£3,500,000 from Partizan Belgrade on 17/7/95) PL 65+2/20 FLC 7+1/1 FAC 8/1 Others 2

MILTON Simon Charles

Born: Fulham, 23 August 1963
Height: 5'10" Weight: 11.5
Club Honours: Div 2 '92

A series of niggling injuries curtailed Simon's season in 1996-97 and did not allow him a settled run in the Ipswich side, most of his appearances coming from the bench. Due a testimonial in 1997-98, he is a player who, when fully fit, is comfortable on either flank from where he can produce good early crosses and is more than capable of scoring explosive goals after bursting through. Is also a sweet striker of the ball.

Ipswich T (£5,500 from Bury T on 17/7/87) F/PL 210+51/48 FLC 14+7/3 FAC 12/1 Others 14+2/3
Exeter C (Loaned on 1/11/87) FL 2/3 Others 1
Torquay U (Loaned on 1/3/88) FL 4/1

Savo Milosevic

MIMMS Robert (Bobby) Andrew
Born: York, 12 October 1963
Height: 6'3" Weight: 14.4
Club Honours: Div 1 '87; CS '86, '87
International Honours: E: U21-3
Released by Blackburn during the 1996 close season, Bobby signed for Crystal Palace on non-contract terms, playing just once in an emergency, before joining Preston last September. An experienced goalie, he continued to demonstrate the talent which saw him play in the Premiership and old first division and rescued his defenders on many occasions. Despite losing his place for a short period in mid season, it was short lived and he returned strongly.
Halifax T (From apprentice on 5/8/81)
Rotherham U (£15,000 on 6/11/81) FL 83 FLC 7 FAC 3 Others 1
Everton (£150,000 on 30/5/85) FL 29 FLC 2 FAC 2 Others 4
Notts Co (Loaned on 13/3/86) FL 2 Others 1
Sunderland (Loaned on 11/12/86) FL 4
Blackburn Rov (Loaned on 23/1/87) FL 6
Manchester C (Loaned on 24/9/87) FL 3
Tottenham H (£325,000 on 25/2/88) FL 37 FLC 5 FAC 2
Aberdeen (Loaned on 16/2/90) SL 6 SC 2
Blackburn Rov (£250,000 on 22/12/90) F/PL 126+2 FLC 15 FAC 9 Others 4
Crystal Palace (Free on 30/8/96) FL 1
Preston NE (Free on 5/9/96) FL 27 FLC 2 FAC 2

MINETT Jason
Born: Peterborough, 12 August 1971
Height: 5'10" Weight: 10.2
Jason, a tough-tackling midfield player, failed to hold down a place at Lincoln in 1996-97 and moved back to his former club, Exeter, in January. Able to be used either in defence or midfield, where he adapted himself more than adequately, his versatility was a big plus for a club suffering from injuries and a lack of squad depth.
Norwich C (From trainee on 4/7/89) F/PL 0+3
Exeter C (Free on 19/3/93) FL 83+5/3 FLC 4 FAC 6 Others 7/2
Lincoln C (Free on 10/7/95) FL 41+5/5 FLC 2+4 FAC 1 Others 4+1
Exeter C (Free on 17/1/97) FL 13

MINTO Scott Christopher
Born: Heswall, 6 August 1971
Height: 5'9" Weight: 12.7
Club Honours: FAC '97
International Honours: E: U21-6; Yth
With the transfer of Terry Phelan to Everton last December, Scott at last had the opportunity to make the Chelsea left-wing back position his own. Since his transfer from Charlton in May 1994, his career has been interrupted by a catalogue of injuries and the 1996-97 season was no exception, starting approximately half of the matches. His goalscoring record with Chelsea could be likened to London buses: you wait ages for the first one and then they come along in pairs, opening his account against Wimbledon at the Bridge in October and three days later scoring again at Burnden Park in a Coca-Cola Cup tie. After a four-month gap, he scored at Derby and four days later sent a screamer past Tim Flowers to salvage a point for Chelsea against

Blackburn. With Dan Petrescu working the right flank, his attacking forays down the left gave Chelsea the perfect balance, enabling the midfield players to switch play and create havoc from either wing. *Stop Press:* Out of contract during the summer, an FA Cup winners medal in his pocket thanks to the 2-0 win over Middlesbrough at Wembley, Scott left for Benfica in early June on a free transfer.
Charlton Ath (From trainee on 2/2/89) FL 171+9/7 FLC 8/2 FAC 8+2 Others 7/1
Chelsea (£775,000 on 28/5/94) PL 53+1/4 FLC 3/1 FAC 9 Others 5+1

MINTON Jeffrey (Jeff) Simon Thompson
Born: Hackney, 28 December 1973
Height: 5'6" Weight: 11.10
This speedy, ball-playing Londoner was an automatic choice for Brighton's midfield in 1996-97 under Jimmy Case and was named as Player of the Month for November by the Evening Argus, but on returning from a short-term lay off he became unsettled when selected as a substitute by new boss, Steve Gritt, and requested a transfer. Jeff subsequently returned to the side and played his part admirably in Albion's nail-biting escape from oblivion.
Tottenham H (From trainee on 11/1/92) FL 2/1 FLC 0+1
Brighton & Hove A (Free on 25/7/94) FL 96+7/16 FLC 8 FAC 6 Others 4

MISON Michael
Born: Southwark, 8 November 1975
Height: 6'3" Weight: 14.0
Restricted mainly to Fulham's reserves in 1996-97, usually as a central defender, although this was a poor season by his standards, he finished on a higher note when loaned to Stevenage Borough for their battle to gain League status. Before returning to the Cottage, he scored several important goals from his favoured midfield position, which should hold him in good stead for Rushden & Diamonds during the coming campaign, having been released in the summer.
Fulham (From trainee on 15/7/94) FL 35+20/5 FLC 7+2/1 FAC 4+1 Others 4+2/1

MITCHELL Andrew (Andy) Barry
Born: Rotherham, 12 September 1976
Height: 6'0" Weight: 12.0
After joining Chesterfield during the 1996 close season from Aston Villa on a trial basis, Andy was awarded a year's contract in August, having proved to be a versatile lad, who could play anywhere in defence or midfield. Utility players are rarely presented with an opportunity to press a claim in one position, though, and this has been the case with Andy, who, despite being a valued squad member, was denied by the fine form of his team mates.
Aston Villa (From trainee on 27/9/93)
Chesterfield (Free on 16/9/96) FL 1+1 Others 1

MITCHELL Graham Lee
Born: Shipley, 16 February 1968
Height: 6'1" Weight: 12.13
A strong central defender, who is comfortable on the ball with good passing technique,

Graham started last season for Bradford as a regular, appearing in eight of the first 11 matches, before signing for Scottish Premier League side, Raith Rovers, on 10 October. More than capable of playing in midfield or at full back if required, previously he had an unfortunate run of injuries.
Huddersfield T (From trainee on 16/6/86) FL 235+9/2 FLC 13+2/1 FAC 27/1 Others 24/1
Bournemouth (Loaned on 24/12/93) FL 4
Bradford C (Signed on 23/12/94) FL 64+1/1 FLC 8 FAC 2 Others 4

MITCHELL James (Jamie)
Born: Glasgow, 6 November 1976
Height: 5'6" Weight: 9.10
Signed from Norwich during the 1996 close season, the inexperienced youngster was given an early opportunity by Scarborough and proved to be a skilful and exciting attacking midfielder who could score his fair share of goals, seven being a more than fair start. With last season being his first in senior football, his potential was there for all to see.
Norwich C (From trainee on 4/7/95)
Scarborough (Free on 2/8/96) FL 23+20/7 FLC 2+2 FAC 3

MITCHELL Paul Robert
Born: Nottingham, 8 November 1978
Height: 5'8" Weight: 10.8
A highly talented local lad, and a second-year Notts County trainee, Paul made his league debut in a 1-1 draw against Burnley at Meadow Lane towards the end of last season, following outstanding performances at youth and reserve level. Can play at right back, as a central defender, and in midfield.
Notts Co (Trainee) FL 1

MITCHELL Paul Robert
Born: Bournemouth, 20 October 1971
Height: 5'10" Weight: 12.0
International Honours: E: Yth; Sch
Released by Bournemouth during the 1996 close season, the full back, cum midfield player, had an unfortunate time with various injuries at Torquay in 1996-97, but showed plenty to suggest that he is good enough to shine at this level. However, despite that, he was given a free at the end of the campaign.
Bournemouth (From trainee on 7/8/89) FL 6+6 Others 1+1
West Ham U (£40,000 on 6/8/93) PL 0+1
Bournemouth (Free on 28/3/96) FL 2+2
Torquay U (Free on 9/8/96) FL 22+2 FLC 2 FAC 0+1 Others 1

MOHAN Nicholas (Nicky)
Born: Middlesbrough, 6 October 1970
Height: 6'1" Weight: 14.0
This strong, domineering Bradford centre back played more games than anyone else at the club in 1996-97 and would have been ever present had it not been for suspension. A great ambassador for City, always being asked to attend social functions for the supporters and schools, his organising of the defence was yet again first class and his attacking presence at corners and free kicks continually made him a constant threat to opposing defenders. Is excellent in the air and a battler.

Middlesbrough (From juniors on 18/11/87) F/PL 93+6/4 FLC 11 FAC 9+1 Others 11
Hull C (Loaned on 26/9/92) FL 5/1
Leicester C (£330,000 on 7/7/94) PL 23 FLC 2 FAC 1
Bradford C (£225,000 on 13/7/95) FL 83/4 FLC 8 FAC 5 Others 5

Nicky Mohan

MOILANEN Teuvo (Tepi) Johannes
Born: Oulu, Finland, 12 December 1973
Height: 6'5" Weight: 13.12
International Honours: Finland: U21
Started as Preston's first choice goalkeeper in 1996-97, but some indifferent form led to him being replaced by Bobby Mimms. Confident on crosses, he was found to be suffering from an undiagnosed hand injury and, after treatment, he spent time on loan at Scarborough and Darlington to give him some experience and restore his confidence. Interestingly, his debut for the Quakers was in a 2-0 success over Cambridge, their first clean sheet for 24 games.
Preston NE (£120,000 from FF Jaro on 12/12/95) FL 6 FLC 1
Scarborough (Loaned on 12/12/96) FL 4
Darlington (Loaned on 17/1/97) FL 16

MOLBY Jan
Born: Kolding, Jutland, 4 July 1963
Height: 6'1" Weight: 14.7
Club Honours: Div 1 '86, '90; FAC '86, '92; CS '86; FLC '95
International Honours: Denmark: 67
Despite being sent off in the opening match against Rochdale last season, and then getting over a hamstring injury, the cultured Swansea player/manager was still a prominent member of the side from midfield. At the same time, having little cash at his disposal, he continued to show confidence in the youngsters and his successes saw him included in the third division PFA side, besides winning a Manager of the Month award. He also scored some important goals, while taking Swans into the play offs.

Liverpool (£575,000 from Ajax on 24/8/84) F/PL 195+23/44 FLC 25+3/9 FAC 24+4/4 Others 16+2/4
Barnsley (Loaned on 22/9/95) FL 5
Norwich C (Loaned on 22/12/95) FL 3 FLC 2/1
Swansea C (Free on 22/2/96) FL 38+2/8 FLC 1 Others 1+1

MOLENAAR Robert
Born: Zaandam, Holland, 27 February 1969
Height: 6'2" Weight: 14.4
When this no-nonsense, tough-tackling defender was signed by Leeds from the Dutch club, FC Volendam, last January, he was virtually unknown outside his native country, despite the fact that at the half-way stage in the Dutch season, he was rated the country's top defender. After making his debut against Leicester only two days after signing, and being voted Man of the Match, Robert continued to turn in some inspired performances in a much improved defence. He also scored his first goal for the club in the victory over Everton in March. An excellent acquisition, he proved to be a highly consistent defender who, after a full pre-season's training, can only get better in 1997-98.
Leeds U (£1,000,000 from FC Volendam on 11/1/97) PL 12/1 FAC 2

MONCUR John Frederick
Born: Stepney, 22 September 1966
Height: 5'7" Weight: 9.10
The stylish West Ham midfielder bounced back after early season injury problems in 1996-97 to give some of his best-ever performances for the Hammers in the vital closing weeks of the campaign. His only goals of the season were both against Leicester City in the home and away games, and both were matchwinners in single-goal victories. And, in introducing more bite to his play to become a ball winner, in addition to his long acknowledged creative skills, his importance to the club was paramount.
Tottenham H (From apprentice on 22/8/84) FL 10+11/1 FLC 1+2
Doncaster Rov (Loaned on 25/9/86) FL 4
Cambridge U (Loaned on 27/3/87) FL 3+1
Portsmouth (Loaned on 22/3/89) FL 7
Brentford (Loaned on 19/10/89) FL 5/1 Others 1
Ipswich T (Loaned on 24/10/91) FL 5+1
Swindon T (£80,000 on 30/3/92) F/PL 53+5/5 FLC 4 FAC 1 Others 4/1
West Ham U (£900,000 on 24/6/94) PL 75+2/4 FLC 10/2 FAC 4/1

MONINGTON Mark David
Born: Bilsthorpe, 21 October 1970
Height: 6'1" Weight: 14.0
Club Honours: AMC '96
A strong Rotherham central defender, Mark was a regular in the team in 1996-97 until being sidelined by injury at the end of February, having willingly adopted a role up front in the closing stages of some games. Good in the air, he topped his half century of Millers' appearances, but, with the team so often under pressure, he got little respite from his defensive duties. Spending the last couple of months either on the treatment table or in the reserves, he looks to be back in time for the coming season.

Burnley (From juniors on 23/3/89) FL 65+19/5 FLC 5 FAC 4+1/1 Others 4+2
Rotherham U (Signed on 28/11/94) FL 60+4/2 FLC 3 FAC 1 Others 3

MONKOU Kenneth (Ken) John
Born: Surinam, 29 November 1964
Height: 6'3" Weight: 14.4
Club Honours: FMC '90
International Honours: Holland: U21
The Southampton centre back had a disappointing time of it in 1996-97, his season disrupted by injury and, even when fit, being kept out of the side by the new signings, Claus Lundekvam and Richard Dryden. Strong, both in the air and on the ground, Ken was perhaps unlucky to be often left out, making just 13 starts, as the management continuously tried to resolve the problems of a defence regularly leaking goals. Comfortable on the ball for a big man, and capable of hitting quality long balls behind the opposition, with a new manager due to arrive at the Dell shortly, following the departure of Graeme Souness, there is every chance he will be given further opportunities to shine.
Chelsea (£100,000 from Feyenoord on 2/3/89) FL 92+2/2 FLC 12 FAC 3 Others 10
Southampton (£750,000 on 21/8/92) PL 138+6/8 FLC 15+1/1 FAC 13/1

MOODY Paul
Born: Portsmouth, 13 June 1967
Height: 6'3" Weight: 14.9
Oxford's top scorer for the previous two seasons, Paul found the going tougher in the higher division in 1996-97 and managed just six goals. Suffering from a string of niggling injuries he often found the going easier when coming off the subs' bench and scored a 90th minute equaliser against Southampton, his former club, in the Coca-Cola Cup. A big striker, he remains a popular player with the United fans.
Southampton (£50,000 from Waterlooville on 15/7/91) F/PL 7+5 FLC 1 FAC 0+1
Reading (Loaned on 9/12/92) FL 5/1 Others 1
Oxford U (£60,000 on 19/2/94) FL 98+38/49 FLC 10+4/4 FAC 7+1/5 Others 3/3

MOONEY Thomas (Tommy) John
Born: Middlesbrough, 11 August 1971
Height: 5'11" Weight: 12.6
Left-sided Watford midfield player, cum striker. Suffered more than his fair share of injuries, including two knee operations during last season, but bounced back quickly and was still the Hornets' leading scorer with 13 goals, his commitment and effort making him one of the club's most popular players.
Aston Villa (From trainee on 23/11/89)
Scarborough (Free on 1/8/90) FL 96+11/30 FLC 11+2/8 FAC 3 Others 6/2
Southend U (£100,000 on 12/7/93) FL 9+5/5 FLC 1+1 Others 2+3
Watford (Signed on 17/3/94) FL 110+8/24 FLC 11/1 FAC 5+1/1 Others 1

MOORE Alan
Born: Dublin, 25 November 1974
Height: 5'10" Weight: 10.7
Club Honours: Div 1 '95
International Honours: Ei: 8; U21-4; Yth; Sch

Alan must have spent most of last season pondering on what might have been, highly talented though he undoubtedly is, after failing to make the breakthrough into the Middlesbrough first team and spending more time on the subs' bench than he would have wished for. When called upon to do so, he never failed to deliver the goods and also served his country superbly well when called up for national service. A very skilful winger, easily capable of providing match-winning moments on his day, he is still young enough to enjoy the very bright and successful future predicted for him.
Middlesbrough (From trainee on 5/12/91) F/PL 92+18/14 FLC 8+5/1 FAC 3+2/2 Others 3+1

MOORE Darren Mark
Born: Birmingham, 22 April 1974
Height: 6'2" Weight: 15.6
Big Darren made an immediate impact at Belle Vue in 1995-96, his sterling displays at the heart of Doncaster's defence soon gaining support of the locals. Rock-like, his form last season remained as impressive as ever, his tackling ability and aerial strength breaking down many an opposing attacking move, it being no surprise when he was named as the supporter's Player of the Year.
Torquay U (From trainee on 18/11/92) FL 102+1/8 FLC 6 FAC 7/2 Others 8/2
Doncaster Rov (£62,500 on 19/7/95) FL 76/7 FLC 4 FAC 1 Others 3/1

MOORE Ian Ronald
Born: Birkenhead, 26 August 1976
Height: 5'11" Weight: 12.0
International Honours: E: U21-7; Yth
The son of former Tranmere coach and current Rotherham manager, Ronnie, Ian was in and out of the Rovers' side in 1996-97, and spent a month on loan at Bradford in September, playing six games. Despite winning two England U21 caps, by his standards it was a poor season with regard to scoring goals, not finding the back of the net at all between February and October, especially disappointing when you bear in mind that he is good both in the air and on the ground and blessed with seemingly boundless energy. Transferred to Nottingham Forest in March, being bought for the future by Stuart Pearce, Ian made five appearances before the campaign closed and will most certainly be in contention for a place in the side in 1997-98 as Forest try to get back to the Premiership at the first time of asking.
Tranmere Rov (From trainee on 6/7/94) FL 41+17/12 FLC 3+2/1 FAC 1+1 Others 0+1
Bradford C (Loaned on 13/9/96) FL 6
Nottingham F (£1,000,000 on 15/3/97) PL 1+4

MOORE Neil
Born: Liverpool, 21 September 1972
Height: 6'1" Weight: 12.9
Signed from Everton in January, having been unable to make the side in 1996-97, it was an inauspicious start at Norwich for Neil, when suffering a back injury in his first outing in City colours and a sending off versus Bristol City reserves. Arrived at Carrow Road with a reputation as a central defender who could also play in a holding midfield role, but was released from his short-term contract after just two games as his difficulties with injuries and suspension continually led to his unavailability. Recognised as a good all-round defender who is aggressive and strong in the air, the current Norwich manager, Mike Walker, had, in fact, earlier given the Liverpudlian his Premier League debut when he was running the show at Goodison.
Everton (From trainee on 4/6/91) PL 4+1 FLC 0+1
Blackpool (Loaned on 9/9/94) FL 7 Others 1
Oldham Ath (Loaned on 16/2/95) FL 5
Carlisle U (Loaned on 25/8/95) FL 13 Others 2
Rotherham U (Loaned on 20/3/96) FL 10+1
Norwich C (Free on 8/1/97) FL 2

MORALEE Jamie David
Born: Wandsworth, 2 December 1971
Height: 5'11" Weight: 11.0
Freed by Watford during the summer of 1996, Jamie signed for Crewe prior to the start of last season and made his debut on the opening day wearing the number nine shirt. A talented striker with good skills, who moves off the ball well, he was sidelined for nearly three months before getting back into the side and playing eight out of nine mid-term games. Unfortunately, still to open his scoring account, his campaign came to an end as a further injury set in.
Crystal Palace (From trainee on 3/7/90) FL 2+4
Millwall (Free on 3/9/92) FL 56+11/19 FLC 3+1/1 FAC 1 Others 3+1
Watford (£450,000 on 13/7/94) FL 40+9/7 FLC 6+1 FAC 5
Crewe Alex (Free on 8/8/96) FL 7 FAC 2

MOREIRA Joao Manuel Silva
Born: Angola, 30 June 1970
Height: 6'2" Weight: 14.0
A close season signing from Benfica, Joao missed the start of 1996-97 through injury and fitness problems, before making his first full Swansea appearance against Bristol City in the FA Cup and taking Man of the Match honours. A strong, attacking left-sided defender, he soon became a favourite with the club's supporters due to his exciting overlapping displays.
Swansea C (£50,000 from Benfica on 3/7/96) FL 10 FLC 0+1 FAC 2 Others 5

MORGAN Alan Meredith
Born: Aberystwyth, 2 November 1973
Height: 5'9" Weight: 11.4
International Honours: W: U21-2; Yth; Sch
Having made his league debut for Tranmere in 1995-96, Alan was hoping that further opportunities would have been more forthcoming last season. In the event, a 13 minute stint from the subs' bench at home to Port Vale at the start of the campaign was the sum total for this versatile player who can perform effectively anywhere on the park with the exception of goal. Had a spell on loan at Portadown of the Irish League in January, appearing once before returning to Prenton.
Tranmere Rov (From trainee on 8/5/92) FL 0+5/1

MORGAN Philip Jonathon
Born: Stoke, 18 December 1974
Height: 6'1" Weight: 13.0
International Honours: E: Yth: Sch
Third in the goalkeeping pecking order at Stoke last season behind Carl Muggleton and Mark Prudhoe, and yet to make an appearance for the club since joining from Ipswich, Philip was loaned out to Chesterfield in October. Very brave, and a more than useful shot stopper, he played two games, keeping clean sheets in both of them, before returning to the Potteries as injuries to Andy Leaning and Billy Mercer cleared up. Also kicks long and accurately.
Ipswich T (From trainee on 5/7/93) PL 1
Stoke C (Free on 6/7/95)
Chesterfield (Loaned on 14/10/96) FL 2

MORGAN Ryan Stephen
Born: Bristol, 12 July 1978
Height: 6'0" Weight: 11.2
Ryan, a left-sided midfielder, made an early breakthrough after just a handful of reserve matches to make his league debut for his hometown club, Bristol Rovers, at Watford last March. A former youth trainee at Norwich City, he joined Rovers to complete his training, but then spent three months of the season out after recovering from glandular fever. Following his debut, he was rewarded with a full professional contract and is expected to challenge strongly for a league place in the future.
Bristol Rov (From trainee on 25/3/97) FL 1

Simon Morgan

MORGAN Simon Charles
Born: Birmingham, 5 September 1966
Height: 5'10" Weight: 12.5
International Honours: E: U21-2
Fulham's inspirational skipper missed just two league matches in 1996-97 and, with the Cottagers failing to score in either, those two results probably cost him the championship medal he so richly deserved. Consistent to a fault, he returned to score twice in the penultimate game against Hull City and

again finished the campaign as the driving force in midfield, netting nine times in all. Originally a centre back, Simon is now the club's second longest-serving player.

Leicester C (From apprentice on 15/11/84) FL 147+13/3 FLC 14/1 FAC 4+1 Others 3
Fulham (£100,000 on 12/10/90) FL 267+4/42 FLC 19/1 FAC 13/1 Others 15/4

MORGAN Stephen (Steve) Alphonso
Born: Oldham, 19 September 1968
Height: 5'11" Weight: 13.0
Club Honours: Div 3 '97
Released by Coventry during the 1996 close season, the hard-tackling left back, who can play in midfield if required, suffered a disappointing time at Wigan when hampered by injuries in 1996-97. After scoring a spectacular long-range effort in the home match against Hull City, a recurring achilles problem which eventually needed surgery, was to end his first campaign at the club prematurely, a blow that was dampened somewhat when his 23 league games saw him win a third division championship medal.

Blackpool (From apprentice on 12/8/86) FL 135+9/10 FLC 13/2 FAC 16/1 Others 10+1/1
Plymouth Arg (£115,000 on 16/7/90) FL 120+1/6 FLC 7 FAC 6 Others 5
Coventry C (£110,000 on 14/7/93) PL 65+3/2 FLC 5/3 FAC 5
Bristol Rov (Loaned on 1/3/96) FL 6 Others 2
Wigan Ath (Free on 10/7/96) FL 18+5/1 FLC 2 Others 1

MORLEY Trevor William
Born: Nottingham, 20 March 1961
Height: 5'11" Weight: 12.1
Club Honours: Div 4 '87
International Honours: E: SP-6
Trevor enjoyed an outstanding season for Reading in 1996-97, scoring 23 goals and being elected the fans' Player of the Season, by a huge margin. His goals included eight penalties, but he was a brave leader of the attack despite suffering some horrendous injuries, including one against Barnsley which may rule him out for up to six months. Scored a memorable hat trick at Elm Park against Bolton, the first division champions elect, in February.

Northampton T (£20,000 from Nuneaton Borough on 21/6/85) FL 107/39 FLC 10/4 FAC 6/2 Others 7
Manchester C (£175,000 on 22/1/88) FL 69+3/18 FLC 7/3 FAC 1 Others 2
West Ham U (£500,000 on 28/12/89) F/PL 159+19/57 FLC 10+1/5 FAC 14+5/7 Others 5+1/1
Reading (Free on 1/8/95) FL 50+4/26 FLC 3/1 FAC 4/2

MORRIS Andrew (Andy) Dean
Born: Sheffield, 17 November 1967
Height: 6'4" Weight: 15.12
Known as Bruno, Andy had one of his best seasons for some time in 1996-97, enjoying a relatively injury-free run, by his standards, and coming up with some vital goals for Chesterfield. Playing a crucial role in many games, where his height and presence were used to unsettle opposing defences and create chances for others, none more so, perhaps, than in the FA Cup match with Wrexham, where his excellent flick on the

half-way line set Chris Beaumont off to score the winner, he delighted everyone by signing a new contract that will take him into a richly-deserved testimonial season.
Rotherham U (From juniors on 29/7/85) FL 0+7 FLC 0+1
Chesterfield (Signed on 12/1/88) FL 222+39/55 FLC 15+2/8 FAC 15+2/4 Others 18+4/3
Exeter C (Loaned on 4/3/92) FL 4+3/2

Andy Morris

MORRIS Christopher (Chris) Barry
Born: Newquay, 24 December 1963
Height: 5'11" Weight: 11.11
Club Honours: SPD '88; SC '88, '89; Div '95
International Honours: E: Sch. Ei: 35
Disappointed not to have been offered more opportunities for Middlesbrough in the Premiership last season, Chris has always given nothing less than 100 per-cent effort in every appearance in a Boro shirt, and should be most upset that he was not included in the recent publication of the Boro's best 50 players, deserving nothing less than that. Released at the end of a long and difficult campaign, at his best, a brilliant overlapping wing back, he displayed skills that were nothing short of breathtaking, while his dedication, concentration, and will to win every ball, won him admirers everywhere.

Sheffield Wed (Signed on 1/10/82) FL 61+13/1 FLC 5+5/1 FAC 7+5
Glasgow Celtic (£125,000 on 10/8/87) SL 157+6/8 SLC 16+1 SC 22/1 Others 9
Middlesbrough (Signed on 14/8/92) F/PL 75+7/3 FLC 12 FAC 6 Others 4/1

MORRIS Jody
Born: Hammersmith, 22 December 1978
Height: 5'5" Weight: 9.7
International Honours: E: U21-3; Yth; Sch

Continued his meteoric rise when Ruud Gullit gave him his full Chelsea league debut in the second match of last season against Middlesbrough in preference to several more experienced players. He was then named in England's U21 squad against Moldova whilst still five months short of his 18th birthday, before an ankle injury sustained in the next league match against Coventry forced his withdrawal. Returned for the Coca-Cola Cup first-leg tie at Bloomfield Road and scored his first senior goal, a neatly-taken equaliser after Blackpool had taken an early lead, and then made his delayed U21 debut as a second-half substitute in the goalless draw against Poland at Molineux in October. A series of niggling injuries sidelined him for five months and he did not return to first-team action until the March Premiership fixture at Derby, when he came on as a late substitute. Assuming that he steers clear of further injuries, this talented young playmaker will be challenging strongly for a first-team place next season in a Chelsea midfield that is looking increasingly powerful.
Chelsea (From trainee on 8/1/96) PL 6+7 FLC 2/1

MORRIS Mark John
Born: Morden, 26 September 1962
Height: 6'1" Weight: 14.2
Club Honours: Div 4 '83
A hugely experienced central defender, Mark was signed by Brighton manager, Jimmy Case, last November from Bournemouth, following a spell on loan at Gillingham, and installed as skipper in the absence of George Parris. Scored what proved to be the decisive goal in a crucial 3-2 win at Hartlepool on his impressive debut, and was an automatic choice in the number five shirt until suffering ruptured ankle ligaments in the 3-2 home defeat by Darlington early in December. Returned to first-team duty in late March in time for the critical run in to the season and was elected Player of the Month for April by the Evening Argus.
Wimbledon (From apprentice on 26/9/80) FL 167+1/9 FLC 11 FAC 11 Others 1+1
Aldershot (Loaned on 5/9/85) FL 14 FAC 1
Watford (£35,000 on 21/7/87) FL 41/1 FLC 5/1 FAC 7
Sheffield U (£175,000 on 11/7/89) FL 53+3/3 FLC 5 FAC 5 Others 2
Bournemouth (£100,000 on 31/7/91) FL 190+4/8 FLC 15/2 FAC 17/1 Others 9
Gillingham (Loaned on 23/9/96) FL 6 FLC 2
Brighton & Hove A (Free on 31/10/96) FL 11+1/1 FAC 2

MORRIS Stephen (Steve)
Born: Liverpool, 13 May 1976
Height: 5'10" Weight: 12.0
Club Honours: WC '95
Steve continued to hover on the fringe of the Wrexham first team in 1996-97 without being able to warrant a permanent place in the side. Injuries also hampered this enthusiastic forward runner, who is always aware of the half chance with his busy play featuring strongly in his game.
Wrexham (Free from Liverpool juniors on 5/9/94) FL 24+18/9 FLC 1+1 FAC 6/2 Others 4+2

MORRISON Andrew (Andy) Charles
Born: Inverness, 30 July 1970
Height: 5'11" Weight: 13.10

Transferred to Huddersfield during the 1996 close season, Andy became the club's record buy from Blackpool. A no-nonsense centre half, the fans warmed to his combative style during the early part of the campaign, only to be disappointed by his long lay off due to injury, which led to him making only a handful of appearances. Hopefully free of injury, big things are expected of him this coming season. Equally at home in midfield, and a player who can always be expected to get the odd goal or two, he got on the scoresheet in his second game against Charlton at Leeds Road, a header from a corner that sealed a 2-0 victory.

Plymouth Arg (From trainee on 6/7/88) FL 105+8/6 FLC 10+1/1 FAC 6 Others 2+1
Blackburn Rov (£500,000 on 5/8/93) PL 1+4 FAC 1
Blackpool (£245,000 on 9/12/94) FL 47/3 FAC 2 Others 4
Huddersfield T (£500,000 on 4/7/96) FL 9+1/1 FLC 2

MORRISON David Ellis
Born: Waltham Forest, 30 November 1974
Height: 5'11" Weight: 12.10

Out injured at the start of last season, the left-sided midfielder did not come into the Peterborough side until the end of November, following a spell on loan at Rushden & Diamonds, and was just beginning to find some form when he was sold to Leyton Orient in transfer deadline week. An excellent crosser with both feet, he quickly got into the action and is bound to become a vital part of the side in 1997-98.

Peterborough U (£30,000 from Chelmsford C on 12/5/94) FL 59+18/12 FLC 4+1/1 FAC 5+3 Others 6+2
Leyton Orient (£25,000 on 21/3/97) FL 8

MORRISSEY John Joseph
Born: Liverpool, 8 March 1965
Height: 5'8" Weight: 11.9
International Honours: E: Yth

The son of former Everton star of the '60s, John was in and out of the Tranmere side throughout last season, only getting a regular run in the last six weeks. In his 11th season at Prenton Park, this mesmerising and skilful right winger continued to outwit the opposition, to the delight of the Rovers' fans, and to supply numerous threatening crosses into the box. However, he had a lean time as regards scoring himself, only finding the back of the net twice since August. Is due a testimonial at the end of the 1997-98 season.

Everton (From apprentice on 10/3/83) FL 1 Others 0+1
Wolverhampton W (Free on 2/8/85) FL 5+5/1 FLC 1
Tranmere Rov (£8,000 on 2/10/85) FL 364+45/48 FLC 33+2/1 FAC 27+1/5 Others 39+3/6

MORROW John James
Born: Belfast, 20 November 1971
Height: 5'7" Weight: 10.0
International Honours: NI: B-1; Yth

Having been at Glasgow Rangers for eight years, playing just six times, the pint-sized

winger signed for Oldham during the 1996 close season and made his debut when coming off the bench in the opening game of 1996-97 against Stoke at Boundary Park. Unfortunately, although highly skilled and reminiscent of George Best in many ways, especially with his two-footed dribbling ability, that was where the comparison ended. Following a couple of appearances, it was noticeable that he was just too frail for the physical elements of the first division and, come the summer, was allowed to return to Scotland on a free after serving less than 12 months of a three-year contract.

Glasgow Rangers (Free from Linfield on 29/7/88) SL 5 Others 0+1
Oldham Ath (Free on 13/8/96) FL 1+1

Steve Morrow

MORROW Stephen (Steve) Joseph
Born: Belfast, 2 July 1970
Height: 6'0" Weight: 12.2
Club Honours: FAYC '88; FLC '93; ECEC '94
International Honours: NI: 27; B-1; U23-2; Yth; Sch

A transfer deadline day signing for QPR last March, initially on loan, Steve came in from Arsenal, replacing Alan McDonald in the centre of defence in partnership with Steve Yates, and scoring with a tremendous 25 yarder on his debut at Bolton. Although a regular Northern Ireland international, he had never been more than a squad player at Highbury, but had impressed as a versatile operator who could fill a number of roles well, specifically in the centre of defence, at left back, or in central midfield. With a few games now under his belt at Rangers, he should be a major influence to a side looking to get back to the Premiership this coming season.

Arsenal (From trainee on 5/5/88) F/PL 39+23/1 FLC 7+4/2 FAC 5+2 Others 1+4
Reading (Loaned on 16/1/91) FL 10
Watford (Loaned on 14/8/91) FL 7+1 Others 1
Reading (Loaned on 30/10/91) FL 3
Barnet (Loaned on 4/3/92) FL 1
Queens Park R (£1,000,000 on 27/3/97) FL 5/1

MORTIMER Paul Henry
Born: Kensington, 8 May 1968
Height: 5'11" Weight: 11.3
International Honours: E: U21-2

Paul, a skilful left-sided Charlton midfield player was unfortunate to miss most of last season through injury. Comfortable on the ball, with good vision, and the ability to run at defences and score spectacular goals, he came back into the side at the end of the campaign and could strike up an effective partnership with Mark Kinsella if he can stay free from injury this time round.

Charlton Ath (Free from Farnborough T on 22/9/87) FL 108+5/17 FLC 4+1 FAC 8 Others 3+1
Aston Villa (£350,000 on 24/7/91) FL 10+2/1 FLC 2
Crystal Palace (£500,000 on 18/10/91) F/PL 18+4/2 FLC 1 FAC 1 Others 3
Brentford (Loaned on 22/1/93) FL 6 Others 2
Charlton Ath (£200,000 on 5/7/94) FL 49+7/10 FLC 2 FAC 3/1

MOSES Adrian Paul
Born: Doncaster, 4 May 1975
Height: 5'10" Weight: 12.8
International Honours: E: U21-1

Adrian was without doubt the most improved player at Barnsley last season. Up to the turn of the year, he was a valuable squad player who filled in at the back on a number of occasions, but following the injury that saw Steve Davis sidelined for the remainder of the campaign he was given the opportunity to claim the centre-back position and did so with such success that he was eventually called into the England U21 squad, having already represented the Football League U21s. Good in the air and a strong tackler, with added confidence, his distribution improved immeasurably.

Barnsley (From juniors on 2/7/93) FL 49+7/3 FLC 2 FAC 4

MOSS David Albert
Born: Doncaster, 15 November 1968
Height: 6'2" Weight: 13.7

A big strong, experienced player who could operate in midfield or up front, David signed for Scunthorpe during the 1996 close season, having been released by Chesterfield. Combining playing with a job outside football, unfortunately, for Irons' fans, his stay lasted just five games and a single goal, before a lucrative job offer took him to Scotland and a contract with Partick Thistle.

Doncaster Rov (Signed from Boston U on 10/3/93) FL 18/5 FLC 2 Others 0+1
Chesterfield (Free on 8/10/93) FL 59+12/16 FLC 2/1 FAC 2+1 Others 3
Scunthorpe U (Free on 1/7/96) FL 4 FLC 1/1

MOSS Neil Graham
Born: New Milton, 10 May 1975
Height: 6'2" Weight: 13.3

Having been at Southampton since

December 1995 without getting a first-team goalkeeping opportunity, he finally made his Premiership debut against Nottingham Forest at the Dell last September, due to Dave Beasant being indisposed, and was unfortunate to concede an early goal before settling in. Came back for a further four games shortly afterwards, keeping two clean sheets, before a similar slip befell him in injury time at Coventry and it was back to the reserves for the remainder of the campaign. Still a youngster as far as 'keepers go, once he can match experience with undoubted ability he should not look back.

Bournemouth (From trainee on 29/1/93) FL 21+1 FLC 1 FAC 3+1 Others 2
Southampton (£250,000 on 20/12/95) PL 3 FLC 2

MOUNTAIN Patrick Douglas
Born: Pontypridd, 1 August 1976
Height: 6'0" Weight: 12.0
International Honours: W: U21-2; Yth
Having starred for Barry Town in their historic UEFA Cup win over Budapest of Hungary, Patrick joined Cardiff on non-contract forms prior to the start of 1996-97 to provide goalkeeping cover in the event of an emergency. When the call came in December, following an injury to Tony Elliott, he was found to be ready and played eight times, providing some good displays, before giving way to the returning 'keeper. Was also twice capped for the Welsh U21 side, when appearing against Holland and Turkey.

Cardiff C (From trainee on 31/7/95) FL 5 FAC 1 Others 2

MOUNTFIELD Derek Neal
Born: Liverpool, 2 November 1962
Height: 6'1" Weight: 13.6
Club Honours: FAC '84; CS '84, '85; Div 1 '85, '87; Div 3 '95; ECWC '85
International Honours: E: B-1; U21-1
Strong in the air and difficult to pass on the ground, the vastly experienced Walsall defender once again proved a great marshaller of the defence in 1996-97 and it was unfortunate that he took a couple of knocks late in the season, causing him to miss a few games and to be substituted in others. Freed during the summer, he was absent on only four occasions, which was not a bad record for a player in his 35th year with well over 500 league and cup games behind him.

Tranmere Rov (From apprentice on 4/11/80) FL 26/1 FLC 2 FAC 1
Everton (£30,000 on 2/6/82) FL 100+6/19 FLC 16/3 FAC 17/2 Others 14+1/1
Aston Villa (£450,000 on 6/6/88) FL 88+2/9 FLC 13/2 FAC 6/1 Others 11/5
Wolverhampton W (£150,000 on 7/11/91) FL 79+4/4 FLC 4/1 FAC 2 Others 2
Carlisle U (Free on 3/8/94) FL 30+1/3 FLC 4+1 FAC 4/1 Others 6/1
Northampton T (Free on 6/10/95) FL 4
Walsall (Free on 6/11/95) FL 70/1 FLC 2 FAC 7 Others 3

MOWBRAY Anthony (Tony) Mark
Born: Saltburn, 22 November 1963
Height: 6'1" Weight: 13.2
International Honours: E: B-2

The groin injury which he sustained last February 1996 was to be the most significant factor in Tony's Ipswich season, taking a long time to completely heal and twice re-occurring after what was initially thought to be successful convalescence. When the problem was finally sorted out, Chris Swailes and Tony Vaughan were in such good form that he was unable to dislodge them. Throughout all the trauma associated with a long-term injury, the strong central defender retained a public presence, attending all first-team games in his role as club captain and could always be seen encouraging his team mates. Good in the air, positionally sound, and a great motivator, hopefully, he will be back to strength this coming term.

Middlesbrough (From apprentice on 27/11/81) FL 345+3/25 FLC 28+2/2 FAC 23/1 Others 23+1/1
Glasgow Celtic (£1,000,000 on 8/11/91) SL 75+3/6 SLC 7 SC 5 Others 6
Ipswich T (£300,000 on 6/10/95) FL 27/2 FLC 1 FAC 4 Others 3/1

MOWBRAY Darren Karl
Born: Middlesbrough, 24 January 1978
Height: 6'0" Weight: 12.6
A teenage defender who had trials with Scarborough towards the end of the 1995-96 season, having been at Middlesbrough as a trainee, Darren signed up with the club and was a regular in the reserves last season, also making four first-team appearances and never looking out of place when called upon. The younger brother of former Middlesbrough player, Tony, he was released on a free transfer in the summer.

Scarborough (Free from Middlesbrough juniors on 9/8/96) FL 2+1 FLC 1

David Moyes

MOYES David William
Born: Glasgow, 25 April 1963
Height: 6'1" Weight: 12.12
Club Honours: SPL '82; AMC '86; Div 3 '96
International Honours: S: Yth; Sch
Preston's assistant manager was not expected to figure in the first team picture in 1996-97, but injuries and loss of form saw him bring his experience to the team. A superb timer of headers, he no longer has his former pace, but his organisational ability compensates for this and he is a fine example to any young defender. Still scores his share of goals every year, including the 50th senior goal of his career against Bury in March.

Glasgow Celtic (From juniors in 1980) SL 19+5 SLC 7+1 Others 2+1
Cambridge U (Free on 28/10/83) FL 79/1 FLC 3 FAC I Others 3
Bristol C (£10,000 on 10/10/85) FL 83/6 FLC 6 FAC 5 Others 15
Shrewsbury T (£30,000 on 30/10/87) FL 91+5/9 FLC 4 FAC 3/1 Others 5
Dunfermline Ath (Signed on 1/8/90) SL 105/13 SLC 7/1 SC 5
Hamilton Academical (£42,500 in August 1993) SL 5
Preston NE (Free on 20/9/93) FL 134/15 FLC 5/1 FAC 11/1 Others 13+1/1

Carl Muggleton

MUGGLETON Carl David
Born: Leicester, 13 September 1968
Height: 6'2" Weight: 13.4
International Honours: E: U21-1
The athletic Stoke 'keeper, was in and out of the side throughout 1996-97, but again proved himself to be an excellent shot stopper with penalty saves to his credit during the campaign. Lost his place to Mark Prudhoe after conceding 32 goals in 18 games, including four at home to Sheffield United, but came back strongly despite the team having a difficult spell.

Leicester C (From apprentice on 17/9/86) FL 46 FAC 3 Others 5
Chesterfield (Loaned on 10/9/87) FL 17 Others 2
Blackpool (Loaned on 1/2/88) FL 2
Hartlepool U (Loaned on 28/10/88) FL 8 Others 2
Stockport Co (Loaned on 1/3/90) FL 4
Stoke C (Loaned on 13/8/93) FL 6 FLC 1 Others 2

Glasgow Celtic (£150,000 on 11/1/94) SL 12 SC 1
Stoke C (£150,000 on 21/7/94) FL 63 FLC 7 Others 4
Rotherham U (Loaned on 1/11/95) FL 6 Others 1
Sheffield U (Loaned on 28/3/96) FL 0+1

MULLIN John
Born: Bury, 11 August 1975
Height: 6'0" Weight: 11.10

Essentially a reserve, John showed the Sunderland fans that he has been steadily improving with some good displays when called upon by Peter Reid in 1996-97. Although making only nine league starts, he scored one of the most celebrated goals at Roker all season – the winner against champions, Manchester United, in March. With Sunderland finding themselves back in the Nationwide League, the leggy striker could be pushing for a permanent slot in the first team next term.
Burnley (From trainee on 18/8/92) FL 7+11/2 FAC 2
Sunderland (£40,000+ on 12/8/95) P/FL 14+6/2 FLC 1 FAC 2+1

MUNDEE Denny William John
Born: Swindon, 10 October 1968
Height: 5'10" Weight: 13.0

Denny's ability to perform a variety of roles proved a great asset to Brighton in 1996-97, though he was at his best in the central midfield slot. The team's penalty expert, he converted three spot kicks that enabled the Seagulls to grab vital points, but was badly missed in the final two months of the struggle to stave off relegation to the Conference after a back problem was diagnosed as a slipped disc.
Swindon T (Free from Queens Park R juniors on 21/8/86)
Bournemouth (Free on 29/3/88) FL 76+24/6 FLC 3+2 FAC 9+2/4 Others 5+1/2
Torquay U (Loaned on 7/9/89) FL 9
Brentford (Free on 12/8/93) FL 64+20/16 FLC 1+4 FAC 3 Others 5+3/2
Brighton & Hove A (Free on 19/10/95) FL 58+3/7 FAC 6 Others 4/1

MURPHY Daniel (Danny) Benjamin
Born: Chester, 18 March 1977
Height: 5'9" Weight: 10.8
International Honours: E: Yth; Sch

Another established Crewe youngster who came through the youth scheme, and a former England schoolboy and youth international, Danny has now played over 100 games for the club with 35 goals to his credit. Expected by many shrewd judges in the game to go right to the top, the midfield architect of many of the team's attacking moves missed just one league match from his midfield role and was a key player in the Wembley play-off final that saw Alex promoted to the first division at the expense of Brentford. Was also recognised by his fellow professionals when elected to the PFA award-winning second division team.
Crewe Alex (From trainee on 21/3/94) FL 110+24/27 FLC 7 FAC 7/4 Others 15+2/4

MURPHY James (Jamie) Anthony
Born: Manchester, 25 February 1973
Height: 6'1" Weight: 13.10

Although Jamie originally joined Doncaster

Rovers from Blackpool as a utility player, he spent most of last season at right back. Also played a couple of matches in a midfield role, before being restored to his defensive duties, where he was always keen to get forward in support of the front men.
Blackpool (From juniors on 23/8/90) FL 48+7/1 FLC 4/1 FAC 3 Others 2+3
Doncaster Rov (Free on 14/9/95) FL 47+7 FLC 2 FAC 1 Others 2

MURPHY John James
Born: Whiston, 18 October 1976
Height: 6'1" Weight: 14.0

A product of the Chester youth policy, this hard-shooting central striker's appearances in 1996-97 were restricted to just five starts due to injury. Having scored City's opening goal of the campaign at Brighton, he will be looking for more luck this time round. Is a player with good aerial ability.
Chester C (From trainee on 6/7/95) FL 5+29/4 FLC 2+2/1 FAC 0+1 Others 2+1

MURPHY Matthew (Matt) Simon
Born: Northampton, 20 August 1971
Height: 5'11" Weight: 12.2

Once again, Matt was a regular on the Oxford subs' bench, not making his first start until the end of last January. Amazingly, he has now appeared in over 50 games as sub, over half of those last season, but still has a good goalscoring record, which would obviously be improved with more starts.
Oxford U (£20,000 from Corby T on 12/2/93) FL 37+51/15 FLC 2+5/1 FAC 2+3 Others 3+3/3

MURPHY Shaun Peter
Born: Sydney, Australia, 5 November 1970
Height: 6'1" Weight: 12.0
Club Honours: AIC '95
International Honours: Australia: 9

The tall, dark-haired central defender, who can also play in midfield, gave some outstanding displays for the Australian Olympic squad that won the bronze medal in 1996 before coming back as a regular in the Notts County side at the start of 1996-97. However, in missing just one of the first 17 league games it was a surprise when he signed for West Bromwich at the turn of the year, making an impressive debut in the FA Cup tie at Chelsea. Good in the air and on the ground, Shaun proved to be a reliable and impressive figure in Albion's back four for the rest of the campaign.
Notts Co (Signed from Perth Italia on 4/9/92) FL 100+9/5 FLC 5+2 FAC 6/1 Others 12+1/1
West Bromwich A (£500,000 on 31/12/96) FL 16+1/2 FAC 1

MURRAY Paul
Born: Carlisle, 31 August 1976
Height: 5'9" Weight: 10.5
International Honours: E: U21-2; Yth

Having only played one game for QPR prior to the start of 1996-97, the young midfielder had an excellent season, making 31 starts and scoring five times, including a brilliant solo effort at home to Portsmouth when he came off the subs' bench to embark on a driving run from midfield to bend a superb 25 yarder round the 'keeper. Apart from

selection for the England U21 side in March, another highlight for Paul would have been Rangers' remarkable fight back from 4-0 down at Port Vale to 4-4, a game which saw him chip the goalie from a tight angle in the 88th minute for the club's third. Is comfortable on the ball and has great composure for one so young.
Carlisle U (From trainee on 14/6/94) FL 27+14/1 FLC 2 FAC 1 Others 6+1
Queens Park R (£300,000 on 8/3/96) P/FL 27+6/5 FLC 2 FAC 3

MURRAY Robert (Rob) James
Born: Hammersmith, 21 October 1974
Height: 5'11" Weight: 12.7
International Honours: S: U21-1

Starting last season in the centre of Bournemouth's defence with Owen Coll, after losing his place he made numerous substitute appearances before coming back as a striker to replace the injured Steve Fletcher. A very strong player, Rob is obviously versatile and equally comfortable as a striker or defender.
Bournemouth (From trainee on 11/1/93) FL 88+55/11 FLC 6+5 FAC 2+6 Others 2+4/2

MURRAY Scott George
Born: Aberdeen, 26 May 1974
Height: 5'10" Weight: 11.0

With Gary Charles out injured, Scott started last season in the Aston Villa right-back berth at Sheffield Wednesday, but that was to be his only game before he was replaced by the new signing, Fernando Nelson. Excellent on the ball when going forward, he came back later in the campaign to sit on the bench without getting onto the pitch and, with Charles fit again, the youngster could well be down the batting order for 1997-98. However, he is highly thought of by the management and still remains one for the future.
Aston Villa (£35,000 from Fraserburgh on 16/3/94) PL 4

MURRAY Shaun
Born: Newcastle, 7 December 1970
Height: 5'8" Weight: 11.2
International Honours: E: Yth; Sch

Despite Bradford having to fight an uphill battle in order to maintain its first division status in 1996-97, Shaun had an exceptional season, especially after taking over the number seven shirt from Chris Waddle when the latter moved on to Sunderland in March. Although on a week-to-week contract, the skilful midfielder always entertained and won several Man of the Match awards during the closing weeks, his ability on the ball being vital to keeping possession and building up attacks. Needless to say, he is a great favourite of the crowd.
Tottenham H (From trainee on 10/12/87)
Portsmouth (£100,000 on 12/6/89) FL 21+13/1 FLC 2+1/1 FAC 1+3 Others 2+2
Scarborough (Signed on 1/11/93) FL 29/5 FAC 2 Others 2
Bradford C (£200,000 on 11/8/94) FL 76+16/8 FLC 5+2/1 FAC 3+2 Others 4/2

MURTY Graeme Stuart
Born: Middlesbrough, 13 November 1974
Height: 5'10" Weight: 11.10

A knee injury caused Graeme to miss the final three months of last season, after he had proved to be a useful and versatile player who was able to fit in at either left or right-full back, or in midfield for York. Scored one of the goals that knocked Everton out of the Coca-Cola Cup and was at his best when operating wide on the right where his pace and endeavour caused problems to opposing defenders.

York C (From trainee on 23/3/93) FL 74+9/6 FLC 8/1 FAC 3+1 Others 5+2

MUSCAT Kevin Vincent
Born: Crawley, 7 August 1973
Height: 6'0" Weight: 12.8
International Honours: Australia: 9

Despite being born at nearby Crawley, Kevin was brought up in Australia, and it was from South Melbourne that he arrived at Crystal Palace last August, immediately prior to the start of 1996-97. A strong, tough-tackling defender, and the captain of the Australian side who is a must for Terry Venables' World Cup plans, he made his debut on the opening day at Birmingham and missed just three games throughout a campaign that saw the club ultimately achieve promotion to the Premiership following the 1-0 Wembley play-off win over Sheffield United. Equally at home on the right or left-hand side of defence, and comfortable in pushing forward to provide extra attacking options, he also scored three goals.

Crystal Palace (£35,000 from South Melbourne on 16/8/96) FL 42+2/2 FLC 3/1 FAC 2 Others 2

MUSSELWHITE Paul Stephen
Born: Portsmouth, 22 December 1968
Height: 6'2" Weight: 12.9
Club Honours: AMC '93

Having began last season in Port Vale's reserve team after Arjan van Heusden was preferred in goal for the first 16 games, he made his first appearance against Crystal Palace at Vale Park in October and, although unfortunately conceding two early goals, held his place for the remainder of the campaign until being left out for the final game. A commanding 'keeper, his performances improved as the season went on and in February he won the Nationwide Save of the Month award for one particular stop at Birmingham City.

Portsmouth (From apprentice on 1/12/86)
Scunthorpe U (Free on 21/3/88) FL 132 FLC 11 FAC 7 Others 13
Port Vale (£20,000 on 30/7/92) FL 203 FLC 10 FAC 18 Others 19

MUSTOE Robin (Robbie)
Born: Witney, 28 August 1968
Height: 5'11" Weight: 11.12
Club Honours: Div 1 '95

The engine room of Middlesbrough's fighting midfield, Robbie enjoyed an inspirational season in 1996-97, a season that saw him take over the role of captain during the enforced absence of Nigel Pearson through injury. His never-say-die spirit, aggression, and absolute professionalism continually inspired his colleagues to greater heights during a time of turmoil for the club, while his injury at Wembley that forced him to leave the field during the FA Cup final must have been the most difficult career situation he has ever had to endure, and that he did so with such dignity spoke volumes for his integrity. On a brighter note, his many Man of the Match awards during the campaign bear testimony to his commitment to the Boro and his legion of fans will ensure that he gets a big hand in 1997-98.

Robbie Mustoe

Oxford U (From juniors on 2/7/86) FL 78+13/10 FLC 2 FAC 2 Others 3
Middlesbrough (£375,000 on 5/7/90) F/PL 202+9/15 FLC 32+1/7 FAC 17 Others 12+1/1

MUTCH Andrew (Andy) Todd
Born: Liverpool, 28 December 1963
Height: 5'10" Weight: 11.3
Club Honours: Div 4 '88, Div 3 '89; AMC '88
International Honours: E: B-3; U21-1

Again a big favourite with the Stockport fans in 1996-97, due to his knack of scoring timely and important goals, including the tap in, his first touch after coming on as a sub, which knocked Southampton out of the Coca-Cola Cup, he was mainly used to good effect from the bench. Other timely strikes for the experienced front runner came in the shape of a threesome in the two Coca-Cola games against Chesterfield and winners against Doncaster (FA Cup) and Burnley in an important end of season league game.

Wolverhampton W (Signed from Southport on 25/2/86) FL 277+12/96 FLC 14/4 FAC 11+1/1 Others 23/4
Swindon T (£250,000 on 16/8/93) F/PL 34+16/6 FLC 6+1/3 FAC 4/1 Others 3/2
Wigan Ath (Loaned on 24/8/95) FL 7/1
Stockport Co (Free on 15/3/96) FL 26+18/8 FLC 3+1/4 FAC 1+2/1 Others 3+1

MYERS Andrew (Andy) John
Born: Hounslow, 3 November 1973
Height: 5'10" Weight: 12.11
Club Honours: FAC '97
International Honours: E: U21-4; Yth

Andy started 1996-97 in the left-wing-back position for Chelsea, in preference to Scott Minto, and in the fifth Premiership match of the season, scored his first goal for five years with a fierce drive – the clincher at Hillsborough that wrecked Sheffield Wednesday's 100 per-cent league record. A back injury forced him out of the side but, later in the season, he showed his versatility when turning in some good performances as a left-sided central defender, until carried off against Sunderland in March with a nasty thigh injury. An exceptionally fast player, with a good left foot, this latest injury was yet another setback for him and the fact that he has played only 80 matches in the five seasons since his debut sums up his bad luck. Despite being an unused sub at Wembley, Andy picked up an FA Cup winners medal following Blues' 2-0 win over Middlesbrough.

Chelsea (From trainee on 25/7/91) F/PL 62+9/2 FLC 1+1 FAC 9 Others 3

MYERS Christopher (Chris)
Born: Yeovil, 1 April 1969
Height: 5'10" Weight: 11.10

Another Exeter player dogged by injuries last season, Chris found first-team chances hard to come by, despite being a creative and tenacious midfielder, and he was released during the summer.

Torquay U (From trainee on 16/6/87) FL 8+1 (Free to Dawlish during 1988 close season)
Torquay U (Free from Barnstaple T on 22/8/90) FL 88+8/7 FLC 8+2/1 FAC 3 Others 5+3
Dundee U (Signed on 5/8/93) SL 4+2 SLC 3+2
Torquay U (Loaned on 8/12/93) FL 6
Wrexham (Free on 8/1/96)
Scarborough (Free on 22/1/96) FL 8+1
Exeter C (Free on 28/3/96) FL 38+3/2 FLC 2 FAC 2

NASH Carlo James
Born: Bolton, 13 September 1973
Height: 6'5" Weight: 14.1
Spotted keeping goal for Clitheroe against Brigg Town in the 1996 FA Vase final, despite letting three goals in that day he must have impressed Crystal Palace, who signed him during the close season. A part-time model, Carlo made his debut in the 6-1 win at Reading in September and played in three more matches, including another 6-1 victory, before holding down a regular place at the expense of young Chris Day. Ever present for the final 18 league games of 1996-97, having impressed with his handling, especially when coming for crosses, he was an integral part of the side that were promoted to the Premiership following the 1-0 play-off victory at Wembley over Sheffield United. Again showing a calm presence, he gave notice that he will not be out of his depth at the highest level.
Crystal Palace (£35,000 from Clitheroe on 16/7/96) FL 21 FLC 1 Others 3

NASH Martin
Born: Regina, Canada, 27 December 1975
Height: 5'11" Weight: 12.5
International Honours: Canada: 6
As Stockport's first international since 1924, the Canadian star winger found it difficult to break into the first team in 1996-97, after arriving at the club last November, but early glimpses of this young talent suggested that he had the pace and crossing ability to make a big impact in the near future. Scored the winner at Burnley in the AWS competition on his full debut for County.
Stockport Co (Free from Regina on 27/11/96) FL 0+3 FLC 0+1 Others 2+1/1

NAYLOR Anthony (Tony) Joseph
Born: Manchester, 29 March 1967
Height: 5'7" Weight: 10.8
A diminutive striker with Port Vale, Tony achieved a personal best by topping the scoring charts with 20 goals in 1996-97. Lethal in the box, he often operated away from home as a lone striker, but managed a hat trick in a 3-1 victory at Charlton. And, although his form dipped slightly after Christmas, which led to him being dropped as Lee Mills took over the scoring mantle, he returned with three brilliant goals in the last two home games to almost fire the club into play offs.
Crewe Alex (£20,000 from Droylsden on 22/3/90) FL 104+18/45 FLC 7+2/5 FAC 9/7 Others 12/9
Port Vale (£150,000 on 18/7/94) FL 99+16/37 FLC 8/4 FAC 7/1 Others 5+1/3

NAYLOR Dominic John
Born: Watford, 12 August 1970
Height: 5'10" Weight: 13.3
Club Honours: FAYC '89
An attacking left-wing back, signed from Gillingham last August, Dominic proved to be a Leyton Orient bargain with his ability to attack opposing defenders and supply excellent crosses in 1996-97. Taking over as club captain after the injuries to Alvin Martin, having also been appointed the club's penalty taker, he missed just two games in an impressive start.
Watford (From trainee on 20/9/88)
Halifax T (Loaned on 6/12/89) FL 5+1/1 Others 1+1 (Free to Hong Kong in October 1990)
Barnet (Free on 12/8/91) FL 50+1 FLC 2 FAC 5/1 Others 4
Plymouth Arg (Free on 16/7/93) FL 84+1 FLC 2 FAC 8 Others 4+1/1
Gillingham (Free on 11/8/95) FL 30+1/1 FLC 2/1 FAC 3 Others 1
Leyton Orient (£25,000 on 15/8/96) FL 44/3 FLC 2 FAC 2 Others 1

NAYLOR Glenn
Born: Poole, 11 August 1972
Height: 5'10" Weight: 11.10
A skilful forward who signed for Darlington last September, having been on loan from York City in 1995-96, Glenn finished as the club's second highest goalscorer. Opening the scoring in his first full match at Cambridge, he struck some vital goals as the club struggled, including his first ever hat trick at Colchester.
York C (From trainee on 5/3/90) FL 78+33/30 FLC 2+4 FAC 4+1/2 Others 3+4
Darlington (Loaned on 13/10/95) FL 3+1/1 Others 1+1
Darlington (Signed on 26/9/96) FL 30+7/10 FAC 2/1 Others 1

NAYLOR Richard Alan
Born: Leeds, 28 February 1977
Height: 6'1" Weight: 13.7
Originally a central defender when he first joined Ipswich as a youngster, Richard was played up front in the youth team when there was a shortage of strikers and never looked back. A very determined character, he certainly made his presence felt on the field of play in 1996-97, making his full debut at Birmingham and scoring his first goal in the Coca-Cola Cup tie against Gillingham - a lovely strike on the run as he controlled a through ball and fired it into the net. Unfortunate to be forced to sit out the last quarter of the campaign because of knee problems, he is certain to figure prominently this coming term.
Ipswich T (From trainee on 10/7/95) FL 19+8/4 FLC 1+3/1 FAC 0+1

NAYLOR Stuart William
Born: Wetherby, 6 December 1962
Height: 6'4" Weight: 12.10
International Honours: E: B-3; Yth
Having joined Bristol City from West Bromwich on a free transfer just prior to the start of last season, this former England U21 goalkeeper enjoyed an excellent campaign until injury ruled him out for the concluding matches. A good shot stopper, he made a number of penalty saves during the campaign and although not as accomplished with the ball at his feet as City's other 'keeper, Keith Welch, he nevertheless became very popular at Ashton Gate, missing very few games until being replaced by the latter for the final eight matches, following an injury. Kept 13 clean sheets, including six in succession during October.
Lincoln C (Free from Yorkshire Amateurs on 19/6/80) FL 49 FLC 4 FAC 2 Others 6
Peterborough U (Loaned on 23/2/83) FL 8
Crewe Alex (Loaned on 6/10/83) FL 38
Crewe Alex (Loaned on 23/8/94) FL 17 FLC 2 FAC 2 Others 3
West Bromwich A (£100,000 on 18/2/86) FL 354+1 FLC 22 FAC 13 Others 20
Bristol C (Free on 13/8/96) FL 35 FLC 4 FAC 4 Others 1

NDAH George Ehialimolisa
Born: Dulwich, 23 December 1974
Height: 6'1" Weight: 11.4
International Honours: E: Yth
Another player who had come through the Crystal Palace youth network, despite being troubled with injuries ever since turning professional six years ago, George has still managed nearly 100 appearances, while scoring 10 goals. Having shown the determination to succeed, the tall, exciting striker, with the ability to operate on either flank, signed a new three-year contract last November and consolidated his place on the Palace bench when making 22 appearances as a sub, normally as a shock tactic. Scored three goals, including an 83rd minute equaliser at Manchester City, coming in one of his eight starts. Is the brother of Jamie, currently at Barnet.
Crystal Palace (From trainee on 10/8/92) F/PL 31+44/8 FLC 7+5/1 FAC 3+1/1 Others 4+1
Bournemouth (Loaned on 13/10/95) FL 12/2 Others 1

NDAH Jamie Jidefor Ogoegbunan
Born: Camberwell, 5 August 1971
Height: 6'1" Weight: 12.4
A tall, pacy centre forward who joined Barnet from Torquay on a free transfer last February, Jamie scored on his debut at Doncaster and finished the campaign with three more under his belt. Had started 1996-97 quite promisingly at Torquay, scoring in his first game of the season, but with the goals drying up and the advent of Rodney Jack, he was allowed to move on. Released during the summer, he is the brother of Crystal Palace's George.
Torquay U (£20,000 from Kingstonians on 22/8/95) FL 25+3/4 FLC 2+1 FAC 1+1 Others 1
Barnet (Free on 7/2/97) FL 12+2/4

NDLOVU Peter
Born: Buluwayo, Zimbabwe, 25 February 1973
Height: 5'8" Weight: 10.2
International Honours: Zimbabwe: 13
Peter had a frustrating season in 1996-97, suffering a knee injury whilst on international duty with Zimbabwe in the summer of 1996 and, following an operation, did not appear for Coventry until the middle of October. After a handful of substitute appearances and two starts he was again hit by more knee problems and needed a further operation. However, after some stirring reserve appearances he re-appeared on the bench and was used as sub in ten out of 12 successive games before starting at

Anfield where he looked his most liveliest of the season. Following this, he kept up his good form in the win over Chelsea and scored his first goal of the season against Southampton. Peter has been at Highfield Road for six years now and next term could be a crucial one for him.

Coventry C (£10,000 from Highlanders on 16/8/91) F/PL 141+36/37 FLC 10/2 FAC 5+4/2 Others 0+1

NEAL Ashley James
Born: Northampton, 16 December 1974
Height: 6'0" Weight: 13.8

Unable to get a look in at Liverpool, the son of Phil, the former England full back, was loaned to Brighton last September and had to endure a torrid league baptism in the leaky Seagull's defence, playing eight consecutive matches during which only one point was gathered, before returning to Anfield. Transferred to Huddersfield in December, but failing to get a game there, the uncompromising, hard-tackling full back signed for Peterborough on non-contract terms and played the last four games of the campaign in a side doomed for the third division.

Liverpool (From trainee on 27/4/93)
Brighton & Hove A (Loaned on 27/9/96) FL 8
Huddersfield T (Free on 13/12/96)
Peterborough U (Free on 27/3/97) FL 4

NEIL James (Jimmy) Darren
Born: Bury St Edmunds, 28 February 1976
Height: 5'8" Weight: 10.5

A right-sided Grimsby defender, and junior professional, Jimmy's senior opportunities were limited last season, which surprised many supporters in view of the club's continuing injury problems in defence. Having had a useful spell on loan at Grantham, this highly promising youngster will soon be back.

Grimsby T (From trainee on 13/7/94) FL 1+1

NEILL Lucas Edward
Born: Sydney, Australia, 9 March 1978
Height: 6'1" Weight: 12.0
International Honours: Australia: U21

Proved to be Millwall's most outstanding player last season, showing his versatility by playing in both full-back roles and also in midfield, his good all-round skills, ball control, tackling, and tireless energy, ensuring him time away on international duty with Australia and the club's Player of the Year award. Scored the match winner against Burnley with a stunning shot from outside the box.

Millwall (Free from AIS on 13/11/95) FL40+12/4 FLC 1+1 FAC 2 Others 1

NEILSON Alan Bruce
Born: Wegburg, Germany, 26 September 1972
Height: 5'11" Weight: 12.10
International Honours: W: 5; B-2; U21-7

The Southampton defender started last season at right back before being in and out of the side as the manager continually shuffled players and changed formations in order to secure the rearguard. An excellent passer of the ball, who brings confidence to the back third of the field, Alan's greatest strength has always been in getting into forward positions to create chances for others. And, although yet to score for Saints, it was his right-wing cross that presented Egil Ostenstad with the opportunity to strike the only goal in the vital bottom of the table clash at Sunderland that ultimately ensured Premiership survival, before reverting to the bench for the final two matches. Added to his Welsh caps when coming back into the side for the World Cup qualifier in Holland.

Newcastle U (From trainee on 11/2/91) F/PL 35+7/1 FLC 4 Others 4
Southampton (£500,000 on 1/6/95) PL 39+8 FLC 5 FAC 1+1

NELSON Fernando
Born: Portugal, 5 November 1971
Height: 6'2" Weight: 12.3
International Honours: Portugal: 5

Having been signed from Sporting Lisbon during the 1996 close season, Fernando made his debut for Aston Villa in the third game of the new campaign when coming on as a sub at Villa Park against Derby. From then on he was a regular in the right-wing back position, settling in well and hardly missing a game for the remainder of 1996-97, despite a thigh strain, which saw him sidelined for three matches, his longest spell out of action. A Portuguese international, who continued to add to his caps in the World Cup qualifiers, he proved to be a sound defensive player with excellent powers of recovery, although it was his ability to go forward that caught the eye, especially when running at defenders and cutting inside to get a shot in. Never managed a goal, however.

Aston Villa (£1,750,000 from Sporting Lisbon on 26/7/96) PL 33+1 FLC 2 FAC 0+1 Others 2

NELSON Garry Paul
Born: Braintree, 16 January 1961
Height: 5'10" Weight: 11.10
Club Honours: Div 4 '81

Having been released by Charlton during the summer of 1996, Torquay United's new player/coach was a fine example to those around him last season. At 36 years of age, his tireless running and enthusiasm, coupled with an eye for goal, soon made him a crowd favourite and he did not let his work for the media affect his vast contribution to the running of the club.

Southend U (From juniors on 9/7/79) FL 106+23/17 FLC 3+1/1 FAC 6+2
Swindon T (£10,000 on 17/8/83) FL 78+1/7 FLC 4/1 FAC 5 Others 5/1
Plymouth Arg (£15,000 on 12/7/85) FL 71+3/20 FLC 4 FAC 7/2 Others 3
Brighton & Hove A (£80,000 on 17/7/87) FL 132+12/46 FLC 7 FAC 7/6 Others 8/6
Notts Co (Loaned on 8/11/90) FL 0+2
Charlton Ath (£50,000 on 16/8/91) FL 147+38/37 FLC 17+1/2 FAC 8+3/1 Others 7+1
Torquay U (Free on 8/8/96) FL 30+4/8 FLC 1+1 FAC 1

NETHERCOTT Stuart David
Born: Ilford, 21 March 1973
Height: 6'0" Weight: 13.8
International Honours: E: U21-8

An extremely robust defender with terrific ability and accuracy in heading a ball, Stuart found places sparse in the Tottenham back four in 1996-97 and, with the introduction of John Scales and Ramon Vega to address a leaky defence, he had little opportunity to demonstrate the form that had won him international honours at U21 level and made him a frequent first-team member. Minor injuries also hindered his efforts to hold a regular place, along with Colin Calderwood and Sol Campbell finding top form. Definitely more to come from a valuable player to have in any squad.

Tottenham H (From trainee on 17/8/91) PL 31+23 FAC 5+3/1
Maidstone U (Loaned on 5/9/91) FL 13/1 Others 1
Barnet (Loaned on 13/2/92) FL 3

Gary Neville

NEVILLE Gary Alexander
Born: Bury, 18 February 1975
Height: 5'10" Weight: 11.10
Club Honours: FAYC '92; PL '96, '97; FAC '96; CS '97
International Honours: E: 22; Yth (UEFAC '93)

A hard-tackling Manchester United full back, who is equally as effective in the centre of defence, Gary emerged as one of England's great heroes during 'Euro '96.' His biggest battle at Old Trafford, however, was in vying for the regular right-back slot with his brother, Phil. Having started last season on the substitutes' bench against Wimbledon and Everton, he came on during the third game against Blackburn and stayed for the next 14 matches. Although this period also included a lean spell for the United defence, when they conceded 13

goals in three games during mid October, he remained on the top of his form and, despite a short spell out of the side in November, he was an ever present during the important run in to the end of the campaign. The fact that he played against Porto with a disabling injury, that required a pre-match injection, showed the depth of his commitment – it later ruled him out of England's friendly against Mexico in March. His only goal of the campaign - his first-ever for United - against Middlesbrough in May, allowed the team to earn a vital point and set the seal on another championship success. Having signed a new five-year contract in September, he remarked, "I'm delighted. I would have signed a ten-year contract if it had been put in front of me. United are the only club I ever wanted to play for, and it's a dream every time I play for them." Another honour came his way when he was selected for the PFA award-winning Premiership side.

Manchester U (From trainee on 29/1/93) PL 77+4/1 FLC 4+1 FAC 12+1 Others 12+4

NEVILLE Philip (Phil) John
Born: Bury, 21 January 1977
Height: 5'11" Weight: 12.0
Club Honours: FAYC '95; PL '96, '97; FAC '96: CS '97
International Honours: E: 6; U21-7; Yth; Sch

A superb Manchester United right back, who is equally as adaptable as a central defender, Phil had a nightmare start to last season, a period punctuated by injuries. Having undergone an ankle operation after just three matches of the new campaign, which kept him out for six weeks, he suffered a hamstring injury during the warm up of United's Champions' League game against Juventus at Old Trafford. Then, after just one first team outing against Sunderland in December, he went down with glandular fever, an illness which could so easily have ended his career. Having lost a stone and a half in just four days, he recalled, "They were the worse four days of my life." Although his recovery was slow, and required the use of a heart monitor during training, he regained his place in the squad for the Premiership game against Arsenal in February. With his problems now firmly behind him, Phil looks to be back at his best, and with a new five-year contract signed in September and another championship medal in his pocket, plus further international honours at both full and U21 levels, his long-term future at Old Trafford is well and truly secured.

Manchester U (From trainee on 1/6/94) PL 37+7 FLC 2+1 FAC 7+1 Others 4+2

NEVIN Patrick (Pat) Kevin Francis Michael
Born: Glasgow, 6 September 1963
Height: 5'6" Weight: 11.9
Club Honours: S Div 2 '82, Div 2 '84; FMC '86
International Honours: S: 28; B-4; U21-5; Yth
Plagued with a variety of niggling injuries, which caused lengthy and enforced absences from the Tranmere first team, the chairman of the PFA suffered the ignominy

of being sent off for the only time in his career when playing at the Valley against Charlton in February, having come on as substitute. A skilful, old-fashioned winger, who can play on either flank, and loves to run at the full back, he later appealed and had the satisfaction of seeing the decision overturned. Also an excellent ambassador for both his club and the PFA, Pat started his own web-site during the course of the season and continues to expand his non-playing career with broadcasts on both local and national radio, with frequent forays into journalism.

Clyde (Signed from Gartcosh in 1981) SL 60+13/17 SLC 5+3 SC 10/3
Chelsea (£95,000 on 14/7/83) FL 190+3/36 FLC 25+1/5 FAC 8+1/1 Others 13/4
Everton (£925,000 on 13/7/88) FL 81+28/16 FLC 10+1/2 FLC 12+6/2 Others 9+3/1
Tranmere Rov (Loaned on 4/3/92) FL 8
Tranmere Rov (£300,000 on 18/8/92) FL 181+12/30 FLC 16/5 FAC 8/2 Others 14/2

NEWELL Michael (Mike) Colin
Born: Liverpool, 27 January 1965
Height: 6'2" Weight: 12.0
Club Honours: AMC '85; PL '95
International Honours: E: B-2; U21-4

A strong-running striker, Mike transferred from Blackburn to Birmingham during the 1996 close season, with the expectations of his new manager, Trevor Francis, that he and Paul Furlong would score 40 goals between them in 1996-97. Unfortunately, it did not work out like that as Mike asked for a transfer after just ten weeks, citing difficulty in settling at St Andrews. Following that, he went on loan to West Ham (December) when Hammers' manager, Harry Redknapp, was desperately searching for a forward who could score goals, but in failing to find the net in seven games, he returned to City. It was the same at Bradford during another seven-game loan spell in March and, with just three goals during the campaign, he had his leanest spell for ages.

Crewe Alex (Free from Liverpool juniors on 28/9/83) FL 3
Wigan Ath (Free on 31/10/83) FL 64+8/25 FLC 6/1 FAC 8/6 Others 5+1/3
Luton T (£100,000 on 9/1/86) FL 62+1/18 FAC 5/1
Leicester C (£350,000 on 16/9/87) FL 81/21 FLC 9/5 FAC 2 Others 4
Everton (£850,000 on 27/7/89) FL 48+20/15 FLC 7+3/4 FAC 6+4 Others 6/2
Blackburn Rov (£1,100,000 on 15/11/91) F/PL 113+17/28 FLC 14+2/8 FAC 9+2/6 Others 9+1/6
Birmingham C (£775,000 on 26/7/96) FL 11+4/1 FLC 4/2 FAC 0+1
West Ham U (Loaned on 21/12/96) PL 6+1
Bradford C (Loaned on 17/3/97) FL 7

NEWELL Paul Clayton
Born: Woolwich, 23 February 1969
Height: 6'1" Weight: 14.7
After having such a good run in the previous season, Darlington losing just twice in 24 games, he suffered two injuries and a loss of form leading to the deployment of three on-loan 'keepers during 1996-97. Appearing in only half the games possible, at his best, he is an excellent shot stopper who stands up well to opposing forwards.

Southend U (From trainee on 17/6/87) FL 15 FAC 2 Others 1
Leyton Orient (£5,000 on 6/8/90) FL 61 FLC 3 FAC 3 Others 4
Colchester U (Loaned on 12/8/92) FL 14 FLC 2
Barnet (Free on 26/7/94) FL 16 Others 1
Darlington (Free on 29/1/96) FL 41 FLC 4 FAC 2 Others 4

NEWLAND Raymond (Ray) James
Born: Liverpool, 19 July 1971
Height: 6'3" Weight: 13.10
The first-choice goalkeeper at the start of the 1996-97 campaign, Ray lost his Torquay place through injury in September and did not return until April when he gave some superb displays to confirm United's place in the Football League, before being released in the summer.

Plymouth Arg (Free from St Helens on 3/7/92) FL 25+1 FLC 1 FAC 2
Chester C (Free on 18/7/94) FL 9+1 Others 2
Torquay U (Free on 12/1/96) FL 28 FLC 2

Ricky Newman

NEWMAN Richard (Ricky) Adrian
Born: Guildford, 5 August 1970
Height: 5'10" Weight: 12.6
A versatile Millwall defender, Ricky produced sterling work in the Lions' midfield last season. Quick in the tackle and good in the air, he was captain until Alan McLeary took over. Is a good man to have in your team.

Crystal Palace (From juniors on 22/1/88) F/PL 43+5/3 FLC 5 FAC 5+2 Others 2
Maidstone U (Loaned on 28/2/92) FL 9+1/1
Millwall (£500,000 on 19/7/95) FL 73+4/4 FLC 5 FAC 4 Others 2

NEWMAN Robert (Rob) Nigel
Born: Bradford on Avon, 13 December 1963
Height: 6'2" Weight: 13.4
Club Honours: AMC '86
Norwich's Rob improved immeasurably during last season, so much so he was close

to winning the Player of the Year trophy. Strong in the air and tackle, he marked most opponents out of the game and won new-found acclaim of the Barclay Choir after a period in the apparent doldrums. His one goal was a close-range tap in when City were losing 3-0 to Barnsley and, in staying clear of a major injury, he missed just two games. Although a player who can get forward especially for set plays, he is predominantly a defender who can defend, often being the last of the line, his spirit remaining indomitable.

Bristol C (From apprentice on 5/10/81) FL 382+12/52 FLC 29+1/2 FAC 27/2 Others 33/5
Norwich C (£600,000 on 15/7/91) F/PL 171+19/14 FLC 21+1/2 FAC 13/1 Others 7

NEWSOME Jonathan (Jon)
Born: Sheffield, 6 September 1970
Height: 6'2" Weight: 13.11
Club Honours: Div 1 '92

Jon will have been disappointed with the number of games he played for Sheffield Wednesday in 1996-97, especially in the light of having regained his place he then injured his ankle in the FA Cup tie with Wimbledon, which kept him out for the remainder of the season. Although a tall centre back, who adds some height to the defence and looks to be a good player whom many feel could gain international honours, he will have to battle with Dejan Stefanovic for the other centre back spot alongside Des Walker in 1997-98. Always a danger in the opponents penalty area, he scored with a header in the home 1-1 draw against Southampton last November.

Sheffield Wed (From trainee on 1/7/89) FL 6+1 FLC 3
Leeds U (£150,000 on 11/6/91) F/PL 62+14/3 FLC 3 FAC 3+1 Others 5
Norwich C (£1,000,000 on 30/6/94) P/FL 61+1/7 FLC 9 FAC 5/1
Sheffield Wed (£1,600,000 on 16/3/96) PL 18/2 FLC 1 FAC 3

NEWTON Edward (Eddie) John Ikem
Born: Hammersmith, 13 December 1971
Height: 5'11" Weight: 12.8
Club Honours: FAC '97
International Honours: E: U21-2

Having missed the climax of the previous season, following a freak collision with his own goalkeeper which resulted in a broken leg, Eddie regained full fitness and reclaimed his first-team spot last December, playing 14 consecutive matches which coincided with Chelsea's best form of the season. His unselfish workrate, sound tackling and thoughtful distribution in central midfield made him an indispensable part of the team and he must have been close to an international call up. But then his injury jinx came back to haunt him, again in the most unfortunate of circumstances. Whilst warming up for the Premiership fixture at Derby in March, he badly injured his knee in the pre-match kick about and missed seven matches, including the sixth round FA Cup tie at Portsmouth. This came shortly after an unfortunate late own goal in the fifth round which gave Leicester City a draw. Returned just in time to play in the

semi final against Wimbledon and his steadying influence was crucial as Chelsea overcame their local rivals to give Eddie his second appearance in the Final, his goal in a 2-0 win over Middlesbrough erasing the painful memories of the 1994 Final when a penalty was awarded against him.

Chelsea (From trainee on 17/5/90) F/PL 121+19/8 FLC 12+1/1 FAC 15+2/1 Others 5
Cardiff C (Loaned on 23/1/92) FL 18/4

Eddie Newton

NEWTON Shaun O'Neill
Born: Camberwell, 20 August 1975
Height: 5'8" Weight: 11.0
International Honours: E: U21-3

A right-sided Charlton midfielder, who can also play at right back, Shaun proved to be one of the fastest players in the first division last season, being at his most dangerous when going past players on the right and getting telling crosses into the penalty area. Won three long awaited England U21 caps during the term and firmly established himself in the Athletic side, scoring some valuable goals, including two headers against Huddersfield at The Valley, the second one from 30 yards out! Also represented the Football League U21 side that played the Italian Serie "B" equivalent in February, scoring in a 1-1 draw.

Charlton Ath (From trainee on 1/7/93) FL 101+30/10 FLC 12/2 FAC 4+2 Others 4+1/1

NICHOLSON Shane Michael
Born: Newark, 3 June 1970
Height: 5'10" Weight: 12.2
Club Honours: GMVC '88

Naturally left footed, West Brom's Shane was doing very well at full back before suffering a serious leg injury 20 games into last season, subsequently missing practically the rest of the campaign except for a handful

of reserve team outings. An extremely versatile player, his ability to hit the target from outside the penalty helps keep opposing defenders on their toes.

Lincoln C (From trainee on 19/7/88) FL 122+11/6 FLC 8+3 FAC 6/1 Others 7+1
Derby Co (£100,000 on 22/4/92) FL 73+1/1 FLC 4 FAC 4/1 Others 5
West Bromwich A (£150,000 on 9/2/96) FL 34+2 FLC 2 Others 2

NICHOLLS Kevin John Richard
Born: Newham, 2 January 1979
Height: 6'0" Weight: 11.7
International Honours: E: Yth

The young Charlton midfield player made his league debut as substitute against Ipswich last September and his full debut against Burnley in the Coca-Cola Cup just three days later. With good ball control, and an accurate passer of the ball, Kevin made only spasmodic appearances during the season, but scored a spectacular long-range goal in the opening minute of his first full league game against Barnsley at The Valley. A good prospect for the future, he is in the same mould as former team mate, Lee Bowyer.

Charlton Ath (From trainee on 29/1/96) FL 3+3/1 FLC 1+1

NICHOLLS Mark
Born: Hillingdon, 30 May 1977
Height: 5'9" Weight: 9.10

A promising young striker who made his Chelsea senior bow at Blackpool as a half-time substitute for Steve Clarke in the Coca-Cola Cup last season, he intelligently cut the ball back from the byeline for Mark Hughes to thrash home the third goal from the edge of the penalty area. Despite causing a sensation when he was preferred to Gianluca Vialli for the league match at Filbert Street in October, he was kept under wraps for virtually the rest of the season, before returning to first-team action as a substitute at Derby in March. Is a consistent goalscorer for the reserve side and clearly one for the future.

Chelsea (From trainee on 1/7/95) PL 3+5 FLC 0+2

NICOL Stephen (Steve)
Born: Irvine, 11 December 1961
Height: 5'10" Weight: 12.8
Club Honours: Div 1 '84, '86, '88, '90; FAC '86, '89, '92; EC '84; CS '89
International Honours: S: 27; U21-14

In his second season with Sheffield Wednesday in 1996-97, again Steve was a great calming influence for the younger players in the side. Nowadays, his experience makes up for his lack of pace and when playing he did not come in for more than the occasional sub game until the second half of the season and he did not let himself or his manager down. Still very competititve, a good passer, and able to play in defence or midfield, most of his games were at full back and he was a regular in the last few weeks of the season. Now aged 35, he is in the veteran stage of his career.

Ayr U (From juniors in 1979) SL 68+2/7 SLC 16/1 SC 3
Liverpool (£300,000 on 26/10/81) F/PL 328+15/36 FLC 42/4 FAC 50/3 Others 32+2/3
Notts Co (Free on 20/1/95) FL 32/2 FLC 1 FAC 1 Others 3/1
Sheffield Wed (Free on 25/11/95) PL 37+5 FLC 0+2 FAC 2+1

Allan Nielsen

NIELSEN Allan
Born: Esbjerg, Denmark, 13 March 1971
Height: 5'8" Weight: 11.2
International Honours: Denmark: 10

An attacking midfielder, Alan signed for Spurs from leading Danish side, Brondby, a few weeks into last season. Unfortunately, an injury meant he could not put together a good run of games at a time when he was beginning to show top-class form, but six goals, that included headers and powerful drives both from inside and outside the box, and the ability to run for the whole 90 minutes, keep possession well, and act as a pivotal player to support the strikers and close down opponents, soon made him a favourite. Adding width and depth in midfield, strong in the challenge, with great tenacity, Alan is the ideal ball winner, performing in a similar workhorse role to his colleagues, Gary Mabbutt and David Howells. All in all, it was an excellent start for the Danish international.
Tottenham H (£1,650,000 from Brondby on 3/9/96) PL 28+1/6 FLC 2+1 FAC 1

NIELSEN John Schmidt
Born: Arhus, Denmark, 7 April 1972
Height: 5'8" Weight: 11.5

An all-action Dane, John arrived at Southend in the 1996 close season and immediately made himself a favourite with the fans, his tireless running and strong tackling making him a vital element in the midfield, and his volleying ability leading to a couple of stunning goals. Missed the latter part of the campaign due to injury, but should return all fired up for 1997-98.
Southend U (Free from Ikaast on 2/8/96) FL 17+7/3 FLC 2/1 FAC 1

NIELSEN Thomas
Born: Arhus, Denmark, 25 March 1972
Height: 6'1" Weight: 13.7

The second of Shrewsbury's 1996 close season Danish imports, Thomas came into the side either at full back or in central defence, proving to be a strong tackler and comfortable in the air. Still to fully establish his place as a regular, although 22 starts were a fair beginning to the rigours of English football, one of his main assets being a throw-in capability that was almost worth a corner.
Shrewsbury T (Free from Arhus Fremad on 20/8/96) FL 19+3/1 FLC 1+1 FAC 0+1 Others 2

Roger Nilsen

NILSEN Roger
Born: Tromso, Norway, 8 August 1969
Height: 5'10" Weight: 12.6
International Honours: Norway: 28

Having started last season in the centre of Sheffield United's defence, following the decision of Gary Ablett to sign for Birmingham, the acquisition of David Holdsworth enabled him to revert to left back, with occasional centre-back appear-

ances when the formation demanded. Volunteered to take over in goal against Norwich City when there was no sub 'keeper on the bench – his first ever competitive appearance between the posts (unfortunately, there was no fairy tale ending as he conceded two goals and United lost). Regained his place in the Norwegian international squad during the campaign, his club form demanding he be recognised.
Sheffield U (£550,000 from Viking Stavanger on 2/11/93) P/FL 125+2 FLC 5 FAC 4+2 Others 2+1

NIVEN Stuart Thomas
Born: Glasgow, 24 December 1978
Height: 5'11" Weight: 12.8
International Honours: S: Yth

Having made his Ipswich debut at Sheffield United last September and his home debut in front of the BSkyB cameras against Charlton two games later, and put in two solid displays, he was called up to the Scotland U18 side and played against his Town team-mate, Keiron Dyer, when England played Scotland. An attacking midfielder who is more comfortable on the right-hand side of the pitch, Stuart is a good passer and comes forward confidently.
Ipswich T (From trainee on 21/9/96) FL 2

NIXON Eric Walter
Born: Manchester, 4 October 1962
Height: 6'4" Weight: 15.7
Club Honours: AMC '90

Eric shared the Tranmere goalkeeping duties more or less on a 50-50 basis with Danny Coyne in 1996-97, enjoying a prolonged run from January right up to the end of the season. Although going on loan to Bradford City in September, he returned after one month and had a dream recall to the first team when playing a key role in the 2-1 defeat of his former club and boyhood idols, Manchester City, at Maine Road. Was appointed club goalkeeping coach in July 1996 and continues to be a huge influence on all the youngsters at Prenton Park, as well as being a perennial crowd favourite.
Manchester C (£1,000 from Curzon Ashton on 10/12/83) FL 58 FLC 8 FAC 10 Others 8
Wolverhampton W (Loaned on 29/8/86) FL 16
Bradford C (Loaned on 28/11/86) FL 3
Southampton (Loaned on 23/12/86) FL 4
Carlisle U (Loaned on 23/1/87) FL 16
Tranmere Rov (£60,000 on 24/3/88) FL 341 FLC 34 FAC 19 Others 45+1
Reading (Loaned on 9/1/96) FLC 1
Blackpool (Loaned on 5/2/96) FL 20 Others 2
Bradford C (Loaned on 13/9/96) FL 12

NOEL-WILLIAMS Gifton Ruben Elisha
Born: Islington, 21 January 1980
Height: 6'1" Weight:11.10
International Honours: E: Yth

Tall, well-built centre forward who, at the age of 16 years and 314 days, became Watford's youngest-ever first team scorer when coming off the bench at Vicarage Road to get the second goal in a 2-2 draw against Blackpool. He also has the distinction of being the first Watford player with a double-barrelled surname! Mobile, he leads the line well, and as engaging and confident off the field as on, Gifton is a

member of the England U18 squad.
Watford (From trainee on 13/2/97) FL 9+16/2 FLC 0+1 FAC 2/1

NOGAN Kurt

Born: Cardiff, 9 September 1970
Height: 5'10" Weight: 12.7
International Honours: W: U21-2

An automatic choice as striker and scoring regularly up to Christmas, Kurt's Burnley career then fell apart with a much-publicised contractual dispute, followed by problems off the field, which inevitably led to the club selling him. Signed by Preston for a knockdown fee, he quickly impressed with his skill on the ball, pace, and awareness, and was unlucky not to score twice on his debut at Blackpool. Although yet to find the net for North End, his partnership with Lee Ashcroft and David Reeves has the promise of goals written all over it.
Luton T (From trainee on 11/7/89) FL 17+16/3 FLC 1+3/1 Others 1+1
Peterborough U (Free on 30/9/92) Others 1
Brighton & Hove A (Free on 17/10/92) FL 97/49 FLC 10/7 FAC 5+1 Others 7/4
Burnley (£250,000 on 24/4/95) FL 87+5/33 FLC 8/5 FAC 3 Others 5/4
Preston NE (£150,000 + on 13/3/97) FL 5+2

NOGAN Lee Martin

Born: Cardiff, 21 May 1969
Height: 5'10" Weight: 11.0
International Honours: W: 2; B-1; U21-1

A regular in the Reading line up for the first half of last season, a loss of form and confidence saw the striker dropped and go out on loan to Notts County in February. Despite having no luck at all in front of goal, at a time when the Magpies were desperate, Lee impressed the fans with his intelligent and selfless running before returning to Elm Park. Quick off the mark and a difficult man to mark, he scored just six goals throughout the campaign.
Oxford U (From trainee on 25/3/87) FL 57+7/10 FLC 4+1 FAC 2+1/1 Others 4+1/1
Brentford (Loaned on 25/3/87) FL 10+1/2
Southend U (Loaned on 17/9/87) FL 6/1 FLC 2 Others 1/1
Watford (£350,000 on 12/12/91) FL 97+8/26 FLC 5+2/3 FAC 2/1 Others 1+2
Southend U (Loaned on 17/3/94) FL 4+1
Reading (£250,000 on 12/1/95) FL 71+20/26 FLC 5+1/1 FAC 2 Others 3/2
Notts Co (Loaned on 14/2/97) FL 6

NOLAN Ian Robert

Born: Liverpool, 9 July 1970
Height: 6'0" Weight: 12.1
International Honours: NI: 5

An ever present in the Sheffield Wednesday side last season, Ian was also called up to represent Northern Ireland in their World Cup qualifiers despite his Liverpool upbringing. Although a right-footed player, he spent most of 1996-97 in the left-back berth but, despite playing out of his normal position, he has been a vital member of the side since joining the club. A very consistent player who likes to get forward to help the attack, he did manage one goal in the last campaign – a vital one in a draw at Tottenham.

Preston NE (From trainee on 31/8/88)
Tranmere Rov (£10,000 from Marine, via Northwich Victoria, on 2/8/91) FL 87+1/1 FLC 10/1 FAC 7 Others 9
Sheffield Wed (£1,500,000 on 17/8/94) PL 109/4 FLC 10 FAC 8

NORMAN Anthony (Tony) Joseph

Born: Deeside, 24 February 1958
Height: 6'2" Weight: 14.5
International Honours: W: 5; B-1

The veteran Huddersfield goalkeeper was a more than able deputy for first-choice Steve Francis, playing a handful of games in 1996-97, when called upon due to injury and keeping two clean sheets, before being released during the summer. Doubled up as the goalkeeping coach and also acted as a radio summariser on local commentaries.
Burnley (From juniors on 1/8/76)
Hull C (£30,000 on 14/2/80) FL 372 FLC 22 FAC 26 Others 13
Sunderland (Signed on 29/12/88) FL 198 FLC 8 FAC 14 Others 7
Huddersfield T (Free on 7/7/95) FL 7 FLC 1 FAC 1

NORTON David Wayne

Born: Cannock, 3 March 1965
Height: 5'8" Weight: 11.12
International Honours: E: Yth

Released by Northampton during the summer of 1996, David moved to Hereford and was soon appointed club captain, missing just one league game and leading the team by example from right back in 1996-97. Tough tackling, and cool under pressure, he will be an extremely valuable asset in 1997-98 as United try to fight their way out of the Conference.
Aston Villa (From apprentice on 23/3/83) FL 42+2/2 FLC 8 FAC 2+1 Others 2
Notts Co (£30,000 on 24/8/88) FL 22+5/1 FLC 3+1 Others 4+1
Rochdale (Loaned on 18/10/90) FL 9 Others 2
Hull C (Loaned on 10/1/91) FL 15
Hull C (£80,000 on 16/8/91) FL 134/5 FLC 7 FAC 7/1 Others 1
Northampton T (£25,000 on 15/8/94) FL 78+4 FLC 4 FAC 3 Others 4
Hereford U (Free on 12/8/96) FL 45/1 FLC 2/1 FAC 1 Others 1

NOTEMAN Kevin Simon

Born: Preston, 15 October 1969
Height: 5'10" Weight: 12.2

Despite ending last season as Chester's second highest goalscorer with ten from 32 starts, Kevin was given a free transfer during the summer. Earlier, the speedy winger again used his pace to good purpose down City's left flank until the arrival of Sam Aiston, on loan from Sunderland, left him on the sidelines and effectively ruled him out of further contention. A player with an eye for goal, his last two strikes for the club, both at the Deva, was the winner against Mansfield and another in a 1-1 draw against Carlisle.
Leeds U (From trainee on 13/6/88) FL 0+1 Others 1
Doncaster Rov (£10,000 on 10/11/89) FL 105+1/20 FLC 4/1 FAC 5+1/2 Others 11/1
Mansfield T (£25,000 on 27/3/92) FL 77+18/15 FLC 7/1 FAC 3 Others 5+1
Doncaster Rov (Free on 4/8/95) FL 4/1 FLC 2
Chester C (Free on 1/9/95) FL 57+11/18 FLC 0+1/1 FAC 3+1 Others 1+2

NTAMARK Charles (Charlie) Batmbog

Born: Paddington, 22 July 1964
Height: 5'10" Weight: 11.12
International Honours: Cameroon: 31

This popular Cameroon international completed seven seasons at Walsall in 1996-97 and played his 300th game for the club against Wrexham, when an otherwise excellent display was marred by him being instrumental in the visitors' match winner. He was also unlucky a few weeks later when he was booked in the 1-1 draw at Brentford, after which the referee admitted he had made a mistake. Through thick and thin, Charlie, in a mainly defensive role, once again proved himself a class player and a popular figure with fans.
Walsall (Free from Boreham Wood on 22/8/90) FL 256+20/12 FLC 17+1/1 FAC 23 Others 18+1/1

NUGENT Kevin Patrick

Born: Edmonton, 10 April 1969
Height: 6'1" Weight: 13.3
International Honours: Ei: Yth

One of Bristol City's unsung heroes, this hard-working centre forward fought his way back into the side towards the end of last season to play a prominent part in the run in to claim a place in the play offs. Rather surprisingly to some, he formed an excellent partnership with Shaun Goater, setting up many chances with his close control and passing ability. In making up for lack of pace with an ability to lead a line well, coupled to good heading power, Bristol City did well in signing this likeable player from Plymouth Argyle in September 1995.
Leyton Orient (From trainee on 8/7/87) FL 86+8/20 FLC 9+3/6 FAC 9/3 Others 9+1/1
Plymouth Arg (£200,000 on 23/3/92) FL 124+7/32 FLC 11/2 FAC 10/3 Others 5+3
Bristol C (Signed on 29/9/95) FL 48+22/14 FLC 2+2 FAC 3+2/1 Others 2+1

NWADIKE Chukweumeka (Chuk) Ibezimife

Born: Camberwell, 9 August 1978
Height: 6'0" Weight: 12.7

A Wolves' professional recruit from the trainee ranks during the 1996 close season, he failed to make any impression at Molineux in the opening months of 1996-97 and was transferred to Shrewsbury in December. Subsequently, the central defender made a substitute appearance during an injury crisis and was then given his first start in the final game of the campaign, where he gave a good account of himself. Is certainly one for the future.
Wolverhampton W (From trainee on 3/7/96)
Shrewsbury T (Free on 10/12/96) FL 1+1

NYAMAH Kofi

Born: Islington, 20 June 1975
Height: 5'8" Weight: 10.12

A mid-season signing from Kettering Town in 1996-97, Kofi made a handful of substitute appearances on his return to the Football League with Stoke, but failed to serve notice of the quick left-footed wing play that had brought him to the club's attention.
Cambridge U (From trainee on 19/5/93) FL 9+14/2 FLC 0+2 FAC 3+1/1 Others 4) Free to Kettering T during 1995 close season
Stoke C (£25,000 on 24/12/96) FL 0+7

OAKES Michael Christian
Born: Northwich, 30 October 1973
Height: 6'1" Weight: 12.6
International Honours: E: U21-6
Michael made the most of the injuries to Mark Bosnich to show that he is also a very capable goalkeeper in his own right when he appeared in half of Aston Villa's matches in 1996-97. A good pair of hands and a confident kicker of the ball, he had waited a while for his chance and is banking on becoming the number-one choice at the Birmingham club before very much longer. His league debut came on the opening day of the campaign and he was either in the team or on the bench for all but one of Villa's games last season. Is the son of Alan, the former Manchester City wing half and appearance record holder.
Aston Villa (From juniors on 16/7/91) PL 18+2 FLC 2 Others 2
Scarborough (Loaned on 26/11/93) FL 1 Others 1

OAKES Scott John
Born: Leicester, 5 August 1972
Height: 5'10" Weight: 11.13
International Honours: E: U21-1
Moving from a side relegated to division two back to the Premiership was always going to be a tough assignment and so it proved for the former Luton midfielder, cum striker. Although having just a few starts in a Sheffield Wednesday side that did well in the league in 1996-97, when he did play he was impressive, skilful and constructive in midfield, and showed himself to have a good shot. Opened his scoring account for the club in a 1-1 draw at Sunderland and having settled back into top flight football he must look forward to the new campaign with more confidence.
Leicester C (From trainee on 9/5/90) FL 1+2 Others 1
Luton T (Signed on 22/10/91) FL 136+37/27 FLC 3+3/1 FAC 12+2/5 Others 3+3/1
Sheffield Wed (£425,000 + on 1/8/96) PL 7+12/1 FLC 0+1

OAKLEY Matthew
Born: Peterborough, 17 August 1977
Height: 5'10" Weight: 12.1
International Honours: E: U21-1
The Southampton winger who can operate on either flank, became much more of a regular in 1996-97 when making 23 starts in the Premiership, despite a spell out due to injury in February and March. A good passer with plenty of vision, his forceful play gets him into excellent attacking positions, something which saw him hit the net three times during the campaign and score his first-ever league goal, at Wimbledon, in September. Able to get a lot of distance on long throws, an ability which created additional opportunities for his team mates, his good form also saw him selected for the England U21 side.
Southampton (From trainee on 1/7/95) PL 28+11/4 FLC 6+1 FAC 2+2/1

OATWAY Anthony (Charlie)
Born: Hammersmith, 28 November 1973
Height: 5'7" Weight: 10.10
Although not quite as impressive as the previous season this aggressive midfielder was still a great favourite with the Torquay fans in 1996-97 for his total commitment to the cause. Scored his first goal for the club at home to Swansea in October, the opener in a 2-0 win for United.
Cardiff C (Free from Yeading on 4/8/94) FL 29+3 FLC 2/1 FAC 1+1 Others 3+1
Torquay U (Free on 28/12/95) FL 63+2/1 FLC 2 FAC 1

O'BRIEN Andrew James
Born: Harrogate, 29 June 1979
Height: 6'3" Weight: 11.9
International Honours: E: Yth
Nicknamed "Rash" for the way he sticks to opponents, the young defender signed pro forms for Bradford last October, after coming through the club's youth scheme as a trainee. Having made his first-team debut at QPR just 12 days earlier, and showing himself to be a great prospect, Andrew went on to play 24 more times before the season came to a halt, scoring his first goal for the club in a 2-0 home win over Oxford. Slotting in well with Nicky Mohan as an integral part of the defence, he looked to be a player who could go right to the top and was justly voted Young Player of the Year.
Bradford C (From trainee on 28/10/96) FL 18+4/2 FAC 3

O'BRIEN Liam Francis
Born: Dublin, 5 September 1964
Height: 6'1" Weight: 13.7
Club Honours: Div 1 '93
International Honours: Ei: 16; U23-1; Yth; Sch
Liam was delighted to find himself recalled to the Eire squad by the new manager, Mick McCarthy, in the 1996 close season, and jetted off on their tour of the United States. The nearest that Tranmere had to an ever present in 1996-97, he made 46 first team starts and scored one goal in the process, proving to be a consistent and dependable performer. A good striker of the ball who can spray 40-yard passes around and is dangerous at set pieces, his preferred position is just in front of the back four, from where he can act as playmaker.
Manchester U (£60,000 from Shamrock Rov on 14/10/86) FL 16+15/2 FLC 1+2 FAC 0+2
Newcastle U (£250,000 on 15/11/88) F/PL 131+20/19 FLC 9/1 FAC 12+2/1 Others 9+2/1
Tranmere Rov (£300,000 on 21/1/94) FL 114+4/7 FLC 11 FAC 4+1/1 Others 5+1

O'BRIEN Roy Joseph
Born: Cork, 27 November 1974
Height: 6'1" Weight: 12.0
International Honours: Ei: Yth; Sch
Released by Arsenal during the 1996 close season, having suffered from long-term injuries, Roy trialled at Wigan for a couple of weeks before arriving at Bournemouth on a monthly contract and making his league debut at Gillingham early in October. A quick and determined all-round central defender who is excellent in the air and a

good tackler, he was unfortunately stretchered off awaiting a medial ligament repair. Back in training with the club, the young Irishman will be hoping that the knee stands up in pre-season.
Arsenal (From trainee on 6/7/93)
Wigan Ath (Free on 12/8/96)
Bournemouth (Free on 23/8/96) FL 1

O'CONNELL Brendan
Born: Lambeth, 12 November 1966
Height: 5'10" Weight: 12.1
A hard-working midfielder signed from Barnsley during the summer of 1996, Brendan quickly settled into the Charlton side, winning over the Valley faithful with his non-stop running and tenacious tackling. Took over the captaincy of the side midway through the season, and led the team by example, playing in a more forward role just behind the sole striker for several games towards the end of the campaign.
Portsmouth (From apprentice on 1/7/85)
Exeter C (Free on 4/8/86) FL 73+8/19 FLC 3+1/2 FAC 3 Others 4
Burnley (Free on 1/7/88) FL 62+2/17 FLC 6/3 FAC 3/1 Others 5/2
Huddersfield T (Loaned on 30/11/89) FL 11/1
Barnsley (£50,000 on 23/3/90) FL 212+28/35 FLC 10+1/1 FAC 14/1 Others 7+1/2
Charlton Ath (£125,000 on 26/7/96) FL 33+5/2 FLC 2 FAC 2

O'CONNOR Gary
Born: Newtongrange, 7 April 1974
Height: 6'2" Weight: 13.0
International Honours: S: Yth; Sch
Gary had a lengthy run in Doncaster's goal in 1996-97, following the injury to Dean Williams, but suffered a shoulder injury of his own in late January which allowed the latter to reclaim the first team 'keeper's shirt. Although a promising player, he was released during the summer.
Heart of Midlothian (Signed from Dalkeith Thistle on 6/3/92) SL 3
Berwick R (Loaned on 19/2/93) SL 39 SLC 1 SC 1 Others 1
Doncaster Rov (£25,000 on 17/1/96) FL 26 FAC 1 Others 1

O'CONNOR Mark Andrew
Born: Thundersley, 10 March 1963
Height: 5'7" Weight: 10.10
Club Honours: Div 3 '87
Mark made a remarkable comeback from the broken leg he received in that infamous game against Fulham in November 1995. At one time it looked as if his career might be over, but he returned for Gillingham, surprisingly, against his old club, Bournemouth, last October. Often used as an attacking wing back, he still looked more comfortable in an attacking midfield role on the right, where his ball control and neat passing made him a dangerous player. In March, he was given a new two-year contract.
Queens Park R (From apprentice on 1/6/80) FL 2+1
Exeter C (Loaned on 7/10/83) FL 38/1 FAC 2/1 Others 3/1
Bristol Rov (£20,000 on 13/8/84) FL 79+1/10 FLC 8/1 FAC 7/1 Others 4/1
Bournemouth (£25,000 on 27/3/86) FL 115+13/12 FLC 5+3 FAC 7 Others 4+1

Gillingham (£70,000 on 15/12/89) FL 107+9/8 FLC 8 FAC 7+1 Others 6+2/1
Bournemouth (Free on 5/7/93) FL 56+2/3 FLC 7+1 FAC 4 Others 1
Gillingham (Free on 4/8/95) FL 36+4/1 FLC 3 FAC 5

O'CONNOR Martyn John
Born: Walsall, 10 December 1967
Height: 5'9" Weight: 12.8

Signed by Peterborough during the 1996 close season from Walsall, Martyn never really settled with Posh, even missing two penalties during his short-lived stay. A strong, hard-working midfielder with exceptional stamina that allows him to work from box to box, he had turned down Brum prior to leaving for London Road, but when Trevor Francis came back for him in November he failed to repeat the same mistake twice, signing for Birmingham then and there and quickly settling in at the heart of midfield where he gave some pretty impressive performances. Also scored four goals, two of them being crucial, against Grimsby and Southend, when Blues were struggling to pull away from those teams at the foot of the first division. Is tipped as a possible future captain for City.
Crystal Palace (£25,000 from Bromsgrove Rov on 26/6/92) FL 2 Others 1+1
Walsall (Loaned on 24/3/93) FL 10/1 Others 2/1
Walsall (£40,000 on 14/2/94) FL 94/21 FLC 6/2 FAC 10/2 Others 3/1
Peterborough U (£350,000 on 12/7/96) FL 18/3 FLC 4 FAC 2
Birmingham C (£500,000 + on 29/11/96) FL 24/4

O'CONNOR Paul Daniel
Born: Easington, 17 August 1971
Height: 5'11" Weight: 13.5

An eventful season for Hartlepool's part-time goalkeeper who began 1996-97 with the job description that he was with the club just to provide cover for the more experienced Stephen Pears. However, with the latter's long-term injury, he took the opportunity to make the goalkeeping position his own, being especially impressive towards the end of the campaign when under great pressure, and will be particularly remembered for two point-blank saves in the important game at Darlington.
Leicester C (From trainee on 1/3/89 - Free to Nuneaton Borough in November 1990)
Hartlepool U (Free from Blyth Spartans on 19/4/96) FL 31 FAC 1 Others 1

OGRIZOVIC Steven (Steve)
Born: Mansfield, 12 September 1957
Height: 6'5" Weight: 15.0
Club Honours: FAC '87

The longstanding goalkeeper broke George Curtis' record appearances for Coventry at Elland Road on Boxing Day 1996 and by the end of 1996-97 had played over 550 times for City, had been an ever present, and had enjoyed an excellent season. At the time of writing, he had won nine Man of the Match awards, his brave performance at Arsenal being typical of Oggy, as he ended up being carried off with concussion and a broken nose after a collision with Ian Wright. The big away games also seemed to inspire him to higher levels of performance. In the FA Cup at Blackburn he made numerous saves, including a penalty from Chris Sutton, and then at Anfield he made three world class saves to help City to a great win. However, he saved a rare boob for the Sky TV game against Arsenal when he failed to hold an innocuous through ball and in trying to retrieve the situation brought down Ian Wright, who converted the resulting penalty. Voted Player of the Year by the London Supporters Club and Sports Argus, his contract has another year to run and it is highly likely that he will start between the sticks this coming season.
Chesterfield (Signed from ONRYC on 28/7/77) FL 16 FLC 2
Liverpool (£70,000 on 18/11/77) FL 4 Others 1
Shrewsbury T (£70,000 on 11/8/82) FL 84 FLC 7 FAC 5
Coventry C (£72,000 on 22/6/84) F/PL 478/1 FLC 45 FAC 32 Others 11

Steve Ogrizovic

O'HALLORAN Keith James
Born: Dublin, 10 November 1975
Height: 5'10" Weight: 12.3
International Honours: Ei: U21-3; Yth; Sch

Not a member of the Middlesbrough first-team squad in 1996-97, due to the heavy influx of foreign stars at the club, the central midfielder settled down to playing in the reserves before going on loan to Cardiff at the end of November in an effort to get his career back on the rails. Strong and determined, and a good tackler, Keith started well but lost his way a little, the third division not quite suiting him, before returning to the Riverside. Released at the end of March, he moved back to the Republic to play his football there, having played for the national U21 side earlier in the campaign.
Middlesbrough (Signed from Cherry Orchard on 6/9/94) P/FL 3+1 FAC 2 Others 1
Scunthorpe U (Loaned on 25/3/96) FL 6+1
Cardiff C (Loaned on 29/11/96) FL 8 Others 2

OHANDJANIAN Demis
Born: Manchester, 1 May 1978
Height: 5'8" Weight: 10.10

After joining Doncaster on a non-contract basis from Curzon Ashton last February, Demis made his league debut when coming on as a substitute during Rovers' away game at Northampton just two weeks later. Particularly fast on the ball, he is not afraid to battle up front despite his diminutive size.
Doncaster Rov (Free from Curzon Ashton on 7/2/97) FL 0+1

O'HANLON Kelham Gerrard
Born: Saltburn, 16 May 1962
Height: 6'1" Weight: 13.1
Club Honours: Div 4 '89
International Honours: Ei: 1; U21-1

Previously at Dundee United, the former Preston goalkeeper returned to the club early last season as coach. His sterling displays in the reserves, whilst North End's young goalies were away on loan, led to him making a return to first team action when Bobby Mimms had a dip in form and he quickly showed he had lost none of the ability he demonstrated in his first spell at the club.
Middlesbrough (From apprentice on 21/5/80) FL 87 FLC 4 FAC 6
Rotherham U (Free on 7/8/85) FL 248 FLC 22 FAC 18 Others 16
Carlisle U (£25,000 on 5/8/91) FL 83 FLC 6 FAC 3 Others 5
Preston NE (£25,000 on 20/7/93) FL 23 FLC 2 FAC 2 Others 1
Dundee U (£30,000 on 16/9/94) SL 31 SC 4 Others 3
Preston NE (£12,000 on 6/9/96) FL 13 Others 2

O'KANE John Andrew
Born: Nottingham, 15 November 1974
Height: 5'10" Weight: 12.2
Club Honours: FAYC '92; Div 2 '97

A talented Manchester United right back, who is excellent on the ball and a natural athlete, John became an instant hero when going on loan to Bury last October, scoring a last-minute winner on his debut against Bristol Rovers at Gigg Lane and getting another, also from the bench, against York. However, when United suffered an injury crisis in November, he was recalled and made a promising full debut at Middlesbrough, also playing in the Coca-Cola Cup against Leicester. With those tasks over, and following an injury to Bury skipper, David Pugh, he returned to Gigg Lane in January, where he performed as a left-wing back, his 11 full appearances entitling him to a second division championship medal as the Shakers fought their way to the title.
Manchester U (From trainee on 29/1/93) PL 1+1 FLC 2+1 FAC 1 Others 1
Bury (Loaned on 25/10/96) FL 2+2/2
Bury (Loaned on 16/1/97) FL 9/1 Others 1

OLDFIELD David Charles
Born: Perth, Australia, 30 May 1968
Height: 5'11" Weight: 13.4
International Honours: E: U21-1

An intelligent attacker who finally won over Luton fans in 1996-97, David prefers to play behind the front line, although he was cast as a striker at the start of the season and responded with some early goals. He then formed an outstanding partnership with the prolific Tony Thorpe and, whilst his own strike rate dropped away, his contribution in terms of holding up the ball, creating opportunities, and non-stop chasing, more than compensated. Scored his first ever hat trick in February after a period out through injury and finished the campaign with all three goals in the play-off semi finals against Crewe. Unfortunately, it was not enough to see Town through to the finals and this classy player will be plying his skills in the second division again in 1997-98.

Luton T (From apprentice on 16/5/86) FL 21+8/4 FLC 4+2/2 FAC 0+1 Others 2+1/2
Manchester C (£600,000 on 14/3/89) FL 18+8/6 FLC 2+1/2 Others 0+1/1
Leicester C (£150,000 on 12/1/90) F/PL 163+25/26 FLC 10+1/1 FAC 6/3 Others 11+3/2
Millwall (Loaned on 24/2/95) FL 16+1/6
Luton T (£150,000 on 21/7/95) FL 54+18/8 FLC 7/2 FAC 1 Others 4+2/3

O'LEARY Kristian Denis
Born: Neath, 30 August 1977
Height: 6'0" Weight: 13.4
International Honours: W: Yth

Featured well for Swansea last season, either at centre back or full back, despite being troubled by ankle problems throughout the campaign. Showed his versatility during the Torquay game in giving a commanding midfield display and scoring his first league goal, and with 15 appearances for the club now under his belt, Kristian should figure strongly in any midfield permutation in 1997-98.

Swansea C (From trainee on 1/7/96) FL 10+3/1 FLC 1 FAC 1+1

OLIVER Michael
Born: Cleveland, 2 August 1975
Height: 5'10" Weight: 12.4

A creative Darlington midfielder signed from Stockport County during the 1996 close season, Michael impressed with his strong running and skill, scoring some spectacular goals after bursting through from midfield. Had a spell out of the side towards the end of the season, but came back well, scoring the winner against Carlisle, a result that moved the club four places up the table.

Middlesbrough (From trainee on 19/8/92) Others 0+1
Stockport Co (£15,000 on 7/7/94) FL 17+5/1 FLC 0+2 FAC 2 Others 1
Darlington (Free on 30/7/96) FL 34+5/9 FLC 4 FAC 2 Others 0+1

OLIVIERA Raul Miguel Silva
Born: Lisbon, Portugal, 26 August 1972
Height: 6'2" Weight: 13.2
International Honours: Portugal: U21

A strong and powerful centre back, having been in dispute with Farense (Portugal), Raul spent a month on trial at Newcastle last February before joining Bradford until the end of the season. However, after making

his first-team debut against Wolves, standing in for the suspended Nicky Mohan, the Alan Hansen lookalike made way for the returning Mohan following a 3-1 defeat at Portsmouth and eventually returned home.

Bradford C (Signed from Farense on 21/3/97) FL 2

OMIGIE Joseph Eghodalo
Born: Hammersmith, 13 June 1972
Height: 6'2" Weight: 13.0

Tall and awkward Brentford central striker. In and out of the side in 1996-97, Joe scored his first goal for the club at Bristol Rovers (AWS) and his first in the league at Plymouth, both coming in December. Still used predominately as a sub, he often came on to shake a game up.

Brentford (Free from Donna FC on 26/8/94) FL 10+13/1 FAC 0+3 Others 2+1/1

OMOYINMI Emmanuel (Manny)
Born: London, 28 December 1977
Height: 5'6" Weight: 10.7
International Honours: E: Sch

Another promising youngster from the West Ham academy of youth, Manny is a right winger with pace, dribbling, and goal-scoring abilities, and one of the stars of the Hammers' Youth Cup side of 1996. After a useful spell early last season on loan to Bournemouth, where he made his league debut, he returned to regular reserve-team football at Upton Park and was called up once for Premier League action, making his Hammers' debut in March as a substitute at Leeds, when coming on for the closing minutes of the game.

West Ham U (From trainee on 17/5/95) PL 0+1
Bournemouth (Loaned on 30/9/96) FL 5+2

O'NEILL Brian
Born: Paisley, 6 September 1972
Height: 6'1" Weight: 12.4
International Honours: S: 1; U21-7; Yth; Sch

Brian, a midfielder, came to Nottingham Forest on loan from Celtic for the remaining two months of last season, and proved to be a tough-tackling player who was also capable of playing at centre back. Having made a sub appearance at Middlesbrough, he started the Leeds game at the City Ground and quickly improved with clever touches and the ability to work openings for himself.

Glasgow Celtic (Free from Porirua Viard U on 10/7/91) SL 91+27/8 SLC 6+4/1 SC 10/9 Others 8+3/1
Nottingham F (Loaned on 18/3/97) PL 4+1

O'NEILL John Joseph
Born: Glasgow, 1 January 1974
Height: 5'11" Weight: 12.0

Having joined Bournemouth at the end of 1995-96, John found it difficult to get a first-team place last season, making just seven starts and numerous substitute appearances, despite being top scorer for the reserve side. Able to play either up front or in midfield, he scored his first league goal for the club in the last home game of the campaign, a 2-1 win against Wrexham.

Queens Park (From school on 25/7/91) SL 70+21/30 SLC 2+1 SC 2 Others 0+1
Glasgow Celtic (Signed on 16/5/94) SL 0+2
Bournemouth (Free on 29/3/96) FL 9+15/1 FLC 0+2 FAC 0+1

O'NEILL Keith Padre Gerard
Born: Dublin, 16 February 1976
Height: 6'2" Weight: 12.7
International Honours: Ei: 9; U21-1; Yth; Sch

Keith and Darren Eadie, when working in Tandem for Norwich, and on form, appeared at times in 1996-97 almost unstoppable. Their youthful pace and skill frequently looked set to destroy defences, but dogged by injuries, damaged left ankle ligaments, a double hernia operation, a bout of flu, the list was almost endless for Keith as he played a couple, missed a couple, with the longest spell out stretching to 11 matches and Norwich City supporters can only hope that the flourishing strike partnership continues this coming season unhampered. A Republic of Ireland international, he is pacy and dangerous from the left flank, his accurate crosses often causing havoc in opponents' penalty areas.

Norwich C (From trainee on 1/7/94) P/FL 35+11/7 FLC 6+1 FAC 2

O'NEILL Michael Andrew Martin
Born: Portadown, 5 July 1969
Height: 5'11" Weight: 11.10
International Honours: NI: 31; B-1; U23-1; U21-1; Yth; Sch

Michael had an unfortunate season after joining Coventry City from Hibernian in the summer of 1996. Although the Northern Ireland international winger started the first game of 1996-97, he was substituted at half time when the system was not working and then spent the rest of the campaign either injured or in the reserves. Will be hoping for a fresh start in 1997-98.

Newcastle U (Signed from Coleraine on 23/10/87) FL 36+12/15 FLC 2 FAC 3+2/1 Others 1
Dundee U (Signed on 15/8/89) SL 49+15/11 SLC 3+2/1 SC 2 Others 3+2/1
Hibernian (Signed on 20/8/93) SL 96+2/19 SLC 9/3 SC 6/2
Coventry C (£500.000 on 26/7/96) PL 1

ONUORA Ifem (Iffy)
Born: Glasgow, 28 July 1967
Height: 6'1" Weight: 13.10

Possibly one of the bargain buys in the lower divisions of the Nationwide League in 1996-97. Cost just £25,000 from Mansfield Town at the beginning of the season, he started out wide for Gillingham, but when the unfortunate injury to Leo Fortune-West occurred, he was moved to a central attacking position and celebrated by scoring a first-half hat trick against Rotherham on 21 September. Following that, it was goals all the way, many of them spectacular efforts, which was why he had two in the top ten of Sky's choice for many months. Quick off the mark, he has deceptive pace over ten yards and is always a handful for opposing defences.

Huddersfield T (Signed from Bradford University on 28/7/89) FL 115+50/30 FLC 10+6/4 FAC 11+3/3 Others 13+3/3

Mansfield T (£30,000 on 20/7/94) FL 17+11/8 FAC 0+1 Others 1
Gillingham (£25,000 on 16/8/96) FL 37+3/21 FLC 6/1 FAC 2/1

ONWERE Udo Alozie
Born: Hammersmith, 9 November 1971
Height: 6'0" Weight: 11.7

Freed by Lincoln during the summer of 1996, the hard-tackling midfielder joined Blackpool last September for the season's duration, although spending most of his time in the reserves. Always popular with the fans, Udo had more than his fair share of injuries and was released at the end of the campaign.
Fulham (From trainee on 11/7/90) FL 66+19/7 FLC 4+2 FAC 1+1 Others 9
Lincoln C (Free on 12/8/94) FL 40+3/4 FLC 5 FAC 1 Others 4/1 (Free to Dover Ath in August 1996)
Blackpool (Free on 13/9/96) FL 5+4 FLC 1 FAC 1 Others 0+2

ORD Richard John
Born: Murton, 3 March 1970
Height: 6'2" Weight: 13.5
Club Honours: Div 1 '96
International Honours: E: U21-3

A left-sided centre back, "Dickie" enjoyed a testimonial at Sunderland in 1996, but also suffered relegation from the Premiership for the second time after being one of the club's most consistent performers last season, having turned in excellent displays in the two away derbies at Newcastle and Middlesbrough. However, he also blotted his copybook somewhat by picking up unnecessary red cards in two matches. Excellent in the air, a good tackler, and surprisingly skilful for a big man, Richard obviously hopes for a quick return to the Premiership as he has already proved that he has the ability to compete at the top level.
Sunderland (From trainee on 14/7/87) P/FL 210+19/7 FLC 17+5 FAC 11+1/1 Others 5+1
York C (Loaned on 22/2/90) FL 3

Richard Ord

ORIE Eric Alexander
Born: Utrecht, Holland, 25 July 1968
Height: 5'10" Weight: 11.6

A Dutch left winger, or wide midfielder, Eric trialled at Blackpool on non-contract forms at the beginning of last season, making his debut at Scunthorpe in the Coca-Cola Cup and departing eight days later. Next stop was Grimsby, but, although he was there for several months, there were no appearances and he went home in March.
Blackpool (Free from Vienna on 19/8/96) FLC 1
Grimsby T (Free on 28/8/96)

ORLYGSSON Thorvaldur (Toddy)
Born: Iceland, 2 August 1966
Height: 5'11" Weight: 11.3
International Honours: Iceland: 41

Always seeming to be in the wars, Oldham's plucky Icelandic midfielder missed the end of last season due to a calf strain, being forced to sit on the sidelines as the Latics ultimately slipped out of the first division. Not only a strong tackler, but a good passer also, there was no doubting that he was missed. Equally effective in central midfield or on the wide right, where he can make strong runs into opposition territory, Toddy is also a dead-ball expert.
Nottingham F (£175,000 from KA Akureyri on 9/12/89) F/PL 31+6/2 FLC 5+1/2 FAC 1 Others 0+1
Stoke C (Free on 5/8/93) FL 86+4/16 FLC 7/1 FAC 6/1 Others 7/1
Oldham Ath (£180,000 on 22/12/95) FL 38+5/1 FLC 4+1 FAC 3+1

ORMEROD Brett Ryan
Born: Blackburn, 18 October 1976
Height: 5'11" Weight: 11.4

Having scored 28 goals for non-league Accrington, the young striker was snapped up by Blackpool last March and made his league debut just a week later when coming off the bench at Chesterfield with eight minutes left on the clock. Three more subs' appearances followed before the campaign came to a close and big things are expected from him this coming term.
Blackpool (£50,000 from Accrington Stanley on 21/3/97) FL 0+4

ORMEROD Mark Ian
Born: Bournemouth, 5 February 1976
Height: 6'0" Weight: 12.11

After four years on Brighton's staff as understudy to the consistent Nicky Rust, this young goalkeeper made his long-awaited debut in the absence of the injured Rust in a 3-2 home win over Scarborough last season. Mark's handling and instinctive shot stopping quickly gained the confidence and admiration of the Goldstone crowd and he subsequently enjoyed a lengthy run in the side, having a superb match in the vital 1-1 draw at Hereford in the last match of the campaign, a result which enabled the Seagulls to retain their Football League status.
Brighton & Hove A (From trainee on 21/7/94) FL 21 Others 1

ORMONDROYD Ian
Born: Bradford, 22 September 1964
Height: 6'4" Weight: 13.9

Unable to claim a regular place at Bradford at the start of 1996-97, the tall, gangling forward arrived at Oldham towards the end of September and immediately got down to business, notching up eight goals in quick succession. Unfortunately, just when it looked likely that Latics' might avoid the drop into the second division, an ankle injury put him out of action for the last dozen matches, apart from the odd subs' appearance, and the club's hopes seemed to sink with him. Not a prolific scorer, but one who can be relied upon to pick up valuable goals.
Bradford C (Signed from Thackley on 6/9/85) FL 72+15/20 FLC 12+2/4 FAC 7/2 Others 7+2/1
Oldham Ath (Loaned on 27/3/87) FL 8+2/1
Aston Villa (£600,000 on 2/2/89) FL 41+15/6 FLC 4+2/2 FAC 5/2 Others 6+1
Derby Co (£350,000 on 19/9/91) FL 25/8 FLC 3 FAC 3/1
Leicester C (Signed on 11/3/92) F/PL 67+10/7 FLC 6/2 FAC 1+1 Others 11/3
Hull C (Loaned on 27/1/95) FL 10/6
Bradford C (£75,000 on 13/7/95) FL 28+10/6 FLC 7/3 FAC 2+1/1 Others 2+2
Oldham Ath (Free on 20/9/96) FL 26+4/8 FAC 1

Simon Osborn

OSBORN Simon Edward
Born: Croydon, 19 January 1972
Height: 5'10" Weight: 11.4

The Wolves' midfielder scored with a lovely free kick past QPR, and though he played in nine of the first ten games he was unable to train in between. Minor surgery on his knee then kept him out for seven matches, but he came back in fine form as Wanderers scored

three in the second half against Manchester City, probing for the early ball then making telling passes. It seemed that when Simon played well so did the team, and in December he scored a penalty at Tranmere and a brace against Oxford, before the New Year saw him strike a superb right-footed free kick at Sheffield. Had played 26 consecutive games when he limped off against Norwich in April and was hardly seen after that, except for the play offs, when he still appeared to lack match fitness.

Crystal Palace (From trainee on 3/1/90) F/PL 47+8/5 FLC 11/1 FAC 2 Others 1+3
Reading (£90,000 on 17/8/94) FL 31+1/5 FLC 4 Others 3
Queens Park R (£1,100,000 on 7/7/95) PL 6+3/1 FLC 2
Wolverhampton W (£1,000,000 on 22/12/95) FL 54+2/7 FLC 1/1 FAC 5 Others 2

O'SHEA Daniel (Danny) Edward
Born: Kennington, 26 March 1963
Height: 6'0" Weight: 13.4
Club Honours: Div 3 '91
Capable of playing in central defence or in midfield, Danny is also the club's player/coach. A steadying influence, although first team outings were limited last season, when called upon he always gave 100 per cent.

Arsenal (From apprentice on 23/12/80) FL 6 FLC 3
Charlton Ath (Loaned on 23/2/84) FL 9
Exeter C (Free on 24/8/84) FL 45/2 FLC 2 FAC 2 Others 2
Southend U (£5,000 on 9/8/85) FL 116+2/12 FLC 8 FAC 5+1 Others 6
Cambridge U (Free on 18/8/89) FL 186+17/1 FLC 18+1 FAC 15+3 Others 12+2/1
Northampton T (Free on 23/3/95) FL 73+7/1 FLC 6 FAC 3 Others 3+2

OSTENSTAD Egil
Born: Haugesvad, Norway, 2 January 1972
Height: 6'0" Weight: 12.6
International Honours: Norway: 4
Signed last October from Viking Stavanger, the Norwegian side, as a ready-made replacement for Neil Shipperley, the outgoing centre forward, his form for Southampton was such that he was voted Player of the Year, having proved immensely popular with the fans. Very fast and mobile, and often acting as the lone striker, he scored 14 goals as well as creating chances for others by his purposeful running, both on and off the ball. Obviously, with the Saints' Premiership place ultimately saved, some of his strikes proved crucial, none more so than his 14th of the season at Sunderland, a goal which virtually relegated the home team, while, at the same time, preserving Saints' future among the top flight. Another memorable day for him came against Manchester United at the Dell in October, when Saints upset the formbook by winning 6-3, Egil scoring a hat trick in a magnificent day out. All in all, an excellent campaign for the Norwegian international.

Southampton (£800,000 from Viking Stavanger on 3/10/96) PL 29+1/10 FLC 6/3 FAC 1/1

OSTER John Morgan
Born: Boston, 8 December 1978
Height: 5'9" Weight: 10.8
International Honours: W: U21-4; Yth

From a Wales U18 debut to being named in the full international squad inside ten months is the unlikely story of this young left-sided Grimsby midfielder in 1996-97. Not only that, his U21 debut came before his initial appearance at league level. With speed, ball control, and the ability to deliver telling balls into the box, John shows footballing maturity far beyond his years and is predicted to be the best yet produced through the club's youth scheme. His excellence has certainly been noticed, leading to widespread interest at Premier League level, Kenny Dalglish and Terry McDermott being amongst several faces espied at Blundell Park.

Grimsby T (From trainee on 11/7/96) FL 21+3/3 FAC 0+1/1

John Oster

O'SULLIVAN Wayne St John
Born: Akrotiri, Cyprus, 25 February 1974
Height: 5'10" Weight: 11.2
Club Honours: Div 2 '96
International Honours: Ei: U21-2
After seemingly establishing himself as a first-team player in Swindon's 1995-96 division two championship team, Wayne must have been disappointed to find his place usurped by the newcomer, Scott Leitch, at the beginning of the past campaign. Nevertheless, he always remained at least on the fringe of the team and was a useful squad player to have on call to deputise for any injured or suspended midfield players, his first appearances of the season being at left back when replacing the injured Jason Drysdale before the arrival of Gary Elkins. Normally a defensive midfielder, his only goal of the campaign was a header at Loftus Road in a Coca-Cola Cup second leg tie,

where the Robins surprisingly overturned a 2-1 deficit from the home leg to record a 3-1 victory and qualification for a third round tie at Old Trafford. Is an attacking player who has a habit of checking back when on the left flank in order to cross dangerous inwingers.

Swindon T (From trainee on 1/5/93) FL 65+24/3 FLC 11/1 FAC 1+3 Others 3+2

O'TOOLE Gavin Francis
Born: Dublin, 19 September 1975
Height: 5'9" Weight: 11.0
International Honours: Ei: U21-2; Yth; Sch
Unable to get a first-team game at Coventry in 1996-97, the young Irishman was loaned out to Hereford in November, playing just once on the wide right in a 2-0 defeat at Cardiff before returning to Highfield Road. Recognised at Coventry as an excellent passer with great vision, although the terrier-like midfielder gave 100 per-cent effort, the game was too frenetic for him to be judged fairly. Had earlier been capped at U21 level for the Republic of Ireland.

Coventry C (From trainee on 5/7/93)
Hereford U (Loaned on 21/11/96) FL 1

OTTO Ricky
Born: Hackney, 9 November 1967
Height: 5'10" Weight: 11.10
Club Honours: Div 2 '95; AMC '95
An extremely fast Birmingham left winger with tremendous skill, Ricky has yet to show what he is capable of at St Andrews, making just one start last season as an experimental centre forward, and was allowed to go out on loan to Charlton (September) and Peterborough (February). A popular signing for Athletic, he immediately made his debut in the televised game at Ipswich and made nine appearances before returning after two months due to there being a surplus of wingers on their books at the time. At Peterborough it was six goals in 17 games as he mesmerised second division defences and, while it was reported that Barry Fry had splashed out £800,000 to make him his record signing for Posh, according to Football League records, he is still with Brum.

Leyton Orient (Free from Haringey Borough on 7/11/90) FL 41+15/13 FLC 3 FAC 2+1 Others 5+1/2
Southend U (£100,000 on 9/7/93) FL 63+1/17 FLC 3 FAC 1 Others 8/2
Birmingham C (£800,000 on 19/12/94) FL 25+21/6 FLC 3+3 FAC 2/1 Others 8/1
Charlton Ath (Loaned on 19/9/96) FL 5+2 FLC 2
Peterborough U (Loaned on 6/2/97) FL 15/4 Others 2/2

OTTOSSON Ulf Peter
Born: Sweden, 2 July 1968
Height: 5'10" Weight: 11.10
With Degefors from the age of seven he moved in the mid 1990s to Grupo Desportivo de Chaves and then Norrkoping. Although already 28, but with a pedigree of scoring goals, including some in the European Cup Winners Cup, Ulf signed for Norwich last January on a temporary basis and, following an enshrouded game, the local paper remarked "out of the fog the Ulf

man came as Red Hottosson and scored twice on his Canary debut in a reserve match". This encouraging all-action display augered well for the future, but his loan period was terminated after two months, his only goal being a memorable on-the-run blast into the roof of the net at Sheffield United.

Norwich C (Loaned from Norrkoping on 13/1/97) FL 4+3/1 FAC 0+1

OVERSON Vincent (Vince) David
Born: Kettering, 15 May 1962
Height: 6'2" Weight: 15.0
Club Honours: Div 3 '82, Div 2 '93; AMC '91, '92

Signed from Stoke last August, although he performed well in his familiar hard-man defensive role when available, Vince had a disappointing season at Burnley, spending most of it sidelined through various injuries. A strong and uncompromising central defender, with great aerial strength, he may have a chance at Turf Moor if he is able to recover his fitness.
Burnley (From apprentice on 16/11/79) FL 207+4/6 FLC 9/1 FAC 19 Others 10
Birmingham C (Free on 11/6/86) FL 179+3/3 FLC 11+1 FAC 8 Others 11/1
Stoke C (£55,000 on 29/8/91) FL 167+3/6 FLC 13/1 FAC 10 Others 23
Burnley (Free on 15/8/96) FL 6+2 FLC 1 Others 1

OWEN Gareth
Born: Chester, 21 October 1971
Height: 5'8" Weight: 12.0
Club Honours: WC '95
International Honours: W: B-1; U21-8
Wrexham's Gareth continued to frustrate the critics who felt that he had the ability to have far more influence on proceedings at the Racecourse in 1996-97. Unfortunately, injuries again hampered him, but an in-form Gareth Owen always appeared to enhance Wrexham's performances from his central midfield role. Has a cracking shot when unleashed, and with his long-passing game and strong foraging a feature of his play, he is always more comfortable in an attacking role.
Wrexham (From trainee on 6/7/90) FL 174+40/21 FLC 7+1 FAC 16+5 Others 29+1

OWEN Michael James
Born: Chester, 14 December 1979
Height: 5'9" Weight: 10.4
Club Honours: FAYC '96
International Honours: E: Yth; Sch

An outstanding young Liverpool striker and reckoned to be very much in the mould of a young Robbie Fowler, Michael started last season as an associated schoolboy before signing professional forms at the end of last year. Making excellent progress, he was given a first-team debut when coming off the bench at Wimbledon in the 57th minute and scoring in 74th, when slotting the ball in from just inside the area. With pace and a desire to get into shooting positions, he started the game at Sheffield Wednesday, thus finishing the season on a high.
Liverpool (From juniors on 18/12/96) PL 1+1/1

OWERS Gary
Born: Newcastle, 3 October 1968
Height: 5'11" Weight: 12.7
Club Honours: Div 3 '88
1996-97 was a great season for Bristol City's midfielder and captain, who was an ever present in the side that fought its way into the play offs, only to lose to Brentford at the semi-final stage. Scored many crucial goals and was back at his best as the zest and invention that had been so apparent when he first arrived at Ashton Gate returned after his disappointing form of 1995-96.
Sunderland (From apprentice on 8/10/86) FL 259+9/25 FLC 25+1/1 FAC 10+2 Others 11+1/1
Bristol C (£250,000 on 23/12/94) FL 101+3/8 FLC 5/1 FAC 9 Others 7/2

Michael Owen

P

PAATELAINEN Mika (Mixu) Matti
Born: Helsinki, Finland, 3 February 1967
Height: 6'0" Weight: 13.11
International Honours: Finland: 51

The Finnish international striker missed the majority of last season through injury, although he returned to the Bolton subs' bench for the majority of the first dozen games, scoring in the 2-1 win over Manchester City in April which confirmed Bolton as first division champions. Unfortunately, "The Moose", a typical strong centre forward who provides some experienced cover for Bolton's regular front-line pairing of Nathan Blake and John McGinlay, failed to play in the requisite number of league games that would have brought him a first division championship medal, but that will not stop him looking forward to Premiership football in 1997-98.
Dundee U (Signed from Valkeakosken in October 1987) SL 101+32/33 SLC 7+2/5 SC 20+1/8 Others 8+1/1
Aberdeen (Signed on 31/3/92) SL 53+22/23 SLC 6/3 SC 7+1/1 Others 3/1
Bolton W (£300,000 on 29/7/94) P/FL 58+11/15 FLC 8+1/2 FAC 1+1 Others 3/1

PACK Leonard (Lenny) John
Born: Salisbury, 27 September 1976
Height: 5'10" Weight: 12.9

Unable to break into the Cambridge team early last season, although he made a few appearances as substitute, the young midfielder had a spell on loan at Baldock. Unfortunately, back at the Abbey, a groin injury saw him miss most of what was left of the campaign, although he did play for the reserves before being released during the summer.
Cambridge U (From trainee on 20/7/95) FL 5+10 FLC 1+1 Others 1

PAGE Robert John
Born: Llwynpia, 3 September 1974
Height: 6'0" Weight: 12.5
International Honours: W: 3; U21-6; Yth; Sch

The Watford central defender was appointed club captain at the start of last season at the age of only 21. Dominating in the air, and a strong tackler, Robert led by example and gained a personal reward when winning his first full Welsh cap, making an outstanding debut versus Turkey, before going on to play against Belgium and Scotland. Also scored his first goal for the club, the opener in a 2-1 home win against Torquay in the AWS.
Watford (From trainee on 19/4/93) FL 59+5 FLC 4 FAC 5+1 Others 3/1

PAINTER Peter **Robert (Robbie)**
Born: Wigan, 26 January 1971
Height: 5'11" Weight: 12.2

A big hit when on loan from Darlington last October, he netted four times in five games and formed a fruitful partnership with Steve Whitehall, after Rochdale had struggled to find the net in early season games. However, following his permanent transfer, the goals dried up, though, and he spent a while relegated to the bench. Is a hard working player who will always follow up.
Chester C (From trainee on 1/7/88) FL 58+26/8 FLC 2+2 FAC 7+1/3 Others 3+3
Maidstone U (£30,000 on 16/8/91) FL 27+3/5 FLC 2 FAC 1+1 Others 0+2
Burnley (£25,000 on 27/3/92) FL 16+10/2 FLC 2 FAC 1
Darlington (Signed on 16/9/93) FL 104+11/28 FLC 2+4/1 FAC 5+1/2 Others 9/3
Rochdale (Signed on 10/10/96) FL 21+6/7 FLC 2 Others 1

PALLISTER Gary Andrew
Born: Ramsgate, 30 June 1965
Height: 6'4" Weight: 14.13
Club Honours: FAC '90, '94, '96; CS '90, '93, '94, '97; ECWC '91; ESC '91; FLC '92; PL '93, '94, '96, '97
International Honours: E: 22; B-9

A superb Manchester United central defender, whose pace makes him difficult to pass, Gary started last season in fine fettle, with no early signs of the back injury problems that plagued him during the previous campaign. However, after showing up well in his first four Premiership games, he sustained a knee injury against Leeds in September, missing just one match, before aggravating his old back injury whilst playing for England against Poland in mid October. Returning in time for the important Champions' League game against Rapid Vienna, injury again ruled him out in late December. Although he missed United's short-lived FA Cup campaign, he returned to bolster the defence for the vital assault on the Premiership and European Cup and it was during this spell that he scored his only goal of the season against Southampton, before netting two at Liverpool that all but sealed United's fourth championship in five years. Another promising aspect was his solid partnership with Ronny Johnsen, which looks set to dominate like the glory days of Pallister and Steve Bruce.
Middlesbrough (Free from Billingham T on 7/11/84) FL 156/5 FLC 10 FAC 10/1 Others 13
Darlington (Loaned on 18/10/85) FL 7
Manchester U (£2,300,000 on 29/8/89) F/PL 281+3/12 FLC 36 FAC 35/1 Others 38+1/1

PALMER Carlton Lloyd
Born: Rowley Regis, 5 December 1965
Height: 6'2" Weight: 12.4
International Honours: E: 18; B-5; U21-4

Captained Leeds early last season, when he operated in both defence and a defensive midfield position, contributing greatly with his non-stop running and tackling, even if appearing somewhat unorthodox in style. However, following the arrival of the new manager, George Graham, and amid media speculation of unrest and he was dropped for the game at Tottenham in March and subsequently handed in a written transfer request. At his best an excellent team player, hopefully, all will have been resolved during the close season.
West Bromwich A (From apprentice on 21/12/84) FL 114+7/4 FLC 7+1/1 FAC 4 Others 6
Sheffield Wed (£750,000 on 23/2/89) F/PL 204+1/14 FLC 31/1 FAC 18/2 Others 8+1/1
Leeds U (£2,600,000 on 30/6/94) PL 100+2/5 FLC 12 FAC 12/1 Others 4/1

Carlton Palmer

PALMER Lee James
Born: Croydon, 19 September 1970
Height: 6'0" Weight: 13.0

Almost a regular in the left-back slot for Cambridge in 1995-96, Lee was unable to command a first-team place in 1996-97, making only one full appearance. Spent the latter months of the season on loan at Woking, and then at Dover, before being released in the summer.
Gillingham (From trainee on 28/7/89) FL 109+11/5 FLC 7+1 FAC 7+1 Others 8
Cambridge U (Free on 2/8/95) FL 30+1/1 FLC 2 FAC 1 Others 1

PALMER Stephen (Steve) Leonard
Born: Brighton, 31 March 1968
Height: 6'1" Weight: 12.13
Club Honours: Div 2 '92
International Honours: E: Sch

Defensive Watford midfield player or central defender. One of the mainstays of the side who can be relied on to do a sound job in any position, the one blot on his record in 1996-97 was his sending off at Manchester City in the FA Cup after he had done an effective man-marking job on Georgi Kinkladze. Was unfortunate to be hampered by a groin injury at the end of the season.
Ipswich T (Free from Cambridge University on 1/8/89) F/PL 87+24/2 FLC 3 FAC 8+3/1 Others 4+2
Watford (£135,000 on 28/9/95) FL 75+1/2 FLC 6 FAC 4 Others 3

PARDEW Alan Scott
Born: Wimbledon, 18 July 1961
Height: 6'0" Weight: 12.4

An important figure at Barnet under Ray Clemence in 1996-97, starting 20 of the first 22 fixtures, Alan was out of favour

following Alan Mullery's arrival and, after being switched from midfield into a sweeper role, was released at the end of the campaign. More of a provider for others than a goalscorer, he failed to find the net in his two seasons at the club.
Crystal Palace (£7,000 from Yeovil T on 17/3/87) FL 111+17/8 FLC 9+3/1 FAC 8/1 Others 20/2
Charlton Ath (Free on 21/11/91) FL 98+6/24 FLC 3+1 FAC 9+1/1 Others 6/1
Barnet (Free on 31/7/95) FL 64+3 FLC 6 FAC 2+1 Others 3

PARKER Garry Stuart
Born: Oxford, 7 September 1965
Height: 5'11" Weight: 13.2
Club Honours: FLC '89, '90, '97; ESC '89
International Honours: E: B-1; U21-6; Yth
After starting 1996-97 on the bench for Leicester, Garry ran into outstanding form as the season wore on, despite a family crisis over the premature birth of his daughter. First-choice penalty taker for City, the right-footed midfielder missed one at Scarborough in the first leg of the Coca-Cola Cup second round tie, but then scored in the 90th minute of the return game, via the spot. A player who will not be hurried, with an excellent first touch and passing game, he was outstanding at Wembley and again at Hillsborough, his free kick leading to the winning goal, and the club lifting the Coca-Cola Cup for the first time in its history. Is also a great striker of the ball.
Luton T (From apprentice on 5/5/83) FL 31+11/3 FLC 1+3/1 FAC 6+2
Hull C (£72,000 on 21/2/86) FL 82+2/8 FLC 5 FAC 4 Others 2/1
Nottingham F (£260,000 on 24/3/88) FL 99+4/17 FLC 22+1/4 FAC 16/5 Others 9/3
Aston Villa (£650,000 on 29/11/91) F/PL 91+4/13 FLC 12 FAC 10/1 Others 0+2
Leicester C (£300,000 on 10/2/95) P/FL 72+13/7 FLC 13/1 FAC 7/1 Others 2+1/2

PARKER Paul Andrew
Born: West Ham, 4 April 1964
Height: 5'7" Weight: 11.11
Club Honours: FLC '92; PL '93, '94; CS '93; FAC '94
International Honours: E: 19; B-3; U21-8; Yth
Following a catastrophic catalogue of injuries to centre backs last March, that left Chelsea desperately short of experienced defensive cover, the dilemma was resolved by signing free-agent Paul Parker on a short-term contract until the end of the season. Released by Manchester United the previous summer, Paul, who had spent time at Derby, Sheffield United and Fulham, made his first appearance as a substitute in the televised encounter with Sunderland after Andy Myers was injured. His arrival steadied a side who were in danger of throwing away a three-goal lead, before eventually running out comfortable 6-2 winners. An adaptable defender, who can play either at right back or in central defence, he is cool under pressure and confident on the ball, which fits in perfectly with Ruud Gullit's philosophy of bringing the ball out of defence intelligently, rather than launching long passes for forwards to chase.

Fulham (From apprentice on 15/4/82) FL 140+13/2 FLC 16/1 FAC 11 Others 2
Queens Park R (£300,000 on 18/6/87) FL 121+4/1 FLC 14 FAC 16 Others 5
Manchester U (£2,000,000 on 8/8/91) F/PL 100+5/1 FLC 15 FAC 14+1/1 Others 8+3
Derby Co (Free on 14/8/96) PL 4 FLC 2
Sheffield U (Free on 8/11/96) FL 7+3
Fulham (Free on 10/1/97) FL 3
Chelsea (Free on 7/3/97) PL 1+3

PARKIN Brian
Born: Birkenhead, 12 October 1965
Height: 6'3" Weight: 14.7
Club Honours: Div 3 '90
A vastly experienced goalkeeper signed on a free from Bristol Rovers in the summer of 1996, he lost his Wycombe place to John Cheesewright shortly after John Gregory arrived last October, but regained the jersey in March, only to sit out four games when Martin Taylor arrived on loan from Derby. With excellent reflexes, he pulled off many point-saving stops.
Oldham Ath (From juniors on 31/3/83) FL 6 FLC 2
Crewe Alex (Free on 30/11/84) FL 98 FLC 7 FAC 2 Others 6
Crystal Palace (Free on 1/7/88) FL 20 FLC 3 Others 2
Bristol Rov (Free on 11/11/89) FL 241 FLC 15 FAC 12 Others 23
Wycombe W (Free on 24/7/96) FL 24 FLC 4

Gary Parkinson

PARKINSON Gary Anthony
Born: Thornaby, 10 January 1968
Height: 5"11" Weight: 13.2
Gary was the surprise success of Burnley's season in 1996-97, adapting with style to his new role as a right-sided wing back. Solid in defence and often linking well with Paul Weller or Paul Smith when going forward, he had easily his best campaign since arriving at Turf Moor, despite playing out the whole of it on a week-to-week contract, his efforts being rewarded with selection for the PFA divisional side. *Stop Press:* Transferred to Preston on 30 May.
Middlesbrough (Free from Everton juniors on 17/1/86) FL 194+8/5 FLC 20/1 FAC 17/1 Others 19
Southend U (Loaned on 10/10/92) FL 6

Bolton W (Free on 2/3/93) FL 1+2 Others 4
Burnley (Signed on 27/1/94) FL 134+1/4 FLC 12 FAC 10 Others 6/1

PARKINSON Joseph (Joe) Simon
Born: Eccles, 11 June 1971
Height: 6'0" Weight: 13.0
Club Honours: FAC '95; CS '95
A powerful, tough-tackling midfielder, his ability on the ball is often overlooked, but as a vital and influential member of the Everton midfield, his was always one of the first names on Joe Royle's Everton team-sheet until, like so many of his Goodison team mates last season, succumbing to injury. After missing five matches over Christmas and undergoing surgery, a knee problem flared up again and forced him to sit out the final five matches. The possessor of a powerful shot, Joe was employed almost exclusively as a midfield anchor man and was given little opportunity to add to the three goals he scored the previous campaign.
Wigan Ath (From trainee on 1/4/89) FL 115+4/6 FLC 11/1 FAC 9 Others 8
Bournemouth (£35,000 on 1/7/93) FL 30/1 FLC 4/1 FAC 4 Others 1
Everton (£250,000 on 24/3/94) PL 88+2/3 FLC 5 FAC 9/1 Others 3

PARKINSON Philip (Phil) John
Born: Chorley, 1 December 1967
Height: 6'0" Weight: 11.12
Club Honours: Div 2 '94
Although his 1996-97 season was interrupted several times by injury, including a dislocated shoulder sustained against Swindon, Phil showed that he had lost none of the spirit and determination that made him such an important element of Reading's midfield. His consistency in winning the ball was vital to the team's progress and he was one of six players to captain the side. He also coaches at the club's school of excellence.
Southampton (From apprentice on 7/12/85)
Bury (£12,000 on 8/3/88) FL 133+12/5 FLC 6+1 FAC 4/1 Others 13/1
Reading (£37,500 on 10/7/92) FL 156+22/8 FLC 15+1/1 FAC 8/1 Others 4+2

PARLOUR Raymond (Ray)
Born: Romford, 7 March 1973
Height: 5'10" Weight: 11.12
Club Honours: FLC '93
International Honours: E: U21-12
An invaluable Arsenal squad player, who plays in the engine room, or on the wide right of midfield, Ray's first-team opportunities were limited in 1996-97, making 15 of his 36 appearances from the bench. A good man to have in your team, he has an impressive range of passing skills and, despite picking up injuries, is a strong tackler who harries and chases the opposition into mistakes. Not a regular scorer, normally leaving that to others, having come off the bench in the 87th minute of the home Premiership fixture against Sunderland in September he fired in a 20-yard thunderbolt a minute later for the clincher in a 2-0 win. Always recognisable by his shock of hair.
Arsenal (From trainee on 6/3/91) F/PL 101+35/6 FLC 13+3 FAC 12/1 Others 8+3

PARMENTER Steven (Steve) James
Born: Chelmsford, 22 January 1977
Height: 5'9" Weight: 11.0

Released by QPR during the 1996 close season, Steve, a slightly built but strong left-footed forward, who is adept at holding the ball up, took the opportunities for league football with Bristol Rovers when they were presented in 1996-97. Scoring just two goals, after coming on as substitute in September against Bournemouth in an exciting 3-2 victory, followed by a consolation effort in a 2-1 home defeat by Exeter in a first round FA Cup tie, he finished the campaign with a new role as a wide player on the left, from where he could supply accurate crosses and netted a further goal at Blackpool.
Queens Park R (Free from Southend U juniors on 2/5/95)
Bristol Rov (Free on 15/7/96) FL 10+4/2 FLC 1+1 FAC 0+1/1 Others 0+1

PARRIS George Michael
Born: Ilford, 11 September 1964
Height: 5'9" Weight: 13.0
International Honours: E: Sch

As Brighton's midfield ball winner, George inherited the captaincy at the beginning of last season and was initially as enthusiastic as ever, but his form suffered as the Seagulls endured a dreadful sequence of results in the first half of the campaign and he lost his place in the side soon after the arrival of new boss, Steve Gritt. An all-action battler, with a penchant in getting forward, he was released during the summer.
West Ham U (From apprentice on 9/9/82) FL 211+28/12 FLC 27+3/1 FAC 21/4 Others 7+1/1
Birmingham C (£150,000 on 12/3/93) FL 36+3/1 FLC 2 FAC 1 (Free to Norrkoping during 1996 close season)
Brentford (Loaned on 8/8/94) FL 5 FLC 2/1
Bristol C (Loaned on 1/12/94) FL 6
Brighton & Hove A (Loaned on 9/2/95) FL 18/2
Brighton & Hove A (Free on 29/9/95) FL 55+1/3 FLC 2 FAC 6 Others 6

PARRISH Sean
Born: Wrexham, 14 March 1972
Height: 5'10" Weight: 11.0

Signed by Northampton from Doncaster immediately prior to the start of last season, the central midfielder, an all-action player with a flair for goals, was being watched by the Welsh selectors when he received a facial injury that put him out for several weeks. Unfortunately, no sooner had he returned than he received a broken nose, before coming back strongly to assist in the run for a play-off place and later scoring in the first semi-final leg.
Shrewsbury T (From trainee on 12/7/90) FL 1+2 FLC 1 Others 3 (Free to Telford during 1992 close season)
Doncaster Rov (£20,000 on 28/5/94) FL 64+2/8 FLC 3+1 FAC 2/1 Others 3
Northampton T (£35,000 + on 2/8/96) FL 37+2/8 FLC 3 FAC 1 Others 3/1

PARTRIDGE Scott Malcolm
Born: Leicester, 13 October 1974
Height: 5'9" Weight: 11.2

Unable to get the opportunities at Bristol City in 1996-97 that many thought his

talents deserved, the classy midfielder transferred to Cardiff in February to play in the remaining league programme. At Ninian Park, however, Scott was certainly a welcome addition to the squad, his probing runs down the left, and incisive passing, paving the way for a successful climax that ended in the play offs. Is the son of Malcolm, a former Grimsby star.
Bradford C (From trainee on 10/7/92) FL 0+5 FLC 1+1
Bristol C (Free on 18/2/94) FL 24+33/7 FLC 2+3/1 FAC 1+3
Torquay U (Loaned on 13/10/95) FL 5/2
Plymouth Arg (Loaned on 22/1/96) FL 6+1/2
Scarborough (Loaned on 8/3/96) FL 5+2
Cardiff C (£50,000 on 14/2/97) FL 14+1

PATERSON Jamie Ryan
Born: Dumfries, 26 April 1973
Height: 5'5" Weight: 10.6

A Scunthorpe wing forward who is small and lively and can operate on either flank, Jamie likes to run at opponents, his ball control and speed taking him into crossing positions. Unable to retain a regular place in the side last season, he looks to get back to his best in 1997-98.
Halifax T (From trainee on 5/7/91) FL 34+10/5 FLC 0+1 FAC 1 Others 3
Falkirk (Signed on 11/12/94) SL 1+3
Scunthorpe U (£18,000 on 12/10/95) FL 34+21/2 FAC 4+1/1 Others 3

PATERSON Scott
Born: Aberdeen, 13 May 1972
Height: 6'2" Weight: 12.10

This composed and skilful central defender had the benefit of a lengthy run in the Bristol City side at the end of last season, taking over when Shaun Taylor was injured and did well in minimising the loss of such an inspirational player. His ability both on the ground and in the air, together with his overall air of assurance, suggest that he should have a long and successful career in the game.
Liverpool (£15,000 from Cove R on 19/3/92)
Bristol C (Free on 4/7/94) FL 33+7/1 FLC 3 FAC 2 Others 3

PATTERSON Darren James
Born: Belfast, 15 October 1969
Height: 6'2" Weight: 12.10
International Honours: NI: 10; B-2; U21-1; Yth

Equally at home at centre back or right back, the strong-tackling Darren was unable to dislodge Julian James, Steve Davis or Marvin Johnson from their regular berths in the Luton defence and had to settle for a squad place throughout last season. A mid-term injury and a one match suspension for accumulating 21 disciplinary points did not help his cause, but he did enough on his first team chances to impress the Northern Ireland selectors, who picked him for both their "B" and full international squads. Loaned to Preston in October as defensive cover, he appeared just twice before returning to Kenilworth Road.
West Bromwich A (From trainee on 5/7/88)
Wigan Ath (Free on 17/4/89) FL 69+28/6 FLC 7+1/3 FAC 5+4/1 Others 7

Crystal Palace (£225,000 on 1/7/92) PL 22/1 FLC 4 FAC 6
Luton T (£100,000 on 21/8/95) FL 29+4 FLC 0+1 FAC 2 Others 6
Preston NE (Loaned on 4/10/96) FL 2

PATTERSON Gary
Born: Newcastle, 27 November 1972
Height: 6'1" Weight: 12.5
Club Honours: Div 3 '94

A strong Wycombe central midfielder who likes to push forward, he started the first five games last season, but thereafter found it difficult to establish himself and was loaned out to first Barnet and then Chesterfield in 1997. Played just four times for the former, but stayed with the Spireites until returning to Adams Park at the end of April, spending most of his time on the sidelines until an injury to Tom Curtis presented him with a chance of a place in the engine room. A good tackler who can mix his passes, Gary was released during the summer by Wanderers.
Notts Co (From trainee on 17/7/91)
Shrewsbury T (Free on 2/7/93) FL 52+5/2 FLC 5 FAC 4 Others 3
Wycombe W (£70,000 on 9/12/94) FL 46+13/2 FLC 4 FAC 4+1/1 Others 0+1
Barnet (Loaned on 6/1/97) FL 3 Others 1
Chesterfield (Loaned on 7/2/97) FL 7+2

PATTERSON Mark
Born: Leeds, 13 September 1968
Height: 5'10" Weight: 12.4

Probably the most talented footballer in the Plymouth squad, Mark was a huge loss when he broke his leg in a pre-season friendly against Chelsea. One of the best attacking full backs outside the first division, he returned to the team for the last two months of the 1996-97 campaign, having to be content with a central defensive berth due to the excellent form of stand-in Chris Billy. A tenacious player, the defensive side of his game is enhanced by his tackling and ability to control the ball in tight situations.
Carlisle U (From trainee on 30/8/86) FL 19+3 FLC 4 Others 1
Derby Co (£60,000 on 10/11/87) FL 41+10/3 FLC 5+2 FAC 4 Others 5+1/2
Plymouth Arg (£85,000 on 23/7/93) FL 131+3/3 FLC 3 FAC 8 Others 9

PATTERSON Mark Andrew
Born: Darwen, 24 May 1965
Height: 5'6" Weight: 11.4
Club Honours: FMC '87

A tough-tackling ball winner, Mark produced some gritty performances in Sheffield United's central midfield in 1996-97, though he performed less well when asked to play wide on the left. Never less than 100 per cent committed, however, he took over the captaincy when it was relinquished by Alan Kelly, but, following the signing of Nick Henry, his first-team prospects were reduced and he joined Southend on loan on transfer deadline day, playing four times before returning to Bramall Lane.
Blackburn Rov (From apprentice on 1/5/83) FL 89+12/20 FLC 4/1 FAC 3+1 Others 2+4/1

Preston NE (£20,000 on 15/6/88) FL 54+1/19 FLC 4+1 FAC 4 Others 7/2
Bury (Signed on 1/2/90) FL 42/10 FLC 2 FAC 1 Others 4
Bolton W (£65,000 on 10/1/91) P/FL 158+11/11 FLC 16+4/2 FAC 17/1 Others 9
Sheffield U (£300,000 on 22/12/95) FL 55+1/3 FLC 4 FAC 3
Southend U (Loaned on 27/3/97) FL 4

PATTIMORE Michael Richard
Born: Newport, 15 March 1979
Height: 5'8" Weight: 10.13
International Honours: W: Yth
A trainee defender or sweeper for Swindon Town, and also a Welsh youth international, Michael made his Football League debut as a substitute last March against Stoke City, coming on in the closing minute. Was expected to sign a professional contract for the Robins during the summer.
Swindon T (Trainee) FL 0+1

Derek Payne

PAYNE Derek Richard
Born: Edgware, 26 April 1967
Height: 5'6" Weight: 10.8
Released by Watford during the summer of 1996, Derek moved to Peterborough and made his debut four games into 1996-97. From then on, injuries apart, he was a regular in Posh's midfield, his aggressive, tireless, and hard-working performances bringing him the accolade of the club's Player of the Year at the end of a tough campaign. Small in stature but big in heart sums this player up precisely.
Barnet (£12,000 from Hayes on 1/12/88) FL 50+1/6 FLC 2 FAC 2 Others 3+1
Southend U (Free on 15/7/93) FL 32+3 FLC 2 FAC 1 Others 8/1
Watford (Signed on 21/7/94) FL 33+3/1 FLC 3 FAC 0+1 Others 2
Peterborough U (Free on 8/8/96) FL 36/2 FLC 3 FAC 6 Others 5

PAYTON Andrew (Andy) Paul
Born: Whalley, 23 October 1967
Height: 5'8" Weight: 11.13
Surprisingly allowed to leave Barnsley during the 1996 close season, Andy quickly

set about doing what he does best, scoring goals, this time for Huddersfield. Always looking for an opening, he was the club's top scorer in 1996-97, despite, due to injuries, finding himself having to form an understanding with a number of different strike partners, his 19 goals tally included four doubles against Ipswich, Grimsby, Norwich and Oldham.
Hull C (From apprentice on 29/7/85) FL 116+28/55 FLC 9+2/1 FAC 8 Others 3/1
Middlesbrough (£750,000 on 22/11/91) FL 8+11/3 FAC 1+3
Glasgow Celtic (Signed on 14/8/92) SL 20+16/15 SLC 3+2/5 SC 1+1 Others 3
Barnsley (Signed on 25/11/93) FL 100+8/41 FLC 7/3 FAC 6+1/1
Huddersfield T (£350,000 on 4/7/96) FL 38/17 FLC 5/2 FAC 2

Darren Peacock

PEACOCK Darren
Born: Bristol, 3 February 1968
Height: 6'2" Weight: 12.12
Club Honours: WC '90
Very noticeable because of the pony tail he sports, Darren had another very sound season at the heart of Newcastle's defence in 1996-97, employing skills rather than muscle to dispossess his opponents, and then using the ball intelligently to set his side on the attack. His sharp positional sense also enabled him to make a number of important goal-line clearances. Although selected for the Charity Shield match he began the league campaign on the bench, before being recalled after three games to combat the aerial threat of Sunderland's Niall Quinn. Thereafter, his wholehearted and consistent performances made him a permanent fixture in the side and stimulated speculation that he might exploit a parental qualification to play international football for Wales. However, goals were something of a rarity for him, but he did head the crucial opener in the glorious 5-0 win over Manchester United.
Newport Co (From apprentice on 11/2/86) FL 24+4 FLC 2 FAC 1 Others 1+1
Hereford U (Free on 23/3/89) FL 56+3/4 FLC 6 FAC 6/1 Others 6

Queens Park R (£200,000 on 22/12/90) F/PL 123+3/6 FLC 12/1 FAC 3 Others 2
Newcastle U (£2,700,000 on 24/3/94) PL 112+1/2 FLC 11/2 FAC 10 Others 13

PEACOCK Gavin Keith
Born: Eltham, 18 November 1967
Height: 5'8" Weight: 11.8
Club Honours: Div 1 '93
International Honours: E: Yth; Sch
Now in his second spell with QPR, having been re-signed from Chelsea last December after spending a month on loan, he joined former Blues' team mate, John Spencer, at Loftus Road, thus renewing their double act. Not given a game in 1996-97 at Chelsea, the midfielder soon settled in at Rangers, making his debut at Reading and scoring his first goal at Oldham two weeks later. Ever present for the remainder of the campaign, scoring seven goals in 31 appearances, his great strength is in playing behind the front men, where his ability to run effortlessly and play one-twos often take him into goal-scoring positions. Born into a football family, Gavin is the son of Keith, a former Charlton star.
Queens Park R (From apprentice on 19/11/84) FL 7+10/1 FAC 0+1
Gillingham (£40,000 on 5/10/87) FL 69+1/11 FLC 4 FAC 2 Others 5/1
Bournemouth (£250,000 on 16/8/89) FL 56/8 FLC 6 FAC 2 Others 2
Newcastle U (£275,000 on 30/11/90) FL 102+3/35 FLC 6/5 FAC 6/2 Others 3/4
Chelsea (£1,250,000 on 12/8/93) PL 92+11/17 FLC 6/1 FAC 14+4/9 Others 7
Queens Park R (£1,000,000 on 22/11/96) FL 27/5 FAC 4/2

Gavin Peacock

PEACOCK Lee Anthony (Tony)
Born: Paisley, 9 October 1976
Height: 6'0" Weight: 12.8
Club Honours: AMC '97
International Honours: S: Yth
Hard-working Carlisle forward who claimed a regular first team berth in 1996-97. Powerfully built, and a strong runner who

made his presence felt in opposing penalty areas, he undoubtedly benefited from a longer spell in the first team, scoring nine league goals, including a double against Chester. Still only 20, and with a Scottish U18 cap behind him, he is another whose future in the game looks secure.

Carlisle U (From trainee on 10/3/95) FL 51+23/11 FLC 2+3 FAC 4+1/1 Others 6+4

Lee Peacock

PEACOCK Richard (Rich) John
Born: Sheffield, 29 October 1972
Height: 5'10" Weight: 11.5
The one-time Sheffield Wednesday associate schoolboy began last season as Hull City's most senior forward. Blessed with quick feet, Rich was usually found on the right wing, although often tried on the left, and even as Duane Darby's central partner. A talented practitioner, he is striving to find a more ruthless streak.

Hull C (Signed from Sheffield FC on 14/10/93) FL 105+28/17 FLC 5+1/1 FAC 6/1 Others 3+1

PEAKE Jason William
Born: Leicester, 29 September 1971
Height: 5'11" Weight: 12.10
International Honours: E: Yth; Sch
Signed during the 1996 close season from Rochdale, Jason quickly settled down as Brighton and Hove Albion's midfield play maker, being chosen as Player of the Month for October by the Evening Argus, although by his own high standards he enjoyed only a moderate campaign in a team that struggled from the word go. Admired for his energetic style and fine distribution, there was no lack of effort on his behalf, but he did not find the net until 4 March when he hit a long-range scorcher that earned the Seagulls a precious 2-1 home win over Northampton Town.

Leicester C (From trainee on 9/1/90) FL 4+4/1 Others 1+1
Hartlepool U (Loaned on 13/2/92) FL 5+1/1
Halifax T (Free on 26/8/92) FL 32+1/1 FAC 1 Others 2
Rochdale (Signed on 23/3/94) FL 91+4/6 FLC 3 FAC 5/2 Others 7/1
Brighton & Hove A (Signed on 30/7/96) FL 27+3/1 FLC 2 FAC 2 Others 1

PEARCE Dennis Anthony
Born: Wolverhampton, 10 September 1974
Height: 5'9" Weight: 11.0
The Wolves' left back made four appearances last autumn, highlighted when giving a long, diagonal pass to Steve Bull to run on to and score the only goal of the game at Manchester City. A strong tackler, but sometimes caught out of position, he was not called upon after being replaced against Barnsley in November and was released during the summer.

Aston Villa (From trainee on 7/6/93)
Wolverhampton W (Free on 3/7/95) FL 7+2 FLC 1 FAC 1

PEARCE Ian Anthony
Born: Bury St Edmunds, 7 May 1974
Height: 6'3" Weight: 14.4
Club Honours: PL '95
International Honours: E: U21-3; Yth
After a season away from the game following an operation to remove a piece of floating bone from his foot, Ian returned to the Blackburn side in 1996-97 only to find that his shins were not ready for a renewal of the game. Having made two starts in October, against Stockport (Coca-Cola Cup) and West Ham (Premiership), it was March before he recovered full fitness and, on doing so, was thrust back into the first team when the club decided to play the three-centre back game in tricky away matches. Able to play at full back, in central defence, or up front, he is both skilful on the ground and a strong header of the ball.

Chelsea (From juniors on 1/8/91) F/PL 0+4 Others 0+1
Blackburn Rov (£300,000 on 4/10/93) PL 42+15/2 FLC 4+4/1 FAC 1+2 Others 6+1

Stuart Pearce

PEARCE Stuart
Born: Hammersmith, 24 April 1962
Height: 5'10" Weight: 13.0
Club Honours: FLC '89, '90; FMC '89, '92
International Honours: E: 76; U21-1

The Nottingham Forest left back became the first manager to represent his country after being talked out of retirement to play in England's World Cup qualifiers during last season. The management part came when Stuart was asked to become Forest's player/manager, following the departure of Frank Clark in December. He showed some reluctance at first, but soon picked up the Manager of the Month award in January. Still a committed player, he missed few games, scored five times, and would rather play than manage, but soon received some help come Dave Bassett's appointment as general manager. Woe betide any player not to give his all with Stuart behind him. Sadly, the season ended with relegation after he had led them initially out of the danger zone. A free-kick specialist and heavy tackler, with determination, strength and power, he continued to stand tall.

Coventry C (£25,000 from Wealdstone on 20/10/83) FL 52/4 FAC 2
Nottingham F (£200,000 on 3/6/85) F/PL 401/63 FLC 60/10 FAC 37/9 Others 24/6

PEARCEY Jason Kevin
Born: Leamington, 23 July 1971
Height: 6'1" Weight: 13.12
Having graduated to automatic choice for Grimsby's number-one jersey in 1996-97, following the departure of Paul Crichton to join the growing band of former Mariners at the Hawthorns, he was unfortunate to experience a loss of confidence as the club's struggle against relegation continued, eventually losing his place first of all to loan signing Alan Miller, and eventually to rookie, Andy Love. A brief spell in the reserves enabled him to regain his old form and he put in some sterling performances in the fight against relegation.

Mansfield T (From trainee on 18/7/89) FL 77 FLC 5 FAC 2 Others 7
Grimsby T (£10,000 on 15/11/94) FL 45 FLC 2 FAC 1

PEARS Richard James
Born: Exeter, 16 July 1976
Height: 5'11" Weight: 12.6
Although in and out of the Exeter side in 1996-97, due to injury and inconsistency, Richard worked well, before being released during the summer. Very quick, his goal ratio is good for a player of his age and experience, despite him having few chances to shine last season.

Exeter C (From trainee on 7/7/94) FL 43+17/8 FLC 2+3 FAC 1 Others 2+1

PEARS Stephen (Steve)
Born: Brandon, 22 January 1962
Height: 6'0" Weight: 13.12
An experienced goalkeeper signed by Hartlepool from Liverpool on a three-year contract during the summer of 1996, he looked to be the answer to Keith Houchen's problems, before being sidelined by a troublesome groin strain early on. Made a brief comeback, playing against York City in an FA Cup tie when not fully fit, but then his season was effectively over, the specialists determining whether he can continue playing in 1997-98.

Manchester U (From apprentice on 25/1/79) FL 4
FLC 1
Middlesbrough (Loaned on 1/11/83) FL 12 FAC 2
Middlesbrough (£80,000 on 9/7/85) F/PL 327
FLC 32 FAC 23 Others 28
Liverpool (Free on 14/8/95)
Hartlepool U (Free on 2/8/96) FL 16 FLC 2 FAC 1

PEARSON Nigel Graham
Born: Nottingham, 21 August 1963
Height: 6'1" Weight: 14.5
Club Honours: FLC '91; Div 1 '95

Nigel was on the threshold of undying fame
in the annals of Middlesbrough Football
Club when he looked certain to lead the
team to it's first ever domestic cup glory at
Wembley in 1997. Having missed out on a
huge chunk of the club's most exciting
season ever, through an injury sustained in
the early home match against Wimbledon,
he came back to play a captains' role in
every match in which he appeared, winning
several Man of the Match awards for the
tremendous inspiration and confidence he
gave to his players from the heart of
defence, his control of the area behind the
midfield, and his distribution to his forwards
being immaculate. Having carried the heart-
breaking defeats at the hands of Leicester
and Chelsea in the league and FA Cup finals,
respectively, with great dignity, he emerged
from Boro's relegation season with his
reputation as "Captain Fantastic" intact.
Shrewsbury T (£5,000 from Heanor T on
12/11/81) FL 153/5 FLC 19 FAC 6 Others 3
Sheffield Wed (£250,000 on 16/10/87) F/PL
176+4/14 FLC 17+2/5 FAC 15/1 Others 10
Middlesbrough (£500,000 on 19/7/94) P/FL
86+1//3 FLC 10 FAC 8

Per Pedersen

PEDERSEN Per Werner
Born: Aalberg, Denmark, 30 March 1969
Height: 6'1" Weight: 13.0
International Honours: Denmark: 8

Purchased from Odense last February, the
Danish international striker became
Blackburn's first signing following the sale
of Alan Shearer seven months earlier, and
found it difficult to adjust to the English

game, being confined to the bench unless
Chris Sutton was absent. Although exhibiting a fair turn of pace, composure and the
ability to combine in moves, apart from a
close-range effort at Chelsea, he showed
little evidence of being an out-and-out
goalscorer and the fact that circumstances
never permitted him to be played alongside
Sutton simply suggest that he came as an
alternative to the latter, who suffered with a
multitude of problems throughout the
campaign. Will be looking for better
opportunities under the new manager, Roy
Hodgson.
Blackburn Rov (£2,500,000 from Odense on
22/2/97) PL 6+5/1

PEER Dean
Born: Stourbridge, 8 August 1969
Height: 6'2" Weight: 12.4
Club Honours: AMC '91

Although the Northampton central midfield
player's first team opportunities were
limited last season, each time he was called
on he always gave his best. Made his
reputation on tremendous stamina and
workrate.
Birmingham C (From trainee on 9/7/87) FL
106+14/8 FLC 14+1/3 FAC 2+1 Others 11+1/1
Mansfield T (Loaned on 18/12/92) FL 10 Others 1
Walsall (Free on 16/11/93) FL 41+4/8 FLC 2 FAC
4+2 Others 3
Northampton T (Free on 22/8/95) FL 44+19/2
FLC 3+2/1 FAC 2 Others 5+4

PEHRSSON Magnus Karl
Born: Malmo, Sweden, 25 May 1976
Height: 6'2" Weight: 13.6
International Honours: Sweden: U21

Signed on loan from the Swedish club,
Djurgaardens, at the end of last October, the
tall midfielder came straight into the fray for
Bradford on the left, replacing the
indisposed Marco Sas in a 3-0 home defeat
at the hands of Oldham. Obviously a useful
player, despite being unable to acclimatise
quickly enough, he was recalled to
Stockholm on 30 November and that was it
as far as City were concerned.
Bradford C (Loaned from Djurgaardens on
31/10/96) FL 1

PELL Robert Anthony
Born: Leeds, 5 February 1979
Height: 6'1" Weight:13.1

Starting last season as a striker in the
Rotherham junior side, the young second-
year trainee was moved to the centre of
defence with such effect that he was called
into the first team in April, making his debut
at Wrexham, and following it up with
another promising performance in the home
game against Brentford. Strong in the tackle,
and good in the air, Robert seems to have
found himself, while his ability to deliver
long throws is an additional asset.
Rotherham U (Trainee) FL 2

PEMBERTON Martin Calvin
Born: Bradford, 1 February 1976
Height: 5'11" Weight: 12.6

A hard-working central attacker, Martin
joined Doncaster from Oldham last March,

following a spell on loan with Irish
Leaguers' Ards, after disappointingly
making just four subs' appearances for the
Latics in 1996-97, having earlier impressed
with his deft touches and ability to take on
opponents. Coming into another struggling
side for nine of the final ten games of the
campaign, he scored his one and only goal
in the 3-0 win at Darlington. However, with
a bit of luck he could have scored a hat trick
against Hereford and promises to be up the
charts in 1997-98.
Oldham Ath (From trainee on 22/7/94) FL 0+5
FLC 0+1 Others 0+1
Doncaster Rov (Free on 21/3/97) FL 9/1

PEMBRIDGE Mark Anthony
Born: Merthyr Tydfil, 29 November 1970
Height: 5'8" Weight: 11.12
International Honours: W: 23; B-2; U21-1;
Sch

After starting 1996-97 receiving some
criticism from some sections of the
Sheffield Wednesday fans, Mark soon won
them over in becoming a vital cog in both
the Owls and Wales' midfield, missing just
five games all season, four of them early on.
A very consistent left-sided player, he not
only added strength and power to the side,
but weighed in with seven goals, five of
them coming in four successive games.
Recognised for his left-footed shooting
ability, two long-range efforts certainly
stood out – a volley from fully 30 yards out
that screamed into the net at Chelsea and a
20-yard plus free kick in the home game
against Everton that well beat Neville
Southall.
Luton T (From trainee on 1/7/89) FL 60/6 FLC 2
FAC 4 Others 4
Derby Co (£1,250,000 on 2/6/92) FL 108+2/28
FLC 9/1 FAC 6/3 Others 15/5
Sheffield Wed (£900,000 on 19/7/95) PL 57+2/8
FLC 4/1 FAC 4/1

PENDER John Patrick
Born: Luton, 19 November 1963
Height: 6'0" Weight: 13.12
Club Honours: Div 4 '92, Div 3 '97
International Honours: Ei: U21-5; Yth

John, an outstanding Wigan Athletic central
defender, had the misfortune to suffer a
severe knee injury last January, although it
did not stop him coming back into the side
at the end of a long, hard season to pick up
a third division championship medal, a just
reward for 27 league starts. Again forming a
solid partnership with Colin Greenall, the
well-travelled and experienced campaigner,
has now achieved promotion six times and
his career has not have finished yet.
Wolverhampton W (From apprentice on 8/11/81)
FL 115+2/3 FLC 5 FAC 7/1
Charlton Ath (£35,000 on 23/7/85) FL 41 FLC 1
FAC 1 Others 2/1
Bristol C (£50,000 on 30/10/87) FL 83/3 FLC 11
FAC 8 Others 12
Burnley (£70,000 on 18/10/90) FL 171/8 FLC
11/1 FAC 17/1 Others 21/1
Wigan Ath (£30,000 on 22/8/95) FL 67+3/1 FLC
2 FAC 5 Others 4

PENNEY David Mark
Born: Wakefield, 17 August 1964
Height: 5'10" Weight: 12.0
Club Honours: WC '91

Appointed Swansea captain following the transfer of Shaun Garnett to Oldham last September, the strong, hard-working midfielder again proved to be an excellent professional when giving 100 per-cent commitment throughout the campaign. Always dangerous with his surging runs from deep positions and long-range shooting capability, he even ended 1996-97 as the club's top scorer with 13 league goals, six of them coming from the penalty spot.
Derby Co (£1,500 from Pontefract Collieries on 26/9/85) FL 6+13 FLC 2+3/1 FAC 1/1 Others 1+3/1
Oxford U (£175,000 on 23/6/89) FL 76+34/15 FLC 10+1 FAC 2+2/1 Others 3+1
Swansea C (Loaned on 28/3/91) FL 12/3
Swansea C (£20,000 on 24/3/94) FL 112+7/20 FLC 5+1/2 FAC 7/1 Others 14

PENNOCK Adrian Barry
Born: Ipswich, 27 March 1971
Height: 6'1" Weight: 13.5
Signed from Bournemouth last October, his Gillingham career looked in tatters after a serious injury, but Tony Pulis had faith in him and he continued to improve with every game he played. Surprisingly made his debut at Ipswich (his home town) in the fourth round of the Coca-Cola Cup in November, after injuries to Matt Bryant and Glen Thomas and retained his place. Can play in either central midfield or in central defence, where he is calm and collected.
Norwich C (From trainee on 4/7/89) FL 1
Bournemouth (£30,000 on 14/8/92) FL 130+1/9 FLC 9 FAC 12/1 Others 8
Gillingham (£30,000 on 4/10/96) FL 26/2 FLC 1 FAC 2 Others 1

PENRICE Gary Kenneth
Born: Bristol, 23 March 1964
Height: 5'7" Weight: 10.6
Classy Watford midfield player or striker. With good close control, and an excellent passer of the ball who is adept at setting up chances for others, Gary was unluckily prone to injuries in 1996-97, which prevented him from making more than sporadic appearances. Despite coming back for the last three games, he was released during the summer.
Bristol Rov (Free from Mangotsfield on 6/11/84) FL 186+2/54 FLC 11/3 FAC 11/7 Others 13+2/2
Watford (£500,000 on 14/11/89) FL 41+2/18 FAC 4/1 Others 1/1
Aston Villa (£1,000,000 on 8/3/91) FL 14+6/1
Queens Park R (£625,000 on 29/10/91) F/PL 55+27/20 FLC 5+2/2 FAC 2+2/1 Others 1
Watford (£300,000 on 15/11/95) FL 26+13/2 FLC 2+1 FAC 1 Others 1+1

PEPPER Colin Nigel
Born: Rotherham, 25 April 1968
Height: 5'10" Weight: 12.4
After having hit his best ever seasonal goals' tally of 14 for York in 1996-97, the tough-tackling, hard-running midfielder transferred to Bradford in February, making his debut at home to Manchester City. He then missed two games due to suspension, but returned to open his scoring account in a 2-1 home win over Wolverhampton and followed that up with winners against Stoke and Charlton, both 1-0 home victories,

before getting City out of gaol with two goals in a 3-0 home win over QPR on the final day of the campaign. A real bargain, Nigel sets up as many goals for others as he scores himself with unselfish play, yet another trademark of his game.
Rotherham U (From apprentice on 26/4/86) FL 35+10/1 FLC 1/1 FAC 1+1 Others 3+3
York C (Free on 18/7/90) FL 223+12/39 FLC 16+2/3 FAC 12/1 Others 15+1
Bradford C (£100,000 on 28/2/97) FL 11/5

PEREZ Lionel
Born: Bagnols Coze, France, 24 April 1967
Height: 5'11" Weight: 13.4
The French goalkeeper who joined Sunderland from Bordeaux last August was initially seen as cover for Tony Coton, but was thrust into the spotlight following the former's serious injury in October. Lionel took his opportunity with both hands and ended the season as the club's Player of the Year thanks to some thrilling displays, particularly away at Everton when his penalty save set up a 3-1 win. Despite his heroics, the Rokerites were unable to hang on to their Premiership status but, hopefully, he will play his part in a successful return to the top flight next term.
Sunderland (£200,000 from Bordeaux on 21/8/96) PL 28+1 FLC 1 FAC 2

PERKINS Christopher (Chris) Peter
Born: Nottingham, 9 January 1974
Height: 5'11" Weight: 11.0
Chris developed well in 1996-97, following a change in role at Chesterfield that saw him pushed up from his normal defensive duties to take up more attacking positions, on either the right or left-hand sides. The change clearly made him more of an asset and, although his development may have been overshadowed by the great strides made by the likes of Jon Howard, he continued to work hard to improve.
Mansfield T (From trainee on 19/11/92) FL 3+5 Others 0+1
Chesterfield (Free on 15/7/94) FL 61+9 FLC 2+1/1 FAC 10 Others 7+3

PERKINS Steven (Steve) William
Born: St Helens, 25 April 1975
Height: 6'2" Weight: 14.0
A young lad signed from local league side, Crediton United, Steve made his full debut in front of 15,000 in the penultimate game of last season at Bristol City at the heart of Plymouth Argyle's defence. Has two good feet and looks to have a big future in the game.
Plymouth Arg (Free from Crediton U on 24/2/97) FL 1+3

PERRETT Russell
Born: Barton on Sea, 18 June 1973
Height: 6'3" Weight: 13.2
For a player who had been discarded by Portsmouth back in 1991 when still a youngster, it must have given Russell a warm feeling inside when making the transition from Pompey's reserves to the first team in 1996-97, following the departure of Guy Butters in October. The ball-playing central defender was not going

to let the opportunity slip this time round and once in the side on a regular basis, and forming a solid partnership with Andy Awford, his all-round performances came on in leaps and bounds. Also scored his first goal for the club at Tranmere in October.
Portsmouth (Signed from Lymington on 30/9/95) FL 39+2/1 FLC 2 FAC 4

PERRY Christopher (Chris) John
Born: Carshalton, 26 April 1973
Height: 5'8" Weight: 11.1
This reliable Wimbledon centre half is very popular with the Selhurst Park faithful who believe, like many people, that he will one day be a top-quality England international. Full of pace and perception in 1996-97, Chris was like a rock at the back, and with well-timed tackles and great heading ability he frustrated some of the Premier's best strike forces. And, as the scorer of a priceless equaliser at Gresty Road that gave the Dons a replay in the FA Cup game against Crewe Alexandra, it was a more than satisfactory campaign for the player who supported the club as a child.
Wimbledon (From trainee on 2/7/91) PL 89+9/1 FLC 11 FAC 17/1

PERRY Jason
Born: Newport, 2 April 1970
Height: 5'11" Weight: 10.10
Club Honours: WC '92, '93; Div 3 '93
International Honours: W: 1; B-2; U21-3; Yth; Sch
A Cardiff right back or central defender, Jason came back last season, following a long lay off and missed very few games in helping the club to the play offs. Started the campaign as he meant to finish it, getting to every ball first and making it difficult for attackers, his tigerish tackling and commanding presence often winning the day. Offered a free transfer during the summer, he would have been at the club ten years as a professional this August.
Cardiff C (From trainee on 21/8/87) FL 278+3/5 FLC 22 FAC 14+1 Others 25+1

Jason Perry

PERRY Mark James
Born: London, 19 October 1978
Height: 6'0" Weight: 11.11
International Honours: E: Yth; Sch

Having impressed in the reserves after signing pro forms early in. 1995-96, the young QPR midfielder merely emphasised his potential when making his first-team debut at Barnsley last September and scoring the second goal in a 3-1 win, a header from a corner. Making one further appearance, at home to Port Vale, Mark has proved to be comfortable on the ball, an excellent passer, both short and long, and a good reader of the game. Can also play on the right-hand side of three at the back, where he exhibits fair tackling ability.

Queens Park R (From trainee on 26/10/95) FL 2/1

PESCHISOLIDO Paolo (Paul) Pasquale
Born: Scarborough, Canada, 25 May 1971
Height: 5'4" Weight: 10.12
International Honours: Canada: 27

Signed from Birmingham during the 1996 close season, the small, nippy striker, who is quick off the mark and a fine goalscorer, became a firm favourite with the West Brom fans. Worked well alongside Andy Hunt and Bob Taylor and if it had not been for World Cup international calls (with Canada) he would have surely doubled his goals tally. A real terrier in his approach to the game, and a real handful for defenders, hitting a hat trick in Albion's 4-2 win at Norwich, his pace gets to the heart of the opposition's defence. Is married to the Birmingham City managing director, Karren Brady.

Birmingham C (£25,000 from Toronto Blizzards on 11/11/92) FL 37+6/16 FLC 2/1 FAC 0+1 Others 1+1
Stoke C (£400,000 on 1/8/94) FL 59+7/19 FLC 6/3 FAC 3 Others 5+1/2
Birmingham C (£400,000 on 29/3/96) FL 7+2/1
West Bromwich A (£600,000 on 24/7/96) FL 30+7/15 FLC 1 FAC 1

PETHICK Robert (Robbie) John
Born: Tavistock, 8 September 1970
Height: 5'10" Weight: 11.12

Held down a place in the heart of Portsmouth's team for most of last season, playing in the main as the right-sided attacking wing back, although when Aaron Flahaven was sent off on the opening day of the campaign it was Robbie who went between the sticks. Very strong going forward, and a good passer of the ball, his crossing also improved with his attacking responsibilities.

Portsmouth (£30,000 from Weymouth on 1/10/93) FL 110+25/1 FLC 11+2 FAC 7 Others 3+1

PETRESCU Daniel (Dan) Vasile
Born: Bucharest, Romania, 22 December 1967
Height: 5'9" Weight: 11.9
Club Honours: FAC '97
International Honours: Romania: 61

The epitome of the modern wing back, Dan overcame a bitterly disappointing Euro 96 campaign for Romania to have another outstanding season for Chelsea in 1996-97. Using his experience gained in Serie A, he dovetailed perfectly with the Italian trio of Roberto di Matteo, Gianluca Vialli and Gianfranco Zola, forming a particularly good combination with the latter on the right flank. Clever on the ball, with good positional sense, he has the uncanny abliity to lose his marker and drift infield from the right wing to set up chances for the strikers. He did this superbly against Liverpool in the fourth round FA Cup tie, putting Vialli through for the Blues' third goal with a sweetly-timed pass. He also possesses a fierce shot, scoring cracking goals against Blackpool in the Coca-Cola Cup, Blackburn and Sunderland in the televised 6-2 drubbing. Finished an excellent campaign as the proud possessor of an FA Cup winners medal, following the 2-0 Wembley win over Middlesbrough.

Sheffield Wed (£1,250,000 from Genoa, via Foggia, on 6/8/94) PL 28+9/3 FLC 2 FAC 0+2
Chelsea (£2,300,000 on 18/11/95) PL 56+2/5 FLC 2/1 FAC 13/1

PETTA Robert (Bobby) Alfred Manuel
Born: Rotterdam, Holland, 6 August 1974
Height: 5'7" Weight: 11.3

Bobby joined Ipswich from Feyenord during the summer of 1996 and his impressive form in the pre-season friendlies, particularly against Arsenal in John Wark's testimonial, earned him a place in the side for the opening game at Manchester City. Although able to operate as a winger or as an out-and-out striker, with the ability to get past players, he found it difficult to adjust to the English game and, together with illness and some niggling injuries, he soon became the forgotten man of Portman Road, although much will be expected of him in 1997-98.

Ipswich T (Free from Feyenoord on 12/6/96) FL 1+5 FLC 1

Andy Petterson

PETTERSON Andrew (Andy) Keith
Born: Freemantle, Australia, 26 September 1969
Height: 6'2" Weight: 14.12

Is a good shot stopper who is not afraid to come off his line when necessary and possesses a powerful and accurate kick. Came into the Charlton side for the injured Mike Salmon on New Year's Day and kept his place for the remainder of 1996-97, in giving some superb displays. His save against Crystal Palace, likened to Gordon Banks' from Pele in the World Cup, was the best seen at The Valley for many a season, and earned a standing ovation from the crowd. Was deservedly voted Supporters' Player of the Year.

Luton T (Signed on 30/12/88) FL 16+3 FLC 2 Others 2
Ipswich T (Loaned on 26/3/93) PL 1
Charlton Ath (£85,000 on 15/7/94) FL 38+1 FLC 3 Others 4
Bradford C (Loaned on 8/12/94) FL 3
Ipswich T (Loaned on 26/9/95) FL 1
Plymouth Arg (Loaned on 19/1/96) FL 6
Colchester U (Loaned on 8/3/96) FL 5

PHELAN Terence (Terry) Michael
Born: Manchester, 16 March 1967
Height: 5'8" Weight: 10.0
Club Honours: FAC '88
International Honours: Ei: 37; B-1; U23-1; U21-1; Yth

Eyebrows were raised last January when Everton's Joe Royle signed a 29-year-old left back, who could not force his way into the Chelsea starting line up following a lengthy injury lay off. However, Terry rapidly established himself as a firm favourite amongst Evertonians with a succession of impressive performances, perpetuating his reputation as a speedy left back who loves to overlap and whip in crosses, and being the perfect replacement when Andy Hinchcliffe suffered serious injury. Signed initially as emergency cover for Hinchcliffe, he showed enough in his four months at Everton to suggest he will be anything but a stop gap in 1997-98. Also made two appearances for the Republic of Ireland.

Leeds U (From apprentice on 3/8/84) FL 12+2 FLC 3 Others 2
Swansea C (Free on 30/7/86) FL 45 FLC 4 FAC 5 Others 3
Wimbledon (£100,000 on 29/7/87) FL 155+4/1 FLC 13+2 FAC 16/2 Others 8
Manchester C (£2,500,000 on 25/8/92) PL 102+1/2 FLC 11 FAC 8/1
Chelsea (£900,000 on 15/11/95) PL 13+2 FAC 8+1
Everton (£850,000 on 1/1/97) PL 15 FAC 1

PHILLIPS David Owen
Born: Wegburg, Germany, 29 July 1963
Height: 5'10" Weight: 12.5
Club Honours: FAC '87
International Honours: W: 62; U21-4; Yth

Now in the veteran stage of his career, the Welsh international appeared in more than half of Nottingham Forest's games during last season. Has always been a versatile player and stood in at full back and in a variety of midfield roles during a tough season for his club, which ultimately led to relegation. Despite all of this, David regained his place in the Welsh side and added to his impressive tally of caps. Known for his super diagonal passing, he has two good feet and is a lovely striker of the ball.

Plymouth Arg (From apprentice on 3/8/81) FL 65+8/15 FLC 2+1 FAC 12+1 Others 4/1
Manchester C (£65,000 on 23/8/84) FL 81/13 FLC 8 FAC 5 Others 5/3
Coventry C (£150,000 on 5/6/86) FL 93+7/8 FLC 8 FAC 9/1 Others 5+1/2
Norwich C (£525,000 on 31/7/89) F/PL 152/18 FLC 12 FAC 14/1 Others 8/1
Nottingham F (Signed on 20/8/93) F/PL 116+10/5 FLC 15 FAC 10+2 Others 4

PHILLIPS Gareth Russell
Born: Pontypridd, 19 August 1979
Height: 5'8" Weight: 9.8
International Honours: W: Yth; Sch
Yet another Swansea YTS youngster given an opportunity by Jan Molby in 1996-97, the 17-year-old midfielder came off the bench at Cambridge last November. Still a trainee, Gareth looks to have a good future in the game.
Swansea C (Trainee) FL 0+1

PHILLIPS James (Jimmy) Neil
Born: Bolton, 8 February 1966
Height: 6'0" Weight: 12.7
Club Honours: Div 1 '97
A dependable player for Bolton, Jimmy again had a solid season in 1996-97, despite a considerable challenge for the left-back spot from Bryan Small. Having lost his place in the starting line up to Small for a run of 13 games in the New Year, at a time when Colin Todd was assessing his squad potential, he had returned by the end of the campaign to produce his usual solid and effective performances. One of the few regulars who failed to score in 1996-97, although his foraging runs up the field brought him close on a few occasions, his first division championship medal was a fair return for his endeavours.
Bolton W (From apprentice on 1/8/83) FL 103+5/2 FLC 8 FAC 7 Others 14
Glasgow R (£95,000 on 27/3/87) SL 19+6 SLC 4 Others 4
Oxford U (£110,000 on 26/8/88) FL 79/8 FLC 3 FAC 4 Others 2/1
Middlesbrough (£250,000 on 15/3/90) F/PL 139/6 FLC 16 FAC 10 Others 5/2
Bolton W (£250,000 on 20/7/93) P/FL 160+1/1 FLC 22 FAC 10 Others 9/2

PHILLIPS Kevin
Born: Hitchin, 25 July 1973
Height: 5'7" Weight: 11.0
Watford striker blessed with fast feet and a footballing brain to match. Missed over half of last season when recovering from a troublesome broken shin bone, but made an immediate impact on his comeback, scoring a fine hat trick against Bristol City – the first of his career – in only his third full game. A former non-leaguer, Kevin has become a great favourite with the Watford crowd.
Watford (£10,000 from Baldock on 19/12/94) FL 54+5/24 FLC 2/1 FAC 2 Others 0+2

PHILLIPS Lee
Born: Aberdare, 18 March 1979
Height: 6'1" Weight: 11.9
International Honours: W: Yth
Still a trainee, Lee came into the Cardiff side when Scott Young was unavailable, making his league debut at Hartlepool last February and playing twice more before going back to

the reserves for further experience. Shows great composure for a youngster, preferring the sweeper role, where he is able to read the game well and is comfortable on the ball, to that of centre back. Also a good passer and tackler, his ability was quickly recognised by a call up to the Welsh U21 squad.
Cardiff C (Trainee) FL 2+1

PHILLIPS Lee Paul
Born: Penzance, 16 September 1980
Height: 5'11" Weight: 12.0
The young Plymouth centre forward, who is a strong and lively front runner, became the youngest player in the club's history when, at 16 years and 43 days, he made his debut against Gillingham last October. Appeared twice more as a substitute, before unfortunately breaking his leg and bringing his highly promising start in the Football League to a temporary halt. Once fully recovered, however, Lee is bound to have the scouts flocking to Home Park.
Plymouth Arg (Trainee) FL 0+2 Others 0+1

PHILLIPS Marcus Stuart
Born: Trowbridge, 17 October 1973
Height: 5'10" Weight: 11.4
Made a return to league football, albeit briefly, as a substitute for Oxford at Huddersfield after joining the club from Beazer Homes side, Witney Town, midway through last season. Earlier released by Swindon, and one of very few players to have played for both United and their arch rivals, he made several fine displays in midfield for the reserves before being surprisingly freed in the summer.
Swindon T (From trainee on 1/5/93) FLC 0+1 Others 0+1 (Released in March 1995)
Oxford C (Free from Witney T on 4/2/97) FL 0+1

PHILLIPS Martin John
Born: Exeter, 13 March 1976
Height: 5'10" Weight: 12.8
After his initiation and glowing reports during 1995-96, Martin started last season at Manchester City in the home win over Ipswich Town, but was subbed in the second half. Following that, he made only four sub appearances under managers, Alan Ball and Asa Hartford, although playing regularly for the reserves. While disappointing for both himself and the club, time is still on the side of this ball-playing winger with a direct style, having recently celebrated his 21st birthday.
Exeter C (From trainee on 4/7/94) FL 36+16/5 FLC 1+2 FAC 2+2 Others 1+5
Manchester C (£500,000 on 25/11/95) P/FL 3+12 FLC 0+1

PHILLIPS Wayne
Born: Bangor, 15 December 1970
Height: 5'10" Weight: 11.2
International Honours: W: B-1
As Wrexham's 1995-96 Player of the Year, Wayne continued in impressive form in central midfield right up until the away match with Wycombe Wanderers at the end of last October. However, a bad injury sustained in that match put him out of the game for four months and he did not appear

on the team sheet again until March. With his up-and-down play always a feature, he is quite liable to have a crack at goal, often successfully, while his enthusiastic approach is an example to many young players. Is currently on the fringe of the Welsh squad.
Wrexham (From trainee on 23/8/89) FL 170+17/15 FLC 15+1 FAC 10+2/1 Others 18+5/1

PHILLISKIRK Anthony (Tony)
Born: Sunderland, 10 February 1965
Height: 6'1" Weight: 13.3
International Honours: E: Sch
Playing in a withdrawn role for Cardiff in 1996-97, which proved productive, Tony suffered a couple of injuries and was forced to miss much of the second part of the campaign. These days very much a maker rather than taker of chances, he scored his first goal for the club in the 2-2 home draw against Northampton. Hopefully, he will get an injury free run this time round.
Sheffield U (From juniors on 16/8/83) FL 62+18/20 FLC 4+1/1 FAC 5/1 Others 3+2
Rotherham U (Loaned on 16/10/86) FL 6/1
Oldham Ath (£25,000 on 13/7/88) FL 3+7/1 FLC 0+2/1 Others 1
Preston NE (Signed on 10/2/89) FL 13+1/6
Bolton W (£50,000 on 22/6/89) FL 139+2/51 FLC 18/12 FAC 10/7 Others 13/5
Peterborough U (£85,000 on 17/10/92) FL 37+6/15 FLC 2/1 FAC 4/1 Others 2/1
Burnley (£80,000 on 21/1/94) FL 33+7/9 FLC 4+1
Carlisle U (Loaned on 26/10/95) FL 3/1
Cardiff C (£60,000 on 7/12/95) FL 55+6/5 FLC 2 FAC 2 Others 1+2

PHILPOTT Lee
Born: Barnet, 21 February 1970
Height: 5'10" Weight: 12.9
Club Honours: Div 3 '91
A wide left-sided midfielder who can cross with the best of them, Lee started last season for Blackpool in great form with three goals in the first seven games, before suffering injury problems which restricted his appearances. Can also play at full back if required.
Peterborough U (From trainee on 17/7/86) FL 1+3 FAC 0+1 Others 0+2
Cambridge U (Free on 31/5/89) FL 118+16/17 FLC 10/1 FAC 19/3 Others 15/2
Leicester C (£350,000 on 24/11/92) F/PL 57+18/3 FLC 2+1 FAC 6+2 Others 4+1
Blackpool (£75,000 on 22/3/96) FL 24+12/3 FLC 2/1 FAC 2 Others 0+1

PICKERING Albert (Ally) Gary
Born: Manchester, 22 June 1967
Height: 5'11" Weight: 11.1
Signed by Stoke from Coventry at the start of 1996-97, the attacking right back, who is also strong in the tackle and noted for his flat crosses, appeared to fall out of favour towards the end of the season and consequently lost his place in the side. However, Ally is too good a player to remain on the sidelines and is expected to come back strongly in 1997-98.
Rotherham U (£18,500 from Buxton on 2/2/90) FL 87+1/2 FLC 6 FAC 9 Others 7
Coventry C (£80,000 on 27/10/93) PL 54+11 FLC 5+1 FAC 4/1
Stoke C (£280,000 on 15/8/96) FL 39+1 FLC 4 FAC 1

PIEARCE Steven (Steve)
Born: Birmingham, 27 September 1974
Height: 5'11" Weight: 10.10
Having joined Doncaster from Wolves during the summer of 1996, Steve, a young striker still learning his trade, was given his Football League debut by the Rovers on the opening day of last season. Although in and out of the first team, playing 21 games, most of them from the subs' bench, he scored his first league goal, at Lincoln, in January.
Wolverhampton W (From trainee on 6/7/93)
Doncaster Rov (Free on 15/7/96) FL 8+11/1 FLC 0+1 FAC 0+1

PILKINGTON Kevin William
Born: Hitchin, 8 March 1974
Height: 6'1" Weight: 13.0
Club Honours: FAYC '92
International Honours: E: Sch
A very promising young Manchester United goalkeeper who is good on crosses and stands up well, Kevin improved in confidence during a three-month loan spell with Rotherham, having gone to Millmoor last January. Although playing in 17 successive games and making a string of brilliant saves, none more so than in a match-winning performance at Shrewsbury, his super displays could not stop the Millers from avoiding the drop into the third division. Despite the departure of Steve Cherry, who was not prepared to play second fiddle, it was always intended that he would return to Old Trafford where he is still considered an excellent long-term prospect and he did just that two games from the end of the campaign. Gets real length and distance from his kicks.
Manchester U (From trainee on 6/7/92) PL 2+2 FLC 1 FAC 1
Rochdale (Loaned on 2/2/96) FL 6
Rotherham U (Loaned on 22/1/97) FL 17

PINNOCK James Edward
Born: Dartford, 1 August 1978
Height: 5'9" Weight: 11.5
Top scorer for Gillingham's South-East Counties side in season 1995-96 and for the Capital League side last season, this young trainee made his first-team debut when he came on as substitute in the Auto Windscreen tie at home to Cardiff City. A good-looking prospect, hopefully, there are further opportunities to be had.
Gillingham (Trainee) FL 0+2 Others 0+1

PINTO Sergio Paulo Viera
Born: Escudos, Portugal, 8 January 1973
Height: 5'7" Weight: 10.4
The younger brother of Jaio, the Portuguese international star, Sergio signed for Bradford last October from Boavista with a view to seeing the season out, but on getting homesick he left at the end of March. An extremely tricky and skilful right winger, and a definite crowd pleaser, he made few starts with most of his appearances coming from the bench.
Bradford C (Free from Boavista on 1/10/96) FL 7+11 FAC 1+1

PIPER Leonard (Lenny) Henry
Born: London, 8 August 1977
Height: 5'6" Weight: 9.9
International Honours: E: Yth
An England youth international, he was signed from Wimbledon at the start of 1996-97 and made a sensational start to his first-team career with Gillingham on the opening day of the season when he came on as a substitute and scored a last-minute winner at home to Bristol City. Despite that, his appearances, however, were mainly restricted to the bench. With good close control, he likes to take players on and is possibly one for the future.
Wimbledon (From trainee on 1/6/95)
Gillingham (£40,000 on 22/7/96) FL 4+15/1 FLC 2+2 FAC 1 Others 1/1

PITCHER Darren Edward
Born: Stepney, 12 October 1969
Height: 5'9" Weight: 12.2
International Honours: E: Yth
A tough-tackling Crystal Palace midfielder with excellent workrate, Darren had a disastrous start to 1996-97 when, four games into the campaign, a damaged cruciate knee ligament at Huddersfield put him out of action for seven months. Returned to play two reserve matches, but then suffered another blow when it was revealed that the operation would have to be carried out again. Hopefully, the surgery this time round is more successful and that the unlucky player gets back into the side before too long.
Charlton Ath (From trainee on 12/1/88) FL 170+3/8 FLC 11 FAC 12/3 Others 8
Crystal Palace (£700,000 on 5/7/94) P/FL 60+4 FLC 5+1/1 FAC 10/1 Others 3

PITCHER Geoffrey (Geoff)
Born: Sutton, 15 August 1975
Height: 5'7" Weight: 11.2
Released by Watford in the summer of 1996, Geoff, who plays on the right of midfield, spent some time with Colchester but was not taken on, signing for non-league Kingstonian instead. Returned on trial later in the season and was taken on a short-term contract, making one substitute appearance at home to Mansfield, before being released in the summer.
Millwall (From trainee on 18/3/93)
Watford (Signed on 13/7/94) FL 4+9/2 FLC 1+1 FAC 2 (Free to Kingstonians during 1996 close season)
Colchester U (Free on 17/2/97) FL 0+1

PITMAN Jamie Roy
Born: Trowbridge, 6 January 1976
Height: 5'9" Weight: 10.12
Unfortunately, Jamie was restricted to very few appearances for Hereford in 1996-97, due to injury, and remained sidelined for long periods. Despite being on the small side, he is a good midfield battler who can always be relied upon and will come again.
Swindon T (From trainee on 8/7/94) FL 2+1
Hereford U (Free on 16/2/96) FL 16+5 FLC 2 Others 2

PLATT Clive Linton
Born: Wolverhampton, 27 October 1977
Height: 6'4" Weight: 12.7

After a sensational start to his first-team career at Walsall, with two goals in successive home games in 1995-96, Clive made just two substitute appearances at the beginning of last season, while continuing to impress in the reserve team that just missed promotion from the second division of the Pontins League. Now a pro, having signed during the summer of 1996, the young striker, just like Michael Ricketts, is not being rushed and with power on the ground, coupled to an obvious aerial ability, should break through in 1997-98.
Walsall (From trainee on 25/7/96) FL 0+5/2 FLC 0+1

David Platt

PLATT David Andrew
Born: Chadderton, 10 June 1966
Height: 5'10" Weight: 11.12
International Honours: E: 62; B-3; U21-3
The Arsenal and England central midfield player finally shook off his injury problems in 1996-97 to return to something like his normal form, while making 34 club appearances. Although still primarily used in the midfield holding role, he was, nevertheless, able to get forward more than previously and in one purple patch scored in consecutive April matches against Chelsea, Leicester and Blackburn, as the Gunners battled away in a supreme effort to overhaul Manchester United at the top of the Premiership. Sat on the England bench for a couple of games under Glenn Hoddle last season but, despite not being used, there is every chance that the former captain could be recalled at a later date, injuries allowing. At his best, a midfield dynamo who links with the front men to score goals, often turning up on a defender's blind side to volley home, David still has plenty to offer the game and will relish the challenge of playing in Arsene Wenger's continental shaped side this coming term.

Manchester U (Signed from Chadderton on 24/7/84)
Crewe Alex (Free on 25/1/85) FL 134/55 FLC 8/4 FAC 3/1 Others 7
Aston Villa (£200,000 on 2/2/88) FL 121/50 FLC 14/10 FAC 4/2 Others 6/6 (£5,500,000 to Bari on 20/7/91)
Arsenal (£4,750,000 from Sampdoria, via Juventus, on 14/7/95) PL 54+3/10 FLC 5+1/1 FAC 2 Others 2

PLUMMER Christopher (Chris)
Born: Isleworth, 12 October 1976
Height: 6'3" Weight: 12.9
International Honours: E: U21-5; Yth

Having made a single subs' appearance for QPR in 1995-96, the young central defender was given his first start for the club, following an injury to Steve Yates, at Swindon in the Coca-Cola Cup on 18 September, and played five more consecutive games before going back to the reserves. Looking very poised and comfortable on the ball, his added height giving him options at set pieces, Chris will be looking to build on last season's performances in 1997-98.
Queens Park R (From trainee on 1/7/94) F/PL 4+2 FLC 2

PLUMMER Dwayne Jermaine
Born: Bristol, 12 May 1978
Height: 5'9" Weight: 11.0

A naturally gifted player who has yet to fulfil his potential at Bristol City, this right winger made only two substitute appearances in 1996-97, without demonstrating the form of which he was known to be capable of and it is to be hoped that he will seize all available opportunities in 1997-98 in order to cement his place in the side. Loves running at defenders where he can utilise his pace to get into good attacking positions.
Bristol C (From trainee on 5/9/95) FL 1+12 FLC 1+2 Others 0+1

POBORSKY Karel
Born: Czechoslovakia, 30 May 1971
Height: 5'9" Weight: 11.6
Club Honours: PL '97; CS '97
International Honours: Czechoslovakia: 25

An exciting winger, whose speed earns him the nickname of "The Express Train," Karel arrived at Manchester United from Slavia Prague in the 1996 close season, having given a brilliant showing for Czechoslovakia during 'Euro '96.' Made a promising start to his Premiership career, celebrating his first goal against Leeds in September, then netting one of United's two goals against Swindon in the Coca-Cola Cup, but, with competition for places hotting up, he was confined to the substitutes' bench for several spells, before showing up well during the clubs exciting run in to the end of the campaign. When signing him, Alex Ferguson remarked, "He's got great feet and vision and is also very tenacious. He will give me the variety on the right wing because he's a different type of player from the likes of David Beckham and Terry Cooke." Karel himself was even more optimistic stating, "I want to deliver. In four years time I want everybody

to know the name Poborsky." Was delighted to win a championship medal at the end of his first season in England as United won the Premiership title for the fourth time in five years.
Manchester U (£3,500,000 from Slavia Prague on 8/8/96) PL 15+7/3 FLC 2/1 FAC 2 Others 3+4

POLLITT Michael Francis
Born: Farnworth, 29 February 1972
Height: 6'4" Weight: 14.0

Michael proved to be a very popular second string goalkeeper behind Darren Ward at Notts County in 1996-97, forcing his way into the team on merit after performing brilliantly in the reserves. Tall, and a highly competent handler of crosses, he played in ten games, six of them losing ones, but never let the side down.
Manchester U (From trainee on 1/7/90)
Bury (Free on 10/7/91)
Lincoln C (Free on 1/12/92) FL 57 FLC 5 FAC 2 Others 4
Darlington (Free on 11/8/94) FL 55 FLC 4 FAC 3 Others 5
Notts Co (£75,000 on 14/11/95) FL 8 Others 2

Jamie Pollock

POLLOCK Jamie
Born: Stockton, 16 February 1974
Height: 5'11" Weight: 14.0
Club Honours: Div 1 '95, '97
International Honours: E: U21-3; Yth

A combative midfielder who gives everything and more, and one of Colin Todd's most inspired signings, Jamie joined Bolton at the end of last November, following a nightmare spell with Spanish second division club, Osasuna. Having made his Wanderers' debut in the 2-1 home defeat by Ipswich midway through December, where it was clear that he was not 100 per cent, after working on his fitness he claimed his place in the starting line up in the New Year and was a revelation, scoring in four consecutive games at the end of the month. The winner of a first division championship medal after less than six months at Burnden, his Premiership experience will be inval-

uable to the Trotters on their return to the big time.
Middlesbrough (From trainee on 18/12/91) F/PL 144+11/17 FLC 17+2/1 FAC 13+1/1 Others 4+1 (Free to Osasuna on 6/9/96)
Bolton W (£1,500,000 on 22/11/96) FL 18+2/4 FLC 0+1 FAC 3/2

POLSTON John David
Born: Walthamstow, 10 June 1968
Height: 5'11" Weight: 11.12
International Honours: E: Yth

Ever reliable, he was enjoying one of his best seasons for Norwich in 1996-97 when a groin injury sidelined him from 18 January to 25 April. Although he eased himself back, coming of the bench in early April, he was one of five first teamers not to start 30 league games, a telling factor in City's losing season. Never a prolific scorer, it was mischievously rumoured that his obstinate ailment was partially caused by the sheer shock of scoring crucial goals in two successive games, versus Sheffield United and Grimsby Town. A centre back who is strong both on the ground, and in the air, first and foremost he is basically a defender.
Tottenham H (From apprentice on 16/7/85) FL 17+7/1 FLC 3+1
Norwich C (£250,000 on 24/7/90) F/PL 193+10/8 FLC 18+1/2 FAC 17+1/1 Others 9/1

POOLE Gary John
Born: Stratford, 11 September 1967
Height: 6'0" Weight: 12.4
Club Honours: GMVC '91; Div 2 '95; AMC '95

Following a well publicised on-field incident in Birmingham's colours, the right-sided defender signed for Charlton last November and scored on his debut at Loftus Road with a 25-yard screamer against QPR. A strong tackler, and good when going forward, Gary quickly established himself in his new side and created competition for Steve Brown in the right-back spot, although he missed several games through a knee injury which eventually required an operation.
Tottenham H (From juniors on 15/7/85)
Cambridge U (Free on 14/8/87) FL 42+1 FLC 2 FAC 2 Others 3
Barnet (£3,000 on 1/3/89) FL 39+1/2 FLC 2 FAC 7 Others 6/1
Plymouth Arg (Free on 5/6/92) FL 39/5 FLC 6/2 FAC 2 Others 0+1
Southend U (£350,000 on 9/7/93) FL 43+1/2 FLC 2 FAC 1 Others 6
Birmingham C (£50,000 on 16/9/94) FL 70+2 FLC 13 FAC 7/1 Others 10/2
Charlton Ath (£250,000 on 13/11/96) FL 14+2/1

POOLE Kevin
Born: Bromsgrove, 21 July 1963
Height: 5'10" Weight: 12.11

As the reserve goalkeeper at Leicester and understudy to Kasey Keller throughout 1996-97, Kevin made occasional appearances when the latter was absent on international duty and did not let the team down before being released during the summer. Recognised as an excellent shot stopper in his own right, and sound when coming for crosses, he was a good man to have in the wings and was part of the

defence that heroically held off Wimbledon at Selhurst Park for a 3-1 win.

Aston Villa (From apprentice on 26/6/81) FL 28 FLC 2 FAC 1 Others 1
Northampton T (Loaned on 8/11/84) FL 3
Middlesbrough (Signed on 27/8/87) FL 34 FLC 4 FAC 2 Others 2
Hartlepool U (Loaned on 27/3/91) FL 12
Leicester C (£40,000 on 30/7/91) F/PL 163 FLC 10 FAC 8 Others 12

POOM Mart

Born: Tallin, Estonia, 3 February 1972
Height: 6'4" Weight: 13.6
International Honours: Estonia: 54

The Estonian international goalkeeper had previously been on Portsmouth's books under Jim Smith's management, before having his work permit revoked and moving back home. Very tall and agile, he played a blinder in holding Scotland to a 0-0 draw in their replayed World Cup tie in Monaco, his performances alerting several managers. However, Jim Smith moved quickest and within days he was making his debut for Derby in the tremendous 3-2 win at Old Trafford in April where he looked quite at home. Injured a shoulder soon afterwards, but if he can show the same kind of consistency in 1997-98 he has a great future in the Premier League.

Portsmouth (£200,000 from FC Wil on 4/8/94) FL 4 FLC 3 (Signed by Tallin SC on 9/5/96)
Derby Co (£500,000 on 26/3/97) PL 4

Hugo Porfirio

PORFIRIO Hugo Cardosa

Born: Lisbon, Portugal, 28 September 1973
Height: 5'5" Weight: 10.10
International Honours: Portugal: 6

The young Portuguese international striker, cum winger, joined West Ham on loan from Sporting Lisbon last September for the remainder of the season, making his Premiership debut as a substitute at home to Liverpool. Whilst never an automatic first-choice selection, he remained an essential component of the first-team squad, scoring goals against Blackburn in October and Chelsea in December. However, his best

performance came in a Coca-Cola Cup tie against Nottingham Forest in October when he created two goals for Iain Dowie and scored one himself in a 4-1 victory. The Hammers are hoping to make his transfer permanent for the coming season.

West Ham U (Loaned from Sporting Lisbon on 27/9/96) PL 15+8/2 FLC 2/1 FAC 1+1/1

PORIC Adem

Born: London, 22 April 1973
Height: 5'9" Weight: 11.13

Unable to get a game at Sheffield Wednesday during 1996-97, the stocky midfielder arrived on loan to Southend in February showing himself to be fully committed, especially in the tackling side of the game. His distribution was also good and it was a disappointment to the fans when he was allowed to return to Wednesday the following month.

Sheffield Wed (£60,000 from St George's Budapest on 1/10/93) PL 3+7 FLC 0+2
Southend U (Loaned on 7/2/97) FL 7

PORTER Andrew (Andy) Michael

Born: Holmes Chapel, 17 September 1968
Height: 5'9" Weight: 11.2
Club Honours: AMC '93

The tough-tackling Port Vale midfield player once again played his heart out for the cause, missing just two games throughout 1996-97, a 3-0 defeat at Oldham and a 1-1 draw at home to Stoke. And, in adding his usual aggression to the middle of the park as a foil for the more skilful Ian Bogie, he merely emphasised his value to the team. Scored four goals, including one from the penalty spot, and has now made over 350 senior appearances for the club.

Port Vale (From trainee on 29/6/87) FL 285+31/21 FLC 22 FAC 18+4/3 Others 26+2/1

PORTER Gary Michael

Born: Sunderland, 6 March 1966
Height: 5'6" Weight: 11.0
Club Honours: FAYC '82
International Honours: E: U21-12; Yth

An experienced, very left-footed midfield player who was in his 14th season as a first teamer with Watford in 1996-97. After establishing a promising partnership with Steve Palmer, and scoring a spectacular goal against Walsall, Gary suffered a broken leg and missed the rest of the campaign, just when he was within sight of overtaking Luther Blissett's club record for league appearances. Was released during the summer.

Watford (From apprentice on 6/3/84) FL 362+38/47 FLC 30+2/5 FAC 25+2/3 Others 12+1/2

POTTER Graham Stephen

Born: Solihull, 20 May 1975
Height: 6'1" Weight: 11.12
International Honours: E: U21-1; Yth

A studious left-sided player who can fill in at full back, or in midfield as a wing back, his terrific pace and crossing ability making openings for the front men, having starred for Stoke in 1995-96, Graham became Graeme Souness' first signing when he

moved to Southampton during the 1996 close season. Unfortunately consigned mainly to the subs' bench, making just three starts, despite winning an England U21 cap against Moldova, he moved on to West Bromwich in February, this time as Ray Harford's first signing, but was injured after a handful of outings and sidelined for the last six weeks of the campaign. Hopefully, Graham will be fully fit for the coming term.

Birmingham C (From trainee on 1/7/92) FL 23+2/2 FAC 1 Others 6
Wycombe W (Loaned on 17/9/93) FL 2+1 FLC 1 Others 1
Stoke C (£75,000 on 20/12/93) FL 41+4/1 FLC 3+1 FAC 4 Others 5
Southampton (£250,000 + on 23/7/96) FL 2+6 FLC 1+1
West Bromwich A (£300,000 + on 14/2/97) FL 2+4

POTTS Steven (Steve) John

Born: Hartford, USA, 7 May 1967
Height: 5'8" Weight: 10.11
International Honours: E: Yth

West Ham's longest serving player completed his 13th season as a professional at Upton Park in 1996-97, although no longer an automatic first-team selection, with Slaven Bilic and Marc Rieper being manager Harry Redknapp's favoured partnership in central defence. Despite spending most of the earlier part of the campaign in the reserves, after his recall to first-team duty in February, he held his place to the end of the term, covering for the injured Tim Breacker at right back for the last seven matches. Has now signed a new three -year contract which will enable him to make his 400th first-team appearance for the Hammers', early in 1997-98, his testimonial season.

West Ham U (From apprentice on 11/5/84) F/PL 319+13/1 FLC 31+1 FAC 35 Others 14+1

POUNEWATCHY Stephane Zeusnagapa

Born: Paris, France, 10 February 1968
Height: 6'1" Weight: 15.12
Club Honours: AMC '97

Signed on a free transfer from FC Gueugnon at the start of last season under the Bosman ruling, and valued at £500,000 in his native country, this immensely powerful defender soon became a dominating influence in the Carlisle side with his authority and skilful reading of the game. Fittingly, his finest game was at Wembley in the AWS final, where his classy performance deservedly won him the Man of the Match award.

Carlisle U (Free from Gueugnon on 6/8/96) FL 42/1 FLC 4 FAC 4 Others 7/1

POUTON Alan

Born: Newcastle, 1 February 1977
Height: 6'0" Weight: 12.8

The young York City midfielder became the find of the season at Bootham Crescent in 1996-97 after making his full senior debut in November and having a successful extended first-team run before being injured. A strong, hard-running player with good control, he was at his best in the centre of midfield and will be looking forward to picking up where he left off in 1997-98.

Oxford U (Free from Newcastle U juniors on 7/11/95)
York C (Free on 8/12/95) FL 18+4/1 FAC 3 Others 1

POWELL Christopher (Chris) George Robin
Born: Lambeth, 8 September 1969
Height: 5'9" Weight: 11.7
This consistent and highly talented Derby left-wing back has maintained his progress and hence his place in the Premier League side during 1996-97. Very calm under pressure, his skill at developing counter attacking play down the left flank brought a maturity to his game which Jim Smith had first noted during his time at Southend, and was one of the reasons that he missed just three Premiership games throughout the campaign. Is comfortable with either foot, passes well, and is a shrewd reader of the game.
Crystal Palace (From trainee on 24/12/87) FL 2+1 FLC 0+1 Others 0+1
Aldershot (Loaned on 11/1/90) FL 11
Southend U (Free on 30/8/90) FL 246+2/3 FLC 13 FAC 8 Others 21
Derby Co (£750,000 on 31/1/96) F/PL 54 FLC 1 FAC 3

Chris Powell

POWELL Darryl Anthony
Born: Lambeth, 15 November 1971
Height: 6'0" Weight: 12.3
Versatile Derby midfielder who, although preferring a left-sided role, can adapt himself to any given position in defence or midfield. Signed from Portsmouth, he continued to make progress at Derby, his strength and pace worrying opposing midfielders and defenders alike, while his only goal of the season gave County the lead at Arsenal, a match that eventually ended in a 2-2 draw. Able to play up front if required, Darryl is strong in the tackle, and a good passer, and certainly was not out of place in the Premiership, his 33 appearances being testament to that.
Portsmouth (From trainee on 22/12/88) FL 83+49/16 FLC 11+3/3 FAC 10 Others 9+5/4
Derby Co (£750,000 on 27/7/95) F/PL 64+6/6 FLC 2+1 FAC 3

POWER Graeme Richard
Born: Harrow, 7 March 1977
Height: 5'9" Weight: 10.10
International Honours: E: Yth
A confident, left-footed defender, Graeme made his league debut in the centre of Bristol Rovers' defence against Plymouth Argyle last September, the club's first away victory of the season. Switched to left back for the following ten matches, before reverting again to central defence, by this time Rovers had suffered four consecutive defeats and he lost his place. Is sure to come again.
Queens Park R (From trainee on 11/4/95)
Bristol Rov (Free on 15/7/96) FL 16 FAC 1 Others 1

PREECE Andrew (Andy) Paul
Born: Evesham, 27 March 1967
Height: 6'1" Weight: 12.0
The Blackpool striker started last season on the bench before forcing his way into the side by mid October and eventually retaining his place. Dangerous around the box, often coming to life at critical moments, Andy scored several important goals, including winners at Rotherham (AWS), Shrewsbury, and at home to Bristol City.
Northampton T (Free from Evesham on 31/8/88) FL 0+1 FLC 0+1 Others 0+1 (Free to Worcester C during 1989 close season)
Wrexham (Free on 22/3/90) FL 44+7/7 FLC 5+1/1 FAC 1/2 Others 5/1
Stockport Co (£10,000 on 18/12/91) FL 89+8/42 FLC 2+1 FAC 7/3 Others 12+2/9
Crystal Palace (£350,000 on 23/6/94) PL 17+3/4 FLC 4+2/1 FAC 2+3
Blackpool (£200,000 on 5/7/95) FL 72+10/24 FLC 4+2 FAC 1+3/1 Others 9/1

PREECE David William
Born: Bridgnorth, 28 May, 1963
Height: 5'6" Weight: 11.6
Club Honours: FLC '88
International Honours: E: B-3
An experienced midfielder, David had been tracked by Cambridge for a considerable time before finally joining them last September, on being released by Derby. However, although making an impressive start on his debut against Torquay, he was carried off with a fractured leg bone. A tenacious ball winner, he returned to the first team in November and was influential in midfield as well as taking on coaching duties at the club.
Walsall (From apprentice on 22/7/80) FL 107+4/5 FLC 18/5 FAC 6/1 Others 1
Luton T (£150,000 on 6/12/84) FL 328+8/21 FLC 23/3 FAC 27/2 Others 8+1/1
Derby Co (Free on 11/8/95) FL 10+3/1 FLC 2
Birmingham C (Loaned on 24/11/95) FL 6 Others 1
Swindon T (Loaned on 21/3/96) FL 7/1
Cambridge U (Free on 6/9/96) FL 19+6 FAC 1+1

PREEDY Philip (Phil)
Born: Hereford, 20 November 1975
Height: 5'10" Weight: 11.2
As in 1995-96, this left-sided Hereford player had limited experience last season, playing 14 times, of which just two were starts. A strong and aggressive lad who enjoys attacking runs down the flank, he

twice scored when coming off the bench at Mansfield and Wigan and is still young enough to establish himself.
Hereford U (From trainee on 13/7/94) FL 31+20/4 FLC 4+4 FAC 3+1 Others 1+2/1

PRESSMAN Kevin Paul
Born: Fareham, 6 November 1967
Height: 6'1" Weight: 14.12
International Honours: E: B-2; U21-1; Yth; Sch
Probably the best uncapped goalkeeper in the Premiership, Kevin had yet another very successful season for Sheffield Wednesday in 1996-97, being an ever present and keeping 12 clean sheets, four of them in successive games. A steady, solid and reliable player, and not one to flap under pressure, maybe he will still get a chance to represent England, despite there being a wealth of talented 'keepers about. In this day and age where it is important for goalies to have good kicking ability, his trusted left foot gets good length, even when under pressure.
Sheffield Wed (From apprentice on 7/11/85) F/PL 196 FLC 27 FAC 12 Others 4
Stoke C (Loaned on 10/3/92) FL 4 Others 2

PRESTON Michael John
Born: Plymouth, 22 November 1977
Height: 5'7" Weight: 11.0
Having signed pro forms for Torquay during the summer of 1996, the former YTS winger was given three substitute appearances before a bad injury in a reserve game ended his season prematurely. An excellent prospect, hopefully, he will return as new.
Torquay U (From trainee on 12/7/96) FL 4+6 Others 0+1

PRICE Jason Jeffrey
Born: Pontypridd, 12 April 1977
Height: 6'2" Weight: 11.5
After being included several times in the Swansea squad as a non-playing substitute in 1996-97, Jason was eventually given his opportunity when coming off the bench against Doncaster at the Vetch Field in January, before making a full appearance at Lincoln. Predominately a full back, he also figured well as a central defender with the reserves.
Swansea C (Free from Aberaman on 17/7/95) FL 1+1

PRIEST Christopher (Chris)
Born: Leigh, 18 October 1973
Height: 5'10" Weight: 10.10
In turning in some very useful performances in Chester's midfield during 1996-97, Chris attracted the attention of many scouts from the higher divisions and looks to have an excellent future in the game. Good with the ball, and possessing great stamina, he is very much in keeping with the modern day box-to-box type, with the ability to score useful goals, one such strike procuring a 1-1 draw at Fulham during the run up to the play offs. Unfortunately ended the season on a low when sent off in the play-off semi-final leg at Swansea.

Everton (From trainee on 1/6/92)
Chester C (Loaned on 9/9/94) FL 11/1 Others 2
Chester C (Free on 11/1/94) FL 79+5/15 FLC 3 FAC 3 Others 5

PRIMUS Linvoy Stephen
Born: Forest Gate, 14 September 1973
Height: 6'0" Weight: 14.0
Classy centre half whose pace and positioning was a major reason for Barnet's defensive strength last season. As an ever present, scouts have been flocking to Underhill to watch a player with all the attributes to eventually go on to the highest level. Three goals was not a bad return either, including two headed winners, and he will undoubtedly continue to improve in 1997-98.
Charlton Ath (From trainee on 14/8/92) FL 4 FLC 0+1 Others 0+1
Barnet (Free on 18/7/94) FL 127/7 FLC 9+1 FAC 8/1 Others 4

PRIOR Spencer Justin
Born: Southend, 22 April 1971
Height: 6'3" Weight: 13.4
Club Honours: FLC '97
Signed from Norwich in time for the start of Leicester's 1996-97 Premiership prog- ramme, the central defender excelled in thrilling home wins over Derby and Aston Villa, proving to be solid and reliable. In short, a typical City defender. A bargain buy by Martin O'Neill, Spencer had a major stabilising effect on a defence that was normally under a great deal of pressure, and despite being troubled by a thigh strain in March and a knee injury later on, went on to give exceptional performances at Wembley and Hillsborough, where he must have run Steve Walsh close for the Man of the Match award as the club ultimately lifted the Coca-Cola Cup. Is extremely flexible for a big man, having a fine recovery rate, and always starts favourite to win an aerial battle.
Southend U (From trainee on 22/5/89) FL 135/3 FLC 9 FAC 5 Others 7/1
Norwich C (£200,000 on 24/6/93) P/FL 67+7/1 FLC 10+1/1 FAC 0+2 Others 2
Leicester C (£600,000 on 17/8/96) PL 33+1 FLC 7 FAC 4

PRITCHARD David Michael
Born: Wolverhampton, 27 May 1972
Height: 5'8" Weight: 11.5
His return last November after a year out through injury was a tremendous boost to Bristol Rovers. A reliable and attacking full back, he continued to inspire team mates with his competitive attitude and it was no surprise when he took over the captaincy on the occasions when Andy Tillson was absent. However, having turned down the offer of a new contract with the club, David will be playing his football elsewhere this coming term.
West Bromwich A (From trainee on 5/7/90) FL 1+4 (Free to Telford during 1992 close season)
Bristol Rov (£15,000 on 25/2/94) FL 92 FLC 6 FAC 5 Others 6

PROCTOR Mark Gerard
Born: Middlesbrough, 30 January 1961
Height: 5'10" Weight: 11.12
International Honours: E: U21-4; Yth

An experienced midfielder signed by Hartlepool shortly before the transfer deadline last March, Mark had been out of full-time professional football for a couple of years. However, he proved to be just what was needed, playing an important part in Pool's end of season recovery by slowing the game down and feeding the ball to the forwards. Really only seen as a short-term signing, and a calculated gamble by the manager, Mick Tait, he was sufficiently im- pressive to suggest that he may be retained on a non-contract basis for 1997-98.
Middlesbrough (From apprentice on 14/9/78) FL 107+2/12 FLC 6/1 FAC 10/1
Nottingham F (£440,000 on 4/8/81) FL 60+4/5 FLC 10/3 FAC 2/1
Sunderland (£115,000 on 18/3/83) FL 115+2/19 FLC 13/2 FAC 6 Others 2/2
Sheffield Wed (£275,000 on 3/9/87) FL 59/4 FLC 1 FAC 6/1 Others 3
Middlesbrough (£300,000 on 23/3/89) F/PL 101+19/6 FLC 7+2 FAC 4+3 Others 11+1
Tranmere Rov (Free on 15/3/93) FL 31/1 FLC 1 FAC 1 Others 2+1/1 (Released during 1995 close season)
Hartlepool U (Free from South Shields on 21/3/97) FL 6

PROKAS Richard
Born: Penrith, 22 January 1976
Height: 5'9" Weight: 11.4
Club Honours: Div 3 '95; AMC '97
A hard-tackling Carlisle midfielder who operates just in front of the back four, Richard's first team appearances in 1996-97 were more limited than in the last campaign. An unspectacular player, but a grafter who will run all day for the club if required, despite not being a noted goalscorer, his last-minute effort at Swansea in December snatched all three points for the Cumbrians.
Carlisle U (From trainee on 18/7/94) FL 64+8/2 FLC 3+1 FAC 4 Others 13+3

PRUDHOE Mark
Born: Washington, 8 November 1963
Height: 6'0" Weight: 14.0
Club Honours: GMVC '90; Div 4 '91
Always a firm favourite with the Stoke supporters, Mark had an eventful campaign in 1996-97. Carried off on the first day, his return to first-team duty was short lived and he was publicly unhappy at being dropped. Then, after being loaned out to York and attracting a number of clubs, his season ended after failing a medical with an undiagnosed Achilles injury, and seeing a proposed £150,000 transfer to Bradford City fall through.
Sunderland (From apprentice on 11/9/81) FL 7
Hartlepool U (Loaned on 4/11/83) FL 3
Birmingham C (£22,000 on 24/9/84) FL 1 FLC 4
Walsall (£22,000 on 27/2/86) FL 26 FLC 4 FAC 1
Doncaster Rov (Loaned on 11/12/86) FL 5
Grimsby T (Loaned on 26/3/87) FL 8
Hartlepool U (Loaned on 29/8/87) FL 13
Bristol C (Loaned on 6/11/87) FL 3 Others 2
Carlisle U (£10,000 on 11/12/87) FL 34 FLC 2
Darlington (£10,000 on 16/3/89) FL 146 FLC 8 FAC 9 Others 4
Stoke C (£120,000 on 24/6/93) FL 82 FLC 6+1 FAC 5 Others 7
Peterborough U (Loaned on 30/9/94) FL 6
York C (Loaned on 14/2/97) FL 2

PUGH David
Born: Liverpool, 19 September 1964
Height: 6'1" Weight: 13.0
Club Honours: Div 2 '97
At home in any left-sided position, the Bury skipper, must have been one of the unluckiest players in the Football League during 1996-97. On 20 August, he scored in the Coca-Cola Cup at Notts County and then fractured his left elbow, missing the next six weeks. He regained his place, but then, on 13 January, scored in the Shakers' Auto Windscreens Trophy game against Mansfield only to shatter his right arm in two places during the match. It was an injury which needed an operation and a steel plate inserting in his arm. Happily, the club allowed him to appear as a substitute in the final championship clinching game and, along with stand-in skipper Chris Lucketti, he collected the trophy.
Chester C (£35,000 from Runcorn on 21/7/89) FL 168+11/23 FLC 13 FAC 11+1 Others 9
Bury (£22,500 on 3/8/94) FL 100+2/28 FLC 7/1 FAC 6 Others 9/3

PURSE Darren John
Born: Stepney, 14 February 1977
Height: 6'2" Weight: 12.8
It was a very eventful 1996-97 season for the Oxford centre back who had been signed during the summer from Leyton Orient. Purchased by Denis Smith as one for the future, he came into the side firstly at full back and then alongside either of the regular central defenders in successive games, mixing a series of impressive displays with a few errors, but learning a lot and being selected for the Nationwide squad versus the Italian League. Sadly ended the season suspended for an out-of-character incident.
Leyton Orient (From trainee on 22/2/94) FL 48+7/3 FLC 2 FAC 1 Others 7+1/2
Oxford U (£100,000 on 23/7/96) FL 25+6/1 FLC 4+1 FAC 1

PUTTNAM David Paul
Born: Leicester, 3 February 1967
Height: 5'10" Weight: 12.2
Since joining Gillingham in October 1995, this skilful, left-sided midfielder has made more substitute appearances than starts. He looks good at times and has the ability to go past full-backs with ease, but very often he flatters to deceive. His only moment of celebration in 1996-97 came when he scored the winner against high-flying Barnsley in the second round of the Coca-Cola Cup, after he came on as sub! Prior to being released during the summer, he spent the final two months of the campaign at Yeovil, when he helped the club win the ICIS Premier League.
Leicester C (£8,000 from Leicester U on 9/2/89) FL 4+3 FLC 0+1
Lincoln C (£35,000 on 21/1/90) FL 160+17/21 FLC 13+1/1 FAC 4 Others 8+1
Gillingham (£50,000 on 6/10/95) FL 15+25/2 FLC 1+5/1 FAC 0+5 Others 2

QUASHIE Nigel Francis
Born: Peckham, 20 July 1978
Height: 5'9" Weight: 11.0
International Honours: E: U21-1; Yth
Struck down by illness towards the end of 1995-96, the young central midfielder came back into the QPR side early last September, starting six games before injury ruled him out until the end of March. Desperately unlucky, Nigel returned to the side as a substitute at home to Wolves and then appeared in the final five games, only just beginning to show the kind of exciting form that earmarked him as a player to watch out for. Is strong on the ball with good touch and a willingness to get into areas where he can test the goalkeeper. Completed his season when winning his first England U21 cap against Poland at the end of May.
Queens Park R (From trainee on 1/8/95) P/FL 20+4 FLC 0+1 FAC 2/2

QUIGLEY Michael Anthony
Born: Manchester, 2 October 1970
Height: 5'7" Weight: 11.4
Once again, the injury jinx hit "Quigs" to rob Hull City of his midfield qualities in 1996-97. Struck down by a mystery stomach

virus in the early weeks of the campaign, he returned to find his best form, only to suffer knee, calf, and thigh complaints. A pocket battleship, Michael certainly deserves an injury-free season in 1997-98.
Manchester C (From trainee on 1/7/89) F/PL 3+9 Others 1
Wrexham (Loaned on 17/2/95) FL 4
Hull C (Free on 5/7/95) FL 32+10/2 FLC 2+1/1 FAC 3 Others 1

QUINN Stephen James (Jimmy)
Born: Coventry, 15 December 1974
Height: 6'1" Weight: 12.10
International Honours: NI: 8; B-1; U21-1; Yth
The young Blackpool striker, who continued to be the subject of transfer speculation and a regular in the Northern Ireland squad, was again a consistent scorer last season, even netting his first international goal. With pace and height to unsettle the best of defences, many of his goals in 1996-97 came in the shape of winners or equalisers. Is still an improving player.
Birmingham C (Trainee) FL 1+3
Blackpool (£25,000 on 5/7/93) FL 117+20/32 FLC 7+4/5 FAC 5+1/4 Others 7+3/2
Stockport Co (Loaned on 4/3/94) FL 0+1

QUINN James (Jimmy) Martin
Born: Belfast, 18 November 1959
Height: 6'0" Weight: 11.6
Club Honours: Div 2 '94
International Honours: NI: 46; B-1
Along with Mick Gooding, in 1996-97 he

completed his second full term as Reading's player/manager, though not playing so regularly. However, he made an effective contribution on the field, scoring four times, and giving a brave, if unorthodox, goal-keeping display to help Reading to a 3-2 win over Bolton after Bobby Mihailov had been injured, before resigning his post as the season drew to a close.
Swindon T (£10,000 from Oswestry on 31/12/81) FL 34+15/10 FLC 1+1 FAC 5+3/6 Others 1
Blackburn Rov (£32,000 on 15/8/84) FL 58+13/17 FLC 6+1/2 FAC 4/3 Others 2/1
Swindon T (£50,000 on 19/12/86) FL 61+3/30 FLC 6/8 FAC 5 Others 10+1/5
Leicester C (£210,000 on 20/6/88) FL 13+18/6 FLC 2+1 FAC 0+1 Others 0+1
Bradford C (Signed on 17/3/89) FL 35/14 FLC 2/1 Others 1
West Ham U (£320,000 on 30/12/89) FL 34+13/19 FLC 3/1 FAC 4+2/2 Others 1
Bournemouth (£40,000 on 5/8/91) FL 43+19/19 FLC 4/2 FAC 5/2 Others 2/1
Reading (£55,000 on 27/7/92) FL 149+33/71 FLC 12+4/12 FAC 9/5 Others 6+3/6

QUINN Niall John
Born: Dublin, 6 October 1966
Height: 6'4" Weight: 15.10
Club Honours: FLC '87
International Honours: Ei: 61; B-1; U23-1; U21-5; Yth; Sch
The tall striker became Sunderland's record signing after moving from Manchester City during the 1996 close season and started the campaign very well with three goals in his first seven starts, plus an international appearance for Eire, before an ankle injury in September kept him out until April. When he returned, however, the club were in desperate relegation trouble and although he provided them with some much needed presence in the penalty area, the drop could not be avoided. An old-fashioned type, and one of the finest headers in the game, not only is Niall a target man, but is a consistent scorer himself and will relish getting back to proper match fitness.
Arsenal (From juniors on 30/11/83) FL 59+8/14 FLC 14+2/4 FAC 8+2/2 Others 0+1
Manchester C (£800,000 on 21/3/90) F/PL 183+20/66 FLC 20+2/7 FAC 13+3/4 Others 3/1
Sunderland (£1,300,000 on 17/8/96) PL 8+4/2 FLC 1/1

QUINN Robert John
Born: Sidcup, 8 November 1976
Height: 5'11" Weight: 11.2
International Honours: Ei: U21-2
Another product of the Crystal Palace youth team, Robert started last season well, playing on the opening day at Birmingham and going on to become a regular member of the first team squad when putting 24 appearances under his belt. A strong and tenacious, hard-working defender, who is not only a ball winner but also skilled at getting the ball to the front men, Robert's good form also saw him selected for Republic of Ireland U21 side. Scored his first goal for the club in the home Coca-Cola Cup leg against Bury and followed that up with one in the league against Portsmouth.
Crystal Palace (From trainee on 11/3/95) FL 18+4/1 FLC 2+1/1 Others 2+1

Nigel Quashie

R

RADEBE Lucas
Born: Johannesburg, South Africa, 12 April 1969
Height: 6'1" Weight: 11.8
International Honours: South Africa: 25
Lucas' career flourished at Leeds in 1996-97, more so than any one else, due to the change of management and he was possibly the most improved player at the club. He was seen as one of the finest man markers in the Premiership, a point illustrated by his sterling performances when up against the likes of Eric Cantona, Gianfranco Zola, Matt Le Tissier and Fabrizio Ravanelli and putting the shackles on at a time when the side was struggling to stop conceding goals shortly after George Graham's arrival. Showing speed in recovery and no mean skill on the ball, the South African international was justifiably rewarded for his efforts with a new three-year contract.
Leeds U (£250,000 from Kaizer Chiefs on 5/9/94) PL 47+10 FLC 2+3 FAC 7+2

Lucas Radebe

RADUCIOIU Florin
Born: Romania, 17 March 1970
Height: 5'10" Weight: 11.6
International Honours: Romania: 39
The biggest disappointment of all Harry Redknapp's 1996 summer signings, inasmuch that he could not claim injuries as an excuse, the Romanian international forward simply failed to show the application and commitment required to meet the physical demands of the Premier League. Much was expected and required from West Ham's then record signing fee,

but, in the event, he only made six starts in the Premiership, being unimpressive in all of them, and whilst he did score two quality goals as a substitute at Old Trafford and Roker Park in December, it was too little too late. Redknapp then lost patience and returned him to his previous club, RCD Espanol, in January.
West Ham U (£2,400,000 from Espanol on 14/8/96) PL 6+5/2 FLC 1/1

RAE Alexander (Alex) Scott
Born: Glasgow, 30 September 1969
Height: 5'9" Weight: 11.12
International Honours: S: B-2; U21-8
A midfield schemer with a good goalscoring record, Alex arrived at Sunderland from Millwall in the summer of 1996 and could consider himself extremely unlucky to have made only 15 starts last term when the Rokerites were crying out for goals. In managing to record three strikes in his limited appearances, including a vital penalty in the 2-2 draw with local rivals Middlesbrough at Roker, the tenacious, hard-tackling Scot proved himself popular with Roker fans and hopefully he will get the chance to help the club in their attempt to return to the Premiership.
Falkirk (Free from Bishopbriggs in 1987) SL 71+12/20 SLC 5/1 SC 2+1
Millwall (£100,000 on 20/8/90) FL 205+13/63 FLC 13+2/1 FAC 13/6 Others 10/1
Sunderland (£750,000 on 14/6/96) PL 13+10/2 FLC 2/1

RAHMBERG Marino
Born: Orebro, Sweden, 7 August 1974
Height: 5'11" Weight: 11.12
International Honours: Sweden: 4
Signed on loan from Degerfors in January for ten weeks before returning home to Sweden, the former Swedish international striker never settled to the pace of the English game, making just one subs' appearance in a 4-2 defeat at Leicester before returning home. Arriving as added cover for injuries to Ashley Ward and Marco Gabbiadini, with others standing in as well, he was never really required.
Derby Co (Loaned from Degerfors on 14/1/97) PL 0+1

RAMAGE Craig Darren
Born: Derby, 30 March 1970
Height: 5'9" Weight: 11.8
International Honours: E: U21-3
Richly talented but enigmatic Watford midfield player whose season in 1996-97 was a frustration for both player and fans. Following a knee injury in September which led to a cartilage operation that cost him his first team place, he went on loan to Peterborough in February. Back at Vicarage Road, Craig returned as a striker for the run in, scoring three goals in three games, only to be sent off in the key match against Chesterfield.
Derby Co (From trainee on 20/7/88) FL 33+9/4 FLC 6+1/2 FAC 3+1/1 Others 0+3
Wigan Ath (Loaned on 16/2/89) FL 10/2 Others 0+1
Watford (£90,000 on 21/2/94) FL 99+5/27 FLC 8+1/2 FAC 7
Peterborough U (Loaned on 10/2/97) FL 7 Others 1

RAMASUT Mahan William Thomas (Tom)
Born: Cardiff, 30 August 1977
Height: 5'9" Weight: 10.10
International Honours: W: U21-2; Yth
Following his release by Norwich during the 1996 close season, the tricky two-footed winger made the breakthrough into the Bristol Rovers' side after a handful of reserve matches, when making his league debut on 26 October at Bury, coming on as a substitute. Tom made his full debut three days later against Brentford in a remarkable 2-1 victory, remembered for a bizarre gift of a goal when Bees' 'keeper, Kevin Dearden, was caught out by a phantom whistler. His good form brought him to the attention of the international selectors and he made his Welsh under 21 debut in Holland, winning a second cap against Belgium.
Norwich C (Signed on 28/7/95)
Bristol Rov (Free on 12/9/96) FL 5+6 FAC 1

RAMMELL Andrew (Andy) Victor
Born: Nuneaton, 10 February 1967
Height: 6'1" Weight: 13.12
A true old-fashioned centre forward, Andy scored some important goals for Southend, including the opener, during a difficult season in 1996-97. Good in the air and strong on the ground, he often shared forward duties with Jeroen Boere, but both suffered from lapses in form in a poor side. A wholehearted player, he could never be accused of not giving 100 per cent in the team's cause.
Manchester U (£40,000 from Atherstone U on 26/9/89)
Barnsley (£100,000 on 14/9/90) FL 149+36/44 FLC 11+3/1 FAC 12+1/4 Others 8/1
Southend U (Signed on 22/2/96) FL 32+11/11 FLC 2/1 FAC 1

RAMSAY John William
Born: Sunderland, 25 January 1979
Height: 5'8" Weight: 9.10
The second of Doncaster's YTS boys to gain first-team experience in 1996-97, John came off the subs' bench at Belle Vue against Stockport in the AWS match last December. An attacking midfielder or forward, he is expected to turn professional with the club on his trainee contract running out this coming October.
Doncaster Rov (Trainee) Others 0+1

RANDALL Adrian John
Born: Amesbury, 10 November 1968
Height: 5'11" Weight: 12.4
Club Honours: Div 4 '92, Div 2 '97
International Honours: E: Yth
After just one year with York City, and the club's record signing, the skilful midfielder was transferred to Bury last December, having shown good form earlier in 1996-97 and figuring prominently in the Coca-Cola Cup games against Everton. A more than useful addition to the Shakers' squad as a player who shows great awareness when going forward, he made his debut as a substitute at Gillingham and scored with his first touch. His season then climaxed as Bury won the second division title and he picked up a championship medal after just

19 league games.

Bournemouth (From apprentice on 2/9/86) FL 3 Others 1+2
Aldershot (Signed on 15/9/88) FL 102+5/12 FLC 3 FAC 11/3 Others 10/2
Burnley (£40,000 on 12/12/91) FL 105+20/8 FLC 6/1 FAC 8+2/1 Others 3
York C (£140,000 on 28/12/95) FL 26+6/2 FLC 5 FAC 0+1
Bury (£140,000 on 12/12/96) FL 14+5/3 Others 0+2

RANKINE Simon **Mark**
Born: Doncaster, 30 September 1969
Height: 5'9" Weight: 12.11

Midfielder Mark was bought by Preston from Wolves last September to add bite to midfield. Unfortunately, after making a promising start, a hamstring injury meant his participation in the starting line up became more sporadic and he seemed to suffer from a lack of confidence during the team's poor mid season, his form being affected. Hopefully, he will be able to show the fans the talents which persuaded Gary Peters to bring him to the club.

Doncaster Rov (From trainee on 4/7/88) FL 160+4/20 FLC 8+1/1 FAC 8/2 Others 14/2
Wolverhampton W (£70,000 on 31/1/92) FL 112+20/1 FLC 9+1 FAC 14+2 Others 7+2
Preston NE (£100,000 on 17/9/96) FL 19+4 FLC 2 FAC 2

RAPLEY Kevin John
Born: Reading, 21 September 1977
Height: 5'9" Weight: 10.8

Brentford right winger who signed professional forms during the 1996 close season, having previously been a trainee. After impressing in the reserves last season, Kevin was eventually blooded at Walsall in the penultimate league fixture, when coming off the bench for David McGee, and started the final game against Peterborough. Could be one to watch out for in 1997-98.

Brentford (From trainee on 8/7/96) FL 1+1

RATCLIFFE Simon
Born: Urmston, 8 February 1967
Height: 6'0" Weight: 13.0
Club Honours: Div 3 '92
International Honours: E: Yth; Sch

The workhorse of Gillingham's midfield, he just gets on with doing his job, with the added bonus of being able to score valuable goals, mainly because of his shooting prowess with a strong right foot. None was better than the 35 yarder he hit at Barnsley in the second round of the Coca-Cola Cup, one that he believed was the best of his career.

Manchester U (From apprentice on 13/2/85)
Norwich C (£40,000 on 16/6/87) FL 6+3 FLC 2
Brentford (£100,000 on 13/1/89) FL 197+17/14 FLC 13+3 FAC 9+1 Others 26+2/2
Gillingham (Free on 4/8/95) FL 84/9 FLC 9/2 FAC 5/1

RATTRAY Kevin Winston
Born: Tottenham, 6 October 1968
Height: 5'10" Weight: 11.11
Club Honours: FAT '95

The busy midfielder bought in the summer of 1996 from Gillingham could never quite secure a regular spot in the Barnet side

during 1996-97 and, apart from his 12 starts, spent most of his time on the bench, receiving treatment, on loan at Welling United, or in the reserves. However, with 1997-98 beckoning, he will be hoping for a change of fortune.

Gillingham (£5,000 from Woking on 23/6/95) FL 18+8/3 FLC 1 FAC 2 Others 2
Barnet (£15,000 on 13/9/96) FL 9 FLC 2 Others 1

RAVANELLI Fabrizio
Born: Italy, 11 December 1968
Height: 6'2" Weight: 12.6
International Honours: Italy: 17

Signed from Juventus immediately prior to the start of the 1996-97 campaign, the "White Feather" sent the home crowd into raptures on his debut at the Riverside in Middlesbrough's opening game of the last season when he scored the first ever hat trick there in the Premiership match against Liverpool. It was also the first ever debutant's hat trick and gave the fans a mouth watering feast of the fare that was about to be served up. His shirt over the head routine was to be witnessed by his adoring fans on 28 further occasions as he paraded his tremendous goalscoring opportunism around the country. Truly a striker of world class, the Italian international made giant strides to repay the staggering (for Boro) £7m transfer fee that was a prerequisite of his transfer in the first place, his goals in the league and both domestic cup competitions, establishing him as a striker of repute and ensuring his place in the company of Boro's legendary strikers, George Camsell, Micky Fenton, Charlie Wayman, Brian Clough, Alan Peacock, John Hickton, Bernie Slaven, and John Hendrie. At the time of going to press, with Boro due to play in the first division this coming term, Fabrizio's future career was still undecided.

Middlesbrough (£7,000,000 from Juventus on 15/8/96) PL 33/16 FLC 8/9 FAC 7/6

RAVEN Paul Duncan
Born: Salisbury, 28 July 1970
Height: 6'1" Weight: 12.12
International Honours: E: Sch

Paul had a sound 1996-97 season in West Brom's defence, performing competently alongside a variety of partners, including Paul Mardon, Daryl Burgess, and Shaun Murphy, and even Paul Groves and Julian Darby at times. Strong in the air, resilient on the ground, he received his fair quota of injuries, but always came up fighting.

Doncaster Rov (From juniors on 6/6/88) FL 52/4 FLC 2 FAC 5 Others 2
West Bromwich A (£100,000 on 23/3/89) FL 208+4/14 FLC 12 FAC 8/3 Others 15/1
Doncaster Rov (Loaned on 27/11/91) FL 7

RAWLINSON Mark David
Born: Bolton, 9 June 1975
Height: 5'10" Weight: 11.4

After just four starts for Bournemouth in 1995-96, Mark established himself as a first-team regular towards the latter part of last season, taking over the central midfield role left by club captain, Matt Holland, who moved into defence. Playing in the centre of

midfield, he makes driving runs forward and is a good passer of the ball.

Manchester U (From trainee on 5/7/93)
Bournemouth (Free on 1/7/95) FL 25+19/2 FLC 0+1 FAC 1 Others 2

RAYNOR Paul James
Born: Nottingham, 29 April 1966
Height: 6'0" Weight: 12.11
Club Honours: WC '89, '91

A two-footed midfielder who operated on both sides of the Cambridge defence in 1996-97 as a wing back and missed only a handful of games all season, Paul scored valuable goals, including home winners against Hartlepool and Hull. Is also excellent from dead-ball situations.

Nottingham F (From apprentice on 2/4/84) FL 3 FLC 1
Bristol Rov (Loaned on 28/3/85) FL 7+1
Huddersfield T (Free on 15/8/85) FL 38+12/9 FLC 3 FAC 2+1 Others 1
Swansea C (Free on 27/3/87) FL 170+21/27 FLC 11+1/3 FAC 8+1/1 Others 15+1/3
Wrexham (on 17/10/88) FL 6
Cambridge U (Free on 10/3/92) FL 46+3/2 FLC 5 FAC 1 Others 2+1/1
Preston NE (£36,000 on 23/7/93) FL 72+8/9 FLC 4+1 FAC 7/1 Others 10/2
Cambridge U (Signed on 12/9/95) FL 78+1/7 FLC 1+1 FAC 2 Others 1

READ Paul Colin
Born: Harlow, 25 September 1973
Height: 5'11" Weight: 12.6
International Honours: E: Sch

Signed from Arsenal last January for what appeared to be an initial bargain £35,000, this mobile and opportunist striker in the penalty area made an immediate impact for Wycombe with three goals in his first four games. Although a groin strain sidelined him after seven games and he found it difficult to break back into a resurgent team, he clearly has a big future at Wycombe. Appears to have the knack of being in the right place at the right time.

Arsenal (From trainee on 11/10/91)
Leyton Orient (Loaned on 10/3/95) FL 11 Others 1
Southend U (Loaned on 6/10/95) FL 3+1/1 Others 1
Wycombe W (£35,000 + on 17/1/97) FL 7+6/4

READY Karl
Born: Neath, 14 August 1972
Height: 6'1" Weight: 13.3
International Honours: W: 1; B-2; U21-5; Sch

Started the opening day of last season as QPR's right back at home to Oxford, but due to injury missed the next 11 games before returning to the side at Grimsby and enjoying a prolonged spell at the heart of the defence, prior to being injured and missing the remaining six games, apart from a subs' appearance at Bradford. Able to play anywhere across the back four, good in the air and steady, he was an excellent foil to Alan McDonald as Rangers chased a play-off place. Won his first full Welsh cap when selected for the match against the Republic in February.

Queens Park R (From trainee on 13/8/90) F/PL 77+13/3 FLC 4+2/1 FAC 5

REDFEARN Neil David
Born: Dewsbury, 20 June 1965
Height: 5'9" Weight: 12.8
Club Honours: Div 2 '91

In what turned out to be the greatest season in Barnsley's history, Neil, as captain, led the team from the front in 1996-97, missing just three games. Acclaimed as a true pro, and nicknamed "Mr Perpetual Motion", as the club's leading scorer he also had his best ever season in terms of goals and would have broken the 20 mark had it not been for a couple of missed penalties. A terrific tally when you realise that he sat in central midfield, even allowing for the fact that six of them came from the penalty spot, and he fully deserves Premiership football as a result of his endeavours.

Bolton W (Free from Nottingham F juniors on 23/6/82) FL 35/1 FLC 2 FAC 4
Lincoln C (£8,250 on 23/3/84) FL 96+4/13 FLC 4 FAC 3/1 Others 7
Doncaster Rov (£17,500 on 22/8/86) FL 46/14 FLC 2 FAC 3/1 Others 2
Crystal Palace (£100,000 on 31/7/87) FL 57/10 FLC 6 FAC 1 Others 1
Watford (£150,000 on 21/11/88) FL 22+2/3 FLC 1 FAC 6/3 Others 5/1
Oldham Ath (£150,000 on 12/1/90) FL 56+6/16 FLC 3/1 FAC 7+1/3 Others 1
Barnsley (£150,000 on 5/9/91) FL 252+3/61 FLC 18/4 FAC 14/4 Others 5

Jamie Redknapp

REDKNAPP Jamie Frank
Born: Barton on Sea, 25 June 1973
Height: 6'0" Weight: 12.0
Club Honours: FLC '95
International Honours: E: 8; B-1; U21-18; Yth; Sch

After struggling to retain his Liverpool role in 1996-97, through injury and the good form of Michael Thomas, the classy midfielder finally returned as a regular late on in the campaign, his accurate passing and intelligent distribution shining through. At

the same time, he also regained his England place. Together, with John Barnes, Jamie finished a long, hard campaign at the core of a powerful midfield partnership which, whilst not being the most lethal in terms of tackling, was surely among the most creative and attack minded. Born into a football family, his father Harry manages fellow Premiership side, West Ham, if he can overcome the injury problems there should be no stopping him.

Bournemouth (From trainee on 27/6/90) FL 6+7 FLC 3 FAC 3 Others 2
Liverpool (£350,000 on 15/1/91) F/PL 134+23/16 FLC 22/4 FAC 14+1/1 Others 13+4/1

REDMILE Matthew Ian
Born: Nottingham, 12 November 1976
Height: 6'3" Weight: 14.10

The young Notts County central defender broke into the side in 1996-97, having played just once previously, holding down a place ahead of more experienced players, despite the club being in the second division danger zone throughout the campaign. A local lad, whose father was once on the club's books, he is a colossus who possesses exceptional ball skills and passing ability for one so large. Thought highly of at Meadow Lane and reckoned to be a great prospect.

Notts Co (From trainee on 4/7/95) FL 23/2 FAC 3 Others 2

REDMOND Stephen (Steve)
Born: Liverpool, 2 November 1967
Height: 5'11" Weight: 12.13
Club Honours: FAYC '86
International Honours: E: U21-14; Yth

Solid and dependable as ever in Oldham's rearguard during 1996-97, forming excellent partnerships at different times with both Richard Graham and Shaun Garnett, Steve suffered an horrific injury in the match at Boundary Park against his old club, Manchester City, just before Christmas. With the backbone of the team gone, Latics' slim hopes of first division survival also seemed to go with him, while two operations later it is still not clear whether his knee ligaments are going to hold up to the rigours of league football in 1997-98. A sweet striker of the ball, he scored twice, including the opening goal of the campaign.

Manchester C (From apprentice on 3/12/84) FL 231+4/7 FLC 24 FAC 17 Others 11
Oldham Ath (£300,000 on 10/7/92) P/FL 163+8/4 FLC 18 FAC 7+2 Others 1+1

REED Adam Maurice
Born: Bishop Auckland, 18 February 1975
Height: 6'0" Weight: 12.0

Adam, a young central defender who was transferred to Blackburn in the summer of 1995, returned to Darlington in 1996-97 on three-month's loan towards the end of the season and captained the side in the local derby against Hartlepool. Yet to play in the Premiership with Rovers, he has great aerial strength and positional qualities.

Darlington (From trainee on 16/7/93) FL 45+7/1 FLC 1+1 FAC 1 Others 3
Blackburn Rov (£200,000 on 9/8/95)
Darlington (Loaned on 21/2/97) FL 14

REED Ian Paul
Born: Lichfield, 4 September 1975
Height: 5'9" Weight: 11.4

The Shrewsbury midfielder spent some time on loan at Stafford Rangers in 1996-97, as first team opportunities were limited to just one AWS appearance and three league substitutions, and Ian will be looking to improve on that this time round if he is to make it at Gay Meadow. Is an attacking player with an eye for goal.

Shrewsbury T (From trainee on 4/7/94) FL 10+8/2 FLC 2 FAC 0+1 Others 2

REED Martin John
Born: Scarborough, 10 January 1978
Height: 6'0" Weight: 11.6

A promising young York City central defender who came through the junior ranks, he did well when thrust into first-team action at right back in a game at Stockport last season and could be challenging for a regular place in 1997-98.

York C (From trainee on 4/7/96) FL 2

REES Jason Mark
Born: Aberdare, 22 December 1969
Height: 5'5" Weight: 10.2
International Honours: W: 1; U21-3; B-1; Yth; Sch

In making just one start for Portsmouth in 1996-97, Jason had too few chances to impress, despite having scored the only goal of the game at Grimsby. It therefore came as no surprise when the terrier-like ball winner, and former Welsh international, went out on loan to Exeter where he immediately made a strong impression on the left-hand side of midfield in January. However, although City had planned on putting in an offer for Jason, his time at the club lapsed and he returned to Fratton Park and reserve team football, prior to being released in the summer.

Luton T (From trainee on 1/7/88) FL 59+23 FLC 3+2 FAC 2+1 Others 5+1/2
Mansfield T (Loaned on 23/12/93) FL 15/1 Others 1
Portsmouth (Free on 18/7/94) FL 30+13/3 FLC 2+1 FAC 0+1
Exeter C (Loaned on 31/1/97) FL 7

REEVES Alan
Born: Birkenhead, 19 November 1967
Height: 6'0" Weight: 12.0

A good quality centre back who made only one full start for Wimbledon last term, and that in the Coca-Cola Cup, the tall, blonde Scouse lad is one to watch in the box at set pieces as he can head the ball with immense power and accuracy. An old-fashioned type of defender who did not fit into Joe Kinnear's plans in 1996-97, nobody can doubt his enthusiasm or ability.

Norwich C (Signed from Heswall on 20/9/88)
Gillingham (Loaned on 9/2/89) FL 18
Chester C (£10,000 on 18/8/89) FL 31+9/2 FLC 1+1 FAC 3 Others 3
Rochdale (Free on 2/7/91) FL 119+2/9 FLC 12/1 FAC 6 Others 5
Wimbledon (£300,000 on 6/9/94) PL 52+5/4 FLC 2+1 FAC 8

REEVES David Edward
Born: Birkenhead, 19 November 1967
Height: 6'0" Weight: 12.6
Club Honours: Div 3 '95

Centre forward David was bought from Carlisle to replace Andy Saville in Preston's attack last October and had a fairly successful start to his career at Deepdale. His hit list included an FA Cup hat trick against Altrincham, and his 100th league goal in the 5-1 thrashing at Luton. On the down side, this hard-working, wholehearted player also received a first-half dismissal against Watford. The lack of a regular strike partner did not help him in his efforts to improve Preston's poor scoring rate last year and he looks to put things right in 1997-98.

Sheffield Wed (Free from Heswall on 6/8/88) FL 8+9/2 FLC 1+1/1 FAC 1+1 Others 0+1
Scunthorpe U (Loaned on 17/12/86) FL 3+1/2
Scunthorpe U (Loaned on 1/10/87) FL 6/4
Burnley (Loaned on 20/11/87) FL 16/8 Others 2/1
Bolton W (£80,000 on 17/8/89) FL 111+23/29 FLC 14+1/1 FAC 8+5/5 Others 9+2/7
Notts Co (£80,000 on 25/3/93) FL 9+4/2 FLC 1+1
Carlisle U (£121,000 on 1/10/93) FL 127/47 FLC 9/5 FAC 9/4 Others 23/7
Preston NE (Signed on 9/10/96) FL 33+1/11 FAC 2/3 Others 1

REGIS David (Dave)

Born: Paddington, 3 March 1964
Height: 6'1" Weight: 13.8
Club Honours: Div 2 '93

With the signing and form of Paul Wilkinson at Barnsley, Dave's first team opportunities were limited to just seven subs' appearances and in order to keep match fit he was loaned out first to Peterborough and then Notts County. A powerful and still very quick striker whose physical presence causes problems to defenders, he scored once in seven appearances at Posh, while at Meadow Lane he proved extremely popular with two goals in ten games. A former County player, he is still fondly remembered as the scorer of a Wembley play-off goal.

Notts Co (£25,000 from Barnet on 28/9/90) FL 31+15/15 FLC 0+2 Others 6/2
Plymouth Arg (£200,000 on 7/11/91) FL 28+3/4 FLC 2/3 FAC 1
Bournemouth (Loaned on 13/8/92) FL 6/2
Stoke C (£100,000 on 23/10/92) FL 49+14/15 FLC 2/1 FAC 4+1/2 Others 7+1/2
Birmingham C (£200,00 on 1/8/94) FL 4+2/2 FLC 1
Southend U (Signed on 16/9/94) FL 34+4/9 FLC 1 FAC 1 Others 1+2/1
Barnsley (Signed on 21/2/96) FL 4+12/1 FLC 0+3
Peterborough U (Loaned on 30/9/96) FL 4+3/1
Notts Co (Loaned on 7/2/97) FL 7+3/2

REGTOP Erik

Born: Emmen, Holland, 16 February 1968
Height: 5'8" Weight: 11.6

Signed from the Dutch Premier side, Herenveen, during the 1996 close season, the pacy centre forward played very few games for Bradford before becoming homesick. Despite starting in good fashion at Valley Parade, opening both his and the club's scoring account on the first day of the campaign, a penalty in a 3-1 win over Portsmouth, that was it as far as goals were concerned and, with his family also unable to settle, he moved to the Swiss First Division side, FC St Gallen, on 4 October.

Bradford C (Free from FC Herenveen on 12/7/96) FL 5+3/1

REID Nicholas (Nicky) Scott

Born: Davyhulme, 30 October 1960
Height: 5'10" Weight: 12.5
International Honours: E: U21-6

Now in the twilight of his career, Nicky stepped into the Bury first team on six occasions in 1996-97, deputising early on at left back for the injured Gordon Armstrong, before coming into midfield for a couple of games at the end of the season, prior to being released during the summer. Very much a utility player, but still an excellent passer of the ball, he belies his 36 years.

Manchester C (From apprentice on 4/11/78) FL 211+6/2 FLC 20 FAC 17 Others 8 (Signed for Seattle Sounders on 9/5/82. Transferred back on 24/9/82)
Blackburn Rov (Free on 10/7/87) FL 160+14/9 FLC 13 FAC 6+2 Others 13+1/1
Bristol C (Loaned on 17/9/92) FL 3+1 Others 1
West Bromwich A (Free on 7/11/92) FL 13+7 FAC 2+1 Others 2+1/1
Wycombe W (Free on 4/3/94) FL 6+2 FAC 0+1 Others 5 (Free to Woking during 1995 close season)
Bury (Free from Witton A on 15/12/95) FL 19+6 FLC 1

REID Paul Robert

Born: Oldbury, 19 January 1968
Height: 5'9" Weight: 11.8

An experienced midfielder who spent most of last season on Huddersfield's transfer list, Paul surprisingly left the club on transfer deadline day after successfully forcing his way back in to the side and showing touches of his old form. His move to Oldham saw him line up with the man who brought him to Huddersfield, Neil Warnock, and he repaid his faith when making an immediate impact down the left-hand side. A solid tackler with a good shot in his left foot, he scored a spectacular 35 yarder against Birmingham.

Leicester C (From apprentice on 9/1/86) FL 140+22/21 FLC 13/4 FAC 5+1 Others 6+2
Bradford C (Loaned on 19/3/92) FL 7
Bradford C (£25,000 on 27/7/92) FL 80+2/15 FLC 3/2 FAC 3 Others 5/1
Huddersfield T (£70,000 on 20/5/94) FL 70+7/6 FLC 9/1 FAC 5+1 Others 1
Oldham Ath (£100,000 on 27/3/97) FL 9/1

REID Shaun

Born: Huyton, 13 October 1965
Height: 5'8" Weight: 12.2

Having failed to hold down a place at Bury in 1996-97, Shaun joined Chester on a permanent basis in January, following a period on loan, and proved to be the catalyst behind the club's push for the play offs. A tenacious midfield general, and very much a favourite with City's fans who admired his ball-winning qualities, the only games he missed were through injury. Is very much in the same mould as his brother, Peter, the Sunderland manager.

Rochdale (From apprentice on 20/9/83) FL 126+7/4 FLC 10/2 FAC 5/1 Others 12
Preston NE (Loaned on 12/12/85) FL 3
York C (£32,500 on 23/12/88) FL 104+2/7 FLC 7 FAC 4 Others 5/1
Rochdale (Free on 16/8/92) FL 106+1/10 FLC 8 FAC 5/1 Others 8+1/2
Bury (£25,000 on 5/7/95) FL 20+1 FLC 5 FAC 1 Others 2
Chester C (£30,000 on 25/11/96) FL 27/1 Others 2

REINELT Robert (Robbie) Squire

Born: Loughton, 11 March 1974
Height: 5'10" Weight: 12.7

Having had a mixed time at Colchester in 1996-97, Robbie signed for Brighton last February to add some attacking punch to a side already in dire straits. Did not get off to a great start, being concussed and substituted in the first half of his initial appearance at Carlisle, but quickly settled into the squad. Bagged three crucial goals during the Seagulls' nerve-racking run in to the season, including the priceless equaliser at Hereford on the last day of the campaign, which saw Albion escape being relegated to the Conference.

Aldershot (Trainee) FL 3+2
Gillingham (Free from Wivenhoe T on 19/3/93) FL 34+18/5 FLC 3/1 FAC 5+2/2 Others 5
Colchester U (Signed on 22/3/95) FL 22+26/10 FLC 4+1/2 FAC 1 Others 3/1
Brighton & Hove A (£15,000 on 13/2/97) FL 7+5/3

RENNIE David

Born: Edinburgh, 29 August 1964
Height: 6'0" Weight: 12.0
International Honours: S: Yth;

Released by the Premier League's Coventry during the 1996 close season, the central defender, cum midfielder, was snapped up by Northampton. With a no-nonsense style to his game he is a man you can rely upon, also being a free-kick expert and dangerous at set pieces.

Leicester C (From apprentice on 18/5/82) FL 21/1 FLC 2
Leeds U (£50,000 on 17/1/86) FL 95+6/5 FLC 7 FAC 7/1 Others 1
Bristol C (£175,000 on 31/7/89) FL 101+3/8 FLC 8 FAC 9 Others 5
Birmingham C (£120,000 on 20/2/92) FL 32+3/4 FLC 1 Others 1
Coventry C (£100,000 on 11/3/93) PL 80+2/3 FLC 6 FAC 3+1
Northampton T (Free on 5/8/96) FL 42+1/4 FLC 4 Others 5

RICE Gary James

Born: Zambia, 25 September 1975
Height: 5'9" Weight: 11.12

Another of Exeter's players to have come up through the youth ranks, Gary was a squad player last season, mainly appearing on the left-hand side of defence. He will be looking for a regular spot in 1997-98 if he can see off competition, mainly from Darren Hughes.

Exeter C (From trainee on 7/7/94) FL 31+13 FLC 3 Others 4

RICHARDS Dean Ivor

Born: Bradford, 9 June 1974
Height: 6'2" Weight: 13.5
International Honours: E: U21-4

The Wolves' central defender has undoubted talent but does not seem the same since hurting his knee in a car crash in January 1996, despite being elected by his fellow professionals to the PFA award-winning side. Gave some good displays in his 23 appearances, but was restricted to two games as sub in December, prior to looking the part on his return against Albion the next month, racing into their area to score with a powerful header. However, after one more

game, a turn in training led to a considerable tear. Unfortunately, it was a variation of his knee problem and an operation was required to repair the split, almost a year after the crash. Having failed to recover by May, it now looks likely that the cruciate surgery will keep him out for quite a while yet.

Bradford C (From trainee on 10/7/92) FL 82+4/4 FLC 7/1 FAC 4/1 Others 3+2
Wolverhampton W (£1,850,000 on 25/3/95) FL 65+3/4 FLC 7 FAC 2 Others 2

Dean Richards

RICHARDS Tony Spencer
Born: Newham, 17 September 1973
Height: 6'0" Weight: 13.1

The aggressive Cambridge forward missed the first two games of last season through suspension, before an achilles injury then sidelined him and, without full fitness, more often than not found himself on the bench. There was no doubting that United missed his battling forward play and the fact that they assumed he would obtain more than four goals obviously contributed to the poor goalscoring total at the club. Has great strength on the ball and also puts his head in where it hurts.

West Ham U (From trainee on 14/8/92. Free to Hong Kong R during 1993 close season)
Cambridge U (Signed from Sudbury T on 10/8/95) FL 29+13/5 FLC 1 Others 3

RICHARDSON Barry
Born: Wallsend, 5 August 1969
Height: 6'1" Weight: 12.1

An excellent shot-stopper, despite being let down at times by disciplinary problems, the goalkeeper's superb form saved the Imps on many occasions during the season. Replaced by John Vaughan for the final weeks of the

campaign, as he had been when the pair were at Preston together, his confident play, on occasion, can see him dribbling out of his area.

Sunderland (From trainee on 20/5/88)
Scarborough (Free on 21/3/89) FL 30 FLC 1 Others 1
Stockport Co (Free on 16/8/91)
Northampton T (Free on 10/9/91) FL 96 FLC 4 FAC 5 Others 8
Preston NE (£20,000 on 25/7/94) FL 20 FLC 2 FAC 3 Others 2
Lincoln C (£20,000 on 20/10/95) FL 70 FLC 5 FAC 2 Others 1

RICHARDSON Dominic Kevin
Born: Plymouth, 19 March 1978
Height: 5'11" Weight: 11.6

Having made his Plymouth debut during the previous season, the youth team centre forward, who has scored plenty of goals at junior level, failed to oust his senior colleagues in 1996-97, making no impact at all apart from a solitary substitute appearance in the Auto Windscreen Shield game against Bournemouth. Released during the summer, following a spell on loan at Weston super Mare, there is still plenty of time for this lively youngster to make the breakthrough he is looking for.

Plymouth Arg (From trainee on 8/8/96) Others 0+3

RICHARDSON Ian George
Born: Barking, 22 October 1970
Height: 5'10" Weight: 11.1
International Honours: E: SP-1

Having arrived late in professional football with Birmingham, before coming to Notts County as Colin Murphy's midfield anchor man in 1995-96, Ian continued to make up for lost time in 1996-97, proving himself to be a tough tackler with terrific energy, which carried him from box to box. An aerial danger at set pieces, he scored his first goal for County in a 2-1 home defeat against Luton in February.

Birmingham C (£60,000 from Dagenham & Redbridge on 23/8/95) FL 3+4 FLC 3+1 FAC 2 Others 1+2
Notts Co (£200,000 on 19/1/96) FL 31+3/1 FLC 2 Others 5

RICHARDSON Jonathan (Jon) Derek
Born: Nottingham, 29 August 1975
Height: 6'0" Weight: 12.6

It was another superb season in 1996-97 for Jon in the centre of Exeter's defence, his composure helping the Grecians out on many occasions. Good in the air and on the ground, he had the presence of Noel Blake to help him through difficult times as the team struggled.

Exeter C (From trainee on 7/7/94) FL 127+4/3 FLC 5/1 FAC 5 Others 7

RICHARDSON Kevin
Born: Newcastle, 4 December 1962
Height: 5'7" Weight: 11.7
Club Honours: FAC '84; CS '84, '86; Div 1 '85, '89; ECWC '85; FLC '94
International Honours: E: 1

The veteran Coventry midfielder consistently demonstrated the attributes that have made his career such a successful one in

1996-97, covering miles, chasing, closing people down, and still finding time to deliver the killer ball. He demonstrated the latter skill to great effect in the 2-1 win over Newcastle in December when his probing passes made both goals. Dropped after the Gillingham defeat, and showing great resilience in playing for the reserves without complaint, his recall to the side coincided with the rich vein of form in December and overall was on the losing side less times than any other regular player. Although rested again in the final run in, Kevin played vital substitute roles against Southampton and Arsenal.

Everton (From apprentice on 8/12/80) FL 95+14/16 FLC 10+3/3 FAC 13/1 Others 7+2
Watford (£225,000 on 4/9/86) FL 39/2 FLC 3 FAC 7 Others 1
Arsenal (£200,000 on 26/8/87) FL 88+8/5 FLC 13+3/2 FAC 9/1 Others 3 (£750,000 to Real Sociedad on 1/7/90)
Aston Villa (£450,000 on 6/8/91) F/PL 142+1/13 FLC 15/3 FAC 12 Others 10
Coventry C (£300,000 on 16/2/95) PL 72+3 FLC 8/1 FAC 7

Kevin Richardson

RICHARDSON Lee James
Born: Halifax, 12 March 1969
Height: 5'11" Weight: 11.0

Undoubtedly the most skilful player on Oldham's books, and strong with it, Lee would have been a regular throughout 1996-97, had it not been for a hernia problem that finally resulted in an operation last May. As in previous seasons, he just loved taking penalties, three more going in during the campaign, making a career total of 27 taken and 27 scored. His shooting power was also seen to good effect in the 2-2 home draw against Tranmere, his tremendous right-foot

drive from fully 25 yards crashing in to the top corner for the equaliser. Hopefully, will be fully recovered in time for the 1997-98 start.

Halifax T (From trainee on 6/7/87) FL 43+13/2 FLC 4 FAC 4+2 Others 6
Watford (£175,000 on 9/2/89) FL 40+1/1 FLC 1+1 FAC 1
Blackburn Rov (£250,000 on 15/8/90) FL 50+12/3 FLC 1 Others 2+2
Aberdeen (£152,000 on 16/9/92) SL 59+5/6 SLC 2/1 SC 8/2 Others 3/1
Oldham Ath (£300,000 on 12/8/94) FL 82+6/21 FLC 6/2 FAC 3 Others 4

RICHARDSON Lloyd Matthew
Born: Dewsbury, 7 October 1977
Height: 5'11" Weight: 11.12
International Honours: E: Yth

Having spent over two years as a professional on Oldham's books, Lloyd's debut, when coming off the bench for the second half at Oxford last February, was long overdue. Originally an out-and-out winger, but now a wide midfielder, in the short time he was on the park he looked to be both tricky and confident on the ball and most certainly one to follow in the future. Watch this space....
Oldham Ath (From trainee on 11/10/94) FL 0+1

RICHARDSON Neil Thomas
Born: Sunderland, 3 March 1968
Height: 6'0" Weight: 13.9
Club Honours: AMC '96

As Rotherham's 1995-96 Player of the Year, he soon found himself out of favour last season, despite the fact that he had a reputation of being the best long passer of the ball in the club. Probably more comfortable in the heart of the defence, Neil can also play in a midfield role, but he had to spend three months out on loan at Exeter City in order to give him first-team football. Having equipped himself well at St James' Park he returned to Millmoor and still managed to give of his best when called upon, prior to being released in the summer.
Rotherham U (Signed from Brandon U on 18/8/89) FL 127+14/7 FLC 11+1 FAC 4+1 Others 10+2/1
Exeter C (Loaned on 8/11/96) FL 14 Others 2

RICHARDSON Nicholas (Nick) John
Born: Halifax, 11 April 1967
Height: 6'1" Weight: 12.6
Club Honours: Div 3 '93; WC '93

After starting 1996-97 in good form for Chester, the attacking midfielder suffered an horrendous knee injury during the match at Hartlepool in October and, following surgery to repair two ligaments, he was forced to undergo a lengthy rehabilitation programme which put him out of action for the rest of the season. A skilful player with the ability to get into shooting positions and score spectacular goals, he was badly missed, especially at the play-off stage.
Halifax T (Free from Emley on 15/11/88) FL 89+12/17 FLC 6+4/2 FAC 2+1/1 Others 6/1
Cardiff C (£35,000 on 13/8/92) FL 106+5/13 FLC 4 FAC 6 Others 12+2/2
Wrexham (Loaned on 21/10/94) FL 4/2
Chester C (Loaned on 16/12/94) FL 6/1

Bury (£22,500 on 8/8/95) FL 3+2 FLC 1
Chester C (£40,000 on 7/9/95) FL 45+1/4 FLC 2 FAC 1 Others 2/1

RICHES Steven (Steve) Alexander
Born: Sydney, Australia, 6 August 1976
Height: 6'1" Weight: 12.6

A left winger who joined Leyton Orient from Warringah Dolphins last September, having spent the early part of the season on trial with West Ham and Crewe, Steve showed himself to be a player with tremendous pace. However, finding it difficult to adjust to English football, he had spells with Billericay and Millwall to try and gain valuable experience and will, with experience, surely become a valuable member of the squad.
Leyton Orient (Signed from Warringah Dolphins on 27/9/96) FL 2+3

RICKERS Paul Steven
Born: Leeds, 9 May 1975
Height: 5'10" Weight: 11.0

Despite Oldham failing to avoid the drop into the second division last season, Paul never missed a game and was always in the thick of things in midfield, showing the heart of a lion. Not just an energetic player, but a skilful one also, being comfortable on the ball, tidy in possession, and always looking to start a move. Packs a good shot also, hitting the target four times during the campaign, which included a terrific 30-yard effort at Sheffield United that beat his team mate Gary Kelly's brother, Alan, all ends up for the equaliser in a 2-2 draw, and a home double against Wolves that produced a 3-2 win.
Oldham Ath (From trainee on 16/7/93) FL 72+1/5 FLC 5 FAC 2+1 Others 1+2

RICKETTS Michael Barrington
Born: Birmingham, 4 December 1978
Height: 6'2" Weight: 11.12

After scoring on his Walsall debut on the final day of the previous season, this tall striker scored another coolly-taken goal in a substitute appearance against Shrewsbury last March and, at 18, looks an outstanding prospect, despite his manager being reluctant to rush him into regular league action too soon. With a good football brain, and good feet, coupled with aerial ability, he should not be too long in making the grade.
Walsall (From trainee on 13/9/96) FL 2+10/2 FLC 0+1

RIDEOUT Paul David
Born: Bournemouth, 14 August 1964
Height: 5'11" Weight: 12.2
Club Honours: FAC '95; CS '95
International Honours: E: U21-5; Yth; Sch

Paul thought he had secured a lucrative transfer to the Chinese League with Huan Dao Vanguards towards the end of last season, only to be called back by caretaker manager, Dave Watson, to ease a crippling Everton injury crisis. Having returned to play what Watson later described as "the match of his life" against Tottenham in an unfamiliar midfield role and helping to secure Everton's escape from a relegation

battle, he was allowed to return to China to complete his £250,000 transfer. A much travelled and experienced player, who holds the ball up well and is excellent in the air, the striker figured in only a handful of first-team matches during 1996-97, of which three were in that unusual central midfield role.
Swindon T (From apprentice on 15/8/81) FL 90+5/38 FLC 3/2 FAC 7/1
Aston Villa (£200,000 on 1/6/83) FL 50+4/19 FLC 4+2/3 FAC 1+1 Others 1 (£400,000 to Bari on 1/7/85)
Southampton (£430,000 on 5/7/88) FL 68+7/19 FLC 13/2 FAC 5+2 Others 1
Swindon T (Loaned on 28/3/91) FL 9/1
Notts Co (£250,000 on 16/9/91) FL 9+2/3 FLC 2 FAC 1 Others 2
Glasgow R (£500,000 on 10/1/92) FL 7+5/1 FLC 0+1 FAC 1
Everton (£500,000 on 14/8/92) PL 86+26/29 FLC 11+2/3 FAC 9+1/3 Others 5/1

RIDGEWAY Ian David
Born: Reading, 28 December 1975
Height: 5'8" Weight: 10.6

Having made his debut for Notts County in 1994-95, but not called up for first team duty the following season, Ian appeared eight times in 1996-97, either on the Magpies' right wing or at wing back, before being released during the summer. Proved to be a smart crosser of the ball, however.
Notts Co (From trainee on 15/7/94) FL 3+4 Others 0+2

RIDLER David George
Born: Liverpool, 12 March 1976
Height: 6'1" Weight: 12.2

David is a late starter in the game, being recommended to Wrexham by Karl Connolly, who runs the Merseyside Sunday League side, Rocky's. Having previously played as a midfielder, cum forward, the Racecourse management team converted him into a central defender with no little success. Earlier qualified as a chef and baker, he made an impressive first full league appearance at Deepdale against Preston last March and hopes to "cook up" a selection problem for Brian Flynn in the near future.
Wrexham (Free from Rockys on 3/7/96) FL 7-4 Others 1

RIEPER Marc
Born: Rodoure, Denmark, 5 June 1968
Height: 6'4" Weight: 14.2
International Honours: Denmark: 47

The big Danish international central defender enjoyed another good spell in the heart of the West Ham defence in partnership with Slaven Bilic in 1996-97. Strong in the air, and always a threat at corners, he scored an early season goal, albeit a low shot through a crowd of defenders, which saved a point against Coventry. However, his finest game came at Anfield in January when he not only subdued the Liverpool forwards to secure an unexpected point in a goalless draw, but also broke forward for two excellent pots at goal, both well saved by David James. He lost his way somewhat towards the end of the

campaign, following the return of Steve Potts and Richard Hall, plus the emergence of Rio Ferdinand, and faces fierce competition to hold his place in the coming term.

West Ham U (£500,000 from Brondby on 8/12/94) PL 78+7/4 FLC 6+1 FAC 4

RIGBY Anthony (Tony) Angelo
Born: Ormskirk, 10 August 1972
Height: 5'10" Weight: 12.12
Club Honours: Div 2 '97

Bury's skilful but enigmatic midfielder had to be content with 15 league appearances from the subs' bench in 1996-97 without starting a single game, albeit it was enough to win him a second division championship medal as the Shakers ultimately won the title. Always an exciting player, who the fans feel can do the unexpected, he was allowed to move on loan to Scarborough in February, although the Bury manager, Stan Ternent, made it quite clear that it was purely a means of giving the player match practice. Needless to say, Tony impressed in five games before returning to Gigg Lane.

Crewe Alex (From trainee on 16/5/90)
Bury (Free from Barrow, via Lancaster C and Runcorn & Burscough, on 6/1/93) FL 111+29/18 FLC 5+2/2 FAC 5+2/1 Others 13+3/2
Scarborough (Loaned on 14/2/97) FL 5/1

RIMMER Stuart Alan
Born: Southport, 12 October 1964
Height: 5'7" Weight: 11.0
International Honours: E: Yth

As Chester's all-time record goalscorer with 141 under his belt in all games, Stuart had an indifferent season in 1996-97, playing only 25 league games due to injury and scoring just three times. A skilful player who still has a great turn of speed, despite these setbacks he continued to prove a handful for defenders and, at the same time, provided openings for others. Scored a brace in the 3-0 home FA Cup win over Stalybridge.

Everton (From apprentice on 15/10/82) FL 3
Chester C (£10,000 on 17/1/85) FL 110+4/67 FLC 6/6 FAC 4+3 Others 11+1/3
Watford (£205,000 on 18/3/88) FL 10/1 FLC 0+1/1
Notts Co (£200,000 on 10/11/88) FL 3+1/2 FAC 2 Others 3
Walsall (£150,000 on 2/2/89) FL 85+3/31 FLC 6/4 FAC 5/2 Others 7/7
Barnsley (£150,000 on 5/3/91) FL 10+5/1 Others 1
Chester C (£150,000 on 15/8/91) FL 187+26/59 FLC 13+2/3 FAC 9+2/2 Others 9+4/1
Rochdale (Loaned on 2/9/94) FL 3
Preston NE (Loaned on 5/12/94) FL 0+2

RIOCH Gregor (Greg) James
Born: Sutton Coldfield, 24 June 1975
Height: 5'11" Weight: 12.10

Having been released by Peterborough during the 1996 close season, the son of Bruce Rioch was persuaded to move north to Hull City by Tigers' coach Jeff Lee (also a former Posh left back). Full of aggression, and never lacking enthusiasm, Greg enjoyed joining up with the attack and soon won over the fans; more so with a blockbuster of a free kick against Scarborough in the Coca-Cola Cup.

Luton T (From trainee on 19/7/93)
Barnet (Loaned on 17/9/93) FL 3 FLC 2 Others 1
Peterborough U (Free on 11/8/95) FL 13+5 FLC 2 FAC 2+1 Others 2+1
Hull C (Free on 10/7/96) FL 38+1/1 FLC 2/2 FAC 2 Others 1

RIPLEY Stuart Edward
Born: Middlesbrough, 20 November 1967
Height: 5'11" Weight: 13.0
Club Honours: PL '95
International Honours: E: 1; U21-8; Yth

A recurring injury and the arrival of George Donis reduced Stuart's Blackburn starting contribution in 1996-97 to five and it was a substitute appearance at West Ham in October that signalled the end of his season, apart from coming off the bench for the last three games. At his best, a right winger who, using his pace to good effect, is able to pass defenders in order to get into scoring positions or to get down the line to fire in crosses for the forwards, hopefully, he will be back in 1997-98 fully fit and raring to go.

Middlesbrough (From apprentice on 23/12/85) FL 210+39/26 FLC 21+2/3 FAC 17+1/1 Others 20+1/1
Bolton W (Loaned on 18/2/86) FL 5/1 Others 0+1
Blackburn Rov (£1,300,000 on 20/7/92) PL 147+11/11 FLC 18 FAC 11/2 Others 8+1

RITCHIE Andrew (Andy) Timothy
Born: Manchester, 28 November 1960
Height: 5'10" Weight: 12.9
Club Honours: Div 2 '91
International Honours: E: U21-1; Yth; Sch

With 250 appearances and 105 goals to his credit, "The Prodigal Son" needed no introduction to Oldham fans after returning to Boundary Park last February as player/coach and assistant to Neil Warnock, following a two-year spell at Scarborough. Earlier in 1996-97, the vastly experienced striker produced outstanding early season form for a rejuvenated team and still finished as the Boro's leading marksman, despite being released from his contract to move back to Athletic. Expects to play on in 1997-98.

Manchester U (From apprentice on 5/12/77) FL 26+7/13 FLC 3+2 FAC 3+1
Brighton & Hove A (£500,000 on 17/10/80) FL 82+7/23 FLC 3+1/1 FAC 9/2
Leeds U (£150,000 on 25/3/83) FL 127+9/40 FLC 11/3 FAC 9/1 Others 2+1
Oldham Ath (£50,000 on 14/8/87) F/PL 187+30/83 FLC 18+2/18 FAC 8+2/4 Others 3
Scarborough (Free on 3/8/95) FL 59+9/17 FLC 4+1/2 FAC 4/1 Others 1
Oldham Ath (Free on 21/2/97) FL 4+6

RIVERS Mark Alan
Born: Crewe, 26 November 1975
Height: 6'0" Weight: 11.2

After bursting onto the league scene for Crewe in 1995-96, Mark started last season on the left flank before switching to the right and scoring five goals. Unfortunately laid low by two injury spells, he missed quite a chunk of games prior to forcing his way back into the side from the bench, just in time for the play offs. One goal down at home to Luton in the semi-final first leg, the young centre forward squeezed in an

equaliser that ultimately took Alex to Wembley and first division football.
Crewe Alex (From trainee on 6/5/94) FL 47+13/16 FLC 2+1 FAC 7/2 Others 6+3/3

ROACH Neville
Born: Reading, 29 September 1978
Height: 5'10" Weight: 11.1

A brilliant young Reading striker who scored over 40 goals for the youth and reserve teams before being given his first team opportunity at the end of last season, Neville scored with a delicate chip on his home debut against Oldham, and was rewarded with a two-year contract. Another graduate of the club's youth scheme, he began with Royals when only ten years of age at the school of excellence.
Reading (From trainee on 10/5/97) FL 2+1/1

ROBERTS Andrew (Andy) James
Born: Dartford, 20 March 1974
Height: 5'10" Weight: 13.0
Club Honours: FAYC '91
International Honours: E: U21-5

Having had an excellent 1995-96 season, Andy was again superb in 1996-97, missing just one game and being instrumental in Crystal Palace's run to the Premiership. Cool, calm and collected, his improvement continued, whether he was playing as a sweeper or in midfield, and he also found time to score his first league goals, the second being on the final day of the league programme when he drew the Port Vale 'keeper off his line, before cleverly chipping him. Obviously delighted when Palace defeated Sheffield United in the first division play-off final at Wembley, bearing in mind that he had given Palace the lead in the 1996 final against Leicester only to see it wiped out, it was difficult to know who was more elated – Andy or David Hopkin.
Millwall (From trainee on 29/10/91) FL 132+6/5 FLC 12/2 FAC 7 Others 4/1
Crystal Palace (£2,520,000 on 29/7/95) FL 81+2/2 FLC 6+1 FAC 4 Others 6/1

ROBERTS Anthony (Tony) Mark
Born: Holyhead, 4 August 1969
Height: 6'0" Weight: 13.11
International Honours: W: 2; B-2; U21-2; Yth

Having started last season as QPR's second choice goalie, he eventually received his opportunity when Juergen Sommer was away on World Cup duty with America towards the end of November. Came back into the line up at Reading, which, incidentally, was his 100th league appearance, and in 12 games, was only on the losing side twice, before being replaced by Sommer. Returned to the side again for the last four games, with Sommer back in America, and kept three clean sheets. A good shot stopper and sure kicker, which is vital these days, Tony is sure to lay claim to the 'keeper's jersey in 1997-98. Added to his Welsh caps when coming on as a sub for Neville Southall during the World Cup qualifier at home to Georgia in August.
Queens Park R (From trainee on 24/7/87) F/PL 112 FLC 11 FAC 9+1 Others 2

ROBERTS Benjamin (Ben) James
Born: Bishop Auckland, 22 June 1975
Height: 6'1" Weight: 12.11
International Honours: E: U21-1

A fine all-round sportsman, Ben was thrust into the limelight when Middlesbrough's injury and illness crisis came to a head in the crucial run in to complete Premiership, Coca-Cola Cup and FA Cup games, over a very limited period in 1996-97. So tight was the schedule that the manager, Bryan Robson, was moved to support Manchester United's application to extend the season to relieve the pressure on tired and injured players in order to give a sensible dimension to the very important end of season games that would have a major effect on the final placings for promotion, relegation, and the participation, through various challenge cups, to the lucrative European tournaments. In the circumstances, the young goalkeeper was forced to play whilst suffering from an elbow injury that would normally have seen him in the treatment room rather than on the field of play. However, his performances won acclaim from every source and his esteem as a shot stopper of the highest calibre, which saw him win an England U21 cap, was clearly established, gaining invaluable experience in the torrid atmosphere of the fierce Premiership survival battle and a Wembley FA Cup final. A young man whose name must be marked for future reference, earlier in the season he had played two games on loan at Bradford.

Middlesbrough (From trainee on 24/3/93) Pl 9+1 FLC 1+1 FAC 6 Others 1
Hartlepool U (Loaned on 19/10/95) FL 4 Others 1
Wycombe W (Loaned on 8/12/95) FL 15
Bradford C (Loaned on 27/8/96) FL 2

ROBERTS Darren Anthony
Born: Birmingham, 12 October 1969
Height: 6'0" Weight: 12.4

A hard-running centre forward signed from Chesterfield during the 1996 close season, Darren soon became a Feetham's favourite with his enthusiastic approach, ending 1996-97 as the highest-scoring Darlington player in the league for ten years. Starting where he meant to finish, netting on the opening day, his goals were vital in a season where the club hovered close to the foot of the table.

Wolverhampton W (£20,000 from Burton A on 23/4/92) FL 12+9/5 FLC 0+1 Others 1+1
Hereford U (Loaned on 18/3/94) FL 5+1/5
Chesterfield (Free on 18/7/94) FL 10+15/1 FLC 3/1 FAC 1+1 Others 2+5/3
Darlington (Free on 30/7/96) FL 42+2/16 FLC 4/2 FAC 1 Others 1

ROBERTS Iwan Wyn
Born: Bangor, 26 June 1968
Height: 6'3" Weight: 14.2
International Honours: W: 7; B-1; Yth; Sch

The Wolves' manager, Mark McGhee, returned to Leicester in the 1996 close season to sign Iwan, a proven scorer from the first division. The striker had a frustrating start against Swindon as Wolves crashed out of the Coca-Cola Cup, before getting off the mark at the eighth attempt and arriving with a hat trick on his next outing, being the first man to achieve this in

an Albion versus Wolves derby at the Hawthorns. Unfortunately, after 13 appearances a domestic accident put him out for a spell and, from then on, he and Don Goodman usually challenged for one place. Can be awkward on the floor at times, but thrives on quality crosses, as he proved with powerful, twisting headers against Albion and Tranmere.

Watford (From trainee on 4/7/88) FL 40+23/9 FLC 6+2/3 FAC 1+6 Others 5
Huddersfield T (£275,000 on 2/8/90) FL 141+1/50 FLC 13+1/6 FAC 12/4 Others 14/8
Leicester C (£100,000 on 25/11/93) F/PL 92+8/41 FLC 5/1 FAC 5/2 Others 1
Wolverhampton W (£1,300,000 + on 15/7/96) FL 24+9/12 FLC 2 FAC 0+1 Others 2

ROBERTS Paul
Born: Bangor, 29 July 1977
Height: 5'11" Weight: 11.9
International Honours: W: U21-1

Paul joined Wrexham last December from League of Wales club, Porthmadog, having began his career with Llanystymdwy (the home of David Lloyd George) in the Caernarfon and District League. Progressed to represent the North Wales Coast FA against the Scottish Junior side, before catching the eye of Porthmadog with his scoring prowess and becoming an instant goalscoring sensation, thus prompting the Welsh management team to select him for the U21's versus Holland in October. A pacy player with an eye for goal, and hopefully focused on a successful career, at the time of joining Wrexham he had begun a leisure and tourism course at Bangor College, which had to be curtailed on his signing for the Robins.

Wrexham (£10,000 from Porthmadog on 20/12/96) FL 0+1 FAC 0+1

ROBERTSON Graham Stuart
Born: Edinburgh, 2 November 1976
Height: 5'11" Weight: 10.10

Having joined Millwall from Raith during the summer of 1996, this right-footed striker put in some consistent displays for the reserve side with well taken goals. Despite that, he only made a couple of substitute appearances for the first team, although his fortune could change in 1997-98.

Raith Rov (Free from Balgonie Juniors on 3/8/93)
Millwall (Signed on 21/8/96) FL 0+1 Others 0+1

ROBERTSON John Nicholas
Born: Liverpool, 8 January 1974
Height: 6'2" Weight: 13.2

A solid Lincoln central defender who was kept out of the team for most of 1996-97 by the form of Grant Brown, John scored his first goal in two seasons with the club when he netted in the 3-1 win at Cambridge on Easter Monday. Is a wholehearted, strong-tackling player you can rely on.

Wigan Ath (From trainee on 6/7/92) FL 108+4/4 FLC 12 FAC 8+1 Others 8+1
Lincoln C (£15,000 on 5/12/95) FL 36+2/1 FLC 1 FAC 1 Others 1

ROBERTSON Paul
Born: Manchester, 5 February 1972
Height: 5'7" Weight: 11.6

Having started 1996-97 at left back for Doncaster, playing in the first five games of the season, this pacy defender decided it was time to move on and signed for non-league Witton Albion on 6 September. During his stay at Belle Vue he showed good ability, but suffered at the hands of a huge playing turnover.

Stockport Co (Free from York C juniors on 29/8/89) FL 7+3 FLC 3 Others 3
Bury (Free on 18/7/91) FL 8 FLC 3 (Free to Runcorn on 15/12/92)
Doncaster Rov (Free on 30/10/95) FL 15+5 FLC 1 Others 2

ROBINS Mark Gordon
Born: Ashton under Lyme, 22 December 1969
Height: 5'8" Weight: 11.11
Club Honours: FAC '90; ECWC '91; ESC '91; FLC '97
International Honours: E: U21-6

A would be regular on Leicester's bench in 1996-97, in order to give him some match practice, the right-footed striker was loaned to FC Copenhagen for a spell and scored with some regularity, proving that he had lost none of his predatory instincts. Returned to City's first team to score a spectacular winner in the Coca-Cola Cup quarter-final win at Ipswich and also netted with an overhead kick in the 3-1 league victory at Wimbledon. However, although opportunities remained limited due to the continued excellent form of Steve Claridge and the emergence of Emile Heskey, he made a crucial appearance at Wembley when coming on as a sub to help lay on the late equaliser. Mark also came on deep into extra time in the replay at Hillsborough as City ultimately went on to lift the Coca-Cola Cup.

Manchester U (From apprentice on 23/12/86) FL 19+29/11 FLC 0+7/2 FAC 4+4/3 Others 4+3/1
Norwich C (£800,000 on 14/8/92) PL 57+10/20 FLC 6+3/1 Others 1+1
Leicester C (£1,000,000 on 16/1/95) P/FL 40+16/12 FLC 5+4/5 FAC 4+2 Others 1+1

ROBINSON Carl Phillip
Born: Llandrindod Wells, 13 October 1976
Height: 5'10" Weight: 12.10
International Honours: W: U21-6; Yth

The strong-running, right-footed midfielder was already a Welsh U21 international when he came on as sub for Wolves last April. The aggressive side of his play was soon to the fore and, as he adjusted to the pace of the game, he grew in confidence, being keen to get involved. Also proved himself a good link man with all the required qualities, something that was noticeable when making his full debut in the last fixture of the season.

Wolverhampton W (From trainee on 3/7/95) FL 1+1
Shrewsbury T (Loaned on 28/3/96) FL 2+2 Others 1

ROBINSON Ian Brendan
Born: Nottingham, 25 August 1978
Height: 5'9" Weight: 11.10

The young Mansfield midfielder continued to make progress in 1996-97, but unfortunately suffered a niggling injury in mid

season which kept him sidelined for some time. Despite many fans thinking that Ian was a rising star, he was loaned out to Ilkeston Town in February prior to being released during the summer.

Mansfield T (From trainee on 3/7/96) FL 7+10/1 FLC 1+2

ROBINSON Jamie
Born: Liverpool, 26 February 1972
Height: 6'1" Weight: 12.8
Club Honours: Div 3 '95

For most of 1996-97, Carlisle's defensive unit was virtually self selecting and, apart from the odd game, Jamie found it difficult to break into the first team. He did play in several matches in the early part of the campaign, but for most of the time he had to be content with reserve team soccer, before being released during the summer. A utility player, who is more at home on the left-hand side of the defence, his height makes him useful at both ends of the park.

Liverpool (From trainee on 4/6/90)
Barnsley (Free on 17/7/92) FL 8+1 Others 3
Carlisle U (Signed on 28/1/94) FL 46+11/4 FLC 1+2 FAC 3 Others 7+6/1

ROBINSON John Robert Campbell
Born: Bulawayo, Rhodesia, 29 August 1971
Height: 5'10" Weight: 11.2
International Honours: W: 8; U21-5

A right-sided Charlton midfielder, who is equally at home playing on either wing or at full back, John loves to run at players and is an accurate crosser of the ball, as well as having a powerful shot. Scored some valuable goals, including two in the Coca-Cola Cup tie against Burnley at The Valley in 1996-97 and became a regular in the full Welsh international side. Is a firm favourite of the Addicks' supporters for every good reason.

Brighton & Hove A (From trainee on 21/4/89) FL 57+5/6 FLC 5/1 FAC 2+1 Others 1+2/2
Charlton Ath (£75,000 on 15/9/92) FL 142+7/15 FLC 9+2/4 FAC 7+2/1 Others 5

ROBINSON Leslie (Les)
Born: Shirebrook, 1 March 1967
Height: 5'10" Weight: 12.4

Remained a regular and consistent right back at Oxford, even having two rare appearances as a sub last season, always doing the simple things well and always looking at opportunities to supplement the attack. Missed more games with injuries than in the last few years combined, but, with his no-nonsense displays, he remained a favourite. Closed 1996-97 at just under 250 league games for the club.

Mansfield T (Free from Chesterfield juniors on 6/10/84) FL 11+4 Others 1
Stockport Co (£10,000 on 27/11/86) FL 67/3 FLC 2 FAC 4 Others 4
Doncaster Rov (£20,000 on 24/3/88) FL 82/12 FLC 4 FAC 5 Others 5/1
Oxford U (£150,000 on 19/3/90) FL 243+5/2 FLC 25/7 FAC 13+1 Others 10

ROBINSON Spencer Liam
Born: Bradford, 29 December 1965
Height: 5'7" Weight: 12.7

Liam was only occasionally selected for

first-team duty at Burnley during 1996-97, despite being ever industrious, and, unable to dislodge Paul Barnes and Andy Cooke from the strikers' roles at Turf Moor, was freed at the end of the season. For a player who only three years ago carried the Claret's record transfer tag, there should be no difficulty in finding another club.

Huddersfield T (Free from Nottingham F juniors on 5/1/84) FL 17+4/2
Tranmere Rov (Loaned on 18/12/85) FL 4/3
Bury (£60,000 on 8/7/86) FL 248+14/89 FLC 17+3/6 FAC 9/1 Others 24/4
Bristol C (£130,000 on 14/7/93) FL 31+10/4 FLC 2/1 FAC 5 Others 1
Burnley (£250,000 on 26/7/94) FL 43+20/9 FLC 5+1/2 FAC 5/1 Others 1+1

Mark Robinson

ROBINSON Mark James
Born: Rochdale, 21 November 1968
Height: 5'9" Weight: 11.8
Club Honours: Div 2 '96

Swindon Town's most consistent performer of the 1996-97 campaign, missing only four games of the Robins' 52-match programme, despite the fact he was asked to fill a number of different positions during the season. Having started on the right side of midfield, he then dropped back to his more familiar right-back position, replacing Frederic Darras in September, and stayed there for most of the remainder of the campaign, apart from a spell from November to January when David Kerslake (on loan from Spurs) took over the spot, whilst Mark moved into the unfamiliar position of central defence to cover for the injured Mark Seagraves. His only goal of the season came in August - a free kick to secure the equaliser in a 1-1 draw with Port Vale. Able to strike excellent long passes from the back, he is a quality crosser of the ball.

West Bromwich A (From apprentice on 10/1/87) FL 2 FLC 0+1
Barnsley (Free on 23/6/87) FL 117+20/6 FLC 7+2 FAC 7+1 Others 3+2/1

Newcastle U (£450,000 on 9/3/93) F/PL 14+11 FAC 1
Swindon T (£600,000 on 22/7/94) FL 129/2 FLC 14 FAC 9 Others 6+1

ROBINSON Matthew Richard
Born: Exeter, 23 December 1974
Height: 5'11" Weight: 11.2

A Southampton midfielder, Matthew's appearances in 1996-97 were again limited due to a large number of players on the club's books competing for similar opportunities. Confident and strong running down the left side, he made three successive starts against Liverpool, Middlesbrough, and Newcastle, mainly in a wing-back role, before going back to the bench and then the reserves. Has great touch and a superb left foot.

Southampton (From trainee on 1/7/93) PL 3+10 FAC 1+2

ROBINSON Paul Derrick
Born: Sunderland, 20 November 1978
Height: 5'11" Weight: 11.0

While still only a second year YTS player, this lively Darlington forward made four substitute appearances during last season and looks set for a first team start before too long. Confident and tricky, he signed a two-year professional contract at the end of the campaign.

Darlington (Trainee) FL 0+7 FAC 0+2

ROBINSON Paul Peter
Born: Watford, 14 December 1978
Height: 5'9" Weight: 11.6

Locally-born Watford left back who made his debut at the age of 17 in 1996-97 and went on to make 17 appearances, some in midfield. Strongly built and a doughty tackler, although less assured at the moment in his distribution, Paul is bound to progress even further in 1997-98. Is highly thought of at Vicarage Road.

Watford (From trainee on 13/2/97) FL 8+4 FAC 2+1 Others 2

ROBINSON Phillip (Phil) John
Born: Stafford, 6 January 1967
Height: 5'10" Weight: 11.7
Club Honours: Div 4 '88, Div 3 '89; AMC '88, '91

When signed from Chesterfield during the 1996 close season it was Phil's second spell at Notts County, having previously enjoyed promotion success with Neil Warnock. Although a very experienced midfielder with a number of Wembley appearances to his credit, and an excellent team player who has the ability to contribute vital goals, he was unable to lift a side that was destined for the drop into the third division.

Aston Villa (From apprentice on 8/1/85) FL 2+1/1
Wolverhampton W (£5,000 on 3/7/87) FL 63+8/8 FLC 6 FAC 3/1 Others 8+2
Notts Co (£67,500 on 18/8/89) FL 65+1/5 FLC 6/1 FAC 1+1 Others 9+1
Birmingham C (Loaned on 18/3/91) FL 9 Others 2+1
Huddersfield T (£50,000 on 1/9/92) FL 74+1/5 FLC 4 FAC 8/1 Others 8
Northampton T (Loaned on 2/9/94) FL 14 FLC 1 FAC 1 Others 2

Chesterfield (£15,000 on 9/12/94) FL 60+1/17 FLC 1 FAC 2 Others 8/4
Notts Co (£80,000 on 16/8/96) FL 33+4/2 FLC 2 FAC 4/1

ROBINSON Stephen (Steve)
Born: Lisburn, 10 December 1974
Height: 5'9" Weight: 11.3
International Honours: NI: 1; B-3; U21-1; Yth; Sch
Steve appeared in several positions in Bournemouth's midfield during the 1996-97 season, as well as having a spell as a striker. In showing his abilities in all of these positions and, at the same time, gaining international recognition with Northern Ireland at both full and "B" levels, he proved to be a very busy player who was able to run with the ball as well as score his quota of goals. Will be looking to claim his first full cap before too long.
Tottenham H (From trainee on 27/1/93) PL 1+1
Bournemouth (Free on 20/10/94) FL 100+13/19 FLC 4 FAC 5+1/1 Others 5/1

ROBINSON Steven (Steve) Eli
Born: Nottingham, 17 January 1975
Height: 5'4" Weight: 11.3
An extremely promising homegrown Birmingham wide player, Steve recovered well from a mystery illness that left him weak at the start of last season to impress with some hard-working performances on the right-hand side of midfield towards the latter stages, as the Blues moved into a ten-game unbeaten streak. Busy and effective, but unflashy, he was rewarded with a new two-year contract for his fine efforts and now looks to build on the back of the nine appearances that finally brought him to the public's notice.
Birmingham C (From trainee on 9/6/93) FL 11+4 Others 1
Peterborough U (Loaned on 15/3/96) FL 5

ROBSON Bryan
Born: Witton Gilbert, 11 January 1957
Height: 5'10" Weight: 12.6
Club Honours: CS '83, '93; FAC '83, '85, '90; ECWC '91; PL '93, '94; Div 1 '95
International Honours: E: 90; B-3; U21-7; Yth
Brian Robson's ambitious plans to put Middlesbrough in the top echelons of English and European football were thwarted when his so called "Foreign Legion" of fabulously talented stars failed to deliver performances to match their salaries and signing on fees in 1996-97. The smart southern commentators were unable to hide their amusement, with Juninho standing alone as the only import to demonstrate the will, the passion and the pride, to fight for success. On a playing front, the player/manager looked as good as ever when making his only appearance of the season, at Highbury, controlling the midfield and inspiring all those around him to greater efforts, while taking the Man of the Match award in his stride in the process. Despite all the problems, "Robbo" always conducted himself with aplomb and dignity throughout what, in spite of every carping criticism, will still be regarded by Boro fans as their most

successful season ever. Even relegation could not dampen the elation of two Wembley finals and the club is sure to be revitalised and challenging for promotion this coming term.
West Bromwich A (From apprentice on 1/8/74) FL 194+4/39 FLC 17+1/2 FAC 10+2/2 Others 12/3
Manchester U (£1,500,000 on 5/10/81) F/PL 326+19/74 FLC 50+1/5 FAC 33+2/10 Others 32+2/11
Middlesbrough (Free on 1/5/94) P/FL 23+2/1 FLC 1 FAC 1

ROBSON Glenn Alan
Born: Sunderland, 25 September 1977
Height: 6'0" Weight: 11.7
A youngster signed from Murton last November (north eastern non-league football), Glenn starred in attack for Rochdale's all conquering reserve side (who had 13 straight wins) before earning a call up to the first-team squad as a substitute and making his debut against Hull City in February.
Rochdale (Signed from Murton on 13/11/96) FL 0+3

ROBSON Mark Andrew
Born: Newham, 22 May 1969
Height: 5'7" Weight: 10.2
The skilful left-sided winger was unable to command a regular place in the Charlton side in 1996-97, despite playing well when called upon to do so. Fast and tricky in possession, and an accurate crosser of the ball who likes to run at defenders, often beating them with ease, Mark has a powerful shot, scoring a brilliant free kick at Newcastle in a third round FA Cup replay. Also had the distinction of scoring the club's only penalty of the season against Tranmere at The Valley, prior to being released during the summer.
Exeter C (From apprentice on 17/12/86) FL 26/7 FAC 2 Others 2
Tottenham H (£50,000 on 17/7/87) FL 3+5 FLC 1
Reading (Loaned on 24/3/88) FL 5+2
Watford (Loaned on 5/10/89) FL 1
Plymouth Arg (Loaned on 22/12/89) FL 7
Exeter C (Loaned on 3/1/92) FL 7+1/1 Others 3/1
West Ham U (Free on 14/8/92) F/PL 42+5/8 FLC 2 FAC 2/1 Others 4+1
Charlton Ath (£125,000 on 17/11/93) FL 79+26/9 FLC 4+2 FAC 10/2 Others 2

ROCASTLE David·Carlyle
Born: Lewisham, 2 May 1967
Height: 5'9" Weight: 12.10
Club Honours: FLC '87; Div 1 '89, '91
International Honours: E: 14; B-2; U21-14
The ex-England International midfielder graced the colours of Norwich for only 11 games after joining City on loan from Chelsea last January. With no prospect of figuring in Ruud Gullit's star-studded line up, and trying to resurrect his career, he proved his fitness and was dubbed Rocky II when an additional month's loan gave him the opportunity to show infrequent sublime skills. Outrageous dummies left markers floundering, but he was unable to agree personal terms with Norwich and returned to Stamford Bridge. At his best, David is a skilful right-sided player with great vision

and quick feet who is constantly looking to find space.
Arsenal (From apprentice on 31/12/84) FL 204+14/24 FLC 32+1/6 FAC 18+2/4 Others 9
Leeds U (£2,000,000 on 4/8/92) PL 17+8/2 FLC 0+3 FAC 0+3 Others 2+1
Manchester C (£2,000,000 on 22/12/93) PL 21/2 FAC 2
Chelsea (£1,250,000 on 12/8/94) PL 27+2 FLC 3/1 Others 7+1/1
Norwich C (Loaned on 9/1/97) FL 11

ROCHE Stephen (Steve) Michael
Born: Dublin, 2 October 1978
Height: 5'11" Weight: 11.2
International Honours: Ei: Yth; Sch
Another graduate from the Millwall youth set up. Steve made his first-team debut at left back, although he can also play as an attacking left-sided midfielder. A fine ball winner, with good passing ability, he certainly looks to be one for the future.
Millwall (Free from Belvedere on 6/10/94) FL 4+3

ROCKETT Jason
Born: London, 26 September 1969
Height: 6'1" Weight: 13.6
A strong and dominant centre back, Jason had an outstanding season in 1996-97 for Scarborough, being a key figure in the club's rise away from the lower reaches of the third division. His consistent, whole-hearted performances earned him the Player of the Year and away supporters' Player of the Season awards.
Rotherham U (Signed from British Universities on 25/3/92)
Scarborough (Free on 4/8/93) FL 139+1/9 FLC 9 FAC 6 Others 4

RODDIE Andrew Robert
Born: Glasgow, 4 November 1971
Height: 5'10" Weight: 11.6
International Honours: S: U21-5; Yth; Sch
A former Scottish U21 international with Aberdeen and Motherwell, Andrew was released by the latter last January and trialled on non-contract forms at Notts County, playing on the left wing against Scunthorpe in the AWS competition. Despite making a promising debut when showing up as a skilful operator who got down the line well to deliver crosses to the front men, he returned home shortly after.
Aberdeen (Free from Glasgow U on 16/4/88) SL 5+22/5 SC 0+1
Motherwell (Free on 20/8/94) SL 34+31 SLC 2+1 SC 0+1 Others 1
Notts Co (Free on 27/1/97) Others 1

RODGER Graham
Born: Glasgow, 1 April 1967
Height: 6'2" Weight: 11.13
Club Honours: FAC '87
International Honours: E: U21-4
This right-footed Grimsby central defender is exceptionally strong in the air and very useful in the box during set pieces. Having struggled for his place in 1995-96, he took full advantage of the Mariners' injury problems in central defence to recapture a permanent place in 1996-97, and had probably his best season since joining the club, being rewarded with the team captaincy.

Wolverhampton W (Apprentice) FL 1
Coventry C (Free on 18/2/85) FL 31+5/2 FLC 3+1 FAC 1+1 Others 0+1
Luton T (£150,000 on 1/8/89) FL 27+1/2 FLC 2 Others 3
Grimsby T (£135,000 on 8/1/92) FL 124+11/11 FLC 3 FAC 7 Others 2

RODGER Simon Lee
Born: Shoreham, 3 October 1971
Height: 5'9" Weight: 11.9
Club Honours: Div 1 '94
As Crystal Palace's longest serving professional, 1996-97 began with him injured and ended with him playing at Wembley, while sandwiched between were two loan spells at Manchester City and Stoke. Joining City at the end of October for a period that was extended until Boxing Day, scoring once in eight appearances despite damaging a hamstring, the tough-tackling, hard-working midfielder returned to Selhurst Park before going out to Stoke in mid February, but was soon back at Palace again having failed to resolve the Potter's problems on the left-hand side. Later, when Steve Coppell, who had temporarily taken him to Manchester City, replaced Dave Bassett as manager at Palace, Simon was reintroduced to the side and played in all three play-off games that ended with promotion to the Premiership. Is also good at running the ball while others jockey for position.
Crystal Palace (£1,000 from Bognor Regis T on 2/7/90) F/PL 106+20/5 FLC 15 FAC 2+3 Others 5+2
Manchester C (Loaned on 28/10/96) FL 8/1
Stoke C (Loaned on 14/2/97) FL 5

RODGERSON Ian
Born: Hereford, 9 April 1966
Height: 5'8" Weight: 11.6
In his second spell at Cardiff, Ian failed to nail down a regular place in 1996-97, despite having started the season as an attacking right back. A versatile player who is also able to operate in midfield and up front, he was unable to get back into the side, apart from the odd game, and spent most of his time on the subs' bench prior to being released during the summer.
Hereford U (From juniors on 3/7/85) FL 95+5/6 FLC 7 FAC 4 Others 7+1
Cardiff C (£35,000 on 3/8/88) FL 98+1/4 FLC 8 FAC 10 Others 6+1
Birmingham C (£250,000 on 4/12/90) FL 87+8/13 FLC 7+1/2 FAC 2 Others 11/1
Sunderland (£140,000 on 23/7/93) FL 5+5
Cardiff C (Free on 31/7/95) FL 43+12/1 FLC 5+1/1 FAC 4 Others 4

RODOSTHENOUS Michael
Born: Islington, 25 August 1976
Height: 5'11" Weight: 11.2
After doing very well as a striker in the reserves, and in a loan spell at Telford (December), Michael was given his league debut for West Brom at Bolton last March, coming on as a second-half substitute. Fast over the ground, he has a good first touch and an eye for goal and could go far in the game.
West Bromwich A (From trainee on 19/7/95) FL 0+1

ROGAN Anthony (Anton) Gerard Patrick
Born: Belfast, 25 March 1966
Height: 6'0" Weight: 13.0
Club Honours: SPD '88; SC '88, '89
International Honours: NI: 18
Anton had a great start to the 1996-97 season, scoring seven goals in 13 games for Millwall, mainly brilliant headers from corners and free kicks, his good form seeing him called up for Northern Ireland against Germany. A tenacious left back who loves to get forward, he was unfortunate to pick up a niggling calf injury that was slow mending, causing him to miss some vital games and led to his release during the summer.
Glasgow Celtic (Signed from Distillery on 9/5/86) SL 115+12/4 SLC 12+1 SC 18/1 Others 8
Sunderland (£350,000 on 4/10/91) FL 45+1/1 FLC 1 FAC 8 Others 2
Oxford U (Signed on 9/8/93) FL 56+2/3 FLC 4 FAC 4 Others 2
Millwall (Free on 11/8/95) FL 30+6/8 FLC 1 FAC 2 Others 1

ROGERS Alan
Born: Liverpool, 3 January 1977
Height: 5'10" Weight: 11.8
The exciting young Tranmere left back never failed to impress in his 32 first team appearances in 1996-97, despite his tender years, and he played a key role in Rovers' new formation, first tried at Ipswich, when he was employed as a wing back. Although being sent off in the first game of the season at Southend, Alan is a mature and level-headed player who always gave 100 per cent, whether playing in front of a capacity crowd or the few hundred spectators who watch the reserves. Selected for the Football League U21 side that played the Italian Serie "B" equivalent in February, he enjoyed a prolonged run in the first team in the last quarter of the campaign, missing just one of the last 15 matches. *Stop Press:* Reported to have joined Nottingham Forest for a fee of £2 million.
Tranmere Rov (From trainee on 1/7/95) FL 53+4/2 FLC 1 FAC 1

ROGERS Darren John
Born: Birmingham, 9 April 1970
Height: 6'0" Weight: 13.0
A skilful-left sided Walsall defender, who can also perform equally well in the centre of the defence, following a substitute appearance in last season's opening game he was unfortunately laid low by a cruciate injury. A difficult injury to overcome, Darren surprisingly recovered to play his one full game in the final match at Preston and will obviously be looking to get back to full fitness in 1997-98.
West Bromwich A (From trainee on 5/7/88) FL 7+7/1 FAC 0+1 Others 1/1
Birmingham C (Free on 1/7/92) FL 15+3 FLC 2 FAC 0+1 Others 5
Wycombe W (Loaned on 5/11/93) FL 0+1 Others 1
Walsall (Free on 19/7/94) FL 44+10 FLC 4 FAC 5+2 Others 5

ROGERS David (Dave) Raymond
Born: Liverpool, 25 August 1975
Height: 6'1" Weight: 12.0

Started last season at left back for Chester, but after just six starts was replaced by the returning Iain Jenkins and moved on to non-league Southport in November. Can also play in central defence, his height being an asset.
Tranmere Rov (From trainee on 6/7/94)
Chester C (Free on 7/8/95) FL 18+7/1 FLC 2+2 FAC 0+1 Others 1

ROGERS Lee Julian
Born: Doncaster, 28 October 1966
Height: 5'11" Weight: 12.1
Lee's 1996-97 season got off to the best possible start with a successful testimonial match against Nottingham Forest and although Chesterfield shaped up well in the early promotion chase with him in the side, he was hit by injury in January and did not recover until March, spending a faultless 45 minutes in goal in his second game back. Unfortunately, in all the hoo-ha concerning the Spireites' FA Cup run, he became something of a forgotten man, but he is the sort of determined, mature individual who will use the summer wisely to regain full fitness and will undoubtedly challenge for a first-team place again.
Doncaster Rov (From trainee on 27/7/84) Others 1
Chesterfield (Free on 29/8/86) FL 308+23/1 FLC 17+1 FAC 11+1 Others 27+1

ROGERS Paul Anthony
Born: Portsmouth, 21 March 1965
Height: 6'0" Weight: 12.0
Club Honours: Div 3 '97
International Honours: E: SP-6
Unable to hold down a place at Notts County in 1996-97, the tough, hard-working midfielder went out on loan to Wigan in December and was one of the players instrumental in Athletic's great run of results through January and February. In such excellent form and now vital to the cause, Paul was recruited on a permanent basis in early March, being an ever present following his transfer and scoring three goals in total on his way to a third division championship medal.
Sheffield U (£35,000 from Sutton U on 29/1/92) F/PL 120+5/10 FLC 8+1/1 FAC 4 Others 1
Notts Co (Signed on 29/12/95) FL 21+1/2 FAC 1/1 Others 6
Wigan Ath (£50,000 on 13/12/96) FL 18+2/3

ROGET Leo Thomas Earl
Born: Ilford, 1 August 1977
Height: 6'1" Weight: 12.2
Leo came into the Southend team in 1996-97 when an injury forced Mike Lapper out and he never looked back from there. Dominant in the air, and very quick on the ground, his timing in the tackle saved United on more than one occasion during the season. Certainly one to watch in the future, his only disappointment came when he was sent off in a case of mistaken identity.
Southend U (From trainee on 5/7/95) FL 29+4/1 FAC 1

ROLLING Franck Jacques
Born: Colmar, France, 23 August 1968
Height: 6'1" Weight: 14.0
Club Honours: FLC '97

Franck, a cultured right-footed Leicester central defender, failed to build on his performances of the previous season in 1996-97, despite playing in the early stages of the Coca-Cola Cup run. Desperate for a taste of Premiership action which he finally achieved at Blackburn on the last Sunday of the campaign, he was unfortunate to be in the shadows of a wealth of central defenders at Filbert Street. Comfortable on the ball, and well versed in the continental approach to the game, he can also be used in midfield if required. Released during the summer.

Ayr U (Signed from FC Pau on 8/8/94) SL 35/2 SLC 2 SC 1 Others 4
Leicester C (£100,000 on 4/9/95) P/FL 18 FLC 5 FAC 0+1

ROLLO James (Jimmy) Stuart
Born: Wisbech, 22 May 1976
Height: 5'11" Weight: 11.5
Released by Walsall during the summer of 1996, Jimmy joined Cardiff on non-contract forms at the start of 1996-97. A real livewire of a player who can be used in a number of positions in defence, as well as further afield at wing back, although playing just 11 times, eight of them from the bench, he created a good enough impression to be retained for the coming term.

Walsall (From trainee on 26/5/95) Others 0+1 (Free to Yate T in April 1996)
Cardiff C (Free on 16/8/96) FL 3+7 Others 0+1

ROMANO Serge
Born: Metz, France, 25 May 1964
Height: 5'10" Weight: 11.0
A free signing from Martigues at the beginning of last season, the right back looked a steady footballer, but a touch too fragile for the English game and, in fact, he suffered bruised ribs within five minutes of his Wolves' debut. Replaced during the opening two fixtures, he came on as a sub three times in October, which included his only run out at Molineux, and left in the summer when his contract expired.

Wolverhampton W (Free from Martigues on 16/8/96) FL 1+3 FLC 1

ROPER Ian Robert
Born: Nuneaton, 20 June 1977
Height: 6'3" Weight: 14.0
This homegrown teenage defender, the tallest player on Walsall's books, impressed in the handful of first-team games that he played in 1996-97, his opportunities being limited by the consistency of central defensive partners, Adrian Viveash and Derek Mountfield. Good in the air, as you would expect from someone of his size, in a total of 11 full games and substitute appearances he was only twice on the losing side.

Walsall (From trainee on 15/5/95) FL 8+8 FAC 1+1 Others 1

ROSCOE Andrew (Andy) Ronald
Born: Liverpool, 4 June 1973
Height: 5'11" Weight: 12.0
Club Honours: AMC '96
Previously known as a wide left-sided midfielder, Andy was successfully turned into a left back by Rotherham last season,

where he confounded many people with his ability to adapt. Despite his defensive responsibilities, he still managed to launch many surging runs down the left and took on the mantle of becoming the free-kick specialist without a great deal of luck, often seeing many of his efforts producing brilliant saves from opposing 'keepers. Also specialises as the taker of in-swinging corners from the right.

Bolton W (Free from Liverpool juniors on 17/7/91) FL 2+1 Others 1+1
Rotherham U (£70,000 on 27/10/94) FL 114+5/6 FLC 6 FAC 2 Others 8/2

ROSE Matthew
Born: Dartford, 24 September 1975
Height: 5'11" Weight: 11.1
Club Honours: FAYC '94
International Honours: E: U21-2
A young Arsenal central defender, and a player with potential, Matthew's form last season was promising enough for him to be awarded an England U21 cap against Georgia in a European championship match in November, followed by another against Italy. He also impressed in the Gunners' reserve side, showing good positional sense and awareness on the left-hand side. Later, in January, when standing in for Martin Keown, he appeared in the Premiership side's 2-1 win at West Ham, where he unfortunately conceded an own goal when turning in Slaven Bilic's downward header from a corner. Relatively stylish, and a good tackler with passing skills, he was quoted during the summer as being interested in a move away from Highbury. Stop Press: Signed for Queens Park Rangers on 20 May.

Arsenal (From trainee on 19/7/94) PL 2+3

Ronny Rosenthal

ROSENTHAL Ronny
Born: Haifa, Israel, 11 October 1963
Height: 5'10" Weight: 12.13
Club Honours: CS '90

International Honours: Israel: 54
Ever the enthusiastic striker, cum winger, Ronny, hindered by minor injuries, had little opportunity to establish himself in the Tottenham side in 1996-97, following a change in tactics and an outstanding season's performance by Andy Sinton. Confident on the ball and willing to take opponents on in attack, the Israeli international is a firm favourite at White Hart Lane, having the ability to add sparkle to any game, and still looks to be enjoying his football while maintaining a good level of personal fitness. No one need be reminded that he can pull a magical performance out of the bag at his best, demonstrated in the classic FA Cup sixth round replay defeat of Southampton in 1995. Stop Press: Released during the summer.

Liverpool (Loaned from Standard Liege on 22/3/90) FL 5+3/7
Liverpool (£1,000,000 on 29/6/90) F/PL 27+39/14 FLC 2+7/1 FAC 5+3 Others 2+4
Tottenham H (£250,000 on 26/1/94) PL 55+33/4 FLC 3/1 FAC 7+2/6

Uwe Rosler

ROSLER Uwe
Born: Attenburg, Germany, 15 November 1968
Height: 6'0" Weight: 12.4
International Honours: East Germany: 5
After two seasons in the Premiership, and having become a firm favourite with the Manchester City fans, scoring spectacular goals in unison with support from the likes of Paul Walsh and Niall Quinn, now elsewhere, Uwe had a season of two halves in 1996-97. Prior to the year ending, although he appeared in all games he netted only five league goals, while playing under four different managers, and could be seen foraging alone with no recognised support, which obviously contributed to his loss of form and thoughts of wanting to be away. However, with the present manager in charge since the New Year, Uwe was a

revelation, running hard with the support from the new signings, scoring goals consistently, and back to his exciting and skilful best.

Manchester C (£375,000 from FC Nurnberg on 2/3/94) P/FL 118+5/44 FLC 8+1/5 FAC 12/8

ROWBOTHAM Darren
Born: Cardiff, 22 October 1966
Height: 5'10" Weight: 12.13
Club Honours: Div 4 '90
International Honours: W: Yth

Having signed from Shrewsbury last October, it was the second spell at Exeter for Darren. His experience was much needed up front as he helped to solve City's goal shortage on his arrival and it was an indication of his character that he had several striking partners during the season and managed to hit it off with them all. Enthusiastic, and always dangerous, he had earlier shrugged off ligament problems on his way to the Player of the Year award.

Plymouth Arg (From juniors on 7/11/84) FL 22+24/2 FLC 1 FAC 0+3/1 Others 1+1
Exeter C (Signed on 31/10/87) FL 110+8/47 FLC 11/6 FAC 8/5 Others 5/1
Torquay U (£25,000 on 13/9/91) FL 14/3 FAC 3/1 Others 2
Birmingham C (£20,000 on 2/1/92) FL 31+5/6 FLC 0+1 Others 3+1
Mansfield T (Loaned on 18/12/92) FL 4
Hereford U (Loaned on 25/3/93) FL 8/2
Crewe Alex (Free on 6/7/93) FL 59+2/21 FLC 3/1 FAC 4/3 Others 6+2/1
Shrewsbury T (Free on 28/7/95) FL 31+9/9 FLC 3+2/2 FAC 4/1 Others 1+3
Exeter C (Free on 24/10/96) FL 25/9 FAC 2/1 Others 2/1

ROWBOTHAM Jason
Born: Cardiff, 3 January 1969
Height: 5'9" Weight: 11.6
Club Honours: S Div 1 '95; SLC '95

Signed from Wycombe last October, after five years away from Plymouth, Jason initially came on loan and then on weekly contracts as cover. Having little chance to show his ability, and on the verge of being released, a large number of injuries changed his season as he came in and kept his place on merit to earn a contract. Played in the sweeper role and looked an extremely accomplished defender and, being quick and intelligent, his distribution from the back was a delight to see.

Plymouth Arg (From trainee on 20/7/87) FL 8+1 FLC 0+1
Shrewsbury T (Free on 26/3/92)
Hereford U (Free on 17/10/92) FL 3+2/1 FAC 1
Raith Rov (Free on 31/7/93) SL 47+9/1 SLC 3+2 SC 2+1 Others 1
Wycombe W (£40,000 on 14/9/95) FL 27 FLC 2 FAC 2 Others 2
Plymouth Arg (Loaned on 11/10/96) FL 0+3
Plymouth Arg (Free on 10/1/97) FL 12 Others 1+1

ROWE Ezekiel (Zeke) Bartholomew
Born: Stoke Newington, 30 October 1973
Height: 5'11" Weight: 12.8

Having been freed by Chelsea during the 1996 close season, Zeke signed for Barry Fry's Peterborough. The speedy forward then proceeded to have a stuttering 1996-97 season in keeping with a team facing

relegation for much of the time and was unable to show the form he was capable of, his league subs' appearances outweighing his starts. Good when running at defences, he is bound to worry a few in the third division in 1997-98.

Chelsea (From trainee on 12/6/92)
Barnet (Loaned on 12/11/93) FL 9+1/2 FAC 2/1
Brighton & Hove A (Loaned on 28/3/96) FL 9/3
Peterborough U (Free on 4/7/96) FL 10+12/3 FLC 2 FAC 3+1 Others 0+1

Rodney Rowe

ROWE Rodney Carl
Born: Huddersfield, 30 July 1975
Height: 5'8" Weight: 12.8

Signed from Huddersfield last February, Rodney had a mixed first three months with his new club, York. Having operated as a striker, or on the wide right, and netting perhaps City's best goal of the season in a 3-1 win over Preston, his form fluctuated and spells on the bench, plus a three match suspension, marked the closing weeks. However, putting that behind him, he bounced back and netted in a win at Rotherham which ensured that the club avoided the drop.

Huddersfield T (From trainee on 12/7/93) FL 14+20/2 FLC 0+2 FAC 6+1/2 Others 3/1
Scarborough (Loaned on 11/8/94) FL 10+4/1 FLC 4/1
Bury (Loaned on 20/3/95) FL 1+2
York C (£80,000 on 19/2/97) FL 9+1/3

ROWETT Gary
Born: Bromsgrove, 6 March 1974
Height: 6'0" Weight: 12.10

Considering he was valued at only £300,000 when joining Derby from Everton, Gary, who must go down as one of the bargain buys of the last two years, converted from a sweeper role to central defence and continued to develop in 1996-97. Generally a right-sided player, his strengths are in his

ability to keep possession and impressive timing in the tackle. Enjoying a generally injury-free season by comparison to the previous campaign, missing just three games, on several occasions he was County's Man of the Match and fully justified his place in a side that surprised more than a few shrewd judges.

Cambridge U (From trainee on 10/9/91) FL 51+12/9 FLC 7/1 FAC 5+2 Others 5/3
Everton (£200,000 on 21/5/94) PL 2+2
Blackpool (Loaned on 23/1/95) FL 17
Derby Co (£300,000 on 20/7/95) P/FL 69+1/2 FLC 4 FAC 4+1

ROWLAND Keith
Born: Portadown, 1 September 1971
Height: 5'10" Weight: 10.0
International Honours: NI: 12; B-2; Yth

With Julian Dicks holding down his favoured position of left back for West Ham in 1996-97, Keith had to be content with occasional appearances on the left-hand side of midfield. The highlight of his season was undoubtedly his first goal for the club at Newcastle in November, when he headed home a cross from Tim Breacker to earn a valuable away point for the side. He was also voted Man of the Match in a 2-1 home defeat by Arsenal in January, for his tireless running and excellent crosses. A valuable squad member, who appeared three times for Northern Ireland during the campaign, as well as picking up a "B" cap, he will be looking for more opportunities in 1997-98.

Bournemouth (From trainee on 2/10/89) FL 65+7/2 FLC 5 FAC 8 Others 3
Coventry C (Loaned on 8/1/93) PL 0+2
West Ham U (£110,000 on 6/8/93) PL 57+16/1 FLC 3 FAC 5+1

ROY Bryan Edward
Born: Amsterdam, Holland, 12 February 1970
Height: 5'10" Weight: 10.12
International Honours: Holland: 33

1996-97 was another disappointing season for Nottingham Forest's flying Dutchman, having few opportunities to shine (spending most of the campaign on the bench) in a side in search of attacking flair. Apart from a goal against Wycombe in the Coca-Cola Cup, his only other strikes came when he hit both goals in a 2-1 win over Spurs, but that was not until January! Then, given the chance to briefly link up with fellow Dutch international, Pierre Van Hooijdonk, in March, he was unable to take advantage of the opportunity when continuing to suffer from loss of form. *Stop Press:* With skill in abundance, being fast, tricky, two footed, and having superb balance, Bryan was reported to have joined the German club, Hertha Berlin, for £1.5 million during the close season.

Nottingham F (£2,500,000 from Foggia on 4/8/94) PL 70+15/24 FLC 7+1/2 FAC 10+1/1 Others 6/1

ROYCE Simon Ernest
Born: Forest Gate, 9 September 1971
Height: 6'2" Weight: 12.8

1996-97 was another fantastic season between the sticks at Southend for Simon,

his reflex saves and general handling much admired by fans of many clubs and also by Premiership scouts. Chris Kamara, the visiting manager, pronounced his performance against Bradford as the best goalkeeping display he had ever seen. Unfortunately, lack of defensive cover meant his skills were called into play all too often and despite many goals being conceded, he was rarely faulted.

Southend U (£35,000 from Heybridge Swifts on 15/10/91) FL 110+2 FLC 5 FAC 3 Others 5

Simon Royce

Neil Ruddock

RUDDOCK Neil
Born: Wandsworth, 9 May 1968
Height: 6'2" Weight: 12.12
Club Honours: FLC '95
International Honours: E: 1; B-1; U21-4; Yth

Prior to the Coca-Cola Cup third round match at Charlton last November, Neil had not had a consistent run in the Liverpool defence due to the excellent form of others, notably Dominic Matteo and Mark Wright,

but, from then on, broke into the side on a more regular basis. A player with great physical presence and strength who attacks the ball in the air and whose tackling ability makes him invaluable in tight situations, he also strikes passes diagonally out of defence well. Scored just one goal last term, the first in a 2-0 win at Leeds.

Millwall (From apprentice on 3/3/86) Others 3+1/1
Tottenham H (£50,000 on 14/4/86) FL 7+2 FAC 1+1/1
Millwall (£300,000 on 29/6/88) FL 0+2/1 FLC 2/3 Others 1+1
Southampton (£250,000 on 13/2/89) FL 100+7/9 FLC 14+1/1 FAC 10/3 Others 6
Tottenham H (£750,000 on 29/7/92) PL 38/3 FLC 4 FAC 5
Liverpool (£2,500,000 on 22/7/93) PL 109+4/11 FLC 18+1/1 FAC 11 Others 4+1

RUFUS Richard Raymond
Born: Lewisham, 12 January 1975
Height: 6'1" Weight: 11.2
International Honours: E: U21-6

Classy Charlton central defender who was honoured by being appointed captain of the England U21 team at the start of the 1996-97 season. Good in the air, and a strong tackler, Richard is exceptionally fast and recovers well when beaten, which is rare. He is also very calm under pressure, reads the game well, and is a mainstay of the Athletic defence. Still awaiting his first senior goal for the club.

Charlton Ath (From trainee on 1/7/93) FL 100+3 FLC 7 FAC 4 Others 2

RUSH David
Born: Sunderland, 15 May 1971
Height: 5'11" Weight: 11.4

After falling out of favour at Oxford early last season when having few opportunities to shine, the popular striker battled back to become a regular squad member, prior to signing for York City at the end of January. Unfortunately, David made only three appearances for his new club before injuries and then illness prematurely ended his campaign. One can only hope that with better fortune, he can look forward to happier times at Bootham Crescent in 1997-98.

Sunderland (From trainee on 21/7/89) FL 40+19/12 FLC 1+1 FAC 9/1 Others 1+1
Hartlepool U (Loaned on 15/8/91) FL 8/2
Peterborough U (Loaned on 27/10/93) FL 2+2/1 FLC 1/1
Cambridge U (Loaned on 12/9/94) FL 2
Oxford U (£100,000 on 23/9/94) FL 67+25/21 FLC 3+3 FAC 2+3/1 Others 6+1/2
York C (£80,000 on 31/1/97) FL 1+1 Others 1

RUSH Ian James
Born: St Asaph, 20 October 1961
Height: 6'0" Weight: 12.6
Club Honours: Div 1 '82, '83, '84, '86, '90; FLC '81, '82, '83, '84, '95; FAC '86, '89, '92; EC '84
International Honours: W: 73; U21-2; Sch

A veteran goalscorer and model professional, the former Liverpool legend signed for Leeds on a free transfer in the 1996 close season, ahead of a queue of clubs eager for his services. Then, firstly under Howard Wilkinson and later George Graham, Ian

went on to hit the worst goalscoring drought of his long career, going 15 games without finding the net. However, in some of those games, and during a campaign where the side lacked creativity, he was asked as a favour by Graham to perform on the right-hand side of midfield, and, like the professional he is, did so to help the cause. Looking as hungry and as fit as ever, his commitment and endeavour never waned and he would surely have scored more goals if more chances had been created.

Chester C (From apprentice on 25/9/79) FL 33+1/14 FAC 5/3
Liverpool (£300,000 on 1/5/80) FL 182/109 FLC 38/21 FAC 22/20 Others 31+1/17 (£3,200,000 to Juventus on 1/7/86)
Liverpool (Loaned on 1/7/86) FL 42/30 FLC 9/4 FAC 3 Others 3/6
Liverpool (£2,800,000 on 23/8/88) F/PL 223+22/90 FLC 30/23 FAC 30+6/19 Others 16+1/7
Leeds U (Free on 24/5/96) PL 34+2/3 FLC 2 FAC 2+2

RUSH Matthew James
Born: Hackney, 6 August 1971
Height: 5'11" Weight: 12.10
International Honours: Ei: U21-4

Unfortunately, Matthew spent a long time recovering from a cruciate knee ligament operation, before spending even more time in the Norwich reserve side (apart from two first-team subs' appearances that totalled just 43 minutes), last season in an effort to get back to match fitness and to also give him the confidence to twist and turn without worry. Loaned to Northampton, he had two spells with the third division club, scoring four goals in 15 games, before returning to Carrow Road and securing a permanent transfer to Oldham on transfer deadline day. Scoring on his debut, he showed himself to be very quick in his eight games played and will be hoping that 1997-98 brings him back to top form on the Latics' right wing.

West Ham U (From trainee on 24/3/90) F/PL 29+19/5 FLC 4 Others 2+1
Cambridge U (Loaned on 12/3/93) FL 4+6
Swansea C (Loaned on 10/1/94) FL 13 Others 4
Norwich C (£330,000 on 18/8/95) FL 0+3
Northampton T (Loaned on 28/10/96) FL 6/2
Northampton T (Loaned on 19/12/96) FL 8/1 Others 1/1
Oldham Ath (£165,000 on 27/3/97) FL 6+2/2

RUSSELL Alexander (Alex) John
Born: Crosby, 17 March 1973
Height: 5'8" Weight: 11.7

A regular in Rochdale's midfield at the start of last season, Alex briefly lost his first team place. However, after netting a last-gasp equaliser when coming on as substitute against Barnet, he was given a more attacking role in the absence of the side's regular strikers and netted six times in the space of eight games. Is the son of former Southport stalwart, Alex.

Rochdale (£4,000 from Burscough on 11/7/94) FL 57+14/10 FLC 4 FAC 0+1 Others 2+2

RUSSELL Craig Stewart
Born: South Shields, 4 February 1974
Height: 5'10" Weight: 12.6
Club Honours: Div 1 '96

Having top scored for Sunderland in 1995-

96, Craig was largely confined to the substitutes' bench last term, a situation which must have frustrated the locally-born crowd favourite as the club struggled for goals all season. When selected, his main attributes of strength and pace were often a threat to opposition defences and, despite making only ten Premiership starts, he actually finished as joint-leading scorer with four goals – the most memorable being the equaliser in the 2-2 Roker draw with Middlesbrough.
Sunderland (From trainee on 1/7/92) P/FL 103+44/31 FLC 5+5/1 FAC 6+3/2 Others 2

RUSSELL Keith David
Born: Aldridge, 31 January 1974
Height: 5'10" Weight: 12.0
A left-sided midfielder, cum winger, Keith impressed Blackpool so much when he played for Hednesford against them in the FA Cup earlier last season that they signed him on transfer deadline day. It was hardly a surprise, as he had been largely responsible for the non leaguer's biggest ever victory, his 20-yard strike coming back off the post to be tapped in for an 87th minute winner at Bloomfield Road. Received his first taste of league football at Wycombe as a sub and looked useful.
Blackpool (Signed from Hednesford on 27/3/97) FL 0+1

Kevin Russell

RUSSELL Kevin John
Born: Portsmouth, 6 December 1966
Height: 5'9" Weight: 10.12
Club Honours: Div 2 '93
International Honours: E: Yth
Kevin will be forever remembered by Wrexham fans for his winning last-minute strike against West Ham United in the third round FA Cup replay last January at Upton Park. He followed this up with two in the

next round at Peterborough and was a major influence in the club's cup run. Now a midfielder, "Rooster" has a high workrate and is always involved with attacking movements, which are proof of his former striker role. Nearly 13 years a pro, he shows no sign of slacking.
Portsmouth (Free from Brighton & Hove A juniors on 9/10/84) FL 3+1/1 FLC 0+1 FAC 0+1 Others 1+1
Wrexham (£10,000 on 17/7/87) FL 84/43 FLC 4/1 FAC 4 Others 8/3
Leicester C (£175,000 on 20/6/89) FL 24+19/10 FLC 0+1 FAC 1 Others 5/2
Peterborough U (Loaned on 6/9/90) FL 7/3
Cardiff C (Loaned on 17/1/91) FL 3
Hereford U (Loaned on 7/11/91) FL 3/1 Others 1/1
Stoke C (Loaned on 2/1/92) FL 5/1
Stoke C (£95,000 on 16/7/92) FL 30+10/5 FLC 3 FAC 2 Others 4+1/1
Burnley (£150,000 on 28/6/93) FL 26+2/6 FLC 4/1 FAC 4 Others 1/1
Bournemouth (£125,000 on 3/3/94) FL 30/1 FLC 3/1 FAC 2/1
Notts Co (£60,000 on 24/2/95) FL 9+2
Wrexham (£60,000 on 21/7/95) FL 74+7/7 FLC 3/1 FAC 8+2/3 Others 3

RUSSELL Lee Edward
Born: Southampton, 3 September 1969
Height: 5'11" Weight: 12.0
Lee began last season in Portsmouth's left-back spot, but injury and the form of others meant that he failed to hold down a regular place in the team from the end of October, making just one start thereafter. Also capable of playing in midfield and in central defence, where his ability and strength in the air make him difficult to get the better of, injuries have been his problem. Scored his second and third career goals during the campaign, including the winner against Southend at Fratton Park.
Portsmouth (From trainee on 12/7/88) FL 95+20/3 FLC 8+1 FAC 3+2 Others 5+2
Bournemouth (Loaned on 9/9/94) FL 3

RUSSELL Matthew Lee
Born: Dewsbury, 17 January 1978
Height: 5'11" Weight: 11.5
A skilful young Scarborough midfielder, and son of the club chairman, Matthew graduated through the YTS ranks to challenge for a first-team place in 1996-97, his senior debut coming as a substitute against Leicester in the Coca-Cola Cup, and his first full appearance at Chester near the end of the season. Unfortunately, soon afterwards, he suffered a stress fracture of his left foot in training, but is certain to be back in time for the start of 1997-98.
Scarborough (From trainee on 3/7/96) FL 1+4 FLC 0+1

RUSSELL Wayne Leonard
Born: Cardiff, 29 November 1967
Height: 6'2" Weight: 13.7
The consistency of Marlon Beresford ensured that Burnley's reserve 'keeper had few chances to impress in 1996-97, and his keenness for first team football, which was not realised at Turf Moor, led to him being transfer listed and freed during the summer. An excellent shot stopper, however, Wayne

kept clean sheets in his first two appearances last season, but was unfortunate to be on the end of a five-goal battering at the hands of Wycombe's forwards in mid April.
Burnley (Signed from Ebbw Vale on 28/10/93) FL 22+2 FLC 2 FAC 1

RUST Nicholas (Nicky) Charles Irwin
Born: Cambridge, 25 September 1974
Height: 6'0" Weight: 13.1
International Honours: E: Yth
Unrivalled as Brighton's regular goalkeeper for the previous three seasons, Nicky again assumed the role with distinction during 1996-97 until a rare injury gave young Mark Ormerod his chance. Still only 22, he clocked up his 150th league appearance during the course of the campaign and looks set for a long and successful career. The Seagulls are indeed fortunate to have two young goalkeepers of the class of Rust and Ormerod on the staff.
Brighton & Hove A (Free from Arsenal juniors on 9/7/93) FL 161 FLC 14 FAC 8 Others 9

RYAN Robert (Robbie) Paul
Born: Dublin, 16 May 1977
Height: 5'10" Weight: 12.0
International Honours: Ei: Yth; Sch
A versatile Huddersfield defender who can also play in midfield, Robbie is another youngster who forced his way to the fringe of the first team in 1996-97. A promising player who has been recognised at junior international level, he made his debut when coming off the bench at Ipswich in early September and is one to watch for the future.
Huddersfield T (Free from Belvedere on 26/7/94) FL 2+3

RYAN Timothy (Tim) James
Born: Stockport, 10 December 1974
Height: 5'10" Weight: 11.0
Broke into Doncaster Rovers' first team last September, following a move from non-league Buxton during the summer of 1996. Having virtually made the left back position his own, his main strengths being his pace and strong tackling, he was surprisingly allowed to move on loan to Altrincham in March before having his contract cancelled by mutual consent at the end of the season.
Scunthorpe U (From trainee on 8/4/93) FL 1+1 (Free to Buxton on 28/11/94)
Doncaster Rov (Free on 8/8/96) FL 22+6 FLC 0+1 FAC 1 Others 1

RYDER Stuart Henry
Born: Sutton Coldfield, 6 November 1973
Height: 6'0" Weight: 12.6
International Honours: E: U21-3
After 18 months out with a serious knee injury, Stuart returned in 1996-97 for Walsall's penultimate away game at Gillingham, only to suffer a hamstring strain. A calm young central defender who is extremely comfortable on the ball, he remains, however, a fine prospect for the future with England youth caps already behind him.
Walsall (From trainee on 16/7/92) FL 75+13/5 FLC 4+1 FAC 8 Others 4+1

PANINI

OFFICIAL LICENSEE

 **NUMBER 1 FOR FOOTBALL CARDS & STICKERS**

SADLER Richard Thomas
Born: Dublin, 14 January 1979
Height: 6'2" Weight: 12.10
International Honours: Ei: Yth
An Irish youth international, Richard signed for Millwall prior to the start of the 1996-97 season and proved to be a prolific goal-scorer in the juniors and reserves with his quick pace and flair. Introduced into first team action by John Docherty, he has taken time to adjust to the fast pace of the game, but has already shown that he is dangerous with either foot.
Millwall (Signed from Belvedere on 14/8/96) FL 7+3

SALAKO John Akin
Born: Nigeria, 11 February 1969
Height: 5'10" Weight: 12.8
Club Honours: FMC '91; Div '94
International Honours: E: 5
An enigmatic Coventry winger, John had a mixed season in 1996-97 before suffering a recurrence of an old back injury in January. He did briefly return as a sub in the Leicester home game, but was substituted himself after only 20 minutes on the field and then a knee injury ruled him out for the duration of the campaign. At his best one of the most talented wingers in the country, a great crosser of the ball, and with an ability to go past players, he can often frustrate when giving the impression of being too casual. Was certainly on top form in the Leeds home win, scoring a superb equaliser after running from inside his own half and keeping a steady flow of good crosses to his strikers.
Crystal Palace (From apprentice on 3/11/86) F/PL 172+43/22 FLC 19+5/5 FAC 20/4 Others 11+3/2
Swansea C (Loaned on 14/8/89) FL 13/3 Others 2/1
Coventry C (£1,500,000 on 7/8/95) PL 57+4/4 FLC 7/1 FAC 4/1

SALE Mark David
Born: Burton on Trent, 27 February 1972
Height: 6'5" Weight: 14.4
Having had a disappointing time of it in 1996-97 at Mansfield, due to suspension and niggling injuries, the Colchester manager, Steve Wignall, who had been trying to sign Mark, got his man at the third attempt in March. Known as "Carboot", the target man made an immediate impact and scored three goals in the last four games in the league as United missed the play offs by one point. He would therefore not wish to be reminded of his injury-time equaliser for Mansfield against Colchester in December, which cost the U's the two points needed.
Stoke C (From trainee on 10/7/90) FL 0+2
Cambridge U (Free on 31/7/91. Free to Rocester in December 1991)
Birmingham C (Free on 26/3/92) FL 11+10 FLC 2/1 Others 3+1/2
Torquay U (£10,000 on 5/3/93) FL 30+14/8 FLC 1 FAC 2/1 Others 3+1

Preston NE (£20,000 on 26/7/94) FL 10+3/7 FLC 1+1 FAC 0+1 Others 4
Mansfield T (£50,000 on 31/7/95) FL 36+9/12 FLC 4/1 FAC 2 Others 1
Colchester U (£23,500 on 10/3/97) FL 10/3 Others 2+1

SALMON Michael (Mike) Bernard
Born: Leyland, 14 July 1964
Height: 6'2" Weight: 12.12
Started last season as Charlton's first-choice goalkeeper, but lost his place through injury against Wolves in December and was unable to regain it due to the outstanding form of Andy Petterson. Very laid back in approach, Mike is, nevertheless, a good shot stopper and reasonable on crosses, although it is hard to envisage him replacing Petterson at the start of 1997-98, in view of the latter's recent form.
Blackburn Rov (From juniors on 16/10/81) FL 1
Chester C (Loaned on 18/10/82) FL 16 FAC 2
Stockport Co (Free on 3/8/83) FL 118 FLC 10 FAC 3 Others 3
Bolton W (Free on 31/7/86F) FL 26 FLC 2 FAC 4 Others 4
Wrexham (£18,000 on 7/3/87) FL 100 FLC 4 FAC 4 Others 9
Charlton Ath (£100,000 on 6/7/89) FL 139 FLC 11 FAC 8 Others 6

SAMBROOK Andrew (Andy) John
Born: Chatham, 13 July 1979
Height: 5'10" Weight: 11.7
Still on associate shcoolboy forms at Gillingham, Andy came on as a sub in the penultimate game of last season against Walsall, almost scoring with his first touch, but in the next breath being booked at the other end. A youngster who can play in central defence or at full back, preferring the latter, and reads the game well, being quick, strong in the air, and a good tackler, he disappointed the club in turning down a decent contract to take up a four-year soccer scholarship in America, instead.
Gillingham (Associate Schoolboy) FL 0+1

SAMPSON Ian
Born: Wakefield, 14 November 1968
Height: 6'2" Weight: 13.3
This Northampton central defender, who is reliable and steady, with a strong tackle, has the ability to be in the right place at the right time, as his goals tally shows. Also good in the air, he missed very few games as the club strove for a promotion place, via the play offs.
Sunderland (Signed from Goole T on 13/11/90) FL 13+4/1 FLC 1 FAC 0+2 Others 0+1
Northampton T (Loaned on 8/12/93) FL 8
Northampton T (Free on 5/8/94) FL 115+3/10 FLC 8 FAC 2 Others 11/1

SAMUELS Dean Walter
Born: Hackney, 29 March 1973
Height: 6'2" Weight: 11.10
Bought from non-league Boreham Wood as cover for the injured Sean Devine last December, his improvement came on in leaps and bounds after scoring on his Barnet debut in the AWS at Brentford. With Devine struggling to get back to full fitness, the tall, pacy, tricky striker impressed as a player

who could hold down a regular place in 1997-98.
Barnet (Signed from Boreham Wood on 24/12/96) FL 13+4/1 Others 1/1

SAMWAYS Mark
Born: Doncaster, 11 November 1968
Height: 6'2" Weight: 14.0
Scunthorpe goalkeeper. In failing to find consistent form in 1996-97, errors at crucial times eventually cost him his senior place and he went on loan to York prior to transfer deadline, as cover for Andy Warrington. A good shot stopper, who is often capable of keeping his side in the game, unfortunately, like a great many goalies currently playing, he occasionally experiences difficulties with crosses. Was released during the summer.
Doncaster Rov (From trainee on 20/8/87) FL 121 FLC 3 FAC 4 Others 10
Scunthorpe U (Signed on 26/3/92) FL 180 FLC 10 FAC 16 Others 16

SANDEMAN Bradley Robert
Born: Northampton, 24 February 1970
Height: 5'10" Weight: 10.8
Having joined Rotherham during the summer of 1996, essentially as a right back, he was an automatic choice in that role before accepting a more forward running position. This saw him net a couple of goals, but injuries, and the fact that he dropped out of favour, saw him move on a free transfer to Hereford United on deadline day after turning down a move to Exeter City. Quickly got into the swing of things at Edgar Street, making an impact with his excellent tackling and surging runs up the flank, before coming face to face with the realisation that he would be playing in the Conference in 1997-98.
Northampton T (From trainee on 14/7/88) FL 28+30/3 FLC 2+3 FAC 2 Others 6+1
Maidstone U (£10,000 on 22/2/91) FL 55+2/8 FLC 1 FAC 2 Others 2
Port Vale (Free on 14/8/92) FL 62+7/1 FLC 6+1 FAC 3+1 Others 2
Rotherham U (Free on 15/7/96) FL 20+1/2 FLC 2 FAC 1
Hereford U (Free on 28/3/97) FL 7

SANDFORD Lee Robert
Born: Basingstoke, 22 April 1968
Height: 6'1" Weight: 13.4
Club Honours: AMC '92; Div 2 '93
International Honours: E: Yth
A versatile defender signed from Stoke during the summer of 1996, after being tracked by Howard Kendall for some time, Lee started 1996-97 at left back for Sheffield United but lost his place to Roger Nilsen following the signing of David Holdsworth. Following that, he struggled to hold down a regular spot, although providing valuable cover at full back and centre back when required and could always be relied upon in an emergency. Good in the air, and on the ground, his strength in the tackle makes him a difficult opponent.
Portsmouth (From apprentice on 4/12/85) FL 66+6/1 FLC 11 FAC 4 Others 2+1
Stoke C (£140,000 on 22/12/89) FL 255+3/8 FLC 19 FAC 16/2 Others 31/4
Sheffield U (£500,000 on 22/7/96) FL 25+5/2 FLC 3 FAC 1 Others 1+1

SAN MIGUEL Xabier
Born: Bilbao, Spain, 7 May 1971
Height: 5'10" Weight: 12.0
Signed on non-contract terms from Spanish football last August, the midfielder made his league debut for Cambridge in a 1-1 home draw against Hereford a week later, and appeared once more from the subs' bench, before returning home.
Cambridge U (Free from Spanish lower leagues on 30/8/96) FL 0+1 FLC 1

SANSAM Christian (Chris)
Born: Hull, 26 December 1975
Height: 5'11" Weight: 11.7
Came to the attention of his hometown club after scoring against Hull City's second string for Bradford City reserves, who he had joined on non-contract terms. Jumped at the chance of a Boothferry trial last November, but it was to end in disappointment for the speedy forward when he was released before Christmas.
Scunthorpe U (From trainee on 23/12/93) FL 10+11/1 FAC 2+1 Others 1+4 (Free to Halifax on 16/2/96)
Scarborough (Free on 15/3/96) FL 5+1
Bradford C (Free on 15/8/96) FL 0+1
Hull C (Free on 15/11/96) FL 2+1 FAC 0+1 Others 1

SANSOME Paul Eric
Born: New Addington, 6 October 1961
Height: 6'0" Weight: 13.8
Club Honours: FLT '83
The performances of Simon Royce in goal at Southend during 1996-97 meant that Paul's first-team outings were limited and he eventually went on loan to Gravesend & Northfleet. Despite making just four appearances and conceding eight goals, his handling and shot-stopping capabilities were still excellent. Was appointed reserve team coach in March 1997.
Millwall (Free from Crystal Palace juniors on 18/4/80) FL 156 FLC 12 FAC 13 Others 9
Southend U (£40,000 on 24/3/88) FL 308 FLC 19 FAC 8 Others 16
Birmingham C (Loaned on 9/1/96) FL 1 FLC 1

SAS Marco
Born: Vlaardingen, Holland, 16 February 1971
Height: 6'1" Weight: 12.6
International Honours: Holland: U21
Signed in the 1996 close season from the Dutch side, NAC Breda, Marco came straight into Bradford's team and, despite missing a few games due to illness and injury, impressed the Valley Parade faithful as a skilful centre back who just loved taking the play to the opposition when bringing the ball out of defence and going on surging runs. Brilliant at spraying 50 to 60 yard passes around the ground, his shooting ability from long range also excited the fans, albeit his three goals came from headers and the penalty spot. Should continue to catch the eye in 1997-98.
Bradford C (Free from NAC Breda on 10/7/96) FL 31/3 FLC 2 FAC 1

SAUNDERS Dean Nicholas
Born: Swansea, 21 June 1964
Height: 5'8" Weight: 10.6

Club Honours: FAC '92; FLC '94
International Honours: W: 58
Dean returned to the English game at the start of last season when Nottingham Forest signed him from the Turkish side, Galatasaray. A very quick striker, he did not have the best of times as Forest struggled, and scored just five times in all, but his workrate never faltered and he started in a good partnership with Kevin Campbell. However, when the former Arsenal man was injured, he was forced to play alongside several different partners without forming a good understanding with any of them and, subsequently, his form occasionally suffered. Despite all of that, he missed just four games, retained his place in the Welsh side, and scored in the World Cup qualifiers. Hopefully, in a more settled side in 1997-98, Dean will be back to doing what he does best, in getting in behind defenders and hurting them with his pace.
Swansea C (From apprentice on 24/6/82) FL 42+7/12 FLC 2+1 FAC 1 Others 1+1
Cardiff C (Loaned on 29/3/85) FL 3+1
Brighton & Hove A (Free on 7/8/85) FL 66+6/21 FLC 4 FAC 7/5 Others 3
Oxford U (£60,000 on 12/3/87) FL 57+2/22 FLC 9+1/8 FAC 2/2 Others 2/1
Derby Co (£1,000,000 on 28/10/88) FL 106/42 FLC 12/10 FAC 6 Others 7/5
Liverpool (£2,900,000 on 19/7/91) F/PL 42/11 FLC 5/2 FAC 8/2 Others 6/10
Aston Villa (£2,300,000 on 10/9/92) F/PL 111+1/37 FLC 15/7 FAC 9/4 Others 8/1 (£2,350,000 to Galatasaray on 1/7/95)
Nottingham F (£1,500,000 on 16/7/96) PL 33+1/3 FLC 3 FAC 2/2

Dean Saunders

SAUNDERS Mark Philip
Born: Reading, 23 July 1971
Height: 5'11" Weight: 11.12

After a frustrating start to 1996-97, when injury again halted his progress at Plymouth, Mark returned to fitness to show why he was signed from local non-league football. As a combative midfielder who gets into excellent forward positions, he scored three times, all of them vital to Argyle's cause and, if he can stay injury free, the coming season should be a good one.
Plymouth Arg (Signed from Tiverton T on 22/8/95) FL 26+9/4 FLC 1+1 FAC 0+3 Others 1

SAVAGE David (Dave) Thomas Patrick
Born: Dublin, 30 July 1973
Height: 6'1" Weight: 12.7
International Honours: Ei: 5; U21-5

Moving from his right-sided midfield role at Millwall in 1996-97 to a more central position saw Dave get himself into some excellent goalscoring situations, most notably his one touch and volley for the winning goal against Notts County at the Den. Established as an Eire international, a niggling back injury unfortunately kept this strong-running, pacy player from gaining more caps.
Brighton & Hove A (Signed from Kilkenny on 5/3/91 - Free to Longford T in May 1992)
Millwall (£15,000 on 27/5/94) FL 80+19/5 FLC 8/1 FAC 5+2/2 Others 1/1

SAVAGE Robert (Rob) William
Born: Wrexham, 18 October 1974
Height: 5'11" Weight: 10.7
Club Honours: FAYC '92
International Honours: W: 5; U21-5; Yth; Sch

A hard-working Crewe midfielder with abundant energy, Rob missed only eight games in 1996-97, three of them being in the play offs, the aftermath of which saw the club reach the first division for the first time in its history. His consistent form also saw him continue to add to his Welsh caps during the campaign. Once recognised as a forward player when with Manchester United, his ability to run off the ball well can often be used to good effect in attacking areas of the field.
Manchester U (From trainee on 5/7/93)
Crewe Alex (Free on 22/7/94) FL 74+3/10 FLC 5 FAC 5 Others 8/1

SAVILLE Andrew (Andy) Victor
Born: Hull, 12 December 1964
Height: 6'0" Weight: 12.13
Club Honours: Div 3 '96

Unable to rediscover his 1995-96 goalscoring form for Preston, having scored just once in 16 starts, Andy moved to Wigan last October. While a surprise arrival at Springfield Park, he failed to reproduce the kind of scoring form he was famed for, although injuries which led to surgery meant that the shaven-headed striker never enjoyed an extended run in the side. Strong in the air and with the ability to hold the ball up well, despite scoring only four goals, Andy collected a division three championship medal for the second year running, as the

Latics pipped Fulham for the title on goal difference.
Hull C (Signed on 23/9/83) FL 74+27/18 FLC 6/1 FAC 3+2/1 Others 4+2
Walsall (£100,000 on 23/3/89) FL 28+10/5 FLC 2 Others 1+1
Barnsley (£80,000 on 9/3/90) FL 71+11/21 FLC 5+1 FAC 2+1 Others 4/1
Hartlepool U (£60,000 on 13/3/92) FL 37/14 FLC 4/1 FAC 4/5 Others 3/1
Birmingham C (£155,000 on 22/3/93) FL 51+8/17 FLC 4/1 FAC 1 Others 1
Burnley (Loaned on 30/12/94) FL 3+1/1 FAC 1
Preston NE (£100,000 on 29/7/95) FL 56/30 FLC 6 FAC 2 Others 2/1
Wigan Ath (£125,000 on 25/10/96) FL 17+3/4 FAC 1 Others 1

SCALES John Robert
Born: Harrogate, 4 July 1966
Height: 6'2" Weight: 13.5
Club Honours: FAC '88; FLC '95
International Honours: E: 3; B-2

Although at the heart of Liverpool's defence during last September and October, following the return of Mark Wright and unable to command a regular place in the side, the athletic defender joined Tottenham in early December, amidst controversy about a proposed transfer to Leeds United. Having favoured a move back to London, John made two subs' appearances but did not make his full debut until 1 March at White Hart Lane against Nottingham Forest after recovering from injury. From then on, he demonstrated great aerial ability and terrific pace, with superb accuracy when directing the ball, and the prospect of him playing alongside Ramon Vega, Colin Calderwood and Sol Campbell for a full season in 1997-98 will daunt many of the Premiership's top strikers. Similar in spirit to Gary Mabbutt, this player definitely has the presence and temperament to stamp his authority on the game and make a terrific impression at Spurs.
Bristol Rov (Free from Leeds U juniors on 11/7/85) FL 68+4/2 FLC 3 FAC 6 Others 3+1
Wimbledon (£70,000 on 16/7/87) F/PL 235+5/11 FLC 18+1 FAC 20+1 Others 7+1/4
Liverpool (£3,500,000 on 2/9/94) PL 65/2 FLC 10/2 FAC 14 Others 4+1
Tottenham H (£2,600,000 on 11/12/96) PL 10+2

SCHMEICHEL Peter Boleslaw
Born: Gladsaxe, Denmark, 18 November 1963
Height: 6'4" Weight: 16.0
Club Honours: ESC '91; FLC '92; PL '93, '94, '96, '97; FAC '94, '96; CS '93, '94, '97
International Honours: Denmark (UEFAC '92): 93

A highly influential goalkeeper with great presence, Peter made a superb start to last season with five consecutive clean sheets for Manchester United from the end of September to mid October. Then came a highly forgettable spell when he conceded five goals at Newcastle, six at Southampton, and finally the goal which ended United's 40-year unbeaten home record in European competition against Fenerbahce. With opposing supporters suggesting that he might have to be protected from lumbago, he hardly batted an eyelid. Come the start of December, he answered his critics with a

sublime save against Rapid Vienna, one that was compared with Gordon Banks' legendary effort against Pele in Mexico in 1970, with some even suggesting it was the greatest of all time. Typically, Peter shrugged his huge shoulders and said, "It was no big deal." A month later, in the FA Cup replay against Wimbledon, he appeared to have saved United again, when he put a spectacular last minute bicycle kick into the roof of the net, but it was ruled out for off side. Having missed only one Premiership game throughout 1996-97, against Aston Villa with a stomach bug, his consistency was paramount as United mounted their quest for major honours that ended in them clinching the league title for the fourth time in five years.
Manchester U (£550,000 from Brondby on 12/8/91) F/PL 226 FLC 17 FAC 29 Others 26/1

Peter Schmeichel

SCHOFIELD John David
Born: Barnsley, 16 May 1965
Height: 5'11" Weight: 11.8

Captain of Doncaster, John led the side by example in 1996-97 from his position in central midfield. Solid, rather than spectacular, his form remained largely consistent, despite the team's lowly position, and there was certainly no lack of effort on his part as the Rovers fought to preserve their Football League status.
Lincoln C (Free from Gainsborough Trinity on 10/11/88) FL 221+10/11 FLC 15/4 FAC 5+2 Others 1
Doncaster Rov (Free on 18/11/94) FL 107+3/12 FLC 4 FAC 2 Others 3

SCHOLES Paul
Born: Salford, 16 November 1974
Height: 5'7" Weight: 11.0
Club Honours: PL '96, '97; FAC '96, '97; CS '97
International Honours: E: 3; Yth (UEFAC '93)

A prolific goalscorer who can play as an out-and-out striker or in central midfield, Paul's hopes of a regular first-team place at Manchester United were dashed in the 1996

241

close season by the arrival of so many big-money stars. But, having spent the early part of the campaign on the substitutes' bench, he netted two goals in successive games in October, against Swindon in the Coca-Cola Cup and Southampton in the Premiership. In December, he began one of his most consistent spells in the side, striking United's equaliser in the Premiership game against Sheffield Wednesday and scoring in the FA Cup ties against Spurs and Wimbledon. Having undergone a cartilage operation in February, he made a remarkable recovery and was a vital member of the squad during the hectic run in, his season being made complete with his first major honour in the game, a championship medal, followed by an England call up that saw him starring on the international front.

Manchester U (From trainee on 29/1/93) PL 38+29/18 FLC 6/5 FAC 3+3/3 Others 2+7/1

SCHWARZER Mark
Born: Sydney, Australia, 6 October 1972
Height: 6'4" Weight: 13.6
International Honours: Australia: 4

Signed from Kaiserslautern last November, the big Australian international goalkeeper quickly settled into the Bradford line up to become a Valley Parade favourite before a shock transfer saw him snapped up by Middlesbrough in February. Making his Boro debut against Stockport in the hard-fought Coca-Cola Cup match at Edgeley Park, and playing with supreme confidence, he won over the travelling fans who took him to their hearts in just two minutes when he got down in great style to cover a vicious shot from Luis Cavaco to deny County a goal that would certainly have sealed Boro's fate in the competition. Earlier, his dual nationality, Australian of German descent, had opened the door for him to follow the precedent set by his fellow countryman, former Boro hero, Craig Johnston. Sadly, for the fans, he was FA Cup tied through his Bradford appearance, and injures, allowed him only seven Premiership outings, but it looks odds on that he will star in the coming campaign.

Bradford C (£350,000 from Kaiserslautern on 22/11/96) FL 13 FAC 3
Middlesbrough (£1,500,000 on 26/2/97) PL 7 FLC 3

SCIMECA Riccardo
Born: Leamington Spa, 13 June 1975
Height: 6'1" Weight: 12.9
Club Honours: FLC '96
International Honours: E: U21-5

Many felt that Riccardo would make a big impact on the Aston Villa side last season, but he would have been disappointed just to have made 15 starts, plus a few more as a sub. He was however, often a non-playing sub. An extremely versatile player, who very rarely gave a poor performance, most of his games were as a centre back, which is deemed to be his best position now. A regular in the England U21 side when fit, he missed the last month of the season with injury.

Aston Villa (From trainee on 7/7/93) PL 18+16 FLC 2+3 FAC 5

SCOTT Andrew (Andy)
Born: Epsom, 2 August 1972
Height: 6'1" Weight: 11.5

A player who can fill any number of roles, Andy failed to regain a regular first-team place at Sheffield United in 1996-97, following his recovery from injury the previous campaign, playing just a couple of games before going on loan to Chesterfield in October. Despite making an immediate impact with the Spireites, coming off the bench to net the winner and scoring twice on his full debut the following week, he returned to Bramall Lane keen to force his way back into contention, but again went out on loan, this time to Bury, as the transfer deadline loomed. Very pacy and dangerous, especially down the left side, his only goal for United came at Bradford on Boxing Day.

Sheffield U (£50,000 from Sutton U on 1/12/92) P/FL 38+31/6 FLC 3/1 FAC 2+1 Others 3+1/3
Chesterfield (Loaned on 18/10/96) FL 4+1/3
Bury (Loaned on 21/3/97) FL 2+6

SCOTT Andrew (Andy) Michael
Born: Manchester, 27 June 1975
Height: 6'0" Weight: 12.11

Freed by Cardiff at the end of last season after playing just three times in 1996-97, Andy was unable to do himself justice, having suffered from a whole spate of injuries during his two-year stay at Ninian Park. At his best, a pacy full back who passes the ball well, hopefully, he will be able to attain match fitness and find another club quickly.

Blackburn Rov (From trainee on 4/1/93)
Cardiff C (Free on 9/8/94) FL 14+2/1 FLC 0+1 FAC 1 Others 1

SCOTT Keith
Born: Westminster, 9 June 1967
Height: 6'3" Weight: 14.3
Club Honours: GMVC '93; FAT '93

Despite scoring against Manchester City, Birmingham and Reading, two of them coming while on the pitch as a sub, Keith struggled to command a regular first-team place at Norwich in 1996-97 and was loaned to Watford in February. Seen as the ideal target man by the management there, although scoring twice in eight outings, funds were not forthcoming and he returned to Carrow Road, before taking up a further spell on loan at his old club, Wycombe. Having twice turned down the opportunity previously, he arrived to a heroes welcome and, inevitably, scored in his first game back, until ending a much needed extra dimension to Wanderers' patient passing game.

Lincoln C (Free from Leicester U on 22/3/90) FL 7+9/2 FLC 0+1 Others 1+1
Wycombe W (£30,000 in March 1991) FL 15/10 FLC 4/2 FAC 6/1 Others 2/2
Swindon T (£375,000 on 18/11/93) P/FL 43+8/12 FLC 5/3 Others 3/1
Stoke C (£300,000 on 30/12/94) FL 22+3/3 FAC 2/1 Others 0+1
Norwich C (Signed on 11/11/95) FL 10+15/5 FLC 0+2 FAC 0+2
Bournemouth (Loaned on 16/2/96) FL 8/1
Watford (Loaned on 7/2/97) FL 6/2 Others 2
Wycombe W (Loaned on 27/3/97) FL 9/3

SCOTT Kevin Watson
Born: Easington, 17 December 1966
Height: 6'3" Weight: 14.5
Club Honours: FAYC '85; Div 1 '93

Unable to get a look in at Spurs in 1996-97, the central defender went out on loan to Charlton in December with a view to getting a few games under his belt and immediately made his debut at Crystal Palace. Strong in the air and dangerous at corners with his aerial power, Kevin made three more appearances before returning to White Hart Lane and signing for Norwich in January, following a long-term injury to John Polston. A natural left-footed player, seemingly a rarity these days, and comfortable on the ball, he helped shore up a leaky City defence and looks good for 1997-98.

Newcastle U (From apprentice on 19/12/84) F/PL 227/8 FLC 18 FAC 15+1/1 Others 12+1/2
Tottenham H (£850,000 on 1/2/94) PL 16+2/1 FLC 0+1
Port Vale (Loaned on 13/1/95) FL 17/1
Charlton Ath (Loaned on 20/12/96) FL 4
Norwich C (£250,000 on 21/1/97) FL 9

SCOTT Martin
Born: Sheffield, 7 January 1968
Height: 5'9" Weight: 11.7
Club Honours: Div 4 '89; Div 1 '96

The highly-rated left back's 1996-97 season was ruined by injury and his overlapping wing play was sorely missed by Sunderland in their unsuccessful relegation fight. "Scotty" had started the campaign well enough, scoring in the derby match against Newcastle at Roker in September, but, having recovered from a hernia operation in February, he picked up a leg injury in his comeback match against Leeds that sidelined him until 1997-98. Apart from his obvious attacking capability, Martin's pace and powerful tackling make him difficult to pass.

Rotherham U (From apprentice on 10/1/86) FL 93+1/3 FLC 11/2 FAC 7+2 Others 7/2
Bristol C (£200,000 on 5/12/90) FL 171/14 FLC 10/1 FAC 10 Others 8/1
Sunderland (£750,000 on 23/12/94) P/FL 82/7 FLC 5/1 FAC 5

SCOTT Richard Paul
Born: Dudley, 29 September 1974
Height: 5'9" Weight: 12.8

Strong-tackling Shrewsbury midfielder who likes to get forward. By the standard he set himself in 1995-96, last season was a little disappointing and, after being a regular early on, opportunities seemed to be limited to the subs' bench or in injury situations. Limited appearances also reduced his goalscoring total to just one strike.

Birmingham C (From trainee on 17/5/93) FL 11+1 FLC 3+1 Others 3
Shrewsbury T (Signed on 22/3/95) FL 63+8/8 FLC 5 FAC 6+1/3 Others 7+1/1

SCOTT Robert (Rob)
Born: Epsom, 15 August 1973
Height: 6'1" Weight: 11.10

A strong front runner who often dropped back into right midfield in tactical switches, Rob's long throws and accurate crosses led to several goals in Fulham's promotion

campaign, while he finished up as second top scorer for the club with ten. Obviously a taker of chances as well as a provider, his great pace gets him into good attacking positions.

Sheffield U (£20,000 from Sutton U on 1/8/93) FL 2+4/1 FLC 0+1 Others 2+1
Scarborough (Loaned on 22/3/95) FL 8/3
Northampton T (Loaned on 24/11/95) FL 5 Others 1
Fulham (£30,000 on 10/1/96) FL 57+7/14 FLC 3+1 FAC 1 Others 0+1/1

SCOWCROFT James (Jamie) Benjamin
Born: Bury St Edmunds, 15 November 1975
Height: 6'1" Weight: 12.2
International Honours: E: U21-4

Jamie quickly found himself in regular first team football when he took over from Ian Marshall at Ipswich early last season, scoring 11 goals, including doubles at Sheffield United and Bolton, and one in the second play-off leg at home to the former. The goals at Bolton were a bit of a milestone as they enabled Town to become the first team to win at Burnden Park in 1996-97, the clincher coming in the last minute when he ran on to Jason Cundy's clearance and coolly flicked it over the oncoming goalkeeper. Undoubtedly a player who is going to be heard from more often, his talent was reassured by regular call ups to the England U21 side during the campaign.

Ipswich T (From trainee on 1/7/94) FL 53+11/11 FLC 6+1/1 FAC 3 Others 3+2/1

SCULLY Anthony (Tony) Derek Thomas
Born: Dublin, 12 June 1976
Height: 5'7" Weight: 11.12
International Honours: Ei: U21-8; Yth; Sch

A Crystal Palace midfielder who normally plays on the right-hand side, Tony managed just one appearance in 1996-97 when coming off the bench at Barnsley for the final minute of the game. Hardly much to write home about, despite having an excellent season with the reserves, and he went for a spell on loan with Portadown in March, scoring twice in five games, following which he expected to come back refreshed for the coming term. Is a skilful ball winner who gets forward and links up play well, he represented the Republic of Ireland at U21 level against Iceland in November.

Crystal Palace (From trainee on 2/12/93) FL 0+3
Bournemouth (Loaned on 14/10/94) FL 6+4 Others 2
Cardiff C (Loaned on 5/1/96) FL 13+1

SEABURY Kevin
Born: Shrewsbury, 24 November 1973
Height: 5'9" Weight: 11.11

A versatile Shrewsbury Town player who always gives 100 per cent, Kevin can be used at full back, in midfield, or in central defence. Very popular with the crowd, he consolidated further last season and became a regular, looking at home in any of the roles he fulfilled, either defending or creating and played in central defence in emergencies.

Has a knack of getting back on the goal line just at the right time to make vital clearances.

Shrewsbury T (From trainee on 6/7/92) FL 87+16 FLC 5+1/1 FAC 6 Others 7+2

SEAGRAVES Mark
Born: Bootle, 22 October 1966
Height: 6'0" Weight: 13.4
Club Honours: Div 2 '96
International Honours: E: Yth

1996-97 was an in-and-out season for the Swindon central defender. Following the early departure of his twin centre back, Shaun Taylor, he formed a useful partnership with Ian Culverhouse which, for a time, seemed to be the bedrock of Town's defence. However, injured in October, he probably made a premature return in November with unfamiliar partners and then had to wait until January for his next return. A tri-partite defensive line up with Culverhouse and on-loan Marlon Broomes appeared to restore some defensive stability until a traumatic 7-0 defeat away to champions elect Bolton Wanderers in March and, following another defensive debacle at Oldham on Easter Monday, he was rested for the remainder of the campaign, when it seemed that he was still troubled with injury.

Liverpool (From apprentice on 4/11/83) FLC 1 FAC 1
Norwich C (Loaned on 21/11/86) FL 3
Manchester C (£100,000 on 25/9/87) FL 36+6 FLC 3 FAC 3 Others 2
Bolton W (£100,000 on 24/9/90) FL 152+5/7 FLC 8 FAC 17/1 Others 13/1
Swindon T (£100,000 on 6/6/95) FL 52+4 FLC 8+1 FAC 4+1 Others 2

SEAL David
Born: Penrith, Australia, 26 January 1972
Height: 5'11" Weight: 12.4

Many at Ashton Gate felt that David was not given much of a chance to shine up front last season, especially after Bristol City's top scorer in 1995-96 and in good scoring form for the reserves. Swansea City, though, realised his potential and were on the verge of signing him when he pulled out due to failure to agree terms. Hopefully, Swansea's loss will be the Robins' gain as new manager, John Ward, offers him the opportunity to make a new start.

Bristol C (£80,000 from Eendracht Aalst on 7/10/94) FL 24+27/10 FLC 4+1/3 FAC 1+1 Others 2+1/1

SEALEY Leslie (Les) Jesse
Born: Bethnal Green, 29 September 1957
Height: 6'1" Weight: 13.6
Club Honours: FAC '90; ECWC '91; CS '90

Very experienced goalkeeper who joined Leyton Orient during the summer of 1996 on a free transfer from West Ham, and known for his vocal encouragement of defenders, he soon had the desired affect with six clean sheets in his 14 games before injury and a chance to return to West Ham as a makeweight in the Peter Shilton deal ended his Leyton Orient career last November. Called up at Blackburn, he later came on as a sub at Old Trafford in an emotional return to his former club on the final day of the season.

Coventry C (From apprentice on 1/3/76) FL 158 FLC 11 FAC 9
Luton T (£100,000 on 3/8/83) FL 207 FLC 21 FAC 28 Others 3
Plymouth Arg (Loaned on 5/10/84) FL 6
Manchester U (Loaned on 21/3/90) FL 2 FAC 1
Manchester U (Free on 6/6/90) FL 31 FLC 8 FAC 3 Others 9
Aston Villa (Free on 19/7/91) FL 18 FAC 4 Others 2
Coventry C (Loaned on 25/3/92) FL 2
Birmingham C (Loaned on 2/10/92) FL 12 Others 3
Manchester U (Free on 6/1/93) FLC 1 FAC 0+1
Blackpool (Free on 18/7/94) FL 7 FLC 2
West Ham U (Free on 28/11/94) PL 1+1
Leyton Orient (Free on 17/7/96) FL 12 FLC 2
West Ham U (Free on 29/11/96) PL 1+1

SEAMAN David Andrew
Born: Rotherham, 19 September 1963
Height: 6'4" Weight: 14.10
Club Honours: Div 1 '91; FAC '93; FLC '93; ECWC '94
International Honours: E: 36; B-6; U21-10

1996-97 was an injury ravaged season for the Arsenal and England goalkeeper who was yet again troubled by persistent rib trouble. However, David was still a role model of consistency and, when missing, it was as much for his imposing presence, which means so much to the Gunners, as for his goalkeeping ability. It was also pleasing to see him so well received on the opposition's grounds following his Euro '96 heroics, and now firmly established as England's number one 'keeper his absence at Wembley in the crucial World Cup qualifier against Italy turned out to be a major set back to the national team. Still showing safe hands and quick thinking, he had three spells out of the Arsenal side during the campaign, making 28 appearances and keeping 13 clean sheets, four of them in the final seven games as the side overhauled Liverpool to grab third place in the Premiership and a place in Europe in 1997-98. A good kicker of the ball, often running it out to gain extra distance, his calling is superb, another honour came his way when he was selected for the PFA award-winning Premiership side.

Leeds U (From apprentice on 22/9/81)
Peterborough U (£4,000 on 13/8/82) FL 91 FLC 10 FAC 5
Birmingham C (£100,000 on 5/10/84) FL 75 FLC 4 FAC 5
Queens Park R (£225,000 on 7/8/86) FL 141 FLC 13 FAC 17 Others 4
Arsenal (£1,300,000 on 18/5/90) F/PL 249 FLC 30 FAC 32 Others 28

SEARLE Damon Peter
Born: Cardiff, 26 October 1971
Height: 5'11" Weight: 10.4
Club Honours: WC '92, '93; Div 3 '93
International Honours: W: B-1; U21-6; Yth

Signed during the 1996 close season, having been released by Cardiff, the left back lost his place in Stockport's side to Lee Todd early on in 1996-97 and could not win it back. A steady performer and useful stand-by, Damon is an attacking left-wing back who, in the past, has been close to selection for the Welsh side and is bound to fight his way back into contention for places in 1997-98.

Cardiff C (From trainee on 20/8/90) FL 232+2/3 FLC 9/1 FAC 13 Others 29
Stockport Co (Free on 28/5/96) FL 7+3 FLC 2+1 Others 1

SEBA Jesus
Born: Zaragoza, Spain, 11 April 1974
Height: 5'7" Weight: 10.3
International Honours: Spain: U21

The forgotten Amigo left Wigan Athletic last October after accepting John Deehan's offer to tear up his contract. A former Spanish U21 international, Jesus had failed to win a regular place in 1996-97, the striker being restricted to just two substitute appearances, and after brief trials with Burnley and Bristol Rovers he returned home to re-sign for Real Zaragoza.
Wigan Ath (Free from Real Zaragoza on 10/8/95) FL 8+13/3 FLC 2+1 FAC 0+2 Others 1

SEDGEMORE Benjamin (Ben) Redwood
Born: Wolverhampton, 5 August 1975
Height: 6'0" Weight: 13.11
International Honours: E: Sch

A very talented midfielder whose transfer from Peterborough last September cost Mansfield a fee they could have avoided, had the manager taken him permanently following his loan spell a year earlier when he was at Birmingham. One to watch for the future.
Birmingham C (From trainee on 17/5/93)
Northampton T (Loaned on 22/12/94) FL 1
Mansfield T (Loaned on 25/8/95) FL 4+5 Others 1
Peterborough U (Free on 10/1/96) FL 13+4 FAC 1
Mansfield T (Free on 6/9/96) FL 37+2/4 FAC 1 Others 1

Steve Sedgley

SEDGLEY Stephen (Steve) Philip
Born: Enfield, 26 May 1968
Height: 6'1" Weight: 13.13
Club Honours: FAC '91; CS '91
International Honours: E: U21-11

1996-97 was yet another consistent season for the versatile Ipswich player, who is equally at home in defence or in midfield

and is the club's dead-ball specialist, taking most corners, free kicks and penalties. Towards the end of the year, however, he was troubled by a foot injury, but his attempts to play through the pain did not resolve matters and he was forced to rest it completely in the New Year. Although relinquishing the role of team captain, he nevertheless led by example and was a tremendous influence on the youngsters, particularly when he played alongside them in defensive situations.
Coventry C (From apprentice on 2/6/86) FL 81+3/3 FLC 9/2 FAC 2+2 Others 5+1
Tottenham H (£750,000 on 28/7/89) F/PL 147+17/8 FLC 24+3/1 FAC 22+1/1 Others 5+3
Ipswich T (£1,000,000 on 15/6/94) P/FL 105/15 FLC 10/2 FAC 5 Others 5/1

Scott Sellars

SELLARS Scott
Born: Sheffield, 27 November 1965
Height: 5'8" Weight: 10.0
Club Honours: FMC '87; Div 1 '93, '97
International Honours: E: U21-3

A left-sided Bolton midfielder with sublime skills, in 1996-97, Scott had one of his best seasons. At his best when running at players with the ball and deadly from free-kick situations, his eight goals bear testament to his abilities – abilities which saw him win a number of Man of the Match awards and also saw him cement his place in the Wanderers' starting line up on his way to winning a first division championship medal and the promise of a return to Premiership football.
Leeds U (From apprentice on 25/7/83) FL 72+4/12 FLC 4/1 FAC 4 Others 2/1
Blackburn Rov (£20,000 on 28/7/86) FL 194+8/35 FLC 12/3 FAC 11/1 Others 20/2
Leeds U (£800,000 on 1/7/92) PL 6+1 FLC 1+1 Others 1
Newcastle U (£700,000 on 9/3/93) F/PL 56+5/5 FLC 6+1/2 FAC 3 Others 4/1
Bolton W (£750,000 on 7/12/95) P/FL 62+2/11 FLC 3+1 FAC 3

SELLEY Ian
Born: Chertsey, 14 June 1974
Height: 5'9" Weight: 10.1
Club Honours: FLC '93; FAC '93; ECWC '94

International Honours: E: U21-3; Sch
Having recovered from the badly-broken leg suffered in February 1995, the Arsenal midfield ball winner, also recognised at the club as being second only to Martin Keown in the man-marking area, was loaned out to Southend last December in an effort to help re-establish him. Returned to Highbury after four games to resume his rehabilitation with the reserves and later made a cameo appearance in the 3-0 win at Chelsea in April, looking quite perky during the five-minute run out. Versatile and skilful, and having good vision and a shot to match, with the pre-season training schedule under his belt he should be raring to go in 1997-98.
Arsenal (From trainee on 6/5/92) PL 35+6 FLC 5+1 FAC 3 Others 8+2/2
Southend U (Loaned on 3/12/96) FL 3+1

SERRANT Carl
Born: Bradford, 12 September 1975
Height: 5'11" Weight: 12.1
International Honours: E: Yth

Picked for England U21 squad in May after being Man of the Match for the Football League U21s against the Italian League in February, merely confirmed his new found status at Oldham in 1996-97. A class left back, who is both solid and dependable on the ground and good in the air, his terrific pace allows him to overlap and link well with the midfield and front men, whilst his recovery rate at the back is exceptional. Missing very few games, and then only when unavailable, he is very much a rising star.
Oldham Ath (From trainee on 22/7/94) FL 54+6/1 FLC 5 FAC 3 Others 3

SERTORI Mark Anthony
Born: Manchester, 1 September 1967
Height: 6'3" Weight: 14.2
Club Honours: GMVC '88

A free signing for Scunthorpe during the 1996 close season after being out of contract at Bury, Mark again proved to be a big, solid, and reliable central defender. Strong in the air and assured on the ground, he occasionally played at centre forward in 1996-97 and, at 6'3", was obviously danger-ous at set pieces.
Stockport Co (Signed from East Manchester on 7/2/87) FL 3+1 FLC 1
Lincoln C (Free on 1/7/88) FL 43+7/9 FLC 6 FAC 4/1 Others 5/2
Wrexham (£30,000 on 9/2/90) FL 106+4/3 FLC 8+1 FAC 6 Others 9+1
Bury (Free on 22/7/94) FL 4+9/1 FLC 1 FAC 2+1 Others 1+2/1
Scunthorpe U (Free on 22/7/96) FL 42/1 FLC 2 FAC 3 Others 1+1

SHAIL Mark Edward David
Born: Sandviken, Sweden, 15 October 1966
Height: 6'1" Weight: 13.3
International Honours: E: SP-1

After recovering from an injury that saw him miss the second half of 1995-96, apart from a few early games in 1996-97, this cool, composed Bristol City central defender with good aerial ability had to wait until April before he was once again given a lengthy spell in the side. A good end of term

run in that took the side into the promotion play offs, saw Mark establish himself again and, hopefully, he will remain at Ashton Gate to assist in the 1997-98 promotion drive. Always gave 100 per-cent commitment to the cause.
Bristol C (£45,000 from Yeovil on 25/3/93) FL 94+7/4 FLC 5+1 FAC 10/1 Others 4

SHAKESPEARE Craig Robert
Born: Birmingham, 26 October 1963
Height: 5'10" Weight: 12.5
Primarily right footed, but with a strong left foot as well, Craig is probably most effective at the centre of midfield, although at home on either flank. As Grimsby's midfield ball winner, with the ability to run with the ball he had an indifferent season for the club in 1996-97 and found himself out of favour with the management, making only sporadic appearances at senior level. However, he was given a notable role in defence when both regular wing backs suffered injury towards the end of the campaign, before being released during the summer.
Walsall (From apprentice on 5/11/81) FL 276+8/45 FLC 31/6 FAC 22/6 Others 18/2
Sheffield Wed (£300,000 on 19/6/89) FL 15+2 FLC 3/1 Others 0+1
West Bromwich A (£275,000 on 8/2/90) FL 104+8/12 FLC 6/1 FAC 5/2 Others 5/1
Grimsby T (£115,000 on 14/7/93) FL 84+22/10 FLC 6+1 FAC 5+2 Others 0+1

SHARMAN Samuel (Sam) Joseph
Born: Hull, 7 November 1977
Height: 5'10" Weight: 12.1
Sam returned to Hull City, his hometown club (he lives within walking distance of Boothferry), after being released by Sheffield Wednesday last March. The left back went straight into the Tigers' first team (against third division leaders, Carlisle), giving a most assured display which offered much promise for the future.
Hull C (Free from Sheffield Wed juniors on 11/3/97) FL 2+2

SHARP Kevin Phillip
Born: Ontario, Canada, 19 September 1974
Height: 5'9" Weight: 11.11
Club Honours: FAYC '93; Div 3 '97
International Honours: E: Yth (UEFAYC '93); Sch
A skilful left-sided player with excellent technique, who can provide telling passes and strong running, the ex-England youth star celebrated a half century of league appearances for Wigan Athletic in their championship winning season, scoring two league goals, including the winner at Mansfield Town. His impressive performances at left back late in the campaign may yet see him make the position his own in 1997-98.
Leeds U (£60,000 from Auxerre on 20/10/92) PL 11+6 Others 0+1
Wigan Ath (£100,000 on 30/11/95) FL 50+5/8 FLC 1 FAC 2 Others 0+1

SHARPE John James
Born: Halesowen, 9 August 1975
Height: 5'11" Weight: 11.6
Following a loan spell for Exeter the previous season, John, the brother of Leeds' Lee, signed for City at the start of 1996-97. Unfortunately, the left-sided midfielder could not command a regular first-team spot and moved back to his native Midlands, and non-league football, towards the end of the campaign, his only highlight being the 25-yard belter against local rivals, Plymouth, in the FA Cup.
Manchester C (From trainee on 9/7/93)
Exeter C (Loaned on 1/2/96) FL 9+5/1
Exeter C (Free on 16/8/96) FL 19+2/1 FLC 2 FAC 1/1

Lee Sharpe

SHARPE Lee Stuart
Born: Halesowen, 27 May 1971
Height: 6'0" Weight: 12.7
Club Honours: ECWC '91; FLC '92; PL '93, '94, '96; FAC '94, '96; CS '94
International Honours: E: 8; B-1; U21-8
Signed from Manchester United in the week leading up to last season, Lee smashed Leeds transfer record in what proved to be Howard Wilkinson's last transfer deal for the club. Unfortunately, he suffered his share of injury problems, causing him to be sidelined for the whole of January and February, which was a shame because in a season where creativity was in short supply, he had sparkled both in defence and attack on the left-hand side of the park with his silky skills and his eye for goal. Indeed, he weighed in with some valuable strikes, including a superb curling effort from outside the box to defeat Wimbledon in August, and with his right foot at that! Hopefully, if he can stay free from injury this coming season we will see the real prowess of Lee Sharpe in George Graham's side, whether it be in central midfield, on the wing, or at left back.

Torquay U (From trainee on 31/5/88) FL 9+5/3 Others 2+3
Manchester U (£185,000 on 10/6/88) F/PL 160+33/21 FLC 15+8/9 FAC 22+7/3 Others 18+2/3
Leeds U (£4,500,000 on 14/8/96) PL 26/5 FLC 3/1 FAC 0+1

SHARPLES John Benjamin
Born: Bury, 26 January 1973
Height: 6'1" Weight: 12.8
A talented York central defender, John was sidelined by injury between last October and January before returning in the second half of the season to form a good partnership with Tony Barras in the heart of the defence. Netted only one goal, but it was sufficient to earn a vital win over Blackpool.
Heart of Midlothian (Free from Manchester U juniors on 26/7/91)
Ayr U (Signed on 13/7/94) SL 53/4 SLC 2 SC 2 Others 2
York C (£75,000 on 28/3/96) FL 38/1 FLC 3 FAC 1 Others 1

SHAW Paul
Born: Burnham, 4 September 1973
Height: 5'11" Weight: 12.4
International Honours: E: Yth
An Arsenal striker who proved he could get among the goals in the lower leagues during a series of loan transfers over the past couple of seasons, and very much in the Paul Merson mould, Paul continued his football apprenticeship in 1996-97 when making nine appearances for the Gunners, eight of them from the subs' bench. Interestingly, he scored his opening goals for the club both home and away against Southampton, the game at the Dell being his only start of the campaign. Also able to play in midfield, he has an excellent first touch, so important in a crowded area, and is always looking to get his shots off.
Arsenal (From trainee on 18/9/91) PL 1+11/2 FAC 0+1
Burnley (Loaned on 23/3/95) FL 8+1/4
Cardiff C (Loaned on 11/8/95) FL 6
Peterborough U (Loaned on 20/10/95) FL 12/5 Others 2

SHAW Richard Edward
Born: Brentford, 11 September 1968
Height: 5'9" Weight: 12.8
Club Honours: FMC '91; Div 1 '94
The experienced Coventry defender had a good season in 1996-97 after mixed results the year before, playing in several positions, including central defence, full back and wing back. He always looked most at home in the man-to-man marking role, doing excellent jobs on Andrei Kanchelskis, Steve McManaman and Ian Wright, and is a player who appears to know his strengths and plays to them, leaving the more creative work to his midfield players. He never gives less than 100 per cent and one of these days may break his goal duck with City. Was runner up in the London Supporters' Club Player of the Season poll.
Crystal Palace (From apprentice on 4/9/86) F/PL 193+14/3 FLC 28+2 FAC 18 Others 12+1
Hull C (Loaned on 14/12/89) FL 4
Coventry C (£1,000,000 on 17/11/95) PL 56 FLC 3 FAC 7

SHAW Simon Robert
Born: Middlesbrough, 21 September 1973
Height: 6'0" Weight: 12.0
Now Darlington's longest-serving player, having come through the ranks to make his debut in 1991-92, following three seasons in midfield, he has since held down the right-back spot for most of the past two campaigns. A good passer, who gives himself time on the ball, Simon scored four goals in 1996-97, his best yet.
Darlington (From trainee on 14/8/92) FL 116+29/10 FLC 5+1 FAC 6/2 Others 5+1

SHEARER Alan
Born: Newcastle, 13 August 1970
Height: 6'0" Weight: 12.6
Club Honours: PL '95
International Honours: E: 35; B-1; U21-11; Yth
Alan is the quintessential English centre forward, acting as the focal point for his side's attack, and being so strong and excellent at shielding the ball and laying it off to bring his colleagues into play. Claiming to be as adept at scoring tap ins, as making a habit of scoring spectacular goals from a distance, open play, and set pieces, he joined his hometown club of Newcastle from Blackburn for a world record fee of £15 million just before the start of last season, following a highly successful Euro 96, in which he topped the goalscoring list with five goals in five games. Well aware of the club's history, he requested that he be allowed to wear the number nine shirt, a wish which was granted, and he made his competitive debut for the club in the Charity Shield match. His first goal was a stunning free kick in his home debut against Wimbledon, and he continued to score regularly thereafter, forming an increasingly formidable partnership with Les Ferdinand. Glenn Hoddle also chose him to be captain of the England side, and he first carried this honour in the Moldova game in September. Unfortunately, injury problems resulted in an operation on his right groin at the end of October, following a similar one on his left groin the previous season, but he was soon back in action to continue a hot goal sequence, his strike in the Coca-Cola Cup versus Middlesbrough was his sixth consecutive scoring match, a feat he had achieved twice with Blackburn. A goal in the home game against Arsenal extended this to seven games and equalled Mark Stein's record of scoring in seven consecutive Premiership matches, after which he was elected third in two prestigious polls, the first in December for the European Footballer of the Year, and the other in January for the FIFA World Player of the Year. Scored his first hat trick for Newcastle in the final 13 minutes against Leicester to turn a 3-1 deficit into a 4-3 win. A further injury necessitated another groin operation in March, his third in less than a year, but again he recovered remarkably quickly, making a scoring return against Sunderland. Despite missing seven games, his 25 goals made him the leading Premiership scorer for the third consecutive season and kept him at the top of the all-time list with 137. Elected Player of the Year by his fellow professionals at the PFA annual awards dinner, the second time he has won the award, it was a second successive such honour for United, following Les Ferdinand's success the previous year.
Southampton (From trainee on 14/4/88) FL 105+13/23 FLC 16+2/11 FAC 11+3/4 Others 8/5
Blackburn Rov (£3,600,000 on 24/7/92) PL 132+6/112 FLC 16/14 FAC 8/2 Others 9/2
Newcastle U (£15,000,000 on 30/7/96) PL 31/25 FLC 1/1 FAC 3/1 Others 5/1

SHEARER Lee Sean
Born: Southend, 23 October 1977
Height: 6'3" Weight: 12.0
A young Leyton Orient centre half who played a handful of first team games in 1996-97 before going on loan to Hastings in order to gain more experience, Lee used his height to good effect at set plays and will be looking to become a first-team regular this coming season. Scored the first goal in a friendly with Wales, despite Neville Southall being the 'keeper.
Leyton Orient (From trainee on 6/7/95) FL 14+4/1 FLC 1+1 FAC 1

SHEERIN Joseph (Joe) Earnan
Born: Hammersmith, 8 November 1977
Height: 6'1" Weight: 13.0
Big and strong, and rather similar in style at the same age as another Chelsea centre-forward hero from bygone days, the bustling Bobby Smith, Joe is still a baby-faced trainee, who could have a big future in the game. Obviously, Ruud Gullit thinks so as well as he introduced him from the subs' bench at Wimbledon in one of the final games of last season, albeit blooding the youngster in the 90th minute. Shows no fear and has a great attitude to the game, despite having many injury problems during his time at Stamford Bridge, and could make an impact in the not too distant future.
Chelsea (Trainee) PL 0+1

Alan Shearer

SHEFFIELD Jonathan (Jon)
Born: Bedworth, 1 February 1969
Height: 5'11" Weight: 12.10
Started last season as Peterborough's first choice goalkeeper, but finished third behind Bart Griemink and Mark Tyler, and found himself loaned out to Watford and Oldham without getting a game at either club. Very agile and a good shot stopper, Jon appeared to do nothing wrong at Posh other than be involved in some high-scoring games and will be looking to get back into contention during the current campaign.
Norwich C (From apprentice on 16/2/87) FL 1
Aldershot (Loaned on 22/9/89) FL 11 Others 1
Aldershot (Loaned on 21/8/90) FL 15 Others 1
Cambridge U (Free on 18/3/91) FL 56 FLC 3 FAC 4 Others 6
Colchester U (Loaned on 23/12/93) FL 6
Swindon T (Loaned on 28/1/94) PL 2
Hereford U (Loaned on 15/9/94) FL 8 FLC 2
Peterborough U (£150,000 on 20/7/95) FL 62 FLC 8 FAC 6 Others 5

SHELTON Gary
Born: Nottingham, 21 March 1958
Height: 5'7" Weight: 11.2
International Honours: E: U21-1
As the assistant manager to Kevin Ratcliffe at Chester in 1996-97, Gary combined his managerial duties with those in midfield and was one of the main reasons for the club making it into the play offs. A skilful operator who reads the game well and brings others into the play, while not scoring so frequently these days, one at Rochdale early on in the campaign was enough to secure a 1-0 victory. Still registered as a player at 39 years of age.
Walsall (From apprentice on 1/3/76) FL 12+12 FLC 0+1 FAC 2+2/1
Aston Villa (£80,000 on 18/1/78) FL 24/7 FLC 2+1/1
Notts Co (Loaned on 13/3/80) FL 8
Sheffield Wed (£50,000 on 25/3/82) FL 195+3/18 FLC 19/3 FAC 23+1/3 Others 1
Oxford U (£150,000 on 24/7/87) FL 60+5/1 FLC 7+1/2 FAC 5 Others 1
Bristol C (Signed on 24/8/89) FL 149+1/24 FLC 12 FAC 9 Others 9/3
Rochdale (Loaned on 11/2/94) FL 3
Chester C (Free on 22/7/94) FL 59+7/6 FLC 4+1 FAC 3 Others 2/2

SHEPHERD Paul
Born: Leeds, 17 November 1977
Height: 5'8" Weight: 10.3
International Honours: E: Yth
A local-born midfield player who, like so many other promising youngsters at Leeds, has now gained first-team experience, Paul landed his big chance at Arsenal last October, due to the chronic injury list at that time. An England U18 international, he went on to gain much valuable experience at reserve team level and is certainly one for the future.
Leeds U (From trainee on 15/9/95) PL 1

SHERIDAN Darren Stephen
Born: Manchester, 8 December 1967
Height: 5'5" Weight: 10.12
A vital cog in Barnsley's 1996-97 promotion campaign, missing just seven league matches, Darren was one of the club's unsung heroes. An aggressive battler in midfield, he won more than his fair share of the ball and this, coupled with accurate passing, gave the side the required balance. Only scored twice, but the first, a blistering 25-yard shot in a 3-0 home win against Reading, was definitely one to savour. An accurate passer, he can also play at wing back if required.
Barnsley (£10,000 from Winsford U on 12/8/93) FL 114+6/4 FLC 4+1 FAC 4+1 Others 1+1

SHERIDAN John Joseph
Born: Stretford, 1 October 1964
Height: 5'9" Weight: 12.0
Club Honours: FLC '91; Div 1 '97
International Honours: Ei: 34; B-1; U23-2; U21-2; Yth
Out of favour at Sheffield Wednesday, the vastly-experienced midfield playmaker joined Bolton on loan last November, due to an injury crisis, and after giving some top-class performances and scoring two goals in his vital first two games against Birmingham and Crystal Palace, Colin Todd brought him to Burnden Park permanently on Christmas Eve. Remaining a first team regular until Alan Thompson's return from injury at the end of January, although he did make a number of subsequent appearances as a substitute, he did enough to win a first division championship medal as Wanderers went back to the Premiership at the first time of asking. A superbly skilful player, John must still be regarded as one of the best passers of a ball in the game today.
Leeds U (Free from Manchester C juniors on 2/3/82) FL 225+5/47 FLC 14/3 FAC 11+1/1 Others 11/1
Nottingham F (£650,000 on 3/8/89) FLC 1
Sheffield Wed (£500,000 on 3/11/89) F/PL 187+10/25 FLC 24/3 FAC 17+1/3 Others 4/2
Birmingham C (Loaned on 9/2/96) FL 1+1 FLC 2
Bolton W (£180,000 on 13/11/96) FL 12+8/2 FLC 2 FAC 2

SHERINGHAM Edward (Teddy) Paul
Born: Highams Park, 2 April 1966
Height: 5'11" Weight: 12.5
Club Honours: Div 2 '88; FMC '92
International Honours: E: 28; U21-1; Yth
Widely acclaimed as the most intelligent footballer in the Premiership, Teddy, a natural goalscorer, enjoyed another fine season in 1996-97, Euro '96 having provided the perfect stage for him to endorse his growing reputation – England's group game against Holland seeing him produce his finest international performance to date with two instinctive predatory goals that ensured a conclusive 4-1 victory. Although club form saw him often struggle to produce his best, further hindered by the absence of strike partner, Chris Armstrong, he was Tottenham's top goalscorer and again created as many goals as he scored. The campaign also saw him playing deeper, searching for openings in midfield to create opportunities for attack, and featuring as a key figure in Glenn Hoddle's England selections, scoring in three consecutive appearances for his country – the finest coming against Georgia at Wembley, a superb header gaining three vital points.

Stop Press: Signed for Manchester United at the end of June for a fee of £3.5 million.
Millwall (From apprentice on 19/1/84) FL 205+15/93 FLC 16+1/8 FAC 12/5 Others 11+2/5
Aldershot (Loaned on 1/2/85) FL 4+1 Others 1
Nottingham F (£2,000,000 on 23/7/91) FL 42/14 FLC 10/5 FAC 4/2 Others 6/2
Tottenham H (£2,100,000 on 28/8/92) PL 163+3/76 FLC 14/7 FAC 17/13

SHERLOCK Paul Graeme
Born: Wigan, 17 November 1973
Height: 5'10" Weight: 11.5
As in 1995-96, the Mansfield left-sided defender had an up-and-down season in 1996-97 as injury again decimated his appearances. A player with good shooting ability, especially from long range, he also failed to get on the scoresheet and was released during the summer.
Notts Co (From trainee on 1/7/92) FL 8+4/1 FLC 1 FAC 2 Others 2+1
Mansfield T (£15,000 on 23/3/95) FL 29+10/2 FLC 1+1 FAC 2+1/1 Others 0+1

SHERON Michael (Mike) Nigel
Born: Liverpool, 11 January 1972
Height: 5'9" Weight: 11.13
International Honours: E: U21-16
An electric start to last season saw Mike top the first division goalscoring charts and, at the same time, being linked to a host of clubs, especially QPR and West Ham. Unfortunately, a neck injury sustained before the game at Huddersfield on New Year's Day troubled him for some time and this was reflected by a much-publicised goal drought, also blamed on the constant press speculation over his future at Stoke. Recognised by his fellow professionals when elected to the PFA award-winning first division side, as a striker with both skill and vision there is no reason to doubt that 1997-98 will see him back at his best. *Stop Press:* Was reported to have signed for Queens Park Rangers during the summer, a £2.75 million fee securing the transfer.

Mike Sheron

Manchester C (From trainee on 5/7/90) F/PL 82+18/24 FLC 9+1/1 FAC 5+3/3 Others 1
Bury (Loaned on 28/3/91) FL 1+4/1 Others 2
Norwich C (£1,000,000 on 26/8/94) P/FL 19+9/2 FLC 6/3 FAC 4/2
Stoke C (£450,000 on 13/11/95) FL 64+5/34 FLC 4/5 FAC 1 Others 2

SHERWOOD Timothy (Tim) Alan
Born: St Albans, 6 February 1969
Height: 6'0" Weight: 12.9
Club Honours: PL '95
International Honours: E: B-1; U21-4
The previously enigmatic midfielder thrived in Blackburn's relegation fight last season, his commitment to the cause and energy shining out like a beacon. Permitted to get forward because of the presence of Billy McKinlay, he tried to provide the finishing touch on numerous occasions, but had bad luck in front of goal, apart from four goals, two of them in the Premiership, against Southampton and Everton, proving vital. An extremely determined competitor, Tim picked up the customary collection of yellow cards, but, for the first time, gained the hearts of the Ewood crowd. Also enjoys the passing game.
Watford (From trainee on 7/2/87) FL 23+9/2 FLC 4+1 FAC 9 Others 4+1
Norwich C (£175,000 on 18/7/89) FL 66+5/10 FLC 7/1 FAC 4 Others 5+1/2
Blackburn Rov (£500,000 on 12/2/92) F/PL 191+5/17 FLC 21/1 FAC 11+2/2 Others 10

SHILTON Peter Leslie
Born: Leicester, 18 September 1949
Height: 6'1" Weight: 14.2
Club Honours: Div 2 '71; Div 1 '78; CS '78; EC '79, '80; ESC '79; FLC '79
International Honours: E: 125; U23-3; Yth; Sch
A very experienced former international goalkeeper signed last November from West Ham on a free transfer, he was just four games short of his 1000th league game, which he duly completed four days before Christmas in Leyton Orient's live Sky Sports game against Brighton, where he was given a special award to mark this achievement by the Football Association. Carried on to make another five appearances before injury curtailed nearly all the rest of his season and returned briefly just before the end to play in the reserve team cup final where, even at 47 years of age, he made a series of stops as if he was playing in a major cup final or international. Was released at the end of the campaign.
Leicester C (From apprentice on 1/9/66) FL 286/1 FLC 20 FAC 30
Stoke C (£300,000 on 1/11/74) FL 110 FLC 4 FAC 7
Nottingham F (£270,000 on 15/9/77) FL 202 FLC 26 FAC 18 Others 26
Southampton (£325,000 on 28/8/82) FL 188 FLC 28 FAC 17 Others 9
Derby Co (£90,000 on 7/7/87) FL 175 FLC 18 FAC 10 Others 8
Plymouth Arg (Free on 5/3/92) FL 34 FLC 6 FAC 1 Others 2
Wimbledon (Free on 10/2/95)
Bolton W (Free on 11/3/95) FL 0+1 Others 1
Coventry C (Free on 17/7/95)
West Ham U (Free on 11/1/96)
Leyton Orient (Free on 29/11/96) FL 9 FAC 1

SHIPPERLEY Neil Jason
Born: Chatham, 30 October 1974
Height: 6'1" Weight: 13.12
International Honours: E: U21-7
Following just one goal in 12 outings for Graeme Souness' Southampton in 1996-97, Neil was allowed to move on to Crystal Palace at the end of October. A striker from a footballing family, his father David having played for a number of clubs in the 1970s, and one who had been brought up in the Premiership, the former England U21 star quickly made his mark with a double at Bradford in his second game and went on to strike 11 more, including one in the opening leg of the play offs. A player with great workrate who chases lost causes and packs a good shot in both feet, he will be back in the top flight again in 1997-98, thanks to Palace's 1-0 win over Sheffield United at Wembley.
Chelsea (From trainee on 24/9/92) PL 26+11/7 FLC 4+2/1 FAC 3/1 Others 2
Watford ((Loaned on 7/12/94) FL 5+1/1
Southampton (£1,250,000 on 6/1/95) PL 65+1/11 FLC 5+1/2 FAC 10/5
Crystal Palace (£1,000,000 on 25/10/96) FL 29+3/12 FAC 2 Others 3/1

SHIRTLIFF Peter Andrew
Born: Hoyland, 6 April 1961
Height: 6'2" Weight: 13.3
Club Honours: FLC '91
This experienced Barnsley defender, despite being used mainly for squad duties in 1996-97, showed on his limited opportunities that he had lost none of his organisational expertise and the ability to win the ball both in the air and on the ground. Loaned out to Carlisle in October, Peter came back to do his bit as the club ultimately won promotion to the Premiership and has been offered the job of player/coach for the coming campaign.
Sheffield Wed (From apprentice on 31/10/78) FL 188/4 FLC 17+1 FAC 17+1/1
Charlton Ath (£125,000 on 6/8/86) FL 102+1/7 FLC 10 FAC 5 Others 7/2
Sheffield Wed (£500,000 on 26/7/89) F/PL 104/4 FLC 18/1 FAC 9/2 Others 4
Wolverhampton W (£250,000 on 18/8/93) FL 67+2 FLC 4 FAC 7 Others 5
Barnsley (£125,000 on 25/8/95) FL 44+1 FAC 1
Carlisle U (Loaned on 25/10/96) FL 5

SHORT Christian (Chris) Mark
Born: Munster, Germany, 9 May 1970
Height: 5'10" Weight: 12.2
Club Honours: AIC '95
The Sheffield United right back suffered a disjointed season in 1996-97 due to injuries, but never failed to impress when available and was an effective raider down the right-hand side, putting in some quality crosses. The brother of Everton's Craig, he unluckily missed the play-off final due to suffering a sprained ankle in training prior to the match. Is also a sound defender, with good tackling ability, who can be used in central defence if required.
Scarborough (Free from Pickering T on 11/7/88) FL 42+1/1 FLC 5 FAC 1 Others 3+1
Notts Co (£100,000 on 5/9/90) FL 77+17/2 FLC 7 FAC 4+1 Others 8+1/1
Huddersfield T (Loaned on 23/12/94) FL 6 Others 1
Sheffield U (Signed on 29/12/95) FL 35+4 FLC 3 FAC 3 Others 1+1

SHORT Craig Jonathan
Born: Bridlington, 25 June 1968
Height: 6'2" Weight: 13.8
A tall and commanding centre back, who is comfortable when bringing the ball out of defence at his feet, Craig started 11 of Everton's opening 13 matches in 1996-97, but then found his appearances intermittent. Unluckily dropped in mid November, Everton winning the match he missed 7-1 against Southampton, he then picked up a succession of niggling injuries and when he finally returned to the starting line up in March, he scored a spectacular own goal at The Dell. Obviously looking for a better time in 1997-98, an appearance in the Goodison derby match ended, almost predictably, in injury as he tumbled horribly onto his neck and was stretchered off.
Scarborough (Free from Pickering T on 15/10/87) FL 61+2/7 FLC 6 FAC 2 Others 7/1
Notts Co (£100,000 on 27/7/89) FL 128/6 FLC 6/1 FAC 8/1 Others 16/2
Derby Co (£2,500,000 on 18/9/82) FL 118/9 FLC 11 FAC 7/4 Others 7
Everton (£2,700,000 on 18/7/95) PL 41+5/4 FLC 3 FAC 4 Others 3

SHOWLER Paul
Born: Doncaster, 10 October 1966
Height: 5'11" Weight: 11.6
International Honours: E: SP-2
Signed from Bradford City during the 1996 close season, this left-footed attacking midfielder scored some important goals for Luton Town in 1996-97, but, unfortunately, his frequent reluctance to take on players in preference to passing did not always endear him to the fans. Missed the last two months of the campaign due to a cartilage operation, before returning to play in the crucial second-leg play-off game against Crewe and setting up a goal for David Oldfield after 19 minutes. Lack of match practice forced him to be substituted towards the end of the game, but, by then, Town had lost the tie.
Barnet (Free from Altrincham on 15/8/91) FL 69+2/12 FLC 2 FAC 3+1/1 Others 7
Bradford C (Free on 4/8/93) FL 72+16/15 FLC 8+1/5 FAC 6/2 Others 4+1
Luton T (£50,000 on 19/8/96) FL 21+2/6 FLC 3+1 FAC 3 Others 1+1

SHUTT Carl Steven
Born: Sheffield, 10 October 1961
Height: 5'10" Weight: 12.10
Club Honours: Div 2 '90; Div 1 '92
Despite his age, when called upon, the veteran midfielder, cum forward, ran his socks off for Bradford in 1996-97, his subs' appearances narrowly exceeding his starts, before he joined Darlington on transfer deadline day as part of the deal that took Robbie Blake in the opposite direction. Immediately impressing with his hard-working performances, Carl opened his scoring account in the penultimate game, a tremendous right-footed dipping 20 yarder at Mansfield, followed by another on the final day, and there should be something left in the tank for the coming season.
Sheffield Wed (Free from Spalding on 13/5/85) FL 36+4/16 FLC 3/1 FAC 4+1/4
Bristol C (£55,000 on 30/10/87) FL 39+7/10 FLC 5+2/4 FAC 7+1/4 Others 10+1/4

Leeds U (£50,000 on 23/3/89) F/PL 46+33/17 FLC 6+2/2 FAC 10/1 Others 4+5/4
Birmingham C (£50,000 on 23/8/93) FL 18+8/4 FLC 3
Manchester C (Loaned on 31/12/93) PL 5+1
Bradford C (£75,000 on 11/8/94) FL 60+28/15 FLC 8+2/1 FAC 3+2 Others 5+2/1
Darlington (Signed on 27/3/97) FL 5+1/2

SIGURDSSON Larus Orri
Born: Akureyri, Iceland, 4 June 1973
Height: 6'0" Weight: 12.8
International Honours: Iceland: 11

Continuing to make improvement, the Icelandic international defender was made captain of the Stoke side after the retirement of Ian Cranson in 1996-97. An outstanding marker with excellent tackling skills, Larus reads the game well and this turned out to be another good season for the reliable stopper, and he was regularly watched by Newcastle United, who were, no doubt, impressed by his first class attitude. Is the cousin of the former City midfielder, Toddy Orlygsson.
Stoke C (£150,000 on 21/10/94) FL 113+1/1 FLC 7 FAC 3+1 Others 4

Larus Sigurdsson

SILENZI Andrea
Born: Rome, Italy, 10 February 1966
Height: 6'3" Weight: 11.13
International Honours: Italy: 1

Andrea became one of the most disappointing million pound signings for any club and last season he made just one start and one appearance as a sub for Nottingham Forest, both of them early on. Those two games added up to less than 20 appearances in his two seasons in England and towards the end of the campaign he went back to Italy on a loan spell with Vinezia in order to try and recover some form. Brought to Forest to specifically lend height to the attack, the fact that the club play more to feet was obviously unhelpful to his cause.
Nottingham F (£1,800,000 from Torino on 16/8/95) PL 4+8 FLC 1/1 FAC 2+1/1 Others 1+3

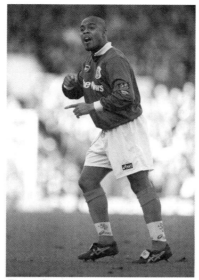

Fitzroy Simpson

SIMPSON Fitzroy
Born: Bradford on Avon, 26 February 1970
Height: 5'7" Weight: 10.7

Played most of last season operating as a wing back on Portsmouth's right flank, missing very few games and being a key member of the side that made an ultimately unsuccessful challenge for the play offs and had an excellent cup run. Once a hard-running left winger, he is ideally suited to his new role, as a hard-working player full of spirit, who can tackle with the best of them. He can also score goals, including one apiece home and away against his old club, Manchester City. However, having scored from the spot against Huddersfield he later missed one in the fifth round FA Cup tie at Leeds but, with Pompey going on to win 3-2, it was soon forgotten.
Swindon T (From trainee on 6/7/88) FL 78+27/9 FLC 15+2/1 FAC 2+1 Others 3+2
Manchester C (£500,000 on 6/3/92) F/PL 58+13/4 FLC 5+1 FAC 4+1
Bristol C (Loaned on 16/9/94) FL 4
Portsmouth (£200,000 on 17/8/95) FL 67+4/9 FLC 5 FAC 5

SIMPSON Karl Edward
Born: Newmarket, 14 October 1976
Height: 5'11" Weight: 11.9

Karl's three Norwich appearances in 1996-97 were in the last trio of games of the season, having suffered an unlucky spell of injuries with pulled hamstrings which had an effect on the thigh that went three times. Canary managements, past and present, have always recognised the signs of genuine talent in his quick-witted feet and dug deep to unearth a new contract during the summer. Is a versatile, well-built youngster who can play up front or in midfield with equal propensity and has an excellent long throw.
Norwich C (From juniors on 4/7/95) FL 2+2 FLC 1

SIMPSON Michael
Born: Nottingham, 28 February 1974
Height: 5'9" Weight: 10.8
Club Honours: AIC '95

With just two games under his belt at Notts County in 1996-97, the hard-working central midfield playmaker with astute passing skills impressed with a loan at Plymouth in October, before signing permanently for Wycombe in January following a temporary spell at the club. Despite losing his place in the final stages of the campaign after a slight drop in form, Michael showed what he was capable of in terms of effort and also scored with a spectacular, curling shot at Bristol Rovers.
Notts Co (From trainee on 1/7/92) FL 39+10/3 FLC 4+1 FAC 2+1 Others 7+3
Plymouth Arg (Loaned on 4/10/96) FL 10+2
Wycombe W (£50,000 on 5/12/96) FL 16+4/1 Others 1

SIMPSON Paul David
Born: Carlisle, 26 July 1966
Height: 5'7" Weight: 11.12
International Honours: E: U21-5; Yth

An experienced Derby left winger with a natural ability to get wide and cross accurately, Paul was used almost exclusively as a late substitute in 1996-97 to keep control of the ball, gaining further match practice during a loan spell at Sheffield United in December in a similar role. An important and valued member of the first-team squad at the Baseball Ground, he relishes free kicks and corners, where he is often able to bend balls around defenders to great advantage.
Manchester C (From apprentice on 4/8/83) FL 99+22/18 FLC 10+1/2 FAC 10+2/4 Others 8+3
Oxford U (£200,000 on 31/10/88) FL 138+6/43 FLC 10/3 FAC 9/2 Others 5/2
Derby Co (£500,000 on 20/2/92) P/FL 133+52/48 FLC 12+1/6 FAC 4+4/1 Others 14+2/2
Sheffield U (Loaned on 6/12/96) FL 2+4

SIMPSON Phillip (Phil) Mark
Born: Lambeth, 19 October 1969
Height: 5'8" Weight: 11.12

A player with a liking for taking opponents on from midfield, as in the previous season, he showed a good engine and the ability to lift the Barnet crowd in 1996-97. Although unfortunate to lose his place for a couple of spells through injury, his ability to score important goals always brought him back into contention when fit.
Barnet (Signed from Stevenage Borough on 27/10/95) FL 53+3/3 FLC 3/2 FAC 3+1/1 Others 1

SINCLAIR David (Dave)
Born: Dunfermline, 6 October 1969
Height: 5'11" Weight: 12.10

Signed by Millwall from Raith during the summer of 1996, this tough-tackling midfielder or centre back never really imposed himself in the first team after suffering an injury to his right ankle in the very first game of last season. It was therefore no surprise when he returned to Scotland with Dundee United in February.
Raith Rov (Free from Kelty U21 in 1990) SL 150+27/10 SLC 9+1 SC 6+1 Others 8+3
Millwall (Signed on 4/7/96) FL 6+2 FAC 0+1 Others 1+1

SINCLAIR Frank Mohammed
Born: Lambeth, 3 December 1971
Height: 5'9" Weight: 12.9
Club Honours: FAC '97

Frank looked destined to spend 1996-97 on the fringes of the Chelsea first team until January when Michael Duberry's unfortunate injury gave him an extended run alongside Frank Leboeuf and Steve Clarke in central defence. Although, along with David Lee and Erland Johnsen, he was kept out of the side by the good form shown by Ruud Gullit's first-choice trio, the popular defender played an important role in Blues' march to their second successive FA Cup semi final, when giving an impressive performance against Wimbledon at Highbury in standing firm under the Dons' aerial bombardment and attacking intelligently down the right flank. A mobile, wholehearted player, with a prodigious spring-heeled leap to head dangerous crosses away from the penalty area, Frank even got upfield in the televised match against Sunderland to score one of his rare goals – nodding home a Gianfranco Zola cross. Made up for his disastrous performance in the 1994 FA Cup final, when picking up an FA Cup winners medal this time round thanks to the 2-0 Wembley win over Middlesbrough.
Chelsea (From trainee on 17/5/90) F/PL 143+4/6 FLC 13/1 FAC 18/1 Others 7/2
West Bromwich A (Loaned on 12/12/91) FL 6/1

SINCLAIR Ronald (Ronnie) McDonald
Born: Stirling, 19 November 1964
Height: 5'11" Weight: 12.3
Club Honours: Div 2 '93
International Honours: S: Yth; Sch

A vastly experienced goalkeeper, Ronnie moved from Stoke to Chester at the start of last season and quickly became a crowd favourite with his shot stopping and agility often keeping the side in the game. Extremely important in the run to the play offs, such was his impact in collecting 17 clean sheets in 44 games, including five in succession, that he was voted City's Player of the Year. Despite being on the small side for a 'keeper, his positional play normally gets him out of trouble.
Nottingham F (From apprentice on 30/10/82)
Wrexham (Loaned on 1/3/84) FL 11 Others 1
Leeds U (£10,000 on 27/6/86) FL 8 FLC 1
Halifax T (Loaned on 1/3/87) FL 4
Halifax T (Loaned on 23/12/88) FL 10 Others 1
Bristol C (Free on 1/9/89) FL 44 FLC 3 FAC 5 Others 3
Walsall (Loaned on 5/9/91) FL 10 Others 1
Stoke C (£25,000 on 21/11/91) FL 78+2 FLC 2 FAC 4 Others 10
Chester C (Free on 12/8/96) FL 37 FLC 1 FAC 3 Others 3

SINCLAIR Trevor Lloyd
Born: Dulwich, 2 March 1973
Height: 5'10" Weight: 12.5
International Honours: E: U21-13; Yth

Considering all the constant speculation surrounding this young man, concerning his future at QPR, you would have thought that 1996-97 would have been an up-and-down season for him, but, instead, he proved remarkably consistent. Always prepared to take full backs on and run at them, his skill and pace making him difficult to contain, he scored four goals, including one that many who witnessed it would say was one of the greatest of all time, an acrobatic overhead kick from fully 20 yards in the FA Cup against Barnsley. Unfortunately injured in the home match against Portsmouth in March and ruled out for the remainder of the campaign, he would have been heartened to have been selected for the division one side at the PFA Awards night.
Blackpool (From trainee on 21/8/90) FL 84+28/15 FLC 8 FAC 6+1 Others 8+5/1
Queens Park R (£750,000 on 12/8/93) P/FL 138+3/13 FLC 11/3 FAC 8/2

SINNOTT Lee
Born: Pelsall, 12 July 1965
Height: 6'1" Weight: 13.7
International Honours: E: U21-1; Yth

An experienced Huddersfield centre back, now approaching the veteran stage, Lee reads the game well and uses his experience to good advantage. Lost his place towards the end of 1996-97, but then regained both that and the captaincy with some assured end-of-season performances, appearing in the final eight games after replacing an out of sorts Kevin Gray. Still good with long passes into the channels.
Walsall (From apprentice on 16/11/82) FL 40/2 FLC 3 FAC 4
Watford (£100,000 on 15/9/83) FL 71+7/2 FLC 6 FAC 11
Bradford C (£130,000 on 23/7/87) FL 173/6 FLC 19 FAC 9 Others 12/1
Crystal Palace (£300,000 on 8/8/91) F/PL 53+2 FLC 9+1 FAC 1 Others 2
Bradford C (£50,000 on 9/12/93) FL 34/1 FLC 2 FAC 2 Others 2
Huddersfield T (£105,000 on 23/12/94) FL 86+1/1 FLC 6 FAC 4 Others 3

SINTON Andrew (Andy)
Born: Newcastle, 19 March 1966
Height: 5'8" Weight: 11.5
International Honours: E: 12; B-3; Sch

This versatile midfielder overcame the previous season's injury problems to produce a terrific overall performance for Tottenham in 1996-97. Although injuries kept many key players out of the Spurs' line up, Andy's experience and tremendous close-ball skills kept enthusiasm and team spirit alive against such as Manchester United, when continually demonstrating the form which had won him his international honours, and, at the age of 31, still made him a key figure in the club's bid to build a championship challenging side. Accuracy in crossing and releasing quick, intelligent balls up and across field continued to be his strength and, much to the delight of fans, he regained his instinct for scoring to become a firm favourite at White Hart Lane.
Cambridge U (From apprentice on 13/4/83) FL 90+3/13 FLC 6/1 FAC 3 Others 2/1
Brentford (£25,000 on 13/12/85) FL 149/28 FLC 8/3 FAC 11/1 Others 14/2
Queens Park R (£350,000 on 23/3/89) F/PL 160/22 FLC 14 FAC 13/2 Others 3/1
Sheffield Wed (£2,750,000 on 19/8/93) PL 54+6/3 FLC 13 FAC 5
Tottenham H (£1,500,000 on 23/1/96) PL 40+2/6 FLC 2 FAC 1

SKELTON Aaron Matthew
Born: Welwyn Garden City, 22 November 1974
Height: 5'11" Weight: 12.6

After another injury ridden season, which saw this talented Luton midfielder make just a handful of appearances during the first half of 1996-97, Aaron was released on a free transfer. Having missed so much of the last three campaigns with various injuries he may have difficulty attracting the interest of another league club which will be extremely unfortunate, because he once again showed excellent touches on his rare appearances.
Luton T (From trainee on 16/12/92) FL 5+3 FLC 0+1 FAC 2 Others 2

SKINNER Craig Richard
Born: Heywood, 21 October 1970
Height: 5'10" Weight: 11.6

Was not involved last season at Wrexham as much as he would have liked, due to injuries and competition for the number seven shirt with Martyn Chalk. Considered by some Wrexham fans as similar in style to former favourite, Brian Tinnion, he is an industrious wide midfield player who drops back to help his defenders as often as possible with a penchant to go on mazy runs.
Blackburn Rov (From trainee on 13/6/89) FL 11+5 FLC 0+1 FAC 1 Others 3/1
Plymouth Arg (Signed on 21/8/92) FL 42+11/4 FLC 4 FAC 5+2/1 Others 3+1
Wrexham (£50,000 on 21/7/95) FL 42+8/7 FLC 1+1/1 FAC 6+1 Others 3

SKINNER Justin
Born: Hounslow, 30 January 1969
Height: 6'0" Weight: 12.0

The Bristol Rovers' central midfielder failed to start last season in the side and was in and out of the team up to Christmas, before managing to re-establish himself with a regular place following the transfer of Marcus Browning. On 31 March against Wrexham, Justin managed to get on the scoresheet for the first time in almost two years and promptly doubled his goal tally in the next home game, scoring the winner against Millwall, which effectively ruled out any chance of relegation for the club. Has now completed over 300 league appearances for his two clubs.
Fulham (From apprentice on 17/11/86) FL 111+24/23 FLC 10+1/4 FAC 5+1 Others 10+1/1
Bristol Rov (£130,000 on 27/8/91) FL 170+13/12 FLC 11 FAC 8+1 Others 14+2/2

SKIVERTON Terence (Terry) John
Born: Mile End, 26 June 1975
Height: 6'0" Weight: 12.6

A tall, rangy defender, who is good in the air and comfortable in midfield as well, he was released by Wycombe at the end of last season, having spent most of the campaign in the reserves. Still a useful man to have at your disposal, he suffered at the hands of new Adams Park signings, Paul McCarthy, Jason Kavanagh, and Michael Forsyth.
Chelsea (From trainee on 19/5/93)
Wycombe W (Loaned on 17/5/95) FL 8+2
Wycombe W (Free on 26/3/96) FL 5+5/1 FAC 0+1

SLADE Steven (Steve) Anthony
Born: Romford, 6 October 1975
Height: 5'11" Weight: 10.10
International Honours: E: U21-4

Signed from Spurs in the 1996 close season, Steve made his QPR debut at Wolves three games into the new campaign and eventually opened his scoring account with two in a week, at Tranmere and Sheffield United, both goals being points winners for Rangers. However, despite showing much promise, following a run of eight games he lost his place when John Spencer arrived from Chelsea and was later loaned out to Brentford in February. A striker with good movement on and off the ball, he came back to play a part in the final six matches, scoring twice after coming off the bench. Also climbs well for the ball.
Tottenham H (From trainee on 1/7/94) PL 1+4 FLC 0+1 FAC 0+2
Queens Park R (£350,000 on 12/7/96) FL 11+6/4
Brentford (Loaned on 13/2/97) FL 4

SLATER Robert (Robbie) David
Born: Ormskirk, 22 November 1964
Height: 5'11" Weight: 13.0
Club Honours: PL '95
International Honours: Australia: 17

Having made just three Premiership appearances for West Ham in 1996-97, The Australian international midfielder was transferred to Southampton in order to add more bite down the flanks. A tigerish red-headed competitor who is happy to operate almost anywhere on the park, and often does on occasions, he weighed in with two important goals in the final 12 matches. Having come off the bench at the Dell with Saints 2-0 down against Everton, he struck the first in a 2-2 fight back and, in the penultimate game of the season, he again fired in the first during a 2-0 win at home to Blackburn, his old club, thus helping to avert the threat of relegation. As it turned out in an extremely tough campaign, his workrate and enthusiasm were every bit as vital as his playing ability.
Blackburn Rov (£300,000 from Lens on 4/8/94) PL 12+6 FLC 1 FAC 1 Others 2
West Ham U (£600,000 on 15/8/95) PL 18+7/2 FLC 3 FAC 1
Southampton (£250,000 on 3/9/96) PL 22+8/2 FLC 5+2 FAC 1

SLATER Stuart Ian
Born: Sudbury, 27 March 1969
Height: 5'9" Weight: 11.6
International Honours: E: B-2; U21-3

Released by Ipswich last October, Stuart had a month on trial at Leicester City before settling down at Watford, proving to be an excellent free-transfer signing for the Hornets. An experienced wide midfield player, he looked particularly comfortable on the ball, showing good control and passing skills, but his slight frame, however, made him vulnerable to robust defending, the result of which saw him troubled with an achilles problem towards the end of the season. Scored his one and only goal for the club in a 2-0 win against Rotherham at Vicarage Road.

West Ham U (From apprentice on 2/4/87) FL 134+7/11 FLC 16+1/2 FAC 16/3 Others 5/2
Glasgow Celtic (£1,500,000 on 14/8/92) SL 40+3/3 SLC 3+2 SC 3 Others 4
Ipswich T (£750,000 on 30/9/93) P/FL 61+11/4 FLC 6 FAC 6 Others 2+2
Leicester C (Free on 24/10/96)
Watford (Free on 28/11/96) FL 13+3/1 FAC 3 Others 1

SLAWSON Stephen (Steve) Michael
Born: Nottingham, 13 November 1972
Height: 6'1" Weight: 12.13

Released by Mansfield during the 1996 close season, Steve had few chances to carve himself a regular place at Rotherham and, after having to spend most of his time playing for the reserves, he was released and moved to non-league football with Kettering. A clever ball player, at his best is also a scorer of spectacular goals.
Notts Co (From trainee on 9/7/91) FL 16+22/4 FLC 1+1 FAC 0+3 Others 3+3/1
Burnley (Loaned on 12/2/93) FL 5/2
Shrewsbury T (Loaned on 31/10/94) FL 6 Others 0+1
Mansfield T (Free on 4/7/95) FL 21+8/5 FLC 2 Others 1+1
Rotherham U (Free on 15/7/96) FL 2+3 FLC 0+1

SMALL Bryan
Born: Birmingham, 15 November 1971
Height: 5'9" Weight: 11.9
International Honours: E: U21-12; Yth

A strong Bolton left back with a terrific turn of pace, Bryan saw little first-team football last season due to the consistency of Jimmy Phillips, but during a 13-game spell in the side in the New Year he produced some confident performances and showed a distinct knack for charging up the field and supplying quality crosses for the front line to latch on to. Is a valuable member of Colin Todd's squad and will continue to mount a serious challenge for the left-back position which Phillips has held for so long, especially with the Premiership looming up.
Aston Villa (From trainee on 9/7/90) F/PL 31+5 FLC 2 FAC 2+1 Others 4
Birmingham C (Loaned on 9/9/94) FL 3
Bolton W (Free on 20/3/96) F/PL 11+1 FLC 1 FAC 3

SMART Allan Andrew Colin
Born: Perth, 8 July 1974
Height: 6'2" Weight: 12.10
Club Honours: AMC '97

This skilful forward joined Carlisle last October as part of the deal that took David Reeves to Preston, following a successful loan spell at Brunton Park the previous year and one at Northampton during the previous month. An all-round performer who can both make and take chances, he ended the term with 11 goals to top United's league scoring chart, despite injury restricting his appearances at the end of the season. At the age of 23, with his best years still ahead of him, his ability will be an undoubted asset in division two come 1997-98.
Preston NE (£15,000 from Caledonian Thistle on 22/11/94) FL 17+4/6 FAC 2/1 Others 1+1
Carlisle U (Loaned on 24/11/95) FL 3+1
Northampton T (Loaned on 13/9/96) FL 1
Carlisle U (Signed on 9/10/96) FL 25+3/11 FAC 4 Others 4+1

SMITH Alexander (Alex) Philip
Born: Liverpool, 15 February 1976
Height: 5'7" Weight: 9.9

Although signed ostensibly as a left back, Alex only occupied this position once, early on last season, and had to wait until February for his second starting line up, in midfield, following the departure of Kevin Horlock. Although he was a fairly regular selection thereafter, either in the centre or left of midfield, it was still not clear whether he has yet found his best position. However, his only goal of the campaign, at West Bromwich in February, proved to be a match winner.
Everton (From trainee on 1/7/94)
Swindon T (Free on 12/1/96) FL 15+11/1

SMITH Benjamin (Ben) Peter
Born: Chelmsford, 23 November 1978
Height: 5'8" Weight: 10.6

Released by Arsenal from their YTS scheme, Ben came to Reading and impressed with his midfield play so much so that he progressed through the reserves and made his first-team debut at Manchester City in the final game of last season as a second-half substitute. Has now been given a one-year contract.
Reading (Free from Arsenal juniors on 16/4/97) FL 0+1

SMITH David
Born: Stonehouse, 29 March 1968
Height: 5'8" Weight: 10.7
International Honours: E: U21-10

After a disappointing 1995-96, Dave came good in 1996-97 and following the arrival of manager Ray Harford, re-established himself in the West Brom first team. Able to play at left back, in midfield, and on the wing (his normal position), he gave a good account of himself each and every time he took the field, before being unfortunately injured in the FA Cup tie at Chelsea and put out of action for four weeks. A hard worker, he has good all-round ability and pace to match.
Coventry C (From apprentice on 7/7/86) F/PL 144+10/19 FLC 17 FAC 6 Others 4+1
Bournemouth (Loaned on 8/1/93) FL 1
Birmingham C (Signed on 12/3/93) FL 35+3/3 FLC 4 FAC 0+1 Others 1
West Bromwich A (£90,000 on 31/1/94) FL 64+16/2 FLC 1+2 FAC 1+3 Others 4+1

SMITH David (Dave) Christopher
Born: Liverpool, 26 December 1970
Height: 5'10" Weight: 12.3

Again virtually a regular in the Oxford midfield in 1996-97, Dave has now appeared in over 130 league games in his three seasons at the club. His goal tally, however, still remains on one, but he came very close to doubling that when, after appearing late in the box, his diving header hit the post. Very important to United, he is the link between the defence and the rest and is also more than capable of playing as a sweeper.
Norwich C (From trainee on 4/7/89) F/PL 13+5 FAC 2+1 Others 1+1
Oxford U (£100,000 on 5/7/94) FL 131+1/1 FLC 16/1 FAC 8 Others 7

SMITH Dean
Born: West Bromwich, 19 March 1971
Height: 6'1" Weight: 12.10
Hereford centre half who formed a good understanding with Trevor Matthewson in the second half of last season. Deservedly the club's Player of the Year, the tall, dominating defender was devastating from set pieces and got into double figures, many of his goals being crucial prior to United being relegated to the Conference. *Stop Press:* Equally effective in the air or on the ground, a Football League tribunal met for the first time under the Bosman ruling to decide that Leyton Orient must pay £42,500 for a player valued by his club at £200,000.
Walsall (From trainee on 1/7/89) FL 137+5/2 FLC 10 FAC 4 Others 10
Hereford U (£75,000 on 17/6/94) FL 116+1/19 FLC 10/3 FAC 7 Others 11+1/4

SMITH James (Jamie) Jade Anthony
Born: Birmingham, 17 September 1974
Height: 5'6" Weight: 10.8
Omitted from the first two matches of 1996-97, the Wolves' right back was included in the next 18 fixtures and the 18 after that saw him alternate with Andy Thompson in the line up. Worked hard on the defensive aspects of his game, despite conceding a penalty at Barnsley, and got forward quickly to find some good attacking positions, while in the second half of the season his crosses also improved. Scored his first goal for the club in the play-off semi final at Crystal Palace, and a very coolly-taken strike it was.
Wolverhampton W (From trainee on 7/6/93) FL 70+6 FLC 5+1 FAC 2 Others 4/1

SMITH Martin Geoffrey
Born: Sunderland, 13 November 1974
Height: 5'11" Weight: 12.6
Club Honours: Div 1 '96
International Honours: E: U21-1; Sch
A skilful left-sided midfielder who, at one time, was reckoned by many to be a future England player, Martin made only seven starts last season and the fans would dearly love to see him given more opportunities. At his best, he can go past defenders with ease, possesses a powerful shot, is good in the air, and is at home either in midfield or up front.
Sunderland (From trainee on 9/9/92) P/FL 75+20/20 FLC 5+3 FAC 7+2/1

SMITH Michael (Mike) Robert
Born: Liverpool, 28 September 1973
Height: 5'11" Weight: 11.7
In and out of Doncaster Rovers' first team since moving to Belle Vue, at his best, he is a hard-working, speedy winger, keen to take players on. Unfortunately, a chronic hamstring injury limited his first team appearances last season and the best is still yet to come.
Tranmere Rov (From trainee on 22/5/92 - Free to Derry C during 1993 close season)
Doncaster Rov (Signed from Runcorn on 5/1/96) FL 24+7/2 FLC 0+1

SMITH Neil James
Born: Lambeth, 30 September 1971
Height: 5'10" Weight: 12.4
Club Honours: FAYC '90
A strong and tireless Gillingham midfielder, he played most of last season as a right-wing back, and always got forward to propel his long throws into the opposition's penalty area. During the course of the season, he made his 200th league appearance for the club and scored the winner at Coventry City in the third round of the Coca-Cola Cup, a goal that had his picture spread across most of the national newspapers the following day, after dreaming that he would score the winning goal.
Tottenham H (From trainee on 24/7/90)
Gillingham (£40,000 on 17/10/91) FL 204+9/10 FLC 14+1/1 FAC 18/2 Others 7+1/2

SMITH Ian Paul
Born: Easington, 22 January 1976
Height: 6'0" Weight: 13.3
Arguably the brightest of Burnley's young prospects, Paul finally achieved regular first-team status in 1996-97. Capable of dazzling skills on either wing, and with a penchant for long-distance shooting, he was moved to left-wing back after an injury to David Eyres and following a dip in form was dropped to sub for the last few matches of the season. Despite that he is already rumoured to be the subject of £1 million plus interest from Premiership clubs.
Burnley (From trainee on 10/7/94) FL 33+15/4 FLC 1+1 FAC 4 Others 2

SMITH Paul William
Born: East Ham, 18 September 1971
Height: 5'11" Weight: 14.0
Right-footed Brentford central midfielder. For the second successive season, Paul was an ever present in the league for the Bees in 1996-97 and kept the side flowing. A good passer and ball winner, and noted for his deep probing runs, he scored the vital first goal in the play-off semi final at Bristol City when controlling a clearance on the edge of the box and shooting home.
Southend U (From trainee on 16/3/90) FL 18+2/1 Others 0+1
Brentford (Free on 6/8/93) FL 159/11 FLC 12/1 FAC 12/3 Others 15/2

SMITH Peter John
Born: Stone, 12 July 1969
Height: 6'1" Weight: 12.7
In 1996-97, Peter again retained the number two shirt that he had worn with distinction in Brighton's back four for the previous two seasons. As enthusiastic as ever, the lanky six footer was at his best going forward to assist in attack, but he had little opportunity to do so as the Seagulls failed to find any sort of form in the first half of the campaign. Missing only a handful of matches through injury and suspension until March, his form then suffered and he lost his place to the experienced John Humphrey. Defensively sound, being a firm tackler, he also has great pace.
Brighton & Hove A (Free from Alma Swanley on 8/8/94) FL 89+10/3 FLC 8+1 FAC 5/1 Others 6+1

SMITH Peter Lee
Born: Rhuddlan, 18 September 1978
Height: 5'10" Weight: 10.8
International Honours: E: Yth

A graduate from the FA School of Excellence, Peter turned professional for Crewe during the 1996 close season and made his first-team debut against Luton at Gresty Road last March, when coming off the bench with just two minutes of the game left. Yet another to watch out for in 1997-98, he is a midfielder with a big future.
Crewe Alex (From trainee on 12/7/96) FL 0+1

SMITH Richard Geoffrey
Born: Lutterworth, 3 October 1970
Height: 6'0" Weight: 13.13
This right-footed, classy central defender unfortunately missed most of last season as Grimsby's defence was decimated by long-term injury to three key players, a situation which contributed greatly to a forgettable nine months for Town fans. Rest assured, however, that he will be back, along with his magnificent long throws.
Leicester C (From trainee on 15/12/88) F/PL 82+16/1 FLC 4 FAC 6/1 Others 12
Cambridge U (Loaned on 6/9/89) FL 4 FLC 1
Grimsby T (Loaned on 8/9/95) FL 8
Grimsby T (£50,000 on 11/3/96) FL 22+2 FLC 1

SMITH Scott David
Born: Christchurch, New Zealand, 6 March 1975
Height: 5'8" Weight: 11.6
Club Honours: AMC '96
An accomplished Rotherham defender who started last season as a first-team choice, Scott soon lost his place and was only used spasmodically before becoming one of the players surplus to the club's requirements and accepting an early release. Failed to find the net during his time at Millmoor.
Rotherham U (From trainee on 1/10/93) FL 30+6 FLC 2 FAC 2+1 Others 2+1

SMITH Gareth Shaun
Born: Leeds, 9 April 1971
Height: 5'10" Weight: 11.0
A natural left footer who normally operates at full back for Crewe, and a dead-ball specialist, Shaun scored his normal quota in 1996-97, including an amazing effort at Brentford in April when his free kick from fully 60 yards flew over the 'keeper for the second goal in a 2-0 win. A few weeks later, with the play offs underway, it was his strike against Luton which took Alex to Wembley to meet a Brentford side who could have well done without meeting up with him again. Having already scored twice against the Bees during the campaign, his third took Alex into the first division for the first time in their history.
Halifax T (From trainee on 1/7/89) FL 6+1 Others 1 (Free to Emley in May 1991)
Crewe Alex (Free on 31/12/91) FL 176+19/24 FLC 5+1 FAC 11+2/3 Others 19+2/3

SMITHARD Matthew Philip
Born: Leeds, 13 June 1976
Height: 5'9" Weight: 10.9
Club Honours: FAYC '93
Having failed to make his mark at Leeds, the young defender signed for Bradford prior to the start of last season and, despite being a regular in the reserves, made just one appearance for the first team, being called

off the bench in October during the 0-0 home draw against Southend. For a player who had impressed earlier in his career with balance, pace, and good feet, it must have been disappointing for him when he was released at the end of March and allowed to join non-league Farsley Celtic.

Leeds U (From trainee on 5/3/93)
Bradford C (Free on 16/8/96) FL 0+1

Richard Sneekes

SNEEKES Richard

Born: Amsterdam, Holland, 30 October 1968
Height: 5'11" Weight: 12.2
International Honours: Holland: U21-2; Yth

With his long flowing blond hair, Richard was not at his best during the first half of 1996-97 and at one stage was left out of West Brom's side. But the new cult hero at The Hawthorns, bounced back after Christmas and began scoring goals – a thing he had done so emphatically during the last two months of the previous season. Playing in the centre of midfield, he was allowed to run from deep positions, always making defenders think hard and long about his next move!

Bolton W (£200,000 from Fortuna Sittard on 12/8/94) P/FL 51+4/7 FLC 11+1/3 FAC 2/1
West Bromwich A (£385,000 on 11/3/96) FL 55+3/18 FLC 2 FAC 1

SNODIN Ian

Born: Rotherham, 15 August 1963
Height: 5'7" Weight: 11.0
Club Honours: Div 1 '87
International Honours: E: B-2; U21-4; Yth

Limited to just 14 games for Oldham in

1996-97, specifically as a stand in for Shaun Garnett, he suffered from a mixture of hamstring and back injuries before being freed during the summer. At his best, Ian has proved over the years to be both a reliable, classy defender, mixing up uncompromising tackling with excellent passing skills, and being equally at home in midfield. Is the brother of Glynn, most recently at Carlisle.

Doncaster Rov (From apprentice on 18/8/80) FL 181+7/25 FLC 9/1 FAC 11+1/1 Others 3
Leeds U (£200,000 on 22/5/85) FL 51/6 FLC 3/2 FAC 1
Everton (£840,000 on 16/1/87) F/PL 142+6/3 FLC 19+4/2 FAC 26/2 Others 3
Sunderland (Loaned on 13/10/94) FL 6
Oldham Ath (Free on 9/1/95) FL 55+2 FAC 1 Others 1

SOLIS Mauricio Mora

Born: Costa Rica, 13 December 1972
Height: 5'8" Weight: 11.10
International Honours: Costa Rica: 29

A Costa Rican international midfielder, signed together with Paulo Wanchope in late March, Mauricio was used only sparingly for Derby as a substitute and will take time to adapt to the English game. However, possessing the high skill factor that one generally associates with Latin American players, County fans will be asking more than a passing interest in 1997-98 as to whether he has the same pedigree as Wanchope and, if so, can it be turned to advantage in the Premiership.

Derby Co (£600,000 from CS Heridiano on 27/3/97) PL 0+2

SOLOMAN Jason Rafael

Born: Welwyn Garden City, 6 October 1970
Height: 6'0" Weight: 12.2
Club Honours: FAYC '89
International Honours: E: Yth

Released by Wycombe during the 1996 close season, Jason appeared in four matches for Wrexham at the commencement of 1996-97, playing alongside Brian Carey in the centre of defence, before moving on to Fulham in November. Despite scoring five times in seven reserve matches for the Cottagers, he only made the first team starting line up once, against Exeter City on Boxing Day, and ended the campaign with Stevenage Borough, showing his versatility when taking over in goal after the regular 'keeper was sent off.

Watford (From trainee on 9/12/88) FL 79+21/5 FLC 9/1 FAC 1 Others 5+1
Peterborough U (Loaned on 13/1/95) FL 4
Wycombe W (Free on 17/3/95) FL 11+2/1 FLC 1
Wrexham (Free on 14/8/96) FL 2 FLC 2
Fulham (Free on 20/11/96) FL 1+3

SOLSKJAER Ole Gunnar

Born: Norway, 26 February 1973
Height: 5'10" Weight: 11.10
Club Honours: PL '97; CS '97
International Honours: Norway: 11

A well-balanced Manchester United striker with a powerful shot in either foot, Ole was the least known of Alex Ferguson's 1996 summer signings when he joined the club from Molde, but what an impact he made to his career. In one memorable week during August, he hit a brace of goals in the

reserves, then scored on his Premiership debut against Blackburn, and having established himself as the club's leading scorer by the end of the year there were so many delightful contributions it was hard to pick out his best. Although he has only been a full-time professional for a year, Alex Ferguson could not hide his astonishment at his progress when he recalled, "I told him, I was expecting him just to bed in during the season, but Ole's got lightening feet and he's made our players sit up through his technique and finishing on the training ground." Although the United boss sees him as a long-term investment, his goal ratio gave the club an instant return and vital strikes in successive games against Leicester and Middlesbrough ensured United of its fourth championship in five years. The Norwegian international is undoubtedly a star of the present as well as the future.

Manchester U (£1,500,000 from Molde on 29/7/96) PL 25+8/18 FAC 0+3 Others 8+2/1

SOMMER Juergen Petersen

Born: New York, USA, 27 February 1969
Height: 6'5" Weight: 15.12
International Honours: USA: 5

At 6'4" one of the tallest goalkeepers in the league, Juergen began last season as QPR's first choice but, while away on international duty with the USA, he lost his place to Tony Roberts. Agile for such a big man, getting down to shots quickly and using his body to block when standing up to forwards, he came back into the side at the end of January before again going off on international duty in early April. Looks sure to contest the number one slot just as keenly with Roberts in 1997-98.

Luton T (Signed on 5/9/91) FL 82 FLC 6 FAC 11 Others 2
Brighton & Hove A (Loaned on 13/11/91) FL 1
Torquay U (Loaned on 31/10/92) FL 10 Others 1
Queens Park R (£600,000 on 29/8/95) P/FL 66 FLC 2 FAC 3

SONNER Daniel (Danny) James

Born: Wigan, 9 January 1972
Height: 5'11" Weight: 12.8
International Honours: NI: B-2

Back from a stint in Europe, Danny settled into the Ipswich side very well and reasonably quickly last season, proving to be a predominantly right-footed central midfield player who was able to create openings for team mates, and the possessor of a reasonable shot himself. Although a regular in the side, initially, he struggled to regain his place after missing several games because of a knee injury, but scored three goals during the season, all of them spectacular. His first being an overhead kick in the Coca-Cola Cup tie with Fulham and towards the end of the campaign, having come on as substitute against Bradford, he scored with a screaming drive from just outside the box, which helped to turn a 2-1 deficit into a 3-2 victory. Towards the end of 1996-97 he was called up to play for Northern Ireland's "B" team and there are hopes that a place in the full squad will be forthcoming this coming term.

253

Ole Solskjaar

Burnley (Free from Wigan Ath juniors on 6/8/90) FL 1+5 FLC 0+1/1 Others 0+2 (Free to Preussen Koln during 1993 close season)
Bury (Loaned on 21/11/92) FL 5/3 FAC 3 Others 1/1
Ipswich T (Free on 12/6/96) FL 22+7/2 FLC 5+1/1 FAC 1

SOUTHALL Neville
Born: Llandudno, 16 September 1958
Height: 6'1" Weight: 14.0
Club Honours: FAC '84, '95; CS '84, '85, '95; Div 1 '85, '87; ECW '85

International Honours: W: 91
After a legendary 16-year career at Everton, time finally began to catch up with the Welsh goalkeeping wizard in 1996-97. He made a record breaking 700th first team appearance for the Blues on the opening day of the season, received an MBE from the Queen in the Birthday Honours list, but then found himself dropped for the first time in 15 years after the FA Cup upset against Bradford. Joe Royle's decision caused some division amongst Everton supporters, who had not seen any evidence of a waning in the talents which once saw Neville rated as the best goalkeeper in the world. Although he regained his place after a three-match absence, the beginning of the end of an outstanding Everton career seemed to be close, especially now the club have Paul Gerrard in attendance.
Bury (£6,000 from Winsford U on 14/6/80) FL 39 FAC 5
Everton (£150,000 on 13/7/81) F/PL 566 FLC 64 FAC 70 Others 37
Port Vale (Loaned on 27/1/83) FL 9

SOUTHALL Leslie Nicholas (Nicky)
Born: Stockton, 28 January 1972
Height: 5'10" Weight: 12.12
A left-sided, attacking Grimsby midfielder whose fast runs down the wing and telling crosses contribute well to the Mariners attack. Also capable of getting amongst the goals himself, hopes that he might retain his regular spot on the left flank established in 1995-96, following the acrimonious departure of Ivano Bonetti, were dashed by the arrival of ex-Forest winger, Kingsley Black, and the subsequent emergence of teenage star, John Oster, in this position. On his limited senior outings in 1996-97, however, Nicky proved himself a tireless worker.
Hartlepool U (Free from Darlington juniors on 21/2/91) FL118+20/24 FLC 6+1/3 FAC 4+4 Others 6+2
Grimsby T (£40,000 on 12/7/95) FL 51+16/6 FLC 2+2/1 FAC 3+2/1

SOUTHGATE Gareth
Born: Watford, 3 September 1970
Height: 6'0" Weight: 12.8
Club Honours: Div 1 '94; FLC '96
International Honours: E: 19
Gareth had reasons to have started last season for Aston Villa in not quite the form he had shown at the end of the previous campaign. Although the thoughts associated with the missed penalty in Euro 96 were still there at the start, he battled away to produce consistent displays, playing mostly as the central of three defenders in the Villa backline. He also had a spell in midfield, a position he had played at his previous club and also captained the side when Andy Townsend was out. While missing ten games through injury, and showing that his disappointments of the summer had been forgotten, his only goal came in Villa's opening home game, the winner against Blackburn, giving him an early chance to celebrate. Good in the air and on the ground, and comfortable when bringing the ball out of defence, he also retained his place in the England squad, playing against Moldova, Poland, Georgia (twice), and Mexico, prior to the summer games.
Crystal Palace (From trainee on 17/1/89) F/PL 148+4/15 FLC 23+1/7 FAC 9 Others 6
Aston Villa (£2,500,000 on 1/7/95) PL 59/2 FLC 9/1 FAC 7 Others 2

SPACKMAN Nigel James
Born: Romsey, 2 December 1960
Height: 6'1" Weight: 13.2
Club Honours: Div 2 '84, Div 1 '88; FMC '86; SPD '90, '91, '92; SLC '91; SC '92

Signed by Sheffield United's Howard Kendall during the 1996 close season as his assistant manager and the "manager on the pitch", the former Chelsea star suffered an injury-hit campaign, however, and struggled to hold down a regular place, although still battling on to produce some effective performances in both midfield and defence. At this best an unspectacular ball winner who rarely captured the headlines when others less capable did, Nigel probably gave his best performance at Wembley in the play-off final where his vast experience came into play.

Bournemouth (Free from Andover on 8/5/80) FL 118+1/10 FLC 5 FAC 7
Chelsea (£40,000 on 20/6/83) FL 139+2/12 FLC 22+1 FAC 8/1 Others 7/1
Liverpool (£400,000 on 24/2/87) FL 39+12 FLC 6+1 FAC 5
Queens Park R (£500,000 on 2/2/89) FL 27+2/1 FLC 2/1 Others 2
Glasgow R (£500,000 on 30/11/89) SL 100/1 SLC 10 SC 9 Others 5
Chelsea (£485,000 on 8/9/92) PL 60+7 FLC 5 FAC 6+3 Others 7
Sheffield U (Free on 11/7/96) FL 19+4 FLC 2 FAC 1 Others 1

SPARROW Paul

Born: Wandsworth, 24 March 1975
Height: 6'1" Weight: 11.4
Club Honours: Div 3 '96

Injured on the first day of pre-season training, Paul was not seen often at right back for Preston during 1996-97. At his best, a strong tackler who likes to overlap and can cross effectively, hopefully, he will return stronger this coming season.

Crystal Palace (From trainee on 13/7/93) FL 1 FLC 0+1
Preston NE (Signed on 8/3/96) FL 19 FAC 1 Others 1

SPEARE James Peter Vincent

Born: Liverpool, 5 November 1976
Height: 6'1" Weight: 13.0

Released by Everton last March, James joined Darlington on non-contract terms and became the fourth 'keeper used in 1996-97 when making his debut in the local derby against Hartlepool in April. Tall and imposing, it was a difficult start, the side going down 2-1.

Everton (From trainee on 1/7/95)
Darlington (Free on 25/3/97) FL 3

SPEARING Anthony (Tony)

Born: Romford, 7 October 1964
Height: 5'6" Weight: 12.2
International Honours: E: Yth

Again mainly used in the left-back position at Peterborough in 1996-97, despite being at the veteran stage, Tony continued as an enthusiastic and willing trier who would do anything the club asked of him. Still into the overlap, and a strong tackler, he was used sparingly in competition with Simon Clark, before being freed during the summer.

Norwich C (From apprentice on 11/10/82) FL 67+2 FLC 5 FAC 4 Others 4
Stoke C (Loaned on 1/11/84) FL 9
Oxford U (Loaned on 1/2/85) FL 5

Leicester C (£100,000 on 12/7/88) FL 71+2/1 FLC 2+1 FAC 1 Others 2
Plymouth Arg (Free on 1/7/91) FL 35 FLC 6 FAC 1 Others 2+1
Peterborough U (Free on 21/1/93) FL 105+6/2 FLC 7 FAC 3+3 Others 8

SPEED Gary Andrew

Born: Deeside, 8 September 1969
Height: 5'10" Weight: 12.10
Club Honours: Div 2 '90, Div 1 '92; CS '92
International Honours: W: 42; U21-3; Yth

A childhood Evertonian, who was once a paper boy for the most successful captain in Goodison history, Kevin Ratcliffe, Gary joined the club he once supported in the summer of 1996 from Leeds. Enjoyed a dream start to his new career, scoring on his debut against Newcastle, and went on to record his best goals return since winning the championship with Leeds in 1992. Playing ostensibly on the left-hand side of midfield, the Welsh international offered strength and vision down that flank, not to mention excellent aerial prowess, his ability in the air making Everton a potent threat at set pieces, particularly when Duncan Ferguson and Andy Hinchcliffe were also in action. Scored his first senior hat trick in the 7-1 defeat of Southampton at Goodison Park, netting his third with a towering header from Hinchliffe's corner.

Leeds U (From trainee on 13/6/88) F/PL 231+17/39 FLC 25+1/11 FAC 21/5 Others 14+3/2
Everton (£3,500,000 on 1/7/96) PL 37/9 FLC 2/1 FAC 2/1

John Spencer

SPENCER John

Born: Glasgow, 11 September 1970
Height: 5'6" Weight: 11.7
International Honours: S: 14; U21-3; Yth; Sch

Signed from Chelsea last November, having spent much of the season on the touchline, with Mark Hughes and Gianluca Vialli

preferred and making just three starts, John made his QPR debut two days later at Reading, scoring in a 2-1 defeat. He then scored nine times in the next 12 appearances, including his first ever hat trick in the 3-1 home win over Barnsley, the team that would eventually be promoted as runners-up to the Premiership. Following that, the goals dried up for a while before he got on the rails again with eight in the last ten games. A skilful and quick-thinking striker who turns defenders to make space for shooting opportunities, he was selected for the Scotland squad in all their World Cup qualifying games.

Glasgow R (From juniors in 1986) SL 7+6/2 SLC 2 Others 1+1/1
Morton (Loaned on 4/3/89) FL 4/1
Chelsea (£450,000 on 1/8/92) PL 75+28/36 FLC 5+4/2 FAC16+4/4 Others 4+1/1
Queens Park R (£2,500,000 on 22/11/96) FL 25/17 FAC 4/1

Dean Spink

SPINK Dean Peter

Born: Birmingham, 22 January 1967
Height: 6'0" Weight: 14.8
Club Honours: Div 3 '94

As the Shrewsbury supporters' Player of the Year, and a very popular club captain, the uncompromising Dean played the majority of last season in central defence. Very competitive, strong in the air, which makes him a danger at set pieces, he is more than happy playing up front as a good target man, although equally happy with the ball at feet. His goals total for 1996-97 was obviously limited by his defensive role.

Aston Villa (£30,000 from Halesowen T on 1/7/89)
Scarborough (Loaned on 20/11/89) FL 3/2 Others 1
Bury (Loaned on 1/2/90) FL 6/1
Shrewsbury T (£75,000 on 15/3/90) FL 244+29/53 FLC 22+2/1 FAC 18+2/6 Others 19+2/3

SPINK Nigel Philip

Born: Chelmsford, 8 August 1958
Height: 6'2" Weight: 14.6
Club Honours: EC '82; ESC '82; FLC '94
International Honours: E: 1; B-2

255

Hardly figured in goal for West Brom in 1996-97 after receiving a leg injury at QPR and losing his place in the team to Paul Crichton. Took some time to regain full fitness after that and late in the season he acted as goalkeeping coach at the Hawthorns. Is still a good man to be able to fall back on.

Aston Villa (£4,000 from Chelmsford C on 1/1/77) F/PL 357+4 FLC 45 FAC 28 Others 25+1
West Bromwich A (Free on 31/1/96) FL 19 FLC 2 Others 2

SQUIRES James (Jamie) Alexander
Born: Preston, 15 November 1975
Height: 6'2" Weight: 13.11

Jamie was never a first choice for Preston last season, either at right back or in his favoured central defensive role and seemed to have lost his way a little after showing great promise as a youngster. Strong in the air and cool under pressure, he is still young enough to succeed and captained the championship-winning reserve side.

Preston NE (From trainee on 26/4/94) FL 24+7 FLC 1 FAC 0+1 Others 4+1

SRNICEK Pavel
Born: Ostrava, Czechoslovakia, 10 March 1968
Height: 6'2" Weight: 14.9
Club Honours: Div 1 '93
International Honours: Czechoslovakia: 8

A goalkeeper, whose quick reflexes enable him to be an able shot stopper, Pavel has become something of a folk hero on Tyneside, having worked hard to improve his ability to cope with crosses into the box and to become more mobile, acting as a sweeper behind his back four. Proud to be a member of the Czech Republic squad which reached the final of Euro 96, although not playing in any of the games, it was noticeable on his return to Premiership football that he seemed to have acquired the European goalkeeping habit of dealing with crosses by punching clear rather than collecting the ball. In vying with Shaka Hislop for the first team jersey at Newcastle throughout last season, he played in the Charity Shield match, was left out for the opening Premiership fixture, recalled for the following game, and then retained his place until the Blackburn defeat at Christmas, after which he was confined to the substitutes' bench. This led to him reluctantly requesting to be made available for transfer, a wish which was granted, although when Hislop fell victim to flu he returned for the final four games, keeping a clean sheet in all of them. Had earlier been seen at his best in the match at Stamford Bridge when ten-men United held on for a 1-1 draw and Pav gave a brilliant display of spectacular and defiant goalkeeping as Chelsea laid siege to his goal.

Newcastle U (£350,000 from Banik Ostrava on 5/2/91) F/PL 147+1 FLC 10+1 FAC 11 Others 17

STALLARD Mark
Born: Derby, 24 October 1974
Height: 6'0" Weight: 12.10

Started last season as part of the regular strike force at Bradford, but due to a drop in form he was loaned out to Preston in February and impressed in four appearances, especially when scoring against Bury, before leaving the club abruptly to sign for Wycombe. A broad-shouldered striker who can fend off challenges with ease, and cool in front of goal, his measured shots invariably on target, he scored on his debut and ended the campaign with four goals in 12 games.

Derby Co (From trainee on 6/11/91) FL 19+8/2 FLC 2+1/2 FAC 2+1 Others 3/2
Fulham (Loaned on 23/9/94) FL 4/3
Bradford C (£110,000 on 12/1/96) FL 33+10/10 FLC 2/1 FAC 0+1 Others 3/2
Preston NE (Loaned on 14/2/97) FL 4/1
Wycombe W (£100,000 on 7/3/97) FL 12/4

STAMP Philip Lawrence
Born: Middlesbrough, 12 December 1975
Height: 5'10" Weight: 12.3
International Honours: E: Yth

An enthusiastic young Middlesbrough midfielder, Phil proved to be full of pride and passion for his hometown team in 1996-97, while desperately anxious to ensure that the fans on the same terraces he occupied as a supporter, shared in the success they have been denied over the years. His commitment was unquestionable, his thirst for success undeniable, and his gutsy performances, covering 35 league and cup appearances, with three goals, one in each competition, under his belt, summed up admirably the brilliant future of this determined and strong-running player. Having kept his feet firmly on the ground amid the heady presence of the influx of international stars with whom he shared the Premiership stage during a tenuous and difficult campaign, shows he is made of the right material.

Middlesbrough (From trainee on 4/2/93) P/FL 35+14/3 FLC 8+2/1 FAC 4+3/1 Others 5+1

STAMPS Scott
Born: Birmingham, 20 March 1975
Height: 5'11" Weight: 11.0

Signed by Colchester the day before the transfer deadline last March, having made 32 appearances for Torquay in 1996-97, predominantly wearing the number 11 shirt, Scott immediately took over the left-back slot from Paul Gibbs and his eight appearances left the United faithful very impressed. With left back being a bit of a problem position for some years now, hopefully, that is now resolved.

Torquay U (From trainee on 6/7/93) FL 80+6/5 FLC 5 FAC 2 Others 2+1/1
Colchester U (£10,000 on 26/3/97) FL 7+1

STANNARD James (Jim) David
Born: Harold Hill, 6 October 1962
Height: 6'2" Weight: 16.2

After his success of 1995-96 at Gillingham, last season was always going to be a difficult act to follow for "Big" Jim. Having suffered with a thigh strain for a large part of the campaign, two goalkeepers had to be brought in on loan, but his performances were still generally good and he looks forward to making the 600th league appearance of his career early in 1997-98. A known shot stopper, he is still surprisingly agile for such a big man.

Fulham (Signed from Ford U on 5/6/80) FL 41 FLC 3 FAC 1
Southend U (Loaned on 17/9/84) FL 6
Charlton Ath (Loaned on 1/2/85) FL 1
Southend U (£12,000 on 28/3/85) FL 103 FLC 6 FAC 4 Others 5
Fulham (£50,000 on 14/8/87) FL 348/1 FLC 22 FAC 13 Others 18
Gillingham (Free on 4/8/95) FL 84 FLC 8 FAC 7 Others 1

STANT Phillip (Phil) Richard
Born: Bolton, 13 October 1962
Height: 6'0" Weight: 13.4
Club Honours: Div 3 '93; WC '93

Unable to gain a regular place at Bury in 1996-97, being picked as a sub most weeks, the proven goalscorer was finally given his chance and responded with a goal in a 2-1 home win over Bristol Rovers. It was to prove his last goal for the Shakers as he ended a frustrating time by initially joining Northampton on loan, scoring twice in five appearances, and then signing permanently for Lincoln in December. Scored in his first four league games for the Imps and the goals kept flowing until the end of a campaign, during which he formed a lethal strike partnership with Gareth Ainsworth.

Reading (Signed from Camberley on 19/8/82) FL 3+1/2
Hereford U (Free from Army on 25/11/86) FL 83+6/38 FLC 3/2 FAC 3/2 Others 11/7
Notts Co (£175,000 on 18/7/89) FL 14+8/6 FLC 2/1 FAC 0+1 Others 3+2
Blackpool (Loaned on 5/9/90) FL 12/5
Lincoln C (Loaned on 22/11/90) FL 4
Huddersfield (Loaned on 3/1/91) FL 5/1
Fulham (£60,000 on 8/2/91) FL 19/5 Others 1
Mansfield T (£50,000 on 1/8/91) FL 56+1/32 FLC 4/1 FAC 2 Others 5
Cardiff C (£100,000 on 4/12/92) FL 77+2/34 FLC 2/2 FAC 6+1/4 Others 10/3
Mansfield T (Loaned on 12/8/93) FL 4/1 FLC 1/1 FAC 1
Bury (£90,000 on 27/1/95) FL 49+13/23 FLC 5+1/4 FAC 1 Others 5
Northampton T (Loaned on 22/11/96) FL 4+1/2
Lincoln C (£30,000 on 26/12/96) FL 22/16 Others 1

STARBUCK Philip (Phil) Michael
Born: Nottingham, 24 November 1968
Height: 5'10" Weight: 13.3

This Sheffield United striker was at the back of the queue at the Lane following the Howard Kendall signings, his only league start in 1996-97 coming at Wolverhampton where he was pulled off for Petr Katchouro, who then began his fine run in the team. Spent a successful spell on loan in Holland with RKC Waalwijk, scoring three goals in five games, and, following his return, a loan to Oldham Athletic on deadline day ended with a ruptured achilles tendon in his first training session and a six-month spell out of the game, before being released at the end of the season.

Nottingham F (From apprentice on 19/8/86) FL 9+27/2 FLC 1+3 FAC 2+5 Others 0+4
Birmingham C (Loaned on 7/3/88) FL 3
Hereford U (Loaned on 19/2/90) FL 6 Others 1
Blackburn Rov (Loaned on 6/9/90) FL 5+1/1
Huddersfield T (£100,000 on 17/8/91) FL 120+17/36 FLC 13+2/4 FAC 5+1 Others 16+3/7
Sheffield U (£150,000 on 28/10/94) FL 26+10/2 FLC 0+2 FAC 1+1
Bristol C (Loaned on 15/9/95) FL 5/1 Others 1

STATHAM Brian
Born: Zimbabwe, 21 May 1969
Height: 5'9" Weight: 11.7
Club Honours: Div 3 '92
International Honours: E: U21-3
As Brentford's right-footed defender or midfield ball winner, Brian returned last December after a year out with a broken leg and played as if he had never been away, becoming a regular in the squad for the rest of the season. Unfortunately sent off in the play-off final at Wembley, it marked a disappointing end for a side that had been in an automatic promotion place for much of the campaign.
Tottenham H (From trainee on 3/8/87) FL 20+4 FLC 2 FAC 0+1
Reading (Loaned on 28/3/91) FL 8
Bournemouth (Loaned on 20/11/91) FL 2 Others 1
Brentford (£70,000 on 16/1/92) FL 148+18/1 FLC 12 FAC 6 Others 22

Steve Staunton

STAUNTON Stephen (Steve)
Born: Dundalk, 19 January 1969
Height: 6'0" Weight: 12.4
Club Honours: FAC '89; CS '89; Div 1 '90; FLC '94, '96
International Honours: Ei: 68; U21-4; Yth
Steve came back fit and well for Aston Villa in 1996-97, following his injury hit time the previous year, and played in the opening dozen games before picking up the first of three injuries in the campaign. A hamstring injury sidelined him for a few games, but he was soon back and scored on his return at Coventry. He then appeared in the centre of defence, with Villa playing with three centre backs in a change from his normal full-back role, but continued to give consistently good displays and always posed a threat when able to get into attacking situations. A left-sided player who likes to get forward to send in telling crosses, Steve continued to be selected for the Republic of Ireland side, playing in four more games and captaining the side in one of them.

Liverpool (£20,000 from Dundalk on 2/9/86) FL 55+10 FLC 6+2/4 FAC 14+2/1 Others 1/1
Bradford C (Loaned on 13/11/87) FL 7+1 FLC 2 Others 1
Aston Villa (£1,100,000 on 7/8/91) F/PL 178+3/15 FLC 17+2/1 FAC 15+1 Others 8

STEELE Timothy (Tim) Wesley
Born: Coventry, 1 December 1967
Height: 5'9" Weight: 11.7
Signed during the summer of 1996 from Hereford, Tim was troubled by injuries during 1996-97 and was freed during the close season, but, nevertheless, gave Exeter fans indication of his ability with a 20-yard effort at Scarborough. A midfield battler who can play on either flank, he was always looking to get forward to deliver dangerous crosses.
Shrewsbury T (From apprentice on 7/12/85) FL 41+20/5 FLC 3+1/1 Others 1+1
Wolverhampton W (£80,000 on 22/2/89) FL 53+22/7 FLC 5/3 FAC 1 Others 4
Stoke C (Loaned on 20/2/92) FL 7/1
Bradford C (Free on 16/7/93) FL 8+3 FLC 2+1/1
Hereford U (Free on 14/1/94) FL 24+8/2 FLC 2 FAC 1+1 Others 1+2
Exeter C (Free on 5/8/96) FL 14+14/3 FLC 1

STEFANOVIC Dejan
Born: Yugoslavia, 28 October 1974
Height: 6'2" Weight: 12.10
International Honours: Yugoslavia: 9
The Yugoslav international's second season in England saw him impress far more and he was a regular in Sheffield Wednesday's centre-back spot in 1996-97, keeping out Jon Newsome for long periods. He also managed two goals, both of them vital – a last minute equaliser at Chelsea and the winner against Sunderland – and despite having seen his compatriot Darko Kovacevic transferred to Spain, Dejan has settled well in Yorkshire and looks a good prospect. A classy player who gives himself time on the ball, being comfortable in possession, he occasionally played at left back during the campaign.
Sheffield Wed (£2,000,000 from Red Star Belgrade on 22/12/95) PL 32+3/2 FLC 1 FAC 2

STEIN Mark Earl Sean
Born: Capetown, South Africa, 29 January 1966
Height: 5'6" Weight: 11.10
Club Honours: FLC '88; AMC '92; Div 2 '93
International Honours: E: Yth
There would be no appearances for Chelsea last season even when he was available for selection, mainly due to the advent of the foreigners, and he was loaned out to Stoke in November for a second spell in an effort to regain match fitness and possibly to find a club who would appreciate his qualities. Obviously relishing the opportunity, after having to train with Blues' youth team, the Potters brought him back to partner Mike Sheron and he did well, scoring four times in 11 appearances. However, City's interest waned when the Premiership side put a price of £1 million on his head. From a footballing family, Brian (Luton) and Eddie (Barnet) both played fairly recently, Mark is a natural goalscorer who can put away half

chances with the best of them, but has found his career stymied by injuries.
Luton T (From juniors on 31/1/84) FL 41+13/19 FLC 4+1 FAC 9/3 Others 3/1
Aldershot (Loaned on 29/1/86) FL 2/1
Queens Park R (£300,000 on 26/8/88) FL 20+13/4 FLC 4/2 FAC 2+1/1 Others 4
Oxford U (Signed on 15/9/89) FL 72+10/18 FLC 4 FAC 2+1 Others 3
Stoke C (£100,000 on 15/9/91) FL 94/50 FLC 8/8 FAC 4 Others 17/10
Chelsea (£1,500,000 on 28/10/93) PL 46+4/21 FLC 0+1 FAC 9/2 Others 2+1/2
Stoke C (Loaned on 22/11/96) FL 11/4

STEINER Robert Herman
Born: Finsprong, Sweden, 20 June 1973
Height: 6'2" Weight: 13.5
Signed on a three-month contract from IFK Norrkoping (Sweden) last October, in 16 games for Bradford, Robert proved to be a strong, bustling forward who was more than capable on the ground and in the air. Sadly for the fans, however, having opened his scoring account with a long-range equaliser in a 3-3 draw at Huddersfield, and with three more strikes already under his belt, he returned to Sweden in early February. *Stop Press:* Signed for City on a permanent basis during the summer, a £500,000 fee securing the deal.
Bradford C (Loaned from Norrkoping on 31/10/96) FL 14+1/3 FAC 1/1

STEPHENSON Paul
Born: Wallsend, 2 January 1968
Height: 5'10" Weight: 12.12
International Honours: E: Yth
A skilful, ball-playing winger, Paul operated for York City on either flank last season, proving to be a match winner and one of the most talented players in the lower divisions. Although his form did at times fluctuate and injuries caused him a few problems, there was no doubting his great value to the club.
Newcastle U (From apprentice on 2/1/86) FL 58+3/1 FLC 3+1 FAC 2 Others 2
Millwall (£300,000 on 10/11/88) FL 81+17/6 FLC 3/1 FAC 9/2 Others 8/1
Gillingham (Loaned on 21/11/92) FL 12/2 Others 2
Brentford (£30,000 on 4/3/93) FL 70/2 FLC 6/1 FAC 1+1 Others 5
York C (Signed on 7/8/95) FL 57+5/3 FLC 6+1 FAC 3 Others 2+2/1

STERLING Worrell Ricardo
Born: Bethnal Green, 8 June 1965
Height: 5'7" Weight: 11.0
Club Honours: FAYC '82
An experienced winger signed on a free transfer from Bristol Rovers in the summer of 1996, Worrell failed to win a regular place at Lincoln in 1996-97 and was placed on the transfer list at the end of the season. At his best, a hard-working, tricky player who can supply accurate crosses for the front men as well as being defensively sound.
Watford (From apprentice on 10/6/83) FL 82+12/14 FLC 7+2/1 FAC 18/2 Others 0+1
Peterborough U (£70,000 on 23/3/89) FL 190+3/28 FLC 15/3 FAC 14/5 Others 14/2
Bristol Rov (£140,000 on 29/7/93) FL 117+2/6 FLC 7/1 FAC 6 Others 15
Lincoln C (Free on 26/7/96) FL 15+6 FLC 3+1 FAC 0+1 Others 0+1

STEVENS Michael Gary
Born: Barrow, 27 March 1963
Height: 5'11" Weight: 12.7
Club Honours: FAC '84; Div 1 '85, '87;
ECWC '85; CS '84, '85; SPD '89, '90, '91,
'92, '93, '94; SLC '89, '91, '94; SC '92
International Honours: E: 46; B-1
Practically an ever present in the Tranmere team in 1996-97, until a badly broken forearm picked up in the away fixture at Charlton in early February, Gary then found himself sidelined until almost the end of the season, when he had several games for the reserves in the Pontins' League. An economical, mature, and neat player, with plenty of top-flight experience both in England and Scotland behind him, he continued to show that he was comfortable either at left back, right back, or as cover in central defence, and, as always, was reliable and versatile in his approach to any game.
Everton (From apprentice on 8/4/81) FL 207+1/8 FLC 30/1 FAC 39/3 Others 10
Glasgow R (£1,000,000 on 19/7/88) SL 186+1/8 SLC 22 SC 22/1 Others 14
Tranmere Rov (£350,000 on 22/9/94) FL 101+1/1 FLC 10 FAC 4 Others 4

STEVENS Ian David
Born: Malta, 21 October 1966
Height: 5'9" Weight: 12.6
Club Honours: AMC '89
Very sharp in the box, good at losing his marker and converting a fair proportion of his chances, both in the air and on the ground, 17 league goals were included in his 19 Shrewsbury strikes for 1996-97, the majority in the first half of the campaign. Never a target man, his goals tended to dry up a little when he was asked to fulfill this role, but, nevertheless, it was his best season yet at Gay Meadow. *Stop Press:* Transferred to Carlisle on 13 May.
Preston NE (From apprentice on 22/11/84) FL 9+2/2 Others 1
Stockport Co (Free on 27/10/86) FL 1+1 FAC 0+1 Others 0+1 (Free to Lancaster C on 27/11/86)
Bolton W (Free on 25/3/87) FL 26+21/7 FLC 1+2 FAC 4/2 Others 3+1
Bury (Free on 3/7/91) FL 100+10/38 FLC 3+1 FAC 2+2 Others 7+1/2
Shrewsbury T (£20,000 on 11/8/94) FL 94+17/37 FLC 2+1 FAC 4+2/2 Others 10+2/12

STEVENS Keith Henry
Born: Merton, 21 June 1964
Height: 6'0" Weight: 12.12
Club Honours: FLT '83; Div 2 '88
With the Millwall captain spending most of last season out of action due to a cruciate knee ligament injury, it was hardly surprising that the defence missed his steadying influence and rugged tackling. Unfortunately, his comeback lasted all of 11 minutes against Bristol City, leaving him just short of 550 competitive games.
Millwall (From apprentice on 23/6/81) FL 448+7/9 FLC 36/1 FAC 28 Others 29

STEWART William Paul Marcus
Born: Bristol, 7 November 1972
Height: 5'10" Weight: 11.0
International Honours: E: Sch
The record signing from Bristol Rovers during the 1996 close season, Marcus

became a hit before he had even kicked a ball, attracting a lot of attention from the Premier League before deciding to join Huddersfield. A very skilful forward, unfortunately his campaign was decimated by injury, during which he showed only glimpses of his true attacking form. Despite that, he still finished as the club's second highest scorer with 11 under his belt, including a hat trick in a 3-0 home win in the Coca-Cola Cup against Wrexham, in just his second outing with his new club. Hopefully injury free, big things are expected of him this coming season.
Bristol Rov (From trainee on 18/7/91) FL 137+34/57 FLC 11/5 FAC 7+1/3 Others 16+1/14
Huddersfield T (£1,200,000 + on 2/7/96) FL 19+1/7 FLC 4/4 FAC 1

STEWART Paul Andrew
Born: Manchester, 7 October 1964
Height: 5'11" Weight: 12.4
Club Honours: FAC '91; CS '91; Div 1 '94, '96
International Honours: E: 3; B-5; U21-1; Yth
The striker was one of four players to top the Sunderland goalscoring charts last term, albeit with only four goals. However, the former England international was at times forced to plough a lone furrow up front and he certainly gave his all in Sunderland's unsuccessful attempt to preserve their Premiership status. A bustling midfielder, cum striker, Paul announced prior to the season's end that he would be seeking a move back to Lancashire in the summer for family reasons.
Blackpool (From apprentice on 13/10/81) FL 188+13/56 FLC 11/3 FAC 7/2 Others 6/1
Manchester C (£200,000 on 19/3/87) FL 51/26 FLC 4/2 FAC 6/1 Others 2/1
Tottenham H (£1,700,000 on 21/6/88) FL 126+5/28 FLC 23/7 FAC 9/2 Others 9
Liverpool (£2,300,000 on 29/7/92) PL 28+4/1 FLC 6 FAC 1 Others 3/2
Crystal Palace (Loaned on 24/1/94) FL 18/3
Wolverhampton W (Loaned on 2/9/94) FL 5+3/2 Others 2
Burnley (Loaned on 8/2/95) FL 6
Sunderland (Loaned on 29/8/95) FL 1+1
Sunderland (Free on 5/3/96) P/FL 30+4/5 FLC 3

STEWART Simon Andrew
Born: Leeds, 1 November 1973
Height: 6'1" Weight: 13.8
A 1996 close season capture from Sheffield Wednesday, the central defender was injured in a summer friendly and was the "missing man" of Fulham's promotion campaign, playing in just four reserve and three first team games throughout. Recognised for his ability to attack the ball and defend solidly, when Simon regains full fitness for 1997-98, hopefully, he can start again.
Sheffield Wed (From trainee on 16/7/92) PL 6 FLC 0+1
Shrewsbury T (Loaned on 11/8/95) FL 4
Fulham (Free on 17/6/96) FL 2+1

STIMAC Igor
Born: Croatia, 6 September 1967
Height: 6'2" Weight: 13.0
International Honours: Croatia: 23
The Derby team captain and experienced Croatian central defender experienced a

season disrupted by injury and suspensions (the latter being blamed on the officials' interpretation of his tackling!) in 1996-97. A tremendous inspiration to the rest of the defence, having the ball control and distribution skills expected of a top continental centre back, a regular international, Igor has signed for Derby till the year 2000. Both calm and invigorating, when he played well County played well, he scored his first Premiership goal in a 2-2 home draw against Sheffield Wednesday, his firmly placed header putting the Rams temporarily in front. Is one of the men that Jim Smith will be building around.
Derby Co (£1,570,000 from Hadjuk Split on 31/10/95) F/PL 48/2 FLC 1 FAC 2

Igor Stimac

STIMSON Mark
Born: Plaistow, 27 December 1967
Height: 5'11" Weight: 12.6
The Southend fans saw very little of Mark during 1996-97, a season that he was badly affected by injuries. Very strong in the tackle, with excellent distribution skills, his overlapping runs were greatly missed and all United fans will be hoping that he can return in the new campaign and find the form he showed when first arriving at the club.
Tottenham H (From apprentice on 15/7/85) FL 1+1
Leyton Orient (Loaned on 15/3/88) FL 10
Gillingham (Loaned on 19/1/89) FL 18
Newcastle U (£200,000 on 16/6/89) FL 82+4/2 FLC 5 FAC 7/1 Others 6
Portsmouth (Loaned on 10/12/92) FL 3+1
Portsmouth (£100,000 on 23/7/93) FL 57+1/2 FLC 9/1 FAC 3 Others 3
Barnet (Loaned on 21/9/95) FL 5 Others 1
Southend U (£25,000 on 15/3/96) FL 17/2

STOCKLEY Samuel (Sam) Joshua
Born: Tiverton, 5 September 1977
Height: 6'0" Weight: 12.0
Arriving at Underhill from Southampton last December, as part of the Maik Taylor

deal, Sam went straight into the Barnet side as a right-wing back. A regular from then on, and very quick and lively, his runs down the flank were a highlight and augured well for both him and the club's future.

Southampton (From trainee on 1/7/96)
Barnet (Free on 31/12/96) FL 21 Others 1

STOCKWELL Michael (Micky) Thomas
Born: Chelmsford, 14 February 1965
Height: 5'9" Weight: 11.4
Club Honours: Div 2 '92
Micky began last season for Ipswich at right back, but, once Gus Uhlenbeek returned to the side, he moved into a right-sided midfield position from where he was able to support the forwards by providing width and also found the time to set into the box to get on the scoresheet himself. His total of nine goals was his best ever and the equaliser at Sheffield United in the first leg of the play-off semi finals, when he collected Jamie Scowcroft's flick, rounded the 'keeper and calmly slotted the ball home, was by far the most important strike of his career. Alas, it was ultimately to be of no avail, but, rest assured, this quick tackling, quick thinking player will be doing much of the same in 1997-98.

Ipswich T (From apprentice on 17/12/82) F/PL 374+21/28 FLC 30+4/3 FAC 22+3/1 Others 20+2/2

STOKER Gareth
Born: Bishop Auckland, 22 February 1973
Height: 5'9" Weight: 10.10
This battling midfielder continued his impressive form for Hereford in 1996-97, so much so that Cardiff moved to prise him away from Edgar Street in January. At City, Gareth merely carried on where he had left off, showing great determination and excellent tackling ability, his gritty performances helping the club reach the play offs. He was also never afraid to go forward, scoring three times, two of them in succession, and one of them coming against his former club.

Hull C (Free from Leeds U juniors on 13/9/91) FL 24+6/2 FLC 3 FAC 2+1 Others 0+2 (Released during 1993 close season)
Hereford U (Signed from Bishop Auckland on 16/3/95) FL 65+5/6 FLC 5+1 FAC 3+1/1 Others 6+1/1
Cardiff C (£80,000 on 29/1/97) FL 17/3 Others 1+1

STOKES Dean Anthony
Born: Birmingham, 23 May 1970
Height: 5'9" Weight: 10.5
A second-choice left back who was limited to just nine starts for Port Vale last season, he did well when he did come in, his strong tackling and pace being particular features, but an injury at Sheffield United in March allowed Allen Tankard to reclaim his place. His main highlight was when playing at Blackburn Rovers in the FA Cup.

Port Vale (Signed from Halesowen T on 15/1/93) FL 48+4 FLC 0+1 FAC 4 Others 5+3

STOKOE Graham
Born: Newcastle under Lyme, 17 December 1975
Height: 6'0" Weight: 12.4

One of the emerging band of Stoke's young players, the midfielder made a small number of substitute appearances in 1996-97, without fully settling into the side. Yet to make a first-team start, Graham is still rated as one of the club's better prospects, and a player who will get a run of games before too long.

Stoke C (Free from Newcastle U juniors on 7/7/94) FL 0+2
Hartlepool U (Loaned on 23/2/96) FL 8

STONE Steven (Steve) Brian
Born: Gateshead, 20 August 1971
Height: 5'9" Weight: 12.7
International Honours: E: 9
A serious knee injury sustained against Leicester in just the fifth game of 1996-97 ruled Steve out of the Nottingham Forest side for the rest of the campaign and he was sorely missed by a team that confronted relegation throughout. Such were his displays in 1995-96, that he had become an England regular and was no doubt missed by his country as well. Aiming to be fit again for the coming season, the fans can only hope that the midfielder will be back to his hard-working best as Forest aim to come back to the Premiership at the first attempt.

Nottingham F (From trainee on 20/5/89) F/PL 136+2/18 FLC 11+1 FAC 8 Others 12/2

STONES Craig
Born: Scunthorpe, 31 May 1980
Height: 5'11" Weight: 11.2
A first year Lincoln YTS player who was given his league debut at 16 when coming on as substitute for the final 18 minutes of the home match with Swansea last April, Craig proved to be a talented midfield lad. Highly regarded by all at Sincil Bank, he is reckoned to have a great future.

Lincoln C (Trainee) FL 0+2

STORER Stuart John
Born: Rugby, 16 January 1967
Height: 5'11" Weight: 12.13
Club Honours: AMC '89
One of the successes of Brighton and Hove Albion's generally traumatic campaign in 1996-97, Stuart's pace, industry, and enthusiasm down the right wing provided excellent support to the main strikers. Named as Player of the Month for March by the Evening Argus, he had a particularly excellent match in the vital 1-0 win over eventual champions, Wigan, in the penultimate home match, and scored the equally crucial winner against Doncaster Rovers in the last-ever fixture at the Goldstone Ground, which enabled the Seagulls to go to Hereford knowing that a draw in the final game would save the club from relegation to the Conference.

Mansfield T (Juniors) FL 0+1 (Freed in March 1984)
Birmingham C (Free from VS Rugby on 10/1/85) FL 5+3 FLC 1
Everton (Signed on 6/3/87)
Wigan Ath (Loaned on 23/7/87) FL 9+3 FLC 4
Bolton W (£25,000 on 24/12/87) FL 95+28/12 FLC 9+2 FAC 7+3/2 Others 5/1
Exeter C (£25,000 on 25/3/93) FL 75+2/8 FLC 4/1 FAC 4+1/1 Others 6
Brighton & Hove A (£15,000 on 2/3/95) FL 67+15/9 FLC 3+1 FAC 3+1 Others 3/1

STOWELL Michael (Mike)
Born: Portsmouth, 19 April 1965
Height: 6'2" Weight: 14.2
Throughout the summer of 1996 it seemed a question of not if he would be replaced, but, simply, who by. Yet he began 1996-97 as Wolves' top goalkeeper and by the end of the campaign he was a contender for their top player award. Has always been a good shot stopper, having a better understanding with colleagues as well as more command of the penalty area these days, Mike played in all 51 matches as the club's only ever present.

Preston NE (Free from Leyland Motors on 14/2/85)
Everton (Free on 12/12/85) Others 1
Chester C (Loaned on 3/9/87) FL 14 Others 2
York C (Loaned on 24/12/87) FL 6
Manchester C (Loaned on 2/2/88) FL 14 FAC 1
Port Vale (Loaned on 21/10/88) FL 7 Others 1
Wolverhampton W (Loaned on 17/3/89) FL 7
Preston NE (Loaned on 8/2/90) FL 2
Wolverhampton W (£250,000 on 28/6/90) FL 278 FLC 18 FAC 14 Others 11

STRACHAN Gordon David
Born: Edinburgh, 9 February 1957
Height: 5'6" Weight: 10.8
Club Honours: SPD '80, '84; SC '82, '83, '84; ECWC '83; ESC '83; FAC '85; Div 2 '90, Div 1 '92; CS '92
International Honours: S: 50; U21-1; Yth; Sch
Gordon became Coventry's manager last November with the team lying in the bottom three and having made just two cameo substitute appearances. His appearance as a sub in his first game in charge against Gillingham failed to stop the second division side winning and between then and April he played only seven minutes as a sub in three games before coming on at Anfield to help clinch a dramatic win. Three days later he made his first start at home to Chelsea and had a brilliant game, inspiring his team to a win and creating the third goal. His appearance at the Dell sparked off City's revival from a two goal deficit and he played 75 minutes against Arsenal, two days later, before leaving the field to a tumultuous ovation. A fiery, right-sided midfielder with a brilliant football brain who sees openings quickly, he still has the drive of a youngster.

Dundee (From juniors in 1971) SL 56+13/13 SLC 11+2/1 SC 7/1 Others 1+1
Aberdeen (£50,000 on 1/11/77) SL 175+8/55 SLC 43+3/20 SC 25/7 Others 30+4/7
Manchester U (£500,000 on 13/8/84) FL 155+5/33 FLC 12+1/1 FAC 22/2 Others 10+2/3
Leeds U (£300,000 on 23/3/89) F/PL 188+9/37 FLC 19/3 FAC 14/2 Others 14+1/3
Coventry C (Free on 22/3/95) PL 13+13 FLC 3+1 FAC 2+1

STRODDER Gary John
Born: Cleckheaton, 1 April 1965
Height: 6'1" Weight: 13.3
A strong, uncompromising Notts County centre half, Gary was former manager, Colin Murphy's first signing as his captain and leader on the field. Highly experienced and thoroughly professional, and an inspiration and mentor to the younger players around him, unfortunately, his sterling displays

were not enough to save County from relegation in 1996-97. Is noted for his aerial power.

Lincoln C (From apprentice on 8/4/83) FL 122+10/6 FLC 7+1 FAC 2+1 Others 5+1
West Ham U (Signed on 20/3/87) FL 59+6/2 FLC 8 FAC 4+2 Others 2
West Bromwich A (£190,000 on 22/8/90) FL 123+17/8 FLC 8+1 FAC 7/1 Others 10
Notts Co (£145,000 on 14/7/95) FL 71/5 FLC 5 FAC 6 Others 6

Graham Stuart

STUART Graham Charles
Born: Tooting, 24 October 1970
Height: 5'9" Weight: 11.10
Club Honours: FAC '95
International Honours: E: U21-5; Yth

A versatile and talented footballer, Graham kicked off last season as striking partner to Duncan Ferguson, a role he had filled with great success at Everton in 1995-96. Unfortunately, in dropping back to right midfield following the sale of Andrei Kanchelskis, and even playing two matches at right-wing back during the height of an injury crisis, his positional switching meant that his goals return did not match his previous season's haul. However, he still remained one of the most important and unsung members of the Everton team and a player who will run his socks off for the cause.

Chelsea (From trainee on 15/6/89) F/PL 70+17/14 FLC 11/2 FAC 5+2/1 Others 3+2/1
Everton (£850,000 on 19/8/93) PL 102+20/21 FLC 6/2 FAC 10+3/5 Others 2+1/1

STUART Jamie Christopher
Born: Southwark, 15 October 1976
Height: 5'10" Weight: 11.0
International Honours: E: U21-4; Yth

1996-97 was a disappointing campaign for Jamie, who started as Charlton's first-choice left back, before suffering a loss of form due to injury problems, which restricted his appearances for the rest of the season. A good tackler, and an assured passer of the ball, he likes to run down the left flank to get in early crosses. Scored his only goal of the season against Southend at The Valley.

Charlton Ath (From trainee on 18/1/95) FL 49/3 FLC 8 FAC 3 Others 0+1

STUART Mark Richard
Born: Chiswick, 15 December 1966
Height: 5'10" Weight: 11.3
International Honours: E: Sch

Following a successful start to his fourth campaign at Rochdale, Mark was again troubled by injuries and, after missing a large part of last season, he regained his scoring touch with four goals in the last three games. Is a tricky winger, cum midfielder, and a specialist at set pieces.

Charlton Ath (From juniors on 3/7/84) FL 89+18/28 FLC 7+3/2 FAC 1/1 Others 9+1
Plymouth Arg (£150,000 on 4/11/88) FL 55+2/11 FLC 4 FAC 3 Others 2/1
Ipswich T (Loaned on 22/3/90) FL 5/2
Bradford C (£80,000 on 3/8/90) FL 22+7/5 FLC 6/1 FAC 0+1 Others 1+1
Huddersfield T (Free on 30/10/92) FL 9+6/3 FAC 2 Others 4/1
Rochdale (Free on 5/7/93) FL 127+11/35 FLC 7+1/1 FAC 5/1 Others 5+3/1

STURGESS Paul Christopher
Born: Dartford, 4 August 1975
Height: 5'11" Weight: 12.5

A strong-tackling, left-sided Charlton defender, his appearances in 1996-97 were restricted, due to injury and the form of Anthony Barness. A good crosser of the ball and comfortable going forward, Paul had an excellent game against Newcastle United in the FA Cup at The Valley and was picked for the Football League representative side which played the Italian League in Italy. Surprisingly released during the summer.

Charlton Ath (From trainee on 1/7/93) FL 43+8 FLC 4+1 FAC 1 Others 5

STURRIDGE Dean Constantine
Born: Birmingham, 26 July 1973
Height: 5'8" Weight: 12.1

A former youth team player now firmly established in the first team at Derby, Dean continued to make progress in the more

testing arena of the Premiership in 1996-97. On the small side, but with great acceleration and pace, and difficult for defenders to force off the ball, he started the season with a double against Leeds before the goals dried up until his partnership with Ashley Ward started to gel. His determination was epitomised by the way he beat both Gary Pallister and Peter Schmeichel to a high ball to force home the winner at Old Trafford in April. However, his best effort was his solo goal at Arsenal when he cut inside from the left wing and crashed in a stunning 25-yard shot off the underside of the bar to secure a vital point. As County's leading scorer with 14 to his credit, his speed off the mark continually took him clear of even the best of defenders, while his finishing under pressure and ability to reach the ball on the ground and in the air merely confirmed his excellence.

Derby Co (From trainee on 1/7/91) P/FL 78+14/32 FLC 1+1/1 FAC 3/2 Others 2+1
Torquay U (Loaned on 16/12/94) FL 10/5

STURRIDGE Simon Andrew
Born: Birmingham, 9 December 1969
Height: 5'5" Weight: 10.13
Club Honours: AMC '91

A nippy striker whose 1996-97 season was cut short by a cruciate knee ligament injury sustained at Barnsley in September, his positive runs and goalscoring returns were dearly missed by Stoke as the campaign wore on. The brother of Dean, currently starring for Derby, Simon is a dribbler with tight control who is not afraid to take on the opposition.

Birmingham C (From trainee on 8/7/88) FL 129+21/30 FLC 10+4/1 FAC 8/2 Others 14/5
Stoke C (£75,000 on 24/9/93) FL 42+25/14 FLC 2 FAC 3+3/1 Others 7+3

Neil Sullivan

SULLIVAN Neil
Born: Sutton, 24 February 1970
Height: 6'0" Weight: 12.1
International Honours: S: 1

Now one of the Premiership's outstanding

goalkeepers after giving many memorable performances for Wimbledon in 1996-97, which included two vital penalty stops in the 4-2 win over Sheffield Wednesday and the 1-1 draw against Middlesbrough, not to mention that superb save in the FA Cup victory over Manchester United, Neil confounded the critics and was called up by Scotland. His assets are good shot stopping, dealing well with crosses, and keeping a cool head under pressure, and, having now secured a regular first-team place, the local lad deserves all the recognition he is getting.
Wimbledon (From trainee on 26/7/88) F/PL 67+1 FLC 7 FAC 15
Crystal Palace (Loaned on 1/5/92) FL 1

SUMMERBEE Nicholas (Nicky) John
Born: Altrincham, 26 August 1971
Height: 5'11" Weight: 12.8
International Honours: E: B-1; U21-3

Having now completed his third full season at Manchester City, Nicky again had a satisfying campaign in contributing much to the build up in the City style on the wing. Utilised in the first half of the season as a deep winger, playing out from defence as he did mainly in 1995-96, since the arrival of Frank Clark in the New Year he was used up front more with his style of play altered to be more direct and to shoot more on reaching the penalty area. This, one feels has improved his game and certainly, since January, it gave more impetus to the team's attacking flair. Scored more goals in 1996-97 than in his previous two seasons, one in particular against his old club Swindon Town, giving him great pleasure. Is the son of the former England star, Mike.
Swindon T (From trainee on 20/7/89) F/PL 89+23/6 FLC 9+1/3 FAC 2+4 Others 7/1
Manchester C (£1,500,000 on 24/6/94) P/FL 115+7/6 FLC 9+2 FAC 12/2

SUMMERBELL Mark
Born: Durham, 30 October 1976
Height: 5'10" Weight: 11.9

Having made the remarkable leap from the juniors to the Middlesbrough first team in unbelievable brevity during 1995-96, the young midfielder continued to astound the establishment in 1996-97 with his undeniable potential. Clearly another young Boro starlet to watch out for in the future, he came into the side for a couple of subs' appearances and will undoubtedly be in line for a step up this coming term.
Middlesbrough (From trainee on 1/7/95) PL 0+3

SUNDERLAND Jonathan (Jon) Paul
Born: Newcastle, 2 November 1975
Height: 6'0" Weight: 12.0

Having been released by Scarborough last December, following just two subs' appearances in 1996-97, the attacking midfielder joined Hartlepool on a non-contract basis at the recommendation of ex-Pool player, Mitch Cook. Made a dream debut for his new club when he scored just eight minutes after coming on as a substitute against Lincoln City, but, although he went on to have a short run in the first team, he was not able to match this spectacular start.

Blackpool (From trainee on 18/7/94) FL 0+2 Others 0+1
Scarborough (Free on 28/3/96) FL 3+5
Hartlepool U (Free on 20/12/96) FL 6+7/1

SUNDGOT Ole Bjorn
Born: Olsmund, Norway, 21 March 1972
Height: 6'1" Weight: 11.4
International Honours: Norway: 1

Having scored 65 goals in 110 games for Molde, while forming an outstanding partnership with Ole Gunnar Solskjaar, now at Manchester United, the out-of-contract Norwegian international striker decided it was time for change and signed for Bradford last November. Good in the air and comfortable on the ball, as you would expect, he made his debut in a 3-0 home defeat by Oldham, but soon settled to score both goals in a 2-1 home win over Ipswich. Unfortunately due for six weeks due to an operation for a double hernia, he was used more from the bench in the latter weeks of the campaign, but was always a threat.
Bradford C (Free from Molde on 1/11/96) FL 11+9/6

SUTCH Daryl
Born: Beccles, 11 September 1971
Height: 6'0" Weight: 12.0
International Honours: E: U21-4; Yth

A success story for Norwich saw Daryl carrying a consecutive 46-game run over to 1997-98. Comfortable when doing man-marking jobs, as he did against Trevor Sinclair and Chris Waddle, it took him six years to reach the milestone of 150 first-team games for City and, in doing so, he defied the season's plague of injury and disciplinary problems. With good pace, great engines, and improved in the air, he excelled in the left-sided wing-back slot, which is not really his position. Also wore eight different numbered shirts as City tried out various formations.
Norwich C (From trainee on 6/7/90) F/PL 92+33/6 FLC 9+3 FAC 6+2 Others 2+3

SUTHERLAND Colin
Born: Glasgow, 15 March 1975
Height: 5'11" Weight: 11.10

Colin is a strong and versatile defender who prefers the left-back role, but can also play centre back, or in midfield. Gave a string of impressive performances after being signed by Scarborough from Clydebank midway through last season, and quickly adapted to full-time football, having previously worked as a joiner, whilst playing part time in the Scottish League.
Clydebank (Free from Kilpatrick Juniors on 24/2/95) SL 42+1/2 SLC 2+1 SC 1 Others 3
Scarborough (Signed on 20/12/96) FL 17+4

SUTTON Christopher (Chris) Roy
Born: Nottingham, 10 March 1973
Height: 6'3" Weight: 13.5
Club Honours: PL '95
International Honours: E: B-2; U21-13

Following a season with little football, Chris was re-injured again during summer of 1996 and was late in starting 1996-97. By the time he was fully fit, Ray Harford had

disappeared and the caretaker manager, Tony Parkes, was asking him to play further upfield for Blackburn as a lone striker. For a time, in the middle of the campaign, he was in fine form, holding the ball up well and distributing it effectively. He also rediscovered his goal touch, but in February caught a virus that caused weight loss, followed by concussion on his return to action. Next it was a groin strain that kept him out, before he came back to become the centre of controversy at Arsenal where, following an injury to the Gunners' Steve Hughes, the ball was put out of play by his team mates and returned to them when play was restarted, only for Chris to quickly close down a defender to force a corner from which an equaliser was scored. The son of former pro, Mike, he can also play in defence, has skill in abundance, is useful in the air, has two good feet, and, strong and direct, knows where the goal is.

Norwich C (From trainee on 2/7/91) F/PL 89+13/35 FLC 8+1/3 FAC 10/5 Others 6
Blackburn Rov (£5,000,000 on 13/7/94) PL 73+5/26 FLC 8+1/5 FAC 4/2 Others 6+3/1

SUTTON Stephen (Steve) John
Born: Hartington, 16 April 1961
Height: 6'1" Weight: 14.11
Club Honours: FLC '89, '90; FMC '89
Signed from Derby during the 1996 close season, the highly experienced goalkeeper moved to Birmingham as cover for Ian Bennett and came into the side in November when the latter was injured, keeping five consecutive clean sheets in six games played. Although producing some fine reflex saves during that spell, and commanding the defence impressively, a broken finger allowed Bennett the chance to return and he took it with both hands. Later, Steve sustained a knee injury which not only ended his season, but also ended his career at St Andrews, City releasing him during the summer.

Nottingham F (From apprentice on 16/4/79) FL 199 FLC 33 FAC 14 Others 11
Mansfield T (Loaned on 10/3/81) FL 8
Derby Co (Loaned on 25/1/85) FL 14
Coventry C (Loaned on 1/2/91) FL 1
Luton T (Loaned on 28/11/91) FL 14
Derby Co (£300,000 on 6/3/92) FL 60+1 FLC 7 FAC 3 Others 11
Reading (Loaned on 19/1/96) FL 2
Birmingham C (Free on 16/8/96) FL 6

SUTTON Wayne Frank
Born: Derby, 1 October 1975
Height: 6'0" Weight: 13.10
Unable to obtain a Premiership opportunity at Derby for one reason or another in 1996-97, Wayne had a spell on loan at Hereford in September with a view to getting himself match fit in order to compete for a first-team place. Unfortunately, he joined the struggling third division club at a very bad time, making seven appearances and being on the winning side just once before returning to the Baseball Ground. An excellent tackler and ball winner who can play both in defence and midfield, he will undoubtedly be looking to make his mark this coming term.

Derby Co (From trainee on 27/10/92) FL 4+3 FAC 1
Hereford U (Loaned on 2/9/96) FL 4 FLC 2+1

SVENSSON Mathias
Born: Boras, Sweden, 24 September 1974
Height: 6'0" Weight: 12.4
International Honours: Sweden: 1
Bustling Swedish striker who seemingly came from nowhere to become a household name on the south coast after giving some great performances for Portsmouth in 1996-97. Having been spotted by the former England coach, Ted Buxton, Mathias joined Pompey midway through last term and soon got into the action, scoring twice on his full league debut and being sent off in his second game. He was also influential in helping the club to the quarter finals of the FA Cup, when turning a Leeds' defender and drilling his shot into bottom corner to put his new club on their way to the quarter finals. Unfortunately, his season ended abruptly when he was carried off unconscious after a collision with Tranmere's Andy Thorn at Fratton Park four games from the end of the campaign. He will be back, have no doubts.

Portsmouth (£200,000 from Elfsborg on 6/12/96) FL 17+2/6 FAC 2+1/1

SWAILES Christopher (Chris) William
Born: Gateshead, 19 October 1970
Height: 6'2" Weight: 12.11
If there was an award for the most improved player at Ipswich last season it would surely have gone to Chris, his performances at the end of the campaign bearing no resemblance to those of the previous term, and proving once again that the confidence gained from an extended run in the first team can do wonders. Playing in the last 20 games, during which time Town lost three times, he was part of the defence which set a club record of five successive clean sheets as the final run in approached, thus guaranteeing a place in the play offs. The tall central defender also found time to notch his first goal for the club, at Swindon, when he headed home Jamie Scowcroft's driven cross.

Ipswich T (From trainee on 23/5/89)
Peterborough U (£10,000 on 28/3/91 - Free to Boston in August 1991)
Doncaster Rov (Free from Bridlington T on 27/10/93) FL 49 FLC 2/1 FAC 1 Others 2
Ipswich T (£225,000 on 23/3/95) P/FL 27+1/1 FLC 2 Others 2

SWALES Stephen (Steve) Colin
Born: Whitby, 26 December 1973
Height: 5'8" Weight: 10.6
1996-97 was a rather disappointing second season for the young Reading full back, of whom great things were expected when he signed from Scarborough. A player with pace and good tackling ability, he never had an extended run in the first team, making only three appearances, all during December, and lacked the height and strength to establish a regular place in the side.

Scarborough (From trainee on 3/8/92) FL 51+3/1 FAC 5 Others 3
Reading (£70,000 on 13/7/95) FL 7+5 FLC 0+1 FAC 1

SWAN Peter Harold
Born: Leeds, 28 September 1966
Height: 6'2" Weight: 15.9
Club Honours: AMC '93
Out of favour at the start of last season, Peter returned in November and made a major impact, often being the dominant figure at the heart of Burnley's defence and always a big handful for opposing strikers. However, following a brief injury absence, he was unable to regain his place and thus missed out on what had looked like a strong challenge for Burnley's Player of the Year awards. Once a striker himself, he is always a danger at free kicks.

Leeds U (From trainee on 6/8/84) FL 43+6/11 FLC 3/2 FAC 3 Others 1+2
Hull C (£200,000 on 23/3/89) FL 76+4/24 FLC 2+3/1 FAC 2 Others 1
Port Vale (£300,000 on 16/8/91) FL 105+6/5 FLC 6 FAC 9/1 Others 12/1
Plymouth Arg (£300,000 on 22/7/94) FL 24+3/2 FLC 2/1 FAC 2
Burnley (£200,000 on 4/8/95) FL 47+2/7 FLC 2 FAC 3 Others 6

SYMONS Christopher (Kit) Jeremiah
Born: Basingstoke, 8 March 1971
Height: 6'2" Weight: 13.7
International Honours: W: 27; B-1; U21-2; Yth
Following on from his 100 per-cent record in 1995-96, Kit had yet another successful season for Manchester City in 1996-97. Appearance wise, his only blemish was in being sent off at Sheffield United in September for what many scribes reported as being an insignificant incident, which caused him to miss a match. His game as a strong central defender with few frills was a feature during the campaign and no more so when he had a strong aide of the likes of Alan Kernaghan and more recently, Paul Beesley, alongside him. A player who moves up for corners to add more pressure in the opponents penalty area, one of his main disappointments was in not finding the net after having several near misses by way of the woodwork. Still a regular member of the Welsh international team, playing in the qualifying games of the World Cup, he also has a skilful side to his game, especially when playing the ball out of defence to set up attacks.

Portsmouth (From trainee on 30/12/88) FL 161/10 FLC 19 FAC 10 Others 13+1/1
Manchester C (£1,600,000 on 17/8/95) P/FL 82/2 FLC 5 FAC 8

SYMONS Paul
Born: North Shields, 20 April 1976
Height: 5'11" Weight: 12.0
A pro since the 1994 close season, the young Blackpool striker made his first team debut in the AWS competition against Rotherham last December. Despite being one of three youngsters given their start that day, and impressing, Paul was freed during the summer.

Blackpool (From trainee on 18/7/94) Others 1

TAGGART Gerald (Gerry) Paul
Born: Belfast, 18 October 1970
Height: 6'1" Weight: 13.12
Club Honours: Div 1 '97
International Honours: NI: 42; U23-2; Yth; Sch

A rock-solid Bolton central defender whose excellence in 1996-97 culminated in automatic selection for the division one team of the season and saw him win a league medal at the same time, his no-nonsense style of play may have earned him a feared reputation as one of football's hard men, but his performances at the heart of the defence proved him to be an assured and proficient player. He also retained his place in the Northern Ireland team, scoring the goal which earned them a shock 1-1 draw in Germany in November. Always a danger from corners and set pieces, scoring four goals during the campaign, Gerry is certain to be a thorn in the side of many Premiership strikers this coming season. Recognised by his fellow professionals, he was elected to the PFA award-winning first division team.
Manchester C (From trainee on 1/7/89) FL 10+2/1 Others 1
Barnsley (£75,000 on 10/1/90) FL 209+3/16 FLC 15/1 FAC 14/2 Others 6/1
Bolton W (£1,500,000 on 1/8/95) F/PL 54/4 FLC 7/1 FAC 4

TAIT Michael (Mick) Paul
Born: Wallsend, 30 September 1956
Height: 5'11" Weight: 12.10
Club Honours: Div 3 '83, Div 4 '91; FMC '88

1996-97 was an eventful season that was not without its problems for Hartlepool's player/manager. As a manager, he achieved his main objective to keep the club in the Nationwide League and has now been rewarded with a longer contract. As a player, however, it was certainly a time when he achieved many personal milestones, playing Nationwide League football at 40, becoming the oldest player ever to play first-team football for Hartlepool, and appearing alongside his son, Lou, in the Hartlepool reserve team. He has now been playing first-team football for 23 seasons and has made 760 Football League appearances, the ninth highest aggregate of all time. Having retained his playing registration for 1997-98, there is every chance that the Nationwide League has not seen the last of this hard-tackling competitor.
Oxford U (From apprentice on 8/10/74) FL 61+3/23 FLC 2+1/1 FAC 2
Carlisle U (£65,000 on 3/2/77) FL 101+5/20 FLC 7 FAC 7/2
Hull C (£150,000 on 6/9/79) FL 29+4/3 FAC 1/1
Portsmouth (£100,000 on 11/6/80) FL 228+12/30 FLC 23+1/1 FAC 13/1 Others 2+1
Reading (£50,000 on 1/9/87) FL 98+1/9 FLC 9/2 FAC 16 Others 9/3
Darlington (Free on 3/8/90) FL 79/2 FLC 5 FAC 4 Others 3

Hartlepool U (Free on 31/7/92) FL 60+1/1 FLC 5/1 FAC 2 (Free to Gretna during 1994 close season)
Hartlepool U (Free on 9/9/94) FL 74+4/2 FLC 6 FAC 2 Others 1

TAIT Paul Ronald
Born: Sutton Coldfield, 31 July 1971
Height: 6'1" Weight: 10.10
Club Honours: Div 2 '95; AMC '95

A product of Birmingham's youth set up, Paul produced some of his best football last season, combining good touches and vision in midfield with a combative nature, before being dropped after Christmas and demanding a transfer. Eventually came off the list to get back into the side and agreed a new contract, which included a testimonial on him reaching ten years at St Andrews this coming term. Now City's longest-serving player, he always gives 100 per-cent effort and when fully fit is a tremendous asset for the club.
Birmingham C (From trainee on 2/8/88) FL 135+35/14 FLC 13+2 FAC 6+2 Others 13+5/4

TALBOT Stuart
Born: Birmingham, 14 June 1973
Height: 5'10" Weight: 11.0

This strong-running Port Vale midfield player was deployed mainly away from home as the team operated a successful 4-5-1 formation in 1996-97, his bursts through the middle helping to support the lone striker, and he ended the campaign with four goals. Although often back on the subs' bench at home, when two strikers played, he was a very important member of the squad and attracted more than a passing interest from Premiership clubs. Won the Young Player of the Year award for last season.
Port Vale (Signed from Moor Green on 10/8/94) FL 35+21/4 FLC 0+3 FAC 2+1 Others 2+3/1

TALBOYS Steven (Steve) John
Born: Bristol, 18 September 1966
Height: 5'10" Weight: 11.10

A free-transfer signing from Wimbledon during the summer of 1996, Steve made four appearances early in 1996-97 but, unable to command a first team place, was later transfer listed. With plenty of stamina and skill, he is a left winger who, in past seasons, has proved adept at crossing and getting into good shooting positions.
Wimbledon (£10,000 from Gloucester C on 10/1/92) PL 19+7/1 FLC 2+1 FAC 1+1
Watford (Free on 25/7/96) FL 2+1 FLC 0+1

TALIA Francesco (Frank)
Born: Melbourne, Australia, 20 July 1972
Height: 6'1" Weight: 13.6
Club Honours: Div 2 '96

Started last season as first-choice 'keeper for Swindon Town and held his place until late October when a calamitous display at home to West Bromwich gifted the visitors two long-range goals and the points. Thereafter having to play second fiddle to the evergreen Fraser Digby, he was out of contract during the summer and was transfer listed after refusing improved terms. Is extremely agile and a good shot stopper who comes out for crosses well.

Blackburn Rov (Free from Sunshine George Cross on 28/8/92)
Hartlepool U (Loaned on 29/12/92) FL 14 Others 1
Swindon T (£150,000 on 8/9/95) FL 31 FLC 5

TALLON Gerrit (Gary) Thomas
Born: Drogheda, 5 September 1973
Height: 5'10" Weight: 12.7

A former Blackburn player, Gary went on loan to Chester last March with a view to a permanent transfer from Kilmarnock, making just one appearance, his Football League debut at home to Brighton. Naturally left footed and skilful, he would have hoped for more opportunities to show the City fans what he could really do.
Blackburn Rov (£30,000 from Drogheda U on 27/11/91)
Kilmarnock (Free on 20/6/96) SL 4 SLC 1
Chester C (Loaned on 26/3/97) FL 1

TANKARD Allen John
Born: Fleet, 21 May 1969
Height: 5'10" Weight: 11.7

Once again Port Vale's regular left back, missing only a handful of games in 1996-97, all through injury, Allen was the bane of many an opposing right winger and his excellent positional sense went a long way to helping the club to one of their highest positions in over 60 years. Managed to get on the scoresheet just the once, at Grimsby Town in January, his third strike in four years at Vale Park and his first away from home. Has excellent pace for a defender.
Southampton (From apprentice on 27/5/87) FL 5 Others 2
Wigan Ath (Free on 4/7/88) FL 205+4/4 FLC 15/1 FAC 13 Others 20
Port Vale (£87,500 on 26/7/93) FL 126+5/2 FLC 14 FAC 11/1 Others 8+1

TANNER Adam David
Born: Maldon, 25 October 1973
Height: 6'0" Weight: 12.1

Once again, Adam only had limited opportunities to play in the Ipswich first team in 1996-97, mainly because of the competition for places, and when he did get in it was in central defence as a result of an injury crisis, rather than in his favoured midfield role. His best run in the team was in December, when he also took on penalty responsibilities in Steve Sedgley's absence, but it all fell apart when he tested positive for cocaine and was suspended for three months by the FA. However, the club stood by him and he received a great reception from the fans when he came on as substitute in the final league game against Birmingham. Adept at hitting long passes to the front men, he has an excellent touch for one so big.
Ipswich T (From trainee on 13/7/92) P/FL 22+14/6 FLC 1 FAC 2 Others 3+1/1

TARICCO Mauricio Ricardo
Born: Buenos Aires, Argentine, 10 March 1973
Height: 5'9" Weight: 11.7
International Honours: Argentine: U23

Mauricio was probably the most consistent player in the Ipswich team during 1996-97 and had a tremendous season, culminating

in him being voted the supporters' Player of the Year by a huge margin - receiving over 75 per cent of the votes cast. Although naturally right footed, he made the left-wing back position his own, his combination play with Paul Mason down the left side being a major part of Town's attacking play. Having scored his first goal for the club against Reading in August with a diving header, he then got the winner in the victory at Stoke, before opening the scoring in the local derby against Norwich with a lovely low shot curled round the 'keeper.

Ipswich T (£175,000 from Argentinos on 9/9/94) FL 77+3/3 FLC 8 FAC 4 Others 5

TATE Craig David
Born: South Shields, 16 October 1979
Height: 5'11" Weight: 10.7

A first year trainee, having only joined Shrewsbury during the 1996 close season, the young striker obviously created quite an impression because he was asked to sit on the bench for the club's final game of the campaign at Gillingham. An exciting prospect, and one of Town's youngest ever first teamers, he came on for the last ten minutes and will undoubtedly be looking for further opportunities in 1997-98.

Shrewsbury T (Trainee) FL 0+1

TAYLOR Gareth Keith
Born: Weston super Mare, 25 February 1973
Height: 6'2" Weight: 12.5
International Honours: W: 6; U21-7

A Sheffield United striker who formed a good understanding with both Andy Walker and Petr Katchouro, Gareth was a regular at the start of last season, before the signing of Jan-Aage Fjortoft led to the loss of his first-team place. Although an injury towards the end of the campaign limited his opportunities, despite the difficulties he retained his place in the Welsh squad, adding to his tally of caps. An excellent targetman, he managed to find the net on 12 occasions, while his sheer physical presence always created problems for opponents.

Bristol Rov (Free from Southampton juniors on 29/7/91) FL 31+16/16 FLC 3+1 FAC 1+1 Others 5
Crystal Palace (£750,000 on 27/9/95) FL 18+2/1 FAC 2/1
Sheffield U (Signed on 8/3/96) FL 36+8/13 FLC 4/1 Others 0+2

TAYLOR Ian Kenneth
Born: Birmingham, 4 June 1968
Height: 6'1" Weight: 12.4
Club Honours: AMC '93; FLC '96

Showed himself to be a very versatile performer for Aston Villa last season when, as well as standing out in his normal midfield role, he also stood in at full back and as back up at centre back. With the club using the wing-back system, it helped in his switch to full back as it gave him the chance to continue with his attacking play. Suffered with a series of niggling injuries, his worst meant missing seven games, but, other than that, he was a regular in the team, even if a few of his early games were as a sub. Always a workhorse, he is one of the unsung heroes of the side.

Port Vale (£15,000 from Moor Green on 13/7/92) FL 83/28 FLC 4/2 FAC 6/1 Others 13/4
Sheffield Wed (£1,000,000 on 12/7/94) PL 9+5/1 FLC 2+2/1
Aston Villa (£1,000,000 on 21/12/94) PL 75+6/6 FLC 7+1/2 FAC 4+1/1 Others 1

TAYLOR Jamie Lee
Born: Bury, 11 January 1977
Height: 5'6" Weight: 9.12

In his fourth season with Rochdale, though still only 20, Jamie had to wait until last April before adding to his first-team appearances as a substitute in a couple of games. A hard-working striker, he was again a regular scorer for the reserves, skippering them to the Pontins League division three championship, before being released during the summer.

Rochdale (From trainee on 12/1/94) FL 10+26/4 FLC 0+1 Others 1+2/1

TAYLOR John Patrick
Born: Norwich, 24 October 1964
Height: 6'3" Weight: 13.12
Club Honours: Div 3 '91

Not involved in team selection at Luton in 1996-97, the veteran striker had a period on loan at Lincoln in September, after an earlier attempt to bring him to Sincil Bank permanently had failed. Made an excellent start, scoring against Cardiff, and ended his five-match spell with another versus Scarborough prior to returning to Town and going out on another temporary transfer, this time to Colchester in November. Again, he got on the scoresheet with five goals in nine games, including two consecutive doubles at Chester and at Layer Road against Lincoln, who must have wished they had kept him following a 7-1 defeat. Finally, at the turn of the year, he signed for another old club, Cambridge, adding vital experience to the forward line, while playing in every remaining game and taking his club tally to 50.

Colchester U (From juniors on 17/12/82)
Cambridge U (Signed from Sudbury T on 24/8/88) FL 139+21/46 FLC 9+2/2 FAC 21/10 Others 12+2/2
Bristol Rov (Signed on 28/3/92) FL 91+4/44 FLC 4/1 FAC 3 Others 5
Bradford C (£300,000 on 5/7/94) FL 35+1/11 FLC 4/2 FAC 2 Others 3
Luton T (£200,000 on 23/3/95) FL 27+10/3 FLC 2 Others 1/1
Lincoln C (Loaned on 27/9/96) FL 5/2
Colchester U (Loaned on 8/11/96) FL 8/5 Others 1
Cambridge U (Free on 10/1/97) FL 18+2/4

TAYLOR Lee Vincent
Born: Hammersmith, 24 February 1976
Height: 5'11" Weight: 12.0

Signed on the eve of last season from non-league Southwark Faweh, one week he was working for Marks and Spencers, the next making his league debut for Shrewsbury in the opening game of 1996-97 at full back. Looking comfortable on the ball, despite inexperience, Lee also operated in central defence quite effectively, especially later on. A good prospect, 1997-98 cannot come soon enough for him.

Shrewsbury T (Free from Southwark Faweh on 14/8/96) FL 13+3 FLC 2

TAYLOR Maik Stefan
Born: Germany, 4 September 1971
Height: 6'5" Weight: 13.8

Ever present for Barnet in 1996-97, making 33 appearances while keeping 13 clean sheets, this imposing goalkeeper caught the eye of Graeme Souness at the beginning of January and immediately went into a Southampton side who were among the favourites to be relegated from the Premiership. That he did so well, especially when you realise that he was playing non-league football just 18 months earlier, had to be partly down to the personal coaching he had received at Barnet under the former England goalie, Ray Clemence. Maintaining his place at the Dell, despite the challenges of Dave Beasant and Neil Moss, and proving to have safe hands and sound positional sense, he contributed enormously to calming a nervous defence that ultimately avoided the drop. Is also a great shot stopper.

Barnet (Free from Farnborough on 7/6/95) FL 70 FLC 6 FAC 6 Others 2
Southampton (£500,000 on 1/1/97) PL 18

TAYLOR Martin James
Born: Tamworth, 9 December 1966
Height: 6'0" Weight: 13.6

Long-serving Derby goalkeeper whose absence from the game with a broken leg sustained in 1995 resulted in his being second choice to Russell Hoult in 1996-97. Played on loan at Crewe and Wycombe in mid term before finally returning to the first team for the FA Cup quarter final with Middlesbrough, where he played well enough to keep his place for a further two games before the signing of Mart Poom signalled the end of his County career and saw him released during the summer. A shot stopper who gets down well, and noted for penalty saves, Martin kept two clean sheets in his six games at Crewe, and three in four at Wycombe, where he impressed the locals with spectacular saves and cool handling. *Stop Press:* Was reported to have signed on a permanent basis for Wanderers in June.

Derby Co (Signed from Mile Oak Rov on 2/7/86) F/PL 97 FLC 7 FAC 5 Others 11
Carlisle U (Loaned on 23/9/87) FL 10 FLC 1 FAC 1 Others 2
Scunthorpe U (Loaned on 17/12/87) FL 8
Crewe Alex (Loaned on 20/9/96) FL 6
Wycombe W (Loaned on 27/3/97) FL 4

TAYLOR Robert (Bob)
Born: Horden, 3 February 1967
Height: 5'10" Weight: 12.0

Bob was not his usual self in the goalscoring stakes in 1996-97, although he still managed to find the net at vital times. Injuries and loss of form, however, meant that he missed a fair proportion of games, but, nevertheless, when on the park he was always a handful for defenders, heading two great goals in a 3-2 win at Birmingham. Strong, and powerful, both on the ground and in the air, he also skippered the team on occasions.

Leeds U (Free from Horden Colliery on 27/3/86) FL 33+9/9 FLC 5+1/3 FAC 1 Others 4+1/1
Bristol C (£175,000 on 23/3/89) FL 96+10/50 FLC 6+1/2 FAC 9+1/5 Others 3/1
West Bromwich A (£300,000 on 31/1/92) FL 200+23/94 FLC 13/5 FAC 6+2/3 Others 16+3/8

Bob Taylor (West Bromwich Albion)

Robert Taylor (Brentford)

TAYLOR Robert Anthony
Born: Norwich, 30 April 1971
Height: 6'1" Weight: 13.8

Brentford striker. A target man with deft flicks from both head and feet, and a good passer of the ball, his goals scored in 1996-97 were down on previous seasons due partially to the fact that he played part of the campaign in a withdrawn Teddy Sheringham-type position behind the main strikers. Scored the fastest ever Golden Goal in the home AWS tie against Barnet after 15 seconds of extra time and also struck twice in both play-off semi finals.

Norwich C (From trainee on 26/3/90)
Leyton Orient (Loaned on 28/3/91) FL 0+3/1
Birmingham C (Signed on 31/8/91)
Leyton Orient (Free on 21/10/91) FL 54+19/20 FLC 1+1 FAC 2+1 Others 2+1
Brentford (£100,000 on 24/3/94) FL 133/43 FLC 12/3 FAC 9/6 Others 13/4

TAYLOR Robert Mark
Born: Birmingham, 22 February 1966
Height: 5'9" Weight: 12.5
Club Honours: Div 3 '94

By his standards, 1996-97 was not his best. Usually a strong midfield influence for Shrewsbury, there were games when he struggled to reach his normal high standards and it is said that when Mark plays well so does the whole side. However, his creative ability continued to be a constant threat and his crosses from the tightest positions on the byline always caused danger.

Walsall (From trainee on 24/7/84) FL 100+13/4 FLC 7+1 FAC 3+4 Others 10
Sheffield Wed (£50,000 on 22/6/89) FL 8+1 FLC 2
Shrewsbury T (£70,000 on 13/9/91) FL 246+4/15 FLC 17 FAC 16 Others 16+2/3

TAYLOR Scott Dean
Born: Portsmouth, 28 November 1970
Height: 5'9" Weight: 11.5
Club Honours: Div 2 '94; FLC '97

A right-footed Leicester midfielder with energy to spare, Scott was not always first choice in 1996-97, often losing out to the greatly experienced Garry Parker. He started well though, in helping to get City off to a solid start on their return to the Premiership, before losing a little confidence, especially in front of goal. A lot of the problem was caused by a long-term knee injury and, having appeared as a sub at Wembley in the Coca-Cola Cup final against Middlesbrough, Scott missed the replay as he had already been booked in for an operation. Hopefully, he will return in fighting form for the coming season.

Reading (From trainee on 22/6/89) FL 164+43/24 FLC 7+5/1 FAC 11+2/3 Others 12+4/1
Leicester C (£250,000 on 12/7/95) P/FL 59+5/6 FLC 7+3 FAC 2+1 Others 3

TAYLOR Scott James
Born: Chertsey, 5 May 1976
Height: 5'10" Weight: 11.4

A highly talented young Bolton striker, who is certainly a name for the future, Scott failed to make many first-team appearances last season, due to the lethal combination of Nathan Blake and John McGinlay, but he scored consistently in the reserves and

proved to be competent when replacing one of the main front men from the bench. He showed this to good effect when coming on for John McGinlay late on and scoring one of the goals in the 6-1 thrashing of Spurs in the Coca-Cola Cup fourth round tie in November. Although one game short of winning a first division championship medal, the disappointment will fade away once into Premiership action in 1997-98. Was also selected for the Nationwide League U21s against the Italian Serie "B" equivalent in February.

Millwall (£15,000 from Staines on 8/2/95) FL 13+15 FLC 0+2/2 FAC 1+1
Bolton W (£150,000 on 29/3/96) P/FL 2+10/1 FLC 0+3/1 FAC 1/1

TAYLOR Shaun

Born: Plymouth, 26 February 1963
Height: 6'1" Weight: 13.0
Club Honours: Div 4 '90; Div 2 '96

The signing of this inspirational central defender from Swindon Town early last September was a master stroke by Bristol City manager, Joe Jordan. Described as a "lion-hearted defender" by the Swindon contributor the previous season, the City fans had no reason to disagree with that statement and it was fitting that Shaun won the Supporters' Player of the Year award to add to three similar awards achieved at the County Ground. His game is all about commitment and if others follow his example then the promotion prize should be achievable in 1997-98.

Exeter C (Free from Bideford T on 10/12/86) FL 200/16 FLC 12 FAC 9 Others 12
Swindon T (£200,000 on 26/7/91) F/PL 212/30 FLC 22+1/2 FAC 14 Others 10/1
Bristol C (£50,000 + on 6/9/96) FL 29/1 FAC 3 Others 3

TEALE Shaun

Born: Southport, 10 March 1964
Height: 6'0" Weight: 14.2
Club Honours: FLC '94
International Honours: E: SP-1

Although an ever present at centre half for Tranmere until the turn of last year, Shaun was dropped for the first game of 1997, and never regained his place. Following that, he spent a month on loan at Preston North End in January and, on his return to Prenton Park, was made available for transfer. However, he remains an uncompromising and tough central defender who would be a steadying influence on any side.

Bournemouth (£50,000 from Weymouth on 22/1/89) FL 99+1/4 FLC 8 FAC 5/1 Others 3
Aston Villa (£300,000 on 25/7/91) F/PL 146+1/2 FLC 15/3 FAC 13 Others 6
Tranmere Rov (£450,000 on 14/8/95) FL54 FLC 8
Preston NE (Loaned on 6/2/97) FL 5

TELFER Paul Norman

Born: Edinburgh, 21 October 1971
Height: 5'9" Weight: 11.6
International Honours: S: B-2; U21-3

Paul had a much improved season for Coventry in 1996-97 and began to justify his large fee, being used as either a right-sided midfield player or, when the system was changed, as a right-wing back, a role he adapted well to. However, in the latter role

he was unable to get as many crosses in, part of his game which is very strong, and on the goalscoring front he netted within three minutes of each other at Gillingham in the Coca-Cola Cup. Is an aggressive ball winner with good distribution.

Luton T (From trainee on 7/11/88) FL 136+8/19 FLC 5 FAC 14/2 Others 2/1
Coventry C (£1,500,000 on 11/7/95) PL 62+3/1 FLC 8/2 FAC 7/1

TEN HEUVEL Laurens

Born: Amsterdam, Holland, 6 June 1976
Height: 6'0" Weight: 12.3

Three subs' appearances gave Barnsley fans only a fleeting glimpse of this highly promising young striker in 1996-97. As the leading scorer for the reserves, Laurens was unlucky in that the established first teamers remained injury free, thus denying him the chance he craved, and he will be undoubtedly looking for more opportunities when the Premiership action gets underway in 1997-98. Is a player who likes the ball to feet and enjoys the passing game.

Barnsley (£75,000 from FC Den Bosch on 12/3/96) FL 1+5

THACKERAY Andrew (Andy) John

Born: Huddersfield, 13 February 1968
Height: 5'9" Weight: 11.0
Club Honours: FAYC '86

The former Rochdale skipper lost his right-back spot to new signing Andy Fensome in 1996-97, but after some months in the shadows reappeared in the first team, playing in midfield. Unfortunately, after switching to the jinxed left-back spot, he followed Wayne Dowell and Dave Bayliss onto the injured list. Released during the summer, this reliable defender also enjoys the attacking side of the game.

Manchester C (From juniors on 15/2/86)
Huddersfield T (Free on 1/8/86) FL 2 Others 0+1
Newport Co (£5,000 on 27/3/87) FL 53+1/4 FLC 3+1 FAC 1 Others 2+1/1
Wrexham (£5,000 on 20/7/88) FL 139+13/14 FLC 10/1 FAC 6 Others 13+2
Rochdale (£15,000 on 15/7/92) FL 161+4/13 FLC 8+1 FAC 7+1/1 Others 10+3/2

THATCHER Benjamin (Ben) David

Born: Swindon, 30 November 1975
Height: 5'10" Weight: 12.7
International Honours: E: U21-3; Yth

Signed from Millwall during the 1996 close season after debating whether to join the Dons or Leicester, Ben is an intelligent defender who can read a dangerous situation well and cope with it in a cool and calculated way. Made a good start to last season, playing for both Wimbledon and the England U21 side in the opening weeks, before picking up an ankle injury that ultimately kept him out for the rest of the campaign. A player that you can always rely on to tackle with precision, and one who is also comfortable in the air, hopefully, he is fully recovered to give it his best shot in 1997-98.

Millwall (From trainee on 8/6/92) FL 87+3/1 FLC 6 FAC 7 Others 1
Wimbledon (£1,840,000 on 5/7/96) PL 9

THIRLBY Anthony (Tony) Dennis

Born: Berlin, Germany, 4 March 1976
Height: 5'9" Weight: 11.5
International Honours: NI: Yth

Following on from one injury after another, Tony was released by Exeter during the 1996 close season and found his way to Torquay on non-contract terms last February, via non-league football. A constructive, creative midfielder at his best, he was given just three games, two of them as a sub, before moving on in March.

Exeter C (From trainee on 4/7/94) FL 27+12/2 FLC 2+2 Others 1 (Released during 1996 close season)
Torquay U (Free from Bideford on 14/2/97) FL 1+2

THOMAS Anthony (Tony)

Born: Liverpool, 12 July 1971
Height: 5'11" Weight: 13.0
Club Honours: AMC '90

Playing for Tranmere throughout 1996-97 on a week-to-week contract, "Thomas the Tank", as he is known, still turned in a number of assured and creative performances for the club. Although his appearances in the first half of the season were few and far between, Tony was an ever present in 1997, playing in either of the full-back positions with increasing composure and competence. It is to be hoped that this provider of such dangerous crosses will have signed a long-term contract with the Prenton Park outfit during the close season.

Tranmere Rov (From trainee on 1/2/89) FL 254+3/12 FLC 23+1/1 FAC 7 Others 26/1

THOMAS David (Dai) John

Born: Caerphilly, 26 September 1975
Height: 5'10" Weight: 11.7

A strong Swansea front runner, who had worked hard during the summer to improve his skill level, Dai came to the fore last season as a first-team regular with ten goals to his credit after scoring the opening goal of the new campaign against Rochdale. Sent off against Barnet at the Vetch and booked for giving a "Ravanelli" impression after scoring, he will, no doubt, be aiming to channel his aggression into goals in 1997-98.

Swansea C (From trainee on 25/7/94) FL 36+20/10 FLC 2 FAC 0+1 Others 5+3/3

THOMAS Geoffrey (Geoff) Robert

Born: Manchester, 5 August 1964
Height: 6'1" Weight: 13.2
Club Honours: FMC '91
International Honours: E: 9; B-3

Wolves badly needed the sort of midfield dynamo Geoff used to be when he came on as a sub in November, and after three years of knee operations and setbacks he played at Crystal Palace the next weekend, heading the winner in fairy-tale fashion. Stayed in the side until January, but could not command a regular place from then on, although, towards the end of the season became more involved, partly due to Neil Emblen's absence. Crowned his comeback with a measured pass to Mark Atkins that set up a play-off goal and gave Wolves a chance of promotion, before being released in the summer.

Rochdale (Free from Littleborough on 13/8/82) FL 10+1/1 Others 0+1
Crewe Alex (Free on 22/3/84) FL 120+5/20 FLC 8 FAC 2 Others 2+1
Crystal Palace (£50,000 on 8/6/87) F/PL 192+3/26 FLC 24/3 FAC 13+1/2 Others 15+1/4
Wolverhampton W (£800,000 on 18/6/93) FL 36+10/8 FLC 1 FAC 1 Others 2

THOMAS Glen Andrew
Born: Hackney, 6 October 1967
Height: 6'1" Weight: 13.3
Able to play in the centre of Gillingham's defence or at left back, Glen made just a handful of appearances last season. Due to play at Ipswich in the fourth round of the Coca-Cola Cup, during training earlier that day, he fell and a branch of a tree nearly blinded him in one eye. Lucky not to lose his sight, hopefully, he can pick up where he left off.
Fulham (From apprentice on 9/10/85) FL 246+5/6 FLC 21 FAC 8 Others 14+1
Peterborough U (Free on 4/11/94) FL 6+2 FAC 0+1 Others 2
Barnet (Free on 23/3/95) FL 22+1 FLC 2 Others 1
Gillingham (£30,000 on 15/1/96) FL 18+7 FAC 1 Others 1

THOMAS Martin Russell
Born: Lymington, 12 September 1973
Height: 5'8" Weight: 11.4
As a wide or central midfielder, Martin's Fulham appearances in 1996-97 were restricted mostly to coming off the subs' bench, due to changed tactics (using wing backs) and the signing of two central midfielders. As committed as ever, he was often brought on to add a fresh pair of legs and to either protect a lead or to go for a winner.
Southampton (From trainee on 19/6/92)
Leyton Orient (Free on 24/3/94) FL 5/2
Fulham (Free on 21/7/94) FL 59+27/8 FLC 6+1 FAC 4/1 Others 5

THOMAS Michael Lauriston
Born: Lambeth, 24 August 1967
Height: 5'10" Weight: 12.4
Club Honours: FLC '87, 95; Div 1 '89, '91; CS '91; FAC '92
International Honours: E: 2; B-5; U21-12; Yth; Sch
Establishing himself in Liverpool's midfield at the beginning of last season following a series of outstanding performances, Michael took the eye with his strong running and powerful tackling. Often involved in the side's attacking movements, his great stamina allowing him to run at defenders to open up space for the more lethal finishers such as Robbie Fowler and Stan Collymore, he also found time to score three times himself, including the winner at West Ham. As in the past, an unsung hero at Anfield, it is his running off the ball that impresses people in the game and 1996-97 was no exception.
Arsenal (From apprentice on 31/12/84) FL 149+14/24 FLC 21+2/5 FAC 14+3/1 Others 5+2/1
Portsmouth (Loaned on 30/12/86) FL 3
Liverpool (£1,500,000 on 16/12/91) F/PL 86+27/8 FLC 6+3/1 FAC 15+2/2 Others 9+2

THOMAS Mitchell Anthony
Born: Luton, 2 October 1964
Height: 6'2" Weight: 13.0
International Honours: E: B-1; U21-3; Yth
After a difficult season in 1995-96, the Luton left back enjoyed a tremendous campaign last season, benefiting from playing in a more organised defence that allowed him to exploit his attacking qualities. He missed only a handful of matches through injury and relished his forays upfield, which resulted in three goals for himself and a contribution in many more. Although now in the veteran stage of his career, his height, strength, and experience, equip him well for soccer at this level and he should be capable of frustrating attackers and terrorising defenders for some time to come.
Luton T (From apprentice on 27/8/82) FL 106+1/1 FLC 5 FAC 18
Tottenham H (£233,000 on 7/7/86) FL 136+21/6 FLC 28+1/1 FAC 12/1
West Ham U (£525,000 on 7/8/91) FL 37+1/3 FLC 5 FAC 4 Others 2
Luton T (Free on 12/11/93) FL 117+8/4 FLC 7+1 FAC 6 Others 3+1

THOMAS Roderick (Rod) Clive
Born: Brent, 10 October 1970
Height: 5'6" Weight: 11.0
Club Honours: FAYC '89; Div 3 '95; AMC '97
International Honours: E: U21-1; Yth; Sch
In what proved to be his last season at Carlisle, having come to the end of his contract, this talented ball player continued to operate on the right flank at the start of 1996-97, but spent much of the latter part of the campaign on the substitutes' bench. On his day, a man who can open up any defence, he scored just three goals, all in cup competitions, including a double strike in the second leg of the Coca-Cola Cup at home to Port Vale, a game which, although ending at 2-2, saw the visitors go through on aggregate.
Watford (From trainee on 3/5/88) FL 63+21/9 FLC 3+2 FAC 0+1 Others 3+1
Gillingham (Loaned on 27/3/92) FL 8/1 Others 1
Carlisle U (Free on 12/7/93) FL 124+22/16 FLC 11+1/3 FAC 9+4 Others 22+4/9

THOMAS Wayne
Born: Walsall, 28 August 1978
Height: 5'11" Weight: 11.10
Having come through Walsall's junior ranks as a trainee to sign pro forms during the 1996 close season, Wayne had two spells in midfield at Bescot, his constructive ability and use of the telling long ball belying his years. His should be very much a name to look out for in the future.
Walsall (From trainee on 25/7/96) FL 14+6 FAC 2

THOMAS Wayne Junior Robert
Born: Gloucester, 17 May 1979
Height: 5'11" Weight: 11.12
Still a Torquay YTS player, having made his first team debut in 1995-96, Wayne can play in a variety of positions (including goal-keeper) and looks to be a very bright prospect. Obviously still growing, central defence probably looks to be his best bet.
Torquay U (Trainee) FL 2+16 Others 0+1

THOMPSON Alan
Born: Newcastle, 22 December 1973
Height: 6'0" Weight: 12.8
Club Honours: Div 1 '97
International Honours: E: U21-2; Yth
The brilliant Bolton midfielder would have undoubtedly played a full season in 1996-97 had injury and suspension not taken their toll in mid term. Supremely confident on the ball, and possessing one of the most lethal shots in English football, as demonstrated by his stunning late winner in the televised game against QPR at the beginning of the campaign, Alan's top-class performances allegedly attracted attention from a host of big names clubs, including Leeds and Nottingham Forest, although it is likely that the Wanderers will want to hold on to one of their star names. Came back with a bang to play in the final 11 league games, scoring four times, as the club stormed to the first division championship and Premier League football in 1997-98. Another honour came his way when he was elected by his fellow professionals to the PFA award-winning first division side.
Newcastle U (From trainee on 11/3/91) FL 13+3 FAC 1 Others 3
Bolton W (£250,000 on 22/7/93) P/FL 110+14/25 FLC 20+1/4 FAC 5+2/2 Others 7+1/1

THOMPSON Andrew (Andy) Richard
Born: Cannock, 9 November 1967
Height: 5'4" Weight: 10.11
Club Honours: Div 4 '88, Div 3 '89; AMC '88
The small, tenacious full back's popularity at Wolves was underlined by the fact that almost 24,000 watched his pre-1996-97 season testimonial with Chelsea. When the serious football began, however, he was given a role in midfield, where he had started his Wanderers' career, but having converted two penalties in September, Andy was hurt in training the following month, a small tear in his patella tendon being revealed. Although returning six weeks later in a more customary defensive role, he was in and out of the team from then on. *Stop Press:* Freed during the summer, it was reported that he had joined Tranmere.
West Bromwich A (From apprentice on 16/11/85) FL 18+6/1 FLC 0+1 FAC 2 Others 1+1
Wolverhampton W (£35,000 on 21/11/86) FL 356+20/43 FLC 22 FAC 20/1 Others 33/1

THOMPSON David Anthony
Born: Birkenhead, 12 September 1977
Height: 5'7" Weight: 10.0
Club Honours: FAYC '96
International Honours: E: U21-2; Yth
A tenacious, hard-working livewire of a central midfielder, and almost two years a professional, David started his first-team career at Liverpool last August when coming off the bench at Anfield against Arsenal (87th minute) and Sunderland (85th minute). With just eight minutes of Premiership football behind him you could hardly say that had arrived, but in that short time he showed himself to have a great deal of commitment to the cause and a strong tackler. Selected twice for the England U21 side, and a regular in the reserves, this

enthusiastic youngster is desperate for a run in the side to show what he can do at a higher level.

Liverpool (From trainee on 8/11/94) PL 0+2

THOMPSON David (Dave) George
Born: Ashington, 20 November 1968
Height: 6'3" Weight: 13.2

The tall Cambridge central defender had a disappointing season in 1996-97, when, after being ever present for the first two months, he was kept out of the first team by the Jody Craddock/Danny Granville defensive pairing, before a thigh strain then put him out of action for the second half of the campaign. Good in the air, he matches that with determination and strong tackling.

Millwall (From apprentice on 26/11/86) FL 88+9/6 FLC 4 FAC 4/1 Others 6
Bristol C (Signed on 18/6/92) FL 17 FLC 4 Others 5+1
Brentford (Free on 1/2/94) FL 9+1/1
Blackpool (Signed on 9/9/94) FL 17 FAC 1 Others 2
Cambridge U (Free on 23/3/95) FL 36+8/2 FLC 4/1 FAC 0+2

THOMPSON David (Dave) Stephen
Born: Manchester, 27 May 1962
Height: 5'10" Weight: 12.10

A useful member of the Rochdale squad in 1996-97, the veteran wing man was a virtually permanent substitute before injury ruled him out of the last couple of months of the season and led to his release during the summer. Only the fourth player to pass 250 league games for Dale, at his best he can run defenders silly.

Rochdale (Free from North Withington on 26/9/81) FL 147+8/13 FLC 7 FAC 7+1 Others 6
Notts Co (£70,000 on 22/8/86) FL 52+3/8 FLC 3+1 FAC 3 Others 2
Wigan Ath (£35,000 on 20/10/87) FL 107+1/14 FLC 5/2 FAC 3+1 Others 6/1
Preston NE (£77,500 on 1/8/90) FL 39+7/4 FLC 1+1 Others 3+1
Chester C (Free on 14/8/92) FL 70+10/9 FLC 4 FAC 5 Others 4
Rochdale (£6,000 on 8/8/94) FL 90+21/11 FLC 4+2 FAC 4+1 Others 10+1

THOMPSON Garry Linsey
Born: Birmingham, 7 October 1959
Height: 6'2" Weight: 14.6
Club Honours: FMC '91
International Honours: E: U21-6

As Northampton's player/coach, Garry was not expected to make many appearances in 1996-97, especially when coming up to 38 years of age and having had almost 20 years in the game. At his best a good old-fashioned striker who unsettled defenders and was strong in the air, following an 11th minute stint from the bench against Leyton Orient in September, he was not called upon again and was released during the summer.

Coventry C (From apprentice on 29/6/77) FL 127+7/38 FLC 12+1/7 FAC 11/4
West Bromwich A (£225,000 on 17/2/83) FL 91/39 FLC 9/5 FAC 5/1
Sheffield Wed (£450,000 on 12/8/85) FL 35+1/7 FLC 2+1/1 FAC 5/1
Aston Villa (£450,000 on 5/6/86) FL 56+4/17 FLC 6/2 FAC 4 Others 3
Watford (£325,000 on 24/12/88) FL 24+10/8 FLC 0+1 FAC 7+1

Crystal Palace (£200,000 on 24/3/90) FL 17+3/3 FLC 0+1/1 Others 0+1
Queens Park R (£125,000 on 19/8/91) F/PL 10+9/1 FLC 3+2/3 Others 1
Cardiff C (Free on 15/7/93) FL 39+4/5 FLC 2 FAC 5+2/1 Others 6+3/3
Northampton T (Signed on 10/2/95) FL 36+14/6 FLC 0+2 Others 0+1

THOMPSON Neil
Born: Beverley, 2 October 1963
Height: 5'11" Weight: 13.7
Club Honours: GMVC '87; Div 2 '92
International Honours: E: SP-4

Signed on a free from Ipswich during the 1996 close season, Neil quickly settled in at left-wing back for Barnsley in 1996-97, his cultured left foot being the source of many attacks. Despite suffering from a number of niggling injuries during the campaign, when fit his presence in the team was always marked and he also scored a number of vital goals, including two in a 4-0 home win over Charlton in April. On his way back to the Premiership after a two year absence, he took over the Reds' penalty duties following Neil Redfearn's abdication.

Hull C (Free from Nottingham F juniors on 28/11/81) FL 29+2
Scarborough (Free on 1/8/83) FL 87/15 FLC 8/1 FAC 4 Others 9/1
Ipswich T (£100,000 on 9/6/89) F/PL 199+7/19 FLC 14+1/1 FAC 17/1 Others 8/2
Barnsley (Free on 14/6/96) FL 24/5 FLC 3 FAC 1

THOMPSON Neil Philip
Born: Hackney, 30 April 1978
Height: 5'11" Weight: 11.6

The young Barnet left back made just one appearance last season, a 0-0 draw at Mansfield in September, before a bad back injury saw him sidelined and ultimately relegated to the reserves. Still a first year professional, this industrious, strong-tackling youngster, who can also play in midfield, was released during the summer.

Barnet (From trainee on 3/7/96) FL 2+1

THOMPSON Steven (Steve) James
Born: Oldham, 2 November 1964
Height: 5'10" Weight: 13.5
Club Honours: AMC '89

1996-97 was another stop-start season for Steve, whose Turf Moor career seems to be drawing to a close following his release during the summer. Probably the best passer of a ball on Burnley's books, injuries apart, he was overlooked for much of the campaign and failed to make the expected impact when recalled following Nigel Gleghorn's absence. Strangely, his only goal for the club was the first in a 2-1 win at Luton on the opening day.

Bolton W (From apprentice on 4/11/82) FL 329+6/49 FLC 27/2 FAC 21/4 Others 39/2
Luton T (£180,000 on 13/8/91) FL 5 FLC 2

Neil Thompson (Barnsley)

Leicester C (Signed on 22/10/91) F/PL 121+6/18 FLC 6/2 FAC 8/1 Others 11+3/4
Burnley (£200,000 on 24/2/95) FL 44+5/1 FLC 2 Others 1+1

THOMPSTONE Ian Philip
Born: Bury, 17 January 1971
Height: 6'0" Weight: 13.0

A forceful, experienced lower division striker who joined Scarborough from Rochdale on a free transfer during the 1996 close season, despite showing glimpses of his undoubted ability, he unfortunately suffered hamstring problems which restricted his progress. Henceforth, he struggled to command a regular first-team place, while scoring just two goals, and was released at the end of February. Came back with Bury on transfer deadline day, but was not called upon for first-team duty.
Manchester C (From trainee on 1/9/89) FL 0+1/1
Oldham Ath (Free on 25/5/90)
Exeter C (Free on 23/1/92) FL 15/3
Halifax T (Free on 14/7/92) FL 31/9 FLC 1+1 FAC 1 Others 2
Scunthorpe U (£15,000 on 25/3/93) FL 47+13/8 FLC 2 FAC 4+2/1 Others 2
Rochdale (Free on 28/7/95) FL 11+14/1 FLC 1/1 FAC 2+2 Others 1+1
Scarborough (Free on 9/8/96) FL 12+7/2 FLC 2 FAC 3 Others 0+1
Bury (Free on 27/3/97)

THOMSEN Claus
Born: Aarhus, Denmark, 31 May 1970
Height: 6'3" Weight: 13.6
International Honours: Denmark: 14

Joe Royle snapped up Claus from Ipswich last January and gave him his Premiership debut in Everton's live televised clash at Arsenal. Equally at home in central defence or in midfield, he was initially bought to strengthen the Blues' squad, but ended up becoming a virtual ever present in the heart of the midfield. A solid tackler and precise passer of the ball, the tall Dane suffered the misfortune of scoring an own goal in the Goodison derby against Liverpool.
Ipswich T (£250,000 from Aarhus on 15/6/94) P/FL 77+4/7 FLC 8/1 FAC 5 Others 2+1
Everton (£900,000 on 18/1/97) PL 15+1

THOMSON Andrew (Andy)
Born: Motherwell, 1 April 1971
Height: 5'10" Weight: 10.13

Another Southend player whose season was badly affected by injuries in 1996-97, the close control and tricky running, not to mention the goals, of Andy were badly missed. However, his commitment to the team's cause could never be questioned and his team mates always appeared to appreciate his appearance in the side, giving them a better target than when he was missing.
Queen of the South (Free from Jerviston BC on 28/7/89) SL 163+12/93 SLC 8/3 SC 7+2/5 Others 9/8
Southend U (£250,000 on 4/7/94) FL 71+18/22 FLC 2+1 FAC 1+2 Others 1+1

THOMSON Andrew (Andy) John
Born: Swindon, 28 March 1974
Height: 6'3" Weight: 14.12

Replacing Lee Russell midway through last season as one of Portsmouth's three centre backs, he worked efficiently alongside either Andy Awford, Russell Perrett or Adrian Whitbread. A tall and powerful, tough-tackling central defender, who, as you might guess, is more than capable in the air, and is a lovely striker of the long ball, apart from giving sterling performances at the back, he also scored his first goal for Pompey at Crystal Palace in January. Incidentally, Andy's looping header not only took the three points, but it was the first time the club had won at Palace in 30 years.
Swindon T (From trainee on 1/5/93) P/FL 21+1 FLC 5/1 Others 3
Portsmouth (£75,000 on 29/12/95) FL 37+7/11 FAC 3+1

Andy Thorn

THORN Andrew (Andy) Charles
Born: Carshalton, 12 November 1966
Height: 6'0" Weight: 11.5
Club Honours: FAC '88
International Honours: E: U21-5

Signed by John Aldridge on a free transfer last September in an attempt to strengthen the Tranmere defence. With John McGreal out injured, Andy quickly stepped into the Rovers' side and scored his only goal for the club after only two minutes of the home game against Crystal Palace, one of his former clubs. Unfortunately, his season was also blighted by injury and he did not enjoy an extended run in the first team, but, not before he had proved to be a vastly experienced and quick-thinking organiser on the field. Is not afraid to coach and encourage his younger colleagues at any level.

Wimbledon (From apprentice on 13/11/84) FL 106+1/2 FLC 7 FAC 9 Others 1
Newcastle U (£850,000 on 1/8/88) FL 36/2 FLC 4/1 Others 3
Crystal Palace (£650,000 on 5/12/89) F/PL 128/3 FLC 19/4 FAC 10 Others 11
Wimbledon (Free on 5/10/94) PL 33+4/1 FLC 2 FAC 3
Heart of Midlothian (Free during 1996 close season) SL 1
Tranmere Rov (Free on 27/9/96) FL 19/1

Peter Thorne

THORNE Peter Lee
Born: Manchester, 21 June 1973
Height: 6'0" Weight: 12.10
Club Honours: Div 2 '96

1996-97 was a fairly disappointing season for the Swindon Town striker, who had to share the role of support striker to Wayne Allison with both Steve Cowe and Steve Finney. However, he enjoyed a purple patch in October with six goals from five games, including a hat trick in a 6-0 thrashing of Huddersfield, and the equaliser at Old Trafford in a Coca-Cola Cup tie with Manchester United, which the Robins lost narrowly to an under strength United team, but only scored twice more in the remainder of the campaign as the manager, Steve McMahon, chopped and changed in search of the best forward line formation. A player who holds the ball up well for fellow forwards, he was out of contract during the summer and transfer listed after refusing improved terms.
Blackburn Rov (From trainee on 20/6/91) Others 0+1
Wigan Ath (Loaned on 11/3/94) FL 10+1
Swindon T (£225,000 on 18/1/95) FL 66+11/27 FLC 5+1/4 FAC 4+2 Others 1+1/1

THORNLEY Benjamin (Ben) Lindsay
Born: Bury, 21 April 1975
Height: 5'9" Weight: 11.12
Club Honours: FAYC '92
International Honours: E: U21-3; Sch

A tricky Manchester United right winger who is essentially left footed, Ben made an encouraging start to last season with solid performances in the Coca-Cola Cup against Swindon and Leicester, and in the Premiership against Middlesbrough and Sunderland. Having suffered a wretched time with injuries during the last few years, his confidence was boosted when Alex Ferguson turned down a £750,000 offer from Huddersfield manager, Brian Horton, in February, stating that, "United are not willing to sell at any price."

Manchester U (From trainee on 29/1/93) PL 1+3 FLC 2
Stockport Co (Loaned on 6/11/95) FL 8+2/1 Others 1
Huddersfield T (Loaned on 22/2/96) FL 12/2

Tony Thorpe

THORPE Anthony (Tony) Lee
Born: Leicester, 10 April 1974
Height: 5'9" Weight: 12.6

After several seasons as a promising attacking midfielder for Luton, Tony finally came of age in 1996-97 as the complete striker, amassing 31 goals during the season – the highest in the division – and scoring with powerful shots, delicate chips, tap ins, headers and penalties. A previous tendency towards nonchalance was completely thrown off as he improved almost match by match, registering three hat tricks and also assisting in creating goals for his colleagues. This tremendous form saw him elected to the PFA second division XI by his fellow professionals and he also won both the Luton Supporters and Players' Player of the Year awards.

Luton T (Free from Leicester C juniors on 18/8/92) FL 66+26/36 FLC 3+3/2 FAC 3+3/2 Others 3+2/1

THORPE Jeffrey (Jeff) Roger
Born: Whitehaven, 17 November 1972
Height: 5'10" Weight: 12.8
Club Honours: Div 3 '95

It was not the first time that Jeff's Carlisle appearances were badly disrupted by injury problems and only in the final few weeks of last season was he fit enough to return to the first team squad and assist in the promotion run in. An enthusiastic left-sided player, whose pace is his main asset, he can either be used in defence or as a wing back who can eat into the opposition. He must be praying for an injury-free 1997-98.

Carlisle U (From trainee on 2/7/91) FL 82+54/6 FLC 6+3 FAC 4+2 Others 7+8/1

THORPE Lee Anthony
Born: Wolverhampton, 14 December 1975
Height: 6'1" Weight: 12.4

Still to make a first team start for Blackpool, despite being top scorer for the reserve side, the young striker yet again made appearances from the bench last season without being able to claim a permanent place. A pro for over three years, he was released during the summer.

Blackpool (From trainee on 18/7/94) FL 2+10 FLC 0+1 FAC 1 Others 1

TIERNEY Francis
Born: Liverpool, 10 September 1975
Height: 5'10" Weight: 11.0
International Honours: E: Yth

A player once thought to be signing for Liverpool, and one who continued to be tracked by Premiership scouts despite not being a Crewe regular in 1996-97, Francis played in a number of attacking roles, including wide on both flanks, as well as being used tactically from the bench. Predominately right footed, his excellent control and coolness appears to give him extra time on the ball.

Crewe Alex (From trainee on 22/3/93) FL 56+27/10 FLC 6 FAC 1+4 Others 5+6/3

TILER Carl
Born: Sheffield, 11 February 1970
Height: 6'4" Weight: 13.0
International Honours: E: U21-13

Unfortunately, Carl started 1996-97 badly at Aston Villa, as the hamstring injury picked up on his debut the previous season kept him out of action until October when he came into the side for a small run of games and scored his only goal, ironically, against his former club, Nottingham Forest. Although the classy centre back remained a member of the first-team squad, he was clearly behind Ugo Egiogu and Gareth Southgate in the pecking order and signed for Sheffield United in transfer deadline week, specifically to cover for the injured Michel Vonk. Following a shaky start, he quickly became the mainstay of the defence, his calmness under pressure often saving the day, and scored the vital goal against Stoke that ensured United of a play-off place.

Barnsley (From trainee on 2/8/88) FL 67+4/3 FLC 4 FAC 4+1 Others 3+1
Nottingham F (£1,400,000 on 30/5/91) F/PL 67+2/1 FLC 10+1 FAC 6 Others 1

Swindon T (Loaned on 18/11/94) FL 2
Aston Villa (£750,000 on 28/10/95) PL 10+2/1 FLC 1 FAC 2
Sheffield U (£650,000 on 26/3/97) FL 6/1 Others 3

TILLSON Andrew (Andy)
Born: Huntingdon, 30 June 1966
Height: 6'2" Weight: 12.10

As the club captain, Andy performed consistently and bravely at the heart of Bristol Rovers' defence in 1996-97, missing just a handful of league games due to injury. It was revealed in April he had played throughout the campaign with a niggling ankle problem which necessitated an operation that was delayed until the club was safe from relegation. Tall, commanding, and a good organiser on the pitch, he turned down the opportunity of a transfer to Oxford United to replace outbound Matt Elliott in order to remain with Rovers. Only two current players have made more appearances for the Pirates.

Grimsby T (Free from Kettering T on 14/7/88) FL 104+1/5 FLC 8 FAC 10 Others 5
Queens Park R (£400,000 on 21/12/90) FL 27+2/2 FLC 2 Others 1
Grimsby T (Loaned on 15/9/92) FL 4 Others 1
Bristol Rov (£370,000 on 7/11/92) FL 157+1/5 FLC 10/1 FAC 7 Others 15/1

TILSON Stephen (Steve) Brian
Born: Wickford, 27 July 1966
Height: 5'11" Weight: 12.10

An excellent season at Southend for Steve was cruelly cut short by a hernia injury last January, his skilful left foot and courage in the tackle, allied with some strong running, had made the left-midfield spot his own and it was a surprise when he was freed during the summer. A volleyed goal, which ultimately proved to be the winner against Grimsby was certainly one to remember.

Southend U (Signed from Witham T on 7/2/89) FL 199+40/26 FLC 9+1 FAC 4 Others 12+1/4
Brentford (Loaned on 16/9/93) FL 2

TIMONS Christopher (Chris) Bryan
Born: Shirebrook, 8 December 1974
Height: 6'1" Weight: 12.6

Released by Mansfield during the 1996 close season, Chris signed for non-league Gainsborough Trinity before coming back into the Football League with Chesterfield last November. Having appeared just once in a weakened side, again at Preston in the AWS competition, the young centre half signed on non-contract terms for Leyton Orient in March and started with a goal in each of his first two games, proving to be a real threat at set plays.

Mansfield T (Signed from Clipstone Colliery on 1/2/94) FL 35+4/2 Others 2+1 (Free to Gainsborough Trinity during 1996 close season)
Chesterfield (Free on 1/11/96) Others 1 (Free to Gainsborough Trinity in August 1996)
Leyton Orient (Free on 21/3/97) FL 6/2

TINKLER Mark Roland
Born: Bishop Auckland, 24 October 1974
Height: 5'11" Weight: 13.3
Club Honours: FAYC '93
International Honours: E: Yth (UEFAC '93); Sch

Unable to get himself anything more than the odd game for Leeds, Mark moved to York just before last March's transfer deadline. The well-built midfield player took a little time to adjust at Bootham Crescent in the tense last few weeks of the season, but his vision and control auger well for the future.

Leeds U (From trainee on 29/11/91) PL 14+11 FLC 1 Others 0+1
York C (Signed on 25/3/97) FL 9/1

TINNION Brian
Born: Stanley, 23 February 1968
Height: 6'0" Weight: 13.0

Not quite up to the standard of the previous season, but such is Brian's ability with his left foot that he was still able to command a place in the Bristol City side throughout most of 1996-97 and although injury threatened to curtail his campaign in early March, he surprised many be returning for the concluding games. Able to play down the left side, whether it be at full back or in midfield, his skill in taking on defenders and providing crosses for the front men was a vital ingredient to the side.

Newcastle U (From apprentice on 26/2/86) FL 30+2/2 FLC 5 Others 1+1
Bradford C (£150,000 on 9/3/89) FL 137+8/22 FLC 12/1 FAC 9/4 Others 7+1/2
Bristol C (£180,000 on 23/3/93) FL 141+8/13 FLC 8 FAC 12+1/3 Others 4+2

TISDALE Paul Robert
Born: Malta, 14 January 1973
Height: 5'9" Weight: 11.13
International Honours: E: Sch

Not called upon by Southampton manager, Graeme Souness, for first-team duty in 1996-97, Paul played two games on loan at Huddersfield in November and December without impressing enough to make the move permanent. At his best a creative player, who can perform with equal ability in midfield or at right back, he was released at the end of the campaign and was looking for a new club during the summer.

Southampton (From juniors on 5/6/91) PL 5+11/1 FLC 0+1 FAC 0+1
Northampton T (Loaned on 12/3/92) FL 5
Huddersfield T (Loaned on 29/11/96) FL 1+1

TODD Andrew (Andy) John James
Born: Derby, 21 September 1974
Height: 5'10" Weight: 12.3
Club Honours: Div 1 '97

The son of the Bolton manager, Andy is a versatile player who appears mainly in defence, although he is equally at ease in a midfield role. His first team starts for Wanderers in 1996-97 were limited to providing cover for Gudni Bergsson, although making a number of substitute appearances during the first half of the season, and he eventually found it hard holding a place on the bench, mainly due to the quality of the squad which his father was assembling. However, his six starts and nine subs' appearances were good enough to win him a first division championship medal as the club roared into the Premiership at the first time of asking.

Middlesbrough (From trainee on 6/3/92) FL 7+1

FLC 1+1 Others 5
Swindon T (Loaned on 27/2/95) FL 13
Bolton W (£250,000 on 1/8/95) P/FL 15+12/2 FLC 3+5

TODD Lee
Born: Hartlepool, 7 March 1972
Height: 5'5" Weight: 10.3

Stockport's chirpy little left back matured into a top-notch attacking defender in 1996-97 and, at the same time, caught the eye of a few Premiership managers for his contributions further up the field. Cool and terrier-like, Lee missed just five league games during County's run to the first division and became a great favourite of the fans.

Stockport Co (Free from Hartlepool U juniors on 23/7/90) FL 214+11/2 FLC 24+2 FAC 17/2 Others 32+1

Lee Todd

TOLSON Neil
Born: Walsall, 25 October 1973
Height: 6'2" Weight: 12.4

Released by Bradford during the summer of 1996, Neil signed for York and, in what proved another difficult campaign for the club, had a very satisfactory first season, finishing top scorer with 17 goals. Good in the air, and with a touch of pace, he had a five-match scoring sequence early in the term, netting in both legs of the Coca-Cola Cup games against Everton. Interestingly, only two of the games he scored in were lost by City, something that merely emphasises his value to them.

Walsall (From trainee on 17/12/91) FL 3+6/1 FAC 0+1/1 Others 1+2
Oldham Ath (£150,000 on 24/3/92) PL 0+3
Bradford C (Signed on 2/12/93) FL 32+31/12 FLC 1+4/1 FAC 3+1/1 Others 2+2/3
Chester C (Loaned on 6/1/95) FL 3+1
York C (Free on 15/7/96) FL 39+1/12 FLC 5/3 FAC 4/2 Others 0+1

TOMLINSON Michael (Micky) Lloyd
Born: Lambeth, 15 September 1972
Height: 5'9" Weight: 11.0

Another player whose season at Barnet in

1996-97 was blighted by injury, Micky is a fast and tricky right winger who, on his day, is capable of winning the game for you. Out again at the end of the campaign, he will be hoping for better fortunes in 1997-98.

Leyton Orient (From trainee on 5/7/91) FL 7+7/1 FLC 4/1 FAC 1 Others 0+1
Barnet (Free on 21/3/94) FL 67+26/4 FLC 4+4/1 FAC 4+4 Others 1+2

TORPEY Stephen David James
Born: Islington, 8 December 1970
Height: 6'3" Weight: 14.13
Club Honours: AMC '94

Despite being criticised by a section of Swansea fans for his lack of aggression last season, perversely, the tall striker was sent off on two occasions and received a number of bookings that saw him miss games due to suspension. Despite all that, there was a great improvement in his all-round ball skills during the campaign, going some way to matching his excellent aerial ability, and making him more than a match for third division defenders. Was still among the goals with 11 to his credit.

Millwall (From trainee on 14/2/89) FL 3+4 FLC 0+1
Bradford C (£70,000 on 21/11/90) FL 86+10/22 FLC 6 FAC 2+1 Others 8/6
Swansea C (£80,000 on 3/8/93) FL 151+11/44 FLC 9+2/2 FAC 10/5 Others 18+3/6

TOWN David Edward
Born: Bournemouth, 9 December 1976
Height: 5'8" Weight: 11.13

Striker. After being on the fringes of the Bournemouth first team for a couple of seasons, David made the breakthrough in the latter stages of 1996-97, being a regular from February. Extremely quick and very sharp in and around the box and striking up a good partnership with Steve Fletcher until the latter was injured, David will look to consolidate his position in 1997-98.

Bournemouth (From trainee on 11/4/95) FL 17+22/2 FLC 0+4 Others 0+2

TOWNSEND Andrew (Andy) David
Born: Maidstone, 23 July 1963
Height: 5'11" Weight: 12.7
Club Honours: FLC '94, '96
International Honours: Ei: 66; B-1

Appearing in all but four of Aston Villa's matches in 1996-97, and notching up his normal couple of goals, one of them a cracker against his old club, Chelsea, at Stamford Bridge, it was yet another consistent season for this hard-running, but equally creative player. As you would have expected, as the captain, Andy continued to contest every midfield battle and must have covered each blade of grass in Villa's cause as the club battled for a top-five Premiership position and a place in Europe for 1997-98, while, on the international front, again a regular for the Republic of Ireland, he scored against Liechtenstein, before breaking his nose in the Iceland game. From a footballing family, his father, Don, played for Charlton and Crystal Palace between 1950 and 1964.

David Town (right)

Southampton (£35,000 from Weymouth on 15/1/85) FL 77+6/5 FLC 7+1 FAC 2+3 Others 3+2
Norwich C (£300,000 on 31/8/88) FL 66+5/8 FLC 3+1 FAC 10/2 Others 3
Chelsea (£1,200,000 on 5/7/90) F/PL 110/12 FLC 17/7 FAC 7 Others 4
Aston Villa (£2,100,000 on 26/7/93) PL 130+1/8 FLC 20/2 FAC 12 Others 10/1

TOWNSEND Quentin Lee
Born: Worcester, 13 February 1977
Height: 6'1" Weight 13.0

Released by Wolves during the 1996 close season, having failed to garner a first-team opportunity at Molineux, the young centre back moved to Hereford, making his debut in the opening game of 1996-97 at Fulham. Although proving to be very solid and reliable, once Dean Smith had been paired with Trevor Matthewson, Quentin failed to get a further look in and was loaned out to non-league Worcester City prior to being released in the summer.

Wolverhampton W (From trainee on 3/7/95)
Hereford U (Free on 12/7/96) FL 6+1 FLC 3

TRACEY Simon Peter
Born: Woolwich, 9 December 1967
Height: 6'0" Weight: 13.8

A goalkeeper whose chances were limited at Sheffield United in 1996-97, due to the outstanding form of Alan Kelly, his seven league appearances came only when the latter was injured. However, when called upon he did not let the side down, but suffered the heartbreak of conceding the last-minute winner in the play-off final against Crystal Palace when he appeared to be wrong footed, although in reality he had little chance of making the save. Having been linked with a move to the Londoners earlier in the season, but unable to agree terms, to lose to them at Wembley was a bitter twist to end the campaign.

Wimbledon (From apprentice on 3/2/86) FL 1 Others 1
Sheffield U (£7,500 on 19/10/88) F/PL 159+2 FLC 7 FAC 10 Others 8
Manchester C (Loaned on 27/10/94) PL 3
Norwich C (Loaned on 31/12/94) PL 1 FAC 2
Wimbledon (Loaned on 2/11/95) PL 1

TREVITT Simon
Born: Dewsbury, 20 December 1967
Height: 5'11" Weight: 12.9

First a knee problem, then a serious groin injury kept Simon out of action from last November after he had played an important role in Hull City's impressive defensive start to 1996-97 from his preferred right-wing-back berth. A player who adds vital experience to a young squad, he scored his first goal for the club with the winner at Wigan.

Huddersfield T (From apprentice on 16/6/86) FL 216+13/3 FLC 23/1 FAC 13 Others 19+1
Hull C (Free on 24/11/95) FL 46+1/1 FLC 2 Others 1

TROLLOPE Paul Jonathan
Born: Swindon, 3 June 1972
Height: 6'0" Weight: 12.6
International Honours: W: 1

The versatile Derby midfield player added an ability to man mark successfully in a central position in 1996-97 to his other abilities as a distributor and midfield link man. His performances at the end of the season when he won back his first-team place earned him a full debut for Wales in the friendly with Scotland in May, having gained valuable match practice in loan spells at both Crystal Palace and Grimsby earlier. Loaned to Grimsby at the end of August, he played seven times, scoring Town's only goal in a 6-1 defeat at Bolton, prior to having a spell at Palace and appearing as a sub on nine occasions before returning to the Baseball Ground. Is the son of the former Swindon record appearance holder, John.

Swindon T (From trainee on 23/12/89)
Torquay U (Free on 26/3/92) FL 103+3/16 FLC 9+1/1 FAC 7 Others 8+1
Derby Co (£100,000 on 16/12/94) F/PL 43+12/5 FLC 1+1 FAC 3+1
Grimsby T (Loaned on 30/8/96) FL 6+1/1
Crystal Palace (Loaned on 11/10/96) FL 0+9

TRUSTFULL Orlando
Born: Amsterdam, Holland, 4 August 1970
Height: 6'0" Weight: 13.0
International Honours: Holland: 2

Another member of the Sheffield Wednesday overseas brigade, Orlando was not always a regular in 1996-97 but he did enough to show promise of him becoming the midfield playmaker for both the Owls and Dutch sides. Having joined the club from Feyenoord in the summer of 1996, after a few games as a sub he became a regular in the side until the end of November, opening his goalscoring account with the first in a 2-0 win against Nottingham Forest at Hillsborough. Following that, however, he struggled for a game before coming back with a bang near the end of the campaign when, after coming on as a sub against Wimbledon, he scored two late goals. A strong, skilful player, who has two Dutch full caps to his name, 1997-98 will be an interesting season for him.

Sheffield Wed (£750,000 from Feyenoord on 24/8/96) PL 9+10/3 FLC 2 FAC 0+1

TUCK Stuart Gary
Born: Brighton, 1 October 1974
Height: 5'11" Weight: 11.7
Another of Brighton and Hove Albion's crop of homegrown youngsters, despite being plagued with niggling injuries, the 22 year old can look back on the traumatic 1996-97 season with a good deal of satisfaction. After returning from a long-term knee injury sustained in the 3-0 defeat at Barnet in August, Stuart blossomed into a first team regular at left back and was named as Player of the Month for February by the Evening Argus. Can also play in the centre of defence if required.
Brighton & Hove A (From trainee on 9/7/93) FL 57+12 FLC 6 FAC 1 Others 5+1

TUCKER Lee Antony
Born: Plymouth, 10 August 1978
Height: 5'8" Weight: 11.0
With Torquay already 3-0 down and with just 23 minutes remaining, the young YTS midfielder made a brief substitute appearance in the last home game of 1996-97 against Wigan, following an injury to Jamie Howell.
Torquay U (Trainee) FL 0+1

TURLEY William (Billy) Lee
Born: Wolverhampton, 15 July 1973
Height: 6'4" Weight: 14.10
Dependable Northampton goalkeeper. His manager, Ian Atkins, claimed to have the two best 'keepers in the third division, and although Billy was reserve to Andy Woodman, when called upon he could always be relied upon. Also helped to spark Kettering Town's revival in the Vauxhall Conference while on loan to them last season.
Northampton T (Free from Evesham on 10/7/95) FL 3

TURNBULL Lee Mark
Born: Stockton, 27 September 1967
Height: 6'0" Weight: 13.0
The tough competitive Scunthorpe midfield anchor man missed the start of the 1996-97 campaign due to a recurrence of knee cartilage trouble, which required an operation, and, on getting back, was unfortunate to suffer further injury, leaving his appearances considerably depleted. Released during the summer, Lee can also be used as a target man.
Middlesbrough (From trainee on 7/9/85) FL 8+8/4 FLC 0+1 Others 1+1/1
Aston Villa (Signed on 24/8/87)
Doncaster Rov (£17,500 on 3/11/87) FL 108+15/21 FLC 3+1/2 FAC 5+1 Others 9+1/2
Chesterfield (£35,000 on 14/2/91) FL 80+7/26 FLC 2+3/1 FAC 3/1 Others 5
Doncaster Rov (Signed on 8/10/93) FL 10+1/1 FAC 2 Others 1
Wycombe W (£20,000 on 21/1/94) FL 8+3/1 FLC 0+1/1 FAC 1 Others 1
Scunthorpe U (£12,000 on 6/3/95) FL 37+10/7 FLC 2 FAC 2 Others 1

TURNER Andrew (Andy) Peter
Born: Woolwich, 23 March 1975
Height: 5'10" Weight: 11.7
International Honours: Ei: U21-7. E: Yth; Sch

Signed from Tottenham early last season, the left winger quickly slotted in at Portsmouth, playing in 23 consecutive games before a loss of form led to him being left out. To be fair, he had been substituted on 12 occasions and from then on he found himself consigned either to the subs' bench or the reserves. Both pacy and skilful, and a player who can get down the line to get across excellent crosses for the front men, or get inside to have a crack himself, Andy scored two goals, including the winner, against Stoke at Fratton Park.
Tottenham H (From trainee on 8/4/92) PL 8+12/3 FLC 0+2/1 FAC 0+1
Wycombe W (Loaned on 26/8/94) FL 3+1
Doncaster Rov (Loaned on 10/10/94) FL 4/1 Others 1/1
Huddersfield T (Loaned on 28/11/95) FL 2+3/1
Southend U (Loaned on 28/3/96) FL 4+2
Portsmouth (£250,000 on 4/9/96) FL 22+2/2 FLC 2+1

TURNER Graham Mark
Born: Bebbington, 4 October 1972
Height: 6'0" Weight: 11.1
The son of the Hereford manager, Graham, Mark joined up with his father on transfer deadline day last March, having been playing in non-league soccer with Telford. A skilful midfielder with good passing abilities, he came into the side on the left flank, showing battling determination, and was unlucky not to score on a number of occasions.
Wolverhampton W (Signed from Paget R on 2/7/91) FL 1
Northampton T (Free on 1/7/94) FL 2+2 Others 1 (Free to Telford on 15/12/95)
Hereford U (Free on 27/3/97) FL 6

TURNER Robert (Robbie) Peter
Born: Gateshead, 18 September 1966
Height: 6'3" Weight: 14.1
A hard tackling and aggressive centre forward, Robbie was unable to command a first team place at Cambridge in 1996-97 and went on loan to Hull City, where he scored twice on his debut at Scarborough. Unfortunately, thoughts of a permanent move disappeared as back trouble restricted appearances and he quit the game in January. Following that, he moved to non-league, Taunton Town, scoring a hat trick on his debut.
Huddersfield T (From apprentice on 19/9/84) FL 0+1 FLC 1
Cardiff C (Free on 19/7/85) FL 34+5/8 FLC 3/1 FAC 1 Others 1
Hartlepool U (Loaned on 2/10/86) FL 7/1
Bristol Rov (Free on 31/12/86) FL 19+7/2 FLC 2 Others 0+1
Wimbledon (£15,000 on 17/12/87) FL 2+8 FLC 1+1 FAC 0+1/1 Others 3+1/1
Bristol C (£45,000 on 27/1/89) FL 45+7/12 FAC 7/3 Others 2
Plymouth Arg (£150,000 on 23/7/90) FL 66/17 FLC 5/1 FAC 3 Others 3/1
Notts Co (£90,000 on 21/11/92) FL 7+1/1 FAC 1
Shrewsbury T (Loaned on 25/3/93) FL 9
Exeter C (Free on 4/2/94) FL 38+7/7 FLC 2/1 FAC 1+1 Others 2/1
Cambridge U (Signed on 19/12/95) FL 12+5/4 FAC 0+2 Others 1
Hull C (Loaned on 14/10/96) FL 5/2

TUTILL Stephen (Steve) Alan
Born: York, 1 October 1969
Height: 5'10" Weight: 12.6
International Honours: E: Sch
It was a disappointing testimonial season for York's local-born stalwart central defender in 1996-97 as injuries, plus the consistent form of Tony Barras and John Sharples limited his senior appearances. Hard tackling and a player with presence, when called upon he gave his usual 100 per cent.
York C (From trainee on 27/1/88) FL 291+8/6 FLC 20 FAC 18+1 Others 22+3/1

TUTTLE David Philip
Born: Reading, 6 February 1972
Height: 6'1" Weight: 12.10
Club Honours: FAYC '90
International Honours: E: Yth
A strong-tackling Crystal Palace central defender who gets the job done on the ground and loses little in the air, David had an excellent season in 1996-97 and was the longest ever present until injury at Charlton in early March caused him to miss several games. Back in time for the second play-off leg at Wolves, following a 4-3 aggregate win, he went forward to play against his old team, Sheffield United, in the final at Wembley, a place in the Premiership at stake. Had an excellent game in the 1-0 defeat of United and will not be out of place this coming term when battling against the likes of forwards such as Mark Hughes and company.
Tottenham H (From trainee on 8/2/90) F/PL 10+3 FLC 3+1 Others 1/1
Peterborough U (Loaned on 21/1/93) FL 7
Sheffield U (£350,000 on 1/8/93) P/FL 63/1 FLC 2 FAC 3
Crystal Palace (Signed on 8/3/96) FL 48+1/3 FLC 3 FAC 1 Others 5

TWYNHAM Gary Steven
Born: Manchester, 8 February 1976
Height: 6'0" Weight: 12.1
A former Manchester United youngster, Gary impressed with his strong running and surges through from Darlington's midfield to score three times in 1996-97. Improving as the season progressed, he showed he had the ability to return to a higher level and has already attracted the attentions of other clubs.
Manchester U (From trainee on 1/7/94)
Darlington (Free on 28/3/96) FL 23+8/3 FLC 4 Others 1

TYLER Mark Richard
Born: Norwich, 2 April 1977
Height: 6'0" Weight: 12.9
International Honours: E: Yth
Having started 1996-97 deputising for Jon Sheffield in the Peterborough goal, Mark had a spell on loan at Yeovil and then found himself standing in for the new signing, Bart Griemink, when the latter fell out of favour. Tall, with good handling and shot-stopping skills, he was given just four opportunities to show what he was made of and did well, keeping a clean sheet in a 2-0 home win against Colchester. Looks a likely one for the future, but needs more match practice.
Peterborough U (From trainee on 7/12/94) FL 7+1 Others 3

273

GEORGE DAVIES CO

SOLICITORS

FOUNTAIN COURT
68 FOUNTAIN STREET
MANCHESTER M2 2FB

Solicitors to the PFA

COMPANY

COMPANY FORMATION
COMPANY DISPUTES
INSOLVENCY

COMMERCIAL

SPONSORSHIP CONTRACTS
TERMS OF BUSINESS
TAXATION

EMPLOYMENT

SERVICE CONTRACTS
INDUSTRIAL TRIBUNALS
DISCRIMINATION CLAIMS

PROPERTY

HOUSE PURCHASE
WILLS AND TRUSTS
INHERITANCE AND INVESTMENT

LITIGATION

PERSONAL INJURY
CRIME

FAMILY

CUSTODY AND DIVORCE
CARE PROCEEDINGS

*George Davies & Co are proud
to have been solicitors to the PFA for over 25 years.*

*Whatever your legal problem telephone us
and we will explain how we can help you.*

INVESTOR IN PEOPLE

0161-236-8992

UHLENBEEK Gustav (Gus) Reinier
Born: Paramaribo, 20 August 1970
Height: 5'8" Weight: 11.1

Gus started 1996-97 for Ipswich with a cream rinse in his hair, presumably to match the club's new colours of cream and black, but pre-season injury problems hampered his training schedule and he was not really match fit, and consequently dropped out of the team. It then took him until December to get back into the side on a regular basis, but once there, he stayed for the rest of the campaign. Initially played wide on the right of midfield, he soon reverted to the role of right-wing back where his pace was used to the full, either in shackling the opposing winger, or in boosting the club's attacking possibilities by running from deep positions. This was best illustrated in the home game against QPR when he received the ball in his own half and proceeded to run through the defence before laying it off to Neil Gregory, who, scored.

Ipswich T (£100,000 from Top Ost on 11/8/95) FL 71+7/4 FLC 5+3 FAC 2+3 Others 6

ULLATHORNE Robert
Born: Wakefield, 11 October 1971
Height: 5'8" Weight: 11.3
International Honours: E: Yth

Robert, a left-sided wing back was signed from Spanish club, Osasuna, last February in a deal which, under the terms of the Bosman ruling, saw Leicester pay Osasuna £500,000 and his former club, Norwich, £100,000, due to the fact that he had exercised his right to a free transfer in Spain, but had then moved on within 12 months. Unfortunately, his City debut, in the Coca-Cola Cup semi final against Wimbledon, lasted just 11 minutes, when a broken ankle put him out for the remainder of the season. Not very big, but full of enthusiasm and the ability to take on defenders to get telling crosses into dangerous areas, he will be looking to make a good start in 1997-98, when, hopefully, fully recovered.

Norwich C (From trainee on 6/7/90) F/PL 86+8/7 FLC 10+2/1 FAC 7+1 Others 1 (Free to Osasuna during 1996 close season)
Leicester C (£600,000 on 18/2/97) FLC 1

UNSWORTH David Gerald
Born: Chorley, 16 October 1973
Height: 6'1" Weight: 14.7
Club Honours: FAC '95; CS '95
International Honours: E: 1; U21-7; Yth

A technically adept left-sided Everton defender, David was a first-team regular in 1996-97, showing signs towards the end of the campaign of rediscovering the form which won him his solitary England cap in 1995. Swift and very strong, he forged a reliable central defensive partnership with Dave Watson. He also showed a remarkable composure in front of goal for a defender,

slotting in several high-pressure penalty kicks and also scoring several times from open play. Successive Everton coaches have never been absolutely convinced of where best to employ his obvious talent, but his best performances last season came on the left-hand side of a three-man defensive triangle and that is where his future may lie.

Everton (From trainee on 25/6/92) F/PL 108+8/11 FLC 5+2 FAC 7 Others 4/1

UNSWORTH Lee Peter
Born: Eccles, 25 February 1973
Height: 5'11" Weight: 11.8

Started last season for Crewe in the number two shirt before being sidelined for nearly two months due to injury. After coming back into the side from the subs' bench, he switched flanks to cover for Shaun Smith, prior to having another spell out of action and then slotting in at right back for the final five games, including the play offs. Now looking to forward to playing in the first division, Lee has excellent speed in recovery and continues to improve.

Crewe Alex (Signed from Ashton U on 20/2/95) FL 44+14 FLC 4+1/1 FAC 3+1/1 Others 8+2

UPSON Matthew James
Born: Stowmarket, 18 April 1979
Height: 6'1" Weight: 11.4

An intelligent young centre back with excellent distribution skills, Matthew captained the Luton Town youth team to the FA Youth Cup semi final and to the championship of the South-East Counties division two, as well as playing regularly for the reserves. As in 1995-96, he made just one league appearance as a substitute in a 1-0 home win against Rotherham last August, but his promise was such that Arsenal paid £1m for his transfer as an investment for the future in May. Furthermore, Hatters stand to make at least as much again depending on future success.

Luton T (From trainee on 24/4/96) FL 0+1 Others 1

UTLEY Darren
Born: Barnsley, 28 September 1977
Height: 6'0" Weight: 11.7

Darren proved to be a more than capable deputy for either of Doncaster's main central defenders when he was called upon in 1996-97. He only signed full-time professional forms at the start of the season, and looks to have an excellent footballing future in front of him, especially if he continues to progress as he has since leaving the Rovers' junior ranks.

Doncaster Rov (From trainee on 9/12/95) FL 20+4/1 FLC 1 FAC 1

VAN BLERK Jason
Born: Sydney, Australia, 16 March 1968
Height: 6'1" Weight: 13.0
International Honours: Australia: 22

Jason was another of Millwall's experienced internationals who saw his 1996-97 season devastated by injuries. Medial ligament, then tendon problems just days before the campaign started meant that this fine left back, who is also capable of playing in midfield, managed only a handful of games

during mid term, before being freed during the summer.

Millwall (£300,000 from Go Ahead Eagles on 8/9/94) FL 68+5/2 FLC 5 FAC 6+1 Others 1+1

VAN DER GOUW Raimond (Rai)
Born: Oldenzaal, Holland, 24 March 1963
Height: 6'3" Weight: 13.1
Club Honours: CS '97

A highly experienced goalkeeper with a safe pair of hands, Rai was signed from Vittesse in the 1996 close season to replace the outgoing Tony Coton as Manchester United's cover for Peter Schmeichel. Although his appearances were restricted to just two Premiership outings, the first against Aston Villa in September, he played in both of United's Coca-Cola Cup ties against Swindon and Leicester and later stood in at the last minute for Schmeichel for the European Cup semi-final leg against Borussia Dortmund in Germany. Despite conceding a deflected goal in the 1-0 defeat, the understudy excelled himself, especially in the first half, and could in no way be blamed for the defeat. Realising that further opportunities will be somewhat rare, he seems content just to wind down his brilliant career in England as a member of United's high-flying squad.

Manchester U (Signed from Vitesse Arnhem on 12/7/96) PL 2 FLC 2 Others 1

VAN DER LAAN Robertus (Robin) Petrus
Born: Schiedam, Holland, 5 September 1968
Height: 5'11" Weight: 13.8
Club Honours: AMC '93

As Derby's club captain, the combative midfield player was troubled by ankle injuries at the beginning of last season and found it difficult to reclaim his place in the side, being one of a number of players farmed out on loan. Assisting Wolves during a spell of seven games he appeared to be just the robust type of player needed at the club, but, with Mark McGhee, manager at Molineux, unable to decide whether to sign him permanently or not, Robin returned to the Derby side for the FA Cup game with Aston Villa and scored the first goal. From then on, his battling performances kept him in the team for the rest of the season, scoring vital Premiership goals against Tottenham and Aston Villa, plus another FAC goal against Coventry, and showing himself to be back at his best, his strong tackling and good engine power made to order for Jim Smith's team.

Port Vale (£80,000 from Wageningen on 21/2/91) FL 154+22/24 FLC 11+1/1 FAC 9+1/1 Others 11+1/1
Derby Co (£675,000 on 2/8/95) F/PL 54+1/8 FLC 4+1 FAC 3+1/3
Wolverhampton W (Loaned on 11/10/96) FL 7

VAN DER VELDEN Carel
Born: Arnhem, Holland, 3 August 1972
Height: 5'8" Weight: 13.7

A Barnsley midfielder who has good skill on the ball and enjoys the passing game, his season never really started in 1996-97. Not included in the new-look team, Carel did not

do enough to force his way in, apart from three appearances, and was soon back in the reserves. Will obviously be looking for more of a chance in 1997-98, especially now that Premiership football has arrived at Oakwell.

Barnsley (£75,000 from FC Den Bosch on 12/3/96) FL 7+2 FLC 1

VAN GOBBEL Ulrich
Born: Surinam, 16 January 1971
Height: 5'11" Weight: 13.8
International Honours: Holland: 9

Signed from Galatasaray, Graeme Souness's old club, last October, Ulrich broke Southampton's transfer record fee in doing so and throughout the campaign proved to be an athletic defender of enormous strength and pace. Nicknamed "Bruno" by the fans for his resemblance to the famous boxer, he could be used either in the centre of defence or out wide as a wing back, his barnstorming runs surprisingly bringing him just two goals, albeit important ones. Out of the side only when injured or suspended, he was sent off at Blackburn, the Dutch international complimented Claus Lundekvam well and should do even better this coming season.

Southampton (£1,300,000 from Galatasaray on 19/10/96) PL 24+1/1 FLC 6/1 FAC 1

VANHALA Jari
Born: Helsinki, Finland, 29 August 1965
Height: 5'10" Weight: 12.4
International Honours: Finland: 21

A former Finnish international striker, having signed non-contract forms for Bradford last December, Jari was immediately given an opportunity to see what he could do, when coming on for the last 18 minutes in a 0-0 home draw against Reading as a sub for Ole Sundgot. However, as quickly as he had arrived, he had departed, leaving Valley Parade after just seven days.

Bradford C (Free from Finnpa on 16/12/96) FL 0+1

VAN HEUSDEN Arjan
Born: Alphen, Holland, 11 December 1972
Height: 6'4" Weight: 12.9

After impressing during pre-season friendlies he started the 1996-97 campaign as Port Vale's number one goalkeeper and did well early on. Unfortunately, results on the field were not too impressive during September and October and, after a run of 16 games, Arjan was replaced by Paul Musselwhite. He did not manage to regain a first-team spot again until being recalled for the final game, but was content enough to sign a new contract at the club.

Port Vale (£4,500 from Noordwijk on 15/8/94) FL 22 FLC 4 Others 2

VAN HOOIJDONK Pierre
Born: Steenbergen, Holland, 29 November 1969
Height: 6'4" Weight: 13.5
International Honours: Holland: 3

Pierre became Nottingham Forest's record signing when he joined them from Celtic last March. A prolific striker for the Scottish

giants, he fell out with the club and wanted a move, but after looking likely to join West Ham, he went to the City Ground instead. Despite linking well with Dean Saunders, the Dutchman failed to hit the net until his sixth game, a 1-1 draw at home to Leeds, but should find the first division more to his liking in 1997-98. A big man with good skills on the ground, as well as being an obvious threat in the air, he reclaimed his place for Holland and scored against Wales in the World Cup qualifiers.

Glasgow Celtic (£1,200,000 from NAC Breda on 7/1/95) SL 63+3/46 SLC 5+1/3 SC 10/9 Others 5+2

Nottingham Forest (£4,500,000 on 11/3/97) PL 8/1

VARTY John William (Will)
Born: Workington, 1 October 1976
Height: 6'0" Weight: 12.4
Club Honours: AMC '97

One of the finds of last season, Will made his league debut on the opening day of 1996-97 and soon became an automatic choice in Carlisle's central defence, where he displayed a maturity that belied his years. Still only 20, this product of the youth team looks to have a bright future in the game and his performances have already attracted the attention of clubs from higher divisions.

Carlisle U (From trainee on 10/7/95) FL 31+1 FLC 4 FAC 2 Others 6+1

VAUGHAN Anthony (Tony) John
Born: Manchester, 11 October 1975
Height: 6'1" Weight: 11.2
International Honours: E: Sch; Yth

Had an early boost to his confidence in 1996-97, scoring twice for Ipswich, both headers from set pieces against Reading, before picking up a nasty rib injury against Portsmouth which caused him to miss several games. Returned in Jason Cundy's absence to partner Chris Swailes and was part of the defence which kept five successive clean sheets in the run in to the play offs. Although he was offered a new contract during the season, he declined to sign it, preferring to keep his options open, and, at the time of writing, was believed to be in negotiation with Manchester City. Excellent in the air and sound on the ground, Tony is expected to go all the way. *Stop Press:* Reported to have completed his £1 million move to Manchester City in mid June.

Ipswich T (From trainee on 1/7/94) P/FL 56+11/3 FLC 4+2 FAC 2 Others 4

VAUGHAN John
Born: Isleworth, 26 June 1964
Height: 5'10" Weight: 13.1
Club Honours: Div 3 '91, '96

Released by Preston during the 1996 close season, the experienced goalkeeper joined the Lincoln manager, John Beck, for the third time when signing at the beginning of 1996-97, having previously served under him at Cambridge and North End. However, apart from four early games and the final seven, when he came in to keep three clean sheets, John spent most of the campaign in

the reserves deputising for Barry Richardson, apart from having a spell on loan at Colchester in February as cover for injuries to Carl Emberson and Garrett Caldwell. Although he performed well in a team that had been unbeaten for 15 matches, he will probably be best remembered for an unfortunate early sending off in a 2-1 AWS home win over Northampton.

West Ham U (From apprentice on 30/6/82)
Charlton Ath (Loaned on 11/3/85) FL 6
Bristol Rov (Loaned on 5/9/85) FL 6
Wrexham (Loaned on 23/10/85) FL 4
Bristol C (Loaned on 4/3/86) FL 2
Fulham (£12,500 on 21/8/86) FL 44 FLC 4 FAC 4 Others 3
Bristol C (Loaned on 21/1/88) FL 3
Cambridge U (Free on 6/6/88) FL 178 FLC 13 FAC 24 Others 16
Charlton Ath (Free on 5/8/93) FL 5+1 FAC 2 Others 1+1
Preston NE (Free on 26/7/94) FL 65+1 FLC 2 FAC 2 Others 5
Lincoln C (Free on 14/8/96) FL 10 FLC 1
Colchester U (Loaned on 3/2/97) FL 5 Others 1

VEART Thomas Carl
Born: Whyalla, Australia, 21 May 1970
Height: 5'11" Weight: 12.8
International Honours: Australia: 20

Crystal Palace's second Australian international (Kevin Muscatt is the other) had not been an instant hit with the fans when joining the club at the latter end of 1995-96, but won them round with some fine displays last season. A hard-working midfielder, who can also link well with the forwards, as an added bonus, Carl cracked in nine goals, including four in successive games during September and October. Obviously hoping to make Terry Venables' World Cup squad, he was surprisingly left on the bench for the three play-off games that culminated in Palace joining the Premiership following their 1-0 win over Sheffield United, his old club. All in all, though, the Aussie had an excellent campaign.

Sheffield U (£250,000 from Adelaide C on 22/7/94) FL 47+19/15 FLC 2+1/1 FAC 2+1/1 Others 2
Crystal Palace (£225,000 on 8/3/96) FL 40+11/6 FLC 3/2 FAC 2/1 Others 2+2/1

VEGA Ramon
Born: Zurich, Switzerland, 14 June 1971
Height: 6'3" Weight: 13.0
International Honours: Switzerland: 20

After an impressive Euro '96 performance at the heart of Switzerlands' defence, Ramon became a target for a host of Premiership and European clubs, ultimately signing for Tottenham last January. His stature and speed make him the ideal defender who can not only organise the back four but be the instigator of sweeping attacks, while his great ability to head the ball saw him feature heavily in set pieces. Also, a keen eye for goal ensured chances to score were well taken. Injury interrupted a promising start, but, as performances showed towards the end of the season, the best is definitely yet to come. In the company of such figures as John Scales, Sol Campbell, and Colin Calderwood, Gerry Francis has created a

defence that, once gelled, will be amongst the strongest in the Premiership.

Tottenham H (£3,750,000 from Cagliari on 11/1/97) PL 8/1

VENISON Barry

Born: Consett, 16 August 1964
Height: 5'10" Weight: 12.3
Club Honours: CS '86, '88, '89, '90; ESC '86; Div 1 '88, '90, '93; FAC '89
International Honours: E :2; U21-10; Yth

A very experienced Southampton defender who can play equally well in midfield, his link-up play and passing excellent, Barry was rejoined at the Dell for the start of last season by his former Galatasaray manager, Graeme Souness. Unfortunately, a continuing back problem restricted the Saints' captain to just two appearances, the opening two games, and he was more recognisable during the campaign for his Sky TV work off the field than for his ability on it.

Sunderland (From apprentice on 20/1/82) FL 169+4/2 FLC 21 FAC 7+1 Others 3/1
Liverpool (£200,000 on 31/7/86) FL 103+7/1 FLC 14+3 FAC 16+5 Others 6+4/2
Newcastle U (£250,000 on 31/7/92) F/PL 108+1/1 FLC 9 FAC 11 Others 4 (£750,000 to Galatasaray during 1995 close season)
Southampton (£850,000 on 25/10/95) PL 23+1 FLC 2 FAC 3

VENUS Mark

Born: Hartlepool, 6 April 1967
Height: 6'0" Weight: 13.11
Club Honours: Div 3 '89

Few people expected this transfer-listed versatile defender to be at Wolves in 1996-97, but injuries meant he played from the opening day, giving his usual wholehearted performances. Capable of whipping in quick left-foot crosses, Mark provided the corner for Geoff Thomas's winner at Crystal Palace and started every game until 24 January, when Adrian Williams made his long-awaited debut. However, in continuing to fill in when (and where) he was needed, though his form was not so consistent as before, following a difficult afternoon at QPR at Easter, just one full appearance ensued.

Hartlepool U (From juniors on 22/3/85) FL 4 Others 0+1
Leicester C (Free on 6/9/85) FL 58+3/1 FLC 3 FAC 2 Others 2+1
Wolverhampton W (£40,000 on 23/3/88) FL 271+16/7 FLC 17+1/1 FAC 15+1 Others 17/2

VIALLI Gianluca

Born: Italy, 9 July 1964
Height: 5'11" Weight: 13.6
Club Honours: FAC '97
International Honours: Italy: 59

Twelve months after Ruudi-mania (and dreadlock wigs) hit Stamford Bridge it was the turn of shaven-headed Vialli-mania when the Juventus player chose to join Ruud Gullit's Chelsea revolution on a free transfer in preference to Arsenal and Glasgow Rangers during the 1996 close season. A national hero in Italy, his exclusion from Arrigo Saachi's Euro 96 squad brought

Barry Venison

bitter criticism of the beleaguered Italian manager and he immediately became a cult-hero to the Chelsea fans. After scoring his first Premiership goal in his third match, a rasping volley against Coventry City which clinched a 2-0 victory, Luca consistently found the net throughout the first three months of the season, including the winning goal at Manchester United, until sustaining a hamstring strain against Everton in December, shortly after heading a superb equaliser. During Luca's absence Ruud Gullit pushed Gianfranco Zola further forward to play alongside Mark Hughes and the new pairing played so well together that the clearly disgruntled Italian could not regain his first-team place, sitting out the next seven matches until the dramatic FA Cup fourth round tie against Liverpool, when he surprisingly replaced Mark Hughes. Two goals down at half time, Gullit gambled by bringing Hughes off the bench and playing three up front and the Blues responded with a scintillating display of attacking football with Gianluca scoring the two deciding goals. However, after the euphoria of this famous victory it was back to the bench as Gullit stuck to his 3-5-2 strategy. An extravagantly gifted player with a wide range of ball skills, flicks and feints, he has a good footballing brain which enables him to lose defenders and create space in the tightest of penalty-box situations and has endeared himself to Chelsea fans with his sheer enthusiasm, workrate and commitment to the team's cause. In coming on for the final two minutes, the Italian got his wish of participating in the FA Cup final, a 2-0 win over Middlesbrough earning him a cup winners medal.

Chelsea (Free from Juventus, via Sampdoria and Cremonese, on 10/7/96) PL 23+5/9 FLC 1 FAC 1+3/2

VICKERS Stephen (Steve)
Born: Bishop Auckland, 13 October 1967
Height: 6'1" Weight: 12.12
Club Honours: AMC '90; Div 1 '95

Voted Player of the Year by the Middlesbrough faithful in 1995-96, Steve built on his tremendous popularity by turning in even more performances of sterling quality last season. His goals against Liverpool in the fifth round of the Coca-Cola Cup merely epitomised his determination and confidence, while a string of star ratings and Man of the Match awards underlined his commitment. A brilliant central defender, whose ball-playing skills and control of the defensive areas were faultless throughout the campaign, he is sure to be one of the men that Bryan Robson builds on to get the club back into the top flight at the first time of asking.

Tranmere Rov (Signed from Spennymoor U on 11/9/85) FL 310+1/11 FLC 20+1/5 FAC 19/3 Others 36/1
Middlesbrough (£700,000 on 3/12/93) P/FL 127+4/7 FLC 14+1/2 FAC 12+1 Others 2

VIERA Patrick
Born: Angola, 25 May 1973
Height: 6'4" Weight: 13.0
International Honours: France: 5

The first signing for Arsene Wenger, ahead of his arrival as the new manager at Arsenal, Patrick joined the club from the Italian giants, AC Milan, at the start of last season and once into the side, making his debut at home to Chelsea, the tall and elegant midfielder quickly settled into the English game. In particular, and somewhat surprisingly, the Frenchman relished the physical side, but it was his visionary passing that really excited the fans, bringing back memories of Highbury legend, Liam Brady. With a fierce shot in either foot, he scored a life-saving equaliser against Derby at Highbury in injury time, a fierce half volley from the edge of a crowded penalty area that beat the 'keeper all ends up, for his first goal in this country. The French international looks to be a quality player and one much needed in the Gunners' changing format.

Arsenal (£3,500,000 from AC Milan on 14/8/96) PL 30+1/2 FLC 3 FAC 3 Others 1

VINCENT Jamie Roy
Born: Wimbledon, 18 June 1975
Height: 5'10" Weight: 11.8

Brought in from Crystal Palace during the summer of 1996, Jamie settled down to be the first-choice left back at Bournemouth and, subsequently, had a very consistent season. His campaign, however, was interrupted by injury early on, before he came back strongly to play his part in a very solid looking back four. Is always keen to get forward and is adept at delivering a dead ball, creating many goalscoring opportunities from set pieces.

Crystal Palace (From trainee on 13/7/93) FL 19+6 FLC 2+1/1 FAC 1
Bournemouth (Loaned on 18/11/94) FL 8
Bournemouth (£25,000 + on 30/8/96) FL 28+1 FLC 0+1 FAC 1 Others 1

VINNICOMBE Christopher (Chris)
Born: Exeter, 20 October 1970
Height: 5'9" Weight: 10.12
Club Honours: SPD '91
International Honours: E: U21-12

Absent through the ankle injury sustained in 1995-96 for most of the first half of last season, Burnley's unluckiest player was then unable to dislodge David Eyres from his new wing-back role. A classy left back, it remains to be seen whether Adrian Heath's system can accommodate him as a first-team player in 1997-98. At his best, has speed and skill in abundance.

Exeter C (From trainee on 1/7/89) FL 35+4/1 FLC 5/1 Others 2
Glasgow R (£150,000 on 3/11/89) SL 14+9/1 SLC 1+2 Others 1
Burnley (£200,000 on 30/6/94) FL 70+2/3 FLC 7 FAC 1 Others 4

VIRGO James Robert
Born: Brighton, 21 December 1976
Height: 5'11" Weight: 12.10

A local lad, James made Brighton and Hove Albion's senior side on just one occasion during 1996-97, but had the distinction of scoring the extra-time, sudden-death winner with a stunning free kick in a 3-2 defeat of Fulham in the Auto Windscreens Shield competition on 17 December. Despite being released during the summer, the young left back is a highly promising defender and should have no difficulty finding another club.

Brighton & Hove A (From juniors on 10/7/95) FLC 0+1 Others 1/1

VIVEASH Adrian Lee
Born: Swindon, 30 September 1969
Height: 6'1" Weight: 11.9

After his first full season in 1996-97, Adrian was voted Player of the Year for the second time in succession and has now proved to be one of Walsall's best-ever free transfer signings. As the club's only ever present, quite apart from his sterling defensive work and skilful use of the ball, he netted ten goals, most of them from headers, and at one stage at the turn of the year he had scored six in eight games. Is a versatile player, who can perform anywhere across the back four with equal ability and passes both long and accurately.

Swindon T (From trainee on 14/7/88) FL 51+3/2 FLC 6+1 FAC 0+1 Others 2
Reading (Loaned on 4/1/93) FL 5 Others 1/1
Reading (Loaned on 20/1/95) FL 6
Barnsley (Loaned on 10/8/95) FL 2/1
Walsall (Free on 16/10/95) FL 77/9 FLC 2 FAC 9/1 Others 4/1

VONK Michel Christian
Born: Alkmaar, Holland, 28 October 1968
Height: 6'3" Weight: 13.3

The Sheffield United centre back who is excellent in the air and can man mark with the best of them, continued where he left off in the previous season in 1996-97, producing some dominant displays in defence. Scored two early goals in the victory at Stoke City with headers from corners, and was most unlucky not to get a hat-trick, before suffering a knee injury against Swindon in November which necessitated a cartilage operation. Further complications when almost fit meant another spell on the sidelines, one of the factors in United's slump in form in the second half of the term. Will hope to be fully recovered for the new campaign, but faces stiff competition for his place.

Manchester C (£300.000 from SVV Dordrecht on 11/3/92) F/PL 87+4/3 FLC 3+2/1 FAC 6+1/1
Oldham Ath (Loaned on 17/11/95) FL 5/1
Sheffield U (£350,000 on 21/12/95) FL 34/2 FLC 4/2 FAC 2

VOWDEN Colin Dean
Born: Newmarket, 13 September 1971
Height: 6'0" Weight: 13.0

1996-97 was not a happy season for the Cambridge central defender, losing his place after three games and only rarely being used as a substitute. Although he was given a free transfer in mid term, his services were still retained by the club until the end of the campaign as defensive cover. Can also play at full back on either flank, if required.

Cambridge U (£15,000 from Cambridge C on 19/5/95) FL 27+3 FLC 3 Others 2

W

WADDLE Christopher (Chris) Roland
Born: Felling, 14 December 1960
Height: 6'2" Weight: 13.3
International Honours: E: 62; U21-1

Released by Sheffield Wednesday last September, Chris moved north of the border with Falkirk, before signing for Bradford a month later. He certainly looked a class act at Valley Parade and, much to the chagrin of the fans, 28 games and seven goals later, the former England striker moved to Sunderland where he immediately set about trying to save the club from relegation. In seven games, his ability at set pieces set up five out of a total of seven goals and he fulfilled a lifelong ambition of scoring at Roker Park in the final home game at the old ground against Everton, having supported the club as a boy. Typically, the goal was a scorching free kick. Initially handed a short-term contract, at the time of going to press, Chris's future was still undecided following the Rokerites' relegation.
Newcastle U (£1,000 from Tow Law on 28/7/80) FL 169+1/46 FLC 8/2 FAC 12/4
Tottenham H (£590,000 on 1/7/85) FL 137+1/33 FLC 21/4 FAC 14/5 Others 4 (£4,250,000 to Marseilles on 1/7/89)
Sheffield Wed (£1,000,000 on 1/7/92) PL 94+15/10 FLC 19 FAC 12+1/3 Others 3+1/1
Falkirk (Free on 13/9/96) SL 3/1
Bradford C (Free on 12/10/96) FL 25/6 FAC 3/1
Sunderland (£75,000 on 20/3/97) PL 7/1

WADDOCK Gary Patrick
Born: Kingsbury, 17 March 1962
Height: 5'10" Weight: 12.5
Club Honours: Div 2 '83
International Honours: Ei: 21; B-1; U23-1; U21-1

Rewarded for his tenacity and ball-winning, defensive midfield skills by being awarded the Luton club captaincy, Gary led the team to the brink of promotion in 1996-97. An excellent reader of the game, he frequently stopped the midfield being overrun and distributed the ball well out of defence, often to players in wide positions, and on the rare occasions when he was unable to make the starting line up, his presence was sorely missed.
Queens Park R (From apprentice on 26/7/79) FL 191+12/8 FLC 21+1/2 FAC 14 Others 1 (Free to Charleroi in December 1987)
Millwall (£130,000 on 16/8/89) FL 51+7/2 FLC 5+1 FAC 5 Others 3/1
Queens Park R (Free on 20/12/91)
Swindon T (Loaned on 19/3/92) FL 5+1
Bristol Rov (£100,000 on 7/11/92) FL 71/1 FLC 2 FAC 2 Others 2
Luton T (Free on 9/9/94) FL 110+5/3 FLC 6 FAC 4 Others 4+1

WALKER Andrew (Andy) Francis
Born: Glasgow, 6 April 1965
Height: 5'8" Weight: 10.7
Club Honours: S Div 1 '85; SPD '88; SFAC '88
International Honours: S: 3; U21-1

The Sheffield United striker spent periods of the 1996-97 on the bench, emerging to score some vital goals for the club and ending the season as the leading scorer with 15. Continued to show an instinct for being in the right place at the right time, as illustrated by the 77th minute goal at Ipswich which took the Blades to Wembley, when he took several touches to finally coolly place the ball into the net. Yet another United player to suffer from injuries through the season, his ability to score important goals is well recognised, his first touch significant, especially in the penalty area, his second being normally deadly.
Motherwell (From Baillieston Juniors on 31/7/84) SL 65+12/17 SLC 2+4/1 SC 9+2/2
Glasgow Celtic (£350,000 on 1/7/87) SL 86+22/40 SLC 9+6/8 SC 8+3/6 Others 5+2/3
Newcastle U (Loaned on 1/9/91) FL 2 FLC 1
Bolton W (£160,000 on 9/1/92) FL 61+6/44 FLC 3/1 FAC 9+3/8 Others 5/2
Glasgow Celtic (£550,000 on 1/7/94) SL 26+16/9 SLC 6+1/2 SC 3+2 Others 2+1/1
Sheffield U (£500,000 on 23/2/96) FL 32+19/20 FLC 2/2 FAC 1 Others 0+2/1

WALKER Desmond (Des) Sinclair
Born: Hackney, 26 November 1965
Height: 5'11" Weight: 11.13
Club Honours: FLC '89, '90; FMC '89, '92
International Honours: E: 59; U21-7

Des had yet another very successful season in the Sheffield Wednesday defence in 1996-97 and, somewhat surprisingly, failed to get back into an England squad whom many thought would have felt the need to call upon his vast experience. One of the most outstanding sweepers of recent years, and one noted for his tremendous pace and coolness under pressure, his distribution remained sound and he rarely gave the ball away as he marshalled the Owls' defence, alongside either Dejan Stefanovic or Jon Newsome, in playing a big part in the club's successful campaign, missing just three games. Interestingly, he again failed to get on the scoresheet, having just one goal in over 400 league games.
Nottingham F (From apprentice on 2/12/83) FL 259+5/1 FLC 40 FAC 27 Others 14 (£1,500,000 to Sampdoria on 1/8/92)
Sheffield Wed (£2,700,000 on 22/7/93) PL 152 FLC 15 FAC 12

WALKER Ian Michael
Born: Watford, 31 October 1971
Height: 6'1" Weight: 12.9
Club Honours: FAYC '90; CS '91
International Honours: E: 3; U21-9; Yth

1996-97 was an indifferent season for the Tottenham goalkeeper and he found it hard to reproduce the form of 1995-96 which established him as England's regular deputy to David Seaman. At his best when displaying the agility and quick reflexes which have become his trade mark at Tottenham, his cool temperament and self confidence took a massive knock in the 7-1 defeat at Newcastle, the 6-2 exit in the Coca-Cola Cup at the hands of first division champions, Bolton, and the media-wide criticism of his part in Gianfranco Zola's goal in England's 1-0 defeat against Italy in the World Cup qualifier at Wembley.

However, starting to find his best form late in the campaign, Ian has the ability and self belief to silence his critics and shine for Spurs in 1997-98.
Tottenham H (From trainee on 4/12/89) F/PL 162+1 FLC 13 FAC 15 Others 2
Oxford U (Loaned on 31/8/90) FL 2 FLC 1

Ian Walker

WALKER James Barry
Born: Nottingham, 9 July 1973
Height: 5'11" Weight: 13.5

The Walsall goalkeeper lost his place for a spell early on last season after being sent off at Chesterfield and then turning an ankle at Bristol City, but came back strongly and played in all of the last 35 games, making a vital penalty save at Wrexham in April. Undeterred by buffetings in a number of matches, his nickname "Whacker" is due to him being a powerful, long kicker of the ball.
Notts Co (From trainee on 9/7/91)
Walsall (Free on 4/8/93) FL 96+1 FLC 4 FAC 11 Others 4

WALKER John
Born: Glasgow, 12 December 1973
Height: 5'6" Weight: 11.6
International Honours: S: Yth

Clever ball control, distribution and positional sense are this young midfielder's greatest assets. After joining Mansfield from Grimsby last season, having impressed greatly when taken on loan early in September, the club wasted no time in giving him a two-and-a-half year contract. Definitely one for the future, he could go far in the game.
Glasgow R (From Clydebank BC on 29/8/90)
Clydebank (Signed on 31/7/93) SL 18+9/2 Others 4+3
Grimsby T (Signed on 19/9/95) FL 1+2/1
Mansfield T (£50,000 on 6/9/96) FL 33+3/3 FAC 2 Others 1

WALKER Justin
Born: Nottingham, 6 September 1975
Height: 5'10" Weight: 12.12
International Honours: E: Yth

Out of contention for a place at Nottingham Forest in 1996-97, as in previous seasons, Justin was loaned to Scunthorpe in transfer deadline week, making his league debut when coming off the bench against Leyton Orient, before going on to play in the remaining eight fixtures of the campaign. A right-sided midfielder who can also play as a wing back, he impressed as a good passer of the ball with either foot. *Stop Press:* Joined United on a permanent basis on 9 May.
Nottingham F (From juniors on 10/9/92)
Scunthorpe U (Loaned on 26/3/97) FL 8+1

WALKER Keith Cameron
Born: Edinburgh, 17 April 1966
Height: 6'0" Weight: 12.8

In contractual dispute with Swansea at the start of last season, the strong-tackling central defender showed his value to the club when, after signing a weekly contract, steadying the defence and producing consistency week in and week out. Despite repeated rumours regarding a move away from the Vetch, Keith showed his character during the home derby game against Cardiff, playing for nearly 85 minutes with a broken bone in his arm.
Stirling A (Signed from ICI in 1984) SL 82+9/17 SLC 5/3 SC 5/2
St Mirren (Signed during 1987 close season) SL 41+2/6 SLC 3 SC 1 Others 3
Swansea C (£80,000 on 23/11/89) FL 222+8/6 FLC 8 FAC 16/1 Others 26

WALKER Raymond (Ray)
Born: North Shields, 28 September 1963
Height: 5'10" Weight: 12.0
Club Honours: FAYC '80
International Honours: E: Yth

A classy Port Vale midfielder who is nearing the end of this playing days, he was limited to 11 starts in 1996-97, mainly in October and November, before regularly appearing on the bench. Having managed to take his number of senior appearances for the club to over 400, Ray was rewarded with a well deserved testimonial in May, prior to being released in the summer. Has also spent some time coaching the first team and looking after the reserves on occasions, which may prove to be the next step of his career.
Aston Villa (From apprentice on 26/9/81) FL 15+8 FLC 2+1 FAC 2
Port Vale (Loaned on 7/9/84) FL 15/1
Port Vale (£12,000 on 5/8/86) FL 322+29/33 FLC 19+2/1 FAC 25+3/5 Others 22+3/3
Cambridge U (Loaned on 23/9/94) FL 5 Others 2

WALKER Richard Neil
Born: Derby, 9 November 1971
Height: 6'0" Weight: 12.0

A product of the Notts County youth team and one of the longest serving players at the club, this strong, left-footed central defender also appeared at full back and occasionally in midfield last season, standing in for Ian Baraclough, Ian Hendon and Shaun Murphy when needed. A dedicated and wholehearted professional, Richard was surprisingly released during the summer.
Notts Co (From trainee on 3/7/90) FL 63+4/4 FLC 10 FAC 1+2 Others 8+1
Mansfield T (Loaned on 23/3/95) FL 4

WALKER Steven (Steve)
Born: Ashington, 2 November 1973
Height: 5'9" Weight: 10.12
International Honours: E: Sch

Signed from non-league Blyth Spartans during the 1996 close season, this speedy right winger made his Doncaster debut at Rochdale last September before falling victim to the competition for places and returning from whence he came at the beginning of October. However, during his short stay at Belle Vue a facet of his play that stood out was his crossing ability.
Doncaster Rov (Signed from Blyth Spartans on 18/7/96) FL 1

WALLACE Raymond (Ray) George
Born: Greenwich, 2 October 1969
Height: 5'6" Weight: 11.4
International Honours: E: U21-4

An energetic and tough-tackling Stoke central midfielder who failed to recapture his excellent form of 1995-96 last season, possibly due to the changing midfield partners he played with. One of three footballing brothers, Rod (Leeds) and Danny (once of England) being the other two, Ray has proved to be extremely versatile, being more than capable of playing at full back, and always shows great commitment to the cause.
Southampton (From trainee on 21/4/88) FL 33+2 FLC 8 FAC 2 Others 2
Leeds U (£100,000 on 8/7/91) F/PL 5+2
Swansea C (Loaned on 20/3/92) FL 2
Reading (Loaned on 11/3/94) FL 3
Stoke C (Free on 11/8/94) FL 105+4/9 FLC 8 FAC 4 Others 11/1
Hull C (Loaned on 16/12/94) FL 7

Ray Wallace

WALLACE Rodney (Rod) Seymour
Born: Greenwich, 2 October 1969
Height: 5'7" Weight: 11.3
Club Honours: Div 1 '92; CS '92
International Honours: E: B-2; U21-11

Like Lucas Radebe, Rod seemed to thrive on the change of management at Leeds in 1996-97, and, despite his infrequent appearances, was the side's top scorer,

bagging a brace against Nottingham Forest in October to give the new manager his first victory, while appearing to keep his goals for the cup competitions, including a spectacular long-range winner in the FA Cup replay with Crystal Palace and the winner over Arsenal in the next round. Although this speedy and direct player could have, on previous occasions, been sold, he stayed and his attitude and application under George Graham was first class, while his ability to come from wide and deep positions was always a problem for the opposition.
Southampton (From trainee on 19/4/88) FL 111+17/45 FLC 18+1/6 FAC 10/3 Others 3+1/2
Leeds U (£1,600,000 on 7/6/91) F/PL 158+23/43 FLC 14+1/6 FAC 12+5/3 Others 1+4/1

Rod Wallace

WALLING Dean Anthony
Born: Leeds, 17 April 1969
Height: 6'0" Weight: 11.10
Club Honours: Div 3 '95; AMC '97

With well over 200 league appearances for Carlisle, "Deano", one of the longest serving players at Brunton Park, was an ever present in 1996-97, apart from one cup match, and can look back on another season in which his committed performances were a key factor in the club's success. Apart from his sterling work in defence, his power in the air again brought him several goals and he was one of four United players named in the third division PFA select side.
Rochdale (Free from Leeds U juniors on 30/7/87) FL 43+22/8 FLC 3 FAC 0+1 Others 1+1 (Free to Kitchener (Toronto), during 1990 close season)
Carlisle U (Free from Guiseley, via Franklin (Toronto), on 1/7/91) FL 224+6/21 FLC 16/2 FAC 14+1/1 Others 35/5

WALSH Gary
Born: Wigan, 21 March 1968
Height: 6'3" Weight: 15.10
Club Honours: ECWC '91; ESC '91; FAC '94
International Honours: E: U21-2

Known to Middlesbrough fans as "Safe Hands", Gary could just as easily have made

the grade in rugby league, the goalkeeper also being a skilful practitioner with the odd-shaped ball. Having spent many years at Old Trafford, understudying Jim Leighton and Peter Schmeichel, before "Robbo" plucked him from relative obscurity to become Boro's number one shot stopper, he gave many brilliant displays last season before injury and illness allowed the new signing, Mark Schwartzer, to deprive him of his coveted position. Tall and commanding, he kept six clean sheets in his 16 first-team appearances and vows to be back.

Manchester U (From juniors on 25/4/85) F/PL 49+1 FLC 7 Others 6
Airdrie (Loaned on 11/8/88) SL 3 SLC 1
Oldham Ath (Loaned on 19/11/93) PL 6
Middlesbrough (£500,000 on 11/8/95) PL 44 FLC 9 FAC 4

WALSH Michael Shane
Born: Rotherham, 5 August 1977
Height: 6'0" Weight: 12.8

A slightly built, but competent and confident ever-improving Scunthorpe right back, Michael continued his improvement in 1996-97 and is currently tipped for a higher grade football. An added bonus is his long throw, which can be as good as a corner kick when launched into opposition areas.

Scunthorpe U (From trainee on 3/7/95) FL 57+7 FLC 2 FAC 5 Others 2

WALSH Steven (Steve)
Born: Preston, 3 November 1964
Height: 6'3" Weight: 14.9
Club Honours: AMC '85; FLC '97

In a richly-deserved testimonial year, Steve, sent off early in the 1996-97 campaign at West Ham, continued to be a major influence at Leicester as club captain. The left-footed central defender hit the post with long-range screamer at Nottingham Forest, before scoring his first ever Premiership goal at home to Everton, having previously missed a penalty at Tottenham. A player who is always in the wars, he suffered a groin injury against Manchester United in the Coca-Cola Cup that resulted in a hernia operation, then required another knee operation before his return, and pressed back into action in the FA Cup tie against Chelsea, despite not being fully recovered, scored the goal that brought City back into the game. Two days later he suffered a further groin injury in the Coca-Cola Cup semi final against Wimbledon, then injured a toe at Goodison Park. Despite these problems, he led his team by example in the Coca-Cola Cup final matches, setting up both the equaliser at Wembley and the winner at Hillsborough, where he deservedly won the Man of the Match award. Due to undergo another groin operation during the summer, he is more than capable of playing up front if required, his aerial ability and aggression giving the club several options.

Wigan Ath (From juniors on 11/9/82) FL 123+3/4 FLC 7 FAC 6 Others 10+2
Leicester C (£100,000 on 24/6/86) F/PL 307+2/47 FLC 31/3 FAC 11/1 Others 22/4

WALTERS Mark Everton
Born: Birmingham, 2 June 1964
Height: 5'9" Weight: 11.8
Club Honours: FAYC '80; ESC '82; SPD '89, '90, '91; SLC '89, '91; FAC '92
International Honours: E: 1; B-1; U21-9; Yth; Sch

Released by Southampton in the summer of 1996, Mark was reunited with a former Liverpool colleague when Steve McMahon signed the mercurial winger for Swindon – although theirs was not a close playing association, only ten games in the same team before the latter's departure. For the first half of last season, he was highly effective for the Robins, both as a goalmaker, with his intelligent crosses, and as a goalscorer. However, after Christmas he was troubled with a persistent thigh injury and made no further first-team appearances from February onwards. With a deficiency of creativity in the existing Robins' squad, a fully fit Mark Walters is vital to Town's prospects next season.

Aston Villa (From apprentice on 18/5/82) FL 168+13/39 FLC 20+1/6 FAC 11+1/1 Others 7+3/2
Glasgow R (£500,000 on 31/12/87) SL 101+5/32 SLC 13/11 SC 14/6 Others 10/2
Liverpool (£1,250,000 on 13/8/91) F/PL 58+36/14 FLC 10+2/4 FAC 6+3 Others 8+1/1
Stoke C (Loaned on 24/3/94) FL 9/2
Wolverhampton W (Loaned on 9/9/94) FL 11/3
Southampton (Free on 18/1/96) PL 4+1 FAC 4
Swindon T (Free on 31/7/96) FL 24+3/7 FLC 4/1 FAC 1

WALTON David (Dave) Lee
Born: Bedlington, 10 April 1973
Height: 6'2" Weight: 14.1
Club Honours: Div 3 '94

A very strong and committed Shrewsbury Town central defender, who always gives 110 per cent, and dangerous at set pieces in the air, his 1996-97 season was interrupted by injury. An automatic choice when fit, he bounced back as if he had never been away. Is certain to be a key member of the side as Town try to come back to the second division at the first time of asking in 1997-98.

Sheffield U (Free from Ashington on 13/3/92)
Shrewsbury T (Signed on 5/11/93) FL 121+1/9 FLC 6 FAC 10/1 Others 11/1

WALTON Mark Andrew
Born: Merthyr Tydfil, 1 June 1969
Height: 6'2" Weight: 14.7
International Honours: W: U21-1

After understudying Brian Gunn at Norwich and playing in the 1992 FA Cup semi final against Sunderland, things went wrong for Mark and he was out of football for 18 months until being invited to Fulham's 1996 summer training. An all-action goalkeeper, he earned himself a contract and vyed for the number one spot with Tony Lange for most of last season, before emerging as first choice in February. Very strong in coming out for crosses, and a good long kicker, he was awarded a further contract before the end of the campaign.

Luton T (From juniors on 21/2/87)
Colchester U (£15,000 on 5/11/87) FL 40 FLC 3 FAC 8 Others 5

Norwich C (£75,000 on 15/8/89) FL 22 FLC 1 FAC 5
Wrexham (Loaned on 27/8/93) FL 6
Dundee (Free on 27/1/94)
Bolton W (Free on 2/3/94) FL 3 (Free to Wrexham on 9/9/94)
Fulham (Free from Fakenham T on 12/8/96) FL 28 FLC 3 Others 1

WALTON Paul Anthony
Born: Sunderland, 2 July 1979
Height: 5'9" Weight: 11.0

After his early promotion to the Hartlepool first team the previous season, this young striker will probably be a little disappointed not to have made a bigger impact in 1996-97. A left-sided forward who can show great speed, he remains a great prospect, however, and has now been offered a full professional contract after completing his two years as a YTS player.

Hartlepool U (Trainee) FL 3+7

WANCHOPE Pablo Cesar
Born: Costa Rica, 31 July 1976
Height: 6'4" Weight: 12.0
International Honours: Costa Rica: 17

A tall and extravagantly skilled Derby striker, Paulo signed from Costa Rica, where he is a full international, on transfer deadline day. Made national TV on his debut with a wonderful solo goal at Old Trafford, a sign of things to come once he makes the adaptation to English football. Few, if any, players have made a more spectacular top-flight debut than his at Old Trafford in April. Not only did he create Derby's opening goal with a knock down to Ashley Ward, but he followed it up with a solo effort after carrying the ball 40 yards into the heart of the United defence and toe poking it past Peter Schmeichel to give Derby a 2-0 lead, thus paving the way for the Ram's first victory at Old Trafford for over 30 years. Not easy to shake off the ball, and already a favourite with the home crowd, he signed for County after being rejected by QPR, following a trial period at Loftus Road. Has already drawn comparisons with Leicester's Emile Heskey.

Derby Co (£600,000 from CS Heridiano on 27/3/97) PL 2+3/1

WANLESS Paul Steven
Born: Banbury, 14 December 1973
Height: 6'1" Weight: 13.4

As Cambridge's "Mr Versatile", the useful midfielder once again found himself in between the posts in 1996-97, when he played the second half of the home game against Swansea and kept a clean sheet. A player who can also be used in defence and up front, Paul was out of the team for a while, but returned to score vital goals and add bite to the midfield in the last part of the season. Full of enthusiasm, he rarely gives opposing forwards much room to work in.

Oxford U (From trainee on 3/12/91) FL 12+20 FLC 0+3/1 Others 2+2
Lincoln C (Free on 7/7/95) FL 7+1 Others 2
Cambridge U (Free on 8/3/96) FL 41+3/4 FLC 1 FAC 1 Others 1

WARBURTON Raymond (Ray)
Born: Rotherham, 7 October 1967
Height: 6'0" Weight: 12.13
Northampton's central defender and club captain, "Mr Dependable", the 1995-96 Player of the Year, missed the start of last season due to an operation. Thankfully, back to his best, he could always be seen lurking around the far post at set pieces, from where he scored several goals as the club moved towards the play offs, including one in the semi-final leg prior to promotion being achieved.
Rotherham U (From apprentice on 5/10/85) FL 3+1 FAC 2 Others 2
York C (Free on 8/8/89) FL 86+4/9 FLC 8/1 FAC 6/1 Others 7
Northampton T (£35,000 on 4/2/94) FL 135/11 FLC 4 FAC 4/1 Others 12/2

Ray Warburton

WARD Ashley Stuart
Born: Manchester, 24 November 1970
Height: 6'1" Weight: 12.4
A much travelled striker, Derby being his seventh club, he formed a dangerous partnership with Dean Sturridge after missing the first two months of last season due to a hernia operation. Strong in the air, and alert to the half chance close to goal, he had difficulty winning over the home crowd before a run of six goals in eight games during March and April convinced them of his worth. Among his strikes was one in the 90th minute at Chelsea, which gave County a 3-2 win, while one home victory over Coventry and a draw at the Baseball Ground against Southampton. Is one of the best front men around when it comes to holding the ball up with his back to the goal.

Manchester C (From trainee on 5/8/89) FL 0+1 FAC 0+2
Wrexham (Loaned on 10/1/91) FL 4/2 Others 1
Leicester C (£80,000 on 30/7/91) FL 2+8 FLC 2+1 FAC 0+1 Others 0+1
Blackpool (Loaned on 21/11/92) FL 2/1
Crewe Alex (£80,000 on 1/12/92) FL 58+3/25 FLC 4/2 FAC 2/4 Others 7/5
Norwich C (£500,000 on 8/12/94) P/FL 53/18 FLC 6/3 FAC 1
Derby Co (£1,000,000 on 19/3/96) F/PL 30+7/9 FLC 1+1 FAC 2/1

WARD Darren
Born: Worksop, 11 May 1974
Height: 5'11" Weight: 12.9
International Honours: W: U21-2
This highly talented Notts County goalkeeper was widely tipped for a Premiership future and seen as a potential long-term successor to Neville Southall in the Welsh side, but slipped back in the pecking order in 1996-97. An outstanding prospect, in a season that saw County relegated, Darren could still be relied upon, keeping nine clean sheets in the first 31 league matches, before losing his place to Michael Pollitt. However, regained form, confidence, and his goalkeeping jersey towards the end of a tough campaign.
Mansfield T (From trainee on 27/7/92) FL 81 FLC 5 FAC 5 Others 6
Notts Co (£160,000 on 11/7/95) FL 84 FLC 6 FAC 7 Others 7

WARD Darren Philip
Born: Kenton, 13 September 1978
Height: 6'0" Weight: 11.8
In making eight appearances in 1996-97, this highly promising centre half merely enhanced the fine impression he had made on his debut the previous season. Already over six feet tall, with a build to match, Darren is strong in the air and not afraid to bring the ball out of defence and definitely looks to be one for the future.
Watford (From trainee on 13/2/97) FL 8 FAC 1

WARD Gavin John
Born: Sutton Coldfield, 30 June 1970
Height: 6'4" Weight: 14.12
Club Honours: Div 3 '93; WC '93
A talented Bolton goalkeeper, providing experienced back up for Keith Branagan in 1996-97, Gavin had a run of 13 games in the first team in the New Year, initially when injury prevented the latter from playing. During this period, he produced some assured and commanding performances, although a couple of poor team displays, including the shock FA Cup defeat by Chesterfield, led to a Branagan recall. Despite failing to regain the number one jersey for the rest of the season, he is sure to be a constant threat to Branagan for the coveted goalkeeping position in 1997-98.
Shrewsbury T (Free from Aston Villa juniors on 26/9/88)
West Bromwich A (Free on 18/9/89)
Cardiff C (Free on 5/10/89) FL 58+1 FAC 1 Others 7
Leicester C (£175,000 on 16/7/93) F/PL 38 FLC 3 FAC 0+1 Others 4
Bradford C (£175,000 on 13/7/95) FL 36 FLC 6 FAC 3 Others 2
Bolton W (£300,000 on 29/3/96) F/PL 15+1 FLC 1 FAC 3

WARD Mark William
Born: Huyton, 10 October 1962
Height: 5'5" Weight: 10.0
Club Honours: Div 2 '95; AMC '95
International Honours: E: SP-1
Released by Huddersfield during the 1996 season, the hard-working central midfielder, who keeps play simple and tackles with the best of them, spent a month as a non-contract player at Wigan Athletic. Unfortunately, a hand injury sustained in the victory over Torquay ended his spell at the club.
Everton (From apprentice on 5/9/80)
Oldham Ath (£10,000 from Northwich Victoria on 19/7/83) FL 84/12 FLC 5 FAC 3
West Ham U (£250,000 on 15/8/85) FL 163+2/12 FLC 20+1/2 FAC 17 Others 6
Manchester C (£1,000,000 on 29/12/89) FL 55/14 FLC 3 FAC 6 Others 3/2
Everton (£1,100,000 on 12/8/91) F/PL 82+1/6 FLC 6/1 FAC 4 Others 1
Birmingham C (£500,000 on 24/3/94) FL 63/7 FLC 6+1 FAC 4 Others 8/1
Huddersfield T (Free on 22/3/96) FL 7+1
Wigan Ath (Free on 27/9/96) FL 5

WARD Mitchum (Mitch) David
Born: Sheffield, 19 June 1971
Height: 5'8" Weight: 10.12
A versatile Sheffield United player who performed well in 1996-97 in midfield, on the wide right and in both full-back positions, wearing seven different shirts in the process. Although one of the first names to appear on the team sheet, and the team penalty taker, Mitch perhaps suffered from the constant change in position, sometimes from match to match, but remained one of the most consistent players throughout a long, hard campaign that ended in disappointment on the Wembley turf, following Crystal Palace's last-minute winner that took them into the Premiership rather than United. Missed a spell of two months in mid term, due to a broken bone in his foot suffered at West Bromwich Albion.
Sheffield U (From trainee on 1/7/89) F/PL 132+16/10 FLC 8+3/2 FAC 7+2/2 Others 5+1/1
Crewe Alex (Loaned on 1/11/90) FL 4/1 FAC 1/1 Others 2

WARD Nicholas John
Born: Wrexham, 30 November 1977
Height: 5'9" Weight: 11.9
Having signed pro forms for Shrewsbury during the 1996 close season, following his YTS apprenticeship, the busy forward was given the opportunity to make his mark, with a mix of full starts and sub appearances, scoring his first goal on New Year's Day. Needs a target man to feed off if the club are to get the full benefit of his abilities.
Shrewsbury T (From trainee on 12/7/96) FL 5+9/1 FAC 0+1 Others 0+2

WARD Peter
Born: Durham, 15 October 1964
Height: 5'11" Weight: 11.10
Central midfielder. A prominent hub in Wrexham's midfield engine room with his

free kicks always a cause for concern among opposition goalkeepers, Peter revelled in the FA Cup run last season and was involved in many of the vital moments. A fine passer of the ball, which fits in well with the passing game that is the hallmark of the club's style of play, he missed a number of games towards the end of the campaign, which did not help the hoped for push towards the play-off positions!

Huddersfield T (Signed from Chester le Street on 7/1/87) FL 24+13/2 FLC 1+1 FAC 2 Others 1
Rochdale (Free on 20/7/89) FL 83+1/10 FLC 5 FAC 7/1 Others 5
Stockport Co (Signed on 6/6/91) FL 140+2/10 FLC 8/1 FAC 7 Others 26/6
Wrexham (£50,000 on 19/7/95) FL 57+1/7 FLC 3 FAC 13/1 Others 1/1

Peter Ward

WARE Paul David
Born: Congleton, 7 November 1970
Height: 5'9" Weight: 11.5
Club Honours: Div 2 '93

This combative Stockport midfielder again had his first-team opportunities restricted in 1996-97, due to the fierce competition for places, and had a spell on loan at Cardiff in a bid for a regular place. Although performing well in his five games, his probing passes being a joy to watch, a permanent move failed to materialise and Paul returned home, leaving County with a more than useful reserve, prior to being released in the summer. Earlier in the campaign he had scored his customary superb goal, a 30-yard cracker that put Chesterfield out of the Coca-Cola Cup.

Stoke C (From trainee on 15/11/88) FL 92+23/10 FLC 7+1 FAC 4+1 Others 12+2/4
Stockport Co (Signed on 8/9/94) FL 42+12/14 FLC 6+1/1 FAC 2 Others 3/1
Cardiff C (Loaned on 29/1/97) FL 5

WARHURST Paul
Born: Stockport, 26 September 1969
Height: 6'1" Weight: 12.10
Club Honours: PL '95
International Honours: E: U21-8

1996-97 was yet another frustrating season for the talented Blackburn utility player. Given the opportunity to start in the strike force (he can play equally well in any number of positions, including midfield and defence), Paul played in the opening four matches (the first as a sub), before pulling a muscle and being out of action until February. Initially relegated to the bench, on his return he started the Manchester United game at Ewood Park and scored, thus completing a curious record of having only scored two goals during the campaign, both of them against the Old Trafford outfit. The son of a former pro, Roy, he has overcome a whole range of serious injuries in the past to make his mark, his athletic frame and spirit getting him through and, no doubt, he will be looking forward to making a 1997-98 start under new manager, Roy Hodgson.

Manchester C (From trainee on 1/7/88)
Oldham Ath (£10,000 on 27/10/88) FL 60+7/2 FLC 8 FAC 5+4 Others 2
Sheffield Wed (£750,000 on 17/7/91) F/PL 60+6/6 FLC 9/4 FAC 7+1/5 Others 5/3
Blackburn Rov (£2,700,000 on 17/8/93) PL 30+27/4 FLC 6+2 FAC 2+1 Others 4+2

WARK John
Born: Glasgow, 4 August 1957
Height: 5'10" Weight: 12.10
Club Honours: FAYC '75; FAC '78; UEFAC '81; SC '86; Div 2 '92
International Honours: S: 29; U21-8; Yth

Despite not intending to play for Ipswich in 1996-97, John was required to turn out on three occasions - at Fulham, QPR and Tranmere - and did not let anyone down, the training he did to prepare himself for his testimonial match against Arsenal standing him in good stead. Having now confirmed that this was indeed his last season as a player, he will be remembered with great affection as one of Town's all-time greats, and a man who scored over 200 goals during three spells at Portman Road.

Ipswich T (From apprentice on 1/8/74) FL 295+1/94 FLC 24+1/12 FAC 36+1/12 Others 25/18
Liverpool (£450,000 on 10/3/84) FL 64+6/28 FLC 6+4/3 FAC 11+2/6 Others 13+2/5
Ipswich T (£100,000 on 4/1/88) FL 87+2/23 FLC 4 FAC 3 Others 9/2
Middlesbrough (£50,000 on 23/8/90) FL 31+1/2 FLC 5 FAC 2 Others 1
Ipswich T (Free on 21/9/91) F/PL 151+3/18 FLC 14+1 FAC 16/2 Others 5

WARNER Michael James
Born: Harrogate, 17 January 1974
Height: 5'9" Weight: 10.10

A right-sided or central midfield player, Michael joined Northampton in 1995-96 and spent some time on loan to non-league Telford, after competing for Great Britain in the Student Games in Japan. Forced his way into the first team last season and appears to have a great future ahead of him.

Northampton T (Free from Tamworth on 10/7/95) FL 1+8 FAC 0+1 Others 1+1

WARNER Robert (Robbie) Mark
Born: Stratford on Avon, 20 April 1977
Height: 5'10" Weight: 11.6

Robbie made an excellent start to his league career at Hereford in 1994-95 before breaking a leg a few games before the end of the campaign, an injury that kept him out of first team action throughout 1995-96. The tough-tackling midfielder finally got back into contention last December, having been on the bench for several weeks, and soon gained a regular place, settling in well and trying hard in difficult circumstances. He will be a key player in the Conference this term.

Hereford U (From trainee on 17/1/95) FL 31+6 FLC 1 FAC 0+1 Others 1

WARNER Vance
Born: Leeds, 3 September 1974
Height: 6'0" Weight: 13.2
International Honours: E: Yth

After coming into the side for the visit to Liverpool, the centre back doubled his Nottingham Forest appearances with a handful of games as cover for others towards the end of last season. Big and strong, a sound tackler, and good in the air, Vance will be looking to breakthrough in 1997-98.

Nottingham F (From trainee on 14/9/91) F/PL 4+1 FLC 1
Grimsby T (Loaned on 2/2/96) FL 3

WARREN Christer
Born: Bournemouth, 10 October 1974
Height: 5'10" Weight: 11.3

An attacking Southampton player who is capable of providing good crosses from either flank and not afraid to get into shooting range, Christer did not seem to fit into the new manager, Graeme Souness' scheme of things and went on loan first to Brighton (October) and, then to Fulham (March), making a Saints' sub appearance in between. Played just three times for Albion before damaged tendons in his left knee saw him back at the Dell for treatment, but had better luck for the Londoners, scoring on his debut (his first league goal) against Scarborough and playing in the last 11 games as part of the side that gained promotion to the second division.

Southampton (£40,000 from Cheltenham T on 31/3/95) PL 1+7 FLC 1
Brighton & Hove A (Loaned on 11/10/96) FL 3
Fulham (Loaned on 6/3/97) FL 8+3/1

WARREN Lee Anthony
Born: Manchester, 28 February 1969
Height: 6'0" Weight: 12.2

A versatile Doncaster Rovers' player who can perform equally well in defence or midfield, Lee missed the first three months of last season with a troublesome foot injury. Appeared to have no further problems with the injury, playing regularly from November onwards and showing much skill.

Leeds U (From trainee on 27/7/87)
Rochdale (Free on 28/10/87) FL 31/1 FAC 1 Others 2
Hull C (£40,000 on 25/8/88) FL 141+12/1 FLC 2 FAC 5+1 Others 3+2/1

Lincoln C (Loaned on 20/9/90) FL 2+1/1
Doncaster Rov (Free on 21/7/94) FL 71+10/2
FLC 2 FAC 1+1 Others 4+1

WARREN Mark Wayne
Born: Clapton, 12 November 1974
Height: 5'9" Weight: 11.2
International Honours: E: Yth
Following the arrival of Tommy Taylor as manager at Leyton Orient, Mark was switched from right back to centre half, where he used his pace to great effect and was not afraid to get forward in support of the forwards. Voted the Supporters Away Player and Player of the Year, he has now played just about everywhere for the Londoners, whether it be as a goalscoring forward or tough-tackling midfielder.
Leyton Orient (From trainee on 6/7/92) FL 83+18/5 FLC 4 FAC 2 Others 8+4/1

WARRINGTON Andrew (Andy) Clifford
Born: Sheffield, 10 June 1976
Height: 6'3" Weight: 12.13
With the departure of goalkeeper, Dean Kiely to Bury on the eve of last season, Andy was thrust into first-team action between the sticks with York. As you would have expected, his confidence was a little shaky in the early weeks and although having outstanding games against Everton, he lost his place in October to Tim Clarke. However, recalled four months later, his confidence restored, he finished the campaign in good form as the Minstermen avoided the drop.
York C (From trainee on 11/6/94) FL 33 FLC 6 FAC 1 Others 3

WASSALL Darren Paul
Born: Birmingham, 27 June 1968
Height: 5'11" Weight: 12.10
Club Honours: FMC '92
Unable to get an opportunity at Derby last season, Darren had two spells on loan, at Manchester City (September) and Birmingham (March), in an effort to get some match practice. An experienced defender, who has bags of pace and is a specialist man marker, he was an ever present during his three-month loan at Maine Road, playing for five different managers, and standing tall alongside Kit Symons at the heart of the defence until damaging his Achilles tendon and being forced onto the sidelines. Back at the Baseball Ground, he was rescued by Birmingham manager, Trevor Francis, who recognised his ability, and performed solidly next to Gary Ablett after Steve Bruce missed most of the final two months of the campaign due to injury. Stop Press: Signed on a permanent basis for Birmingham on 17 May, £100,000 changing hands.
Nottingham F (From apprentice on 1/6/86) FL 17+10 FLC 6+2 FAC 3+1 Others 4+2/1
Hereford U (Loaned on 23/10/87) FL 5 FAC 1 Others 1
Bury (Loaned on 2/3/89) FL 7/1
Derby Co (£600,000 on 15/6/92) FL 90+8 FLC 9 FAC 4 Others 11
Manchester C (Loaned on 11/9/96) FL 14+1 FLC 2
Birmingham C (Loaned on 26/3/97) FL 8

WATERMAN David (Dave) Graham
Born: Guernsey, 16 May 1977
Height: 5'10" Weight: 12.0
A second year Portsmouth professional and former youth team captain, the young defender spent most of last season on the edge of the squad after making his first-team debut when coming off the bench at Grimsby at the end of August. A player who is highly thought of at Fratton Park, Dave made three more subs' appearances and looks to make the breakthrough in 1997-98.
Portsmouth (From trainee on 4/7/95) FL 0+4

WATKIN Stephen (Steve)
Born: Wrexham, 16 June 1971
Height: 5'10" Weight: 11.10
Club Honours: WC '95
International Honours: W: B-2; Sch
The FA Cup has always been Steve's favourite competition, as illustrated by his contribution to Wrexham, and last season was no exception with his forward play significant in the club's run to the quarter finals. His league form did not produce enough goals, however, and he put in a transfer request, feeling a change of club may do him good. Withdrawing this later to concentrate on keeping his place in the side, he held the ball up very well for his colleagues and was always aware of goal chances. An in form Steve Watkin means good news for the fans!
Wrexham (From juniors on 24/7/89) FL 167+30/54 FLC 11+2/4 FAC 16+6/12 Others 17+5/4

WATKINSON Russell
Born: Epsom, 3 December 1977
Height: 5'10" Weight: 11.1
Snapped up by Southampton from non-league Woking at the start of last season, having played in the Surrey side's successful youth team during 1995-96, Russell made his Premiership debut just six matches into the new campaign when coming on in place of Matt le Tissier at the Dell against Tottenham for the final 23 minutes. A strong-running right winger, cum forward, who gets in good crosses, the youngster made two further subs' appearances before going back to the reserves to add to his experience.
Southampton (Free from Woking on 4/9/96) PL 0+2 FLC 0+1

WATKISS Stuart Paul
Born: Wolverhampton, 8 May 1966
Height: 6'2" Weight: 13.7
Having joined Mansfield from Hereford during the 1996 close season, this reliable and dependable defender was soon made club captain and led by example. He was very unfortunate to be suspended for three games when he passed his disciplinary points limit, then was sent off in the penultimate game before his suspension – adding even more to his woes – picking up a further three-game consecutive ban. Took time to win back his place in the senior side afterwards, but when doing so he gave some excellent performances.
Wolverhampton W (From trainee on 13/7/84) FL 2

Crewe Alex (Free on 28/2/86) FL 3
Walsall (Free from Rushall Olympic on 5/8/93) FL 60+2/2 FLC 8/1 FAC 5 Others 2
Hereford U (Free on 16/2/96) FL 19 Others 2
Mansfield T (Free on 17/7/96) FL 30+1/1 FLC 1 FAC 1

WATSON Alexander (Alex) Francis
Born: Liverpool, 5 April 1968
Height: 6'1" Weight: 13.0
Club Honours: CS '88
International Honours: E: Yth
As captain, Alex was the only Torquay player to start every game last season. A great inspiration to all with his aerial power and strength in the tackle, the central defender deservedly won United's Player of the Year award. Is the brother of Everton's Dave.
Liverpool (From apprentice on 18/5/85) FL 3+1 FLC 1+1 FAC 1+1 Others 1
Derby Co (Loaned on 30/8/90) FL 5
Bournemouth (£150,000 on 18/1/91) FL 145+6/5 FLC 14/1 FAC 12/1 Others 5
Gillingham (Loaned on 11/9/95) FL 10/1
Torquay U (£50,000 on 23/11/95) FL 75/3 FLC 2 FAC 3 Others 1/1

WATSON Andrew (Andy) Anthony
Born: Leeds, 1 April 1967
Height: 5'9" Weight: 11.2
Club Honours: WC '91
On a weekly contract at Blackpool at the start of last season, Andy signed for Walsall in September and made his debut against his former club a few days later, laying on a goal for Mark Blake. He then netted against Wycombe in his second game, but rather mixed fortunes followed, having a spell in midfield later on. A striker who can make his own goalscoring opportunities he netted a superb match winner at Bristol Rovers' Memorial ground with a dipping drive, but could never quite put an extended run of form together.
Halifax T (Free from Harrogate T on 23/8/88) FL 75+8/15 FLC 5+1/2 FAC 6/1 Others 7/1
Swansea C (£40,000 on 31/7/90) FL 9+5/1 FLC 0+1 Others 1+1
Carlisle U (£30,000 on 19/9/91) FL 55+1/22 FLC 4/5 FAC 3 Others 1/1
Blackpool (£55,000 on 5/2/93) FL 88+27/43 FLC 6/5 FAC 3+2 Others 7+1/1
Walsall (£60,000 on 5/9/96) FL 22+14/5 FAC 0+3 Others 1

WATSON David (Dave)
Born: Liverpool, 20 November 1961
Height: 6'0" Weight: 13.7
Club Honours: FLC '85; Div 2 '86; Div 1 '87, CS '87, '95; FAC '95
International Honours: E: 12; U21-7 (UEFAC '84)
An aggressive and inspirational centre half in 1996-97, Dave remained as integral and important a member of the Everton set up in his testimonial season, as he had been since his debut ten years earlier. He kicked off the campaign as club captain, and ended it as caretaker/manager, following the departure of Joe Royle! Having suffered a knee injury on the opening day, which sidelined him for two months, on his return he swiftly recaptured the form he had displayed throughout a decade of model consistency at Goodison. Still one of the fittest men at the

club, he has been tipped to take up a coaching role when he eventually hangs up his boots.
Liverpool (From juniors on 25/5/79)
Norwich C (£100,000 on 29/11/80) FL 212/11 FLC 21/3 FAC 18/1
Everton (£900,000 on 22/8/86) F/PL 367+2/23 FLC 35/6 FAC 44/5 Others 16+1/3

WATSON David Neil
Born: Barnsley, 10 November 1973
Height: 6'0" Weight: 12.3
International Honours: E: U21-5; Yth
The number one choice in goal for Barnsley in 1996-97, being ever present in a team that won promotion to the Premiership, the only time the club has been among the elite in 99 years, speaks for itself. Certainly, in keeping 18 clean sheets, his shot stopping remained second to none and he worked hard with great success on improving his ability to deal with crosses – the goalkeepers night-mare. Distribution was also an impressive feature of his play.
Barnsley (From trainee on 4/7/92) FL 142 FLC 13 FAC 5 Others 1

WATSON Gordon William George
Born: Sidcup, 20 March 1971
Height: 5'11" Weight: 12.9
International Honours: E: U21-2
A hard-working Southampton forward, he started last season on the bench under the new manager, Graeme Souness, but once he got going he soon hit the target, scoring three times in six Coca-Cola Cup outings, although Premiership goals were harder to come by. Useful in the air, a good target man, and a striker who chases lost causes, he found his way blocked at the Dell once Egil Ostenstad and Eyal Berkovic had established themselves and was allowed to join Bradford in January. Made a good start, scoring the winner against Port Vale in his second game, but then tragedy struck when he suffered a double fracture of the right leg after just four minutes of the Huddersfield match. Obviously a great disappointment, but Gordon will be back.
Charlton Ath (From trainee on 5/4/89) FL 20+11/7 FLC 2/1 FAC 0+1 Others 1+1
Sheffield Wed (£250,000 on 20/2/91) F/PL 29+37/15 FLC 6+5/3 FAC 5+2/2 Others 2+2/1
Southampton (£1,200,000 on 17/3/95) PL 37+15/8 FLC 6+3/5 FAC 5+1/1
Bradford C (£550,000 on 17/1/97) FL 3/1

WATSON Kevin Edward
Born: Hackney, 3 January 1974
Height: 6'0" Weight: 12.6
After four years without a first-team game at White Hart Lane, the Spurs' midfielder was signed on a free transfer by Swindon in the summer of 1996, and must have been grateful for an early season run in the Robins' first team, during which he scored his first ever Football League goal in a 3-1 victory at Southend - from 25 yards. Although used sparingly thereafter, he was always on the fringe of first-team action, with 20 selections as a substitute and ten times called on and should feel fairly satisfied with his first year at the County Ground. Is a skilful player with some lovely touches on the ball.

Tottenham H (From trainee on 15/5/92) PL 4+1 FLC 1+1/1 FAC 0+1
Brentford (Loaned on 24/3/94) FL 2+1
Bristol C (Loaned on 2/12/94) FL 1+1
Barnet (Loaned on 16/2/95) FL 13
Swindon T (Free on 15/7/96) FL 17+10/1 FLC 1+1 FAC 0+1

WATSON Mark Leon
Born: Birmingham, 28 December 1973
Height: 6'1" Weight: 13.2
Having come to Bournemouth in the deal that took Steve Jones back to West Ham in May 1996, and looking for a foundation to build his career on, the tall striker had a disappointing season making only six starts and 11 substitute appearances, due to him suffering from an ankle injury for a good part of the campaign. Freed during the summer, when he did play, however, he showed speed and strength and the two goals he scored were of the highest quality.
West Ham U (Signed from Sutton U on 9/5/95) PL 0+1
Leyton Orient (Loaned on 4/9/95) FL 0+1/1
Cambridge U (Loaned on 27/10/95) FL 1+3/1 Others 1
Shrewsbury T (Loaned on 2/2/96) FL 1
Bournemouth (Signed on 17/5/96) FL 6+9/2 FAC 0+1 Others 0+1

WATSON Paul Douglas
Born: Hastings, 4 January 1975
Height: 5'8" Weight: 10.10
One of three Fulham signings from Gillingham during the 1996 close season, this predominantly left-footed defender or midfielder was slotted into the right-wing back position in place of Duncan Jupp, who had been sold to Wimbledon. His forays down the right, drag backs and left-footed crosses, led to several goals and his accurate, swinging free kicks were a feature of the Cottagers at their best. Moved to left back in February and was an important part of a defence which conceded just six goals in 15 games, including only one defeat, which ultimately made promotion a certainty.
Gillingham (From trainee on 8/12/92) FL 57+5/2 FLC 4 FAC 6 Others 5+3
Fulham (£13,000 on 30/7/96) FL 44/3 FLC 3/1 FAC 1 Others 3

WATSON Stephen (Steve) Craig
Born: North Shields, 1 April 1974
Height: 6'0" Weight: 12.7
International Honours: E: U21-12; Yth
Steve, a strong, well-built player, who has a fine, delicate touch on the ball, somewhat surprising for a big man, continued to display his versatility, filling a number of roles at Newcastle, although for most of last season he was a fixture at right back, keeping big money buy Warren Barton on the bench. He also played in midfield and in the centre of the defence, where he gave one of his best performances in the rearguard action at Arsenal which led to a vital 1-0 win with ten men, and, on occasion, was pushed forward into a striking position in the closing minutes of matches when Newcastle were in need of goals. However, his only counter came against Coventry when he surged forward from full back, took a pass

from Tino Asprilla, rounded the 'keeper and scored. Having signed a new four-year contract in March, he is sure to figure prominently in the club's push for honours over the next few years and is also tipped for further international honours.
Newcastle U (From trainee on 6/4/91) F/PL 145+27/11 FLC 8+5/1 FAC 10+3 Others 9+4/1

WATTS Julian
Born: Sheffield, 17 March 1971
Height: 6'3" Weight: 13.7
Club Honours: FLC '97
Right-footed Leicester central defender. Scored first goal for the club in 1996-97 with close range effort at home to Chelsea and performed solidly throughout the season, though his place came under threat after Matt Elliott was signed from Oxford. As a valuable squad member who held his form, he was a little unfortunate to miss out on the Coca-Cola Cup final against Middlesbrough, both at Wembley and Hillsborough in the replay, but, with his aerial ability coupled to excellent pace and the instinct to come out of defence with the ball, he could always be relied on.
Rotherham U (Signed from Frenchville CA on 10/7/90) FL 17+3/1 FLC 1 FAC 4 Others 2
Sheffield Wed (£80,000 on 13/3/92) PL 12+4/1 FLC 1 Others 1
Shrewsbury T (Loaned on 18/12/92) FL 9 Others 1
Leicester C (£210,000 on 29/3/96) P/FL 31+4/1 FLC 5+1 FAC 2+1 Others 3

WDOWCZYK Dariusz
Born: Warsaw, Poland, 21 September 1962
Height: 5'11" Weight: 11.11
International Honours: Poland : 51
Reading missed the elegance and composure of the Polish international centre back in 1996-97, as he lost his place through injury as early as October and never returned to the team. Although he still has a year of his contract to run, achilles tendon problems must place his future at Reading in some doubt. Is an outstanding passer of the ball, especially off the left foot.
Glasgow Celtic (£400,000 from Legia Warsaw on 17/11/89) SL 112+4/4 SLC 11 SC 13/2 Others 6+1
Reading (Free on 12/8/94) FL 74+2 FLC 6 FAC 1 Others 3

WEATHERSTONE Simon
Born: Reading, 26 January 1980
Height: 5'11" Weight: 11.0
17-year-old Simon had a brief taste of first-team action for Oxford in 1996-97 when he made his debut as a substitute against Port Vale. A young forward, he had done well in the youth and reserve sides and signed pro forms just prior to the game with over a year of his YT contract still to go.
Oxford U (From trainee on 27/3/97) FL 0+1

WEAVER Luke Dennis Spencer
Born: Woolwich, 26 June 1979
Height: 6'2" Weight: 13.2
International Honours: E: Yth; Sch
An England youth team goalkeeper whose progression through the Leyton Orient ranks in 1996-97 took him to a regular first-team spot a lot sooner than expected, due to injuries to Les Sealey and Peter Caldwell,

Luke performed creditably for such a young goalkeeper, although his inexperience told against him at times and is definitely one for the future. Spent the end of the season training with Manchester United and then on loan with West Ham.

Leyton Orient (From trainee on 26/6/96) FL 9 FAC 1 Others 1

WEAVER Simon Daniel
Born: Doncaster, 20 December 1977
Height: 6'1" Weight: 11.0
Having signed professional forms for Sheffield Wednesday at the end of 1995-96, and in order to further his experience, the young defender was loaned to Doncaster last February. Came straight into the Rovers' side in central defence at Belle Vue against Barnet, thus making his league debut, before reverting to right back for one more game prior to departing for Hillsborough. Predominantly a central defender, Simon is tenacious, good in the air for his height, very quick, and eventually could be a good un.

Sheffield Wed (From trainee on 24/5/96)
Doncaster Rov (Loaned on 14/2/97) FL 2

WEBB Neil John
Born: Reading, 30 July 1963
Height: 6'1" Weight: 13.7
Club Honours: Div 3 '83; FLC '89, '92; FLC '89; FAC '90; ECWC '91; ESC '91
International Honours: E: 26; B-4; U21-3; Yth

The former Nottingham Forest and England midfielder appeared briefly on trial for Grimsby in 1996-97, in an attempt to revive his career, but although he showed he had retained much of his former vision he obviously did not impress former team-mate, Brian Laws, as much as he did the fans and departed after only four games. Is currently playing for non-league Aldershot.

Reading (From apprentice on 14/11/80) FL 65+7/22 FLC 2+2 FAC 2
Portsmouth (£83,000 on 29/7/82) FL 123/34 FLC 9/3 FAC 6/1
Nottingham F (£250,000 on 3/6/85) FL 146/47 FLC 21/4 FAC 13/2 Others 6/4
Manchester U (£1,500,000 on 24/7/89) F/PL 70+5/8 FLC 14/1 FAC 9/1 Others 12/1
Nottingham F (£800,000 on 23/11/92) F/PL 26+4/3 FLC 2+3/1 FAC 6+1/2 Others 1
Swindon T (Loaned on 7/10/94) FL 5+1
Grimsby T (Free on 16/8/96) FL 3+1 FLC 1

WEBBER Damien John
Born: Littlehampton, 8 October 1968
Height: 6'4" Weight: 14.0
Tall Millwall central defender. Showing good control, Damian scored two goals with powerful headers, the second a point saver at home to York in 1996-97. He also delighted the fans in giving an excellent impersonation of Franz Beckenbauer at Watford, when bringing the ball out of defence, dribbling past four players and setting up Stephen Crawford to score.

Millwall (Signed from Bognor Regis on 27/10/94) FL 52+12/4 FLC 2+2 FAC 3+2 Others 2

WELCH Keith James
Born: Bolton, 3 October 1968
Height: 6'2" Weight: 13.7
This accomplished goalkeeper fell out of favour at Bristol City in 1996-97 and it was

not until John Ward took over as the manager and an injury to Stuart Naylor again gave him the chance to demonstrate in the final eight games that he had no equal in his position in the Football and Premier Leagues in dealing with the back pass, his play giving City the benefit of an extra sweeper. Cool and unflappable, it is to be hoped that he settles down with City once more so all at Ashton Gate can continue to appreciate his great skills.

Rochdale (Free from Bolton W juniors on 3/3/87) FL 205 FLC 12 FAC 10 Others 12
Bristol C (£200,000 on 25/7/91) FL 206 FLC 12 FAC 11 Others 12

WELLER Paul Anthony
Born: Brighton, 6 March 1975
Height: 5'8" Weight: 11.0
Paul's performance on the right-hand side of Burnley's midfield improved as last season went on, his confidence growing as he overcame the reservations of a section of the club's support. A skilful young man, but never one to recognise a lost cause, he was the most consistent player in the team's poor run at the end of the campaign and seems certain to improve again next time round.

Burnley (From trainee on 30/11/93) FL 46+10/3 FLC 2+1 FAC 2+2 Others 4

WELLS Mark Anthony
Born: Leicester, 15 October 1971
Height: 5'9" Weight: 11.2
A dogged defender who likes to get forward whenever possible, and a strong tackler and accurate distributor of the ball, Mark turned in some sterling performances for Scarborough last season. Always giving 100 per-cent commitment, he scored only his second goal for the club on the final day of the campaign in a 2-0 win at Hull City, prior to being freed.

Notts Co (From trainee on 3/7/90) FL 0+2 Others 0+1
Huddersfield T (Free on 9/8/93) FL 21+1/4 FLC 4 FAC 3 Others 2+1
Scarborough (Free on 21/7/94) FL 48+14/3 FLC 1+1 FAC 6+1 Others 3

WELSH Stephen (Steve)
Born: Glasgow, 19 April 1968
Height: 6'1" Weight: 12.3
Transferred to Partick Thistle in December 1994, Steve returned to Peterborough during the 1996 close season, having signed a two-year contract, but after just nine games the central defender was on his way back to Scotland due to Posh's financial problems. A wholehearted player, he was sorely missed as the club plummeted towards the foot of the second division table and ultimate relegation.

Cambridge U (Free from Wimborne T on 22/6/90) FL 0+1 Others 2
Peterborough U (Free on 8/8/91) FL 146/2 FLC 20 FAC 8 Others 13
Partick Thistle (£40,000 on 23/12/94) SL 55 SLC 3 SC 1
Peterborough U (Signed on 9/7/96) FL 6 FLC 3

WEST Colin
Born: Wallsend, 13 November 1962
Height: 6'1" Weight: 13.11
The experienced Leyton Orient centre forward started last season well but, with

inexperienced strikers around him, he had to shoulder a lot of the forward play himself. Although remaining a threat and leading the line well, Colin was unfortunate to break his ankle in January, which ruined his chances of finishing top scorer for a fourth successive season. Good in the air and the possessor of a powerful long-range shot.

Sunderland (From apprentice on 9/7/80) FL 88+14/21 FLC 13+4/5 FAC 3+1/2
Watford (£115,000 on 28/3/85) FL 45/20 FLC 2+1 FAC 8/3
Glasgow R (£180,000 on 23/5/86) SL 4+6/2 SLC 2/1 SC 0+1 Others 0+2
Sheffield Wed (£150,000 on 7/9/87) FL 40+5/8 FLC 6/3 FAC 6/1 Others 3/1
West Bromwich A (Signed on 24/2/89) FL 64+9/22 FLC 2 FAC 4/1 Others 2/1
Port Vale (Loaned on 1/11/91) FL 5/1
Swansea C (Free on 5/8/92) FL 29+4/12 FLC 0+1 FAC 5/2 Others 3+2/1
Leyton Orient (Free on 26/7/93) FL 130+5/42 FLC 5/2 FAC 7/2 Others 9/4

Colin West (left)

WEST Dean
Born: Morley, 5 December 1972
Height: 5'9" Weight: 12.2
Club Honours: Div 2 '97

In having yet another impressive campaign for Bury, Dean was one of three ever present for the Shakers in their division two championship season in 1996-97. A whole-hearted player who is at ease in an attacking wing-back role, he popped up with four goals for the club, yet was a member of a defence which let in just seven goals at home all season.

Lincoln C (From trainee on 17/8/91) FL 93+26/20 FLC 11/1 FAC 5/1 Others 5+2/1
Bury (Signed on 29/9/95) FL 78+5/5 FLC 4 FAC 2 Others 1

WESTWOOD Ashley Michael
Born: Bridgnorth, 31 August 1976
Height: 5'11" Weight: 11.3

Club Honours: FAYC '95
International Honours: E: Yth

Now established alongside Steve Maculey in the centre of Crewe's defence since his move from Manchester United, Ashley missed just a couple of games last season and is now only a handful away from the 100 mark. Came back well from an injury suffered at the end of 1995-96 to be an integral part of the team that reached the first division via the play offs, his workrate and positional play excellent. Scored important goals too, including one that took Wimbledon to a FA Cup replay.

Manchester U (From trainee on 1/7/94)
Crewe Alex (£40,000 on 26/7/95) FL 74+3/6 FLC 6 FAC 9/2 Others 10

Ashley Westwood

WETHERALL David
Born: Sheffield, 14 March 1971
Height: 6'3" Weight: 13.12
International Honours: E: Sch

In a season of somewhat mixed fortunes and inconsistency, David began 1996-97, his sixth campaign at Leeds, in the first team, and went on to keep his place following the arrival of the new manager, who rightfully deemed that the defence was his main priority. However, struggling to maintain a good level of consistency and failing to maintain his usual threat at set-piece situations, he was ultimately replaced by Robert Molenaar in the defensive system and had to be content with a squad place as the season neared its end. Highly competitive and good in the air, he is bound to be back in contention for 1997-98.

Sheffield Wed (From trainee on 1/7/89)
Leeds U (£125,000 on 15/7/91) F/PL 141+6/9 FLC 15+1 FAC 14+3/3 Others 4

WHALLEY Gareth
Born: Manchester, 19 December 1973
Height: 5'10" Weight: 11.6

The club captain and a very talented midfielder who passed the 200 appearance mark for Crewe in 1996-97, Gareth's progress in the game continued to be monitored by scouts from higher placed clubs. Hard working, excellent on the ball, his passing accurate, and always looking to set up attacks, his performances in the play-off games, which ultimately saw the club reach the first division for the only time in its history, were of the highest calibre. Also versatile and able to play at full back without difficulty, his good form was recognised by his selection for the PFA award-winning second division team.

Crewe Alex (From trainee on 29/7/92) FL 156+6/8 FLC 9+1/1 FAC 15+1/4 Others 24/3

Gareth Whalley

WHARTON Paul William
Born: Newcastle, 26 June 1977
Height: 5'4" Weight: 9'9"
International Honours: E: Yth

Suffered a dislocated shoulder during the summer of 1996, which caused such a problem that his 1996-97 season extended to just one substitute appearance for Hull City at Leyton Orient. However, come 1997-98, the diminutive right-footed midfielder will be determined to put his disappointment behind him.

Leeds U (From trainee on 27/6/94)
Hull C (Free on 13/2/96) FL 7+3

WHEELER Adam
Born: Sheffield, 29 November 1977
Height: 6'0" Weight: 13.10

Having left Newcastle, where he was a YTS, to sign for Doncaster in April 1996, the teenage goalkeeper made his league debut at Northampton last February, following the unavailabiltiy of Dean Williams and Gary O'Connor. Despite making a competent start to his league career, following his unexpected promotion, he was released during the summer.

Doncaster Rov (Free from Newcastle U Juniors on 15/4/96) FL 1

WHELAN Noel
Born: Leeds, 30 December 1974
Height: 6'2" Weight: 12.3
Club Honours: FAYC '93
International Honours: E: U21-2; Yth (UEFAC '93)

1996-97 was a frustrating season for the young Coventry star of the previous year, his striking partnership with Dion Dublin being not nearly as productive as previously and by November he had scored only one goal, albeit the winner against his old club. But, in a deeper role at Wimbledon, he scored a spectacular goal and, playing up front alongside Darren Huckerby, was successful for a time, having excellent games in the FA Cup, scoring at Woking and Derby, and starring at Blackburn. His league form though was patchy and he was withdrawn to a midfield role after the West Ham home defeat and responded with goals in successive games against Liverpool, Chelsea and Southampton. With super skills on the ground for such a big youngster, and excellent in aerial confrontations, his performances against Southampton and Arsenal were his best of the campaign, his energy level having been raised considerably.

Leeds U (From trainee on 5/3/93) PL 28+20/7 FLC 3+2/1 FAC 2 Others 3
Coventry C (£2,000,000 on 16/12/95) PL 55+1/14 FLC 4 FAC 7/3

WHELAN Philip (Phil) James
Born: Stockport, 7 March 1972
Height: 6'4" Weight: 14.1
International Honours: E: U21-3

By his own standards Phil will look back on what he will consider to be a season of disappointment for Middlesbrough in 1996-97 through personal injuries, and the form of colleagues, whose performances kept him sidelined. That he was denied the opportunity of getting back into the team, apart from 11 appearances, his commanding control of the central defensive area being missed by his fans, who would have been delighted to have had his strong and aggressive presence in the back four more often. A giant of a defender who not only excels in aerial battles, but passes the ball well, he is bound to get further opportunities in 1997-98, injuries permitting that is.

Ipswich T (From juniors on 2/7/90) F/PL 76+6/2 FLC 6+1 FAC 3+1 Others 1
Middlesbrough (£300,000 on 3/4/95) PL 18+4/1 FLC 5 FAC 3

WHELAN Spencer Randall
Born: Liverpool, 17 September 1971
Height: 6'2" Weight: 13.0

The tall Chester central defender who has now made over 200 league appearances for the club was restricted to just 20 starts last season, mainly due to injuries and suspension. Still young enough to make it into the higher leagues, he is particularly

Noel Whelan

strong in the air, as you would expect of a tall man, and deceptively fast in recover. Is also a danger at set pieces.

Chester C (Free from Liverpool juniors on 3/4/90) FL 161+19/4 FLC 9+1/2 FAC 7+3 Others 4+2

WHISTON Peter Michael
Born: Widnes, 4 January 1968
Height: 6'1" Weight: 12.4

1996-97 was probably a season that both Peter and Shrewsbury will want to forget. Asked to play at full back for much of the campaign, it was evident that central defence was his most comfortable position and, on top of that, he lost a number of games through injury, which never allowed him the chance to forge a continuous partnership, something he has shown he can flourish with. His biggest disappointment would be a dubious hat trick of sendings off, all the decisions being very questionable.

Plymouth Arg (Signed on 17/12/87) FL 4+6 FAC 1 Others 1
Torquay U (Free on 21/3/90) FL 39+1/1 FLC 5/1 FAC 1 Others 6
Exeter C (£25,000 on 13/9/91) FL 85/7 FLC 7 FAC 10 Others 10/1
Southampton (£30,000 on 10/8/94) PL 0+1
Shrewsbury T (£50,000 on 11/9/95) FL 54+1/3 FLC 1 FAC 7/2 Others 8

WHITBREAD Adrian Richard
Born: Epping, 22 October 1971
Height: 6'2" Weight: 11.13

Having had a spell on loan at Portsmouth in 1995-96, and unable to secure himself a place in the West Ham rearguard, Adrian arrived back at Fratton Park last October on a more permanent basis. A solid and reliable centre back, in forming an effective partnership with Andy Awford, Andy Thomson and Russell Perrett, his wholehearted performances helped to shore up a defence that had been leaking goals before his arrival. Out for 11 games after Christmas with an injury, he came back well for the last ten matches to add his weight to a side pushing hard for a play-off place.

Leyton Orient (From trainee on 13/11/89) FL 125/2 FLC 10+1 FAC 11/1 Others 8
Swindon T (£500,000 on 29/7/93) P/FL 35+1/1 FAC 2
West Ham U (£650,000 on 17/8/94) PL 3+7 FLC 2+1 FAC 1
Portsmouth (Loaned on 9/11/95) FL 13
Portsmouth (£250,000 on 24/10/96) FL 24 FAC 1

WHITE David
Born: Manchester, 30 October 1967
Height: 6'1" Weight: 12.9
International Honours: E: 1; B-2; U21-6; Yth

Competing with Mitch Ward for a wide-right role at Sheffield United in 1996-97, David had a disappointing season by his own standards, suffering from a series of niggling injuries and admitting that he was not playing to his full potential. However, at his best, he can be expected to delight the crowd when running at defences and, despite them being few and far between throughout a long and hard campaign, his trademark has always been in scoring spectacular goals from prodigious distances and acute angles. Hopefully, will be back to his best in 1997-98.

Manchester C (From apprentice on 7/11/85) F/PL 273+12/79 FLC 24+2/11 FAC 22/4 Others 9/2
Leeds U (£2,000,000 on 22/12/93) PL 28+14/9 FLC 1 FAC 6/1 Others 1+1
Sheffield U (Signed on 17/11/95) FL 55+10/13 FLC 2+1/1 FAC 4 Others 3

WHITE Devon Winston
Born: Nottingham, 2 March 1964
Height: 6'3" Weight: 14.0
Club Honours: Div 3 '90; AIC '95

Idolised by the Notts County fans, the big stalwart centre forward rejoined the club from Watford last March and went straight into the action, wearing his heart on his sleeve every game and showing total commitment in an unsuccessful effort to stave off relegation to the third division. Really a target man, Devon is excellent in the air and will always pick up his share of goals.

Lincoln C (From Arnold FC on 14/12/84) FL 21+8/4 Others 2+1/2 (Free to Boston U in October 1986)
Bristol Rov (Free on 21/8/87) FL 190+12/53 FLC 9/2 FAC 10/3 Others 19/2
Cambridge U (£100,000 on 28/3/92) FL 15+7/4 FLC 4/1 FAC 1 Others 1/1
Queens Park R (£100,000 on 26/1/93) PL 16+10/9 FLC 1+1
Notts Co (£110,000 on 23/12/94) FL 34+6/15 FLC 4/6 FAC 2+1/2 Others 4/1
Watford (£100,000 on 16/2/96) FL 28+10/7 FLC 4 FAC 2/1 Others 1
Notts Co (£20,000 on 14/3/97) FL 7+2

WHITE Jason Gregory
Born: Meriden, 19 October 1971
Height: 6'1" Weight: 12.10

An out-and-out Northampton striker, with pace and ball juggling ability, Jason was the club's top scorer in 1995-96, but struggled to find his form last season, hence spending most of his time on the bench. However, he is still seen as part of the set up, due to the management declining two recent offers for him.

Derby Co (From trainee on 4/7/90)
Scunthorpe U (Free on 6/9/91) FL 44+24/16 FLC 2 FAC 3+3/1 Others 4+4/1
Darlington (Loaned on 20/8/93) FL 4/1
Scarborough (Free on 10/12/93) FL 60+3/20 FLC 2+1 FAC 5/1 Others 1
Northampton T (£35,000 on 15/6/95) FL 55+22/18 FLC 1+4 FAC 3 Others 5+2

WHITE Stephen (Steve) James
Born: Chipping Sodbury, 2 January 1959
Height: 5'11" Weight: 12.6
Club Honours: Div 2 '82

Even at the age of 38, this old campaigner still managed to put much younger strikers to shame in 1996-97, having been snapped up by Cardiff from Hereford on a free during the close season. Continuing to show that extra burst which takes him clear of defenders, and always a danger in crowded areas where he got in where it hurt, Steve ended the campaign as City's leading goalscorer with 14 to his credit. It is therefore no surprise to find him retained for the coming term.

Bristol Rov (Free from Mangotsfield on 11/7/77) FL 46+4/20 FLC 2/1 FAC 3/3
Luton T (£200,000 on 24/12/79) FL 63+9/25 FLC 3+1/1 FAC 2+1
Charlton Ath (£150,000 on 30/7/82) FL 29/12 FLC 2
Lincoln C (Loaned on 28/1/83) FL 2+1
Luton T (Loaned on 24/2/83) FL 4
Bristol Rov (£45,000 on 26/8/83) FL 89+12/24 FLC 8/2 FAC 7+1/2 Others 5+2/1
Swindon T (Free on 8/7/86) F/PL 200+44/83 FLC 21+8/11 FAC 9+2/2 Others 22+6/15
Hereford U (Free on 26/8/94) FL 70+6/44 FLC 5/2 FAC 6/4 Others 9+2/3
Cardiff C (Free on 9/8/96) FL 32+6/13 FLC 2 FAC 2/1 Others 2+2

WHITE Thomas (Tom) Matthew
Born: Bristol, 26 January 1976
Height: 6'1" Weight: 13.6

A central defender, Tom had to wait almost two years after making his league debut for Bristol Rovers before he made another appearance, starting against York City on 18 January 1997. Settled in well and showed growing maturity alongside Andy Tillson, adapting well to the rigours of league football. Good in the air, but less effective on his distribution from the back, he was left out of the team in March, following a disturbing spell of four defeats in March, and was replaced by the experienced Brian Gayle, before returning in the final run in.

Bristol Rov (From trainee on 13/7/94) FL 22+5 Others 0+1

WHITEHALL Steven (Steve) Christopher
Born: Bromborough, 8 December 1966
Height: 5'9" Weight: 11.5

Rochdale's leading scorer for the past few seasons again began successfully in 1996-97, despite the side's erratic form, netting eight times in the first 17 games and striking up a promising partnership with Robbie Painter. Later suffered from niggling injuries and was well short of his best, eventually having an operation for an ankle problem.

Rochdale (£20,000 from Southport on 23/7/91) FL 212+26/75 FLC 10+3/4 FAC 13+2/3 Others 15+1/10

WHITEHEAD Philip Matthew
Born: Halifax, 17 December 1969
Height: 6'3" Weight: 15.4

Now recognised as one of the best 'keepers in Oxford's history, producing a string of fine performances in 1996-97, Phil started last season with another run of clean sheets (the team conceded one goal in six games), although the later stages of the campaign saw the defence, radically changed, doing less to help his impressive record. Big and

strong, with goal-kicking ability, and fully commanding his area, he is much liked and deservedly won United's Player of the Year award.

Halifax T (From trainee on 1/7/88) FL 42 FLC 2 FAC 4 Others 4
Barnsley (£60,000 on 9/3/90) FL 16
Halifax T (Loaned on 7/3/91) FL 9
Scunthorpe U (Loaned on 29/11/91) FL 8 Others 2
Scunthorpe U (Loaned on 4/9/92) FL 8 FLC 2
Bradford C (Loaned on 19/11/92) FL 6 Others 4
Oxford U (£75,000 on 1/11/93) FL 154 FLC 12 FAC 12 Others 3

Dane Whitehouse

WHITEHOUSE Dane Lee
Born: Sheffield, 14 October 1970
Height: 5'9" Weight: 11.10

Sheffield United's first choice left-sided midfielder was unfortunate to sustain another injury hit season in 1996-97, following a hamstring injury suffered in November at Queens Park Rangers, which led to a month on the sidelines. Incidentally, a comeback against Oldham lasted just 17 minutes and produced a further two months of frustration. Despite that, Dane still managed 37 games, all of them starts, from a possible 54, and scored six goals, including a vital equaliser at Tranmere which kept the Blades on track for the play offs. Is a hard-working player.

Sheffield U (From trainee on 1/7//89) F/PL 187+27/36 FLC 15+1/5 FAC 14+3/2 Others 6/2

WHITLEY Jeffrey (Jeff)
Born: Zambia, 14 April 1975
Height: 5'8" Weight: 10.0
International Honours: NI: 2

After just two reserve-team appearances for Manchester City, Jeff was called up for his senior debut at home to Barnsley last September, where he excelled with a performance that had all the hallmarks of a

future star. Unfortunately, in the last minute he gave the game away with a miss-hit back pass. The encouraging thing about the incident was that it did not affect him whatsoever and he went on to play some very mature games, alternating with full and sub appearances to coax him along, and scored his first goal, the winner, at home against Bradford. Zambian born, but with a mixed parentship, he elected to play for Northern Ireland and made his international debut against Belgium in Belfast, when coming on as a substitute for Kevin Horlock, his club mate, prior to playing against Thailand in the summer.

Manchester C (From trainee on 19/2/96) FL 12+11/1 FLC 1

WHITLOW Michael (Mike) William
Born: Northwich, 13 January 1968
Height: 6'0" Weight: 12.12
Club Honours: Div 2 '90, Div 1 '92; FLC '97

Unfortunately, the left-footed, highly dependable Leicester left back's season in 1996-97 was hampered by a medial ligament injury sustained in the Coca-Cola Cup victory over Manchester United in November that sidelined him for several months, following effective contributions during the early weeks. Returned to the bench for the visit to Southampton at the end of March, before being recalled for the Coca-Cola Cup final against Middlesbrough at Wembley, where he performed very solidly and gave a repeat performance in the replay at Hillsborough. Obviously, with little opportunity to make use of his trademark screaming free kicks during the campaign, despite almost finding the net at Sheffield Wednesday with a rasping low drive, he will be raring to go in 1997-98.

Leeds U (£10,000 from Witton A on 11/11/88) FL 62+15/4 FLC 4+1 FAC 1+4 Others 9
Leicester C (£250,000 on 27/3/92) F/PL 141+6/8 FLC 12/1 FAC 6 Others 14

WHITNEY Jonathan (Jon) David
Born: Nantwich, 23 December 1970
Height: 5'10" Weight: 12.3

A tough-tackling Lincoln left back who likes to get forward, this very effective defender's 1996-97 season was curtailed by a cruciate knee ligament injury in November, which put him out of action for an estimated 12 months. A league ever present at that moment in time, Jon overcame injury problems before and intends to be back as good as new.

Huddersfield T (£10,000 from Winsford, via Wigan Ath YTS and Skelmersdale, on 21/10/93) FL 17+1 FLC 0+1 Others 4/1
Wigan Ath (Loaned on 17/3/95) FL 12
Lincoln C (£20,000 on 31/10/95) FL 43+1/5 FLC 5/1 FAC 2 Others 3

WHITTAKER Stuart
Born: Liverpool, 2 January 1975
Height: 5'7" Weight: 9.6

Unable to get a game at Bolton last season, Stuart, an out-and-out left winger, signed for Wigan Athletic on loan in September. However, substituted in the two matches he started, he returned to Burnden Park early

after failing to impress and spent the rest of 1996-97 in Wanderers' Central League side prior to being released in the summer.
Bolton W (Free from Liverpool juniors on 14/5/93) FL 2+1 FLC 0+1
Wigan Ath (Loaned on 30/8/96) FL 2+1

WHITTINGHAM Guy
Born: Evesham, 10 November 1964
Height: 5'10" Weight: 12.2
Guy had another useful season in 1996-97 as a goalscoring right-sided midfielder for Sheffield Wednesday, contributing much to the Owl's excellent season, scoring five goals, and laying on many more, including five against Grimsby in the side's 7-1 cup success. He remains, however, a frustrated striker, but being the dedicated pro that he is he gave many typical, no-nonsense performances, never letting anyone down, in a role that he has now settled into. Missing very few matches, amongst his goal tally was the winner in Wednesday's triumph at Liverpool.
Portsmouth (Free from Yeovil on 9/6/89) FL 149+11/88 FLC 7+2/3 FAC 7+3/10 Others 9/3
Aston Villa (£1,200,000 on 1/8/93) PL 17+8/5 FLC 4+1/1 Others 2+1
Wolverhampton W (Loaned on 28/2/94) FL 13/8 FAC 1
Sheffield Wed (£700,000 on 21/12/94) PL 72+11/18 FLC 5+1/2 FAC 6+1/1

WHITTLE Justin Phillip
Born: Derby, 18 March 1971
Height: 6'1" Weight: 12.12
A determined Stoke centre back, who, having burst into the side in 1995-96, eventually reaffirmed his partnership with Larus Sigurdsson at the heart of the defence last season. Strong in the air, and always one to compete for every ball, he suffered from a lack of composure at times, but that is sure to change with added experience.
Glasgow Celtic (Free from Army during 1994 close season)
Stoke C (Free on 20/10/94) FL 42+3 FLC 2 FAC 1 Others 2

WHITTON Stephen (Steve) Paul
Born: East Ham, 4 December 1960
Height: 6'1" Weight: 13.7
Club Honours: Div 2 '92
A very experienced Colchester midfielder, cum forward, who also doubles as the U's assistant manager, Steve's injury problems in 1995-96 are now gladly behind him, allowing him to show the benefit of nearly 20-years experience. Appearing last season, either at centre forward or, later on, as a central midfielder, he scored the last-minute goal at Cambridge to set United off on the Wembley trail. Also played 45 minutes in goal at WBA in the Coca-Cola Cup after Garrett Caldwell was injured.
Coventry C (From apprentice on 15/9/78) FL 64+10/21 FLC 3+2 FAC 3/2
West Ham U (£175,000 on 11/7/83) FL 35+4/6 FLC 6/2 FAC 1
Birmingham C (Loaned on 31/1/86) FL 8/2
Birmingham C (£60,000 on 28/8/86) FL 94+1/28 FLC 7+1/4 FAC 5 Others 3/1
Sheffield Wed (£275,000 on 3/3/89) FL 22+10/4 FLC 3/4 FAC 0+1 Others 0+1
Ipswich T (£150,000 on 11/1/91) F/PL 80+8/15 FLC 7+1/2 FAC 8+1/2 Others 4
Colchester U (£10,000 on 24/3/94) FL 90+5/20 FLC 6+1 FAC 4/2 Others 7+2/1

Steve Whitton

Chris Whyte

WHYTE Christopher (Chris) Anderson
Born: Islington, 2 September 1961
Height: 6'2" Weight: 13.0
Club Honours: Div 1 '92, Div 2 '95
International Honours: E: U21-4
Joined Oxford on non-contract terms last February before signing for the last few months of the season. Had been playing overseas before having a spell with Leyton Orient but, with United seeking defensive cover, the experienced centre back came in and did a reasonable job. Plunged straight into the side he added some security to the

young defenders at the club, winning several Man of the Match awards. Strong in the air, his reading of the game is extremely sound.
Arsenal (From apprentice on 24/12/79) FL 86+4/8 FLC 14 FAC 5 Others 3+1 (Free to Los Angeles Lazers during 1986 close season)
Crystal Palace (Loaned on 23/8/84) FL 13 FLC 4
West Bromwich A (Free on 25/8/88) FL 83+1/7 FLC 5/2 FAC 5 Others 2
Leeds U (£400,000 on 18/6/90) F/PL 113/5 FLC 14+1/1 FAC 8 Others 11
Birmingham C (£250,000 on 12/8/93) FL 68/1 FLC 12 FAC 4 Others 5+1
Coventry C (Loaned on 9/12/95) PL 1
Charlton Ath (Free on 11/3/96) FL 10+1 Others 2 (Free to Detroit Neon during 1996 close season)
Leyton Orient (Free on 2/1/97) FL 1
Oxford U (Free on 27/2/97) FL 10

WHYTE David Antony
Born: Greenwich, 20 April 1971
Height: 5'9" Weight: 10.7
Club Honours: Div 1 '94
Charlton striker who finished as joint-top scorer, despite figuring in only half of the fixtures in 1996-97. With a powerful shot and good awareness in the box, David was never really able to recapture the form he is capable of and, added to that, was unfortunate to suffer a ruptured achilles tendon in a reserve fixture in April, which could have put him out of the game for six months.
Crystal Palace (Free from Greenwich Borough on 15/2/89) FL 17+10/4 FLC 5+2/2 FAC 0+1 Others 0+3/1
Charlton Ath (Loaned on 26/3/92) FL 7+1/2
Charlton Ath (£450,000 on 5/7/94) FL 65+20/28 FLC 5+2/4 FAC 3+1/1 Others 0+2

WHYTE Derek
Born: Glasgow, 31 August 1968
Height: 5'11" Weight: 12.12
Club Honours: SPD '88; SC '88, '89; Div 1 '95
International Honours: S: 10; B-3; SU21-9; Yth; Sch
Enjoying his fifth term with Middlesbrough in 1996-97, having been the club's record signing when he joined them from Glasgow Celtic in August 1992, "Whytey" is still considered by the national coach, Craig Brown, to be an important asset to the Scottish squad. Has on may occasions raised the efforts and aspirations of his team mates, especially when wearing the captain's arm band, his strong and determined running out of defence and intelligent distribution to his midfielders and strikers leading the way home. Continuing to play a major role in Boro's domestic cup runs, and the "dog fight" to maintain Premiership status, his 29 appearances in a tough and difficult campaign coming in more than handy, he will look to be part of a side that hopes to achieve a Premiership return at the first time of asking.
Glasgow Celtic (From juniors in 1985) SL 211+5/7 SLC 18+1 SC 26 Others 15/1
Middlesbrough (£500,000 on 1/8/92) F/PL 156+3/2 FLC 14+1/1 FAC 4+2 Others 6

WIDDRINGTON Thomas (Tommy)
Born: Newcastle, 1 October 1971
Height: 5'10" Weight: 11.12
At £300,000 Grimsby's most expensive signing, during the 1996 close season, the

ex-Southampton left-sided midfielder proved to be a tough, uncompromising ball winner, making a complete contrast to the cultured Paul Groves, whom he replaced in the number six shirt. Capable of going forward and bagging the odd goal, Tommy is a versatile player who can also perform at full back and in the sweeper role.

Southampton (From trainee on 10/5/90) F/PL 67+8/3 FLC 3+1 FAC 11
Wigan Ath (Loaned on 12/9/91) FL 5+1 FLC 2
Grimsby T (£300,000 on 11/7/96) FL 41+1/4 FLC 2 FAC 1

WILCOX Jason Malcolm
Born: Farnworth, 15 July 1971
Height: 5'11" Weight: 11.10
Club Honours: PL '95
International Honours: E: 1; B-1

Starting last season at Blackburn on a low note when having to undergo a further operation to remove gristle from his knee, he returned with fresh motivation and appeared to have regained the form that brought him international honours. Although his crosses were often not picked up by the new strike force, possibly due to the almost telepathic understanding he had earlier had with Alan Shearer, there was nothing wrong with the rest of his game and he retained his high workrate and the ability to drop deep and cover. Got off the mark with a goal in the 3-0 win over Liverpool in November and followed that up with another in a 2-2 draw at Nottingham Forest a couple of weeks later, but there were no more in the offing. Hopefully, injury free in 1997-98, Jason can get back to his best as a left winger with pace and two useful feet, who can leave defenders in his wake to produce superb, telling crosses.

Blackburn Rov (From trainee on 13/6/89) F/PL 174+14/24 FLC 15+1/1 FAC 13/1 Others 5

WILCOX Russell (Russ)
Born: Hemsworth, 25 March 1964
Height: 6'0" Weight: 12.12
Club Honours: Div 4 '87; Div 3 '96
International Honours: E: SP-3

Russ is a consummate professional, who continued to use his wide experience in Preston's cause last season, despite not always being a first choice in central defence. His wholehearted approach helped to steady the younger players around him and, when he played in the reserves, he was a superb example to all around him. A decisive tackler and strong header, he is the type of player every club needs, both on and off the pitch.

Doncaster Rov (Apprentice) FL 1
Northampton T (£15,000 from Frickley Ath on 30/6/86) FL 137+1/9 FLC 6 FAC 10 Others 8/1
Hull C (£120,000 on 6/8/90) FL 92+8/7 FLC 5 FAC 5/1 Others 5+1
Doncaster Rov (£60,000 on 30/7/93) FL 81/6 FLC 5/2 FAC 3 Others 3
Preston NE (£60,000 on 22/9/95) FL 62/1 FLC 4 FAC 3/1 Others 2

WILDE Adam
Born: Southampton, 22 May 1979
Height: 5'10" Weight: 11.8

Adam was yet another discovery from the Cambridge youth team production line, the attacking left winger made a surprise first-team debut from the bench against Cardiff City in August, before a groin operation kept him on the sidelines for four long months. Having signed a two year professional contract, with full fitness on the agenda, he will be challenging for a first team spot this coming season.

Cambridge U (From trainee on 21/2/97) FL 0+1

WILDER Christopher (Chris) John
Born: Stocksbridge, 23 September 1967
Height: 5'11" Weight: 12.8

A highly competent right back, occasional sweeper, and central defender, Chris was a regular at Notts County in 1996-97, missing just two games before joining Bradford on transfer deadline day. Involved in seven of the final eight games at City, strangely, he left a side doomed for the third division for one ultimately relegated to the second. Effective in possession and a determined leader, Chris is also a free-kick and long-throw specialist.

Southampton (From apprentice on 26/9/85)
Sheffield U (Free on 20/8/86) FL 89+4/1 FLC 8+1 FAC 7 Others 3
Walsall (Loaned on 2/11/89) FL 4 FAC 1 Others 2
Charlton Ath (Loaned on 12/10/90) FL 1
Charlton Ath (Loaned on 28/11/91) FL 2
Leyton Orient (Loaned on 27/2/92) FL 16/1 Others 1
Rotherham U (£50,000 on 30/7/92) FL 129+3/11 FLC 11 FAC 6+1/1 Others 6+1
Notts Co (£150,000 on 2/1/96) FL 46 FLC 2 FAC 4 Others 1
Bradford C (£150,000 on 27/3/97) FL 4+3

WILKES Timothy (Tim) Craig
Born: Nottingham, 7 November 1977
Height: 6'0" Weight: 12.0

A tall, strong centre forward, Tim forced his way into first-team contention at Notts County last season, having given some powerful displays in the reserve side. Following his first-team debut at Plymouth in early September, due to a surplus of strikers on the club's books, he appeared just four more times before being loaned out to Grantham Town in February and then signing for non-league Kettering in March.

Notts Co (From trainee on 29/7/96) FL 3 Others 1+1

WILKINS Raymond (Ray) Colin
Born: Hillingdon, 14 September 1956
Height: 5'8" Weight: 11.2
Club Honours: FAC '83; SPD '90
International Honours: E: 84; U23-2; U21-1; Yth; Sch

After resigning as the QPR player/manager a few weeks into 1996-97, this elegant midfield general made one cameo appearance for Wycombe against Luton, thus becoming the club's oldest ever player (39 years and 358 days), before moving north of the border with Hibernian. Brought back to the English game on a weekly contract at Millwall in January, Ray showed that he could still produce defence-splitting passes, before moving on to Leyton Orient when the Lions went into administration. However, with the third division not really suiting his style he retired after just three games and

will now almost certainly be looking to pass on his vast experience through a managerial position in the game.

Chelsea (From apprentice on 1/10/73) FL 176+3/30 FLC 6+1/2 FAC 10+1/2
Manchester U (£825,000 on 1/8/79) FL 158+2/7 FLC 14+1/1 FAC 10/1 Others 9/1 (£1,500,000 to AC Milan on 1/7/84)
Glasgow R (£250,000 from Paris St Germain on 1/11/87) SL 69+1/2 SLC 10/1 SC 8+1 Others 7
Queens Park R (Free on 30/11/89) F/PL 153+1/7 FLC 13 FAC 13/2 Others 2/1
Crystal Palace (Free on 26/5/94) PL 1
Queens Park R (Free on 17/11/94) P/FL 16+5 FLC 2+1 FAC 1
Wycombe W (Free on 6/9/96) FL 1
Hibernian (Free on 10/9/96) SL 15+1 SLC 1
Millwall (Free on 6/1/97) FL 3 Others 1
Leyton Orient (Free on 27/2/97) FL 3

WILKINS Richard John
Born: Lambeth, 28 May 1965
Height: 6'0" Weight: 12.3
Club Honours: Div 3 '91

The former Colchester favourite, who had moved on when the club dropped into the Vauxhall Conference in 1990, returned to his roots, via Hereford, in the summer of 1996, holding the U's together from the middle of midfield, and doing much of the unglamorous, but necessary work in the engine room. His consistent quality of performance saw him rewarded with the team captaincy in Peter Cawley's absence through injury, an honour he retained when leading the team out at Wembley. Earlier in the AWS campaign, he spent an unbeaten 25 minutes in goal against Northampton, following John Vaughan's sending off.

Colchester U (Free from Haverhill Rov on 20/11/86) FL 150+2/22 FLC 6 FAC 7+2/4 Others 9+3/3
Cambridge U (£65,000 on 25/7/90) FL 79+2/7 FLC 6 FAC 8+1 Others 9
Hereford U (Free on 20/7/94) FL 76+1/5 FLC 6 FAC 6 Others 8/2
Colchester U (£30,000 on 3/7/96) FL 40/2 FLC 3 FAC 1/1 Others 6

Paul Wilkinson

WILKINSON Paul
Born: Louth, 30 October 1964
Height: 6'1" Weight: 12.4
Club Honours: CS '86; Div 1 '87, '95
International Honours: E: U21-4

Freed by Middlesbrough during the summer of 1996, Paul's experience when leading the Barnsley line in 1996-97 made all the difference. In forming a great partnership with former Boro team mate, John Hendrie, he was always available to the defence and midfield when they were under pressure and won more than his fair share, both up front or when defending from set pieces. Still an excellent target man, who again got into double figures, it was his link-up play, however, that was the major factor in the Reds' promotion success.
Grimsby T (From apprentice on 8/11/82) FL 69+2/27 FLC 10/5 FAC 4+2/1
Everton (£250,000 on 28/3/85) FL 19+12/7 FLC 3+1/7 FAC 3/1 Others 6+2/1
Nottingham F (£200,000 on 26/3/87) FL 32+2/5 FLC 3/1 FAC 4+1/1/2 Others 1
Watford (£300,000 on 16/8/88) FL 133+1/52 FLC 4/1 FAC 8+1 Others 8/3
Middlesbrough (£550,000 on 16/8/91) F/PL 161+5/49 FLC 16/8 FAC 14/5 Others 5+1/4
Oldham Ath (Loaned on 26/10/95) FL 4/1 Others 1/1
Watford (Loaned on 1/12/95) FL 4
Luton T (Loaned on 28/3/96) FL 3
Barnsley (Free on 19/7/96) FL 45/9 FLC 4/2 FAC 2

WILKINSON Stephen (Steve) John
Born: Lincoln, 1 September 1968
Height: 6'0" Weight: 11.0
Club Honours: Div 3 '96

After starting 1996-97 for Preston on fire, with seven goals in five games, including a Coca-Cola Cup hat trick at Wigan, his season was effectively ruined by a knee injury which required surgery. Unfortunately, on his return, he was obviously not fit and a second operation was found to be necessary. His constructive forward play and striking ability were sorely missed by the fans and team alike as he remained on 99 league goals from September. Currently the club's programme editor, Steve hopes to enter journalism at the end of his playing career.
Leicester C (From apprentice on 6/9/86) FL 5+4/1 FAC 1
Crewe Alex (Loaned on 8/9/88) FL 3+2/2
Mansfield T (£80,000 on 2/10/89) FL 214+18/83 FLC 13+1/4 FAC 10/2 Others 17/1
Preston NE (£90,000 on 15/6/95) FL 44+8/13 FLC 4/4 FAC 3/1 Others 3

WILLEMS Ron
Born: Epe, Holland, 20 September 1966
Height: 6'0" Weight: 13.0

An experienced Dutch striker, Ron was more of a squad member than an automatic first choice in the Derby line up during 1996-97. Best utilised in an attacking role, playing behind the front two with the ability to lose his marker in the penalty area when played in this fashion, he is an energetic player who can always be relied upon to give 100 per-cent effort when called upon. Despite coming off the bench more times than he had Premiership starts, he scored two important goals, the first in a 2-1 win at Blackburn and the equaliser at Wimbledon.

Also netted twice in three FA Cup games.
Derby Co (£300,000 from Grasshoppers, Zurich, via PEC Zwolle, Twente Enschede and Ajax, on 28/7/95) F/PL 38+11/13 FLC 2/1 FAC 4/2

WILLER-JENSEN Thomas
Born: Copenhagen, Denmark, 19 September 1968
Height: 6'4" Weight: 13.4

Signed from the Danish club, HIK Copenhagen, on non-contract forms last March, having earlier impressed in a trial game, the tall central defender proved to have good ball skills as well as aerial power. Despite suffering from ankle problems during his stay at Swansea, he impressed in seven of the last nine fixtures.
Swansea C (Free from HIK Copenhagen on 14/3/97) FL 7

WILLIAMS Adrian
Born: Reading, 16 August 1971
Height: 6'2" Weight: 12.6
Club Honours: Div 2 '94
International Honours: W: 7

Transferred from Reading to Wolves during the 1996 close season, the centre back's bad year with knee injuries continued on the summer tour of Austria, and cruciate ligament damage was diagnosed, with an operation being needed to reconstruct it. He finally made a quiet debut at Sheffield United in January, that was until his long ball saw Steve Bull run on to score a late winner. The powerful, commanding defender was really looking the part by his fifth appearance, only to limp off with a hamstring problem which forced another period of inactivity. Came back to play in the play offs with mixed fortunes, hitting the bar in one game and scoring with a header in the other, but making errors in both as he tired. However, Wolves did win six of the eight matches he competed in.
Reading (From trainee on 4/3/89) FL 191+5/14 FLC 16/1 FAC 16/2 Others 14/2
Wolverhampton W (£750,000 on 3/7/96) FL 6 Others 2/1

WILLIAMS Andrew (Andy)
Born: Birmingham, 29 July 1962
Height: 6'1" Weight: 12.0
Club Honours: Div 2 '90

An experienced midfielder who can also adapt to play in the sweeper's role, Andy joined Scarborough on the eve of last season following his release by Hull City. However, after appearing in the opening two matches of the campaign as a non-contract player, he turned down the offer of a monthly contract and moved on.
Coventry C (£20,000 from Solihull Borough on 24/7/85) FL 3+6 Others 0+1
Rotherham U (Signed on 16/10/86) FL 87/13 FLC 8 FAC 6 Others 5/2
Leeds U (£175,000 on 11/11/88) FL 25+21/3 FLC 3+3 FAC 2 Others 5+2/2
Port Vale (Loaned on 11/12/91) FL 5
Notts Co (£115,000 on 4/2/92) FL 32+7/2 FLC 3 FAC 1
Huddersfield T (Loaned on 13/9/93) FL 4+2
Rotherham U (Signed on 21/10/93) FL 51/2 FLC 2 FAC 3 Others 4
Hull C (Free on 19/7/95) FL 33+1 FLC 2 FAC 1 Others 2
Scarborough (Free on 16/8/96) FL 1 FLC 1

WILLIAMS Darren
Born: Middlesbrough, 28 April 1977
Height: 5'9" Weight: 11.2

After making just one subs' appearance for York last season, the highly promising teenage midfielder joined Sunderland in October and by the end of the campaign had established himself in the first team. In doing so, Darren showed himself to be an industrious midfielder with an eye for goal, especially against Middlesbrough at the Riverside in April, when his header was enough to take three vital points. Although the Rokerites were eventually relegated, he will have gained valuable experience from his few months in the Premiership and could well go on to become a fixture in the side.
York C (From trainee on 21/6/95) FL 16+4 FLC 4+1 FAC 1 Others 3/1
Sunderland (£50,000 on 18/10/96) PL 10+1/2 FAC 1+1

WILLIAMS Dean Paul
Born: Lichfield, 5 January 1972
Height: 6'0" Weight: 12.8

Dean began last season as Doncaster's first choice goalkeeper, but lost his place following a foot injury in October. A good shot stopper and particularly agile, the injury proved to be a severe one, which kept him out for a number of months before his return to first team action in February. Unfortunately, he then broke a finger in training which brought his campaign to an early close.
Birmingham C (From trainee on 11/7/90) FL 4 FAC 1 (Free to Tamworth in March 1992)
Brentford (£2,000 on 8/8/93) FL 6+1
Doncaster Rov (Free on 12/8/94) FL 77+2 FLC 3 FAC 1 Others 5

WILLIAMS Gareth James
Born: Isle of Wight, 12 March 1967
Height: 6'0" Weight: 12.2

Having been released by Northampton during the summer, this valuable utility player enjoyed a highly successful first season for Scarborough in 1996-97, operating mostly in midfield. When on form, he looked to be outstanding, and was a major factor in the club's much improved form after two years of struggling against relegation.
Aston Villa (£30,000 from Gosport Borough on 9/1/88) FL 6+6 FLC 0+1 FAC 2 Others 0+1
Barnsley (£200,000 on 6/8/91) FL 23+11/6 FLC 1 FAC 1+1 Others 1+1
Hull C (Loaned on 17/9/92) FL 4
Hull C (Loaned on 6/1/94) FL 16/2
Wolverhampton W (Free on 23/8/94) FL 0+1
Bournemouth (Free on 16/9/94) FL 0+1
Northampton T (Free on 27/9/94) FL 38+12/1 FLC 2 FAC 2 Others 5+1
Scarborough (Free on 9/8/96) FL 45/10 FLC 4/1 FAC 3 Others 1

WILLIAMS David Geraint
Born: Treorchy, 5 January 1962
Height: 5'7" Weight: 12.6
Club Honours: Div 2 '87
International Honours: W: 13; U21-2; Yth

Took over from Steve Sedgley as Ipswich team captain at the end of last year and led by example from his central midfield role. Very good at chasing the opposition down, with a penchant to be in the thick of things,

Geraint is never happier than when involved in midfield battles such as those in derby games. Scored only his third goal for the club in the Oldham match when he found himself in the penalty area and was the first to react when Gus Uhlenbeek's fierce drive came back off the post. Not only a destroyer, the Welsh international often sets up attacks with the neatest of passes.

Bristol Rov (From apprentice on 12/1/80) FL 138+3/8 FLC 14 FAC 9+2/2 Others 5
Derby Co (£40,000 on 29/3/85) FL 276+1/9 FLC 26+1/1 FAC 17 Others 11
Ipswich T (£650,000 on 1/7/92) P/FL 194/3 FLC 17+1 FAC 14 Others 4

Geraint Williams

WILLIAMS John Nelson
Born: Birmingham, 11 May 1968
Height: 6'1" Weight: 13.1

A tall, speedy striker who scores spectacular goals, notably in each of Wycombe's two Coca-Cola Cup games against Reading last season, John quickly lost his place but, with Neil Davis cup tied, he was recalled for the FA Cup game at Colchester where he delivered the winner, before obliging with three more goals in the two games against Barnet in the next round. Unhappy that his cup-tie performances could not secure a place in the league team, he left for Hereford in February. Known as "The Flying Postman" he collected three goals in 11 appearances for United, including an amazing one at Lincoln when, on recovering the ball from a defender by the corner flag, he sent it over the 'keeper in one move to bring about a 3-3 draw in the 90th minute.

Swansea C (£5,000 from Cradley T on 19/8/91) FL 36+3/11 FLC 2+1 FAC 3 Others 1
Coventry C (£250,000 on 1/7/92) PL 66+14/11 FLC 4 FAC 2
Swansea C (Loaned on 2/7/94) FL 6+1/2

Notts Co (Loaned on 7/10/94) FL 3+2/2
Stoke C (Loaned on 23/12/94) FL 1+3
Wycombe W (£150,000 on 15/9/95) FL 34+14/8 FLC 4+1/2 FAC 5/4 Others 2
Hereford U (Free on 14/2/97) FL 8+3/3

WILLIAMS Lee
Born: Birmingham, 3 February 1973
Height: 5'7" Weight: 11.13
International Honours: E: Yth

Released by Peterborough during the summer of 1996, Lee hopped over to the Republic to play for Shamrock Rovers last season before deciding to come back to the English game, trialling with Tranmere. Failing to get a game at Prenton, a month later, on transfer deadline day, he signed for Mansfield on a non-contract basis and appeared six times in their midfield, showing himself to be a more than useful passer of the ball and possessing good balance.

Aston Villa (From trainee on 26/1/91)
Shrewsbury T (Loaned on 8/11/92) FL 2+1 FAC 1+1/1 Others 2
Peterborough U (Signed on 23/3/94) FL 83+8/1 FLC 4+1 FAC 5+1/1 Others 7 (Free to Shamrock Rov during 1996 close season)
Tranmere Rov (Free on 26/2/97)
Mansfield T (Free on 27/3/97) FL 3+3

WILLIAMS Mark Stuart
Born: Hyde, 28 September 1970
Height: 6'0" Weight: 13.0
Club Honours: Div 3 '94

As is the case with any team, defensive strength is essential to success and, in "Bomber" Williams, Chesterfield have one of the best (and most underrated) centre halves in the second division. Combining well with Sean Dyche, he is courageous, unflappable, and rock-solid, and has few peers in the air, where his sheer power is as much an asset going forward at set pieces as it is in run-of-the-mill defending. Also possesses a cracking shot from free kicks.

Shrewsbury T (Free from Newtown on 27/3/92) FL 96+6/3 FLC 7+1 FAC 6 Others 6/1
Chesterfield (£50,000 on 7/8/95) FL 84/6 FLC 3 FAC 9/1 Others 5

WILLIAMS Martin Keith
Born: Luton, 12 July 1973
Height: 5'9" Weight: 11.12

Martin played much more regularly and consistently in 1996-97 than in his previous season with Reading and began to find his niche as a creative midfield player who can also burst through defences to score goals. His defending improved too, and he looks to be one of the young players around whom Royals will build their team in the future.

Luton T (Free from Leicester C juniors on 13/9/91) FL 12+28/2 FLC 1 FAC 0+1 Others 2+1
Colchester U (Loaned on 9/3/95) FL 3
Reading (Free on 13/7/95) FL 32+12/4 FLC 2+1 FAC 2

WILLIAMS Michael (Mike) Anthony
Born: Bradford, 21 November 1969
Height: 5'10" Weight: 11.6

Having broken his leg the previous season, Mike must have been hoping for more luck in 1996-97, but suffered with a whole string of injuries and once again failed to make an

impression at Sheffield Wednesday, making just one start against Oxford in the Coca-Cola Cup and one sub Premiership appearance. After being loaned out to Huddersfield to cover a severe injury crisis in October, and in March to Peterborough, the strong-running midfielder was released during the summer.

Sheffield Wed (Free from Maltby MW on 13/2/91) F/PL 16+7/1 FLC 3+2 Others 1
Halifax T (Loaned on 18/12/92) FL 9/1
Huddersfield T (Loaned on 18/10/96) FL 2
Peterborough U (Loaned on 27/3/97) FL 6

WILLIAMS Paul Anthony
Born: Stratford, 16 August 1965
Height: 5'7" Weight: 10.9
Club Honours: FLC '91; Div 1 '94
International Honours: E: B-3; U21-4

A lively, nippy forward, Paul proved very popular at Southend, signing last August after a successful trial spell, having earlier been released by Torquay. Carving out a first-team place for himself for two thirds of the season, he contributed many lightning runs and good crosses, not to mention some more than useful goals. He also acted as a good foil for both Jeroen Boere and Andy Rammell, who both appreciated the support he gave the forward line.

Charlton Ath (£12,000 from Woodford T on 23/2/87) FL 74+8/23 FLC 6/3 FAC 6+1/3
Brentford (Loaned on 20/10/87) FL 7/3 Others 1/3
Sheffield Wed (£700,000 on 15/8/90) F/PL 78+15/25 FLC 10+3/3 FAC 3+2 Others 3
Crystal Palace (Signed on 11/9/92) F/PL 38+8/7 FLC 4+1 Others 2/2
Sunderland (Loaned on 19/1/95) FL 3
Birmingham C (Loaned on 13/3/95) FL 8+3 Others 1/1
Charlton Ath (Free on 29/9/95) FL 2+7
Torquay U (Loaned on 28/3/96) FL 9
Southend U (Free on 30/8/96) FL 24+9/6 FLC 0+1 FAC 1

Paul Williams (Coventry)

WILLIAMS Paul Darren
Born: Burton, 26 March 1971
Height: 6'0" Weight: 14.3
International Honours: E: U21-6

Paul is a hard-tackling Coventry midfield player who can also play in the centre of defence. The clubs best spell of last season, in December, coincided with him playing successfully as a ball winner, where previously opponents had run through the City midfield, while in defence, he seemed more at ease with the three-centre-back system. As always, his wholehearted approach made him popular with the fans, his tussles with Mark Hughes and John Hartson being fascinating, and he was outstanding in the final run in, none more so than against Arsenal when getting the better of Dennis Bergkamp in an excellent battle. Is also the possessor of a fierce shot and dangerous at set pieces.
Derby Co (From trainee on 13/7/89) FL 153+7/26 FLC 10+2/2 FAC 8/3 Others 14+1/2
Lincoln C (Loaned on 9/11/89) FL 3 FAC 2 Others 1
Coventry C (£975,000 on 6/8/95) PL 59+5/4 FLC 6/1 FAC 5

WILLIAMS Paul Richard Curtis
Born: Leicester, 11 September 1969
Height: 5'7" Weight: 10.7

As in the previous season, Plymouth's consistent left-wing back appeared in every league game in 1996-97, again showing great ability in both defending and going forward. Although defensively sound, being a strong tackler with good powers of recovery, it is his attacking capability that makes him ideal for his wing-back role, especially his crossing. Always looking to bring his team mates into the game, he could prove to be a vital link in the club's plans for 1997-98.
Leicester C (From trainee on 1/7/88)
Stockport Co (Free on 5/7/89) FL 61+9/4 FLC 3 FAC 4 Others 7+5/1
Coventry C (£150,000 on 12/8/93) PL 8+6 FLC 1+1 FAC 3
West Bromwich A (Loaned on 19/11/93) FL 5
Huddersfield T (Loaned on 17/11/94) FL 2 Others 1
Huddersfield T (Loaned on 17/3/95) FL 7
Plymouth Arg (£50,000 on 10/8/95) FL 92/4 FLC 4 FAC 6 Others 6/1

WILLIAMS Ryan Neill
Born: Mansfield, 31 August 1978
Height: 5'4" Weight: 9.10
International Honours: E: Yth

The Mansfield striker, who is the smallest player currently performing in the league, showed skill and courage when playing against very physical odds in 1996-97 and added to his England U17 call up the previous season with an U18 cap – the only third division player so honoured.
Mansfield T (Trainee) FL 9+17/3 FLC 2 FAC 0+1

WILLIAMS Scott John
Born: Bangor, 7 August 1974
Height: 6'0" Weight: 12.0
International Honours: W: U21-5; Yth

Scott has probably been Wrexham's unluckiest recent player regarding injuries, not featuring at all during 1995-96 after showing much promise the previous season when a regular in the Wales U21 set up. Made his first full appearance since April 1995 in the away match at Plymouth last March and must now be hoping for an extended run in the squad. Tall and slim, and with time on his side, he shows fine composure for a youngster and can adjust to a number of positions in midfield and defence.
Wrexham (From trainee on 2/7/93) FL 23+6 FLC 1 Others 2+2

Steve Williams

WILLIAMS Steven (Steve) David
Born: Aberystwyth, 16 October 1974
Height: 6'3" Weight: 12.12
International Honours: W: Yth

Unable to get a game for Cardiff in 1996-97 with Tony Elliott going great guns, even when the latter was injured this giant goalkeeper found his way barred by Patrick Mountain. However, having been loaned out to non-league Merthyr in March, he then had to be recalled for the final five games of the campaign when Elliott was again put out of action and, in keeping three clean sheets, Steve certainly did his bit in getting City into the play offs.
Cardiff C (Free from Coventry C juniors on 13/8/93) FL 33 FAC 1 Others 7+1

WILLIAMSON Daniel (Danny) Alan
Born: West Ham, 5 December 1973
Height: 5'11" Weight: 12.3

The young local-born West Ham midfielder was plagued with ankle injury problems throughout last season and was thus unable to build on the progress he had made in 1995-96. Started well, playing the first six games, only to be sidelined for three months until returning to first-team duty in December and enjoying another run of seven games before dropping out again in February. His season ended in March at Chelsea when, making his second comeback (as a substitute), the ankle gave way and he was rushed to hospital for an operation. A player with a good football brain, who shines at the passing game and has plenty of stamina, he will be hoping for better luck, and fitness, in the coming season.
West Ham U (From trainee on 3/7/92) PL 47+4/5 FLC 0+2 FAC 5
Doncaster Rov (Loaned on 8/10/93) FL 10+3/1 FAC 2/2 Others 1

WILLIS Roger Christopher
Born: Sheffield, 17 June 1967
Height: 6'2" Weight: 12.0
Club Honours: GMVC '91
International Honours: E: SP-1

Snapped up on a free from Southend immediately prior to the start of the 1996-97 season, Roger, or "Harry"as he is more commonly known, once again joined up with his old manager, Barry Fry, this time at Peterborough. An attacking player with excellent heading ability who often plays out wide, he started the opener as a regular, getting off the mark in a 2-1 win at Bournemouth, and, having struggled with injuries in recent years, missed very few games. Despite being a member of a side ultimately doomed to relegation, he could not be faulted for effort and was always trying to turn things around.
Grimsby T (Signed from Dunkirk on 20/7/89) FL 1+8 FLC 0+1
Barnet (£10,000 on 1/8/90) FL 39+5/13 FLC 2 FAC 5+1/3 Others 1+4/1
Watford (£175,000 on 6/10/92) FL 30+6/2 FAC 1
Birmingham C (£150,000 on 31/12/93) FL 12+7/5 FLC 0+1
Southend U (Signed on 16/9/94) FL 30+1/7 FAC 1 Others 1
Peterborough U (Free on 13/8/96) FL 34+6/6 FLC 3 FAC 5+1 Others 5

WILMOT Rhys James
Born: Newport, 21 February 1962
Height: 6'1" Weight: 12.0
International Honours: W: U21-6; Yth; Sch

Having been released by Crystal Palace during the 1996 close season and joining Torquay, the experienced goalkeeper was then hampered by a niggling back injury. Then, after putting that behind him and claiming the first team jersey in September he performed with a cool assurance before another serious leg injury put paid to his season at the end of March and led to him being freed in the summer. Big and strong with no frills, he commands the area well.
Arsenal (From apprentice on 8/2/80) FL 8 FLC 1
Hereford U (Loaned on 18/3/83) FL 9
Leyton Orient (Loaned on 27/5/84) FL 46 FLC 4 FAC 4 Others 3
Swansea C (Loaned on 26/8/88) FL 16
Plymouth Arg (£100,000 on 23/2/89) FL 133 FLC 8 FAC 2 Others 4
Grimsby T (£87,500 on 1/7/92) FL 33 FLC 4 FAC 4 Others 2
Crystal Palace (£80,000 on 9/8/94) PL 5+1 FAC 1
Torquay U (Free on 16/8/96) FL 34 FAC 1 Others 1

WILSON Clive Euclid Aklana
Born: Manchester, 13 November 1961
Height: 5'7" Weight: 10.0
Club Honours: Div 2 '89

A defender who is capable of playing on either flank, this full back was another quality performer who found it hard to hold down a regular first-team place at Tottenham in 1996-97, due to injuries and increased competition, following the introduction of John Scales, Ramon Vega and Steve Carr. In the few appearances made, however, he showed he had lost none of his accuracy in delivering crosses best underlined with the goal in the home defeat against Leicester in September, or his enthusiasm to join in the attack, while his cool temperament meant that he would continue to be one of the side's penalty takers. A fully fit Clive still has a great deal to offer at Premiership level and he can go on adding to the 500th appearance made in October against Sunderland.

Manchester C (From juniors on 8/12/79) FL 96+2/9 FLC 10/2 FAC 2 Others 5
Chester C (Loaned on 16/9/82) FL 21/2
Chelsea (£250,000 on 19/3/87) FL 68+13/5 FLC 3+3 FAC 4 Others 10+2
Manchester C (Loaned on 19/3/87) FL 11
Queens Park R (£450,000 on 4/7/90) F/PL 170+2/12 FLC 16/1 FAC 8/1 Others 2+1
Tottenham H (Free on 12/6/95) PL 51+3/1 FLC 4 FAC 4+1/1

WILSON Kevin James
Born: Banbury, 18 April 1961
Height: 5'8" Weight: 11.4
Club Honours: Div 2 '89; FMC '90
International Honours: NI: 42

In his third season at Walsall, and his 18th in the game, Kevin did not have the best of luck in 1996-97, especially when being left out of the team for a game on an icy pitch at Wycombe at the end of December, a decision that ended a run of 137 successive appearances for the club. At times, however, he looked as good as ever, getting the match winner against Preston in October, but was bitterly upset by a cruel sending off in a vital game in April, his first dismissal in nearly 20 years.

Derby Co (£20,000 from Banbury U on 21/12/79) FL 106+16/30 FLC 8+3/8 FAC 8/3
Ipswich T (£100,000 on 5/1/85) FL 94+4/34 FLC 8/8 FAC 10/3 Others 7/4
Chelsea (£335,000 on 25/6/87) FL 124+28/42 FLC 10+2/4 FAC 7+1/1 Others 14+5/8
Notts Co (£225,000 on 27/3/92) FL 58+11/3 FLC 3+1 FAC 2 Others 5+1
Bradford C (Loaned on 13/1/94) FL 5
Walsall (Free on 4/8/94) FL 124+1/38 FLC 8/3 FAC 13/7 Others 6/1

WILSON Paul Anthony
Born: Bradford, 2 August 1968
Height: 5'11" Weight: 12.2

A strong, snappy-tackling Scunthorpe left back, who gave consistently good displays last season, Paul likes to fire in powerful long-range shots. Also more than capable of getting in excellent deep crosses, transfer deadline day surprisingly saw him go to Cambridge on loan with a view to a permanent signing, prior to him being freed during the summer.

Huddersfield T (From apprentice on 12/6/86) FL 15 FLC 1
Norwich C (£30,000 on 23/7/87)
Northampton T (£30,000 on 12/2/88) FL 132+9/6 FLC 10/1 FAC 7 Others 6+3

Halifax T (£30,000 on 19/12/91) FL 45/7 FLC 2 FAC 1 Others 2
Burnley (Signed on 1/2/93) FL 31 FAC 0+1
York C (Signed on 6/10/94) FL 21+1 FAC 2 Others 1
Scunthorpe U (Signed on 9/8/95) FL 77/2 FLC 4 FAC 6 Others 4
Cambridge U (Loaned on 27/3/97) FL 7

WILSON Paul Derek
Born: Doncaster, 16 November 1960
Height: 5'9" Weight: 11.12
International Honours: E: SP

Having played for a number of non-league sides, including Denaby United, Frickley Athletic, Boston United, and Yeovil Town, the former England semi-pro international striker decided to move on, becoming youth development officer at Scunthorpe in February 1996 and signing non-contract forms at the same time. Remarkably, named as a sub during an injury crisis last April, Paul came on for the last 35 minutes at Cardiff, thus becoming the oldest post-war Football League debutant at the age of 36.

Scunthorpe U (Signed from Yeovil T on 2/2/96) FL 0+1

WILSON Paul Robert
Born: Forest Gate, 26 September 1964
Height: 5'9" Weight: 12.0
Club Honours: GMVC '91

The Barnet club captain and the player who epitomises the never-say-die spirit of the club, Paul is a tough-tackling central midfielder who also has nerves of steel when taking penalties. Although four of his five league goals in 1996-97 were from the spot, it was the odd one out that got the biggest cheer, a rasping 25 yarder which beat the goalie all ends up for the Bees' second in the 2-0 Coca-Cola Cup win over Exeter.

Barnet (Signed from Barking on 1/3/88) FL 167+7/16 FLC 10/1 FAC 20+1 Others 8+2

Steve Wilson

WILSON Stephen (Steve) Lee
Born: Hull, 24 April 1974
Height: 5'10" Weight: 10.12

As understudy to Roy Carroll at Hull City, Steve displayed his own notable keeping skills, especially when a gruesome hand injury sidelined the young Irish goalie in the latter stages of the 1996-97 campaign. He later added to his repertoire by coming on as a left-wing sub in an Auto Windscreens Shield tie at Carlisle.

Hull C (From trainee on 13/7/92) FL 93+1 FLC 7 FAC 7 Others 7+1

WILSON Stuart Kevin
Born: Leicester, 16 September 1977
Height: 5'8" Weight: 9.12

A highly promising young midfielder, Stuart made his debut for Leicester as substitute in FA Cup victory over Southend last January and showed much promise during the 27 minutes he was on the pitch. Again came off the bench in the FA Cup tie against Chelsea and again looked very impressive with his speed and crossing ability, scoring his first goal on the final day at Blackburn, and is clearly one to watch for the future.

Leicester C (From trainee on 4/7/96) PL 0+2/1 FAC 0+2

WILSTERMAN Brian Hank
Born: Surinam, 19 November 1966
Height: 6'1" Weight: 12.8

Brian joined Oxford, via NEC, Go Ahead Eagles, and SVV Dordrecht (Holland) last February after a 12-year career in Holland and Belgium, and went straight into the side against Crystal Palace. Despite the team having a nightmare match in a 4-1 defeat, leading to him being replaced for the next game, he showed some good signs and once used to the pace of the English game should settle in well.

Oxford U (£200,000 from Beerschot on 28/2/97) FL 1

WINSTANLEY Craig Jason
Born: Hartlepool, 23 August 1978
Height: 5'11" Weight: 11.7

This young midfielder remained on Hartlepool's books after completing two years as a YTS player during the 1996 close season. Unfortunately, he was unable to make much impact at first-team level, but his four minutes as a substitute against Northampton made him the new holder of Pool's shortest ever league career record. Finished the campaign playing for Unibond League team, Bishop Auckland.

Hartlepool U (From trainee on 24/12/96) FL 0+1

WINSTANLEY Mark Andrew
Born: St Helens, 22 January 1968
Height: 6'1" Weight: 12.7
Club Honours: AMC '89

At one stage in 1996-97, it seemed likely that Mark would be the casualty of Burnley's proliferation of central defenders, but he regained his place when Peter Swan was injured and ended the season as a first choice. The traditional defensive skills of stopping and tackling more than compensate for any absence of flair in his performances,

dependency being the byword.

Bolton W (From trainee on 22/7/86) FL 215+5/3 FLC 19+1 FAC 19 Others 26/3
Burnley (Signed on 5/8/94) FL 123+1/5 FLC 11 FAC 8 Others 4+1

WINSTON Samuel (Sammy) Anthony
Born: Islington, 6 August 1978
Height: 5'9" Weight: 11.2

A young centre forward with a lot of pace, he joined Leyton Orient after being released by Norwich from his YTS in the summer of 1996. Spent much of the early part of last season in the youth team and reserves, before being given his chance in the FA Cup match with Merthyr Tydfil, due to injuries, coming off the bench to score a goal on his debut. After notching his first league goal in the home game with Exeter, he will be looking to become a regular in 1997-98.

Leyton Orient (Free from Norwich C juniors on 15/8/96) FL 3+8/1 FAC 0+2/1

WINTER Steven (Steve) David
Born: Bristol, 26 October 1973
Height: 5'8" Weight: 10.12

The talented Torquay wing back, who can also play in midfield, took a step forward in 1996-97 as he also added a goalscoring touch to his play, with the winner at home against Hereford, his first goal for the club. This was followed by five more, three of them vital, as United maintained its position for another year. Despite the progress, Steve was freed during the summer.

Walsall (From trainee on 13/3/92) FL 14+4 Others 3 (Free to Yate T on 30/6/93)
Torquay U (£10,000 from Taunton T on 25/8/95) FL 72+1/6 FLC 2 FAC 2 Others 1

WINTERBURN Nigel
Born: Nuneaton, 11 December 1963
Height: 5'9" Weight: 11.4
Club Honours: Div 1 '89, '91; FAC '93; FLC '93; ECWC '94
International Honours: E: 2; B-3; U21-1; Yth

Nigel was another Arsenal man who played with renewed vigour in 1996-97 following the arrival of the cultured and articulate French manager, Arsene Wenger. Surprisingly, for him, he had a largely injury-free season, being a Premiership ever present, which had to be a tribute to the timing of the left-wing back's fierce tackling. Not always given the credit he deserved in a Gunners' rearguard noted for its meaness, 32 goals conceded during the campaign being one of the main reasons for the side's rise to third place, he is also quick to get forward to supply accurate crosses to the front men. A wonderful servant of the club, Nigel had a well deserved and well supported testimonial against Glasgow Rangers at the end of the season in recognition of his fine work during the past ten years. Is also noted for his throwing capability.

Birmingham C (From apprentice on 14/8/81)
Wimbledon (Free on 22/9/83) FL 164+1/8 FLC 13 FAC 12 Others 2
Arsenal (£407,000 on 26/5/87) F/PL 345+1/7 FLC 45/3 FAC 33 Others 32

Dennis Wise

WISE Dennis Frank
Born: Kensington, 16 December 1966
Height: 5'6" Weight: 10.0
Club Honours: FAC '88, '97
International Honours: E: 12; B-3; U21-1

The Chelsea skipper could have been forgiven if he had started 1996-97 under a cloud, with press rumours of a close-season rift with Ruud Gullit closely following his exclusion from Terry Venables' Euro 96 squad. The "little fella" responded magnificently, however, playing some of the best football of his career – the arrival of Chelsea's continental stars being a great influence. Despite scoring the Blues' injury-time equaliser in the pulsating 3-3 draw in September at Arsenal, his form dipped in November and he was left out of the side for four matches. His reappearance before the Christmas fixtures coincided with an upturn in the team's form and he led the side to their second FA Cup final in four years, scoring against West Brom in the third round and grabbing a brace in the sixth round against Portsmouth, before putting in a superb performance against his old club, Wimbledon, in the semi final at Highbury. In following Ron Harris to become the second player to captain Chelsea to an FA Cup final win, thanks to the 2-0 Wembley victory over Middlesbrough, and to emphasise his commitment to Chelsea, Dennis signed an extension to his contract which will keep him at the Bridge until 2001.

Wimbledon (Free from Southampton juniors on 28/3/85) FL 127+8/27 FLC 14 FAC 11/3 Others 5
Chelsea (£1,600,000 on 3/7/90) F/PL 211+7/43 FLC 23/6 FAC 25/6 Others 10/3

WITTER Anthony (Tony) Junior
Born: London, 12 August 1965
Height: 6'1" Weight: 13.0

This fast and pacy central defender was sorely missed at the heart of Millwall's defence when he was injured last November, following which the Lions lost their place at the top of the second division. Cool and calm, using both feet comes easy to him and towards the end of a difficult campaign he was almost back at his best.

Crystal Palace (£10,000 from Grays Ath on 24/10/90)
Queens Park R (£125,000 on 19/8/91) PL 1
Plymouth Arg (Loaned on 9/1/92) FL 3/1
Reading (Loaned on 11/2/94) FL 4
Millwall (£100,000 on 14/10/94) FL 89+2/2 FLC 6 FAC 8

WOAN Ian Simon
Born: Heswall, 14 December 1967
Height: 5'10" Weight: 12.4

If 1995-96 was his best season for Nottingham Forest, then last season was probably his most difficult as he struggled to make an impression for most of the campaign and when his left-sided midfield role bought him little success, he moved into the centre to accommodate Chris Allen outside him. However, it was not a change for the good. Despite the problems, Ian missed very few matches, his highlight

Ian Woan

undoubtedly being the FA Cup fourth round tie at Newcastle where he scored twice in Forest's shock win. Those goals were his first of the season and he scored only one more. Hopefully, 1997-98 will see him back at his best with his wide range of passing skills and clever touches on the ball providing the impetus for Forest to come back to the Premiership at their first attempt.

Nottingham F (£80,000 from Runcorn on 14/3/90) F/PL 176+11/30 FLC 15+2/1 FAC 20+1/6 Others 13/2

WOOD Simon Onward
Born: Hull, 24 September 1976
Height: 5'9" Weight: 11.8

After a few weeks of last season it was discovered that Simon, although used by Mansfield as a defender by former manager, Andy King, had only played as an attacker previously. Once this misconception had been redressed, the former Coventry man had a good season, leading the attack for much of the remainder of the campaign. Whilst not tall, he proved to be a very good header of the ball – frequently outjumping much taller opponents. Was released during the summer.

Coventry C (From trainee on 11/11/93)
Mansfield T (Free on 15/3/96) FL 32+9/4 FLC 1 FAC 2/1 Others 1

WOOD Trevor John
Born: Jersey, 3 November 1968
Height: 6'0" Weight: 13.7
International Honours: NI: 1; B-1

Despite making some outstanding saves during his ten first-team appearances for Walsall last season, he was replaced by "Whacker" Walker following a 2-0 defeat at Notts County, before transferring to Hereford to cover an injury to Andy Debont. After settling down, the Northern Ireland international goalie soon showed himself to be one of the best shot stoppers in the lower divisions, especially with his experience and command of the area.

Brighton & Hove A (From apprentice on 7/11/86)
Port Vale (Free on 8/7/88) FL 42 FLC 4 FAC 2 Others 2
Walsall (Free on 18/7/94) FL 69 FLC 4 FAC 7 Others 3
Hereford U (Free on 8/1/97) FL 19

WOODMAN Andrew (Andy) John
Born: Camberwell, 11 August 1971
Height: 6'3" Weight: 13.7

As Northampton's first-team goalkeeper, "Woody" is comfortable on crosses and has pulled off many a good save in his time at the club. Despite there being some speculation that he was about to join a Premier or division one club last season, he remained between the sticks at Sixfields, and was a driving force in the club's promotion run, at one stage keeping four consecutive clean sheets.

Crystal Palace (From trainee on 1/7/89)
Exeter C (Free on 4/7/94) FL 6 FLC 1 FAC 1 Others 2
Northampton T (Free on 10/3/95) FL 99 FLC 6 FAC 3 Others 10

WOODS Christopher (Chris) Charles Eric
Born: Boston, 14 November 1959
Height: 6'2" Weight: 14.12
Club Honours: Div 2 '86; FLC '78, '85; SPD '87, '89, '90, '91; SLC '87, '89, '91
International Honours: E: 43; B-2; U21-6; Yth

Despite his age, Chris continued in 1996-97 to show that he possessed the reflexes required for a top-class goalkeeper, while being technically sound and agile, with safe hands and good with crosses. Having left Sheffield Wednesday during the 1996 close season for a stint in the USA, he came back in November to replace Southampton's out-of-favour Dave Beasant, playing six games, before breaking a leg at Blackburn. Still hoping to extend his career, on recovering, he joined Sunderland on a short-term contract in March as the stand-in 'keeper for Lionel Perez, sitting on the bench for the last six games without being called upon. When in action, it was noticeable that he had not lost the ability to marshal a defence.

Nottingham F (From apprentice on 1/12/76) FLC 7
Queens Park R (£250,000 on 4/7/79) FL 63 FLC 8 FAC 1

297

Andy Woodman

Norwich C (£225,000 on 12/3/81) FL 216 FLC 26 FAC 19 Others 6
Glasgow R (£600,000 on 2/7/86) SL 173 SLC 21 SC 15 Others 21
Sheffield Wed (£1,200,000 on 15/8/91) F/PL 106+1 FLC 13 FAC 10 Others 5
Reading (Loaned on 27/10/95) FL 5 (Free to Colorado Rapids on 10/5/96)
Southampton (Free on 2/11/96) PL 4 FLC 2
Sunderland (Free on 27/3/97)

WOODS Matthew (Mattie) James

Born: Gosport, 9 September 1976
Height: 6'1" Weight: 12.13

Released by Everton during the 1996 close season without receiving any opportunities at Goodison, Mattie joined Chester and made 28 appearances, playing either in defence or midfield. Although used mainly from the bench, he did enough to warrant that he had a future in the game, opening his scoring account with a scorching 25-yard drive against Brighton at the Deva Stadium, and producing several confident displays that extended into the play offs.

Everton (From trainee on 1/7/95)
Chester C (Free on 12/8/96) FL 9+12/1 FLC 0+1 FAC 3 Others 2+1

WOODS Neil Stephen

Born: Bradford, 30 July 1966
Height: 6'0" Weight: 12.11

Grimsby striker. A right-footed, play maker, particularly adept at holding, shielding, and laying off the ball, Neil is very fast in the box and shows quick reactions in front of goal. Had to struggle for his place during the early part of last season, but, following the change of management, regained his regular first-team spot, although finding goals somewhat hard to come by, before being unfortunately sidelined by injury towards the end of the campaign and released during the summer.

Doncaster Rov (From apprentice on 31/8/83) FL 55+10/16 FLC 4/1 FAC 5/2 Others 5+2/3
Glasgow R (£120,000 on 22/12/86) SL 0+3
Ipswich T (£120,000 on 3/8/87) FL 15+12/5 Others 4/1
Bradford C (Signed on 1/3/90) FL 13+1/2
Grimsby T (£82,000 on 23/8/90) FL 174+42/42 FLC 11+1/2 FAC 8+1/2 Others 7/1

WOODS William (Billy)

Born: Cork, 24 October 1973
Height: 6'0" Weight: 12.0
International Honours: Ei: U21-4

A regular member of the Tranmere Pontins' League side in 1996-97, Billy, who also combines accountancy studies with his football career, made his first-team debut at Port Vale at left back in March. However, this was to be his one and only appearance, and the Eire U21 international was released on a free transfer at the end of the season, having earlier spent a month on loan at Blackpool, where he appeared in three games.

Tranmere Rov (£50,000 from Cork Co on 10/7/95) FL 1
Blackpool (Loaned on 10/10/96) FL 3

WOODWARD Andrew (Andy) Stephen

Born: Stockport, 23 September 1973
Height: 5'11" Weight: 13.6
Club Honours: Div 2 '97

Andy will undoubtedly look back on 1996-97 with much pleasure as he finally gained a regular place in Bury's defence in his third season at Gigg Lane. Given his chance in the line up, replacing Preston-bound Michael Jackson, he proved to be a more than capable replacement, grabbing the opportunity with both hands and collecting a second division championship medal as the Shakers pipped Stockport for top spot.

Crewe Alex (From trainee on 29/7/92) FL 9+11 FLC 2 Others 0+3
Bury (Signed on 13/3/95) FL 25+7 FLC 0+1 Others 5

WORRALL Benjamin (Ben) Joseph

Born: Swindon, 7 December 1975
Height: 5'6" Weight: 10.0
International Honours: E: Yth

An energetic young midfielder, and a graduate of the FA's National School of Excellence at Lilleshall, he joined Scarborough in the summer of 1996 following his release by Swindon Town. A regular in the reserve side who always did a good job when called up for senior action, his only first team goal was a late equaliser to secure a 2-2 draw at Exeter early in the campaign.

Swindon T (From trainee on 8/7/94) FL 1+2
Scarborough (Free on 2/8/96) FL 6+9/1 FLC 1+1 Others 0+1

WORTHINGTON Nigel

Born: Ballymena, 4 November 1961
Height: 5'11" Weight: 12.6
Club Honours: FLC '91
International Honours: NI: 66; Yth

Signed from Leeds during the 1996 close season, the experienced left back started 1996-97 in the Stoke first team before an injury let in promising 17-year-old Andrew Griffin during November. Despite being kept out by the youngster, even when fit again, Nigel was still regularly called up for the Northern Ireland international squad who continued to recognise his quality as a hard tackler, good crosser and corner-kick specialist. Was freed during the summer.

Notts Co (£100,000 from Ballymena on 1/7/81) FL 62+5/4 FLC 11 FAC 4
Sheffield Wed (£125,000 on 6/2/84) F/PL 334+4/12 FLC 41/1 FAC 29 Others 9/1
Leeds U (£325,000 on 4/7/94) PL 33+10/1 FLC 4+1 FAC 6+1
Stoke C (Free on 18/7/96) FL 12 FLC 3/1

WOTTON Paul Anthony

Born: Plymouth, 17 August 1977
Height: 5'11" Weight: 12.0

A second year Plymouth professional, Paul is a versatile player who played in midfield last term, proving to be both quick and strong with a good eye for goal. While his performances gave him a good run in the side, keeping out more experienced colleagues, it attracted potential buyers as well and he spent a trial period at Sheffield Wednesday. Also an excellent passer, he should continue to make sound progress in 1997-98.

Plymouth Arg (From trainee on 10/7/95) FL 10+7/1 FAC 2 Others 4/2

Darren Wrack

WRACK Darren
Born: Cleethorpes, 5 May 1976
Height: 5'9" Weight: 12.2

The locally-born Darren returned to his hometown club, Grimsby, in the 1996 close season, as opportunities at Derby had been limited. Unfortunately, he fared little better at Blundell Park in 1996-97, appearing rarely in the first team, before spending a spell on loan at Shrewsbury in February. A lively right-footed winger, with the ability to get wide to put in accurate crosses, he is bound to be given further opportunities.
Derby Co (From trainee on 12/7/94) FL 4+22/1 FLC 0+3 FAC 0+2
Grimsby T (£100,000 + on 19/7/96) FL 5+7/1
Shrewsbury T (Loaned on 17/2/97) FL 3+1 Others 1

WRAY Shaun Warren
Born: Birmingham, 14 March 1978
Height: 6'1" Weight: 12.11

A right-sided forward, and a player still trying to make his way into the Shrewsbury side, Shaun made just one appearance last season, in the home game against Gillingham in October, before going back to the reserves.
Shrewsbury T (From trainee on 1/7/95) FL 1+3

WRIGHT Alan Geoffrey
Born: Ashton under Lyne, 28 September 1971
Height: 5'4" Weight: 9.4
Club Honours: FLC '96
International Honours: E: U21-2; Yth; Sch

An ever present for the second successive season in the Aston Villa left-wing back berth in 1996-97, Alan also weighed in with one goal, a cracking left-foot volley at Wimbledon. With a fit again Steve Staunton looking set to battle for the position, both were fitted in, with Paul McGrath missing out on team selection, as Staunton moved inside. Not the biggest of players, he continued to give everything and his pace and willingness to get forward made him a useful asset, especially the way he linked with Dwight Yorke. Remains one of the best backs in England and could still win international honours.
Blackpool (From trainee on 13/4/89) FL 91+7 FLC 10+2 FAC 8 Others 11+2
Blackburn Rov (£400,000 on 25/10/91) F/PL 67+7/1 FLC 8 FAC 5+1 Others 3
Aston Villa (£1,000,000 on 10/3/95) PL 84/3 FLC 10 FAC 8 Others 2

WRIGHT Ian Edward
Born: Woolwich, 3 November 1963
Height: 5'10" Weight: 11.8
Club Honours: FMC '91; FLC '93; FAC '93
International Honours: E: 27; B-3

The mercurial goalscoring icon showed no sign of losing his touch in 1996-97, when passing personal landmarks galore – 100th league goal for Arsenal when completing a hat trick in a 4-1 home win against Sheffield Wednesday, 200th career league goal, and 150th goal in all competitions for Arsenal – and only Cliff Bastin still stands ahead of him in the Arsenal goalscoring charts, something that will surely fall to the man from south London this coming season. Despite his fragile tolerance lever with referees, Ian is undoubtedly the greatest scoring machine to have graced the famous red and white shirt and, apart from the hat trick against Sheffield Wednesday, his 30 strikes included doubles against Blackburn, Stoke, Liverpool, and Derby in the final game of a long, hard campaign that saw the Gunners attain a UEFA Cup spot after finishing third in the Premiership, one of the outstanding features being his great partnership and understanding with the

Ian Wright

Dutchman, Dennis Bergkamp. Played for England in World Cup qualifiers in Georgia and at Wembley against Italy, and the Mexican friendly, before stepping out in another friendly, this time against South Africa, and scoring the winner. Selected for the PFA award-winning Premiership team, even at the age of 33, he shows no signs of slowing down.

Crystal Palace (Free from Greenwich Borough on 2/8/85) FL 206+19/89 FLC 19/9 FAC 9+2/3 Others 19+3/16
Arsenal (£2,500,000 on 24/9/91) F/PL 190+7/118 FLC 28/28 FAC 15/12 Others 20/16

WRIGHT Ian Matthew
Born: Lichfield, 10 March 1972
Height: 6'1" Weight: 13.4

Ian responded in magnificent fashion to the challenge of regular first-team football in his first season at Hull City, having spent much of his time with Bristol Rovers on the sidelines. A quiet character who is calm under pressure, the right-footed "Wrighty" is a traditional stopper centre back who goes about his work efficiently and effectively.

Stoke C (From trainee on 11/7/90) FL 6 FLC 1+1 Others 1
Bristol Rov (Signed on 23/9/93) FL 50+4/1 FLC 2+1 FAC 2 Others 5+1
Hull C (Free on 2/7/96) FL 40 FLC 2 FAC 3 Others 2/1

WRIGHT Jermaine Malaki
Born: Greenwich, 21 October 1975
Height: 5'9" Weight: 11.9
International Honours: E: Yth

The Wolves' right-footed winger came on four times in 1996-97 as a sub in the first ten matches, but, that apart, he had few opportunities to get his fast crosses in and was not called upon again until the closing minutes of the last league match. A winger from the old school who can play down either flank and delights in running at defenders, Jermaine has still to score his first league goal.

Millwall (From trainee on 27/11/92)
Wolverhampton W (£60,000 on 29/12/94) FL 4+12 FLC 1+3/1 Others 0+1
Doncaster Rov (Loaned on 1/3/96) FL 13

WRIGHT Jonathan (Jon)
Born: Belfast, 24 November 1975
Height: 5'9" Weight: 11.7
International Honours: NI: B-2; Yth

The 29 players used for Norwich in 1995-96 and the 28 last season showed the devastation caused by injuries and suspensions at the club. Despite the opportunities being there, Jon's four meagre appearances were all before Xmas, with the last two being dire -5-1 and 6-1 losses to West Brom and Port Vale, respectively, and he found Danny Mills, Matt Jackson, and Rob Newman ahead of him for the full-back slots. Out of first-team contention, and consigned to being a reserve performer, the young defender was released during the summer.

Norwich C (From trainee on 1/7/94) P/FL 5+2

WRIGHT Mark
Born: Dorchester, 1 August 1963
Height: 6'3" Weight: 13.3
Club Honours: FAC '92
International Honours: E: 45; U21-4

Continuing his comeback to form in 1996-97, Mark ousted both Neil Ruddock and John Scales (since moved to Spurs) as the main Liverpool central defender, his gritty determination, delicate ball control, and powerful heading ability often coming to the Red's rescue during a long and arduous campaign, which ultimately resulted in a place in the UEFA Cup this coming season. A regular fixture in the side, only missing games when injured, he showed the form that first took him to Anfield and, in doing so, went a long way to re-establishing himself as one of the country's best defenders. Capable of attacking the ball at both ends of the park, and an obvious danger at set pieces, and with Pool 3-1 down on aggregate against Paris St Germain in the second leg of the European Cup Winners Cup at Anfield, it was Mark who powered in an 80th minute header to bring the scores to 3-2. Unfortunately, with the forwards unable to find the net again another assault on Europe came to an end – for another year at least. Held in high esteem by his fellow professionals, he was elected to the award-winning Premiership side at the PFA annual dinner.

Oxford U (From juniors on 26/8/80) FL 8+2 FAC 1
Southampton (£80,000 on 25/3/82) FL 170/7 FLC 25/2 FAC 17/1 Others 10/1
Derby Co (£760,000 on 27/8/87) FL 144/10 FLC 15 FAC 5 Others 7
Liverpool (£2,200,000 on 15/7/91) F/PL 150+2/5 FLC 14+2/1 FAC 18 Others 17/1

WRIGHT Matthew Paul
Born: Norwich, 6 January 1978
Height: 6'1" Weight: 11.7

While still an apprentice, this young Torquay central defender performed with good sense and solidity when called upon to deputise for his more experienced colleagues in 1996-97. Such was his impact, the club had no compunction in offering him a six-month contract in January.

Torquay U (From trainee on 9/1/97) FL 7+2 Others 0+1

WRIGHT Richard Ian
Born: Ipswich, 5 November 1977
Height: 6'2" Weight: 13.0
International Honours: E: U21-2; Yth; Sch

Richard confirmed his potential in 1996-97 as the best young 'keeper in the country, establishing himself on the way as Ipswich's number one when keeping Craig Forrest on the sidelines and gaining England U21 caps towards the end of the season. Indeed, he kept five successive clean sheets in the final games of the campaign and also had a clean sheet on his U21 debut during the same period. Missed six games in September after he went to pick up a ball in the Huddersfield game to take a free kick and collapsed with spasms in his back. Not only does his tremendous build allow him the confidence to come for crosses, but he is extremely agile for such a big lad, something that enables him to get down sharply for ground shots. Is also a good kicker.

Ipswich T (From trainee on 2/1/95) P/FL 66 FLC 6 FAC 4 Others 4

WRIGHT Thomas (Tommy) Elliott
Born: Dunfermline, 10 January 1966
Height: 5'7" Weight: 11.4
International Honours: S: U21-1; Yth

Having started last season on the Bradford bench, the attacking midfielder then went down with back and hamstring injuries that put him on the sidelines for two months and, back in harness, he then found himself on the bench again, making 14 subs' appearances without a single start. That all changed, however, in the final two games of the campaign. With City needing to obtain six points to avoid relegation, the little Scot set up Nigel Pepper's winner against Charlton, before taking a major hand on the last day, when making another for Pepper and scoring twice himself in a 3-0 win over QPR. At the time of going to press, the out of contract Tommy was due to be offered improved conditions, but, disappointed at being accused of being unable to play in a system using five at the back, watch this space.

Leeds U (From apprentice on 15/1/83) FL 73+8/24 FLC 3+2/1 FAC 4/3
Oldham Ath (£80,000 on 24/10/86) FL 110+2/23 FLC 7+1/2 FAC 3/2 Others 3
Leicester C (£350,000 on 14/8/89) FL 122+7/22 FLC 7+1 FAC 4 Others 10/7
Middlesbrough (£650,000 on 1/7/92) F/PL 44+9/5 FLC 3+1 FAC 3/1 Others 5+1
Bradford C (Free on 4/7/95) FL 30+15/5 FLC 6+1/2 FAC 1+1 Others 2+1

WRIGHT Thomas (Tommy) James
Born: Belfast, 29 August 1963
Height: 6'1" Weight: 14.5
Club Honours: Div 1 '93
International Honours: NI: 28; U23-1. E: FL Rep

Having joined Manchester City last January on one month's loan from Nottingham Forest, he made his debut in goal at Huddersfield and received very encouraging reports. A regular in all games except in the FA Cup, due to him being cup tied with Forest, he returned to his old club for one league match to help out with an injury problem, but two days later, joined City on a permanent basis. As the current Northern Ireland 'keeper, adding to the number of Irish players at Maine Road, he has stabilised the defence since arriving, having good rapport with his central defenders, which showed in the side's more confident and disciplined play. Earlier in the season, he had an unbroken run of games on loan at Reading in giving confidence to a shaky defence, following an injury to Bobby Mihailov.

Newcastle U (£30,000 from Linfield on 27/1/88) F/PL 72+1 FLC 6 FAC 4 Others 1
Hull C (Loaned on 14/2//91) FL 6
Nottingham F (£450,000 on 24/9/93) P/FL 11 FLC 2
Reading (Loaned on 4/10/96) FL 17
Manchester C (Loaned on 17/1/97) FL 5
Manchester C (£450,000 on 3/3/97) FL 8

XYZ

YATES Dean Richard
Born: Leicester, 26 October 1967
Height: 6'2" Weight: 12.6
Club Honours: AIC '95
International Honours: E: U21-5

A cultured but injury prone Derby central defender, Dean played in the opening game of last season before picking up an achilles tendon injury. Returned to the first team in November before suffering further injury at Wimbledon in January, which then sidelined him to the end of the season. All in all it was a very disappointing season for a player immensely popular with the home supporters as an English defender able to use the ball constructively in a continental style. There was no doubt that County missed his coolness under pressure and passing skills, in what was their first Premiership campaign, but it was good to see him back on the bench for the final two matches.
Notts Co (From apprentice on 14/6/85) FL 312+2/33 FLC 24 FAC 20 Others 36/4
Derby Co (£350,000 on 26/1/95) F/PL 57+2/3 FLC 3 FAC 1

YATES Stephen (Steve)
Born: Bristol, 29 January 1970
Height: 5'11" Weight: 12.2
Club Honours: Div 3 '90

Began last season in the centre of QPR's defence alongside Alan McDonald, but a bad injury sustained during the away game at Barnsley in mid September ruled him out until mid February when he returned for just three matches. A hard-working defender who rarely misses a tackle, and who is also more than capable in aerial battles, Steve made a goalscoring return to the side in a 3-2 win at Oxford on Easter Saturday and remained for the rest of the campaign. Is equally effective in either of the full-back slots.
Bristol Rov (From trainee on 1/7/88) FL 196+1 FLC 9 FAC 11 Others 21
Queens Park R (£650,000 on 16/8/93) P/FL 95+3/2 FLC 5 FAC 5

YEBOAH Anthony (Tony)
Born: Ghana, 6 June 1966
Height: 5'10" Weight: 13.11
International Honours: Ghana: 25

After an explosive start at Elland Road, the Ghanaian international suffered a serious knee injury and, after a summer operation, was sidelined for most of last season. Making his first appearance of 1996-97 at Manchester United in December, he was substituted and subsequently dropped for the next ten games, whereby there was much media speculation of a rift with George Graham. This was heightened by the fact that during a period where he was reported as being unfit, he played in a international match for Ghana, against the club's wishes,

only to worsen the injury. On his return to the first team, and in his fifth appearance at Tottenham in March, matters came to a head, when looking unfit and uninterested he was substituted in the 72nd minute. For the next game at Sheffield Wednesday he withdrew with a mysterious hamstring injury, only to declare himself fit again some four days later for another Ghanaian international match. At his best, an electrifying striker with tremendous shooting ability, hopefully, both he and the club can sort out their differences prior to the start of 1997-98.
Leeds U (£3,400,000 from Eintracht Frankfurt on 5/1/95) PL 44+3/24 FLC 7/3 FAC 6+2/2 Others 4/3

YORKE Dwight
Born: Canaan, Tobago, 3 November 1971
Height: 5'10" Weight: 11.12
Club Honours: FLC '96
International Honours: Trinidad & Tobago: 15

Reaching the 20-goal mark for the second successive term, Dwight top scored for Aston Villa again in 1996-97. The campaign started slowly for the Tobago-born striker,

but he bounced back with a hat trick at Newcastle at the end of September, amazingly finishing on the losing side. After that, goals again came at regular intervals (at one time 14 in 16 games) as Villa retained a top-eight spot. Perhaps he was not as successful as in 1995-96, although having reached those heights he should be able to return to them. However, 20 goals (virtually the total of the rest of the squad, other than Savo Milosevic, put together) in only a reasonable season shows what one of the Premiership's top marksmen is capable of. The pacy striker missed just two matches.
Aston Villa (£120,000 from Signal Hill on 19/12/89) F/PL 164+36/63 FLC 19+2/8 FAC 20+2/11 Others 3/1

YOUNG Christopher William
Born: Manchester, 11 August 1979
Height: 5'10" Weight: 12.6

Having made such a good showing for Mansfield when scoring two goals in the County Cup against Nottingham Forest, Chris was given a league debut at Swansea at the back end of last season, coming off the bench with eight minutes left on the clock in an effort to add more firepower to a side

Dwight Yorke

losing 3-2. A first-year trainee, he is expected to make a useful striker as he develops.

Mansfield T (Trainee) FL 0+1

YOUNG Eric
Born: Singapore, 25 March 1960
Height: 6'3" Weight: 13.5
Club Honours: FAC '88; FMC '91; Div 1 '94
International Honours: W: 21

Although Wolves were willing to release the hard-tackling central defender last season, they found that his experience was useful in the reserves and, following an injury to Dean Richards, he made the first team in October against Port Vale, giving a typically committed display. Released during the summer, at his best Eric was a player you could rely upon, always difficult to pass and always seemingly able to get a foot in. Big and brave in the air, he continued to pose a threat at set pieces.

Brighton & Hove A (£10,000 from Slough T on 1/11/82) FL 126/10 FLC 8 FAC 11/1 Others 2
Wimbledon (£70,000 on 29/7/87) FL 96+3/9 FLC 12 FAC 6+1/1 Others 7
Crystal Palace (£850,000 on 15/8/90) F/PL 161/15 FLC 25/1 FAC 10 Others 8/1
Wolverhampton W (Free on 13/9/95) FL 31/2 FLC 5 FAC 4

YOUNG Neil Anthony
Born: Harlow, 31 August 1973
Height: 5'9" Weight: 12.0

1996-97 was another very good season for Neil as he performed consistently well on the right-hand side of the Bournemouth defence. Always gave 100 per cent and linked well with the more forward players in making many good runs down the right wing and delivering telling crosses. A strong tackler, he has now made over 100 appearances for the Cherries.

Tottenham H (From trainee on 17/8/91)
Bournemouth (Free on 11/10/94) FL 116+1 FLC 5 FAC 6 Others 5

YOUNG Scott
Born: Pontypridd, 14 January 1976
Height: 6'1" Weight: 12.6
International Honours: W: U21-5

Played out of position for part of last season, Scott ended the campaign where he is best suited - in the heart of Cardiff's defence. Dependable and solid, good on the ground and in the air, he also scored his first league goal in the 1-0 win at Chester and will surely be one of the players the club will be looking to in the future. Added to his Welsh U21 caps, with four further appearances in 1996-97.

Cardiff C (From trainee on 4/7/94) FL 87+14/1 FLC 5+1 FAC 4 Others 11+3/1

ZABEK Lee Kevin
Born: Bristol, 13 October 1978
Height: 6'0" Weight: 12.0

A central midfielder, Lee made his league debut for Bristol Rovers in the final league match of last season when coming on as a sub after 57 minutes against Rotherham at the Memorial Ground. One of a remarkable 14 players who made their debuts for Rovers during the club's first season back in Bristol,

following an absence of a decade, the former youth captain is a good distributor of the ball and has scored goals at reserve and junior levels. Rewarded with a pro contract, he will provide strong competition for a first-team place in 1997-98.

Bristol Rov (Trainee) FL 0+1

ZOLA Gianfranco
Born: Sardinia, Italy, 5 July 1966
Height: 5'6" Weight: 10.10
Club Honours: FAC '97
International Honours: Italy: 33

Ruud Gullit pulled off one of the transfer coups of last season when, in November, he snapped up the Sardinian wizard from Parma to complete the trio of Italian internationals at Chelsea. The diminutive Gianfranco settled immediately to the demands of Premiership football and had the Stamford Bridge faithful entranced with his dribbling and ball control during a campaign that ended in glory, following the Londoners' 2-0 Wembley FA Cup final win over Middlesbrough. A former team mate of Diego Maradona at Napoli, he is also an outstanding dead-ball expert, his first goal in English football being a perfect demonstration when he whipped in a vicious, curling free kick against Everton from almost 30 yards. This was followed with four stunning strikes in three matches over the Christmas period which clinched his selection as Carling Premiership Player of the Month for December, just seven weeks after beginning his English career. Carried on in the same vein in the New Year – a wonderful left-foot curler against Liverpool in the FA Cup, a memorable solo run against Manchester United, a stunning volley which opened the scoring in the televised 6-2 victory over Sunderland, and yet another dazzling solo run against Wimbledon in the FA Cup semi final. But the goal that will be remembered most, sadly for England fans, was the powerful shot he thrashed past Ian Walker at Wembley to give Italy victory over England in the World Cup qualifier in February, which severely dented England's chances of reaching the 1998 Finals. A brilliant individual, he is also a totally committed team player, working his socks off to win the ball deep in his own half. Although one third of the league programme had been completed before his arrival in England, such was his impact on English football that he was chosen as the Football Writers' Footballer of the Year.

Chelsea (£4,500,000 from Parma, via Napoli, Torres and Nuorese, on 15/11/96) PL 22+1/8 FAC 7/4

Gianfranco Zola

FA Carling Premiership and Nationwide League Clubs : Summary of Appearances and Goals for 1996-97.

KEY TO TABLES: P/FL = Premier/Football League. FLC = Football League Cup. FAC = FA Cup. Others = Other first team appearances.
Left hand figures in each column list number of full appearances + appearances as substitute. Right hand figures list number of goals scored.

ARSENAL (PREM: 3rd)

Player	P/FL App	P/FL Goals	FLC App	FLC Goals	FAC App	FAC Goals	Others App	Others Goals
Adams	27+1	3	3		3		1	
Anelka	0+4							
Bergkamp	28+1	12	2	1	2	1	1	
Bould	33		3		3		1+1	
Dickov	0+1							
Dixon	31+1	2	3		1		1	
Garde	7+4							
Harper	1							
Hartson	14+5	3	1+2		1+1	1	2	
Helder	0+2						0+2	
Hillier	0+2							
Hughes	9+5	1			2	1		
Keown	33	1	3		3		2	
Linighan	10+1	1					2	
Lukic	15		1		1			
McGowan	1							
Marshall	6+2							
Merson	32	6	3	1	3		2	2
Morrow	5+9		0+2		2			
Parlour	17+13	2	0+1		3		1+1	
Platt	27+1	4	3	1	1		2	
Rose	1							
Seaman	22		2		2		2	
Selley	0+1							
Shaw	1+7	2			0+1			
Vieira	30+1	2	3		3		1	
Winterburn	38		3		2		2	
Wright	30+5	23	3	5	1		2	2

ASTON VILLA (PREM: 5th)

Player	P/FL App	P/FL Goals	FLC App	FLC Goals	FAC App	FAC Goals	Others App	Others Goals
Bosnich	20		1		3			
Curcic	17+5		1		2	1		
Draper	28+1		1+1				2	
Ehiogu	38	3	2		3	1	2	
Farrelly	1+2							
Hendrie	0+4				1+2			
Hughes	4+3							
Joachim	3+12	3	1		1			
Johnson	10+10	4	1		2		1+1	1
McGrath							0+1	
Milosevic	29+1	10	0+1		3		2	
Murray	1							
Nelson	33+1		2		0+1		2	
Oakes	18+2		1				2	
Scimeca	11+6		1+1		3			
Southgate	28		1		3		2	
Staunton	30	2	1		2		2	
Taylor	29+5	2	2	1			1	
Tiler	9+2	1	1		2			
Townsend	34	2	2		3		2	
Wright	38	1	2		3		2	
Yorke	37	17	2	1	2	2	2	

BARNET (DIV 3: 15th)

Player	P/FL App	P/FL Goals	FLC App	FLC Goals	FAC App	FAC Goals	Others App	Others Goals
Adams	1+2		0+1					
Brady	1+6							
Brazil	15+4	2			0+1			
Campbell	36+7	4	1+3	1	2+2	1	1	
Codner	20+4	1	4	1	4			
Constantinou	1							
Devine	30+1	11	4	1	3	4	1	
Dunwell	1		0+1					
Ford	13	1						
Gale	40+3	2	4		4			
Goodhind	1+2							

BARNET cont.

Player	P/FL App	P/FL Goals	FLC App	FLC Goals	FAC App	FAC Goals	Others App	Others Goals
Hardyman	13+3	2	3		4			
Harrison	21						1	
Hodges	28+3	5	0+1		4	2		
Howarth	37+1	1	4		3		1	
McDonald	10+8		2+1		1			
Mills	0+2		0+1					
Ndah	12+2	4						
Pardew	23+3		4		0+1		1	
Patterson	3						1	
Primus	46	3	4		4		1	
Rattray	9		2				1	
Samuels	13+4	1					1	1
Simpson	29+3	2	3	2	3+1	1	1	
Stockley	21						1	
Taylor	25		4		4			
Thompson	1							
Tomlinson	19+11		1+2	1	4			
Wilson	37	5	4	1	4			

BARNSLEY (DIV 1: 2nd)

Player	P/FL App	P/FL Goals	FLC App	FLC Goals	FAC App	FAC Goals	Others App	Others Goals
Appleby	35		4		1			
Bosancic	17+8	1	3+1		2			
Bullock	7+21		1+1		1+1	1		
Davis	24	3	4					
De Zeeuw	43	2	4		2			
Eaden	46	3	4		2			
Hendrie	36	15			2	1		
Hurst	0+1		1					
Jones	12+6				0+2			
Liddell	25+13	8	3		0+2			
Marcelle	26+14	8	3+1		2	1		
Moses	25+3	2			2			
Redfearn	43	17	4	1	2	1		
Regis	0+4		0+3					
Sheridan	39+2	2	1+1		1+1			
Shirtliff	12+1							
Ten Heuvel	0+3							
Thompson	24	5	3		1			
Van der Velden	1+1		1					
Watson	46		4		2			
Wilkinson	45	9	4	2	2			

BIRMINGHAM CITY (DIV 1: 10th)

Player	P/FL App	P/FL Goals	FLC App	FLC Goals	FAC App	FAC Goals	Others App	Others Goals
Ablett	39+3	1	4		3			
Barnett	6							
Bass	11+2				1			
Bennett	40		4		3			
Bowen	19+6	3	1+1		1+2			
Breen	20+2	1	4		1			
Brown	11				1			
Bruce	30+2		4		3	1		
Castle	4+4		4					
Cooke	1+3							
Devlin	32+6	16	3+1	1	3	2		
Donowa	0+4		1					
Edwards	1+2		1					
Finnan	3							
Forster	4+3	3						
Frain	1							
Francis	4+15	1			1+1	2		
Furlong	37+6	10	4	1	2	1		
Gabbiadini	0+2							
Grainger	21+2	3			2			
Holland	28+4				3			
Horne	33		3		3			

BIRMINGHAM CITY cont.

Player	P/FL App	P/FL Goals	FLC App	FLC Goals	FAC App	FAC Goals	Others App	Others Goals
Hughes	10+1							
Hunt	6+6	2	1+2		1			
Jackson	10							
Johnson	28+7		0+2		1+1			
Legg	22+11	4	3+1		2+1			
Limpar	3+1				1			
Newell	11+4	1	4	2	0+1			
O'Connor	24	4						
Otto	1+3							
Poole	9+1		3					
Robinson	6+3							
Sutton	6							
Tait	17+9		0+1		1			
Wassall	8							

BLACKBURN ROVERS (PREM: 13th)

Player	P/FL App	P/FL Goals	FLC App	FLC Goals	FAC App	FAC Goals	Others App	Others Goals
Beattie	1		1					
Berg	36	2	3		2			
Bohinen	17+6	2	2+1		1		1	
Coleman	8		1					
Croft	4+1		2					
Donis	11+11	2	3		0+1			
Duff	1							
Fenton	5+8	1	0+2		0+1			
Flitcroft	27+1	3	2	1	1			
Flowers	36		3		2			
Gallacher	34	10	3	1	2			
Given	2		0+1					
Gudmundsson	0+2							
Hendry	35	1	2		2			
Kenna	37		3		2			
Le Saux	26				2			
McKinlay	23+2	1			2			
Marker	5+2		0+1		0+1			
Pearce	7+5		1+1					
Pedersen	6+5	1						
Ripley	5+8							
Sherwood	37	3	3	1	2	1		
Sutton	24+1	11	2	1	2			
Warhurst	5+6	2			0+1			
Wilcox	26+2	2	2		2			

BLACKPOOL (DIV 2: 7th)

Player	P/FL App	P/FL Goals	FLC App	FLC Goals	FAC App	FAC Goals	Others App	Others Goals
Banks	46		4		2		3	
Barlow	43+3	1	2+2		2		3	
Bonner	25+4	1	4		2		1	
Brabin	30+2	2	3		1		2	
Bradshaw	4+6				1		1	
Brightwell	1+1							
Bryan	34	1	4		1		2	
Butler	41+1		3		1		2	1
Carden	0+1				0+1		1	
Clarkson	17	5						
Darton	8+7	1					2	
Dixon	3+8		2		1		2	
Ellis	41+4	15	4	3	1		2	2
Haddow							1	
Linighan	42	1	3		1		2	
Lydiate	18+2		2+1		1		0+1	
Malkin	8+7	3			2		0+2	
Mellon	43	4	4		1		2	1
Onwere	5+4		1		1		0+2	
Orie			1					
Ormerod	0+4							
Philpott	20+6	3	2	1	2			

BLACKPOOL cont.

	P/FL App	Goals	FLC App	Goals	FAC App	Goals	Others App	Goals
Preece	35+6	10	2+2		0+1		3	1
Quinn	37+1	13	3	3	1	1	2	
Russell	0+1							
Symons							1	
Thorpe	2+7		0+1		1		1	
Woods	3							

BOLTON WANDERERS (DIV 1: 1st)

	P/FL App	Goals	FLC App	Goals	FAC App	Goals	Others App	Goals
Bergsson	30+3	3	3		2			
Blake	42	21	5	3	3	2		
Branagan	36		4					
Burnett	0+1							
Coleman					1			
Fairclough	46	6	5		3			
Frandsen	40+1	5	4+1		2+1			
Green	7+5	1	0+1		2+1	2		
Johansen	24+9	5	3		1+1			
Lee	13+12	2	4		1+1			
McAnespie	11+2		1					
McGinlay	43	24	5	5	1	1		
Paatelainen	3+7	2						
Phillips	36		4					
Pollock	18+2	4	0+1		3	2		
Sellars	40+2	8	3+1		2			
Sheridan	12+8	2	2		2			
Small	10+1		1		3			
Taggart	43	3	5	1	2			
Taylor	2+9	1	0+3	1	1	1		
Thompson	34	11	4	1	1+1	1		
Todd	6+9		1+3					
Ward	10+1	1	1		3			

BOURNEMOUTH (DIV 2:16th)

	P/FL App	Goals	FLC App	Goals	FAC App	Goals	Others App	Goals
Bailey	40	1	2		1		1	
Beardsmore	37+1		2				0+1	
Brissett	16+9	4	1				1	
Christie	3+1							
Coll	16		2		1			
Cotterell	2+7							
Cox	44	8	2		1		1	
Dean	10+2				1			
Ferdinand	10						1	
Fletcher	33+2	7	2	1	1		1	
Glass	35		2		1		1	
Gordon	14+2	1	2		1			
Hayter	0+2							
Holland	45	7	2		1		1	
Howe	7+6							
Marshall	11							
Morris	0+1							
Murray	20+12	1	2		0+1		1	
O'Brien	1							
Omoyinmi	5+2							
O'Neill	7+11	1	0+2		0+1			
Rawlinson	22+3	2					1	
Robinson	34+6	7	1		1		1	
Town	16+10	2	0+1				0+1	
Vincent	28+1		0+1		1			
Watson	6+9	2			0+1		0+1	
Young	44		2		1		1	

BRADFORD CITY (DIV 1: 21st)

	P/FL App	Goals	FLC App	Goals	FAC App	Goals	Others App	Goals
Blake	3+2							
Brightwell	2							
Cowans	23+1		2					
Davison	10							
Dreyer	27+1	1	2		3	3		
Duxbury	33	3	2		3			
Edinho	15	5			1			
Gould	9		2					
Hamilton	24+8		1		3			
Huxford	1+1		0+1					

BRADFORD CITY cont.

	P/FL App	Goals	FLC App	Goals	FAC App	Goals	Others App	Goals
Jacobs	37+2	3	1		3			
Kiwomya	20+7	1	1		3			
Kulcsar	9							
Liburd	33+3	1	1		1+2			
Midgley	0+1				0+1			
Mitchell	6		2					
Mohan	44		2		3			
Moore	6							
Murray	13+4	1						
Newell	7							
Nixon	12							
O'Brien	18+4	2			3			
Oliviera	1							
Ormondroyd	0+1		1					
Pehrsson	1							
Pepper	11	5						
Pinto	7+11				1+1			
Regtop	5+3	1						
Roberts	2							
Sansam	0+1							
Sas	31	3	2		1			
Schwarzer	13				3			
Shutt	10+12	3	1+1		1			
Smithard	0+1							
Stallard	13+9	1	2	1	0+1			
Steiner	14+1	3			1	1		
Sundgot	11+9	6						
Vanhala	0+1							
Waddle	25	6			3	1		
Watson	3	1						
Wilder	4+3							
Wright	2+9	1	0+1		0+1			

BRENTFORD (DIV 2: 4th)

	P/FL App	Goals	FLC App	Goals	FAC App	Goals	Others App	Goals
Abrahams	5+3	2	1+2					
Anderson	46	1	4		2		4	
Asaba	44	23	4		3		5	1
Ashby	40	1	4		3		3+1	
Bates	37	2	4		3		6	
Bent	29+5	3	4		2		4+1	1
Canham	13	1	2		1		0+2	
Dearden	44		4		3		5	
Dennis	9+3							
Fernandes	2						1	
Forster	25	10	3	1	3	1	1	1
Goddard-Crawley	0+1							
Harvey	2+12		0+2		0+2		1	
Hurdle	28+3		4		2		4	
Hutchings	23+5	2	0+1		1		4	
Janney	1+1		1					
McGhee	44+1	1	2+1		3	1	6	
McPherson	2+1						1+1	
Omigie	7+6	1			0+3		2+1	1
Rapley	1+1							
Slade	4							
Smith	46	1	4		3	1	5	1
Statham	11+8				1		5	
Taylor	43	7	4	1	3	2	6	3

BRIGHTON & HOVE ALBION (DIV 3: 23rd)

	P/FL App	Goals	FLC App	Goals	FAC App	Goals	Others App	Goals
Adekola	1							
Allan	31		2				1	
Andrews	1+6	1						
Baird	34+1	13	2		1+1		1	
Fox M	0+2							
Fox S	5+7						1	
Hobson	35+2	1	2		2		2	
Humphrey	11							
Johnson	21+8		0+1				1+1	
McDonald	40+5	4	2		2		2	1
McGarrigle	9+4				2		0+1	

BRIGHTON & HOVE ALBION cont.

	P/FL App	Goals	FLC App	Goals	FAC App	Goals	Others App	Goals
Martin	1							
Maskell	37	14	2		2	1	2	1
Mayo	22+2				0+1		1+1	
Minton	22+3	3	2		1			
Morris	11+1	1			2			
Mundee	27+2	4			2		2	
Neal	8							
Ormerod	21						1	
Parris	17+1	1	2		2		2	
Peake	27+3	1	2		2		1	
Reinelt	7+5	3						
Rust	25		2				1	
Smith	26+4	1	2				2	
Storer	37+5	6	1+1		2			
Tuck	27		1				1	
Virgo							1	1
Warren	3							

BRISTOL CITY (DIV 2 : 5th)

	P/FL App	Goals	FLC App	Goals	FAC App	Goals	Others App	Goals
Agostino	34+10	9	2+2	1	4	5	2+1	
Allen	13+1						3	
Barnard	44	11	4	1	4		4	1
Bent	17+5	3	1		1		2+1	
Blackmore	5	1						
Brennan	7+1							
Carey	40+2		3		4		0+2	
Cundy	6	1						
Doherty					0+1			
Edwards	31		4		2+1		3	
Goater	39+3	23	4	1	3		4	1
Goodridge	19+9	6	3		3+1	1	0+3	
Hewlett	33+3	2	3+1		2+1	2	4	
Kuhl	22+9		2+2		4	2	1	
Langan							1	
McLeary	1+2		3					
Naylor	35		4		4		1	
Nugent	19+17	6	2+2		1+2	1	2+1	
Owers	46	4	4	1	4		4	2
Partridge	0+6		0+1	1				
Paterson	15+4		1		1		2	
Plummer	0+2							
Seal	0+12		0+1					
Shail	10+1						2	
Taylor	29	1			3		3	
Tinnion	30+2	1	4		4		3+1	
Welch	11						3	

BRISTOL ROVERS (DIV 2: 17th)

	P/FL App	Goals	FLC App	Goals	FAC App	Goals	Others App	Goals
Alsop	10+6	3					1	
Archer	18+3	2	2	1	1			
Beadle	36+6	12	1		1			
Bennett	6+5	1						
Browning	24+2	2	2		1		1	
Clapham	4+1							
Clark	26+1	1	2				1	
Collett	44				1		1	
Cureton	33+5	11	2		1			
French	3+1		0+1		0+1			
Gayle	7							
Gurney	21+3	2	2	1			1	
Harris	5+1	2			1		1	1
Hayfield	12+5						1	
Higgs	2							
Holloway	29+2	1	2		1			
Lockwood	36+3	1	2		1		0+1	
Low	0+3		0+2				1	
Martin	25		2					
Miller	22+3	2	2		1			
Morgan	1							
Parmenter	10+4	2	1+1		0+1	1	0+1	
Power	16				1		1	
Pritchard	26		1					

BRISTOL ROVERS cont.

	P/FL App	Goals	FLC App	Goals	FAC App	Goals	Others App	Goals
Ramasut	5+6				1			
Skinner	29+5	2			0+1		0+1	
Tillson	38	2	2		1		1	
White	18+3							
Zabek	0+1							

BURNLEY (DIV 2: 9th)

	P/FL App	Goals	FLC App	Goals	FAC App	Goals	Others App	Goals
Barnes	39+1	24	2		3	1		
Beresford	40		2		4		2	
Brass	37+2		2+1		3+1		2	
Carr-Lawton							0+1	
Cooke	19+12	12	1+2	1	1+2		1	
Eyres	36	3	4	3	4	1	2	
Gleghorn	32+1	4	4		4	1	2	
Guinan	0+6						1	
Harrison	32+3		2		4		0+1	
Heath	0+2							
Hodgson	1							
Hoyland	24+1	2	4		2			
Huxford	2+7						1	
Little	5+4				1+1		0+1	
Matthew	29+3	6	3	1	2	1	1	
Nogan	30+1	10	4	2	2		1	1
Overson	6+2		1				1	
Parkinson	43	1	4		4		1	
Robinson	3+5		1+1				1	
Russell	6		2					
Smith	30+7	4	1+1		4		2	
Swan	16+1	2			2		2	
Thompson	14+5	1	2				1+1	
Vinnicombe	6+2							
Weller	22+9	2	1+1		2+2		2	
Winstanley	34+1		4		2		0+1	

BURY (DIV 2: 1st)

	P/FL App	Goals	FLC App	Goals	FAC App	Goals	Others App	Goals
Armstrong	16+16	2	2		0+1		1+1	
Battersby	9+2	2						
Bimson	1		1					
Butler	40+1	2	4		1		3	1
Carter	28+12	12	4	1	1		3	2
Daws	46	2	4		1		3	1
Hughes	14+8		4				0+1	
Jackson	31	3	4	1	1		3	
Jepson	24+7	9	3		0+1		1+1	2
Johnrose	43	4	3+1		1		3	1
Johnson	34+10	8	3+1		1		2+1	1
Kiely	46		4		1		3	
Lucketti	38				1		3	1
Matthews	22+5	5	1+3		1		3	
O'Kane	11+2	3					1	
Pugh	16+2	2	1	1	1		1	1
Randall	14+5	3					0+2	
Reid	6+1		1					
Rigby	0+15		1				0+2	
Scott	2+6							
Stant	3+5	1	0+1					
West	46		4		1		1	
Woodward	16+7		0+1				2	

CAMBRIDGE UNITED (DIV 3: 10th)

	P/FL App	Goals	FLC App	Goals	FAC App	Goals	Others App	Goals
Ashbee	16+2							
Barnwell-Edinboro	35+5	6	2		2	1	0+1	
Barrett	45		2		2		1	
Beall	33+3	2	2		2	1	1	
Benjamin	1+6	1	0+1					
Brazil	1	1	1					
Craddock	41	1			2		1	
Foster	7							
Granville	37		2		2		1	
Hay	0+4							
Hayes	19+6		0+1		2		1	

CAMBRIDGE UNITED cont.

	P/FL App	Goals	FLC App	Goals	FAC App	Goals	Others App	Goals
Hyde	38	7	1		2		1	
Joseph M E	5+3		1				0+1	
Joseph M N	44		2		2		1	
Kyd	22+7	7			2	1		
McGleish	10	7	1					
Marshall	1							
Pack	0+1							
Palmer	0+1		1					
Preece	19+6				1+1			
Raynor	43+1	4	1+1		2		1	
Richards	14+9	4	1				1	
San Miguel	0+1		1					
Taylor	19+2	4						
Thompson	15+7	2	2	1	0+2			
Turner	2+5	1			0+2		1	
Vowden	5+1		1					
Wanless	27+3	3	1		1		1	
Wilde	0+1							
Wilson	7							

CARDIFF CITY (DIV 3: 7th)

	P/FL App	Goals	FLC App	Goals	FAC App	Goals	Others App	Goals
Baddeley	4+5						1	
Bennett	5+9	1	2		1+1		0+1	
Burton	5	2					1	
Coldicott	6							
Dale	28+5	8	1	1	2		4	2
Davies	6	2						
Eckhardt	34+1	5	1		2		4	1
Elliott	36		2		1			
Flack	1							
Fleming	9+1							
Fowler	37	5	2		2		3	1
Gardner	19+9	1	0+1		1		2+1	
Haworth	20+4	9			0+1		2	1
Jarman	27+5		2		1		2+1	
Lloyd	27+4	1	2				3	
McStay	1							
Michael	0+1							
Middleton	40+1	4	0+1		2	1	3+1	
Mountain	5				1		2	
O'Halloran	8						2	
Partridge	14+1							
Perry	35		2		1		4	
Phillips	2+1							
Philliskirk	27+6	1	2		2		1+2	
Rodgerson	15+6		2		2		1	
Rollo	3+7						0+1	
Scott	1+1		0+1					
Stoker	17	3					1+1	
Ware	5							
White	32+6	13	2		2	1	2+2	
Williams	5						2	
Young	32	1	2		2		4	

CARLISLE UNITED (DIV 3: 3rd)

	P/FL App	Goals	FLC App	Goals	FAC App	Goals	Others App	Goals
Archdeacon	46	7	4	1	4	2	6	4
Aspinall	39+1	5	2	1	4		6	
Bass	3							
Caig	46		4		4		7	
Conway	22+3	9	4		4	1	5	3
Currie	5+4		0+1					
Delap	25+7	4	3+1		0+3		7	
Dobie	0+2	1						
Edmondson	19+1		2		3	1	2	
Freestone	3+2	2					2	
Hayward	43	8	4	1	4		7	
Heath	0+1							
Hopper	13+7	1			2	1	2+1	
Jansen	4+15	1	0+1		0+3		1+3	
Kerr	0+1							
McAlindon	3+9	2			0+1	1	0+2	1
Peacock	37+7	9	2+2		4	1	5+1	

CARLISLE UNITED cont.

	P/FL App	Goals	FLC App	Goals	FAC App	Goals	Others App	Goals
Pounewatchy	42	1	4		4		7	1
Prokas	10+3	1	0+1				1+2	
Reeves	8	3	3	1				
Robinson	6+1		1+1		1			
Shirtliff	5							
Smart	25+3	11			4		4+1	
Thomas	23+13		4	2	0+4		2+4	1
Thorpe	2+3							
Varty	31+1		4		2		6+1	
Walling	46	2	3		4		7	2

CHARLTON ATHLETIC (DIV 1: 15th)

	P/FL App	Goals	FLC App	Goals	FAC App	Goals	Others App	Goals
Allen	13+5	4	3	2				
Balmer	28+4	2	3					
Barness	45	2	4		2			
Bright	4+2	2						
Brown	22+5		2		1			
Chapple	25+1	2	3		2			
Jones K	14+5				1+1			
Jones S	2							
Kinsella	37	6			1	1		
Leaburn	40+4	8	4	1	2			
Lee	7+1	3						
Lisbie	4+21	1	0+3		0+1			
Mortimer	10+1	1	2					
Newton	39+4	3	4	1	2			
Nicholls	3+3	1	1+1					
O'Connell	33+5	2	2		2			
Otto	5+2		2					
Petterson	21		1		2			
Poole	14+2	1						
Robinson	41+1	3	3	2	0+1			
Robson	8+7	3			2	1		
Rufus	33+1		2		2			
Salmon	25		3					
Scott	4							
Stuart	10	1	3					
Sturgess	1+2		1+1		1			
Whyte	18+4	7	1+2	2	2			

CHELSEA (PREM: 6th)

	P/FL App	Goals	FLC App	Goals	FAC App	Goals	Others App	Goals
Burley	26+5	2	3		1+3	1		
Clarke	31		3		7			
Clement	1							
Colgan	1							
Di Matteo	33+1	7	3		7	2		
Duberry	13+2	1	2		1			
Forrest	2+1							
Granville	3+2							
Grodas	20+1		1		5			
Gullit	6+6	1			0+1			
Hitchcock	10+2		2		2			
Hughes M	32+3	8	2	1	6+1	5		
Hughes P	8+4	2			2			
Johnsen	14+4		1		1+3			
Kharine	5							
Leboeuf	26		2		7	1		
Lee	1	1	1	1				
Minto	24+1	4	2	1	6			
Morris	6+6		2	1				
Myers	15+3	1						
Newton	13+2				5	1		
Nicholls	3+5		0+2					
Parker	1+3							
Petrescu	34	3	2	1	6			
Phelan	1+2		0+1					
Sheerin	0+1							
Sinclair	17+3	1			6			
Spencer	0+4		3	2				
Vialli	23+5	9	1		1+3	2		
Wise	27+4	3	2		7	3		
Zola	22+1	8			7	4		

	P/FL App	Goals	FLC App	Goals	FAC App	Goals	Others App	Goals
CHESTER CITY (DIV 3: 6th)								
Aiston	14		1				2	
Alsford	43	2	2		3		3	
Brown G	0 + 1				0 + 1			
Brown W	2							
Cutler	5							
Davidson	40	2	1		2		3	
Fisher	19 +10	1	2		3		1	
Flitcroft	30 + 2	6	0 + 1		2		3	
Giles					0 + 1			
Helliwell	8 + 1	1						
Jackson	32	1	2		2		1	
Jenkins	39		1		3		3	
Jones	3 +14	1					0 + 1	
Knowles	2		1					
McDonald	22	6					3	1
Milner	38 + 8	12	2		3	2	2 + 1	
Murphy	4 + 7	1	1					
Noteman	30 + 5	9	0 + 1	1	2 + 1		0 + 1	
Priest	30 + 2	2			2		3	
Reid	27	1					2	
Richardson	9		2					
Rimmer	22 + 3	3	2		3	2	1 + 2	
Rogers	4 + 1		2		0 + 1			
Shelton	18 + 4	3	2		1			
Sinclair	37		1		3		3	
Tallon	1							
Whelan	18 + 7	1			1 + 2		1 + 1	
Woods	9 +12	1	0 + 1		3		2 + 1	
CHESTERFIELD (DIV 2: 10th)								
Allison	0 + 2							
Beaumont	29 + 4	1	2		3 + 2	1	1	
Bowater	0 + 1							
Carr	12				3 + 2		1	
Curtis	40	3	1		8	1		
Davies	28 + 6	3	1 + 1		7	4		
Dunn	10 + 1				0 + 1			
Dyche	36		2		6	1		
Ebdon	11 + 1	1						
Gaughan	14 + 4		1	1	0 + 1		1	
Hanson	3	1						
Hewitt	36 + 1	1	1		8	1	1	
Holland	24 + 1	3	2		7			
Howard	26 + 9	9	2		7	2		
Jules	41 + 1		2		8		1	
Law	4 + 3	1	1					
Leaning	9						1	
Lomas	0 + 2						0 + 1	
Lormor	25 +11	8	2	1	3	1	1	
Lund	7 + 3				1			
Mason	1 + 1							
Mercer	35		2		8			
Mitchell	1 + 1						1	
Morgan	2							
Morris	19 + 8	4	0 + 1		5 + 1	1	1	
Patterson	7 + 2							
Perkins	26 + 4		0 + 1		7		1	
Rogers	14 + 3		1					
Scott	4 + 1	3						
Timons							1	
Williams	42	3	2		7	1		
COLCHESTER UNITED (DIV 3: 8th)								
Abrahams	27 + 2	7			1		5 + 1	2
Adcock	26 +10	11	3 + 1	1	0 + 1		6	2
Barnes	11		1				1	
Betts	10	1	4					
Buckle	24						5	3
Caldwell	6		2					
Cawley	28	1	4		1		3 + 1	
Duguid	10 +10	3	0 + 2		0 + 1		1 + 1	
Dunne	23 +12		3	1	1		2 + 1	

	P/FL App	Goals	FLC App	Goals	FAC App	Goals	Others App	Goals
COLCHESTER UNITED cont.								
Emberson	35		2		1		6	
Forbes	1	1						
Fry	31 +11	6	2 + 2	1	1		6 + 1	1
Gibbs	18 + 2				1		5 + 1	
Greene	44	2	4		1		6	1
Gregory	32 + 6	1	1 + 1		1		7	
Haydon	0 + 1	1						
Kelly	2 + 1							
Kinsella	7	2	3	1				
Lock	1 + 5	1					0 + 1	
Locke	22 +10	4	3 + 1		1		4 + 3	
McCarthy	34 + 1		3				5	
Pitcher	0 + 1							
Reinelt	8 +13	3	4		2	1		
Sale	10	3					2 + 1	
Stamps	7 + 1							
Taylor	8	5					1	
Vaughan	5						1	
Whitton	36 + 3	6	2 + 1				5	1
Wilkins	40	2	3		1	1	6	
COVENTRY CITY (PREM: 17th)								
Boland	0 + 1							
Borrows	16 + 7		4		3			
Breen	8 + 1							
Burrows	17 + 1		2					
Daish	20	1	3	1				
Dublin	33 + 1	13	3 + 1		1			
Ducros	1 + 4							
Evtushok	3							
Filan	0 + 1							
Genaux	3 + 1							
Hall	10 + 3		2		3			
Huckerby	21 + 4	5			4	2		
Isaias	0 + 1							
Jess	19 + 8		1		4	2		
McAllister	38	6	4	1	4			
Ndlovu	10 +10	1			0 + 3			
Ogrizovic	38		4		4			
O'Neill	1							
Richardson	25 + 3		4		4			
Salako	23 + 1	1	4		1			
Shaw	35		3		4			
Strachan	3 + 6		0 + 1		0 + 1			
Telfer	31 + 3		4	2	4			
Whelan	34 + 1	6	4		4	2		
Williams	29 + 3	2	2		4			
CREWE ALEXANDRA (DIV 2: 6th)								
Adebola	27 + 5	16	1	1	2 + 1	1	4	
Anthrobus	10							
Bankole	3							
Barr	29 + 5	4			2		2	
Billing	9 + 6				1 + 1		3	
Charnock	24 + 8	1			2		6	
Ellison	3	2	1					
Garvey	9 + 7		0 + 1		1 + 1	1	1 + 2	
Gayle	4		2					
Johnson	8 + 3	1					0 + 3	
Kearton	30				4		6	
Launders	6 + 3		1 + 1					
Lightfoot	16 + 9	1			1 + 1	1	1 + 2	
Little	3 +14		0 + 1		2		4	2
Macauley	40 + 2	2	2		4	1	5	
Mautone	3							
Moralee	7				2			
Murphy	44 + 1	10	2		4	3	6	2
Rivers	23 + 4	6	2		2		4 + 1	1
Savage	41	1	2		4		3	
Smith P	0 + 1							
Smith S	34 + 4	4	2		4	1	4 + 1	2
Taylor	6							

	P/FL App	Goals	FLC App	Goals	FAC App	Goals	Others App	Goals
CREWE ALEXANDRA cont.								
Tierney	18 +14	3	2		1 + 1		1 + 2	1
Unsworth	28 + 1		2				5	
Westwood	43 + 1	2	2		4	1	6	
Whalley	38	3	1		4		6	
CRYSTAL PALACE (DIV 1: 6th)								
Andersen	7 + 7	1	3		1			
Boxall	4 + 2		0 + 1					
Cyrus	1							
Davies	5 + 1						1	
Day	24		2		2			
Dyer	39 + 4	17	2 + 1		2	1	3	
Edworthy	42 + 3		3	1	2		3	
Freedman	33 +11	11	2 + 1	1	0 + 1		0 + 2	2
Gordon	26 + 4	3			2		3	
Harris	0 + 2		0 + 2					
Hopkin	38 + 3	13	2	2	2		3	2
Houghton	18 + 3	1	2				1	
Linighan	19	2					3	
McKenzie	4 +17	2	1		0 + 2			
Mimms	1							
Muscat	42 + 2	2	3	1	2		2	
Nash	21		1				3	
Ndah	5 +21	3	1 + 1		2			
Pitcher	3							
Quinn	17 + 4	1	2 + 1	1				
Roberts	45	2	3		2		3	
Rodger	9 + 2						3	
Scully	0 + 1							
Shipperley	29 + 3	12			2		3	1
Trollope	0 + 9							
Tuttle	39	2	3		1		2	
Veart	35 + 4	6	3	2	2	1	0 + 1	
DARLINGTON (DIV 3: 18th)								
Atkinson B	25 + 5	4	4		0 + 1		1	
Atkinson J	2 + 3							
Barbara	1 + 5	1					1	1
Barnard	35 + 2		4		2		1	
Blake	28 + 2	10	4	1	2		0 + 1	
Brumwell	31 + 7	1	4		2	1	0 + 1	
Brydon	17 + 8		0 + 1		0 + 1		1	
Byrne	1 + 1							
Carss	20 + 9		3		1		1	
Collins	0 + 1							
Crosby	42	1	4		2	1	1	
Devos	7 + 1				1			
Faulkner	2 + 2							
Gregan	16		4		1			
Hope M	1							
Hope R	20							
Hunt	0 + 1							
Innes	1 +14		0 + 1					
Kelly	13 +10	2	0 + 1					
Key	0 + 3				1			
Laws	10				1			
Lowe	5 + 2							
Lucas	7							
McCelland	1							
Moilanen	16							
Naylor	30 + 7	10			2	1	1	
Newell	20				2		1	
Oliver	34 + 5	9	4		2		0 + 1	
Painter	2 + 4		0 + 4	1				
Reed	14							
Roberts	42 + 2	16	4	2	1		1	
Robinson	0 + 3				0 + 1			
Shaw	34 + 4	3	1		2	1	1	
Shutt	5 + 1	2						
Speake	3							
Twynham	21 + 8	3	4				1	

DERBY COUNTY (PREM: 12th)

Player	P/FL App	Goals	FLC App	Goals	FAC App	Goals	Others App	Goals
Asanovic	34	6	1		3			
Carbon	6+4		1		0+1			
Carsley	15+9		1+1		4			
Cooper			0+2					
Dailly	31+5	3	2		4			
Flynn	10+7	1			2			
Gabbiadini	5+9		1		0+1			
Hoult	31+1		2		3			
Laursen	35+1	1	2		2			
McGrath	23+1				2			
Parker	4		2					
Poom	4							
Powell C	35		1		3			
Powell D	27+6	1	1		3			
Rahmberg	0+1							
Rowett	35	2	2		3+1			
Simpson	0+19	2	2	1	0+3			
Solis	0+2							
Stimac	21	1	1		1			
Sturridge	29+1	11	1	1	3	2		
Taylor	3				1			
Trollope	13+1	1			3			
Van der Laan	15+1		1+1		2+1	3		
Wanchope	2+3	1						
Ward	25+5	8	1+1		2	1		
Willems	7+9	2			3	2		
Yates	8+2							

DONCASTER ROVERS (DIV 3: 19th)

Player	P/FL App	Goals	FLC App	Goals	FAC App	Goals	Others App	Goals
Anderson	6							
Beirne	1							
Birch	26+1	2	2		1		1	
Bullimore	4							
Clark	8+12	2	1		0+1		1	
Coady	1							
Colcombe	9+3	1	1		1		0+1	
Cramb	40+1	18	2	1	1	1	1	1
Cunningham	11							
Dixon	13+3	3	2		1		1	
Doling	3+2							
Donnelly	0+2							
Esdaille	16+2	1						
Fahy	0+5							
Gore	35+1	1	2		1		1	
Gray	1						1	
Ireland	27	2						
Larmour	3+17		0+2					
Lester	5+6	1						
McDonald	33	2	2		1			
Marquis	3							
Messer	0+1							
Mike	5	1						
Moore	41	5	2				1	
Murphy	30+1		2		1			
O'Connor	18				1		1	
Ohandjanian	0+1							
Pemberton	9	1						
Piearce	8+11	1	0+1		0+1			
Ramsay							0+1	
Robertson	3+1		1					
Ryan	22+6		0+1		1		1	
Schofield	42	7	2		1		1	
Smith	12+6	2	0+1					
Utley	19+4	1	1		1			
Walker	1							
Warren	21+4				0+1			
Weaver	2							
Wheeler	1							
Williams	27		2					

EVERTON (PREM: 15th)

Player	P/FL App	Goals	FLC App	Goals	FAC App	Goals	Others App	Goals
Allen	0+1							

EVERTON cont.

Player	P/FL App	Goals	FLC App	Goals	FAC App	Goals	Others App	Goals
Ball	2+3							
Barmby	22+3	4			2	1		
Barrett	36		2		2			
Branch	13+12	3	0+1		1			
Cadamarteri	0+1							
Dunne	6+1				1			
Ebbrell	7							
Ferguson	31+2	10	1		2	1		
Gerrard	4+1							
Grant	11+7		1		0+2			
Hills	1+2							
Hinchcliffe	18	1	2					
Hottiger	4+4		1					
Kanchelskis	20	4	2	1	2	1		
Limpar	1+1		1					
Parkinson	28		2		1			
Phelan	15				1			
Rideout	4+6		1+1	1	1			
Short	19+4	2	1		1			
Southall	34		2		2			
Speed	37	9	2	1	2	1		
Stuart	29+6	5	1		2			
Thomsen	15+1							
Unsworth	32+2	5	2					
Watson	29	1			2			

EXETER CITY (DIV 3: 22nd)

Player	P/FL App	Goals	FLC App	Goals	FAC App	Goals	Others App	Goals
Baddeley	8+3							
Bailey	32+3	2	2		2		2	
Bayes	41		2		2		1	
Birch	2							
Blake	46	6	2		2		2	
Braithwaite	26+12	5	2		0+2		1+1	
Chamberlain	22+4	3	2		1		2	
Crowe	10	5						
Dailly	8+9		1		2		1	
Flack	20+7	4			2	1	2	
Fox	5						1	
Gayle	10							
Ghazghazi	1+5		0+1					
Hare	16+9	1	0+1		2		1	
Hodges	16+1							
Hughes	33+3	1	2		1		1	
McConnell	20+14		0+2		1+1			
McKeown	3							
Medlin	7+4	1					0+2	
Minett	13							
Myers	31+2	2	2		2			
Pears	6+2	1	1+1					
Rees	7							
Rice	9+6						2	
Richardson N	14						2	
Richardson J	42+1	1	2		2		2	
Rowbotham	25	9			2	1	2	1
Sharpe	19+2	1	2		1	1		
Steele	14+14	3	1					

FULHAM (DIV 3: 2nd)

Player	P/FL App	Goals	FLC App	Goals	FAC App	Goals	Others App	Goals
Adams	2+1		1				1	
Angus	28+4	1	2+1				1	
Blake	40+1	7	4		1		0+1	
Brooker	0+26	2	0+1	1	0+1		1	
Carpenter	34	5			1			
Cockerill	27+5	1	3		1			
Conroy	40+3	21	4	2	1		1	
Cullip	23+6	1	4		1		1	
Cusack	44+1	2	4		1		1	1
Davis	0+1							
Freeman	32+7	9	2				1	
Hartfield	1+1							
Herrera	26		4		1			
Lange	18		1		1			

FULHAM cont.

Player	P/FL App	Goals	FLC App	Goals	FAC App	Goals	Others App	Goals
Lawrence	13+2							
McAree	5+4	1	1					
Marshall			0+1					
Mison	1+3		0+2				0+1	
Morgan	44	8	4	1	1		1	
Parker	3							
Scott	36+7	9	3+1		1		0+1	1
Soloman	1+3							
Stewart	2+1							
Thomas	6+20		1+1				1	
Walton	28		3				1	
Warren	8+3	1						
Watson	44	3	3		1		1	

GILLINGHAM (DIV 2: 11th)

Player	P/FL App	Goals	FLC App	Goals	FAC App	Goals	Others App	Goals
Akinbiyi	19	7						
Armstrong	10		2				1	
Bailey	16+14	2	5+2		0+1		1	
Bryant	38+1		6		2			
Butler	29+9	9	4+1	1	3		1	
Butters	30				3			
Carpenter	1							
Chapman	20+3	1	5		1+2		1	
Ford	2+2		3		0+1		1	
Fortune-West	7	2	1		1			
Galloway	6+3	1						
Gould	3							
Green	28+1	2	2		3			
Harris	19+2	1	6		1+1		0+1	
Hessenthaler	38	2	7		3		1	
Humphrey	9		3				1	
Manuel	3+8				1		1	
Marshall	5		1				1	
Morris	6		2					
O'Connor	18+4		1		3			
Onuora	37+3	21	6	1	2		1	
Pennock	26	2	1		2			
Pinnock	0+2						0+1	
Piper	4+15	1	2+2		1		1	1
Puttnam	5+9	1	1+5	1	0+2		1	
Ratcliffe	43	6	7	2	2			
Sambrook	0+1							
Smith	42	1	6+1	1	2			
Stannard	38		6		3			
Thomas	4+6				1		1	

GRIMSBY TOWN (DIV 1: 22nd)

Player	P/FL App	Goals	FLC App	Goals	FAC App	Goals	Others App	Goals
Appleton	10	3						
Black	19+5		2		1			
Childs	19+8	1	2		1			
Fickling	20+7	2	0+1		1			
Forrester	4+9	1	0+2					
Gallimore	36+6	1	2		1			
Handyside	8+1	1	2					
Jobling	24+4				1			
Laws	3							
Lee	2+5	2			1			
Lester	16+6	5			0+1			
Lever	20+1							
Livingstone	23+9	6	1+1					
Love	3							
McDermott	29	1	2					
Mendonca	45	18	2	1	1			
Miller	3							
Neil	0+1							
Oster	21+3	3			0+1	1		
Pearcey	40		2		1			
Rodger	27+1	2			1			
Shakespeare	23+3	2	2					
Smith	12+2	1						
Southall	23+11	4	0+2					
Trollope	6+1	1						

GRIMSBY TOWN cont.

	P/FL App	Goals	FLC App	Goals	FAC App	Goals	Others App	Goals
Walker	0+1							
Webb	3+1		1					
Widdrington	41+1	4	2		1			
Woods	21+3	1	1		1			
Wrack	5+7	1						

HARTLEPOOL UNITED (DIV 3: 20th)

	P/FL App	Goals	FLC App	Goals	FAC App	Goals	Others App	Goals
Allon	27+3	9	2	2	1		1	
Baker	6	2						
Barron	16							
Beech	42	8	2	1	2		1	
Bradley	12	1						
Brown	6	1						
Clegg	24+11	2	1		2		1	
Cooper	33	9	2		1		1	
Cullen	5+1							
Davies	30+2	1	2	1			1	
Elliott	2+2							
Gallagher							0+1	
Halliday	28+3	8	1+1		2			
Hislop	23+4				2		1	
Homer	0+1							
Horace	0+1							
Houchen	2+3		1+1					
Howard	26+6	7	1		1		1	
Hutt							0+1	
Ingram	34+3	1	2		2		1	
Irvine	2+2	1			0+1		0+1	
Knowles	7							
Lee	23+1		0+1		2		1	
Lucas	7							
McAuley	38	1	2		2		1	
McDonald	9		2					
McGuckin	21+1		1+1		2			
Mike	7	1						
O'Connor	30				1		1	
Pears	16		2		1			
Proctor	6							
Sunderland	6+7	1	1					
Tait	16+3		1		1			
Walton	2+2							
Winstanley	0+1							

HEREFORD UNITED (DIV 3: 24th)

	P/FL App	Goals	FLC App	Goals	FAC App	Goals	Others App	Goals
Agana	3+2	2						
Bartlett	0+3							
Beeston	9	2						
Brough	32+7	1	4		1		1	
Cook	17+3		0+2		1		1	
Cross	5	1					1	
Debont	27		4		1		1	
Downing	16		3					
Ellison	0+1							
Fishlock	29+1	1	2					
Forsyth	12							
Foster I	4+15		2+1				0+1	
Foster A	42+1	16	4	1	1		1	
Hargreaves	42+2	3	3+1		1		1	
Hibbard	5+2	1	1		1			
Jordan	1							
Kottila	11+2	1						
Law	14				1			
McGorry	7	1						
Mahon	10+1	1	4					
Matthewson	35	2			1		1	
Norton	45	1	2	1	1		1	
O'Toole	1							
Pitman	4+4		2					
Preedy	2+7	2	0+3		0+1		0+1	
Sandeman	7							
Smith	42	8	4	2	1		1	
Stoker	25+2	3	3+1		1		1	

HEREFORD UNITED cont.

	P/FL App	Goals	FLC App	Goals	FAC App	Goals	Others App	Goals
Sutton	4		2+1					
Townsend	6+1		3					
Turner	6							
Warner	16+5		1		0+1		1	
Williams	8+3	3						
Wood	19							

HUDDERSFIELD TOWN (DIV 1: 20th)

	P/FL App	Goals	FLC App	Goals	FAC App	Goals	Others App	Goals
Baldry	2+5							
Beresford	6	1						
Browning	13							
Bullock	26+1	1	4		2			
Burnett	33+2		3		1+1			
Collins Sam	3+1		1+1					
Collins Simon	10+6		2+2	1	0+2			
Cowan	42	3	5	1	1			
Crosby	19+5	2			2	1		
Dalton	17+12	4	1+2					
Davies	3							
Dunn	1+4							
Dyson	18+5		0+2		2			
Edmondson	10							
Edwards	24+9	3	4+1	1	2	1		
Facey	1+2							
Francis	42		5		1			
Glover	11							
Gray	36+3	1	4					
Heary	2+3				1			
Illingworth	2+1							
Jenkins	33		5		2			
Kaye	0+1							
Lawson	8+10	3	1+3		1+1			
Makel	19	3	3					
Morrison	9+1	1	2					
Norman	4				1			
Payton	38	17	5	2	2			
Reid	20+2		4		1+1			
Rowe	1+6		0+1					
Ryan	2+3							
Sinnott	29+1		2					
Stewart	19+1	7	4	4	1			
Tisdale	1+1							
Williams	2							

HULL CITY (DIV 3: 17th)

	P/FL App	Goals	FLC App	Goals	FAC App	Goals	Others App	Goals
Allison	11		0+1					
Brien	29+3	1	2		3		2	
Brown	7+19	1	0+1		2			
Carroll	23		2		1		1	
Darby	40+1	13	2		3	6	2	1
Davison	9						1	
Dewhurst	20+2				2		1	
Dickinson	0+1							
Doncel	22+4	2	2		1+1		1	
Ellington	0+2						0+1	
Elliott	3							
Fewings	3+9							
Gilbert	15+4	1	1		0+1		1+1	
Gordon	19+1	4	1+1	1	1		1	
Greaves	23+7	2			1		1	
Joyce	45	5	2		3	1	2	1
Lowthorpe	13+1	1					1	
Mann	24+8	2	1		1+2	1	2	
Marks	7+3				2		1	
Mason	4+2	3					0+1	
Maxfield	10+7		1+1		1		0+1	
Peacock	34+6	4	1		3	1	1	
Quigley	23+6	1	1+1	1	3		1	
Rioch	38+1	1	2	2	2		1	
Sansam	2+1				0+1		1	
Sharman	2+2							
Trevitt	21+1	1	2					

HULL CITY cont.

	P/FL App	Goals	FLC App	Goals	FAC App	Goals	Others App	Goals
Turner	5	2						
Wharton	0+1							
Wilson	14+1				2		0+1	
Wright	40	2			3		2	1

IPSWICH TOWN (DIV 1: 4th)

	P/FL App	Goals	FLC App	Goals	FAC App	Goals	Others App	Goals
Creaney	6	1						
Cundy	13	2	2		1			
Dyer	2+11				1		1+1	
Forrest	6		2					
Gregory	10+7	6	0+1				1+1	
Gudmundsson	2+6	2					1+1	1
Howe	2+1		1					
Jean	0+1							
Marshall	2		1	1				
Mason	41+2	12	6	3			1	
Mathie	11+1	4	5	5				
Milton	8+15		3+2	1				
Mowbray	8		1					
Naylor	19+8	4	1+3	1	0+1			
Niven	2							
Petta	1+5		1					
Scowcroft	40+1	9	6	1	1		2	1
Sedgley	39	7	6	1			2	
Sonner	22+7	2	5+1	1	1			
Stockwell	42+1	7	6+1	1	1		2	1
Swailes	23	1	2				2	
Tanner	10+6	4	1		1			
Taricco	41	3	5		1		2	
Thomsen	10+1		4		1			
Uhlenbeek	34+4		3+3		1		2	
Vaughan	27+5	2	4+2				2	
Wark	2		1					
Williams	43		6		1		2	
Wright	40		5		1		2	

LEEDS UNITED (PREM: 11th)

	P/FL App	Goals	FLC App	Goals	FAC App	Goals	Others App	Goals
Beeney	1							
Beesley	11+1		1		1			
Blunt	0+1		0+1					
Bowyer	32	4			4	2		
Boyle	0+1							
Couzens	7+3	1	3					
Deane	27+1	5			4	1		
Dorigo	15+3				4			
Ford	15+1	1	3					
Gray	1+6		2					
Halle	20				3			
Harte	10+4	2	2+1	1	1			
Hateley	5+1							
Jackson	11+6				4			
Jobson	10		3					
Kelly	34+2	2	3		4			
Kewell	0+1							
Laurent	2+2							
Lilley	4+2							
Martyn	37				4			
Molenaar	12	1			2			
Palmer	26+2		2		3			
Radebe	28+4		1		3			
Rush	34+2	3	2		2+2			
Sharpe	26	5	3	1	0+1			
Shepherd	1							
Tinkler	1+2							
Wallace	17+5	3	3	3	4	2		
Wetherall	25+4		2+1		1+1			
Yeboah	6+1							

LEICESTER CITY (PREM: 9th)

	P/FL App	Goals	FLC App	Goals	FAC App	Goals	Others App	Goals
Campbell	4+6		0+2		2			
Claridge	29+3	12	8	2	4	1		
Elliott	16	4			2			

LEICESTER CITY cont.

	P/FL App	Goals	FLC App	Goals	FAC App	Goals	Others App	Goals
Grayson	36		7	2	3			
Guppy	12+1							
Heskey	35	10	8+1	2	3			
Hill	6+1		1+1					
Izzet	34+1	3	8	1	3			
Kaamark	9+1		3		2			
Keller	31		8		4			
Lawrence	2+13		3+4	2	1+1			
Lenhart			0+1					
Lennon	35	1	7	1	2			
Lewis	4+2		2					
Marshall	19+9	8			4	2		
Parker	22+9	2	9	1	4	1		
Poole	7		1					
Prior	33+1		7		4			
Robins	5+3	1	3+3	1	1+1			
Rolling	1		2					
Taylor	20+5		4+3		1+1			
Ullathorne			1					
Walsh	22	2	8		2	1		
Watts	22+4	1	5+1		2+1			
Whitlow	14+3		4					
Wilson	0+2	1			0+2			

LEYTON ORIENT (DIV 3: 16th)

	P/FL App	Goals	FLC App	Goals	FAC App	Goals	Others App	Goals
Ansah	0+2							
Arnott	28+3	3	2		2		1	
Atkins	5							
Ayorinde	6+6	2	1+1		1			
Baker	15+5				0+1			
Caldwell	3							
Castle	4							
Channing	40	5	1		2	1	1	
Chapman	31+9	2	0+1		1+1		1	
Clapham	6							
Fortune-West	1+4							
Garland	13+8		1		2			
Griffiths	13	6						
Hanson	15+10	3	1+1					
Heidenstrom	3+1							
Hendon	28	1	2		2		1	
Hodges	3							
Howes	3+2							
Hyde	13							
Inglethorpe	10+6	8			0+1		0+1	
Joseph	15						1	
Kelly	6+3	1	1					
Ling	39+5	1	2		2		1	1
McCarthy	3+1		1					
McGleish	28	7			1		1	
Martin A	16+1		2					
Martin D	8		2					
Morrison	8							
Naylor	44	3	2		2			
Riches	2+3							
Sealey	12		2					
Shearer	7+1				1			
Shilton	9				1			
Timons	6	2						
Warren	25+2	1			2		1	
Weaver	9				1		1	
West	22+1	3	2	1	2		1	1
Whyte	1							
Wilkins	3							
Winston	3+8	1			0+2	1		

LINCOLN CITY (DIV 3: 9th)

	P/FL App	Goals	FLC App	Goals	FAC App	Goals	Others App	Goals
Ainsworth	46	22	6	2	1		1	
Alcide	38+4	8	4+2	2	1		1	
Austin	44		6				1	
Barnett	33+3		3		1		1	
Bimson	13+2						1	

LINCOLN CITY cont.

	P/FL App	Goals	FLC App	Goals	FAC App	Goals	Others App	Goals
Bos	18+5	1	6	3	1	1	1	
Brown G	34	1	5		1		1	
Brown S	9+6	2	0+3					
Cort	5+1	1						
Dennis	23+5	2	1+2				1	
Fleming	37		6	1	1		1	
Foran	1+1							
Holmes	27+1	4	4	2				
Hone	26+3		5+1	1	1			
Martin	29+5	4	5	1	1		0+1	
Minett	2+2		0+4				0+1	
Richardson	36		5		1		1	
Robertson	15+1	1	1		1			
Stant	22	16						
Sterling	15+6		3+1		0+1		0+1	
Stones	0+2							
Taylor	5	2						
Vaughan	10		1					
Whitney	18	3	5	1	1			

Phil Stant (Lincoln City)

LIVERPOOL (PREM: 4th)

	P/FL App	Goals	FLC App	Goals	FAC App	Goals	Others App	Goals
Babb	21	1	3		1		4+1	
Barnes	34+1	4	3		2		7	3
Berger	13+10	4	3	1	1+1		6	2
Bjornebye	38	2	4		2		8	2
Carragher	1+1	1	0+1					
Collymore	25+5	12			2	2	4+1	2
Fowler	32	18	4	5	1	1	7	7
Harkness	5+2						3	
James	38		4		2		8	
Jones L	0+2							
Jones R	2		1					
Kennedy	0+5		0+1		0+1		0+1	
Kvarme	15				1			
McAteer	36+1	1	4		2		8	
McManaman	37	7	4	2	2		8	1
Matteo	22+4		3		2		7	
Owen	1+1	1						
Redknapp	18+5	3	1	1	1		4+3	
Ruddock	15+2	1	2				2+1	
Scales	3		1				2+1	
Thomas	29+2	3	4		1		5+1	

LIVERPOOL cont

	P/FL App	Goals	FLC App	Goals	FAC App	Goals	Others App	Goals
Thompson	0+2							
Wright	33		3	1	2		5	1

LUTON TOWN (DIV 2: 3rd)

	P/FL App	Goals	FLC App	Goals	FAC App	Goals	Others App	Goals
Alexander	44+1	2	6		3		3+1	
Davis K							1	
Davis S	43+1	8	6		3		4	1
Douglas	2+7		0+1		1			
Evers	1						1	
Feuer	46		6		3		3	
Fotiadis	9+8	3	0+2				1+2	
Grant	8+17	2	4	2	0+2		2+1	1
Guentchev	15+12	1	3+2		1+1		2	
Harvey	1+1							
Hughes	36	4	6	1	3	1	2	
James	44	1	6	1	3		2	
Johnson	44		6		2	1	2	
Kiwomya	5	1						
Linton	3+4		1		1		1	
McGowan	2							
McLaren	13+11		0+1				2	
Marshall	9+15	4			2+1	3	2+2	
Oldfield	31+7	6	5	2			2+2	3
Patterson	8+2				1		4	
Showler	21+2	6	3+1		3		1+1	
Skelton	2+1				2		1	
Thomas	42	3	6		1		3	
Thorpe	39+2	28	3+1	2	2	1	2	
Upson	0+1							
Waddock	38+1	2	5		2		3	

MANCHESTER CITY (DIV 1: 14th)

	P/FL App	Goals	FLC App	Goals	FAC App	Goals	Others App	Goals
Atkinson	7+1	2						
Beagrie	0+1				0+1			
Beesley	6							
Brannan	11	1						
Brightwell	36+1	2			2			
Brown	7+4		1+1		1			
Clough	18+5	2	2					
Creaney	1+4	1			0+1			
Crooks	8+7		0+1		2			
Dibble	12+1		2					
Dickov	25+4	5	2		0+1			
Foster	3							
Frontzeck	8+3		1					
Greenacre	0+4							
Heaney	10+5	1			2		1	
Hiley	2+1							
Horlock	18	4						
Immel	4							
Ingram	13+5		1		3			
Kavelashvili	6+18	2	0+1					
Kernaghan	9+1				2			
Kinkladze	39	12	1		3			
Lomas	35	3	2		3			
McGoldrick	33		1		3			
Margetson	17				3			
Phillips	1+3		0+1					
Rodger	8	1						
Rosler	43+1	15	2	1	3	1		
Summerbee	43+1	4	2		3	2		
Symons	44		2		3			
Wassall	14+1		2					
Whitley	12+11	1	1					
Wright	13							

MANCHESTER UNITED (PREM: 1st)

	P/FL App	Goals	FLC App	Goals	FAC App	Goals	Others App	Goals
Appleton			1+1					
Beckham	33+3	8			2	1	11	3
Butt	24+2	5					9+1	1
Cantona	36	11			3		11	4
Casper	0+2		2		1		0+1	

MANCHESTER UNITED cont.

Player	P/FL App	P/FL Goals	FLC App	FLC Goals	FAC App	FAC Goals	Others App	Others Goals
Clegg	3+1		1		1			
Cole	10+10	7			2+1		2+3	1
Cooke			0+1					
Cruyff	11+5	3	1				3+1	
Davies			0+2					
Giggs	25+1	3			3		7+1	2
Irwin	29+2	1			3		9	
Johnsen	26+5				2		9	
Keane	21	2	2		3		7	1
McClair	4+15		2		1+2		0+3	
May	28+1	3	2		1		8+1	1
Neville G	30+1	1	1		3		10+1	
Neville P	15+3		1				3+2	
O'Kane	1		1					
Pallister	27	3			1		9	
Poborsky	15+7	3	2	1	2		3+4	
Schmeichel	36				3		10	
Scholes	16+8	3	2	1	2	2	1+4	
Solskjaer	25+8	18			0+3		8+2	1
Thornley	1+1		2					
Van der Gouw	2						1	

MANSFIELD TOWN (DIV 3: 11th)

Player	P/FL App	P/FL Goals	FLC App	FLC Goals	FAC App	FAC Goals	Others App	Others Goals
Bowling	46		2		2		1	
Christie	8							
Clarke	17+2	2			0+1		0+1	
Clifford	3		1					
Cresswell	5	1						
Doolan	41	6	2		2	1	1	
Eustace	41+1	4	1		2	1	1	
Ford	25+2	2			2	1	1	
Hackett	35+1	1	2		1		1	
Hadley	31+5	4	1		2		1	
Harper	37+3	2	2		2		1	
Helliwell	4+1	1						
Holbrook	0+1							
Hurst	5+1						0+1	
Ireland	5+1		2		0+1			
Kerr	9		1					
Kilcline	30+1	3	1		2		1	
Martindale	5	2						
Robinson	3+5		1+1					
Sale	12+6	5	2		1			
Sedgemore	37+2	4			1		1	
Sherlock	14+5		0+1		0+1			
Walker	33+3	3			2		1	
Watkiss	30+1	1	1		1			
Williams L	3+3							
Williams R	4+12		2		0+1			
Wood	23+8	3	1		2	1	1	
Young	0+1							

MIDDLESBROUGH (PREM: 19th)

Player	P/FL App	P/FL Goals	FLC App	FLC Goals	FAC App	FAC Goals	Others App	Others Goals
Barmby	10	1						
Beck	22+3	5	6+1	4	5+1	2		
Blackmore	14+2	2	2+1		4+1			
Branco	1+1		2	2				
Campbell	0+3							
Cox	29+2		7		3	1		
Emerson	32	4	8	2	5	1		
Festa	13	1	4		5	1		
Fjortoft	2+3	1	1		0+2	1		
Fleming	30		7	1	4+1			
Freestone	0+3				0+1			
Hendrie			1+1					
Hignett	19+3	4	6	1	6	2		
Juninho	34+1	12	7	1	6	2		
Kinder	4+2	1	1		2+1			
Liddle	5				1			
Miller	10		2					
Moore	10+7		1+3		1+1			
Morris	3+1		2					

MIDDLESBROUGH cont.

Player	P/FL App	P/FL Goals	FLC App	FLC Goals	FAC App	FAC Goals	Others App	Others Goals
Mustoe	31	2	8		7			
Pearson	17+1		5		3			
Ravanelli	33	16	8	9	7	6		
Roberts	9+1		1+1		6			
Robson	1							
Schwarzer	7		3					
Stamp	15+9	1	4+2	1	3+2	1		
Summerbell	0+2							
Vickers	26+3		5+1	1	5+1			
Walsh	12		3		1			
Whelan	9		2					
Whyte	20+1		3+1	1	3+1			

MILLWALL (DIV 2: 14th)

Player	P/FL App	P/FL Goals	FLC App	FLC Goals	FAC App	FAC Goals	Others App	Others Goals
Aris							0+1	
Berry	13+1							
Bircham	6							
Bowry	26+2	1	2		2			
Bright	3	1					1	
Cadette	7	1						
Canoville	0+2							
Carter	46		2		2		1	
Crawford	40+2	11	1		2	1	2	3
Dair	21+3	1	2		2		1	2
Dolby	15+6	2	1+1		0+1		2	
Doyle	19+9	1	1				1+1	
Fitzgerald	7							
Harle	12+9	1	1+1		1		1	
Hartley	35+9	4	1+1		2		1	
Hockton	0+2							
Huckerby	6	3						
Iga	0+1						1	
Lavin	7+2				1+1		1	
McLeary	15							
McRobert	3+1						0+1	
Malkin	7+2	2	2	1				
Neill	35+4	4	1+1		2		1	
Newman	39+2	3	2		2		2	
Robertson	0+1						0+1	
Roche	4+3							
Rogan	26+2	8	1		2		1	
Sadler	7+3							
Savage	32+3	3	1		2	1	1	1
Sinclair	6+2				0+1		1+1	
Stevens	6		2					
Van Blerk	2+2				0+1		1+1	
Webber	25+1	2	1		1		2	
Wilkins	3						1	
Witter	33		2		1			

NEWCASTLE UNITED (PREM: 2nd)

Player	P/FL App	P/FL Goals	FLC App	FLC Goals	FAC App	FAC Goals	Others App	Others Goals
Albert	27	2	2		2		8+1	1
Asprilla	17+7	4	2				6+1	5
Barton	14+4	1	1		1+1		4+2	
Batty	32	1	2		3		8	
Beardsley	22+3	5	2	1	3		7	2
Beresford	18+1				3		4+1	
Clark	9+16	2	1		2+1	1	2+3	
Crawford	0+2							
Elliott	29	7	2		1+1		4+1	
Ferdinand	30+1	16	1		2+1	1	5	4
Gillespie	23+9	1	1		1+1		6+3	
Ginola	20+4	1	2		2		7+1	1
Hislop	16		1		3		2	
Howey	8	1					1	
Kitson	0+3		0+2				0+1	
Lee	32+1	5	1		2	1	9	
Peacock	35	1	2		3		9	
Shearer	31	25	1	1	3	1	5	1
Srnicek	22		1				7	
Watson	33+3	1	0+1		2+1		5+1	

NORTHAMPTON TOWN (DIV 3: 4th)

Player	P/FL App	P/FL Goals	FLC App	FLC Goals	FAC App	FAC Goals	Others App	Others Goals
Burns	6		1				6	
Clarkson	45		4		1		6	
Colkin	1+5		1+3		0+1		0+2	
Cooper	37+4	10	3		1		1	
Frain	13						6	1
Gayle	9+4	1					5	2
Gibb	6+12	1	3+1				0+1	
Grayson	32+8	12	3+1		1		5	
Hunter	26+10	6	4		1		4	
Kirby	0+1							
Lee	12+17	7	1	2	0+1		3+2	
Lyne	1							
Maddison	34		3+1		1		2+1	
Martin	10+2						3	2
O'Shea	29+6		4		1		1+1	
Parrish	37+2	8	3		1		3	1
Peer	7+14	1	1+2				1+4	
Rennie	42+1	4	4				5	
Rush	14	3					1	1
Sampson	43	4	4		1		6	1
Smart	1							
Stant	4+1	2						
Thompson	0+1							
Turley	1							
Warburton	35	4			1		5	1
Warner	1+8				0+1		1+1	
White	15+17	2	1+3		1		2+2	
Woodman	45		4		1		6	

NORWICH CITY (DIV 1: 13th)

Player	P/FL App	P/FL Goals	FLC App	FLC Goals	FAC App	FAC Goals	Others App	Others Goals
Adams	45	13	2	2	2	1		
Akinbiyi	3+9		0+2					
Bellamy	0+3							
Bradshaw	11+6		0+1					
Broughton	3+5	1						
Carey	8+6		0+1		1+1			
Crook	33+4	2	2		1			
Eadie	42	17	2		2			
Fleck	33+3	4	2		1			
Forbes	3+7				1			
Gunn	39		2		2			
Jackson	19	2			2			
Johnson	24+3	5	1	1	1			
Marshall	7							
Milligan	37	1	2		2			
Mills	27+5		2		1			
Moore	2							
Newman	44	1	2		2			
O'Neill	23+3	6	2		1			
Ottosson	4+3	1			0+1			
Polston	27+4	2	2		1	1		
Rocastle	11							
Rush	0+2							
Scott Keith	5+8	3			0+2			
Scott Kevin	9							
Simpson	1+2							
Sutch	43+1	3	1		2			
Wright	3+1							

NOTTINGHAM FOREST (PREM: 20th)

Player	P/FL App	P/FL Goals	FLC App	FLC Goals	FAC App	FAC Goals	Others App	Others Goals
Allen	16+8				1	1	1	
Bart-Williams	16	1	3		2			
Blatherwick	7		2		1			
Campbell	16+1	6			3			
Chettle	31+1	1			3			
Clough	10+3	1						
Cooper	36	2	3	1	3			
Crossley	33		3		3			
Fettis	4				0+1			
Gemmill	18+6	2	2+1		0+2			
Guinan	0+2	1						
Haaland	33+2	6	2+1		3			

NOTTINGHAM FOREST cont.

Player	P/FL App	P/FL Goals	FLC App	FLC Goals	FAC App	FAC Goals	Others App	Others Goals
Howe	0+1							
Jerkan	14							
Lee	5+8	1	2+1	1	0+1			
Lyttle	30+2	1	2		3			
McGregor	0+5				0+1			
Moore	1+4							
O'Neill	4+1							
Pearce	33	5	2		2			
Phillips	24+3		2		2			
Roy	8+12	3	2+1	1	2+1			
Saunders	33+1	3	3		2	2		
Silenzi	1+1							
Stone	5							
Van Hooijdonk	8	1						
Warner	2+1							
Woan	29+3	1	3		3	2		
Wright	1							

NOTTS COUNTY (DIV 2: 24th)

Player	P/FL App	P/FL Goals	FLC App	FLC Goals	FAC App	FAC Goals	Others App	Others Goals
Agana	17+6	3			2+1	1		
Arkins	13+2	1	1+1		1+1	1		
Baraclough	36+2	2	2		3		1	
Battersby	6+12	1	1		0+3			
Cunnington	6+2							
Derry	37+2	2	2		4			
Diuk	0+1							
Dudley	6+4	2						
Farrell	10+4	1			3		1	
Finnan	18+5				4		1	
Gallagher	1						1+1	
Galloway	4+1				0+1		1	
Hendon	12							
Hogg	35		1		2		1	
Hunt	5+4				0+1		2	1
Jones	21+6	3	1	1	2	1		
Kennedy	20+2		1		2+1	1	0+1	
Ludlam	1							
Martindale	16+12	6	2		2		2	1
Mendez	2+1							
Mitchell	1							
Murphy	16		1					
Nogan	6							
Pollitt	8						2	
Redmile	23	2			3		1	
Regis	7+3	2						
Richardson	16+3	1	2				2	
Ridgeway	3+3						0+2	
Robinson	33+4	2	2		4	1		
Roddie							1	
Rogers	0+1						2	
Simpson	1							
Strodder	28	2	2		3			
Walker	13+3				1+2		2	
Ward	38		2		4			
White	7+2							
Wilder	37		2		4		1	
Wilkes	3						1+1	

OLDHAM ATHLETIC (DIV 1: 23rd)

Player	P/FL App	P/FL Goals	FLC App	FLC Goals	FAC App	FAC Goals	Others App	Others Goals
Allott	0+5	1						
Banger	16+7	5	4	1	1			
Barlow	26+9	12	3+1					
Beresford	24+9		2+2		0+1			
Duxbury	11+1	1						
Fleming	44		4		1			
Foran	0+1							
Gannon	1							
Garnett	22+1	1			1			
Graham	16+3	1	2		1			
Halle	18+2	3	5					
Hallworth	4		2					
Henry	21+1	1	3+1		1			

OLDHAM ATHLETIC cont.

Player	P/FL App	P/FL Goals	FLC App	FLC Goals	FAC App	FAC Goals	Others App	Others Goals
Hodgson	11+1							
Holt	0+1							
Hughes	7+1		0+1					
Kelly	42		3		1			
McCarthy	17+4	4	3	2	0+1			
McNiven D	2+6		0+2					
McNiven S	11+1		1		1			
Morrow	1+1							
Orlygsson	23+4	1	4+1		0+1			
Ormondroyd	26+4	8			1			
Pemberton	0+3		0+1					
Redmond	24	2	5					
Reid	9		1					
Richardson Lee	27+4	4	4	1	1			
Richardson Lloyd	0+1							
Rickers	45+1	4	5		1			
Ritchie	4+6							
Rush	6+2	2						
Serrant	34+6		5		1			
Snodin	14							

OXFORD UNITED (DIV 1: 17th)

Player	P/FL App	P/FL Goals	FLC App	FLC Goals	FAC App	FAC Goals	Others App	Others Goals
Aldridge	18+12	8	5+2	1	1			
Angel	15+9	2	2+1					
Beauchamp	36+9	7	8		1			
Elliott	26	4	8		1			
Ford M	42	4	8	1	1			
Ford R	29+4		5+1	1	1			
Gabbiadini	5	1						
Gilchrist	38	2	5		1			
Gray	41+2	2	7		1			
Jackson	3							
Jemson	44	18	7	5	1			
Marsh	6+2	1						
Massey	15+14	3	3+3		0+1			
Moody	19+19	4	3+4	2	0+1			
Murphy	5+25	3	0+3		0+1			
Phillips	0+1							
Purse	25+6	1	4+1		1			
Robinson	36+2		7		1			
Rush	4+11	1	0+2					
Smith	45		8		1			
Weatherstone	0+1							
Whitehead	43		8		1			
Whyte	10							
Wilsterman	1							

PETERBOROUGH UNITED (DIV 2: 21st)

Player	P/FL App	P/FL Goals	FLC App	FLC Goals	FAC App	FAC Goals	Others App	Others Goals
Basham	4+1		1		0+1			
Billington	2+3		1+1					
Bodley	31		3		5		4	
Boothroyd	24+2	1	2		4+1		4	
Bullimore	2+4							
Carruthers	13+1	4			3	2	2	
Carter	3+5		0+2		0+1			
Charlery	36+1	5	4	1	6	6	5	1
Clark	30+4	2			6		3	
Cleaver	6+7	1			0+1		1	
Desouza	8	2						
Donowa	16+6	1					4+1	2
Drury	5	1	1					
Ebdon	12+8	1	2+1		2+2			
Edwards	25				4		5	
Etherington	1							
Farrell	4+3	3	1+1	1				
Foran	2+2							
Grazioli	0+4		0+2		0+3	1		
Griemink	27				4		4	
Griffiths	2+10	1	0+2	1	1+1	1	0+1	
Heald	34+2	2	4		5+1		3	1
Houghton	26+6	8	2+2		5	1	0+1	
Huxford	7							

PETERBOROUGH UNITED cont.

Player	P/FL App	P/FL Goals	FLC App	FLC Goals	FAC App	FAC Goals	Others App	Others Goals
Inman	0+3		1		0+1			
Le Bihan	2						2+1	
Linton	8							
McGleish	0+1							
McKeever	2+1		1					
Morrison	4+7	2			3+2		2+1	
Neal	4							
O'Connor	18	3	4		2			
Otto	15	4					2	2
Payne	36	2	3		6		5	
Ramage	7						1	
Regis	4+3	1						
Rowe	10+12	3	2		3+1		0+1	
Sheffield	16		4		2			
Spearing	11+2				0+1		2	
Tyler	3						1	
Welsh	6		3					
Williams	6							
Willis	34+6	6	3		5+1		5	

PLYMOUTH ARGYLE (DIV 2: 19th)

Player	P/FL App	P/FL Goals	FLC App	FLC Goals	FAC App	FAC Goals	Others App	Others Goals
Barlow	38+2	1	1		3		3	
Billy	44+1	3	2		3	1	2+1	
Blackwell	4							
Clayton	0+1							
Collins	11+1	1						
Corazzin	22+8	5	1+1		0+2	1	2	
Curran	20+2		1+1		1		1	
Dungey	6						3	
Evans	33	12	2		3	3	3	
Grobbelaar	36				3			
Heathcote	41+1	1	2		3		3	
Illman	12+13	4			2		1+1	1
James	34	1			3		1	
Leadbitter	17+2		2		3		1	
Littlejohn	33+4	6	2		1+2	2	3	
Logan	19+9	4	2				3	
Mauge	29+6	3	1		3	2	1	
Patterson	11+1							
Perkins	1+3							
Phillips	0+2						0+1	
Richardson							0+1	
Rowbotham	12+3						1+1	
Saunders	22+3	3	1		0+2		1	
Simpson	10+2							
Williams	46	2	2		3		2	
Wotton	5+4	1			2		2	2

PORTSMOUTH (DIV 1: 7th)

Player	P/FL App	P/FL Goals	FLC App	FLC Goals	FAC App	FAC Goals	Others App	Others Goals
Allen	3+1				0+1			
Awford	37+2		4		4			
Bradbury	38+4	15	1+2		4	2		
Burton	12+9	1	2	2	0+1	1		
Butters	7		2					
Carter	23+4	1	4	1				
Cook	6+2							
Dobson	4+2		1		0+1			
Durnin	16+18	3			2			
Flahaven	24							
Hall	36+6	13	3+1		4	2		
Hillier	21	2			4	1		
Igoe	22+18	2	3+1		0+2			
Knight	22				4			
McLoughlin	33+3	5	4		4	2		
Perrett	31+1	1	2		4			
Pethick	27+8		4		4			
Rees	1+2	1						
Russell	18+2	2	4					
Simpson	40+1	4	4		4			
Svensson	17+2	6			2+1	1		
Thomson	22+6	1			3+1			
Turner	22+2	2	2+1					

PORTSMOUTH cont.

	P/FL App	P/FL Goals	FLC App	FLC Goals	FAC App	FAC Goals	Others App	Others Goals
Waterman	0 + 4							
Whitbread	24				1			

PORT VALE (DIV 1: 8th)

	P/FL App	P/FL Goals	FLC App	FLC Goals	FAC App	FAC Goals	Others App	Others Goals
Aspin	32 + 1		4		1			
Bogie	28 + 3	1	4	1	0 + 1			
Corden	5 + 7		1					
Foyle	9 +28	3	4 + 1	1	0 + 1			
Glover	40 + 2	2	5		1			
Griffiths	24 + 2		4		1			
Guppy	34	6	5		1			
Hill	36 + 2	1	5					
Holwyn	5 + 2							
Jansson	10 + 1	1			1			
Koordes	7 + 6							
McCarthy	45	4	6	2	1			
Mills	22 +13	13	3 + 3	2				
Musselwhite	33		2		1			
Naylor	40 + 3	17	5	3	1			
Porter	44		6		1			
Stokes	8 + 2				1			
Talbot	25 + 9	4	0 + 3					
Tankard	37	1	6		1			
Van Heusden	13		4					
Walker	9 + 8		2 + 1					

PRESTON NORTH END (DIV 2: 15th)

	P/FL App	P/FL Goals	FLC App	FLC Goals	FAC App	FAC Goals	Others App	Others Goals
Ashcroft	26 + 1	8			2	3	0 + 1	
Atkinson	12 + 5		3	1	0 + 1		2	1
Barrick	30 + 6		4		1			
Beckford	0 + 2				1			
Bennett	10 + 6	3			1		1	1
Brown	5 + 1		0 + 1					
Bryson	32 + 9	3	3		1 + 1		2	
Cartwright	14	1					1	
Davey	30 + 7	6	4	1	0 + 1		2	
Gage	16				1			
Gregan	21	1					1	
Holt	8 +11	3	2	1	1 + 1			
Jackson	7							
Kay	7		3					
Kidd	33 + 2		3 + 1		2		1	
Kilbane	32 + 4	2	4		1			
Lucas	2		1					
McDonald	12 +10		0 + 2	1	2			
McKenna	4 + 1	1					2	
Mimms	27		2		2			
Moilanen	4		1					
Moyes	26	4	1		2		0 + 1	
Nogan	5 + 2							
O'Hanlon	13						2	
Patterson	2							
Rankine	19 + 4		2		2			
Reeves	33 + 1	11			2	3	1	
Saville	12	1	4					
Sparrow	6				1		1	
Squires	6 + 3		1		0 + 1		2	
Stallard	4	1						
Teale	5							
Wilcox	35		4		2		1	
Wilkinson	8 + 2	3	2	4	1		1	

QUEENS PARK RANGERS (DIV 1: 9th)

	P/FL App	P/FL Goals	FLC App	FLC Goals	FAC App	FAC Goals	Others App	Others Goals
Barker	38	4	2		2			
Brazier	22 + 5	2	2	1	2			
Brevett	44		2		4			
Challis	2							
Charles	6 + 6	1	0 + 1					
Dichio	31 + 6	7	2	1	2 + 2			
Gallen	2	3						
Graham	16 + 2		2		2			
Hateley	8 + 5	1			2 + 2	2		

QUEENS PARK RANGERS cont.

	P/FL App	P/FL Goals	FLC App	FLC Goals	FAC App	FAC Goals	Others App	Others Goals
Impey	26 + 6	2	2	1	1 + 1			
Jackson	7							
McDermott	6	2						
McDonald	38 + 1	2	2		3	1		
Maddix	18 +7				2			
Mahoney-Johnson	0 + 2							
Morrow	5	1						
Murray	26 + 6	5	2		3			
Peacock	27	5			4	2		
Perry	2	1						
Plummer	4 + 1		2					
Quashie	9 + 4		0 + 1					
Ready	28 + 1				4			
Roberts	13				3			
Sinclair	39	3	2		4	1		
Slade	11 + 6	4			1			
Sommer	33		2		1			
Spencer	25	17			4	1		
Wilkins	4							
Yates	16	1			1			

READING (DIV 1: 18th)

	P/FL App	P/FL Goals	FLC App	FLC Goals	FAC App	FAC Goals	Others App	Others Goals
Bass	0 + 2							
Bernal	41		1 + 1		2			
Bibbo	5				1			
Blatherwick	6 + 1							
Bodin	37	1	2		2			
Booty	14		2		2			
Brown	5							
Caskey	26 + 9		1		2	1		
Gilkes	27 + 5	1	0 + 1		2			
Glasgow	2 + 2				0 + 1			
Gooding	40 + 3		2		2			
Hammond	1							
Holsgrove	12 + 2	2	1		2			
Hopkins	17 + 1		1		1			
Hunter	26 + 1	2	1		1			
Lambert	20 +11	5			2	1		
Lovell	17 + 9	5	1		0 + 1			
McPherson	39	2			1			
Mautone	15							
Meaker	15 +10	1						
Mihailov	8		2		1			
Morley	36 + 1	22	1		2	1		
Nogan	21 +11	6	1 + 1					
Parkinson	15 + 9	1	1 + 1					
Quinn	10 +14	3	1 + 1	1				
Roach	2 + 1	1						
Smith	0 + 1							
Swales	3							
Wdowczyk	8		2					
Williams	21 + 8	3	2		2			
Wright	17							

ROCHDALE (DIV 3: 14th)

	P/FL App	P/FL Goals	FLC App	FLC Goals	FAC App	FAC Goals	Others App	Others Goals
Bailey	13 + 2				1		1	
Bayliss	22 + 2		1		1		1	
Brown	5							
Cecere	2 + 2	1	0 + 1		1		1	
Deary	37 +1	5	2	1	2	1	1	
Dowell	6 + 1							
Farrell	37 + 3	2	2		2			
Fensome	38 + 2		2		2			
Formby	12 + 4	1	1					
Gouck	22 + 6	3			1			
Gray	46		2		2		1	
Hill	43	3	2		2		1	
Johnson	46	4	2		2	1	1	
Lancaster	1 + 5		1					
Leonard	39	4	2		1			
Martin	0 + 1							

ROCHDALE cont.

	P/FL App	P/FL Goals	FLC App	FLC Goals	FAC App	FAC Goals	Others App	Others Goals
Painter	21 + 6	7			2		1	
Robson	0 + 3							
Russell	35 + 4	9	2				1	
Stuart	28 + 3	7	2		1			
Taylor	0 + 1							
Thackeray	17		0 + 1		0 + 1	1	0 + 1	
Thompson	9 +19	1	0 + 2		0 + 1		0 + 1	
Whitehall	27 + 8	9	1	1	2		1	

ROTHERHAM UNITED (DIV 2: 23rd)

	P/FL App	P/FL Goals	FLC App	FLC Goals	FAC App	FAC Goals	Others App	Others Goals
Bain	10 + 2							
Barnes	2							
Berry	19 +11	4	1 + 1		0 + 1		1	
Blades	9	1					0 + 1	
Bowman	13							
Bowyer	10 + 1	2					1	
Breckin	42	3	2		1		1	
Cherry	20		2				1	
Clarke	1 + 1						1	
Crawford	11							
Dillon	11 + 2	1						
Dobbin	17 + 2		0 + 1		1		1	
Druce	16 + 4	4			1			
Farrelly	7				1			
Garner	30	2	2				1	
Gayle	19 + 1				1		1	
Glover	16 + 6	1	2		1		0 + 1	
Goodwin	7 + 1	3	2		1		1	
Hayward	32 + 2	4	1 + 1					
Hurst	25 + 5	3	1					
James	0 + 3							
Jean	7 +11	6						
Landon	7 + 1							
McDougald	14 + 4	2			1		1	
McGlashan	28 + 3		1 + 1		1	1	1	
McKenzie	6 + 5							
Monington	28		1		1		1	
Pell	2							
Pilkington	17							
Richardson	10 + 4	1	1					
Roscoe	39 + 4		2		1		1	
Sandeman	20 + 1	2	2		1			
Slawson	2 + 3		0 + 1					
Smith	9 + 2				0 + 1			

Andy Roscoe (Rotherham United)

SCARBOROUGH (DIV 3: 12th)

	P/FL App	Goals	FLC App	Goals	FAC App	Goals	Others App	Goals
Bennett G	46	9	4	2	3		1	
Bennett T	4+1	1						
Bochenski	5+14	1	2+1				0+1	
Brodie	23+1	5						
Brooke	28+6	2	3		1+1		1	
Burridge							1	
Currie	16	6						
Daws	4+2		1	1	1+1		1	
Hanby	1+3		2					
Hicks	36+2	1	3		3		1	
Ironside	39		4		3			
Kay	34				2	1		
Knowles	12+5		3+1		1		1	
Lucas	19+9		4		2+1		1	
McElhatton	26+2	1	1		2+1		1	
Martin	3				0+1			
Midgley	6	2						
Mitchell	23+20	7	2+2		3			
Moilanen	4							
Mowbray	2+1		1					
Rigby	5	1						
Ritchie	26+5	9	2+1	2	3	1	1	
Rockett	40	5	3		1			
Russell	1+4		0+1					
Sunderland	0+2							
Sutherland	17+4							
Thompstone	12+7	2	2		3		0+1	
Wells	22+8	1	1+1		2+1		1	
Williams A	1		1					
Williams G	45	10	4	1	3		1	
Worrall	6+9	1	1+1				0+1	

Chris Hope (Scunthorpe United)

SCUNTHORPE UNITED (DIV 3: 13th)

	P/FL App	Goals	FLC App	Goals	FAC App	Goals	Others App	Goals
Baker	21	9			3	5	2	
Borland	0+2							
Bradley	22	1	2		1			
Clarke	15							
Clarkson	28	13	2	1	3	2	1	
D'Auria	39	3	2		3	1	1+1	
Dunn	3							
Eyre	41+1	8	2		3		1	
Forrester	10	6						
Francis	1+4		0+1					
Garcia	7+6	1			2		1	
Gavin	10+1	1	1				1+1	
Hope	46	3	2		2		2	2
Housham	31+3	3	0+1		2		2	
Jackson	0+4	1					0+1	
Jones	9+2	5						
Knill	29		2		1		2	
Laws	2+2						2	
Lucas	6						2	
McAuley	9							
McFarlane	7+7	3	2		0+2			
Moss	4		1	1				
Paterson	11+18				1+1		1	
Samways	25		2		3			
Sertori	42	1	2		3		1+1	
Turnbull	11+3	1						
Walker	8+1							
Walsh	32+4				3		1	
Wilson P A	37	1	2		3		2	
Wilson P D	0+1							

SHEFFIELD UNITED (DIV 1: 5th)

	P/FL App	Goals	FLC App	Goals	FAC App	Goals	Others App	Goals
Anthony	0+2							
Beard	9+7				1			
Bettney	0+1							
Ebbrell	1							
Fjortoft	15+2	10					3	1
Hartfield	1+1				0+1			
Hawes	0+2							
Henry	9						2	
Hodgson	12+1	1	1+1		1			
Holdsworth	37				1		3	
Hutchison	38+3	3	3+1				2+1	
Katchouro	28+12	12	2+2	1	1		3	1
Kelly	39		4		1		2	
Nilsen	32+1		2		0+1		2+1	
Parker	7+3							
Patterson	34+1	1	4		1			
Sandford	25+5	2	3		1		1+1	
Scott	4+4	1			1			
Short	22+2		3				1+1	
Simpson	2+4							
Spackman	19+4		2		1		1	
Starbuck	1+1		0+2					
Taylor	26+8	11	4	1			0+2	
Tiler	6	1					3	
Tracey	7						1	
Vonk	17	2	4	2				
Walker	20+17	12	2	2	1		0+2	1
Ward	34	4	4				3	
White	31+6	6	2+1	1	1		3	
Whitehouse	30	6	4				3	

SHEFFIELD WEDNESDAY (PREM: 7th)

	P/FL App	Goals	FLC App	Goals	FAC App	Goals	Others App	Goals
Atherton	37	2	2		4			
Blinker	15+18	1	2		1			
Briscoe	5+1							
Booth	32+3	10	2		4	3		
Bright	0+1							
Carbone	24+1	6			2			
Clarke	0+1							
Collins	8+4	1			1			

SHEFFIELD WEDNESDAY cont.

	P/FL App	Goals	FLC App	Goals	FAC App	Goals	Others App	Goals
Donaldson	2+3	2						
Hirst	20+5	6	1		0+2			
Humphreys	14+15	3	1+1		3+1	2		
Hyde	15+4	2	1		4	1		
Newsome	10	1	1		3			
Nicol	19+4		0+2		2+1			
Nolan	38	1	2		4			
Oakes	7+12	1	0+1					
Pembridge	33+1	6	1		4	1		
Pressman	38		2		4			
Sheridan	0+2							
Stefanovic	27+2	2	1		1			
Trustfull	9+10	3	2		0+1			
Walker	36				4			
Whittingham	29+4	3	2	1	3	1		
Williams	0+1		1					

SHREWSBURY TOWN (DIV 2: 22nd)

	P/FL App	Goals	FLC App	Goals	FAC App	Goals	Others App	Goals
Anthrobus	33	6	2		2		2+1	1
Bennett	2+2	3						
Bent	6							
Berkley	20+4		1+1		0+1		3	1
Blamey	6							
Briscoe	0+1							
Brown	17+2	1					3	
Cope	3							
Currie	25+12	2	1+1		2			
Dempsey	37+3		0+1		2		3	
Edwards	23				2		1	
Evans	42	6	1		2		3	3
Gall	23		2				2	
Nielsen	19+3	1	1+1		0+1		2	
Nwadike	1+1							
Reed	0+3						1	
Rowbotham	11+3	1	1+1	1				
Scott	20+7	1	2		1+1		1+1	
Seabury	34+4		1+1		2		1	
Spink	39+2	4	2		2		2	
Stevens	41	17	2		2	1	2	1
Tate	0+1							
Taylor L	13+3		2					
Taylor R	33+4	1	2		2		1+1	
Walton	23+1	1	1		1		3	
Ward	5+9	1			0+1		0+2	
Whiston	26+1	1	1		2		2	
Wrack	3+1						1	
Wray	1							

SOUTHAMPTON (PREM: 16th)

	P/FL App	Goals	FLC App	Goals	FAC App	Goals	Others App	Goals
Basham	1+5							
Beasant	13+1		4		1			
Benali	14+4				1			
Berkovic	26+2	4	5+1	2	1			
Charlton	24+3		5+1	1	0+1			
Dia	0+1							
Dodd	23		3					
Dryden	28+1	1	6	3				
Evans	8+4	4						
Heaney	4+4	1						
Hughes	1+5		1+1					
Le Tissier	25+6	13	6	3	1			
Lundekvam	28+1		7+1		1			
Maddison	14+4	1	2+2		1			
Magilton	31+6	4	6+2	2	1			
Monkou	8+5		5+1					
Moss	3		2					
Neilson	24+5		5					
Oakley	23+5	3	6+1		0+1			
Ostenstad	29+1	10	6	3	1	1		
Potter	2+6		1+1					
Robinson	3+4				1			
Shipperley	9+1	1	1+1					

SOUTHAMPTON cont

	P/FL App	P/FL Goals	FLC App	FLC Goals	FAC App	FAC Goals	Others App	Others Goals
Slater	22+8	2	5+2		1			
Taylor	18							
Van Gobbel	24+1	1	6	1	1			
Venison	2							
Warren	0+1							
Watkinson	0+2		0+1					
Watson	7+8	2	4+2	3	0+1			
Woods	4		2					

SOUTHEND UNITED (DIV 1: 24th)

	P/FL App	P/FL Goals	FLC App	FLC Goals	FAC App	FAC Goals	Others App	Others Goals
Boere	27+9	9	1+1		0+1			
Byrne	23+9	1	1		1			
Clarke	7							
Codner	3+1							
Dublin	46		2		1			
Dursun	0+1							
Gridelet	34+7	1	1					
Hails	32+5		2		0+1			
Hanlon	1+1							
Harris	43+1		2		1			
Jones	0+1							
Lapper	23+5	1	1					
McNally	32+2		2		1			
Marsh	35	5	2		1			
Nielsen	17+7	3	2	1	1			
Patterson	4							
Poric	7							
Rammell	26+10	9	2	1	1			
Roget	25				1			
Royce	43		1		1			
Sansome	3		1					
Selley	3+1							
Stimson	7+2							
Thomson	14+3	5			0+1			
Tilson	27+1	1	2		1			
Williams	24+9	6	0+1		1			

STOCKPORT COUNTY (DIV 2: 2nd)

	P/FL App	P/FL Goals	FLC App	FLC Goals	FAC App	FAC Goals	Others App	Others Goals
Angell	30+4	15	8+2	3	3	1	4+1	1
Armstrong	38+1	9	11	3	4	1	3	
Bennett	43	3	11	2	4		4+1	
Bound	4		1				1	
Cavaco	19+8	5	7+1	2	3		3+2	1
Charlery	8+2							
Connelly	45		11	1	4		5+1	
Cooper	11+1	3					1	
Cowans	6+1						0+1	
Dinning	12+8	2	2+2		0+3		4+1	1
Durkan	36+5	3	9		4	3	4+2	
Edwards							2	
Flynn	46	2	11	1	4	1	5	
Gannon	38+2	4	9+2	1	4		4	
Jeffers	25+9	3	6+2		1+1		3	
Jones L							0+1	
Jones P	46		11		4		4	
Kiko	0+3						1+1	
Landon	0+2				0+1			
Marsden	34+1	2	9		4		4	1
Mike	0+1						1+1	
Mutch	15+18	4	3+1	4	1+2	1	3+1	
Nash	0+3		0+1				2+1	1
Searle	7+3		2+1				1	
Todd	39+2		9+1		4		6	
Ware	4+4		1	1			1	

STOKE CITY (DIV 1: 12th)

	P/FL App	P/FL Goals	FLC App	FLC Goals	FAC App	FAC Goals	Others App	Others Goals
Beeston	17+1							
Carruthers	0+1		0+1					
Cranson	6							
Da Costa	1+1		1+1					
Devlin	13+8		3		1			
Dreyer	12	1	3					

STOKE CITY cont

	P/FL App	P/FL Goals	FLC App	FLC Goals	FAC App	FAC Goals	Others App	Others Goals
Forsyth	40	8	3		1			
Flynn	5							
Gayle	8+4	1	2					
Griffin	29+5	1	0+1		1			
Kavanagh	32+6	4	2		1			
Keen	5+11	1	2+2					
Macari	15+15	3	0+3		0+1			
MacKenzie	5+17	1			0+1			
McMahon	31+4	3	3+1		1			
McNally	3							
Muggleton	33		4					
Nyamah	0+7							
Pickering	39+1		4		1			
Prudhoe	13		0+1		1			
Rodger	5							
Sheron	41	19	4	5	1			
Sigurdsson	45		4		1			
Stein	11	4						
Stokoe	0+2							
Sturridge	5							
Wallace	45	2	4		1			
Whittle	35+2		2		1			
Worthington	12		3	1				

SUNDERLAND (PREM: 18th)

	P/FL App	P/FL Goals	FLC App	FLC Goals	FAC App	FAC Goals	Others App	Others Goals
Agnew	11+4	2	2		1			
Aiston	0+2				0+2			
Ball	32	3	2+1	1	1			
Bracewell	38		2		1			
Bridges	10+15	3	1+1		2			
Coton	10		2					
Eriksson	1							
Gray	31+3	3	2		2	1		
Hall	32		3		2			
Howey	9+3							
Johnston	4+2	1						
Kelly	23+1		1+1		2			
Kubicki	28+1		1		2			
Melville	30	2	3		2			
Mullin	9+1	1	1		2			
Ord	33	2	3		2			
Perez	28+1		1		2			
Quinn	8+4	2	1	1				
Rae	13+10	2	2	1				
Russell	10+19	4	1+2		1+1			
Scott	15	1	2	1				
Smith	6+5		1		0+1			
Stewart	20+4	4	3					
Waddle	7	1						
Williams	10+1	2			1+1			

SWANSEA CITY (DIV 3: 5th)

	P/FL App	P/FL Goals	FLC App	FLC Goals	FAC App	FAC Goals	Others App	Others Goals
Ampadu	25+4	4	1		2		4	
Appleby	8+3	1	2				1	
Brayson	11	5						
Brown	13+8	3	1+1		1		1+2	
Casey	3+7							
Chapple	10+8		1+1				1+1	
Clode	16+2	1	1		2		0+2	
Coates	38+2	3	1		2		5	
Edwards	36		1		2		5	
Freestone	45		2		2		5	
Garnett	6		2					
Heggs	5+9	2			1		2+1	1
Hills	11							
Jenkins	21+2	2			1		1	
Jones L	1							
Jones S	46	1	2		2		4	
King	2				0+1		0+1	
Lacey	9+1		1					
McDonald	3+7							
McGibbon	1							

SWANSEA CITY cont

	P/FL App	P/FL Goals	FLC App	FLC Goals	FAC App	FAC Goals	Others App	Others Goals
Molby	26+2	6	1				1+1	
Moreira	10		0+1		2		5	
O'Leary	9+3	1	1		1+1			
Penney	44	13	2		2		5	
Phillips	0+1							
Price	1+1							
Thomas	31+5	9	2		0+1		5	2
Torpey	37+2	9	1+1		2	1	5	1
Walker	31	1					5	
Willer-Jensen	7							

SWINDON TOWN (DIV 1: 19th)

	P/FL App	P/FL Goals	FLC App	FLC Goals	FAC App	FAC Goals	Others App	Others Goals
Allen	5+5	1	2					
Allison	39+2	11	4	2	1			
Anthony	3							
Broomes	12	1						
Bullock	12+1	1						
Collins	3+1				1			
Coughlan	3							
Cowe	28+10	6	3+1		1			
Culverhouse	31		4		1			
Darras	30+5		4					
Digby	31				1			
Drysdale	13+1		2		0+1			
Elkins	19+4	1	2		1			
Finney	8+12	2	1+1					
Gooden	7+6	1						
Holcroft	2+1							
Horlock	28	8	5		1			
Hulbert			0+1					
Kerslake	8							
King	5							
Leitch	36		5	1	1			
McMahon	2+1							
Mildenhall	0+1							
O'Sullivan	16+9		2	1	0+1			
Pattimore	0+1							
Robinson	43	1	4		1			
Seagraves	27+1		4+1		1			
Smith	13+5	1						
Talia	15		5					
Taylor	2		1+1					
Thorne	24+7	8	2+1	2				
Walters	24+3	7	4	1	1			
Watson	17+10	1	1+1		0+1			

TORQUAY UNITED (DIV 3: 21st)

	P/FL App	P/FL Goals	FLC App	FLC Goals	FAC App	FAC Goals	Others App	Others Goals
Adcock	0+1		0+1					
Baker	10	4	2	3				
Barrow	45+1		2		1		1	
Bedeau	3+5	1						
Chandler	4							
Crane	0+2						1	
Gittens	33	3	2		1		1	
Gregg	1							
Gregory	5							
Hancox	6+5		2		1			
Hapgood	0+1							
Hathaway	21+14	1	0+1		0+1			
Hawthorne	25+9	2	0+1		1		1	
Hinshelwood	7+2							
Hockley	0+2							
Hodges	0+1							
Howells	2+2							
Jack	30+3	10	2				1	
Laight	6+4	1			1			
McCall	23+1	1	2				1	
McFarlane	19	3						
Mitchell	22+2		2		0+1		1	
Ndah	9+3	1			0+1		1	
Nelson	30+4	8	1+1		1			
Newland	11		2					

TORQUAY UNITED cont.

	P/FL App	P/FL Goals	FLC App	FLC Goals	FAC App	FAC Goals	Others App	Others Goals
Oatway	39+ 2	1	2		1			
Preston	0+ 2						0+1	
Stamps	30	3			1		1	
Thirlby	1+ 2							
Thomas	1+11						0+1	
Tucker	0+ 1							
Watson	46	1	2		1		1	1
Wilmot	34				1		1	
Winter	36+ 1	6	1		1			
Wright	7+ 2						0+1	

Rodney Jack (Torquay United)

TOTTENHAM HOTSPUR (PREM: 10th)

	P/FL App	P/FL Goals	FLC App	FLC Goals	FAC App	FAC Goals	Others App	Others Goals
Allen	9+ 3	2	2+1	2	1			
Anderton	14+ 2	3	3	2				
Armstrong	12	5	3	1				
Austin	13+ 2				1			
Baardsen	1+ 1							
Calderwood	33+ 1		4		1			
Campbell	38		4	1	1			
Carr	24+ 2		3		1			
Clapham	0+ 1							
Dozzell	10+ 7	2	1					
Edinburgh	21+ 3		2		1			
Fenn	0+ 4							
Fox	19+ 6	1	3+1					
Howells	32	2	4		1			
Iversen	16	6						
Mabbutt	1							
McVeigh	2+ 1	1						
Nethercott	2+ 7							
Nielsen	28+ 1	6	2+1		1			
Rosenthal	4+16	1						
Scales	10+ 2							
Sheringham	29	7	3	1				
Sinton	32+ 1	6	2		1			
Vega	8	1						
Walker	37		4		1			
Wilson	23+ 3	1	4					

TRANMERE ROVERS (DIV 1: 11th)

	P/FL App	P/FL Goals	FLC App	FLC Goals	FAC App	FAC Goals	Others App	Others Goals
Aldridge	32+11	18	4	2	1			
Bonetti	9+ 4	1	2	1				
Branch	22+13	5	3+1	1	0+1			
Brannan	31+ 3	6	3+1		1			
Challinor	4+ 1							
Cook	30+ 6	3	4		1			
Coyne	21		4					
Higgins	21+ 1	2	3		1			
Irons	34+ 7	5	3+1		0+1			
Jones G	13+17	6	1+1					
Jones L	8	5						
McGreal	24		1+1		1			
Mahon	14+11	2	0+2					
Morgan	0+ 1							
Moore	14+ 7	3	0+1		0+1			
Morrissey	21+10	1	3	1	1			
Nevin	10+11	2			1			
Nixon	25				1			
O'Brien	41	1	4		1			
Rogers	28+ 3		1					
Stevens	31		3		1			
Teale	25		4					
Thomas	28+ 2		1		1			
Thorn	19	1						
Woods	1							

WALSALL (DIV 2: 12th)

	P/FL App	P/FL Goals	FLC App	FLC Goals	FAC App	FAC Goals	Others App	Others Goals
Beckford	3+ 5							
Blake	35+ 3	4	1		0+2		1	
Bradley	21+ 5		2		2		1	
Butler	20+ 3	1	2					
Daniel	8+ 2		2		2		1	
Donowa	6	1						
Evans	27+ 1		1		2		1	
Hodge	32+ 5	4			4		0+1	
Keates	1+ 1							
Keister	30+ 6	1			4			
Lightbourne	45	20	2	1	4	4	1	
Marsh	28+ 2		2		4			
Mountfield	42		2		4		1	
Ntamark	36+ 2	1	2		4		1	
Platt	0+ 1		0+1					
Ricketts	2+ 9	1	0+1					
Rogers	1+ 1							
Roper	5+ 6							
Ryder	0+ 1							
Thomas	14+ 6				2			
Viveash	46	9	2		4	1	1	
Walker	36		2		4		1	
Watson	22+14	5			0+3		1	
Wilson	36+ 1	7	2		4	2	1	
Wood	10							

WATFORD (DIV 2: 13th)

	P/FL App	P/FL Goals	FLC App	FLC Goals	FAC App	FAC Goals	Others App	Others Goals
Andrews	16+ 9	4	3	1	0+2		2	1
Armstrong	15							
Bazeley	38+ 3	3	3		4	3	3	1
Chamberlain	4							
Connolly	12+ 1	2	1		2+1	4	1	1
Easton	17	1			2+1		2	
Flash	0+ 1							
Gibbs	43+ 2	1	4		4		3	
Johnson C	1				0+1			
Johnson R	35+ 2	2	2		2+1		2	
Lowndes	0+ 3		0+1					
Ludden	18+ 2		3		1		2	
Millen	42	2	3		3		1	
Miller	42		4		4		3	
Mooney	33+ 4	13	4		3		1	
Noel-Williams	9+16	2	0+1		2	1		
Page	35+ 1		4		4		3	1
Palmer	40+ 1	1	4		4		3	

WATFORD cont

	P/FL App	P/FL Goals	FLC App	FLC Goals	FAC App	FAC Goals	Others App	Others Goals
Penrice	22+10	1	2+1		1		1+1	
Phillips	13+ 3	4					0+2	
Porter	6		2	1				
Ramage	10+ 1	3	1+1					
Robinson	8+ 4				2+1		2	
Scott	6	2					2	
Slater	13+ 3	1			3		1	
Talboys	2+ 1		0+1					
Ward	7				1			
White	19+ 3	3	4		2	1	1	

WEST BROMWICH ALBION (DIV 1: 16th)

	P/FL App	P/FL Goals	FLC App	FLC Goals	FAC App	FAC Goals	Others App	Others Goals
Agnew	21+ 1				0+1			
Ashcroft	2+ 3		0+1					
Bennett	0+ 1							
Burgess	33	1	1		1			
Butler	12+ 5				0+1			
Coldicott	13+ 6	3						
Crichton	30				1			
Cunnington	0+ 4		0+2					
Darby	13+ 4							
Donovan	17+15		0+2	1				
Gilbert	11+ 7	1	2					
Groves	27+ 2	4	2	1	1			
Hamilton	39	5	2	1	1			
Holmes	37+ 1	1	2		1			
Hunt	42+ 3	15	1	1	1			
Joseph	0+ 2							
McDermott	6							
Mardon	11+ 3		2					
Miller	12							
Murphy	16+ 1	2			1			
Nicholson	16+ 2		2					
Peschisolido	30+ 7	15			1			
Potter	2+ 4							
Raven	33	1	1		1			
Rodosthenous	0+ 1							
Smith	21+ 3	2			1			
Sneekes	42+ 3	8	2		1			
Spink	4		2					
Taylor	16+16	10	2		0+1			

WEST HAM UNITED (PREM: 14th)

	P/FL App	P/FL Goals	FLC App	FLC Goals	FAC App	FAC Goals	Others App	Others Goals
Bilic	35	2	5	1	1			
Bishop	26+ 3	1	5		2			
Bowen	15+ 2	1	3					
Boylan	0+ 1							
Breacker	22+ 4		3		2			
Cottee	2+ 1		2	1				
Dicks	31	6	5	2	2			
Dowie	18+ 5		5	2				
Dumitrescu	3+ 4		2+1					
Ferdinand	11+ 4	2	0+1		1			
Futre	4+ 5							
Hall	7							
Hartson	11	5						
Hughes	31+ 2	3	4		2			
Jones	5+ 3		0+1		2			
Kitson	14	8						
Lampard	3+10		1+1		1			
Lazaridis	13+ 9	1	3+1					
Lomas	7							
Mautone	1		2					
Miklosko	36		3		2			
Moncur	26+ 1	2	4					
Newell	6+ 1							
Omoyinmi	0+ 1							
Porfirio	15+ 8	2	2	1	1+1	1		
Potts	17+ 3		1					
Raducioiu	6+ 5	2	1		1			
Rieper	26+ 2	1	4		1			
Rowland	11+ 4	1						

WEST HAM UNITED cont.

	P/FL App	P/FL Goals	FLC App	FLC Goals	FAC App	FAC Goals	Others App	Others Goals
Sealey	1+1							
Slater	2+1							
Williamson	13+2		0+1		2			

WIGAN ATHLETIC (DIV 3: 1st)

	P/FL App	P/FL Goals	FLC App	FLC Goals	FAC App	FAC Goals	Others App	Others Goals
Biggins	20+13	3	1+1		1		0+1	
Bishop	20+1		1				1	
Butler J	20+4				1		1	
Butler L	46		2		1		1	
Carragher	12+6		2		0+1			
Diaz	26+13	6	0+1		0+1			
Greenall	46	2	1+1	1	1		1	
Johnson	37	3	2		1		1	
Jones	39+1	31	1+1	1	1		1	1
Kilford	24+11	8	1		1			
Kirby	5+1							
Lancashire	15+9	9	2	4				
Love	0+3							
Lowe	31+11	6	2		1		1	
McGibbon	10	1						
Martinez	38+5	4	2		1		0+1	1
Morgan	18+5	1	2				1	
Pender	27+2		2		1		1	
Rogers	18+2	3						
Saville	17+3	4			1		1	
Seba	0+1		0+1					
Sharp	30+5	2	1		1		0+1	
Ward	5							
Whittaker	2+1							

Vinny Jones (Wimbledon)

WIMBLEDON (PREM: 8th)

	P/FL App	P/FL Goals	FLC App	FLC Goals	FAC App	FAC Goals	Others App	Others Goals
Ardley	33+1	2	4+1		5			
Blackwell	22+5		8		6			
Castledine	4+2	1	1		1			
Clarke	4+7	1	2+4		1			
Cort	0+1							
Cunningham	36		7		7			
Earle	32	7	6		7	4		
Ekoku	28+2	11	5	1	6			
Euell	4+3	2	1					
Fear	9+9		4	1				

WIMBLEDON cont.

	P/FL App	P/FL Goals	FLC App	FLC Goals	FAC App	FAC Goals	Others App	Others Goals
Gayle	34+2	8	7	3	6	2		
Goodman	6+7	1	1		0+3			
Harford	3+10	1	0+5		0+2			
Heald	2		1					
Holdsworth	10+15	5	4+1	2	3+3	2		
Jones	29	3	7		7			
Jupp	6		1		0+2			
Kimble	28+3		8		6			
Leonhardsen	27	5	6+1	1	7			
McAllister	19+4		0+1		2+3			
Perry	37	1	7		7	1		
Reeves	0+2		1+1					
Sullivan	36		7		7			
Thatcher	9							

WOLVERHAMPTON WANDERERS (DIV 1: 3rd)

	P/FL App	P/FL Goals	FLC App	FLC Goals	FAC App	FAC Goals	Others App	Others Goals
Atkins	44+1	4	2		1		2	1
Bull	43	23	2		1		2	
Corica	33+3	2	2		1			
Crowe	5+1							
Curle	20+1	2					2	
Dennison	9+5				1			
Dowe	5+3							
Emblen	27+1				1			
Ferguson	10+6	3	1		0+1	1	2	
Foley	0+5	1					0+2	
Froggatt	27	2	2					
Gilkes	5	1						
Goodman	19+8	6			1		1	
Law	4+3							
Leadbeater	0+1							
Osborn	33+2	5	1	1	1		2	
Pearce	4							
Richards	19+2	1	2					
Roberts	24+9	12	2		0+1		2	
Robinson	1+1							
Romano	1+3		1					
Smith	36+2		1+1		1		2	1
Stowell	46		2		1		2	
Thomas	15+7	3			1		2	
Thompson	26+6	2	2				1	
Van der Laan	7							
Venus	36+4		2		1			
Williams	6						2	1
Wright	0+3		0+2					
Young	1							

WREXHAM (DIV 2: 8th)

	P/FL App	P/FL Goals	FLC App	FLC Goals	FAC App	FAC Goals	Others App	Others Goals
Bennett	15	5			0+1			
Brace	26	1	2		4		1	
Brammer	17+4	1	0+1		0+2		1	
Carey	38		2		9		1	
Cartwright	3				1			
Chalk	34+9	1	2		6		1	
Connolly	27+3	14	2		8	1	1	
Cross	11+7	2	0+1					
Gardner							0+1	
Hardy	13		1		6			
Hughes	20+3	3			9	6	0+1	
Humes	34	4			8	1		
Jones B	14+8		0+1		1+1		0+1	
Jones L	2+4							
Jones P	6							
McGregor	37+1	1	1		8			
Marriott	43		2		8		1	
Morris	10+7	4			5	2	1	
Owen	12+11	1	1		4+2		1	
Phillips	26	5	2					
Ridler	7+4						1	
Roberts	0+1				0+1			
Russell	37+4		1		5+2	3	1	
Skinner	21+6	4	0+1	1	3+1			

WREXHAM cont.

	P/FL App	P/FL Goals	FLC App	FLC Goals	FAC App	FAC Goals	Others App	Others Goals
Soloman	2		2					
Ward	24	1	2		9	1		
Watkin	24+2	7	2		5+3	3		
Williams	3+1							

WYCOMBE WANDERERS (DIV 2: 18th)

	P/FL App	P/FL Goals	FLC App	FLC Goals	FAC App	FAC Goals	Others App	Others Goals
Bell	46	2	4		4		1	
Brown	28+6	6	4		2+1		0+1	
Carroll	42+1	9	4		4	1		
Cheesewright	18				4		1	
Cornforth	8+2							
Cousins	36+1		3		4		1	
Crossley	7+2				2		0+1	
Davis	13						1	
Desouza	29+4	5	4		4	2	1	
Evans	38+4	2	4	1	1+1			
Farrell	17+10	1	4		1+2			
Forsyth	22+1	2			1		1	
Harkin	0+4				0+2			
Kavanagh	27				2		1	
Lawrence	12+1	1	4		1		0+1	
McCarthy	36+4		4	1	4		1	
McGavin	33+2	8	1		4	1	1	
McGorry							1	1
Mahoney-Johnson	2+2	2						
Markman	0+2							
Parkin	24		4					
Patterson	6+3		2		2+1			
Read	7+6	4						
Scott	9	3						
Simpson	16+4	1					1	
Skiverton	2+4				0+1			
Stallard	12	4						
Taylor	4							
Wilkins	1							
Williams	11+8	1	2+1	2	4	4		

YORK CITY (DIV 2: 20th)

	P/FL App	P/FL Goals	FLC App	FLC Goals	FAC App	FAC Goals	Others App	Others Goals
Atkin	6+6		1					
Atkinson	13+1				3		2	
Barras	46	1	5		4	1	2	
Bull	33+8	2	4+1	1	4			
Bushell	26+5	3	1+1	1	1		1	
Campbell	5+6	1			0+2		2	
Clarke	17		1		4		1	
Cresswell	9+8		1+2		0+1		1	
Gilbert	9		1					
Greening	0+5							
Hall	12+1		2		1			
Harrison	0+1						0+1	
Himsworth	32+1	2	4		4	1	2	1
Jordan	7+8	1			0+1		1	
McMillan	46		5		3		2	
Murty	25+2	2	5	1	3+1		1+1	
Naylor	0+1		0+1					
Pepper	26+3	12	4+1	1	3	1	1	
Pouton	18+4	1			3		1	
Prudhoe	2							
Randall	13+3	2	5		0+1			
Reed	2							
Rowe	9+1	3						
Rush	1+1						1	
Sharples	28	1	3		1		1	
Stephenson	33+2	1	4+1		3		1+1	
Tinkler	9	1						
Tolson	39+1	12	5	3	4	2	0+1	
Tutill	13+2		1		3+1		1	
Warrington	27		4				1	
Williams	0+1							

PFA AWARDS 1997

Players' Player of the Year
ALAN SHEARER

Young Player of the Year
DAVID BECKHAM

Special Merit Award
PETER BEARDSLEY

DIVISIONAL AWARDS

Carling Premier League

David Seaman	Arsenal
Gary Neville	Manchester United
Stig Inge Bjornebye	Liverpool
David Beckham	Manchester United
Tony Adams	Arsenal
Mark Wright	Liverpool
Roy Keane	Manchester United
David Batty	Newcastle United
Alan Shearer	Newcastle United
Ian Wright	Arsenal
Steve McManaman	Liverpool

Nationwide League Division 1

Alan Kelly	Sheffield United
Nick Eaden	Barnsley
Steve Froggatt	Wolverhampton Wanderers
Georgiou Kinkladze	Manchester City
Gerry Taggart	Bolton Wanderers
Dean Richards	Wolverhampton Wanderers
Alan Thompson	Bolton Wanderers
Trevor Sinclair	Queens Park Rangers
Mike Sheron	Stoke City
John McGinlay	Bolton Wanderers
Darren Eadie	Norwich City

Nationwide League Division 2

Kevin Miller	Watford
Gary Parkinson	Burnley
David Eyres	Burnley
Danny Murphy	Crewe Alexandra
Mike Flynn	Stockport County
Steve Davis	Luton Town
Gareth Whalley	Crewe Alexandra
Chris Marsden	Stockport County
Tony Thorpe	Luton Town
Carl Asaba	Brentford
Bryan Hughes	Wrexham

Nationwide League Division 3

Tony Caig	Carlisle United
Ian Hendon	Leyton Orient
Owen Archdeacon	Carlisle United
Roberto Martinez	Wigan Athletic
Dean Walling	Carlisle United
Jody Craddock	Cambridge United
Warren Aspinall	Carlisle United
Gareth Ainsworth	Lincoln City
Graeme Jones	Wigan Athletic
Mike Conroy	Fulham
Jan Molby	Swansea City

THE TIMES
ITF
INTERACTIVE TEAM FOOTBALL

IN ASSOCIATION WITH

SKY **sports**
interactive

Listed below are the players' final scoring totals in *The Times* Interactive Team Football at the end of the 1996-97 season

(qualification – a minimum of 10 ITF qualifying appearances. Figures include a player's 1996-97 appearances for any previous ITF club)

GOALKEEPERS

			Appearances
40	N Martyn	Leeds	42
36	D Seaman	Arsenal	24
31	M Bosnich	Aston Villa	23
30	S Kerr	Celtic	25
29	A Goram	Rangers	28
20	P Srnicek	Newcastle	23
20	G Walsh	Middlesbrough	13
17	M Oakes	Aston Villa	18
10	D James	Liverpool	41
9	T Coton	Sunderland	10
8	P Schmeichel	Man United	41
8	G Marshall	Celtic	11
7	M Taylor	Southampton	18
4	A Maxwell	Dundee U	10
2	N Sullivan	Wimbledon	44
1	J Lukic	Arsenal	16
-4	F Grodas	Chelsea	19
-5	G Rousset	Hearts	37
-7	T Flowers	Blackburn	39
-8	B Roberts	Middlesbrough	11
-11	I Walker	Tottenham	39
-12	M Watt	Aberdeen	10
-14	N Walker	Aberdeen	19
-15	K Pressman	Sheffield W	42
-18	S Hislop	Newcastle	19
-20	K Keller	Leicester	34
-20	L Miklosko	West Ham	39
-20	S Howie	Motherwell	34
-27	D Lekovic	Kilmarnock	36
-28	D Beasant	Southampton	15
-28	K Hitchcock	Chelsea	14
-30	J Leighton	Hibernian	38
-36	N Southall	Everton	37
-38	L Perez	Sunderland	31
-41	R Hoult	Derby	36
-42	S Ogrizovic	Coventry	43
-49	M Crossley	Nottingham F	37
-59	I Westwater	Dunfermline	32
-78	S Thomson	Raith Rovers	24

FULL BACKS

67	A Wright	Aston Villa	41
55	M Malpas	Dundee U	31
51	G Kelly	Leeds	39
50	F Nelson	Aston Villa	33
49	N Winterburn	Arsenal	40
48	D Robertson	Rangers	24
45	S Bjornebye	Liverpool	40
43	S Staunton	Aston Villa	31
43	M Perry	Dundee U	41
43	C Perry	Wimbledon	45
40	G Halle	Leeds	22
39	D Irwin	Man United	34
38	J McNamara	Celtic	34
38	L Dixon	Arsenal	32
38	R Elliott	Newcastle	31
36	S Watson	Newcastle	37
34	D Petrescu	Chelsea	40
34	G Neville	Man United	36
32	H Berg	Blackburn	39
31	T McKinlay	Celtic	27
30	K Cunningham	Wimbledon	43
30	G Le Saux	Blackburn	28
25	P Atherton	Sheffield W	41
25	G Locke	Hearts	12
24	N Pointon	Hearts	28
23	J Dicks	West Ham	34
22	I Nolan	Sheffield W	42
22	J Beresford	Newcastle	21
20	A Haaland	Nottingham F	37
20	T Dorigo	Leeds	19
20	W Barton	Newcastle	16
19	J Kenna	Blackburn	40
17	A Kimble	Wimbledon	34
15	E Barrett	Everton	39
14	A Hinchcliffe	Everton	19
14	C Blackmore	Middlesbrough	19
13	J Edinburgh	Tottenham	24
12	A Dow	Hibernian	18
12	C Wilson	Tottenham	25
10	S Grayson	Leicester	38
10	S Pearce	Nottingham F	35
10	S Clarke	Chelsea	38
9	B Thatcher	Wimbledon	10
9	S McMillan	Motherwell	1
8	C Fleming	Middlesbrough	36
8	C Powell	Derby	39
8	S McKimmie	Aberdeen	15
7	G Hall	Sunderland	35
7	P Neville	Man United	15
7	S Nicol	Sheffield W	22
7	D Austin	Tottenham	15
7	W Miller	Hibernian	34
6	D Stefanovic	Sheffield W	28
6	F Benali	Southampton	16
6	M Hall	Coventry	14
6	M Whitlow	Leicester	16
5	D Kubicki	Sunderland	31
5	D Lyttle	Nottingham F	34
5	G MacPherson	Kilmarnock	39
4	M Scott	Sunderland	15
4	S Charlton	Southampton	25

3	S Minto	Chelsea	30
3	T Breacker	West Ham	25
2	M Bowen	West Ham	16
-3	T Phelan	Everton	17
-4	J Dodd	Southampton	21
-4	K Rowland	West Ham	12
-4	N Jerkan	Nottingham F	14
-4	S Carr	Tottenham	21
-5	C Miller	Dunfermline	19
-9	A Tod	Dunfermline	38
-10	B Borrows	Coventry	19
-11	N Cox	Middlesbrough	33
-12	D Burrows	Coventry	17
-14	D Kirkwood	Raith Rovers	15
-16	P Bonar	Raith Rovers	9

CENTRAL DEFENDERS

75	U Ehiogu	Aston Villa	41
56	R Gough	Rangers	29
52	S Pressley	Dundee U	41
50	M Keown	Arsenal	36
44	M MacKay	Celtic	23
44	G Southgate	Aston Villa	31
42	D Wetherall	Leeds	27
41	S Bould	Arsenal	36
40	J Bjorklund	Rangers	30
40	T Boyd	Celtic	36
39	T Adams	Arsenal	29
39	D May	Man United	29
36	F Leboeuf	Chelsea	33
34	P Ritchie	Hearts	29
32	C Hendry	Blackburn	38
32	D Peacock	Newcastle	39
32	R Scimeca	Aston Villa	17
30	D McPherson	Hearts	29
29	L Radebe	Leeds	30
29	M Wright	Liverpool	36
26	D Matteo	Liverpool	26
26	P Albert	Newcastle	29
25	D Walker	Sheffield W	39
25	R Johnsen	Man United	32
24	A McLaren	Rangers	19
24	M Van Der Gaag	Motherwell	30
24	P Babb	Liverpool	22
23	R Molenaar	Leeds	13
22	A Stubbs	Celtic	23
22	S Campbell	Tottenham	40
21	M Reilly	Kilmarnock	38
18	G Petric	Rangers	18
18	R Ord	Sunderland	34
17	C Calderwood	Tottenham	35
17	S Bilic	West Ham	37
17	S Walsh	Leicester	24
16	B McAllister	Wimbledon	21
16	D Blackwell	Wimbledon	29
16	E Johnsen	Chelsea	15
16	R Montgomerie	Kilmarnock	25
15	J Newsome	Sheffield W	12
14	K Ball	Sunderland	33
12	A Melville	Sunderland	33
12	D Unsworth	Everton	34
12	N Ruddock	Liverpool	13
11	D Watson	Everton	30
11	G Pallister	Man United	29
10	J Laursen	Derby	37
10	M Elliott	Leicester	17
10	M Rieper	West Ham	27

10	R Ferdinand	West Ham	14
9	B Welsh	Hibernian	17
9	S Chettle	Nottingham F	36
8	J Watts	Leicester	26
7	A Neilson	Southampton	26
7	J Scales	Tottenham	14
6	C Short	Everton	21
6	G Festa	Middlesbrough	17
6	N Pearson	Middlesbrough	19
5	S Potts	West Ham	19
5	A Myers	Chelsea	17
5	L Daish	Coventry	19
4	A Kombouare	Aberdeen	11
4	F Sinclair	Chelsea	23
4	J McLaughlin	Hibernian	11
3	B Kvarme	Liverpool	15
3	C Lundekvam	Southampton	27
2	C Woodthorpe	Aberdeen	16
2	R Dryden	Southampton	28
2	R Jobson	Leeds	11
2	R Shaw	Coventry	40
1	C Cooper	Nottingham F	39
1	M Duberry	Chelsea	15
0	B O'Neil	Celtic	10
0	S Prior	Leicester	33
-1	B Martin	Motherwell	38
-3	G Hunter	Hibernian	16
-4	P McGrath	Derby	26
-4	P Whelan	Middlesbrough	10
-6	B Irvine	Aberdeen	23
-6	M Millar	Dunfermline	19
-6	S Vickers	Middlesbrough	33
-9	U Van Gobbel	Southampton	24
-10	D Whyte	Middlesbrough	23
-10	I Stimac	Derby	23
-13	D Craig	Raith Rovers	14
-19	I Den Bieman	Dunfermline	23
-19	S Dennis	Hibernian	23

MIDFIELD PLAYERS

75	B Laudrup	Rangers	35
71	Juninho	Middlesbrough	41
69	M Gayle	Wimbledon	41
68	R Earle	Wimbledon	40
67	R Winters	Dundee U	33
66	G Speed	Everton	40
63	R Di Matteo	Chelsea	41
62	D Beckham	Man United	38
62	G McAllister	Coventry	43
61	J Albertz	Rangers	33
61	P Gascoigne	Rangers	26
60	P Di Canio	Celtic	31
59	S McManaman	Liverpool	39
58	L Bowyer	Leeds	36
57	P Merson	Arsenal	34
56	J Barnes	Liverpool	38
55	N Ardley	Wimbledon	39
54	A Smith	Dunfermline	33
53	A Asanovic	Derby	38
53	O Leonhardsen	Wimbledon	33
52	M Pembridge	Sheffield W	36
51	A Townsend	Aston Villa	37
49	J McIntyre	Kilmarnock	32
48	H French	Dunfermline	36
48	J McAteer	Liverpool	39
47	D Lennon	Raith Rovers	38
47	D Wise	Chelsea	34
47	L Sharpe	Leeds	26
47	P Bracewell	Sunderland	40
47	R Lee	Newcastle	33
47	T Sherwood	Blackburn	40
46	A Sinton	Tottenham	32
46	J Magilton	Southampton	35
46	M Gray	Sunderland	35
45	D Platt	Arsenal	29
44	A Nielsen	Tottenham	29
44	Emerson	Middlesbrough	38
44	I Taylor	Aston Villa	29
43	D Windass	Aberdeen	31
43	M Izzet	Leicester	36
43	P McGinlay	Hibernian	30
43	R Giggs	Man United	29
42	G Rowett	Derby	37
41	B Carbone	Sheffield W	26
41	P Vieira	Arsenal	34
40	J Wilcox	Blackburn	29
39	C Burley	Chelsea	30
39	C Dailly	Derby	36
39	D Howells	Tottenham	33
39	M Hughes	West Ham	34
39	M Thomas	Liverpool	31
39	R Mustoe	Middlesbrough	38
39	S Donnelly	Celtic	23
38	V Jones	Wimbledon	37
37	C Hignett	Middlesbrough	25
37	G Parker	Leicester	27
37	I Woan	Nottingham F	34
37	N Butt	Man United	23
37	N Lennon	Leicester	36
36	P Telfer	Coventry	36
36	P Williams	Coventry	34
35	C Robertson	Dunfermline	33
35	G Flitcroft	Blackburn	28
35	K Richardson	Coventry	30
34	I Bishop	West Ham	29
34	M Draper	Aston Villa	27
34	R Wallace	Leeds	21
34	S Fulton	Hearts	28
33	E Berkovic	Southampton	27
33	E Jess	Coventry	25
33	G McSwegan	Dundee U	17
33	T Rougier	Raith Rovers	29
32	A Thom	Celtic	19
32	C Palmer	Leeds	31
32	D Batty	Newcastle	36
32	D Phillips	Nottingham F	29
32	J Dolan	Dundee U	35
32	J Redknapp	Liverpool	22
32	J Salako	Coventry	26
32	M Oakley	Southampton	23
32	R Van Der Laan	Derby	19
31	J Parkinson	Everton	28
31	P Berger	Liverpool	15
30	D Fleming	Dunfermline	25
30	K Poborsky	Man United	19
29	G Hyde	Sheffield W	19
29	L Bohinen	Blackburn	21
29	P Grant	Celtic	24
28	D Powell	Derby	34
28	I Kiriakov	Aberdeen	28
28	K Gillespie	Newcastle	24
28	R Fox	Tottenham	22
27	J Moncur	West Ham	25
27	P Stamp	Middlesbrough	20
27	T Tzvetanov	Aberdeen	24
26	A Millen	Raith Rovers	31
26	A Mitchell	Kilmarnock	23
26	D Bowman	Dundee U	26
26	R Parlour	Arsenal	20
26	S Thomson	Raith Rovers	22
25	R Slater	Southampton	26
24	B McKinlay	Blackburn	25
24	D Ginola	Newcastle	23
24	E Newton	Chelsea	21
24	L Clark	Newcastle	16
24	S Curcic	Aston Villa	19
24	S Glass	Aberdeen	21
23	R Keane	Man United	23
22	C Bart-Williams	Nottingham F	19
22	P McStay	Celtic	16
21	J McInally	Dundee U	17
21	S Taylor	Leicester	22
20	D Anderton	Tottenham	15
19	D Hannah	Celtic	16
19	I Harte	Leeds	13
19	J Cruyff	Man United	12
19	M Ford	Leeds	15
19	S Lazaridis	West Ham	15
18	R Blinker	Sheffield W	19
18	S Gemmill	Nottingham F	21
17	D Williamson	West Ham	16
17	J Dozzell	Tottenham	11
17	O Trustfull	Sheffield W	12
16	C McCart	Motherwell	17
16	G Donis	Blackburn	11
16	S Agnew	Sunderland	13
15	C Thomsen	Everton	15
15	S Hughes	Arsenal	10
14	A Rae	Sunderland	15
14	J Philliben	Motherwell	13
13	W Collins	Sheffield W	10
12	S Flynn	Derby	13
11	B McClair	Man United	11
11	P Fear	Wimbledon	11
11	S Valikarri	Motherwell	11
11	T Grant	Everton	12
10	I Cameron	Hibernian	10
10	P Bernard	Aberdeen	11
7	A McManus	Hearts	12

STRIKERS

92	J Cadete	Celtic	35
87	A Shearer	Newcastle	35
84	F Ravanelli	Middlesbrough	39
79	D Yorke	Aston Villa	38
71	I Wright	Arsenal	31
68	R Fowler	Liverpool	34
66	P Wright	Kilmarnock	34
61	L Ferdinand	Newcastle	32
61	O Solskjaer	Man United	31
59	A Booth	Sheffield W	36
58	M Hughes	Chelsea	40
58	S Claridge	Leicester	33
56	J Robertson	Hearts	27
56	K Gallacher	Blackburn	36
55	E Ostenstad	Southampton	30
54	C Cameron	Hearts	40
54	T Coyne	Motherwell	27
53	D Jackson	Hibernian	34
52	E Cantona	Man United	41
52	E Ekoku	Wimbledon	35

52	G Zola	Chelsea	29
52	S Collymore	Liverpool	28
50	D Sturridge	Derby	32
49	P Van Hooydonk	Nottingham F	29
48	E Heskey	Leicester	38
48	I Marshall	Leicester	24
47	D Bergkamp	Arsenal	29
47	D Ferguson	Everton	35
47	N Barmby	Everton	36
46	D Dublin	Coventry	32
46	S Milosevic	Aston Villa	29
45	D Saunders	Nottingham F	36
45	M Le Tissier	Southampton	26
44	G Vialli	Chelsea	25
42	A Ward	Derby	27
42	C Sutton	Blackburn	26
42	M Beck	Middlesbrough	28
41	A McCoist	Rangers	15
41	B Deane	Leeds	32
41	B Dodds	Aberdeen	27
41	N Whelan	Coventry	38
39	G Whittingham	Sheffield W	32
38	G Stuart	Everton	34
38	O Coyle	Motherwell	24
37	D Huckerby	Coventry	26
36	I Rush	Leeds	37
36	T Sheringham	Tottenham	29
35	P Duffield	Raith Rovers	26
34	K Campbell	Nottingham F	19
34	P Kitson	West Ham	15
32	P Beardsley	Newcastle	26
32	S Iversen	Tottenham	15
29	J Hartson	West Ham	26
27	D Holdsworth	Wimbledon	13
26	D Hirst	Sheffield W	21
26	S Petrie	Dunfermline	26
24	A Cole	Man United	13
24	F Asprilla	Newcastle	18
24	T Johnson	Celtic	17
23	K Wright	Hibernian	20
22	R Humphreys	Sheffield W	17
21	G Durie	Rangers	16
21	K Olafsson	Dundee U	14
21	P Scholes	Man United	19
20	C Russell	Sunderland	13
20	D Kelly	Sunderland	25
19	C Armstrong	Tottenham	12
19	P Stewart	Sunderland	21
19	R Willems	Derby	11
18	D Arnott	Motherwell	13
18	M Branch	Everton	13
17	I Dowie	West Ham	20
16	M Bridges	Sunderland	13
15	B Roy	Nottingham F	11
14	A Moore	Dunfermline	14
12	S Booth	Aberdeen	13
11	P Ndlovu	Coventry	11
9	S Guppy	Leicester	11

MANAGERS

77	T Burns	Celtic
76	W Smith	Rangers
73	A Ferguson	Man United
67	R Gullit	Chelsea
62	T McLean	Dundee U
62	R Evans	Liverpool
57	J Kinnear	Wimbledon

56	D Pleat	Sheffield W
53	B Little	Aston Villa
47	A Wenger	Arsenal
43	J Jefferies	Hearts
41	B Robson	Middlesbrough
40	J Smith	Derby
38	M O'Neill	Leicester
33	G Graham	Leeds
32	B Paton	Dunfermline
31	R Aitken	Aberdeen
27	A McLeish	Motherwell
27	G Francis	Tottenham
26	H Redknapp	West Ham
26	K Dalglish	Newcastle
25	T Parkes	Blackburn
24	G Strachan	Coventry
23	G Souness	Southampton
22	P Reid	Sunderland
14	J Duffy	Hibernian
4	S Pearce	Nottingham F

MOST POPULAR CHOICES

The most popular choices in each category in a starting line-up were:

GOALKEEPERS

David James	Liverpool	42577
Peter Schmeichel	Man United	20804
Mark Bosnich	Aston Villa	17797
David Seaman	Arsenal	15722
Andy Goram	Rangers	13713
Ian Walker	Tottenham	11562
Gordon Marshall	Celtic	10798
Nigel Martyn	Leeds United	9257
Tim Flowers	Blackburn	7739
Mark Crossley	Nottingham F	7352
David James	Liverpool	6792

Most in demand through transfers

Michael Oakes	Aston Villa	4401
David Seaman	Arsenal	3309
Tony Coton	Sunderland	2529
Andy Goram	Rangers	2437

FULL BACKS

Stig Inge Bjornebye	Liverpool	31169
Claudio Branco	Middlesbrough	26869
Gary Neville	Man United	21563
Dan Petrescu	Chelsea	16426
Steve Harkness	Liverpool	15513
John Brown	Rangers	13642
Andy Hinchcliffe	Everton	13339
Lee Dixon	Arsenal	11751
David Robertson	Rangers	11746
Stuart Pearce	Nottingham F	9505

Most in demand through transfers

Stig Inge Bjornebye	Liverpool	22040
Lee Dixon	Arsenal	2943
Martin Scott	Sunderland	2935
Chris Perry	Wimbledon	2863

CENTRAL DEFENDERS

Frank Leboeuf	Chelsea	29028
Sol Campbell	Tottenham	20863
Richard Gough	Rangers	18900
Ugo Ehiogu	Aston Villa	18741
Michael Duberry	Chelsea	13573
Gareth Southgate	Aston Villa	12804
David Unsworth	Everton	12064
Malky MacKay	Celtic	10920
Gary Pallister	Man United	9958
David May	Man United	9439

Most in demand through transfers

Frank Leboeuf	Chelsea	11500
Dominic Matteo	Liverpool	7632
Richard Gough	Rangers	4601
Ugo Ehiogu	Aston Villa	4032

MIDFIELD PLAYERS

Andreas Thom	Celtic	36304
Stuart McCall	Rangers	34314
Jordi Cruyff	Man United	25845
David Beckham	Man United	20389
Roberto Di Matteo	Chelsea	19640
Brian Laudrup	Rangers	17373
Juninho	Middlesbrough	17323
George Donis	Blackburn	16395
Andy Townsend	Aston Villa	15791
Anders Limpar	Everton	12965

Most in demand through transfers

Patrick Berger	Liverpool	9090
Marcus Gayle	Wimbledon	8647
Juninho	Middlesbrough	7165
David Beckham	Man United	6516

STRIKERS

Fabrizio Ravanelli	Middlesbrough	31718
Robbie Fowler	Liverpool	21750
Gianluca Vialli	Chelsea	18911
Ian Rush	Leeds United	17696
Dean Holdsworth	Wimbledon	14476
Alan Shearer	Newcastle	13721
Ally McCoist	Rangers	13496
Pierre Van Hooydonk	Nottingham F	13005
Dean Saunders	Nottingham F	12637
Eric Cantona	Man United	10998

Most in demand through transfers

Fabrizio Ravanelli	Middlesbrough	15643
Ole Gunnar Solskjaer	Man United	7254
Ian Wright	Arsenal	7013
Jorge Cadete	Celtic	6433

MANAGERS

Ruud Gullit	Chelsea	34694
Walter Smith	Rangers	21804
Tommy Burns	Celtic	12694
Kevin Keegan	Newcastle	12650
Bryan Robson	Middlesbrough	12607
Alex Ferguson	Man United	11412
Gerry Francis	Tottenham	7280
Joe Kinnear	Wimbledon	6758
Roy Evans	Liverpool	5966
Brian Little	Aston Villa	5954

Most in demand through transfers

Joe Kinnear	Wimbledon	3469
Ruud Gullit	Chelsea	2382
Walter Smith	Rangers	2350
Tommy Burns	Celtic	2204